HOGAN AND M
ADMINISTRATIVE LAW

HOGAN AND MORGAN'S ADMINISTRATIVE LAW

FOURTH EDITION

STUDENT VERSION

DAVID GWYNN MORGAN
LL.M. (LOND.), PH.D. (N.U.I.)
PROFESSOR EMERITUS OF LAW AT UNIVERSITY COLLEGE CORK

With contributions from
PAUL DALY
REPLACEMENT PROFESSOR OF LAW AT UNIVERSITY OF OTTAWA, B.C.L.,
LL.M. (NUI); LL.M. (PENN.); PH.D. (CANTAB.); OF THE BAR OF NEW YORK

ROUND HALL  THOMSON REUTERS

Published in 2012 by
Thomson Reuters (Professional) Ireland Limited
(Registered in Ireland, Company No. 80867.
Registered Office and address for service:
43 Fitzwilliam Place, Dublin 2, Ireland)
trading as Round Hall

Typeset by
Gough Typesetting Services
Dublin

Printed by
MPG Books

ISBN 978-1-85800-687-1

A catalogue record for this book
is available from the British Library

First edition, 1986
Second edition, 1991
Third edition, 1998
Fourth edition, first print, 2010
Fourth edition, student version, 2012

To Deirdre, Gwendolen, Daniel and Gareth

PREFACE

As elaborated later in this Preface, the present book is a student version—that is updated and somewhat abbreviated—of its parent, the Brehon volume, which published in late 2010. It comes at a bleak time in the affairs of the Irish State. While our administrative law has developed, in many respects, since the Third Edition was published in 1998, when all seemed right in the world, the last four disastrous years have exposed massive regulatory failures both in Ireland and elsewhere. The administrative lawyer and the political scientist must both, therefore, ask the fundamental question of how administrative law can be remodelled as a part of a wider political and economic reform to ensure that failure on such a dismal scale never happens again.

Much of our public law is very old and goes back to the days when intervention by the State (or Crown) in the affairs of the citizen was exceptional. This era gave birth to a number of legal doctrines which are no longer appropriate in modern conditions. One prime example is the non-delegation (*delegatus non potest delegare*) doctrine. This is a precept which dates at least from the era when public administration consisted mainly of a handful of secretaries working behind the scenes in a Royal Palace; and is out of line with the realities and assumptions of the twenty-first century. As outlined in Chapter 11, Parts E and F, the law has attempted to accommodate such developments as the *Carltona* doctrine in the case of Ministers and their Departments; or statutory exclusions elsewhere. However, the draftsman has not always been cognisant of this elephant trap and there remain public bodies in relation to which the doctrine might yet claim a victory, to no-one's legitimate advantage.

As regards the law relating to fair procedures in public administration, there is truth in the basic theory here, namely, that fair procedure encourages an appropriate substantive result; and also that the dignity of the individual requires fair procedure. At the same time, as mentioned in Chapters 11–14, there are points at which this has, perhaps, been taken too far. The principle called the second rule of constitutional justice (*audi alteram partem*) is quintessentially a rule developed for litigation before a court. Its imposition in the field of public administration has sometimes taken even conscientious public servants by surprise (in a way which evokes the old line that the people "speak a language that the stranger never knew"). It must be said that there is something unexpected about the notion that an individual affected by any administrative action must be empowered to make their own case, rather than leaving it to the public servants familiar with the area to take all relevant circumstances into account and deal justly with the individual citizen. In addition, there is a tension between this notion that the person affected must be allowed to make their own case and, on the other hand, the developing concept that the administrator is responsible for supplying all relevant facts, precedents and other information.

The judiciary has been alert to implement the *zeitgeist* in favour of the dignity of the individual by establishing a "rights-based" jurisprudence, recognising the fundamental rights of the citizen against the public administrator. In line with this, as can be seen in Chapter 15 on the Control of Discretionary Powers, there have been constructive developments. By virtue of *Meadows v Minister for Justice, Equality and Law Reform* [2010] 4 I.R. 701, there appears to have been some dilution of the exacting standards, which a court was required to apply before quashing an administrative decision, on grounds of irrationality.

So far as the Order 84 leave procedure, outlined in Chapter 16, is concerned, the Oireachtas has finally listened to the criticisms of scholars and practitioners alike and has, in the Planning and Development (Amendment) Act 2010, significantly modified the bi-furcated leave procedure contained in s.50 of the Planning and Development Act 2000. But was an opportunity lost to rework entirely the Order 84 procedure (modified only slightly in 2011), by the abolition of the leave procedure itself? This would mean that applications for judicial review would simply follow the procedure now prescribed for procurement cases by Ord.84A, so that an applicant would be required to file a grounding statement and affidavit without the necessity for leave itself. The same sort of conservatism has greeted suggestions to replace the historically distinct orders for judicial review, by a single comprehensive remedy like the US "petition for review".

Apart from substance, the organisation and presentation of the law is almost equally important. Yet, in the chapters concerning Fair Procedure and that on the Control of Discretionary Powers, numerous instances are noted in which the law has sprouted unnecessary complexity. This may have arisen because (possibly through an omission by counsel) a judgment has started reasoning from first principles, without adverting to the fact that this particular area is not a green-field site; and there is in fact already in existence a well-developed construct of law. As a result, this book contains examples of significant blocs of law in which a profusion of labels obscures what could be a rather straightforward core of substance. Connected to this is a lack of respect for precedent: frequently one notices a failure by one High Court judge to follow the decision of another, on the same point. The outcome is a divergent line of authority. Yet precedent is the fundamental discipline by which uniformity and an absence of judicial individualism is instilled into the law. It is the principal technique by which the Rule of Law is respected by the judiciary. Another related point is that, as Lord Bingham has remarked[1]:

> "The judges are quite ready to criticize the obscurity and complexity of legislation … [But] we may agree with Justice Heydon of the High Court of Australia that judicial activism taken to extremes can spell the death of the rule of law: it is one thing to move the law a little further along a line on which it is already moving or to adapt it to deal with modern views and practice; it is quite another to seek to recast the law in a radically innovative and adventurous way, because that is to make it uncertain and unpredictable, features which are the antithesis of the rule of law."

There have also been significant statutory changes since the Third Edition, including a restatement of law on the selection and dismissal of civil servants, by no means an unimportant field, in the light of recent events. There have also been many reforms in the field of local government. In the area of public inquiries, at a time of public economy, recent experience shows that inquiries are now more likely to take the form of a commission of investigation, rather than a tribunal of inquiry. More widely,

---

[1]   Bingham, *The Rule of Law* (Penguin Books, 2010). The reference to Justice Heydon is to his article in *Quadrant* (January–February 2003).

the number of public bodies (including administrative tribunals, as well as what were formerly called state-sponsored bodies) had increased exponentially during the gallop of the Celtic Tiger and a culling is now promised. Indeed, this is rather anticipated here by the pruning of Chapter 4 on public bodies, more drastically than other chapters.

Apart from the specific disclaimer below, one ought to emphasise the limits of this book. The boundary with constitutional law, on which there are many excellent works, is fairly rigorously observed. And on the other border-line, public law is now a huge sprawling area, including the bodies of law relating to: welfare, tax, asylum and immigration and licensing systems, such as planning or broadcasting, as well as the traditional step-brother of criminal procedure. Plainly, we are not attempting to deal with the *substance* of these vast areas. Thus, the reader will find little on refoulement or broadcasting, and only a sketch of planning law. And, even as regards *procedure and machinery*, we are only able to indicate general issues such as, the relationship between courts and tribunals; the limits on the proper use of licensing powers; or how tribunals of inquiry differ from commissions of investigation.

Another limitation is that what is on offer is a synthesis of judicial review cases from all subject areas and we do not analyse the cases in the context of their own area. One justification for this policy choice is that, on the whole, the traditional approach of a judge pondering some problem of constitutional justice or delay in the application for judicial review, in the field of (say) immigration, does not hesitate to borrow from the field of planning, albeit with sensitivity to any special considerations which are relevant.

Readers may reasonably ask what is the comparison between the present book and the Brehon volume which appeared in late 2010. One answer is that this is about two-thirds the length (bear in mind Hemingway's remark that the test of a book's worth is how much good stuff one can throw away). The footnotes have been somewhat slimmed down. The material has been thoroughly updated and the excisions have facilitated relocation, to bring into closer association material which belongs together. But to ease cross-reference, the division into chapters and their numbering is the same here as in the parent volume. Where reference is made to the parent, the abbreviation "H & M" is used, in contradistinction from the Third (1998) Edition which is referred to as the "Third Edition". In determining where to apply the surgeon's knife I have retained topics of central importance in most courses, while excising more outlying material, such as: public procurement; the "shall-may" dichotomy in statutory interpretation; or restitution. On the positive side, I have added, especially at the start of chapters, more introductory material, on the basis that many readers will be strangers to the territory. A fair reviewer of the first edition remarked that: "the authors operate all the time from first principles … they have an awareness of the social and political context of many of the rules they discuss and a mild scepticism which enables them to be pragmatic about the technicalities they are laying before the readers."[2] This quality has, I hope, been retained.

As ever, I should be grateful to readers who draw attention to errors and omissions. May I stress, however, that no liability is accepted by the author, in this

---

[2] The quotation is from C. Gearty, "Administrative Law in the 1980s" (1987) 9 D.U.L.J. 21 at 26. Elsewhere, Conor Cruise O'Brien has pointed out that when writers receive a favourable review, they refer to it as "fair".

regard and this book should not be regarded as a substitute for legal advice.

It is a pleasure to record the friends and colleagues who have given every assistance with the book in whichever form. Two people merit special mention. First, Paul Daly was initially employed as a research assistant to Gerard Hogan and myself. However, it soon became clear that his contribution was going way beyond that of the usual research assistant. As a result of his mature legal understanding; his resourcefulness in unearthing legal sources; and his capacity to write new material into an existing framework, so much more difficult than starting from scratch, a good proportion of the new material was originated by Paul. And this is acknowledged by putting his name on the title page. Secondly, Sheila Cunneen word processed almost all of David Gwynn Morgan's part of the parent volume and then gave great assistance in converting the material to the present version. Going way beyond word-processing, her gift for the correct word and sentence structure; rigorous exclusion of cliché and repetition; good cheer; talent for organising a great mass of material; and quickness at seeing through a false argument were all indispensible.

I should also like to thank Mary Foley, Mary McGrath, David Maguire and Helen Mulcahy (from the UCC Library) for efficient and cheerful help beyond the call of duty. Catherine Phelan handled a huge volume of material with characteristic efficiency. I also thank Conleth Bradley SC, Michael Howard SC, James O'Reilly SC, Garrett Simons SC, (Professor) Gerry Whyte, as well as countless others for drawing attention to particular points. At Round Hall, Catherine Dolan, Frieda Donohue and Nicola Barrett showed endless ability, patience and forbearance in dealing with such a large project. I am hugely indebted to them

And I am especially grateful to my spouse, Deirdre, for her love and support through the years and not least, for putting up with the intrusion into family life which a project of this kind necessarily entails.

As regards the changes made, after 2010, to the original volume, in creating the present book, it should be emphasised that these are entirely my work; Mr Justice Gerard Hogan having no hand, act or part in them. That said, it is appropriate to acknowledge that almost all of the text appeared, at some point, in the parent book. May I add that Mr Justice Hogan is an exceptional person in terms of ability, industry, generosity and commitment; no-one ever had a better colleague. And I am happy to find this view widely shared. For instance, Conleth Bradley SC remarks in the Preface to his distinguished (2000) book on Judicial Review: "I make one exception of not individually naming colleagues and associates to whom I offer a collective thank-you ... Gerard Hogan S.C. has been and remains an enormously influential figure in the development of Irish public law."

David Gwynn Morgan
St David's Day, March 1, 2012

TABLE OF CONTENTS

TABLE OF CASES

IRELAND

Duff v Dunne [2004] IEHC 151; unreported, High Court, July 6, 2004 .... 10–73n
Duff v Mangan [1994] 1 I.L.R.M. 91 .... 16–40n
Duff v Minister for Agriculture [1997] 2 I.R. 22 .... 15–138n, 15–141, 15–161, 18–04n,
                                                18–25n, 18–47, 18–67, 18–72n, 19–50n, 20–44n
Duggan v An Taoiseach [1989] I.L.R.M. 710 .... 16–85n, 16–92, 19–52n
Dumbrell v Governor of Mountjoy, unreported, Supreme Court, December 2, 1993 .... 15–72n
Dundalk Town Council v Lawlor [2005] IEHC 73; [2005] 2 I.L.R.M. 106 5–146
Dunleavy v Dún Laoghaire Rathdown County Council [2005] IEHC 381 19–21, 19–44n, 19–66
Dunne v Donohoe [2002] IESC 35; [2002] 2 I.R. 533;
      [2002] 2 I.L.R.M. 200 ....7–08n, 11–61, 14–133n, 15–138
Dunne v Minister for Environment, Heritage and Local Government (No. 1) [2006] IESC 49;
      [2007] 1 I.R. 194; [2007] 1 I.L.R.M. 264 ....2–11n, 2–19, 2–21, 2–23, 16–101n
Dunne v Minister for Environment (No. 2) [2007] IESC 60;
      [2008] 1 I.R. 775 .... 16–33, 16–36, 16–37
Dunne v Minister for Fisheries and Forestry
      [1984] I.R. 230 .... 11–30n, 11–34n, 11–36n, 11–37n, 11–44n
Dunne Ltd v Dublin County Council [1974] I.R. 45 .... 11–91n
Dunnes Stores Ireland Co. Ltd v Houlihan [2003] IEHC 619 .... 11–49n
Dunnes Stores v Maloney [1999] 3 I.R. 542; [1999] 1 I.L.R.M. 119 .... 14–168, 15–06n
Dunnes Stores v Ryan [2002] 2 I.R. 60 .... 15–06n
Dunraven Estates Ltd v Commissioners of Public Works [1974] I.R. 113 .... 10–42, 11–80
DVTS v Minister for Justice, Equality and Law Reform [2007] IEHC 305;
      unreported, High Court, July 4, 2007 .... 10–86n

East Donegal Co–Operative Livestock Marts Ltd v Attorney General
      [1970] I.R. 317 .... 2–49n, 2–56n, 7–08, 7–46, 7–48, 7–50, 7–52, 10–32n, 10–90,
                      14–133n, 14–179n, 15–01n, 15–39, 15–42, 15–138n, 15–157n, 16–112, 16–126
East Wicklow Conservation Community Ltd v Wicklow County Council
      [1997] 2 I.L.R.M. 72 .... 5–46n
Eastern Health Board v Farrell [2000] 1 I.L.R.M. 446 (HC); [2001] IESC 96;
      [2001] 4 I.R. 627 10–12
Eastern Health Board v Fitness to Practice Committee [1998] 3 I.R. 399 ... 6–121, 6–125, 6–126
Eastern Health Board v MK [1999] 2 I.R. 99 .... 20–10n
Easy Readers Ltd v Bord na Radharchmhastori [2003] IEHC 67 .... 17–03n
Ebonwood Ltd v Meath County Council [2004] 3 I.R. 34; [2004] 1 I.L.R.M. 305 5–118
Edobar v Ryan [2005] 2 I.L.R.M. 113 .... 6–72n
Edobor v Refugee Appeals Tribunal [2005] IESC 15; [2006] 2 I.R. 11 10–32
Efe v Minister for Justice, Equality and Law Reform
      [2011] 2 I.L.R.M. 411 ....10–92, 15–09n, 15–69, 15–72, 15–112n, 15–113
Egan v Minister for Defence, unreported, High Court, Barr J.,
      November 24, 1988 .... 16–09n, 19–37, 19–66
Eircell v Leitrim County Council [2000] 1 I.R. 479 ....14–11n, 14–142n
Eircom Plc v Director of Telecommunications Regulation [2003] 1 I.L.R.M. 106 .... 16–32n
Electricity Supply Board v Gormley [1985] I.R. 129 .... 14–62, 16–100n, 18–31n, 18–33
Ellis v O'Dea [1990] I.L.R.M. 87 .... 15–26n
Elwyn (Cottons) Ltd v Master of the High Court [1989] I.R. 14 .... 16–06n
Emerald Meats Ltd v Minister for Agriculture and Food [1997] 2 I.L.R.M. 275 .... 18–68n
English v Health Service Executive [2008] IEHC 398 .... 7–01n
Eogan v University College Dublin [1996] 1 I.R. 390;
      [1996] 2 I.L.R.M. 302 .... 17–03n, 17–20, 17–26n, 19–31n, 19–43n, 19–66
EOK v DK (witness: immunity) [2001] 3 I.R. 568 .... 18–102n
EPI v Minister for Justice, Equality and Law Reform [2009] 2 I.R. 254 .... 13–75n
Esat Digifone v South Dublin County Council [2002] IEHC 173; [2002] 3 I.R. 585 .... 11–38n
Eviston v Director of Public Prosecutions [2002] 3 I.R. 260 (HC);
      [2003] 1 I.L.R.M. 178 (SC) 15–168n, 16–66n, 16–126n
Ezeani v Minister for Justice, Equality and Law Reform [2011] IESC 23 .... 14–02n

Fairleigh Ltd v Temple Bar Renewal Ltd [1999] 2 I.R. 508 .... 15–66n, 15–140
Fairyhouse Club Ltd v An Bord Pleanála, unreported, High Court,
      Finnegan J., July 18, 2001 .... 14–19n, 14–101n

NORTHERN IRELAND

GREAT BRITAIN

EUROPEAN

EUROPEAN COURT OF HUMAN RIGHTS

OTHER JURISDICTIONS

TABLE OF LEGISLATION

CONSTITUTIONAL PROVISIONS

STATUTES

Acts of the Parliament of Great Britain, Ireland and the United Kingdom (pre-1922)

Acts of the Irish Free State and Ireland (post-1922 Acts)

STATUTORY INSTRUMENTS

TREATIES OF THE EUROPEAN COMMUNITY/UNION

LEGISLATION OF THE EUROPEAN COMMUNITIES/EUROPEAN UNION

INTERNATIONAL TREATIES AND CONVENTIONS

CHAPTER 1

INTRODUCTION

A. FLAVOUR OF ADMINISTRATIVE LAW

1–01   Administrative law is conventionally defined as the law regulating the organisation, composition, functions and procedures of public authorities[1]; their impact on the citizen; and the restraints to which they are subject. By public authorities, we mean (to list the examples principally covered in this book): the Government in the sense—which is the one employed in Art.28 of the Constitution—of the 15 Ministers who are the central directorate of the executive; a Minister in his Department; and public bodies like the Property Registration Authority or RTÉ and local authorities.[2] There are other public bodies—such as the Universities; the Garda Síochána; or the Defence Forces—which there is no space to cover specifically here, apart from noticing that the general ideas and rules of administrative law apply to them. In addition, there are certain entities or associations, historically private, yet which over the past decade or so are increasingly coming under public control, which have always discharged public (or "quasi-public") functions; for example, professional associations, like the Medical Council. Such bodies have been characterised as "domestic governments" and it has accordingly seemed appropriate to the courts and legislature to extend to them, certain of the characteristic principles of administrative law, for example, the rules of constitutional justice, a point detailed at Chapter 17, Parts B and C.

1–02   Administrative law is clearly a public law subject, that is to say, its focus is relations between the individual and the state, in contrast with private law (for example, the law of contract or tort), which regulates relations mainly between private individuals. Classification of administrative law as public law raises the difficult question of the boundary and, be it said, the substantial overlap, with constitutional law. One point of distinction stems from the fact that administrative law focuses on the executive and the other two major organs (legislature and judicature) are important only so far as they impact on the executive—by contrast, constitutional law covers all three organs equally. The second point of distinction is that, generally speaking, matters of principle are fixed by constitutional law; whereas administrative law looks to questions of detail and to matters of function more than structure. Thirdly, constitutional law includes as a major component the

---

[1]   Of course large public companies may be as much in need of control by the law as public authorities. Companies are, in fact, controlled by company law and labour law and an interesting book remains to be written comparing these controls with those imposed by administrative law. For the present, see Ch.17 on The Scope of Public Law.

[2]   See Ch.5, Part A.

law of fundamental rights, i.e. those legal rights which are regarded as so essential to decent, dignified life as a human being that they are established by the Constitution and prevail over all other types of law. This source of higher law is augmented now by the European Convention on Human Rights and the law of the European Union. With administrative law, fundamental rights are less central. However, very often in cases involving the administrative actions of the executive the fundamental rights, established by these higher sources, have to be invoked. Thus, there is a substantial, if adventitious, connection and at various points[3] we shall note the fundamental rights as part of the controls upon administrative actions.

1–03 In the mid-nineteenth century, following the Industrial Revolution, and with the rise of political democracy, there was a vast increase in the activity of the executive and its intervention in the affairs of the citizen. This has taken various forms, including the regulation of land use and commercial transactions; the provision of social welfare benefits and free or subsidised health and education services; and the management of the economy by such measures as the control of prices and incomes, levying of taxes and paying grants or subsidies.

1–04 Since administrative law is the law regulating the administration of the executive arm of government, one might have expected such trends to be reflected in the development of administrative law as a coherent subject. Yet, the reality is that in the common law world, administrative law only came to be acknowledged and studied as a unified discipline[4] since (at the earliest in Britain) the end of the Second World War. There are at least three reasons for this, the first of which is historical and is common to Ireland and Britain. The parliamentary victory in the British Civil War in the seventeenth century led to the eradication of the central executive machinery built around the Privy Council. The organs which evolved to fill these gaps did so in a cramped, ad hoc way. It is to this historical factor that is owed such features of our system of administrative law as: the absence of the specialised administrative courts which exist on the continent; the distorting fiction that public law is simply a special case of private law; the crab-like growth of our system of judicial review, proceeding from the baseline of the ultra vires

---

[3] See, e.g. para.10–38.
[4] The first lectures on administrative law in Irish universities were given as indicated: TCD (1946, F. C. King); UCD (early 1950s, P. McGilligan); UCG (1975, J.M.G. Sweeney); UCC (1978, D. Gwynn Morgan); QUB (1953). For works on Irish administrative law (or aspects thereof), see: Stout, *Administrative Law in Ireland* (Dublin: IPA, 1985); Casey, "Ireland" (written in English) in Hegen (ed.), *Gesichte der Verwaltungsrecht wissenschaft in Europa* (Frankfurt am Main, 1982); Koekkoek, "Ierland" (written in Dutch) in Prakke and Kortmann (eds), *Het bestuursrecht van de landen der Europese Gemeenschappen* (Kluwer, 1986); Collins and O'Reilly, *Civil Proceedings and the State in Ireland* (Dublin: Round Hall Press, 1989); Hogan, "Judicial Review – The Law of the Republic of Ireland" in Hadfield (ed.), *Judicial Review: A Thematic Approach* (Dublin: Gill and Macmillan, 1995); Hogan, "Irland" in Schwarze (ed.), *Das Verwaltungsrecht unter europaischem Einfluss: Zur Konvergenz der mitgliedstaatlichen Verwaltungsrechtsordnungen in der Europaischen Union* (Baden-Baden, 1996); Bradley, *Judicial Review* (Dublin: Round Hall, 2000); Coffey, *Administrative Law* (Dublin: Round Hall, 2009); de Blacam, *Judicial Review* (Haywards Heath: Tottel, 2009); Delany, *Judicial Review of Administrative Action: A Comparative Analysis* (Dublin: Round Hall, 2009). For the administrative law of Northern Ireland, see Hadfield, "Judicial Review in Northern Ireland: A Primer" (1991) 42 N.I.L.Q. 332 and Maguire, "The Procedure for Judicial Review in Northern Ireland" in Hadfield (ed.), *Judicial Review: A Thematic Approach* (1995).

doctrine; the formal significance of the legislature in the control of governmental administration; and the late development of professionalism in the public service. At the local level too, the institutions of government were not tailor-made for their tasks. Before the nineteenth century, the principal institution was the amphibious justices of the peace, who also acted as local courts of law. When, as a result of the seventeenth century Civil War, the justices were released from the control of the Privy Council (exercised by way of the Court of the Star Chamber), they could only be called to account by the Court of King's Bench. It seemed natural simply to apply to the justices in their administrative role the same remedies as those which controlled them in their judicial duties. By another apparently natural development, the courts extended these remedies and, with them, the substantive law for the control of the justices' administrative action, so as to apply to all the other organs of the State, as these grew up.

1–05   The second factor was the enormous, ideological influence of the early twentieth-century scholar, Dicey. His principal tenet was that ministers and other state organs ought to be subject to the same law, administered by the same courts, as a private individual and that this ideal was achieved in the British system of law. Contrasted with this was the French institution of the *droit administratif* in which specialised tribunals applied law to the acts of the executive and, it was implied, gave the executive an easy ride. From such an outlook, it was a short step to the conclusion that a system of administrative law, which acknowledged the unique position of the state and systematically granted it special powers and subjected it to special controls, was anathema. It followed that to embark on—and possibly implicitly approve—a study of such elements of administrative law as there happened to be in British law was to court disaster.

1–06   The third reason why administrative law has been so slow to develop as a coherent, unified whole, is that the territory which it covers is so voluminous and diverse. The subject really consists of general principles, with the substantive details being contained in such subjects as: planning law; immigration law; housing and public health law; social welfare law; licensing law; revenue law; and economic law. Throughout this work, we shall be examining material which could be relocated in one or other of these categories. This is a feature which distinguishes administrative law from discrete subject-blocs like tort or criminal law, where a single book can cover more or less the whole area and where the overlap with neighbouring subjects is less significant. The result of this feature is that the most fruitful approach in explaining administrative law is to describe the leading principles and to observe their operation in specimen cases. A typical case could well involve law from its own substantive area, coupled with a general administrative law point.

1–07   Administrative law may be regarded as made up of two components: the instruments of government and the instruments of control. The instruments of government—ministers and departments, public bodies, local authorities—are, or should be, designed to enable administrators, working under the control, direct or indirect, of elected politicians, to take decisions and provide services which are in the best interests of the community. The powers of these agencies are delineated by the law, albeit a law which allows them a great deal of latitude. The law is administered by the instruments of control: the tribunals; the Ombudsman; and, most important of all, the courts, enforcing a bloc of law known as judicial review.

B. Two Distinctions

1–08   The major difficulty inherent in administrative law is the sheer diversity of the decisions, powers, functions, etc. (these words mean more or less the same) which it comprehends. Here are some examples of typical governmental decisions: a local authority's decision to build a concert hall or theatre under the Local Government Act 1960; the making of a statutory instrument regulating the procedure of a tribunal; the making of a development plan by a local planning authority; a decision whether to grant planning permission in respect of a particular building; assessment of capital gains following the sale of a piece of land; award of a social welfare benefit; allocation of a corporation house. In ordering these disparate functions and in understanding the controls which administrative law imposes on them, we shall be assisted by two sets of distinctions: first, policy and administration; and secondly, legislative and individual decisions.

Policy–administration

1–09   Put briefly, administration[5] assumes that there is already in existence a principle and that all the administrator has to do is to establish the facts and circumstances and then apply the principle. It is part of the essence of good administration that the principle must be fairly clear and precise so that, in any given situation, the result should be the same, whether it is administrator A or administrator B who has taken the decision. For, in its purest form, administration requires only a knowledge of the pre-existing principle and an appreciation of the facts to which it is being applied; it is an intellectual process involving little discretion. By contrast, policy-making is largely discretionary; the policy-maker must decide, as between two alternatives, the one which he considers best in the interest of the community. He must take into account all the relevant factors and which factors are relevant is, to a considerable extent, left to him. In doing this, the policy-maker will have to draw on his own values and, in light of this, it is no coincidence that the words policy and politics come from the same Greek root (*polis*, meaning city). For each word relates to choice in the affairs of the community and it is natural, in a democracy, that major policy questions should be taken by elected politicians (often on the advice of senior public servants), whether ministers or, at local government level, elected councillors. As Mendes-France observed: "To govern is to choose." According to the democratic ideal, one elected politician is chosen in preference to another politician just because it is his policy which finds favour with the electorate.

1–10   Applying the policy–administration dichotomy to the list of governmental functions given earlier, we can say that matters such as: building of a concert hall; making of procedural regulations; making of a development plan are policy matters, whereas the grant of planning permission; assessment of capital gains; award of a welfare benefit; and allocation of a corporation house are acts of administration. Indeed, the planning functions afford particularly neat illustrations

---

[5]   Administration is one of these awkward words which takes its meaning from the word to which it is opposed, i.e. in this Part, to "policy". Unfortunately for clarity, it can also be used in other senses as when it is opposed to legislation or when an administrative decision is contrasted with a quasi-judicial decision.

in that the development plan is the pre-existing standard on which the administrator bases his decision whether to grant permission for a specific development. The making of the development plan is policy and the determining of individual planning applications is administration. It must, of course, be admitted that such classifications overestimate the neatness of reality: policy and administration really represent the opposite poles of a spectrum and most decisions fall at some intermediate point along the range. It would, for instance, be plainly wrong to suppose that a planning officer deciding whether to grant planning permission for a small bungalow in an area zoned as "primarily agricultural" would not have to use some of his own discretion.

1–11 Clearly the question of whether a decision is one of policy or of administration will depend in part on the wording of the statute or other instrument creating the decision. For instance, the former s.5(1) of the Aliens Act 1935 provides that the Minister for Justice may, "if and whenever he thinks proper", expel an alien.[6] Plainly, this is a policy decision. However, the present formulation of this test, in the Immigration Act 1999 s.3(2), which is designed to cater for far more would-be immigrants than were anticipated in 1935, moves the law closer to the administrative end of the scale.[7] While still leaving considerable discretion to the Minister, the new law sets out the grounds on which the Minister's power may be exercised; for instance, that a person is serving or has served a term of imprisonment.

Legislative–individual decisions

1–12 The second major distinction in the field of governmental decision-making lies between legislative and individual decisions. A legislative decision affects a potentially unlimited category of persons or situations which share the specified common characteristics; whereas an individual decision is directed to, and affects only, some particular individual(s). It will be seen immediately that an Act of the Oireachtas is an example of a legislative decision. Nor is the Act the only example, for the meaning of "legislation" invoked here is wider than the artificially-restricted meaning imposed upon "law-making" in the context of Art.15.2.1°,[8] which provides that only the Oireachtas may "make laws for the State". The definition used here is intended to comprehend any rule; for instance, a statutory instrument or bye-law.

1–13 Before a legislative decision has any effect in a particular instance, an individual decision is necessary in order to "concretise", that is, apply the rule to the particular situation to which it is relevant. One way in which this may be done is by the application of a law by a court. But it often happens that law, especially public law, is applied not by a court but by an administrative agency and, of the list of examples given earlier, the grant of planning permission (local planning authority: county or city manager); the assessment of capital gains (the Revenue Commissioners); and the award of a social welfare benefit (deciding officer in the Department of Social Protection), are all instances of individual decisions taken by the administrative agency indicated in brackets.

---

[6] For control of a discretionary (policy) decision, see Ch.15, Parts A–C.

[7] The law had to be changed as a result of *Laurentiu v Minister for Justice, Equality and Law Reform* [1999] 4 I.R. 26; [2000] 1 I.L.R.M. 1: see S. Egan (1999) No.22 *Irish Current Law Statutes Annotated.*

[8] See further, Ch.2, Part B.

1–14 We can summarise the relationship between the two sets of distinctions by saying that a legislative decision is inevitably a policy decision. On the other hand, an individual decision will usually be nearer the administrative end of the spectrum in that it is the product of the application of some (more or less) precise standard—and examples of this were listed in the preceding paragraph. However, in some cases, an individual decision will be the direct result of the decision-maker's discretion and such individual policy decisions include, for example, the building of a concert hall; a public inquiry's decision to investigate a particular field; or the diplomatic recognition of a foreign government.

Application of the two sets of distinctions

1–15 The significance of these two types of classification lies in the part they have played in influencing the design of the organs and procedures of government administration and of the controls which are exercised over this administration. Much of the remainder of the book consists of illustrations of this observation. Thus, here we can only advert to a few examples of it and direct the reader to the place where they are amplified. For example, consider the design of governmental structures at the local government level: broadly speaking, the reserved functions, which are the preserve of the elected councillors, deal with policy matters; whereas the executive functions, which are vested in the top official, the county or city manager, consist of administrative acts. For historical reasons, the picture is not so clear when one examines the ministers and departments, though here, too, there is an approximate observation of the distinction.[9]

1–16 Where there are existing legal rules, the control exercised over the decision will be necessarily stricter. In the first place, as regards institutions of control, in this situation it happens that the legislature will be more likely to have established a tribunal to take the decision and/or to have created an appeal to a court in respect of the decision. Secondly, even where this has not been done, a court may intervene, by way of judicial review, on the ground of error of law. Policy decisions may, it is true, be reviewed by a court—but it is only in a very clear case that they will be struck down, and at an earlier stage in the development of administrative law, courts have been heard to say that they must leave policy questions to be dealt with through the agency of ministerial responsibility to the legislature. These results flow from the idea that elected persons or bodies take policy decisions, whilst courts customarily take decisions on the basis of pre-existing principles.

1–17 Reinforcing the trend noted in the previous paragraph is the fact that administrative decisions are always individual decisions. It is because individual decisions have a direct effect on individual rights that they are more stringently controlled than legislative decisions; for example, it is probable that a narrow category of decision must be taken by a minister personally rather than through his civil servants. Again, where the significant procedural safeguard of constitutional justice is concerned, we find that these rules are less likely to apply to policy than to administrative decisions and usually do not apply to legislation. Finally, the Ombudsman's jurisdiction is *formally* confined to "action[s] taken in the

---

[9]   See Ch.3, Part A.

performance of administrative functions",[10] thereby excluding legislative, though not other types of policy, decision.

C. THE POINT OF IT ALL

1–18   The title of this Part is intended to allude to a field of enquiry which is (largely) beyond the scope of this book; yet which it is necessary to mention, in order to identify the space within which the book is set. Because administrative law is the law governing the functioning of the executive organ of the state, its contours are shaped—much more than any other field of law—by the character of the state. Or, as the same thought has been put by a distinguished English writer[11]:

> "For some ... the main object of [administrative law] is to protect the individual rights. Others place greater emphasis upon rules that are designed to ensure that the administration effectively performs the tasks assigned to it. Yet others see the principal object of administrative law as ensuring governmental accountability and fostering participation by interested parties in the decision-making process.
>
> None of these are right or wrong in some absolute sense. All are however incomplete. An adequate understanding of the nature and purpose of administrative law requires us to probe further into the way in which our society is ordered. It requires the articulation of the type of democratic society in which we live and some vision of the political theory which that society espouses. The role of more particular legal topics that constitute administrative law, such as natural justice and judicial review, can only be adequately assessed within such a framework."

1–19   The second paragraph of this quotation may be briefly teased out in various ways. In the first place, we may dismiss as archaic the "public philosophy" devised by the British in the nineteenth century, which aimed at enhancing the collective well-being, because this would now be regarded as transforming the state into an "elective dictatorship". The effect of this would be to leave the executive organ largely free from control during the four or five-year period between general elections. Plainly, in an era suspicious of authority and in which the state is servicing a highly individualistic society, this is no longer acceptable. Next, assuming that administrative organs must be controlled, many questions arise and, it should be stressed, may arise at either the policy-making or policy-delivery stage. First, what values or policies are to underpin the system of control? The candidates include the following:

- participation in the design of laws and policies by those affected by them, however widely or narrowly defined;
- openness and accessibility of the administrative system to citizens, including certainty and precision in the articulation of administrative decisions;

---

[10]   Ombudsman Act 1980 s.4(2). The assertions made in this and the preceding paragraph are substantiated in the appropriate Chapters.

[11]   Craig, *Administrative Law*, 6th edn (London: Sweet and Maxwell, 2008), para.1–001.

- respect for fair procedure and the human rights of those affected by administrative decisions;
- accountability and, if a mistake is made, sanctions against the responsible public representatives or officials;
- efficiency, economy and promptness in the delivery of public services and generally protecting the community interest.

Obvious questions arise as to whether there is any tension among these values and, if so, where an appropriate balance might be struck in the many different contexts occurring in public administration.

1–20   Next, once the values and objectives have been settled, by what enforcement machinery are they to be implemented? At present, the institutional models in operation include the following: public representatives; courts; internal grievance systems; tribunals or regulators; public inquiries; and Ombudsmen. In practice, probably making the appropriate choice at this stage is likely to matter as much as the preference adopted in regard to the previous question, about substantive policies and values. Finally, are the enforcement agencies themselves to be controlled and, if so, how: "Who should guard the guardians?" (*Quis custodies custodiet?*).

1–21   These questions have been pitched at a high level of generality, so that no reference has been made to the various substantive fields (identified at para. 1–06) of which administrative law may be a partner. However, the answer to these questions will depend on which of the substantive fields is under consideration. Both the values engaged and the institution by which they are enforced will vary according to whether the substantive field is: land use planning; trade—or professional— licensing; welfare benefits; tax liability; citizenship, immigration or refugees.

1–22   Unfortunately, despite these queries and choices, there has been very little discussion of the character of the Irish State or, consequently, the values underlying its administrative law. This reticence has been true of both the legislature and the courts, each of which are significant players in determining the nature and shape of administrative law. Since neither has been very articulate about its values and policies—which often are somewhat divergent from each other—small wonder that there has been no effective dialogue.

1–23   Further, it is only recently the academic community has started to take an interest in this field.[12] The present work too does not, primarily, delve into the character of the state and fundamental questions surrounding it; though sometimes and subterraneously there are glimpses of such queries. A particular obstacle to a discussion lies in the dominance of the traditional separation of powers doctrine in the Constitution and the great emphasis placed on it by judicial exegesis: "The doctrine has failed to justify or explain the emergence of an interventionist administrative State, in which public power is (in reality) exercised on a

---

[12]   Though, for green shoots in this area, see, for instance: Murphy and Twomey, *Ireland's Evolving Constitution 1937–1997* (Oxford: Hart Publishing, 1998); Gwynn Morgan, *A Judgment Too Far? Judicial Activism and the Constitution* (Cork University Press, 2001); Whyte, *Social Inclusion and the Legal System* (Dublin: IPA, 2002); and Carolan and Doyle (eds), *The Irish Constitution: Governance and Values* (Dublin: Thomson Round Hall, 2008).

decentralised and largely discretionary basis."[13] The reason is that the traditional doctrine (without embarrassment) traces its lineage back to the time of Aristotle, in fifth century BC Athens; whereas the interventionist administrative state is less than two centuries old. As a result, the conventional constitutional approach has been to try to explain away the administrative state rather than to devise a sensible and realistic theory to accommodate it. An incidental pedagogical point is that it is unfortunate that the separation of powers in usually covered in one bloc of law (constitutional law); with judicial review of administrative action in a discrete area (administrative law). They need to be seen as a unity and evaluated by reference to their joint success, or otherwise, in tackling such issues as: discretion-arbitrariness in public administration; fair procedure; accountability and conflict of interest (the latter being a big subject which is calling out for book length treatment).

1–24 A sceptic might respond to these theoretical questions by asking whether there is a sufficiently distinctive Irish cast to such issues to warrant a discussion which will only attract a minority of scholars (given that so many will be focusing on more popular fields like human rights). A practical rejoinder to such a query would be to point to a significant contemporary example of where the discussion we did not have would have been of practical use. This is the way in which the gallop of the Celtic Tiger swept us into the present inflation of over 400 public bodies, with next to no thought about this change to our institutional architecture. A not unrelated question is the extent to which the law on judicial review contributed to the spectacular failure of regulation in the banking, commercial and planning area, which came to light in the financial crisis of 2008–2009. Leaving aside possible philosophical objections and issues relating to the separation of powers, one might also raise the question, to what extent, for example, could it be said that the courts' omission actively to review actions or inactions of the regulatory authorities contributed to the errors which led to the crisis? For example, the question arises whether, assuming that an appropriate case had been brought before them, the courts either could or should have done anything to ameliorate a situation in which planning permission was granted too freely for speculative development, a factor which indirectly contributed to economic collapse? One recent post mortem[14] remarks:

> "... there has been a catastrophic failure of the planning system ... Planning should provide checks and balances to the excesses of development and Act, for the common good, even if that means taking unpopular decisions. However, during the Celtic Tiger period, a laissez faire approach to planning predominated at all levels of governance ... As a result not only was there an unsustainable growth in property prices, but this was accompanied by a property building frenzy ...".

1–25 This document goes on to refer to "charges of localism, cronyism and clientism". Undoubtedly, a good part of the cause for the crisis which has overtaken the country rests on bad policy, both at formation and application level. This book is only very indirectly concerned with policy, but it has a good deal to say about

---

[13] Carolan, *The New Separation of Powers* (Oxford: OUP, 2009), p.253.
[14] Kitchin et al, *A Haunted Landscape: Housing and Ghost Estates in Post Celtic Tiger Ireland* (National Institute for Regional and Spatial Analysis, 2010), p.2. For the Ombudsman's attempt at improvement regarding too free grant of planning permission, see paras 9–38 to 9–39.

the design, procedure and composition of the public institutions which make and/ or apply policy, including, critically, the regulation of private enterprise. It also considers the controls on these bodies and their staff. No one would suggest that flaws in the law are the only factors underlying this failure. However, equally, given the increasing influence of legal controls in modern Ireland, it must be true that the performance of the law had a role in this failure and that, correspondingly, an improvement is necessary to prevent a recurrence. For the moment, however, we must leave these difficult questions for others to ponder, as we begin our account of what our administrative law currently is and not what it might or should be.

CHAPTER 2

SOURCES OF ADMINISTRATIVE LAW

A. THE RULE OF LAW AND ADMINISTRATIVE LAW

2–01 The twin concepts of the rule of law[1] and the separation of powers are the fundamental principles underlying Irish administrative law.[2] Both the structure of our system of government and the basis of judicial review of administrative action are founded on these principles. Because of their fundamental character, a comprehensive analysis of these constitutional doctrines more properly belongs to a textbook on constitutional law. However, some of the major aspects of these principles may be sketched here and other more detailed instances of their practical impact will be mentioned throughout this book.[3] At the heart of the rule of law[4] there are four interrelated notions.

(1) Principle of legality

2–02 By this principle, "every executive or administrative act which affects legal rights, interests or legitimate expectations must be legally justified".[5] And:

"Where the rule of law governs relations between government and citizens,

---

[1] For an excellent historical and contemporary treatment, see Bingham, "The Rule of Law" (London: Penguin, 2011). See also Jowell, "The Rule of Law and its Underlying Values" in Jowell and Oliver (eds), *The Changing Constitution*, 6th edn (Oxford: OUP, 2007).

[2] The centrality of the rule of law was also affirmed in *A v Governor of Arbour Hill Prison* [2006] IESC 45; [2006] 4 I.R. 88 at 127 and described as a "cornerstone of the Irish legal system" in *Maguire v Ardagh* [2002] IESC 21; [2002] 1 I.R. 385 at 567.

[3] See especially, paras 2–14 to 2–33.

[4] The Supreme Court has described the rule of law as having three components: "(a) everyone is subject to the law, (b) the law must be public and precise, and, (c) the law must be enforced by some independent body, principally the court system"; *Maguire v Ardagh* [2002] IESC 21; [2002] 1 I.R. 385 at 567. When these three ideas are joined by the principle of legality, the basic conception of the rule of law is complete. For grander theories of the rule of law see, e.g. Allan, *Constitutional Justice: a Liberal Theory of the Rule of Law* (Oxford: OUP, 2001) and Dyzenhaus, *The Constitution of Law: Legality in a Time of Emergency* (Cambridge: Cambridge University Press, 2006).

[5] *Browne v Attorney General* [2002] IEHC 47 per Kearns J.

an individual person or company will reasonably expect that decisions purporting to be made under governmental authority will be clothed with the necessary legislative powers."[6]

2–03   The main way in which this principle is implemented is the ultra vires doctrine, elaborated below.[7] By this precept, not only must the administrative authority concerned show that it possesses legal authority by reference to the wording of the statute, but in addition, the courts will review the exercise of discretionary power according to settled principles of reasonableness, proper motives and compliance with constitutional justice.[8]

(2) Everyone, including the Government and its servants, is subject to the law

2–04   Smyth J. put the point stridently in *Flood v Lawlor*:

"Respect for the rule of law is enjoined on all citizens and persons within the State, *a fortiori* on all who seek to promulgate, interpret or enforce the law. 'Tis a trite saying that 'no one, no matter how high, is above the Law,' but like many a platitude its correlative profundity is oft times lost in its superficial truth. Equality before the law is the rightful expectation of all who come before the courts. In the matter of the obligation of citizens and persons within the state to observe those orders applicable to them, there are no Untouchables."[9]

2–05   This principle received graphic affirmation in cases such as: *Macauley v Minister for Posts and Telegraphs*[10] (where a statutory provision requiring the prior permission, or *fiat*, of the Attorney General before an action could be taken against a Minister of State was found to be unconstitutional); *Byrne v Ireland*[11] (holding that the former Crown immunity from suit had not survived the enactment of the Constitution); and *Howard v Commissioners of Public Works*[12] (holding that the common law rule whereby the State was presumed not to be bound by the application of statute had not survived the enactment of the Constitution).

(3) Legality determined by independent judges

2–06   The legality of executive or administrative acts (and "the proper balance to be struck between [fundamental] rights and interests")[13] is to be determined by judges who are independent of the Government: "An independent judiciary guarantees that the organs of the state conduct themselves in accordance with

---

6   *Albatros Feeds v Minister for Agriculture and Food* [2006] IESC 52; [2007] 1 I.R. 221 at 233 per Fennelly J. For an example of reasoning inspired by the principle of legality, see Denham J.'s dissenting judgment in *DPP v Fagan* [1994] 2 I.R. 265. Cf. *Bode (A Minor) v Minister for Justice* [2007] IESC 62.
7   See Ch.10, Parts A to D.
8   See below, Chs 14 and 15.
9   [2001] IEHC 553.
10   [1966] I.R. 345.
11   [1972] I.R. 241.
12   [1994] 1 I.R. 101.
13   *Mahon v Keena and Kennedy* [2007] IEHC 348.

the rule of law."[14] The principle of judicial independence is enshrined in Art.34.1 of the Constitution,[15] and the courts have always jealously safeguarded their powers to review administrative action. Thus, legislative attempts to prevent—or even altogether to curb—review of administrative action have been viewed with disfavour by the judiciary:

> "It would be contrary to the very notion of a state founded on the rule of law, as this state is, and one in which, pursuant to Article 34 justice is administered in courts established by law, if all persons within this jurisdiction, including non-nationals, did not, in principle, have a constitutional right of access to the courts to enforce their legal rights ... It may be that in certain circumstances a right of access to the courts of non-nationals may be subject to conditions or limitations that would not apply to citizens. However, where the state or state authorities make decisions which are legally binding on, and addressed directly to, a particular individual within the jurisdiction, whether a citizen or non-citizen, such decisions must be taken in accordance with the law and the Constitution. It follows that the individual legally bound by such a decision must have access to the courts to challenge its validity. Otherwise the obligation on the state to act lawfully and constitutionally would be ineffective."[16]

(4) Law is public and precise

2–07   The law must be public and precise, so that it is ascertainable and its operation predictable:

> "Certainty of legal principle is the opposite end of the spectrum to the arbitrary decision making that characterises a totalitarian society. A judge, tribunal, or quasi-judicial tribunal, cannot divert from its duty to discover the law and then to apply it. The law cannot be made up. It must be applied whether it is attractive or unattractive; subject only to the power of the Superior Courts to declare a law unconstitutional as a last resort ...".[17]

---

[14]   *Curtin v Dáil Éireann* [2006] IEHC 14; [2006] 2 I.R. 556 at 617. See also, *DPP v Independent Newspapers* [2003] IEHC 624; [2003] 2 I.R. 367 at 378. In *White v Dublin City Council* [2004] IESC 35; [2004] 1 I.R. 545 at 573, the Supreme Court felt it "inherent in the principle of respect for the rule of law that citizens should have the right to challenge the legality of decisions, made under public law, by administrative bodies". See also, the remarks of Denham J. in *CK v JK* [2004] IESC 21; [2004] 1 I.R. 224 at 250: "In a society based on the rule of law it would certainly be a major gap in its fabric if persons who have been wronged ... were to be left without remedy" and in *Bula Ltd (In Receivership) v Crowley* [2003] IESC 28; [2003] 2 I.R. 430 at 465 per Barr J.

[15]   *JM Kelly: The Irish Constitution*, 4th edn (Dublin: Lexis Nexis Butterworths, 2003), pp.663–728. See generally, *Buckley v Attorney General* [1950] I.R. 67; *Re Haughey* [1971] I.R. 217; *State (McEldowney) v Kelleher* [1983] I.R. 289; and *Curtin v Dáil Éireann* [2006] IESC 14; [2006] 2 I.R. 556.

[16]   *In re Art.26 and the Illegal Immigrants (Trafficking) Bill 1999* [2000] 2 I.R. 360 at 385 per Keane C.J. But while the Oireachtas may regulate the right of access to the courts for legitimate reasons and on proportionate grounds, it may not confine the grounds of challenge to an administrative decision affecting constitutional rights simply to those of bad faith or want of reasonable care: see *Blehein v Minister for Health and Children* [2008] IESC 40; [2009] 1 I.R. 275 (holding s.260 of the Mental Treatment Act 1961 to be unconstitutional).

[17]   *Galway Mayo Institute of Technology v Employment Appeals Tribunal* [2007] IEHC 210 per

2–08   This principle allows the citizen to arrange his or her behaviour to conform to the law. It underlies a number of important rules of statutory construction such as: the presumption against retrospectivity; the principle that taxing statutes must be strictly construed; the presumption against unclear changes in the law; and the rule against excessive delegation of power by the legislature.[18]

B. Separation of Powers and Delegated Legislation

2–09   Article 6 of the Constitution assumes that the powers of government are of three types: legislative, executive and judicial. Article 6 does not in terms prescribe a separation of powers, but the effect of other constitutional provisions—most notably, Arts 15, 28 and 34—is to "entrench the different arms of government in varying degrees and prescribe their sovereignty in their own areas, without, however, hermetically insulating the different powers from one another in all respects".[19] As this quotation indicates, the distribution of powers is, however, an imperfect one. The central exception, indeed, constitutes the main feature of our governmental system, namely that the fused legislature–executive and the strength of the party whip system mean that the Oireachtas is almost completely under the control of the government of the day. It is only the judiciary which enjoys a secure position vis-à-vis the other branches of government. This is one of the many points where the separation of powers and the rule of law coincide.

2–10   Four aspects of the separation of powers are of particular importance for administrative law. These concern: delegated legislation (Art.15.2.1°); ouster and preclusive clauses; tribunals and whether they fall foul of Arts 34.1 and 37 (which collectively forbid the Oireachtas to vest judicial functions in bodies other than courts, save only where the functions are of a limited kind); and executive privilege.

2–11   All but the first of these matters is examined elsewhere[20]. Accordingly, it remains to consider here the provisions of Art.15.2.1° and its impact on delegated legislation.[21] While Art.15.2.1° vests the Oireachtas with exclusive power of legislation, it is nevertheless permissible for the Oireachtas to delegate power to make regulations which will give effect to the principles and policies contained in the parent Act. The question therefore is whether the parent Act has actually

---

Charleton J. For criticism of excessive reliance by administrators on non-statutory rules whose existence "is known only to a handful of officials and specialists" and which are not "readily available to the public, see the comments of Costello P. in *McCann v Minister for Education* [1997] 1 I.L.R.M. 1.

[18]   Each of these principles is treated in Ch.10 Part B.

[19]   *JM Kelly: The Irish Constitution*, 4th edn (Dublin: Lexis Nexis Butterworths, 2003), pp.108–140. See, too, Gwynn Morgan, *The Separation of Powers in the Irish Constitution* (Dublin: Round Hall Sweet & Maxwell, 1997), *passim*.

[20]   See generally, paras 11–67 to 11–83 (ouster clauses); and paras 6–47 to 6–58 (Arts 34 and 37); and *JM Kelly: The Irish Constitution* (2003), paras [6.1.136]–[156] (executive privilege).

[21]   For a theoretical discussion see Carolan, "Democratic Control or 'High-Sounding Hocus Pocus'? – a Public Choice Analysis of the Non-Delegation Doctrine" (2007) 29 D.U.L.J. 111.

sanctioned the delegation of a power which goes beyond the mere giving effect to its principles and policies.[22]

2–12   In the modern era, two lines of cases have developed under Art.15.2.1°. The first relates to the extent of permissible delegations of legislative power, by reference to the "principles and policies" test; the other to so-called "Henry VIII" clauses, which purport to permit a provision of primary legislation to be modified by executive diktat.[23]

Principles and policies test

2–13   The classic test for a permissible delegation of power was laid down by the Supreme Court in *Cityview Press Ltd v An Comhairle Oiliúna*.[24] Rejecting a challenge to provisions of the Industrial Training Act 1967, which gave the respondents the power to fix the amount of a levy to be collected from industrial enterprises for the purpose of training apprentices, O'Higgins C.J. held that the regulation would be valid if it were: "... a mere giving effect to principles and policies which are contained in the statute itself."[25]

2–14   It appeared briefly as if the principles and policies test laid down in *Cityview* might prove to have far-reaching consequences for legislative drafting. To take just one recent case, in *Laurentiu v Minister for Justice*,[26] the Supreme Court invalidated s.5(1)(e) of the Aliens Act 1935 (and art.13 of the Aliens Order made thereunder), on the basis that the Oireachtas in delegating to the executive the power to regulate immigration, had failed to specify any criteria by which the Minister might fulfil his role of deporting aliens. The impugned section allowed the Minister to "make provision for the exclusion or the deportation and exclusion of such aliens from Saorstát Éireann and provide for and authorise the making by the Minister of orders for that purpose". The court took the view, however, that no principle or policy had been specified in the provision. A remarkable feature of its decision was that the court did not limit itself to holding that the regulations in question were ultra vires; rather, the provision of the parent legislation itself was

---

[22]   The case law on this significant provision includes: *Pigs Marketing Board v Donnelly* [1939] I.R. 413. See also, *National Union of Railwaymen v Sullivan* [1947] I.R. 77; *de Búrca v Attorney General* [1976] I.R. 38; *State (Devine) v Larkin* [1977] I.R. 24; *State (Gilliland) v Governor of Mountjoy Prison* [1987] I.R. 201; *McDaid v Sheehy* [1991] 1 I.R. 1; *Laurentiu v Minister for Justice* [1999] IESC 47; [1999] 4 I.R. 26; *In re Art.26 and the Planning and Development Bill 1999* [2000] 2 I.R. 320; *Leontjava v DPP* [2004] IESC 37; [2004] 1 I.R. 591; *In re Art.26 and the Health (Amendment) (No.2) Bill 2004* [2005] IESC 7; [2005] 1 I.R. 105; *Dunne v Minister for the Environment, Heritage and Local Government* [2006] IESC 49; [2007] 1 I.R. 194; *Clarke v South Dublin County Council* [2008] IEHC 84. See also, *JM Kelly: The Irish Constitution* (2003), pp.234–252 and Gwynn Morgan, *The Separation of Powers* (1997), Ch.11.

[23]   The derivation of the name lies in the fact that Henry VIII was regarded as the personation of executive autocracy. See Barber and Young, "The Rise of Henry VIII Clauses and the Implications for Sovereignty" [2003] P.L. 112; Maddox, "The Legality of Henry VIII Clauses" (2004) 9(5) B.R. 188; Marshall, "Metric Measures and Martyrdom by Henry VIII Clause" (2002) 118 L.Q.R. 493.

[24]   [1980] I.R. 381.

[25]   [1980] I.R. 381 at 399.

[26]   [1999] IESC 47; [1999] 4 I.R. 26.

held to be unconstitutional. Not even the presumption of constitutionality could intervene to save it.

2–15   However, *Laurentiu* was distinguished by the Supreme Court in *Leontjava v Director of Public Prosecutions*.[27] The relevant part of this case concerned the validity of the Aliens Order 1946, as amended. In the first instance art.15 of the 1946 Order required foreign nationals to produce identity documents on request by State officials. Keane C.J. distinguished *Laurentiu* on the basis that: "[t]he policy enunciated is plain: the desirability of regulating the registration, change of abode, travelling, employment and occupation of aliens while in the State and the further desirability of regulating 'other like matters.'" Here, the legislature, far from abdicating its responsibility, had specified "the matters which it considered required regulation". It was perfectly permissible, then, for the legislature to permit the Minister "to put in place specific regulatory provisions".[28]

2–16   Article 15.2.1 may be regarded as the constitutional form of control over excessive delegated authority. The other type of control is the common law notion of ultra vires, dealt with more fully elsewhere,[29] and the second argument in *Leontjava* drew on this principle. The Aliens Order allowed an immigration officer to limit the amount of time a foreign national granted leave to land might remain in the State. The ostensible authority for the regulations was s.5(1) of the Aliens Act 1935, which in subss.(b) and (d) permitted the Minister to impose conditions in respect of landing in or entering, or leaving the state. Keane C.J. held as to the limitation of time, that the regulation was ultra vires the parent Act because there was "no indication of any intention on the part of the legislature to impose conditions requiring aliens to leave on the expiration of specified time or to confer on immigration officers powers of the kind actually granted by Article 5(6)".[30]

2–17   This is not to say that the principles and policies test does not have any teeth left. In *Delargy v Minister for the Environment*,[31] the primary legislation was the Road Traffic Act 1961 s.56(1) which made motor insurance a mandatory requirement for those operating motor vehicles. The obligation did not extend to "exempted persons". This term was defined in s.65 of the Act, which also permitted the Minister to specify certain classes of vehicle to which compulsory insurance cover would attach. By virtue of the regulations promulgated under s.65, motorbike

---

27   [2004] IESC 37; [2004] 1 I.R. 591. See generally, Fanning, "Reflecting on the Legislative Process Following Leontjava v DPP" (2004) 39 Ir. Jur. 386. For another case in which it was held that sufficiently clear policies and principles were present in the Statute, see *Cronin v Competition Authority* [1998] 1 I.R. 265.

28   [2004] 1 I.R. 591 at 624.

29   See Ch.10, Parts A to D.

30   Moreover, it was suggested that even if such an intention was present, expressly or implicitly, the Minister did not have the authority to "re-delegate" the power on to an immigration officer "[e]ven if s.5(1)(b) could be read as conferring such a power, either expressly or by implication, there is no indication of any intention on the part of the legislature to confer the power on any person other than the Minister, *e.g.*, an immigration officer": [2004] 1 I.R. 591 at 622. There is no explanation as to why this is the case. The leading English authority on the point, *R. v Secretary of State for the Home Department, Ex p. Oladehinde* [1991] 1 A.C. 254 at 302–304, suggests that quite extensive powers can be delegated by the minister in immigration matters, as long as the officials to whom the powers are delegated are of an appropriate rank and the exercise of the powers does not conflict with their other statutory duties.

31   [2005] IEHC 94.

pillion passengers, such as the applicant, were excluded from compulsory insurance cover. However, the parent Act was vague as to the appropriate principle to guide the promulgation of regulations:

> "The legislature in the present case permits the Minister to make a distinction between various classes of vehicles but does not provide any guidance whatsoever as to the principle upon which the Minister is to draw that distinction. The Minister has been given the power to introduce a provision which makes a difference between a case where one person injured by the negligence of another without the means to satisfy a judgment, can be compensated and a case where a person similarly injured with the same level of fault on the part of a similarly situated defendant cannot be so compensated … What the Minister has done is not merely regulatory or administrative only but is an attempt to arbitrarily restrict cover to a category of otherwise insured passengers."

2–18   The regulations were held to be ultra vires and Murphy J. also invalidated the regulations by reference to Art.40 of the Constitution. Indeed, one might query whether Murphy J.'s real difficulty with the regulations was the arbitrary distinction drawn within them, rather than the absence of any guiding principle in the parent Act. Arguably this is a case of Art.15.2.1° being (wrongly) used to invalidate delegated legislation which was objectionable for reasons unrelated to the vagueness of the primary legislation.

Discretion and legislative power

2–19   Before going on to "Henry VIII clauses", we should note *Dunne v Minister for Environment, Heritage and Local Government (No.1)*[32] which draws a distinction between the exercise of discretionary power and delegation of legislative power. This case concerned a challenge on Article 15.2.1° grounds to the constitutionality of s.8 of the National Monuments (Amendment) Act 2004. Section 8 provided that the consent of the Minister would not be required to carry out an upgrade of the M50 motorway that affected a national monument, and, further, that any such works would be carried out on the directions of the Minister. In considering whether to issue directions, the Minister is "not restricted to archaeological considerations but he is entitled to consider the public interest" even though damage to a national monument might result. Further, while the Minister could have regard to, inter alia, "the preservation, protection or maintenance of the archaeological, architectural, historical or other cultural heritage or amenities of, or associated with the national monument", he could also take into account "any social or economic benefit that would accrue to the State or region or immediate area in which the national monument is situated as a result of the carrying out of the road development", amongst other considerations.

2–20   The Minister made directions under s.8 with regard to the Carrickmines Castle archaeological site. The plaintiff argued that, as s.8(2)(a) did not confine the Minister to a consideration of archaeological issues but allowed him to take into account the public interest, the parent section provided no principle or policy to

---

[32]   [2006] IESC 49; [2007] 1 I.R. 194.

guide the Minister in balancing the public interest. This contention was, however, rejected by the Supreme Court, since in the words of Murray C.J.:

> "The Court is satisfied that section 8 … does not give rise to delegated legislation at all. Rather, the section is concerned with the making of an administrative decision which consists of the giving of directions. This is an entirely different legal concept as the exercise of a statutorily conferred discretion is not governed by the provisions of Article 15 of the Constitution, but is instead subject to the requirements of administrative law. In that regard, the exercise of those powers by the Minister is subject to the necessarily implied constitutional limitation of jurisdiction in all decision- making which affects rights or duties, namely, the decision maker must not flagrantly reject or disregard fundamental reason or common sense in reaching his decision … Thus understood, the exercise by the Minister of his powers under section 8 is a discretion which is open to challenge by way of judicial review proceedings in the ordinary way."[33]

2–21   Similarly, in two other recent cases the Supreme Court adjudged a delegation to have fallen on the discretion, rather than the legislative, side of the line.[34] But a potential problem with the *Dunne* formulation is that it is over-reliant on a distinction between legislation and discretion. The essence of the matter is surely not the logical distinction between secondary legislation and a one-off exercise of discretion (which distinction smacks of the worst excesses of the separation of powers): an exercise of discretion, for example, the establishment or location of a motorway or hospital, may make at least as great an impact on the lives of citizens as secondary legislation. Accordingly, even if, for historical reasons, the blocs of law involved are different, the objective should be the same in each case, namely that the decision-maker takes a rational, principled, approach. The use of the discretion–legislation distinction may be unhelpful inasmuch as it clouds the proper issue of discussion, which is whether the scope of the delegation is excessive and whether the decision-maker is sufficiently constrained by principle. In any event, notwithstanding the emphasis on the distinction, the presence of principles and policies in the legislation seems still to have been central to the reasoning in *Dunne*. However, *Dunne* and the other cases which drew on the distinction certainly indicate a judicial reluctance to wield Art.15.2.1° aggressively.

Henry VIII clauses

2–22   In *Cooke v Walsh*[35] and *Harvey v Minister for Social Welfare*,[36] the Supreme Court addressed the problem of "Henry VIII" clauses.[37] In both cases, the court

---

[33]   [2006] IESC 49; [2007] 1 I.R. 194 at 209. As an alternative basis for its decision, as to the *Cityview* claim, the court identified quite detailed principles and policies in the legislation.

[34]   *In re Art.26 and the Health (Amendment) (No.2) Bill 2004* [2005] IESC 7; [2005] 1 I.R. 105 at 168–172; *Casey v Minister for Arts, Heritage and the Gaeltacht* [2004] IESC 14; [2004] 1 I.R. 402 at 421–422.

[35]   [1984] I.R. 71. See also, *Lovett v Minister for Education* [1997] 1 I.L.R.M. 89 and Barron J. in *O'Connell v Ireland* [1996] 1 I.L.R.M. 187.

[36]   [1990] 2 I.R. 232.

[37]   See generally, "The Legality of Henry VIII Clauses" (2004) 9(5) B.R. 188; Cousins, "Overlapping Benefits: the Rise and Fall of Legislative Control" (1992) 14 D.U.L.J. 193. See also, *McDaid v Sheehy* [1991] 1 I.R. 1 and Hogan, "A Note on the Imposition of Duties

employed the presumption of constitutionality to save the offending parent sections in the principal Acts, but invalidated the regulations made thereunder as ultra vires.[38] In *Harvey* itself, the Supreme Court struck down as ultra vires regulations adopted under s.75 of the Social Welfare Act 1952, because they had purported to vary or alter the terms of s.7 of the 1952 Act. And the court so ruled, despite the fact that the section expressly authorised the making of regulations of this type.

2–23   *Mulcreevy v Minister for the Environment*[39] was another instalment in the Carrickmines saga. The problem was similar to that in *Dunne*: the State wished to undertake an infrastructure project which would necessarily involve removing some of the remains of a national monument. The relevant legislation required that, for work to proceed under these circumstances, the consent of the Minister, the Commissioners of Public Works and the local authority would each have to be obtained. The latter pair could only consent if it was "in the interests of archaeology to do so or the Minister [for Arts, Culture and the Gaeltacht] has approved of the giving of that consent". Thus:

> "[t]hey could grant the joint consent themselves only where it was in the interests of archaeology to do so. In any other case, their consent was ineffective unless it was approved of by the Arts Minister."[40]

2–24   Subsequently, by what approximated to an omnibus regulation, the power of the Commissioners under this provision, along with many others, was transferred to the respondent. The effect in the instant case was:

> "... to replace the hierarchy of controls requiring the consent or approval of three entirely distinct and independent statutory bodies with different remits, the Commissioners, the local authority and the Arts Minister, by a different system of control, requiring the approval or consent of two bodies only, the local authority and the Arts Minister".[41]

2–25   The Supreme Court reversed a High Court decision not to grant leave to apply for judicial review and Keane C.J. strongly suggested that the ministerial order purporting to consent to the removal of remains from the national monument was ultra vires.

2–26   Cutting in a different direction, however, *Minister for Justice v Tighe*[42] indicates a certain judicial reluctance to interfere with Henry VIII clauses. Section 24 of the Criminal Justice Act 1994 provided that certain restraint orders[43] "may be made only on an application by the D.P.P.". This provision was modified by a subsequent regulation permitting applications to be made by or on behalf of

---

Act 1957" (1985) 7 D.U.L.J. (n.s) 134; *Report of the Constitution Review Group* (Pn. 2632, 1996), pp.39–40.
[38]   Even though the power to make regulations expressly contemplated the variation or alteration of the terms of s.7.
[39]   [2004] IESC 5; [2004] 1 I.R. 72.
[40]   [2004] IESC 5; [2004] 1 I.R. 72 at 84.
[41]   [2004] IESC 5; [2004] 1 I.R. 72 at 85.
[42]   [2008] IEHC 118.
[43]   Orders preventing the defendant from dealing with property the subject of the order.

designated foreign countries. Another provision in the Act, s.46(6), allowed the Government to "make such modifications of this Act as appear to it to be necessary for the purpose of adapting to confiscation co-operation orders, any of the provisions of this Act relating to confiscation orders, in particular in relation to enforcement". Here, the Minister had relied on the modification to make an application on behalf of the British Government to prevent the respondent from dealing in certain named properties. The question arose then whether the modification, effected by regulation, was valid. Feeney J. held that the modification fell within the terms of s.46(6) because it was "necessary or expedient for the specific purpose envisaged within the legislation". Indeed, the Act itself "indicated a particular intention to modify the provisions providing for the making of domestic restraint orders to cover international restraint orders arising from international co-operation". Thus, the regulations amounted to "to the giving effect to the principles and policies" in the Act and the Minister's application could proceed. Although *Tighe* veers away from *Harvey*, it can be distinguished: in *Tighe* the authorisation to make regulations was contained in a general provision and did not permit the making of a regulation which would have compromised another provision of the statute; indeed, it probably made the statute's overall aims easier to achieve.

2–27   Henry VIII clauses remain popular with the Oireachtas. A typical example, which resembles the provision at issue in *Tighe*, is s.269 of the Planning and Development Act 2000:

> If any difficulty arises during the period of three years from the commencement of this Act in bringing any provision of this Act into operation or in relation to the operation of any provision, the Minister may by regulations do anything which appears to the Minister to be necessary or expedient for the purposes of removing the difficulty, bringing that provision into operation, or securing or facilitating its operation.[44]

2–28   A different example is s.8(5) of the Employment Permits Act 2006, which provides that "the period that shall be specified in the employment period ... shall not exceed 2 years ... or such longer period as may be specified by regulations ...". Because it admits of a power to extend a period beyond the time specified in a statute, this is technically a Henry VIII clause. However, its rather innocuous nature and its approval by the Oireachtas suggest that the courts might do best to leave well enough alone.

2–29   As regards the attitude of the courts: in summary, after an initial spurt of enthusiasm in *Laurentiu*, the judges have ceded ground on both the *Cityview* and *Harvey* fronts, although they seemingly remain ready to strike on occasion.

---

[44]   Such "enabling" provisions have drawn adverse comment in the Oireachtas: "[t]here is a growing practice of putting enabling legislation through these Houses so that a substantial amount of legislation which has a serious impact on people's rights and liberties goes through secondary legislation without proper scrutiny." 622 *Dáil Debates* Col.1222, June 28, 2006 (Deputy Howlin). See also, 167 *Seanad Debates* Col.1051, July 4, 2007 (Senator Ryan).

European Communities Act 1972: the implementation of directives by ministerial order

2–30   In nearly all cases, implementing measures will be necessary, in the form of domestic legislation, in each Member State in order to give a European Communities directive full force and effect.[45] One of the principal methods of implementing directives in this jurisdiction is contained in s.3 of the European Communities Act 1972, which enables a Minister of State to implement such directives by statutory order. Section 3(2) states:

> Regulations made under this section may contain such incidental, supplementary and consequential provisions as appear to the Minister to be necessary for the purposes of the regulations (including provisions repealing, amending or applying, with or without modification, other law, exclusive of this Act).

The possible impact of Art.15.2.1 on this provision and its progeny has given rise to a good deal of case law, which is surveyed elsewhere.[46]

C. Sources of Administrative Law

2–31   The legal sources of administrative law are various and heterogeneous —and many real-life administrative law problems involve issues drawn from more than one source—but five principal domestic sources can be identified: the Constitution, primary legislation, common law, delegated legislation and administrative circulars. In addition, Irish courts are increasingly influenced by the general principles of law established by the jurisprudence interpreting the European Convention on Human Rights and EU law. EU law is referred to at various points elsewhere in the book[47] and the ECHR is covered at Part D of this chapter and in Chapter 12, Part A. As regards the domestic sources, Parts E and F are devoted to a consideration of the last two of the principal sources of administrative law: delegated legislation and the use of circulars and non-statutory administrative schemes. As regards the first three sources, most of the material in the remainder of the book comes from the Constitution, common law or primary legislation and, accordingly, here we need give only the following overview of the inter-play these sources.

---

[45] Community directives, unlike Community regulations, are not usually directly enforceable, i.e. they do not immediately become part of the domestic law of each Member State. However, the European Court of Justice has made it clear that the implementation of EU directives may in certain cases be superfluous, but in such cases Member States must ensure that their nationals are aware of such rights under such a directive: *Commission v Germany* (C-29/84) [1985] E.C.R. 1661. Of course, as was made clear by the Supreme Court in *Maher*, Community regulations may also require some implementing measures at the national level. See *Azienda Agricola Monte Arcosu v Regione Autonoma della Sardegna* (C-403/98) [2001] E.C.R. I-103.

[46] See Hogan and Morgan, *Administrative Law in Ireland*, 4th edn (Dublin: Round Hall, 2010) (hereinafter referred to as "H & M"), paras 2–36 to 2–50. See also, *JM Kelly: The Irish Constitution* (2003), paras. 4.2.31–44. See also, *Browne v Attorney General* [2003] IESC 43; [2003] 3 I.R. 205; *T v Minister for Justice, Equality and Law Reform* [2009] IEHC 529.

[47] See Fair Procedures (paras 12–04 to 12–19), Control of Discretionary Power (paras 15–113 to 15–119), Damages and Legitimate Expectation (para.18–04).

Constitution

2–32   The Constitution has been used in order to make an impact at a number of points in the public administration system.[48]

- The extension of procedural protection, in large part through the establishment of constitutional justice.
- Buttressing the control of discretionary powers in the various ways outlined in the chapter on that subject.
- The invoking of the separation of powers to establish that it is the judiciary, not the responsible Minister, who decide the extent of executive privilege against the disclosure of official evidence.
- The use of Art.34.3.1° to prohibit the exclusion of judicial review and to restrain time limits in this field.
- Invocation of Art.34.1, coupled with Art.37.1, to ensure that it is only a court and not a tribunal which administers justice, save in the exercise of limited functions of a non-criminal character.

Primary legislation

2–33   By far, the greatest volume of administrative law is provided by primary legislation. In a way, this is the Cinderella of the subject, since it lacks the intellectual coherence of concepts such as ultra vires or constitutional justice. In addition, the drafting of common law statutes, with its emphasis on detail, normally does not make general principles very evident. Further, statutes are more commonly treated as part of the substantive public law subjects—welfare, taxation, immigration and naturalisation, trade regulation and planning —which are in the next field to administrative law. However, even in a general administrative law text, the reader will catch many glimpses of statutes. In addition, primary legislation has been the main source of what might be termed organic administrative law, i.e. the law on the structure and functions of the law relating to government administration, ministers and departments, local authorities and public bodies.

2–34   Primary legislation has been of lesser importance as far as the field of judicial review is concerned, as there are few statutory provisions containing principles of general application in this sphere. But apart from judicial review, the other institutions of control of administrative action—such as the Ombudsman, tribunals and Freedom of Information Acts—are the product of statute.

Common law

2–35   The law of judicial review is, of course, very largely a creation of the common law in the form of rules of statutory interpretation for there is no Irish equivalent of the United States Administrative Procedure Act 1946. Accordingly, key principles—such as the scope of error of law[49] and the doctrine of reasonableness,[50]

---

[48]   See paras 12–38 to 12–44; 15–82 to 15–112; Ch.20, Part E; Ch.11, Part A and paras 6–44 to 6–54, respectively.
[49]   See below, Ch.10, Part G.
[50]   See below, Ch.15, Part B, especially paras 15–59 to 15–60.

legitimate expectations[51] and proportionality[52]—have been formulated entirely by the judiciary. The development of these principles has, in turn, been buttressed and extended by the Constitution.[53] In addition, common law doctrines such as the rule that the State is presumed not to be bound by the application of statute,[54] state immunity[55] and executive privilege[56] have been declared to be unconstitutional and constitutional principles have been introduced to support other far-reaching judicial developments.

D. European Convention on Human Rights

2–36 One should emphasise that what follows is an overview and there is a more detailed consideration of the effect of the Convention on one important subsection, namely art.6.1 on the procedure of administrative agencies, at paras 12–04 to 12–18. The incorporation of the European Convention on Human Rights into Irish law has not had as radical an effect[57] as Britain's Human Rights Act 1998.[58] Nevertheless, under s.2(1) of the European Convention on Human Rights Act 2003, judicial review of administrative action must now take account of the Convention:

> "In interpreting and applying any statutory provision or rule of law, a court shall, in so far as is possible, subject to the rules of law relating to such interpretation and application, do so in a manner compatible with the State's obligations under the Convention provisions."

2–37 Further, s.4 obliges Irish courts when interpreting Convention provisions to take judicial notice of decisions of the Strasbourg court, the European Commission of Human Rights and the Committee of Ministers.

2–38 Section 5 provides for declarations of incompatibility, according to which a court declares that "a statutory provision or rule of law is incompatible with the State's obligations under the Convention provisions". The Taoiseach must subsequently "cause a copy of any order containing a declaration of incompatibility

---

[51] See below, Ch.19.

[52] See below, paras 15–83 to 15–92.

[53] See below, especially at paras 15–82 to 15–112.

[54] *Howard v Commissioners of Public Works* [1994] 1 I.R. 101.

[55] *Byrne v Ireland* [1972] I.R. 241.

[56] *Murphy v Dublin Corporation* [1972] I.R. 215.

[57] For appraisal, see: O'Connell et al., *The European Convention on Human Rights Act 2003: a Preliminary Assessment of Impact* (Dublin: Solicitors Bar Association, 2006); O'Connell, "The Irish Constitution and the E.C.H.R.: Belt and Braces or Blinkers?" (2000) *Irish Human Rights Review* 90 at 97; O'Connell, "Ireland" in Blackburn and Polakiewicz (eds), *Fundamental Rights in Europe: the European Convention on Human Rights and its Member States, 1950-2000* (Oxford: OUP, 2001), p.423; Hogan, "The Belfast Agreement and the Future Incorporation of the European Convention of Human rights in the Republic of Ireland" (1999) (4)4 B.R. 205.

[58] In contrast to the United Kingdom, courts are not expressed to be organs of the State which are obliged to comply with the Convention. This reduces the possibility of the Convention having horizontal effect and might impact on the courts' duties in other areas. However, a government representative suggested during the Act's passage through the Oireachtas that courts are nonetheless obliged to comply with the Convention: 173 *Seanad Debates* Col.979 June 19, 2003 (Deputy Lenihan).

to be laid before each House of the Oireachtas within the next 21 days on which that House has sat after the making of the order". Crucially, however, s.5(2)(a) imports a key restriction by providing that a declaration "shall not affect the validity, continuing operation or enforcement of the statutory provision or rule of law in respect of which it is made".

2–39 Any assessment of the impact of the Convention in Ireland is of necessity premature.[59] That the Convention has not yet entirely "taken off" in the Irish context is not a surprise. It should first be noted that the common accusation that the Irish legal profession was relatively unwilling to beat a path to Strasbourg, is somewhat misplaced. Rather, our own relatively vibrant corpus of constitutional jurisprudence obviated the need of most litigants to travel to the continent for redress.[60]

2–40 Another reason is that the 2003 Act has been held not to have retrospective effect, although this factor is naturally fading.[61] More importantly, the mode of incorporation in Ireland at sub-constitutional level ensured that the Convention would, more often than not, remain of secondary importance to the Constitution itself.[62] A supporter of stronger incorporation has lamented how:

> "... the Act will not radically change the status quo. No doubt, it may assist in some cases by enabling the judiciary to read legislation in a way that conforms to the principles in the Convention. However, aside from the possible application of s.3, it will not provide an independent cause of action in contentious cases or guarantee an all-important remedy to the litigant".[63]

2–41 In particular, the declaration of incompatibility provided for by s.5 can be viewed as "a species of booby prize",[64] because it does not provide an especially effective remedy. On the one hand, a finding of unconstitutionality amounts in Ireland to a "judicial death certificate"[65] with *erga omnes* force, generally

---

[59] "If hundreds of years after the event was too soon for the Chinese Premier, Zhou Enlai, to assess the impact of the French Revolution, 2006 is almost certainly too soon to reach any definitive conclusions as to the likely impact of the ECHR Act 2003." O'Connell et al., *The European Convention on Human Rights Act 2003: a Preliminary Assessment of Impact* (2006), p.i.

[60] Hogan, "Incorporation of the E.C.H.R.: Some Issues of Methodology and Process" in Kilkelly (ed.), *The E.C.H.R. and Irish Law* (Bristol: Jordan Publishing Ltd, 2004), p.14.

[61] *Fennell v Dublin City Council* [2005] IESC 33; [2005] 2 I.L.R.M. 228. See also, *JD v Residential Institutions Redress Committee* [2008] IEHC 350.

[62] However, a stronger incorporation would have raised serious issues of compatibility with the Constitution. Hogan, "Incorporation of the E.C.H.R.: Some Issues of Methodology and Process" in Kilkelly (ed.), *The E.C.H.R. and Irish Law* (2004), pp.18–21. Cf. Egan, "The European Convention on Human Rights Act 2003: A Missed Opportunity for Domestic Human Rights Litigation" (2003) 25 D.U.L.J. 230 at 239–245.

[63] Egan, "The European Convention on Human Rights Act 2003: A Missed Opportunity for Domestic Human Rights Litigation" (2003) 25 D.U.L.J. 230 at 246.

[64] Marshall, "Two Kinds of Incompatibility: More about Section 3 of the Human Rights Act" [1999] P.L. 377 at 382. See also, Hogan, "Incorporation of the E.C.H.R.: Some Issues of Methodology and Process" in Kilkelly (ed.), *The E.C.H.R. and Irish Law* (2004), pp.21–28; "The Value of Declarations of Incompatibility and the Rule of Avoidance" (2006) 28 D.U.L.J. 408 at 415–417.

[65] *Murphy v Attorney General* [1982] I.R. 241 at 307 per Henchy J.

rendering the statutory provision void ab initio.[66] On the other hand, a declaration of incompatibility merely invites the Oireachtas to "consider its position" and pass repealing legislation, while the legislation remains in force pending such repeal. Moreover, the incorporation of the Convention as a sub-constitutional instrument suggests that a court is duty bound to consider constitutional issues first, only turning to the Convention as a last resort.[67] This is underscored by the Supreme Court's decision in *McD v L*,[68] which stressed that the Convention was not directly effective in Irish law, but rather simply, in accordance with Art.29.6 of the Constitution, had effect only to the extent to which the Oireachtas had so provided via the European Convention on Human Rights Act 2003.

2–42   In addition, as Fennelly J. noted in *McD v L*:

> "[The European Court of Human Rights] has the prime responsibility of interpreting the Convention. Its decisions are binding on the contracting states. It is important that the Convention be interpreted consistently. The courts of the individual states should not adopt interpretations of the Convention at variance with the current Strasbourg jurisprudence."

The Irish courts thus enjoy less freedom in the interpretation of the Convention than in the case of the Constitution.

2–43   Notwithstanding these sceptical remarks, cross-fertilisation between the Convention and the Constitution may well occur.[69] In addition, Irish courts have traditionally been heavily influenced by events in Britain, where the still-gathering momentum of the Human Rights Act 1998 provides a ready source of information and insight about the application of the Convention in a domestic setting. In particular, if the protections of the Convention are extended by the British courts, Irish litigants may well bring similar challenges.[70] Again, although achieving a declaration of incompatibility may, in some circumstances, only be a pyrrhic victory, the alternative technique of "reading down" legislation has been utilised quite extensively. This can be a potent weapon. The high water mark in the United

---

[66]   cf. *A v Governor of Arbour Hill Prison* [2006] IESC 45; [2006] 4 I.R. 88.

[67]   This reversal of the usual sequence is explained in Hogan, "The Value of Declarations of Incompatibility and the Rule of Avoidance" (2006) 28 D.U.L.J. 408 at 417–421. See *Law Society v Competition Authority* [2006] IEHC 455; [2006] 2 I.R. 262. Cf. *Carmody v Minister for Justice, Equality and Law Reform* [2005] IEHC 10; [2010] 1 I.R. 635. Indeed, to do otherwise than to consider the Constitution first might have adverse consequences for the applicant: "Ironically, the danger here is that the claim under the [2003 Act] might be *successful*, and that the court might then decide that this is sufficient to dispose of the case and accordingly not address the constitutional argument. ... In such circumstances the lawyer might have wished that he had simply omitted the claim under the [2003 Act] and, instead, gone for gold by aiming for a declaration of constitutional invalidity." Simons, *Planning and Development Law*, 2nd edn (Dublin: Thomson Round Hall, 2007), p.857 (emphasis in original).

[68]   [2009] IESC 81.

[69]   See, e.g. the ready adoption of the equality of arms ("égalité des armes") principle by the Supreme Court in *JF v Director of Public Prosecutions* [2005] IESC 24; [2005] 2 I.R. 174; *Carmody v Minister for Justice, Equality and Law Reform* [2009] IESC 71; [2010] 1 I.R. 635.

[70]   O'Connell et al., *The European Convention on Human Rights Act 2003: a Preliminary Assessment of Impact* (2006), p.29.

Kingdom is probably *Ghaidan v Godin-Mendoza*.[71] The applicant challenged, under art.14 of the Convention, a provision that gave the survivor of a heterosexual couple—but not of a homosexual couple—a statutory tenancy. The House of Lords held that art.14 had been infringed but rather than grant a declaration of incompatibility, effectively re-wrote the offending provision such that it guaranteed a statutory tenancy to the survivor of a homosexual couple.[72] It may be difficult, if the underlying law is similar, for the Irish courts to resist issuing declarations of incompatibility or taking the more pro-applicant step of utilising the power of s.2(1) to interpret statutory provisions as conforming to the Convention.[73]

2–44	Against that backdrop, the Irish judiciary might be tempted to import Convention values into the Constitution. For example, art.8, which has been influential in human rights litigation in Britain, might inspire the Irish courts to be more generous in their interpretation of the constitutional articles dealing with the family and private property.[74] This conclusion is bolstered by obiter dicta in the pre-incorporation case of *Lobe and Osayande v Minister for Justice, Equality and Law Reform*.[75] The point at issue, stated neatly, was whether the Minister could lawfully refuse asylum to and deport the parents of minors who had been born in Ireland. Denham J. cited the judgment of Lord Phillips M.R. in *R. (Mahmood) v Secretary of State for the Home Department*[76] as "a useful analysis of the law in a neighbouring jurisdiction".[77] Hardiman J. also found this judgment of use because the "approach of balancing family and state rights closely reflects the approach in the Irish cases".[78] However, the suggestion of cross-fertilisation was made most strongly by Fennelly J. in his dissenting opinion:

> "It is also important at all times to bear in mind that the Convention merely lays down minimum standards. It is open to the Member States to adopt stricter ones. In other words, it is not valid to deduce from the fact of compatibility with the Convention, that the impugned act complies with the

---

[71]	[2004] UKHL 30; [2004] 3 W.L.R. 113 (HL).

[72]	See generally, Kavanagh, "The Elusive Divide Between Interpretation and Legislation under the Human Rights Act 1998" (2004) 24 O.J.L.S. 273.

[73]	The Interpretation Act 2005 s.5 only permits of departures from the "literal" rule of statutory interpretation where a provision is unambiguous if an absurd result would otherwise be reached. This might cut down the scope of operation of the 2003 Act, at least where the statute is unambiguous on its face. On the possibility of "tension between a literal interpretation and the giving of effect to the Convention": see Simons, *Planning and Development Law* (2007), pp.852–855.

[74]	Egan, "The European Convention on Human Rights Act 2003: A Missed Opportunity for Domestic Human Rights Litigation" (2003) 25 D.U.L.J. 230 at 234–236. For example, the provisions considered in *Harrow London Borough Council v Qazi* [2003] UKHL 43; [2004] 1 A.C. 983; *Connors v United Kingdom* (2005) 40 E.H.R.R. 9; *Kay v Lambeth Borough Council* [2006] UKHL 10; [2006] 2 A.C. 465; and *Birmingham City Council v Doherty* [2008] UKHL 57; [2008] 3 W.L.R. 636, some of which were held to be incompatible with art.8, seem to have counterparts in Irish law. See Lyall, *Land Law in Ireland*, 2nd edn (Dublin: Round Hall Sweet & Maxwell, 2000), p.1062. These may be vulnerable to challenge. See also, Biehler, *International Law in Practice: an Irish Perspective* (Dublin: Thomson Round Hall, 2005), pp.236–238 (discussing extradition law) and Simons, *Planning and Development Law* (2007), Ch.14 (discussing planning law).

[75]	[2003] IESC 3; [2003] 1 I.R. 1.

[76]	[2000] EWCA Civ 315; [2001] 1 W.L.R. 840.

[77]	[2003] IESC 3; [2003] 1 I.R. 1 at 57.

[78]	[2003] IESC 3; [2003] 1 I.R. 1 at 143.

Constitution. It may, conversely, be possible to argue persuasively that an act which does not satisfy the minimum standards of the Convention should not lightly be considered compatible with the more rigorous demands of the Constitution."[79]

2–45 At the same time, Irish courts would, however, do well to recall Lord Bingham's sage warning of the dangers of "emasculation (by over-judicialisation)" of administrative law if the Convention is given too broad an interpretation.[80] As McCarthy J. has observed:

"[A] great many applications for judicial review, in fact, raise issues of constitutional rights in one form or another, such as breach of the principles of constitutional justice, say, in relation to a planning decision or the grant or refusal of a licence or the dismissal of an office holder."[81]

2–46 McCarthy J.'s comments were made in the constitutional context but they extend equally to the Convention and the possibility of cross-fertilisation. If administrative law is not to become a litigant's charter, then the courts should exercise some restraint in identifying breaches of Convention or constitutional rights.[82]

E. DELEGATED LEGISLATION

2–47 Delegated legislation is made by some person or body other than the Oireachtas, to which the Oireachtas had delegated its legislative functions in a strictly limited area or field of operation. While the delegate is usually a Minister, it is sometimes a local authority, professional body,[83] or other specialist body possessing particular expertise.[84] Delegated legislation is now an established feature of our law; it could scarcely be otherwise given the growth of the modern state. There are several practical reasons which justify the existence of delegated legislation. Parliamentary time is scarce and the Oireachtas could not reasonably

---

[79] [2003] IESC 3; [2003] 1 I.R. 1 at 198–199.

[80] *R. (Begum) v Tower Hamlets LBC* [2003] UKHL 5; [2003] 2 A.C. 430 at [5].

[81] *N v Minister for Justice* [2008] IEHC 8.

[82] The English courts have made an interesting and sustained attempt to fend off the possibility of permitting proportionality challenges to the taking of repossession proceedings by local authorities against tenants whose right to occupy a particular property has lapsed. First, in *Kay v Lambeth Borough Council* [2006] UKHL 10; [2006] 2 A.C. 465 and then in *Birmingham City Council v Doherty* [2008] UKHL 57; [2008] 3 W.L.R. 636, their Lordships have attempted to distinguish between the traditional public law grounds of review and full proportionality review. An intervening decision of the Strasbourg Court, *McCann v United Kingdom* [2008] E.C.H.R. 385, suggested that the English approach was too restrictive, but *McCann* was distinguished—and indeed criticised—by the House of Lords in *Doherty*. The applicant in *Kay* has now made an application to Strasbourg.

[83] See, e.g. Solicitors Act 1954 s.66 (as inserted by s.76 of the Solicitors (Amendment) Act 1994) which provides that the Law Society may make regulations with the concurrence of the President of the High Court governing solicitors' accounts.

[84] For example, orders made by the Joint Labour Committee under the Industrial Relations Act 1946 fixing minimum wages for certain industries. These orders are not affected by the national minimum wage policy; save that the national minimum wage applies universally. See National Minimum Wage Act 2000 s.42.

be expected to legislate for every administrative detail. It is, therefore, content to state the general principles in legislation and to allow the details to be regulated by ministerial order. There is also a need for flexibility and the law must be capable of rapid adjustment to meet changing circumstances. There is, however, as we have seen in our exegesis of Art.15.2.1° in Part B, a constitutional limit on the length to which delegated legislation may be taken,[85] as well, of course, as the common law ultra vires principle.[86]

Statutory Instruments Act 1947

2–48   The Statutory Instruments Act 1947 is designed to ensure the publication of all items of delegated legislation, thus rendering academic any doubts as to whether the Rules Publication Act 1893 applied to Ireland.[87] The term "statutory instrument" is defined by s.1(1) as meaning every "order, regulation, rule, scheme or bye-law" made in the exercise of a statutory power. However, the Act then goes on to make the quite unnecessary distinction between statutory instruments to which the Act primarily applies, and other statutory instruments to which the Act's provisions may apply. In fact, the phrase "primarily applies" is something of a misnomer, for the Act does not apply in a secondary sense to other delegated legislation. In other words, if the Act does not primarily apply to certain instruments, then they fall outside the scope of the Act. The Statutory Instrument Act 1947 applies[88] to statutory instruments made after January 1, 1948 by either the President, Government, Minister, Minister of State, an authority having for the time being power to make rules of court, or "any person or body, whether corporate or unincorporate, exercising throughout the State any functions of government or discharging throughout the State any public duties in relation to public administration".[89]

---

[85]   See the following comments of Walsh J., in the introduction to Humphreys, *Index to Irish Statutory Instruments* (1988) (Vol. 1), pp.xiii–xiv: "As the State becomes more and more involved, both directly and indirectly, in almost every aspect of our social and economic life it was inevitable that a great deal of regulations would be required. This is particularly so in a state which is as centralised as Ireland … Our own constitutional jurisprudence has shown that the Courts are ready to strike down any unauthorised delegation of legislative power while at the same time recognising that in the complex and frequently changing situations which confront the modern state there is a necessity for subordinate legislation."

[86]   See paras 2–19 to 2–30.

[87]   In *State (Quinlan) v Kavanagh* [1935] I.R. 249, Kennedy C.J. had assumed that the Rules Publications Act 1893 applied to Ireland, but in *Re McGrath and Harte* [1941] I.R. 69, Sullivan C.J. pointed out that this Act had not been adapted for publication in this jurisdiction. In fact, the 1893 Act was repealed by s.7 of the 1947 Act.

[88]   The certificate of the Attorney General to the effect that in his opinion a particular instrument is one to which the Act primarily applies is conclusive: s.2(2). Legislation might also provide that a particular order shall be treated as a statutory instrument to which the 1947 Act primarily applies. See, e.g. Prisons Act 2007 s.18(2) (construction of new facilities) and Defence Act 1954 s.240B(2), as inserted by the Defence (Amendment) Act 2007 s.71. In some instances, later legislation expressly provides that the 1947 Act does not "primarily apply", for example, s.32 of the Civil Service Commissioners Act 1956.

[89]   The instrument must also be one which is required by statute to be laid before both or either Houses of the Oireachtas or is of such a character as affects the public generally or any particular class or classes of the public (1947 Act s.2(2)) and must not be a statutory instrument, which is required by statute to be published in *Iris Oifigiúil* (1947 Act s.2(1)). This last requirement should be distinguished from the normal requirement under s.3(1) of the 1947 Act, which is that *notice of making* should be published in *Iris Oifigiúil*.

2–49   This last category would include, for example, state-sponsored bodies and the Commissioners of Public Works, but not local authorities. In addition, the Attorney General is given power to exempt from the provisions of the Act a particular instrument or type or class of instrument on the grounds that it or they are only of local or personal or temporary application or for "any other reason".[90]

2–50   The significance of the Statutory Instrument Act 1947 is as follows. Section 3(1) of the 1947 Act (as inserted by s.1 of the Statutory Instruments (Amendment) Act 1955) requires that a copy of each statutory instrument must be sent to certain listed libraries[91] within 10 days of its being made; that "notice of the making thereof and of the place where copies thereof may be obtained shall be published in the *Iris Oifigiúil*" and that each instrument must also be published by the Stationery Office.[92] This has been described as a "modest standard of publication".[93] Section 3(2) of the 1947 Act provides that in civil cases the validity or effect or coming into operation of any statutory instrument shall not be affected by non-compliance with these publication requirements.

2–51   As far as criminal cases are concerned,[94] s.3(3) provides that where a person has been charged with the offence of contravening a provision in a statutory instrument to which the Act applies, the prosecution must prove that notice of the making of the order has been published at the date of the alleged offence unless the prosecutor can satisfy the court that reasonable steps have been taken to bring the purport of the statutory instrument to the attention of the public.[95]

---

[90]   Statutory Instruments Act 1947 s.2(3) and (4). Notice of exemption must be published in *Iris Oifigiúil*. The compatibility of this exemption procedure with the equality guarantee contained in Art.40.1 of the Constitution may be questioned, having regard to the decision of the Supreme Court in *East Donegal Co-operative Ltd v Attorney General* [1970] I.R. 317. For a more extensive discussion of the 1947 Act, see Jackson, "Delegated Legislation in Ireland" [1962] P.L. 417.

[91]   Section 3(1) of the Statutory Instruments Act 1947 (as amended by the Statutory Instruments (Amendment) Act 1955 s.1) lists the libraries in question: the National Library, the Law Library, the Library of the Law Society, the library of the Southern Law Association and the Libraries of the Dublin, Cork, Limerick, Waterford and Galway Chambers of Commerce, but not the Oireachtas Library.

[92]   There are a number of specific statutory provisions which provide for a special exemption from these publication requirements, e.g. ss.8(3), 12, 49 and 51 of the Roads Act 1993.

[93]   *Campbell v Minister for Agriculture* [1999] 2 I.R. 245 at 254 per Murphy J.

[94]   There is more on the important question of the notice taken of the requirement of publication before Statutory Instruments may be applied in criminal cases in H & M, paras 2–72 to 2–76.

[95]   The Statutory Instruments Act 1947 s.3 thus preserves the common law principles recognised in cases such as *Lim Chin Aik v R.* [1963] A.C. 160. It may be, however, that a failure to publish a statutory instrument will mean that an individual is not "on notice" as to the requirements imposed by the statutory instrument. See, e.g. "Hundreds of speed summonses struck out on technicality", *Irish Times*, November 20, 2008. This District Court case, admittedly, apparently related to failure to publish a bye-law rather than a statutory instrument in *Iris Oifigiúil*. The Court of Justice considers that publication of legislative measures is a key element of legal certainty and that failure to effect formal publication is fatal to the enforceability of such measures against private citizens: see, e.g. *ROM Projecten* (C-158/06) [2007] E.C.R. I-5719; *Skoma Lux* (C-161/06) [2007] E.C.R. I-10841 and *Gottfried Heinrich* (C-345/06) [2009] 3 C.M.L.R. 7. But the principles in *Heinrich* do not apply to laws enacted and promulgated in this jurisdiction: see *Minister for Justice, Equality and Law Reform v Adach* [2010] IESC 33.

2–52 It might be thought that the requirement of a prosecutor satisfying the court of the taking of reasonable steps could be satisfied by the invocation of the common law doctrine of judicial notice. The effect of judicial notice would be to remove from the prosecution the burden of proving the existence of the statutory instrument. Some authority supports this view. In *State (Taylor) v Wicklow Circuit Judge*,[96] the respondent had been administering the Road Traffic Act 1933 for many years and on this basis Davitt J. was prepared to accept that the trial judge was entitled to take judicial notice of the ministerial order without the need for formal proof of its making. An alternative view was expressed, however, in *People v Kennedy*.[97] There, the Court of Criminal Appeal held that orders made under the Emergency Powers Act 1939 were not in the same position as a statute, because they were not in the public domain. Accordingly, upon a prosecution for contravention of a ministerial order, the order would have to be proved in evidence.[98] This requirement as to proof was preferred by the Court of Criminal Appeal in *People (DPP) v Cleary*.[99]

2–53 So far we have considered the need for publication in the particular context of criminal cases. As regards the position generally there is some English authority for the proposition that delegated legislation does not come into force until it is published.[100] The point is, however, dealt with by s.16(3) and s.16(4) of the Interpretation Act 2005 which provides:

> (3) Subject to subsection (4), every provision of a statutory instrument comes into operation at the end of the day before the day on which the statutory instrument is made.
>
> (4) Where a statutory instrument or a provision of a statutory instrument is expressed to come into operation on a particular day (whether the day is before or after the date of the making of the statutory instrument and whether the day is named in the instrument or is to be fixed or ascertained in a particular manner), the statutory instrument or provision comes into operation at the end of the day before the particular day.

2–54 The idea, however, that delegated legislation should have the force of law in advance of its publication (even if this period is relatively short) would seem to be inimical to constitutional values such as legal certainty and the rule of law. In addition to the publication requirement in most cases, the parent statute (rather than the 1947 Act) will state that the statutory instrument must be "laid" before the Houses of the Oireachtas within a specified period—generally, 21 sitting days. But such authorities as there are suggest that failure to comply with this "laying" requirement does not invalidate the statutory instrument.[101]

---

[96] [1951] I.R. 311. See also, *DPP v Collins* [1981] I.L.R.M. 447; Stevenson, "Proof of Legislation in Litigation" (1983) 19 Ir. Jur. (N.S) 95.

[97] [1946] I.R. 517. See also, *People v Griffin* [1974] I.R. 416.

[98] [1946] I.R. 517 at 520–521.

[99] [2005] IECCA 51; [2005] 2 I.R. 189.

[100] *Johnson v Sargant* [1918] 1 K.B. 101. See Lanham, "Delegated Legislation and Publication" (1974) 37 M.L.R. 510.

[101] *Premier Meat Packers Ltd v Minister for Agriculture*, unreported, High Court, July 28, 1971. See also, *R. v Sheer Metalcraft Ltd* [1951] 1 Q.B. 586. Probably on the basis of these authorities, the Attorney General's Office has also advised that failure to lay does not render a statutory instrument invalid: *Report of Senate Select Committee on Statutory Instruments* (T.162) (Pr. 4685), p.15. On mandatory/directory requirements, see Ch.11, Part H.

Judicial control

2–55 In the first place, as described in Part B of this chapter, the delegation of power must not be in breach of Art.15.2.1°, and, as described in later chapters, the courts must examine the validity of any delegated legislation according to the standard criteria of vires or reasonableness. As executive or administrative bodies do not possess an inherent legislative power, the validity of delegated legislation falls to be tested against the background of what is authorised by the parent statute, either expressly or by necessary implication, in just the same way as any administrative action effecting only an individual change. The judicial role was aptly described by Fennelly J. in *Kennedy v Incorporated Law Society of Ireland*[102]:

> "The delegatees of statutory power cannot be allowed to exceed the limits of the statute or, as here, the secondary legislation conferring the power. The rationale for this is simple and clear. The Oireachtas may, by law, while respecting the constitutional limits, delegate powers to be exercised for stated purposes. Any excessive exercise of the delegated discretion will defeat the legislative intent and may tend to undermine the democratic principle and, ultimately, the rule of law itself. Secondly, the courts have the function of review of the exercise of powers. They are bound to ensure respect for the laws passed by the Oireachtas. A delegatee of power which pursues, though in good faith, a purpose not permitted by the legislation by, for example, combining it with other permitted purposes is enlarging by stealth the range of its own powers. These principles, in my view, must inform any test for deciding whether a power has been exercised ultra vires."[103]

2–56 Granted that a statutory instrument is intra vires, the next question is the meaning of the statutory instrument and this is, essentially, a matter of statutory interpretation. This commonly involves a number of standard presumptions, explained in Chapter 10, Part D which are employed by the courts and these apply in the same way to delegated as to primary legislation. Thus, for example, the Oireachtas is presumed not to have delegated the power: to raise taxes[104]; to oust the jurisdiction of the courts to encroach upon the liberty of the citizen[105]; to give retrospective effect to delegated legislation[106]; to effect a substantial alteration

---

[102] [2002] 2 I.R. 458.
[103] [2002] 2 I.R. 458 at 486.
[104] *Attorney General v Wilts United Dairies Ltd* (1921) 39 T.L.R. 781; *Ryanair v Aer Rianta* [2003] 2 I.R. 143.
[105] *State (O'Flaherty) v O'Floinn* [1954] I.R. 295; *Murphy v PMPA Insurance Co. Ltd* [1978] I.L.R.M. 25; *State (Lynch) v Ballagh* [1986] I.R. 203; *Maguire v Ardagh* [2002] 1 I.R. 385 at 767–777.
[106] *People (DPP) v Cawley* [2003] 4 I.R. 321; *Dublin City Council v Fennell* [2005] IESC 33; [2005] 2 I.L.R.M. 228; *In re Art.26 and the Health (Amendment) (No.2) Bill 2004* [2005] IESC 7; [2005] 1 I.R. 604; *In re Tipperary Fresh Foods Ltd* [2005] IEHC 96; [2005] 1 I.R. 551. See, in particular, *Aer Rianta CPT v Commissioner for Aviation Regulation* [2003] IEHC 707. But cf. *Re McGrath and Harte* [1941] I.R. 68 and *Minister for Agriculture v O'Connell* [1942] I.R. 600. The Joint Oireachtas Committee on the Secondary Legislation of the European Communities has drawn attention to the fact that the European Communities Act 1972 does not authorise the making of delegated legislation with retrospective effect.

in the general law[107] or to infringe any provisions of the Constitution.[108] Subject to these presumptions, the task of the courts is to ascertain the true intent of the enabling Act.[109]

2–57 Many of the challenges to the vires of delegated legislation have been to Rules of Court. The various Rules Committees for the District Court, Circuit Court and the Superior Courts have been given statutory jurisdiction to make rules concerning the "practice and procedure" of their respective courts. Several cases turn on the question of whether a particular rule is properly a matter of practice and procedure[110] because the power to make rules "does not extend to making rules regarding substantive law".[111] However, *Hillary v Minister for Education*[112] was a more typical administrative law case. The respondent had purported by order to confer additional functions on the Commission to Inquire into Child Abuse.[113] The additional functions related to vaccine trials that had been conducted in State-run institutions between 1940 and 1987. The question for the High Court was whether the trials came within the statutory definition of "abuse" contained in s.4(4) of the Commission to Inquire into Child Abuse Act 2000, which centred on such behaviour as "the wilful, reckless or negligent infliction of physical injury on, or failure to prevent such injury to, the child".

2–58 Relying on a report prepared by the chief medical officer of the Department

---

[107] *Minister for Industry and Commerce v Hales* [1967] I.R. 50 at 76; *Re Macks Bakeries Ltd* [2003] 2 I.R. 396; *Visual Impact and Displays Ltd v Murphy* [2003] 4 I.R. 451 at 453; *Cahill v O'Driscoll* [2005] IEHC 179.
[108] There is a presumption that statutory powers (including the power to make delegated legislation) granted by an Act of the Oireachtas do not authorise the donee of such powers to infringe the Constitution: *East Donegal Co-operative Ltd v Attorney General* [1970] I.R. 317. For recent examples of the courts' treatment of challenges to the constitutionality of statutory instruments, see *Laurentiu v Minister for Justice, Equality and Law Reform* [1999] 4 I.R. 26 and *Leontjava v DPP* [2004] IESC 37; [2004] 1 I.R. 591.
[109] The importance of giving effect to the intention of the Oireachtas was stressed by Murphy J. in *Humphrey v Minister for the Environment*: "[i]t does not seem to have been *in the contemplation of the legislature* to delegate to the Minister such a right [to impose what amounted to taxes] let alone allow the Minister to delegate to a local authority." [2001] 1 I.R. 263 at 294 (emphasis added). See too, *Minister for Industry and Commerce v Hales* [1967] I.R. 50 at 83.
[110] The power of the Superior Courts Rules Committee to make Rules of Court governing "pleading, practice and procedure generally" is contained in s.36 of the Courts of Justice Act 1924, as applied by ss.14(2) and 48 of the Courts (Supplemental Provisions) Act 1961.
[111] *Southern Hotel Sligo Ltd v Iarnród Éireann* [2007] IEHC 254.
[112] [2004] IEHC 250; [2005] 4 I.R. 333. Other non-Rules examples include: *United States International Tobacco Co. v Attorney General* [1990] 1 I.R. 394 (s.65 of the Health Act 1947 confined the Minister to declaring that certain medical preparations were to be "restricted articles", and the Minister could not avail of this section to restrict the sale of non-medical articles such as tobacco sachets); *O'Neill v Minister for Agriculture* [1998] 1 I.R. 539 (quantitative and geographic licensing system held to be invalid in absence of express statutory authorisation); *Humphreys v Minister for Environment* [2001] 1 I.R. 263 (regulations prescribing quantitative restrictions on the numbers of taxi licences held invalid); *Kennedy v Incorporated Law Society of Ireland (No.3)* [2001] IESC 103; [2002] 2 I.R. 458 (respondent body did not have the power to appoint an accountant to investigate allegations of fraud made against the applicant); *BUPA Ireland Ltd v Health Insurance Authority (No.2)* [2008] IESC 52; [2009] 1 I.L.R.M. 81 (risk equalisation regulations impacting significantly on applicants' constitutional property rights held not to be justified by oblique words in statute).
[113] Commission to Inquire into Child Abuse Act 2000 (Additional Functions) Order 2001 (S.I. No. 280 of 2001).

of Health, the respondent argued that the giving of consent for the trials by the children's guardians may not have been in their best interests and thus amounted to abuse. Ó Caoimh J., however, held that the statutory instrument was ultra vires the primary legislation:

> "In considering the report itself and the passages opened by counsel, I am satisfied that nothing disclosed therein suggests that the conduct of the trials, the subject of the report, was such that they can be said in any way to amount to "abuse" as defined in the Act of 2000."

Procedure

2–59   One practical problem relates to the methods by which a statutory instrument may be challenged. The normal rule is that the validity of the statutory instrument should be challenged directly in High Court plenary proceedings, but this question can also be raised in Order 84 judicial review proceedings if it arises *collaterally* in a challenge to the validity of an administrative decision.[114] Strictly speaking, it would seem that the validity of a statutory instrument cannot be *directly* challenged[115] in judicial review proceedings.[116] While in theory, at least, the invalidity of a statutory instrument can be raised by way of defence,[117] in practice this is likely to be confined to cases of patent invalidity in civil cases[118] or to criminal cases.[119] Even in the latter case, any decision of the trial judge would not have *erga omnes* effect and would bind only the parties before the trial judge.[120]

2–60   Notwithstanding this principle, the majority of challenges arise in judicial review proceedings, where the challenge can be linked directly to a challenge to the validity of an administrative decision. While there is some authority for the proposition that the invalidity of a statutory instrument can be challenged by way of case stated,[121] this line of thinking would probably have to give way to the modern view that, save perhaps in the clearest of cases, any such challenge must directly invoke the original jurisdiction of the High Court.[122]

---

[114] As happened in, e.g. *BUPA (Ireland) Ltd v Minister for Health and Children (No.2)* [2008] IESC 68.

[115] i.e. other than in cases where the challenge arises *collaterally* to a direct challenge to an administrative decision.

[116] This is because the making of a statutory instrument involves the exercise of legislative (rather than administrative) type powers and, hence, the decision maker is (probably) not amenable to either certiorari or prohibition. As there is thus no "decision" of a kind amenable to being prohibited or being quashed by certiorari, one is (probably) not entitled to seek a declaration of invalidity under Ord.84: see H & M, paras 16–32 to 16–33.

[117] See, e.g. *Listowel U.D.C. v McDonagh* [1968] I.R. 312.

[118] See, e.g. the comments of Geoghegan J. in *Dublin City Council v Williams* [2010] IESC 7.

[119] *Blanchfield v Harnett* [2002] IESC 41; [2002] 3 I.R. 207.

[120] [2002] IESC 41; [2002] 3 I.R. 207 at 224.

[121] As happened in *Minister for Industry and Commerce v Hales* [1967] I.R. 50.

[122] cf. the reasoning of the Supreme Court in *Dublin City Council v Williams* [2010] IESC 7, where the court held, per Geoghegan J., that complex questions bearing on the validity of waste charges "are wholly inappropriate to be dealt with in the District Court by way of defence to a simple claim for the charges."

Categories of delegated legislation

2–61   We have already seen that s.1(1) of the Statutory Instruments Act 1947 defines a statutory instrument as meaning "an order, regulation, rule, scheme or bye-law" made in the exercise of a statutory power.[123] What is the meaning of these various terms?

Order

2–62   An order may be contrasted with regulations and rules in that it refers (or, at any rate, ought to refer) to the single exercise of an administrative power in relation to a particular person or situation.[124] Examples include commencement orders bringing statutes into force, judicial appointments and compulsory purchase orders. However, the nomenclature employed in the case of delegated legislation is not consistent and there are many examples of delegated legislation which are referred to as "orders" when, strictly speaking, they should be designated as regulations.

Regulations and Rules

2–63   In contrast to orders, the categories of regulations or rules each have a definite legislative character. The term "Rules" is usually reserved for orders describing and regulating the procedure of courts, tribunals, or other statutory bodies, whereas regulations are generally of a substantive nature.

Schemes

2–64   Schemes, like orders, tend to be administrative in character, but this nomenclature is often employed where the instrument involves a system of figures or gradations, or where it prescribes the details of fees or charges. A good example is provided by statutory instruments made under s.48 of the Planning and Development Act 2000.[125] Under this provision, planning authorities may impose conditions on planning permission which require grantees to pay contributions towards local infrastructure and facilities provided by a local authority. The amount of contributions is to be calculated by reference to "a development contribution scheme made under this section". For example, the Offaly County Council Development Contribution Scheme 2004 provides for a contribution of €4,500 in the case of houses and €30 per square metre of floor area in the case of commercial

---

[123] Section 1(1) was briefly considered in *Makumbi v Minister for Justice, Equality and Law Reform* [2005] IEHC 403. Section 22(7) of the Refugee Act 1996 permitted the Minister to revoke an order made under that section. However, the order at issue was made under delegated legislation. Finlay Geoghegan J. held that the power of revocation contained in s.22(7) applied only to orders made under that section, which were statutory instruments. Because the order at issue had been made under delegated legislation and not pursuant to a statutory power, it was not a statutory instrument, and the power of revocation could not, by definition, apply to it.

[124] See *Report of the Senate Select Committee on Statutory Instruments* (T.162) (Pr. 4685), p.15.

[125] For litigation on the requirements of this section, see *Construction Federation Industry v Dublin City Council* [2005] IESC 16; [2005] 2 I.R. 496.

or industrial development. Contributions are to be index-linked. A number of exemptions are also provided for.[126]

Bye-laws

2–65 As their title implies, bye-laws have a legislative character, but differ from regulations in that they are restricted in their ambit or field of application. Bye-laws are typically made by local authorities in respect of their own functional area, but other examples include bye-laws made for the purposes of the election of representatives to certain industry boards[127] and bye-laws made by cultural institutions,[128] railway companies and airport authorities.[129] There are special rules governing the publication of draft bye-laws to enable representations to be made by members of the public in respect of any of the proposals.[130].

One element of what constitutes a bye-law was explained by Lord Russell in *Kruse v Johnson*[131]:

> "An ordinance affecting the public, or some portion of the public, imposed by some authority clothed with statutory powers ordering something to be done or not to be done, and accompanied by some sanction or penalty for its non-compliance."[132]

2–66 This definition was approved by Walsh J. in *State (Harrington) v Wallace*.[133] Here the question was whether certain sheep-dipping regulations made by Cork County Council could properly be regarded as bye-laws so as to determine whether they were "reserved functions"[134] and, thus should have been made by the councillors rather than by the county manager. Walsh J. agreed that not every administrative regulation made by a local authority could be regarded as a bye-law and where the regulation did not itself contain a sanction, it could not be regarded as a bye-law. Here the regulations did contain a criminal sanction for non-observance and this fact, coupled with the local character of the regulations, was enough to make them bye-laws.[135]

2–67 While other legislation vests local authorities with power to make bye-laws in relation to specific subjects, especially in relation to environmental and public

---

[126] See also, Land Act 2005 s.3(1) and Land Purchase Annuities Redemption Scheme Regulations 2005 (S.I. No. 830 of 2005) and Land Purchase Annuities Redemption Scheme (Amendment) Regulations 2006 (S.I. No. 352 of 2006). The details of pension arrangements in the public service are often regulated by means of schemes: see, e.g. Central Bank and Financial Services Authority of Ireland Superannuation Scheme (S.I. No. 99 of 2008).
[127] See, e.g. Building Control Act 2007 s.69(1).
[128] See, e.g. National Gallery of Ireland Act 1928 s.5.
[129] See, e.g. State Airports Act 2004 s.15(1) (airport authority given general authority to make "bye-laws in relation to a State airport which it manages or controls").
[130] Local Government Act 2001 ss.200, 202.
[131] [1898] 2 Q.B. 91.
[132] [1898] 2 Q.B. 91 at 96.
[133] [1988] I.R. 290.
[134] See paras 5–34 to 5–39.
[135] An individual guilty of contravening a bye-law is liable to a fine "not exceeding £1,500 or such lesser amount as may be specified in the bye-law in respect of such contravention." Local Government Act 2001 s.205(1). (Naturally the fine would now be payable in euro: see Euro Changeover (Amounts) Act 2001.)

health matters,[136] a local authority's general power to make bye-laws (which is a reserved power, i.e. for the councillors and not the manager)[137] is now principally derived from Pt 19 of the Local Government Act 2001. Although s.199(1) and (2) of the 2001 Act define in broad terms a local authority's power to make a bye-law, this power is nonetheless essentially confined to two types of categories: (a) the regulation or control of land, services or any other "thing whatsoever provided by or under the control or management" of the local authority; and (b) the regulation or control of "any activity or matter" or the suppression of any nuisance. Thus, the making of bye-law prohibiting the playing of certain games in a local park owned by the council would fall within the former category; a bye-law controlling the behaviour of dogs within its functional area would fall within the latter. In *Clarke v South Dublin County Council*,[138] Hanna J. noted "the very broad scope of the areas which those bye-laws may embrace" and took the view that the prohibition of the consumption of intoxicating liquor in a local authority park fell into the former category: "It would be absurd to suggest that the Oireachtas did not intend local authorities to have a wide area of discretion in ordering conduct, inter alia, in public parks." By s.199(7), the appropriate Minister may by regulation prescribe matters or classes of matters in respect of which local authorities shall not be entitled to make a bye-law.

2–68   An unsuccessful effort was made by the applicant in *Clarke v South Dublin County Council*[139] to open a new front in the fight against excessive delegations of power. The applicant attempted to invoke something like the American doctrine of pre-emption (according to which action may not be taken in a particular area by a state government if the federal government has already legislated in the area). Here, the respondent local authority had passed a bye-law making it an offence to consume alcohol in a place maintained by the local authority. The applicant had been charged with an offence under the bye-law. Hanna J. rejected the notion of an equivalent of the pre-emption doctrine and dismissed the applicant's claim that the bye-law was ultra vires. On the contrary, the Act contained "a broad area of principles and policies empowering the local authority in question to make bye-laws encompassing the wide range of the scope of its governance".

Parliamentary control

2–69   Many hundreds of statutory instruments are promulgated each year, some of them of a very far-reaching nature. In an attempt to deal with this difficulty the Oireachtas often seeks to retain some measure of parliamentary control.[140] The parent statute typically provides that every regulation made pursuant to that

---

[136] Examples include Public Health (Ireland) Act 1878 s.54 (empowering local authorities to make bye-laws regulating the keeping of animals so as to prevent injury to health); Casual Trading Act 1995 s.6 (giving local authorities powers to make bye-laws "in relation to the control, regulation, supervision and administration of casual trading in its functional area"); and Litter Pollution Act 1997 s.21(1) (as substituted by the Protection of the Environment Act 2003 s.57) (enabling a local authority to prevent the creation of and to control litter).

[137] Local Government Act 2001 s.199(5). See also, Ch.5.

[138] [2008] IEHC 84.

[139] [2008] IEHC 84.

[140] For perspectives from the United Kingdom, see Hayhurst and Wallington, "The Parliamentary Scrutiny of Delegated Legislation" [1999] *Public Law* 547; Hazell, "Who is the Guardian of Legal Values in the Legislative Process: Parliament or the Executive?" [2004] *Public Law* 495;

Act must be laid before each House of the Oireachtas. Either House may then pass a resolution within 21 sitting days annulling any such regulation but without prejudice to anything previously done thereunder.[141] Such authorities as there are suggest that failure to comply with this "laying" requirement does not invalidate the statutory instrument.[142] However, the authorities are rather old and given that the object of the 1966 Act is to enable the Houses of the Oireachtas to examine a statutory instrument with a view to its possible annulment, it could be argued that the "laying requirement" is mandatory, and not merely directory.[143] There is also no requirement that a statutory instrument should be laid in front of the Houses (or published in Iris Oifigiúil) before it comes into force.[144]

2–70 While this procedure might be of some value in permitting the discussion of a contentious statutory instrument (though, in fact, seldom—if ever—is a resolution even proposed and one has never been passed), it ignores the reality of a government majority in both Houses of the Oireachtas, so that this method of control remains largely theoretical. One might also mention that while this annulment procedure has been described by O'Higgins C.J. as a "valuable safeguard", it cannot authorise that which is not otherwise sanctioned by Art.15.2.[145] Occasionally a statute may require that confirming legislation is passed within a particular stated period[146]; or that the draft instrument will not come into force unless confirmed by resolution of each House of the Oireachtas[147]; or provide for an appeal by any person aggrieved against the making of the instrument to the courts.[148]

2–71 There is no parliamentary examination of domestic statutory instruments. The Senate Select Committee on Statutory Instruments' last report was published in respect of the 1978–81 period. (This Committee was briefly replaced by the Joint Oireachtas Committee.). As noted below, by virtue of s.4 of the European Communities Act 1972 (as amended), the Joint Committee on European Scrutiny performs the statutory function of reviewing statutory instruments made pursuant to the European Communities Act 1972.[149]However, the Ombudsman has sought,

---

Himsworth, "The Delegated Powers Scrutiny Committee" (1995) *Public Law* 34; Himsworth, "Subordinate Legislation in the Scottish Parliament" (2002) *Edinburgh Law Review* 356.

[141] See, e.g. Dormant Accounts Act 2001 s.4(4). The "laying" procedure is regulated by statute: see Houses of the Oireachtas (Laying of Documents) Act 1966.

[142] *Premier Meat Packers Ltd v Minister for Agriculture*, unreported, High Court, July 28, 1971. See also, *R. v Sheer Metalcraft Ltd* [1951] 1 Q.B. 586.

[143] This view is reinforced by *O'Neill v Minister for Agriculture and Food* [1998] 1 I.R. 539; [1997] 2 I.L.R.M. 435.

[144] *J & J. Haire & Co Ltd v Minister for Health and Children* [2010] 2 I.R. 615 at para.[59].

[145] *Cityview Press v AnCo* [1980] I.R. 381.

[146] See, e.g. Provisional Collection of Taxes Act 1927 s.4.

[147] See, e.g. Dentists Act 1985 s.9(3); Electoral Act 1997 s.72(6); Dormant Accounts Act 2001 s.4(3); Local Government Act 2001 s.27(5).

[148] See, e.g. Fisheries (Consolidation) Act 1959 s.11(1)(d) (right of appeal to the High Court); Casual Trading Act 1995 s.6(8) (right of appeal by a person aggrieved to the District Court against the making of bye-laws regulating casual trading).

[149] The current committee was established in 2007 and works in tandem with the Joint Committee on European Affairs. From 2002 to 2007, the scrutiny function was performed by a sub-committee of the Joint Committee on European Affairs. Originally, the scrutiny function was exercised by the Oireachtas Joint Committee on Secondary Legislation of the European Communities. However, "[i]n practice the Committee made very little contribution to the democratic scrutiny of EC measures. It was under-resourced and constantly overloaded with a backlog of measures". Walsh, "Parliamentary Scrutiny of E.U. Criminal Law in Ireland"

to some extent, to step into the breach. In her report on Nursing Home Subventions, the Ombudsman was critical of the use of delegated legislation, and suggested some straightforward, practical reforms:

> "In the shorter term, establishing a mechanism for monitoring secondary legislation is an obvious step worth taking. Such monitoring might have to be done, initially at least, on a selective basis. This could be done by ensuring that, in the case of certain Bills, the section dealing with the making of regulations by the relevant Minister would provide that an affirmative resolution from each of the Houses of the Oireachtas would be needed before any such regulations would come into effect. This would be particularly the case where the regulations in question confer entitlements, require payments by, or otherwise impose penalties on members of the public. There is something to be said for having the Committee, which dealt with the passage of the legislation, also deal with monitoring the making of the regulations. In this context, what was done in the case of the Ombudsman Act, 1980 may be of interest. When the Ombudsman Act was passed it contained, at section 4(10), the 'standard' provision in relation to the making of regulations whereby public bodies could be added to, or deleted from, the list of public bodies subject to investigation by the Ombudsman. When the Act was implemented in 1984 with the appointment of the first Ombudsman, the then Minister introduced the Ombudsman (Amendment) Bill. This, when enacted, provided that any regulation under section 4(10) required an affirmative resolution by each of the Houses of the Oireachtas. It was considered that any proposed amendments to the Ombudsman's jurisdiction were worthy of consideration by the two Houses."[150]

2–72   Save in the case of statutory instruments made under the European Communities Act 1972 there is currently no functioning parliamentary scrutiny of delegated legislation. Indeed, even in the case of instruments made under the 1972 Act, it does not appear that the Oireachtas Committee on European Affairs has made any headway in performing such scrutiny. The problem is all the more pressing given the increased volume of delegated legislation.[151] This is in contrast with the position which obtained between 1948 and 1983 when this function was discharged, in relation to domestic statutory instruments, by a Senate Select Committee on Statutory Instruments. This function was then vested in the Joint Oireachtas Committee on Legislation during the 1983–1987 period.

(2006) 31 Eur.L.R. 48 at 60. For a discussion of the work of this Committee, see McMahon and Murphy, *European Community Law in Ireland* (Dublin: Butterworths, 1989) at paras 14.13 and 16.12 and Robinson, "Irish Parliamentary Scrutiny of European Community Legislation" (1979) 16 C.M.L.Rev. 9. For more detail on the scrutiny of EU secondary legislation, see H & M, paras 2–121 to 2–130.

[150] Office of the Ombudsman, *Report on Nursing Home Subventions* (January 2001), p.71. See generally, above Ch.8.

[151] For adverse comment in the Oireachtas on the increased resort to delegated legislation, see 579 *Dáil Debates* Col.391, February 3, 2004 (Deputy J. Bruton); 622 *Dáil Debates* Col.1222, June 28, 2006 (Deputy Howlin).

F. Administrative (Non-Statutory) Circulars or Rules

Introduction

2–73   One of the most remarkable features of the many diverse government schemes and licensing arrangements currently in existence is the extent to which they are derived from administrative (i.e. non-statutory) circulars and rules.[152] Thus, our system of public administration now teems with a growth of enigmatic rules (for we are not speaking here of individual executive orders) which are neither primary nor delegated legislation.[153] The names given to these instruments include: circulars (of diverse types), codes of practice, notes of guidance, "instructions" and administrative guidelines. However, the nomenclature in this area is not of great importance since the distinction between the different instruments has never been made clear and there is little consistency. Accordingly, the term "administrative rules" is used to refer collectively to the family. The more important questions in regard to these rules are: first, why they have been developed and what are their advantages and disadvantages (questions addressed in this section); and, secondly, what is their legal status and what (direct or indirect) effects do they have (questions examined in the succeeding sections).

2–74   Probably the easiest type of this species to justify is that which emerges where some statutory discretion has been conferred upon a public body and the body chooses to indicate the conditions on which it is going to exercise its discretion by issuing a circular. In other words, such an instrument constitutes a useful and much used means of—to use US parlance—"structuring discretion" and publicising how it will be exercised.[154] A contemporary example here is supplied by the guidelines produced by the Revenue Commissioners[155] for determining whether a work in respect of which a tax exemption under s.2 of the Finance Act 1969 has been

---

[152]   For literature on this topic, see: Baldwin, *Rules and Government* (Oxford: OUP, 1995); Baldwin and Houghton, "Circular Arguments: the Status and Legitimacy of Administrative Rules" (1986) *Public Law* 231; Black, "Talking about Regulation" [1998] *Public Law* 77; Black, "Enrolling Actors in Regulatory Systems: Examples from U.K. Financial Services Regulation" (2003) *Public Law* 63; Craig, *Administrative Law*, 6th edn (London: Sweet & Maxwell, 2008), pp.715–757; Etherington, "'Mandatory Guidance' for Dealing with Contaminated Land: Paradox or Pragmatism?" (2002) 23 *Statute Law Review* 203; Ganz, "Quasi-Legislation: Recent Developments in Secondary Legislation" (1987) 14 C.L.J. 108; Ganz, "Delegated Legislation: a Necessary Evil or Constitutional Outrage?" in Leyland and Woods (eds), *Administrative Law Facing the Future: Old Constraints and New Horizons* (Blackstone Press, 1997), p.60; Hogan, "The Legal Status of Administrative Rules and Circulars" (1987) 22 Ir. Jur. (N.S) 194; Hadfield, "The Doctrine of Legitimate Expectations" (1988) 39 N.I.L.Q. 103; O'Reilly, "Coping with Community Legislation – a Practitioner's Reaction" (1996) 17 *Statute Law Review* 15; Page, *Governing by Numbers: Delegated Legislation and Everyday Policymaking* (Oxford: Hart Publishing, 2001); Wade and Forsyth, *Administrative Law*, 9th edn (Oxford: OUP, 2004), pp.857–873.

[153]   The term "tertiary legislation" is employed in Baldwin, "Informal Legislation" (1986) *Public Law* 267.

[154]   Davis, *Discretionary Justice: a Preliminary Inquiry* (Louisiana State University Press, 1969), Ch.4.

[155]   Section 195(12)(a) of the Taxes Consolidation Act 1997 provides that the Arts Council and Minister for the Arts shall, with the consent of the Minister for Finance, draw up such guidelines. The guidelines have been produced in booklet form by the Revenue Commissioners and are issued to every applicant for such artists' tax relief. Other than this they have not been published in any way. In particular, they have not been published either in *Iris Oifigiúil* or as a statutory instrument, although it is strongly arguable that such guidelines fall within the

sought is, in fact, an "original and creative work" possessing "cultural or artistic merit" within the meaning of this section. In other instances a public authority is required to have regard to guidelines issued by the appropriate government department.[156] Thus, this usage is, in many ways, beneficial to the persons affected by the discretion. Nevertheless, this may seem to the administrator to be a case of "damned if you do; damned if you don't". For a difficulty arises here from the fact that the law—with its emphasis on process, rather than substance—is concerned to ensure that discretion is exercised as authorised by the legislature, rather than that discretion is limited. This difficulty will be considered in a later chapter,[157] under the heading of "fettering a discretionary power". In a succeeding section of this chapter, we shall address the question of whether the reasonableness or vires of a decision should be judged by reference to the terms of a relevant circular.

2–75   In a second type of instrument—often known as a code of practice—the arrangement affords a way of allowing a trade, commercial or professional group which is affected by the rule to be involved in devising its content. A good example here is provided by the "guidance notes" issued by the Pensions Board for the guidance of pensions' administrators.[158] Another example is supplied by the very detailed guidelines issued by the Garda Commissioner as to the practical application and operation of the Firearms Acts 1925–2009.[159] In this genus, there is a range of possibilities with the "softest law" (for the entire area of administrative rules is sometimes known as "soft law") occurring in the form of voluntary codes.[160] Here the thinking is that "persuasion may be preferable to compulsion".[161] Yet the courts will not permit guidance notes to alter the law and decisions which are based on guidance notes which inaccurately state the law will be quashed.[162] Frequently, as, for example, in *The Rules of the Road*, there is the advantage that non-technical language can used to explain complex legal issues to the general public.

---

definition of a statutory instrument provided by the Statutory Instruments Act 1947 s.1(1), for which see paras 2–48 to 2–49.

[156] See, e.g. Planning and Development Act 2000 s.28 (local authorities required in the performance of their functions to have regard to guidelines issued by the Department of Local Government); Residential Tenancies Act 2004 s.183 (Private Residential Tenancies Board to have regard to guidelines issued by the Minister); State Airports Act 2004 s.9(4)(c) (airport authorities required to have regard to "any policy, financial or other guidelines" given by the Minister in relation to the performance of their statutory functions).

[157] See Ch.15, Part E.

[158] See, e.g. *Guidance Notes on Disclosure of Information* (May, 2007); *Guidance Notes on Compulsory and Voluntary Reporting to the Pensions Board* (October, 2005); and *Guidance Notes on Member Participation in the Selection of Trustees* (December, 1993).

[159] *Garda Commissioner's Guidelines as to the Practical Application and Operation of the Firearms Acts, 1925-2009* (September 2009). These guidelines are exceptionally detailed and involve an extensive analysis of the legislation and the relevant case-law. The guidelines themselves were issued in accordance with s.3A of the Firearms Act 1925, as inserted by s.31 of the Criminal Justice Act 2006 (as amended by s.29 of the Criminal Justice (Miscellaneous Provisions) Act 2009).

[160] See, e.g. Consumer Protection Act 2007 s.88: "[A] person representing one or more traders may submit a code of practice to the Agency for its review or approval". See also, the slightly less voluntary Data Protection Act 1988 s.13, as substituted by Data Protection (Amendment) Act 2003 s.14; Industrial Relations Act 1990 s.42; Licensing of Indoor Events Act 2003 s.9; Public Service Management (Recruitment) Act 2004 s.23; Disability Act 2005 ss.25, 30 and 50.

[161] Ganz, "Delegated legislation: A necessary evil or Constitutional outrage?" (1997), pp.97–98.

[162] See *Sherwin v An Bord Pleanála* [2007] IEHC 227; [2008] 1 I.L.R.M. 31 at 48.

2–76 There is some evidence that government departments issue administrative rules and circulars in preference to legislation almost as a matter of policy. The main culprits here appear to be the Departments of Agriculture and Food,[163] and the Environment, and, even after an apparently new legislative dawn ushered in by the Education Act 1998, the Department of Education.[164] It is quite remarkable, for example, that there is often no legislation underpinning various schemes administered by the Department of Agriculture, or requiring the Minister to secure parliamentary approval for a significant change in policy.

2–77 From the perspective of public administrators (we shall come to the view of lawyers below), the use of circulars undoubtedly carry advantages: the procedure is convenient, whereas a statutory structure might prove to be inflexible. Parliamentary time is scarce and there may be difficulties in securing the assistance of a parliamentary draftsman to prepare the appropriate legislation or even a statutory instrument. Thus, one study of the method of implementing Community legislation in the various Member States found that Irish officials did not like to have to implement directives by means of primary legislation "because it requires extensive consultation with interested organisations, adequate attention from the Parliamentary Draftsman, discussion in Cabinet and parliamentary time".[165]

---

[163] Thus, prior to the European Communities (Milk Quotas) Regulations 1994 (S.I. No. 70 of 1994), virtually the entire milk quota system was administered by a series of administrative circulars: see generally, O'Reilly, "Coping with Community Legislation" (1996) 17 *Statute Law Review* 15. This also meant that such circular letters and notices (at 22) dealt with such matters as: "... reductions in quotas granted to individual producers in exercise of discretion conferred by Community legislation; the leasing of land and quota; the operation of a 'claw back' which is applied to leases of land; and the leasing of dairy cows by 'SLOM' or 'Mulder' producers to fulfil a SLOM quota allocation granted on a provisional basis. No formal record exists of these circulars or notices. It is difficult to imagine a less transparent system."

Not surprisingly, in *Lawlor v Minister for Agriculture* [1990] 1 I.R. 356, 366, Murphy J. expressed astonishment at the informal manner in which the milk quota regime was operated by the Department of Agriculture.

[164] See, e.g. *Sheedy v Information Commissioner* [2005] IESC 35; [2005] 2 I.R. 272 (Department of Education inspections of schools still governed by departmental circulars). There is still some force in the comments made by Costello J. in a bygone era. In *O'Callaghan v Meath VEC*, unreported, High Court, November 20, 1990, he suggested: "It is a remarkable feature of the Irish system of education that its administration by the Department of Education is largely uncontrolled by statute or statutory instruments and many hundreds, perhaps thousands, of rules and regulations, memoranda, circulars and decisions are issued and made by the Department and the Minister (dealing sometimes with the most important aspects of educational policy) not under any statutory power but merely as administrative measures. The measures are, not of course, illegal. But they have no statutory force and the sanction which ensures compliance with them is not a legal one but the undeclared understanding that the Department will withhold financial assistance in the event of non-compliance."

See also, *O'Shiel v Minister for Education and Science* [1999] 2 I.R. 321 at 328; *Prendergast v Higher Education Authority* [2008] IEHC 257. The Department of Education has long been identified as a sinner in this respect: "A striking characteristic of the legal framework for education in Ireland for many years was an almost complete absence of legislation. Along with the principle of State subsidiarity in education, the reasons for this can also be traced back to the Supreme Court decision in *Re Article 26 and the School Attendance Bill, 1942* [1943] I.R. 334, where the heavy emphasis placed on parental rights by the Court resulted in the striking down of the Bill as unconstitutional." O'Mahony, *Educational Rights in Irish Law* (Dublin: Thomson Round Hall, 2006), p.179. Internal citations omitted.

[165] Laffan, Manning, Kelly, "Ireland" in *Making European Policies Work: the Implementation of Community Legislation in the Member States* (European Institute of Public Administration, 1986), p.383.

Furthermore, although the production of delegated legislation was found to be less time-consuming than an Act of the Oireachtas, this nevertheless brought its own difficulties:

> "The drafting of statutory instruments is not a simple procedure. A proposed legal instrument makes its way slowly from the sponsoring department, to the Attorney-General's office, and finally to the Parliamentary Draftsman. This process is repeated until all interests are satisfied with the statutory instrument. Delays are generated not only by policy conflict, but also because of bureaucratic blockages in the system."[166]

2–78   The disadvantages of this proliferation of such administrative rules from the point of view of a conventional constitutional system of laws scarcely need emphasis. Despite the fact that administrative circulars may create legal rights and obligations and are subject to judicial review, their legal status defies exact classification. In a seminal article published in 1944,[167] Sir Robert Megarry described such legislation as a form of "quasi-legislation" and this seems as good a description as any of the effect in practice of such circulars. But no legal system can be content with a situation whereby public authorities and Government Departments habitually resort to circulars in an attempt to regulate legal rights.[168] The confusion resulting from the habitual use of such circulars has frequently been judicially deplored[169] and in *McCann v Minister for Education*,[170] Costello P. made the following plea for reform:

> "If administrative ministerial rules and regulations were dated; if they were identified by reference to the sub-head in the Book of Estimates to which they relate; if amendments bore the same reference and were dated by reference to the ministerial order which made them; if a register was kept of the original measure and amendments to it; if the original measure and amendments were regularly consolidated and meanwhile made available in loose leaf form to

---

[166] Laffan, Manning, Kelly, "Ireland" in *Making European Policies Work: the Implementation of Community Legislation in the Member States* (1986), p.392.

[167] Megarry, "Quasi-Legislation" (1944) 60 L.Q.R. 125.

[168] Sir Robert Megarry's comments ("Quasi-Legislation" (1944) 60 L.Q.R. 125 at 127) apply a fortiori to our modern legal system: "A system under which the practitioner may have to search Hansard, the Stationery Office list of official publications and the weekly law papers to find out how far up-to-date text-books and the statute book itself can be relied upon as stating the effective law will commend itself to few."

In response, Ganz, "Quasi-Legislation", sardonically observed (at p.2), the practitioner "would have to look a great deal further afield today". In *Kylemore Bakery Ltd v Minister for Trade, Commerce and Tourism* [1986] I.L.R.M. 526, Costello J. observed (at 530) that "these non-statutory schemes have the advantage of flexibility so that they can easily be adapted to changing circumstances but ... their informality can create considerable problems when it becomes necessary to ascertain legal relationships arising from them when a dispute in their administration occurs". See also, the similar comments of O'Hanlon J. in *McKerring v Minister for Agriculture* [1989] I.LR.M. 82 and Murphy J. in *Lawlor v Minister for Agriculture* [1990] 1 I.R. 356 at 366. See also, Tomkin, "Implementing Community Legislation into National Law: the Demands of a New Legal Order" (2004) 4(2) *Judicial Studies Institute Journal* 130 at 150.

[169] See, e.g. *Patchett v Leathem* (1949) 65 T.L.R. 69; *McCann v Minister for Education* [1997] 1 I.L.R.M. 1.

[170] [1997] 1 I.L.R.M. 1.

members of the public, this would be one way of obviating the danger of injustice which is inherent in the present highly informal procedures."[171]

2–79   While it is true that administrative practices would be greatly improved if these suggestions were acted on, the fact remains that the habitual use of circulars as a means of quasi-legislation is unsatisfactory. Such a practice was roundly condemned by Streatfield J. in a notable passage which is also pertinent to this jurisdiction:

> "Whereas ordinary legislation, by passing through both Houses of Parliament or, at least, lying on the table of both Houses, is thus twice blessed, this type of so-called legislation is at least four times cursed. First, it has seen neither House of Parliament; secondly, it is unpublished and is inaccessible even to those whose valuable rights or property may be affected; thirdly, it is a jumble of provisions, legislative, administrative, or directive in character, and sometimes difficult to disentangle one from the other; and, fourthly, it is expressed not in the precise language of an Act of Parliament or an Order in Council but in the more colloquial language of correspondence, which is not always susceptible of the ordinary canons of construction."[172]

2–80   In addition, the limited circulation of such circulars and their general inaccessibility may mean that the reliance on such circulars could be contrary to the guarantee of fair procedures, since it might well be thought that "any rule which is applied on the basis of an internal memorandum which is not available to the public may lack the characteristic of true law and could possibly be challenged on that ground".[173] These principles would certainly seem to have considerable relevance as far as the operation of the Tuberculosis and Brucellosis Schemes are concerned, since *McKerring v Minister for Agriculture*.[174] O'Hanlon J. found it remarkable that the only guidance regarding the grant scheme was to be found in the conditions on the back of the cattle movement permit and any changes in these conditions "were notified to the farming community by way of newspaper advertisement".[175] The issue of fair procedures arising from the restricted publication of this circular had not, however, been argued before him.

The legal status of administrative rules: general principles

2–81   The major conceptual problem of the legal status of circulars and other administrative rules is, as yet, imperfectly explored. Naturally, non-statutory schemes

---

[171] [1997] 1 I.L.R.M. 1 at 5.

[172] *Patchett v Leathem* (1949) 65 T.L.R. 69 at 70.

[173] Byrne, (1987) 22 Ir. Jur. (N.S) 326–327. See also, the comments of Scott L.J. in *Blackpool Corporation v Locker* [1948] 1 K.B. 349 at 361: "The very justification for that basic maxim [that ignorance of the law is no excuse] is that the whole of our law, written or unwritten, is accessible to the public – in the sense, of course, that, at any rate, its legal advisers have access to it, at any moment, as of right." See also, the comments of Costello P. in *McCann v Minister for Education* [1997] 1 I.L.R.M. 1 at 15

[174] [1989] I.L.R.M. 82.

[175] [1989] I.L.R.M. 82 at 83–84. See discussion by the Court of Justice of this issue in the context of notification of changes in the milk quota regime in *Mulligan v Minister for Agriculture and Food* (C-313/99) [2002] E.C.R. I-5719.

can be impugned as unconstitutional on the basis that they infringe constitutional provisions.[176] In addition, the following principles can be suggested.

2–82   First, circulars and the rest of their family are not law. This would follow from the fundamental character of the common law. For, if delegated legislation which is, at least, contemplated in primary legislation, cannot make law which goes beyond principles laid down in the parent Act, then the same restriction must certainly apply in the case of circulars. As a consequence, it is axiomatic that the public authority which issued such a circular may not rely on that circular as against the private citizen in order to affect or prejudice his strict legal rights nor may such a circular be relied on by one citizen against another.[177]

2–83   Secondly, and in reverse, the general proposition that circulars et al. are not law raises the question of whether a citizen may invoke a circular as against the public authority. The answer is that although, as stated, a circular may not alter the law, it may, and often has been, regarded as the basis of a legitimate expectation. There is nothing unique to circulars in this, as a legitimate expectation can be created in a variety of ways, ranging from an official letter to an express oral representation. The decided cases tend to show, however, that circulars are a common source of legitimate expectations.[178]

2–84   Thirdly, as mentioned in the first point, although circulars do not in themselves have a legal status, they tend to have enormous impact as many individuals will assume that the circulars have an official legal standing. Accordingly, the courts will, exceptionally, entertain proceedings challenging the vires of a circular. In line with what just has been said, in strict law such a circular is of no more potency than (say) an opinion of counsel which a public authority had reason to disseminate to the public at large. However, for the sorts of reasons just mentioned, such a circular has immense practical weight and the courts properly assume the jurisdiction to declare that any statement of law contained therein is erroneous in law.

2–85   We elaborate below on the first and third of these propositions, the second proposition being covered separately at paras 19–25 to 19–28. It ought to be noted, too, that, in the United Kingdom, there has been some development (mainly at

---

[176] *Rooney v Minister for Agriculture (No. 2)* [2004] IEHC 305; *O'Shiel v Minister for Education* [1999] 2 I.R. 321. As Laffoy J. said in the latter case (at 354): "[T]he proper constitutional scope of Article 42 cannot be diminished by administrative measures and that, in so far as the rules purport to do so, they are invalid to that extent. It seems to me that as a matter of fundamental principle that proposition must be correct."

[177] A slightly different contention was made by the plaintiffs in *O'Shiel v Minister for Education* [1999] 2 I.R. 321. The plaintiffs claimed that the failure of the Department of Education to fund certain non-denominational primary schools was a breach of Art.42 of the Constitution. The Department's refusal to fund was based on the failure of the school to meet teacher qualification standards and to teach Irish adequately. One element of the claim was that because the regulations governing recognition of schools by the Department were "merely administrative rules", rather than laws promulgated under Art.15.2.1°, they could not "adversely affect constitutional rights." [1999] 2 I.R. 321 at 349. Laffoy J. did not confront this proposition directly, but accepted that constitutional rights could not be infringed by administrative rules. See generally, Daly, "'Political Questions' and Judicial Review in Ireland" (2008) 8(2) *Judicial Studies Institute Journal* 116.

[178] See in particular, *Keogh v Criminal Assets Bureau* [2004] 2 I.R. 159; *Power v Minister for Social and Family Affairs* [2006] IEHC 170; [2007] 1 I.R. 543.

an academic level)[179] in determining the legal consequences, in terms of legal effects, of circulars and other administrative rules by drawing certain distinctions. Among these are: whether the rule or circular is (even implicitly) authorised by or contemplated in, primary or secondary legislation, so that it is not entirely lacking in legitimate means of support[180]; its terminology or whether it otherwise "looks like law"[181] (clarity, precision, justiciability, etc.); and the subject-matter and surrounding context. As yet in this jurisdiction the judiciary have not attempted to discriminate amongst the various types of administrative rules, so as to assign to "soft law" different levels of "softness". Accordingly, we shall not pursue this issue of sub-categorisation any further here.

Can administrative rules alter existing law?

2–86 Recent years have witnessed an increasing number of statutes which expressly permit or require regulatory authorities to issue codes and guidelines, some of which have the effect of an attempt to amend the law. An example here is s.19(1) of the Broadcasting Act 2001 (unaffected by the Broadcasting Act 2009), which now requires the Broadcasting Authority of Ireland, upon being directed to do so by the Minister, to draw up:

(a) a code specifying standards to be complied with, and rules and practices to be observed, in respect of the taste and decency of programme material, the subject of a broadcasting service or sound broadcasting service, and, in particular, in respect of the portrayal of violence and sexual conduct in such material, and

(b) a code specifying standards to be complied with, and rules and practices to be observed, in respect of advertising, teleshopping material, sponsorship and other forms of commercial promotion employed in any broadcasting service or sound broadcasting service (other than advertising and other activities as aforesaid falling within *paragraph (c)*)

...

2–87 A Code has been promulgated under the terms of this section[182] and some examples drawn from the Code may be conveniently examined to illustrate its amorphous legal character. The word "advertising" or "advertisement" is not defined in the primary legislation. The Code defines it as:

"Any form of announcement broadcast in return for payment or for similar consideration or broadcast for self-promotional purposes by a public or private undertaking in connection with a trade, business, craft or profession

---

[179] See further, Baldwin and Houghton, "Circular Arguments: the Status and Legitimacy of Administrative Rules" (1986) *Public Law* 231 at 245–252.

[180] Examples of this type of circular include the programme material guidelines contemplated by the Broadcasting Act 2001; the artists' tax exemption guidelines issued under the Finance Act 1994; and the various codes provided for by the Disability Act 2005.

[181] Thus, many non-lawyers probably assume that the *Rules for National Schools* (1965)—which is replete with formal legal terminology—has some form of official statutory foundation.

[182] *The Broadcasting Commission of Ireland General Advertising Code* (2007).The quotations in the text are from pp.3–5.

in order to promote the supply of products or services, including immovable property, activities, rights and obligations, in return for payment."

2–88 Later in the Code, a whole host of activities are excluded from this definition, including charity appeals and advertisements for the National Symphony Orchestra. The Code also defines (for the purposes of restricting or prohibiting them) "misleading advertising", "comparative advertising", "surreptitious advertising", "subliminal advertising", "teleshopping", "product placement", "virtual advertising", "interactive advertising" and "split-screen advertising". It might be said that these definitions are not guided, let alone warranted, by any "principle or policy" contained in the existing broadcasting legislation. On the other hand, the Broadcasting Authority of Ireland is an expert body established, inter alia, to promulgate and uphold good broadcasting standards. It is doubtful that the Oireachtas has the time or expertise to define and regulate different types of advertising. The Authority is also relatively more flexible and adaptable than the Oireachtas which counsels in favour of giving it a wide remit in an era notable for the rapid rate of technological change.

2–89 A more troubling example is provided by s.8.1 of the Code which not only regulates the advertising of alcohol, but goes so far as to prohibit certain types of alcoholic drink. One might certainly query whether such sweeping prohibitions ought rather to have been a matter for the Oireachtas and the elected representatives.

2–90 As in the case of other administrative circulars, two questions arise in regard to this circular. First, is it binding at law? Secondly, what safeguards—consultation, discussion, publication, etc.—should be or have been applied to it? As regards the first question, the fact that the Code is mandated by the statutory provision quoted earlier militates in favour of its being law. The term "voluntary", which appeared in the Code's predecessor,[183] is not present. Indeed, broadcasters are asked to note that "it is their obligation to comply with the provisions of this Code".[184] At the very least, the code is highly authoritative, if not legally binding. However, to return to the question of safeguards, while the code may have been the subject of informal consultation, this type of secondary legislation—for this, in reality, is what the code is—does not even comply with the minimum safeguards imposed in the case of most secondary legislation, i.e. publication under the terms of the Statutory Instruments Act 1947[185] or being subject to the power of annulment by resolution

---

[183] *Codes of standards, practice and prohibitions in advertising, sponsorship, and other forms of commercial promotion in broadcasting services* (1995).
[184] *The Broadcasting Commission of Ireland General Advertising Code* (2007), p.2.
[185] One question this raises is whether this code does in fact fall within the scope of the Statutory Instruments Act 1947. The query takes us back to the definition of a statutory instrument as "an order, regulation, rule, scheme or bye-law" made in the exercise of a statutory power. As to the second element of the test—statutory power—the 1990 Act states, in s.4(1) that the Commission "shall, upon being directed by the Minister to do so ... prepare a code ...". It might be said that this concerns a statutory *duty*, as opposed to a statutory power as mentioned in the 1947 Act. However, while it is generally true that the power to make a statutory instrument is usually discretionary rather than mandatory, this is by no means unexceptional: see, e.g. Irish Takeover Panel Act 1997 s.8(2). In any case, the power-duty distinction does not seem a rational policy basis upon which to determine whether a rule falls within the Act. The more difficult question is in regard to an element of the definition, namely, whether a code comes

of either House of the Oireachtas. Moreover, as just noted, some features of the code are arguably ultra vires the parent legislation. Furthermore they would seem not to comply with the "principles and policies" test.

2–91 Leaving aside the particular category of administrative rules which are mentioned in statute law and which have been examined in the preceding section, principle and authority seem to argue that administrative rules are not law and, thus, cannot change that procedural or substantive law.[186] Take, for example, Devitt J.'s comment in *Carberry v Yates*[187] (a Circuit Court decision) that a ministerial circular prescribing the teaching of Irish as a compulsory requirement of the primary curriculum was unlawful. He described it as a ministerial "ukase for which there is not any statutory authority".[188] The abolition of corporal punishment by circular provides a particularly good example of an attempt to change substantive law through administrative rules. This was purportedly done in 1982 by a circular emanating from the Department of Education,[189] but it is difficult to see how such a circular could have been legally effective for this purpose.[190] There is a further point: at common law, it was permissible for a parent and those in loco parentis (such as a teacher) to administer reasonable corporal punishment to a child. It seems clear that this common law right[191] can only be altered by an Act of the Oireachtas and not by circular.

---

within the term "order". The answer perhaps should be in the negative if—but only if—the code is not legally binding in the way that an order is, an escape exit that seems to have been blocked off by the omission of the word "voluntary" from the new Code.

[186] One might think that "such rules may supplement the law in allowing concessions to which there is no legal entitlement or in laying down the conditions on which discretionary benefits will be granted." Turpin and Tomkins, *British Government and the Constitution*, 6th edn (Cambridge: Cambridge University Press, 2007), p.477. The authors of this leading British textbook give the example of extra-statutory concessions adopted by the Inland Revenue. However, the Revenue Commissioners, in a submission to the Commission on Taxation, rejected the possibility of such concessions being allowed in Ireland: "There is a major difference in relation to extra-statutory concessions between Ireland and the United Kingdom. In Ireland, the Revenue Commissioners are bound by both legislation and the Constitution. This precludes us from making general extra-statutory concessions. Any such concessions would have to be provided for in legislation. We would apply an extra-statutory concession in an individual case under the care provisions. Since general extra-statutory concessions are not allowed, they do not exist and cannot be published." *http://www.gov.ie/committees-99/c-publicaccounts/sub-ctte/991011/page4.htm* [Last accessed: November 14, 2008].

[187] (1935) 69 I.L.T.R. 86.

[188] (1935) 69 I.L.T.R. 86 at 88. Subsequent attempts to reverse this decision through legislation failed: see Osborough, "Education in the Irish Law and Constitution" (1978) 13 Ir. Jur. (N.S) 145 at 176–180.

[189] Rule 130 of the *Rules for National Schools* (1965) (which provided for corporal punishment in certain circumstances) was amended by Circulars 9/82 and 7/88. The change in practice was announced in the Dáil by the Minister for Education (Professor O'Donoghue) in March 1982: see 333 *Dáil Debates* Cols 1430–1431.

[190] It may be, however, that teachers could lawfully be bound as a matter of contract to observe the terms of this circular and, furthermore, pupils might possibly be in a position to assert that this circular (directed as it was to the public at large) created a legitimate expectation that they should not be subjected to corporal punishment.

[191] It is difficult to find judicial authority for this proposition, but this fact was conceded by the British Government in *Campbell and Cosans v United Kingdom* (1983) 4 E.H.R.R. 293 at 297. This concession would appear to be undoubtedly correct. In *A v United Kingdom* (1999) 27 E.H.R.R. 611, the defence of reasonable chastisement (to a charge of assault occasioning actual bodily harm) was held by the Strasbourg Court to be a violation of art.3 of the European

2–92   A series of High Court decisions also tend to support the view that circulars cannot change the law.[192] For example, in *Crawford v Centime Ltd*,[193] Clarke J. also indicated that the Revenue Commissioners' Guidelines could not change the law:

> "Counsel for the Revenue indicated that such an entitlement might derive from the so-called "care and management" provisions of the Taxes Acts (see for example s.849 Taxes Consolidation Act, 1997) which place the care and management of the operation of tax in the hands of the Revenue. As the matter was not fully debated I should not express any concluded view on this issue save to indicate that I would have significant doubt as to whether the care and management provisions of the Taxes Acts could be construed in a constitutional manner such as would entitle the Revenue Commissioners to impose absolute criteria, the effect of which might be to require a person to bear tax (or, as in this case, not obtain a refund) to which they are, *prima facie* entitled under the Taxes Acts in the absence of a specific statutory entitlement to impose such criteria which conforms with the requirements of the jurisprudence of the courts in relation to principles and policy. In saying that, however, I would wish to make clear that it is entirely appropriate for the Revenue Commissioners to issue guidelines which make clear to taxpayers the way in which the Revenue will exercise any discretion which the law confers as to the manner in which the Taxes Acts may be applied. Such guidelines have the merit of informing taxpayers as to how Revenue discretion is likely to be exercised and achieve the desirable end of making it more likely that any discretion which the Revenue may enjoy will be exercised in a similar manner in like cases. It is, however, the elevation of any such guidelines to matters which are applied as if they have the force of law that is open to serious question. That is particularly so where, as here, and for the reasons which I have analysed above, the criteria appear, in many respects, to be inconsistent with the law."[194]

2–93   But while Revenue Guidelines cannot change the law, there may be circumstances where published Revenue statements may serve to create a legitimate expectation which the individual taxpayer may be able to enforce, especially where these statements relate to Revenue procedures rather than substantive tax law.[195]

Convention on Human Rights, but its decision acknowledged the possibility of the right to chastise existing at common law.

[192] See also, *Colman (JJ) Ltd v Commissioners of Customs and Excise* [1968] 1 W.L.R. 1286. By contrast, in *Crowley v Ireland* [1980] I.R. 112, Kenny J. said that the use by the Minister of unqualified teachers in an industrial dispute would be a breach of the *Rules for National Schools* (1965) and hence an unlawful use of public funds. But this would appear to attach to the Rules a form of legal status which is not warranted, unless one takes the view that the Dáil when voting money supply must be taken to have implicitly only authorised the spending of monies in the manner envisaged by the Rules.

[193] [2005] IEHC 325; [2006] 1 I.L.R.M. 543. For earlier examples, see *Donohue v Dillon* [1988] I.L.R.M. 654; *Grehan v North Eastern Health Board* [1989] I.R. 422; *Devitt v Minister for Education* [1989] I.L.R.M. 639. See further, paras 19–25 to 19–28 and paras 19–49 to 19–58.

[194] [2006] 1 I.L.R.M. 543 at 560.

[195] See, e.g. *Keogh v Criminal Assets Bureau* [2004] IESC 32; [2004] 2 I.L.R.M. 481 and see paras 19–104 to 19–109.

2–94 Finally, following from the foregoing, it is a fortiori that memoranda of understanding or informal agreements between the State and its employees cannot alter the terms of delegated legislation. The point was put forcefully by Hardiman J. in *Curley v Governor of Arbour Hill Prison*,[196] in response to a contention that the Prison (Disciplinary Code for Officers) Rules 1996 was to be construed subject to an agreement concluded by the Department of Justice and staff representatives:

> "There is, in my opinion, no warrant whatever for regarding the instrument or any part thereof as being 'subject to' the memorandum of understanding. This is not a question of construction but a matter of principle. The statutory instrument (whatever its antecedents in industrial relations negotiations may have been) is on the face of it a legitimate piece of delegated legislation ... In my view, no document which is not of a legislative nature can be regarded as in any way affecting the provisions of such an instrument. It is of high importance that a lay person be able to distinguish readily between documents having the force of law and all others. The view advanced by the applicant would make it difficult to do this with certainty."[197]

Judicial review of administrative circulars

2–95 It now seems clear that administrative circulars may be subject to judicial review. The following three situations can be identified for the sake of description and have yielded a fair amount of case law.

Circulars stating the law

2–96 The first concerns circulars which, at any rate, purport not to change the law but merely to state it.[198] It not infrequently happens that government departments will issue a circular by way of guidance for the benefit of bodies such as local authorities and schools. There have also been instances where bodies such as the Competition Authority[199] and the Medical Council[200] have issued formal notices

---

[196] [2005] IESC 49; [2005] 3 I.R. 308.

[197] [2005] IESC 49; [2005] 3 I.R. 308 at 317. Cf. *McLeod v Minister for Justice*, unreported, High Court, Murphy J., December 21, 2001.

[198] See, e.g. *McNamee v Buncrana U.D.C.* [1983] I.R. 213, where the Supreme Court made reference to a circular issued by the Department of the Environment which (incorrectly, as it happened) sought to explain the duties of housing authorities in the wake of the earlier decision of the Supreme Court in *McDonald v Feeley*, unreported, Supreme Court, July 23, 1980.

[199] The Authority is empowered to do so by s.30(1)(d) of the Competition Act 2002 and has issued notices in a number of areas. See, e.g. *Notice in respect of Vertical Agreements and Concerted Practices* (2003); *Notice in respect of the Review of Non-Notifiable Mergers and Acquisitions* (2003); and *Notice in respect of Guidelines for Merger Analysis* (2002). See generally, Hyland, "Legal Status of Notices Issued by the Competition Authority" (1993) 11 I.L.T. 240.

[200] See Medical Practitioners Act 2007 s.12(1). In the wake of the (highly controversial) decision of the Supreme Court in *Attorney General v X* [1992] 1 I.R. 1, the Medical Council issued guidelines (*A Guide to Ethical Conduct and Behaviour and to Fitness to Practice*, 4th edn (Dublin: Medical Council, 1994)) which might have been thought to contradict the tenor (at least) of the Supreme Court decision. This meant that some doctors were worried that if they "undertook terminations, they might be liable legally ...", Tomkin and Hanafin, *Irish Medical Law* (Dublin: Round Hall Press, 1995), p.186. See also, Bowers, "New Legal Risk for Irish Doctors on Abortion" (1993) 10 *Irish Medical News* 186. In such circumstances, it

containing what purport to be authoritative statements of the law. It would be unrealistic to pretend that such circulars have only the same status and influence as counsel's opinion or a legal textbook and, it seems, that even this type of circular is amenable to judicial review in a suitable case.[201]

Circulars creating administrative machinery

2–97 This category refers to circulars which purport to create some form of administrative machinery by which to adjudicate on individual rights or liabilities. As examples of this category being subjected to judicial review, one could refer to the Rules for National Schools[202] or the scheme governing the Criminal Injuries Compensation Tribunal,[203] each of which has been judicially interpreted and construed on several occasions.[204]

Circulars structuring discretion

2–98 The more common type of administrative rule is one already referred to (at the commencement of this section) which structures and indicates how a statutory discretion is to be exercised by a public body. Thus, in a number of cases involving civil service discipline,[205] it has been assumed, albeit without consideration, that the decision of the Minister for Finance could be reviewed by reference to the terms of such a circular. Since such a circular constitutes an

---

might well have been open to a doctor (or any other person with an interest) to seek judicial review of the guidelines on the ground that they attempted by directive to prevent or frustrate patients exercising such rights as were enunciated by the Supreme Court in the *X* case. See, now, *A Guide to Ethical Conduct and Behaviour and to Fitness to Practice*, 6th edn (Dublin: Medical Council, 2004), p.36: "The Council recognises that termination of pregnancy can occur when there is real and substantial risk to the life of the mother." The Council also note (at 44) the "fundamental difference between abortion carried out with the intention of taking the life of the baby, for example for social reasons, and the unavoidable death of the baby resulting from essential treatment to protect the life of the mother" and the importance of providing post-abortion care for those who travelled abroad to undergo the procedure.

[201] For the theoretical basis for this assertion of judicial power, see *Gillick v West Norfolk and Wisbech Health Authority* [1986] A.C. 112. See also the comments of Hyland, "Legal Status of Notices Issued by the Competition Authority" (1993) 11 I.L.T. 240 at 240–241. Note that a circular issued by the Competition Authority which purported to deal with potential conflicts of interest as between the same lawyers representing different clients has been quashed: see *Law Society of Ireland v Competition Authority* [2005] IEHC 455; [2006] 2 I.R. 262.

[202] The cases where the *Rules for National Schools* (1965) have been construed include: *Cotter v Aherne* [1976–1977] I.L.R.M. 248; *Crowley v Ireland* [1980] I.R. 102; and *O'Shiel v Minister for Education* [1999] 2 I.R. 321.

[203] The cases where the Criminal Injuries Compensation Rules have been considered include: *State (Hayes) v Criminal Injuries Compensation Tribunal* [1982] I.LR.M. 210; *State (Creedon) v Criminal Injuries Compensation Tribunal* [1988] I.R. 51; and *Tomlinson v Criminal Injuries Compensation Tribunal* [2005] IESC 1; [2006] 4 I.R. 321.

[204] In *White v Glackin*, unreported, High Court, Costello P., May 19, 1995, the applicant claimed that he had acquired a legitimate expectation that the procedures to be followed at a particular Garda disciplinary inquiry would conform to those specified in a circular issued by the Garda Commissioner entitled "Notes on Disciplinary Procedures under Garda Síochána (Discipline) Regulations 1989". Costello P. did not, however, find it necessary to decide whether the terms of the circular could give rise to a legitimate expectation as he concluded that the applicant's case depended on a misconstruction of the circular in question.

[205] See H & M, Ch.3, e.g. *Reidy v Minister for Agriculture*, unreported, High Court, June 9, 1989.

instruction as to how a statutory discretion should be exercised it is subject to the same disciplines—vires, reasonableness, etc. as an ordinary administrative action in the exercise of a discretion. If the circular satisfies these tests, well and good, if not, then again it is in the same position as the individual administrative action and will be invalidated.

2–99 In one early case, *Maunsell v Minister for Education*,[206] Gavan Duffy J. held that the defendants had misconstrued r.82 of the 1932 Rules for the National Schools in the course of taking an administrative decision against the plaintiff teacher and rejected the argument that he had no jurisdiction to do so because of the non-statutory nature of the Rules in question.[207] However, prior to the decision of Murphy J. in *Greene v Minister for Agriculture*,[208] the question of the courts' jurisdiction to review the legality of such administrative schemes had never received elaborate judicial consideration in this jurisdiction. Murphy J. did not appear to question his entitlement to subject such a scheme to judicial review on ordinary grounds of vires, reasonableness, etc. The plaintiffs in *Greene* succeeded in their claim that the manner in which the means test was imposed in a ministerial circular dealing with headage payments to farmers as a form of grant-aid discriminated against married couples and thus was contrary to Art.41. The important point here is that while Murphy J. said that Art.15.4.1°[209] had no relevance, as this ministerial scheme was not a "law" within the meaning of that subsection, nonetheless, he could intervene to declare the offending portion of the scheme to be unconstitutional.

---

[206] [1940] I.R. 213.

[207] Moreover, in another case involving a challenge to an administrative decision taken on foot of a circular, *Mulloy v Minister for Education* [1975] I.R. 88, the Supreme Court held that a departmental circular which discriminated against priests and members of religious orders was discrimination on the grounds of religious belief or status, contrary to Art.44.2.4°. No question was raised in this case as to the court's jurisdiction to make such a pronouncement in view of the non-statutory (and presumably non-binding) nature of such a Departmental circular.

[208] [1990] 2 I.R. 17. *A contra, McCann v Minister for Education* [1997] 1 I.L.R.M. 1 at 10.

[209] Which provides that: "The Oireachtas shall not enact any law which is any respect repugnant to this Constitution or any provision thereof."

CHAPTER 3

THE DÁIL, MINISTERS, DEPARTMENTS AND CIVIL SERVANTS

3–01   The object of this chapter is to sketch the constitutional and legal framework within which the administration of central government proceeds. Part A deals with control of Ministers and Departments by the Dáil,[1] emphasising recent reform, whilst Part B focuses on the legal dimension of a Minister and Department. Part C covers the selection of a civil servant, dealing at the outset with the definition of a "civil servant". Part D covers dismissal and discipline. Each Part connects with the wider question of public bodies and their staff, which is treated briefly in the following chapter.

A. FORMAL CONTROL BY THE DÁIL

3–02   Following the British model[2] the members of the Government (Cabinet) are formally responsible to the Dáil, though not the Senate,[3] in two ways.

Collective Government responsibility

3–03   The Constitution makes the Government collectively responsible to the Dáil. This means that, after an election, the Dáil elects a Government and also that it can remove and, without reference to the people, replace it with a new Government. However, its power to elect a replacement Government is restricted by the provision that even a Taoiseach who has been defeated in the Dáil may advise a dissolution followed by a general election and, thus far, no President has seen fit to reject such

---

[1]   No attempt is made to deal with the Dáil's role in law-making or as the "Grand Inquest of the Nation", these being matters of constitutional law, on which see MacCarthaigh and Manning, *The Houses of the Oireachtas* (Dublin: IPA, 2010); Gallagher, "The Oireachtas: President and Parliament" in Coakley and Gallagher (eds), *Politics in the Republic of Ireland*, 5th edn (Dublin: PSAI, 2010).

[2]   Though at the inception of the State, some efforts were made to modify this model: see Kohn, *The Constitution of the Irish Free State* (London: Allen & Unwin, 1932), Pt VI, Ch.2; Chubb, *Cabinet Government in Ireland* (Dublin: IPA, 1974).

[3]   The Government is not formally responsible to the Senate in the way that it is to the Dáil. Informally, the Senate's position in regard to publicising and criticising the Government's activities and policy decisions is similar to, though less important than, that of the Dáil.

advice.[4] Moreover, all the Dáil's powers over the Government are conditioned by the basic fact of political life, which is that a Government can almost always command the support of a majority of deputies, because deputies are elected principally on the basis of which party they have pledged themselves to support in the Dáil. Such is the strength of the whip-system that the legislature cannot be regarded as speaking with a voice independent of the executive and, so, it is realistic to characterise the central element in the Irish governmental system as a fused executive-legislature. The principal form of responsibility is collective.

3–04 The epithet "collective" means, first, that the Government, as a collective authority, speaks with one voice and, secondly, that if the Taoiseach resigns from office (or is removed), the other members of the Government also leave office.[5] In other words, the Government stands, or falls, as a single, united entity. This collective responsibility and the strict party system in the Dáil complement each other.

Individual ministerial responsibility

3–05 As is well known, the individual ministerial doctrine—which relied upon a model of Parliament which existed, only for a brief period in mid-nineteenth century Britain, before the growth of the party system and "big government"—has received mainly lip-service and there have been very few resignations for breach of the doctrine since 1922.[6] A governmental decision is seldom so grave that an error in relation to it would warrant the bringing down of a Government. Thus, although from the broad constitutional perspective, collective responsibility is the more important element, it is the individual ministerial doctrine[7] which might seem to be of greater significance in checking undesirable governmental action. According to the individual ministerial doctrine, if a Minister commits certain types of error then there is an obligation on him, and on him alone, to resign. In appropriate circumstances, so the theory runs, a Minister is supposed to resign of his own accord; but if he fails to do this, he must certainly resign if a vote of no confidence in him is passed by the Dáil. The type of error which attracts this duty may be: a personal act of dishonour or indiscretion; a failure of policy; or an act of maladministration within his Department—the latter of which will be considered in greater detail in the next paragraph. Here we need note only that the seven most

---

[4] See generally, Arts 13.1; 13.2; 28.4.1°; and 28.10. The former President, Mary Robinson, however, indicated that she would be quite prepared to reject such advice in appropriate circumstances: *The Irish Times*, November 27, 1994. For a discussion of the President's powers in these circumstances, see Hogan, "Legal and Constitutional Issues arising from the 1989 General Election" (1989) 24 Ir. Jur. 157.

[5] Articles 28.4.2° and 28.11.1°.

[6] It is possible, though uncommon, for an individual minister to resign, by virtue of the collective responsibility doctrine, when the Minister resigning disagrees with the rest of the Government. For the only such event in recent times see 346 *Dáil Debates* Cols 1822–1828 (resignation of Deputy Frank Cluskey because he believed that the terms on which the Government was taking over the assets of the former private company, Dublin Gas, were too generous).

[7] There is no reference to this doctrine in the Constitution. However, it has been accepted that the rule exists as a convention derived from the relationship of Ministers to the Dáil: see, e.g. 187 *Dáil Debates* Cols 19–59 (March 7, 1961) (second stage of the Mental Treatment (Detention in Approved Institutions) Bill 1961); 256 *Dáil Debates* Cols 1473–1501 (November 9, 1970); Cols 1732–1766 (November 10, 1970) (motion of no confidence in Minister for Agriculture, consequent on the Arms Trial).

recent cases of ministerial resignation have been for what may be broadly termed "indiscretions".[8]

3–06   In particular, there have been few if any resignations because of what might be regarded as the principal focus of administrative law, namely acts of maladministration within the Minister's department. The main reason for the failure of the doctrine is the lack of a non-partisan agency to determine conclusively when a Minister should resign and then, if necessary, to enforce this sanction: as is the case with the collective responsibility doctrine, the Dáil is prevented from playing this part because of the strict party system. There are other reasons for the failure: the single sanction of resignation affords no gradation of sanctions to deal with the varied offences of widely varying culpability which may arise; again, resignation would not even be available as a sanction where the responsible Minister had left office before the error came to light. Moreover, a particular difficulty arises in relation to a type of error which is common in the area of administrative law, namely, abuse of power or an act of maladministration, occurring during the course of administration. For in any Department of State, there will be hundreds or thousands of civil servants serving under a Minister and such an error may be wholly the fault of a civil servant.[9] Where the Minister is not personally involved in the error, is it not dogmatic to expect his head to roll?[10] We shall return to survey how these considerations play out in practice in considering the case studies at paras 3–15 to 3–25.

3–07   The view that the existing model reflects a reality which was designed in mid-nineteenth century Britain when Departments of State were so much smaller than those of today, and by now is no longer appropriate, had long been championed by reformers.[11] It led eventually to the Public Service Management Act 1997, examined later in this Part. Even writing more than 15 years after the Act became law, it is unclear how much impact the Act will make on a system whose roots go back for a century and a half. Most probably, its effect will be gradual, occurring as and when the political elite and public become accustomed to the changes.

---

[8]   In the first, the Minister (Deputy H. Coveney) resigned but was immediately re-appointed as a Junior Minister, the reason being that he had inquired whether his family business could put in a tender for a contract being awarded by a state body. In the second episode, a Junior Minister resigned (Deputy P. Hogan) because his political adviser had made an advance disclosure of Budget information. Thirdly, a Minister (Deputy M. Lowry) resigned because an extension to his house had been paid for by a businessman. Fourthly, a Minister (Deputy R. Burke) resigned because he had received a large donation for his election campaign in circumstances which were considered to be inappropriate. Next, a Junior Minister (Deputy R. Molloy) resigned because he had made representations in relation to the sentence in a rape case. Sixthly, a Minister (Deputy W. O'Dea) resigned because of an alleged falsehood in an affidavit he had signed. Finally, a Junior Minister (Deputy T. Sargent) resigned of alleged interference in the bringing of a prosecution. See newspapers for: May 22, 1995; February 3, 1995; December 1, 1996; October 8, 1997; April 11, 2002; February 19, 2010; and February 25, 2010, respectively. An earlier example involved the resignation of a Parliamentary Secretary in 1946 because of allegations of a conflict of interest between his official duties and a firm in which he had an interest: see *Report of the Tribunal appointed by the Taoiseach on November 7, 1947* (P.No. 8576).

[9]   See 187 *Dáil Debates* Cols 19–59.

[10]   Murray, "A Working and Changeable Instrument" (1982) 30 *Administration* 43 at 52; Murray, "Irish Government Further Observed" (1983) 31 *Administration* 284 at 288–298.

[11]   See, as early as the *Devlin Report*, Prl. 792 (1969), Note on Administrative Law and Procedure.

Accordingly it will be described later in this Part, after the traditional doctrine has been scrutinised.

Consequences of individual ministerial doctrine

3–08   Although the ministerial responsibility doctrine is such an ineffective rule, and, as noted, has been formally qualified, its existence (real or supposed) has had a formative influence upon the machinery for the control of Ministers and Departments in the following ways:

1. It remains the formal position that a Minister is responsible to the Dáil for most of the activities going on within his or her Department. In part, as a result of this, the Dáil attempts to shadow too wide an area of government activities and has insufficient time and attention for what should be its principal concern, namely major matters of policy. Thus, one element of ministerial responsibility to the Dáil is the Minister's duty to answer questions on behalf of his Department. A large proportion of these questions relate to the personal minutiae of constituents and discussion of these issues tends to crowd out the examination of policy issues; though there have been some improvements in this regard.

2. Another effect of the doctrine is to "politicise" every decision taken in a Department by converting every decision—however minor, technical or inherently non-controversial—into a potential bone of contention in a parliamentary dog-fight, which may affect the credit of the entire Government. One consequence of this was that the caution of an already-cautious civil service was increased in order to obey the supreme obligation of "protecting the Minister". Thus, for instance, files were pushed up from one level of the civil service hierarchy to another so that issues had to be resolved at a higher level than would otherwise be considered necessary. Another result is "'the representations' system [which] helps to perpetuate the misconception that everything can be 'fixed'".[12]

3. The personification of the entire activity of the Department in its Minister (politically, by the ministerial responsibility doctrine and, legally, through the Ministers and Secretaries Act 1924) left no formal position for anyone else, even senior management. The effect of this arrangement was to militate against personal responsibility and initiative on the part of civil servants.[13]

4. In the past, courts have offered it as a reason (or pretext) to justify a refusal to review some administrative actions that "this is a matter for which the Minister is responsible to Parliament".[14] This traditional and

---

[12]   *Devlin Report*, Prl. 792 (1969), p.448. This practice reached its climax in the circumstances which led to *Brennan v Minister for Justice and Attorney General* [1995] 1 I.R. 612. Here the facts were that—to take the typical year of 1993—over 4,000 petitions were made to the Minister for Justice to use her powers, under the Criminal Justice Act 1951, to commute or remit fines; and well over half of these were successful.

[13]   See, e.g. *Delivering Better Government* (May 2, 1996), p.22: "… the existing structures and reporting systems encourage a risk-averse environment where taking personal responsibility is not encouraged …".

[14]   See, e.g. *Liversidge v Anderson* [1942] A.C. 206 (a case involving individual liberty): *Raymond*

unrealistic view is not part of the thinking of the contemporary Irish judiciary.[15] Nevertheless, it was an influence in shaping the doctrine of judicial review which exists in Ireland today.

5.   To set against these disadvantages, it should be said that the ministerial responsibility doctrine is necessary in order to justify the eminently practical *Carltona* doctrine by which duties and powers vested in a Minister may be performed or exercised by officials in his Department. As it was put in *Carltona v Commissioners of Works*[16]:

> "Constitutionally the decision of such an official is, of course, the decision of the minister. The minister is responsible. It is he who must answer before Parliament for anything that his officials have done under his authority ... The whole system of departmental organisation and administration is based on the view that ministers, being responsible to Parliament, will see that important duties are committed to experienced officials. If they do not do that, Parliament is the place where complaint must be made against them."

The Public Service Management Act 1997: balance between the Minister and his civil servants

3–09   The kernel of the Act[17] is s.4(1), which is a qualification of the individual ministerial doctrine. This provision seeks to remedy the mismatch between the responsibility and authority[18] of the civil service by giving "the authority, responsibility and accountability" in respect of a large area of departmental[19] administration to the principal civil servant in the Department. This position, formerly the "Secretary", is retitled, by s.1, the "Secretary General".[20] It is a little

---

     v Attorney General [1982] Q.B. 839 at 847 on political responsibility for decisions of the DPP.

[15] Indeed in Ireland, this argument has been turned on its head in *Brennan v Minister for Justice and Attorney General* [1995] 1 I.R. 612, where Geoghegan J. stated (at 629): "There has been a long-established practice that the Minister does not answer questions in Dáil Éireann relating to individual instances of the exercise of this power. That being so, the only way that the Minister can in practice be held accountable for the proper exercise of the power is by means of judicial review in an appropriate case."

[16] [1943] 2 All E.R. 560 at 563. The final, rather dated, sentence in this passage is an example of the point made in para.4 above. On *Carltona*, see further Ch.11, Part F.

[17] For a surprisingly short discussion, see: 478 *Dáil Debates* Cols 469–493: 150 *Seanad Debate* Cols 1260–1305; [1997–1998] I.C.L.S.A. No.27 – Introduction and General Note). Specifically on the Secretary General, see paras 3–32 to 3–36.

[18] Cp. "Power without responsibility, the prerogative of the harlot throughout the Ages". This was Stanley Baldwin's (British Prime Minister, 1923–1924, 1924–1929 and 1935–1937) line (written for him by his cousin Rudyard Kipling) about the position of the press barons of his era.

[19] Though note that as well as the provision, mentioned in the text, regarding Departments of State, each of the "Scheduled Offices" (i.e. offices or branches of the public service listed in the Schedule (e.g. Office of the Comptroller and Auditor General or Director of Public Prosecutions) or added to it, by Government order) is to have its managerial "Head" in an equivalent position to the Secretary General But this is subject, in the case of those listed in Pt 1 of the Schedule, to the consent of the appropriate constitutional personage, e.g. the Ceann Comhairle, in the case of the Oireachtas : s.2. For the sake of simplicity, the above account refers only to the Secretary General and Departments and does not refer to the possibilities concerning scheduled offices.

[20] The new title has been bestowed because it was deemed more appropriate to the principal

difficult to say what a court would make of these significant[21] words—"authority, responsibility and accountability". These are political science terms, which seem uncharacteristically fluffy by the standards of normal statutory language. It is hard to predict their effect. (One should add that it is not only the Secretary General who is to receive such responsibility: in the case of "specific elements" it may also be applied *mutatis mutandis* to other officers lower down the hierarchy: ss.4(1)(c) and 9.)

3–10 There is another development which facilitates holding the Secretary General responsible for departmental administration: by the Committees of the Houses of the Oireachtas (Compellability, Privileges and Immunities of Witnesses) Act 1997 s.3, an Oireachtas Committee is empowered to direct any person (including civil servants), though subject to certain other exceptions, to appear before it to answer questions; though, in practice, civil servants have appeared voluntarily.[22] However, there is a working assumption that, if a person is directed to appear, they have to have the right of constitutional justice, including legal representation,[23] and s.15(1) of the Committees of the Houses Act 1997 precludes a civil servant from "questioning or expressing an opinion on the merits of any policy of the Government or a Minister".

3–11 But, there are the following six substantial restrictions and qualifications on this transfer of authority:

1. Even in respect of the functions identified in s.4(1), the Secretary General is made accountable to the Minister, by s.6.
2. Despite what is said in ss.4 and 9 (regarding the transfer of authority), the Minister is to remain "responsible [presumably to the Dáil] for the performance of functions ... assigned to the Department pursuant to [the Ministers and Secretaries Code]".[24] And there is no suggestion here that the Minister's responsibility is confined in any way.
3. Sections 4(1), 6 and 7 make it clear that the Government or the responsible Minister may give directions,[25] provided (in the case of the Ministers) that they are in writing to the Secretary General as regards any of his obligations (save for those in the personnel field below the grade of Principal).
4. Section 4(1) of the Act states that it is for the Minister to "determin[e] matters of policy", a protean, although difficult term. Despite this, it is

---

official in the Department. The Minister for Public Expenditure and Reform (Deputy Quinn) related how, on a visit to the Irish Senate by the Japanese Minister for Industry and Trade, the term "Secretary" had been translated as "ever-lasting typist". See Mullarkey, *Report of the Working Group on the Accountability of Secretaries General and Accounting Officers* (July 2002).

21 Though cp. Oscar Wilde: "Don't use big words; they mean so little."
22 See Public Service Management Act 1997 s.10.
23 See Gwynn Morgan, "Enforcing Public Accountability" (2009) 27 *Irish Law Times* 71 at 73–74.
24 1997 Act s.3.
25 It seems that there is distinct authority (in ss.6 and 7), for both Government and Ministerial directions. In relation to the former (which would be most unusual), nothing is said about writing. The Explanatory Memorandum for the 1997 Act (at p.2) states that "directions provided for in section 7 are ... to be confidential documents".

scarcely necessary to add that, in addition to administration, senior civil servants also bear a major duty to assist in policy formation, a point illustrated in the case studies below.

5.   Linked with this is the fact that, by s.4(1)(b), the Secretary General must prepare a "Strategy Statement". As defined in s.5 of the Act, the "strategy statement" must:

   "(a) [C]omprise the key objectives, outputs and related strategies (including use of resources) of the Department of State or Scheduled Office concerned.

   (b) be prepared in a form and manner in accordance with any directions issued from time to time by the Government ...

   (c) be submitted to and approved by the relevant Minister of the Government with or without amendment."

6.   A "Strategy Statement" for each Department must be made every three years and it must be published by being laid before each House of the Oireachtas. Progress reports on implementation must be provided annually or as specified by the Government.[26] The idea of the Strategy Statement has two consequences. First, it gives the Secretary General some formal authority/accountability, in the policy field. Secondly, from the point of view of accountability to the Dáil/public, it requires the Department itself to set down criteria. There can be no complaint, therefore, if its performance is judged against those criteria.

3–12   Even when these qualifications are taken into account, there may be less to the Act than meets the eye. For, even under the traditional system, most of the time, Ministers leave the normal running of the Department to civil servants; and this is true (to mention the central distinction drawn by the Act) not only of administration but frequently of policy too. In addition, as we have just seen, the new scheme allows Ministers ample instruments of control and authority. Moreover, to shift from the concept of authority to responsibility, even under the new régime, the Minister will usually continue to carry the can. This is the central feature of the constitutional system and the Act would make only a slight modification to it: politicians are known by name to the public and are, as a group, rather unpopular with it. Through the media, the public have access to the doings of politicians which, especially if they are discreditable, make rather good copy. By contrast, most civil servants remain anonymous.

3–13   Next, one might ask whether the new system established by the 1997 Act is unconstitutional. This contention is based on Art.28.4.2°[27] which provides that, "the Government shall be collectively responsible [to the Dáil] for the Departments ... administered by the members of the Government". It is eminently sensible to take

---

[26]   For the strategy statement, see s.5. Section 5(2) provides that all strategy statements must be laid before the Oireachtas.

[27]   It seems clear that the 1997 Act does not violate Art.28.2 which provides: "The executive power of the State shall ... be exercised by or on the authority of the Government". Leaving aside the issue of whether responsibility for any instances of that delphic term, the "executive power of the State" has been delegated, it seems clear that the Minister retains sufficient elements of control (listed in the text) to meet the requirement that it be exercised "on the authority of the Government".

   There was a brief discussion of the possibility of unconstitutionality in the Senate Debate: 150 *Seanad Debate* Cols 1260–1305.

this as implying that as a member of the Government, each individual Minister is to administer his Department and to be responsible for so doing. The case in favour of unconstitutionality is grounded on the divergence between the constitutional precept that the apparent Minister is "responsible" and the central provision in s.4(1) of the 1997 Act, quoted above, which states that it is the Secretary General who bears "authority, responsibility and accountability" in respect of a large area of departmental administration. As against this, however, there is the cumulative effect of certain cautious features of the Act, most of which have already been noticed at paras 3–11 to 3–12. In the first place, the Secretary General's autonomous authority is confined within fairly narrow bounds: apart from *advising* on policy, (as in the traditional system) he is confined to "managing the Department" within the terms of the Strategy Statement and the other controls mentioned. For the Minister retains significant controls by way of: the power of giving directions; the Secretary General's accountability to him; and his own responsibility for policy. Most important of all is the Act's firm statement that the Secretary General is accountable to the Minister, which the Minister remains responsible to the Dáil.

3–14 Many of these ministerial controls are cast in curiously "political" and ambiguous language. They do serve, however, (and may have been included partly for this reason) to equip the Attorney General to argue, in any constitutional action, that ultimate responsibility remains with the Minister. Furthermore, any lawyer assessing the chances of success in such an action would be influenced by the lack of precedents (Irish or foreign) in this area, coupled with the fact that, in such a peculiarly political area, a court would be inclined only to intervene in an extreme case. The 1997 Act does not make the Secretary General accountable to the Dáil. (However, somewhat qualifying this, Oireachtas Committees may cross-examine the Secretary General on his performance). In short, the danger of unconstitutionality seems slight.

Case studies

3–15 Against this background, we must consider how, in practice, responsibility for policy and administration (categories offering much overlap) is divided between Ministers and civil servants. First, take two extreme, and therefore fairly straightforward, situations, each of which was decided before the 1997 Act. The first of these occurred in 1961, in the context of the involuntary detention of mental patients. According to the relevant statute, the Minister for Health's permission had to be renewed after every six month period of detention. The junior civil servant whose task it was to pass on the applications for the Minister's permission fell ill and failed to perform this task, with the result that almost 300 patients were illegally detained. Yet the Minister convincingly brushed aside calls for his resignation as unrealistic on the ground that an appropriate system of administration with properly qualified people had been provided.[28]

---

[28] An opposition deputy (Mr Sweetman) stated: "[The Minister] is the person whose duty it is to see and to ensure that the Department is administered properly in accordance with the directions given to it by this House from time to time ... [I]t is the Minister who must stand over the actions of the civil servants of Parliament."

The inference he drew was that the Minister ought to resign. The Minister (Mr McEntee) refused because "... in these matters there must be some realism. It is all very well to say that constitutional justice theory requires that the Minister should accept full responsibility for

3–16 Another Government, albeit of a different political stripe, took a similar line in an episode in 1996. Officials in the Department of Justice failed to write the necessary letter to inform a member of the Special Criminal Court that he had been "de-listed" by the Government and, so, was no longer a member of the court. As a result of this omission, the judge continued to exercise his functions, as a member of the court—the most significant of which was refusing certain bail applications[29]—for some three months. Neither ensuing Opposition attacks on the Minister for Justice nor Government spokespersons' rebuttal offered much by way of development of the principle under discussion. The Taoiseach remarked that, "[w]hilst Ministers in this or previous governments may not have been punished for the misdeeds of officials, in this Government, Ministers ... have been willing to take responsibility for *personal* errors".[30] The Minister for Justice suggested[31] that there was a difference between accountability, in the sense that a Minister had to give information to the Dáil and, on the other hand, culpability, meaning that a Minister had to resign, and that the latter only arose if a Minister, personally, had made some error. The Opposition's response was to the effect that the Minister was indeed personally responsible just because she had failed to establish a reliable system for dealing with correspondence.

3–17 As a matter of common sense and principle, each of these matters—the involuntary detentions and the failure to relay the "de-listing"—should surely have been regarded as fairly low-level administration. This was the responsibility of the civil service and not the Minister, although as we have seen, in theory this distinction did not exist at the time; but is now more or less established by the 1997 Act.

3–18 Next, take two more complex episodes. The first of these occurred before the Act and, even in the one which post-dated the Act, it is clear that the governmental culture is taking a while to come into line with the Act. The first episode arose from the fact that, during the period 1986–1998, certain financial institutions were using bogus non-resident accounts in order to avoid the payment of Deposit Interest Retention Tax (DIRT). The Comptroller and Auditor General drew up a special report which formed the basis of a Dáil Public Accounts subcommittee hearing in 1999. We are not concerned here with the sins of the banks (which were the main focus of the Reports) but only with the narrow question of responsibility as between Ministers and civil servants within the Department of Finance for the fact

---

everything the department does ... Am I to accept responsibility for the fact that an officer of my Department suffers a breakdown ...? Is there anything I could possibly have done to ensure that this would not have occurred?"

This exchange will be found at 187 *Dáil Debates* Cols 19–59 (March 7, 1961).

[29] The Minister for Justice then ordered the release of the illegally detained prisoners. However, the prisoners were immediately re-arrested and re-charged upon their release and the legality of this procedure was upheld: see *Hegarty v Governor of Limerick Prison* [1998] 1 I.R. 412; and *Quinlivan v Governor of Portlaoise Prison* [1998] 1 I.R. 456.

[30] 47 *Dáil Debates* Col 651 (November 12, 1996) (Emphasis added). (He went on to refer to the resignations mentioned earlier.) See also, Col.563 et seq. (November 7, 1996) and Col.1567 et seq. (November 21, 1996). See also, 446 *Dáil Debates* Col.1136 (October 27, 1994) and 447 *Dáil Debates* Col.346 (November 16, 1994) each of which concerned the similar question of the Attorney General's responsibility for failure of his senior civil servant to process an extradition warrant promptly.

[31] 471 *Dáil Debates* Col.669 (November 12, 1996).

that the Revenue Commissioners were allowed not to enforce the law in relation to the levying of DIRT.

3–19   Senior civil servants explained their failure to direct the Revenue Commissioners (assuming they had this power) to enforce the law on the basis that it might have led to massive flight of capital from Ireland and they "sensed" that their (successive) Ministers would not have wished this. No Minister or former Minister was examined by the Committee. But the senior civil servants who were examined[32] said that, despite the absence of written communications, Ministers were aware of this omission and supported it. While the Committee reached no firm conclusion on this point, they seem to have accepted the implication that an unlawful failure to collect tax, on such a massive scale, was a matter of policy and, in consequence, the responsibility of the Minister for Finance. However, there was no explicit condemnation or any other sanction of either Minister or civil servant, the Report being, as mentioned, mainly concerned with the behaviour of the banks.

3–20   The final episode concerns the fact that, up to 2004, where a person was in a long-stay care Health Board institution, the Health Board was deducting out of that person's welfare benefits, an amount of money which went towards paying for their stay, despite the fact that the patients in question had the right to free in-patient services under the Health Act 1970 s.53. There is no need here to follow the convoluted circumstances of the imposition of the deduction and the intermittent querying of its legality. Suffice it to say that the episode commences with a circular of 1976, and, as early as 1978, there was legal advice to the effect that the deductions were unlawful unless appropriate amending legislation was brought in[33]: something which did not happen until 2004.[34] The Minister under whom this practice commenced was Deputy Brendan Corish (1973–1977). The Minister in the post in 2004 was Mary Harney, the sixteenth Minister to have been in office whilst this practice continued (who took action on the matter within three months of taking up her position). The reason why the necessary legislation was so delayed was because of a strong feeling, at any rate among senior civil servants, that to bring the appropriate legislation to public attention would be politically unpopular.

3–21   This episode was the subject of a report by the Joint Oireachtas Committee on Health and Children and, to assist it, the Committee had first commissioned a report, by John Travers, former Chief Executive Officer of Forfás, which is published as an Appendix to the Committee's Report.[35] The Committee Report split

---

[32]   Committee of Public Accounts, *Sub-Committee On Certain Revenue Matters*, Parliamentary Debates, Verbatim Transcript, Vol.3, Pt 1 (Aug.–Sept. 1999). The make-up of the Sub-Committee is interesting. In line with the Convention of the Constitution governing the parent PAC, there was an equal number of Government and Opposition Deputies, with the Chairperson being a senior Opposition Deputy.

[33]   This view was confirmed by later reports of the Ombudsman (*Special Report of the Ombudsman*, January 2001), see para.9–117, and the Human Rights Commission (*Older People in Longstay Care*, April 2003).

[34]   The legislation passed by the Dáil and Seanad, the Health (Amendment) Bill 2004, sought to legitimise the deductions with retrospective as well as prospective effect. This retrospective element was held unconstitutional in *Re Art. 26 and the Health (Amendment) Bill 2004* [2005] 1 I.R. 105.

[35]   *Report on Certain Issues of Management and Administration in the Department of Health*

on a Government versus Opposition basis,[36] with the Government majority having an obvious motivation to put as much blame as possible on the civil service. (About the time of the release of the Report, the Secretary General in the Department of Health and Children was moved from this position, though with no loss of salary, to be Chairperson of the Higher Education Authority.[37])

3–22 Our concern here is with the allocation of responsibility for the failure to bring in legislation, as between successive Ministers for Health and, on the other hand, Secretaries General. Unhelpfully, for anyone trying to discern principle in a tangled area, scant guidance can be discerned in either the Committee Report or the Travers Reports; much less any reference to the fundamental concepts of the 1997 Act. The principle which emerges from the two reports, though somewhat darkly, is that the Minister should take responsibility for the "political" matters and the Secretary General for the administrative aspects of a Department's performance. In evidence to the Committee, Mr Travers remarked[38]:

> "The conclusion I came to was that there was an overall corporate failure in the Department to deal adequately with the matter. If it is broken down into two parts, I am of the view that the failure was greater on the part of the administrators than it was on the part of the politicians. I did not exclude the politicians from responsibility for these matters, I said that the politicians should have probed more deeply over the years ... this probing was not done ...".

3–23 The following comments may be offered. The first issue is whether the unlawful deduction should be characterised as an act of "administration" or "policy" (or, as the Reports put it, "politics"). On the operational level, making a deduction for a payment is plainly a low-level act of administration. But, when one takes it into account that this was an act of illegality, involving thousands of people over a 30-year period, motivated by a judgment that the legislation could be unpopular with the public, then should it not be regarded as a matter of policy? As such, it should normally have been something for which the Minister was responsible. However, in this case, the Minister's response was that she (and presumably her predecessors) did not know until a very late stage, because the civil servants did not tell her. And, as noted earlier, apart from administration, senior civil servants also bear a duty to assist in policy matters.

3–24 As regards this duty, the Committee did not reach a clear finding as to whether there was adequate communication between the Secretary General and the Minister. The view expressed by Mr. Travers on this was[39]:

& *Children associated with the Practice* [sic] *of Charges for Persons in Long-Stay Care in Health Board Institutions and Related Matters* (June 2005). The Travers Report was published as an Appendix to the Committee's Report. The Committee's Report was based, in part, on the examination of Mr Travers, Mr Kelly, (the Secretary General of the Department of Health and Children, during 2000–2005) and other witnesses.

[36] *The Irish Times*, June 10, 2005, p.2.
[37] See M. Kelly, "Steering a policy course" in McAuliffe and McKenzie (eds) *The Politics of Healthcare – achieving real reform* (Dublin: Liffey Press, 2007), pp.23–25.
[38] Committee Report, p.14.
[39] Committee Report, p.137. The element of Marx Brother comedy, never far from this episode, came to the surface in the question of whether the legal difficulty in regard to the charges

"If ... a comprehensive analysis had been clearly and forthrightly set out and presented to Ministers, it is difficult to believe that the appropriate actions to rectify matters would not have been taken [in] a situation which appears to have trundled along in somewhat of an administrative and operational fog for far too many years. The responsibility to prepare and present such an analysis rested clearly and unambiguously on the officials of the Department."

3–25 This passage, with its many unstated assumptions, may have been directed really not at the civil servants' duty to administer, but rather to their undoubted other duty to alert the Minister to the need for a possible policy change and to advise on the content of the new policy. Nevertheless, even under the 1997 Act, the Minister bears responsibility for policy. Stemming from this, two alternative questions arise. Did successive Ministers, as was claimed, actually not know? Accepting that this is so, the other question which arises is: *should* the Minister not have known?[40] As to this second question, despite the rather cloudy analysis in the passage, Mr. Travers assumed that a Minister had a duty to "probe". This duty was not elaborated. But it may be taken as meaning that, given the continuity between politics and administration, not to mention the Minister's constitutional authority referred to earlier, a Minister retains an obligation to keep him or herself in some sort of contact with what is going on in the Department. This obligation was not honoured in this episode.

Concluding comment

3–26 There is a confusion between: traditional Ministerial responsibility; the terms of the 1997 Act; and the apparent understanding of politicians of their system (as disclosed in the DIRT and Residential Charges episodes). The snag with the 1997 Act is that it is detached from reality, in that, in making the Minister responsible for policy, it fails adequately to acknowledge that a senior civil servant has always had a good deal to do in regard to policy: alerting the Minister (where necessary) to the fact that a policy decision is called for; preparing a draft policy for the Minister (or Government) to approve; and overseeing implementation of the policy. There is a subsidiary point which was of particular relevance in the case of residential charges: which of the ministerial incumbents should be held responsible, especially given that the Minister in post at the time the lapse came to light had been there such a short time?

---

had been effectively "mentioned to the Minister" during a brief conversation on the stairs on the fringe of a MAC/CEO (Management Advisory Committee of the Department and Chief Executive Officers of the Health Boards) meeting, at the Gresham Hotel, on December 16, 2003.

Two sub-plots in relation to communication between the Civil Service and Ministers were first, the civil service's resistance to writing down important matters (in this case doubts about the charge's legality), because of the danger that this material might be published by virtue of the Freedom of Information legislation (on which, see also, Dáil PAC *Sub-Committee on Certain Revenue Matters*, Vol.3, Pt 1, p.64); and whether informing a special adviser counted as communicating with the Minister.

40 The unlawfulness of the deductions had undoubtedly, surfaced intermittently, notably in prominent newspaper headlines, in 2001, at the time of the Ombudsman's Special Report, *Investigation by the Ombudsman of Complaints regarding payment of Nursing Home Subventions by Health Boards* (January 2001).

3–27 In summary, on a broad level, both episodes—DIRT and Residential Charges—had a good deal in common: in each, there was a failure to observe the law by civil servants, because they "perceived" that the Minister would prefer it; whilst the Minister pleaded ignorance. Each, at first glance, may have seemed to involve administration: merely withholding payments or not collecting taxes. But, in our view, because of the long-running unlawfulness affecting thousands of cases, each must be seen as involving policy. In neither episode, was the analysis by the Dáil PAC or Joint Oireachtas Committee anything but superficial. In the DIRT episode, the PAC Sub-Committee seems to have accepted, correctly though tacitly and without following through the implications, that the Minister was responsible for what, it has been argued here, was a policy mistake. In the case of the residential charges, the Government majority on the Committee found it convenient neither to use the old nineteenth century model of ministerial responsibility, nor to apply the 1997 Act faithfully, because either would have meant imposing responsibility on the Minister. No doubt, it will be a long time before politicians, civil servants, media and public—indeed everyone apart from a handful of lawyers—lose from their cognitive map, the model of a Department's operation which had prevailed since the nineteenth century.

Position of the Secretary General

3–28 The Secretary General is the senior civil servant in a Department. Because of his ascendancy, the Secretary General's terms and conditions differ from those of subordinates in a number of ways. Unlike other civil servants who are appointed by the Minister, "the principal officer" (as the 1924 Act s.2(2) styles the office) of each of the Departments is appointed by the Government, on the recommendation of the Ministerial head of the Department. Similarly, dismissal is a matter for the Government.[41] It is only in rare cases that a Secretary General has been dismissed.[42] However, conduct that in the case of a civil servant of a lesser rank might merit only demotion or a reduction in pay could irreparably damage the relationship between the Secretary General and a Minister, and as a result it might be considered necessary to dismiss him/her.

3–29 The Secretary General has the following three main functions, as regards each of which his convoluted relationship with the Minister has to be taken into account:

    1.   As regards administration, s.4(1) of the Public Service Management Act 1997, makes more explicit the duties of Secretaries General and their accountability for the exercise of those duties. The central aspect of administration involves ensuring that the systems and procedures are in place to enable the Department to discharge its functions and to enable the Minister to answer for the performance of those functions to the Dáil. Particular instances of "administration" include: human resources, procurement or financial policy. These functions are especially close to

---

[41] Civil Service Regulation Act 1956 s.2(1)(a). Section 15 of the 1956 Act relating to disciplinary measures (short of dismissal) does not apply to Secretaries General or any other officers holding positions to which they were appointed by the Government.

[42] One such case is DJ O'Donovan in 1951: O'Toole and Dooney, *Irish Government Today* (Dublin: Gill and Macmillan, 2009), p.170.

the Secretary General, in view of his or her role as Accounting Officer (item 3 below) and the further consideration that a lot of the rules in these areas tend to be settled generically throughout all departments, by senior officials in the Department of Public Expenditure and Reform.

But, as noted, there are several qualifications on the Secretary General's authority and accountability. First, s.3 of the 1997 Act reaffirms that, notwithstanding any assignment of functions in the Act, a Minister of the Government retains overall control of his/her Department of State and is responsible and accountable to the Oireachtas for the administration of that Department. As noted in the earlier discussion of the 1997 Act, the Minister may also give written directions to a Secretary General in relation to all the Secretary General's obligations, apart from the management of staffing issues below the grade of Principal. With the result, on one view, that "... the nature of the relationship between a Secretary General and a Minister – though similar in a number of respects – is not fully akin to that of a Chief Executive and Chairman in the private sector. Ministers provide political leadership and authority in a government department. Secretaries General are expected to provide managerial leadership and authority".[43]

2. The Secretary General also has an important role as main policy adviser to the Minister[44]: how could it be otherwise, given that the Secretary General would probably have been conversant with the subject-matter, at several levels, over a career of 20 or 30 years; whereas Ministers come and go every five or so years. By the 1997 Act s.4(1)(b), the preparation of the Strategy Statement which constitutes a framework for the Department's policy must be agreed between the Secretary General and the Minister. The Secretary General is also responsible for preparing progress reports on its implementation. In addition, by s.10, a Secretary General or other officials may also be required to appear before the relevant Oireachtas Committee in relation to the Strategy Statement.[45]

3. The Secretary General also has an independent role as the Accounting Officer for the Department. The Exchequer and Audit Departments Act 1866 required all Departments to produce annual accounts, known as the Appropriation Accounts, for the first time. It established the position of C&AG with responsibility, inter alia, to audit the accounts of Government Departments and report to Parliament accordingly. The 1866 Act was amended by the Comptroller and Auditor General (Amendment) Act 1993 which, significantly for the Accounting Officer, gives the C&AG powers to carry out value-for-money examinations in regard to economy and efficiency in the use of resources and the management systems used to evaluate effectiveness.

3–30 The 1866 Act also introduced a framework of accountability in which,

---

[43] Evaluation of the SMI – PA Consulting (March 2002), p.86, quoted in the Mullarkey Report, p.29.

[44] 1997 Act s.4(1)(d).

[45] The Orders of Reference, in respect of Oireachtas Committees, make specific reference to the consideration of Strategy Statements. The Mullarkey Report, para.4.7, states (possibly wrongly) that, in appearing before these Committees, Secretaries General appear "on behalf of the Minister".

under s.22, senior officials were designated Accounting Officers by the Treasury and were charged with the responsibility to prepare the Appropriation Accounts. By virtue of this responsibility they were also required to give evidence in relation to the accounts before the Public Accounts Committee (established in 1861). The equivalent here is the Dáil Public Accounts Committee.

3–31   After the First World War it became established policy, agreed between the PAC and the Treasury, that (what are now) Secretaries General should be Accounting Officers for their Department. It was considered that they were the only ones with sufficient authority within Departments to discharge the role. By this stage it had also been recognised that finance was an essential element in all policy questions and that financial responsibility had wider implications for efficient management. Thus, even before the 1997 Act, this was regarded (possibly there was a Constitutional Convention to this effect) as a personal responsibility of the Secretary General.[46]

3–32   The special nature of the Accounting Officer's responsibilities requires that specific procedures be followed where there is a difference of opinion between the Accounting Officer and the Minister. In these circumstances, Public Financial Procedures provide that the Accounting Officer should inform the Minister in writing of this view and the reasons for it and suggest a consultation with the Department of Public Expenditure and Reform. If, notwithstanding this, the Minister gives contrary directions in writing, the Accounting Officer should comply with them after informing the Department of Public Expenditure and Reform. The papers should be sent to the C&AG when the directions have been carried out. It should be emphasised that this procedure has rarely had to be operated.

B. LEGAL STRUCTURE OF THE MINISTERS AND DEPARTMENTS[47]

3–33   Before Independence, the separate executive, which was the great anomaly of the Act of Union 1800 (which fused the British and Irish Parliaments), consisted of about 50 units described variously as "departments", "boards" or "offices". Ireland, it was said, had "as many boards as would make her coffin".[48] The administrative units, some of which were merely the Irish branches of a mainland Department, enjoyed a variety of relationships with the Lord Lieutenant (the formal

---

[46]   There was a traditional view that Accounting Officers would be sanctioned by being held personally liable to refund expenditure that the PAC deemed to be improper. However, in the UK the Treasury has stated (in 1980) that they had legal advice that this view had no basis in law; nor did existing Parliamentary procedure appear to provide any mechanism for its enforcement. Similarly, according to the Mullarkey Report, para.7.29 (where this matter is discussed), the principle of personal liability would appear to have no legal basis in relation to Accounting Officers in Ireland, although the position is different in local government where the possibility of surcharging the councillors or manager does exist. See also, Lord Sharman, *Holding to Account: The review of Audit and Accountability for Central Government* (Her Majesty's Stationery Office, 2001).

[47]   There is a good account, from a political scientist's perspective, of some of the material covered in this Part in O'Malley and Martin, "The Government and the Taoiseach" in Coakley and Gallagher (eds), *Politics in the Republic of Ireland* (2010).

[48]   McDowell, *The Irish Administration* (London: Routledge and Keegan Paul, 1964); McColgan, "Partition and the Irish Administration 1920–1922" (1980) 28 *Administration* 147.

head of the executive) and the Chief Secretary (a sort of Minister for Irish Affairs who represented the Irish administration in the House of Commons).

3–34 The objective of the post-Independence Government was to sweep away this detritus. Until the growth of public bodies, examined in Chapter 4, Part A, there was a simple and uniform system in which most of the central executive power of the State flowed directly through the members of the Government, so that the Dáil could exercise control over the entire administration (for, in the heady days of the establishment of the State, it was hoped that the Dáil would wield substantial influence over Governments). On the legal plane, a complementary change was made by the Ministers and Secretaries Act 1924 (a code contemplated at Art.28.12 of the Constitution)[49] which is the chief organic law determining the framework of the executive arm of government.[50]

3–35 We discussed the Public Service Management Act 1997 (which deals with a Minister's political responsibility to the Dáil) in Part A because the Act is most likely to make its impact in the field of political, rather than legal, responsibility. By contrast, the present Part deals with the legal structure of the Department, including the positions of the Minister and civil servants. This law might be relevant, for instance, in respect of whether the correct person has taken (or been involved) in a decision. Here, the changes contained in the 1997 Act, and discussed in Part A, have probably had no effect.

3–36 To elaborate, although the 1997 Act has enlarged the status and responsibility to the Dáil of the Secretary General, it has not altered the Minister's position as corporation sole with complete legal responsibility for the affairs of his Department and associated branches or offices.[51] Consequently, the Minister, or "Ireland", remains the appropriate party to litigation. However, the 1924 Act established—to take one example—the Minister for Justice and Equality (then known as the Minister for Home Affairs) as a statutorily-created corporation sole.[52] The corporation sole is distinct from the temporary incumbent of the office. Linked with this development was the practice of vesting almost all central government functions[53]

---

[49] Article 28.12 states "The following matters shall be regulated in accordance with law, namely, the organization of, and distribution of business amongst, Departments of State …". In *Lovejoy v Attorney General* [2008] IEHC 225 (ex tempore), Birmingham J. stated: "A further point is that the entitlement to assign responsibilities to individual ministers and to assign responsibilities between departments is a matter for legislation, by virtue of Article 28.12 of the Constitution. That legislation is provided for by the *Ministers and Secretaries Act of 1924*. Thus, that the Minister for Justice should have such a role does not, in my view, raise constitutional issues …".

[50] Ministers and Secretaries Act 1924 s.9.

[51] Section 13 of the Public Service Management Act 1997 allows the Government to confer corporate status ("declare … to be a corporation sole") on: the Attorney General; Comptroller and Auditor General; Director of Public Prosecutions; or the Ombudsman. But this power does not extend to branches or officers of Departments like (for example) the Revenue Commissioners.

[52] 1924 Act s.2(1). On the Minister as corporation sole, see further, Ch.20, Part C. See too, Public Service Management Act 1997 s.13.

[53] There are a few functions which, in order to mark their importance or to add lustre, are vested in the President or the Government. In addition, a very few functions are vested in designated civil servants. The principal example is the deciding officer-appeals officer in the Department of Social Protection: see Chapter 6, Part D.

in the appropriate Minister.[54] The 1924 Act provides that, "each Department and the powers, duties and functions thereof shall be assigned to and administered by the Minister"[55] but that whenever any power is vested by statute in a Minister, the administration entailed in the exercise of that power is deemed to be allocated to the Department of that Minister.[56] The result of these provisions is that the Minister is not only head of the Department; he also personifies the Department, in law; and, as corporation sole, bears responsibility in law for its every action, (a responsibility which extends to branches, for example the Revenue Commissioners in the case of the Minister for Finance). And this is so, although most of these actions are performed by Departmental civil servants, rather than the Minister himself, so that the words quoted amount to a statutory formulation of what the British call the *Carltona* doctrine.[57]

3–37 The Ministers and Secretaries Act 1924 "establish[ed] the several [11 in the original 1924 Act] Departments of State amongst which the administration and business of the public services in [the State] shall be distributed". As of the establishment of the Fine Gael-Labour Government in 2011, there have been 16 Ministers and Departments, as listed in the footnote.[58] The Act also gives a generalised description of the duties of the Departments which it establishes, of which the following may be taken as representative:

> "The Department of [Justice and Equality, originally titled 'Home Affairs'] shall comprise the administration and business generally of public services in connection with law, justice, public order and police, and all powers, duties and functions connected with the same … and shall include in particular the business, powers, duties and functions of the branches and officers of the public service specified in the Second Part of the Schedule to this Act [which includes the Courts, the Public Record Office and the Registry of Deeds] and of which Department the head shall be, and shall be styled, an t-Aire Dlí agus Cirt or (in English) the Minister for Justice."

3–38 Despite this sort of generalised description, it is the case that almost all

---

[54] Though this is subject to the overriding imperative contained in Art.28.4 of the Constitution that "The Government … shall be collectively responsible for the Departments of State administered by the members of the Government". See also, Ministers and Secretaries Act 1924 s.5: "Nothing in this Act contained shall derogate from the collective responsibility of the [Government] as provided by the Constitution notwithstanding that members of the [Government] may be appointed individually to be Ministers, heads of particular Departments of State". It is thus open to the Government to direct a Minister as to how a decision should be taken, although the decision has been statutorily vested in a Minister.

[55] 1924 Act s.1.

[56] Ministers and Secretaries (Amendment) Act 1939 s.6(3). See also, Art.28.12 of the Constitution. For *delegatus non potest delegare* and the *Carltona* doctrine, see Ch.11, Parts E and F.

[57] *Carltona v Commissioners of Works* [1943] 2 All E.R. 560.

[58] The full list of Departments of State was as follows: Agriculture, Food and the Marine; Arts, Heritage and the Gaeltacht; Children and Youth Affairs; Communications, Energy and Natural Resources; Defence; Education and Skills; Environment, Community and Local Government; Finance; Foreign Affairs and Trade; Health; Jobs, Enterprise and Innovation; Justice and Equality; Public Expenditure and Reform; Social Protection; the Taoiseach; Transport, Tourism and Sport. On the development of the landscape of Government Departments, see H & M, Ch.4, Appendix; and Coakley and Gallagher (eds), *Politics in the Republic of Ireland* (2010), Appendix 4.

governmental functions are created by a specific statute. Indeed, a good swathe of the Statute Book is taken up with the functions and powers allocated to Ministers and there are numerous examples throughout this book. Such a specific statute would prevail against the job-description given in the 1924 Act, (of which that of the Minister for Justice has just been quoted) even if it involved vesting a function in what would seem, according to that Act, to be an inappropriate Department.

3–39 What then is the legal (as opposed to the informational) purpose of a statutory job-description of the type just quoted? In the first place, a Minister is a corporation sole[59] and, as such, s/he has the capacity to contract, but only for the purpose of the authorised function or purposes incidental thereto. The description in the 1924 Act[60] would be significant in divining what these purposes were and, thus, in determining whether a particular contract was ultra vires the Minister's power. In addition, the description might be helpful in fixing the scope of a civil servant's employment in the context, for instance, of a tort action against the State.[61] It might also be invoked by the Comptroller and Auditor General, if he were deciding whether some item fell outside an imprecisely worded vote. And in the context of the Dáil, the statutory description is an indication of the matters for which a Minister is responsible.

3–40 Where a new Department, with its ministerial head, is established, then a statute (called a Ministers and Secretaries (Amendment) Act) often has to be passed. A statute is necessary because the creation (or dissolution) of a corporation sole requires an Act of the Oireachtas. The Ministers of (for example) Supplies,[62] Health,[63] Social Welfare,[64] or the Gaeltacht,[65] were not created by the Ministers and Secretaries Act 1924 and so each had to be created by its own amending statute. A statute was also passed when the office of Minister for Supplies was dissolved.[66] However, a new statute is not always necessary because of the device of "the shell of the corporation sole". This expression is intended to capture the practice by which a corporation sole, constituted by a Ministers and Secretaries Act as the legal home for one Minister and Department, becomes used for a new Minister and Department. To elaborate: under the Ministers and Secretaries (Amendment) Act 1939, the Government has extensive complementary powers, exercisable by order: first, to transfer powers between Ministers and the administration of a public service between Departments; secondly, to alter the name of any Department or the title of any Minister. The Government is also empowered to make "such adaptations of enactments as shall appear to the Government to be consequential on anything done under [these powers]".[67] Thus, drawing on these powers, it is possible, without a

---

[59] On the intricate topic of the corporation sole, see also, Coakley and Gallagher (eds), *Politics in the Republic of Ireland* (2010), Appendix 4.
[60] Section 1. For the replacement of the title "Ministry" by "Department" in 1924, see Fanning, *The Irish Department of Public Expenditure and Reform, 1922–1958* (Dublin: IPA, 1978), p.39.
[61] See paras 20–45 to 20–49.
[62] Ministers and Secretaries (Amendment) Act 1939.
[63] Ministers and Secretaries (Amendment) Act 1946.
[64] Ministers and Secretaries (Amendment) Act 1946.
[65] Ministers and Secretaries (Amendment) Act 1956.
[66] Minister for Supplies (Transfer of Functions) Act 1945 s.3.
[67] 1939 Act s.6(1). The words quoted in the text constitute a rare example of a "Henry VIII clause". Notice also s.6(1)(e) of the 1939 Act, the neglected provision which empowers the

fresh Act, for the Government to transpose a corporation sole originally established as the legal manifestation of one Minister and Department into the legal haven for a fresh Minister and Department. An example of the "shell of the corporation sole" in use is provided by the transfer of the corporation sole originally intended for the Minister for the Public Service (which was terminated in 1987), so as to be used by the newly created Minister for Tourism and Transport.[68]

3–41   In order to illustrate some of these themes, one can outline developments in the structure of Government, which concerned the Minister for Finance. Save for the 1973–1987 and 2011– periods, the personnel and organisation functions for the public service (a wider term than the civil service, see Chapter 4, Part C) had always been vested in the Minister for Finance. Because the Public Service Pay and Pensions Bill accounts for such a large share of public expenditure, this function had always been regarded as an intrinsic element in the control of government expenditure. However, in order to promote a more positive attitude towards matters of organisation and personnel, the Ministers and Secretaries (Amendment) Act 1973 established the Minister for the Public Service as a separate office; though it was only during the period 1982–1986 that the flesh-and-blood incumbent of the office of Minister did not also hold a second portfolio. Then in 1987, the Office of the Minister for the Public Service was terminated and its functions and personnel were restored to the Minister for Finance.

3–42   The second change came with the Ministers and Secretaries (Amendment) Act 2011 which established the Minister for Public Expenditure and Reform as a corporation sole. Under this legislation the empire of Finance was again divided. By ss.8 and 9, the Minister for Finance's functions in the following fields were transferred to the new Minister: the purchase of commodities and goods by a Department of State; functions relating to salaries and pensions; expenses of members of staff of public service bodies; remuneration; and appointment of members of public service bodies (including the civil service). In addition, by s.10, it becomes a function of the Minister to "formulate and develop in consultation with other Ministers of the Government and public service bodies, the policies required to further modernise and develop public service and enable the efficient and effective provision of services by service providers …". In the case of any doubt as to which Minister the Government places in charge of any particular function, the question is to be "determined by the Taoiseach".[69]

Government, by order "to prescribe the organisation of any Department of State and for that purpose to create units of administration within such Department of State".

[68]   See: Public Service (Transfer of Departmental Administration and Ministerial Functions) Order 1987 (S.I. No. 81 of 1987); Public Service (Alteration of Name of Department and Title of Minister) Order 1987 (S.I. No. 83 of 1987). (For an explanation of this, see Second Edition of this book at pp.61–62.) Another example of such a shell is afforded by the Minister for Equality and Law Reform, as explained in H & M, Ch.4, Appendix. Coakley and Gallagher (eds), *Politics in the Republic of Ireland* (2010), Appendix 4, contains examples of Departments which still exist in theory as a "legal shell"—that is without any staff or functions. This comes about because there were times in the fairly recent past when there were 17—or even 18—Ministers (with the same human incumbent acting as Ministers at the head of two Departments); whereas, as of 2011, there are 16.

[69]   2011 Act s.24. This provision does not go on to say, presumably because of Art.34.3.1 of the Constitution (see paras 11–02 to 11–03), that the Taoiseach's decision shall be final.

Ministers of the Government and Ministers of State

3–43   The Constitution regards the status of a Member of the Government as distinct from that of a Minister, although the positions are almost always occupied by the same person. Thus, while Art.28.1 of the Constitution[70] fixes the maximum number of members of the Government at 15, there have been many occasions when there were as many as 17, and now 16, Ministers. However, no difficulty arose from this apparent mismatch, because the Taoiseach is free to allocate more than one Department to the same member of the Government.[71] The Taoiseach may also (though seldom does) appoint a member of the Government who has no responsibility for a Department; that is a Minister without portfolio.[72]

3–44   The Ministers and Secretaries Act 1924 provided for the appointment by the Executive Council of a maximum of seven "parliamentary secretaries" to act as junior Ministers.[73] In 1977, this provision was repealed and replaced by a measure allowing for the appointment of "Ministers of State" (a change of title explained in the footnote)[74] from among members of either House to a maximum figure of initially 10 and then 15 (1980), 17 (1995) and 20 (2007).[75] However, as an economy measure, in 2009, the number of Ministers of State actually appointed was reduced to 15 with no need to amend the statute. The increase in the number of junior Ministers was explained in the Dáil (in 1977) on the grounds of the greater volume of government business by comparison with that in 1924.[76]

3–45   In spite of this change of name, the function of these junior Ministers remains the same, that is, to assist the Minister at the head of the Department to which they are assigned by their appointment.[77] One should write "Department or

---

[70]   By the Irish Free State Constitution, Art.55 (as amended), there was a maximum of 12 members of the Government, though (at various times) 9, 10 or 11 were actually appointed.

[71]   Ministers and Secretaries (Amendment) Act 1946 s.4, replacing the Ministers and Secretaries Act 1924 s.3 which had significantly limited wording. For example, as of 2011, the Departments of Defence and Justice and Equality are headed by the same person. In earlier decades, it used to be common for the Departments of Health and Social Welfare to be assigned to the same Minister.

[72]   Ministers and Secretaries (Amendment) Act 1939 s.4. The device of a Minister without portfolio has only been availed of twice: once during 1939–1945 when a Minister for the Co-ordination of Defensive Measures was appointed; and, secondly, for a few months in 1977, during a period when a Minister for Economic Planning and Development was appointed before the office had been constituted by the Ministers and Secretaries (Amendment) Act 1977.

[73]   Ministers and Secretaries Act 1924 s.7.

[74]   Since the functions of a Minister of State are largely the same as those formerly performed by a parliamentary secretary, the change is merely a matter of "image", the need for which has been explained on the grounds that the title "parliamentary secretary" gave people, both at home and internationally, the impression that a very junior Minister was involved.

[75]   Ministers and Secretaries (Amendment) (No. 2) Act 1977 s.1; Ministers and Secretaries (Amendment) (No. 2) Act 1980 s.2; Ministers and Secretaries (Amendment) Act 1995; Ministers and Secretaries (Ministers of State) Act 2007.

[76]   301 *Dáil Debates* Cols 59–62 (Nov. 2, 1977) (Mr Colley).

[77]   However, one should note a further point. In recent years, when the Government has included a small party whose support in the Dáil warrants only a single seat, it has been perceived as a disadvantage that the sole Minister would have no party colleague with whom to discuss Government matters. To meet this difficulty, a party colleague (the so-called "super junior") who is a Minister of State has been given the right to attend Government meetings (Deputy Pat Rabbitte, 1995–1997, Deputy Molloy, 1997–2002). But this practice was not repeated

Departments" since their appointment can and sometimes does, straddle more than one Department. Likewise, more than one Minister of State may be assigned to the same Department. A Government order[78] may be made on the request of a Minister, delegating to his Minister of State all the Minister's powers and duties under a particular Act or, more narrowly, any particular statutory power or duty.[79]

C. Appointment and Selection of Civil Servants

Definition of "civil servant"

3–46   The constitutional history of the status of a civil servant in independent Ireland (in Britain, formerly known as "Crown Servants") is authoritatively sketched in Costello P.'s judgment in *Gilheaney v The Revenue Commissioners*.[80] This deals with: the position of civil servants transferred from the British Government in Ireland to the Provisional Government of 1921–1922; those transferred from the Provisional Government to the Irish Free State Government; the (temporary) Civil Service Regulation Act 1923; the (permanent) Civil Service Regulation Act 1924; and the Civil Service Regulation Act 1956.[81] This history makes it clear that civil servants were "… holders of an office and not employees … and that their tenure was a tenure at will".[82] Partly on the basis of this history, the definitions summarised in the following paragraph have been developed.

3–47   It is necessary to define the terms "civil servant" and "civil service" precisely: for these terms are used in various statutes which provide no definition for the terms and there are also some marginal public posts whose constituent statute does not make it clear even whether or not they are civil servants.[83] Most important, the term "civil servant" is used to mark out the scope of both the Public Service Management (Recruitment and Appointments) Act 2004 (which regulates the selection of, amongst others, civil servants) and the Civil Service Regulation Act 1956–2005 (which deals with the terms and conditions of civil servants). A

---

in the 2002–2007 Government and, during 2007, it was unnecessary given the Green Party actually had two Ministers of the Government. (Despite the fact that there are several Labour Ministers in the Fine Gael-Labour Government of 2011–, one of the Ministers of State has, nevertheless, been named as a "Super Junior"). No change had been made in law to reflect this phenomenon, nor, probably, was any necessary.

[78] For example, Enterprise, Trade and Employment (Delegation of Ministerial Functions) Order (S.I. Nos 329 and 330 of 1997) by which separate tranches of functions, dealing with, respectively, insurance and employment, were delegated to the two Ministers of State at the Department of Enterprise, Trade and Employment.

[79] Ministers and Secretaries (Amendment) (No. 2) Act 1977 s.2. See also, Ministers and Secretaries (Amendment) Act 1939 s.9(2)(e) (where a function is delegated, the Minister of the Government retains concurrent power with the Minister of State).

[80] [1996] E.L.R. 25.

[81] [1996] E.L.R. 25 at 32–35. The 1956 Act is now amended by the Civil Service Regulation (Amendment) Act 2005, explained below.

[82] [1996] E.L.R. 25 at 33–35. This distinction was not relevant in *Gilheaney* itself. But see Ch.14, Part E.

[83] Though modern statutes frequently state explicitly that the posts they create are to be civil servants, e.g. Law Reform Commission Act 1975 s.10(6)(b); Ombudsman Act 1980 s.10(2); Staff of the Houses of the Oireachtas Act 1959 s.3; Presidential Establishment Act 1938 s.6. The Ministers and Secretaries Act 1924 s.2(2) does not do this but it is clear that the positions which it contemplates meet the tests for a civil servant given in the text.

masterly sketch of the terms was given by Kingsmill Moore J. in *McLoughlin v Minister for Social Welfare*[84]:

> "The words 'civil service' and 'civil servant' though in frequent use on the lips of politicians and members of the general public, are not terms of legal art. The British Royal Commission on the Civil Service which reported in 1931 stated that 'there is nowhere any authoritative or exhaustive definition of the civil service.' The phrase seems to have been first used to describe the non-combatant service of the East India Company, and was well established in English political language by the middle of the nineteenth century.
>
> Though it may be difficult to frame an exact definition, it does not seem in any way impossible to reach an approximation to the meaning of the words sufficient to meet the requirements of the present case. In Britain civil servants were servants of the Crown, that is to say, servants of the King in his politic capacity, but not all servants of the Crown were civil servants. Those who used the strong arm – military, naval and police forces – were excluded from the conception, for the service was civil, not combatant; and so also, by tradition, were judges and holders of political offices. Civil servants were paid out of monies voted by parliament and if permanent, had the benefit of the Superannuating Acts. In theory, as servants of the King, they held their positions at pleasure but in practice they were treated as holding during good behaviour ...
>
> The bulk of British civil servants working in Ireland were taken into the service of Saorstat Éireann and the phrase, with the ideas attached to it, was assimilated into Irish political life. Soon it made its appearance in the Irish statute book and, after the passing of our present Constitution, in statutes of the Republic. Borderline cases have been dealt with by special legislation. Persons have been deemed to be civil servants for one purpose and deemed not to be civil servants for another. But, if we substitute 'State' for 'King' the summary which I have already given corresponds to the present conception of civil servants in Ireland.
>
> I have no doubt that Mr. McLoughlin is a civil servant. He is a state servant engaged in administering one of the most important of State functions, that of justice: he is paid out of monies voted by the Oireachtas: the situation which he holds was dealt with by a scheduling order under section 10 of the Civil Service Regulation Act, 1924, and such an order could only be properly applicable to a post in the civil service–for its effect is to exclude a situation in the civil service from the operation of the Act."

3–48 Partly in the light of this evolution, we can suggest the following guidelines in defining a civil servant. First, civil servants are paid out of monies provided annually, through the Appropriation Act, by the Oireachtas.[85] Secondly, they serve the various organs of State created by the Constitution, including the President, the Dáil and Senate, the Attorney General, the Comptroller and Auditor General, the Taoiseach and the other Ministers who are in charge of Departments of State. To this list must be added other offices, like the Ombudsman, which, although

---

[84] [1958] I.R. 1 at 14–15. Quoted with approval in *Central Bank of Ireland v Gildea* [1997] 2 I.L.R.M. 391 at 397–398 by Keane J.

[85] Civil Service Regulation Act 1956 s.18.

established by Act of Parliament,[86] rather than by the Constitution, are plainly constitutional in nature.

3–49 As might be expected from the term "servant", the actual incumbents of these offices themselves—for instance, the Ministers or the Comptroller and Auditor General or the Ombudsman—are not usually[87] created civil servants and other political appointees are also excluded from the category of "civil servants". So, too, are those who exercise the military, police or judicial function. Although it involves an element of circularity, it should be noted that civil servants are public officials who are subject to the terms and conditions, outlined in this and the following Part. Finally, the Civil Service Regulations Act 1956 s.20 provides that "for the purposes of this Act", the question of whether a person is a civil servant "shall be decided by the Minister [for Finance], whose decision shall be final".[88]

3–50 The framework of rules governing the appointment, selection, dismissal and conditions of employment of civil servants is largely statutory[89]. However, by way of warning, in connection with the description which follows, it must be emphasised that there are also several extra-statutory rules, often contained in circulars, which in practice often make a greater impact than the statute and which are beyond the scope of a general work. All units of the public sector are heavily unionised and also have to operate in an intense political and media spotlight. Thus, the usual effect of these extra-statutory rules has been designed to shift the balance in the individual civil servant's favour, as regards the terms of employment.

3–51 Apart from the specialised provisions regarding selection and dismissal, which are covered later in this Part, the basic legal provision in respect of civil servants is the provision which is now s.58(1)(a) of the Public Service Management (Recruitment and Appointments) Act 2004,[90] which provides as follows:

> (1) The Minister shall be responsible for the following matters:
>> (a) the regulation and control of the Civil Service,
>> (b) the classification, re-classification, numbers and remuneration of civil servants,
>> (c) the fixing of
>>> (i) the terms and conditions of service of civil servants, and
>>> (ii) the conditions governing the promotion of civil servants.
> (2) The Minister may, for the purpose of subsection (1) of this section, make such arrangements as he thinks fit and may cancel or vary those arrangements.

---

[86] Ombudsman Act 1980 s.2.

[87] The Director of Public Prosecutions is an exception: see Prosecution of Offences Act 1974 s.2(4).

[88] But see paras 11–02 to 11–03 on this sort of provision.

[89] For this and the following Part, see O'Toole and Dooney, *Irish Government Today* (Dublin: Gill and Macmillan, 2009), Ch.6 on the Civil Service.

[90] What used to be the Civil Service Regulation Act 1956 s.17(1)(b), largely repeated in the Public Service Management (Recruitment and Appointments) Act 2004 s.58(1)(a); Ministers and Secretaries Act 1924 s.2(2). This section replaced the Ministers and Secretaries Act 1924 s.3(2) and the Civil Service Regulation Act 1924 s.9. On the history, see *Gilheany v Revenue Commissioners* [1996] E.L.R. 25 at 33–35.

3–52 It is under this provision that the Minister for Public Expenditure and Reform: fixes a civil servant's conditions of employment including such matters as: pay-scale, hours of work and holidays; issues personnel circulars altering these conditions; creates new posts; or divides civil servants into classes and grades.[91]

Appointment and selection

3–53 In the first place, it must be noted that, under the provision just quoted, decisions regarding the creation of new posts in the civil service, including their numbers and the grade at which they are located, are taken by the Minister for Public Expenditure and Reform. (However, since administrative budgets were established in 1991, there has been a substantial delegation of this function.)

3–54 Next, we should mark the fact that there is usually a distinction between selection and appointment. The Secretary General is appointed by the Government on the recommendation of the Minister responsible for the Department concerned[92] and no other body is involved. Otherwise, the position is more complicated: the civil servants in a Department are *formally* appointed by the Minister of that Department or (in the case of staff below Principal level) the Secretary General or his delegate.[93] But there is a critical distinction between appointment and selection for, save in some exceptional cases, the appointing agency is obliged to appoint the candidate who has been selected, under a scheme established by the Public Service Management (Recruitment and Appointments) Act 2004,[94] as explained below.

Selection for basic recruitment posts

3–55 Selection for most of these posts was initially vested in the independent Civil Service Commissioners,[95] first set up in 1923,[96] but later constituted under the Civil

---

[91] *Inspector of Taxes v Minister for the Public Service* [1986] I.L.R.M. 296 at 300.
[92] Ministers and Secretaries Act 1924 s.2(2).
[93] Ministers and Secretaries Act 1924 s.2(2); Public Service Management Act 1997 s.4(1)(h).
[94] 2004 Act ss.34, 57(5), 57(6).
[95] Civil Service Commissioners Act 1956 ss.13(1) and 14(1). In the 1920s, soon after the establishment of the Civil Service Commissioners, a Minister refused to accept the candidate selected by the Commissioners. However, they persisted and the Minister eventually accepted their selection. So far as is known, the Commissioners' other decisions were accepted, without demur.
[96] Civil Service Regulation Act 1923; Civil Service Regulation Act 1924. See also, Fanning, *The Irish Department of Public Expenditure and Reform 1922–1958* (Dublin: IPA, 1978), pp.63–72. Lee, *Ireland 1912–1985* (Cambridge: Cambridge University Press, 1989), p.107 comments: "Perhaps the major achievement of the early years, and it remains one of the most remarkable achievements in the history of the state, was the creation of a Civil Service Commission, consisting of the Ceann Comhairle (Speaker), and two civil servants, to preside over the public appointments process. The new government was naturally deluged with importunities for jobs. The scope for casualness in the appointments process was considerable. The Civil Service Commission did the state great service in setting ethical standards. Given the scope for corruption permitted by the feeble sense of public morality, the imposition of a high degree of integrity in appointments to the central administration verged on the miraculous. The same considerations did not apply to promotion within the civil service, where the criterion of seniority soon took precedence over that of merit even among men themselves originally appointed on grounds of merit. Nevertheless, this was at the time a relatively venial transgression of the code of strict personal integrity which would be rightly regarded as one of the glories of the civil service."

Service Commissioners Act 1956. The object of this system was to prevent jobbery and nepotism. The same spirit animates the new regime established by the Public Service Management (Recruitment and Appointments) Act 2004.[97] The new scheme replaced those formerly existing under both the Civil Service Commissioners and their equivalent at local government level, the Local Appointments Commission, and thus embraces employees in most positions in the civil service and Garda Síochána, as well as certain managerial, professional and technical posts in local authorities and the Health Service Executive.

3–56   Under the 2004 Act, there is a two-level system. At the top, the Commission for Public Service Appointment is the regulator for public service recruitment; which sets general standards for recruitment to the civil service and the public service and regulates compliance with those standards. The Act now casts as statute the former convention governing the selection of civil servants[98]: the Commission is composed of five ex officio members, namely the Ceann Comhairle; the Secretary General to the Government; the Secretary General, Public Service Management and Development, Department of Public Expenditure and Reform; the Chairman of Standards in Public Office Commission; and the Ombudsman.[99]

3–57   The actual work of recruitment—fixing criteria for selection[100] to the particular position, advertising, short-listing, interviewing, etc.—is done, at the second level, by "licence holders".[101] The main licence-holder is the Public Appointments Service ("PAS"). The difference in status between the PAS and other recruitment licence-holders is shown by the fact that, by s.43(1), the Commission "shall grant a recruitment licence to [the PAS] with effect from the establishment date" whereas "the Commission *may* grant a licence to [any other] applicant".

3–58   The fact that the PAS is not the only licence-holder is significant. In line with the policy of devolution of authority (which existed in the period 2003–2008), and the related notion of geographical decentralisation, public bodies which choose to become licence-holders will be allowed to undertake their own recruitment and so tailor it to their needs and to recruit locally.[102] In addition, there was a feeling among

---

[97]   578 *Dáil Debates* Cols 96–147 (January 21, 2004); 587 Cols 1500–1515 (June 23, 2004): 177 Cols 472–506 (June 30, 2004). See also, the Commission's Annual Report for 2005 (incorporating 2004).

[98]   On which see, Third Edition, p.84. As initiated, s.12 of the Bill which became the 2004 Act would have provided that three members of the Commission would be ex officio Commissioners with up to six other Commissioners appointed by the Government. However, the Bill was amended "to remove any suspicion that any influence may be brought to bear on the appointment of the commission ... to maintain the highest standards of integrity in public service recruitment" (Tom Parlon, Minister of State, Department of Public Expenditure and Reform), 177 *Seanad Debates* Col.47 (June 30, 2004).

[99]   2004 Act ss.11 and 12.

[100]   Any condition which attempted to confine a post to Irish citizens only would violate EU law: *Re Colgan* [1997] 1 C.M.L.R. 53, a decision of the Northern Ireland High Court and *European Commission v Luxembourg* (C-473/93) [1996] 3 C.M.L.R. 981 regarding the EU principle of equality of treatment and the scope of public service derogation in art.48(4) of the EU Treaty. (*Colgan* also involved equality of treatment in domestic law.) For a case involving knowledge of the Irish language, see *State (Cussen) v Brennan* [1981] I.R. 181 at 305 and *Groener v Minister for Education* [1990] I.L.R.M. 335.

[101]   2004 Act s.34.

[102]   See Deputy Parlon, 578 *Dáil Debates*, Col 96 (January 21, 2004)).

some public bodies that the Civil Service and Local Appointments Commissions had been inflexible; and so might the PAS. Finally, in the world of nearly full employment, in which the 2004 Act was passed, when a job for life in the public service was no longer regarded as a pearl beyond price, more frequent competitions were necessary to catch the market. Nevertheless, the obvious difficulty which might seem to arise would be that permitting individual public bodies to recruit might lead to the varying standards and even favouritism, which it was the achievement of the Civil Service Commissioners and Local Appointment Commission to prevent. Here is one reason why it was considered necessary to establish the Commissioner as a regulator: in case of any malfunctioning, whether by the PAS or other licence-holders, the independent Commission acts as a watchdog.

Selection outside the 2004 Act

3–59 There are various exceptional initial appointments[103] which are outside the system established by the 2004 Act, in that the Commissioners–PAS (or other licence-holders) are not involved. In addition to the appointment of Secretaries General of Departments (just covered) and promotions (paras 3–60 to 3–63), these exceptions include the following posts:

1. A number of positions which are special in various ways are identified in s.7(1) as not attracting the Act. These exceptional positions include: appointments made by the President or Government; or officers of the Oireachtas; or unestablished appointments, as "service officer, service attendant, night-watchman, cleaner or analogous employment". In addition, by s.7(2), there are other positions to which the Act's provisions do not apply but to which they may be extended by order of the Minister for Public Expenditure and Reform. Among these are: industrial civil servants; and civilians employed for the construction of barracks, placing of buoys or certain other specified technical purposes. The significant point is that the method of recruitment to posts in either category is left to the individual Department.

2. The Commissioners may, on the request of the Minister in whose Department the post arises and with the consent of the Minister for Public Expenditure and Reform, declare that posts of a specified grade are "an excluded unestablished position" (s.8). In this case recruitment is by the individual Department. The safeguard is that "excluded position" must be publicised by a notice in *Iris Oifigiúil* (though s.8(7) states that failure to so publish shall not affect the validity of the order making a position "excluded"). *Iris Oifigiúil* is a bi-weekly publication of official governmental information and, presumably, if there is anything interesting in it, the news media would bring this to public attention.

3. Special advisers and programme managers used to be appointed under a forerunner of exception 2, and in some cases were appointed not merely for the life of the Government which appointed them but as permanent civil servants. Many people including the Civil Service trade unions

---

[103] There has been a complicated series of changes affecting female former civil servants who, by virtue of the Civil Service Regulation Act 1956 s.10, had been forced to retire on marriage, as described in the Third Edition, p.85.

objected to this, in part because it undermined the tradition of a neutral civil service which could be relied upon to serve any "political master". In response to this sort of concern, the Public Service Management Act 1997 s.11, was enacted. This established the concept of "a special adviser" whose duty is: providing advice; "monitoring, facilitating and securing the achievement of government objectives that relate to the Department [and] ... performing such other function as may be directed by the Minister or Minister of State". The numbers of special advisors are limited to two for each Minister and one for each Minister of State; but not at all limited in the case of the Taoiseach or Tánaiste. Their term of office ceases with that of the Minister.

Promotional posts: the Top Level Appointments Committee

3–60 Most of what has been said so far relates to basic recruitment posts. We turn now to the important issue of promotion. Section 57(1) of the 2004 Act provides that the Public Appointments Service shall, at the request of the Minister for Public Expenditure and Reform and after consulting with the Minister in whose Department the promotional post is located, hold a competition to fill the position. Alternatively, by s.57(3), the Minister for Public Expenditure and Reform may allow the promotional post to be filled internally by the Department in which the post is located.

3–61 However, by far the most important qualification on the 2004 Act, in the field of promotion, is that, under s.7(2), senior positions which fall under the jurisdiction of the Top Level Appointments Committee are exempted from the scope of the Act. The jurisdiction of this Committee extends to posts at Assistant Secretary level or above (including non-general service grades) in all Departments, subject to the significant exceptions.[104] Its main purpose was to get away from the tendency, which (because of the public service trade unions) existed before the Committee was established in 1984, for a post to go automatically to a senior, if not the most senior, contender from within the same Department. The main element in the Top Level Appointments Committee system is inter-departmental competition for the posts to which it applies. The Committee is also supposed, where this is possible, to make its decision irrespective of a candidate's background; in other words, to overlook the dual structure of professional and general service streams.

3–62 The Committee consists of: the Secretary to the Government; the Secretary (Public Service Management and Development); Department of Public Expenditure and Reform (Chairman); Secretary General to the Government; two Secretaries General of Departments and a person drawn from the private sector, each chosen by the Taoiseach after consultation with the Minister for Public Expenditure and Reform; and, in the case of the appointment of a Secretary, the outgoing incumbent.

---

[104] What are probably the six most important posts at Secretary General level are excluded from the process: Department of Public Expenditure and Reform; Public Service Management and Development; Taoiseach; Government; Foreign Affairs; and Chairman of the Revenue Commissioners. In addition, Assistant Secretary posts in the Department of Foreign Affairs, including Ambassador posts at this level are not filled through TLAC.

3–63 No information has been published as to whether the Committee's recommendations have been accepted in all cases. However, it seems likely that this has been the case.[105] Nevertheless, since the system is not established by statute,[106] we may briefly entertain the question: what if the Minister or Government fail to appoint the person who has been selected by TLAC? The likelihood is that, in such a situation, a court would hold that the candidate who succeeded before TLAC would have a legitimate expectation that s/he would be appointed. To take a different point, the Secretary of the Department in which the vacancy exists may nominate two applicants who appear before the committee without having to be interviewed by the Civil Service Commissioners, which is a preliminary part of the process for the other candidates. Additionally, in the case of a post of Secretary General, since 1987 the Committee has been required to recommend three candidates, without ranking them so that the Government may choose among them.

D. DISMISSAL AND DISCIPLINE

Dismissal

3–64 Under the Civil Service Regulation Act 1956 s.5, every established civil servant (a category which includes most civil servants) "shall hold office at the will and pleasure of the Government". While, as indicated below, this provision has been significantly qualified by the Civil Service Regulation (Amendment) Act 2005, this extreme test remains (in theory at any rate) part of the law. The inspiration behind this remarkable provision is the legally insecure position of the British Crown servant. This owes its origin to the exigencies of British history— frequently in the military and/or colonial context—which were thought to require the power of immediate dismissal of a Crown servant unhampered by any fear of legal consequences; and also to the authoritarian culture which underlay the Royal Prerogative. The policy reason for this was the idea that the Crown had to be able to dismiss servants, unhampered by any fear of legal consequences.

3–65 On a full literal reading, s.5 is undoubtedly unconstitutional, on two counts. First, as regards the substance of the power to dismiss, plainly if it were exercised in a discriminatory or arbitrary way (say because the civil servant had red hair), it would violate Art.40.1. Secondly, as to procedure, removal would have to observe the rules of constitutional justice. Thus, for instance, the civil servant would have to be told why their dismissal was contemplated and allowed an opportunity to argue the Government out of it.[107]

---

[105] Murray, "The Top Level Appointments Committee" (1988) 9 *Seirbhís Phoiblí* 1 at 10, refers to a rumour that one recommendation involving an Assistant Secretary post was accepted only after an initial refusal. Otherwise, we have heard no report of refusals.

[106] Perhaps to allow for flexibility in case the new Committee did not work, the TLAC is established, not by a statute, but just by a memorandum which was laid before the Oireachtas. This is simply a way of publishing the document authoritatively. But a memorandum is not, strictly speaking, one of the conventional sources of law. For legitimate expectations, see Ch.19.

[107] See the analogous case of *Garvey v Ireland* [1981] I.R. 75 at 95–97. This concerned the removal of the Commissioner of the Gardaí, by a new Government, after the Government which had appointed him lost office. Held: since he was not told the reason why he was being removed, his removal was invalid.

3–66   In practice, for political or trade union reasons, the only few dismissals[108] to occur have always been within the Constitution: dismissals only occur on plainly justifiable grounds, often where a crime of dishonesty at work has been proved before a court. As to procedure, the pre-2005 practice was to inform the civil servant as to why his or her dismissal is contemplated and to allow an opportunity to put his or her side of the case to the entire Government, though by written submission.

3–67 However, the historic relic contained in the 1956 Act has been significantly altered by ss.6 and 7 of the Civil Service (Amendment) Act 2005.[109] The new law retains the former test ("every established civil servant shall hold office at the will and pleasure of the Government"); with the constitutional doubts and practical difficulties mentioned. But it makes a significant change to the dismissing agency: "where the Government so authorises", civil servants below the grade of Principal may be dismissed by the Secretary General.[110] Above that level (again, "where the Government so authorises"), they may be dismissed by a Minister, but only on the recommendation of the Secretary General. The only exceptions are civil servants who are appointed directly by the Government (that is, Secretaries General) who may be dismissed only by the Government.

3–68   There is a further point, namely that almost all civil servants have now been brought within the protection of the Unfair Dismissals Act 1977–2001. Formerly, many categories of *public* service employees, including civil servants, were excluded from the protection of the Unfair Dismissal Act 1977. However, these categories were significantly reduced by the Unfair Dismissals Act 1993. A further notable extension occurred when all but a few of even *civil* servants were brought within the protection of the legislation, by the Civil Service Regulation (Amendment) Act 2005. (Those public servants still outside the legislation include: the members of the defence forces and of the Gardaí[111]; and a few rare birds such as local authority managers[112]; or persons employed by or under the State who are still dismissable by the Government.)[113]

3–69   There is plainly a contradiction between the extreme formula "will and pleasure of the Government" (assuming that this test has been in some way delegated to the person who actually dismisses) and the requirement, imposed by the Unfair Dismissals legislation, that "substantial grounds" are needed to justify dismissal; or that a dismissal may be "deemed" to be unfair if made for trade union membership or on a number of other specified grounds. A further difficulty of alignment arises from the nonchalant way in which the Unfair Dismissals regime was extended to

---

[108] The percentage of established civil servants who have had to be dismissed has always been unnaturally low by comparison either with employees in the private sector or even with unestablished civil servants.

[109] The Civil Service Regulation (Amendment) Act 2005 s.7, substitutes a new section, s.5, in the 1956 Act. This new section then refers the reader to (the new) s.6(1)(a)–(c), which has been inserted by s.5 of the 2005 Act.

[110] Redmond, *Dismissal Law in Ireland*, 2nd edn (Dublin: Tottel Publishing, 2007), para.3.21, comments on the changes outlined in this paragraph: "The *quid pro quo* for what amounts to an encroachment on this category of worker's hitherto security of tenure was the provision of a remedy under Unfair Dismissals legislation."

[111] Unfair Dismissals Act 1977 s.2(1)(d), (e).

[112] Local Authorities (Officers and Employees) Act 1926.

[113] Civil Service Regulation (Amendment) Act 2005 s.2.

most civil servants: is the position now that a dismissed civil servant may choose between the traditional proceedings of judicial review and those under the Unfair Dismissals legislation; or is s/he confined to the latter option?

3–70 In addition, the Minimum Notice and Terms of Employment Act 1973 now applies to almost all civil servants.[114] And, from the initial establishment of the legislation, all categories of civil servant were within the Anti-Discrimination (Pay) Act 1974, the Employment Equality Act 1977 (both of which have now been superseded by the Employment Equality Act 1998) and the Maternity Protection Act 1981 (now the Maternity Protection Act 1994).

Discipline

3–71 What sanctions[115] are available and who within a Department is responsible for the disciplinary function? The position is now regulated by the Civil Service Regulation Act 1956, as amended by the Civil Service Regulation (Amendment) Act 2005 ss.6 and 9–11; considerably supplemented by the Civil Service Disciplinary Code Circular.[116] Section 6 of the 2005 Act imposes responsibility and authority for managing all matters regarding the performance, conduct and discipline of civil servants below Principal level, on the Secretary General; while the Minister retains the appropriate authority for civil servants at Principal level or above.[117]

3–72 The Circular lays down a formal disciplinary procedure with four stages: verbal warning, written warning, final written warning and implementation of further disciplinary action. Where dismissal is proposed, the Personnel Officer must make a recommendation to the appropriate authority and provide him/her with a written report on the circumstances. A decision to take disciplinary action may be appealed within 10 days, to the Civil Service Disciplinary Code Appeal Board. Despite the name, the powers of the Board are more those of review and it is empowered to issue a "recommendation" not a determination.

3–73 Section 10 of the 2005 Act[118] specifies the following disciplinary actions: placing the civil servant on a lower rate of remuneration (including the withholding of an increment)[119]; reducing the civil servant to a specified lower grade or rank;

---

[114] Civil Service Regulation (Amendment) Act 2005 Pts 6 and 7.

[115] Civil servants who go on strike commit a criminal offence (although it might be considered impolitic to prosecute): Offences Against the State Act 1939 s.9(2). *The Report of the Commission of Inquiry on Industrial Relations* (Pl. 114), paras 787–789, recommended the amendment of this provision "to remove any doubt that it might apply to legitimate trade union activities in the public service".

[116] Circular 14/2006 (replacing Circular 1/92), which applies to all new disciplinary cases post-July 2006. For detail, see Redmond, "The New Civil Service Disciplinary Code" (2007) 4 *Irish Employment Law Journal* 42, on which the material in the text draws heavily. According to the legislation, the dividing line fixing the Secretary General's sole jurisdiction runs below Principal; whereas the Circular is made, by para.12, to apply to "Principal and below". Note that there is also a Circular of Grievance Procedures on civil servants—Circular 11/2001.

[117] Civil Service Regulation (Amendment) Act 2005 s.6; Public Service Management Act 1997 ss.4(1)(h), 9(1)(f).

[118] The Circular, para.16, establishes a number of other disciplinary actions, including: formal written notes placed on the officer's personnel file; debarment from competition; transfer to another office; and withdrawal of concessions or allowances.

[119] The granting of the annual salary increase is usually automatic but a civil servant's conditions

suspending the civil servant, in principle[120] without pay. Dismissal also counts as a disciplinary action, for the purpose of attracting the procedures specified in the Circular.[121] Finally, a civil servant will not be paid his remuneration for any period of unauthorised absence.[122]

3–74 The following helpful analysis of how the various forms of indiscipline are dealt with in the Civil Service Regulation Act 1956, has been made by McGuinness J. in *Fuller v Minister for Agriculture*,[123] of which the facts are given below:

> "[Sections] 13 to 16 stand together in a coherent and interrelated scheme which deals with general discipline in the civil service. Section 13 provides for the sanction of suspension where grave misconduct or grave irregularity appear to have occurred, where it seems that the public interest might be prejudiced, or where a charge against a civil servant is being investigated. Section 14 deals in considerable detail with the remuneration of a civil servant who is under suspension. Section 15 goes on to set out, again in detail, the disciplinary measures that can be taken against a civil servant who has been guilty of misconduct, irregularity, neglect or unsatisfactory behaviour in relation to his official duties. Prominent among the graded penalties which may be imposed on the defaulting civil servant is a reduction of the rate of remuneration of the civil servant concerned. These three sections, therefore, deal with the situation where a civil servant is in default of his or her duty. In this statutory context, it seems to me, the legislature goes on to provide [in s.16] for what might be described as the ultimate default – the situation where the civil servant simply fails to come to work at all. In that case the sanction is the ultimate one of complete deprivation …".

3–75 A number of the cases show the courts taking a very literal approach to the legislation. In particular, they will require a public body's action to be authorised by specific statutory sanction, and will not countenance any notion of deducing, from a series of individual powers, an umbrella power which would then make good any gaps between individual powers.[124] These generalisations are illustrated by the facts in *Fuller v Minister for Agriculture*.[125] The central provision here was s.16(1) of the Civil Service Regulation Act 1956, which, in its amended form, provided that "[a] civil servant shall not be paid remuneration in respect of any

---

of employment provide that it may be withheld if the Minister of the particular Department considers it appropriate.
[120] In fact, the fangs of this power are, to some extent, drawn by the 2005 Act s.9 (which provides for the remuneration of civil servants suspended from duty).
[121] For cases on what were probably "holding suspensions" pending an inquiry, rather than substantive sanctions, see *Flynn v An Post* [1987] I.R. 68 at 75, 80–81; *Deegan v Minister for Public Expenditure and Reform* [2000] E.L.R. 190 at 199–200.
[122] 1956 Act s.16, as amended by the 2005 Act s.11.
[123] *Fuller v Minister for Agriculture* [2005] 1 I.R. 529 at para.51. Notice that, of the provisions referred to in the passage quoted, ss.14–16 of the 1956 Act have now been amended by ss.9–11 of the 2005 Act. However, these amendments do not affect the structure explained in the passage.
[124] However, in the reverse situation—where such an approach would tell in favour of the individual—it has sometimes been adopted. See, for instance, *McDonald v Dublin Corporation*, unreported, Supreme Court, July 23, 1980.
[125] [2005] 1 I.R. 529. The rule laid down in *Fuller* is reversed by the Civil Service Regulation (Amendment) Act 2005 s.11.

period of unauthorised absence from duty". The applicants were established civil servants. An industrial dispute arose between the union and the Minister concerning promotional opportunities and the applicants engaged in limited industrial action consisting—significantly—of attendance at their place of work but refusing to deal with telephone and fax queries and counter queries. Following written and verbal warnings, the applicants were removed from the payroll.

3–76 The applicants brought judicial review which succeeded in both the High Court and, on appeal, the Supreme Court. McGuinness J.'s judgment, for the Supreme Court, stated, "… the words of s. 16(1), 'unauthorised absence from duty' [cannot] be interpreted, in accordance with the established canons of construction, to mean the refusal of the applicants, despite their physical presence at their place of work, to perform what the respondents describe as their 'core duties'".[126] (The possible view that "absence from duty" means something different from "absence from the work-place" was not really explored.)

3–77 The court's literal interpretation was fortified by reading s.16(1) in the context of other sections and this analysis is contained in the passage quoted earlier. Building on a similar line of analysis, the unreported High Court (Carroll J.) judgment had observed, in a passage quoted with approval by the Supreme Court[127]:

> "In the normal way, if there was no union involvement with industrial action and a civil servant decided that he/she would not perform certain duties, it seems to me that this would fall under s. 15 as neglect of official duties and could be dealt with accordingly and the civil servant would have the opportunity to make representations under s. 15(5). But the respondents have ruled out using the powers given by s. 15, probably on a pragmatic basis because they believe it would escalate the industrial dispute. In doing so they ruled out a remedy otherwise available to them."

3–78 What this perceptive analysis (especially the final sentence) shows is that there may be extraneous pressures which militate against what may be the safest legal route. Yet, the courts are not sympathetic to the fact that public administrators are under this sort of pressure.

---

[126] [2005] 1 I.R. 529 at para.47.
[127] [2005] 1 I.R. 529 at para.30.

CHAPTER 4

PUBLIC BODIES, ETC.

A. Introduction

4–01   The principle objective of the Ministers and Secretaries Act 1924 was, as has been seen, to provide that all the central, executive power of the State should flow through Ministers responsible to the Dáil. Nevertheless, even at Independence, there were a few independent public bodies,[1] among them the Commissioners of Irish Lights, the Royal Irish Academy and, until recently, the 18th Century Registry of Deeds, which lately[2] married the 19th Century Land Registry, to form the 21st Century Property Registration Authority. And, by 1927, the first four post-Independence examples of what were then called "state-sponsored bodies" and would now be called "public or state bodies". The functions of these four bodies give some idea of the work of the state-sponsored sector: the Electricity Supply Board was set up to provide public financing of a huge investment project which, it was believed, could not be privately financed; the Agricultural Credit Corporation was constituted to make loans to farmers and to promote the co-operative movement; the Dairy Disposal Co. Ltd was set up to acquire, and thus prevent a foreign takeover of, Newmarket Creameries; and the purpose of the Medical Registration Council—whose functions were passed on to the newly

---

[1]   See Fitzgerald, *State-Sponsored Bodies* (Dublin: IPA, 1963); *Industrial Policy* (Dublin: The Stationery Office, 1984); NESC, *Enterprise in the Public Sector* (Dublin: The Stationery Office). The public debt crisis of the late 1980s, coupled with the backwash from the Thatcher Era in Britain, naturally attracted a good deal of writing on the present topic in the late 1980s and early 1990s, for instance: Covery and McDowell, *Privatisation: Issues of Principle and Implementation in Ireland* (Dublin: Gill and Macmillan, 1990); Zimmerman, "Irish State-Sponsored Bodies: The Fractionalisation of Authority and Responsibility" (1986) 7(2) *Seirbhís Phoiblí* 27; Sweeney, "Public Enterprise in Ireland: A Statistical Description and Analysis", a paper given to the Statistical and Social Enquiry Society of Ireland on February 15, 1990.
    More recently, see Gray (ed.), *International Perspectives on the Irish Economy* (Dublin: Indecon Economics Consultants, 1997), Chs 5 and 6; Fitzgerald and McCoy (eds), *Issues in Irish Energy Policy* (1993, ESRI Paper No. 20); FitzGerald and Johnston (eds), *Energy Utilities and Competitiveness* (1995, ESRI Paper No. 24); Organisation for Economic Co-operation and Development, *Public Management Reviews: Ireland, Towards an Integrated Public Service* (2008), pp.293–318; Collins and Quinlivan, "Multi-level Governance" in Coakley and Gallagher (eds), *Politics in the Republic of Ireland* (London: Routledge, 2005); McGauran, Verhoest and Humphreys, *The Corporate Governance of Agencies in Ireland*, CPMR Research Report No. 6 IPA, 2005); Clancy and Murphy, *Outsourcing Government: Public Bodies and Accountability* (Tasc at New Island, 2006); MacCarthaigh, *National Non-commercial State Agencies in Ireland*, IPA Research Paper No. 1 (2010); Jackson, "Irish Public Assets: Establishment, Control and Privatisation" (2010) 5 *International Journal of Public Policy* 74.

[2]   See Registration of Deeds and Titles Act 2006.

constituted Medical Council in 1978[3]—was to regulate the practice of medicine in the State. During the Celtic Tiger era, there was a substantial increase in the number of these peripheral entities—by now there are, depending on how one counts, about 400 in number.

Definitions

4–02 Put simply, the term "public body" embraces any entity which is financed partly or wholly by monies provided through a Minister. From a functional position, the bodies may be classified as: Ministers and Departments; local/regional authorities; tribunals; educational units; Garda Síochána; defence forces; regulatory authorities; commercial state-sponsored bodies; and non-commercial state-sponsored bodies (although popular parlance[4] seems to exclude from the term the first three of these entities; in any case, these three are covered more fully in Chapters 3, 5 and 6).

4–03 What public bodies (apart from Ministers and Departments) have in common is that they discharge specialised, national functions, sometimes of a governmental and sometimes of a commercial nature, yet which are set at a distance from Ministers and the Civil Service. This last point is a central feature in the concept of the public body. For, on the one hand, these agencies exercising public functions are owned by the State and rely, in the case of non-commercial bodies, substantially on state finance; and are controlled by boards whose members are selected by the Government or a Minister. Yet, on the other hand, they are subject to a lesser degree of control, by the responsible Minister and the Dáil, than would apply to the activities of a Department of State.[5] As was said by the Minister when piloting the Bill to constitute the ESB through the Dáil:

> "[T]here are going to be no Parliamentary questions with regard to this Board. There are going to be no complaints from a Deputy that his area is not served at such a rate as some other Deputy … this Board is not going to be regarded as a machine for wiping off all political obligations of this, that and the other Deputy."[6]

4–04 Broadly speaking, two sets of questions arise: the first is, essentially, public policy—what should be done and why is the law as it is; and the other field, to be covered in Part B, is black letter law—of interest to a lawyer advising a client. As regards the first point, various advantages, depending on the function of the particular public body, are thought to be gained by casting certain specialised public functions as independent public bodies rather than as units of Departments

---

[3] Now established by the Medical Practitioners Act 2007.

[4] See, e.g. Clancy and Murphy, *Outsourcing Government: Public Bodies and Accountability* (Tasc at New Island, 2006), p.16 and Appendix II, "List of Public Bodies". This book has useful Appendices I and II giving a list of 500 public bodies, 315 executive agencies, 85 advisory bodies, 14 task forces and the remainder defying classification. See also, McGauran, Verhoest and Humphreys, *The Corporate Governance of Agencies in Ireland* (CPMR Research Reports, 2005), Appendix II.

[5] Chapter 3, Parts A and B.

[6] 18 *Dáil Debates* Col.1919 (March 15, 1927). See also, 470 *Dáil Debates* Col.433 (October 16, 1996).

of State. Their activities are—so far as day-to-day performance is concerned—put beyond control by the Dáil, though it must be said that the cut and thrust of politics is such that this formal position is not always respected. They are removed from the hierarchy of the civil service, which is thought to limit initiative. The public bodies raise common problems of accountability, patronage, staffing, control, organisation, legal status and, particularly, relationship with the parent Minister and Department.[7]

4–05   The major problem is accountability: with the exception of commercial state-sponsored bodies, which now have to contend with private enterprise competitors, "profit motive" is not significant. What then are the means by which they can be made accountable to the public?[8] Dáil questions to a Minister may be turned away by the Ceann Comhairle on the basis that they engage questions of "day-to-day operations", for which the Minister, with whom a public body is most closely associated, is not responsible.[9] But, in the relevant Joint Oireachtas Committee for the field embracing a public body, questions may be directed to the heads of the public body. And, with the exception of commercial state bodies, the audit of other public bodies is carried out by the Comptroller and Auditor General.[10] A device for facilitating more precise accountability, which has become popular over the past decade or so, is a strategic statement or plan.[11] This then provides a standard against which the performance of the public body may be judged and a hook on which opposition Deputies or Senators or the news media may hang unfavourable publicity. In the case of some of the larger or more sensitive public bodies, there are now specialised institutional watchdogs (themselves public bodies). For example, in the case of the HSE—the Health Information and Quality Authority; Prisons—Inspector of Prisons and Visiting Committees for individual prisons; the Gardaí—Garda Síochána Ombudsman Commission (Individual Complaints); and the Garda Inspectorate (Efficiency of the Gardaí in the light of available resources).[12]

B. Terminology and Classification

Terminology

4–06   Both concepts and terminology are treacherous here.[13] Unease at this

---

[7]   On all of which, see H & M, Ch.4, Parts B–F.
[8]   See H & M, Ch.4, Part E; MacCarthaigh, "Parliamentary Scrutiny of Departments and Agencies" in MacCarthaigh and Manning (eds), *The Houses of the Oireachtas* (Dublin: IPA, 2010).
[9]   Though note that the HSE has a parliamentary affairs division, which is designed to respond to questions from Deputies.
[10]   Comptroller and Auditor General (Amendment) Act 1993. A further exception is local authorities: see Ch.5, Part D.
[11]   e.g. Comhairle Act 2000 s.8. For other examples involving Departments and local authorities, see paras 3–11 and 5–27 to 5–28.
[12]   See Health Act 2007 ss.8 and 9; Prisons Act 2007 s.31; Prisons (Visiting Committees) Act 1925; Garda Síochána Act 2005.
[13]   There is a further point of characterisation in which public bodies are not mired: they are probably not exercising "the executive power of the State" so as to engage the separation of powers, as expressed in Art.28.2 of the Constitution.

terminological thicket was expressed by MacMenamin J. in *Health Service Executive v Commissioner of Valuation.*[14] He doubted:

"... whether the terms 'state' 'office of state' or 'semi-state body' can now satisfactorily define or describe all the vast range of statutory bodies or authorities now in existence must be seriously doubted. Certainly, the term semi-state body, absent a statutory definition, is not helpful in an area of law where taxonomy is at a premium".[15]

4–07   A number of different expressions exist. In addition, each of the terms in use is defined afresh in each new statute in which the expression is used. While, because it is in common usage, the term "public body" has been utilised in this Part, statute law uses the following terms:

4–08   The narrowest of these is "state authority", which is used to mean only a Minister and the Commissioner of Public Works in Ireland (or, in some cases, a few other entities).[16]

4–09   Ranging more widely, we come to some two dozen statutes, mainly recent, using the term "public body".[17] Most potential definitional difficulties have been avoided, in that the draftsperson of a new public law statute has usually[18] been careful to indicate, by the use of a list in a Schedule to the particular Act, which entities fall within the legislation. It is usually used widely, to embrace, first, Ministers (although popular parlance tends not to regard Ministers and Departments as being "public bodies"). It also includes local authorities, and "... a body ... established (i) by or under any enactment other than the Companies Acts ... or (ii) under the Companies Acts financed wholly or partly by means of monies provided by a Minister ...".[19] In other words, pretty well any entity which is commonly thought of as "sort of public" would come within this definition.

---

[14]   [2008] IEHC 178.

[15]   [2008] IEHC 178 at para.63.

[16]   See, e.g. State Authorities (Development and Management) Act 1993 s.1; Planning and Development Act 2000 s.2; National Development Finance Agency Act 2002 Sch.; and State Authorities (Public Private Partnership Arrangements) Act 2002 Sch.

[17]   See, e.g. Prevention of Electoral Abuses Act 1923; Transport Act 1958; Ethics in Public Office Act 1995 Sch.1; Freedom of Information Act 1997; Prevention of Corruption (Amendment) Act 2001; Arts Act 2003; Official Languages Act 2003 Sch.1 (on which see *CAO v Minister for Community, Rural and Gaeltacht Affairs* [2010] IESC 32); Public Service (Management and Recruitment) Act 2004; Dormant Accounts (Amendment) Act 2005 s.3(i).

[18]   Unusually among recent statutes, the Pharmacy Act 2007 s.71 uses the term "public body or authority" without defining it.

[19]   Freedom of Information Act 1997 Sch.1. This particular formulation has an analogue in most statutory definitions of "public body". What emerges is that there are rather broad areas of overlap. For instance, most include commercial state bodies. However, in most of the definitions, e.g. Arts Act 2003 s.2(1), something like the wording quoted in the text from the Freedom of Information Act 1997 is utilised. It seems likely that a commercial state body would be included under (i) if it were established under its own Act, or under (ii) where it was a "statutory company" established under the Companies Acts.

  Worth noticing is the fact that the actual operational definition for Freedom of Information purposes is not that in the Act, which is quoted in the text, but the one used in the Freedom of Information Act 1997 (Prescribed Bodies) Regulations 2006 (S.I. No. 297 of 2006). The definition in the Regulations is narrower, in that it omits the categories cited in the text and, therefore, *does not* catch commercial state bodies. In the case of the Official Languages Act

4–10   A further point to note is that the term "public body" is not confined to what may be called executive agencies. It often extends to entities whose task is to police the executive–legislature and to prevent it from abusing its authority and which have, in another jurisdiction, been felicitously called "politically neutral zones".[20] For example, the Comptroller and Auditor General, Director of Public Prosecutions or Ombudsman (though not the courts). As more recent members of the group, one might add: the Referendum Commission; the Ethics in Public Office Commission[21]; and the Houses of the Oireachtas Commission, which services and maintains the Oireachtas.

4–11   Other expressions which have been used infrequently are the term "public authority"[22]; and "state body" (used in the Health Act 2004 and the National Treasury Management (Amendment) Act 2000 respectively).

4–12   The Financial Emergency Measures in the Public Interest Act 2009 and Financial Emergency Measures in the Public Interest (No. 2) Act 2009 were enacted in order to provide for the payment of an additional contribution towards the cost of a pension and to reduce remuneration, respectively. In each case, the persons who are within the scope of this legislation are said to be "public servants".[23] This term is defined as those who are employed by what are called "public service bodies". These bodies are identified (slightly differently in the case of each Act), by reference to a very broad list of bodies which excludes commercial state bodies itself. Also excluded are judges and the President. However, members of the Oireachtas and the European Parliament are included.

Borderline between public bodies and private persons

4–13   But the particular terminology used, in relation to a public body, does not always settle the question of whether the public body falls within the scope of some public law control. This, as we shall see from the case law in this Part, depends on more general concepts. While normally, public bodies are subject to the ordinary law, for example, as to torts or tax, there are a number of contexts in which they enjoy some special position. The specific question is: in what type of circumstances does it make a difference whether a particular entity is classified as a "public body"? These problems of categorisation are coming more increasingly before the courts. The following three situations may be identified.

4–14   (1) Various statutes employ some such term as "public authority" or "public

---

      2003, this is done by itemising by name most of the commercial state bodies, rather than by
      the use of any equivalent formulation.
[20]   De Smith, *The New Commonwealth and its Constitutions* (London: Stephens, 1964), p.136.
[21]   Originally established as the Public Offices Commission by the Ethics in Public Office Act
      1995 and subsequently re-constituted as The Standards in Public Office Commission by the
      Standards in Public Office Act 2001.
[22]   In *Health Service Executive v Commissioner of Valuation* [2008] IEHC 178, MacMenamin
      J. stated: "The term 'public authority' has a wide range of meanings in the interpretation
      section of the Health Act 2004 (section 2(2)). These include a Minister of the Government,
      the Commissioners of Public Works in Ireland, a local authority, a harbour authority, a board
      or other body established by or under statute, a company in which all the shares are held by
      or on behalf of a Minister of the Government or cognate bodies."
[23]   The term is also used in the Ministers and Secretaries (Amendment) Act 2011 s.3.

body", sometimes without offering any assistance by way of definition of the critical term. The question could arise as to whether some particular state body is within the term. The net question in *The General Medical Services (Payments) Board v Minister for Social Welfare*[24] was whether an employee of the plaintiff board was insurable for the Social Welfare Act 1952 at the ordinary rate of contribution or at the special rate applicable to employment by a "public authority" pursuant to art.5(1)(c) of the Social Welfare (Modification of Insurance) Regulations 1956. In short, the question for the High Court was whether the plaintiff board was a public authority. Hamilton J. commenced by observing that "… it is surprising that there does not exist any general definition of what is or what is not a public authority either in statute or in court decisions".[25] Later, the judge adopted the following definition taken from *Halsbury's Laws of England*:

"A public authority is a body, not necessarily a county council, municipal corporation or other local authority, which has public or statutory duties to perform and which performs these duties and carries out its transactions for the benefit of the public and not for private profit."[26]

4–15   The judge also summarised the function and status of the plaintiff board as follows:

"The plaintiff board is a board established by a ministerial order made in pursuance of the powers given to the Minister for Health by section 11(2) of the Health Act 1970, which Act was enacted by the legislature, *inter alia*, to provide for the establishment of bodies for the administration of the health services; it is one of the bodies established for the administration of the health services; its function is admittedly a limited one namely:

(a)   The calculations of payments to be made for the services provided by the health boards under section 58 and section 59(1) of the Health Act 1970.

(b)   The verification of the accuracy and reasonableness of claims in relation to such services.

(c)   The compilation of statistics and other information in relation to such services and the communications of such information to persons concerned with the operation of such services.

It cannot make a profit and its members do not receive any remuneration."[27]

The judge's conclusion that the plaintiff was, indeed, a public authority, then flowed naturally from the definition quoted earlier.

4–16   The most informative case of this type is *Central Applications Office v*

---

24   [1976–1977] I.L.R.M. 210.
25   [1976–1977] I.L.R.M. 210 at 211. Many of the authorities opened to the judge by counsel were concerned with the interpretation of s.1 of the Public Authorities Protection Act 1893 (which is no longer law here or in England).
26   [1976–1977] I.L.R.M. 210 at 217. The quotation is from *Halsbury's Laws of England*, 3rd edn Vol.30, p.682. This passage does not really address the difficulties with the concept of a public body.
27   [1976–1977] I.L.R.M. 210 at 215.

Minister for Community, Rural and Gaeltacht Affairs,[28] in which the High Court and the Supreme Court each held that the CAO was a "public body" for the purpose of the Official Languages Act 2003. Writing for the Supreme Court, Fennelly J. considered, first, whether the CAO performed functions which previously stood vested in a body under public ownership or control. Following a survey of the history of the establishment of the CAO, he concluded, as a matter of fact, that each of the individual Universities originally carried out separately the procedures of processing applications and admitting students. While both application and admission may have been part of the same process, each was performed in respect of each educational institution for its own purposes. Then, in 1976, the functions of processing applications and admitting students were separated, the first thereafter being effected by the CAO, whilst the latter was reserved to each higher educational institution separately. Thus, the function of the CAO was a new one. The significance of this ruling is that it meant that it could not fall within the definition laid down in the relevant regulations which referred to "a body ... performing functions which previously stood vested in a body ... under public ownership or control".[29]

4–17   (2) In most domestic legal systems, as a matter of comity, the courts regard "foreign states" as being exempt from their jurisdiction. Thus, in *Gibbons v Údarás na Gaeltachta,*[30] the question arose before the New York courts in the course of an action for breach of contract and fraudulent misrepresentation allegedly arising from a joint venture agreement partially concluded in New York, as to whether Údarás, a state body, which acts as a promotional agency for the Gaeltacht, fell within the ambit of this immunity.[31] The courts rejected the agency's claim for sovereign immunity, emphasising its view of the Údarás operation as being "no different ... from the promotional activities engaged in by a private public relations firm".

4–18   (3) Probably the most significant category concerns European Union law,[32] which draws on the notion of public character or service in order to determine the scope of various laws. These questions are complicated by the need to maintain uniformity from Member State to Member State, since the issue should be regarded as a mixed question of Community and national law. Significantly, it has been remarked that "in *Sotgiu*, the ECJ made it clear that it and not the respective member states would define the scope of the exception".[33]

---

[28] [2008] IEHC 309 (MacMenamin J.); [2010] IESC 32 (Fennelly J.). See also, *The General Medical Services (Payments) Board v Minister for Social Welfare* [1976–1977] I.L.R.M. 210.

[29] Official Languages Act 2003 (Public Bodies) Regulations 2006 (S.I. No 150 of 2006), para.1(5)(c). The Minister's alternative argument also failed on an equally literal interpretation.

[30] 549 F.Supp. 1094 (S.D.N.Y. 1982). An identical conclusion as to the agency's immunity was reached in *Gilson v The Republic of Ireland* 682 F. 2d. 1022 (D.C. Cir. 1982).

[31] This immunity was created by s.1605 of the US Foreign Sovereign Immunities Act.

[32] On this subject, see an excellent monograph by Curtin, "The Province of Government: Delimiting the Direct Effect of Directives in the Common Law Context" (1990) 15 E.L. Rev. 195; Fahey, "Preliminary Reference from the Circuit Court: The 'Emanation of the State' Doctrine in the Irish Courts" [2004] 22 I.L.T. 6.

[33] Craig and de Búrca, *EU Law, Text, Cases and Materials*, 4th edn (Oxford: OUP, 2008), p.764. See also, Wyatt and Dashwood's *European Union Law*, 5th edn (London: Sweet and Maxwell, 2006), paras 18–17 to 18–19; *Sotgiu v Deutsch Bundespost* [1974] E.C.R. 153.

4–19   Two examples of EU categories will be mentioned here.[34] The first arises from the fact that art.54 of the Treaty on the Functioning of the European Union (TFEU), which establishes the right to free movement of workers, permits a derogation in the case of "the public service". The European Court of Justice has stressed the need for a restrictive interpretation of the exemption from such a fundamental principle. Thus in several rulings, the Court has confined this exemption to posts involved in activities which are peculiar to public service, such as the armed forces, the judiciary, the diplomatic corps and local authorities, in contradistinction to activities such as health care or education, which may also be performed by the private sector. What this means, in the context of state bodies, is that commercial bodies are excluded from the exemption because they involve industrial or commercial enterprises, whereas several of the non-commercial bodies are within the exemption because they entail distinctively public functions, such as economic regulation.

4–20   The second reason for classification required by European Union law arises when an EU Directive has either not been implemented by a Member State after the requisite time allowed for implementation has passed or has been inaccurately translated into its national law. It has now been established that, while such Directives do not operate against a private person, they do—if they are unconditional and sufficiently precise—have direct effect against the State concerned, on the basis that the State is estopped from benefiting from the consequence of its own default.[35] This ruling immediately raises the question of the extent of "the State" and, in particular, whether it would embrace a state-sponsored body. (Unhelpfully here, the word "state" is used in the wide sense of a public body and not in the narrow sense in which it was employed in the next section.)

4–21   The leading authority here is *Coppinger v Waterford County Council*,[36] in which the plaintiff had been injured by reason of a collision with a council truck which had not been fitted with rear-underrun protections. A common law negligence action failed. However, in another cause of action, Geoghegan J. found that the State had been in breach of Community law in the manner in which it had implemented certain directives[37] by not providing for such rear-underrun protection. But, given that the defendant was a local authority, the central part of the ruling was the following test: the provisions of a directive capable of having direct effect may be relied upon against "… a body, whatever its legal form, which has been made responsible, pursuant to a measure adopted by the State, for providing a public service under the control of the State and has for that purpose special powers beyond those which result from the normal rules applicable in relations between

---

[34] For a major example not covered here, i.e. competition law, see H & M, Ch.4, Parts H and I.

[35] Case 152/84, *Marshall v Southampton and South-West Hampshire Area Health Authority (Teaching)* [1987] E.C.R. 723.

[36] [1998] 4 I.R. 220. See Travers, "The Liability of Local Authorities for Breaches of Community Directives by Member States" (1997) 22 E.L. Rev. 173.

[37] Council Directive 70/221, as amended by Council Directive 79/490. The Irish implementing regulations are contained in the Road Traffic (Construction, Equipment and Use of Vehicles) (Amendment) Regulations 1985 (S.I. No. 158 of 1985).

individuals".[38] On this test, Geoghegan J. ruled that the County Council was part of the State for the purposes of holding it liable for a breach of Community law.[39]

Distinction between the State and other public bodies

4–22   The borderline, just discussed, arises where the policy of the relevant law is such that, in defining its scope, a distinction is drawn between public bodies in the broadest sense on one hand and, on the other hand, private persons or companies. A second relevant borderline concerns the division which is sometimes utilised by the law, between the central spine of the executive (that is, Ministers and certain other high constitutional personages like the President, DPP or Ombudsman) and more peripheral public agencies. *Health Service Executive v Commissioner of Valuation*[40] is the case which provides the most comprehensive recent examination of this borderline. The facts were straightforward. The Valuation Act 2001 s.15 exempts from rates a building occupied by "the State including ... any Department or office of State, Defence Forces or the Garda Síochána or used as a prison or place of detention shall not be rateable". On appeal from the Tribunal to the High Court, the High Court upheld the view of the Valuation Tribunal that the Health Service Executive was an office of the State and, consequently, that its property was not rateable. In determining whether the HSE was part of the State, MacMenamin J. found that four criteria were relevant:

4–23   (i) *Nature and function*. Here the judge outlined the statutory functions of the HSE and concluded: "In short its function is to determine in accordance with Government policy the manner and actual implementation of health policy and health services."[41]

4–24   (ii) *Control and integration*. Here the judge quoted the statutory provisions in the Health Act 2004, which empower the Minister to give "general written directions" to the executive and remarked:

> "The emphasised terms are clear indicia of the extent of direct central control. They are not mere guidelines or a general policy remit, on a core issue of government, found in the case of many semi-state bodies. They are indicia of a high level of integration between policy formulation, control and performance. The suggestion [made by counsel for the Commissioner for Valuation] of a statutory dichotomy between the provision of the health service and the 'engine', which provides that service, is, I find, artificial and demonstrably so, when the Act of 2004 is analysed."[42]

---

[38]   This passage, which Geoghegan J. quoted with approval at 226, is from *Foster v British Gas Plc* [1990] 2 C.M.L.R. 833 at 856–857.

[39]   [1998] 4 I.R. 220 at 226. Note that in *Chapelizod Residents' Association Ltd v Dublin Corporation*, unreported, High Court, October 23, 1997, Smyth J. appeared to disagree with these views, saying that he did not consider a local authority to be an emanation of the State. This, however, was in the context of a challenge to the constitutionality of the exemption granted to local authorities from the planning process by s.4 of the Local Government (Planning and Development) Act 1963.

[40]   [2008] IEHC 178.

[41]   [2008] IEHC 178 at para.[36].

[42]   [2008] IEHC 178 at para.[40].

4–25 (iii) *Control of expenditure and source of funding.* The judge noted that:

"The HSE is one of 40 public state bodies or authorities [sic] identified in the Appropriation Act, along with 12 government departments, the defence forces, An Garda Síochána, the prison service and 23 other bodies which receive appropriations directly … Each of the bodies identified in the Schedule to the Act is entirely integral to the functions of the State or an office of State. No semi-State body is identified in the Schedule."[43]

4–26 (iv) *Staffing arrangements and funding.* Here the judge noted that the Chief Executive Officer of the HSE, as well as its other employees, is recruited in accordance with the Public Service Management (Recruitments and Appointments) Act 2004 and the Minister's approval is required for their terms and conditions. The judge commented: "Each of these features is indicative of its status of being highly akin to a government department."[44]

4–27 MacMenamin J. summarised his conclusions in this way[45]:

"[The HSE] is not a semi-State body, however defined. It is impossible to state that its functions are peripheral from the central activities of government. They are at its epicentre. Furthermore the Executive has features which are otherwise unique to Government departments or bodies which are very closely integrated into the process of government. Whether or not some of those statutory authorities are 'independent' in their functions such as the Attorney General or the Director of Public Prosecutions is not material; what is essential is the degree of integration of such authorities to the core functions of government …".

4–28 A somewhat similar, though much broader, issue than that examined in the *Health Service Executive* case would be to ask whether one of these state agencies, such as RTÉ or An Bord Pleanála, would be regarded as part of the State for the purposes of any former prerogative right (e.g. the privilege against disclosure of evidence). Since the issue of whether the prerogative came at all to independent Ireland is controversial,[46] we need not pursue this question too far. However, one can say that, given the historical development of the prerogative, coupled with the Irish courts' dislike of special privileges and, in particular, the tenor of the reasoning in *Re Irish Employers' Mutual Insurance Association Ltd*,[47] it seems

---

[43] [2008] IEHC 178 at paras [44]–[45].

[44] [2008] IEHC 178 at para.[58].

[45] [2008] IEHC 178 at para.[60]. Curiously, the judge's conclusions were cast as a response to the query whether the HSE is a semi-state body, despite the fact that the issue in the Valuation Act 2001, quoted earlier, is whether the HSE is an element of the State.

[46] *Byrne v Ireland* [1972] I.R. 241.

[47] [1955] I.R. 176. The facts of the case were that the Commissioners of Public Works had taken out insurance with a company which subsequently went into liquidation. The Commissioners claimed that the monies due to them from the company should, as a matter of prerogative right, be paid in priority to the debts due to other creditors. For present purposes, the relevant question was whether, assuming that this prerogative existed, the Commissioners would be characterised as sufficiently part of the State to be able to invoke it. It was held that, in general, the Commissioners were to be regarded as servants of the State. However, where the Commissioners were performing work on behalf of local authorities, then they were not acting

unlikely to succeed. In this case, dealing with the criteria for the inclusion (or not) of a state body as a beneficiary of the prerogative, which involved, be it noted, the Commissioners of Public Works, who are less autonomous than a state-sponsored body, Kingsmill Moore J. stated:

> "The degree of direction and control which is exercised by the executive over the conduct of the work may afford an indication as to whether the Commissioners in executing the work are acting as servants of the State."[48]

C. Staff: Public Servants, Civil Servants

4–29 It remains to differentiate between the civil service staff of the Ministers and Departments, and the staff of other public bodies. The widest term used for employees (though not usually in legislation) is the "public sector", a category which embraces not merely civil servants[49] but all those who are employed, directly or indirectly, by some public body. The end 2012[50] target was 294,000. Of these, about 36,000 were civil servants. A slightly narrower term than the "public sector"[51] is the "public service"[52] (that is the public sector less the employees of commercial state-sponsored bodies). The public service comprises those employees whose salary and pension bill (€18 billion, that is, 38 per cent of the Government's total current expenditure; or 10 per cent of Gross Domestic Product) is paid for, directly or indirectly, out of public funds.

4–30 Against this background, one can summarise[53] the status and categories of the various types of employee in the public sector, in the following propositions: (1) at the centre are the civil servants, who service the central Government Departments and certain other major organs of State, such as the President or the Oireachtas; (2) civil servants—the majority—dealing with the Departments are known as civil servants of the Government, whereas those who serve the other

---

as servants of the State. See also, *Re Maloney* [1926] I.R. 202 at 206; *Irish Land Commission v Ruane* [1938] I.R. 148 at 152–157, 161 (Irish Land Commission characterised as a servant of the State).

[48] *Re Irish Employers' Mutual Insurance Association Ltd* [1955] I.R. 176 at 192. This judgment contains the most scholarly and thorough analysis available of a difficult area.

[49] O'Toole and Dooney, *Irish Government Today* (Gill and Macmillan, 2009), Chs 6 and 13; Millar and McKevitt, "The Irish Civil Service System" in Bekke and van der Meer (eds), *Civil Service Systems in Western Europe* (Edward Elgar Publishing, 2000).

[50] For the earlier, Celtic Tiger, era see Foley, "Size, Cost and Efficiency of the Public Service" (2009) 57 *Administration* 69 at 81–91.

[51] Those employed in the public service are made up roughly as follows: civil servants (36,000); Defence (11,000); Garda Síochána (14,000); Education—all sectors (100,000); regional, including local authorities (40,000); non-commercial state-sponsored bodies (12,000); Health (111,000). The total of these figures is somewhat different from the figure in the text, because certain categories are not included. In addition, there are a further 42,000 employees in the commercial state-sponsored bodies, who are regarded as being in the public sector, though not the public service, because their remuneration is generally paid out of commercial income, rather than public funds.

[52] For a rare statutory example of the use of "public service", see Ministers and Secretaries (Amendment) Act 1973 ss.1, 3 and 5 (setting up the Minister for the Public Service and the Public Service Advisory Council).

[53] For more detail, see H & M, paras 3–49 to 3–70 and 3–106 to 3–151.

organs are styled civil servants of the State[54]; (3) all civil servants are servants of the State, but (in the reverse direction) there are servants of the State who are not civil servants, for instance, members of the defence forces; (4) at the furthest extreme are those employees who serve independent public bodies, such as local authorities, state sponsored bodies or independent tribunals. These are not even servants of the State and each public body has its own particular regime of terms and conditions. These distinctions, although they may seem legalistic—and indeed are often swept aside in Governmental decision-making by the exigencies of media and popular pressure—are of significance in regard to the substance and processes of employment.

---

[54] The great authority on this distinction is *McLoughlin v Minister for Social Welfare* [1958] I.R. 1, analysed at H & M, paras 3–56 to 3–58.

CHAPTER 5

LOCAL GOVERNMENT AND PLANNING LAW

A. HISTORICAL INTRODUCTION AND MODERN DEVELOPMENTS

Pre-1922 developments

5–01   Until the enactment of the Local Government Act 2001, the "basic structure of [Irish] local government remained that enacted by the British parliament in 1898".[1] In that year the Local Government (Ireland) Act 1898 was passed, and this legislation effected a major reorganisation of the system which had operated prior to that date. Until 1898 the functions of local government had been discharged by a range of diverse and often single-function bodies, of which only the most important can be mentioned. First, the construction, repair and maintenance of roads and bridges lay in the hands of the grand jury, who also had a supervisory function in relation to other public works.[2] The grand jury was appointed by the assize judge, who was required to approve the grand jury's "presentments", i.e. expenditure proposals. The grand jury raised revenue by means of taxes on local landowners, and these taxes were known as the "grand jury cess". The corrupt[3] and undemocratic nature of this system led to reform, which was to come when the grand juries were relieved of their local government functions by the Local Government (Ireland) Act 1898.

5–02   Secondly, the poor law and sanitary services were administered, in most parts of the country, by boards of guardians. The poor law union was an area 10 miles in radius around each of the 130 market towns,[4] and the guardians were elected

---

[1]   Alexander, "Local Government in Ireland" (1979) 27 *Administration* 3 at 7. What follows is necessarily a brief and very selective account of the principal features of local government law. Readers who desire a fuller treatment of this complicated subject are referred to Street, *The Law Relating to Local Government* (Dublin: Stationery Office, 1955); Roche, *Local Government in Ireland* (Dublin: IPA, 1982); Chubb, *The Government and Politics of Ireland* (London: Longman, 1991), Ch.15; Butler (ed.), *Keane's Local Government in the Republic of Ireland* (Dublin: First Law, 2003); and Callanan and Keogan (eds), *Local Government in Ireland: Inside and Out* (Dublin: IPA, 2004).

[2]   The grand jury system, which originated in the Grand Jury Act 1634, had been reorganised by the Grand Jury (Ireland) Act 1836.

[3]   See generally, Roche, *Local Government in Ireland* (Dublin: IPA, 1982), pp.29–43.

[4]   See Alexander, "Local Government in Ireland" (1979) 27 *Administration* 3 at 29–43. The numbers were increased to 163 after the Famine.

by the poor-law ratepayers. Local ratepayers also sat, ex officio, on the board of guardians. Because the guardians—unlike the grand juries—were permanent bodies holding regular meetings, their functions were extended by legislation throughout the nineteenth century.[5] By 1840 there were also 68 borough corporations to certain of which the powers of grand juries had been transferred. Ten of these (Dublin, Cork, Belfast, Limerick, Waterford, Londonderry, Sligo, Kilkenny, Drogheda, and Clonmel) were retained as municipal boroughs by s.12 of the Municipal Corporations (Ireland) Act 1840. Borough status was later granted to Wexford (by petition, 1845); Dún Laoghaire (by petition, 1930) and Galway (by private Act of the Oireachtas, 1937).

5–03 Further reform came with the passage of the Local Government Act 1871, which gave a centralised body—the Local Government Board—control over the activities of local boards. By the end of the 19th century the local guardians enjoyed wide powers and "were loaded with the administration of public and personal health services and the provision of housing that went far beyond the relief of destitution".[6] Side by side with the boards of guardians system, town commissioners were elected in the towns which had adopted the Towns Improvement (Ireland) Act 1854 or which had been appointed under the Lighting of Towns (Ireland) Act 1828 or other local Acts.[7] The town commissioners had functions in relation to lighting, draining, paving, water supplies, land acquisition, railways, and in some cases, policing.

5–04 Major reform of this system was not to come until the Local Government (Ireland) Act 1898. This Act set up a two-tier system of local government, organised along county lines.[8] Each county was to have a county council, apart from Tipperary which is divided into North and South Ridings.[9] The Local Government (Dublin) Act 1993 provided for the dissolution of the existing Dublin County Council and Dún Laoghaire Corporation and their replacement by the creation of three new counties: Fingal, South Dublin and Dún Laoghaire–Rathdown.

5–05 Returning to the 1898 Act: Dublin, Cork, Belfast, Waterford and Londonderry were made county boroughs in which the corporations were to have the functions of a county council, together with those functions which as borough councils they had previously enjoyed. In addition, Galway was established as a county borough by s.5 of the Local Government (Re-organisation) Act 1985.[10] Each county was divided into local districts, under either an urban or rural district council. In rural areas, the public health functions of the boards of guardians were transferred to the rural district councils. The power to levy the poor law rates was assigned to the county councils, but the boards of guardians were still responsible for the administration of the poor law system, including the provision of medical

---

[5]   See, e.g. Births and Death Registration Act 1863 which required the compilation of mortality statistics.
[6]   Chubb, *The Government and Politics of Ireland* (London: Longman, 1991), p.268.
[7]   Some towns had elected representatives by virtue of local Acts: see *Vanston's Law of Municipal Towns* (1990), pp.6 and 358.
[8]   See generally, Roche, *Local Government in Ireland* (Dublin: IPA, 1982), pp.32–36.
[9]   For the reasons why Tipperary was divided into North and South Ridings, see App. IX to Roche, *Local Government in Ireland* (1982).
[10] For commentary, see Hogan, (1985) I.C.L.S.A. 7–01.

relief. Finally, and perhaps most importantly, the franchise was extended to all adult male ratepayers.[11] This extension of the franchise not only ensured that local government was to be more representative in nature, but also created a form of local politics in Ireland which, in the following 20 years or so, was to be the backbone of the nationalist struggle for Irish independence.

Post-1922 developments

5–06 The first major piece of local government legislation following the establishment of the Irish Free State in 1922 was the Local Government (Temporary Provisions) Act 1923. This was enacted at a time when the country was split between pro- and anti-Treaty factions. Against this background, it seemed natural to the Government of the day to promote a policy of taking greater control over local authorities, many of which were controlled by the anti-Treaty forces. For example, the Minister for Local Government's power to "dissolve and transfer functions to any body or persons or person he shall think fit" which had hitherto applied only to boards of guardians was extended to all local authorities.[12] And, indeed, this power was to be frequently availed of in the next few years.[13] Secondly, "Sinn Féin policy on local government, from which much of the reform thinking of this time derives, was aimed at clearing away most, if not all, of the undergrowth of small local bodies at sub-county level."[14]

5–07 Accordingly, boards of guardians (outside Dublin) were abolished by the 1923 Act, replacing them with boards of health, which were statutory committees of county councils.[15] In the same vein of thinning out the undergrowth of small bodies, the Local Government Act 1925 abolished rural district councils and their functions were assigned to the appropriate county council.[16] Health and sanitary functions were discharged by the boards of health until these were abolished in 1940 and their functions became the direct responsibility of the county councils.[17] Eventually, by the Health Act 1970, the health functions (but not the sanitary functions) were transferred to eight regional health boards.[18] Even this reform was considered over time to have been unsuccessful, since the influence of local politics on the allocation of scarce resources within the health system remained undimmed. The health boards were ultimately swept away by the Health Act 2004 which created the Health Service Executive (and it was announced in 2011 that the HSE is to be given a new corporate governance).

---

[11] The Local Government Act 2001 s.12 provides that all Irish citizens and all other persons "ordinarily resident in the State" who have reached 18 years and who are not otherwise disqualified shall be eligible "for election or co-option to and membership of a local authority". See previously, Local Government Act 1994 s.5.
[12] 1923 Act s.12.
[13] In 1923 five authorities were dissolved. The corresponding figures for 1924 and 1925 were 13 and five respectively.
[14] Roche, *Local Government in Ireland* (1982), p.52.
[15] 1923 Act ss.3–7 and Local Government Act 1923 ss.9 and 10.
[16] Local Government Act 1925 s.3.
[17] County Management Act 1940 s.36.
[18] In the end, however, the influence of local politics on the administration of the health system (and, especially, the allocation of resources) was thought to be too great and the health boards were replaced by the Health Service Executive: see Health Act 2004.

5–08 The Local Authorities (Officers and Employees) Acts 1926–1983 provided that most major local authority officers could be appointed only on the recommendation of the Local Appointments Commissioners.[19] But the Local Appointments Commissioners has now been dissolved by s.5 of the Public Service Management (Recruitment and Appointment) Act 2004, and its functions transferred to the Public Appointments Service. This process of selection by an independent body was a desirable reform, and guards against the political and other forms of patronage which are an all-too-common feature of Irish life. Another major step in the same direction was the introduction of the management system by the County Management Act 1940.[20] This constitutes the most far-reaching change in the local government system since the passing of the Local Government (Ireland) Act 1898, and is described in Part B.

5–09 1971 saw the publication of a White Paper[21] on local government reorganisation and this was the first comprehensive review of local government since 1922. The White Paper proposed the abolition of the ultra vires rule; new legislation on the modernisation of the constitution, membership and procedure of local authorities; new accounting and auditing procedures; and the concentration of central government controls on "key points" only, while at the same time allowing local authorities "the greatest possible discretion in the exercise of their powers".

5–10 These proposals were not implemented until two or three decades later and the trend of centralisation continued with the Local Government (Financial Provisions) Act 1978 which effectively abolished domestic rates. The difficulties faced by local authorities were rendered even more acute by the Supreme Court's decision in *Brennan v Attorney General*[22]—which held that the method of collecting rates on agricultural land was unconstitutional—and made urgent reform of the local government system imperative.[23]

5–11 The financial position of local authorities was alleviated to an extent by the passage of the Local Government (Financial Provisions) (No. 2) Act 1983[24] which substantially extended the power of the local authority to charge for certain

---

[19] For the present position, see O'Beirne, "Human Resources" in Callanan and Keogan (eds), *Local Government in Ireland: Inside and Out* (Dublin: IPA, 2004), pp.305–309.

[20] On which see Part B. The management system had earlier been imposed by a series of separate Acts on Cork, Dublin, Limerick and Waterford county boroughs. See Roche, *Local Government in Ireland* (1982), pp.100–104. For the background to the development of the management system see Chubb, *The Government and Politics of Ireland* (1991), pp.275–278 and O'Halpin, "The Origins of City and County Management" in *City and County Management 1929-1990: a Retrospective* (Dublin: IPA, 1991), pp.1–21.

[21] *Local Government Reorganisation: Proposals for the reorganisation of the existing structure of local government and for modifications and improvements in the operation of the system* (1971).

[22] [1984] I.L.R.M. 355.

[23] The Supreme Court observed that as the anomalous method of valuing agricultural land contained in the Valuation (Ireland) Act 1852 was used as the basis for assessing rates, then the method of collecting such rates (s.11 of the Local Government Act 1946) infringed the plaintiff's property rights as guaranteed by Art.40.3 of the Constitution and was unconstitutional.

[24] See O'Hagan, McBride and Sanfey, "Local Government Finance: the Irish Experience" [1985] B.T.R. 235.

essential services (e.g. water supply and refuse collection), but this was recognised as a (highly controversial) stop-gap measure and one which was not intended to be a substitute for a radical overhaul of the entire local government system. Some significant reforms were effected by the Local Government Act 1991 (which significantly diluted the ultra vires rule) and the Local Government Act 1994 (which recast and modernised much pre-1922 legislation in relation to such matters as the making of bye-laws). The Local Government (Financial Provisions) Act 1997 abolished services charges and rate support grants, but local authorities were instead given a lucrative source of independent revenue by the assignment of the proceeds of motor tax revenue.[25] The Local Government Act 1998 introduced the Local Government Fund, which consisted of the proceeds of motor tax revenue and an annual exchequer contribution. But the major piece of legislation is now the Local Government Act 2001 which, as well as making changes, consolidated much of the existing structural-constitutional law of local governement. Next, in reaction to the crisis in the public finances, and perhaps as a precursor to the introduction of a general property tax, the Local Government (Charges) Act 2009 required home owners to pay a fixed sum of €200 per house (other than their principal private dwelling) to the local authority.[26] In addition, the Local Government (Household Charge) Act 2011 introduced a "household charge" for residential property (whether or not principal private dwelling).

Functions

5–12   Over the centuries, local authorities gathered accretions of diverse statutory functions and powers of varying importance. This may be illustrated by listing the eight programme groups in which they are categorised, by the Public Bodies (Amendment) Order 1975 for estimates of expenditure purposes: housing and building; road transportation and safety; water supply and sewerage; environmental protection; recreation and amenity; miscellaneous services; agriculture, education, services, health and welfare; and development incentives and controls. To take some particular examples local authorities have responsibility for such matters as: the maintenance and improvement of local roads; the protection of the environment; litter; waste management; fire services; vocational education; higher education grants; the licensing of gaming and amusement halls; the maintenance of a register of all multi-storey buildings in its functional area; casual trading; the compilation of electoral registers; and miscellaneous functions relating to the administration of justice, such as the appointment of coroners.[27] In Part G of this chapter, we shall briefly examine one specimen function—planning control. Before this, however, two preliminary points must be made. First, in recent years the Oireachtas has sought, on the one hand, to add to the responsibilities of local authorities[28]; while

---

[25]   The former Minister for the Environment (Mr B. Howlin TD) estimated that in 1996 the motor tax revenue exceeded the combined income from domestic water and service charges and rate support grant by IR£12million: 478 *Dáil Debates* Col.1016 (April 30, 1997). These changes had been foreshadowed in the White Paper, *Better Local Government: A Programme for Change* (1996), Ch.5.

[26]   Section 3(3). Section 3(5) provides, however, that this figure may be revised by the Minister for Environment, Heritage and Local Government having regard to price inflation in the meantime.

[27]   See generally, Local Government Act 2001 Sch.12.

[28]   See. e.g. Local Government Act 2001 s.269 (replacing Local Government Act 1991 s.52, giving power to the Minister to remove certain controls in earlier enactments which required

at the same time in other areas it has been decided that some of their functions should be given to other, nationally based bodies.[29]

5–13 The demarcation line in respect of responsibility for each function as between any lower-tier authority (town council) and the county council is a question of some complexity. This is a difficult matter depending as it does on transfers from grand juries and an intricate analysis of "the tortuous labyrinth of an unexplored administrative code".[30] However, as a generalisation, it may be said that, leaving aside former town commissioners, each type of authority bears responsibility in law for each type of function within its own functional area. The major exception to this is that the maintenance and construction of all county roads shall be the responsibility of the county councils, even if the roads run through an urban district council.[31] But besides this exception, there are a number of cases where, because of the inadequate size and resources of the lower-tier authority, the formal position created by the legislation would be thoroughly impracticable. To circumvent this difficulty, s.85 of the Local Government Act 2001 provides that the power of one authority may be exercised on its behalf by another authority. This device has been frequently used to enable a county council to exercise many of the functions of the lower-tier authorities, for instance, urban roads and aspects of water supply.

Control by Minister for the Environment, Heritage and Local Government

5–14 The powers of the elected representatives have not only been eroded from below by the management system, as discussed in Part B, but also reduced from above by the ascendancy of the Minister. For local authorities are subject to extensive and diverse controls exercised by the Minister,[32] of which there is one at almost every aspect of a local authority's in respect of functions. Local authorities, for instance, enjoy a general power to borrow money, but subject to the control of the Minister.[33]

5–15 In more specific matters, the Minister for the Environment enjoys a power of consent or veto,[34] for example, with regard to the making of bye-laws. Section 199(7) of the 2001 Act allows the Minister to prescribe matters or classes of matters

---

ministerial control and consent) and the Local Government Act 1991 (Removal of Controls) Regulations 1993 (S.I. No. 172 of 1993); Local Government (Financial Provisions) Act 1997 s.9 (power to raise revenue by raising levels of motor taxation within certain prescribed limits).

[29] For example, the evolution in responsibility for health services, (outlined in para.5–07) and the transfer of responsibilities for national roads to the National Roads Authority by the Roads Act 1993 and of responsibilities for the maintenance of courthouses to the Courts Service by the Courts Service Act 1998 are good examples.

[30] *Devanney v Dublin Board of Assistance* (1949) 83 I.L.T.R. 113 per Gavan Duffy J.

[31] By virtue of the Roads Act 1993 Pt III the National Roads Authority now has responsibility for primary roads.

[32] Such powers can also be delegated. See Local Government Act 2001 (the "2001 Act") s.236.

[33] 2001 Act s.106(3)(a).

[34] Section 158(1)(d) of the 2001 Act provides that the Minister may "at any time direct that any of the functions conferred on a local authority ... shall, in relation to an employment or employments for which he or she is the appropriate Minister, be exercisable either generally or in relation to a particular local authority or to specified local authorities, only with his or her consent, or subject to such other conditions or requirements as may be so directed."

in respect of which local authorities are not entitled to make a bye-law. Section 201(2)(a) allows the Minister to designate "any matter or classes of matters in relation to which a bye-law requires the approval of that Minister and any such bye-law made subsequent to the commencement of such regulations shall not come into operation unless so approved". In relation to a bye-law coming within the specified class, the Minister may approve the bye-law, approve the bye-law with amendments, or refuse to approve the bye-law.[35] In addition, a number of provisions in the 2001 Act give the Minister power to make regulations for local authorities.[36] Even when this is not the formal legal position, substantially the same result is achieved (in terms of uniformity throughout the country and ministerial ascendancy) by the Department issuing circulars containing model bye-laws or other regulations which most local authorities are pleased to adopt. On occasion the Minister has a power to give directions. For example, s.15(1) of the Roads Act 1993 provides that a road authority must comply with any direction in relation to "the maintenance or construction of public roads"[37] which is given by the Minister.

5–16   The Minister is even entitled to penetrate to the very heart of local democracy by removing the elected members[38] on any number of specific grounds. Section 216(1) of the 2001 Act provides that:

> The Minister may by order remove from office the members of a local authority if and whenever:
> (a) the Minister, after holding a public local inquiry into the performance by a local authority of its functions, is satisfied that such functions are not being duly and effectually performed, or;
> (b) a local authority refuses or neglects to comply with a judgment, order, or decree of any court, or
> (c) a local authority fails to comply with a requirement made by notification under subsection (1) of section 10A [because an estimate of expenses is thought by the Minister to be insufficient to meet the local authority's financial needs], within 21 days after the date of notification ...

5–17   Where the elected members are dismissed, the Minister may appoint one or more persons to act as commissioners for the local authority.[39] The commissioner discharges the reserved functions of the elected members in the interim period

---

[35]   2001 Act s.201(4).
[36]   e.g. s.44(3) (local authority meetings); s.54(1)(a) (delegation of functions to committees); s.106(5) (borrowing of money); s.118(1) (audit procedure); and s.160(1) (qualifications for employment).
[37]   For further examples of this type of power, see Housing Act 1966 s.111; Local Government (Financial Provisions) Act 1978 s.15.
[38]   An earlier version of this power was employed in 1969 to dismiss the members of Dublin Corporation where the Council had deliberately struck a rate less than the full amount required to meet the demand for health services: Roche, *Local Government in Ireland* (1982), p.123. The members of Naas U.D.C. were dismissed in similar circumstances in 1985. See *The Irish Times*, August 3, 1985.
[39]   2001 Act s.218. But whether this power is constitutionally valid in the light of the requirements of Art.28A.2 which presupposes the continued existence (and, presumably, the continuation in office) of directly elected local authorities must remain an open question, although the decision of Birmingham J. in *O'Doherty v Attorney General* [2009] IEHC 516 might be thought to lend some support to the constitutionality of this provision.

pending the next elections. However, one should note that, as already noted, the Minister no longer has the power to order that local elections be postponed.[40]

5–18   Naturally, the very existence of these powers presupposes that they will be exercised on an informed basis. Accordingly, the Minister may require a local authority "to make to him any return or report or furnish him with any information in relation to their functions which he may consider necessary or desirable."[41] Moreover, the Minister may even cause a local inquiry to be held for the purpose of any of his powers or duties.[42] In reality, of course, even without particular legal warrant, a Minister's or departmental civil servant's suggestion will carry enormous weight because of the relationship of ascendancy and subservience within which it is made.

Constitutional amendment, recent legislation and possible future reforms

5–19   The promise of constitutional recognition for local government was eventually implemented via the Twentieth Amendment of the Constitution Act 1999.[43] The new Art.28A provides:

1.   The State recognises the role of local government in providing a forum for the democratic representation of local communities, in exercising and performing at local level powers and functions conferred by law and in promoting by its initiatives the interests of such communities.
2.   There shall be such directly elected local authorities as may be determined by law and their powers and functions shall, subject to the provisions of this Constitution, be so determined and shall be exercised and performed in accordance with law.
3.   Elections for members of such local authorities shall be held in accordance with law not later than the end of the fifth year after the year in which they were last held.
4.   Every citizen who has the right to vote at an election for members of Dáil Éireann and such other persons as may be determined by law shall have the right to vote at an election for members of such of the local authorities referred to in section 2 of this Article as shall be determined by law.
5.   Casual vacancies in the membership of local authorities referred to in section 2 of this Article shall be filled in accordance with law.

5–20   Viewing Art.28A in tandem with s.63(1)(a) of the Local Government Act 2001, which states that one of the functions of local authorities is "to provide a forum for the democratic representation of the local community ... and to provide civic leadership for that community", one local government expert has identified

---

[40]   See para.5–19.
[41]   2001 Act s.222.
[42]   2001 Act s.212.
[43]   The promise had been included in the *Better Local Government* White Paper in 1996. The insertion of a dedicated article in the Constitution had been mooted previously, most notably by the Barrington Committee in its 1991 report, *Local Government Reorganisation and Reform* (Pn. 7918, 1991) and by the *Report of the Constitution Review Group* (Pn. 2632, 1996), pp.428–431.

rather expansively a "concept of general competence [which] recognises that local government should not limit itself to speaking out on a restricted number of statutory functions."[44] A recent Government report has said of the 2001 Act that "[i]n addition to policy making reforms, [it] gave legal recognition to important 'softer' roles of the elected representative, for example, the recognition of civic leadership, the representational role of councillors and the role of local government in community development".[45]

5–21   Whether Art.28A has any substantive implications for the power of local authorities is, however, debatable. Local government may only exercise powers granted by the Oireachtas, as was previously the case.[46] The position post-Art.28A was aptly summarised thus by Charleton J.:

> "Every local authority is a creature of statute, the exercise of its powers is enabled under the Constitution but those powers do not arise out of the exercise of local government authority and history. Rather, the powers of local government to raise funds, to spend them, or to set up schemes to disburse them appropriately arise from specific statutory provisions. This is because local government did not exist as a lawful exercise of authority without the devolution of power to it by central government. So, it is always a central question as to what power was devolved. The doctrine of legal formalism is particularly apposite in the context of local government powers as those powers must firstly be granted by statute and, secondly, exercised in accordance with it."[47]

Perhaps the most important element in Art.28A is the requirement that elections to local authorities be held at least every five years.[48]

5–22   At the level above local government, the 1990s saw two new creatures emerge onto the landscape: the regional authority and the regional assembly. Eight regional authorities came into operation in 1994[49] covering the Border, Dublin, Mid-

[44] Callanan, "The Role of Local Government" in Callanan and Keogan (eds), *Local Government in Ireland: Inside and Out* (Dublin: IPA, 2004), p.10. See also, Callanan, "Institutionalising Participation and Governance? New Participative Structures in Local Government in Ireland" (2005) 83 *Public Administration* 909.
[45] Department of the Environment, Heritage and Local Government, *Stronger Local Democracy: Options for Change* (Dublin, 2008), p.30.
[46] *Clarke v South Dublin County Council* [2008] IEHC 84; [2008] 4 I.R. 84. See also, *PJ Farrell v Limerick County Council* [2009] IEHC 274; [2010] 1 I.L.R.M. 99 where McGovern J. rejected the argument that a county manager had breached Art.28A by rejecting the validity of a resolution passed by local authority members.
[47] *Prendergast v Higher Education Authority* [2008] IEHC 257; [2009] 1 I.L.R.M. 47. It is not clear, however, that the situation in this regard would have been any different had Art.28A never been enacted.
[48] See the comments of Laffoy J. in *Ring v Attorney General* [2004] IEHC 14; [2004] 1 I.R. 185 at 201–202. Note, though, that in *O'Doherty v Attorney General* [2009] IEHC 316, Birmingham J. upheld the constitutionality of s.19 of the Local Government Act 2001 (which provides for the filling of casual vacancies by party nomination), the provisions of Art.28A.2 notwithstanding.
[49] Local Government Act 1991 s.43; Local Government Act 1991 (Regional Authorities) (Establishment) Order 1993 (S.I. No. 394 of 1993), as amended by Local Government Act 1991 (Regional Authorities) (Establishment) Order 1999 (S.I. No. 226 of 1999); Local Government Act 1991 (Regional Authorities) (Establishment Order) 1999 (Amendment) Order 2006 (S.I.

East, Midland, Mid-West, South-East, South-West and West regions. Only members of local authorities in these regions may be members of the regional authorities: a number of their members are appointed by each local authority.[50] Two regional assemblies were established in 1999, the Southern and Eastern Regional Assembly on the eastern seaboard and the Border, Midland and Western Regional Assembly. The assemblies were established under the same legislation as the authorities and have similar membership requirements.[51]

5–23 The authorities have next to no executive powers but their general function is "to promote co-ordination of the provision of public services in the Authority's region".[52] The assemblies are discussion chambers and are "to promote co-ordination of the provision of public services in the assembly's region"[53] and to oversee the implementation of EU programmes.[54] However, a more pressing reason for their establishment was to access a tranche of European funding:

> "The purpose ... was to seek to retain EU Objective 1 designation for the newly constituted fifteen-county region [in the west] on the grounds that, at the time, it had not exceeded the specified per capita income threshold for Objective 1 status."[55]

5–24 The Local Government Act 2001 introduced a number of reforms as to the framework of local government. At the upper level, county councils remained so designated, but county borough councils (Cork, Dublin, Galway, Limerick and Waterford) became city councils. At the lower level, the distinct designations of non-county borough corporation, town commissioners and urban district council were removed, leaving only town councils. At the same time, however, the powers granted to town councils may vary, without the town's official designation reflecting this. Essentially, a town council retains the legal powers appropriate to its former category. The result is that former non-county boroughs[56] or former UDCs each have the same powers; and greater powers than former town commissioners. All elected members are to be known as councillors, with the result that the title alderman, which designated the first member elected for a particular ward, was jettisoned.[57] Section 185 of the 2001 Act provides for the possible establishment of new town councils, pursuant to a petition by a proportion of the qualified electors in the area of the proposed new town council. Conversely, s.187 permits a town council to apply

---

No. 690 of 2006); and Local Government Act 1991 (Regional Authorities) (Establishment Order) 1993 (Amendment) Order 2006 (S.I. No. 691 of 2006).

[50] 1993 Order art.5.

[51] Local Government Act 1991 (Regional Authorities) (Establishment) Order 1999 (S.I. No. 226 of 1999).

[52] Callanan, "Regional Authorities and Regional Assemblies" in Callanan and Keogan (eds), *Local Government in Ireland: Inside and Out* (2004), p.433.

[53] 1993 Order art.14(1).

[54] 1993 Order art.15, as amended by Local Government Act 1991 (Regional Authorities) (Establishment) Order 1999 (S.I. No. 226 of 1999) and Local Government Act 1991 (Regional Authorities) (Establishment Order) 1999 (Amendment) Order 2006 (S.I. No. 690 of 2006).

[55] O'Sullivan, "Local Areas and Structures" in Callanan and Keogan (eds), *Local Government in Ireland: Inside and Out* (2004), p.67.

[56] The five existing borough councils (Clonmel, Drogheda, Kilkenny, Sligo and Wexford) retain their titles, but their powers and functions are those of larger town councils.

[57] See generally, O'Sullivan, "Local Areas and Structures" in Callanan and Keogan (eds), *Local Government in Ireland: Inside and Out* (2004), pp.50–55.

to the Minister to have the council dissolved. If the Minister dissolves the town council, the relevant county council is its successor; in other words, the members of the town councils would lay down their (political) lives for their county.

5–25 One of the most eye-catching innovations of the 2001 Act was the statutory recognition of Strategic Policy Committees (SPC) and Corporate Policy Groups (CPG), initially suggested by *Better Local Government*. These bodies are required to be set up in city and county councils. Although they are now on a statutory footing, the detail of the organisation of SPCs and CPGs is found in departmental guidelines. The initial guidelines were released in 1997 and revised guidelines were published in 1999.[58] The membership of SPCs is drawn from elected members of local authorities and lay members. The chairperson of each SPC is an elected member and is expected to preside at approximately four meetings a year. Each SPC consists of at least nine members. Two-thirds are councillors and the remaining members must be representatives of sectoral interests; their selection is a matter for local interest groups, not the elected members. The sectors represented on SPCs are agriculture/ farming; environmental/conservation/culture; development/construction; business/ commercial; trade union; and community/voluntary/disadvantaged.

5–26 The remit of SPCs is "to consider matters connected with the formulation, development, monitoring and review of policy which relate to the functions of the local authority and to advise the authority on those matters".[59] The number of SPCs required by various local authorities may vary. The four main areas to be covered are economic development and planning policy; environmental policy; transportation and infrastructural policy; and housing policy, social and cultural development. Each SPC is supported by the local authority's Director of Services for the particular functional area. The key idea is that SPC members are to be involved in the formulation of policy from an early stage and are able to bring their acumen to bear on the subject before it is submitted to the local authority for a final decision on its adoption or rejection. Thus, in theory, SPCs enhance local democracy by in the first place permitting local interest groups to participate in local governance, and secondly, allowing councillors to develop their expertise and therefore play a more proactive role in the formulation of policy.[60] The hope is that "[t]his configuration, anchored in the main local government services, would facilitate networking and information exchange among SPC chairs and among Directors of Services and would facilitate linkage with Government departments and

---

[58] Department of the Environment, Heritage and Local Government, *Strategic Policy Committees—Revised Guidelines* (1999), replacing Department of the Environment, Heritage and Local Government, *Strategic Policy Committees: Guidelines for Establishment and Operation* (1997).

[59] 2001 Act s.48(1).

[60] Callanan, "Institutionalising Participation and Governance? New Participative Structures in Local Government in Ireland" (2005) 83 *Public Administration* 909 at 916. A number of studies have been conducted on the operation of SPCs. See Institute of Public Administration, *Review of the Operation of Strategic Policy Committees* (Dublin, 2004); Institute of Public Administration, *Changing Local Government: a Review of the Local Government Modernisation Programme* (Dublin, 2004); Ó Broin, "Participation at the Periphery: Community Participation in Reformed Local Government Structures" (2002) 1 *Journal of Irish Urban Studies* 1.

other State agencies".[61] In each city or county council, the SPCs are supplemented by a CPG. Here the chairperson of the local authority acts as chair of a group comprising the chairs of each SPC:

"The CPG will link the work of the different SPCs, act as a sort of cabinet and provide a forum where policy positions affecting the whole Council can be agreed for submission to the full Council."[62]

A CPG's statutory remit is to "advise and assist the elected council in the formulation, development, monitoring and review of policy for the local authority and for that purpose propose arrangements for the consideration of policy matters and the organisation of related business by the elected council".[63] The CPG is to take a broader view of the local authority's operations than the SPCs: it co-ordinates the work of the SPCs and may request an SPC to develop policy in a particular area.

5–27 A major function of the CPG is to draft, in consultation with the manager, a "corporate plan" for the local authority area. The plan:

"… shall be prepared on the basis of an organisational wide strategic approach encompassing the various activities of the local authority concerned and shall include:
- (a) a statement of the principal activities of the local authority,
- (b) the objectives and priorities for each of the principal activities and strategies for achieving those objectives,
- (c) the manner in which the authority proposes to assess its performance in respect of each such activity, taking account of relevant service indicators and of the need to work towards best practice in service delivery and in the general operation of the local authority,
- (d) human resources activities (including training and development) to be undertaken for the staff of the local authority and, where appropriate for the elected council,
- (e) the organisational structure of the local authority, both elected council and staff, including corporate support and information technology and the improvements proposed to promote efficiency of operation and customer service and in general to support the corporate plan,
- (f) such other matters as may be set out in guidelines issued [by the Minister]."[64]

5–28 The final adoption of the plan is a reserved function of the local authority. The CPG must also be consulted by the manager before the preparation of a draft

---

[61] Department of the Environment, Heritage and Local Government, *Strategic Policy Committees—Revised Guidelines* (1999), p.8.

[62] Department of the Environment, Heritage and Local Government, *Strategic Policy Committees—Revised Guidelines* (1999), p.6.

[63] 2001 Act s.133(2)(a).

[64] See also, Department of the Environment, Heritage and Local Government, *Guidelines for Local Authorities in the Preparation of Corporate Plans 2004-2009* (Dublin, 2004); Institute of Public Administration, *Corporate Policy Groups: Review, Analysis and Future Recommendations* (Dublin, 2006).

annual budget.[65] But whether the CPG policy has been successful in moving towards a "cabinet" style system of local government has been strongly questioned:

> "The cabinet type governance of local authorities, envisaged under *Better Local Government*, has not developed to its potential. Part of the reason for this may be the annual turnover in chair of the council. In relation to the chairing of Strategic Policy Committees, the intention in law is that the position be filled for at least 3 years. However, not all councils operate this system (and it is not of course possible to have 2 terms within the 5 year life of councils). It is suggested therefore that, to strengthen cabinet governance and balance the position of a directly elected mayor, SPC chairs should also be appointed for the term of the council. This should mean that the natural/political leaders of the various groupings in the council will take on and retain key leadership roles. It is envisaged that the present system of distribution of chairs should continue, with positions being allocated in accordance with councillor groupings, though an argument could be made for appointments to be made as part of the normal political negotiation process between parties."[66]

5–29   The 2001 Act also provides for City and County Development Boards (CDB) in each city and county area. The membership of CDBs comprises all members of the relevant CPG, representatives of public bodies which operate in the local authority area, representatives of the social partners and representatives of any publicly funded local development boards. The aim is that "CDBs will play a pivotal role in developing the relationship between public service planning at county/city and regional authority levels".[67] Provision is also made in s.52 of the 2001 Act for the establishment of joint committees by two or more local authorities, but "[t]he use of joint committees has not been widespread in recent years".[68]

5–30   A number of recent reforms have aimed at enhancing the status of local representatives. The most controversial was the abolition of the so-called dual mandate, in other words, the practice whereby members of the Oireachtas were also councillors. So widespread was the practice that "138 of the 226 members elected to the Dáil or Seanad in 2002 were members of local councils".[69] Unsurprisingly, given the numbers involved, legislative reform was difficult to achieve. However, the Local Government (No. 2) Act 2003 did successfully abolish the dual mandate[70]: the quid pro quo for the querulous backbenchers was the removal from the Bill of a provision allowing for chairpersons (or mayors) of local authorities to be directly

---

[65]   2001 Act ss.102(4) and 133(4)(a).

[66]   Department of the Environment, Heritage and Local Government, *Stronger Local Democracy: Options for Change* (Dublin, 2008), p.54.

[67]   Keyes, "Community and Enterprise" in Callanan and Keogan (eds), *Local Government in Ireland: Inside and Out* (2004), p.294. See also, Department of the Environment, Heritage and Local Government, *A Shared Vision for County/City Development Boards: Guidelines on the CDB Strategies for Economic, Social and Cultural Development* (Dublin, 2000).

[68]   O'Sullivan, "Local Areas and Structures" in Callanan and Keogan (eds), *Local Government in Ireland: Inside and Out* (2004), p.64.

[69]   Kenny, "Local Government and Politics" in Callanan and Keogan (eds), *Local Government in Ireland: Inside and Out* (2004), p.113.

[70]   The constitutionality of this change was upheld by Laffoy J. in *Ring v Attorney General* [2004] IEHC 14; [2004] 1 I.R. 185.

elected (a prospect which would possibly have reduced the status of TDs in the eyes of voters). Local authorities are also now statutorily obliged to supply members of the Oireachtas with appropriate information regarding local authority matters, including supplying the agenda and minutes of local authority meetings.[71] As of early 2012 elected chairpersons or mayors remain on the political agenda.[72]

5–31 A second significant reform was the decision to pay salaries to local authority members. Previously, councillors were entitled to an annual allowance and some other expenses, but s.142 of the 2001 Act permitted the payment of an annual salary. Under the Local Government (Representational Payment For Members) Regulations 2001[73] the initial annual salary of city and county councillors was €11,000, with lower sums payable to other local representatives. The salary is linked to the salary of senators and is to be altered proportionately with any alteration in senatorial salaries.[74]

Despite the reforms of the past 10 or 15 years and the slew of reviews going back much earlier, anxious debate continues over the role of local government and some of the concerns are captured in the following observations:

> "The weak nature of local political democracy and poor articulation of the values of localism means that there can be a lack of understanding at central government level of differences in service delivery or prioritisation at local level. This view applies at both political and administrative levels of central government. This view from the centre has also affected belief in the ability of local authorities to deliver new services. It has encouraged Government to by-pass local authorities in favour of separate local development bodies and it does not encourage decentralisation of power. This approach has arguably served to keep the local government sector much weaker than it should be."[75]

5–32 Yet, in the end, it may be that it will be the need for general financial prudence generated by the economic catastrophes of 2008–2009 that will ultimately drive the political will for greater reform and efficiency. A wholesale culling of the numbers of local authorities, at city or county council level, from 34 to 22, coupled with the abolition of regional authorities and town councils was recommended by the *Report of the Special Group on Public Service Numbers and Expenditure Programmes*.[76] A White Paper on the future of local government is also imminent.

---

[71] Local Government Act 2001, s.237A (as inserted by Local Government (No. 2) Act 2003 s.3).

[72] For a former Government's enthusiasm, see Department of the Environment, Heritage and Local Government, *Stronger Local Democracy: Options for Change* (Dublin, 2008), pp.39–54. It is said that the present Minister (Mr Phil Hogan), is also in favour of this development.

[73] S.I. No. 552 of 2001.

[74] S.I. No. 552 of 2001 art.6(3).

[75] Department of the Environment, Heritage and Local Government, *Stronger Local Democracy: Options for Change* (Dublin, 2008), p.32.

[76] Prn. A9/0988 (2009), Vol.2, Ch.8.

B. The Management System

5–33   The essence of the management system, the unique form of local governments first introduced into Ireland in 1929 in Cork and (thereafter) made of general application,[77] is that certain functions (known as "reserved functions") may, as a matter of law (practice is rather different) be exercised by the elected members, while all other functions ("executive functions") are discharged by a salaried officer, known as "the City [or County] Manager".[78] The Manager's status vis-à-vis the local authority is enhanced by the provisions regarding his appointment and renewal. Selection is a reserved function of the local authority, but exercisable only on a recommendation by the Public Appointments Service, meaning that in effect the councillors have at most a power of veto.[79] In addition, a Manager can only be removed from office with the sanction of the Minister for the Environment, Heritage and Local Government.[80] Detailed provisions as to the tenure of a Manager are contained in the Local Government (Tenure of Office of Managers) Regulations 2003.[81] The tenure period is five years, except in the case of Dublin City Council, where it is six years, and may be extended by the Manager for a further three years upon notifying the Minister in the prescribed form. If the Manager at any point reaches the retirement age, his or her tenure ceases. The Manager may also be removed from office following the passage of a resolution, of which at least 21 days' notice has been given, by a three-quarters' majority of the councillors. No Manager has as yet been removed. But a few have been suspended, a process which requires a resolution of the same type as for a removal, but no ministerial consent.[82] However, the elected members do have the power of giving the Manager binding directions as to the manner in which certain executive functions shall be discharged.[83] Given the need for consistency between a county council and any lower authority within its area, it is most important that a County Manager is ex officio made Manager for every elective body within the county.[84]

Distinction between reserved and executive functions

5–34   Some of the reserved functions of local authorities are listed in Sch.14 to the Local Government Act 2001. The list is not exhaustive; many such functions are granted by other legislation.[85] Section 149(4) of the 2001 Act states that, every power, function or duty of a local authority or elected body which is not declared to be a reserved function[86] shall be an "executive function".[87] Previously, all executive functions had to be performed by the Manager by way of a signed order

[77]   *Cullen v Wicklow County Manager* [2011] 1 I.R. 152 at para.[4].
[78]   On the relationship between the Manager and the elected members, see the discussion in Department of the Environment, Heritage and Local Government, *Stronger Local Democracy: Options for Change* (Dublin, 2008), pp.55–61.
[79]   2001 Act s.145(1)(a).
[80]   2001 Act s.146(7)(a).
[81]   S.I. No. 47 of 2003.
[82]   2001 Act s.146.
[83]   Local Government Act 2001 ss.136–140.
[84]   2001 Act s.144(3)(a).
[85]   For miscellaneous examples, see below, para.5–35.
[86]   Or in the new term specified by s.131(2)(c) of the 2001 Act, a power exercisable by resolution.
[87]   See, to similar import, s.19(1) of the County Management Act 1940.

in writing,[88] but this requirement was significantly modified by s.150 of the 2001 Act which obliges the Manager to perform executive functions by written order where required to do so by statute, where the Minister has designated a function to be an executive function, or where the Manager considers the function "to be of sufficient importance to be done by order". A register must be kept of all such orders made by him for inspection by the elected representatives at a council meeting.[89] It is of practical importance that the Manager has extensive powers of delegation to any employee of the relevant local authority.[90] The Manager may by order amend or revoke the delegation at any time and, in a departure from previous practice, holds the power concurrently with the delegate and may exercise it during the period of delegation.[91]

5–35 There is no comprehensive method of characterising the functions which the legislature has chosen to make reserved rather than executive; nevertheless, it is generally true to say that the latter are of an administrative nature. Reserved functions tend to deal with political and policy-making matters, or involve quasi-legislative or financial powers. Unsurprisingly, the making of bye-laws is always a reserved function.[92] However, contemporary policy is often to cast quasi-legislative functions as executive functions. There is, though, a nod in the direction of the traditional democratic practice of making them reserved, in that s.131(3)(a) of the 2001 Act provides that the Minister for the Environment may by order direct that certain functions or powers should become reserved functions.[93] The determination of an annual valuation rate is also expressly reserved[94] but the administrative act of assessing rates in individual cases is vested by the Valuation Act 2001 in the Commissioner of Valuation. Accordingly the power of elected local representatives to levy finance is not affected but the authority to execute that policy decision lies elsewhere. Draft estimates of expenditure must be prepared by the Manager, after consultation with the corporate policy group of the local authority.[95] The estimates must then be adopted (possibly with amendment) at a full meeting of the council at which the Manager "is present".[96] Naturally, too, dignified and representational

---

[88] County Management Act 1940 s.19.
[89] 2001 Act s.151(3) and (4).
[90] 2001 Act s.154(2).
[91] 2001 Act s.154(4). See generally, Bailey, "Delegation and Concurrent Exercises of Power" [2005] J.R. 84.
[92] 2001 Act Sch.14, Ref. No. 15.
[93] See, e.g. County Management (Reserved Functions) Order 1985 (S.I. No. 341 of 1985) making of domestic service charges under ss.2 and 8 of the Local Government (Financial Provisions) (No. 2) Act 1983; Local Government Act 1991 (Reserved Functions) Order 1993 (S.I. No. 37 of 1993) making of a contribution under s.40 of the Local Government (Sanitary Services) Act 1948; making of arrangements under s.96(1) of the Road Traffic Act 1961; entry into an agreement under s.7 of the Local Authorities (Traffic Wardens) Act 1975; the making of a contribution under s.29 of the Local Government (Water Pollution) Act 1977; the making of a plan under art.4 of the European Communities (Waste) Regulations 1979; the making of a scheme under s.279(5) of the Social Welfare (Consolidation) Act 1993; entry into arrangements under s.15(2)–(4) of the Control of Dogs Act 1986 (other than the provision of services of staff); the making of a decision to provide a public abattoir under s.19(1) of the Abattoirs Act 1988; and the consideration of a request to make a boundary change under s.30(3) of the Local Government Act 1991).
[94] 2001 Act Sch.14, Ref. No. 4.
[95] 2001 Act ss.102(4) and 133(4)(a).
[96] 2001 Act s.103(2)(a).

functions, such as conferring civic honours,[97] entering into "twinning" arrangements with other towns and areas,[98] electing a member of the council to represent it on a public authority or nominating a presidential candidate are also reserved functions.[99] Section 12(6) of the Planning and Development Act 2000 provides that a development plan is to be amended or accepted by resolution of a local authority.[100]

5–36 In some instances, however, it has been considered that the effectiveness of the operation of the relevant statutory function would be frustrated if the power were to continue to be assigned to the elected members. Thus, in the sensitive area of waste management, s.22(10) of the Waste Management Act 1996 now provides[101] that the "review, variation or replacement of a waste management plan" shall be an executive function.[102]

5–37 A curious and amusing example of the legal relationship between the Manager and the elected members is provided by *Waterford Corporation v O'Toole*.[103] The defendant was interested in the life and works of the composer William Vincent Wallace[104] and he sought to erect on his own hotel premises two stone plaques commemorating the composer which had come into the possession of the Corporation. The City Manager agreed to the defendant's proposal that he should take possession of the plaques for this purpose. This decision was subject to ratification by the council, but Mr O'Toole was given to understand that this would be a mere formality. In fact, the Corporation refused to give their consent to this arrangement and the Corporation subsequently sought the return of the plaques which, by this time, had been embedded in concrete. The question arose as to whether the City Manager had power to make these arrangements with the defendant. Finlay J. held that such ratification was not required:

> "[A]s a matter of law, the disposal or, more properly, the erection and display of these plaques on any particular premises was not a reserved function and it was within the power of the City Manager to have made any arrangement he liked with Mr. O'Toole in regard to the plaques without obtaining the ratification or approval of the City Council."

---

[97] 2001 Act s.74(3).

[98] 2001 Act s.75(2).

[99] 2001 Act Sch.14, Ref. No. 2; Presidential Elections Act 1993 s.16(1).

[100] See also, Housing (Traveller Accommodation) Act 1998 s.7 (the adoption of an accommodation programme or the amendment or replacement of an accommodation programme); European Communities (Water Policy) Regulations 2003 (S.I. No. 722 of 2003) (the making of a river basin management plan); Health Act 2004 s.8 (entering into an agreement with the Health Service Executive to allow the Executive to perform a function on behalf of the local authority under s.8); Water Services Act 2007 s.36 (making, replacement or revision of a water services strategic plan).

[101] It had previously been a reserved function: see Waste Management Act 1996 s.22(10)(d) (as inserted by Waste Management (Amendment) Act 2001 s.4).

[102] The making of such a plan is also an executive function: see Waste Management Act 1996 s.22(10)(a) (as inserted by Waste Management (Amendment) Act 2001 s.4).

[103] Unreported, High Court, Finlay J., November 9, 1973.

[104] William Vincent Wallace was born in Waterford in 1812 and died in France in 1865 after an eventful and colourful career. No less a figure than Wagner was compared unfavourably with Wallace by many local enthusiasts, but, alas, *Die Walküre* has proved more durable than *Maritana*.

5–38   However, Finlay J. further found on the facts, that as Mr O'Toole was aware that the City Manager had not intended to transfer the plaques without such consent, in the absence of such consent, a condition of Mr O'Toole's bailment failed. As a result, he committed a detinue of the goods.[105]

5–39   Section 149 of the 2001 Act, in the guise of its predecessor in the County Management Act 1940, appears to have received judicial consideration in only one other case: *State (Harrington) v Wallace*.[106] Schedule 2 to the 1940 Act provided, inter alia, that the "making, amending or revoking of a bye-law" shall be a reserved function. Cork County Council promulgated certain sheep-dipping regulations and the question arose as to whether these regulations were a bye-law within the meaning of the 1940 Act. Walsh J. accepted that if they were not, then they would be invalid in that the making of such regulations would not have been a reserved function within the meaning of the Act and that such powers could only have been exercised by the County Manager. However, Walsh J. decided, without much discussion, that on their true construction the regulations were in fact bye-laws.[107] This case illustrates what, in any event, are unexceptionable propositions, namely, that it is unlawful for the City or County Manager to exercise reserved functions, and conversely, that subject to one important statutory exception presently to be considered, the elected representatives may not usurp the executive functions of the Manager.

5–40   Moreover, it may be tentatively suggested that the elected members may not delegate their reserved powers to the Manager. This point is illustrated by *Grange Developments Ltd v Dublin County Council (No. 2)*,[108] where the terms of the Dublin City development plan (the making of which is a reserved function) purported to invest the City Manager with a power to grant undertakings to grant planning permissions where this was considered by him to be expedient so as to avoid a claim for compensation under the Local Government (Planning and Development) Act 1963. Both Murphy J. and the Supreme Court considered that the effect of this clause was to attempt to give the Manager power to rewrite the terms of the development plan as and when it seemed convenient to do so and that this represented an illegal delegation of powers. As Murphy J. said:

> "As the making of a development plan and any variation of such plan is a reserved function by virtue of s.19(7) of the 1963 Act, it seems to me that the wide-ranging powers conferred on the executive authority by the 1983 development plan is an illegal and invalid intrusion on that power."[109]

---

[105] The Corporation was awarded £1 nominal damages for detinue and Finlay J. refused on discretionary grounds to order the return of the plaques, since the cost and likely damage of removing the plaques from the concrete structure in which they were now embedded would be out of all proportion to their intrinsic value.

[106] [1988] I.R. 290.

[107] Walsh J. considered ([1988] I.R. 290 at 294) that it "would be hard to improve on" the definition of a bye-law given by Lord Russell in *Kruse v Johnson* [1898] 2 Q.B. 91 at 96: "An ordinance affecting the public, or some portion of the public, imposed by some authority clothed with statutory powers ordering something to be done or not to be done, and accompanied by some sanction or penalty for its non-observance."

[108] [1986] I.R. 246.

[109] [1986] I.R. 246 at 312.

5–41   It should be noted that the exercise of a reserved function by the elected members does not, in general, involve any special procedures:

> "A reserved function can be carried out by a local authority by any lawful method of procedure which is contained in the rules of its proceedings and does not require any specific majority or number of persons voting in favour of it. [It may also] be carried out by a local authority without the necessity for any specific notice of its intention so to do to be given to the county manager or to anyone else."[110]

5–42   One of the exceptions to this generalisation concerns the making or amendment of a development plan where, as mentioned elsewhere,[111] strict statutory procedures must be followed. Accordingly, the *Grange Developments* ratio might be distinguished in a case involving a different area.

5–43   As a matter of practicality, an inflexible operation of the "separation of powers" between the elected members and the Manager would plainly be unworkable. It is certainly not the case that the Manager is consigned to a purely administrative role: the council will rely on the Manager's expertise for advice and guidance, and the Manager's "contribution to the development of local policy is considerable".[112]

5–44   This last formulation substantially understates the point, since policy is almost entirely developed by the Manager, who can draw on the advice of his expert staff. In contrast, the interest of many councillors is focused on constituency cases. As to the balance of authority between the Manager and councillors: a Manager has the right to attend council meetings and it is his duty to advise the council, generally and particularly, in regard to the exercise of its functions.[113]

5–45   In the other direction, apart from the power to pass a resolution under s.140 of the 2001 Act, which is elaborated below, the councillors have a number of powers: in the first place, the councillors' right to information has been improved. In relation to either any, or every, performance of a specified executive function (other than staffing), the councillors may by resolution direct that before the Manager exercises that function, he must inform them of the manner in which he proposes to perform that function.[114] Secondly, even without a resolution, the Manager must inform the councillors before any works are undertaken or expenditure for work is committed.[115] This question arose in *O'Reilly v O'Sullivan*[116] where the Dún Laoghaire–Rathdown County Manager took action to develop a particular site as a temporary halting site for Travellers without informing the councillors. Keane J., however, noted that this right was abridged in cases of emergency[117] (such as

---

[110] *P&F Sharpe Ltd v Dublin City and County Manager* [1989] I.R. 710 at 716 per Finlay C.J.
[111] See paras 5–160 to 5–163.
[112] *Report of the Public Services Organisation Review Group* ("the Devlin Report") (1969, Prl. 792), para.25.2.12.
[113] Local Government Act 2001 ss.132(3) and 152.
[114] Local Government Act 2001 s.138(2).
[115] Local Government Act 2001 s.138(1).
[116] Unreported, Supreme Court, February 26, 1997.
[117] The analogue to s.2(9) of the City and County Management (Amendment) Act 1955 is s.138(4)

had arisen in the present case) and the following passage graphically demonstrates the extent to which fundamental democratic principles have been abridged at local level:

> "[Counsel for the applicant] has urged that the section should not be construed so as to enable the Manager to frustrate what he described as the democratic right of the elected members to be informed and (where appropriate) to direct that particular works should not be carried out. That submission, however, overlooks the fact that the Oireachtas, since the enactment of the County Management Act 1940 has maintained in place a system of local government under which the powers of the elected members are heavily circumscribed. Since the Constitution at no point requires the assignment to elected local authorities of any of the powers of central government, it follows that the extent of any of the powers vested in such bodies remains at all times a matter for the Oireachtas. If the legislature were of the view that the effective use of the powers given to housing authorities by the 1988 Act might be inhibited by political considerations … and that the rights and privileges of the elected members under s.2 of the 1955 Act should be correspondingly abridged, that was a matter for them."[118]

5–46 Thirdly, s.139 of the 2001 Act (previously s.3 of the City and County Management (Amendment) Act 1955) provides that the elected representatives may direct that the works be not proceeded with, save where such works are works "which the local authority … are required by or under statute or by order of a court to undertake".[119] In addition, s.136 of the 2001 Act requires that a manager shall whenever requested by an elective authority or joint body, or its chairman, provide:

> … all information that may be in the possession or procurement of such manager in regard to any act, matter or thing relating to or concerning any

---

of the 2001 Act and the analogue to s.27 of the Housing Act 1988 is s.138(5) of the 2001 Act.

[118] However, the court quashed the Manager's order since there was no evidence that the Travellers who had been offered accommodation were "homeless persons" within the meaning of s.2 of the Housing Act. Keane J.'s observations regarding the lack of constitutional protection with regard to the assignment of local authority functions were uttered before the enactment of the 20th Amendment of the Constitution Act 1999 and the insertion of Art.28A. But it would not appear that Art.28A has changed this position: see *PJ Farrell v Limerick City Council* [2009] IEHC 274.

[119] In *East Wicklow Conservation Community Ltd v Wicklow County Council* [1997] 2 I.L.R.M. 72, the respondents had treated as a nullity a section 3 direction requiring them not to build a waste disposal site at a particular place. The question arose as to whether these were works which the authority was required to do by or under statute. The Supreme Court held that these works came within the exception to s.3, even though it was clear that the authority was under no *specific* statutory obligation to perform the works at that *particular site*. In a judgment whose conclusion is by no means self-evident, Blayney J. held that since by virtue of s.55 of the Public Health (Ireland) Act 1878 an authority is required to provide "fit buildings or places for the deposit of any matters collected by them", the proposed works were ones which the local authority was bound to carry out. This may be true, but it still does not meet the applicant's fundamental objection that as the authority was under no obligation to build the waste site at that particular place, the works did not fall within the statutory duty exception to s.3. Thus, *East Wicklow* provides another example of the fundamental lack of democratic accountability at local level.

business or transaction of such local authority or body which is mentioned in the request.

5–47 In *Cullen v Wicklow County Manager*,[120] McCracken J. held that the word "information" in the section's predecessor was not confined to written matters but has a "very wide and general meaning". This meant that the Chairman of the County Council was entitled pursuant to this section to have access to all documents pertaining to litigation involving the Council in respect of an alleged contravention of the relevant development plan.

Section 140 of the 2001 Act

5–48 The City and County Management (Amendment) Act 1955 was passed after a series of departmental circulars designed to enhance the status of the councillors vis-à-vis the Manager had been ignored by many Managers. This Act, as we shall see, strengthened the position of the councillors, but in recent times, the key provisions, now ss.138, 139 and 140 of the Local Government Act 2001, have been rather reduced by judicial decisions. The most important of these provisions, s.140 of the 2001 Act, previously s.4 of the City and County Management (Amendment) Act 1955, enables the elected members to give the Manager directions as to how certain of his executive functions shall be performed.[121] Section 140(2) of the 2001 Act provides:

> [A]n elected council or joint body may by resolution require any particular act, matter or thing specifically mentioned in the resolution and which the local authority or the manager concerned can lawfully do or effect, to be done or effected in the performance of the executive functions of the local authority.

5–49 The power of the local authority to pass such a resolution is, however, subject to a number of important qualifications.[122] Special notice must be given,[123] compliance with which is especially stringent in the planning field, a point to which we shall return below.[124] Furthermore, s.140(10) states that the Manager may not be stripped of an entire executive function by means of a general resolution.[125] So, for example, while a section 140 resolution may validly direct that a particular

---

[120] [1996] 3 I.R. 474.

[121] Of course, in addition to formal s.140 motions, councillors sometimes pass ordinary resolutions which concern executive functions. These motions do not bind the manager and simply amount to "formal recommendations ... as to the performance by him of any particular executive function": *Browne v Dundalk U.D.C.* [1993] 2 I.R. 512 at 520 per Barr J.

[122] Interestingly, with regard to the vexed question of water charges, s.75(9) of the Waste Management Act 1996, as inserted by the Protection of the Environment Act 2003 s.52, prohibits the use of s.140 for any purposes inconsistent with s.75, presumably to prevent opportunistic local politicians from campaigning on an electoral platform to abolish waste collection service charges or dispensing with a charge for particular constituents.

[123] Section 140 of the 2001 Act requires that notice of the resolution must specify a day not later than seven days after the receipt of the notice by the Manager for the holding of the meeting at which the resolution is to be considered.

[124] See below, paras 5–53 to 5–54.

[125] In addition, such resolutions do not extend to the exercise or performance of the Manager's executive functions in relation to the control, remuneration, etc of the council's officers or servants. See 2001 Act s.131(5).

planning permission should be granted, it may not require that all applications of that type should be acceded to. On the other hand, it has now been authoritatively (though obiter) stated that this procedure may be used to compel the Manager to do any particular act, matter or thing, even where this has a negative outcome, for instance to refuse a planning permission application.[126] Significantly, a resolution of this nature can only require the performance of an executive function in a lawful manner, and it is clear that a resolution which required the Manager to act in an unreasonable or arbitrary manner, or in a manner contrary to the requirements of constitutional justice, would be ultra vires.[127]

5–50 A significant and growing difficulty with the practical operation of s.140 was highlighted by the Supreme Court (O'Donnell J.) in *Cullen v Wicklow County Council*.[128] The judgment starts colourfully with the observation that "[i]t is difficult to credit, even now, that virtual civil war raged in Wicklow County Council ... over a proposal to convert a milking parlour into a pet crematorium at Red Cross, County Wicklow".[129] This battle had led on to a section 140 resolution, directing the County Manager not to grant planning permission for the conversion. In fact, however, this was merely part of the background, since the actual issue before the court at this late stage was a dispute regarding costs. Nevertheless, O'Donnell J. took the opportunity to make some general observations regarding the operation of s.140. The judge noted, first, that the decision in *P&F Sharpe Ltd v Dublin Corporation*[130] (the facts of which are in para.5–54) had meant that, in the case of every such resolution, a Manager was obliged to form a view as to the validity of the resolution, not merely by reference to the objective procedural criteria by which the resolution was passed; but also by reference to a more contestable ground, such as irrationality or a failure to take into account relevant considerations. O'Donnell J. stated:

> "[When it is recalled that] the court in *P and F Sharpe Ltd* had emphasised that not only had the planning process become even more technical and complex, but that any decision taken was one which had to be addressed judicially (whether by the manager or by the council members), it is clear that there was considerable scope for challenge to any decision in the planning area made by the councillors pursuant to [section 140] and correspondingly increased opportunity for friction between the management and elected representatives ... It is a matter that might repay reconsideration, both judicial and legislative, since there is in my view, in principle, little to be gained by constituting the executive of the local authority as a shadow court of judicial review, and much to be lost, in increased stress upon the executive and its advisors ... and increased aggravation to elected members in seeing their decisions in effect quashed by the executive. Ironically, it might also be said that [section

---

[126] See the important comments of O'Donnell J. in *Wicklow County Council v Wicklow County Manager* [2011] 1 I.R. 152 at paras 56–62; Butler (ed.), *Keane's Local Government in the Republic of Ireland* (Dublin: First Law, 2003), pp.27–28.

[127] See, e.g. *McDonald v Feeley*, unreported, Supreme Court, July 23, 1980; *P&F Sharpe Ltd v Dublin City and County Manager* [1989] I.R. 701; *Child v Wicklow County Council* [1995] 2 I.R. 447.

[128] [2011] 1 I.R. 152.

[129] [2011] 1 I.R. 152 at para.[3].

[130] [1989] I.R. 701.

140] motions are less potentially harmful in the area of planning than in any
other area of the local authority function, since there is an independent and
relatively rapid appeal process …".

5–51 Sure enough, whereas pre-*Sharpe* there had been few, if any, examples
of County Managers refusing to comply with a resolution under s.140 (or its
predecessor), the decision in *Sharpe*, as O'Donnell J. noted, gave rise to a number
of such refusals and, consequently, cases in which the High Court was invited to
determine whether the Manager was entitled to refuse to comply. O'Donnell J.'s plea
for judicial quietism or legislative reform is, with respect, very sensible (although,
given the activism of the judiciary, it is difficult to see how an appropriately nuanced
provision, stipulating what factors a Manager should, or should not, take into
account to ground a refusal to comply could be worded). At the most general level,
one might comment that this is one of those situations[131] in which uncertainty and
tension arise because there is what might be called a provisional decision on a public
law issue followed by a delay of several months, at least, before the authoritative
ruling from a court. Such situations are likely to grow as law, whether legislation
or judge-made, becomes more intrusive and intensive.

5–52 These questions might have arisen—but ultimately did not—in the aftermath
of the long-running *Grange Developments* case, where a suggestion was made
that Dublin County Council would use its powers to order the Manager not to pay
over a sum of money, even though the Supreme Court had refused to put a stay on
judgment.[132] It is arguable that a section 4 motion could not have been used for this
negative purpose. On the one hand, in *P&F Sharpe Ltd v Dublin City Manager*,
Finlay C.J. said in passing that the power applied to the whole range of "executive
functions, namely, those associated with the granting or refusing of planning
permissions".[133] On the other hand, s.140 omits any reference to a negative act or
deed and, because it represents an exception to the separation of powers between
the Manager and the elected members, it is to be expected that—like all statutory
exceptions—it will be strictly construed. Also, the section refers to any act which
the local authority or the Manager can "lawfully do". Thus, the mechanism of a
section 140 motion cannot be used to achieve an unlawful object and the Manager
may decline to obey a section 140 resolution where it is clear that the resolution
would require the performance of an illegal act.[134]

---

[131] For other somewhat similar situations, see Ch.11, Part E.
[132] *The Irish Times*, March 22, 1989.
[133] [1989] I.R. 701 at 714.
[134] Where the case involves an "obvious and patent illegality, the Manager would be not only
entitled, but in duty bound to refuse to comply with the directions given to him by the
Council"; [1989] I.R. 701 at 708 per O'Hanlon J. While this view has been consistently
followed in other cases (see, e.g. *Griffin v Galway City and County Manager*, unreported,
High Court, October 31, 1990; *Flanagan v Galway City and County Manager* [1990] 2 I.R.
66; *Kenny Homes & Co Ltd v Galway City and County Manager* [1995] 1 I.R. 178; *Child v
Wicklow County Council* [1995] 2 I.R. 447; *PJ Farrell v Limerick City Council* [2009] IEHC
274, it has now been doubted by O'Donnell J. in his hugely important judgment in *Wicklow
County Council v Wicklow County Manager* [2010] IESC 49. Furthermore, a section 140
motion cannot be used to compel the Manager to breach an otherwise valid contract: *Browne
v Dundalk U.D.C.* [1993] 2 I.R. 512. In addition, s.112 of the 2001 Act provides that if the
proposed resolution would involve an illegal payment, or would likely result in a deficiency
or loss of the authority's funds, then the names of the persons voting for such a proposal must
be recorded, and those voting in favour of the resolution are liable to be surcharged. In the

Section 140 in the planning context

5–53   Most section 140 resolutions arise in the context of the granting, rather than the refusal, of planning permission and s.34(6)(c) of the Planning and Development Act 2000 prescribes a special procedure where the Manager is of opinion that the granting of such permission pursuant to a section 140 resolution would materially contravene the provisions of the development plan. In such a case the Manager must ensure that the provisions of s.34(6)(a) of the 2000 Act are complied with, which include, inter alia, the publication of a newspaper notice indicating the intention of the authority to grant the permission,[135] the invitation of submissions from members of the public within four weeks of the publication of such newspaper notice and, finally, the passage of a resolution by three-quarters of the local authority. In addition, the required notice in relation to the resolution must be signed by not less than three-quarters of the total number of the members elected for the electoral area or areas concerned. It is further necessary that three-quarters of the total number of members of the local authority vote in favour.[136]

5–54   The general scope of the powers conferred by s.140's predecessor was considered by the Supreme Court in the important case of *P&F Sharpe Ltd v Dublin City and County Manager*.[137] In this case the applicants had obtained planning permission to erect a large housing development in the vicinity of a dual carriageway. The applicants then sought permission for access to the dual carriageway from the housing estate. Despite the fact that there were several reports before the City Council strongly recommending against acceding to this request for road safety reasons, a section 4 motion requiring the City Manager to grant the permission in the terms sought was carried. The City Manager, however, refused to comply with the resolution on the ground that he considered that it was ultra vires and mandamus proceedings were then commenced by the applicants.

5–55   The central aspect of the court's decision was that the granting of planning permission involved the exercise of quasi-judicial powers and that a planning authority was required to act reasonably and exclude all irrelevant considerations. In the context of a section 4 resolution this did not mean that the Manager was required to exercise a discretion independently of the members, but rather that:

> "[T]he obligation to act in a judicial [sc. quasi-judicial] manner is by virtue of the service of notice of intention to propose a resolution under section 4 of the 1955 Act transferred from the County Manager to the elected members. They must act in a judicial manner before reaching any conclusion on the

---

Child case, Costello P. said (at 452) that if a County Manager "decides that a s.4 resolution is *ultra vires* there is … authority to the effect that he is entitled to ignore it without applying to the court to have it quashed", and this view was affirmed by McGovern J. in *PJ Farrell v Limerick City Council* [2009] IEHC 274. But for a suggestion (in a different context) that the decision-maker might be obliged to apply to the High Court to have the decision quashed, see the (inconclusive) discussion in the judgment of Geoghegan J. in *Hegarty v Governor of Limerick Prison* [1998] 1 I.R. 412, discussed in paras 11–84 to 11–95.

[135]   For a case raising evidential issues concerning proof of whether the appropriate newspaper notices were circulated in the context of a resolution rescinding the application of Pt III of the Gaming and Lotteries Act 1956, see *Re Murphy's Application* [1987] I.R. 667.

[136]   Planning and Development Act 2000 s.34(7), as amended by the Local Government Act 2001 Sch.4.

[137]   [1989] I.R. 701.

resolution. If, however, having done so they resolve to give a direction to the County Manager, I have no doubt but that the proper construction of section 4 is that he carries that out as part of his statutory duty as a mere executive duty and is not entitled, provided the resolution is valid and lawful, to exercise any separate or independent discretion as to whether or not he will obey it. If, of course, the elected members do not resolve to operate section 4 of the 1955 Act, the County Manager's duty to act in a judicial manner in considering the application for permission revives."[138]

5–56   Here it was also significant that the uncontradicted evidence pointed to the fact that the access road would have involved a material contravention of the development plan. At a minimum—and in line with the special statutory procedures envisaged by s.26(3)(c) of the Local Government (Planning and Development) Act 1963, the predecessor of s.34(6)(a) of the 2000 Act—this meant that "specific public notice of their intention to consider this resolution" should have been given. Since this had not been done, the section 4 resolution was a nullity in law. It followed that if the elected members still wished to put down such a resolution in relation to the access road, they would be required to serve a fresh notice on the Manager. The Manager would then be required to implement the special statutory procedure under s.26(3) of the 1963 Act and, once that was done, it would be open to the elected members "to consider this application anew, having served the appropriate notices and having heard and considered all matters concerning it".[139]

C. The Doctrine of Ultra Vires

The traditional ultra vires rules as applied to statutory corporations

5–57   Corporations could be created at common law by virtue of the royal prerogative, but even prior to 1922, the tendency was very much to favour the creation of corporations by statute. Nowadays, it is unlikely that any corporations can be regarded as existing on any basis other than by statute. As Art.28A of the Constitution now makes clear, local authorities exist by virtue of statute.[140]

5–58   Accordingly, prior to the enactment of the Local Government Act 1991 the doctrine of ultra vires applied quite rigidly in the case of all local authorities. This meant that enabling legislation has tended in the past to be very specific and, even after the relaxation of the ultra vires rules, the parliamentary draftsman has remained cautious. This is evident from the present law contained in ss.63 to 67 of the Local Government Act 2001 (formerly the Local Government Act 1991).

---

[138] [1989] I.R. 701 at 718. Note also the comments of O'Donnell J. to the effect that "it is difficult to pass a valid [section 140] resolution on planning matters": *Wicklow County Council v Wicklow County Manager* [2010] IESC 49.

[139] [1989] I.R. 701 at 718.

[140] Borough corporations were originally created by royal charter but their status as statutory corporations was recognised and confirmed by s.12 of the Municipal Corporations (Ireland) Act 1840. County councils and urban district councils (now town councils) were designated as statutory corporations by art.13(1) of the Local Government (Application of Enactments) Order 1898 and s.65 of the Local Government Act 1955 is to the same effect as far as Town Commissioners (now town councils) are concerned.

The incidental powers doctrine

5–59 Even before the relaxation of the ultra vires rule, express statutory authorisation was not necessary, for it was—and still is—enough if the powers in question may be necessarily inferred from the terms of the enabling statute:

> "Whatever may be fairly regarded as incidental to, or consequential upon, those things which the legislature has authorised, ought not (unless expressly prohibited) to be held by judicial construction to be *ultra vires*."[141]

5–60 Many of the reported cases turn on the question of whether the actions of the local authority may be said to be reasonably incidental to the powers expressly conferred, and a number of miscellaneous examples, many from the local government field are given in Chapter 10, Part C. One good example is provided by *Re Cook's Application*[142] which concerned the legality of certain actions taken by the Unionist majority of Belfast City Council in opposition to the Anglo-Irish Agreement of 1985. The applicants—who were Alliance Party councillors—challenged the vires of resolutions which had been passed by the Council delegating its functions to the Town Clerk and affixing a banner, bearing the legend "Belfast says No", to the City Hall. These resolutions had been passed as part of the Council's campaign against the Anglo-Irish Agreement, but this campaign, it was submitted, did not constitute a local government function and, consequently, these functions were ultra vires. Both Hutton J. and the Northern Irish Court of Appeal held, in the first instance, that the ultra vires doctrine applies, not only to the exercise of powers and the expenditure of monies by a council, but also to a council resolution.[143] However, it was held these acts were intra vires the Council because the workings of the Agreement could affect functions, such as transport, parks and recreation, which are either the functions of, or are incidental to, the functions of Belfast City Council.[144] On the other side of the line, in *Hazell v Hammersmith and Fulham Council*,[145] the House of Lords held that, where, as in this case, there had been no attempt by a local authority's financial officers to match the Council's debts and investments, the authority had, by entering into sophisticated transactions on the spot and capital markets, simply engaged in speculative trading. This was held not to be incidental to the defendant's borrowing powers, having regard, in particular, to the statutory context in which such powers operated.[146]

---

[141] *Attorney General v Great Eastern Ry Co* (1880) 5 App. Cas. 473 at 478 per Lord Selborne L.C.

[142] [1986] N.I. 242.

[143] [1986] N.I. 242 at 252.

[144] [1986] N.I. 242 at 254 and 276. But the Council was held to have acted ultra vires in other respects.

[145] [1992] 2 A.C. 1.

[146] As Lord Templeman stressed (at 31): "… a local authority is not a trading or currency or commercial operator with no limit on the method or extent of its borrowings or with powers to speculate." It may be noted that in the wake of this decision the Oireachtas enacted two statutes, Financial Transactions of Certain Companies and Other Bodies Act 1992 and the Borrowing Powers of Certain Bodies Act 1996, designed to confirm the power, subject to ministerial control, of statutory bodies to engage in interest rate swaps and other (now-standard) debt management practices. Thus, s.2(2) of the 1992 Act vests the Minister for Finance with regulatory powers to prevent essentially speculative transactions under the guise of hedging. It should be stressed that *neither* Act applies to local authorities. This exclusion was justified by the then Minster for Finance (Mr B. Ahern TD) in the case of the 1992 Act on the grounds

Relaxation of the ultra vires rule

5–61   The Local Government Act 1991,[147] which significantly reduced the rigours of the ultra vires rule, is now substantially reproduced in the Local Government Act 2001. The 2001 Act addresses the ultra vires issue in three ways. In the first place, s.66(3) deals with the objective of the action which is in question. It shifts the focus from any specific statute (or powers incidental thereto) which will usually be concerned with a relatively narrow objective and places it, instead, on the wider concept of what can appropriately be performed by the authority. Section 66(3) is as follows:

> (a) Subject to this section, a local authority may take such measures ... as it considers necessary or desirable to promote the interests of the local community.
>
> (b) For the purposes of this section a measure, activity or thing is deemed to promote the interests of the local community if it promotes, directly or indirectly, social inclusion or the social, economic, environmental, recreational, cultural, community or general development of the administrative area (or any part of it) of the local authority concerned or of the local community (or any group consisting of members of it).

5–62   Secondly, whereas s.65(1) deals with the object of a local authority's act, the other relevant provision, s.66(3)(a), is directed to the character of the permissible acts necessary to implement the object. Section 66(3) provides that:

> (a) Subject to this section, a local authority may take such measures, engage in such activities or do such things in accordance with law (including the incurring of expenditure) as it considers necessary or desirable to promote the interests of the local community.

5–63   Section 66(4) provides that, without prejudice to the generality of subs.(3) and for the purposes of giving effect to that subsection, a local authority may:

> (a) carry out and maintain works of any kind,
> (b) provide, maintain, manage, preserve or restore land, structures of any kind or facilities,
> (c) fit out, furnish or equip any building, structure or facility for particular purposes,
> (d) provide utilities, equipment or materials for particular purposes,
>   ...
>   (i)   enter into such contracts and make such other arrangements (including the incorporation of one or more than one company) as the authority considers necessary or expedient.

This battery of powers is further augmented by s.65(1) by which "[a] local authority

---

that the amount of local authority debt was relatively small and that local authorities did not engage in swaps: 424 *Dáil Debates* Col.420.
[147] Section 8(1) of the Local Government Act 1991, the predecessor to s.65(1), is "framed in extraordinarily broad and general terms": *Huntsgrove Developments Ltd v Meath CC* [1994] 2 I.L.R.M. 36 at 53 per Lardner J.

may do anything ancillary, supplementary or incidental to or consequential on or necessary to give full effect to ... a function conferred on it by this or any other enactment ...".

Rational use of resources: s.69 of the Local Government Act 2001

5–64 The third aspect of the 2001 Act introduces (or restates) some restrictions on a local authority's powers. Section 69 of the 2001 Act is a potentially highly important provision which deserves to be set out at length:

(1) Subject to *subsection (2)*, a local authority, in performing the functions conferred on it by or under any other enactment, shall have regard to —
  - (a) the resources, wherever originating, that are available or likely to be available to it for the purpose of such performance and the need to secure the most beneficial, effective and efficient use of such resources,
  - (b) the need to maintain adequately those services provided by it which it considers to be essential and, in so far as practicable, to ensure a reasonable balance is achieved, taking account of all relevant factors, between its functional programmes,
  - (c) the need for co-operation with, and the co-ordination of its activities with those of other local authorities, public authorities and bodies whose money is provided (directly or indirectly) either wholly or partly by a Minister of the Government the performance of whose functions affect or may affect the performance of those of the authority so as to ensure efficiency and economy in the performance of its functions,
  - (d) the need for consultation with other local authorities, public authorities and bodies referred to in *paragraph (c)* in appropriate cases,
  - (e) policies and objectives of the Government or any Minister of the Government in so far as they may affect or relate to its functions,[148]
  - (f) the need for a high standard of environmental and heritage protection and the need to promote sustainable development, and
  - (g) the need to promote social inclusion.
(2) A local authority shall perform those functions which it is required by law to perform and this section shall not be construed as affecting any such requirement.

5–65 This section restates or supplements the general limitations imposed by the law on judicial review. First, it provides a statutory context by reference to which the reasonableness of any local authority action or inaction may be judged. Thus, to take a particularly strong example, the effective abdication of local authority functions[149] would be plainly unreasonable in law in this particular statutory context, since any such authority would be failing to have proper regard to s.69(1)(b). Likewise, an

---

[148] A roughly analogous duty to keep itself informed of Government policies is imposed on An Bord Pleanála by s.143 of the Planning and Development Act 2000.
[149] Re Cook [1986] N.I. 242. See H & M, para.5–60.

authority which engaged in extravagant spending on entertainment[150] or which hazarded the Council's finances by excessive spending on a risky or speculative project[151] might well be said to be acting unreasonably in law by reference to s.69(1)(a).[152] Likewise, a local authority which acted in defiance of Government policy and objectives would be acting ultra vires s.69(1)(e).[153]

5–66 Secondly, s.69(1) might yet have considerable relevance for cases such as *Ward v McMaster*,[154] where a local authority had been sued in respect of the alleged negligent exercise of a statutory function. It may be that, for example, where the authority elects (assuming, of course, that it has a discretion in the matter) for policy reasons not to undertake a particular task (e.g. the inspection of a newly constructed house), it can rely on s.69(1) to justify its stance on the ground that it needs to conserve its resources in order that it may provide other, more essential services. An argument of this kind was very much visible in the slightly different context of the provision of certain services by a health board in *McC v Eastern Health Board*.[155] In this case, a dramatic and sudden rise in the number of prospective adopters of Chinese infants, coupled with a shortage of suitably trained personnel, meant that the length of time required for a statutory assessment[156] was now more than a year and half. The Supreme Court held that in the circumstances there had been no breach of a statutory duty to carry out the duty "as soon as practicable" and there is here at least a hint in the judgment of Keane J. that a statutory body is not obliged to divert resources in order to deal with sudden and unexpected demands.[157]

5–67 Finally, the language of s.69(2) indicates that s.69(1) cannot be prayed in aid to justify an authority from failing to perform its statutory duty, even if s.69(1) can assist in providing a backdrop from which it may be determined whether the body in question has abused a statutory power.

5–68 An even stricter attitude is taken towards the question of ultra vires where the authority's action involves the imposition of financial charges. If a local authority is vested with a discretionary power, then by virtue of the (rebuttable) presumption against the imposition of taxes, charges, etc it may not lawfully impose a charge as a condition of exercising that power unless this is clearly authorised by statute.[158] While the Local Government (Financial Provisions) (No. 2) Act 1983 sought to

---

[150] *R. (Bridgeman) v Drury* [1894] 2 I.R. 489.
[151] cf. the comments of Lord Templeman in *Hazell v Hammersmith and Fulham L.B.C.* [1992] 2 A.C. 1, quoted above, fn.146.
[152] Or to put it another way, an authority which did not have regard to the need for efficiency and the effective use of resources would be acting ultra vires s.69(1)(a).
[153] As in *Glencar Explorations Plc v Mayo CC* [1993] 2 I.R. 237 (mining ban included in development plan in defiance of stated Government policy). See also, *Keane v An Bord Pleanála* [1997] 1 I.L.R.M. 508 (planning authority entitled to give planning permission for the construction of large international radio mast when this project represented Government policy and was the subject of an international agreement).
[154] [1988] I.R. 337.
[155] [1996] 2 I.R. 296.
[156] Required by s.8(1)f the Adoption Act 1991 to be conducted "as soon as practicable".
[157] See also, the comments to the same effect of Keane J. in *Brady v Cavan County Council* [1999] 4 I.R. 99.
[158] *City Brick and Terra Cotta Co Ltd v Belfast Corporation* [1958] N.I. 44; *Commissioners of Customs and Excise v Cure and Deeley Ltd* [1962] 1 Q.B. 340; *McCarthy & Stone (Developments) Ltd v Richmond Upon Thames L.B.C.* [1992] 2 A.C. 48; *State (Finglas*

provide a comprehensive, contemporary legal basis for such charges, there have been quite a number of decided cases in which such service charges have been found to be ultra vires as a result of such a strict construction.[159]

5–69   In summary, therefore, the effect of the reforms effected by ss.6 and 8 of the 1991 Act and carried forward by ss.65 and 66 of the 2001 Act is, broadly speaking, that local authorities have a general competence to do things which are conducive to their statutory powers and functions, save that in doing so they may not contravene an express statutory prohibition or statutory condition.

D. THE AUDIT SYSTEM

5–70   One should note that a local authority owes a fiduciary duty to its ratepayers,[160] and it seems that a ratepayer may take judicial review to restrain proposed expenditure which is ultra vires the local authority.[161] However, there are three more specific forms of control. The longest-established of these is the power of surcharge, which because it comes last in the financial cycle, will be reached last here. The other two controls are: the requirement that each local authority prepares annual financial plans giving the public adequate information and committing the local authority to a specified pattern of expenditure; and the audit system, which operates ex post facto to expose financial irregularities and inefficiencies.

(1) Financial plans

5–71   With the enactment of the Local Government Act 2001, all local authorities must prepare annual financial plans in accordance with ministerial regulations. Sections 107 and 108 of the 2001 Act require local authorities to prepare annual financial statements at the close of each financial year. The detailed rules as to the preparation of the statements are laid down in the Local Government (Financial Procedures and Audit) Regulations 2002, which prescribe the procedures to be followed, and the Accounting Code of Practice and guidelines specified by the Department of the Environment, Heritage and Local Government, which prescribes the more technical accounting rules.

5–72   The local authority must also prepare an annual budget in advance of each financial year. The procedure here is that the manager draws up a draft budget, having consulted the Corporate Policy Group, which is then considered by the local authority at a dedicated budget meeting.[162] As seen above, the adoption of a budget is a reserved function which *must* be carried out. The local authority may

---

Industrial Estates Ltd) v Dublin County Council, unreported, Supreme Court, February 17, 1983; *BUPA (Ireland) Ltd v Health Insurance Authority* [2008] IESC 42.

[159]   See paras 5–107 to 5–110.

[160]   *Prescott v Birmingham Corporation* [1955] Ch. 210; *Bromley L.B.C. v Greater London Council* [1983] 1 A.C. 789.

[161]   *R. (Bridgeman) v Drury* [1894] 2 I.R. 489; *Arsenal F.C. v Ende* [1977] A.C. 1. But see *Weir v Fermanagh County Council* [1913] I.R. 193.

[162]   2001 Act ss.102 and 103.

126 Administrative Law

decide to amend the budget submitted to it by the Manager but it "shall" adopt a budget in the budget meeting.[163]

(2) Local government audit

5–73   The 2001 Act also established a central government agency to oversee the discharge by local authorities of their functions from a financial point of view. This is known as the Local Government Audit Service (LGAS) and its "purpose is to provide an independent appraisal of the discharge by management of [its] function[s] and to inform the public of the results of such a review".[164]

5–74   The LGAS is a unit of the Department of the Environment, Heritage and Local Government. It oversees 193 bodies throughout the State.[165] For the purposes of fulfilling its statutory functions, the Service has divided local authorities into 22 local government audit districts, grouped on a geographic basis, to each of which a local government auditor is detailed.[166] The Service as a whole is overseen by a Director of Audit. The LGAS has, as permitted by ss.117 and 118 of the 2001 Act, drawn up a Code of Audit Practice to govern the auditing of local authorities.

5–75   All those who were previously local government auditors, who are the essential elements of LGAS, retain their title in the new service.[167] All local government auditors must be members of a recognised accountancy body and despite the executive's role in their appointment, they are said to be independent:

> "While local government auditors are appointed by the Minister for the Environment, [Heritage] and Local Government and are organisationally subject to the overall control of the Minister, they are, in the performance of their professional functions, independent both of the Minister and of the bodies audited."[168]

5–76   The principal objective of the audits is "to form an opinion on whether the annual financial statement of the audited body presents fairly its financial position and its income and expenditure for the period under audit in accordance with the accounting requirements applicable to the body concerned".[169] Interestingly, the auditor's role might be said to go beyond merely overseeing the financial management of a local authority. Under the heading of "Legality", the Code of Audit Practice demands that "the local government auditor shall carry out such tests as are considered appropriate in order to be satisfied as to whether the transactions conform with the statutory or other authorisation under which they purport to be carried out".[170] The auditor may also assess the procedures put in place by local

---

[163] 2001 Act s.103(7)(a) and (7)(b).
[164] Davis, "Local Government Finance: the Financial Process" in Callanan and Keogan (eds), *Local Government in Ireland: Inside and Out* (2004), p.348; 2001 Act Pt 12.
[165] City, county, borough and town councils, regional authorities, regional assemblies, motor taxation offices and miscellaneous bodies including harbour commissioners.
[166] LGAS, *Activity Report* (2006), p.5.
[167] 2001 Act s.116(6).
[168] LGAS, *Code of Audit Practice*, p.3.
[169] LGAS, *Code of Audit Practice*, p.6.
[170] LGAS, *Code of Audit Practice*, p.18.

authorities to secure value for money, and their arrangements for internal review of these procedures.

5–77 At the conclusion of an audit, the auditor must issue an audit opinion on the local authority's financial statement and may issue an audit report.[171] The audit opinion, as to whether the statement is a fair and accurate reflection of the local authority's financial affairs, will either be qualified or unqualified. A qualified opinion will be issued wherever "there is a limitation on the scope of the audit examination, for whatever reason, or [the auditor] disagrees with the treatment or disclosure of a matter in the financial statement". The auditor should also "specify the nature of the circumstances giving rise to the qualification".[172] The auditor's power to prepare an audit report arises from "any matter or matters which come to his or her notice during the course of the audit", but it may not be issued without consultation "with the manager or chief officer ... in respect of the matters the subject of such report and shall consider and record the comments of the manager or chief officer, as the case may be, which are of material significance to such matters."[173] After the opinion and, in some cases, report have been issued, the local authority's own audit committee, which s.122 of the 2001 Act permits it to establish, may review the auditor's assessment.[174]

5–78 Recent reforms have extended the auditor's remit to include value for money audits. An administrative unit known as the Local Government (Value for Money) Unit has now been established within the Department of the Environment.[175] The unit consists of a number of departmental officials and local government auditors[176] and the Minister for the Environment may request them to carry out:

> ... a study of systems, practices and procedures (including systems, practices and procedures employed outside the State), being a study which they consider will enable them to make recommendations ... with respect to measures that could be taken to—
>> (a) secure the provision by local authorities of services in a more economical, efficient and effective manner,
>> (b) improve the manner in which the local authorities are managed.[177]

5–79 To date, the Value for Money Unit has carried out a number of studies, on topics as diverse as photocopying, water production and distribution, waste collection, advertising, performance management and internal audit:

> "These studies make a number of recommendations with regard to good

---

[171] 2001 Act s.120(1)(a) and (1)(c).

[172] LGAS, *Code of Audit Practice*, p.24.

[173] 2001 Act s.120(2)(a) and (4).

[174] The Indecon Report expressed some concern that not all local authorities had elected to establish audit committees; Indecon International Economic Consultants, *Indecon Review of Local Government Financing* (Dublin, 2005).

[175] Local Government (Financial Provisions) Act 1997 s.14(2). In fact, the unit has been operating since 1993, but s.14 establishes it on a statutory footing. See the comments of the former Minister for the Environment (Mr B. Howlin TD) 478 *Dáil Debates* Col.1021 (April 30, 1997).

[176] Local Government (Financial Provisions) Act 1997 ss.14(3),15.

[177] Local Government (Financial Provisions) Act 1997 s.14(4).

practice. Many local authorities have VFM sections, which add to and complement these studies and help introduce good practice in individual local authority sections."[178]

The VFM Unit has also drawn up a list of national performance indicators:

"... to help local authorities to determine how well they are doing in the delivery of services. The list of service indicators includes the cost of providing specific services ... measures of a local authority's efficiency ... and measures of a local authority's financial performance ... Local authorities are also expected to draw up their own local indicators to monitor their performance."[179]

(3) The power of surcharge

5–80   Section 112 of the 2001 Act provides for the imposition of surcharges on local authority members where in the exercise of a reserved function "illegal payment is to be made out of the funds of the local authority or joint body, or a deficiency or loss is likely to result in or to such funds ...". However, some of the details regarding this (rarely used) power remain in the original 19th century legislation. Section 12 of the Local Government (Ireland) Act 1871, as amended by s.4(2) of the Local Government Act 1994, entitles the auditor to raise a surcharge in respect of payments which are "contrary to law, or which he deems unfounded". The phrase "contrary to law" clearly deals with ultra vires payments,[180] but the phrase "one which he deems unfounded" has given rise to some difficulty. Is the phrase "unfounded" simply a synonym for ultra vires, or does it extend to expenditure on the part of the local authority which in the circumstances is "unnecessary and extravagant?" The weight of authority now supports the latter construction.[181]

5–81   Section 20 of the Local Government (Ireland) Act 1902 also enables the auditor to impose a charge on any member or officer of a local authority in respect of "any deficiency or loss incurred by his negligence or misconduct". It is now clear that the negligence referred to in the section is the ordinary standard of negligence applied in civil cases and that this need not involve "any element of moral culpability or gross negligence".[182]

---

[178] Davis, "Local Government Finance: the Financial Process" in Callanan and Keogan (eds), *Local Government in Ireland: Inside and Out* (2004), p.349. See most recently Value for Money Unit, LGAS, *Follow Up Report on the Development of Internal Audit in Local Authorities* (Dublin, 2006). This followed previous reports in 2000 and 2001.

[179] Davis, "Local Government Finance: the Financial Process" in Callanan and Keogan (eds), *Local Government in Ireland: Inside and Out* (2004), pp.349–350. See also, Indecon International Economic Consultants, *Indecon Review of Local Government Financing* (Dublin, 2005), pp.xv–xvi.

[180] *R. (Bridgeman) v Drury* [1894] 2 I.R. 489; *Ferguson v Moore O'Ferrall* [1903] 2 I.R. 141.

[181] *State (Raftis) v Leonard* [1960] I.R. 381.

[182] *Downey v O'Brien* [1994] 2 I.L.R.M. 130 at 136 per Costello J. In this case it had been alleged that the chairman of a harbour commissioners had negligently sold the body's shares in a joint venture company at undervalue. Costello J. said (at 136) that under s.20 of the 1902 Act the auditor was "required to consider whether the chairman ... owed a duty of care to the harbour commissioners, the nature of that duty (if it existed), whether it was breached and whether the commissioners thereby suffered loss." See *Pentecost v London District Auditor* [1951] 2 K.B. 759. Note, however, the comments of Carswell J. in *Re Baird* [1989] N.I. 56

5–82 Before the Management-system, the councillors were the persons who in law authorised expenditure. And it is the person who authorises an illegal payment who may be surcharged and consequently, formerly, it was the councillors who were surcharged. However, as a result of the establishment of the management system, it is the Manager who authorises the payment and he would have been surcharged had there been no adjustment of the law. Because of the nature of reserved functions, their exercise does not generally lead directly to expenditure, or, at any rate, the expenditure of significant sums. However, it is possible for the elected representatives to take over an executive function via a section 140 motion. Accordingly, s.112 of the 2001 Act provides that councillors who vote in favour of any reserved function (such as a section 140 motion) involving the making of an illegal payment are liable to be surcharged instead of the Manager.[183]

5–83 By virtue of s.12 of the Local Government (Ireland) Act 1871, a person aggrieved by an auditor's decision to surcharge has two distinct remedies. First, he or she may apply to the High Court for an order of statutory certiorari. The High Court's jurisdiction in such cases is—in contrast to ordinary certiorari applications—plenary in nature, and is not confined to issues of law, but can also deal with issues of fact.[184]

5–84 If the person aggrieved adopts this first alternative and the surcharge is confirmed by the High Court, then he may apply to the Minister by way of administrative appeal, who is empowered to remit the surcharge "if [he] is of opinion that the circumstances of the case make it fair and equitable that this should be done". The second alternative is that the person aggrieved may apply directly to the Minister to inquire into and to decide upon the lawfulness of the reasons stated by the auditor.[185]

5–85 Although in some respects a local government auditor may be compared to a company auditor, his functions are altogether more onerous. Although not bound by any statutory rules of procedure, he must, as already mentioned, act in an independent manner[186] and he is obliged to give all interested parties a fair hearing, and to give them an opportunity to show why they should not be surcharged.[187] The

---

at 70 that the standard of proof in surcharge cases should be "high because of the gravity of the accusation and its consequences". See also, *Lloyd v McMahon* [1987] A.C. 561; *Porter v Magill* [2001] UKHL 67; [2002] 2 A.C. 357.

[183] Section 112 of the 2001 Act also provides that in the case of an attempt to do an ultra vires action, the Manager "shall object and state the grounds of his or her objection, and, if a decision is taken on the proposal, the names of the members present and voting for and against the decision and abstaining from voting on the decision shall be recorded in the minutes of the meeting."

[184] *R. (King-Kerr) v Newell* [1903] 2 I.R. 335; *R. (Ferguson) v Moore O'Ferrall* [1903] 2 I.R. 141; *Walsh v Minister for Local Government* [1929] I.R. 377 (Murnaghan J. (*dubitante*)); *State (Raftis) v Leonard* [1960] I.R. 381. An appeal also lies (by virtue of s.12) to the Minister against the making of a surcharge.

[185] Local Government Act 1946 s.68(8).

[186] *R. (Local Government Board) v McLoughlin* [1917] 2 I.R. 174; *State (Deane and Walsh) v Moran* (1954) 88 I.L.T.R. 37.

[187] *State (Dowling) v Leonard* [1960] I.R. 421; *R. (Butler) v Browne* [1909] 2 I.R. 333; *R. (Kennedy) v Browne* [1907] 2 I.R. 505. Cf. the comments of Costello J. in *Downey v O'Brien* [1994] 2 I.L.R.M. 130 at 150 where he rejected the suggestion that the surcharge should be quashed on the ground that the auditor had failed to comply with the rules of natural justice:

auditor is entitled to take evidence on oath, and he can also compel the attendance of any person at an extraordinary audit and issue the equivalent of a *subpoena duces tecum* to that person.[188]

5–86 The 2001 Act and other reforms thus tend to mix the old with the new. The streamlined financial procedures and the new audit system are modern creatures, yet they exist side by side with the archaic surcharge provisions which date from the Victorian era and which, perhaps surprisingly, were not reformed and then re-enacted in the 2001 Act. For practical purposes, the surcharge is not of great importance, especially given the frequency and rigidity with which the new statutory controls operate, which may explain the lack of enthusiasm for updating the legislation (most of the case law being pre-Independence.) Nonetheless, it still dangles like a sword of Damocles over any councillors who might—through expediency or something worse—be tempted by illegality.

E. THE RATING SYSTEM

5–87 As has been well said:

> "Ireland has a relatively simple and flexible system compared to countries with more elaborate federal, regional and local government systems such as Germany or Italy. This is an advantage of our system. However, the financing of local government in Ireland tends to be more centralised than other countries."[189]

5–88 The annual expenditure for the local government system, in 2009, was €8.5 billion (down from €10 billion in 2007); compared with a GNP of €160 billion in 2009. Of this, €4.5 billion was revenue and the remainder capital expenditure. Until relatively recently, the rating system was the principal source of revenue for local authority expenditure and even now commercial rates account for 23 per cent of local authorities' annual current spending.[190] The other major source of local government income is the Local Government Fund established by the Local Government Act 1998. The Fund, managed and controlled by the Minister,[191] consists of an annual Exchequer grant (the original amount was £20 million, to be index linked, which in 2007 gave a figure of €550 million); which is coupled with the proceeds of motor taxation.[192] The Fund "attempts to provide higher allocations to local authorities where estimated needs are greater than estimated resources. A detailed model called the Needs and Resources Model undertakes this task based

"[The auditor] took considerable care to inform all the commissioners ... of his grave concerns at what had happened ... [H]e explained in considerable detail, what, in effect, were the complaints of wrong-doing he was advancing and that he warned each ... that the possibility of the imposition of a charge could arise. He gave to each an opportunity to answer the complaints and I fail to see how there was any unfairness in the procedures which he adopted."
[188] Local Government Act 1941 s.86.
[189] Indecon International Economic Consultants, *Indecon Review of Local Government Financing* (Dublin, 2005), p.62.
[190] Indecon International Economic Consultants, *Indecon Review of Local Government Financing* (Dublin, 2005), p.23.
[191] Local Government Act 1998 s.3(2).
[192] Local Government Act 1998 s.4.

on returns from local authorities. The effectiveness of this equalisation process is an on-going challenge".[193]

Business rates

5–89   As mentioned in Part A, traditionally the main source of a local authority's income was rates. However, a few decades ago, this source was severely restricted. First, the levying of rates on buildings used for domestic purposes was ended by the Local Government (Financial Provisions) Act 1978 (implementing a popular general election promise). Next, in *Brennan v Attorney General*,[194] the Supreme Court held that the system of collecting agricultural rates was unconstitutional. The court observed that the method of collecting rates contained in s.11 of the Local Government Act 1941 was based on the anomalous Griffiths poor law valuation of agricultural land in 1852 and that the use of such an outdated system combined with the absence of any effective review mechanism constituted, in the circumstances, an unjust attack on the plaintiff's property rights. In each case, at first, the Government compensated local authorities for the entire lost income; but, quite soon, the compensation started to reduce. The net result is that the only types of rates remaining are those on business premises. One basic point is worth mentioning: statutes imposing liability for rates are "subject to the same general principles of interpretation as a taxation or penal statute" and as such, impositions and exemptions alike must be strictly construed.[195]

Machinery and procedure

5–90   The first step in the procedures prescribed by the 2001 Act is that the Commissioner of Valuation (an official related to the Department of Finance but, by convention, independent) may, after consultation with the Minister for the Environment, direct that the property in a particular area be valued[196] and then must publish a valuation list and issue valuation certificates to the occupiers of relevant properties.[197] This power must be exercised reasonably regularly: the period of time between publications of valuation lists for a particular area must be "not less than 5 years and not more than 10 years".[198] In addition, there are two interim mechanisms for revision: an interest holder in a relevant property or an occupier of property or a rating authority can apply to the Commissioner under s.27 (as would happen, for instance, in the case of a new shop); or the Commissioner may exercise a right of appointment "of his or her own volition".[199]

5–91   The occupier of a property which is the subject of valuation or a proposed revision has the right to make representations to the revision officer (of the

---

[193] Indecon International Economic Consultants, *Indecon Review of Local Government Financing* (Dublin, 2005), p.18.
[194] [1984] I.L.R.M. 355.
[195] See, e.g. *Kinsale Yacht Club v Commissioner of Valuation* [1994] 1 I.L.R.M. 457; *Nangles Nurseries v Commissioner of Valuation* [2008] IEHC 73. See also, *Slattery v Flynn* [2002] IEHC 199; [2003] 1 I.L.R.M. 450.
[196] Valuation Act 2001 s.19.
[197] Valuation Act 2001 ss.21–24.
[198] Valuation Act 2001 s.25.
[199] Valuation Act 2001 s.28(2).

Commissioner) and the revision officer is obliged to consider these representations and may amend the valuation certification accordingly.[200] There is next a right of appeal to the Commissioner (but this time a fresh revision officer), exercisable by an occupier, a rating authority or the holder of an interest in the property, within 40 days of the impugned valuation.[201]

5–92   There is a possibility of a further appeal (again on the merits) to the Valuation Tribunal, but the right must be exercised within 28 days of the Commissioner's decision.[202] Section 35 provides that the grounds of appeal must be specified, a point emphasised by MacMenamin J. in his judgment in *Nangles Nurseries v Commissioner of Valuation*.[203] There the Tribunal had adjudicated on the question of whether a container store was a relevant property that is not rateable even though the point was not raised in the notice of appeal or the appeal hearing. Consequently, "the Tribunal fell into error" and the High Court remitted the question. The Tribunal has wide powers to amend the terms of any decision taken by the Commissioner but must make its decision within six months,[204] although one recent High Court decision described the time limit as directory rather than mandatory.[205]

5–93   An appeal lies from the Tribunal's decision, by s.39 of the 2001 Act on a point of law, by way of case stated, to the High Court, which has extensive powers "to reverse, affirm or amend the determination in respect of which the case has been stated". The High Court also has power to "remit the matter to the Tribunal with the opinion of the Court thereon, or make such other order in relation to the matter as the Court thinks fit". The Commissioner is under a duty to make amendments pursuant to decisions of the Tribunal and the superior courts[206] and has a discretion to make consequent changes to the valuation of properties similar to the one the subject of appeal.[207] The courts, however, will often defer to the decision of the Tribunal as a specialist body and will generally intervene only on the basis "of an identifiable error of law or an unsustainable finding of fact".[208]

Method of valuation

5–94   Section 48 of the Valuation Act 2001 states that the valuation of individual units of property shall be calculated "by estimating the net annual value of the property and the amount so estimated to be the net annual value of the property shall, accordingly, be its value". Net annual value is defined as:

[200] Valuation Act 2001 ss.26 and 29. It does not appear, however, that the holder of an interest in the property has a right to make representations at this stage. This may raise constitutional concerns, although the interest holder possibly would have a right to be informed and consulted, as a matter of constitutional justice. See generally, Ch.8, Part C.
[201] Valuation Act 2001 ss.30 and 31.
[202] Valuation Act 2001 s.34(2).
[203] [2008] IEHC 73 at paras 66–71. For another recent case on appeal to the tribunal, see *Cork County Council v Valuation Tribunal* [2010] 1 I.R. 57.
[204] Valuation Act 2001 s.37.
[205] *Cork County Council v Valuation Tribunal* [2007] IEHC 311.
[206] Valuation Act 2001 s.38.
[207] Valuation Act 2001 s.40.
[208] *Premier Periclase Ltd v Commissioner of Valuation*, unreported, High Court, Kelly J., February 24, 1999; *Bulmers Ltd v Commissioner of Valuation* [2008] IESC 50; [2009] 1 I.R. 503; [2009] 1 I.L.R.M. 337. For a general discussion of deference to expert bodies, see below, paras 11–123 to 11–124.

"... the rent for which, one year with another, the property might, in its actual state, be reasonably expected to let from year to year, on the assumption that the probable average annual cost of repairs, insurance and other expenses (if any) that would be necessary to maintain the property in that state, and all rates and other taxes and charges (if any) payable by or under any enactment in respect of the property, are borne by the tenant."[209]

5–95   How is the hypothetical rent to be arrived at? As a preliminary, one should note that, because of the difficulties of ensuring that the majority of valuations were up to date, which obtained prior to the passage of the Valuation Act 1988, a practice had evolved from about 1947. This practice consisted of fixing the valuation at about one-third of the net rental value and of giving revised valuations broadly in line with the general run of figures, for similar properties in the areas involved. This practice had no statutory foundation and was held to be illegal on at least two occasions[210] by the High Court. In response, s.49(1) of the Valuation Act 2001 now provides that when a valuation is revised, the "determination shall be made by reference to the values, as appearing on the valuation list relating to the same rating authority area as that property is situate in, of other properties comparable to that property".[211]

Rateable hereditaments and relevant property

5–96   Section 61 of the Poor Relief (Ireland) Act 1838 Act provides that rates are to be levied on the "occupier"[212] of "rateable hereditaments". The property must be beneficially occupied[213] and property in the occupation of the general public will, accordingly, be held not to be rateable. The word "occupier" has, however, been given a special extended meaning by virtue of ss.14 and 23 of the Local Government Act 1946 and the term now includes the owner of the building where it is unoccupied.[214] These sections also provide for rebates where the building is

---

[209] Section 50 contains an exception for "a method of valuation relying on the notional cost of constructing or providing the property ...".

[210] *Scholfield v Commissioner of Valuation*, unreported, High Court, July 24, 1972; *Munster & Leinster Bank Ltd v Commissioner of Valuation* [1979] I.L.R.M. 246.

[211] A special regime for the valuation of "public utility undertakings" exists under s.53 of the Valuation Act 2001. This provision allows the Minister to order that certain types of public utility undertakings shall henceforth be valued on a global valuation basis. Thus far, six global valuation orders have been made under the 2001 Act, against BT Ireland, O2 Ireland, Meteor Mobile Communications Limited, Vodafone Ireland, Eircom and Bord Gáis Éireann.

[212] Defined by s.124 of the 1838 Act as including "every person in the immediate use or enjoyment of any hereditaments rateable under this Act, whether corporeal or incorporeal ...". In *Dublin County Council v Westlink Toll Bridge Ltd* [1996] 1 I.R. 487 at 497, O'Flaherty J. said that the rateability attached to "the occupier of the hereditament rather than the beneficiary of the profit or use derived from the hereditament". See also, *Dublin Corporation v Dublin Cemeteries Committee*, unreported, Supreme Court, November 12, 1975.

[213] This does not mean that the occupier must derive a pecuniary benefit therefrom. In *Sinnott v Neale* (1948) Ir. Jur. Rep. 10 the owner of an uninhabited island which was used solely as a bird sanctuary was held to be in rateable occupation.

[214] The test as regards occupancy is the de facto position, and, accordingly, mere licenses or even trespassers may be liable for rates if they have the unrestricted use and enjoyment of the hereditament: see *Carroll v Mayo County Council* [1967] I.R. 364. However, in *Aer Rianta Cpt v Commissioner of Valuation*, unreported, Supreme Court, November 6, 1996, Murphy J. held that an oil company which had entered into an agreement with the Minister for Transport to manage a fuel depot at Shannon Airport as his agents were simply providing a "service

unoccupied because of the execution of repairs, alterations or additions[215] or where the owner is bona fide unable to find a tenant at a reasonable rent. The occupation of the hereditament must be permanent and not merely transitory in nature.[216] This legislation, though elderly, has not been repealed and still is the legal basis for the actual levying of rates. However, the Valuation Act 2001 provides for the valuation of relevant property.

5–97   A preliminary point of terminology bears noting. The 2001 Act provides that "relevant property" shall be rateable and that "relevant property" is to be construed in accordance with Sch.3. However, Sch.4 is a list of "relevant property" that is not rateable or, one might say, is exempt. The difficulty this formulation presents (perhaps more theoretical than practical) is that because "relevant property" is to be construed in accordance with Sch.3, the list in Sch.4 cannot be "relevant property".[217] There are thus two categories of property: relevant property that is rateable; and relevant property that is not rateable.

5–98   Schedule 3 to the 2001 Act contains a lengthy list of the properties considered to be "relevant property" and rateable. They may be rated if the property:

> (a) is occupied and the nature of that occupation *is such as to constitute rateable occupation of the property, that is to say, occupation of the nature which, under the enactments in force immediately before the commencement of this Act (whether repealed enactments or not), was a prerequisite* for the making of a rate in respect of occupied property, or (b) is unoccupied but capable of being the subject of rateable occupation by the owner of the property.[218]

5–99   As noted above, the key distinction is between relevant property that is rateable and relevant property that is not rateable.

---

function" for the depot, so that in these special circumstances they were not in rateable occupation. Note also the comments of Geoghegan J. in the High Court in *Dublin County Council v Westlink Toll Bridge Ltd* [1994] 1 I.R. 77 at 83 to the effect that the defendants were in "paramount occupation" of the rateable hereditament (a toll bridge) and not merely as an agent for the local authority "as would be so, for instance, in the case of a caretaker".

[215] This includes the demolition of the premises. See *Carlisle Trust Ltd v Commissioner of Valuation* [1965] I.R. 456.

[216] Butler (ed.), *Keane's Local Government in the Republic of Ireland* (Dublin: First Law, 2003), p.347. In *Telecom Éireann v Commissioner for Valuation* [1994] 1 I.R. 66, O'Hanlon J. said (at 71) that the "essential ingredients of rateable occupation" were that it must be: "(1) Exclusive, in the sense that the person using the hereditament can prevent any other person from using it in the same way; (2) Of value or benefit to the occupier, but not necessarily of financial benefit; (3) Not for too transient a period." While O'Hanlon J.'s conclusion in respect of the particular facts was reversed on appeal by the Supreme Court ([1998] 1 I.L.R.M. 64), the principles he enunciated remain nonetheless valid; see *Dublin County Council v Westlink Toll Bridge Ltd* [1994] 1 I.R. 77; *Iarnród Éireann v Commissioner of Valuation*, unreported, High Court, Barron J., November 27, 1992.

[217] For a wrestle with this and an apparent scrivener's error, see *Health Service Executive v Commissioner of Valuation* [2008] IEHC 178.

[218] Emphasis added.

Exemptions

5–100 The subject of rating exemption as it existed prior to the enactment of the 2001 Act was described as "one of considerable difficulty and obscurity, even by the standards of our law of local government".[219] The purpose of the Act was, amongst other things, "to re-cast or review the categories of properties *not* liable for rates, that is those which are to be exempt from liability".[220] The general principle appears to be that any ratepayer relying on an exclusion must demonstrate clearly that he comes within its terms.[221] Schedule 4 to the Act now lists 19 categories of property as being not rateable, including domestic premises and also, for example: agricultural land and farm buildings, land developed for sport, burial grounds and constituency offices of members of the Oireachtas and European Parliament. Exemptions for religious worship, charitable uses and caring for the sick, discussed below, are also retained. However, the former exemption for machinery was jettisoned: plant is now taken into account in valuation.[222]

5–101 One notable change is that the exemption for property used for "public purposes" has been removed. However, "it is still possible to discern some similar lineaments"[223] in the 2001 Act's differently crafted exemption for property "directly occupied by the State".[224] Not a great deal of case law has gathered around the 2001 exemptions[225] so it may be helpful to detail briefly previous decisions in this area.

Charitable purposes

5–102 The exemption for charitable purposes in the Valuation Act 2001 is not as convoluted as that contained in the Poor Relief Act 1838. A proviso in s.63 of the older legislation exempted buildings used "exclusively for religious worship, or for the education of the poor, cemeteries, burial grounds and hospitals or other buildings used exclusively for charitable or public purposes". However, the 2001 Act simply exempts any building occupied by "a charitable organisation that uses the land, building or part exclusively for charitable purposes and otherwise than for private profit".[226]

Service charges

5–103 By 1983, following the effective abolition of rates on domestic dwellings

[219] Keane, *Local Government in the Republic of Ireland* (Dublin: Incorporated Law Society of Ireland, 1982), p.289.
[220] *Nangles Nurseries v Commissioner of Valuation* [2008] IEHC 73 at para.12 per MacMenamin J. (emphasis in original).
[221] *Carribmolasses Ltd v Commissioner of Valuation* [1994] 3 I.R. 189; *Bulmers Ltd v Commissioner of Valuation* [2008] IESC 50; [2009] 1 I.L.R.M. 337 (semble).
[222] Valuation Act 2001 s.51(1)(a).
[223] *Health Service Executive v Commissioner of Valuation* [2008] IEHC 178 at para.67 per MacMenamin J.
[224] Valuation Act 2001 s.15(3).
[225] For a survey of the case law, see H & M. Most of the recent decisions on this point still concern the application of the old law. See, for example, *Marconi Communications Optical Network v Commissioner of Valuation* [2007] IEHC 114; *Bulmers Ltd v Commissioner of Valuation* [2008] IESC 50; [2009] 1 I.L.R.M. 337.
[226] Valuation Act 2001 Sch.4, Ref. No. 16.

and agricultural land, the financial state of so many local authorities had become so parlous that it was considered desirable that they should have the power to impose charges in respect of a diverse number of services provided by them. The Local Government (Financial Provisions) (No. 2) Act 1983[227] was designed to this end. By extending the power of local authorities to impose such charges, even though such power was not contained in the substantive statute authorising the service, it was intended to restore some measure of fiscal autonomy to local government. However, the charges have proved to be controversial, and this legislation was never really regarded as an adequate substitute for some proper form of local taxation. Originally, the making of service charges was an executive function for the Manager. This was itself unusual given the usual distinction between the Manager and the councillors and suggests that it was anticipated that service charges would be unpopular with the people whom the councillors represented. However, by virtue of the County Management (Reserved Functions) Order 1985,[228] the making of domestic service charges was made a matter for the elected representatives.

5–104   Section 2(1) is the key section of the 1983 Act. It provides that:

> … any existing enactment which requires or enables a local authority to provide a service but which, apart from this subsection, does not empower the authority to charge for the provision of the service shall be deemed so to empower that authority.

5–105   Section 3 provides that the amount of such charges shall be such as "the authority considers appropriate", and further states that the charge shall be paid by the occupier (unless the premises is not owned by a local authority and comprise more than one dwelling, when the owner shall be liable).

5–106   Ministerial control is provided for under s.4. The Minister is empowered to exclude certain classes of services from the scope of section 2 charges, but no such order appears to have been made to date. However, s.5 empowers a local authority via the Manager (since this is an executive function) to waive "all or portion of a charge" if it is satisfied that "it is appropriate to do so on the ground of personal hardship", a power which has been extensively used to exempt, for example, the old and the unemployed.[229]

---

[227]   Historically, an inequitable division prevailed as between the urban and rural dwellers. Section 65A of the Public Health (Ireland) Act 1878 (as inserted by s.7 of the Local Government (Sanitary Services) Act 1962) provided for the payment of water charges by (essentially) rural consumers. But this obligation was later extended to all consumers by s.8 of the Local Government (Financial Provisions) (No. 2) Act 1983, although the decision whether to levy such charges rested with the local authority. By virtue of the Local Government (Delimitation of Water Supply Disconnection Powers) Act 1995, the right of local authorities to withdraw supply in respect of defaulting consumers was itself terminated (unless a court order was obtained).

[228]   S.I. No. 341 of 1985.

[229]   Any doubt about the power of local authorities to charge for services that they are required or enabled by statute to provide was removed by the Local Government (Financial Provisions) Act 2000. Confusion had arisen because the 1983 Act only made provision for the levying of charges under statutes that pre-dated the 1983 Act, a restriction removed by the 2000 Act. The latter Act however does not have any similar saving effect for post-2000 enactments and, as a consequence, a power to levy charges in respect of certain services which a local authority is authorised or required to provide must be specified in all post-2000 enactments. Accordingly,

5-107   The validity of the imposition of service charges has been challenged in a series of cases, all of which illustrate the principle that, as the 1983 Act is, in effect, a taxing statute, it must be strictly construed. *Athlone U.D.C. v Gavin*[230] concerned the validity of a charge of £60 levied on every domestic dwelling for water, refuse and sewage services for a particular year. Finlay C.J. held that the charge was invalid in that s.2(1) of the 1983 Act conferred a power to make a charge for a single service and could not, said Finlay C.J., be construed "as enabling a local authority to fix a single charge for a number of services".[231]

5-108   Finally, s.8 amends the provisions of s.65A of the Public Health (Ireland) Act 1878 and allows for the imposition of water charges. These are made payable on an instalment basis and the strict construction approach was continued in *Dublin Corporation v Ashley*.[232] Here the local authority had sought to impose water charges payable on demand and not on instalment, as contemplated by these statutory provisions. Finlay C.J. said that the word "instalment" when applied to payment meant "part of the payment and could not be construed as the entire of it". Accordingly, the County Manager had acted ultra vires in seeking to provide for the fixing of a charge "payable in one single amount".[233] Water charges have always been especially unpopular and, as a result of the Local Government (Financial Provisions) Act 1997 s.12(2), the right to impose water charges in respect of any domestic dwellings have now been terminated. The Indecon Report on local government finance shied away from recommending domestic water charges, although it did recommend charges in respect of non-principal private residences.[234]

5-109   A more recent controversy has been over the imposition of charges for refuse collection. The question of waste collection service charges arose in *O'Connell v Cork Corporation*.[235] Here the local authority had introduced a "sticker system" according to which adhesive labels would be supplied to persons who had paid the requisite fee for waste collection. The adhesive labels were to be placed on the person's bin. Any bin presented for collection which did not have a sticker would not be collected. The applicant alleged that the system breached s.33 of the Waste Management Act 1996, which obliged the local authority to "collect, or arrange for the collection of, household waste within its functional area" unless certain limited exceptions applied. Under s.35, however, the local authority was permitted to enact bye-laws "regarding the presentation of waste for collection" and to refuse to collect waste if these were not complied with. The Supreme Court held that the "sticker system" did not fall within the power to make bye-laws on the presentation of waste. Geoghegan J. noted in particular that s.35 was quite specific as to the

---

the Waste Management Act 1996 s.75, as inserted by the Protection of the Environment Act 2003 s.52, provides that "a local authority may make a charge in respect of the provision of any waste service by, or on behalf of, that authority".

[230] [1985] I.R. 434.

[231] [1985] I.R. 434 at 442. See also, *O'Donnell v Dún Laoghaire Corporation (No. 1)* [1991] I.L.R.M. 301 (where orders which failed to specify the dates on which instalment payments were to be made were held to be invalid).

[232] [1986] I.R. 781.

[233] [1986] I.R. 781 at 786.

[234] Indecon International Economic Consultants, *Indecon Review of Local Government Financing* (Dublin, 2005), pp.183–186.

[235] [2001] IESC 89; [2001] 3 I.R. 602.

content of such bye-laws. They were to pertain to the types of waste that might be presented for collection; precautions to be taken prior to presenting particular types of waste for collection; the size, colour and shape of bins; the location where waste could be presented for collection; and the time of collections:

> "It was never intended that the power to make bye-laws, the breach of which would exempt the corporation could include a so-called presentation type bye-law the substantive purpose of which was to facilitate the collection of charges."[236]

The outcome, then, was that local authorities could not refuse to collect waste from households that had not paid the prescribed fees, although they would be able to pursue the householders through the ordinary means of debt collection. However, this decision was overturned by subsequent legislation. The Protection of the Environment Act 2003 inserted a new s.33(6) into the Waste Management Act 1996, providing that the statutory duty to collect waste lapses where a person has not paid a prescribed charge.

5–110 An intriguing recent case is *Rossborough v Cork City Council*,[237] where the essential point of contention was that the local authority had changed from a weekly to a fortnightly bin collection but the householder was not informed of the change prior to paying an annual charge for what she thought was a weekly collection. Accordingly, she made a claim in contract in the Small Claims Court seeking repayment of half the sum of money she had paid for the waste collection services. Clarke J. noted that while public bodies may in many cases be under a statutory duty to perform a particular function, the existence of a duty did not per se rule out the possibility of a contractual agreement being reached between such a public body and an individual citizen. In this instance, however, Clarke J. held that there was no contract ("the statute contemplates the possibility of a local authority entering into contracts with those who might collect waste on its behalf, but not with householders within its functional area, whose waste might be collected"),[238] and the limited cases in the area pointed to the same conclusion. Clarke J. did suggest, obiter, that if such a contract existed for the provision of service for, say, one year it might not have been permissible for the respondent to vary the level or intensity of provision during the course of that year; but in the absence of a contract, this observation did not avail the householder in the present case.

F. Planning Control

5–111 Although the legislation for planning control[239] has been in existence in

---

[236] [2001] 3 I.R. 602 at 621.
[237] [2008] IEHC 94; [2008] 4 I.R. 572.
[238] [2008] IEHC 94 at para.6.6.
[239] See generally, the comprehensive discussions in Simons, *Planning and Development Law*, 2nd edn (Dublin: Thomson Round Hall, 2007); Scannell, *Environmental and Land Use Law* (Dublin: Thomson Round Hall, 2006); Dodd, *Planning Regulations 2001–2005: Annotated and Consolidated* (Dublin: Thomson Round Hall, 2005); and Scannell, "The Catastrophic Failure of the Planning System" (2011) 33 D.U.L.J. 303. The last publication (which is informed by the fact that the author is both a scholar and a practitioner in the field) is an excellent,

Ireland since 1934,[240] it was not until the coming into force of the Local Government (Planning and Development) Act 1963 that a comprehensive scheme of planning control or licensing[241] was established. Local authorities were designated by this Act as planning authorities for their functional area,[242] and were now obliged to produce, and regularly to update, a development plan. Furthermore, enforcement powers and the power to restrain unauthorised developments were greatly increased.

5–112   But even this legislation proved to be defective in a number of important respects. An appeal lay to the Minister for Local Government, who in practice was susceptible to local political pressures[243] and who often granted permissions which materially contravened the development plan.[244] Moreover, the enforcement powers, while frequently utilised, proved cumbersome in dealing with the growing problem of unauthorised developments. The Local Government (Planning and Development) Act 1976 sought to deal with these problems. It transferred the Minister's appellate functions to an independent tribunal, known as An Bord Pleanála. In addition, the enforcement controls were strengthened, and the Act envisaged a greater role for third-party objectors. Further detailed changes were made both to the planning process and to An Bord Pleanála by legislation enacted in 1982,[245] 1983,[246] 1992[247] and 1993,[248] the frequency of which statutes indicates

---

though depressing account, covering all relevant areas, including: drafting and accessibility of legislation; administration (by local planning authorities and An Bord Pleanála); performance of elected members; and planning gain.

[240] Town and Regional Planning Act 1934; Town and Regional Planning (Amendment) Act 1939. For an account of this legislation (which was repealed in its entirety in 1963) see Miley and King, *Town and Regional Planning in Ireland* (Dublin: Incorporated Law Society of Ireland, 1951).

[241] For licensing in general, see Ch.7.

[242] Local Government (Planning and Development) Act 1963 (the "1963 Act") s.2(2).

[243] This was held to be ultra vires by the Supreme Court in *State (Pine Valley Developments Ltd) v Dublin County Council* [1984] I.R. 407. This decision was reversed by the Local Government (Planning and Development) Act 1982 s.6 but ministerial involvement in the planning process is now circumscribed by s.30 of the Planning and Development Act 2000, which forbids the Minister from exercising "any power or control in relation to any particular [planning] case …". Any such involvement would probably constitute a breach of art.6 of the European Convention on Human Rights which requires decisions affecting "civil rights and obligations" to be taken by an "independent and impartial tribunal". See *R. (Alconbury) v Secretary of State for the Environment* [2001] 2 All E.R. 925. In addition, art.10a of the EIA Directive (Directive 85/337, as amended) requires, inter alia, that a decision to grant a "development consent" (i.e. in an Irish context, planning permission) must be subject to a review procedure, which may either be a court of law or an independent and impartial tribunal. In *Cairde Chill an Disirt Teo v An Bord Pleanála* [2009] IEHC 76; [2009] 2 I.L.R.M. 89, Cooke J. observed (at para.33) that the Board undoubtedly satisfied this requirement of impartiality.

[244] Compare the comments of Henchy J. in *State (Pine Valley Developments Ltd) v Dublin County Council* [1984] I.R. 407 at 425.

[245] Local Government (Planning and Development) Act 1982.

[246] Local Government (Planning and Development) Act 1983. This Act aimed to augment the impartiality of the Board and to reduce political interference with its operations. See Stevenson, "Planning Appeals in the Republic of Ireland" (1985) 7 *Urban Law and Policy* 170.

[247] Local Government (Planning and Development) Act 1992. This effected a number of miscellaneous changes, including inserting important provisions concerning An Bord Pleanála's procedures, the method of challenging the validity of planning decisions and a new version of the planning injunction powers.

[248] Local Government (Planning and Development) Act 1993. This was enacted in the wake of the Supreme Court's decision in *Howard v Commissioners of Public Works* [1994] 1 I.R. 101 and subjected State authorities to the ordinary planning process.

the legal, commercial and political sensitivity of this area, as does the plethora of case law. The law in this area is now governed, however, by the comprehensive Planning and Development Act 2000 and the Regulations promulgated thereunder, together with the Planning and Development (Strategic Infrastructure) Act 2006 and a further amending Act in 2010.

5–113   While undoubtedly the most important function of a planning authority—the granting or refusing of planning permission—is an executive function, which is vested in the City or County Manager, nevertheless the elected representatives do have an important say in the planning process. It is the task of the local councillors to make a development plan,[249] and they may also revoke or modify a planning permission although this power may now only be exercised where "the development ... no longer conforms with the provisions of the development plan".[250] In addition, the councillors may declare any particular area to be one of special amenity.[251]

The development plan

5–114   A development plan drawn up by a local authority must "set out an overall strategy for the proper planning and sustainable development" of the area,[252] and follow certain objectives. The objectives listed in s.10(2) of the 2000 Act are:

 (a)   the zoning of particular areas for particular purposes;
 (b)   the provision of facilities for transport, energy and communications, water supplies, waste recovery and disposal and waste water services;
 (c)   the conservation and protection of the environment;
 (d)   the integration of planning and sustainable development with the social, community and cultural requirements of the area and its population;
 (e)   the preservation of the character of the landscape;
 (f)   the protection of structures of special architectural, historical, archaeological, artistic, cultural, scientific, social or technical interest;
 (g)   the preservation of the character of architectural conservation areas;
 (h)   the development and renewal of areas in need of regeneration;
 (i)   the provision of accommodation for the travelling community ...

5–115   In addition, without prejudice to these objectives, Sch.1 to the 2000 Act contains further legitimate objectives grouped under five headings: Location and Pattern of Development; Control of Areas and Structures; Community Facilities; Environment and Amenities; and Infrastructure and Transport.[253]

---

[249] Section 9(1) of the 2000 Act requires a development plan to be adopted. Section 12(6) provides that this is a reserved function. While the making of the development plan is, of course, subject to judicial review, the courts "must be very slow to interfere with the democratic decision of any local, elected representatives entrusted with making such decisions by the legislature": *Malahide Community Council Ltd v Fingal County Council* [1997] 3 I.R. 383 at 397 per Lynch J.
[250] 2000 Act s.44.
[251] 2000 Act s.202.
[252] 2000 Act s.10(1). See also, Department of the Environment, *Sustainable Development: a Strategy for Ireland* (Dublin, 1997).
[253] See generally, Department of the Environment, Heritage and Local Government, *Development Plans: Guidelines for Planning Authorities* (Dublin, 2007), pp.16–55.

5–116 Given the complexities of modern governance, no planning authority is an island and a number of provisions provide for co-operation between planning authorities.[254] In addition, Pt 2, Ch.IV of the 2000 Act also makes provision for ministerial involvement in the making of the plan. The Minister may issue general guidelines and, more broadly, issue policy directives[255] (although, as we saw above, the Minister is precluded from involvement in individual planning decisions[256]). Again, if the Minister considers that any draft development plan or development plan:

> ... fails to set out an overall strategy for the proper planning and sustainable development of the area of a planning authority or otherwise significantly fails to comply with [the] Act, the Minister may, for stated reasons, direct the authority to take such specified measures as he or she may require to ensure ... compliance ...[257]

5–117 The accommodation of regional and local influences is covered at paras 5–123 to 5–126.

Making the development plan

5–118 The 2000 Act introduced a new framework for the making of development plans.[258] Section 9 requires that a development plan be produced by a planning authority every six years. A number of features are of particular interest:

(i) The possibility of extending the time period for review by ministerial order, provided for by previous legislation,[259] no longer exists:

> Not later than 4 years after the making of a development plan, a planning authority shall give notice of its intention to review its existing development plan and to prepare a new development plan.[260]

Such notice must be widely circulated to public bodies and local authorities and published in one or more newspapers which circulate in the area to which the development plan relates. A period of at least eight weeks must then be allowed for consultation and the planning authority is obliged to hold public meetings and seek written submissions on the development plan; it may also invite oral submissions.[261] Pursuant

---

[254] 2000 Act ss.9, 27 and 34(2).

[255] See, e.g. Department of the Environment, Heritage and Local Government, *Development Management: Guidelines for Planning Authorities* (Dublin, 2007). But these guidelines cannot change the law and any decision based on an erroneous statement of the law contained therein may be quashed as a result: see *Sherwin v An Bord Pleanála* [2007] IEHC 227; [2008] 1 I.R. 561 at 580 per Edwards J.

[256] 2000 Act s.30.

[257] 2000 Act s.31.

[258] For an excellent diagram of the plan making procedure, see Department of the Environment, Heritage and Local Government, *Development Plans: Guidelines for Planning Authorities* (Dublin, 2007), pp.61–63.

[259] See *Blessington Heritage Trust v Wicklow County Council* [1998] IEHC 8; [1999] 4 I.R. 571.

[260] 2000 Act s.11.

[261] 2000 Act s.11(3).

to this reform, "[p]eople now have the opportunity to be proactive by making positive contributions to the preparation of the plan instead of being confined to the reactive submission of objections to the draft plan when published [as was the previous position]".[262]

(ii) The Manager must then prepare a report with his response to the submissions or observations which report is then submitted to the elected members. The planning authority may then issue directions to the Manager after the submission of the Manager's report. Then the Manager must prepare a draft development plan.[263]

(iii) The draft plan is to be put on public display, with strict time periods also applying. Once again, a period within which observations and submissions can be received is provided for and the Manager must prepare a report on any observations and submissions. The level of detail required in such a report was considered by the High Court in *Sandyford Environmental Planning and Road Safety Group v Dún Laoghaire–Rathdown County Council*.[264] Here the Manager had distilled the 71 observations received into bullet points under five headings. No individual entry ran for more than three lines. In addition, the Manager had responded in general, rather than specific, terms to the observations. The applicant alleged, in particular, that the entirety of the observations should have been circulated to the elected members and that the summaries of the observations were inadequate. McKechnie J. held that a general duty to circulate all observations would run counter to the plain language of the statute, which envisages only a summary of the observations being made available. The method of summary here was acceptable because the Manager "is not bound to use any formula or follow any specified method. There is within the section scope for a variety of presentations, some of which by choice may be far more extensive than others."[265] As to the legal effect of the draft development plan, Peart J. suggested in *Ebonwood Ltd v Meath County Council*[266] that the participatory process would be compromised if considerations not part of the adopted development plan could be taken into account in determining whether to grant planning permission.

(iv) The elected members must then, having considered the draft development plan and the Manager's report, amend or accept a development plan.[267]

---

[262] Grist, "Planning" in Callanan and Keogan (eds), *Local Government in Ireland: Inside and Out* (2004), p.229. According to departmental guidelines, "consultation should reach out to those whose views may not have been canvassed in the past, and not just to those who have traditionally participated in the process"; Department of the Environment, Heritage and Local Government, *Development Plans: Guidelines for Planning Authorities* (Dublin, 2007), p.4. The undoubted emphasis on public participation in the planning process in the 2000 Act may not be motivated simply by republican idealism. In *Central Dublin Development Association v Attorney General* (1975) 109 I.L.T.R. 69, Kenny J. accepted (at 90) that development plans were not unconstitutional, because "[a] plan of development for each city and town is necessary for the common good".

[263] 2000 Act s.11(4) and (5).

[264] [2004] IEHC 133. The report considered here concerned a proposed variation of a development plan but the statutory provisions pertaining to reports on the preparation, adoption and variation of a development plan are the same in all relevant respects.

[265] [2004] IEHC 133 at para.53.

[266] [2004] 3 I.R. 34; [2004] 1 I.L.R.M. 305.

[267] 2000 Act s.12(6).

However, if an amendment would constitute a "material alteration" of the draft, a further period of public notice and comment applies, at the end of which the elected members shall make the plan with or without the proposed amendment, although on this occasion they may make further modifications to the amendment without the need for further consultation.[268] Procrastination, from the elected members' point of view, would be foolish; if no development plan has been made within two years of the initial giving of notice, the Manager shall complete the plan-making process (albeit including any components already accepted by the members).[269] A failure to comply with the statutory timetable does not mean that a development plan will be void,[270] but may allow a court to issue an order of mandamus against a non-compliant planning authority.[271]

(v) Within two years after the adoption of a development plan, the Manager is required to issue a report to the planning authority on the progress made in securing the plan's objectives.[272] (It has been suggested[273] that this entire procedure is overly rigid and does not take account of the differences between small and large planning authorities.)

5–119 The planning authority is, first, bound by the terms of the development plan, and secondly, is not entitled to grant a permission which materially contravenes the terms of the development plan (although as we saw at paras 5–53 to 5–54 it may in certain circumstances override these restrictions). The development plan was described by McCarthy J., speaking generally, as:

"… an environmental contract between the planning authority, the Council and the community, embodying a promise by the Council that it will regulate private development in a manner consistent with the objectives stated in the plan, and, further the Council itself shall not effect any development which contravenes the plan materially."[274]

5–120 This is a matter which was considered by O'Hanlon J. in *O'Leary v Dublin County Council*,[275] where the issue was whether the respondents were entitled to provide a halting site for members of the travelling community in a location which had been designated as an area of high amenity in the development plan.

---

[268] 2000 Act s.12(6).

[269] 2000 Act s.12(14).

[270] 2000 Act s.12(16), as amended by Planning and Development (Amendment) Act 2002 s.7.

[271] Simons, *Planning and Development Law*, 2nd edn (2007), p.33. In a High Court case under the previous legislation, McGuinness J. held that the time-limit provisions were mandatory in character and quashed an amendment to a development plan because it was adopted outside the time limit: see *Blessington Heritage Trust v Wicklow County Council* [1998] IEHC 8; [1999] 4 I.R. 571.

[272] 2000 Act s.15(2).

[273] Grist, "Planning" in Callanan and Keogan (eds), *Local Government in Ireland: Inside and Out* (2004), pp.229–230.

[274] *Attorney General (McGarry) v Sligo Corporation* [1991] 1 I.R. 99 at 113.

[275] [1988] I.R. 150. For similar cases, see *Grange Developments Ltd v Dublin County Council* [1986] I.R. 246; *Roughan v Clare County Council* [1989] I.R. 701; *Byrne v Fingal County Council* [2001] 4 I.R. 565 at 583; [2002] 2 I.L.R.M. 321. See generally, Simons, "Travellers: Planning Issues" (1997) 4(1) I.P.E.L.J. 8 and "Unauthorised Travellers' Halting Sites" (1997) 4(2) I.P.E.L.J. 53.

O'Hanlon J. accepted that this proposal constituted a material contravention of the development plan and observed that the "praiseworthy motives of the County Council" were not sufficient to absolve them from compliance with the planning law. He added that:

> "I think that the requirements of the planning law have to be applied with the same stringency against the local authority, in this case, as would be the case if the proposal came from a private developer."[276]

5–121 In a more recent case involving traveller accommodation, however, there was found to be no material contravention. In *Byrne v Fingal County Council*[277] the relevant development plan provided for the provision of accommodation for travellers, but also undertook "to follow a consultation procedure with the Travelling Community and with the local community in the neighbourhood of any such proposed site". Here the planning authority had effectively taken the decision before it met with the local community. McKechnie J. held that a failure to consult could never amount to a material contravention. Nevertheless, on the facts of the case, carrying out the consultation was a "condition precedent" and the proposed development could not proceed until the consultation had been completed.[278]

5–122 Even though a local authority is absolutely bound by the terms of its own development plan, the elected members are entitled to grant a permission which effects a material contravention of the plan following the passing of a special resolution to that effect.[279] It follows naturally that the Manager can also be required to grant planning permission if directed by a valid resolution under s.140 of the Local Government Act 2001, where the proposed development would not materially contravene the development plan.

Regional planning guidelines

5–123 Planning authorities do not make development plans in a vacuum. For one thing, as noted above, a planning authority must:

> … have regard to the development plans of adjoining planning authorities and shall co-ordinate the objectives in the development plan with the objectives in the plans of those authorities except where the planning authority considers it to be inappropriate or not feasible to do so.[280]

---

[276] [1988] I.R. 150 at 154. For criticism of what is alleged to be "judicial radicalism", see Simons, *Planning and Development Law*, 2nd edn (2007), pp 7–8. Simons describes this view as a "private-sector comparator test … [which] came close to open defiance of the statutory provision which exempted local authority development from the requirement to obtain planning permission".

[277] [2001] IEHC 141; [2001] 4 I.R. 565; [2002] 2 I.L.R.M. 321.

[278] [2001] 4 I.R. 565 at 583.

[279] In addition, An Bord Pleanála is entitled to grant a planning permission which materially contravenes the terms of the development plan in certain defined circumstances: see Planning and Development Act 2000 s.37(2).

[280] 2000 Act s.9(4). In addition, s.9(5) states that the likely effect of the development plan on adjoining planning authorities is a relevant consideration in the making of a development plan. See also, Planning and Development (Regional Planning Guidelines) Regulations 2003

5–124   More generally, the eight regional authorities established in 1994[281] have the power under s.21 of the 2000 Act to make regional planning guidelines (either after consultation with affected planning authorities or when directed to do so by the Minister), either for the region as a whole or parts of the region. They are directed to take a longer-term view than planning authorities: s.23 of the 2000 Act defines their goal as "to provide a long-term strategic planning framework for the development of the region" within a timeframe of 10 to 20 years, though the framework must be reviewed every six years.[282] They must also consider the National Spatial Strategy.[283] To some extent the factors to be taken into account here overlap with those to be taken into account by planning authorities in the preparation of development plans, but with the significant addition of projected population trends and settlement and housing strategies; economic and employment trends; and the location of industrial and commercial development.[284]

Local area plans

5–125   The 2000 Act also permits a planning authority to adopt local area plans "for any particular area within its functional area …".[285] But in the case of towns with a population in excess of 2,000 the planning authority must make a local area plan in respect of the town.[286] The plan is to consist of a written statement of objectives for the area and may include objectives for zoning.[287] The particular focus of local area plans is to assist "those areas which require economic, physical and social renewal and [those] areas likely to be subject to large scale development within the lifetime of the plan",[288] a focus which may be bolstered by ministerial regulations requiring that local area plans "be prepared in respect of certain classes of areas or in certain circumstances …".[289] The planning authority is obliged to consult with local residents, public sector agencies, NGOs, local community groups and commercial and business interests before preparing, amending or revoking a local area plan.[290] A further indication of the importance placed on public participation in the planning process by the 2000 Act is a provision allowing planning authorities to "enter into an arrangement with any suitably qualified person or local community group for the preparation, or the carrying out of any aspect of the preparation, of a local area plan".[291] Obviously, a local area plan must comply with the provisions

---

(S.I. No. 175 of 2003); Department of the Environment, Heritage and Local Government, *Implementing Regional Planning Guidelines: Best Practice Guidance* (Dublin, 2005).

[281]   The power to establish such authorities is contained in s.43 of the Local Government Act 1991. See Local Government Act 1991 (Regional Authorities) (Establishment) Order 1993 (S.I. No. 394 of 1993).

[282]   Planning and Development Act 2000 s.26.

[283]   Planning and Development (Regional Planning Guidelines) Regulations 2003 (S.I. No. 175 of 2003) art.7(3)(c).

[284]   2000 Act s.23(2).

[285]   2000 Act s.18(1).

[286]   2000 Act s.19(1)(b).

[287]   2000 Act s.19(2), as substituted by the Planning and Development (Amendment) Act 2002 s.8.

[288]   2000 Act s.19(1)(a).

[289]   2000 Act s.19(3).

[290]   2000 Act s.20(1).

[291]   2000 Act s.18(6).

of the governing development plan.[292] In line with this, it lapses if it becomes inconsistent, by virtue of the variation of a development plan.[293]

5–126   In summary:

"New frameworks for planning at national, regional, county and city levels have been provided with the National Spatial Strategy, Regional Planning Guidelines and the revised arrangements for preparing development plans under the provisions of the Planning and Development Act 2000. However, to be effective each layer of the planning system must reinforce and support the others. Development plans should take on board and implement relevant national and regional policies in a manner consistent with the NSS and regional guidelines if the planning system as a whole is to function effectively. Similarly, good development plans will inform policies at regional and national level. It is intended that guidance will also be prepared for planning authorities on Local Area Plans which will complete the suite of guidance for each layer in the planning framework."[294]

Planning permission and planning conditions

5–127   The major provision governing the grant of planning permission is s.34 of the 2000 Act, which provides that when an application is made, the local planning authority may decide to grant permission "subject to or without conditions, or to refuse it." The provision continues:

(2)(a) When making its decision ... the planning authority shall be restricted to considering the proper planning and sustainable development of the area, regard being had to—
  (i)   the provisions of the development plan,
  (ii) the provisions of any special amenity order relating to the area ...
  (iv) where relevant, the policy of the government, the Minister [for Environment, Community and Local Government]
  (v)   any matter referred to in *subsection (4)* ...

5–128   In a most important provision, the section goes on to amplify the last mentioned item. Section 34(4) states that, without prejudice to the generality of s.34(1) (which states that "the authority may decide to grant the permission subject to or without conditions"), the conditions attached may include "all or any" of a list of specified conditions[295]:

---

[292] 2000 Act s.19(2), as amended by the Planning and Development (Amendment) Act 2002 s.8.
[293] 2000 Act s.18(4)(b).
[294] Department of the Environment, Heritage and Local Government, *Development Plans: Guidelines for Planning Authorities* (Dublin, 2007), p.3.
[295] Simons, *Planning and Development Law*, 2nd edn (2007), pp.193–195 suggests that conditions should generally meet five criteria: first, "a condition should be relevant to planning and, in particular, to the permitted development"; secondly, "a condition must be precise"; thirdly, "a condition must not be unreasonable" and in particular "a condition should not seek to extract an unauthorised 'planning gain' from the developer"; fourthly, "in practice a planning permission will often contain conditions requiring certain matters to be attended to 'prior to commencement of development'"; and finally, "where an activity is subject to licensing ... a

(4) Conditions under subsection (1) may ... include all or any of the following—

    (a) conditions for regulating the development or use of any land which adjoins, abuts or is adjacent to the land to be developed and which is under the control of the applicant, so far as appears to the planning authority to be expedient for the purposes of or in connection with the development authorised by the permission;

    (b) conditions for requiring the carrying out of works (including the provision of facilities) which the planning authority considers are required for the purposes of the development authorised by the permission;

    (c) conditions for requiring the taking of measures to reduce or prevent—

        i. the emission of any noise or vibration from any structure or site comprised in the development authorised by the permission which might give reasonable cause for annoyance either to persons in any premises in the neighbourhood of the development or to persons lawfully using any public place in that neighbourhood, or

        ii. the intrusion of any noise or vibration which might give reasonable cause for annoyance to any person lawfully occupying any such structure or site;

    (d) conditions for requiring provision of open spaces;

    (e) conditions for requiring the planting, maintenance and replacement of trees, shrubs or other plants or the landscaping of structures or other land;

    (f) conditions for requiring the satisfactory completion within a specified period, not being less than 2 years from the commencement of any works, of the proposed development (including any roads, open spaces, car parks, sewers, watermains or drains or other public facilities), where the development includes the construction of 2 or more houses;

    (g) conditions for requiring the giving of adequate security for satisfactory completion of the proposed development ...

5–129 The planning authority may not invoke s.34(1) as a justification for the imposition of a more restrictive condition where such a condition would come within the scope of, but ultimately not be permitted under, one of the subparagraphs of s.34(4). As Hardiman J. commented in *Ashbourne Holdings Ltd v An Bord Pleanála*[296]:

"[I]f ... a particular condition is within the scope of one of [the] subparagraphs but does not meet its requirements, it would appear to contradict the

---

planning authority and An Bord Pleanála are expressly precluded from imposing conditions which are for the purposes of controlling emissions ...". See also, Scannell, *Environmental and Land Use Law* (2006), pp.169–174. On the statutory conditions permitted to be imposed by the 2000 Act, see Simons, *Planning and Development Law* (2007), pp.196–213. On "planning gain", see *Ashbourne Holdings Ltd v An Bord Pleanála* [2003] IESC 18; [2003] 2 I.R. 114.
[296] [2003] IESC 18; [2003] 2 I.R. 114.

intendment of [section 34(1)] to permit the condition to be imposed under the authority of general words."[297]

5-130   Moreover, continuing on a theme of requiring that the power to impose conditions be strictly construed, Hardiman J. held that the advantage aimed to be achieved by the imposition of a condition "must be to the proposed development and not to any wider area".[298] The planning authority is required to give reasons in respect of each condition imposed.[299] The authority may provide by condition that certain "points of detail" (typically matters such as contributions and detailed technical matters) are to be agreed subsequently between the developer and the authority.[300] However, principles of legal certainty[301] require that the authority must nonetheless "lay down criteria by which the developer and the planning authority can reach agreement".[302]

5-131   The discretionary power to refuse or to attach conditions is, of course, governed by ordinary principles of administrative law. The conditions imposed must fairly and reasonably relate to the proposed development, and the reasons given in support of the condition must be capable of justifying the imposition of the condition.[303] Not only that, but the courts will quash the decision to attach conditions—even where the conditions are valid on their face—where it has been

---

[297]   [2003] 2 I.R. 114 at 127.

[298]   [2003] 2 I.R. 114 at 129.

[299]   2000 Act s.34(10)(a). The object of this provision is to enable the applicant to obtain "such information as may be necessary and appropriate for him firstly to consider whether he has got a reasonable chance of succeeding in appealing against the decision of the planning authority and, secondly, to enable him to arm himself for the hearing of such appeal"; *State (Sweeney) v Minister for the Environment* [1979] I.L.R.M. 35 at 37 per Finlay P. In *O'Donoghue v An Bord Pleanála* [1991] I.L.R.M. 750, Murphy J. said (at 757): "It is clear that the reason given by the [Board] must be sufficient first to enable the courts to review it and, secondly, to satisfy the persons having recourse to the tribunal that it has directed its mind adequately to the issue before it. It has never been suggested that an administrative body is bound to provide a discursive judgment as a result of its deliberations, but on the other hand the need for providing the grounds of the decision ... could not be satisfied by recourse to an uninformative, if technically correct, formula. For example, it could hardly be regarded as acceptable for the [Board] to reverse a decision of a planning authority stating only that 'they considered the application to accord with the proper planning and development of the area of the authority.'" For the issue of the general duty of an administrative body to give reasons, see Ch.14, Part D.

[300]   2000 Act s.34(5).

[301]   The conditions must not be so vague as would effectively frustrate a third party's right of appeal. Thus, as Blayney J. said in *Boland v An Bord Pleanála* [1996] 3 I.R. 435 at 472, conditions which were expressed to be subject to the agreement of the developer and the planning authority must be such that having regard to "very detailed instructions set out in the conditions", no member of the public "could reasonably have objected to them" and so the Board in imposing conditions in this form could not thus be said to be "interfering with or prejudicing any right of the public".

[302]   *Boland v An Bord Pleanála* [1996] 3 I.R. 435 at 467 per Hamilton C.J. In both *Boland* and *McNamara v An Bord Pleanála* [1996] 2 I.L.R.M. 339, conditions of this kind were upheld on the ground that in each case they left matters of technical detail to be agreed, subject to criteria specified in the condition itself. This approach was foreshadowed by the judgment of Murphy J. in *Houlihan v An Bord Pleanála*, unreported, High Court, October 4, 1993 where on the facts one of the conditions concerning effluent discharge was held to be ultra vires as delegating too wide a discretion to the planning authority. See also, *Kenny v Dublin City Council (No. 3)* [2009] IESC 19.

[303]   *Killiney and Ballybrack Residents Association Ltd v Minister for Local Government (No. 2)*

shown that the decision has been actuated by improper motives, or that the planning authority has rejected legitimate considerations, or has introduced irrelevant considerations, or has otherwise manifested unreasonableness in arriving at its decision[304] or if the conditions are void for uncertainty.[305] In addition, the courts may quash a condition which disproportionately interferes with private rights of the developer.[306]

5–132 The question of fair procedures and constitutional justice, which is central to the planning process, is considered elsewhere.[307]

Default permission

5–133 An applicant may also obtain planning permission in default. Section 34(8)(f) of the 2000 Act applies where an application has been made to a planning authority in accordance with the regulations for the time being in force,[308] and no decision has been made within the appropriate period (which starts at the date of application and runs for eight weeks).[309] If these conditions are satisfied, a decision by the planning authority to grant permission shall be regarded as having been granted on the last day of the period. It is of some practical significance that if the planning authority requires the developer to provide further information on a number of specified grounds, the time limit is extended.[310] The purpose of these default provisions may be said to be to compel the planning authority to direct its mind to the planning application and to adjudicate upon such application within the appropriate period.[311]

[1978] I.L.R.M. 78; *Ashbourne Holdings Ltd v An Bord Pleanála* [2003] IESC 18; [2003] 2 I.R. 114.

[304] *State (Fitzgerald) v An Bord Pleanála* [1985] I.L.R.M. 117; *P&F Sharpe Ltd v Dublin County Council* [1989] I.R. 701; *Flanagan v Galway County Council* [1990] 2 I.R. 66; *Kenny Homes & Co Ltd v Galway City and County Manager* [1995] 1 I.R. 178.

[305] *Irish Asphalt Ltd v An Bord Pleanála*, unreported, High Court, Costello P., July 28, 1995.

[306] *In re Part V of the Planning and Development Bill, 1999* [2000] IESC 20; [2000] 2 I.R. 321; [2001] 1 I.L.R.M. 81. See also, *McDonagh & Sons Ltd v Galway Corporation* [1995] 1 I.R. 191; *State (O'Hara and McGuinness) v An Bord Pleanála*, unreported, High Court, May 8, 1986.

[307] See below, para.12–14.

[308] The following are the regulations currently in force: Planning and Development Regulations 2001 (S.I. No. 600 of 2001), as amended by Planning and Development Regulations 2002 (S.I. No. 70 of 2002); Planning and Development (No. 2) Regulations 2002 (S.I. No. 149 of 2002); Planning and Development Regulations 2003 (S.I. No. 90 of 2003); Planning and Development (Strategic Environmental Assessment) Regulations 2004 (S.I. No. 436 of 2004); European Communities (Environmental Assessment of Certain Plans and Programmes) Regulations 2004 (S.I. No. 435 of 2004); Planning and Development Regulations 2005 (S.I. No. 364 of 2005); Planning and Development Regulations 2006 (S.I. No. 685 of 2006); Planning and Development Regulations 2007 (S.I. No. 83 of 2007); Planning and Development (No. 2) Regulations 2007 (S.I. No. 135 of 2007); Planning and Development Regulations 2008 (S.I. No. 235 of 2008); Planning and Development (Amendment) Regulations 2008 (S.I. No. 256 of 2008).

[309] 2000 Act s.34(8) and (9).

[310] 2000 Act s.34(8) and (9).

[311] *Mulloy v Dublin City Council* [1990] 1 I.R. 90 at 97 per Blayney J. Simons, *Planning and Development Law*, 2nd edn (2007), p.895, suggests that the default planning permission procedure constitutes a breach of arts 6 and 8 and the First Protocol of the European Convention on Human Rights. This presupposes, however, that the default grant of a planning permission

5–134   It is now clear that even a decision which is ultra vires (and thus liable to be set aside as a nullity) is still a "decision" for the purposes of s.34(8)(f), and thus the applicant cannot claim that "no decision" has been given in such a case and that he is consequently entitled to permission in default.[312] Moreover, a default permission cannot arise where this would result in the obtaining of a permission which would contravene the terms of the development plan[313] or would be otherwise ultra vires.[314]

5–135   The system of default planning permission has also been the subject of some judicial criticism.[315] While there also have been some judicial indications in the past that the entitlement to default permission should be strictly interpreted in view of its potential unsatisfactory consequences,[316] the better view would appear to be that it would be inappropriate for the courts to widen the restrictions beyond the circumstances of either "material non-contravention or something so close to that as to be required to be treated in the same way",[317] a point recently confirmed by the Supreme Court.[318] It remains a very doubtful question, however, whether the present system could ever be applied to an application for permission which is subject to the requirements of the Environment Impact Assessment Directive 85/337, since it is necessarily implicit in the Directive that each such application will be considered on its merits by the planning authority.[319]

5–136   In situations where there is a grant of planning permission but it is claimed (perhaps in enforcement proceedings) that the developer has exceeded its terms, a great deal turns on the interpretation of its wording. It is beyond the scope of this work to go into the particular decisions on this sort of point. However, one should note the general principle that a planning permission is a public document which is not personal to the grantee, but rather enures for the benefit of the land. It follows:

---

amounts to the determination of "civil rights and obligations" for the purposes of art.6(1) ECHR.

[312]   *State (Abenglen Properties Ltd) v Dublin Corporation* [1984] I.R. 381.

[313]   *Calor Teo v Sligo County Council* [1991] 2 I.R. 267 (no default permission as proposed development would have constituted a fire hazard in contravention of the terms of the development plan); *Walsh v Kildare County Council* [2000] IEHC 103; [2001] 1 I.R. 483 (no default permission as proposed housing would have involved a material non-compliance with waste disposal requirements of development plan); *Maye v Sligo County Council* [2007] IEHC 146; [2007] 4 I.R. 678 (similar principle).

[314]   See, e.g. *Abbeydrive Development Ltd v Kildare County Council (No. 2)* [2010] IESC 8.

[315]   See, e.g. the comments of Blayney J. in *Molloy v Dublin County Council* [1990] 1 I.R. 90 at 97; but note the comments of Clarke J. in *Maye v Sligo Borough Council* [2007] 4 I.R. 678 at 682.

[316]   See, e.g. *McGovern v Dublin Corporation* [1999] 2 I.L.R.M. 314 at 319 per Barr J.

[317]   *Maye v Sligo Borough Council* [2007] 4 I.R. 678 at 693 per Clarke J.

[318]   *Abbeydrive Ltd v Kildare County Council (No. 1)* [2009] IESC 56; [2010] 1 I.L.R.M. 187. Here Fennelly J. acknowledged that while the default system might lead to "inappropriate results" by reason of, inter alia, the inability of the planning authority to impose appropriate conditions on the grant of permission, it was nevertheless ([2010] 1 I.L.R.M. 187 at 194) "a legislative provision to which, where its conditions have been satisfied, the courts have a duty to give effect."

[319]   See, e.g. the comments of Kearns P. in *Abbeydrive Development Ltd v Kildare County Council (No. 2)* [2010] IESC 8 and see further, *Commission v Belgium* (C-320/00) [2001] E.C.R. I-4591 and Scannell, *Environmental and Law Use Law* (2006), p.183.

"... as a consequence that a planning permission is to be interpreted objectively, and not in the light of subjective conditions peculiar to the applicant or those responsible for the grant of planning permission. A planning permission is to be given its ordinary meaning as it would be understood by members of the public without legal training, as well as by developers and their agents, unless such documents, read as a whole, necessarily indicate some other meaning."[320]

5–137 But while purely subjective interpretations of the permission are precluded, some flexibility in terms of departure from the literal words are permitted where the permission is "unclear, ambiguous or contradictory".[321] Likewise, minor and de minimis deviations from the terms of a permission which are not material are permissible,[322] as are planning conditions which allow the fine details of plans, drawings and other elements to be approved by the planning authority.[323]

An Bord Pleanála

5–138 An applicant or any person who made written observations or submissions in relation to the application may, on payment of a fee, appeal against the decision of the planning authority to An Bord Pleanála.[324]

5–139 The Board must in most cases determine appeals according to the same considerations that planning authorities are permitted to take into account.[325] The Board is also under a general obligation to take account of the policy of the Government, the Minister, state authorities and planning authorities.[326] In addition, if the planning authority refused permission on the basis that the permission would amount to a material contravention, the Board may grant permission but only on

---

[320] Simons, *Planning and Development Law*, 2nd edn (2007), p.217 and quoted by approval by Fennelly J. in *Kenny v Dublin City Council (No. 3)* [2009] IESC 19. See also, *Readymix (Eire) Ltd v Dublin City Council*, unreported, Supreme Court, June 30, 1974 and *Gregory v Dun Laoghaire Rathdown County Council*, unreported, Supreme Court, July 28, 1997.

[321] *Kenny v Dublin City Council (No. 3)* [2009] IESC 19 at para.34 per Fennelly J. See also, *Gregory v Dun Laoghaire Rathdown County Council*, unreported, Supreme Court, July 28, 1997.

[322] As Fennelly J. observed in *Kenny v Dublin City Council (No. 3)* [2009] IESC 19 at paras 19–20: "There will inevitably be small departures from some or even many of the plans and drawings in every development ... It seems improbable that any development is ever carried out in exact and literal compliance with the terms of the plans and drawings lodged. If there are material departures from the terms of a permission, there are enforcement procedures. However, planning laws are not intended to make life impossible for developers, for those executing works such as architects, engineers, contractors or for the planning authorities in supervising them."

[323] *Boland v An Bord Pleanála* [1996] 3 I.R. 435; *Kenny v Dublin City Council (No. 3)* [2009] IESC 19.

[324] 2000 Act s.37(1). So also may a neighbour, though if not involved at the local planning authority stage; but only where the neighbour can demonstrate that the planning permission, as granted, differed materially from the planning permission as sought because of conditions imposed by the planning authority: s.37(6) of 2000 Act.

[325] 2000 Act s.37(1)(b).

[326] 2000 Act s.143.

specified grounds.[327] The Board is required to act judicially and several of the cases considered in later chapters have the planning process as their subject matter.[328]

5–140   The procedures governing planning appeals are contained in Pt VI, Ch.3 of the 2000 Act.[329] The Board has a discretion to hold an oral hearing of an appeal[330] which, in practice, is sparingly exercised. Section 129 prescribes the procedures to be followed in respect of submissions and observations by other parties; s.130 deals with submissions and observations by persons other than parties[331]; and s.131 enables the Board to request submissions or observations. Next, s.132(1) deals with the power of the Board to require the submission of documents:

> Where the Board is of opinion that any document, particulars or other information may be necessary for the purpose of enabling it to determine an appeal or referral, the Board may, in its absolute discretion, serve on any party, or on any person who has made submissions or observations to the Board in relation to the appeal or referral, as appropriate, a notice under this section—
>> (a) requiring that person … to submit to the Board such document, particulars or other information as is specified in the notice, and
>> (b) stating that, in default of compliance with the requirements of the notice, the Board will, after the expiration of the period so specified and without further notice to the person … dismiss or otherwise determine the appeal or referral.

5–141   These procedures also recognise the need for speedy decision-making and administrative finality. Thus, s.126 imposes a duty on the Board "to ensure that appeals … are disposed of as expeditiously as may be" and normally within 18 weeks. This period may be modified in certain specified circumstances.[332] Notice is required to inform the parties of the reasons for the delay. Again in favour of finality (and also here procedural fairness), s.127(3) prohibits any appellant or person making the referral from elaborating upon the grounds of appeal or referral.[333]

5–142   The Board is also entitled to refer any point of law to the High Court for determination.[334] As a general rule, a party aggrieved by a planning decision should first exhaust his appellate remedies by appealing to An Bord Pleanála. However,

---

[327] 2000 Act s.37(2)(b).
[328] See, e.g. *O'Keefe v An Bord Pleanála* [1993] 1 I.R. 39 and *Ashbourne Holdings Ltd v An Bord Pleanála* [2003] IESC 18; [2003] 2 I.R. 114.
[329] Special procedures apply in respect of developments "of strategic economic or social importance to the State or the region in which it would be situate" or which would contribute to the fulfilment of the National Spatial Strategy or any regional planning guidelines or which would have a significant effect on the area of more than one planning authority: 2000 Act s.37A et seq as inserted by the Planning and Development (Strategic Infrastructure) Act 2006 s.3.
[330] 2000 Act s.134.
[331] Thus curing the striking anomaly disclosed in *State (Haverty) v An Bord Pleanála* [1987] I.R. 485.
[332] 2000 Act s.126(3)(a), (4) and (5).
[333] Section 129(4) of the 2000 Act contains a provision analogous to s.127(3) in the case of submissions made by persons other than parties to the appeal.
[334] 2000 Act s.50, as amended by the Planning and Development (Strategic Infrastructure) Act 2006 s.13.

where the applicant wishes to impugn the vires of a planning decision, it may be that he may now apply directly to the High Court for judicial review of that decision at least in certain circumstances.[335]

Enforcement

5–143 The planning code may be enforced in a number of ways between which there is substantial overlap as regards the situations to which they apply:

Criminal sanction

5–144 By virtue of s.151 of the 2000 Act a person who carries out any development in respect of which permission is required without or in contravention of such permission (known as "unauthorised development") is guilty of an offence. The prosecution may proceed summarily or by way of an indictment.[336]

Enforcement notice

5–145 The planning authority may choose to take the less drastic step of issuing an enforcement notice if a development is being carried out in the absence of planning permission, or contrary to the requirements of conditions attached to the permission. Save for exceptional cases,[337] a warning letter must be issued prior to an enforcement notice. A warning letter can come to be issued in two ways. First, if the planning authority, acting *sua sponte*, takes the view that land is being, is likely to be, or may have been developed in an unauthorised manner. Secondly, if a representation which is not frivolous or vexatious is made in writing to the planning authority.[338] Thus the planning authority has, in fact, very little discretion to refuse to issue a warning letter where complaints are made by third parties. But "[t]he actual legal effect of a warning letter is minimal."[339] It merely triggers the procedure under s.153 of the 2000 Act under which the planning authority considers whether to issue an enforcement notice. This decision must be taken "as soon as may be after the issue of a warning letter".[340]

5–146 The enforcement notice[341] shall, in cases where no planning permission has been granted, order work to cease (or not to commence); shall, in cases where planning permission has been granted, order work to conform to the permission; and, in either case, may "require ... within a specified period ... where appropriate,

[335] See, e.g. *P&F Sharpe Ltd v Dublin City and County Manager* [1989] I.R. 701; *Tennyson v Dún Laoghaire Corporation* [1991] 2 I.R. 527. But there may well be cases where the real issue concerns planning merits and where the courts will defer to An Bord Pleanála (if an appeal is pending), even if the judicial review of the planning authority's initial decision also raises issues of law. See *Healy v Dublin County Council*, unreported, High Court, April 28, 1993.
[336] 2000 Act ss.156(1) and 157. The maximum penalty prescribed here is a fine of approximately €12 million plus two years' imprisonment, together with a maximum daily fine of IR£10,000 in respect of each continuing offence. Although, see also, s.32 which may create a separate offence; Simons, *Planning and Development Law*, 2nd edn (2007), pp.302–303.
[337] 2000 Act s.155.
[338] 2000 Act s.152.
[339] Simons, *Planning and Development Law*, 2nd edn (2007), p.291.
[340] 2000 Act s.153(1).
[341] 2000 Act s.154.

the removal, demolition or alteration of any structure and the discontinuance of any use and, in so far as is practicable, the restoration of the land to its condition prior to the commencement of the development".[342] If the steps specified in the notice have not been taken within six months (or a specified shorter period), the planning authority itself may enter on the land and demolish any unauthorised structures and restore the land to its previous condition.[343] In *Dundalk Town Council v Lawlor*,[344] the High Court decided that the provisions pertaining to the content of the notice had not been complied with. O'Neill J. held that because failure to comply with an enforcement notice is a criminal offence, the requirements contained in an enforcement notice must be stated clearly and precisely. Here, in the first place, a time period "immediately commencing on the date of the service of this notice" was inadequate because it failed to specify an end to the time period within which works could be completed. Thus there was no "specified period" as required by s.154(5)(b). Secondly, an obligation to "[c]ease all excavation site clearance works and return site to its previous condition" was also deficient in that it did not contain any detail as to whether, for example, the topsoil and sod which had been removed—thus giving rise to the issuing of the enforcement notice—should have been replaced.[345]

Section 160 planning injunction

5–147   The planning injunction is undoubtedly the most effective method of ensuring compliance with the planning code. Section 160 of the 2000 Act[346] authorises the High Court or Circuit Court to restrain unauthorised development of land and to ensure "so far as practicable" that the land "is restored to its condition prior to the commencement of any unauthorised development ...". However, in practice, the Circuit Court is not much used because of an assumption that there would usually be an appeal from the Circuit to the High Court so: why not start in the High Court?

5–148   Section 160(1) expressly provides that an applicant need not satisfy ordinary locus standi requirements:

> "We are all, as users and enjoyers of the environment in which we live, given a standing to go to the Court and to seek an order compelling those who have been given a development permission to carry out the development

[342] 2000 Act s.154(5).
[343] 2000 Act s.154(6).
[344] [2005] IEHC 73; [2005] 2 I.L.R.M. 106.
[345] Simons, *Planning and Development Law*, 2nd edn (2007), pp.299–300 suggests that the enforcement notice mechanism is in breach of the European Convention on Human Rights. In the first place the absence of an appeal and procedural safeguards from the planning authority's decision to issue an enforcement notice breaches art.6 and the restrictions on judicial review in this context mean that the breach cannot be cured. Secondly, the interference with individual property rights protected by the First Protocol is disproportionate. Also, in some cases, art.8's protection of the family home might be unjustifiably infringed. One of the key components of Simons' argument is the presence of confusion as to whether notice can be served if the development is, despite the absence of permission, unobjectionable. This, he suggests (at p.302), leaves an administrative decision-maker with an over-broad discretion which may also violate the Constitution.
[346] See generally, Scannell, *Environmental and Land Use Law* (2006), pp.240–244; Simons, *Planning and Development Law*, 2nd edn (Dublin: Thomson Round Hall, 2007), pp.306–337.

in accordance with the terms of that permission. And the Court is given a discretion sufficiently wide to make whatever order is necessary to achieve that objective."[347]

5–149   An applicant under s.160 has thus no obligation to show that he or she has suffered any damage beyond that which all citizens suffer once the planning legislation has been breached and public amenities thereby impaired.[348] In *Leen v Aer Rianta Cpt*[349] it was not relevant to the issue of standing that the applicant's true motivation in seeking the injunction seemed to be to prevent the use of Shannon Airport by the United States military.[350] The new legislative formulation:

"... [brought] coherence to the planning injunction remedy ... Under the new section [160], the court can issue a planning injunction even where a development for which the required permission obtained is not being worked on. Moreover, the anomaly whereby a person carrying out development without permission was in a better position than a person who obtained a permission but was not carrying out the development in accordance [therewith] is now reformed."[351]

5–150   Section 160(1) expressly permits an injunction to be granted against an anticipatory breach.[352] Section 160(2), moreover, allows the court to "order the carrying out of any works, including the restoration, reconstruction, removal, demolition or alteration of any structure or other feature". It has been said that it would require "exceptional circumstances" for the court to refrain from exercising its powers under this section,[353] but it is clear that in the final analysis the court has something approximating to the traditional equitable discretion to issue or not to issue an injunction.[354]

---

[347]   *Morris v Garvey* [1983] I.R. 319 at 323 per Henchy J., discussing the predecessor to this provision.

[348]   *Avenue Properties Ltd v Farrell Homes Ltd* [1982] I.L.R.M. 21. A competitor would also appear to have sufficient standing to seek such relief: *Robinson v Chariot Inns Ltd* [1986] I.L.R.M. 621.

[349]   [2003] IEHC 101; [2003] 4 I.R. 394.

[350]   Although the section 160 procedure is a highly successful innovatory feature, first introduced by the Local Government (Planning and Development) Act 1976, the rather lax language of the original section gave rise to certain anomalies. See, e.g. *Dublin City Council v Kirby* [1985] I.L.R.M. 325; *Loughnane v Hogan* [1987] I.R. 322.

[351]   Cooney, (1992) I.C.L.S.A. at 14-01 and 14-21 to 14-22.

[352]   See *Ampleforth Ltd v Cherating Ltd* [2003] IESC 27. In effect, s.160 reverses *Mahon v Butler* [1997] 3 I.R. 369; [1998] 1 I.L.R.M. 284.

[353]   *Stafford and Bates v Roadstone Ltd* [1980] I.L.R.M. 1; *Morris v Garvey* [1983] I.R. 319.

[354]   See, e.g. *Cork County Council v Cliftonhall Ltd* [2001] IEHC 85; *Grimes v Punchestown Development Ltd* [2002] IESC 79; [2002] 1 I.L.R.M. 409; *Leen v Aer Rianta Cpt* [2003] IEHC 101; [2003] 4 I.R. 394. Scannell, *Environmental and Land Use Law* (2006), pp.242–244 lists the following factors as likely to influence the court in exercising its discretion: the technicality or triviality of the breach; the impact of the unauthorised development on the applicant; the hardship to the developer; the conduct of the developer; the conduct of the applicant; the public interest; the attitude of the planning authority; the extent to which European Law is involved; and whether the order would pre-determine the issue. See also, Simons, *Planning and Development Law*, 2nd edn (2007), pp.324–334; Keeling, "Defending Section 160 Planning Injunctions" (2004) 11 I.P.E.L.J. 54; and Cooney, "Judicial Discretion and the Planning Injunction" in Breen, Kerr and Casey (eds), *Liber Memoralis* (Dublin: Round Hall Sweet & Maxwell, 2001).

CHAPTER 6

TRIBUNALS

A. Introduction

If the reader wishes to get a flavour of typical tribunals in operation, they should consult Part D of this chapter on Social Welfare Appeals or Chapter 5, Part G on An Bord Pleanála.

6–01   One may begin an explanation of the nature of tribunals[1] by listing a few examples (most of which are considered further below). First, in the fields of (broadly speaking) liberty, there are the Mental Health Tribunals,[2] which adjudicate on involuntary detention, and the Refugee Appeals Tribunal[3] (hearing appeals from the Refugee Applications Commissioner).[4] Secondly, for taxation and compulsory acquisition, there are: Appeal Commissioners[5]; the Valuation Tribunal[6]; and arbitrators appointed by the Land Values Reference Committee under various statutes to fix compensation for land compulsorily acquired.[7] Tribunals which resolve disputes arising from the running of the welfare state include the appeals officers in the Department of Social Protection. In the information/privacy areas, there are the Information Commissioner[8] and the Data Protection Commissioner[9] and in the broad criminal justice field, there are the Criminal Injuries Compensation

---

[1]   See generally, O'Toole and Dooney, *Irish Government Today* (Dublin: Gill and Macmillan, 2009), Ch.9 and Grogan, *Administrative Tribunals in the Public Service* (Dublin: IPA, 1961).
[2]   Mental Health Act 2001 Pt III.
[3]   Refugee Act 1996 s.15, as amended by the Immigration Act 1999 s.11.
[4]   Refugee Act 1996 s.6.
[5]   Taxes Consolidation Act 1997 s.850 and Pt 40.
[6]   Valuation Act 2001 s.12.
[7]   Acquisition of Land (Assessment of Compensation) Act 1919, as amended by Acquisition of Land (Reference Committee) Act 1925.
[8]   Freedom of Information Act 1997 Pt IV.
[9]   The Data Protection Act 1988 s.9 and Sch.2, examined in Clark, *Data Protection Law in Ireland* (Dublin: Round Hall Press, 1990), Ch.8.

Tribunal,[10] the Garda Síochána Ombudsman Commission,[11] the Parole Board,[12] and the Legal Aid Board.[13] Other tribunals exist to discipline employees in the public service, for instance the Gardaí[14] and members of the defence forces.[15] Note too, the Prisoners Appeals Tribunal,[16] which deals with prison discipline.

6–02 But probably the largest number of tribunals have been set up to control and regulate, whether at first instance or appellate stage, various types of commercial-financial businesses in the public interest. The administrative technique by which these controls are implemented is often by way of a licensing system, a subject which is covered in more detail in Chapter 7. These include: the Private Security Authority and the Private Security Appeals Board[17]; the Irish Film Classification Office (formerly the Censorship of Films Board)[18]; An Bord Pleanála[19]; the Mining Board[20]; and the Bookmakers Appeal Committee.[21] In addition, there are a number of bodies established in the past decade and known collectively as "regulators". Each of these includes the function of a licensing tribunal but goes beyond this in that it has functions in the field of general surveillance and standards setting. This group comprises Commissions for Energy, Aviation, and Communications Regulation.[22] Then there are the Broadcasting Authority of Ireland[23]; the Competition Authority[24];

[10] *Scheme of Compensation for Personal Injuries Criminally Inflicted* (1974) (Prl. 3658). See Osborough, "The Work of the Criminal Injuries Compensation Tribunal" (1978) 13 Ir. Jur. (N.s) 320.
[11] Garda Síochána Act 2005. It is curious that the term "Ombudsman" was chosen, in view of the fact that in its powers and procedures, the Commission is more of a tribunal than an Ombudsman. This is a testament to the popularity of the brand.
[12] Established on an administrative basis in 2001 (replacing the Sentence Review Group). See *Annual Report of the Parole Board 2002* (2003), pp.4–6.
[13] Civil Legal Act 1995 s.3; *Scheme of Legal Aid and Advice* (1979, Prl. 8534), pp.7–11. For an analysis of the state of affairs prior to the establishment of the Board on a statutory footing, see Whyte, "And Justice for Some" (1984) 6 D.U.L.J. (N.s) 88.
[14] Garda Síochána Act 2005. This was preceded by the disciplinary mechanism established by the Garda Síochána (Discipline) Regulations 1989 (S.I. No. 94 of 1989) and the Garda Síochána (Complaints) Act 1986; for the latter see the 2nd edition of this book, pp.230–231.
[15] Defence Act 1954 ss.178, 179; Rules of Procedure (Defence Forces) 1954 (S.I. No. 243 of 1954) r.6.
[16] Prisons Act 2007 Pt 3.
[17] The Private Security Services Act 2004 Pts 2–5 and Schs 1and 2.
[18] Censorship of Films Act 1923 s.1. See also, Video Recordings Act 1989 s.10 (covering censorship of video/DVD recordings) as amended by the Civil Law (Miscellaneous Provisions) Act 2008. See too, Censorship of Publications Act 1946 s.2. Nowadays the Censorship of Publications Board is rarely used.
[19] Planning and Development Act 2000 Pt VI. See Stevenson, "Planning Appeals in the Republic of Ireland" (1985) 7 *Urban Law and Policy* 170.
[20] Minerals Development Act 1940 s.33.
[21] This Committee is chaired by a judge or practising barrister or solicitor of at least seven years' standing and it hears appeals from the Irish Horseracing Authority in relation to course betting permits and course-betting representative permits: see Irish Horseracing Industry Act 1994 Pt VI.
[22] Electricity Regulation Act 1999; Energy (Miscellaneous Provisions) Act 2006; Aviation Regulation Act 2001 s.10; Communications Regulation Act 2002 s.13. On these regulators, see H & M, Ch.6, Part E.
[23] Broadcasting Act 2009.
[24] Competition Act 2002.

the Director of Corporate Enforcement[25]; and the National Transport Authority[26] (regulation of both taxis and buses). The most significant member of this group was formerly known as the Irish Financial Services Regulatory Authority, but following the banking collapse of 2008–2009, it was recast as the Central Bank of Ireland Commission.[27]

6–03   As can be seen from the previous paragraphs, the majority of the tribunals operate in the field of public law, assisting in the dirigiste and welfare aspects of the State's responsibilities. However, when creating a statutory innovation in the private law area, the Oireachtas sometimes choose to vest responsibility for implementing the scheme in a tribunal, rather than a court. Examples include: An Bord Uchtála[28]; the Labour Court[29]; the Employment Appeals Tribunal[30]; the Equality Authority[31]; the Rent Tribunal[32]; the Pensions Tribunal[33]; the Controller of Patents, Designs and Trade Marks[34]; and the Irish Takeover Panel.[35] Most radically, the Private Residential Tenancies Board has been established to take over the administration of the law in relation to residential tenancies, which had been vested in the courts since tenancies developed six centuries ago.[36]

6–04   A further anomaly is that, while most tribunals have been established by statute, others—for instance, the Criminal Injuries Compensation Tribunal, the Motor Insurers' Bureau of Ireland and the (former) Stardust Compensation Scheme—are established merely by administrative scheme. The extra-statutory character of these tribunals does not, however, preclude judicial review of their decisions. This question was raised in *State (Hayes) v Criminal Injuries Compensation Tribunal*,[37] where Finlay P. held that the High Court would review a decision of the tribunal in appropriate cases, such as where the principles of constitutional justice had been violated, or where the scheme of compensation had been misinterpreted.[38]

---

[25]   The Company Law Enforcement Act 2001.
[26]   Taxi Regulation Act 2003 s.10, as amended by the Public Transport Regulation Act 2009 Pt 4.
[27]   The Central Bank and Financial Services Authority of Ireland Act 2003.
[28]   Adoption Act 1952 s.8.
[29]   Industrial Relations Act 1946 s.10(1). This is one of the provisions of the original Act still retained.
[30]   Redundancy Payments Act 1967 s.39, as amended by s.1 of the Unfair Dismissals Act 1977. The Employment Appeals Tribunal has replaced the former Redundancy Payments Tribunals which had been established under the 1967 Act.
[31]   See Employment Equality Act 1998, renaming the Employment Equality Agency as the Equality Authority.
[32]   Housing (Private Rented Dwellings) (Amendment) Act 1983 ss.2–4. For an account of the procedure in the Rent Tribunal, see de Blacam, *The Control of Private Rented Dwellings* (Dublin: Round Hall Press, 1984), pp.55–62.
[33]   Pensions Act 1990 Pt II.
[34]   Patents Act 1992 s.6.
[35]   The Irish Takeover Panel Act 1997 includes many state-of-the-art features of an administrative agency, e.g. the panel is constituted as a company (s.3); it makes some of its own substantive rules (like a US administrative agency) (s.8); it may act on its own initiative or at the request of a party to a takeover (s.10).
[36]   Residential Tenancies Act 2004 Pt VIII.
[37]   [1982] I.L.R.M. 210.
[38]   See also, *Ryan v Compensation Tribunal* [1997] 1 I.L.R.M. 194 (Hepatitis C Tribunal).

6–05   We ought to mention here a sub-group which are sometimes called (in a further example of the vague terminology endemic in this field) "domestic tribunals". Any profession, trade union, organisation or even club may have rules for dealing itself with the discipline of its own members. Quite often, in the interest of fairness, a domestic tribunal will be set up to apply these disciplinary rules so as to determine whether the member is guilty of some transgression, and if so, what the punishment should be. In some cases the rules will be statutory in origin. Examples are those relating to the legal, medical and dental professions and most recently, veterinary practice and a dozen or so professions falling within the aegis of the Health and Social Care Professionals Council.[39] In other cases, the basis of the tribunal's authority is not statute but the agreement of their members. Notable examples include trade unions[40] and sports associations, like the GAA.[41] In either category, the tribunal will certainly be subject to some, if not all, of the substantive principles of judicial review, though they may have to be invoked by way of plenary proceedings rather than an application for judicial review.[42] The rationale for this intervention is almost certainly that, while these bodies may not be formally or completely "public" in nature, they make such a crucial impact on their members and on the rest of the community that their affairs warrant the attention of the court. In *Abbott v Sullivan*,[43] Denning L.J. said of trade union committees:

> "These bodies, which exercise a monopoly in an important sphere of human activity, with the power of depriving a man of his livelihood, must act in accordance with the elementary rules of justice. They must not condemn a man without giving him an opportunity to be heard in his own defence: and any agreement or practice to the contrary would be invalid."[44]

6–06   Although Denning L.J. was in dissent, it is these views which represent the modern law.[45] However, notwithstanding this principle, in practice, a court will sometimes resile from interfering in certain cases with the internal affairs of a tribunal whose authority derives from contract.[46]

6–07   As with Cleopatra, so with tribunals: "[a]ge cannot wither them nor custom stale their infinite variety." This lack of uniformity extends even to the nomenclature. Not only do the names of tribunals differ: "board", "commission", "tribunal", "officer", "registrar", "controller", "referee" and "umpire" have each been used for different tribunals; in addition, various titles have been used for the entire species. Thus one finds tribunals described as administrative tribunals, special tribunals,

---

[39]   See respectively, Solicitors (Amendment) Act 1960 Pt II (as amended by the Solicitors (Amendment) Act 1994); Medical Practitioners Act 2007 Pts VII and VIII; Dentists Act 1985 Pt II; Veterinary Practice Act 2005 Pt VII; Health and Social Care Professionals Act 2005.

[40]   See Kerr and Whyte, *Irish Trade Union Law* (Professional Books, 1985), pp.100–102.

[41]   See website: *http://www.gaa.ie/files/archives/official_reports/central_committees_2006-2009. doc*: Central Hearings Committee (CHC) and Central Appeals Committee (CAC).

[42]   On these two points, see Ch.17, Part A.

[43]   [1952] 1 K.B. 189.

[44]   [1952] 1 K.B. 189 at 198.

[45]   See, e.g. *NEETU v McConnell* (1983) 2 J.I.S.L.L. 97 and *Connolly v McConnell* [1983] I.R. 172.

[46]   *McGrath and O'Ruairc v Trustees of Maynooth College* [1979] I.L.R.M. 166; *Ryan v VIP*, unreported, High Court, January 10, 1989.

statutory tribunals, or even, quasi-judicial tribunals. Modern usage is adopted here; we simply use the term "tribunals".

Definition

6–08   Before going further, we ought to mention the commonly accepted definition of the term "tribunal". It is: a body, independent of the Government or any other entity but at the same time not a court, which takes decisions affecting individual rights, according to some fairly precise (and usually legal) guidelines and by following a regular and fairly formal procedure. We enlarge on these elements in Part C of this chapter and will have to emphasise that tribunals come in all shapes and sizes, so that not every entity commonly regarded as a tribunal will possess all of these attributes and certainly not to the same extent.

6–09   Such a definition leads straightaway to the question: why does it matter whether or not a body is classified as a tribunal? It should be made clear, first of all, that the term "tribunal" is not a "term of art", which establishes definite legal consequences. Rather it is a label popularised by academic lawyers as an organising principle for books, lectures, etc and as a basis for comparisons. But secondly, and more importantly, a court exercising the power of judicial review over a public body may be more likely to insist on rigorous standards of constitutional justice, reasonableness, etc if it takes the view that the body before it possesses the attributes of a tribunal. However, the question of whether or not the body is stamped with either the name "tribunal" or one of its commonly used synonyms will be of secondary importance in guiding a court to such a decision.

6–10   It follows that, in a large number of judicial review cases, the body whose decision is under review happens to be a tribunal. However, in general, such cases will be considered together with similar cases involving different respondents in the appropriate chapter on judicial review and not here.

B. Why a Tribunal?

6–11   Not only is uniformity lacking from tribunal to tribunal, there is also a lack of consistency as to whether a tribunal should be created at all. If one leaves aside local authorities, state-sponsored bodies and other specialist institutions, it may be said that an individual decision may be vested in any one of at least three different types of body: a Minister and his department, a court, or a tribunal. In part this is because there is a lack of any inherent correlation between the character of a particular type of decision and a particular forum. This can be illustrated by the fact that, as it happens, in regard to three important functions, a decision is taken in the first instance by a body which is part of the executive arm of government; thence an appeal may be taken to a tribunal, with a further right of appeal from the tribunal to a court. One can see this pattern in the areas of planning, social welfare, tax law and rating valuation.[47] In a slightly different hierarchy, the grant of an

---

[47]   In the case of planning and social welfare there is an appeal on a point of law only, to the High Court. For taxation, there is a full appeal to the Circuit Court with a further appeal to the High Court. See further, para.6–33.

aquaculture licence is vested in the responsible Minister; but with a *de novo* appeal to the Aquaculture Licences Appeal Board, which has a high level of institutional independence.[48] In any case, we now review the policy questions underlying the choice between a tribunal and each of the two most obvious alternatives.

Tribunal or Minister?

6–12 It would certainly make for consistency if the following demarcation line for functions between a Minister and a tribunal were consistently observed by the Oireachtas: matters should be allocated to a tribunal where they require a decision to be taken independently of the executive by the determination of facts according to a fairly formalised procedure, and the application to the facts of a reasonably precise set of rules. In short, a tribunal would take all quasi-judicial decisions. This would leave to the Minister and his department decisions containing a high policy content, which are not susceptible to regulation by a code of law.[49]

6–13 In fact, this division of functions as between a tribunal and a Minister fails as an adequate description of reality at two points. First, by no means all of the decisions of a type suitable for resolution by a tribunal are actually vested in a tribunal. Dealing with the question of allocation of functions in Britain, the Council on Tribunals remarked frankly:

> "[T]he choice is influenced by the interplay of various factors – the nature of decision, accidents of history, departmental preferences and political considerations – rather than by the application of a set of coherent principles."[50]

This is at least as true in Ireland as it is in Britain. Occasionally, functions which one would expect to be located in a tribunal are, for historical or other reasons (such as a shortage of public funds at the time when the function happens to be established), vested in a court, or more often, in a Minister.

6–14 Nevertheless, sometimes practice follows theory. And the theory is that as compared with a Minister, tribunals possess various advantages. The first of these was adverted to by Henchy J. in *State (Pine Valley Developments Ltd) v Dublin County Council*.[51] Speaking in the context of an "aberrant" and ultra vires grant

---

[48] Fisheries (Amendment) Act 1997 Pt III and Sch. See too, Education for Persons with Special Educational Needs Act 2004 s.4 (issue of special educational needs determined first by Health Service Executive or National Council for Special Education, but then on appeal to Special Education Appeals Board).

[49] This allocation of functions would be in line with the proposals contained in the *Report of the Public Services Organisation Review Group* (the "Devlin Report"): see Prl.792, App.1.

[50] *The Functions of the Council on Tribunals* (1980) (Cmd. 7805), para.1.7.

[51] [1984] I.R. 407. For the advantages of An Bord Pleanála over the Minister for Local Government, see Stevenson, "Planning Appeals in the Republic of Ireland" (1985) 7 *Journal of Urban Law and Policy* 170. For an early, unsuccessful Private Members Bill which would have constituted a "Planning Appeal Board", chaired by a judge with another member drawn from a panel nominated by the Minister and a third drawn from a panel nominated by the Local Appointments Commission, see 23 *Dáil Debates* Cols 227–253, 517–549 and 795–808 (March 6, 13 and 20, 1968). This proposal was advanced in order to prevent corruption, which the Fine Gael member proposing the measure linked with the Fianna Fáil Builder's

of outline planning permission by the Minister for Local Government, Henchy J. said that the Minister had:

> "... ignored the rights of the respondent planning authority and of those who were entitled to get notices and to be heard before such a material contravention could take place. It is no wonder that Parliament, in its wisdom, by the [Local Government (Planning and Development) Act 1976] transferred to an independent appeal board the appellate power which had been vested by the [Local Government (Planning and Development) Act 1963] in an individual who might be influenced in his decisions by political pressures or other extraneous or unworthy considerations."[52]

6–15   Another example of where it is better, for reasons of fear of political unpopularity, for a Minister not to be involved and for a tribunal to take their place, concerns the Mental Health (Criminal Law) Review Board. Historically, when a person was found guilty but insane under the Trial of Lunatics Act 1883, the court was obliged to commit the defendant to the Central Mental Hospital and the question of whether and when the person was sufficiently recovered to be released was determined by the Lord Lieutenant of Ireland. After independence, this function was transferred to the Minister for Justice. In *Re Gallagher's Application*,[53] it was argued that the release of such a person was an aspect of "the administration of justice" and, by Art.34.1, had therefore to be vested in a court. But this argument was rejected by the Supreme Court, on the ground that this function was not an administration of justice. However, whatever the possibly inflexible attitude of the separation of powers,[54] the case highlighted the fact that it was undesirable for such a politically sensitive function to be vested in a Minister, who is likely to be damned if he did and damned if he did not. The first solution to this was the establishment of a non-statutory ad hoc committee, which was to advise the Minister as to whether the person still suffered from his mental disorder and would be a danger to himself or others. Then, by usual progression, the advisory committee was replaced by a Mental Health (Criminal Law) Review Board, established by the Criminal Law (Insanity) Act 2006. Its function is to review the cases of persons committed to designated centres, following a finding of unfitness to be tried or a verdict of not guilty by reason of insanity.[55]

6–16   Secondly, a tribunal is less affected by the election of a new political party to government than a Minister and Department would be and thus there may be some gain in consistency; a quality very desirable in an area in which the policy content is usually low. Finally, the amorphous quality of a department of state with its various activities and interests may mean that an individual would be more

---

Association, *Taca*. As legislative precedents, the lay commissioners of the Land Commission and the Appeals Officer of the Department of Social Welfare and the Redundancy Payment Appeal Tribunal were cited.

[52]   [1984] I.R. 407 at 425.

[53]   [1991] 1 I.R. 31.

[54]   Contrast the attitude taken by the European Court of Human Rights in *V v United Kingdom* (1999) 30 E.H.R.R. 121.

[55]   A broadly similar explanation could be offered for the setting up of the Parole Board, established on an administrative basis in 2001 (with a promise, hitherto unfulfilled, of being placed on a statutory footing), to replace the Sentence Review Group.

confident that his arguments had been fully taken into account by a tribunal.[56] In short, tribunals are regarded as more likely to be non-partisan and to provide greater safeguards for the individual than would be the case with a Minister. It follows that a tribunal is often created where the area of government administration involved requires interference with valuable private property rights, for example planning, taxation or compulsory acquisition.

6–17   There is a qualification to the principle that decisions for which guidelines are provided are vested in tribunals. By definition, this principle is largely correct for "court-substitute tribunals" but not for "policy-orientated tribunals".[57] For the purpose of the latter is to allow policy, in a narrow field, to be worked out case by case by a specialist body, free of day-to-day interference by party politics and party politicians. The family of regulators, indentified in para.6–02, provides examples, as does An Bord Pleanála. The Labour Court, which is vested, inter alia, with the function of making "recommendation[s] setting forth its opinion on the merits of the [trade] dispute and the terms on which it should be settled",[58] provides another example of a "policy-orientated tribunal" at work. In truth though, many tribunals possess elements of each category of tribunal.

Tribunal or court?

6–18   The other general perspective from which to survey tribunals is by a comparison with the courts. Since most Irish tribunals are of the court-substitute type, could their functions not simply have been vested in a court of the appropriate level? The short answer is that the growth of tribunals is largely due to the perceived failure of the legal system to respond in a flexible manner to new challenges. Thus, the creation of one of the first modern tribunals—the court of referees system, established under the National Insurance Act 1911 to hear national insurance claims—occurred because of the dissatisfaction with the handling of workmen's compensation cases by the County Court.

6–19   The first of the advantages which tribunals are generally supposed to carry is that they are regarded as quicker and cheaper for all the parties concerned. Their simpler procedure means that it is often unnecessary for a lawyer to appear.[59] For instance, in recommending a guardianship board for vulnerable adults instead of

---

[56]   e.g. the establishment of an independent Refugee Applications Commissioner to determine asylum applications and a similar independent Refugee Appeal Tribunal to hear appeals from decisions of the Commissioner was probably prompted by concerns that the former system, whereby all such applications were determined by the Minister for Justice, lacked "transparency": Refugee Act 1996 ss.6 and 15, as amended by Immigration Act 1999 s.11.

[57]   Farmer, *Tribunals and Government* (London: Weidenfeld and Nicolson, 1984), Ch.8.

[58]   Industrial Relations Act 1946 s.68(1), as inserted by s.19 of the Industrial Relations Act 1969.

[59]   On legal representation before a tribunal, see paras 14–47 to 14–53. Cf. *Employment Appeals Tribunal Sixteenth Annual Report* (1983, Pl. 2733), p.4: "While the procedures of the Tribunal were intended to be informal, speedy and inexpensive, the increasing involvement by the legal profession, particularly in claims under the Unfair Dismissals Act 1977, has tended to make the hearings more formal, prolonged and costly, with an over-emphasis on legal procedures and technicalities." According to the 1983 Report, 19.7 per cent of employees and 23.9 per cent of employers opted for legal representation. The 2008 Annual Report recorded a total of 1,538 cases relating to the Unfair Dismissal Acts, in which employees were represented in 813 (54 per cent) and employers in 682 (44 per cent); and 3,919 cases relating to other pieces

the present High Court wards of court jurisdiction, the Law Reform Commission remarked[60]:

> "[A tribunal would] provide an informal non-intimidating approach to decision-making whilst maintaining procedural safeguards ... Such a body has the potential for greater speed in hearing cases and making determinations whilst maintaining the flexibility of sitting at different locations around the country."

6–20 Although a tribunal may not adopt procedures which are unfair or which imperil a just result, it is nonetheless, to a large degree,[61] master of its own procedures, and enjoys a considerable discretion as to whether to depart from the strict rules of evidence or permit legal representation or cross-examination of witnesses. These features, together with the frequent absence of an adversarial framework,[62] the fact that the proceedings are often held in private,[63] and the less formal atmosphere of a tribunal combine to make an appearance before a tribunal a less daunting experience than the "day in court". This was the reason for the creation of the Rent Tribunal to administer the new system of rent assessment in respect of a group of elderly and often vulnerable tenants who had been within the protection of the former Rent Restrictions Act 1960.[64] The tenants preferred the tribunal to the daunting prospect of a courtroom, with its criminal connotation.

6–21 Secondly, traditionally tribunals have tended to take a less rigid attitude to questions of statutory interpretation and to precedent.[65] Although traditionally many tribunals did not publish their decisions, much less their reasons, some change is now occurring, for instance in the planning field; documents relating to decisions of An Bord Pleanála, including inspectors' reports, must be made available to members of the public.[66] The Employment Appeals Tribunal has always maintained a public register of its decisions. And, in a far-reaching development, the Freedom of Information Act 1997 s.16 requires the publication of decisions likely to be

---

of legislation, in which employees were represented in 1,332 (32 per cent) and employers in 923 (23 per cent).

[60]   *Report on Vulnerable Adults and the Law* (LRC 83–2006), para.6.39.

[61]   See paras 6–69 to 6–78.

[62]   See paras 6–34 to 6–36.

[63]   Contrast Art.34.1, which requires that the administration of justice by courts shall be in public, save in "such limited and special cases as may be prescribed by law".

[64]   *Blake v Attorney General* [1982] I.R. 117. For an account of this decision, and the flurry of legislative activity which followed in its wake, see McCormack, "*Blake-Madigan* and its Aftermath" (1983) 5 D.U.L.J. (N.S) 205. Put briefly, the initial response of the legislature—the Housing (Private Rented Dwellings) Act 1982—vested the rent assessment function in the District Court. However, because of the concern aroused among the tenants by the prospect of a courtroom, this jurisdiction was transferred to the newly created Rent Tribunal by the Housing (Private Rented Dwellings) (Amendment) Act 1983. See generally, 344 *Dáil Debates* Cols 2514–2544 (July 7, 1983). A further example of a tribunal being substituted for a court occurred in the field of rating valuation. Until the Valuation Act 1988, an appeal lay from a determination of the Commissioner of Valuation to the Circuit Court. An appeal now lies to the Valuation Tribunal. From the Tribunal there is an appeal on a point of law (just as, before, there was an appeal from the Circuit Court) to the High Court and thence to the Supreme Court. See generally, Valuation Act 2001 Pt VII and Sch.2.

[65]   For the requirement on tribunals to publish precedents and reasons, see paras 12–24 to 12–25; and 14–14 to 14–20.

[66]   Planning and Development Act 2000 s.146(3).

of precedential value. This development naturally encourages the following of precedents; in particular, where points of law are concerned, tribunals must apply the law. An example of this, admittedly from the tax field, is that of McCarthy J. in *McGrath v McDermott*,[67] where the Supreme Court was considering a decision of the Appeal Commissioners. This decision had purported to adopt the doctrine of "fiscal nullity" (a British principle by which financial transactions, which had no purpose other than the avoidance of tax and which did not involve a real loss, should be disregarded). The court struck down the Commissioners' decision because they had either ignored or been unaware of the relevant decisions of the Supreme Court.

6–22 Thirdly, many tribunals possess a particular expertise. This would be true, for example, in the case of long-established bodies such as An Bord Pleanála, the Appeal Commissioners for Income Tax and the Employment Appeals Tribunal. More recent examples are afforded by the Mental Health (Criminal Law) Review Board[68] and the Mental Health Tribunal[69] (as well as the Guardianship Board, which has been proposed by the Law Reform Commission).[70] Broadly speaking, each of these tribunals has to do with mental health; thus, the advantage of these tribunals over a court is that the tribunal may have a medically qualified member, rather than being confined to the less convincing technique of building in medical expertise by way of expert medical witnesses. As the Law Reform Commission pointed out, one way of having the best of both worlds is to make a judge the chairperson of a (usually) three-person tribunal, with a doctor as member.

6–23 But there are disadvantages too in involving experts, notably that, in a relatively small jurisdiction like Ireland, there is a possibility that a specialist member of a tribunal would know the parties before it or, more likely, experts involved with them. One example of this is the Mental Health Tribunal, each panel of which has three members, one of whom must be a practising psychiatrist. Other psychiatrists critically involved before the tribunal are the admitting psychiatrist and the one who examines the patient for the tribunal. There are obvious possibilities of previous relationship, possibly violating the "no bias" rule of constitutional justice.

6–24 Finally, it will often be appropriate for an agency to include not only a regulatory–licensing tribunal but also to possess a number of standard-setting, information-collecting promotional or advisory functions, along the lines of United States "administrative agencies". Evoking the separation of powers, such bodies are sometimes referred to, in the United States, as the "fourth organ of government". In Ireland, a leading example is the Labour Court, which combines general arbitration functions in the field of industrial relations with quasi-judicial (or indeed, possibly judicial) functions under employment legislation.[71]

---

[67] [1988] I.R. 258 at 278.
[68] Criminal Law (Insanity) Act 2006 s.11.
[69] Mental Health Act 2001 Pt III.
[70] *Report on Vulnerable Adults and the Law* (LRC 83–2006), especially para.6.39. See also, Mental Capacity and Guardianship Bill 2008, a Private Member's Bill introduced in the Seanad.
[71] See, e.g. *Synopsis of Determinations Made by the Labour Court in Employment Rights*

6–25   Another example is the Pensions Board constituted by Pt II of the Pensions Act 1990. The Board is not only a tribunal, it also bears the functions of: devising guidelines on the duties of the trustees of pensions schemes; encouraging the provision of training schemes for them; advising the Minister for Social Protection; and monitoring the operation of the Act and pensions developments generally.[72]

6–26   Where a court, rather than a tribunal, was involved in such a combination of roles, it has been argued successfully elsewhere in the common law world that the arrangement contravened the equivalent of Art.34.1 of the Constitution.[73] In Ireland, this argument would probably not succeed, but such an arrangement would certainly be regarded as undesirable and unconventional.

6–27   Apart from Article 34.1, there might be thought to be another constitutional difficulty, in the situation in which a multi-functional body combines quasi-judicial decision-making with (say) public advocacy or standard setting. This point was raised in *Corcoran v Holmes*.[74] The facts were that a demonstration had taken place in Dublin city centre at which there were clashes between demonstrators and members of An Garda Síochána. After the demonstration, the Garda Síochána Complaints Board (the second respondent) received complaints against the applicant, a member of the Gardaí who had been on duty on that day. Following a meeting of the Board, a press release was issued and the chairman gave an interview, the gist of both being that the Board was concerned about the lack of co-operation it had received from Garda members during the course of its investigation. On foot of these remarks, the applicant brought judicial review proceedings to prevent any steps to discipline him, on the ground that the disciplinary tribunal was apparently biased.

6–28   The Supreme Court gave two reasons for rejecting the applicant's contention that the disciplinary tribunal was apparently biased. The first was that the public complaints made by the Board and its chairman were not directed at the applicant but at other members of the Gardaí for failing to co-operate in the investigation. The second reason is of more general interest. To appreciate it, one needs to bear in mind the careful statutory design of the disciplinary tribunal. It was required to consist of two members of the Board "who had not been concerned with the matter referred to the Tribunal" plus a member of the Gardaí who was not a member of the tribunal.[75] Against this statutory background, McCracken J. stated:

Cases in 2007. A further example is the Environmental Protection Agency, established by the Environmental Protection Agency Act 1992 Pt II.

[72]   Pensions Act 1990 s.10. For another well-developed example, see the Private Residential Tenancies Board, established by the Residential Tenancies Act 2004 Pt VIII.

[73]   Legislation which vested a court with non-judicial arbitral functions in the area of industrial relations was held to be contrary to s.71 of the Commonwealth Constitution in *Attorney General of Australia v R. and the Boilermakers' Society of Australia* [1957] A.C. 288. In *Re Neilan* [1990] 2 I.R. 267 at 278, Keane J. described the present issue as "… one of no little difficulty".

[74]   [2007] 1 I.L.R.M. 23.

[75]   Garda Síochána (Complaints) Act 1986 Sch.2 r.1. Because of this third member, it might be thought that the composition of the tribunal was biased in favour of the Garda before it. But the argument that this slant, in favour of the individual and effectively against the community, violates constitutional justice has only seldom (see paras 13–01 to 13–02) been made.

"The statements made in the present case ... by the chairman, were general statements made on a matter of public concern. The board is entitled to make public statements in such circumstances, and indeed it might be said that in certain situations has a duty to do so ... Of course the board is a body corporate and the views must be seen as emanating from a body corporate. What must not be lost sight of, however, is that the proposed tribunal will not be a body corporate, but will be an *ad hoc* body consisting of three individuals, none of whom will have taken part in the decision to refer the appellant's behaviour to the tribunal, and none of whom will have been at the meeting which authorised the public statements. The only perceived bias about which the appellant is entitled to complain would be the perceived bias of the members of the tribunal who are making the decision relating to him."[76]

6–29   This case leaves hanging the question explored later[77] of how well informed about (say) the design of the complaints board a reasonable person is expected to be.

C. Common Features

6–30   We must now elaborate on the remarks, made above in para.6–08, about the types of features which distinguish a tribunal.

Rule bound

6–31   As far as one can generalise about tribunals, it can be said that they take decisions in regard to which the range of options is sufficiently narrow and predictable for it to be crystallised in the form of a reasonably precise set of rules or at least a specific catalogue of factors. This is in contrast with the wide discretionary power which, for instance, permits a Minister to exercise a particular power if he deems it "necessary in the public interest".[78] Yet on the other hand, law administered by a tribunal is more likely than law administered by a court to include a range of factors which tends to create a discretion and so to be expressed in terms of standards as opposed to rules. It is, however, a discretion which must be exercised reasonably, objectively and judicially. In other words, in this respect, as in others, tribunals occupy an intermediate position between ministers and courts. To take some examples: first, An Bord Uchtála must not make an adoption order unless it is satisfied "that the applicant is of good moral character, has sufficient means to support the child, and is a suitable person to have parental rights and duties in respect of the child".[79] Secondly, in awarding contracts, the Broadcasting Authority of Ireland "shall have regard to", inter alia, the following factors[80]:

(a) the character, expertise and experience of the applicant ...;

---

[76] [2007] 1 I.L.R.M. 23 at 30–31.
[77] See paras 13–47 to 13–49.
[78] See, e.g. the Insurance Act 1989 s.22A(10), as substituted by the Central Bank and Financial Services Authority of Ireland Act 2003 Sch.1 Pt VIII. For controls on discretionary powers, see Ch.15.
[79] Adoption Act 1952 s.13(1).
[80] Broadcasting Act 2009 s.66(2); formerly Radio and Television Act 1988 s.6(2).

(b) the adequacy of the financial resources ... and the extent to which the application accords with good business and economic principles;
(c) the quality, range and type of the programmes proposed to be provided ...;
(k) any other matters which the Contract Awards Committee considers to be necessary to secure the orderly development of sound broadcasting services.

6–32 Even where the wording of the statutory test administered by the tribunal is vague, the effect of the open, formal procedure, together with an accumulation of informal precedents (mentioned earlier) would have the effect of restricting its discretion.

Appeals

6–33 Since decisions taken by tribunals are, first, bound by fairly precise rules and secondly, involve questions of individual rights, it might be predicted on the basis of earlier discussion that a statutory appeal[81] would be created from a tribunal to a court. Indeed, provision is often made for an appeal to the High Court, usually confined to points of law.[82] In certain other cases, an appeal will lie to a specialised appellate tribunal.[83] Thus, for example, the position of the taxpayer is protected by lavish opportunities to appeal, which include an appeal de novo from the Revenue Commissioners to the Appeal Commissioners for Income Tax. From a decision of the Appeals Commissioners the taxpayer (though not the Revenue Commissioners) may appeal de novo to the Circuit Court. Either party may ask for a case stated on a point of law from the decisions of the Appeal Commissioners or the Circuit Court.[84]

Accusatorial versus inquisitorial style

6–34 There are two factors which it might be expected would make it likely

---

[81] See generally, the discussion of appeals in Ch.11, Part D and the developing jurisprudence of the superior courts in determining the scope of statutory appeals. Contrast the Competition Act 2002 ss.15 and 24.
[82] See, e.g. Adoption Act 1952 s.20(1); Industrial Relations (Amendment) Act 2001 s.11; Industrial Relations (Miscellaneous Provisions) Act 2004 s.12(2); Disability Act 2005 s.20; Social Welfare Consolidation Act 2005 s.327; Employees (Provision of Information and Consultation) Act 2006 s.15(9). cf. Trade Marks Act 1996 s.79 and Water Services Act 2007 s.92. It was held in *Canty v Private Residential Tenancies Board* [2008] IESC 24; [2008] 4 I.R. 592 that, by virtue of the express words of the Residential Tenancies Act 2004 s.123(4) "[t]he determination of the High Court ... shall be final and conclusive", there was no further appeal from the High Court to the Supreme Court.
[83] e.g. the Private Security Act 2004 s.40(3) and Sch.2 creates an appeal from the Private Security Authority to the Private Security Appeals Board. Again, by the Seanad Electoral (Panel Members) Act 1947, an appeal lies to a judicial referee from a decision of the returning officer on the eligibility of a candidate for a particular electoral panel. See 1947 Act ss.36–38. In *Ormonde and Dolan v MacGabhann,* unreported, High Court, July 9, 1969, Pringle J. held that the plaintiffs were entitled to bypass this judicial referee procedure in order to seek a declaration from the High Court that they had the proper and appropriate qualifications for nomination on the Labour Panel.
[84] Taxes Consolidation Act 1997 s.840. See also, the Planning and Development Act 2000 s.50(1), which allows An Bord Pleanála to refer a question of law to the High Court.

that many tribunals would follow the inquisitorial model. First, as regards subject matter, the accusatorial model is appropriate in ordinary civil proceedings where the court is usually deciding a *lis inter partes* involving two identifiable private parties, each with opposing interests. By contrast, there is often only one individual interest at a hearing before a tribunal, as, for instance, in an application for a grant or a licence. On the other side, there is or may be that nebulous thing, the "public" or "community" interest, which may, according to the circumstances, consist of divergent interests some of which may even pull in the same direction as the individual interest.

6–35 There is, secondly, a practical factor militating in favour of the inquisitorial system, namely, that the accusatorial system works best when the adversaries are equally experienced and informed. This requirement will often not be met in the case of tribunals where the private individuals involved are usually not legally represented.

6–36 Yet, despite these natural features, in the case of many tribunals, a form of adversarial system has been imposed by the law. First, the rules of constitutional justice—which are imposed by judges with the court system in mind, as a role-model—militate against a proactive involvement in the debate by the tribunal itself. In line with this, in certain tribunals it has been thought necessary to establish a *legitimus contradictor* so as to avoid any appearance that the decision-maker is contending against the individual before the tribunal (despite the fact that the reality would probably have been that the decision-maker was seeking to elucidate all relevant facts). Thus, for example, the responsible Inspector of Taxes may appear in front of the Appeal Commissioners to argue in support of his earlier decision (though, in practice, in a major case, the Revenue Commissioners' argument would be put by counsel); and the deciding officer in the Department of Social Protection appears to defend his decision, in an appeal to the appeals officer.

Independence

6–37 Tribunals exercising public law powers are required to strike an even balance between the individual on the one hand, and the administrative authorities who represent the public interest on the other; they should be guided only by the law and their own non-partisan discretion. At times, queries have been raised as to whether certain tribunals measure up to these standards. In the first place, tribunals lack the tradition, status and institutional arrangements necessary to promote independence which the courts have long enjoyed. Moreover, the fact that all the cases before a particular tribunal often involve the same administrative agency may breed a certain cosiness. And, on the other side, there may (especially if the private party involved is a significant business) be an element of what the Americans call "agency capture", meaning that an administrative agency's own reputation and indirectly, prosperity, may become tied up with the perceived performance of the field it is supposed to be regulating. Accordingly, it may not bring an entirely detached assessment of the public interest to bear on its duties.

6–38 The greater the pressure likely to be placed on the tribunal, the more important that it should be, and be seen to be, independent. There has recently[85] been great concern about the treatment of members of the public by individual Gardaí and the adjudication of complaints made against the Gardaí. The outcome was the establishment of the Garda Síochána Ombudsman Commission, by the Garda Síochána Act 2005[86] (which, as already mentioned, is chaired by a superior court judge) as a replacement for the Garda Síochána Complaints Board.[87] In order to give it added lustre, the three members of the new Commission are appointed by the President, on the nomination of the Government and the passage of resolutions by the Dáil and the Seanad recommending their appointment.

6–39   Particular doubt had existed about the independence of the deciding officer/appeals officer system for determining social welfare claims because it is manned by serving civil servants operating within a Department of State[88] and thus, for instance, the decisions of both the deciding officer and the appeals officer have been placed within the scope of the Ombudsman's jurisdiction.[89] Deciding officers are selected by the Minister for Social Protection at executive or staff officer level and they hold this position at the pleasure of the Minister. Deciding officers appear to regard themselves as subject to departmental directions and policy considerations. After some years as a deciding officer a civil servant will generally return to service within the Department. Later he may be appointed, usually at assistant principal grade, as an appeals officer by the Minister and again holds his position at pleasure.[90]

6–40   Lack of independence in an appeals officer's performance is demonstrated by what is now a rather venerable case, *McLoughlin v Minister for Social Welfare*.[91] In this case the question arose as to whether the plaintiff was employed "in the civil service of the Government" for social insurance purposes. The appeals officer considered that he was bound to adhere to the terms of a minute from the Minister for Finance which, in effect, directed the officer to find that the plaintiff was so employed.

6–41   This decision was reversed by the Supreme Court, with O'Daly J. stating that the appeals officer had abdicated his duty to act in an impartial and independent fashion:

> "The Appeals Officer said that he was bound to adhere to a direction, purporting to have been given to him by the Minister for Finance, an observation which disclosed not a concern for the niceties of the probative value, but the belief that a public servant in his position had no option but

---

[85]   See, e.g. *Shortt v Garda Commissioner* [2007] IESC 9; [2007] 4 I.R. 587 per Hardiman J.

[86]   Parts 3 and 4. See Conway, "An Garda Síochána Act 2005 – Breaking Down The Thick Blue Wall?" (2005) 23 I.L.T. 297; "The Garda Síochána Ombudsman Commission" (2004) 22 I.L.T. 125. This Act also establishes a Garda Inspectorate; Garda Síochána Act 2005 Pt 5. See Ch.4.

[87]   Garda Síochána (Complaints) Act 1986. For criticism of the Boards, see Walsh, *The Irish Police* (Dublin: Round Hall Sweet & Maxwell, 1998), pp.267–269.

[88]   Though for some recent improvements, see para.6–92.

[89]   Ombudsman Act 1980 s.5(1)(a).

[90]   See generally, Social Welfare Consolidation Act 2005 ss.299 and 304; and Clark, "Social Welfare Insurance Appeals" (1978) 13 Ir. Jur. (N.S) 165.

[91]   [1958] I.R. 1. See further, on this case, H & M, paras 2–141 and 3–53 to 3–56.

to act on the direction of a Minister of State. Such a belief on his part was an abdication by him from his duty as an Appeals Officer. That duty is laid upon him by the Oireachtas and he is required to perform it as between the parties that appear before him freely and fairly as becomes anyone who is called upon to decide on matters of right or obligation."[92]

6–42 The conventional legal wisdom enshrined in *McLoughlin* is now generally respected. Thus to take one among many examples,[93] s.3 of the Fisheries (Amendment) Act 2003, states that:

The licensing authority shall be independent in the exercise of his or her functions under this Act subject to –
  (a) the law for the time being in force ... and
  (b) such policy directives in relation to sea fishing boat licensing as the Minister may give in writing from time to time.

6–43 Moreover, the scope of the possible policy directives is carefully circumscribed in the remainder of this provision. Thus they may require certain prohibitions or conditions only in order to protect or allow the sustainable exploitation of aquatic species and may not enable "the Minister to exercise any power or control in relation to any particular case or group of cases". In addition, the directive must be laid before each House and published in *Iris Oifigiúil*.

Constitution: Articles 34.1 and 37

6–44 Doubts about the independence of tribunals were probably part of the inspiration for the constitutional rule, Art.34.1, which provides that (subject to certain exceptions) "justice shall be administered in courts established by law by judges ..." and not by tribunals. Article 37.1[94] provides an exception to the pure milk of the separation of powers principle in that it permits the Oireachtas to vest "limited functions and powers of a judicial nature in matters other than criminal matters" in a body which is not a court. The wording of Art.34.1 and Art.37 includes three highly problematic concepts: the distinction between judicial and non-judicial powers; what is a "limited" judicial function; and what is a "criminal matter". These are matters of constitutional definition which are discussed in constitutional law books.[95] It is not intended to attempt to cover the same ground here but merely to outline some of the leading cases in order to alert the reader to the issues. One should note though, that even if Art.34.1 did, at one time, pose

---

[92] [1958] I.R. 1 at 27.
[93] cf. the Patents Act 1992 s.6(3), which states: "The Patents Office shall be under the control of the Controller [of Patents, Designs and Trade Marks] who shall be independent in the discharge of the functions conferred on him by this Act or any other enactment." See also, Transport (Railway Infrastructure) Act 2001 s.42(9); Disability Act 2005 s.8(4); Consumer Protection Act 2007 s.7(3).
[94] See, e.g. *Madden v Ireland*, unreported, High Court, May 22, 1980 and *Melton v Censorship Board* [2003] 3 I.R. 623 at 634. In the present context, note further that Art.37.2 was enacted by the Sixth Amendment of the Constitution Act 1979 to quieten doubts raised by the Supreme Court's decision in *M v An Bord Uchtála* [1977] I.R. 287.
[95] See Hogan and Whyte, *JM Kelly: The Irish Constitution*, 4th edn (Dublin: Lexis Nexis, 2003), pp.610–638 and 1024–1038; and Gwynn Morgan, *The Separation of Powers in the Irish Constitution* (Dublin: Round Hall Sweet & Maxwell, 1997), Ch.5.

a constitutional threat to certain tribunals, recent developments suggest that this danger has substantially reduced.

6–45   In the first place, it must be emphasised that there are several tribunals which are plainly out of danger because they do not administer justice. An example is An Bord Pleanála: it has been held,[96] first, that the Minister for Local Government (who was the forerunner of this tribunal, as the appellate agency for planning permissions) was not administering justice because such a large measure of policy discretion is involved; and secondly (to take another of the Board's powers), that although the function of determining what is "development" or "exempted development" constitutes an administration of justice, it falls within the Article 37 exception.

6–46   The high-water mark of the tide in favour of using Art.34.1 to strike down a tribunal was *Re Solicitors' Act, 1954*,[97] in which the power of the Disciplinary Committee of the Incorporated Law Society to strike off solicitors who had been found guilty of serious disciplinary offences was held to be an administration of justice. Moreover, the Supreme Court also held that even if there were a full appeal, by way of rehearing from the Disciplinary Committee's decision to the High Court, this appeal would not restore constitutionality to the Committee's decision.

6–47   In order to avoid the difficulties disclosed by the *Re Solicitors' Act, 1954* decision, certain crucial features were included when the medical disciplinary system was restructured, in what is now the Medical Practitioners Act 2007. First, the Medical Council does not have the power to strike off a doctor, although it does have the significant power and duty of making an elaborate inquiry as a result of which it may decide that the doctor should be struck off. Secondly, if it does so decide, then the doctor has the right to apply within 21 days to the High Court, which may either cancel or confirm the decision. Finally, the Council bears the onus of proving before the court, in the usual way, any contested facts.

6–48   The disciplinary system constituted by the 1978 Act was upheld in *Re M* by Finlay P. (as he then was) in the High Court. The *Re Solicitors' Act, 1954* decision was distinguished in *Re M* on the basis that one criterion for an "administration of justice" is that it must be "final and conclusive", as opposed to recommendatory. Since the Medical Council's decision was not blessed with the quality of conclusiveness it was held that the Council was not "administering justice".[98] This

---

[96]   *Central Dublin Development Association v Attorney General* (1975) 109 I.L.T.R. 69 at 93–96 per Kenny J.

[97]   [1960] I.R. 239. See also, the remarkable comments of McKenzie J. in *Government of Canada v Employment Appeals Tribunal* [1992] 2 I.R. 484 at 488.

[98]   [1984] I.R. 479. Designed according to the same specification and to meet the same constitutional imperative—satisfying Art.34.1 of the Constitution—as the medical disciplinary system is the nurses' disciplinary system constituted by the Nurses Act 1985. This system came up for constitutional scrutiny before the Supreme Court in *Kerrigan v An Bord Altranais* [1990] 2 I.R. 396. Following the statutory procedure, allegations against the plaintiff had been heard by the Fitness to Practice Committee of the Board in an oral inquiry which lasted for 12 sittings. The Committee's report, finding that the plaintiff was guilty of professional misconduct, was submitted to the Board which gave the plaintiff an opportunity to be heard and then decided that her name should be erased from the Register of Nurses. Nevertheless the Supreme Court held (at 403) that before the High Court could confirm this decision, the High Court must hold a full oral hearing (at any rate where, as in the instant case, there were disputed questions of fact).

authority appears to represent a legislative development of the law as enunciated in the *Re Solicitors' Act, 1954* decision. It is now possible, if the correct formula be used—that is, "confirmation" by the High Court rather than appeal—to allow some involvement by the relevant professional body. Nevertheless, it must be said, as a criticism of the influence of the separation of powers in this area, that it does seem desirable that the relevant factual points and professional standards should be allowed to be settled—as they are even in the United States—by a tribunal including experienced members of the profession, who are appointed or elected to represent the entire profession. For there seems little danger in Ireland, where the independence of the professions is a fundamental tenet, that a disciplinary tribunal would be less independent of the executive branch than are the courts.

6–49 However, shares in *Re Solicitors' Act 1954*-style application of Art.34.1 fell significantly as a result of *Keady v Garda Commissioner*.[99] *Keady* concerned the question of whether the Garda Disciplinary Tribunal—that is, a public service employment tribunal—was administering justice. Accordingly, what was said about tribunals for disciplining professionals or other self-employed persons was, strictly speaking, obiter. Nevertheless, the theme which emerges most strongly from each of the two written judgments is a concern to confine the *Re Solicitors' Act, 1954* line of authority strictly to solicitors, on the basis that "historically the act of striking solicitors off the roll was reserved to judges".[100]

6–50 A similar message emerges from *Minister for Social, Community and Family Affairs v Scanlon*.[101] In the following, brief passage from *Scanlon*, the Supreme Court dismissed a submission that a deciding officer (in the then Department of Social, Community and Family Affairs) who was revising an earlier decision on the basis of new evidence was exercising an "administration of justice". Giving judgment for the court, Fennelly J. stated[102]:

> "Implicit in this submission is the consequence that *all deciding and appeals officers are exercising judicial functions*. I am quite satisfied that this argument is devoid of merit. Such decisions are inherently administrative. They deal with the administration of the statutory social welfare code. The fact that such officers are bound to act judicially [to follow the principles of constitutional justice] does not alter the character of their functions."

6–51 The curtness with which an argument—which, after all, was built upon a vast corpus of precedent and analysis throughout the common law world—was dismissed is consistent with the apparent narrowing in *Keady* of the width of the "administration of justice".

6–52 Despite these authorities, the draftsman has opted for caution in the most recent professional disciplinary systems: the Health and Social Care Professionals Act 2005[103] and the Veterinary Practice Act 2005[104] still require the involvement

---

[99] [1992] 2 I.R. 197.
[100] [1992] 2 I.R. 197 at 210–211. See also, McCarthy J. at 205.
[101] [2001] 1 I.R. 64.
[102] [2001] 1 I.R. 64 at 87.
[103] Sections 69 and 70.
[104] Section 80.

of the High Court in the imposition of any disciplinary sanction, other than an admonishment or a censure.[105]

6–53   In summary, the high tide of judicial adherence to Art.34.1 has ebbed and it would now be wrong to contend, if it were ever true, that Art.34.1 constitutes a timebomb, ticking away under the Irish system of tribunals.

6–54   The same theme—that of independence of tribunals—emerges from art.6.1 of the European Convention of Human Rights which states:

> In the determination of his civil rights and obligations or any criminal charge against him, everyone is entitled to a ... hearing ... by an independent and impartial tribunal.

The significance of art.6.1 is discussed in a wider context than tribunals, in the chapter on Fair Procedure.[106]

Appointment and removal of members of tribunal

6–55   The type of institutional arrangements designed to create independent pedestals for judges are largely absent in the case of tribunals. Thus, in the case of a typical tribunal, the chairman and other members will be selected by the Minister. The term of office is usually fixed at a maximum of three to five years.[107] Members are generally eligible for reappointment.[108] However, in certain other cases, the appointment is intended as a full-time career post.[109]

6–56   Frequently, no statutory qualifications are laid down for appointment. However, there are exceptions: in some cases the chairman must be a lawyer.[110]

---

[105] On the other hand, a "registered electrical contractor" may have their membership revoked without the involvement of a court: Energy (Miscellaneous Provisions) Act 2006 s.4, inserting a new s.9D(6)(e) and (f) into the Electricity Regulation Act 1999. This is a curious type of class distinction.

There is also relevant material in a LRC *Consultation Paper on the Law and the Elderly* (LRC CP23–2003), paras 1.50–1.53 and the equivalent report, (LRC 83–2006), paras 6.15–6.19. The Consultation Paper made a central recommendation that there should be a guardianship board which would take over the functions presently carried out by the High Court as part of its wards of court jurisdiction, and expressed the view that there would be no constitutional difficulty with this. The Report emphasised the point that the wards of court jurisdiction was one of those originally given to the courts, especially before the 20th century, when courts were often given jurisdiction which today would be characterised as part of public administration, because, in the days before "big government", there was nowhere else suitable.

While David Gwynn Morgan was, at an earlier stage, Director of Research at the LRC, he had left before the Report was prepared and so this is not a case of "All my words come back to me/in shades of mediocrity" (Homeword Bound, Paul Simon).

[106] See paras 12–05 to 12–19.

[107] For a difficulty in this area, see Residential Tenancies (Amendment) Act 2009 s.2 and 193 *Seanad Debates* 406–407 (January 28, 2009).

[108] See, e.g. Minerals Development Act 1940 s.33; Adoption Act 1952 s.8 and Sch.1 art.2; Housing (Private Rented Dwellings) (Amendment) Act 1983 ss.2 and 3; Local Government (Planning and Development) Act 1983 ss.5 and 7; Pensions Act 1990 Sch.1.

[109] See, e.g. Controller of Patents, Designs and Trade Marks: see Patents Act 1992 s.97.

[110] See, e.g. Private Security Services Act 2004 Sch.2 art.3(1) (chairperson of the Private Security

The two ordinary members of the Mining Board[111] must be property arbitrators, and in the case of the Private Residential Tenancies Board, the members of the Board must be "persons who, in the Minister's opinion, have experience in a field of expertise relevant to the Board's functions". But neither they nor the members of the tribunal determining a particular case need have any more definitive (for example, legal) qualifications.[112]

6–57 However, in the 2000s there has been a steadily growing concern with the informal way in which appointments are made, though without as yet much legislative or governmental response.[113]

6–58 Removal[114] of members of tribunals is generally a matter for the responsible Minister. The power to remove members is generally confined to specific grounds, such as ill health, stated misbehaviour or where the removal appears to the Minister to be necessary for the effective performance of the Board's functions.[115] In fact, dismissals are rare, and the most spectacular dismissals in recent times—those of the members of An Bord Pleanála in 1983—were brought about directly by an Act of the Oireachtas.[116]

"Balanced" or "representative" tribunals

6–59 There is a distinction between a situation in which members are appointed for their particular expertise and where they are appointed as representatives of interest groups, in order to constitute a "balanced" or "representative" tribunal. For instance, in the case of the Labour Court[117] and the Employment Appeals Tribunal,[118] the employers and employees are represented equally. The most sophisticated attempt in this direction involves An Bord Pleanála. The Minister for the Environment prescribes certain organisations which are variously representative of six categories of interest groups.[119] These groups are: professions or occupations relating to

---

Appeals Board must be a practising barrister or solicitor of at least 7 years' standing); Refugee Act 1996 s.15 Sch.2 (chairperson of the Refugee Appeal Tribunal must be a practising solicitor or barrister of at least 10 years' standing).

[111] Minerals Development Act 1979 s.41.

[112] Residential Tenancies Act 2004 ss.102, 153(2).

[113] McGauran, Verhoest and Humphreys, *The Corporate Governance of Agencies in Ireland*, CPMR Research Report 6 (Dublin: IPA, 2005), para.10.3; Clancy and Murphy, *Outsourcing Government* (TASC at New Island, 2006), paras 48–51. Now, however, the Commission for Aviation Regulation members may only be appointed if they have been selected, after competition, by the Commission for Public Service Appointments (Aviation Regulation Act 2001 s.11(4); Taxi Regulation Act 2003 s.14(2)).

[114] Usually, there is no other form of discipline, apart from removal. However, the Private Security Services Act 2004 Sch.2 para.3(3) empowers the chairperson of the Private Security Appeals Board to require a member of the board to attend for interview and may then inform the member that s/he has misconducted himself or herself.

[115] See, e.g. Mineral Developments Act 1940 s.33(3) (Mining Board); Adoption Act 1952 s.3(1) (An Bord Uchtála); Planning and Development Act 2000 s.106(15) (An Bord Pleanála); Sea-Fisheries and Maritime Jurisdiction Act 2006 s.48(11) (Sea-Fisheries Protection Consultative Committee); Consumer Protection Act 2007 s.10(12) (Consumer Protection Agency). See also, however, Pensions Act 1990 Sch.1 para.5.

[116] Local Government (Planning and Development) Act 1983 s.10.

[117] Industrial Relations Act 1969 s.2.

[118] Redundancy Payments Act 1967 s.39(4).

[119] Planning and Development Act 2000 ss.102–108.

physical planning; organisations concerned with protection and preservation of the environment; organisations concerned with economic development or the development of land; local government; persons nominated by trade unions or bodies representing farmers; and charities or other voluntary bodies including organisations with a special interest in the Irish language, arts, or culture, or representative of those with disabilities. The Minister is then required to choose one member of the Board from among the names nominated by each category of organisation. The seventh ordinary member is chosen from among the civil servants in the Department of Environment, Local Government and Heritage.[120]

6–60   Given the state of orthodox law, such "balanced" tribunals may not be without their dangers. Such tribunals are designed on the basis that, where there are divergent interests, it might seem fair that these interests should have their representatives on the tribunal. We have seen many examples of such a tribunal in Irish law. Classic examples of this come from the employment field, in the form of the Labour Court or the Employment Appeals Tribunal. In the case of professional disciplinary tribunals, the professions involved have always been represented, indeed, until recently, monopolised such tribunals. Now (as explained at paras 6–66 to 6–68), lay persons have their representatives.

6–61   Nevertheless, the conventional view is that constitutional justice requires that each member of a tribunal must be impartial; rather than that the leaning of one member to one side could be regarded as cancelling out the leaning of another member in the opposite direction. There appears to be no case in which this precise argument has been taken. But given the far-reaching impact on Ireland's system of tribunals which a successful argument of this type would have, it is probable that a judge would recoil from this "appalling vista" and would rely heavily on the doctrine of necessity[121] to avoid reaching such a result.

6–62   While *O'Driscoll v Law Society*[122] did not involve an attack on a "balanced" tribunal, as such, the facts are instructive in this context: a firm of solicitors had been accused of overcharging clients for services rendered in cases before the Residential Institutions Redress Board[123] and disciplinary action was initiated by the Complaints and Client Committee of the respondent. It happened that one member of the Committee was also the Director of Consumer Affairs and had been quoted, accurately, in a newspaper article, as saying "I think it is nothing less than scandalous if solicitors are taking money over and above the fees which they are also getting." The applicants sought successfully to have decisions taken by the Committee quashed, on the ground of pre-judgment. McKechnie J. stated:

> "Given her specific area of interest, it would be difficult to believe that she did not carry into the discussions of such committee, the views as previously expressed by her on this topic."[124]

---

[120] Appointment of the Chairman of An Bord Pleanála is by way of a similar, if not quite identical, process: see s.104 of the Act.

[121] See paras 13–61 to 13–66.

[122] [2007] IEHC 352.

[123] On which, see H & M, paras 6–125 to 6–139.

[124] [2007] IEHC 352 at para.57.

6–63   He went on to say:

> "*I do not accept that her comments were truly general* in the sense in which
> that word is normally understood. The issue here was one of overcharging.
> Whilst it may have involved more than one firm of solicitors, nonetheless
> it was in reality a discrete and confined issue, affecting a particular group
> of clients who were together bonded by their former experience and by a
> common tribunal to which their applications were made. The fact that [the
> Director] did not target any single firm of solicitors is in my view of little
> value. I therefore reject each of these suggestions as in any way establishing
> a position of neutrality on the part of [the Director]. In my opinion, she used
> strong language and gave the appearance of declaring a definite position on
> the issue ... I therefore think that a reasonable person could believe that she
> had firmly established a view and placed that view on public record."[125]

6–64   This case, of course recalls the facts of the *Corcoran* case described at paras
6-27 to 6–28. There, the (unsuccessfully) alleged source of bias was the fact that
the Complaints Board was not merely a complaints tribunal but was also involved
in issuing statements about good practice in the field. It should be emphasised that
in *O'Driscoll*, the source of the bias was not principally that one of the members
was the Director of Consumer Affairs, but the content of her statement in the media.
But, as a matter of common experience, such statements are more likely—though
by no means inevitable—where persons with a particular position are appointed.

6–65   As against this, from one perspective—that of the person affected, whose
vantage point is the important one for the reasonable person test of bias—the
source of the bias is unimportant; what really counts is the impact on the reasonable
individual. And, in *Corcoran*, the Supreme Court held that a reasonable person
would not suspect bias. A second point is that, even if the composition of a tribunal
is not ideal, there may be a defence to a complaint of bias, by way of the doctrine of
necessity, covered in paras 13–61 to 13–66. One should, however, qualify that by
referring to the fact that there would usually be options in deciding which member
should sit on which tribunal hearing and such options are usually operated to avoid
"conflicted" members from sitting. In short, what *Corcoran* and *O'Driscoll* each
show is that this is an area of law in which there are quite a few competing interests,
whose balancing requires some thought, from those who are designing, and those
who are operating, the tribunals.

Lay members

6–66   In the case of professional associations, the overall board will usually
include a majority of members of the profession, and it used to be the case that
where the disciplinary committee was concerned, all of the members were from
the profession. However, increasingly, it is being accepted that there should be a
significant and even majority representation of lay persons other than members
of the profession being regulated. Thus, s.34(3) of the Pharmacy Act 2007 states
that whereas at least one-third of the members shall be registered pharmacists, a
majority shall be persons other than pharmacists (at least one of whom must be a

---

[125] [2007] IEHC 352 at para.58 (emphasis added).

person "appointed to represent the interest of the public", an expression which is not explained).[126] Likewise, s.20 of the Medical Practitioners Act 2007 requires that at least one-third of the membership of the Fitness to Practice Committee shall be medical practitioners, but the majority "shall consist of persons who are not medical practitioners". Finally, the composition of the Solicitors' Disciplinary Tribunal was amended[127] but only to the extent of requiring the President of the High Court, when appointing this tribunal, to appoint no more than 20 practising solicitors and no more than 10 persons, neither solicitors nor barristers, nominated by the Minister for Justice and Law Reform. However, under the Legal Services Regulation Bill 2011, there would be a lay majority.

6–67 The injection, long overdue, of lay persons to professional disciplinary bodies stems from the idea that practitioners or experts may possibly have some partisan feeling for their professional brothers or sisters and also that the laity may have something positive to contribute. The issue of the involvement of either professional or lay members on a disciplinary tribunal could give rise to a legal action from either of two directions, each of which would be grounded on the "no bias" principle of constitutional justice. First, the person being disciplined might claim that they were unpopular with their professional peers, possibly because of attracting unfavourable publicity to the profession or of having unorthodox professional views. In consequence, they might be able to claim that there should have been a lay element to the tribunal. Alternatively, a person affected by the alleged professional misconduct might claim that, since dog doesn't eat dog, their complaint of professional misconduct would not be fairly considered.

6–68 Rather surprisingly, the recent case which we have on this issue is of the first type. It is *O'Dowd v Commissioner of An Garda Síochána*,[128] which arose out of episodes of Garda misconduct in Donegal. In particular, the applicant Garda had investigated a road fatality and his role in the investigation subsequently became the subject of several internal Garda investigations in respect of which he failed to co-operate for almost two years and which resulted in the setting up of a disciplinary inquiry. The episodes mentioned had attracted widespread condemnation, leading to a public inquiry. Against this background, the applicant argued unsuccessfully that, at the disciplinary board, he would be made a scapegoat for the sins of the Gardaí of Donegal, and his contention was fortified by reference to the fact that there was no lay person on the disciplinary tribunal. Thus it was claimed there was objective bias. It is a little unclear from the High Court's (Smyth J.) judgment as to which of the respondent's various arguments carried the day. However, the court emphasised that there was no evidence of actual pre-judgment by any member of the board. In addition, the court noted the respondent's arguments that a police force was not like a professional body, and different considerations had to apply

---

[126] See Health and Social Care Professionals Act 2005 s.8(3); Veterinary Practice Act 2005 s.16(1). Of the Pharmacy Council comprising 21 persons, 11 must be persons who "are not and never have been" pharmacists (Pharmacy Act 2007 s.10). By s.17 of the Medical Practitioners Act 2007, out of a Council comprising 25, 11 will almost certainly be lay persons and the number may be as high as 13, the uncertainty arising from the fact that two members must be nominated by the Health Service Executive as representative of "the management of the public health sector".
[127] Solicitors (Amendment) Act 2002 s.8.
[128] [2004] 2 I.R. 516 esp. at paras 28–37.

to its internal discipline, because of the Gardaí's essential role in preserving law and order.[129]

Procedure

6–69 Although subject to the overriding principles of constitutional justice (explained below), procedure is, in the first instance, laid down by the constituent statute, and is generally supplemented by procedural rules made pursuant to statutory instrument or contained in the schedule to the constituent statute or both.[130] These provisions typically deal with matters such as the following: how many members constitute a quorum and a majority; the circumstances in which an oral hearing is required; whether the tribunal has the power to subpoena witnesses and to administer oaths; whether the witness commits an offence if he gives false evidence; and whether the witness enjoys the same privileges as a witness before a court. The provisions may also specify whether certain types of hearings are to be in public or in private[131]; whether the tribunal may sit in divisions; and whether it may delegate its powers to a smaller group of members. These issues aside, the tribunal is generally authorised to regulate its own procedure,[132] though sometimes the consent of the Minister is required.[133]

6–70 In the case of modern tribunals, the constituent statute often states that "[a] witness ... before a tribunal shall be entitled to the same privileges and immunities as a witness before a court".[134] This, be it noted, is a rather restricted protection in that it only covers actions against witnesses in respect of evidence given by them. However, even in the case of statements not within this limited protection or alternatively, where the tribunal enjoys no statutory protection whatsoever, it was

---

[129] It was also noted that the Regulations allowed a Garda to object to members of the board and that there was a right to appeal to an appeal board, which did include lay persons. For a discussion of these points in a more general context, see paras 13–67 to 13–72 and 14–152 to 14–158.

[130] See, e.g. Valuation Act 2001 Sch.2; Criminal Law (Insanity) Act 2006 s.12(6).

[131] For discussion of whether constitutional justice necessarily requires that there be a public hearing, see paras 14–57 to 14–58. For statutory references to this aspect, see the Irish Takeover Panel Act 1997 s.11(2) and s.14(2); Industrial Relations (Miscellaneous Provisions) Act 2004 s.9(8); Disability Act 2005 s.15(9); Safety, Health and Welfare at Work Act 2005 s.28(6); Employees (Provision of Information and Consultation) Act 2006 Sch.3 r.1(8); Employment Permits Act 2006 Sch.2 r.1(8).

[132] See, e.g. Adoption Act 1952 Sch.1; Residential Tenancies Act 2004 s.109. In *State (Casey) v Labour Court* (1984) 3 J.I.S.L.L. 135 at 138, O'Hanlon J. observed that the Labour Court was given a discretion by s.21 of the Industrial Relations Act 1946 to regulate its own procedures in relation to the taking of evidence on oath. Accordingly, neither the parties nor the High Court could dictate to the Labour Court the manner in which it conducts its own procedures "once it exercises its powers in accordance with the statute from which it derives its authority to act". See also, the following obiter dictum of Costello P. regarding the Hepatitis C Compensation Tribunal in *Ryan v The Compensation Tribunal* [1997] 1 I.L.R.M. 194 at 204: "Evidence can be given in writing by means of medical reports, or vive voce. Witnesses are not sworn. They are not subject to cross-examination. The Tribunal is, in my opinion, free to accept or reject any evidence adduced before it and is free to conclude that the evidence or some of it is exaggerated." For a similar attitude to tribunal procedures, see *Keane v An Bord Pleanála*, unreported, High Court, June 20, 1995.

[133] See, e.g. Criminal Law (Insanity) Act 2006 s.12(6).

[134] Committees of the Houses of the Oireachtas (Compellability, Privileges and Immunities of Witnesses) Act 1997 s.11; National Minimum Wage Act 2000 s.28(6); Veterinary Practice Act 2005 s.78(9).

probable that, at common law, proceedings before a tribunal would attract qualified privilege on the ground that the performance of a public duty is involved[135]: this view is now probably confirmed in the Defamation Act 2009 ss.18–19.

6–71 But irrespective of what the constituent statute may say or what administrative practice may develop, a tribunal is always subject to constitutional justice in its more stringent form, and so it is the courts that have the last word on such questions as whether an oral hearing should have been held.[136] The impact of constitutional justice is demonstrated by a British parallel. Out of the three examples, cited by Professor Wade and Dr Forsyth,[137] of amendments to draft procedural regulations secured by the British Council on Tribunals, all three changes have been effected in Ireland by way of the courts.

6–72 It is surprising though that there have been so few cases concerning the particular procedural rules of individual tribunals. However, such cases are starting to come to court. One Supreme Court case, *GE v Refugee Appeals Tribunal*,[138] has recently been decided which raises a common problem, namely the assignment of cases and the independence of tribunal members. The situation arose out of the fact that there was a serious backlog in the cases decided by one particular member of the RAT. Specifically, in the two appeals which formed the subject matter of the judicial review in *GE*, oral hearings had been held in March and May 2003 but, by March 2004, neither case had been determined. In response, the chairperson of the tribunal had purported to re-assign the cases, for re-hearing before another member of the tribunal. In doing this, the chairperson stated that he was acting under the Refugee Act 1996 Sch.2 para.13[139] which states that "the chairperson shall assign to each division [of the Tribunal] the business to be transacted by it."

6–73 Giving judgment for the Supreme Court majority, which reversed the High Court, Fennelly J. held that this statutory power did indeed include authority to remove a case from one division and assign to another. Fennelly J. went on to state that this power, like any other statutory administrative power, must be exercised fairly and in accordance with the rules of constitutional justice but this did not mean that the power should be confined to any particular circumstances, for example, illness or other incapacity (to take situations mentioned in the High Court and in Kearns J.'s dissenting judgment).[140]

---

[135] *Royal Aquarium Society v Parkinson* [1892] 1 Q.B. 431 at 443, 454.
[136] "Tribunals exercising quasi-judicial functions are frequently allowed to act informally—to receive unsworn evidence, to act on hearsay, to depart from the rules of evidence, to ignore courtroom procedures and the like—but they may not act in such a way as to imperil a fair hearing or a fair result": per Henchy J. in *Kiely v Minister for Social Welfare* [1977] I.R. 267 at 281. This is a major subject which is also considered at para.14–46.
[137] Wade and Forsyth, *Administrative Law* (Oxford: OUP, 2004), Ch.23. The three changes are: disclosure to both sides of information given to the tribunal; a right to representation; and the duty to give reasons. For the Irish position, see Ch.14.
[138] [2006] 2 I.R. 11: also reported under the name *Edobar v Ryan* [2005] 2 I.L.R.M. 113.
[139] As inserted by the Immigration Act 1999 s.11.
[140] Kearns J. ([2006] 2 I.R. 11 at 28–29), however, would have made a radical qualification on the power to reassign: "Where a division of the tribunal has business assigned to it, it is a startling proposition and one that requires some considerable justification to suggest that, without good and sufficient reason, the case sent for determination and actually heard by the member/division can be removed from that member/division ... While no contention has been advanced on behalf of the second respondent [the member to whom the cases were first

6–74   On one view, there was only a difference of degree between the majority, who said that the power to assign could not be exercised "unreasonably" and the dissenting judge who said that it could not be exercised "without good and sufficient reason"; whereas Kearns J. put more weight on the need for independence, even in a situation in which there was no actual threat to it.

6–75   The second case concerning tribunal procedure also involved an aspect of independence, namely immunity from suit. The case is *Beatty v Rent Tribunal*.[141] The background to it lay in an earlier case in which it had been held that, in determining a rent under the Housing (Private Rented Dwellings) Act 1982, the tribunal had breached the rules of constitutional justice.[142] On foot of the earlier case, the landlord made a claim, in the Supreme Court, against the tribunal for damages in negligence, for loss of rental income arising from the invalid rent review.

6–76   In the Supreme Court, Geoghegan J. (with whom Denham and Hardiman JJ. agreed) focused on the question of whether a tribunal could rely, as a defence, on some equivalent of judicial immunity. Geoghegan J. stated that the Rent Tribunal was:

> "... a statutory body exercising statutory [adjudicative] duties in the public interest ... [P]roviding it is purporting to act *bona fide* within its jurisdiction, it enjoys an immunity from an action in ordinary negligence ... The immunity of a statutory tribunal arises at common law and may be removed only if statute says so."[143]

6–77   Unfortunately, the judgment uses the term "tribunal" without the need to give a definition, which would have been useful in view of the multifarious forms which tribunals may take. As regards the width of the immunity, throughout the judgment it is assumed to be the same as for a court. Although, as mentioned, Fennelly and McCracken JJ.'s judgments took a broader view of the case than Geoghegan J. and sought to ground the concept of immunity on a sense of what was just and reasonable in the public interest, in the context of damages against

---

assigned] that his independence has been interfered with, by the purported re-assignment, the court must look beyond the facts of the present case to other cases where that consideration might well arise. Where a member/division of the tribunal actively resists the withdrawal and re-assignment of a case ... one can readily imagine that considerations of independence can and will then be under intense focus."

Kearns J. fortified his stance by reference to his own judgment in *Boland v Garda Síochána Complaints Board* [2004] IEHC 239; unreported, High Court, Kearns J., November 28, 2003, where the facts were similar, save that a different tribunal was involved in the two cases. Kearns J. did not go into the question of *jus tertii*, on which see paras 16–235 to 16–238, despite the fact that there was no suggestion that a question of independence arose in the instant case. No one took the point that the Tribunal may have been under a duty to determine the case without too long a delay: see para.14–67.

[141]   [2006] 2 I.R. 191.

[142]   For various reasons: the presence of the tenant and the absence of the landlord during the tribunal's inspection of the premises gave rise to an appearance of bias; the applicant landlords were not allowed adequate time to respond to a valuation report submitted by the notice party; absence of adequate reasons for the determination.

[143]   [2006] 2 I.R. 191 at 195–196. Fennelly and McCracken JJ., in separate assenting judgments, relied mainly on a different ground.

public authorities,[144] their judgments are also of interest here. For they regarded the fact that the tribunal was "adjudicating" as a relevant factor to suggest that it should be immune from liability.[145]

6–78   A more general point of interest here is to what extent precedents developed in respect of one tribunal may be applied to another. In other words, is there a "common law" of tribunals? The answer is probably that, although different tribunals have different governing statutes and different subject matters, depending on the issue a precedent may be of value across the field; for example, the two cases just outlined engage the general theme of independence and so are likely to be of wide influence.

D. The Social Welfare Appeals System

6–79   A study of the detailed substantive operation of a tribunal would extend beyond the bounds of administrative law and into the particular substantive field of law in which the tribunal was operating. For example, the substance of social welfare law[146] turns on the interpretation of such phrases as "capable of work [and] available for work" (unemployment benefit); "accident arising out of and in the course of employment" (occupational injury benefits); or whether a claimant has submitted to the necessary medical examinations (maternity benefit).[147] We cannot go into these substantive issues. But in order to give some flavour of the operation of tribunals, we include the following brief account of the Social Welfare Appeals system.

6–80   In 2008, claims worth an aggregate of €17.8 billion (which is 33.4 per cent of current public expenditure or 11.4 per cent of GNP) were made on the Minister for Social Protection[148] in respect of such social welfare payments as disability benefit; unemployment benefit and assistance; occupational injuries benefit; and old-age pensions.[149] This represented a 15 per cent increase on the corresponding figure for 2007 and at the time of writing a further rise seemed inevitable in view of the

---

[144]   See paras 18–54 to 18–55 and 18–76.

[145]   Fennelly J. stated: "I believe the respondent performs a role akin to that of an arbitrator, the existence of a remedy in damages might tend to compromise the independence of the respondent by inhibiting its judgment in performing its essentially adjudicative role" ([2006] 2 I.R. 191 at 216). McCracken J. stated, at 220: "While [members of the Tribunal] are not judges and, therefore, cannot be acting in a strictly judicial capacity, nevertheless their function is adjudicative."

[146]   The principal statutory provisions and regulations include the following: Social Welfare Consolidation Act 2005; Social Welfare (Appeals) Regulations 1998 (S.I. No. 108 of 1998); and Circuit Court Rules (Social Welfare Appeals) 2007 (S.I. No. 10 of 2007). See generally, Cousins, *Social Welfare Law* (Dublin: Thomson Round Hall, 2002).

[147]   Social Welfare Consolidation Act 2005 s.62(5)(a) (unemployment benefit); s.70(1) (occupational injuries benefits); s.47(1) (maternity benefit).

[148]   Formerly, the Minister for Social and Family Affairs, before that briefly, Community and Family Affairs and, earlier, Social Welfare.

[149]   *Statistical Information on Social Welfare Services 2008*. There are a number of other schemes which are administered by the Health Service Executive and which, therefore, fall outside these particular appeal procedures. These include supplementary welfare allowances (Social Welfare Consolidation Act 2005 Pt 3 Ch.9, especially s.194). See also, *H v Eastern Health Board* [1988] I.R. 747.

prevailing economic gloom. The substantive basis for these vast schemes, which is covered below, is consolidated: initially in 1981, then in 1993 and, currently, in the Social Welfare (Consolidation) Act 2005.[150] The claims are settled by deciding officers, with an appeal to an appeals officer, and we turn now to deal with these officials, of which at any rate the appeals officer is conventionally regarded as a tribunal.

Deciding officer

6–81   In practice most applicants will, first, be advised by junior Department of Social and Family Affairs officials as to their entitlement to the benefit which has been claimed. If the advice is in the negative, then the applicant can insist that a deciding officer adjudicate upon the claim.[151] This officer may make various inquiries (e.g. to former employers of the applicant) but there is no oral hearing and in general, no attempt is made to observe the rules of constitutional justice. Such a failure (in a situation where the effect of the decision of the deciding officer is to terminate payments to persons already in receipt of social welfare benefits or assistance) was the subject of the judgments of Barron J. in *State (Houlihan) v Minister for Social Welfare*[152] and of O'Hanlon J. in *Thompson v Minister for Social Welfare*.[153] In *Houlihan*, the applicant was alleged to have fraudulently obtained social welfare benefits, but since the decision to disqualify her from benefit was based on facts which had not been brought to her attention, Barron J. held that the decision could not stand. He added that the claimant "… should know fully the extent of the case being made against her and that no decision should be made until she has been given proper opportunity to deal fully with a case".[154]

6–82   In *Thompson v Minister for Social Welfare*, the deciding officer ruled that the applicant should be disqualified from receiving unemployment benefit for a six-week period because of the latter's refusal to participate in a career advice programme. O'Hanlon J. held that, in such circumstances, before a deciding officer terminates the payments of an applicant who has been in receipt of unemployment assistance for some time, "… he should inform the person concerned that the position is being reviewed by him; the grounds upon which he is considering disallowing further payment; and the person concerned should be given an opportunity to answer the case made against him".[155] Because of the failure of the deciding officer to satisfy these requirements, "however informally", his decision had to be set aside for non-compliance with constitutional justice.

---

[150] The 2005 Act s.362(2) continues in force all instruments made and documents issued under its precursor, the 1993 Consolidation Act; and the equivalent (s.302 of the 1993 Act) had done the same for instruments made and documents issued, under the 1981 Act.

[151] The deciding officer has a seldom-used power to refrain from deciding the case himself, but to seek the assistance of an appeals officer: Social Welfare Consolidation Act 2005 s.303.

[152] Unreported, High Court, July 23, 1986.

[153] [1989] I.R. 618.

[154] [1989] I.R. 618 at 621.

[155] However, on receiving the news of the decision, the applicant sought and obtained an interview with the deciding officer. The officer explained why he proposed to review the applicant's entitlement and made inquiries of the applicant as to why he had refused to attend a training course. O'Hanlon J. held that, at this point, the deciding officer had sufficiently complied with fair procedures, so that the disqualification decision, which took effect only later, was not invalid.

6–83   It is also noteworthy that in *Corcoran v Minister for Social Welfare*,[156] the High Court was prepared to consider a challenge (albeit an unsuccessful one) based on substantive "unreasonableness" against the termination by a deciding officer of the plaintiff's unemployment assistance.[157]

Appeals officer

6–84   The regulations contain the following broad statement: "[t]he procedure at the hearing shall be such as the appeals officer may determine",[158] which is however subject to a number of detailed provisions, as well of course as constitutional justice. An appeal against a refusal is supposed to be filed with the Chief Appeals Officer within 21 days, although, in practice, this time limit is not strictly adhered to, since the Minister has a discretion to admit late claims. The appeal is initiated by a "notice of appeal" (which states the relevant facts and arguments on which the applicant proposes to rely) and is accompanied by any documentary evidence.[159] If a replying statement is filed, it will generally be confined to a summary of the original basis of the decision under appeal and the applicant will generally be permitted to have access to this document. The appeals officer hears the case de novo.[160]

6–85   The appeals officer is given a broad discretion to decide whether to grant an oral hearing, save that the Minister has power to direct that a particular case shall be heard orally, where he considers that this is warranted in the circumstances.[161] In fact, oral hearings (at 50 to 60 venues throughout the country) are held in a substantial number of appeals.[162]

6–86   Each appeals officer decides an average of about 1,000 cases each year, and many oral hearings are disposed of in less than 15 minutes. The appellant usually appears in person but "may, with the consent of the appeals officer, be

---

[156] [1991] 2 I.R. 175 at 180 per Murphy J.: "If [the deciding officer] drew [from the motor car which the applicant owned] the inference that the applicant had a more substantial income … which would result in the applicant exceeding the … permitted figure, that such a decision could not be described as unreasonable …".

[157] Unfortunately, none of these cases considered a general principle which might have been considered relevant here, that where an appeal is available and not used, a court's discretion should be exercised against granting review. See paras 16–72 to 16–80. Nor was it thought even worth querying whether a want of constitutional justice at the original stage may be made good by its availability on appeal. See paras 14–152 to 14–158.

[158] Social Welfare (Appeals) Regulations 1998 (S.I. No. 108 of 1998) art.18.

[159] Social Welfare (Appeals) Regulations 1998 (S.I. No. 108 of 1998) arts 9–12.

[160] Social Welfare Consolidation Act 2005 s.311(3).

[161] Social Welfare (Appeals) Regulations 1998 (S.I. No. 108 of 1998) arts 13 and 14; but see Social Welfare Consolidation Act 2005 s.326. In *Kiely v Minister for Social Welfare (No. 2)* [1977] I.R. 267 at 278, Henchy J. stated that if there were "unresolved conflicts in the documentary evidence, as to any matter essential to a ruling of the claim, the intention of these Regulations is that those conflicts shall be resolved by an oral hearing." See also, *Galvin v Chief Appeals Officer* [1997] 3 I.R. 240 where Costello P. held that the respondent had breached fair procedures in not holding an oral inquiry to resolve conflicts of fact regarding the payment of insurance contributions. But this approach tends to overlook the fact that in practice "[m]ost, if not all, of the documentary evidence will be adduced by the deciding officer who may fail to set out clearly the appellant's view of the appeal": Clark, "Social Welfare Insurance Appeals" (1978) 13 Ir. Jur. (N.S) 265 at 274.

[162] Some recent figures are: 59 per cent (2008); 63 per cent (2007); 65 per cent (2006); 67 per cent (2005); 69 per cent (2004).

represented at the hearing by any member of his or her family or by any other person".[163] Depending on the circumstances, a failure on the part of the appeals officer to accede to a request to grant legal representation in an appropriate case would probably amount to an unreasonable exercise of his discretion and/or a violation of the principles of constitutional justice.[164]

6–87 A linked question concerns payment of legal costs. *O'Sullivan v Minister for Social Welfare*[165] sets down fairly firmly that the conventional requirement of reasonableness applies. The facts were that, purporting to apply his statutory discretion, an appeals officer had awarded IR£30 expenses for the attendance of the (successful) appellant's solicitor; but had refused an application for costs. Barron J. stated:

> "The basic question must be was it reasonable to have legal representation? If it was, then there may be reasons for awarding costs even if the appeal fails. In such circumstances, where the appeal succeeds then costs should be allowed save where the principles of fairness require otherwise ... Where it is reasonable to expect legal representation, then it would *prima facie* be unfair to refuse costs to a successful appellant. In the instant case there are no valid grounds indicated upon which costs should have been refused."[166]

6–88 In addition, there was an alternative ground for the applicant's success, which is of general interest. This arose from the fact that there was in existence an agreement between the appeals officer and the Law Society that, where a solicitor's attendance had been permitted, an agreed sum should be paid, though only by way of expenses, not costs. Following conventional judicial review principles it was said that this agreement had "fettered the exercise of [the appeals officer's] discretion".[167] In *O'Sullivan*, the earlier case of *Corcoran v Minister for Social Welfare*[168] was distinguished on the basis that that case had held only that there was no *right* for an appellant to be paid his costs. Moreover, in *Corcoran* the appellant had been unsuccessful. Apart from the case law just mentioned, where legal representation is permitted, it used to be the case that solicitors and counsel were awarded costs in accordance with a scale rate, but the regulations now leave the position anything but clear.[169]

6–89 The appeals officer may take evidence on oath.[170] He may require a person to attend or to produce documents and if the person fails to comply with such a

---

[163] Social Welfare (Appeals) Regulations 1998 (S.I. No. 108 of 1998) art.15(2).

[164] The decision as to whether to grant legal representation is said to be at the discretion of the appeals officer; Social Welfare (Appeals) Regulations 1998 (S.I. No. 108 of 1998) art.15; *R. v Home Secretary, Ex p. Tarrant* [1985] Q.B. 251; *Flanagan v University College Dublin* [1988] I.R 724; *Gallagher v Revenue Commissioners (No. 2)* [1995] 1 I.R. 55. But cf. the comments to the contrary of Murphy J. in *Corcoran v Minister for Social Welfare* [1991] 2 I.R. 175 at 183. See also, paras 14–47 to 14–56.

[165] [1997] 1 I.R. 464.

[166] [1997] 1 I.R. 464 at 467.

[167] [1997] 1 I.R. 464 at 467.

[168] [1991] 2 I.R. 175.

[169] Social Welfare Consolidation Act 2005 s.316. For an unidentified High Court case on legal costs, see Social Welfare Appeals Office Annual Report for 1995 (Pn 7783), p.19.

[170] Social Welfare Consolidation Act 2005 s.313.

request, the appeals officer may, on serving notice to such a person, apply to the District Court for an order requiring attendance or production of documents, as the case may be.[171] In addition, the appeals officer may admit "any duly authenticated written statement or other material as *prima facie* evidence of any fact or facts in any case in which he or she thinks it appropriate".[172] The decision of the appeals officer is sent to the Minister. The applicant will then receive a memorandum of the Minister's decision. In the case of unsuccessful appeals, reasons must be given.[173] (The memorandum is in standard form, and, in the case of unsuccessful appeals, sets forth a list of alternative reasons for the decision. The reasons which are inapplicable are deleted.) The fact that appeals officers' decisions are not published means that there is no system of stare decisis, but the annual reports contain about 10 pages comprising approximately 20 synopses of substantive decisions in the area. In addition, the website (*www.socialwelfareappeals.ie*) contains a selection of case studies grouped by topic; and freedom of information requests to the office are running at about 50 annually in recent years (with a spike to 66 in 2008).

6–90   The Chief Appeals Officer is empowered to appoint an assessor to sit with an appeals officer in an appropriate case.[174] The role of the medical assessor under the analogous Social Welfare (Occupational Injuries) Act 1966 (repealed by the 2005 Consolidation Act) was examined by the Supreme Court in *Kiely v Minister for Social Welfare (No. 2)*.[175] In the view of Henchy J. (who appears to have adopted the procedure in a court of law, as a role model) the regulations envisaged that the medical assessors' role should be a strictly limited one: the assessors should not take any active part in the proceedings; their task was simply to give information on medical matters when requested to do so by the appeals officer.

6–91   The number of appeals of all types is given in the Annual Reports: in all, 13,845 appeals were dealt with in 2007,[176] and 15,724 in 2008.[177] Other numerical information given in the reports shows, for example, that nearly half of the appeals in recent years had a favourable outcome for the appellant in that they were either fully or partially allowed or resolved by way of a revised decision of a deciding officer. In addition the average time taken to process all appeals was about 20 weeks.

---

[171]   Social Welfare Consolidation Act 2005 s.314. Wilful disobedience of the notice is an offence carrying a fine not exceeding €1,500.

[172]   Social Welfare (Appeals) Regulations (S.I. No. 108 of 1998). For comment on an earlier version, see *Kiely v Minister for Social Welfare* [1977] I.R. 267 at 279 per Henchy J. Another forerunner, Social Welfare (Appeals) Regulations 1990 (S.I. No. 344 of 1990) art.17(3), gave a wider discretion than the present provision to the appeals officer to admit evidence in writing on a prima facie basis.

[173]   Social Welfare (Appeals) Regulations 1998 (S.I. No. 108 of 1998) art.19(3)(b).

[174]   Social Welfare Consolidation Act 2005 s.309.The Social Welfare (Consolidation) Act 1981 s.298(12)(c) stated that the parties may waive the absence of an assessor. There is no equivalent of this provision in the 2005 Act. Nor was there in the 1993 Act, yet Clarke (p.294) remarked that "in practice appeals are heard without an assessor if the appellant waives the need for the assessor ...".

[175]   [1977] I.R. 267.

[176]   6,531 (47 per cent) had a favourable outcome to the applicant, 5,626 (41 per cent) had an unfavourable outcome and the remaining 1,688 (12 per cent) were withdrawn.

[177]   7,523 (48 per cent) had a favourable outcome to the applicant, 6,135 (39 per cent) an unfavourable outcome and the remaining 2,066 (13 per cent) were withdrawn. The Office put the increase, caused by a surge in applications, down to prevailing unfavourable conditions in the economy.

6–92   How independent is this system?[178] The system is administered by civil servants working in the Department of Social Welfare whose independence is not guaranteed by law and who, perhaps, are influenced by departmental policy considerations. It is true that some attempt has been made to ameliorate this perceived lack of independence. The Chief Appeals Officer (himself a creation of the Social Welfare Act 1952 and appointed by the Minister) is "responsible for the distribution, amongst the appeals officers, of the references [sc. appeals] to them and for the prompt consideration of such references", and also for determining whether assessors should sit with an appeals officer in a particular case and referring questions of law to the High Court.[179] Further reform came with the establishment of the Social Welfare Appeals Office in 1991, of which the Chief Appeals Officer is head.[180] An appeal now formally lies to the Chief Appeals Officer instead of the Minister.

6–93   There are more than 50 staff in the Office, including the Chief Appeals Officer, Deputy Chief Appeals Officer and about 20 appeals officers. Under the regulations, meetings of appeals officers are held three or so times a year. The main purpose of these meetings is to promote best practice, ensure consistency among appeals officers and discuss recent developments, including new regulations and court decisions.[181] The Chief Appeals Officer is obliged to produce an annual report on the working of the appeals officers, which report must be laid before both Houses of the Oireachtas.[182] In addition, an independent Social Welfare Tribunal was established for a very limited category of decisions, namely:

> "[where] in relation to a stoppage of work or a trade dispute, a deciding officer or an appeals officer has decided that a person is disqualified ... for receipt of unemployment benefit ... or assistance, that person may ... apply to the Social Welfare Tribunal."[183]

Review of deciding officer's or appeals officer's decision

6–94   In the first place, a deciding officer may review an earlier decision of a deciding officer or even an appeals officer if there is new evidence, or if the earlier decision was based on a mistake of law or fact, or more significantly, if there has been a change in circumstances. It is also open to an appeals officer to review the earlier decision of an appeals officer, though on slightly narrower grounds than in the case of a deciding officer. By virtue of these provisions, a deciding officer (or where appropriate, an appeals officer) is entitled not only to increase but even to

---

[178] The claim has been made by the Office that: "The independence of Appeals Officers under the law has always been carefully observed and protected by successive Ministers for Social Welfare and by the Department of Social Welfare ..."; Annual Report for 1991, p.5. But see, to the opposite effect, the Ombudsman's comment (1993 Report, p.64). For the narrow category of institutional bias, see paras 13–23 to 13–29.

[179] Social Welfare Act 1952 s.43.

[180] Social Welfare Act 1990 Pt V.

[181] Social Welfare (Appeals) Regulations (S.I. No. 108 of 1998) art.7.

[182] 2005 Act s.308.

[183] 2005 Act s.331.

reduce or disallow payments, save that the latter order will not have retrospective effect, except in the case of fraud.[184]

6–95   Secondly, the thorny s.327 of the Social Welfare Consolidation Act 2005 probably has the effect of creating an appeal on a point of law[185] from a decision of an appeals officer to the High Court. However, read literally, the scope of this appeal would seem to be extraordinarily narrow in that a question arising "in relation to a claim for benefit" would be excluded, and the decision of the appeals officer rendered "final and conclusive".[186] As Lynch J. observed in *Kinghan v Minister for Social Welfare*[187] (interpreting a precursor of s.327), such a literal interpretation would have the effect of excluding appeals in:

> "... the vast majority of questions that might arise under the provisions of the [social welfare legislation], leaving only a minority of cases where persons claim not to be within the Act and therefore not liable to pay contributions under the Act nor entitled to benefits thereunder."

6–96   Indeed, s.320 of the 2005 Act goes further and purports to exclude, even from judicial review (the formula "final and conclusive" is used), virtually all decisions of an appeals officer.[188] It is significant that the scope of the decisions so excluded is defined to be coterminous with the extent of the decisions from which no appeal is allowed. In sum, apart from the negligible area conjectured in the passage quoted from *Kinghan*, there would be neither appeal nor review. The demarcation line postulated in *Kinghan* would appear to be based on the rather quaint view that there should be an appeal in all cases where the citizen was required to make payments to the State, but not where the appellant was a mere recipient of the State's largesse. In *Kinghan's* case, Lynch J. reacted against such a construction of (the earlier equivalent of) s.327, saying that the matter excluded should be construed narrowly so as not to oust the jurisdiction of the High Court "save where such ouster is clear". One might add the comment that this does not go far enough in that it appears that the judge's view was based exclusively on the common law presumption against ouster of the High Court and did not take into account the effect of Art.34.3.1° of the Constitution. In any event, the apparent effect of *Kinghan* is that an appeal now lies to the High Court by virtue of s.327

[184] 2005 Act ss.301–302, 317–319. See also, *Lundy v Minister for Social Welfare* [1993] 3 I.R. 406.
[185] The Chief Appeals Officer is entitled to refer "any question" arising from a decision of the appeals officer to the High Court (i.e. this reference is not confined to points of law), provided that the question does not fall within s.320: 2005 Act s.307. A welcome innovation is that, where the Chief Appeals Officer certifies that the ordinary appeal procedures "are inadequate to secure the effective processing of such appeal", the appeal is then transferred to the Circuit Court which may affirm the decision or substitute the decision of the deciding officer in accordance with this Act and upon the same evidence as would otherwise be available to the Appeals Officer: Social Welfare Consolidation Act 2005 s.307. By virtue of s.307(3), no appeal lies from the decision of the Circuit Court "on an appeal under this section".
[186] Section 327 refers the reader on to s.320. As it happens, s.300(2)(a) is the principal provision to which s.320 applies, for s.300(2)(a) refers to a question arising "in relation to a claim for benefit", which is a very wide category indeed.
[187] Unreported, High Court, November 25, 1985. This case concerned identical provisions of the earlier Social Welfare (Consolidation) Act 1981.
[188] The "final and conclusive" clause contained in s.320 could not, however, bar judicial review by the High Court: see paras 11–02 to 11–03.

of the 2005 Act in respect of all decisions of an appeals officer, the provisions of s.320 notwithstanding.[189]

6–97 As an alternative, an appeals officer's decision may be challenged by way of judicial review, as is testified to by a growing number of such cases. We have just referred to some of these, in the context of constitutional justice and legal costs. Another good example is *McHugh v Minister for Social Welfare*.[190] Here the applicant, who was in receipt of an unmarried mother's allowance, as a result lost a disability benefit based upon her contribution, yet would not have lost unemployment benefit, which was regarded as the equivalent for jobseekers. This difference was held by the Supreme Court to be so illogical, arbitrary or unfair as to be ultra vires the parent section of the Social Welfare (Consolidation) Act 1981. In a field particularly rich in delegated legislation, a number of other cases have involved Art.15.2.1°.[191] Another case engaging a general principle is *Scanlon v Minister for Social, Community and Family Affairs*.[192] This case considered whether the terms of the legislation were such that retrospective effect should be given to a legislative change regarding the recovery of overpayment of social welfare benefit. It was held, first, that this was the result required by the legislation and that it was not unconstitutional; and secondly that the appeals officer was not "administering justice" so that Art.34.1 was not engaged.

6–98 In *State (Power) v Moran*,[193] Gannon J. ruled that an absence of probative evidence to support a decision of an appeals officer was not an error affecting jurisdiction, and the decision could not be impeached in certiorari proceedings. This restrictive interpretation of the scope of jurisdictional error is out of line with some of the modern authorities.[194] However, in the subsequent decision of *Foley v Moulton*[195] the same judge was at pains to stress that, in *Foley*, the appeals officer had based his decision on "evidence which was reasonably capable of supporting the determination he made",[196] which perhaps, may be said to raise the inference that Gannon J. would have quashed the decision had it not been so based. *Murphy v Minister for Social Welfare*[197] provides some further evidence that the courts are now more willing to scrutinise decisions of deciding and appeals officers in judicial review application, for here Blayney J. had little hesitation in quashing a decision of an appeals officer who had answered "the wrong question", and thereby erred in law. Similarly, as far as challenges to the validity of social welfare legislation on

---

[189] Note that in *Foley v Moulton* [1989] I.L.R.M. 169 the respondents accepted that an appeal could be made to the High Court under s.299 of the 1981 Act (which was similar to s.327 of the 2005 Act) on all questions of law.

[190] [1994] 2 I.R. 139.

[191] *Healy v Minister for Social Welfare* [1999] 1 I.L.R.M. 72; *Harvey v Minister for Social Welfare* [1990] 2 I.R. 232; and *State (Kenny) v Minister for Social Welfare* [1986] I.R. 693.

[192] [2001] 1 I.R. 64.

[193] [1976–1977] I.L.R.M. 20.

[194] See Ch.10, Part E. But cf. *Galvin v Chief Appeals Officer* [1997] 3 I.R. 240, where Costello P. held that incorrect inferences, which had not been based on evidence, constituted errors within jurisdiction and could not be quashed in judicial review proceedings.

[195] [1989] I.L.R.M. 169.

[196] [1989] I.L.R.M. 169 at 176.

[197] [1987] I.R. 295.

constitutional[198] and European Community law[199] grounds are concerned, judicial deference has not been much in evidence.

6–99   However, pulling in the other direction is the fact that the courts have sometimes been reluctant to interfere with the decisions of specialists such as appeals officers,[200] especially if this means interfering with a long-standing interpretation of the relevant regulations.[201] This was certainly the approach taken in *Henry Denny & Sons (Ireland) Ltd v Minister for Social Welfare*.[202] In this appeal under s.271 of the 1993 Act, the equivalent of s.327 of the 2005 Act, the Supreme Court upheld an appeals officer's conclusion that a supermarket demonstrator was actually employed by the appellant. The appeals officer's findings of fact could not be disturbed "unless they were incapable of being supported by the facts or were based on an erroneous view of the law [because the courts] should be slow to interfere with the decisions of expert administrative tribunals".

6–100   Many cases in this area turn upon an interpretation of the social welfare legislation, and consequently are not of interest in the present work. Some of the others, which depend upon general principles, are treated in the later chapters dealing with general judicial review.

E. Internal Grievance Systems

6–101   Just as a generation ago, tribunals were the Cinderella of our system for the control of public administration; this doubtful sobriquet has now been transferred to "internal grievance remedies". This term is intended to capture (more or less) formal machinery for settling individual grievances against some unit of public administration.[203] Such arrangements may be internal in the sense that they are administered by machinery which is part of the same institution responsible for the alleged grievance. However, especially given what was said earlier about the indefiniteness of the ground covered by the term "tribunal", in the following notes about a field which is likely to grow, the dividing line suggested by "internal" has not been taken too rigidly.[204]

6–102   In the age of the rights-conscious citizen, the wisdom and economy of

---

[198]   See, e.g. *H v Eastern Health Board* [1988] I.R. 747 and *Hyland v Minister for Social Welfare* [1988] I.R. 624.

[199]   See, e.g. *McDermott and Cotter v Minister for Social Welfare* [1987] I.L.R.M. 324.

[200]   Note the manner in which Gannon J. refused to disturb a finding by an appeals officer in *Foley v Moulton* [1989] I.L.R.M. 169 to the effect that the claimant was co-habiting with a man and was thus disqualified from receiving a widow's pension by virtue of s.92(3) of the Social Welfare (Consolidation) Act 1981.

[201]   *R. v National Insurance Commissioner, Ex p. Stratton* [1979] Q.B. 361 at 369 (Lord Denning).

[202]   [1998] 1 I.R. 34 at 37–38 (Hamilton C.J.).

[203]   Sainsbury, "Internal Reviews and Weakening of Social Security Claimants' Rights of Appeal" in Richardson and Genn (eds), *Administrative Law and Government Action* (Oxford: Clarendon Press, 1994), pp.287–307; Birkinshaw, *Grievances, Remedies and the State* (London: Sweet and Maxwell, 1985).

[204]   An example of a hybrid system concerns freedom of information, which is administered by way of internal review by the public body which, itself, should have provided reasons; with an external review by the Information Commissioner: Freedom of Information Act 1997 s.14.

a robust grievance process which provides accessible remedies is coming to be appreciated. There is great wisdom in the maxim "exhaust your local remedies first", and in 1998 the Ombudsman published a guide to internal complaints systems, *Settling Complaints*.[205] For example, the Disability Act 2005 employs a multi-layered appeals process internal to the Health Service Executive: an initial assessment as to whether or not an applicant is disabled within the meaning of the statute is performed by an Assessment Officer[206]; but an unhappy applicant then has recourse to a Complaints Officer[207]; and if still dissatisfied, may appeal to an Appeals Officer.[208] A variant on this approach is employed by the Education for Persons with Special Educational Needs Act 2004 (which, in contrast to the Disability Act 2005, applies only to those under 18). There, an initial assessment may (on the request of a child's parents, the principal at the child's school or the National Council for Special Education) be made under the auspices of the National Council for Special Education. There is then an appeal lying to an independent and separate Special Education Appeals Board.[209] An interesting feature for the remedy of individual grievances, common to both schemes, is a provision allowing the matter to be referred for mediation between the aggrieved party and the agency concerned.[210]

6–103 One common pattern is illustrated by the case of employment permits, where the review is undertaken by a more senior officer, appointed by the Minister for that purpose.[211] Part IX of the Health Act 2004 establishes a similar complaints system. If anyone provided with a health or personal social service by the Health Service Executive claims that it does not accord with "fair and sound administrative practice",[212] the person may make a complaint to an internal complaints officer, who is someone "designated ... by the Executive for the purpose of dealing with complaints ...".[213] One should add that there is also an independent agency, the

---

[205] In his 2000 Report, p.38, the Ombudsman states: "... I also have a role in promoting higher standards of public administration. One of the ways in which I approach the latter role is to encourage public bodies to set up internal complaints systems. My Office now spends a considerable amount of time advising public bodies on the broad principles which underpin effective complaints systems."
    See the Ombudsman's *Annual Reports* for: 1997, pp.15–21; 1998, pp.6–7, 28; 1999, p.37; 2002, pp.5,19; 2004, pp.23–25; and 2006, pp.21–22, 29–30.
[206] Disability Act 2005 ss.8–10.
[207] Disability Act 2005 ss.14 and 15.
[208] Disability Act 2005 s.16.
[209] Education for Persons with Special Educational Needs Act 2004 ss.4, 12, 19 and 36. See generally, O'Mahony, *Educational Rights in Irish Law* (Dublin: Thomson Round Hall, 2006), pp.184–204, 259–264. The possibility of an overlap between the Disability Act 2005 and the Education for Persons with Special Educational Needs Act 2004 and co-ordination of the two measures in such cases is provided for in the former: see ss.8(3), (9), 11. In the case of a disagreement between the Health Services Executive and the National Council for Special Education, the Executive may appeal to the Special Education Appeals Board (s.11). The Education for Persons with Special Educational Needs Act 2004 addresses the provision of education for persons with special educational needs who are under the age of 18, whereas the Disability Act 2005 is confined to those who are over the age of 18 (s.11(6)).
[210] Education for Persons with Special Educational Needs Act 2004 s.38; Disability Act 2005 s.19.
[211] Employment Permits Act 2006 s.13.
[212] Section 46 of the 2004 Act, which curiously defines this term in exactly the same way as the concept of maladministration in the Ombudsman Act 1980.
[213] Section 45 of the 2004 Act.

Health Information and Quality Authority, whose functions is to consider complaints against the HSE.

Independence

6–104 The big query which has been raised regarding internal complaints systems concerns their independence. Take, for instance, the appeals officers in the Department of Agriculture, Food and the Marine,[214] who operate under a chief appeals officer, known as the Director of Agricultural Appeals. This is a system established by the Agriculture Appeals Act 2001, to entertain appeals against the Minister's decision in respect of certain agricultural or rural enterprise schemes, specified in the Schedule to the Act. The Act states that "the Appeals Officers shall … be independent in the performance of their functions" and they must, if requested by the appellant, hold an oral hearing. The Director is selected following a competition held either by the Top Level Appointments Committee or under the Commission for Public Appointments.[215] On the other hand, the appeals officers are selected either by the Minister from among his civil servants or, under the public service appointments regime, from among civil servants in other Departments. There is no provision for security of tenure and the appeals officers are not part of a separate institution. Thus, it is uncertain whether to regard this as internal or independent. The criticism has also been made that, since the jurisdiction of appeals officers is generally limited to the adjudication of individual cases, they do not have the power to set departmental or agency policy. If robust feedback procedures are not in place, one might find similar problems recurring.[216]

6–105 Concerns about the independence of appeals officers arise in part from the fact that they operate within the agency about which the complaints are made, and thus, they may well find themselves adjudicating on the decisions of close colleagues or superiors. Much hinges, therefore, on the level of the organisation in which appeals officers are placed, and who determines their prospects for promotion. American Administrative Law Judges ("ALJs"), though nominally employed within a particular agency, jealously guard their independence and their interests are represented by a number of union-type organisations.[217] In contrast to this protection, the formulation in Irish legislation is declaratory only, usually stating merely that "[t]he appeals officer shall be independent in the performance of his or her functions under this Act."[218]

---

[214] For equivalent debate regarding arrangements in the Department of Social Protection, see paras 6–37 to 6–43 and 6–92.

[215] See paras 3–55 to 3–63.

[216] Compare "Improving the Delivery of Quality Public Services", *National Economic and Social Forum Report No. 34* (2006), pp.112–117.

[217] e.g. the Federal Administrative Law Judges Conference, the Association of Administrative Law Judges, which represents only Social Security ALJs, and the Forum of United States Administrative Law Judges. Professional organisations that include both state and federal ALJs include the National Association of Administrative Law Judiciary, the ABA National Conference of Administrative Law Judiciary, and the National Association of Hearing Officers.

[218] This drew the ire of Deputy Healy during the Dáil Debates, on the measure which became the Health Act 2004: "Part 9 deals with complaints but an independent complaints procedure is required, not one that is operated by any body established under this legislation. Those who have legitimate complaints about the health service should have access to an independent complaints procedure, rather than to someone who is part of the system. The perception would

6–106   What seemed to be an example of a lack of independence arose in a case centring on the mechanism established by the Education Act 1998 s.29. This establishes an appeal where a primary or post-primary school board expels a student. The appeal is to an appeals committee, which is appointed ad hoc by the Minister for each appeal. Where an appeal is upheld, the Secretary General (not, be it noted, the Minister) may give, to the school board of management, such directions as appear to him expedient to remedy the matter. This is a sensible provision. In paras 13–35 to 13–36, we draw attention to the fact that normally, following a successful judicial review, the case must in principle go back to the public body which it has just reviewed for this decision to be retaken. There are rather obvious dangers to this arrangement, especially where a relatively small institution like a school with a single person at its head, is involved. The Act meets this type of difficulty by in effect empowering the Secretary General to implement the appeals committee's view. Yet in one episode, the Secretary General interpreted his power as allowing him effectively to reinstate the school's original decision and thus overrule the appeals committee's decision. This episode resulted in a successful complaint to the Ombudsman.[219]

F. Overlap between Courts, Tribunals and Other Bodies

6–107   There are now so many public bodies with statutory authority to make decisions which impact on the rights of citizens that it is inevitable that there should be situations in which more than one of these public bodies is involved in the same situation. The courts and the flock of tribunals which are under discussion in this chapter are only the most important examples. In addition, there are ombudsmen (now several in number); public inquiries; and internal grievance/disciplinary systems. Situations may easily be imagined in which there is competing jurisdiction or inconsistency between several of these bodies.[220] In fact, so far the situations which have actually arisen have concerned some form of overlap between a court and a disciplinary tribunal.

6–108   Here we shall focus on the following four discrete areas: (1) where it is argued that publicity from an earlier public inquiry or tribunal would prejudice a later criminal trial; (2) where it is sought to rely on the outcome of a court case in later proceedings before a tribunal; (3) where conduct, by professional witnesses, in or around court proceedings, is the basis of a misconduct charge before a professional disciplinary tribunal; (4) controversy as to the appropriate forum—tribunal or court

---

be that such a person would not have the same feeling for dealing with genuine individual complaints about the various health services provided. A redress board should be established to deal with complaints deemed to be well-founded. People who have gone through the health service and have come out at the other end with serious disability or trauma should be able to seek redress"; 593 *Dáil Debates* Col.1084 (November 26, 2004).

[219]   2004 Report, pp.14–15: "The Secretary General may have exceeded his powers under the Act and may have based his decision on irrelevant grounds". The Ombudsman's report states that the decision "should assist in enhancing the independence of the appeals structure established under the Education Act, 1998".

[220]   "That way madness lies; let me shun that", Shakespeare, *King Lear*, Act III, sc. iv. King Lear was contemplating his daughters' ingratitude.

(1) Publicity from earlier public inquiry or tribunal could prejudice a subsequent criminal trial

6–109   This heading refers to a situation in which there is first a public inquiry or tribunal and then there is a subsequent criminal trial concerning conduct which was also the subject matter of the inquiry.[221] The most likely scenario[222] is that it is claimed that bad publicity generated by the public inquiry may render a later trial unfair. It is inherently likely that the entity involved would be a public inquiry, rather than a tribunal, because of the blaze of publicity which often attends a public inquiry. This situation arose in *Goodman v Hamilton*.[223] The applicant claimed that it was a ground for preventing the Hamilton Tribunal of Inquiry into the beef industry from going ahead, that the publicity flowing from it would render any later criminal trial (which never in fact seemed likely) unfair. Finlay C.J. stated simply that this was not a ground for preventing the tribunal from going ahead, since[224]:

> "… If a person charged with a criminal offence can for any reason establish that due to pre trial publicity a fair trial is impossible, the courts have jurisdiction to prevent an injustice occurring."

In other words, "the horse does not jump until it gets to the stile". More broadly, there is a general bloc of law in respect of publicity which might undermine fairness at a trial, which is not particular to public inquiries. The courts have a duty to apply this law, but to do so at a time when the trial becomes imminent.

(2) Relying on the outcome of a court case in later proceedings before a tribunal

Acquittal by the court

6–110   As Geoghegan J. remarked, giving judgment for the Supreme Court in the most recent case in this field, *Garvey v Minister for Justice, Equality and Law Reform*, it is "an age old question on which there are decisions of this court that are not all that easy to reconcile"[225] whether a public employee can be subject to disciplinary proceedings if the alleged misconduct constitutes a criminal offence of which the employee has already been acquitted on the merits. The facts in *Garvey* provide a typical example. It was alleged that the applicant, a prison officer, had injured a prisoner by kicking him in the face. Disciplinary proceedings were initiated and the applicant was suspended. Next, criminal charges arising out of the assault were brought, but after a five week trial and jury deliberation lasting 16 hours,

---

[221] For discussion, see the Law Reform Commission, *Public Inquiries, including Tribunals of Inquiry* (LRC CP22–2003), Ch.11 "Downstream Proceedings".

[222] Another possibility is that it is sought to use information which was obtained at the inquiry at the trial. Here, it has been held that, because of the privilege against self-incrimination, it must be proved again before the court: see LRC CP22–2003, paras 11.03–11.32.

[223] [1992] 2 I.R. 542 at 591. Note further, *Murphy v Flood* [1999] 3 I.R. 97.

[224] The same issue was dealt with rather briefly in *O'Dowd v Commissioner of An Garda Síochána* [2004] 2 I.R. 516 at 528; *White v Morris* [2007] 4 I.R. 445.

[225] [2006] 1 I.R. 548 at 550. See also, *McGrath v Commissioner of An Garda Síochána* [1989] I.R. 241; [1991] 1 I.R. 69; *McCarthy v Commissioner of An Garda Síochána* [1993] 1 I.R. 489; *AA v The Medical Council* [2002] 3 I.R. 1; *Shine v Fitness to Practice Committee of the Medical Council* [2009] 1 I.R. 283 at para.35. These authorities are analysed in H & M, paras 6–153 to 6–162.

he was acquitted on the merits. In a case considered further below, he secured an order to prevent that disciplinary process from going ahead.

6–111 The first case to be examined is *Mooney v An Post*[226] in which the applicant postman had been acquitted of an offence of dishonesty. To amplify: An Post had obtained confidential information about the applicant from a person who could not be called as a witness at the trial. Effectively, An Post then laid a trap for the applicant which, in its belief, he had fallen into, and the criminal charges were based on that evidence. He was acquitted by the jury. Yet, in the view of An Post, there still remained a simple question of whether he was suitable to be retained as a postman. Writing for the Supreme Court and ruling that the disciplinary proceedings could go ahead, Barrington J. drew attention to a major policy consideration in this area. He stated:

> "[I]t would be absurd if a party who had failed to establish a proposition beyond all reasonable doubt should, by that fact alone, be debarred from attempting to establish the same proposition on the balance of probabilities."[227]

6–112 The most recent Supreme Court case is *Garvey v Minister for Justice*,[228] mentioned above. The court distinguished *Mooney*, in that what was involved in *Garvey* was a simple issue of credibility, namely, whether the applicant had kicked the prisoner in the face. In comparison, addressing the point made in *Mooney* regarding the differing standards of proof employed by a court and a disciplinary committee, Geoghegan J. in *Garvey* stated[229]:

> "It is true, of course, that it is possible that a jury merely had a reasonable doubt but I do not think that that speculative possibility, *by itself*, justifies a rejection of the contention by the applicant that, given the nature of the criminal trial he faced, the issues involved and the fact that essentially it is all a matter of internal dispute between prison officers, it would be oppressive and an unfair procedure now to unravel the verdict of the jury by way of disciplinary inquiry. I mentioned early on in this judgment that if the applicant was a member of An Garda Síochána such a disciplinary inquiry would be forbidden by the relevant statutory regulations. If the Minister for Justice, Equality and Law Reform, who is responsible for the security of the State on the civil side, considered it reasonable to include such a regulation I am at least impressed by that ... Such an understanding was not considered unreasonable or a threat to the security of the State. Conduct which could amount to a criminal offence on the part of the prison officer [as in *Mooney*] and in respect of which he is in fact acquitted in a criminal prosecution may in its surrounding circumstances involve other aspects which would be contrary to good order within the prison service but would not be the *actus reus* of the criminal offence. That might be an example of a situation where a disciplinary inquiry following an acquittal would be perfectly justified. I

---

[226] [1998] 4 I.R. 288.
[227] [1998] 4 I.R. 288. Geoghegan J. in *Garvey* (at 557) stated that (contrary to the view indicated in the headnote) this was "not isolated as a main ground of decision".
[228] [2006] 1 I.R. 548.
[229] [2006] 1 I.R. 548. The quotes are both at 557–558.

merely give that as an example and I do not want to limit the circumstances
in which such an inquiry would be justified."

6–113 Geoghegan J. thus emphasised that all depends upon the circumstances.
He continued his line of thought as follows:

"It is clear, however … that there can be circumstances where such a
disciplinary inquiry is oppressive and impermissible. I have come to the
conclusion that this case falls within that category. By now every aspect of the
case must have been discussed within the prison service whether at Governor
level or prison officer level … In this claustrophobic atmosphere I believe
that … it would be a 'basically unfair procedure' to conduct a disciplinary
inquiry on what in effect are identical allegations to the criminal charges
based on essentially the same evidence and the same witnesses."

6–114 Thus, it can be seen that, in the present leading authority, *Garvey*, the
earlier case of *Mooney* was confined very much to its own rather special facts.
However, on the other side, despite this and the similarity in outcome between
Garvey and the earlier cases of *McCarthy* and *AA*,[230] the reasoning in *Garvey*
seems to be strikingly different. For the earlier cases came close to holding that, if
a disciplinary charge were based on the same actus reus as the crime of which the
accused was acquitted, with no difference of context or circumstances, then the
acquittal in the criminal trial would be in effect a bar to disciplinary proceedings.
However, while the lengthy passage quoted from *Garvey* is not entirely clear, it
seems that the position is now less definite. First, in the view of Geoghegan J. in
Garvey, "[t]here is no necessary preclusion *per se* of such a double process."[231] On
the other hand, to repeat the last quotation, "… there can be circumstances where
such a disciplinary inquiry is oppressive … in this claustrophobic atmosphere". In
Garvey itself, the oppressive character lay in what was tantamount to a breach of the
"no bias" rule, by virtue of pre-judgment. It may be that, in the future, applicants
will need to be able to identify some such definite source of oppression.

Conviction by the court

6–115 So far, we have been considering situations in which the earlier court trial
resulted in an acquittal. What if the situation were that the court had convicted and
the question was whether the conviction could be relied on in later disciplinary
tribunal proceedings? To take a stark example, a doctor is convicted of raping a
patient and the Medical Council wishes to adopt the conviction as its only ground
for visiting a disciplinary sanction on the doctor. Now in some disciplinary regimes,
the governing legislation specifically identifies a criminal sanction as a ground,
of itself, for a professional sanction. Thus, for example, s.57(1) of the Medical
Practitioners Act 2007—in contrast to s.45(1) of the Medical Practitioners Act
1978—provides expressly that conviction, whether within or outside the State, for
an indictable offence, is to be a ground for disciplinary action.

[230] See fn.224.
[231] [2006] 1 I.R. 548 at 556. Despite this, Laffoy J. in *McGlinchey v Ryan*, unreported, High
Court, July 21, 2010 at paras 8, 9 and 10, in effect preferred the line taken by Ó Caoimh J. in
AA to that of the Supreme Court in *Garvey*.

6–116   The question might be raised whether it is constitutional for a tribunal to accept a court conviction in this way, without requiring the substance of the charge to be established (by calling witnesses, etc) before the tribunal itself. The obvious answer is that, given that the charge had been contested before the court, the person being disciplined would already have received ample constitutional justice at a trial before an independent judge and/or jury, which had found the charge proved beyond reasonable doubt.[232]

6–117   What next if the governing legislation does not specify a criminal offence as a basis for professional misconduct, but only uses some such general formulation as "unprofessional conduct"? In this situation, may the disciplinary body still rely on the conviction? It is suggested that, so far as the question of constitutional protection is concerned, the position is the same as in the situation, already discussed, in which criminal conviction was expressly provided for; the differing statutory language does not affect this. However, when one simply focuses on the legislative requirements, it is possible that the position is different. It could be contended by the person brought before the disciplinary tribunal that the statute requires the issue of professional misconduct to be adjudicated upon by the tribunal itself, rather than simply adopting the ruling of a court. This is an open question. It might be that the question is analogous to the issue of whether a criminal conviction should be accepted, in later civil proceedings, as being itself evidence of the facts on which it was based.[233] The answer to this issue was held to be no, in the well-known English case of *Hollington v Hewthorn*.[234]

Disciplinary proceedings followed by criminal trial

6–118   Finally, what if the sequence is the reverse of the situations just considered, in that the facts are that there had been successful disciplinary proceedings and the subject matter of these proceedings is later made the subject of a criminal prosecution? For example, in a High Court case,[235] a prisoner had been disciplined for having a mobile phone in his prison cell and lost 56 days' remission. Subsequently, it was held that the issue of double jeopardy did not arise and the prison disciplinary procedure was no basis for preventing a criminal trial based on the same facts, from going ahead.

---

[232] cf. the position in *Borges v Fitness to Practice Committee* [2004] 1 I.R. 103, where the applicant had earlier been found to have committed professional misconduct not by an Irish court but by an English medical tribunal; for the facts see paras 14–44 to 14–46.

[233] However, in *McGrath* [1991] 1 I.R. 69 at 74, Hederman J. rejected the appropriateness of such an analogy: "The disciplinary hearing is more serious in its consequences than a mere civil action." (See, to similar effect, McCarthy J. at 75 and Geoghegan J. in *Garvey* [2006] 1 I.R. 548 at 556). But, as against this, it may be said that the real question is whether any unfairness is done by accepting the verdict of the criminal court.

[234] [1943] 1 K.B. 587 (subsequently reversed by legislation in England, though not Ireland). The only Irish authority on the point of which we know is *Kelly v Ireland* [1986] I.L.R.M. 318 at 327, which expressly left open the question of whether *Hollington* represents the law of Ireland.

[235] *Gilligan v District Judge Haughton*, unreported, High Court, Ryan J., *The Irish Times*, September 10, 2010.

(3) Where conduct, by professional witnesses, in or around court proceedings, is the basis of a misconduct charge before a professional disciplinary tribunal

6–119   In general, we have surprisingly little authority as to how the conventional legal privileges against the disclosure of evidence—for instance, privilege based on professional relationship or marriage—apply in respect of proceedings before a tribunal. Instead, we have three cases in a surprisingly narrow area. What the cases have in common is that the source of the confidentiality/privilege, on which it is sought to rely before the tribunal, is that the information has been generated in, or on foot of, earlier court proceedings.

6–120   The first of these cases, *MP v AP*,[236] arose in the wake of a grant of judicial separation before the High Court, followed by a settlement relating to custody and access. Under this settlement, in the event of any disagreement, the first recourse of the parties would be a joint meeting with a psychologist, who was the applicant in the instant case. The applicant had expressed a view on certain factual matters, which was favourable to the wife. This resulted in a complaint by the husband to the applicant's professional body, the Psychological Society. The applicant responded by seeking a High Court order that he need not deal with the complaint. He succeeded on two alternative grounds,[237] of which the one which is of general interest is that, as Laffoy J. stated:

> "There is ample authority to support the proposition advanced by counsel for the applicant that a witness is protected from civil proceedings ... in respect of his evidence in the witness box and statements made in preparing evidence ... While no authority has been cited which supports the proposition that an expert witness is immune from disciplinary proceedings ... in respect of evidence he has given ... having regard to the public policy considerations which underlie the immunity from civil proceedings – that witnesses should give their evidence fearlessly and that a multiplicity of actions in which the value or truth of their evidence would be tried over again should be avoided – in my view, such a witness or potential witness must be immune from such disciplinary proceedings or investigation. However, I consider that it is not necessary to make a declaration that the Society cannot conduct any enquiry ... because such enquiry is precluded by section 34 of the Act of 1989."[238]

6–121   In the second case, *Eastern Health Board v Fitness to Practice Committee*,[239] the earlier case of *MP* was distinguished,[240] though not on the same grounds on which *Eastern Health Board* was itself distinguished in the later case of *RM*.[241] The situation was broadly similar to *RM*, but the applicant practitioner lost. The respondent disciplinary body had directed the applicant to produce records in its

---

[236] [1996] 1 I.R. 144.
[237] The alternative ratio was that it would be contrary to s.34 of the Judicial Separation and Family Law Reform Act 1989, which provides that "proceedings under this Act shall be heard otherwise than in public", if disciplinary proceedings connected with these in camera proceedings were to be heard in public.
[238] [1996] 1 I.R. 144 at 155–156 (although she indicated in the final sentence of the passage that, on the facts, it was obiter).
[239] [1998] 3 I.R. 399.
[240] [1998] 3 I.R. 399 at 423–424.
[241] [2001] 2 I.L.R.M. 369.

possession which had been the subject of earlier court proceedings in relation to the alleged abuse of minors. Because of the involvement of minors, these proceedings were held in camera.[242] Now the respondent wished to investigate an allegation that the doctor, a specialist in the diagnosis of child sexual abuse, who had carried out the examination of the children had committed an act of medical misconduct. Barr J.'s basic proposition was that:

> "A statutory imperative that proceedings of a particular nature be held in private ... does not imply that there is an absolute embargo on disclosure of evidence in all circumstances ... [Such a] major far-reaching change in the law, which sets aside established practice, could not arise merely by implication derived from a mandatory statutory requirement that certain proceedings shall be held in private, but, in my view, would require specific statutory authority."[243]

6–122   In addition, the High Court stipulated:

> "There is an established practice at common law recognised in England and in this jurisdiction (see *PSS v Independent Newspapers (Ireland) Ltd.* (Unreported, High Court, May 22, 1995)), that the court in proceedings held *in camera* has a discretion to permit others on such terms as the judge thinks proper to disseminate (and in appropriate cases to disseminate himself/herself) information derived from such proceedings where the judge believes that it is in the interest of justice so to do ... In given circumstances the judge may find that a crucial public interest, such as the prosecution of crime or the protection of vulnerable children, takes precedence over the interest of the protected person in nondisclosure of the information in question. [On the facts of the case] there [was] an imperative public interest that the [complaints against the applicant] be fully investigated by the respondent, as the body having statutory authority to carry out such inquiries ...".[244]

6–123   Accordingly, the High Court found for the respondent, though on the basis that the Medical Council's investigation should be conducted in camera.

6–124   The final case, *RM v OM*,[245] concerned a similar situation to the earlier two—attempted disciplinary procedure arising from conduct around a court case. The applicant barrister succeeded in a case arising out of a complaint to the Barristers' Professional Conduct Tribunal. The barrister who was the object of the complaint had acted as the complainant's counsel in divorce proceedings. Roderick Murphy J. held that the in camera provision in respect of divorce, were in substance, the same words as in the equivalent section in respect of separation proceedings, which was before the court in *MP*. In each case, they implied an absolute embargo on the production in later proceedings, such as those before the Barristers' Tribunal, of information which had been introduced in the divorce proceedings. Furthermore, the learned judge stated that, since breach of the rule

---

[242]   Courts (Supplemental Provisions) Act 1961 s.45(1)(c).
[243]   [1998] 3 I.R. 399 at 428.
[244]   [1998] 3 I.R. 399 at 429–430.
[245]   [2001] 2 I.L.R.M. 369.

may be regarded as a contempt of court, it cannot be waived, even by agreement between all the parties to the court proceedings. The significance of this last point would arise in a scenario in which both the parties supported the disciplinary proceedings, which might well be against a third party.

6–125   In *RM*, the *Eastern Health Board* case was distinguished (and *MP* followed) on the basis that there the subject of the in camera proceedings before the court was not divorce or separation proceedings, but related to minors. But none of the cases focus on the drafting of the in camera provisions in the particular statute. And the reasoning in *Eastern Health Board* (with its emphasis on balancing public and private interests and the fact that it would be possible for the tribunal to hear evidence in camera, as will be the case with most tribunals) certainly seemed not to be based on a particular in camera rule. Indeed, in *Eastern Health Board*, the judge gave a list of 12 statutes which provide for hearings in private, suggesting that they should each lead to the same result.

6–126   Probably, therefore, there is a more realistic and simpler basis for a distinction. *MP* and *RM* both looked like situations in which the real object of the complaint was to continue the dispute before the court but in another forum; whereas, in *Eastern Health Board* the proceedings before the Medical Council were brought because there was genuine concern regarding the performance of the doctor in respect of a number of medical examinations.

(4) Controversy as to the appropriate forum: tribunal or court

6–127   The question which arises is in which forum—a specialised tribunal or the courts—a legal issue should be resolved. As mentioned below, on the constitutional plane, all points are ultimately matters for the court by way of judicial review. However, that is in reference to the ultimate question. Here we are concerned with which body takes the initial decision. Since the question may arise in more than one context, there is, as yet and probably never can be, a simple, general answer; too much depends on the statutory matrix and other particular circumstances.

6–128   One form in which the question has arisen is where a licensing function is vested in a tribunal, whilst a prosecution for carrying on the activity without a licence or beyond the scope of the licence, is, as always, a matter for a court. The problem takes a sharp focus in the planning field, by virtue of s.5 of the Planning and Development Act 2000, which states:

> If any question arises as to what, in any particular case, is or is not development … any person may … request in writing from the relevant planning authority [An Bord Pleanála] a declaration on that question …

6–129   This provision was considered by the Supreme Court in *Grianán an Aileach Interpretative Centre Company Ltd v Donegal County Council (No. 2)*.[246] The plaintiff had been granted planning permission by the defendant for a development described as "a visitors centre" and understood by the defendant to be primarily a visitors centre to interpret a nearby monument. However, it soon became clear that

---

[246] [2004] 2 I.R. 625. On this subject, see also paras 17–53 to 17–57.

the plaintiff was taking a catholic approach to the expression "visitors centre",[247] so much so that the defendant complained to Bord Fáilte, which threatened to cut the plaintiff's funding. The plaintiff's response was to obtain a declaration from the High Court[248] that the specified activities fell within the range of permissible uses. The defendant appealed to the Supreme Court, submitting successfully—and here is the important point—that the High Court had no jurisdiction to grant such relief.

6–130 The immediate issue before the court was whether the proposed uses were authorised by the planning permission granted. But this inevitably drew with it the question of whether what was being proposed would constitute a "material change of use"; otherwise, no permission would have been required in the first place.[249] Thus, the main theme in Keane C.J.'s judgment for the Supreme Court was the effect of s.5 of the 2000 Act. He ruled that even though the plaintiff had not brought the issue to the planning authority or An Bord Pleanála, the High Court should not have entertained the matter because its jurisdiction was, in effect, denied by s.5, for in determining the question, the High Court had put the planning authority in a position where it could not exercise its statutory jurisdiction without finding itself in conflict with a High Court determination.[250]

6–131 Two comments may be made. First, it is true, as Keane C.J. acknowledged,[251] that a person carrying out a development which they claim is not a material change of use is not obliged to refer the question to the planning authority and may, instead, resist enforcement proceedings on the ground that permission was not acquired. In that situation, the court hearing the enforcement proceedings would itself have to determine whether there had been a material change of use, or whether a development was sanctioned by the existing planning permission.[252] Another situation in which a court (rather than a planning authority

---

247 The plaintiff gave details of a number of proposed inter-cultural activities, including: music throughout the ages in New Orleans; an evening of Irish-Scots music; a Caribbean Christmas, a Victorian Christmas and a "themed Dickensian Christmas". Unhappily, there was nothing from Wales.

248 [2003] 3 I.R. 572.

249 In *Palmerlane v An Bord Pleanála* [1999] 2 I.L.R.M. 514, the applicant had been granted permission to use the premises as a retail shop but then began to use premises for the sale of hot food for consumption off the premises. A dispute arose as to whether this new use was within the terms of the planning permission. This was referred to An Bord Pleanála, which declined to entertain the reference on the basis that the board was not empowered to construe the terms of the planning permission. In judicial review proceedings, the High Court ruled that An Bord Pleanála must accept the reference since deciding whether a new activity amounts to development beyond the terms of the planning permission necessarily requires the permission to be interpreted. A similar analysis was adopted in *McMahon v Dublin* [1996] 3 I.R. 509. Outside the planning context, the same approach was adopted, again by Keane C.J., in *Criminal Assets Bureau v Hunt* [2003] 2 I.R. 168 at 183.

250 This conclusion was buttressed by quoting from Finlay C.J.'s judgment in *O'Keeffe v An Bord Pleanála* [1993] 1 I.R. 39 at 71: "The legislature has … placed questions of planning … within the jurisdiction of the planning authorities and [An Bord Pleanála], which are expected to have special skill and competence", though it should be noted that this passage was directed at decisions on planning policy, at least as much as planning law.

251 [2004] 2 I.R. 625 at 638–640.

252 e.g. *O'Connor v Kerry* [1988] I.L.R.M. 660. Notice though *Dublin City Council v Liffey Beat Ltd* [2005] 1 I.R. 478 at 492, discussed further at Ch.14, Part C, in which it was stated that "… although the instant proceedings comprise enforcement proceedings within the jurisdiction of this court, I am nonetheless satisfied that the fundamental principle identified by Keane C.J. [in *Grianán an Aileach*] applies with equal force to the facts of these proceedings …

or An Bord Pleanála) would be involved would be where, in a private law action, a commercial or conveyancing document included a term requiring compliance with planning permission.

6–132   But these situations are different from that in *Grianán an Aileach* in that they involve concrete factual situations, with the planning permission offering a standard—usually a reasonably definite standard—against which to judge them. By contrast, in the situation in *Grianán an Aileach*, there was little or no help to be gained from the existing planning permission. Indeed, what was required was tantamount to the re-writing of the permission and the court would be "drawn into a role analogous to that of a planning authority granting permission".[253]

6–133   Secondly, in *Grianán an Aileach*, as we have said, the point at issue was agitated first in a court. The more natural situation is that proceedings commence before the licensing agency, so that, even without s.5 or an equivalent, the nature of the situation would be such that the agency would have to settle, at least provisionally, any relevant legal points. One should emphasise, though, that Art.34.3.1° of the Constitution has been interpreted to mean that exclusive jurisdiction may be given to a lower court or tribunal; but provided that the High Court's subsequent power of judicial review is retained.[254] The consequence of this, in the circumstances of a case like *Grianán an Aileach*, is that *after* the planning authorities have reached their decision on the issue, the applicant could then seek review by the High Court.

[I]t is not the function of the courts to seek to resolve questions involving planning policy by 'acting, in effect, as a form of planning Tribunal.'"
[253] [2004] 2 I.R. 625 at 639.
[254] *Tormey v Attorney General* [1985] I.R. 289.

CHAPTER 7

GENERAL PRINCIPLES
OF LICENSING

A. INTRODUCTION

7–01 Licensing[1] is one of the most common techniques[2] by which the dirigiste State regulates activities which are potentially harmful to its citizens. The governing legislation establishes specified activity or acts as criminal offences (triable in the usual way), unless authorised by licence and carried out within the terms of the licence, issued by some official authority. McMahon J. offers an excellent introductory description:

> "The state increasingly and for a variety of reasons controls entry into various economic activities in modern society. Although no general regulatory legislation exists for industrial or commercial activities there are many examples in Ireland of specific legislation which regulates or restricts specific activities of a commercial or industrial character. Such specific regulatory legislation usually commences by establishing a licensing authority or a registration authority and persons who are unregistered or unlicensed are prohibited from carrying on the named activity. The legislation normally

---

[1] The meaning explained in this paragraph describes the use of the term "licence" as used in public administration. As used in private law, the term also means permission, for instance, to come on the land of another, but with the implication that the remedy for performing the action without permission is merely a civil wrong and not an offence.

[2] Apart from licensing, there are other techniques for administrative regulation. For instance: (i) a direction to refrain from doing some act or series of acts. Examples of this include the making of a prohibition order under the Censorship of Publications Acts 1929–1967 or the making of an order by the Central Bank under s.21 of the Central Bank Act 1971 (as inserted by s.38 of the Central Bank Act 1989 and amended by the Central Bank and Financial Services Authority of Ireland Act 2004 Sch.1 Pt I) directing that the holder of a banking licence shall not carry on banking business; (ii) in some administrative regulatory systems, the onus is placed upon the private individual to "declare" or "certify" that what he is doing is not potentially injurious. For example, under ss.2, 3 and 12 of the Local Government (Multi-Storey Buildings) Act 1988, if a local authority serves notice on the owner of a building with five or more storeys, the owner must submit to the local authority a certificate signed by a "competent person" (a chartered engineer, etc) certifying, inter alia, that the building is constructed in accordance with the appropriate codes of practice and standards. Failure to submit a certificate, or the submission of a false certificate, is an offence. For litigation concerning a self-regulatory system, albeit at an interlocutory stage, see *JRM Sports Ltd (Trading as Limerick Football Club) v Football Association of Ireland* [2007] IEHC 67; (iii) for "the directing power" (to borrow US parlance), see Stout, *Administrative Law in Ireland* (Dublin: IPA, 1985), pp.373–419.

specifies that certain conditions are to be fulfilled before a person is to be on the register. Such conditions might require the applicant to have a certain level of knowledge (education and training requirements), and/or be of good character and/or be financially sound and/or be of a certain age. There may also be requirements as to the condition and quality of premises used in the activity and requirements regarding the keeping of proper records and accounts. Traditional public policy considerations that justify such regulation typically related to public safety, public health and welfare, public morality, public security as well as the stability of financial institutions and good order at local government level. Sometimes a less rigorous system may be preferred by the state for various reasons and the state's interest may then take the form of a softer model to allow for greater flexibility in the administration of the system and to engage the participants in a more voluntary and more participatory way."[3]

7–02   How does the Oireachtas decide which activities ought to be licensed? Broadly speaking (as will be seen from the examples given below), they involve acts which are not in themselves harmful in the same way as ordinary crimes (such as murder or larceny). Indeed, they are activities which, if carried out in the appropriate circumstances by a suitably qualified person, will usually be beneficial (or, at any rate, neutral) to the community. On the other hand, if performed by the wrong person or in the wrong circumstances (such as medical treatment carried out by an unqualified practitioner), they may be positively harmful. Thus, in contrast with traditional crimes, licensing is preventative rather than curative: a licensing régime is not content to wait until a vendor of land has his money misappropriated by an auctioneer or estate agent. Rather, it strikes at an earlier point in time by seeking to ensure that only persons of good character are granted a licence and by criminalising unlicensed auctioneering.[4]

7–03   Despite their diversity, each licensing system is located at an economic, political or social pressure point and is likely to be involved in substantial controversy and litigation. Before going further, we ought to emphasise by way of a government health warning, that this chapter does not advert to particular licensing systems, but merely attempts to delineate such administrative law principles as are common to the field of licensing. We turn next to consider the stage at which a licence is granted or refused; revoked; and enforced.

Licensing stage: grant or refusal

7–04   Consonant with the haphazard design of our system of government administration, the task of licensing (which usually includes the powers to grant and to revoke) may be vested in any one of at least five different types of agency. In the first place, this function may be vested in a court, generally the District Court, but occasionally the Circuit Court, and examples here include: selling intoxicating

---

[3]   *English v Health Service Executive* [2008] IEHC 398. The difference, so far as there is one, between licensing and registration is explained at paras 7–28 to 7–31.
[4]   See Auctioneers and House Agents Acts 1947–1973.

liquor[5]; running dance halls[6]; and auctioneering.[7] Secondly, control over a number of activities is vested in the local authorities. These activities are generally in the environmental or public health field and include: land use[8]; discharge of effluent[9]; waste collection[10]; air pollution[11]; dog breeding[12]; and running a caravan park[13] or abattoir.[14] Sometimes, however, local authorities are given licensing functions in matters of social concern to the community, such as casual trading or gaming halls.[15] Thirdly, the licensing functions may be allocated to the relevant Minister, as, for example, in the case of: livestock marts[16]; bull breeding[17]; tour operators[18]; or the operation of licensed health insurance schemes.[19]

7–05 Fourthly, licences which have a security or policing dimension (such as firearms,[20] bookmaking[21] and house-to-house and street collections)[22] are handled by the Gardaí. Fifthly, in some cases, the allocation of licences has been considered sufficiently important to warrant the vesting of these functions in a tribunal (an autonomous agency which may also bear functions other than licensing but in the same substantive field: for examples, see paras 6–24 to 6–26.

7–06 One should emphasise that, because of the variety of different cases to which any licensing system will have to apply, there is a need for flexibility. This need is accommodated by empowering the licensing agency to grant a licence not only absolutely but also subject to specified conditions. In practice, licences are seldom, if ever, granted free of conditions. In addition, the governing legislation will invariably provide for some form of appeal against an adverse decision, including refusal of a grant or the imposition of conditions to which the applicant objects. Sometimes the right of appeal will lie to another administrative agency.[23] More often it will lie

---

5   Licensing Acts 1833–2004.

6   Public Dance Halls Acts 1935–2003.

7   Auctioneering and House Agents Acts 1947–1973.

8   Planning and Development Act 2000 s.34. See further, paras 5–138 to 5–142.

9   Local Government (Water Pollution) Act 1977 s.4(1)(b), as amended by Protection of the Environment Act 2003 s.15.

10   Waste Management Act 1996 ss.33 and 34.

11   Air Pollution Act 1987 Pt III.

12   Dog Breeding Act ss.9–11.

13   Local Government (Sanitary Services) Act 1948 s.34(4).

14   Abattoirs Act 1988 s.9.

15   See also, Casual Trading Act 1995 s.6 (local authorities given extension powers to control casual trading). See also, Pt III of the Gaming and Lotteries Act 1956; Control of Horses Act 1996 Pt II (which enables a local authority to adapt bye-laws strictly controlling the keeping of horses where "it is satisfied that horses in that area should be licensed having regard to the need to control the keeping of horses, the need to prevent nuisance, annoyance or injury to persons or damage to property by horses and such other matters as it considers relevant").

16   Livestock Marts Act 1967 s.3.

17   Control of Bulls for Breeding Act 1985 s.3.

18   Transport (Tour Operators and Travel Agents) Act 1982 s.6.

19   Health Insurance Act 1994 Pt IV.

20   Firearms Acts 1925–2000.

21   Betting Act 1931 s.6.

22   Street and House to House Collections Act 1962 ss.5, 6, 9–11.

23   See, e.g. Video Recordings Act 1989 s.10 (appeal to Censorship of Films Appeals Board); Irish Horseracing Industry Act 1994 Pt V (appeals to Bookmakers' Appeal Committee in respect of course-betting permits); Planning and Development Act 2000 Pt VI (appeals to An Bord Pleanála in respect of planning decisions made by local authorities); Dog Breeding Establishments Act 2010 ss.9–11.

to the District Court,[24] the Circuit Court[25] or even to the High Court.[26] In *Cashman v Clifford*[27] Barron J. rejected the argument that, when hearing such appeals from licensing authorities, the courts were merely discharging administrative functions and were not thereby administering justice, so that Art.34.1 of the Constitution was not attracted.[28] Here the applicant had challenged the validity of s.13 of the Betting Act 1931 which had established an appeal to the District Court against a decision of the Garda Superintendent refusing a licence, but had also provided—and here is the important point—that only the Garda Síochána and the Revenue Commissioners and "no other person" were entitled to be heard on the appeal. Barron J. held that the exclusion of other potential objectors (such as the applicant, who was already a bookmaker in the area) represented an unconstitutional interference with the administration of justice. In the result, the provision was found to be invalid.[29] But, rather surprisingly, the judgment does not rely on violation of the principles of constitutional justice.

7–07 Since a licence is granted usually only for a fixed period, frequently a year,[30] it will usually have to be renewed, often annually. Strictly speaking, such a renewal could be regarded as the grant of a new licence. However, this is not usually how it is thought of by the parties in practice, an area explained at para.7–42.

7–08 The general law of judicial review (covered in Chapters 10–15) naturally looms very large in this area.[31] It applies to the refusal of a renewal (a renewal is,

---

[24] See, e.g. Betting Act 1931 s.13; Street and House to House Collections Act 1962 s.13; Health (Nursing Homes) Act 1990 s.5; Veterinary Practice Act 2005 s.114(8).

[25] See, e.g. Consumer Credit Act 1995 s.93(13) (appeal to the Circuit Court against decision of Director of Consumer Affairs to refuse to grant moneylender's licence); National Beef Assurance Scheme Act 2000 s.17 (appeal to the Circuit Court against decision on a bull-breeding licence).

[26] See, e.g. Transport (Tour Operators and Travel Agents) Act 1982 s.9(3) (appeal to the High Court against refusal or revocation of tour operator's licence by Minister). For an unsuccessful appeal against a revocation under the 1982 Act (the revocation being based on breach of a condition of a licence), see *Balkan Tours Ltd v Minister for Communications* [1988] I.L.R.M. 101; Competition Act 2002 s.15 (appeal against a declaration of the Competition Authority that certain agreements, decisions or concerted practices are not anti-competitive in nature); Building Control Act 2007 ss.26, 40 and 54 (appeals against adverse decisions of appeals boards of bodies regulating architects, quantity surveyors, building surveyors).

[27] [1989] I.R. 122.

[28] Barron J. followed the earlier decision of the Supreme Court in *State (McEldowney) v Kelleher* [1983] I.R. 289, where that court had declared unconstitutional a section of the Street and House to House Collections Act. However, the authority of these cases is suspect because in neither was the precise point mentioned in the text—whether Art.34.1 of the Constitution does apply where a court is exercising a regulatory function—really addressed. The result reached in each of these could have been achieved by invoking the *audi alteram partem* rule, without bringing in Art.34.1. For further criticism, see Gwynn Morgan, *The Separation of Powers in the Irish Constitution* (Dublin: Round Hall Sweet & Maxwell, 1997), pp.147–151.

[29] See also, *White v Dublin City Council* [2004] 1 I.R. 545.

[30] See paras 7–26 to 7–27.

[31] These matters are dealt with in later chapters. See, e.g. *East Donegal Co-Operative v Attorney General* [1970] I.R. 317; *International Fishing Ltd v Minister for the Marine (No. 2)* [1991] 2 I.R. 93; *TV3 v IRTC* [1994] 2 I.R. 439; *Shanley v Galway Corporation* [1995] 1 I.R. 396; *Slevin v Shannon Regional Fisheries Board* [1995] 1 I.R. 460; *Madden v Minister for the Marine* [1997] 1 I.L.R.M. 136; *Dunne v Donohue* [2002] 2 I.R. 533; *NWR FM Ltd v Broadcasting Commission of Ireland* [2004] 4 I.R. 50; *Cork Opera House Plc v Revenue Commissioners* [2007] IEHC 388 (legitimate expectations); *Goodison v Sheahan* [2008] IEHC 127; *McCarron v Kearney* [2008] IEHC 195. In regard to a public body's obligation, as part of the law of

in theory, the granting of a fresh licence) or even possibly the refusal of an initial grant.[32] For example, *Goodison v Sheehan*[33] is a case on the renewal of a licence. The applicant had been the holder for many years of firearms certificates, granted under the Firearms Act 1925. Under s.4 of the Act, the only ground on which a request for a licence could be refused was that the applicant owning a firearm would be a danger to public safety or to peace. However, the reason given for the refusal in the instant case was that the respondent was not satisfied that this particular pistol could be used without danger to the public. On this basis, the High Court (Peart J.) held that the refusal was ultra vires. But one should emphasise that the particular feature of this decision was not just that the applicant had a blameless track record, but rather that the licensing system against which he was to be judged had been unchanged over many years and there was no element of competition or scarcity as regards these licences.

7–09   Again, in *O'Leary v Maher*,[34] an applicant who had had a gun licence in respect of one weapon for some years was refused a new licence in respect of a gun of higher calibre. He successfully sought judicial review. Focusing on the terms of the governing legislation, Clarke J. stated:

> "The Firearms Acts 1925 indicates that it is the applicant who must be certified as fit by the superintendent to possess or use a firearm. It is not the firearm itself which is licensed to the owner but rather the owner who is authorised to possess ... the particular firearm."

Revocation

7–10   The governing legislation invariably includes a power to revoke the licence, usually if prescribed violations of its terms are established. Revocation[35] is a

---

judicial review, not "to take irrelevant factors into account", a particular example which may arise in the present context is that factors relevant to one licence (e.g. planning permission) may not be taken into account in deciding whether to issue a different type of licence (e.g. a slaughterhouse licence): see *Doupe v Limerick Corporation* [1981] I.L.R.M. 456 at 462.

[32]   *East Donegal Co-Operative v Attorney General* [1970] I.R. 317 at 344–347 (obiter). For the statutory procedure to be followed in a revocation under the Livestock Marts Act 1967, see ss.3 and 6 of the Act.

[33]   [2008] IEHC 127 (May 2, 2008).

[34]   [2008] IEHC 113 at para.42.

[35]   A rather unfortunate case, arising from the revocation of a licence, is *Sheehan v District Judge Reilly* [1992] 1 I.R. 368. The applicant had been granted a public music and singing licence (under the Public Dance Halls Act 1935) by the respondent. However, because of the numerous objections to the grant of the licence—the gist of which was that the premises created a public nuisance in the neighbourhood—a condition (which was the central point in the case) had been imposed on the licence, namely that the objectors had liberty to re-enter the proceedings on 48 hours' notice. Five days after the grant of the licence and on the hearing of what was in effect their further objection, the licence was revoked.

A critical point in the case is that as a matter of statute, namely s.51(9) of the Public Health (Amendment) Act 1890, as amended by the Licensing (Combating Drug Abuse) Act 1997 s.11, the power of revocation was predicated upon the holder of the licence becoming liable to a penalty as therein provided. Since the terms of the licence contained no condition the breach of which would have given the respondent jurisdiction to revoke the licence or even re-hear the case, the applicant's claim for judicial review was successful. Barron J. stated: "The reality seems to be that the respondent was not fully satisfied that the applicant was entitled to either licence. For this reason, he inserted the condition in each order giving liberty to re-enter. In

catastrophe for the licence holder and powers to revoke, at the absolute discretion of the licensing authority, while once common,[36] are rarely, if ever, conferred today. Appeals in respect of the grant stage have already been mentioned. Sometimes the statute prescribes separate regimes with a more generous appeal in the case of revocation.[37] But, sometimes, the provisions for an appeal are similar.[38] In addition, the revocation of a licence is subject to a fairly stringent application of the principles of judicial review of administrative action, including, for instance, legality, reasonableness or the rules of constitutional justice.

Enforcement stage

7–11   There is less to say with regard to enforcement, since, in principle, this attracts the usual rules of criminal law and procedure. As a general rule, the governing statute will provide for criminal offences triable summarily before the District Court, and/or on indictment before the Circuit Court. In addition, in more modern legislation, the licensing agency may be given a special prosecuting role in summary prosecutions.[39] However, in practice, presumably because there is no readily identifiable victim, the punishments imposed tend to be small if not

---

the event, he became satisfied that his original doubts were justified and revoked the licences. I think that having granted the licences, the respondent was *functus officio*. The matter could only have come before him again upon a prosecution as provided for in the respective Acts which, if successful, would have given him jurisdiction to revoke the licences."

[36]   See, e.g. Road Transport Act 1932 s.17(3) ("The Minister may at any time on his own motion and at his absolute discretion revoke an occasional passenger licence"); Voluntary Health Insurance Act 1957 s.22(1) ("The Minister may, in his absolute discretion, revoke a health insurance licence.") The latter subsection has, in any event, been repealed: see Health Insurance Act 1994 s.5.

[37]   See, e.g. Patents Act 1992 Pt II Ch.VIII; Planning and Development Act 2000 ss.37 and 44; Employment Permits Act 2006 ss.12 and 16 (but note that the machinery for appealing against a refusal or a revocation of an employment permit is substantively the same; Employment Permits Act 2006 ss.13 and 17).

[38]   See, e.g. Slaughter of Animals Act 1935 s.27; Irish Horseracing Industry Act 1994 s.57; Taxi Regulation Act 2003 s.35. See also, Insurance Act 1989 s.22A, as inserted by Central Bank and Financial Services Authority of Ireland Act 2003 Sch.1, which allows the Bank to issue regulations governing the "refusal, suspension or revocation" of an application for authorisation to carry on certain reinsurance business; Prisons Act 2007 ss.6 and 7, which prescribes different regimes but largely similar substantive criteria for the certification and revocation of certification of prisoner custody officers.

[39]   But not in prosecutions on indictment. In fact, the function of prosecuting on indictment in respect of all offences (apart from the few, responsibility for which remains with the Attorney General) is vested in the Director of Public Prosecutions: Prosecution of Offences Act 1974 s.3(1); Criminal Justice (Administration) Act 1924 s.9. There appears to be a policy that the independent and specifically established office of the DPP should bear responsibility for all prosecutions on indictment. However, a rather radical judgment was made in *TDI Metro v Delap (No. 2)* [2000] IESC 62; [2000] 4 I.R. 520 at 535 per Geoghegan J.: a conviction under the Local Government (Planning and Development) Act 1963 had been quashed by the High Court because the local authority, which initiated the prosecution, had never been granted the statutory power to prosecute indictable—as opposed to summary—offences. The Supreme Court, however, reversed the High Court on the basis that this was an overly narrow interpretation of the legislation: "[I]t would be strange if the Oireachtas intended that although the planning authority would be the normal prosecuting authority for the summary offences it could not deal with minor incidents of indictable offences clearly thought fit to be tried summarily."

altogether derisory.[40] They rarely have a deterrent effect and may, indeed, be regarded as simply additional "overheads" of running the unlawful activity.

7–12   Accordingly, recent legislation tends to rely more heavily on civil remedies in aid of enforcement. Thus the licensing agency or some other person with locus standi is entitled to seek an injunction against the unlicensed operator. Here we ought to note that, while even if nothing is said in the statute, as a matter of common law, an injunction may probably be sent to enforce a substantive statutory obligation,[41] several recent statutes expressly provide for an injunction. The best known example is in the field of planning control, where such a remedy is specifically made available by s.160 of the Planning and Development Act 2000.[42]

7–13   The next question is: who has standing to seek an injunction? Plainly, the Attorney General always has standing. But it used to be a vexed question as to whether, in the absence of statutory provisions conferring such a right of objection, a competitor has any remedy against an unlicensed rival. Certainly, a competitor has sufficient standing to seek judicial review of the decision actually to grant a licence to the rival where he alleges that the requisite statutory formalities have not been complied with.[43] But what if the situation is the more common one in which the competitor has no licence and yet the business is trading: where the Attorney General does not take action, can a private individual seek an injunction to restrain the activities of an unlicensed rival? The traditional English authorities,[44] with their rather outdated attitude to standing, were to the effect that a licensed operator did not have standing to complain about the activities of an unlicensed rival. However,

---

[40]   See, e.g. the comments of Costello J. in *Attorney General v Paperlink Ltd* [1984] I.L.R.M. 373 at 392 and those of O'Hanlon J. in *Parsons v Kavanagh* [1990] I.L.R.M. 560 at 567 (where he referred to the unchanged monetary penalties provided by the Road Transport Acts 1932–1933 and commented that with "the fall in the value of money in the meantime, they appear to me at the present time to be somewhat derisory as against possible breaches of the Acts.")

[41]   "Whenever Parliament has enacted a law and given a particular remedy for breach of it, such remedy being in an inferior court, nevertheless, the High Court always has a reserve power to enforce the law so enacted by way of an injunction or other suitable remedy. The High Court has jurisdiction to ensure obedience to the law whenever it is just and convenient to do so"; per Lord Denning in *Attorney General v Chaudry* [1971] 1 W.L.R. 1614 at 1624. This statement was quoted with approval by Costello J. in *Attorney General v Paperlink Ltd* [1984] I.L.R.M. 373. See also, *Attorney General (O'Duffy) v Appleton* [1907] 1 I.R. 252; *O'Connor v Williams* [1996] 2 I.L.R.M. 382; *MMDS Television v South East Deflector Association Ltd*, unreported, High Court, April 8, 1997; and *Attorney General v Lee*, unreported, High Court, June 6, 2002.

[42]   On the planning injunction, see paras 5–147 to 5–150. For further examples of a "statutory injunction", see Local Government (Water Pollution) Act 1977 s.11; Fire Services Act 1981 s.20A, as inserted by Licensing of Indoor Events Act 2003 s.30; Waste Management Act 1996 s.57, as amended by Protection of the Environment Act 2003 s.48; Central Bank Act 1997 s.74; Carriage of Dangerous Goods by Road Act 1998 s.8(8); Railway Safety Act 2005 s.78(9).

[43]   *Irish Permanent Building Society v Caldwell (No. 2)* [1981] I.L.R.M. 242. Cf. *Ryanair Holdings Plc v Irish Financial Services Regulatory Authority* [2008] IEHC 231 (July 10, 2008).

[44]   *RCA Corporation v Pollard* [1983] Ch. 135 at 153. But see, *a contra*: *Re Island Records* [1978] 3 All E.R. 824 and *Rickless v United Artists* [1987] 1 All E.R. 679.

in *Parsons v Kavanagh*,[45] confirmed in *Lovett v Gogan*,[46] it was held that these common law principles must yield, in this jurisdiction, to the constitutional right to earn a livelihood. Accordingly, a competitor may take such a case.[47] In addition, there seems to be no reason in principle not to apply these constitutional authorities to a situation in which the rival trader seeks damages rather than an injunction.

7–14   The lack of a licence, where one is required, may have various consequences in private law. These consequences may amount to an indirect sanction against the failure to obtain a licence. A well known example is the principle that a contract in respect of the unlicensed activity may not be enforceable.[48] But this area of law is not well developed.[49] On the other hand, the holding of a licence gives an entitlement to do that which is prohibited only by the legislation establishing the need for the licence: it does not absolve from other forms of illegality. A fairly typical case of this type is *Casey v Minister for Arts, Heritage, Gaeltacht and the Islands*,[50] which centred on a condition in a licence to land passengers on Skellig Mhichíl. The Supreme Court held that the Minister had an implied power to impose a condition restricting the number of boats that might land passengers on the site: the argument that this condition amounted to an attack on the plaintiff's constitutional right to earn a livelihood was roundly rejected by Murray J.:

> "What is clear is that the applicant wishes to carry on a quite legitimate business of using his boat for tourist or commercial pleasure purposes. There is no complaint that he is restricted in carrying on such a business other than

---

[45]   [1990] I.L.R.M. 560. Moreover, in *Robinson v Chariot Inns Ltd* [1986] I.L.R.M. 621 it was held that a competitor has sufficient standing to seek an injunction pursuant to s.27 of the Local Government (Planning and Development) Act 1976 restraining the unauthorised use by a business rival of his property. In *Pierce v The Dublin Cemeteries Committee* [2006] IEHC 182, Laffoy J. held that the applicant had locus standi to seek declaratory and injunctive relief against a public body which had allegedly acted ultra vires in engaging in commercial activity. This was upheld on appeal (unreported, Supreme Court, May 28, 2009). The facts were fairly typical. The plaintiff, who was a rival trader, sought a declaration that a private Act of the Oireachtas (the Dublin Cemeteries Committee Act 1970) did not empower the defendant to sell monuments or headstones or to offer inscription services. In the Supreme Court, the case turned more on the basis of whether the plaintiff had an alternative remedy (without the fundamental issue of standing itself being discussed) and the court held that, in the circumstances, a claim under the Competition Act 1991 would not amount to a real alternative remedy. As the judge pointed out, there is an overlap between the issue of standing and the question of whether an alternative remedy is available, which is usually discussed in the context of a discretion to send an order at the end of judicial review proceedings.

[46]   [1995] 3 I.R. 132. These authorities are reviewed more fully at para.18–16. See also, *O'Connor v Williams* [1996] 2 I.L.R.M. 382 and *MMDS Televisions Ltd v South East Deflector Association Ltd*, unreported, High Court, April 8, 1997.

[47]   See paras 16–122 to 16–123.

[48]   See Peel, *Treitel's Law of Contract*, 12th edn (London: Sweet & Maxwell, 2007), para.11–021; *Re Moneylenders Act 1933 and Lynn, Applicants* (1940) 74 I.L.T.R. 96.

[49]   In *Plant v Oakes* [1991] 1 I.R. 185, the issue before the High Court was whether the use of one room in a house for business activity (doing the books for a nearby garage) brought the tenancy in respect of the house within the category of being used "wholly or partly for the purpose of carrying on a business", thus attracting the right to a new occupational lease under Pt II of the Landlord and Tenant (Amendment) Act 1980. The significant point here is the fact that the High Court ruled in favour of the tenant, despite the fact that no planning permission in respect of change of use of the house, from domestic to business usage, had been sought or obtained. See also, *Terry v Stokes*, unreported, High Court, March 13, 1986.

[50]   [2004] 1 I.R. 402.

that he has not been given permission by the respondent to land his customers at Skellig Michael [*sic*]. Skellig Michael belongs to the State not to the applicant. In complaining that his constitutional rights have been breached he is in effect saying that he has a constitutional right to land his customers on Skellig Michael as part of his pleasure or tourist business.

I think one only has to state this proposition to see that it cannot be right. It seems to me that the applicant has misconceived the nature and ambit of the right to earn a livelihood. To engage in such a lawful business activity for the purpose of earning a livelihood is something which a citizen is entitled to do as of right. It is self-evident that the right to carry on such a business does not entitle the citizen to have access, as of right, to the property of third parties and use it for business purposes. It does not matter whether the property, in this case a national monument, is privately owned or owned by the State."[51]

7–15 The first point here is the fundamental one, that a licence only entitles the holder to do that which would otherwise be forbidden by the licensing legislation. It certainly does not go further, e.g. to authorise interference with private rights, in this case the State's ownership of Skellig Mhichíl; or, to take another example, to empower the development of land belonging to a neighbour of the grantee of planning permission. The second point is that constitutional rights, for instance in this case the right to earn a livelihood, are not unqualified.

7–16 A further type of enforcement procedure is sometimes provided by statute, in the form of a "concretising" directive (often called a "notice"). With this technique, the licensing authority must give the offender precise instructions as to how the law (including any conditions attached to a licence) has been broken and what must be done to put matters right. Where such a notice is invoked, if and when its terms have been defied for a specified time period, then an offence is committed.[52]

B. CHARACTERISTICS OF LICENCES

7–17 Having considered both the licensing and enforcement stages, we may now proceed to identify some discrete aspects of licensing, which are also of general interest in administrative law.

A licence depends very much on its own governing legislation

7–18 Earlier the point was made that in any concrete situation involving licensing, the particular legislation will usually be of greater significance and the issue will often come down to one of statutory interpretation,[53] involving a fairly minute

---

[51] [2004] 1 I.R. 402 at paras 51–53.

[52] Again an example is provided by the planning legislation: see enforcement notice and warning letter, authorised by the Planning and Development Act 2000 Pt VII, described at paras 5–145 to 5–146. See also, Data Protection Act 1988 s.10, as amended by Data Protection (Amendment) Act 2003 s.11.

[53] See, e.g. *Re Application of Pies Ltd* [1994] 3 I.R. 179 (meaning of "in the immediate vicinity" in the context of transfer of a liquor licence); *Lovett v Gogan* [1995] 3 I.R. 132 (whether, in order for a person to operate an occasional road passenger service, so as to require a licence, under

exercise in legal interpretation of both the terms of the licence and of the parent statute. Rich examples of the particularity of licensing regulations may be found in the voluminous law relating to planning permission[54]; liquor licensing[55]; private broadcasting licences (or franchises)[56]; or casual trading licences.[57]

7–19   The most basic way in which the statute affects matters is by determining the precise activity for which a licence is required, and the extent of activity authorised by a particular licence. This observation may be illustrated by *Bemis v Minister for Arts, Heritage, Gaeltacht and the Islands.*[58] The case was taken by the owner of the wreck of the Lusitania, who wished to obtain a licence to dive, survey and explore the foundered ship. One of the issues that arose concerned the fact that there were two governing Acts, the National Monuments Act 1930, which required a licence for digging or excavation around a national monument, and the National Monuments (Amendment) Act 1987, which required a licence for submarine activities around a national monument. The applicant took the view that only the 1987 Act was relevant to his application. The Supreme Court (Macken J.) rejected this interpretation of the two pieces of legislation.[59] Thus, an application for a licence for submarine activities could be granted under the 1987 Act; but, if intrusive works within the meaning of the 1930 Act were proposed to be carried out (such as the raising of bags of silt from around the wreck, as counsel for the respondent suggested), a separate licence would have to be sought. Again, "… a licence under section 26 of the National Monuments Act 1930 [licence to dig or excavate] could not constitute a permission to do any of the acts prohibited by s.

---

the Road Transport Act 1932 ss.2, 7 and 12, that person has to own the bus involved); *O'Rourke v Grittar* [1995] 1 I.R. 541 (exchange of one type of licence for another); *Slevin v Shannon Regional Fisheries Board* [1995] 1 I.R. 460 (fishing licences); *O'Connell v Environmental Protection Agency* [2003] 1 I.R. 530 (whether an environmental impact assessment had to be conducted before obtaining an integrated pollution licence); *Brady v Environmental Protection Agency* [2007] 3 I.R. 232 (conditions attached to an integrated pollution control licence); *Director of Public Prosecutions v Callaghan* [2008] IEHC 24 (meaning of "day" in licensing legislation); *Goodison v Sheahan* [2008] IEHC 127 (refusal to issue a firearms certificate on the grounds of "public safety" quashed). For further examples, see *Scrollside v Broadcasting Commission of Ireland* [2007] 1 I.R. 166 (broadcasting legislation); *McCarron v Kearney* [2008] IEHC 195 at para.15 (firearms legislation). See also, *Re Lyons* [2004] IEHC 301 (policy of An Garda Síochána to oppose the granting of licences for licensed premises in certain geographical areas).

[54] See paras 5–131 to 5–132.

[55] Licensing Acts 1833–2004. See further, Cassidy, *Cassidy on the Licensing Acts*, 3rd edn (Dublin: Clarus Press, 2009).

[56] See Cassidy, *Cassidy on the Licensing Acts*, 3rd edn (2009), pp.331–332 and pp.672–673.

[57] The Casual Trading Act 1995 is a kind of double-jointed control system by which control in respect of different factors is imposed at different points. Under the 1995 Act, a person selling goods in a public place must in the first place have a casual trading licence which is granted (or not) by a local authority by reference to the personal qualities of the applicant. A local authority may also designate an area as a "casual trading area". If it does so (though not otherwise), then a casual trader must hold not only a licence but also a casual trading permit, which latter control enables the local authority to specify the place which the trader may occupy on specified days: see further, 1995 Act ss.2–4; *Shanley v Galway Corporation* [1995] 1 I.R. 396; *Byrne v Tracey* [2001] IEHC 239.

[58] [2007] 3 I.R. 255. See also, *Donnelly v Commissioner of An Garda Síochána* [2008] 1 I.R. 153.

[59] [2007] 3 I.R. 255 at para.53 ("… [h]aving regard in particular to the absence of any indication in the Act of 1987 that the provisions of section 26 of the Act of 1930 were no longer to apply, or were not to apply …").

3(3) of the [National Monuments (Amendment) Act 1987 which include tampering with any part of a wreck or archaeological object] ...".

A licence is generally personal to the grantee and is not assignable

7–20   As a general rule, a licence is personal to the holder, since it was only granted on proof of the applicant's suitability of character, skill, qualifications, etc. This is so, even if it is not explicitly stated in the statute (as it is, for example, in s.13(1) of the Abattoirs Act 1988 which provides that "(t)he holder of an abattoir licence shall not transfer the licence to any other person ..."). Despite the general principle of non-assignability, there are occasional exceptions. For instance, taxi plates were freely traded, as if they were commodities[60] (though, as far as we know, this practice was not tested in court). In a second category of cases, the governing legislation provides that the grant of the licence does not depend on the personal suitability or qualifications of the applicant but instead attaches to the land, business, etc involved, irrespective of the owner.[61] A grant of planning permission is an example in point, for s.39(1) of the Planning and Development Act 2000 provides that:

> Where permission to develop land or for the retention of development is granted under this Part, then, except as may be otherwise provided by the permission, the grant of permission *shall enure for the benefit of the land* and of all persons for the time being interested therein. (Emphasis added)

7–21   The planning permission attaches to the land and any subsequent purchaser will take the lands with the benefit of that permission.[62] Indeed, such is the effect of s.39(1) that a planning permission has been judicially described as an "appendage to the title of the property".[63] But, naturally, even in this sort of case, the licence or permission may not be severed and sold independently.

7–22   There is a third category of case in which the licence attaches to the premises; but the applicant must also demonstrate suitability to hold the licence in question. This is the case with the Licensing Acts, which require attestation as to the suitability of both the licensed premises and the applicant before a licence is granted.

7–23   Where the licence attaches to the land, it cannot be sold independently from the land. This is illustrated by a series of decisions on the Licensing Acts, of which two cases may serve as examples. In *Re Sherry-Brennan*,[64] a bankrupt publican

---

[60]   See *Hempenstall v Minister for the Environment* [1993] I.L.R.M. 318.

[61]   Such as a register for bulls under s.3(1) of the Control of Bulls for Breeding Act 1985.

[62]   See, e.g. *Pine Valley Developments Ltd v Minister for the Environment* [1987] I.R. 23, where the plaintiffs purchased lands with the benefit of development permission for £550,000. The planning permission was ultimately found to be invalid and the plaintiffs sued the Minister for the Environment and Ireland for damages, since the market value of the lands without the permission was far less. However, the action failed for other reasons.

[63]   *Readymix (Éire) Ltd v Dublin County Council*, unreported, Supreme Court, July 31, 1974 at p.4 per Henchy J. The same judge made similar observations in *Pine Valley Developments Ltd v Minister for the Environment* [1987] I.R. 23 at 42. See also, *Grianán an Aileach Interpretative Centre Company Ltd v Donegal County Council* [2003] 3 I.R. 572; *Altara Developments Ltd v Ventola Ltd* [2005] IEHC 312.

[64]   [1979] I.L.R.M. 113.

was the owner of licensed premises in respect of which a judgment mortgage and other charges had been registered in the Land Registry. The premises were sold. However, the Official Assignee claimed to be entitled to retain the notional value of the licence (as reflected in the enhanced purchase price) for the benefit of the unsecured creditors, basing himself on the argument that the licence (as distinct from the premises itself) was not captured by the judgment mortgage and the other charges. Hamilton J. rejected this submission, stating that:

> "As a licence cannot be regarded as a property capable of separation from the licensed premises, I am satisfied that the licence is subject to the same charges and incumbrances as the property and hold that it is incapable of passing to the Official Assignee in priority to incumbrances registered against the property to which it is attached."[65]

7–24   And in *Macklin v Graecen & Co*,[66] a specific performance action, the Supreme Court held that a purported sale of a seven-day publican's licence, in isolation from the premises, was void and inoperative. Griffin J. said:

> "For almost 100 years it has been accepted that a licence to sell intoxicating liquor is inalienable and must be attached to the premises. The law on the matter has been stated succinctly by O'Connor's, *Irish Justice of the Peace* as follows: – 'The doctor cannot sell his degree, because it is attached to himself; on the other hand, the holder of a licence cannot sell the licence to any other person, unless such other person also buys the premises. The licence *per se* is inalienable. It must always, so long as it exists at all, remain attached to the premises.'"[67]

7–25   This principle of non-assignability is reflected in another (though soon to be obsolescent) licensing system involving land, namely, milk reference quantities or quotas (which are set to be abolished across the European Union in 2015).[68] As

---

[65]   [1979] I.L.R.M. 113 at 117. Hamilton J.'s reasoning was affirmed on appeal by the Supreme Court.

[66]   [1983] I.R. 61.

[67]   [1983] I.R. 61 at 66. The quotation was from O'Connor's *Irish Justice of the Peace* (Dublin: Ponsonby, 1915), Vol.2, p.368. See also, *Brennan v Dorney* (1887) 21 L.R. Ir. 353. In some cases, however, the legislation may explicitly permit the transfer of the licence to another authorised person (see, e.g. Pawnbroking Act 1964 s.9(1) (as inserted by the Consumer Credit Act 1995 s.153) (transfer of pawnbroking licence subject to consent of Director of Consumer Affairs); Environmental Protection Agency Act 1992 s.91 (transfer of integrated pollution licence permitted provided notice given to the Environmental Protection Agency); Water Services Act 2007 s.88(2)(j) (provision for the promulgation of ministerial regulations governing the transfer of water services licences)). However, where the licensing régime involves a trade or business, the governing statute will usually permit other persons (such as close relatives or personal representatives) to carry on the business of the licence holder on a temporary basis in circumstances such as illness, incapacity, death, etc. So the Abattoirs Act 1988 s.13(2) provides that: "Where the holder of an abattoir licence dies, the licence shall continue in full force and effect for the benefit of the licence holder's personal representative, or, as the case may be, his spouse or any other member of his family, for the period of four months, or for the period then unexpired of the term of the licence, whichever is the longer, after the death of the licence holder and shall then expire."

[68]   "New rules to open door to dairying: Milk quota for beef and tillage farmers", *Farmers Journal*, July 19, 2008.

a general rule, it may be said that a milk quota is land based[69] and that it "attaches to land used for milk production by a producer".[70] However, exceptions have been carved out of this principle "in order to continue the restructuring of milk production and improve the environment …".[71]

A licence will generally only be granted for a limited duration

7–26   Since it is of the essence of licensing statutes that they are intended to provide and maintain essential standards regulating the conduct of trade, business or activity in the public interest, it follows that, in the absence of an express statutory provision to the contrary, a licence will generally be deemed to have been granted for a limited duration.

7–27   Some statutes take care to state explicitly that the licence granted is not of indefinite duration. Thus s.59(2) of the Broadcasting Act 2009 provides that a broadcasting licence "shall be valid only for such period of time as a broadcasting contract between the [Broadcasting Authority of Ireland] and a broadcasting contractor is in force."[72] But what of the situation where the licensing provisions are not explicit on this point? This was considered in *Dublin Corporation v Judge O'Hanrahan*,[73] where the renewal of a gaming licence had been granted by the respondent judge, in face of a statutory resolution passed by the applicants rescinding the licensing provisions of the Gaming and Lotteries Act 1956. The notice party sought to justify the decision on the basis that, once a gaming licence had been granted, it attached to the property in perpetuity and that the effect of the rescission resolution was simply to prevent the grant of new licences. Johnson J. agreed that there was nothing in the 1956 Act which expressly declared that the certificate in question was an annual certificate, but said that it was implicit in the statutory framework that a licence subsisted from year to year. Consequently, the notice party's annual licence had lapsed and, because of the resolution, they were unable to apply for a new one. It would seem, therefore, that where the parent Act is not explicit on the question, the duration of the licence may be deduced from the surrounding statutory background.

Registration

7–28   It is noteworthy that although the use of different nomenclature is not, of

---

[69]   *Lawlor v Minister for Agriculture* [1990] 1 I.R. 356. See Geoghegan, "The Superlevy, Sales, Lease and Clawbacks" and Laffoy, "Milk Quotas as Security for Loans" in Robinson (ed.), *Milk Quotas: Law and Practice* (Irish Centre for European Law, 1989), pp.21 and 27 respectively.

[70]   European Communities (Milk Quota) Regulations 2008 (S.I. No. 227 of 2008).

[71]   Council Regulation 1234/2007 of October 22, 2007 establishing a common organisation of agricultural markets and on specific provisions for certain agricultural products, pp.5–6.

[72]   See also, e.g. Wildlife Act 1976 s.42(6), as substituted by Wildlife (Amendment) Act 2000 s.48(e) (authorisation to destroy wild birds that are causing damage); Casual Trading Act 1995 s.4(8) (casual trading licence to last for a maximum of 12 months, unless previously revoked); Package Holidays and Travel Trade Act 1995 ("… licence … to remain in force for such periods as the Minister thinks fit and specifies in the licence").

[73]   [1988] I.R. 121. This view was confirmed by Griffin J. in *Re Camillo's Application* [1988] I.R. 104.

itself, decisive,[74] where the Oireachtas uses the word "registration" (as opposed to "licence"), it generally intends that the entry on the register should be effected automatically and indefinitely; though without prejudice to a possible refusal to register the applicant on the grounds of unfitness to practise and subject to a power of amendment, revocation or erasure. In this sense, registration is an act of recording which is required of persons carrying out certain types of activity, by some scheme of public administration, and which may be permitted as a matter of right, provided that certain (often formal) conditions are satisfied.[75]

7–29   The object of registration is often to facilitate monitoring and the legislation generally provides that the register is open to the public for inspection without a fee.[76] The expression "registration" is usually employed by the legislation governing the professions and connotes an indefinite permission to practise the profession in question, provided—and it is a significant proviso—that they hold the necessary professional qualifications. One such example is provided by the Medical Practitioners Act 2007 ss.46–49 which provide that the Medical Council "shall register ... a medical practitioner ... [who has specified qualifications]".

7–30   In general, an entry in the Medical Register is intended to be of indefinite duration and, indeed, provision is made for the practitioner to apply to have his name removed from the register, and also for the Registrar to erase the name of a practitioner in the case of death. The Act[77] has served as a model for other regulatory legislation, such as the Nurses Act 1985, Dentists Act 1985, Health and Social Care Professionals Act 2005 and Veterinary Practice Act 2005.

7–31   The scheme of the Solicitors Acts 1954–1994 is somewhat different in that there is an additional step, namely that each solicitor on the "roll of solicitors" (the equivalent of registration) must also apply annually for a practising certificate.[78] Although s.61 of the 1994 Act empowers the Law Society to refuse to renew the practising certificate for what are essentially disciplinary reasons, nevertheless

---

[74]   The term "registration" may also be used as a synonym for licensing: see s.17(2) and (3) of the Data Protection Act 1988, as amended by the Data Protection (Amendment) Act 2003 s.17; s.10(3) and (4) of the Building Societies Act 1989; s.4 of the Health (Nursing Homes) Act 1990; Pt III of the Tourist Traffic Act 1939, as amended by the Tourist Traffic Act 1995; Health and Social Care Professionals Act 2005; Dog Breeding Establishment Act 2010 Pt 2.

[75]   See, e.g. Registration of Potato Growers and Potato Packers Act 1984; Control of Bulls for Breeding Act 1985; Control of Dogs Acts 1986 and 1992; Copyright and Related Rights Act 2000. In exceptional cases, the onus of compiling the register is put on the public authority rather than the person registered: see, e.g. Local Government (Multi-Storey Buildings) Act 1988 s.2(1).

[76]   For some diverse examples, see, e.g. Solicitors Act 1954 s.9(2) (as inserted by Solicitors (Amendment) Act 1994 s.65) (roll of solicitors "available for public inspection during office hours without payment"); Local Government (Water Pollution) Act 1977 s.9 (register of licences granted); Video Recordings Act 1989 s.14 (register of certificated video works); Casual Trading Act 1995 s.13 (register of casual trading licences); Planning and Development Act 2000 s.7(6)(a) (planning register); Private Security Services Act 2004 s.33(1) (Private Security Register). Occasionally, an inspection fee is prescribed: see, e.g. s.7 of the Insurance Act 1989, as substituted by the Central Bank and Financial Services Authority of Ireland Act 2003 Sch.1 Pt VIII; Control of Horses Act 1996 s.11(2).

[77]   Although the 1978 Act itself has now been superseded by an essentially similar arrangement in the Medical Practitioners Act 2007 ss.46, 47.

[78]   Solicitors Act 1954 s.48, as inserted by Solicitors (Amendment) Act 1994 s.55(2).

the entry on the roll (again subject to the disciplinary provisions of the legislation concerning refusals) lasts indefinitely and the necessity to obtain annually a practising certificate is little more than a revenue-raising mechanism for the Society.

The refusal or revocation of a licence must be in the public interest and not a punishment

7–32   The refusal or revocation of a licence will generally only be justified where this is established as being itself directly in the public interest to protect the public from injurious action by the putative licence holder and not as a punitive measure. A good example of the application of this principle may be found in *Re Crowley*,[79] where the applicant solicitor had been refused a practising certificate by the Law Society. It appeared that the applicant had engaged in "touting" for business on one occasion in the past and this was relied on by the Society as justification for the refusal of the certificate. Kingsmill Moore J. held that, save in cases where the solicitor is actually being charged with a disciplinary offence, the refusal or withdrawal of a certificate could only be justified where this was in the public interest. The judge went on to admit that there might be circumstances where the public interest required that a solicitor should be restrained from practising; but he added that: "[s]uch action is only justified as a necessary precaution against the likelihood of future misdoing reasonably to be inferred from past conduct."[80] Again, in *Ingle v O'Brien*[81] Pringle J. held that simply because the applicant taxi driver was convicted in the District Court of carriage offences did not entitle the licensing authorities, ipso facto, to revoke the applicant's licence.

7–33   In other cases, the licensing legislation itself will stipulate circumstances in which the licence will automatically lapse. Thus, s.28(1) of the Intoxicating Liquor Act 1927 provides that upon the recording of a third licensing conviction on a licence, the licence is thereby automatically forfeited. Sections 2 and 3(3) of the Licensing (Combating Drug Abuse) Act 1997 are in similar terms—even if more drastic in their effect. They provide that: "Any person who has been convicted of a drug trafficking offence shall be disqualified for ever from holding any intoxicating liquor licence, any public dancing licence or any public music and singing licence …".[82]

The terms of the licence must be construed by reference to public and objective standards

7–34   Since a licence is a public document, the governing legislation often provides

---

[79]   [1964] I.R. 106. See also, *Balkan Tours Ltd v Minister for Communications* [1988] I.L.R.M. 101.

[80]   [1964] I.R. 106 at 129. This approach also finds support in the judgment of Walsh J. for the Supreme Court, though in the different context of Art.38 in *Conroy v Attorney General* [1965] I.R. 411 where it was held that disqualification for drunk driving, coupled with the loss of a driving licence, was not to be regarded as a punishment. As Walsh J. explained (at 441), "[o]ne must not lose sight, however, of the real nature of the disqualification order which is that it is essentially a finding of unfitness of the person concerned to hold a driving licence."

[81]   (1975) 109 I.L.T.R. 7.

[82]   See also, s.17(3) of the 1997 Act.

that the licence is open to public inspection or, even, that the terms of the licence must be publicly displayed.[83] A corollary of this is that the terms of the licence must be objectively construed and any private arrangements or understandings as between the licensing authority and the licence holder are not admissible. This is illustrated by *Readymix (Eire) Ltd v Dublin County Council*,[84] where it was argued that the planning permission granted by the local authority should be construed as having the meaning agreed by the planning officials and the developer. The Supreme Court rejected that submission, with Henchy J. observing:

> "The Act does not in terms make the register the conclusive or exclusive evidence record of the nature and extent of a permission, but the scheme of the Act indicates that anybody who acts on the basis of the correctness of the particulars in the register is entitled to do so. Where the permission recorded in the register is self-contained, it will not be permissible to go outside it in construing it. But where the permission incorporates other documents, it is the combined effect of the permission and such documents which must be looked at in determining the proper scope of the permission ... Since the permission notified to an applicant and entered in the register is a public document, it must be construed objectively as such, and not in the light of subjective considerations special to the applicant or those responsible for the grant of permission."[85]

In sum, a licence is a self-contained public document and must be construed as such.

C. ARE LICENCES CONSTITUTIONAL PROPERTY RIGHTS? CHANGES IN LICENSING REGIMES

7–35 Licence holders have long been protected from the arbitrary refusal or revocation of their licence. Thus, the applicant is entitled to a fair hearing before his application is refused or revoked,[86] he is entitled to reasons if the licence is refused[87] and, indeed, there may in some circumstances, be an argument that he has acquired a legitimate expectation that the licence will be renewed.[88]

7–36 But does the protection of licences go any further than this? For example, is there a right of renewal of licence? Such particular questions are discussed below. For the moment, we shall discuss the main conceptual framework within which

---

[83] See, e.g. Medical Practitioners Act 2007 s.43(7) ("A registered medical practitioner shall, as soon as may be after the practitioner has received the certificate referred to in subsection (5) and if it is practicable to do so, cause the certificate to be displayed: (a) at the principal place where the practitioner practises medicine, and (b) at all times during which the practitioner's registration continues and at no other time."); Casual Trading Act 1995 s.5(1) (obligation on licensee to display casual trading licence).
[84] Unreported, Supreme Court, July 31, 1974.
[85] Unreported, Supreme Court, July 31, 1974 at p.4 of the judgment. But contrast *Liffey Beat*, at paras 15–48 to 15–50 and Ch.6, fn.131.
[86] *International Fishing Vessel Ltd v Minister for Marine* [1989] I.R. 149.
[87] *State (Pheasantry Ltd) v District Justice Donnelly* [1982] I.L.R.M. 512; *Deerland Construction Ltd v Aquaculture Licences Appeals Board* [2008] IEHC 289.
[88] See Ch.19 generally and para.19–13 in particular.

these particular questions are considered, namely whether licences are some species of property right. The judicial consensus on this point is that either licences are not property rights, but only privileges; or, if they are property rights, then, in the public interest, they may be altered. There is not much practical difference between these two positions. Supporting the first alternative, Carroll J. in *State (Pheasantry Ltd) v Donnelly*[89] described a licence as merely "a privilege granted by statute and regulated for the public good".[90] In the *Pheasantry* case, the applicants challenged the constitutionality of s.28 of the Intoxicating Liquor Act 1927 whereby the licence attaching to licensed premises is forfeited when three convictions are duly recorded and indorsed on the licence. Carroll J. agreed that the rights protected by Art.40.3 included the licence in conjunction with the premises, but she could not agree that the forfeiture provisions were, thereby, unconstitutional:

> "The licence is a privilege granted by statute and regulated for the public good. It is, *ab initio*, subject to various conditions, one of which is the inherent possibility of automatic forfeiture under section 28. If the conditions necessary for statutory forfeiture are fulfilled, this is brought about through the licensee's own default. There is no constitutional right to a liquor licence or a renewal thereof. There are only such rights as are given by statute subject to limitations and conditions prescribed by statute."[91]

7–37 Admittedly, this analysis was made in the context of the right to jury trial, under Art.38 of the Constitution, which makes the right depend upon the severity of the sanction, which in this case included forfeiture of the licence. However, this general line of thought has attracted a judicial consensus in a number of cases[92] in the licensing field. The logical consequence of this line of judicial reasoning is that the Oireachtas could constitutionally terminate a particular licensing system where this was established to be in the public interest and prohibit the previously licensed activity without payment of any compensation to the existing licence holders, even though such licensees might have invested heavily in that particular licensed business. It was probably a consequence of this, that when Dublin Corporation rescinded the operation of Pt III of the Gaming and Lotteries Act 1956 in 1986 (thus effectively closing all existing gaming halls), the former licence holders refrained from making any claim for compensation.

7–38 As mentioned, there is a line of cases which lean more in the favour of there being a property right, but then undermine this by holding that there is a wide discretion to change it in the public interest. In *Hempenstall v Minister for the Environment*,[93] the Minister made regulations which had the effect of removing a moratorium (which the Minister had imposed earlier) on the granting of new taxi licences. These regulations, it was claimed by the applicants, who were licensed taxi owners, constituted an unjust attack on their property rights in that it diminished

---

[89] *State (Pheasantry Ltd) v District Justice Donnelly* [1982] I.L.R.M. 512.
[90] *State (Pheasantry Ltd) v District Justice Donnelly* [1982] I.L.R.M. 512 at 516.
[91] *State (Pheasantry Ltd) v District Justice Donnelly* [1982] I.L.R.M. 512 at 516.
[92] See *Permanent Motorists Protection Society Ltd v Attorney General* [1983] I.R. 339; *Cafolla v Attorney General* [1985] I.R. 486; *Hand v Dublin Corporation* [1989] I.R. 26; *Maher v Minister for Agriculture* [2001] 2 I.R. 139.
[93] [1993] I.L.R.M. 318. On licensing and the constitutional right to a livelihood see, *Shanley v Galway Corporation* [1995] 1 I.R. 396 at 404–406.

the capital value of the "taxi plates" (a phrase explained below). Even on the assumption that the factual basis was correct, the claim failed. It was accepted, in the first place, that the applicants' taxi licences were constitutionally protected property rights. However, Costello J. (as he then was) held that there had been no unjust attack, since regulation was in the public interest. More particularly[94]:

> "Property rights arising in licences created by law (enacted or delegated) are subject to the conditions created by law and to an implied condition that the law may change those conditions
>
> ...
>
> [A] change in the law which has the effect of reducing property values cannot in itself amount to an infringement of constitutionally protected property rights. There are many instances in which legal changes may adversely affect property values (for example, new zoning regulations in the planning code and new legislation relating to the issue of intoxicating liquor licences) and such changes cannot be impugned as being constitutionally invalid unless some invalidity can be shown to exist apart from the resulting property value diminution. In this case no such invalidity can be shown. The object of the exercise of the ministerial regulatory power is to benefit users of small public service vehicles. It has not been shown or even suggested that the minister acted otherwise than in accordance with his statutory powers. Once he did so then it cannot be said that he has 'attacked' the applicants' property rights thereby, because a diminution in the value may have resulted."

7–39 A similar approach was taken by Carney J. in *Gorman v Minister for the Environment*.[95] Here, the respondent had introduced the Road Traffic (Public Service Vehicles) (Amendment) (No.3) Regulations 2000,[96] which entirely abolished national quantitative restrictions on the granting of taxi licences.[97] The applicants challenged the abolition as an unconstitutional interference with their property rights in their taxi licences, due to the massive reduction in the value of the licences caused by the respondent's action. Relying heavily on the reasoning of Costello J. in *Hempenstall*, Carney J. held that, although the applicants had a property right in their licences, an ability to vary the licensing scheme "must be necessarily implied if the Minister of State is not to be unduly hampered in exercising his powers under

---

[94] [1993] I.L.R.M. 318 at 324–325. This approach may also be found in the jurisprudence of the Court of Justice. It is true that Advocate General Jacobs once famously observed of milk quotas (*Wachauf v Bundesamt für Ernahärung* (C-5/88) [1991] 1 C.M.L.R. 328 at 342, that: "[The argument has been advanced] that a quota is nothing more than an instrument of market management and cannot be considered as a kind of intangible asset in which property rights can arise ... While this might correspond to the intention of the Community legislation, it does not reflect economic reality ... In a market which is effectively ossified by the introduction of quotas, such a 'licence' is bound to acquire an economic value."
     However, the Court of Justice has consistently rejected the "milk quota as property right" argument, most notably in the Irish development farmers case, *Duff v Minister for Agriculture* (C-63/93) [1996] E.C.R. I–569 at para.30.

[95] [2001] 2 I.R. 414.

[96] S.I. No. 367 of 2000.

[97] In the earlier case of *Humphrey v Minister for the Environment* [2001] 1 I.R. 263, a previous set of regulations, which increased the number of taxi licences in Dublin, was struck down as ultra vires, on particular statutory grounds. The set of regulations impugned in *Gorman* were introduced in the aftermath of the *Humphrey* decision.

statute in the public interest".[98] Moreover, dramatic changes in the licensing regime had previously taken place, and the respondents themselves had previously "reaped the benefits of legislative change" and it was not open to them to "complain about such changes in the law having a detrimental effect on the value of their licences".[99] With regard to the applicants' claim that a system of compensation should be put in place, Carney J. held that it would be incongruous to compensate them for dangers of which they were well aware; that the interference with their property rights was minimal because they could still dispose of their licences (albeit at lower prices); that the payments made for licences achieved their purpose at the time, which was effectively to purchase a job; and that there was no "automatic right to compensation in all circumstances".[100]

7–40 A field in which the constitutional nature of licences might be significant is that of the renewal of licences. In most fields of licensing, the situation as it operates on the ground is that, provided an existing licence holder's conduct does not go seriously awry, then—whatever the legal theory about a fresh licence having to be granted—"his licence" will be renewed, more or less automatically. Thus, from the perspective of a newcomer wishing to break into the field, unless new licences are being issued, the only way to do so will be to purchase the property which is necessary for the occupation, which will often bring with it, as part of the transaction, the necessary licence. A well-known example is the purchase of a public house which will usually carry with it the necessary licence and the reasonable assumption that, at the end of the year, it will be renewed in favour of the purchaser. Again, trading in taxi plates is actually authorised by law "provided only that the Commissioner is satisfied that he would grant a licence to the new owner if an application for the grant of a licence under Article 6 [which lays down conditions for the grant of a licence *ab initio*] were made to him at that time by the new owner."[101]

7–41 This is a far cry from a theoretical world in which licences would be awarded on a competitive basis, without reference to whether an applicant already had an established business or was a newcomer, but simply by reference to the criterion of which applicant would give a better or more economic service to the public. In other words, practical reality, as most people affected take it to be, is a long way from the theory. Against this background, three types of query arise:

Could an existing licence-holder complain if his licence were not renewed but instead re-allocated to a newcomer on the basis of superior merit?

7–42 The argument in favour of there being a freedom to effect such a change is

---

[98] *Gorman v Minister for the Environment* [2001] 2 I.R. 414 at 430. See similarly, Murray J.'s comments in *Maher v Minister for Agriculture* [2001] 2 I.R. 139 at 229, in response to the submission that the applicants held property rights, which had been infringed by Regulations transposing a Council Regulation, in their milk quotas.

[99] *Humphrey v Minister for the Environment* [2001] 1 I.R. 263 at 430.

[100] *Humphrey v Minister for the Environment* [2001] 1 I.R. 263 at 431. See similarly, *NWR FM Ltd v Broadcasting Commission of Ireland* [2004] 4 I.R. 50.

[101] Road Traffic (Public Service Vehicles) (Licensing) Regulations (S.I. No. 292 of 1978). In 1997 the Minister for Enterprise and Employment referred the question of whether the number of taxi plates ought to be increased to the Competition Authority. See now, Annual Reports of the Commission for Taxi Regulation.

afforded a secure foothold in the opening sentence in the passage from *Hempenstall* quoted earlier ("[p]roperty rights arising in licences ... are subject to the conditions created by law ..."). Does it not follow, it might be argued, that if a licence is limited in duration to one year, that no property right enures after this year has expired? The countervailing argument is as follows. Even if there is doubt[102] (in view of the one-year limit of the licence) as to whether there is here a classic legitimate expectation that the licence should be renewed, nevertheless such is the necessary investment by a licence holder in premises, staff, experience and/or qualifications, etc that one would expect that some expectation or property right would be discerned.[103] In addition, despite what was said earlier, the licence holder might well be able in these extreme circumstances to rely upon the constitutional property right.[104] (In contrast with the situation in *Hempenstall*, the interference by the licensing authority would not be with the surrounding circumstances, which affected the value of the right; but rather would amount to a direct interference with the utility of the former licence holder's premises, stock and employment contracts.) The argument seems to be well balanced.

Ought the number of licences to be increased if the public interest requires it?

7–43   This is obviously a contention which an applicant who wished to break into a particular line of business (or even someone who, in the Dublin of the 1990s, had had difficulty in finding a taxi) might wish to advance. In *Hempenstall* and *Gorman*, it was held that it was open to the licensing agency to increase the number of taxi plates. But does the law go further and actually require this to be done in an appropriate case? In principle there seems to be no reason why the usual controls, by way of judicial review, should not be applied to the determination of the number of licences as they do to other functions. These would require the licensing agency fixing numbers to take into account relevant factors, including the interests of: existing licence holders; would-be licence holders; consumers; and (perhaps in an appropriate case) environmentalists. The various interests would have to be balanced against each other reasonably. The public interest in competition would have to be given due weight. All this might militate in favour of an increase, in appropriate circumstances. However, one should sound a note of caution: this function is very much at the policy end of the policy–administration spectrum, depending as it does on a complex of social, commercial, economic, political, etc factors. Accordingly, it is only in an extreme case that a judge would be prepared to intervene in this field.

---

[102] It is notable that in *Hempenstall* the figure of £44,000 for the market value of taxi licences in Dublin was quoted without any observation being made to the fact this figure pre-supposed that the purchaser could expect that the licence would, in effect, last for several years and then be sold on. One had the feeling that this observation went without saying, as it does in popular discourse.

[103] The uncertainty and unsatisfactory nature of the law in this area is paralleled elsewhere, e.g. if I have an annual contract with an insurance company, can the insurance company refuse to renew it, perhaps because they wish to deny me the no-claims bonus?

[104] *Tara Prospecting Ltd v Minister for Energy* [1993] I.L.R.M. 771 (see para.19–39) would not be a relevant authority here, because that was a case in which the Minister exercised his discretion to change his policy regarding environmental standards, rather than as here preferring a new licence holder to an existing licence holder.

Can the number of licences be restricted if the public interest requires it?

7–44 We turn below to EU law, but commence our analysis with Irish administrative law. In the first place, one should distinguish the unusual cases where the governing legislation explicitly allows the licensing authority to impose a restriction on the number of licences to be granted.[105] For example, it used to be the case that there were statutory restrictions on the making of pharmacy contractor agreements. They could not be made unless the chief executive of the relevant health board was of the opinion, inter alia, that "there is a definite public health need for the supply of community pharmacy services in the particular catchment area to which the application relates."[106]

7–45 However, the Regulations in question were revoked in 2002[107] and an indication of the changed legislative landscape (as far as restrictions of competition are concerned) is contained in the Pharmacy Act 2007, s.12 of which requires the Pharmacy Council to submit a draft code of conduct to the Competition Authority for its opinion on whether the proposed code would be "likely to result in competition being prevented, restricted or distorted."[108]

7–46 Nevertheless, apart from situations where there is an express restriction as to the number of licences, may a licensing authority observe a restriction on the number of licences? In the first of the relevant cases, *East Donegal Co-operative Livestock Mart Ltd v Attorney General*,[109] the plaintiffs attacked the licensing provisions of the Livestock Marts Act 1967 on the ground, inter alia, that they would enable the Minister to use his discretion to limit the number of marts in operation. This submission was rejected by Walsh J. in a passage which, however, concedes the underlying thrust of the argument. He stated:

> "The proper conduct of the business concerned, the standard of hygiene and veterinary standards in relation to such places and to provision of adequate and suitable accommodation and facilities for such auctions ... Nowhere in the Act is there anything to indicate that one of the purposes of the Act is to limit or otherwise regulate the number of auction marts as distinct from regulating the way in which business is conducted in auction marts. In the absence of any such indication in the Act, the Minister is not authorised by the Act to limit the number of businesses ...".[110]

---

[105] Murphy J. interpreted s.6(1) of the Radio and Television Act 1988 in this manner in *Dublin and County Broadcasting Ltd v Independent Radio and Television Commission*, unreported, High Court, May 12, 1989, and s.66 of the Broadcasting Act 2009 largely re-enacts the provisions of the 1988 Act. See, to similar effect, Intoxicating Liquor Act 1960 s.14; *Re Matter of Thank God it's Friday Ltd* [1990] I.L.R.M. 228.

[106] Article 5(1) of the Health (Community Pharmacy Contractor Agreement) Regulations 1996 (S.I. No. 152 of 1996).

[107] Health (Community Pharmacy Contractor Agreement) Regulations 1996 (Revocation) Regulations 2002 (S.I. No. 28 of 2002).

[108] Compare Sea-Fisheries and Maritime Jurisdiction Act 2006 s.12 (restriction on catching, retention on board or landing of certain types of fish may be imposed "for the proper management and conservation and rational exploitation of the State's fishing quota and fishing effort under the common fisheries policy").

[109] [1970] I.R. 317.

[110] [1970] I.R. 317 at 342–343.

7–47 In *Re Application of Power Supermarkets Ltd*,[111] the Supreme Court addressed the question of whether the Circuit Court could take the economic consequences to other publicans in the area into account in deciding whether or not to grant an off-licence to a major supermarket chain. Walsh J. said that this was an irrelevant factor in the exercise of the judge's discretion:

> "The object of the [Intoxicating Liquor Acts] was to safeguard the public interest by preventing a proliferation of licensed premises and not to shelter existing publicans from competition. To decide that a licence ought not to be granted because the competition it would offer to existing licences would be economically disadvantageous to the holders of those licences is not a ground which is contemplated by the code and therefore is not one which can be said to be an exercise of judicial discretion."[112]

7–48 It is notable that, in contrast to *East Donegal*, while rejecting the argument founded on the economic consequences to other publicans, Walsh J. did accept (in the context of the Intoxicating Liquor Acts) the possibility of a restriction upon the number of licences provided that it was in "the public interest".[113] In short, this was a rather different view from that given in *East Donegal*, albeit one either expressly or necessarily contemplated by such legislation.

7–49 It might have been thought that, in certain circumstances, there could be a causative link between preventing excessive competition and maintaining adequate standards so that the use of licensing to prevent competition might be regarded as acceptable on the ground that it tended to maintain standards. This link may indeed have been what Walsh J. had in mind by the use of the phrase "in the public interest" in *Power Supermarkets*. This appears to have been the line of thought adopted by Budd J. in *O'Neill v Minister for Agriculture*.[114] The ostensible issue in the case was the Minister's refusal to grant the applicant a licence (under the Livestock (Artificial Insemination) Act 1947 and regulations made thereunder) to

---

[111] [1988] I.R. 206.

[112] [1988] I.R. 206 at 210–211.

[113] In *Re Connellan's Application*, unreported, High Court, October 19, 1973 an objection was raised to the grant of a declaration that the applicant's premises was fit to be licensed under s.15 of the Intoxicating Liquor Act 1960. The objectors intended to build a community centre immediately adjacent to the applicant's premises and the centre would only be economically viable if it had the sole right to sell intoxicating liquor in that area. However, Finlay J. said (at p.7) that this consideration was not one which could properly be taken into account by the Circuit Court: "No matter how much I might, as a matter of social policy, favour the provision of a community centre and favour a situation in which it could from a monopoly sale of intoxicating liquor in its own area fund itself in an economic and profitable way, I do not consider that the licensing code gives me a discretion to implement that view."

The judge went on to observe that as the objects of the Licensing Acts were to restrict the proliferation of public houses and to increase standards generally, it was in these respects essentially "a negative or restrictive code" and could not properly be construed as "a positive weapon of social policy". Thus, one should remark that here the facts were more extreme than in *East Donegal* in that the social policy which the licensing agency sought to serve was not even the efficient operation of licensed premises (a policy which might be contemplated in the 1960 Act: see, e.g. *Re Lyons* [2004] IEHC 301 (policy of An Garda Síochána to oppose the granting of licences for licensed premises in certain geographical areas)), but rather an altogether extraneous policy.

[114] Unreported, High Court, Budd J., July 5, 1995.

run a course to train personnel in the artificial insemination of cattle. However, as Budd J. remarked:

"... the reality behind the case was a challenge to the present system of state-authorised regional monopolies in that the State has authorised the granting of the exclusive right to provide an A.I. field service in each region to one of eight or nine regional monopolists ... [It is argued by the applicant that] Departmental policy, which places geographical and quantitative restrictions on the number of licences granted [is] firstly, contrary to Irish law and, secondly, contrary to EC competition law."[115]

7–50 As regards Irish law (the principles of EU competition law will be considered later[116]), Budd J. recounted the *East Donegal* and *MacGabhann*[117] cases from each of which he was to diverge. All he said by way of distinguishing these authorities was to refer to "the need for a close scrutiny of the content and actual wording of the statute and regulations under analysis."[118] He could perhaps have added that his judgment was the first Irish case in which the present point had received elaborate analysis. In any event, Budd J. concluded:

"After careful scrutiny it seems to me that the evolution of the regime of exclusive contiguous areas of operation divided up between the licensees was done with the agreement of the farming community through the involvement of the co-ops owned by the farmers and was a reasonable way of achieving the Minister's objectives of ensuring a quality A.I. service throughout the land, supported by progeny testing and the keeping of appropriate records. Section 7(2) of the 1947 Act empowered the Minister to attach conditions as he thinks fit to a licence. The conditions attached with regard to a defined operative area are *intra vires* the Minister."[119]

7–51 In *O'Neill*, the High Court was reversed by the Supreme Court. But, before coming to the Supreme Court's judgments, it is instructive to compare *O'Neill* with another roughly contemporaneous High Court case (which, however, did not go to the Supreme Court), *Carrigaline Community Television Broadcasting Company Ltd v The Minister for Transport, Energy and Communications*[120] (neither case being referred to in the other). Whilst the outcomes of the two cases were different, it may be that they can be distinguished. In *Carrigaline*, too, the licensing agency had refused the plaintiff a licence on the broad ground of protecting the quality of the service provided by existing licence holders. Specifically, in *Carrigaline*, the Minister was pursuing a policy of refusing licences (under the Wireless Telegraphy Act 1926 s.5, providing for a licence to keep wireless telegraphy apparatus) to those, like the plaintiff, who were transmitting their signals in the VHF waveband because (the Minister claimed) to do so would risk overcrowding that waveband. Instead,

---

[115] Unreported, High Court, Budd J., July 5, 1995 at p.12.
[116] See paras 7–58 to 7–60.
[117] *MacGabhann v The Incorporated Law Society of Ireland* [1989] I.L.R.M. 854.
[118] Unreported, High Court, Budd J., July 5, 1995 at p.27. This was the main ground on which *MacGabhann* was distinguished. See, to like effect, the distinguishing of *East Donegal* [1970] I.R. 317 at 25 in *MacGabhann*.
[119] Unreported, High Court, Budd J., July 5, 1995 at p.90.
[120] [1997] 1 I.L.R.M. 241.

the Minister was confining licences to persons who owned a Microwave Multipoint Distribution System (MMDS). Plainly there are two inter-related points here.[121] The first is the reasonableness of the policy, as to which the court held—apparently as a finding of fact—that "the evidence establishes overwhelmingly that the provision of four national programmes services in the VHF band does not represent the optimum use of that band". And as to the second point, which is the ground on which the case may be compared with *O'Neill*, Keane J. stated:

"... the Minister was undoubtedly entitled to adopt the policy of protecting and encouraging the development of the cable [MMDS] infrastructure which had been recommended by the Downes Committee. There was, however, no evidence whatever that the existence of the plaintiff's rebroadcasting system had affected to even the slightest degree the economic viability of the cable system operated in Cork City by Cork Communications for the past thirteen years. There was no evidence that the signals transmitted by the plaintiffs were received to any significant extent in Cork city and the evidence was that they discouraged any attempt to transmit them to that area ... [T]here was also no evidence whatever to justify the suggestion that the granting of the MMDS licences on a basis which would exclude any other form of retransmission would encourage the extension of the cable system to other towns and villages thereby facilitating, as it was claimed, the establishment of the 'information highway'."[122]

7–52   The significant point is that here, as Budd J. had held in *O'Neill* (and in contrast to *East Donegal*), it was accepted by Keane J. that a policy of protecting one category of licence holder (at the expense of another) could be pursued provided (it is probably legitimate to assume) that the selection of the favoured group depended upon some factor related to the public interest.

7–53   However, the Supreme Court in *O'Neill* took a significantly different line from that of the High Court in *O'Neill* or *Carrigaline*. The applicant succeeded and the High Court was reversed, on a number of points, of which the one of relevance here was expressed as being whether the Minister, in granting licences was entitled to "adopt a particular policy". In answering this question in *O'Neill*, Keane J. commenced by quoting the following from his own judgment in the High Court in *Carrigaline*:

"It is clear that, in the case of at least some licensing regimes, questions of policy cannot play any part. This would be the case, for example, with television reception licences and driving licences, provided that in the latter case, certain conditions of eligibility are met. At the other extreme, questions of policy must obviously affect the granting or refusal of planning permission and indeed in that area the authority is obliged by statute to adopt a specific set of policy objectives in the form of a development plan. The licensing regime established under the 1926 Act as amended by subsequent legislation belongs to an intermediate category. In the case of this and similar licensing regimes, the adoption by the licensing authority of a policy could have

---

[121] See further, discussion of this coincidence at para.15–148.

[122] [1997] 1 I.L.R.M. 241 at 297.

the advantage of ensuring some degree of consistency in the operation of the regime, thus making less likely decisions that might be categorised as capricious or arbitrary. But it is also clear that inflexible adherence to such a policy may result in a countervailing injustice. The case law in both this jurisdiction and the United Kingdom illustrates the difficulties involved in balancing these competing values."[123]

7–54 Unfortunately, this passage does not directly address the question of whether the licensing may, as a general matter, limit the number of licences. Instead, the burden of the passage is the distinct principle against fettering a discretionary power by a policy rule.[124] Later on in the judgment in *O'Neill*, Keane J. quoted the Department of Agriculture's policy justification for the adoption of the exclusivity scheme:

"... to ensure a comprehensive quality service ... to all farmers; also veterinary controls in respect of animal welfare, health and good conception rates and the provision of high genetic merit semen ... to all breeders with large and small herds. The regional monopoly system [is] ... a mechanism to ensure that all farmers would have access to an available service."[125]

7–55 Keane J.'s comment on this was:

"There is no indication in the 1947 Act that these undoubtedly laudable objectives constituted the underlying policy of the Act, with two qualifications. The evidence in the High Court established, and common sense would have in any event suggested that it was the case, that the major reason for introducing statutory controls over AI in 1947 was because of the desirability of controlling disease and improving the general quality of the national herd. The system of control spelled out is negative rather than positive: the practice of AI may only be carried on where a licence is granted. There is nothing in the Act to suggest that the Oireachtas intended that, for the reasons given in the passage from the High Court judgment already cited, the Minister should divide the country into a number of regions, in respect of which only one licence was to be granted."[126]

---

[123] [1997] 1 I.L.R.M. 241 at 284. In *Carrigaline* itself, in addressing the general question posed in the passage, Keane J. stated (at 286): "In the present case, the minister, while under a duty to consider all applications for licences made to him in a fair and impartial manner, was also entitled, and indeed obliged to have regard to what might be described as certain policy considerations. First, he was obliged to have regard to the principles of good frequency management ... Secondly, he was bound to ensure that the objectives enshrined in other legislation, including the reception on a national basis of the two existing RTÉ programme services and of the contemplated TV3 and Telefís Na Gaeilge programme services, were not frustrated by the exercise of his licensing functions. Thirdly, he was obliged to have regard to the obligations of the State under international conventions ...".

[124] See Third Edition, pp.668–675.

[125] [1997] 2 I.L.R.M. 435 at 441.

[126] [1997] 2 I.L.R.M. 435 at 441–442. Notice that Keane J. later remarked: "The evidence in the High Court established overwhelmingly that some scheme of this nature was essential if the practice of artificial insemination was to be both controlled and facilitated in the interests of an industry of paramount importance in the Irish economy. This court is solely concerned, however, with the legality of the scheme."

7–56 The other judge to give a written judgment, Murphy J., said something similar, fortifying it with a reference to "the manner in which [the licensing scheme] affects the property or other constitutional rights of the citizens" and a substantial nod in the direction of Art.15.2.1°.[127] However, it may be significant that in *O'Neill* Murphy J. condemned the scheme as ultra vires on the basis that it was "so radical in qualifying limited number of persons and disqualifying all others who may be equally competent from engaging in business." This passage carries the hint that had the facts been otherwise, so that the Minister had abandoned the exclusivity scheme, but nonetheless had regard to the adequacy of demand for artificial insemination service by imposing a variable quota, a different outcome might have been possible, especially if a clear nexus between the quota of licences granted and the quality of service could have been demonstrated. This was certainly the view of Carroll J. in *Navan Tanker Services Ltd v Meath County Council*[128] where she held that a local authority could have regard to the adequacy of demand and impose a quota on the number of vehicle testers applying for a statutory licence. The scheme in *Navan Tanker Services* was more flexible and less radical than that actually operated in *O'Neill*—in that it was not rigidly exclusive and the quota appeared to be kept under constant review—so that the decisions are not necessarily incompatible with each other. Similarly, the scheme in *Casey v Minister for Arts, Heritage, Gaeltacht and the Islands*,[129] whereby the Minister used a general statutory power to limit the number of persons who might land passengers on Skellig Michael, survived constitutional challenge, despite the fact that the number of available permits was fixed at 19 in 1995 and not revisited. However, the sensitive nature of Skellig Michael, the preservation of which had been the subject of a number of expert reports, may have been a factor.[130]

7–57 The only general inference to be drawn from this divergent case law is, perhaps, that the courts will be slow to infer from the general words in a statute a licensing system which can be used to control numbers or, at any rate, an exclusive régime (which was in issue in both *O'Neill* and *Carrigaline*). Furthermore, and separately, often such schemes as that which were held invalid by the Supreme Court in *O'Neill* or by Keane J. in *Carrigaline* may, when they were first put in place, have raised no legal objections. However, if there is a failure to adjust the scheme in the light of changed circumstances, it may become unreasonable and thus open to challenge.

7–58 In *O'Neill*, one of the grounds on which the applicant assailed the exclusive AI licensing system was EU competition law (the first occasion on which such a point has been taken in regard to an Irish licensing system). Budd J. summarised the position as follows:

"The nub of the challenge is to both the geographical area condition

---

[127] [1997] 2 I.L.R.M. 435 at 447–450. On Art.15.2.1°, see paras 2–11 to 2–21.

[128] Unreported, High Court, December 19, 1996.

[129] [2004] 1 I.R. 402.

[130] It may be significant that Murray J. felt constrained to note (at para.15), that the documents granting access "were not permits or licences in the formal sense but more in the nature of written permission from the respondent as the person in whom ownership of the island is vested and as the Minister vested with statutory responsibility for the preservation and maintenance of national monuments."

imposed in the licence and the restriction to one licence per area. There is no allegation that the 1947 Act or the 1948 Regulations [Livestock (Artificial Insemination) Regulations 1948] are contrary to the E.C. Treaty and so the Act and regulations are unscathed. The real attack is on the administrative practice of delimiting an area exclusively for the operations of one A.I. licensee as being contrary to Articles 86 and 90(1). It is conceded that the existing A.I. licence stations are undertakings to which Ireland has granted exclusive rights within the meaning of Article 90 and that the administrative practice of imposing geographical restrictives and one licence per area are measures within the meaning of Article 90(1). It is accepted that the A.I. licensees are undertakings in a dominant position in a substantial part of the common market (as in *Crespelle*) and that the granting of exclusivity may affect trade between Member States. The market in this case is the A.I. field service element of the A.I. business. Applying the principle in *Crespelle* (which concerned as it happened, the French A.I. régime and in which the claimant also failed) the creation by the State of regional monopolies is not contrary to Articles 86 and 90(1): the applicant to succeed must also prove that in exercising the exclusive rights the A.I. licensees cannot avoid abusing their dominant position (see paragraphs 18 and 20 of *Crespelle*). It may be helpful if I pose the questions:

1. Are the alleged abuses of their dominant position by the A.I. licensees the direct consequence of the present administrative practice?
2. Are the existing A.I. stations, in merely exercising the exclusive right granted to them, unable to avoid abusing their dominant position?

The applicant has contended that, firstly, the A.I. stations were not catering for certain market needs and thus were limiting production, markets or technical development to the prejudice of consumers and secondly, that the A.I. stations were not using semen of the best genetic merit or the best technology."[131]

7–59 On the points of fact indicated at the end of this passage, Budd J. found against the applicant. More broadly, it emerges from the passage quoted that, according to the High Court, arrangements such as that under attack in *O'Neill* do not necessarily violate EU law. Because the Supreme Court held, as we have seen, for the applicant in *O'Neill* on other grounds, the court did not consider the EU point and the High Court judgment remains the governing authority in this jurisdiction.

7–60 In *Carrigaline*, there was also an argument grounded on EU law. Here, too, the defendant was able to find shelter under art.90(1) of the Treaty, with Keane J. holding:

"It was argued on behalf of the plaintiffs that the Minister could not rely on

---

[131] Unreported, High Court, July 5, 1995 at pp.101–102. The reference in this passage to *Crespelle* is to *Société Civile Agricole du Centre d'Insemination de la Crespelle v Cooperative d'Élevage et d'Insemination Artificielle du Departement de la Mayenne* (C-323/93) [1994] E.C.R. I-5077. It is, of course, merely coincidence that *Crespelle* too concerned regional artificial insemination monopolies. In this case (considered in more detail in H & M, paras 4–158 to 4–161, the Court of Justice found that this exclusive scheme was not necessarily incompatible with EU law.

this ruling or the subsequent ruling of the court to the same effect in ERT [1991] ECR 2925 because the Minister's action in granting the licence to a commercial body on an exclusive basis could not be regarded as an action taken in the public interest for considerations of a non-economic nature.

This is, in my view, a wholly unsustainable argument. Whether the Minister was right or wrong in the view he took that the granting of the MMDS licenses on an exclusive basis was the best method of ensuring the widespread reception of multi-channel television and the protection and development of the cable infrastructure, it was unarguably a decision taken in what he saw as the public interest in ensuring that as many people as possible had access to the widest range of television broadcasting and that the cable infrastructure was protected and developed."[132]

---

[132] [1997] 1 I.L.R.M. 241 at 291.

CHAPTER 8

PUBLIC INQUIRIES

A. "DECISION INQUIRIES"

8–01   The best known type of public inquiry forms the main subject matter of this chapter: it is the one which is given the task of investigating the causes and circumstances of accidents, natural disasters, corruption or other matters of general public concern. There is, however, a distinct type of statutory inquiry—to which we have given the title "decision inquiry". This is the "standard device for giving a fair hearing to objectors before the final decisions made, usually by a Minister or local authority, on some question affecting citizens' rights or interests".[1] It is this type of inquiry which is statutorily required before the taking of certain categories of decision including: the siting of a new burial ground[2]; the removal or suspension of persons holding office under the Vocational Education Acts[3]; the removal of members of the HSE[4] or a local authority[5]; the making of a compulsory purchase order by a local authority[6]; or the determination of certain planning appeals and whether to proceed with major construction projects.[7]

8–02   Traditionally, it was thought that the principles of constitutional justice should not apply in the case of persons conducting a decision inquiry. However, this argument has been rejected by the Irish courts. In *State (Shannon Atlantic Fisheries Ltd) v McPolin*,[8] an inspector had been appointed to investigate the causes of the wrecking of the applicant's fishing vessel. The inspector took depositions from members of the ship's crew, but he did not interview the owners of the vessel or give them an opportunity of refuting the allegations against them. The inspector's findings of fact impugned the good name and reputation of the ship owners and Finlay P. ruled that the inspector's report should be quashed for breach of the *audi alteram partem* rule. Finlay P. continued:

---

[1]   Wade and Forsyth, *Administrative Law*, 10th edn (Oxford: OUP, 2009), p.801. The historical roots of this type of inquiry go back to enclosures of land.

[2]   Public Health (Ireland) Act 1878 s.163. See also, Transport (Dublin Light Rail) Act 1996 s.8.

[3]   Vocational Education Act 1930 s.27(2).

[4]   Health Act 2004 s.14(2).

[5]   Local Government Act 2001 ss.212–214, 216. See also, Harbours Act 1946 s.164 (local inquiry into performance by harbour authority of their "powers, duties and functions" and other related matters).

[6]   See, e.g. Housing Act 1966 s.76 and Sch.3 (Compulsory Purchase Order Procedure), as amended by Housing (Miscellaneous Provisions) Act 1992 ss.31, 38(5).

[7]   Planning and Development Act 2000 Pt VI. See also, 2000 Act s.37, as amended by Planning and Development (Strategic Infrastructure) Act 2006 s.3.

[8]   [1976] I.R. 93. The inquiry was held pursuant to s.465 of the Merchant Shipping Act 1894.

"The fact that it is not the investigating officer but the Minister for Transport and Power who must decide, having regard to the content of the report, whether any further action should be taken by him in relation to prosecutions under the Act seems to me not to affect the true decision-making role of the person carrying out the preliminary inquiry."[9]

8–03   A "decision inquiry" and a "public inquiry" each has many of the characteristics of a tribunal: in each, while much of the procedure is left to the chairman of the inquiry, he must act subject to the procedural requirements imposed by the particular statute and the overriding requirements of constitutional justice. Again, either type usually takes the form of hearings where the witnesses give evidence under oath and are subject to cross-examination by the opposing parties. One should add that, since each type of inquiry is a public body, each is subject to judicial review. However, there are certain differences between a tribunal and an inquiry of either type. First, an inquiry's conclusions do not bind the Minister or other responsible decision-making authority, though in practice it would be rare for the Minister to depart from the conclusions of a decision inquiry. Secondly, whilst a tribunal is a decision-making body, a public inquiry may be better regarded as an instrument of public participation in government. Next, an inquiry is set up ad hoc for each episode examined, whereas a tribunal enjoys a continuous existence. But the main point of distinction between a "decision inquiry" and a "public inquiry" is that a public inquiry's conclusion and recommendations are at large, simply because its conclusions cannot be anticipated in advance.

B. Public Inquiries

8–04   The object of a public inquiry[10] is simply to ascertain authoritatively the facts in relation to a particular matter of legitimate public interest, which is identified in the terms of reference. As mentioned, these days the subject is usually some accident, failure of public body or big business or other discrete matter of grave public concern. In the early years of the State, public inquiries were utilised in a wider variety of circumstances, for instance to inquire into policy issues such as retail prices, the ports and harbours of the State, the marketing of butter, pig production, the grading of fruit and vegetables, the law and practice relating to town tenancies, the state of public transport, the supply and distribution of milk in the Dublin Area and cross-channel ferry rates.[11] But by now such broad policy inquiries are dealt with in other ways, for instance, by standing public agencies,

---

[9]   [1976] I.R. 93 at 98.

[10] See Law Reform Commission, *Public Inquiries including Tribunals of Inquiry* (LRC CP22–2003); Report (LRC 73–2005), which contain useful information on several areas, untouched here. For instance, they give an exegesis of the foundation statutes of various types of inquiry, including company inspectors, the Commission to Inquire into Child Abuse and Oireachtas inquiries, as well as Tribunals of Inquiry. In addition, they cover common themes like the process for drafting the terms of reference; membership (must chairpersons of inquiries be judges?); reserve members; replacement members; down-stream criminal or civil proceedings going over the same ground as an inquiry; right to broadcast inquiry proceedings; and the establishment of a Central Inquiries Office to retain an institutional memory of public inquiries, including a database of records and information, so that each does not have to start from scratch.

[11] For a useful list of 58 inquiries, inspections, investigations, etc held since independence, see

such as the (research or reform functions of) the Private Residential Tenancies Board, Law Reform Commission, or Road Safety Authority.

8–05 It would almost be possible to write a history of the public woes of modern Ireland, centring upon the subject matter of public inquiries. Thus: (i) the advent of planning and other regulatory control, coupled with the intersection between public life and big business, would be portrayed by the Beef Tribunal, the McCracken Tribunal (inquiring into alleged payments by Dunnes Stores), the Moriarty Tribunal (inquiring into the conduct of two politicians) or the Flood/Mahon Tribunal; (ii) accidents claiming several lives (often contributed to by the slackness of regulatory bodies) would be represented by the Whiddy Oil Terminal Tribunal, Stardust Tribunal, and Tribunals investigating the Blood Transfusion Service Board's use of Hepatitis C-contaminated blood; (iii) the Kerry Babies Tribunal would portray the troubled changes in sexual mores of the 1980s; (iv) incompetence or worse in the Garda Síochána would be illustrated by the Barr and Morris Tribunals; and (v) child sex abuse was the subject of the (non-statutory) Report into Ferns Diocese, the Commission to Inquire into Child Abuse in Industrial Schools, and the Commission of Investigation into the Dublin Archdiocese.[12]

8–06 Public inquires may be set up under a variety of legislative codes; or, in some cases,[13] none. First, there is specialised legislation regulating inquiries into

---

Law Reform Commission, *Consultation Paper on Public Inquiries including Tribunals of Inquiry* (LRC CP22–2003), Appendix A.

[12] References to some inquires, including those alluded to in the paragraph above, are as follows: (i) allegations against politicians (*Report of the Tribunal appointed by the Taoiseach on November 7, 1947* (P. No. 8576) (sale of Locke's distillery); *Report of the Tribunal appointed by the Taoiseach on 4 July 1975* (Prl. 4745) (allegations against Minister for Local Government); *Report of the Tribunal of Inquiry into the Beef Processing Industry 1994* (Prl. 1007); *Report of the Tribunal of Inquiry (Dunnes Payments) 1997* (Pn. 4199). The Tribunal of Inquiry into certain payments to politicians was set up in 1997, under the chairmanship of Mr Justice Moriarty. The Tribunal of Inquiry into certain planning matters and payments was set up in 1997, under the chairmanship of Mr Justice Flood, who was replaced, on his retirement, by Judge Mahon); (ii) accidents (*Report of the Tribunal of Inquiry: Disaster at Whiddy Island, Bantry, Co. Cork* (1980, Pl. 8911); *Report of the Tribunal of Inquiry: Fire at the Stardust, Artane, Dublin* (Pl. 853); *Report of the Tribunal of Inquiry into the Blood Transfusion Service Board* (Pn. 3695); *Report of the Tribunal of Inquiry into the Infection with HIV and Hepatitis-C of Persons with Haemophilia* (2002, Pn. 12074)); (iii) *Report of the Tribunal of Inquiry: The "Kerry Babies" case* (Pl. 3514, 1985); (iv) Garda practices: *Coghlan shooting inquiry: Tribunal Report* (1928) J.34; *Death of Liam O'Mahony: Report of the Tribunal appointed by the Minister* (1967, Pr. 9790); Barr Tribunal of Inquiry into fatal shooting at Abbeylara, 2002, *Tribunal of Inquiry into the facts and circumstances surrounding the fatal shooting of John Carthy at Abbeylara, Co. Longford* (2000); Tribunal of Inquiry into certain Gardaí activities in Donegal (2002); (v) *Report on clerical sexual abuse in the Irish Catholic Diocese of Ferns* (Prn. A5/1774); (Ryan–Laffoy) *Commission to Inquire into Child Abuse* (2010); *Report by [Murphy] Commission of Investigation into the handling by Church and State authorities of allegations and suspicions of child abuse against clerics of the Catholic Archdiocese of Dublin 2009*, paras 2.25–2.36.

[13] e.g. *Report of the Chief Justice into the circumstances leading to the early release from prison of Philip Sheedy* (1999).

accidents involving railways,[14] shipping[15] or aeroplanes.[16] Secondly, the Companies (Amendment) Act 1990 Pt II (as amended by the Company Law Enforcement Act 2001 Pt III) empowers the Minister for Enterprise, Trade and Innovation to appoint an inspector to investigate a company for the purpose of determining the identity of "the true persons", who are financially interested in it or who are able to shape its policy. Sometimes, an episode (for example, involving a possible conflict of interest), which engages the wider public interest, will also happen to come within the scope of this provision. Investigations of this type occurred in the case of Greencore and Bord Telecom.[17] Again, under the Local Government Act 2001 s.212, the Minister for the Environment, Heritage and Local Government is empowered to establish a public local inquiry, for either the specific purpose of considering the removal of councillors (as noted in Part A); or with no specified outcome (as contemplated in this Part). Next, complementing its general historic role as the entity which holds the executive organ of government to account (Art.28.4), the Oireachtas has been endowed by specific legislation empowering it to hold inquiries, the Committees of the Houses of the Oireachtas (Compellability, Privileges and Immunities of Witnesses) Act 1997. However, the decision of the Supreme Court in *Maguire v Ardagh*[18] means, in effect, that Oireachtas Committees are precluded from making adjudications that affect a private individual's rights, including the right to good name and reputation.

8–07   The most dignified and high-powered inquiries are constituted under the Tribunals of Inquiry (Evidence) Acts 1921–2004,[19] soon to be consolidated as the Tribunals of Inquiry Act, a measure referred to here as the "2005 Bill". An inquiry of this type is set up by a Minister, following the passage of identical resolutions by each House of the Oireachtas to the effect "that it is expedient that a tribunal be established for inquiry into the following matter of urgent public importance

---

[14]   See, e.g. Transport (Dublin Light Rail) Act 1996 s.8; Railway Safety Act 2005 s.64. For an example of an inquiry held under the terms of the precursor of this section (Regulation of Railways Act 1871 s.7), see *Report of the Investigation into the Accident on the CIÉ Railway at Buttevant, Co. Cork on 1 August, 1980* (Prl. 9698, 1981).

[15]   Merchant Shipping Act 1894 s.465. This section was invoked by the Minister for the Marine to set up an inquiry chaired by a District judge with nautical assessors charged with an investigation into the deaths of four lifeboat officers off Ballycotton, Co. Cork: see *The Irish Times*, September 24, 1990. For a case arising from this tragedy, see *Haussman v Minister for the Marine* [1991] I.L.R.M. 382.

[16]   Air Navigation and Transport Act 1936 s.60, as amended by Air Navigation and Transport Act 1988 ss. 24 and 53 and Air Navigation (Notification and Investigation of Accidents and Incidents) Regulations 1997 (S.I. No. 205 of 1997). For an example of an inquiry held pursuant to these provisions, see *Accident to Reims Cessna F.182 Q in the Blackstairs Mountains, Co. Wexford on 7 September, 1983* (Department of Communications, 1984).

[17]   The several cases arising out of the investigation are reported at [1993] 3 I.R. 1–151. For the Companies Act 1990 s.14, see Courtney, *The Law of Private Companies* (Tottel: Dublin, 2002), Ch.14.

[18]   [2002] 1 I.R. 385. See also, O'Dowd, "Knowing How Way Leads on to Way: Reflections on the Abbeylara Decision" (2003) 38 Ir. Jur. (N.S) 162; LRC CP22–2003, paras 4.22–4.45; Rabbitte, "A Tribunal of Inquiry or an Investigation by Dáil Committee?" (1998) 4 B.R. 114. In October 2011, a proposed constitutional amendment (Thirtieth Amendment of the Constitution (Houses of the Oireachtas Inquiries) Bill 2011), which would have substantially reversed *Maguire* was rejected at referendum, probably because the public felt that it went too far in exempting Oireachtas' inquiries from judicial review.

[19]   The 1921 Act has been amended in 1979, 1997, 1998 (twice), 2002 and 2004. The Tribunals of Inquiry Bill 2005, referred to throughout the footnotes of this chapter, was at the time of writing (late 2011) still at committee stage in the Dáil.

...".[20] By inveterate convention, though not law, such an inquiry is always chaired by a (serving or retired) judge of one of the superior courts.[21] To risk a prediction, it seems likely that, for reasons explained in Part C, public inquiries will be less often established under the 1921 Act/2005 Bill, in the future, than has been the case in the recent past. Likely to be of most importance in the foreseeable future are those inquiries established under the Commissions of Investigation Act 2004, covered in Part C.

8–08 Because an inquiry is primarily concerned with fact finding, most important inquiries will be clothed with the following powers. The first is the power to "subpoena" witnesses,[22] by which is meant that refusal by a witness—whether to appear, to answer questions or to produce relevant documents—is made a criminal offence, heard in the usual way by the District or Circuit Court. A related power is the power to administer the oath so that telling a lie is also an offence.

8–09 Next, privilege against defamation action and other less likely consequences (e.g. breach of confidentiality or offences under the Official Secrets Act 1963), in respect of statements by witnesses (as well as members of the inquiry, lawyers, etc) is usually granted by the legislation constituting an inquiry.[23] In addition—and this may entail some overlap—there is now[24] a general statutory provision giving absolute privilege against defamation, where a statement is made in the case of most public inquiry proceedings or report; and qualified privilege in respect of a fair and accurate report of proceedings, in public, of a public inquiry. There is a connection between these immunities and the obligations on witnesses to appear and answer, for it has always been accepted that it would be unfair to oblige a witness to answer questions truthfully and then to leave him exposed to the risk of defamation action if he does so.[25]

---

[20] Tribunals of Inquiry (Evidence) Act 1921 s.1(1) (but see the slight change in the 2005 Bill s.3). Notice the Tribunals of Inquiry (Evidence) (Amendment) (No. 2) Act 1998 s.2 which permits the amending of terms of reference; 2005 Bill s.7.

[21] Beatson, "Should Judges Conduct Public Inquiries?" (2005) 121 L.Q.R. 221.

[22] Section 4 of the Tribunals of Inquiry (Evidence) (Amendment) Act 1979 provides that the Tribunal "may make such orders as it considers necessary for the purposes of its functions", and it is invested with all such "powers, rights and privileges of the High Court" in that regard (see also, Tribunals of Inquiry (Evidence) (Amendment) Act 1997). In the case of inquiries held at the instance of the Minister for the Environment (under the Local Government Act 2001 ss.212–213), the inspector conducting the inquiry enjoys a statutory power to subpoena witnesses and to take evidence on oath. Similar provisions exist in respect of other statutory inquiries. See, e.g. Regulation of Railways Act 1871 s.7(3); Air Navigation and Transport Act 1936 s.60.

[23] 1921 Act s.1(3) and (4); 1997 Act s.2; 2002 Act s.6(7); 2005 Bill s.32. In addition, by virtue of s.5 of the 1979 Act, statements made during the course of a hearing before a Tribunal of Inquiry are inadmissible in all subsequent criminal prosecutions (with the exception of perjury). A perjury prosecution was commenced after the publication of the Report of the Tribunal into the Whiddy Island disaster; the charge was dismissed (*Goodman International v Hamilton* [1992] 2 I.R. 542 at 605).

[24] Defamation Act 2009 ss.17 and 18 and Sch.1. For a justification in a constitutional context of the absolute nature of this immunity in civil proceedings, see *Cooney v Bank of Ireland* [1996] 1 I.R. 157.

[25] Gwynn Morgan, *Constitutional Law of Ireland* (Dublin: Round Hall Press, 1990), pp.161–162 and 241. This association between privilege and subpoena does not necessarily operate in reverse. In the case of the Select Committee on Legislation and Security of Dáil Éireann (Privilege and Immunity) Act 1994, privilege was bestowed on witnesses. However, (for

C. COMMISSIONS OF INVESTIGATION

8–10   The basic question is whether an inquiry should be held in public, so that the citizens can follow every twist of the evidence; or does it suffice that the final report is published? This is a policy and not a constitutional question, for, because of the Constitution's slant in favour of the individual and against the community, there is no right to an inquiry ("the public's right to know about its Government and big business"?) express or implicit in the Constitution. Nor is there any equivalent of Art.34.1 of the Constitution which stipulates, in regard to courts, that "justice shall be administered in public". Nevertheless, it remains an important policy issue. As Keane C.J. remarked:

> "One of the objects and indeed probably the main object of an inquiry, is to seek to allay public concern arising from matters comprised in the terms of reference of the Tribunal and affecting ... the conduct of public life ... That object of course will be defeated if the inquiry as a general rule is to be conducted in private rather than in public."[26]

8–11   But, if the proceedings of an inquiry are held in public, then anyone whose reputation may be affected by the evidence heard before it would have to be allowed their "*Re Haughey*"[27] rights, including the right to legal representation. Now a major legal and political point of contention concerns whether the legal costs of any party permitted representation should be paid, more or less automatically, by the State; or whether this question should be at the tribunal's discretion, taking into account all relevant matters, including any substantive finding made by the tribunal regarding that party's conduct. To summarise[28] a rather untidy body of law, the legislature has provided fairly clearly that a Tribunal of Inquiry should take into account any substantive ruling made that a party has, in the field under investigation, misconducted themselves. Despite this, many chairpersons of Tribunals of Inquiry have assumed that, provided that a party has not misbehaved before the tribunal, their costs should be paid by the State irrespective of whether the tribunal has, in effect, established facts which amount to misconduct in the field under investigation. And this has recently been confirmed by the Supreme Court in *Murphy v Flood*.[29] This result, which was rather surprising in view of the plain words of the Tribunals of Inquiry (Evidence) (Amendment) Act 1997 s.3, was grounded on the basis that, for a tribunal to decline to order the State to pay parties' legal costs, on the basis of substantive misconduct, would be to impose a penalty. It was held that this would violate Art.34.1 of the Constitution. This is a rather strict interpretation of the separation of powers, bearing in mind the fact that the chairperson of the tribunal is invariably a judge.[30]

---

political reasons) no subpoena power was given: on this Act, see Gallagher, (1994) *Irish Current Law Statutes Annotated* 32–02.

[26]   *Flood v Lawlor*, unreported, Supreme Court, November 24, 2000. See, to like effect, *Redmond v Flood* [1999] 3 I.R. 79 at 88: "It is of the essence of such enquiries that they be held in public for the purpose of allaying the public disquiet which led to their appointment."

[27]   [1971] I.R. 217 at 241. See paras 14–39 to 14–40.

[28]   For a fuller account, see LRC CP22–2003, paras 12.37–12.46; LRC 73–2005, Ch.7.

[29]   [2010] 3 I.R. 136.

[30]   Admittedly, the judge of a tribunal of inquiry is sitting in an "extra curial" role. However, in reaching the decision noted in the text, the Supreme Court leant very heavily on what might be called policy argumentation, rather than strict reference to precedent; and it is surprising

8–12   In any case, it seems probable that, because of the *Re Haughey* rights to constitutional justice, inquiries at which evidence is taken in public (e.g. Tribunals of Inquiry) are likely to be a rarity in the future. The question then becomes how to design a form of inquiry which minimises the right to representation of persons whose conduct is under consideration. In response to this line of enquiry, the Law Reform Commission offered a model for an inquiry which was likely to attract the least right to representation compatible with the Constitution. It reached the following conclusion[31]:

> "(i)   [The inquiry] would be held in private (though the report emanating from the inquiry may be published). The obvious advantage of this is that accusations against a person, made by possibly prejudiced witnesses and often amplified by the mass media, would not be bruited forth to the world immediately. At most, if the inquiry finds the accusations to be substantiated, a version of them will appear in the final report, together with the inquiry's measured judgment. (There is a less obvious point: the privacy and low-key ambience of a private inquiry is more likely to encourage co-operation. The psychological environment within which those involved in inquiries operate is, we have been told by participants, a significant factor);
>
> (ii) Where appropriate, the inquiry report would emphasise the flaw or malfunctioning of the institution, big business or profession involved, rather than the sins of an individual wrong-doer. There is an analogy here with the way in which the Ombudsman goes about his work, avoiding the identification of the particular public servant who was responsible for maladministration.
>
> (iii) As well as the conclusions, where a point is disputed, the report would include comments on, or even disagreement with those conclusions by any person whose good name or conduct they call into question. Thus, each side of the argument is recorded."

8–13   The Commissions of Investigation Act 2004 accords fairly well with what might be regarded as the LRC's specifications and it has been frequently used,[32] despite its brief existence. The new inquiries—Commissions of Investigation—

---

that the realistic point that judges are appointed as chairpersons, not by coincidence but because of their status as judges, was not taken into account. Secondly, from the point of view of technical law, it is also strange that the precedent of the *State (Plunkett) v Registrar of Friendly Societies* [1998] 4 I.R. 1 at 5, in which it was held that an order for costs was not part of the administration of justice, was not referred to.

31   LRC CP22–2003, para.10.07.

32   See Spencer, "A New Era of Tribunalism: the Commissions of Investigation Act 2004" (2005) 10(3) B.R. 80. As of early 2012, there had been six Commissions of Investigation, namely: an inquiry into the Dublin and Monaghan Bombings under the chairmanship of Patrick McEntee SC (Commission of Investigation (Dublin and Monaghan Bombings) Order 2005 (S.I. No. 222 of 2005)); an inquiry into the Dean Lyons case under the chairmanship of George Birmingham SC (Commission of Investigation (Dean Lyons Case) Revised Order 2006 (S.I. No. 69 of 2006)); an inquiry into clerical abuse in the Dublin Archdiocese under the chairmanship of Judge Yvonne Murphy (Commission of Investigation (Child Sexual Abuse) Order 2006 (S.I. No. 137 of 2006)); an inquiry into the death of Gary Douch in Mountjoy Prison under the chairmanship of Gráinne McMorrow SC (Commission of Investigation (Death of Gary Douch in Mountjoy Prison) Order 2007 (S.I. No. 371 of 2007)); and an inquiry into conditions at Leas Cross Nursing Home under the chairmanship of Derry O'Donovan SC (Commission of

which it authorises have two major features, which have been assumed to mean that it is not necessary for a person whose conduct is under investigation to be a party to the proceedings and to have *Re Haughey* rights. These features are that, in general, the proceedings are held in private[33] and that, before a report is published, such a person is allowed to protest against any want of fair procedure.

8–14   To elaborate: the Act provides for the establishment of commissions of investigation to investigate any matters of "significant public concern". These are intended to be alternatives to, or, if it ultimately proves necessary to investigate a matter further, precursors to, a Tribunal of Inquiry.[34] The Act requires the terms of reference to be stated as precisely as possible. They must set out the events, activities, circumstances, systems, practices or procedures to be investigated together with the relevant dates, locations and individuals.[35] The Commission is under a statutory duty to seek, and to facilitate, the voluntary cooperation of persons whose evidence is required by the commission (s.10). However, a Commission does have power to direct a person to attend to give evidence or to provide a document (s.16); and disobedience thereto is an offence (s.16); so too is making a false statement (s.18). A Commission may, having regard in particular to the need to observe fair procedure, establish or adopt rules and procedures for receiving and recording evidence and submissions (s.15).

8–15   Prior to sending a copy of a draft report to the responsible Minister, a Commission must send a copy of it to any person who is identified, setting out the periods for making submissions or applying to the High Court for an order to amend the draft report. Then, if the person believes that the Commission has not "observed fair procedures" (that is the only ground given in the legislation), that person may make a written submission setting out the reasons why the draft should be amended or apply to the court for an order directing that the draft be amended.[36]

Investigation (Leas Cross Nursing Home) Order 2007 (S.I. No. 304 of 2007)); Commission of Investigation (Banking Sector) Order 2010 (S.I. No. 454 of 2010).
[33]   It was held in *Byrne v Ireland* [2011] 1 I.R. 190 that the Commission of Investigation Act 2004 does not afford the plaintiff a right to access the archive of the Commission, when (as usual) evidence is given in private, pursuant to s.11(3) of the Act.
[34]   Commissions of Investigation Act 2004 s.3(1).
[35]   Commissions of Investigation Act 2004 s.5.
[36]   Commissions of Investigation Act 2004 ss.34, 35.

CHAPTER 9

THE PUBLIC SERVICE OMBUDSMAN

A. INTRODUCTION

9–01   Over the past 30 years, the (Public Service) Ombudsman[1] has become a significant part of the constitutional framework, with two complementary tasks. The first is to secure redress when an individual suffers harm or loss, through some act of governmental maladministration. The great majority of complaints are settled informally; it is only the gravest or those in which the public body is not cooperative which receive a formal investigation, following the procedure laid down in the Ombudsman Act 1980 ss.4–6. The Ombudsman's second task is to act as a champion of good administrative practice, and as a repository of information and wisdom on the subject.

9–02   The Office was established by the Ombudsman Act 1980[2] which is soon to be (moderately) amended when the Ombudsman (Amendment) Bill 2008 (referred

---

[1]   A complete summary of the Ombudsman's jurisprudence (which is available in the fairly detailed Annual Reports) would probably be a little more than the reader needs. References to "Reports" are to the Ombudsman's Annual Report for the year indicated. For other literature, see: H & M, Ch.9; Zimmerman, "The Office of Ombudsman in Ireland" (1989) 27 *Administration* 258; Zimmerman, "The Irish Ombudsman-Information Commissioner" (2001) 39 *Administration* 78.

[2]   The idea of an Irish Ombudsman was first suggested, authoritatively, as part of the package of reforms proposed by the *Devlin Report*, Report of Public Services Organisation Review Group 1966–1969 (Prl. 792), App. I, pp.447–458. See also, 280 *Dáil Debates* Cols 1199–1206, 1257–1284 (May 6 and 7, 1975). Eventually, an All-Party Informal Committee on Administrative Justice was set up. The Committee held 10 meetings in 1976 and 1977. It received three submissions including one (dated October 29, 1976) from a well-qualified group convened by the Institute of Public Administration and chaired by Mr Justice Hamilton. See also, Private Member's Bill No. 20 of 1979. The 1980 Act was brought into force as from July 7, 1983; Ombudsman Act 1980 (Commencement Day) Order 1983 (S.I. No. 424 of 1983). See further, 345 *Dáil Debates* Col.605 (October 25, 1983).
  The first Ombudsman was not appointed until January 1984. He was Mr Michael Mills (former political correspondent), who retired at the statutory age of 67 and was succeeded, on November 1, 1994, by Mr Kevin Murphy (formerly a senior civil servant at the head of the public service management and development in the Department of Finance). (For debate of Mr Murphy's appointment, see 443 *Dáil Debates* Cols 959–986 (June 1, 1994) and 140 *Dáil Debates* Cols 1401–1435 (June 15, 1994).) The third and present Ombudsman, Ms Emily O'Reilly (a former political correspondent) was appointed in 2003.
  The fact that the Ombudsman is now a woman naturally raises the question of whether one should speak of an "Ombudsperson" or "Ombudswoman" or simply "Ombuds". The word "Ombudsman" derives from the accusative form of a particular phrase in Old Swedish. It is,

to here as "the 2008 Bill") becomes law.[3] In this chapter, we follow the general practice in Ireland of simply speaking of "Ombudsman", despite the fact that the present Ombudsman is a woman. However, we also use the term "she", where something particular to Ms O'Reilly's time in office comes up.

9–03 The mistakes of large, hierarchical organisations are hard to correct, especially when they have been endorsed by senior management and the need for an Ombudsman is evident when one contemplates the various alternative methods available to remedy maladministration. One possibility would be judicial review. But the High Court—and usually it is only the High Court which has jurisdiction—is a relatively expensive and inaccessible place. The result is that relatively few instances of maladministration surface as court cases. Next, public representatives have traditionally seen it as their principal duty to use their moral authority, behind the scenes, to remedy the grievances of individual constituents against governmental services, a fact reflected in the title of Basil Chubb's classic study of public representatives, "Going about Persecuting Civil Servants".[4] Yet this is not a desirable approach, either from the viewpoint of the effective and economic settlement of grievances or from the wider perspective of the health of the body politic. Finally, there are a growing number of tribunals to oversee government administration (covered in Chapter 6); but these exist only in particular areas, if and when provided for by legislation.

9–04 Testimony to the fact that the Ombudsman principle is an idea whose time

---

in that sense, not gender specific. But see the concerns expressed in the Constitution Review Group Report (Pn. 2632, 1996), p.425.

[3] As of early 2012, this Bill had completed all stages in the Dáil and was on the *Seanad* Order Paper.

[4] "Going about Persecuting Civil Servants: The Role of the Irish Parliamentary Representative" (1963) 11 *Political Studies* 272. cf. the views of the Minister for Finance reported in the *Irish Times*, November 12, 1966 (and quoted in Kelly, "Administrative Discretion and the Courts" (1966) 1 Ir. Jur. (N.S) 209 at p.211): "There is hardly anyone without a direct personal link with someone, be he Minister, T.D., clergyman, county or borough councillor, who will interest himself in helping a citizen to have a grievance examined and, if possible, remedied. My own experience is that members of the Dáil are extremely assiduous and persistent in taking up individual cases and raising them by way of that truly democratic device, the parliamentary question. The basic reason therefore why we do not need an Ombudsman is that we already have so many unofficial but nevertheless effective ones."

Professor Kelly went on to comment on this passage as follows: "In the large perspective of European social and legal history this utterance is a fascinating testimony to the survival in 20th century Ireland of the primitive system of clientship and patronage. This phenomenon was, in the distant past, a sure sign of a society where a weak man had no hope of justice without the aid of a strong one, and its general replacement in civilised countries by a regular, strong and impartial process of law is a major social milestone. It is disheartening to find this primitive doctrine being not alone practised, but also blandly preached from the topmost minaret of the Irish administrative structure.

All this would be unimportant if, in fact, the Minister's preferred system of controls were effective (as was claimed). But it is not, and in the nature of things cannot be. It is very probable that some ignorant poor old man, denied some modest grant or pension because of his own failure to make his position clear, will get redress without question if a deputy or parish priest writes a letter for him. But what machinery can these informal patrons invoke to extract from an unwilling Minister the real history behind a planning application?" However, for a different view, see Gallagher and Komito, "The Constituency role of Dail Deputies" in Coakley and Gallagher (eds), *Politics in the Republic of Ireland*, 5th edn (Dublin: PSAI Press, 2010).

has come is provided by the way in Ireland (as elsewhere)[5] this constitutional species has thrived and spread to fresh fields. In discrete areas, we now also have an Ombudsman for the Defence Forces[6] and Children,[7] as well as the Garda Síochána Ombudsman Commission.[8] And, in effectively the private law field, there is: the Financial Services Ombudsman Bureau, whose function is to investigate, mediate and adjudicate complaints from customers against financial institutions, including now credit institutions and insurance companies[9]; the Pensions Ombudsman, established by the Pensions (Amendment) Act 2002 s.5, vested with the authority to "investigate and determine ... complaints and disputes" concerning occupational pension schemes and Personal Retirement Savings Accounts; and (with a slightly different approach) the Legal Services Ombudsman, who does not deal directly with complaints but rather *oversees* the handling of complaints against lawyers, by the Law Society of Ireland or the Bar Council.[10] However because this is a book about the law relating to public administration, we shall confine ourselves primarily to the (public service) Ombudsman, referred to here as "the Ombudsman", unless the context indicates otherwise.

9–05   A number of additional[11] supervisory roles have been vested in the Office of the Ombudsman. The Disability Act 2005 s.40 gives a role to the Ombudsman in examining complaints about non-compliance with the sectoral plans which have to be drawn up to indicate how public bodies will meet their obligations in providing services to disabled persons. The same person who is Ombudsman[12] has also been

---

[5]   In the United Kingdom, the field of investigation which, in Ireland, is vested in a single Office is divided among a number of entities: the Parliamentary Commissioner for Administration; the English Commissions for Local Administration; Health Service Commissioner for England; Public Service Ombudsman for Wales; Scottish Public Services Ombudsman; Local Government Commissioners; the Northern Ireland Parliamentary Commissioner; and the Northern Ireland Commissioner for Complaints.

[6]   The Ombudsman (Defence Forces) Act 2004 is similar to the Ombudsman Act 1980 save that ss.11 and 12 provide that the Ombudsman may be called before a Committee of the Oireachtas. Notice that in the 1999 Report, p.37, the Ombudsman disapproved suggestions for a separate Tax Ombudsman on the ground that a single Ombudsman can take an overview and apply common standards.

[7]   The Ombudsman for Children Act 2002 establishes a jurisdiction to investigate complaints by children against public bodies. The 2002 Act amended s.5 of the 1980 Act to exclude examination of a complaint by the Ombudsman, where the matter is appropriate for the Ombudsman for Children. On co-operation between the two Ombudsmen, see 2009 Report, p.29.

[8]   Garda Síochána Act 2005. One should emphasise that the Defence Forces Ombudsman investigates complaints by members of the force, whereas the Garda Ombudsman investigates complaints against members of the force.

[9]   Central Bank and Financial Services Authority Ireland Act 2004, as amended.

[10]   The Legal Services (Ombudsman) Act 2009. However, if the Legal Services Regulation Bill 2011 becomes law, the functions of this Ombudsman will be discharged by the Legal Services Regulation Authority.

[11]   However, note that, while the Ombudsman's general supervisory power includes administrative action where there has been a failure to use the Irish language, the Official Languages Act 2003 establishes its own Commissioner to monitor compliance with that Act.

[12]   In addition, the Ombudsman is ex officio a member of: the Standards in Public Office Commission (established by the Ethics in Public Office Act 1995, as amended by the Standards in Public Office Act 2001); the Constituency Commission (established by the Electoral Act 1997); the Referendum Commission (established by the Referendum Act 1998); and the Commission for Public Service Appointments (established by the Public Service Management (Recruitment and Appointment) Act 2004).

appointed to the Office of Information Commissioner, established by the Freedom
of Information Act 1997.[13] The Act extends to all government departments and, by
now, to almost all public bodies, a total of about 400.[14] On the substantive level, the
Act gives an entitlement (subject to certain exemptions) to see records, to be given
assistance, to be given reasons for decisions and to have rights of appeal explained.
As monitor and regulator of this scheme, the Information Commissioner has a range
of functions and powers. These include: promoting good practice; reporting, both
to the Oireachtas and to the bodies concerned; monitoring performance by public
bodies of their obligations; and making binding appeal decisions. It is a point of
distinction from the modus operandi of the Ombudsman that the 1997 Act gives a
citizen direct access to the public body, without the need for any intermediary such
as the Ombudsman. In other words, the Information Commissioner is involved only,
as an appellate agency, where the public body disputes any claim to entitlement
under the Act.[15] The Ombudsman also has functions under the Access to Information
on the Environment Regulations 1993.[16]

Constitutional setting

9–06   The Ombudsman must be, and be seen to be, independent of the Government
or any other body or person. Thus the Office has been provided with a similar,
though not identical, institutional pedestal to that occupied by the higher judiciary.
The Ombudsman derives some limited support for independence from the fact that
staff are to be civil servants of the State,[17] and that the Office has its own separate
vote in the estimates. The Ombudsman Act 1980 contains a declaration that "[t]he
Ombudsman shall be independent in the performance of his functions",[18] and it has
been authoritatively suggested[19] that the Office should be put on a constitutional
basis. He or she is to be appointed by the President, acting on a recommendation
contained in a resolution passed by both Houses of the Oireachtas. No qualifications
are laid down for the incumbent, save that he or she must be no more than 61
years of age (at the time of first appointment), and must retire at the age of 67.[20]

---

[13]   Note that this coincidence is not required by law.
[14]   See paras 12–23 to 12–29.
[15]   See Information Commissioner Annual Report for 1998, p.7.
[16]   S.I. No. 133 of 1993, made under the Environmental Protection Agency Act 1992 ss.6 and
       110 to give effect to EC Directive 90/313 [1990] OJ L158/56, p.56. See further, 1993 Report,
       pp.47–48; 1994 Report, pp.6, 26–30 and 45–50.
[17]   See *McLoughlin v Minister for Social Welfare* [1958] I.R 1 at 16.
[18]   See 2008 Bill s.15 (use of title of "Ombudsman" to be an offence unless authorised: by or under
       legislation; with Minister's consent; or pre-dating July 9, 2008). The essential point is that the
       term "Ombudsman" should be confined to positions which satisfy the essential requirement
       of being independent of the administrative bodies whose operation they overview; otherwise
       there is a danger of the currency being devalued. For allegations concerning pressure brought
       to bear by insurance companies on the first Insurance Ombudsman (Pauline Marrinan-Quinn),
       see press coverage on February 8, 1998.
[19]   Report of the Constitution Review Group (Pn. 2632, 1996), pp.425–428. A majority of the
       All-Party Oireachtas Committee (Pn. 3795, 1997), p.81 agreed.
[20]   The Ombudsman Act 1980 s.2(3), (7). Yet the Government offered, as the reason for its
       hesitancy in appointing Mr Mills for a second term, the fact that Mr Mills would be 67 in
       1994, part of the way through his second term, although the statutory restriction is directed
       at the incumbent's age at the time of his appointment for his first term. This justification was
       coupled with the claim that s.2(3) and (7) was lacking in clarity: 394 *Dáil Debates* Cols 1675
       and 1816 (December 14 and 15, 1989). An interesting point of speculation concerns the position
       which would have arisen had there been a gap of even a few days between the end of Mr

The Ombudsman cannot be a public representative, or a member of the Reserve Defence Force, or hold any other paid Office or employment apart from that of Ombudsman. The Ombudsman may be removed from Office only "for stated misbehaviour, incapacity or bankruptcy", and then only on resolutions passed by each House of the Oireachtas. The term of Office is six years and a holder is eligible for a second or subsequent term. The Ombudsman is to be paid the same salary and expenses as a High Court judge.[21] The Civil Service Regulation (Amendment) Act 2005 s.20 gives the power of appointing staff in the Ombudsman's Office to the Ombudsman, though the Minister for Public Expenditure and Reform determines the number of staff.[22] Following the "Lost at Sea" debacle, outlined below, a Joint Oireachtas Committee on Investigation, Oversight and Petitions has been set up as a formal channel of consultation and communication between the Oireachtas and the Ombudsman.[23]

9–07 There have been three types of major public disputes between the Ombudsman and the Government. First, in 1988, at a time of crisis in public expenditure, the Ombudsman's staff numbers were radically reduced, much more so than those of other public bodies.[24] Secondly, and about the same time, the Government would have preferred not to appoint the first office holder, Michael Mills, to a second term[25]; but was, after strenuous efforts, eventually persuaded to do so.

9–08 Thirdly, there has been considerable controversy over the "Lost at Sea" scheme. Before going on, it should be said that if the response to any recommendation is not "satisfactory", the Ombudsman's classic response has been to make a "special report" on the case to the Houses of the Oireachtas.[26] This term is used in the sense of a report which is separate from the annual report (thereby attracting greater publicity), but which, like an annual report, is laid before the Houses of the Oireachtas. There are three situations in which a special report

---

Mills' first appointment and his re-appointment. Could it then have been argued that he would not have been eligible on the basis of s.2(7) which states "A person shall be not more than 61 years of age upon *first* being appointed ..." (emphasis added). For then the Government might have contended that the policy underlying the words "upon first being appointed" is such that they were intended to benefit only a person who was actually an incumbent at the time of re-appointment, rather than someone who came in from outside.

[21] 1980 Act ss.2, 3, 10(2). For the Ombudsman's Superannuation Scheme, made under s.3(2), see S.I. No. 70 of 1987.

[22] Ombudsman Act 1980 s.10(1)(a). The Minister for Finance is the "appropriate authority" for the purpose of the Civil Service Regulation Act 1956 but almost all his powers as such have been delegated to the Ombudsman: 1980 Act s.10(4); 1985 Report, Ch.10.

[23] Prn. A12/0001 (2012)). For "Lost at Sea", see para.9–08.

[24] See *Irish Times*, January 4, 1988; February 11, 1988; June 4 and 7, 1988; May 13, 1988; *Sunday Independent*, June 12, 1988 ("The Ombudsman and Hypocrisy"); *Cork Examiner*, November 6, 1988 ("Watchdog with no Teeth"); 380 *Dáil Debates* Col.1423 (May 12, 1988); Appendix to 1987 Report (Pl. 5258). The details of this and the second episode are in the 3rd edn, pp.341–342. This episode is fascinatingly described in Mills, *Hurler on the Ditch: Memoir of a Journalist who Became Ireland's First Ombudsman* (Blackrock, Co. Dublin: Currach Press, 2005), pp.142–147.

[25] See 394 *Dáil Debates* Cols 1669–1676 and 1806–1820 (December 14 and 15, 1989); *Sunday Tribune*, December 17, 1989. Mills, *Hurler on the Ditch* (2005), pp.147–150.

[26] Section 6(5), (7). The Ombudsman's functions under s.6(5), (7) (together with those in the personnel field) are the only ones which he is not empowered to delegate to his officers: s.10(3).

has been used. The first is where the public body has defied the Ombudsman's recommendation and the report is published to generate publicity[27] so as to persuade the public body to think again.[28] The most recent and ongoing example was in 2009, when the Ombudsman was forced to publish a special report,[29] because her recommendation arising out of the "Lost at Sea" scheme was not accepted. This scheme gave the owners of fishing boats lost at sea the opportunity to apply to the Minister for Agriculture and Fisheries for grant aid. The complainants were a family who had lost a boat (as well as two family members). Their application had been rejected by the Minister, on the grounds that they had missed the deadline. The Ombudsman's report criticised several aspects of the administration of the Scheme, including the advertising procedure, which she found had not been extensive enough. She recommended compensation of almost €250,000. The Department, however, rejected her recommendation. On the only earlier occasion in 2002 when such a special report had had to be published, the matter was referred by the Dáil to the Public Accounts Committee, which recommended a result which was "satisfactory to all parties" and, in substance, represented a victory for the Ombudsman. However, in respect of the Lost at Sea complaint, the matter was referred to the Oireachtas Committee on Agriculture, Fisheries and Food, which by a (government-party) majority voted to reject the Ombudsman's decision.[30] The second situation in which a special report has been used is to publicise the staffing cutbacks outlined in para.9–07. Thirdly, special reports have been used to highlight particular issues or areas of public administration.[31]

B. Jurisdiction

(This Part may need to be read with Part C "Exemptions from Jurisdiction".)

9–09   The restrictions upon the type of complaint which the Ombudsman is empowered[32] to scrutinise may be examined under five heads. First, the public bodies whose actions may be investigated must be one of those specified. Secondly, the action must have "adversely affected" some person. Thirdly, the complainant must have a sufficient interest in the matter. Fourthly, the action must have been taken in the performance of "administrative functions", though this, as we shall

---

[27]   1993 Report, p.2. See, to similar effect, 1986 Report, p.5; 1989 Report, p.11. Notice too, that in 1993 Report, p.10, the Ombudsman remarked that he had been "preparing to submit a special report" in regard to compensation for late payment for social welfare benefits, but the issue was then resolved.

[28]   The earliest of these reports was *Report of Investigation of Complaints against the Department of Social Welfare regarding Arrears of Contributory Pensions* (March 14, 1997). Another concerned the Revenue Commissioners' refusal to return overpayments of tax: *Special Report on Redress for Taxpayers*; 2002 Report, pp.35–37.

[29]   Lost at Sea Scheme (December 2009) (Prn. A9/1507).

[30]   Initially, the Dáil rejected a motion to refer the matter to a Committee. Then, following protests, the matter was referred: *The Irish Times*, March 10 and March 25, 2010. For the report, see Joint Oireachtas Committee on Agriculture, Fisheries and Food, *Third Report on Ombudsman's Special Report* (Prn. A10/1500, October 20, 2010), p.7 (five lines of rationalisation); possibly the Committee's attitude was affected by the involvement of the Minister.

[31]   For examples, see fn.180 and H & M, paras 9–117 to 9–118.

[32]   Even where all five conditions are satisfied, the Ombudsman still has a discretion whether to exercise his jurisdiction: see 1980 Act s.4(2) and (8).

see, must be taken with a pinch of salt. Finally, the action must be affected by one of the defects specified. These five requirements will now be examined.

(1) Public bodies within field of investigation

9–10   The bodies against whom a complaint may be made have always included all the Departments of State, but not the Government itself, or any of the public bodies listed in the Second Schedule.[33] The Ombudsman's bailiwick has been extended to include An Post; local authorities (excluding the "reserved functions" exercised by elected representatives); and the HSE (replacing the health boards)[34]; and the 2008 Bill will bring in a further 95 or so public bodies, as specified in Sch.1.[35]

9–11   A particular topic of debate concerns the Ombudsman's attempt to have the Office's remit extended to public voluntary hospitals which provide services for the HSE. There has been no legislation doing this expressly, but the Ombudsman has nonetheless asserted, on the basis indicated in the footnote,[36] that these bodies now come within her jurisdiction.

9–12   A second restriction, relevant to the broad health area, also concerns an exclusion from the Ombudsman's jurisdiction of "[p]ersons when acting on behalf of health boards [now HSE] and (in the opinion of the Ombudsman) solely in the exercise of clinical judgment in connection with the diagnosis of illness or the care or treatment of a patient ...".[37] Several complaints have been ruled not to fall foul of this restriction. One example arose out of a mix-up in relation to a prescription which resulted in the complainant receiving twice the prescribed dosage. Despite the exclusion of matters relating to the exercise of clinical judgment, the Ombudsman considered that he could nevertheless establish whether and how the alleged mix-up had occurred and the steps taken to ensure that it did not happen again.[38]

---

[33]   Ombudsman Act 1980 s.4(2), (4) and Schs 1 and 2; s.4(10), as amended by Ombudsman (Amendment) Act 1984 s.1. See 356 *Dáil Debates* Cols 1300 et seq (November 7, 1984). See also, Ombudsman Act 1980 (First Schedule) (Amendment) Order 1984 (S.I. No. 332 of 1984); Ombudsman Act 1980 (First Schedule) (Amendment) Order 1985 (S.I. No. 66 of 1985); Ombudsman Act 1980 (Second Schedule) (Amendment) Order 1985 (S.I. No. 69 of 1985); Agriculture Appeals Act 2001 s.18; British–Irish Agreement Act 1999 s.50; and Health (Repayment Scheme) Act 2006 s.23. For a complaint involving a government decision, see 1988 Report (Pl. 5991), p.71.

[34]   Ombudsman Act 1980 (First Schedule) (Amendment) Order 1984 (S.I. No. 332 of 1984); 356 *Dáil Debates* Col.852 (February 27, 1985). The Ombudsman's jurisdiction now encompasses the HSE, as successor to the various health boards: see Health Act 2004 s.54 and Sch.6 Pt 8.

[35]   For protest at the tardiness of this extension, see, e.g. 1997 Report, p.9; 2000 Report, p.36; 2004 Report, p.26; 2006 Report, p.6.

[36]   2004 Report, pp.26–27; 2005 Report, p.9. The Ombudsman's jurisdiction which is grounded on a failure to enquire by the HSE (which is undoubtedly within the Ombudsman's ken) appears to have been accepted in practice (see H & M, para. 9–10), and the Ombudsman has undertaken "a series of initiatives to develop an awareness among these organisations as to their responsibilities under the new procedures": 2006 Report, p.31. See also, 2000 Report, p.33.

[37]   The clinical judgment exception was removed in the UK by the Health Service Commissioners (Amendment) Act 1996 ss.1, 2 and 6.

[38]   1997 Report, pp.30 and 32. Another complaint concerned whether a discharge had taken proper account of the patient's mobility (2001 Report, p.27).

(2) "Adversely affected"

9–13 It must appear to the Ombudsman that the action has or may have "adversely affected" some person. This wide phrase is not defined and, as far as the Reports show, the concept has only been invoked once. This was in a case in which he came close to finding that a health board ought to have paid the costs of the complainant's treatment at the Mayo Clinic but then concluded:

> "The financial costs had been met from a fund created by public subscription so no adverse financial effects were suffered by the complainant's family. In the circumstances, it was not open to me under the Ombudsman's Act to make a finding or recommendation on the question of finance."[39]

(3) Complainant

9–14 The Ombudsman Act 1980 provides that if, as in almost all cases, the investigation is initiated by way of complaint (rather than by the Ombudsman using his rarely invoked power to act of his own motion) the complainant must have, in the Ombudsman's opinion,[40] "a sufficient interest in the matter".[41] Nevertheless, it seems that the Ombudsman has taken the view that the provision enables him to entertain complaints submitted by, for instance, family members, social workers,[42] and professional advisers.[43] The parish priest is the classic interlocutor but he has faded from view in recent Annual Reports.

9–15 Given a local politician's role as a solver of individual constituents' problems, one might ask, where a complaint is too complex for a politician's office to resolve, how many constituents are directed to the Ombudsman. In fact, only a very few complaints travel via public representatives.[44] For instance, the Ombudsman reported in 2006 that 39 per cent of Deputies and 52 per cent of Senators had not referred any complaints to the Office in the previous 12 months. Respondents to the Ombudsman's survey of Oireachtas members indicated "unfamiliarity with the Ombudsman's role and complaint examination procedures".[45]

---

[39] 1987 Report, p.54. See also, *R. v Local Commissioner, Ex p. Eastleigh B.C.* [1988] Q.B. 855; Jones, "The Local Ombudsman and Judicial Review" (1988) *Public Law* 608.

[40] Ombudsman Act 1980 ss.4(2)(a), 4(3), 9.

[41] There is another definite, though possibly far-fetched, restriction: neither the person affected nor the complainant may be a department or other body specified in the First or Second Schedule: 1980 Act ss.4(2)(a) and 3(a), (9) (to be replaced by the 2008 Bill Schedule, Pts 1 and 2 and 1980 Act s.4(4A), inserted by the 2008 Bill s.6). See also, Ombudsman Act 1980 (Second Schedule) (Amendment) Order 1985 (S.I. No. 69 of 1985) extending this Schedule.

[42] In his 1992 Report, p.2 the Ombudsman refers to development in the co-operation between his Office, the National Social Service Board and the Citizens Advice Bureau.

[43] Indeed, in at least one complaint, it has been recommended that the public body pay the complainant's legal costs: 1991 Report, p.105.

[44] The 1992 Report states as follows at p.2: "Many public representatives appear to be hesitant about bringing their constituents' complaints to my Office ... it is almost always the same nucleus of Deputies, Senators and local Councillors who continually send in complaints." See further, 1993 Report, p.110 and 1990 Report, pp.3–4. Where the complaint is received via a public representative, the Ombudsman's practice is to keep him in touch with developments, e.g. by copying him in on correspondence.

[45] 2006 Report, p.30; see *A Digest of Cases: a Selection of Significant Cases Completed by the Ombudsman in 2000-2001*, pp.35–36 for a complaint made by a "public representative".

(4) "Taken in the performance of administrative functions"

9–16   The requirement that the "action" be "taken in the performance of administrative functions"[46] could well be regarded as excluding other categories; but in fact it has been significantly ignored. For example, "quasi-judicial" decisions—broadly, those which have a high law content and which directly affect a single individual—have been taken to fall within the Ombudsman's jurisdiction, for instance, decisions in regard to housing grants or welfare benefits. Again, notwithstanding the statutory restriction to "administrative functions", the Ombudsman has been prepared to appraise what might be called, at any rate, low-level policy questions.[47] And he has also been prepared to intervene in commercial or business dealings, for example (when Bord Telecom was in existence) telephone billing.[48] In an interesting comparison, the Ombudsman has remarked that:

> "[T]he consumers of faulty goods and services are entitled to refunds or other protection. In my view, the consumers of public services should in principle be treated no differently to private sector consumers. They have a right to expect that, if they pay a charge for a service, the service will be of good quality and fit for the purpose intended. The legislation enabling local authorities to supply water for domestic purposes and to charge for water for domestic purposes envisages that a domestic water supply will not just be fit for drinking but that it will also be suitable for washing and sanitation."[49]

9–17   It might be thought that this restriction to "administrative functions" would at least have the effect of excluding actions taken by the executive which are incidental to the judicial function, for instance, a department deciding whether to prosecute for breach of some specialist legislation for which it is responsible. The Ombudsman dealt in the 2000 Annual Report with a number of cases where such questions were raised. In the first, An Post argued that the summary prosecution of individuals under s.77(b) of the Postal and Telecommunications Services Act 1983 for not having a television licence falls outside the Ombudsman's remit because it relates to the enforcement of the criminal law. In a rather gnomic statement, the Ombudsman simply said "[t]he advice I received in relation to this case was that the matter did fall within my jurisdiction …".[50]

---

[46]   For definitions of "action" (to include, inter alia, failure to act) and "functions" see Ombudsman Act 1980 s.1.

[47]   See further, paras 9–27 to 9–34.

[48]   There used to be many examples, for instance: 1992 Report, pp.133–134; 1993 Report, pp.117–118; 1994 Report, p.41. See also, 1993 Report, p.110 (discounts given to business users of local authority dumps); 1990 Report, p.289 (compensation for damages to a parcel carried by An Post, even though the terms of the insurance excluded liability in the circumstances).

[49]   1994 Report, p.68.

[50]   2000 Report, p.7. An Post certainly seemed to have a strong argument here; but presumably because the focus was on the preliminary bar to jurisdiction, no details were given as to what the Ombudsman was requested to investigate.

   Similar concerns arose with regard to the issuance of fixed penalty notices (also known as "on-the-spot" fines) by local authorities for minor contraventions of the Litter Pollution Act 1997 and the Road Traffic Act 1994 (2000 Report, pp.7–8). On this occasion, he also sidestepped s.5(1)(a)(ii) of the 1980 Act, which prevents the Ombudsman from investigating an action where a person has a right of "appeal, reference or review to or before a court". His dexterity was doubtless aided by the fact that there is no appeal from most of the decisions within the investigation and prosecution fields.

9–18 In another case, the Ombudsman was prepared to review a local authority's failure to initiate legal proceedings. This arose from the fact that a person was generating a great deal of noise and disturbance manufacturing aluminium windows in his house. The local authority admitted to the Ombudsman that it "could and should have taken action under housing legislation". Because of its failure to do so, neighbours were compelled to take action at law. Accordingly the Ombudsman approved the payment of £3,000 by the local authority to cover the costs of the action and for damage caused to the neighbours' boundary fence.[51]

The bad rule

9–19 Another difficult question arises where the adverse consequences of an administrative action can be traced back, not to any error by the administrator, but to the content of a statute, statutory instrument or extra-legal rule (contained in, for example, a circular), which had determined the way the administrative decision had to be taken. If it is some such rule which is the source of, say, unfairness, has the Ombudsman jurisdiction? In the first place, where the maladministration is dictated by an Act of the Oireachtas or a common law rule, the Ombudsman accepts that he has no authority to deal with the case.[52]

9–20 Next, what is the position in regard to statutory instruments and administrative circulars, which are, after all, legislation or quasi-legislation,[53] rather than administration? Here the Ombudsman has taken a more robust attitude. In the first place, we may clear out of the way the easy case, namely the classic situation where the rule is normally fair but an exceptional case presents itself. In cases of this sort, the Ombudsman has recommended that "[t]he Council should take a more flexible compassionate and less legalistic approach"[54] and such recommendations have been accepted.

9–21 But what if the rule is inherently bad? A significant discussion of the important question of the bad rule arose in the course of an investigation into the refusal, by the Department of Social Welfare, to pay arrears of pensions to persons who were later than the specified period (six months) in applying for their pension.[55] This withholding was said, by the Department, to flow inevitably from the relevant

---

[51] 1992 Report, pp.26–27. For prosecutions in the planning field, see H & M, paras 9–81 to 9–83.

[52] 2006 Report, p.36. However, in the 1998 Report, p.18, the Ombudsman highlighted a case where a tax statute, which had been administered fairly, was perhaps itself unfair.

[53] As to the classification of statutory instruments and circulars, see above, Ch.2.

[54] See a complaint in which a disabled person's grant was eventually paid despite the legal requirement (not fulfilled in this case) that the builder have a tax clearance certificate (2003 Report, p.9); and another case in which the claimants had been reared as adopted children and inherited property on the death of their parents, yet, because of problems associated with the "adoption", they were not given the tax-free threshold entitlement which a child would have had in relation to the parents' estate. On the Ombudsman's recommendation the Revenue Commissioners eventually allowed the same tax-free entitlement as if the adoption were legally valid (2001 Report, p.26). See also, 2001 Report, p.29.

[55] *Report of Investigation of Complaints against the Department of Social Welfare regarding Arrears of Contributory Pensions* (March 14, 1997). Hereafter, "Report of March 14, 1997".

statutory instrument. Dealing with this preliminary aspect of the complaint, the Ombudsman stated[56]:

> "Section 4(2) of the Ombudsman Act, 1980 refers to actions 'taken in the performance of administrative functions' and I am advised that I would be precluded from enquiring into legislative actions. A legislative action is the making of a law; it is not the application of that law to individual cases or categories of cases. A question I may be faced with, therefore, is: may I criticise in an investigation report the particular provisions of statutory regulations? I certainly may if I consider the regulations are *ultra vires* the primary legislation because in such an event the decisions in individual cases would be 'taken without proper authority'. But what if the decisions in individual cases were fully in accordance with the provisions of the statutory regulations and did not involve the unreasonable use or withholding of Ministerial discretion? Here the position is more complex but I am satisfied that I may criticise the particular provisions of a statutory regulation if they result in decisions in individual cases which are 'contrary to fair or sound administration'. By this I mean that, in their application, they have an adverse effect which I consider to be unfair and unreasonable."

9–22 The way that the British PCA has adopted to blunt the edge of the investigation of the "bad rule" precept is that he will ask the body which has made the bad rule to review it. If, as would be unlikely, they fail to do so, then that would be regarded as a case of "constructive maladministration". However, if they do so and confirm the rule, then the British PCA can do no more.[57] But, as can be seen from the above quotation, in particular the last two sentences, the Irish Ombudsman now appears to go beyond the position in Britain. Accordingly, if delegated legislation is substantively unfair it is open to the Ombudsman to review it. This is discussed most fully in Appendix 2 of the *Report on the Non-Payment of Arrears of Contributory Pensions* (from which the above quotation was taken). Three reasons are given for this result. The first of these, which is explained in the last two sentences of the extract quoted above, appears to overlook the likelihood that the question of "fair or sound administration" must, by virtue of the meaning of the word "administration", indicate that the underlying law is to be taken as a "given". The second reason is that, for the purpose of Art.15.2.1° of the Constitution, delegated legislation does not constitute "law". But, with respect, this is a rather artificial categorisation which was devised by the judges for the particular purpose of reconciling delegated legislation with the Constitution. Thirdly, since 1987 (when no Joint Oireachtas Committee on Legislation was re-established), there has

---

[56] Report of March 14, 1997, pp.11–12. Strictly speaking, this statement was—as it were—obiter dicta because the Minister had a long-established, though rarely-exercised, "extra-statutory" discretion on the basis of "equity" (Social Welfare (Consolidated Payments Provisions) Regulations 1994 arts 100–107) to pay arrears, in respect of a period before the six months permitted by the statutory instrument. The legal basis of a non-statutory discretion may be doubtful, given that the expenditure of public moneys requires substantive (i.e. legislation apart from the Estimates and Appropriation Act) statutory authority. Notwithstanding this rather legalistic point (which is not even mentioned in the Report), the Ombudsman avoided the need to take a position on the issue under discussion here ("the bad rule"), by recommending that the Department assist the complainants, on the basis that their situations fell within "the equity".

[57] See Gregory, "The Select Committee on the PCA 1967–80" (1982) *Public Law* 49 at 70.

been no committee of the legislature to review the substance (or anything else) of delegated legislation.[58] The Ombudsman argued, accordingly, that, since there is no other adequate forum for reviewing delegated legislation, he should be able to remedy that deficiency. But this sounds like a policy—rather than a legal—argument for extending the Ombudsman's jurisdiction. Possibly, the Ombudsman might succeed in getting it established, as an informal convention, that she can review the content of statutory instruments. But this would involve quite a stretch from her statutory jurisdiction.

(5) Types of defect

9–23   The British Parliamentary Commissioner Act 1967 relies heavily on a term which it does not define; namely, the term "maladministration". In contrast, the Irish legislation does not use this term, yet provides what might be regarded as a definition of it: for s.4(2)(b) of the 1980 Act gives a list of defects which may attract the Ombudsman's attention. The Ombudsman may investigate any action where it appears to the Ombudsman:

> (b)   that the action was or may have been—
>> (i)   taken without proper authority,
>> (ii)   taken on irrelevant grounds,
>> (iii)   the result of negligence or carelessness,
>> (iv)   based on erroneous or incomplete information,
>> (v)   improperly discriminatory,
>> (vi)   based on an undesirable administrative practice, or
>> (vii) otherwise contrary to fair or sound administration.

9–24   The 2008 Bill s.7 augments these requirements, by providing that, in making decisions on rights and benefits, a public body must "consistent with its resources" deal with people fairly and in a timely manner.[59]

9–25   In view of the vagueness of some of these categories; the discretion in their application which is vested in the Ombudsman; and the informal attitude adopted by the Ombudsman (whose Reports, it is worth noting, do not usually identify any particular statutory ground),[60] we shall not use these statutory categories as an organising principle here. However, the following tentative observations may be made in respect of them. In the first place, we shall see throughout this section that there is a substantial overlap between some of the items in the statutory catalogue and the grounds on which a court would exercise its power of judicial review of an administrative action.[61] Thus, head (v) "improperly discriminatory" is similar to Art.40.1[62] of the Constitution which would be available to a court reviewing an

---

[58]   For expansion on the points in this paragraph, see H & M, paras 2–112 to 2–126.

[59]   Though, as we shall see at paras 9–27 to 9–34 and 9–46, this is a requirement which the Ombudsman has long operated.

[60]   In the Annual Report of 1995, the Ombudsman set out the *Principles of Good Administration*. In 1996, he published a checklist highlighting standards of best practice, *The Ombudsman's Guide to Standards of Best Practice for Public Servants*, which was updated in 2002 (2002 Report, Ch.2). See further, Third Edition at pp.349–350.

[61]   The question of this overlap is discussed further at H & M, paras 9–72 to 9–77.

[62]   "All citizens shall, as human persons, be held equal before the law. This shall not be held

administrative action. Again, heads (i) ("taken without proper authority") and (ii) ("taken on irrelevant grounds") establish grounds which would also be available in a court reviewing an administrative action. Take, for instance, a complaint arising from a (former) health board's refusal to pay Disabled Persons' Maintenance Allowance to persons attending secondary school because this meant that they were not available for employment. The Ombudsman upheld the complaint because the statute created an entitlement to payment provided only that three factors—which related to the applicant's age, means and level of disability—were satisfied.[63] In conventional legal parlance, the health boards had taken irrelevant considerations into account.

9–26 However, the remaining heads create wider powers than their judicial equivalents. Thus, in head (iii) ("the result of negligence or carelessness"), since negligence is mentioned, "carelessness" must mean something going beyond negligence. It may be that the "duty of care" or "remoteness of damage" elements do not have to be established or, at least, not to the same standard as for negligence. In any case, given the under-developed state of the law on public authority torts, it is useful to have a flexible alternative to negligence *stricto sensu*. And head (iv) ("based on erroneous or incomplete information") is clearly wider than the embryonic and limited "no-evidence" rule in the field of judicial review of administrative acts. Likewise, as we shall see, head (vii) ("otherwise contrary to fair or sound administration") goes beyond constitutional justice. In any case, as noted below its meaning will be extended by the 2008 Bill s.7.

Policy/fairness/merits

9–27 We are, in this section, drawing no distinction, since the Ombudsman does not do so, between two types of decision: on the one hand, policy decisions which potentially affect a large number of cases and, on the other hand, the exercise of a discretion which immediately affects only a single situation.

9–28 As we shall see, it is clear from his annual reports that the Ombudsman is more prepared than a court would be to review questions of merits or judgment. He has been prepared—to quote a characteristic phrase used by the first incumbent in various public talks—"to push the boat out". In his 2000 Annual Report,[64] unusually, the Ombudsman offered some general reflections on how he would exercise his jurisdiction. He laid emphasis on the importance of "background rights" or "values" lying behind the taking of administrative decisions, such as "the need to uphold the autonomy, dignity, respect, status and security of individuals". He expressed the desire "to develop these concepts by reference to future cases because it seems to me that it would be well worthwhile trying to assist public bodies to adopt a more values-based approach when dealing with people now that a human rights approach to service provision is becoming necessary".

9–29 The Ombudsman has been prepared to intervene on such broad bases

---

to mean that the State shall not in its enactments have due regard to differences of capacity, physical and moral, and of social function."

[63] 1985 Report, p.32. For a close parallel (in the context of judicial review) to the facts in the text, see *State (Keller) v Galway County Council* [1958] I.R. 142.

[64] 2000 Annual Report, pp.12–21. The quotations later in the text are from pp.13 and 14.

as consistency, equity, flexibility, or preventing anomalies. There are examples in diverse fields, including: where welfare payments had been made as from the date of certification of eligibility by the health board rather than the date of application[65]; where a widow's pension had been very substantially reduced in view of her "means" which were taken to include a judgment debt, which she had, in practice, very little hope of enforcing[66]; or where there was an absolute entitlement under the Urban Fuel Scheme which, at the relevant time, operated in 17 urban districts, whereas the National Fuel Scheme, which applied elsewhere, was discretionary.[67]

9–30   As we shall see in the context of judicial review of administrative action, a more sharply focused version of fairness may be characterised as "proportionality". This has been elaborated by the Ombudsman in the following way:

> "Public bodies still tend to administer their schemes and programmes in a rigid manner, even minor breaches of a scheme [e.g. delay] or minor failures to meet qualifying conditions tend to attract the same penalties as major ones. In short the principle of proportionality has not yet been given sufficient recognition."[68]

9–31   One might think that it was implicit in both the nature of the Ombudsman's role and the statutory list of deficiencies quoted earlier, that the Ombudsman has authority to intervene only where there is some specific defect in the process or reasoning leading up to the decision, rather than simply where she differs from the result. In short, she must not usurp the position of the body in which the decision in question has been vested. In one of the minority of cases where the Ombudsman was influenced by this limitation, he rejected a complaint against the Revenue Commissioners. The facts were that the Commissioners had refused to grant a cartographer a tax exemption under the Finance Act 1969 for producing work which is "original and creative" and displays "cultural and artistic merit". The complainant claimed that the Revenue Commissioners had taken no account of evidence of his work's artistic merit. The Ombudsman's view was that:

> "Having studied and consulted on the case at length I came to the conclusion that no fault could be found with the efforts of the Revenue Commissioners to arrive at a decision in a fair and reasonable way. I might not agree with the decision but I have no authority to set up an alternative source of assessment to challenge the advice given to the Commissioners."[69]

9–32   Many policy differences, of course, come down in the end to money. In

---

[65]   2000 Annual Report, pp.31, 52.

[66]   1989 Report, see pp.73–74. See also, 1986 Report, p.48; 2001 Report, p.30.

[67]   1985 Report, p.33; 1991 Report, p.21; 1992 Report, p.26. See also, 1996 Report, p.20.

[68]   1995 Report, p.14; 1993 Report, p.59: "I find it hard to accept that the penalty imposed should, in many cases, be so severe. It would appear that the penalty being imposed in this kind of case is totally out of proportion to whatever 'fault' may have occurred. The principle of proportionality is a feature of European Union law and one which may well evolve as a feature of our public law. The present arrangements would appear to be out of step with this principle." For another example, see 1990 Report, pp.64–66.

[69]   1984 Report, p.46. See also, 1985 Report, p.30.

some cases, the Ombudsman has been prepared to recommend the payment of substantial sums of money, for example: orthodontic treatment[70]; the education of a deaf child[71]; and under the Treatment Abroad Scheme.[72] On the other hand, in another case (probably involving greater expenditure) concerning allegedly inadequate refuse collection arrangements, he found that "the Council's justification for those arrangements was reasonable in light of their financial constraints and I consider that it outweighed the inconvenience experienced by the complainant as a result of these arrangements".[73]

9–33 And the Ombudsman has accepted the need for a fairly administered queue in appropriate circumstances:

> "I could not pursue other cases because the medical records available to me indicated that the health boards concerned were not unreasonable in putting the patients on a waiting list with other children requiring similar treatment, at a time when sufficient financial resources were not available to the boards to enable them to provide early treatment."[74]

9–34 That said, what one should emphasise is that frequently, the Ombudsman has upheld a complaint merely because he took a different view as to the appreciation of the facts from the public body, for example as to whether the complainant was "available for work", in the context of a claim for unemployment benefit.[75]

Without lawful authority

9–35 A large proportion—as many as 20–30 per cent of the cases summarised in the Annual Reports (although these are not typical of the entire case load)—have been regarded by the Ombudsman as requiring her to take an explicit view on actual legal[76] issues.[77] This often involves the interpretation of legislative or administrative

---

[70] 1989 Report, pp.50–59. It is striking that this Report quotes from the Health Board's response to the Ombudsman, that "[it] may well be that the policy itself is open to criticism or even to legal challenge but that, of itself, does not imply that it is necessarily a matter where change is incumbent on the Board as a result of the Ombudsman's observations". The Ombudsman's Report, however, makes no comment on this contention.

[71] 1989 Report, p.43.

[72] 1989 Report, p.64; see also, 1987 Report, p.53.

[73] 1989 Report, p.91. See also, 1987 Report, p.32; 1992 Report, pp.35–36; 2009 Report, p.63; and 1991 Report, pp.70–71; 1990 Report, p.83

[74] 1987 Report, p.28; see also, 1989 Report, p.60.

[75] 1986 Report, p.49; 1988 Report, p.80 (whether complainant was sharing the house with another person, in the context of rent assessment for a local authority house); 2001 Report, p.30 (Local authority refusal to exercise its discretion to corporation-house tenants who were itinerants for reasons of good estate management ruled not to be soundly based, on the ground that the family was not likely to indulge in anti-social activity and the neighbourhood was sparsely habited).

[76] By the 2008 Bill s.12, the Ombudsman will be able to refer any question of law to the High Court for determination.

[77] 1988 Report, p.22 ("I appreciate that this is not a sensible position to adopt but it would appear to be what is provided for in the legislation"). See also, 1997 Report, pp.22–23 (successful complaint against Department of Arts, Heritage, Gaeltacht and the Islands arising out of a refusal of a Gaeltacht housing building grant because the house was a second house); 2004 Report, p.19 (successful complaint against Tipperary Town Council arising out of its policy not to include single persons with no dependents on its housing list); 2004 Report, pp.20–21

schemes which have scarcely been considered by the courts.[78] Let us list some examples: whether under the Higher Education Grant Scheme certain moneys should be treated as capital or income or whether a step-parent's means were to be counted as the means of a "guardian"[79]; whether a Disabled Persons' Maintenance Allowance is payable as from the date of application and not the date of award[80]; the proper assessment of spouses income for the purpose of Disabled Persons' Maintenance Allowance.[81] In addition, the Ombudsman has made recommendations in a case about senior citizens in long-stay institutions, on the basis that "there would appear to be no statutory ground for a means-testing system which includes the income of the family as well as that of the patient".[82]

9–36 Sometimes, a complaint is based on private law grounds, rather than the public body's statutory duties. Surprisingly, the Ombudsman does not acknowledge that this distinction creates any limit on his jurisdiction. For instance, there have been complaints about: trespass to land (damage to a garden wall done by the Department of Posts)[83]; unlawful impounding of cattle in a County Pound[84]; negligent conveyancing by a local authority[85]; and trespass to goods involving the unlawful seizure of a van by the Revenue Commissioners.[86]

Negligence or carelessness

9–37 One set of cases of this type involved the Land Registry's practice of returning original deeds in letters which have been registered at the lowest registered post fee so that the maximum compensation payable was way below the probable value of the loss.[87] Another successful complaint arose out of a breakdown in

---

(failure by Northern Area Health Board to provide a service to a patient in a nursing home even though such provision was mandatory under the Nursing Home Regulations 1993); 2006 Report, p.17 (attempt by local authority to levy rates arrears against a house owner rather than the occupier, even though there was no statutory authority to pursue the owner of the premises); *A Digest of Cases: a Selection of Significant Cases Completed by the Ombudsman in 2000-2001*, pp.29–30 (health board making payment of a nursing home subvention conditional on the provision of information to the board by an applicant's relatives).

[78] For examples of an especially rough and ready legal analysis by the Ombudsman, see 1992 Report, pp.72 and 119–120.

[79] 1987 Report, p.71; 1989 Report, p.85; 1985 Report, p.28, respectively. On interpretation of this Scheme, see also, 1991 Report, pp.59–62; 1992 Report, pp.75–77 and 93–94; 1993 Report, pp.37–39; 1994 Report, p.23.

[80] 1985 Report, p.31. On the Disabled Persons' Grant Scheme, see 1990 Report, pp.45–52.

[81] 1992 Report, pp.39–42. On this point, the Ombudsman waited for the decision in *H v Eastern Health Board* [1988] I.R. 747. For another issue in regard to DPMA, see 1993 Report, pp.100–101. On Carers' Allowance, see 1993 Report, pp.26–27. See also, 1990 Report, pp.76–77; 1994 Report, p.24 and p.71; 1997 Report, p.28; 2006 Report, pp.13–15.

[82] 1992 Report, p.34. See also, 1992 Report, pp.14, 39, 42; 1991 Report, pp.72–73; 1993 Report, p.49.

[83] 1987 Report, pp.94–95; see also, 1989 Report, p.90.

[84] 1993 Report, p.39. See also, 1993 Report, pp.83–84 (improper procedures operated by the Registrar of Companies in striking a company off the Register); 1997 Report, p.28 (house improvement grant under the Housing (Gaeltacht) Act 1929); 1997 Report, p.33 (interpretation of nursing home subvention regulations).

[85] 1988 Report, p.80. See also, 2005 Report, pp.22–23 (Council's legal department's delay in conveyancing work); 2001 Report, p.31 (river erosion caused by Council's drainage works); 2009 Report, pp.67–68.

[86] 1989 Report, pp.34–38.

[87] 1987 Report, pp.26–27. See also, 1992 Report, pp.66–69 (incompetent plumbing in water

communications between two sections of South Dublin County Council, resulting in a failure either to protect a complainant's right of residency in a local authority dwelling (which had been the family home), or to include the complainant on the housing list.[88]

Corruption?

9–38 The focus of the Ombudsman's enquiry is ordinarily on the consequence for the complainant rather than the motivation of the responsible officials. Thus, most of his investigations are relatively informal and, as a matter of policy, do not identify the responsible public servant. (To do so would lead to constitutional justice for the public servants and huge expense for the Ombudsman's Office.) Nevertheless, there was at least one complaint which seemed to carry a suspicion of dishonesty. This concerned an agreement between a local council and the complainant landowner. In return for a payment of €1,270, the landowner granted the council a way-leave (right of way) for a pipe of specified diameter to run across his land. The sole purpose of the way-leave was said to be to drain a public road. However, as constructed, the pipe was for a larger diameter than that authorised in the way-leave. Next, three sites in the vicinity of the complainant's land were purchased and a house built on each by the council official who had negotiated the way-leave, a second council official and a builder. Contrary to the undertaking given to the complainant, outlets from these houses were connected to the pipe. Finally, the builder was granted planning permission for the construction of 65 houses on the same lands and sewerage waste water from these, too, was to use the way-leave. The complainant maintained that, had he known that the Council were going to allow a housing development to be connected to the pipe, he would not have agreed to the original way-leave.

9–39 In a lengthy ruling, the Ombudsman concluded following his investigation (the full details of which were deliberately not published) that there was no evidence of impropriety on the part of the Council officials. However, "the sequence of events … gives rise to serious concern. In particular the Council did not have in place adequate administrative procedures for handling infrastructure projects which would allow it to withstand or refute an allegation, however remote, of a potential or perceived conflict of interest between the Council's staff, developers and third parties".[89] The Ombudsman recommended that compensation of €38,000 be paid by the Council and also sent a copy of his report to the Department of the Environment and Local Government.

Error of fact or novel considerations

9–40 The Ombudsman's investigators are often people who, either from long experience in the Office or because they have earlier worked in the particular sector of the public service which they are overseeing, have an excellent knowledge of the

---

supply to complainant's house) and pp.134–135 (Bord Telecom cutting away part of a tree to make way for telephone poles); 1993 Report, pp.91–92 (passport application mislaid by the Department of Foreign Affairs).

[88] 2006 Report, p.26.

[89] 2000 Report, pp.27–29.

territory under scrutiny.[90] In a surprising number of cases, investigation—some of it very resourceful and imaginative—by a member of the Ombudsman's staff has led to the discovery of new facts or information, or cast a fresh light on the existing information, and this has led to a change of heart in the responsible authority.[91] In one complaint, involving an application for a contributory widow's pension, it was discovered that the complainant had paid the appropriate number of social insurance contributions, but they had been paid under her maiden name (something which the Department had not checked, although they had the complainant's maiden name). The complainant was awarded (in 1988) £13,000 back-payment plus £6,000 for loss of purchasing power.[92]

9–41 A less typical example focused on an inadequate investigation by a health board into standards of care in a private nursing home (since the nursing home itself, being private, was beyond the Ombudsman's jurisdiction). The Ombudsman found two factual errors which had caused distress to the complainant. The complainant's mother had been admitted to a private nursing home, and the complainant claimed that the standard of care was inadequate. An initial investigation by the health board took the view that the complainant's mother had been suffering from Alzheimer's disease and that any difficulties she had experienced in passing urine were unrelated to any defects in the catheter. On intervention by the Ombudsman, however, the health board accepted that these two factual claims were incorrect: there was no documentary evidence to support the finding that the complainant's mother had Alzheimer's; and the catheter had become blocked during the night. In view of the "stress, anxiety, frustration, and inconvenience the complainant suffered as a result of the deficiencies of [the] investigation", a payment of £750 was made.[93]

Fair procedure

9–42 A great number of complaints to the Ombudsman fall into a category which might broadly be called "procedure". Procedural defects naturally include breaches of constitutional justice.[94] One example concerned the drawing of a map setting

---

[90] *A Digest of Cases: a Selection of Significant Cases Completed by the Ombudsman in 2000-2001*, p.34. The 2009 Report, p.53 states: "... it emerged from our examination of the matter that there was additional medical evidence on the Department's file which differed substantially from the medical evidence examined by both the Deciding Officer and the Appeals Officer."

[91] In one set of cases, a fund of money overlooked by the public authority was discovered. It had been set aside in the care of the Public Trustee, for the future maintenance of embankments (1994 Report, pp.23–24). See also, 1996 Report, pp.15–16, 31 and 32. Again, Dublin Corporation claimed that it was unable to issue, by computer, polling cards with the complainant's name and address in Irish without going to considerable expense. "When the Office became aware that Cork Corporation had overcome a similar problem without any major difficulty, Dublin Corporation was asked to review its decision." It did so: 1997 Report, p.28.

[92] 1988 Report, p.63. See 1985 Report, pp.56–57; 1993 Report, pp.112–113; 1999 Report, p.17; 2005 Report, p.15.

[93] 2000 Report, pp.33–34.

[94] Another complaint arose when Disability Benefit was suspended by the Department of Social Welfare because the complainant had failed to attend an examination by a medical referee. The point on which the Ombudsman focused was that "if the Department had advised in time that it did not regard his request as reasonable then he would have clearly understood that failure to attend would have resulted in suspension" (1991 Report, p.95). See, to similar effect, *Thompson v Minister for Social Welfare* [1989] I.R. 618. See also, 1993 Report, pp.85–88 (in

out the boundaries of a Special Protection Area under the Birds Directive 79/409. The Ombudsman found that it was improper to invite submissions from interested parties without fully informing them of the facts on which such submissions were being sought.[95] Another straightforward example concerned the fact that a tenancy offer made to the complainant had been withdrawn on the basis of allegations of antisocial behaviour. These allegations were not put by the Council to the complainant; coupled with which, no appeals procedure was available.[96]

9–43 Another element of constitutional justice to which the Ombudsman has contributed concerns the duty to give reasons. One complaint[97] of this type arose because the complainant had, in 1981–1992, failed in a claim for Deserted Wife's Benefit before the deciding officer, on the ground that she had not obtained maintenance from her husband. However, she had failed before the appeals officer, on the distinct ground that she had not proved constructive desertion. But the complainant had not been made aware of this new argument against her. In 1997 the Ombudsman recommended that the appeals officer's decision of 1982 ought to be reviewed and that she be awarded £24,000 in arrears. Similarly, as a result of the Ombudsman's prompting, farmers are now given details of the assessment of their means where this assessment has led to a reduction in their social welfare payments.[98]

9–44 The Ombudsman will also provide a remedy where there has been a breach of particular (procedural) regulations. An example of this which has come up on a number of occasions concerns the closure of pedestrian rights of way in residential areas in violation of the statutory procedure which requires advertising in the press (or, where there is an objection, an oral hearing). There is one notable feature of these cases, namely that there is a strong public sentiment both for and against closure: in other words, this is a form of the "third party situation".[99] As to this feature, the Ombudsman observed that "... [a]dherence to the established procedures would allow both sides to air their views on closure proposals and would be in accordance with the principles of fair and sound administration".[100]

9–45 On a slightly different point, the Ombudsman has sometimes required full written communication:

> "I felt that it was not satisfactory that the Health Board should rely entirely on verbal communications in a matter of such importance. I felt that the Board should, at least, communicate with parents in writing where a child's dental condition is to be monitored and assessed ...".[101]

---

a claim under the Suckler Cow Scheme, a farmer was not informed that the Department of Agriculture doubted that the animal was a suckler). See also, 1989 Report, p.48; 1993 Report, p.63; 1996 Report, p.30.

[95] 2005 Report, p.16.

[96] 2009 Report, pp.69–71.

[97] 1997 Report, p.25. The case is not put as plainly as this in the report. See also, 1995 Report, p.18.

[98] 1987 Report, p.68; 1988 Report, p.65; 1989 Report, p.73.

[99] i.e. where an Ombudsman's decision in favour of the claimant could have an unfavourable effect on the interest of some other private individual: see H & M, paras 9–108 to 9–110.

[100] 1991 Report, p.37.

[101] 1992 Report, p.112.

Of particular importance, in terms of process, is record keeping. In the health field, the Ombudsman has emphasised the requirement to keep proper records.[102]

9–46   Other instances of bad procedure are delay[103] (which is rather common), and bureaucratic bad manners, which at worst shade into "the insolence of Office".[104] Speaking generally about the performance of the Revenue Commissioners, the Ombudsman made the following observation:

> "Coping with harsh economic realities ... is a traumatic experience, particularly for widows and pensioners. Both are extremely vulnerable and dependent. When sharp cryptic demands for payments are issued from the computer system no account is taken of the age or circumstances of the recipient. The elderly are easily frightened and upset by authoritative demands for payment. It may be that such categories are difficult to identify but some thought should be given as to how the problem might be overcome in order to avoid unnecessary distress to the weak and elderly in our community."[105]

9–47   There are also a group of cases in which the Ombudsman has ruled that the level of service through the Irish language is inadequate.[106]

9–48   From the opposite direction, we find a number of cases in which typically the complainant has been refused some grant or other advantage on the ground that he has missed a deadline.[107] Here the Ombudsman—although "accepting that [in the absence of an Act of the Oireachtas] the Department has to devise its own administrative procedures"[108]—has in effect suggested that a public body ought to overlook breaches of administrative rules or practices by the complainant, where such breaches do not affect the spirit of the particular legislation or scheme.

Information about rights

9–49   The obligation to give information, in the Ombudsman's view, extends not only to a decision taken in respect of a complainant but also as regards the state of the investigation,[109] even though nothing conclusive may yet have happened. A specific example is that an applicant is entitled to information about their position on

---

[102] *Investigation Report on the care of a Patient at Sligo General Hospital* (July 2005). See also, 2004 Report, pp.19–20; and 2006 Report, pp.15–17 and 25–26. In the 2004 Report, pp.9–10, the Ombudsman's intervention resulted in the South Western Area Health Board introducing a form for logging details of telephone calls regarding medical card applications.

[103] By s.1(1) of the 1980 Act, the Ombudsman's jurisdiction includes "failure to act". According to the 1984 Report, Ch.7, 10 per cent of all complaints to the Ombudsman involved delay.

[104] Shakespeare, *Hamlet*, Act III, Scene 2.

[105] 1984 Report, p.18. See also, 1987 Report, p.25 and 1992 Report, p.48 (on the proper procedure for removing a child from foster parents). Note also the 1990 Report, p.86 ("I considered it was a most undesirable administrative practice, to ask any person, but particularly a recently bereaved widow, to sign a contract for accounts which had never been issued").

[106] 1996 Report, p.22.

[107] 1991 Report, p.84: 1990 Report, pp.93–94; 1994 Report, pp.20, 32–33, 45 and 60. *A contra* 1992 Report, p.118. See also, 1991 Report, p.78; 1990 Report, p.77; 1992 Report, p.104.

[108] 1992 Report, p.108. This statement was actually made in a wider context.

[109] For a significant example involving a failure by the HSE to communicate to a crèche that a complaint made against the crèche (centring on child protection) had been found, after investigation, to be groundless, see 2009 Report, pp.33–34. See also, p.25 (Department of

a housing waiting list.[110] In addition, the Ombudsman has treated it as axiomatic that when the complainant has been given incorrect advice[111] (whether as to the facts or law or administrative practice), that he or she should be given a remedy.[112] A typical example arose out of the refusal by the Department of Agriculture and Food to pay the complainant farmer a grant in respect of a piggery. The Ombudsman stated:

> "... taking into account especially the advice given to the complainant by ACOT and the misleading information given to him in the out-of-date form, I found that the decision of the Department of Agriculture and Food to refuse to pay the complainant the grants was *contrary to fair and sound administration*."[113]

9–50   This approach has also been followed in a case where the advice was correct when given, although circumstances later changed, thus rendering the advice bad.[114] Going further, the Ombudsman has stated that "[a]s a general point, I consider that where entitlements are concerned, the onus is on public bodies to send a reminder to people who have not replied to the original notification."[115] The same applies where the public body fails to reply.[116]

9–51   In a number of complaints the Ombudsman appears to have drawn upon a broad principle that the State is under a positive duty to supply the citizen with relevant information about his rights, whether this involves legal advice or facts about his own personal situation.[117] The Ombudsman shows no sympathy whatsoever with the traditional legal principle (which was actually put to him unavailingly on one occasion, by the Department of Social Welfare)[118] that "ignorance of the law is

---

Social and Family Affairs neglected to inform separated man that, because of change of circumstances, he was no longer under an obligation to pay maintenance to his wife).

[110] 2003 Report, pp.23–24.

[111] Again, the Ombudsman has censured the Departments of State involved for their failure, over a period of five years, to reply to letters from a public servant, inquiring what her pension rights would be: 1985 Report, p.63; 1985 Report, p.28.

Notice, likewise, the following strong statement in 1993 Report, p.35, in respect of a different area of administration: "[T]here are basic deficiencies in the information available about the existence and operation of the Treatment Abroad Scheme. This lack of information is evident not only among patients and members of their families, who might need to avail of the scheme but also, unfortunately, among medical and administrative personnel in the health boards. I am concerned also that the operation of the scheme is not sufficiently transparent, that practices differ between health boards and that staff, including medical staff, are not sufficiently familiar with schemes in order to advise or direct the patients at the appropriate time to the relevant administrative scheme."

[112] 1991 Report, p.12B.

[113] 1990 Report, pp.35–42 (emphasis added). Note again, the unusual use of the precise words of the statutory heads of maladministration. This approach was followed even in a case in which the information was correct when given but subsequently revised: 1993 Report, pp.54–55.

[114] 1993 Report, pp.54–55.

[115] *Report of Investigation of Claims* (1997), p.55. See also, 1992 Report, p.80. See also, 1994 Report, pp.16–17, 19–20.

[116] 1992 Report, p.80. See also, 1994 Report, pp.16–17, 19–20.

[117] For several examples in this field, see 1990 Report, pp.42–44; 1995 Report, p.23; 1998 Report, p.114; 2004 Report, pp.15–16; 2006 Report, pp.22–23; *A Digest of Cases: a Selection of Significant Cases Completed by the Ombudsman in 2000-2001*, pp.44–45; 2004 Report, p.15.

[118] 1987 Report, p.68.

no defence".[119] There have also been a number of cases in which welfare agencies have been censured for failing to mention to the complainant alternative benefits (to those sought) which might have applied to him.[120] Thus, "... the Department has agreed that it could treat an existing claim for one payment as satisfying the requirement to have claimed some other higher-rate payment".[121] A particular instance of the failure to supply information concerns the need to notify a person, with whom there is a dispute, about the availability of grievance procedures.[122]

9–52   A tendency seems to have developed among some public bodies of requiring that a person who wishes to obtain information from them should submit a freedom of information request. In regard to this practice, the Ombudsman has commented that "I will exercise extreme vigilance in ensuring that the public are given full and prompt access to information to which they are entitled in the normal course without being forced to resort to the formalities [and expense] of the FOI Act."[123]

Communication/access

9–53   One finds in the Reports, as general comments upon the performance of public bodies, strictures against: the use of "language which, although technically accurate, is not capable of being understood by members of the public"[124]; Bord Telecom's predilection for "standard replies produced by word processor [which] do not respond to the specific point made by the complainant"[125]; and Disabled Persons' Maintenance Allowance regulations which "are unsatisfactory in their lack of clarity".[126] Furthermore:

> "I would urge public bodies to appreciate that the general public do not have the same level of familiarity with schemes and services as the staff of the bodies themselves ... If some action is required on the part of the recipient, this should be stated very clearly. If a prescribed format or application form exists for particular schemes or services, it should be included within the correspondence."[127]

---

[119] Indeed the Ombudsman has remarked: "The experience of my Office over 12 years has been that the vast majority of ... late claimants say that they were poorly informed about their social insurance rights ... The Department has been taking the line that ... ultimately ignorance of the law is not an acceptable excuse for having failed to claim in time. I feel that, in the context of social insurance, this is not a reasonable position to adopt"; *Report of Investigations of Complaints 1997*, pp.62–63.

[120] 1985 Report, p.23; 1990 Report, p.82 ("[p]arents whose children are in receipt of Domiciliary Care Allowance up to a limit of 16 years of age should be informed that payment is about to end and that it is necessary to [apply] for D. P. M. A. [as a successor grant]"). See also, 2000 Report, p.27; 2001 Report, p.22 for a failure of the Department of Social, Community and Family Affairs to advise claimants fully of the negative implications of switching from one social welfare payment to another; 2009 Report, pp.52–53.

[121] 1997 Report, p.25.

[122] 2003 Report, pp.14–15.

[123] 2003 Report, p.34.

[124] 1986 Report, p.15. Cf. Lon Fuller's remark: "I may be clearly wrong; but at least I shall be wrong clearly."

[125] 1986 Report, p.23.

[126] 1988 Report, p.25.

[127] 1994 Report, p.37.

Grievance procedure

9–54 A strong theme which has emerged recently is that the Ombudsman is concerned not only with the initial mistake but also, granted the initial mistake, what sort of an effort the public body itself made to respond adequately to a complaint made to it.[128] One case which arose out of a death in Sligo General Hospital was as much concerned with the inadequate manner in which the hospital dealt with the family's complaint as with the shortcomings in the standard of care and attention afforded to their patient.[129]

9–55 A particularly difficult situation arises—and one must have some sympathy with the public body— where, though the putative complainant is initially parleying with the public body, the public body suspects that the complainant may be trying to lay the ground for future litigation. In such a case, the Ombudsman has remarked:

> "I find that, when there is conflict between a public body and a client which may involve a claim for compensation or possible legal action, the public body may tend, as a matter of course, to adopt an adversarial approach. Little consideration is given to the merits of the case, the public body puts up its defences and the client is left with no option but to take the matter to court or, if appropriate, to my Office. I acknowledge that a public body has a duty to defend its own interests and those of the taxpayer but a primary duty as a public body is to ensure that it responds to its clients in a proper, fair and impartial manner. This means that it is required to consider fully the merits of any case and not to force clients unnecessarily to resort to the courts or to my Office to achieve their rights."[130]

9–56 In commenting, it is hard to be definite about the situation envisaged here, in which probably even the complainant and public body involved would not know how matters might end. The type of conduct which the Ombudsman seems to be condemning here is where a public body refuses to entertain a complaint on the ground that if a person is aggrieved, then the situation is such that he or she could (and therefore should?) bring the matter before a court. The passage quoted (including the last few words about the complainant not being forced "to resort … to my Office") fits in with the Ombudsman's policy, covered at para.9–84, of championing internal complaints procedures. In one of the cases, which the Ombudsman gives as an example of this type, the complainant's house had been damaged by flooding caused, he found, by the neglect of Galway County Council.[131] The local authority's response was that since it had successfully defended, before the courts, claims for compensation of a similar nature to those which had come before the Ombudsman, it would not pay compensation. Our comment is that, if correct, there might be something to be said for the local authority's attitude which was: why should one landowner be compensated, when others had been told, by the

---

[128] 2005 Report, p.8. See also, 1998 Report, pp.9–11.

[129] 2005 Report, p.10.

[130] 1996 Report, p.17. The precept of not adopting an adversarial stance is mentioned explicitly in the "Principles of Good Administration", on which see fn.50.

[131] It was in the 1995 Report (p.3) that the Ombudsman first took to disclosing the identity of local authorities and health boards, save where doing so could identify the complainant. (This was Mr Murphy's first full year of tenure.)

courts, that they had no entitlement? However, as a matter of fact in this particular case, the local authority had *not* successfully defended all compensation claims. Consequently, the Ombudsman's view was that here the local authority had been too quick to rely upon the court judgment as a justification and consequently had not really considered the complaint at all.[132]

C. EXEMPTIONS FROM JURISDICTION

9–57   Even within the subject area thus staked out, six categories of case are exempted from the Ombudsman's jurisdiction.

9–58   (1) The Ombudsman is excluded where there is a right of appeal in respect of the decision to a court.[133] However, the Ombudsman is, naturally, prevented from hearing a case where the person aggrieved has actually initiated "civil legal proceedings".[134] Even then, the Ombudsman will not be excluded if "the proceedings have been dismissed for failure to disclose a cause of action or a complaint justiciable by that court".[135] This limitation upon the matters over which the Ombudsman lacks jurisdiction evidently arises because (as noted above) the grounds on which complaints may be made to the Ombudsman are wider than those which apply to a court, and it is thought to be harsh to prevent a case going to the Ombudsman on the basis that the case has been before a court, if the grounds of complaint anyway fall outside the court's jurisdiction.

9–59   Pursuing a similar line of reasoning, it might be asked whether a complainant ought to lose his chance of going to the Ombudsman if his court case had failed because it was out of time, or because he had adopted the wrong procedure, or for any other reason unrelated to the merits. If the provision is read strictly, such a person would not be within the Ombudsman's jurisdiction. There is, however, an equitable proviso which permits the investigation of actions "if it appears to the Ombudsman that special circumstances make it proper to do so",[136] even though those actions would otherwise be excluded (under either this, or the next, exemption). This proviso would probably enable the Ombudsman to investigate in

---

[132]   1996 Report, p.19.

[133]   Section 5(1)(a)(ii). See also, Ch.11, Part D.

[134]   Section 5(1)(a)(ii). ("Civil legal proceedings" is probably (if only from its context) intended to include both civil actions and applications for judicial review.)

    See further, 1988 Report, p.26, where the Ombudsman remarked: "I have refrained from making a recommendation in the case for the moment as there is a case before the Supreme Court involving similar circumstances and the same issues. In view of this I accept that the Health Boards should await the final judicial decision before deciding on the case I investigated". See also, 1992 Report, p.40 where the Ombudsman (in a series of complaints on the assessment of income for DPMA purposes where the applicant's spouse has income either from employment or a social welfare payment) anticipated the High Court's decision in *Healy v Eastern Health Board* [1988] I.R. 747. See also, 1992 Report, pp.121, 135; and 1993 Report, p.112; 1996 Report, p.24.

[135]   Section 5(1)(a)(ii). See, e.g. 2009 Report, p.2: "The complainant … withdrew the legal proceedings which she had lodged so as to allow my Office to deal with the case. She was seeking clear answers with regard to her late father's treatment, an apology for the shortcomings in his treatment and assurances that lessons had been learned within the hospital system."

[136]   Proviso to s.5(1).

a case in which the court had turned the complainant away for some reason other than the merits of his claim.

9–60 Finally, one might interpolate: what is the position where a complainant goes first to the Ombudsman, and subsequently has recourse to a court? If he is unsuccessful before the Ombudsman, there appears to be nothing, in principle, against his going to a court. (Quaere: whether the delay caused by the reference to the Ombudsman would count against the litigant?) By contrast, what is the position if he were successful (whether partially or completely) before the Ombudsman? Presumably, if compensation had been paid by the public body then this would go to reduce the value of his loss, for the purpose of assessing damages before a court, and, if the case took the form of an application for judicial review, then possibly the recourse to the Ombudsman would be a ground on which the court would exercise its discretion against granting a remedy. A point of principle here is that, where the (Public Service) Ombudsman is concerned, probably no plea of res judicata could be invoked to stop the litigant in his tracks to a court.[137]

9–61 (2) The Ombudsman has no jurisdiction over a decision from which an appeal lies to "a person other than a Department of State or other person specified in Part I of the First Schedule", irrespective of whether any appeal has actually been taken.[138] The effect of the phrase quoted is that, if the appeal lies to a Minister or civil servant[139] in a Department, the Ombudsman retains jurisdiction over decisions. Thus subject to the local remedies rule (see (v) below), the Ombudsman has jurisdiction over claims for social welfare benefit. The reason for this is that

---

[137] At the moment, the only guidance we have on this is the admittedly negative authority of the central passage from Kelly J.'s judgment in *Murray v Trustees of Irish Airlines* [2007] 2 I.L.R.M. 196 at 204 which is as follows: "From this short survey of the relevant statutory provisions it is clear that they contain a self-contained statutory code. They invest the [Pensions] ombudsman with a wide jurisdiction, powers akin to that of this court in many respects, and the ability to make a binding determination which establishes a legal right. That legal right is capable of enforcement in the manner prescribed by the Act. I am satisfied … that the Pensions Act has created a specific jurisdiction for the determination of issues, which established the existence of a legal right, and that there cannot be inferred from these provisions an intention to exclude the principle of *res judicata* … A party, such as Mr. Murray, who is aggrieved with the determination of the trustees, may, at his option, avail himself of the services of the Ombudsman or bring proceedings in an appropriate court for declaratory or other relief. He may not do the latter when in receipt of an adverse determination from the Ombudsman. That is so because the determination of the Ombudsman is *res judicata* of the dispute in question …".

The big question here is whether this ruling as to res judicata would apply so as to bar judicial review, where other Ombudsmen were involved, rather than the Pensions Ombudsman. One possible point of distinction may probably be eliminated, namely that, in the case of the Pensions Ombudsman, an appeal on a point of law to the High Court is expressly provided for in the Pensions Act. In itself, this is undoubtedly a factor which would probably militate against permitting judicial review. However, Kelly J.'s judgment offers, clearly as a separate and stronger reason for the conclusion that judicial review is not available, the fact that the Ombudsman has "powers akin to that of this court in many respects and the ability to make a binding determination, which establishes a legal right" ([2007] 2 I.L.R.M. 196 at 204). This cannot be said of most Ombudsmen, other than the Pensions Ombudsman.

[138] Section 5(1)(a)(iii). By the 2008 Bill s.8, this would be replaced by a provision barring the Ombudsman where there is "… an appeal, reference or review to or before a person, other than a reviewable agency [s.4] who is independent in the performance of his or her function …".

[139] See definition of "Department of State" at s.1(2).

such claims are heard by deciding officers in the Department of Social Protection or appeals from deciding officers, which are heard by appeals officers (again within the Department).[140]

9–62   By contrast, on the other side of the line, the exclusion of cases where there is an appeal to someone other than a Department means, for instance, that, subject to what is said in the following paragraph, the Ombudsman is excluded from planning cases (either at the initial or appeal stage) because of the appeal to An Bord Pleanála. Similarly, he may not review decisions of the Revenue Commissioners since there is an appeal to the Appeals Commissioners. Nevertheless the Ombudsman has investigated a large number of complaints against the Revenue Commissioners in respect of other matters, for instance delay in sending out tax rebates or statements of allowance and excessive zeal in investigating suspected evasion.[141] He has also investigated complaints against the Customs and Excise area, at a time where there was no appeal in respect of the area.

9–63   Likewise, despite the existence of An Bord Pleanála, the Ombudsman is not shut out in the case of procedural or other incidental matters, in relation to planning. Examples include a local planning authority's failure to inform applicants on how to apply for a refund of a planning fee[142] and failure to inform complainants of a local authority decision so that they were not in time to appeal to An Bord Pleanála.[143] Another category relates to access to planning files: complaints have arisen when files have not been made available to a member of the public or where papers are not in the file, or if a person who wants a copy of document from a planning file is charged an exorbitant fee.[144]

9–64   Another field in which (despite the confinement to "administrative functions" mentioned earlier) the Ombudsman has heard many complaints concerns planning enforcement. This is "the Cinderella area of planning with very few local authorities prepared to allocate the resources needed to curb unauthorised development ...".[145] During the building boom, the Ombudsman remarked:

> "... [W]hat is being lost sight of is the very real adverse effect that building development can have on persons living in the neighbourhood of such developments ... Very many local authority planning sections are understaffed. As a result, the emphasis is on processing applications for planning permissions as opposed to policing breaches of planning permissions ... I find there is a marked reluctance on the part of local authorities to take

---

[140] For an example of an appeals officer's decision being effectively overturned on the merits by way of a recommendation to the chief appeals officer, see 2005 Report, pp.11–12. Notice that s.5(1)(a)(iii) is fortified by s.1(1) which defines "action" to include "decision" and s.1(2) which defines "Department of State" "to include not only a Minster but also his officers", i.e. civil servants. See also, s.5(2).
[141] Compare 2001 Report, pp.39–40.
[142] 1992 Report, pp.69–72.
[143] 1991 Report, p.39.
[144] 2003 Report, p.32. See also, 2005 Report, p.30, noting that the charge for photocopying planning documents varies significantly from one local authority to another and had reached as much as €1 per A4 sheet in Mayo.
[145] 2003 Report, p.32; 2001 Report, pp.8, 20; 2002 Report, p.28.

developers to court. Local authorities have discretion [which] ... is very frequently exercised in favour of the developer."[146]

9–65 More generally, the Ombudsman has remarked that he has an important role in maintaining public confidence in the planning system, going on to describe a complaint in which a complainant, refused planning permission, had discovered a letter on the file from a public representative who had quite independently of the complainant written to the Council "please keep me advised of any relevant developments re P.P. Ref. No ...". The complainant believed the case had been discussed with officials of the local authority and was convinced this had influenced the outcome. Following a thorough examination, the Ombudsman concluded that the public representative had played no role in the decision to refuse planning permission. However, he also noted that in the circumstances "this might not have been clear to a member of the public reading the planning file. Public representatives are of course entitled to make representations ... but local authorities must ensure ... its procedures for dealing with public representatives provide for maximum transparency".[147]

9–66 The "third party" difficulty[148] was (unusually) acknowledged in one of the many planning cases in which it arose. This occurred when the developer stated that, although he proposed to build in accordance with an existing permission, he had modified the plans. Although there was no fresh permission, the Council accepted the revised plans on the basis of what the Ombudsman called "the *de minimis* rule, *viz.* that the law does not concern itself with trivialities. Under this rule local authorities permit the alteration of accepted plans where the alterations are seen as minor". However, the Ombudsman concluded that, in reality, the changes were by no means minor. But the snag lay in what action to recommend, given the interest of the developer:

"I reluctantly accepted that, as the Council had given written approval for the development, its chances of success in an action to prevent the developer from proceeding would be weak. In any event, the house had been substantially completed by the time my examination began. But as a result of the Council's decision, third parties, including the complainant, were deprived of their statutory right to object to the development and to appeal to An Bord Pleanála. As it was not possible to restore these rights to the individuals concerned, the Council offered compensation of £200 to them, a figure which I accepted as reasonable in the particular circumstances involved ... I will take a very critical approach in future if similar practices come to light."[149]

9–67 (3) The Ombudsman does not have jurisdiction over actions relating to "national security or military activity or (in the opinion of the Ombudsman) arrangements regarding participation in organisations of states or governments"; "the administration of the law relating to aliens or naturalisation"; or the exercise of

---

[146] 2000 Report, pp.6–7. The 2009 Report, p.15, promises a special report into a complaint against Meath County Council about unauthorised developments.
[147] 2003 Report, pp.31–32.
[148] See H & M, paras 9–108 to 9–110.
[149] 1999 Report, p.31. For discussion of the law implicit in the statement made by the Ombudsman in the first sentence of this extract, see Ch.19 on Legitimate Expectations.

the power of pardon and the administration of prisons or other similar institutions.[150] In addition, the Ombudsman is forbidden to investigate recruitment or appointment to any of the bodies listed in Sch.1[151] (in other words, as a civil servant or other category of public servant).

9–68   (4) A Minister of the Government may prevent or restrain the Ombudsman from investigating any action of that Minister's Department (or of a person "whose business and functions are comprised" in that Department) simply by making a written request to that effect, setting out in full the reasons for the request.[152] The safeguard, which is designed to prevent Ministers from drawing too freely on this blank cheque, is publicity: not only must the communication to the Ombudsman be in writing, but it must be passed on by the Ombudsman to the complainant and must also be recorded in the reports which the Ombudsman has to lay before the Oireachtas.[153] This device has not yet been used.

9–69   (5) The Ombudsman has a jurisdiction not to hear a complaint if he considers that it is "trivial or vexatious"; that the complainant has not exhausted his local remedies; or that the subject matter of the complaint has been, is being, or will be, sufficiently investigated in another investigation by the Ombudsman.[154] In addition, the complaint must be made within 12 months of the time of the action or—and this could be a significant extension—the time when the complainant became aware of the complaint, whichever is the later. However, an exception to this rule may be allowed where "it appears to the Ombudsman that special circumstances make it proper to do so".[155]

D. Appraisal

9–70   It is instructive to characterise the Ombudsman as a form of "alternative dispute resolution" in the public law field. The somewhat fluid or elusive character of the Office is captured in the following remark:

> "My Office variously finds itself acting as conciliator, as facilitator, as investigator, as presenter of complainants' cases, as enabler ... Of course, ultimately, my Office must take a view on the merits of the particular complaint. In seeking solutions to the problems presented in complaints

---

[150]   Section 5(1)(b), (e)(i), (ii) and (iii). The 2008 Bill s.8 adjusts s.5 to take account of the other changes in the 2008 Bill.

[151]   Section 5(1)(c).

[152]   Section 5(3). 321 *Dáil Debates* Cols 867–869 (May 28, 1980). See also, All-Party Report, ss. II, VII.

[153]   Sections 5(3), 6(7).

[154]   Section 4(5), (6). The rule regarding local remedies is reformulated in the 2008 Bill s.6.

[155]   Section 5(1), proviso. In addition, the action must not have taken place before the commencement of the Act (s.5(1)(g)). The Act was brought into force on July 7, 1983, by statutory order, made under s.12(2). Section 5(2) provides that notwithstanding the time limits in the text, the Ombudsman may "investigate insurability and entitlement to benefit under the Social Welfare Acts 1952 to 1979" (now the Social Welfare (Consolidation) Act 1993: see 1993 Act s.3(9)). Even apart from specific provision the Ombudsman observes a general "continuing effect" doctrine by which he is prepared to investigate circumstances or facts occurring before the time limit, if these are relevant to decisions taken after the time limit.

the ultimate step is a written investigation report with formal findings and recommendations. This arises in a small minority of cases only. The vast majority of complaints are concluded on the basis of a relatively informal, but nonetheless fair, procedure. The methodology of the Office in seeking the conciliatory resolution of disputes where possible is in sharp contrast with the adversarial nature of the courts. In addition where the complaint centres on an issue of fairness rather than of legality, the Office may provide a remedy not available at law."[156]

9–71   The Ombudsman has been deliberately designed to effect as little change as possible in existing constitutional relationships: there has, for instance, been no alteration in the relationship between the individual public servant, the State and a member of the public affected by an official action. The 1980 Act contains no provision making the State or a public servant liable where there was no liability before 1980. The major conceptual innovation introduced by the Act is to provide a remedy against the public body in the case of maladministration, even if this falls short of a breach of law. The emphasis is on compensation and not punishment. The legislation is not designed to pillory or even identify the "guilty" public servant, assuming (as will often not be the case) that there is a single culprit.

Ombudsman compared with the courts

9–72   Professor Bradley has written about the British Ombudsman[157]:

"I am in no doubt that the Ombudsman's methods enable him to get closer to reconstructing the administrative history of a citizen's case than does High Court procedure."

The reasons for this assessment apply in Ireland too. These reasons include the facts that the Ombudsman follows an inquisitorial, flexible and private process of inquiry with unrestricted access to departmental files, that this usually occurs in a non-confrontational milieu; and that the investigators are almost all themselves former public servants.[158] Finally, the system for devising a remedy—the interplay of recommendation from the Ombudsman and response from the public body[159]—is more likely to yield a result satisfactory to all parties than would the polarised concepts administered in a court.

9–73   Successive Ombudsmen have seen themselves as the tribune of the people.

---

[156] 1999 Report, p.10.
[157] "Role of Ombudsman in Relation to Citizens' Rights" (1980) C.L.J. 304 at 322. See 1989 Report, p.30.
[158] See, e.g. 1992 Report, p.1: "Examining files is a long and painstaking process; but it is a task for which the staff of my Office are specially prepared. The key leading to a solution may sometimes be found only after files have been examined several times. If there is a flaw in a case, however, it is unlikely to escape the attention of a number of examiners. One case was recently brought to the office which had remained unresolved over a period of six years. In this time, social workers, a doctor, a priest, a solicitor and public representatives had become involved, without success. When it was brought to the attention of my office, and the files were examined, it emerged that one crucial piece of evidence had been overlooked throughout the period. When this evidence was pinpointed, the case was quickly resolved."
[159] Ombudsman Act 1980 ss.6–8.

The Irish version of the Ombudsman is "Fear a Phobal" (literally, "the Man of the People") although the translation used in the Act is simply "Ombudsman".[160] The Office of Ombudsman has been deliberately designed and utilised to promote maximum usage, with a high public profile. Publications are attractively presented and the annual reports over-represent successful applicants.[161] Public bodies have been censured where they have failed to provide web site information regarding Ombudsman contact details.[162]

9–74   In contrast to a court, the Ombudsman is a self-starter. She may for instance perceive an administrative error which is different from the one about which the complainant is complaining. In one such case, the Ombudsman was sent a letter by a mother complaining about the assessment of means for the purposes of a higher education grant in respect of her son. This contained a passing reference to the fact that the daughter had been unable to avail of a *Trí Gaeilge* scholarship because she wished to study medicine and the written scholarship rules did not include medicine; yet there was an unwritten rule which allowed for the scholarship to be paid to medical students. The Ombudsman pursued this point without being asked.

9–75   Where the Ombudsman upholds a complaint, the Ombudsman's recommendation may, in appropriate circumstances, require the public body to carry out a review of similar cases to that of the applicant, in order to see whether any other persons should be entitled to the same remedy.[163] For instance, a

---

[160]   In the 1993 Report, p.54, the Ombudsman opined that "the loss of any social welfare payment for as much as six days can be significant". See also, 1992 Report, pp.14–15. See also, 1992 Report, pp.109–110; 1994 Report, pp.31 and 61.

[161]   As of 1995, the Reports are available on the internet and computer diskette. The 1989 Report, p.71 states that "[t]he cases chosen for this part of my report are mainly cases where I have been successful in having decisions of public servants reversed. I must emphasise that they are not meant to give an unbalanced view of the efficiency or effectiveness of any one organisation. They have been selected purely because they highlight interesting issues and they can be presented fairly and accurately in summary form". The Reports are naturally aimed at a fairly diverse audience, including the public bodies which are under the Ombudsman's surveillance, potential complainants, the news media and commentators. Reports could be improved if their accounts of cases were less factual and more contextual and analytic—so as to give greater guidance.
      For Oireachtas debate, see, e.g. 467 *Dáil Debates* Cols 742–746 (June 20, 1996); 467 *Dáil Debates* Cols 1873–1875 (June 27, 1996). One deputy commented that the complaints to the Ombudsman were low by comparison with the number of callers to the deputy's Constituency Office.
      According to a British writer, Seneviratne, *Ombudsmen in the Public Sector* (Buckingham, Philadelphia: Open University Press, 1994), p.16: "There is a danger that complainants, and the public at large, may have expectations of ombudsmen which are too high. Any publicity about the institution must guard against raising expectations that are unrealistic."

[162]   2008 Report, pp.41–42.

[163]   A good example concerns the developments arising out of the overpayment of local authority house loans investigation. See special report into the matter which was published in July 2000 and laid before the Oireachtas in accordance with s.6(7) of the 1980 Act (Local Authority Housing Loans (Overpayment) Report 2000). This followed individual complaints in 1998 (1998 Report, p.18) and 1999 (1999 Report, p.16).
      See, e.g. 2001 Report, pp.39–40 ("… in view of the large number of people who have approached my Office about this matter, I intend to look at it again, when the legislative proposals have been published"); 2003 Report, pp.24–25 (circular letter sent to all local authorities reminding them that a Council, and not the borrower, bears the cost of legal work in certifying title to a property on which the Council is making a loan) and pp.30–31 (tax refunds totalling €900,000); 2006 Report, pp.13–15 (Health Service entitlements for retired

complaint[164] arose because a charge had been levied in respect of community care home residence. The charge was means tested and it was levied, in this case, on the basis of the income of the resident's spouse's means, rather than the resident's own resources. This was unlawful and the Ombudsman recommended a refund, which amounted to €8,300. In addition, the HSE was requested to initiate a review of other persons in a similar position. As a result, 81 such cases were discovered and refunds totalling €400,000 made.

Maladministration and the law

9–76   As has been demonstrated throughout this chapter, to assert that the Ombudsman and the courts are involved in different types of regulation in that the Ombudsman is concerned with "maladministration" whereas the courts deal with judicial review or causes of action is merely playing with words.[165] Indeed, so far from its being the Ombudsman's business "to operate beyond the frontier where the law stops"[166] (e.g. rudeness or delay), a substantial number of the complaints for which he has provided a remedy could have come before a court. In part, this is because during the past three or so decades, the rising tide of public law has engulfed the island of "maladministration". This coincidence can be demonstrated by reference to: legitimate expectations[167]; the liability of public authorities[168]; the *audi alteram partem* rule[169]; taking irrelevant factors into account[170]; failing to implement the ruling in a High Court case[171]; and the duty to give reasons for decisions[172]—each of which has been the subject of both Ombudsman and court decisions. In some cases, it is only in terminology that there is a difference from a court.

Fair procedure/constitutional justice and the Ombudsman

9–77   We are not here going into the Public Service Ombudsman's procedure: he has always taken care to avoid identifying the particular public servants responsible for an act of maladministration so as to minimise the chance of constitutional justice being invoked. However in the case of Ombudsmen who investigate complaints against commercial or private entities, judicial review to enforce fair procedure has been sought. The principal authority is *Davy v Financial Services Authority*.[173]

Irish public servants living abroad; apart from the original complainant, refunds made to 51 other families).

[164]   2008 Report, para.6.4.2; 2009 Report, p.12.

[165]   See further, Craig, *Administrative Law*, 3rd edn (London: Sweet & Maxwell, 2008), pp.139–141; Crawford (1985) *Public Law* 246 at 262.

[166]   A phrase used by Professor Wade in the 1967 and 1971 editions of *Administrative Law* but not in later editions.

[167]   See 1985 Report, p.55; 1987 Report, pp.13, 17, 75, 80, 81, 88 and 96; 1988 Report, pp.39, 70, 78; 1989 Report, pp.82 and 86; 2009 Report, pp.55–56.

[168]   See 1989 Report, p.93—recipient of a grant complained that renovations which a council engineer certified, for the purposes of the grant, to have been completed, were unsatisfactory. ("Council decided, while not accepting any liability in the case, to pay £1,000 to cover any possible defects in the work.") See also, p.372.

[169]   See 1989 Report, p.41.

[170]   1996 Report, p.27.

[171]   1996 Report, pp.14–15.

[172]   See 1988 Report, p.88; 1985 Report, p.23; and 1997 Report, p.27.

[173]   [2008] 2 I.L.R.M. 507 (HC); [2010] IESC 30; [2010] 3 I.R. 324.

The facts were that, following a complaint by a credit union against the applicant (who was, in the words of the judgment, a "stockbroker"), the Financial Services Ombudsman had made a finding against the applicant. In the instant judicial review proceedings, the applicant made a number of points; but we shall focus on those which could apply to all Ombudsmen.[174] First, it was contended successfully that it was unfair of the Ombudsman to have refused its requests for discovery of communications from the complainant to the Ombudsman. Giving judgment for the Supreme Court, Finnegan J. held that[175]:

> "Procedures before the Ombudsman are to be informal. The discovery process of the Courts is not to be imported into these procedures. However access to documents may be necessary in the interests of fairness to enable a party to establish or answer a complaint. It is within the Ombudsman's power to require a complainant to produce documents in the light of the information before him and determine whether the documents are necessary to enable a financial service provider to deal with the complaint. In the present case the request was couched in very wide terms: none, some or indeed all of the documents may be necessary if [the applicant] is not to be unfairly disadvantaged. The Ombudsman must consider the request in this light and where fairness so demands, he should direct that documents be furnished."

9–78   Secondly, while the relevant legislation did not contemplate a full oral hearing, it was conceded by the Ombudsman that he did have power to direct an oral hearing. And the Supreme Court ruled that, in the circumstances, "... the calling of experts on each side is an undesirable feature of a proceeding which is designed by an Act of the Oireachtas to be informal and expeditious. At times, however, it may be inescapable and it seems to me that this may be one of them".[176] In *Davy*, the critical fact was that the officers of the Credit Union to whom the complainant Financial Services Provider had given oral advice should be made available for cross-examination, because there was controversy as to what had been said at an oral interview.

9–79   Thirdly, in his ruling, the Ombudsman had referred to his own experience of credit unions. The applicant contended that it was unfair of the Ombudsman to draw on his own knowledge. Finnegan J. rejected the need for this scrupulous and contentious aspect of constitutional justice[177]:

---

[174] There were a number of other points which are particular to the Financial Services Ombudsman, identified in H & M, paras 9–96 to 9–99.

[175] [2010] IESC 30 at 39.

[176] [2010] IESC 30 at 42–43. See also, High Court, [2007] 2 I.L.R.M. 507 at paras 24, 52.
        See also, *Murray v Trustees of Irish Airlines* [2007] 2 I.L.R.M. 196 in which, although the Pensions Ombudsman's refusal to hold an oral hearing was not challenged, Kelly J. did remark obiter, at 199: "It is not every case that requires an oral hearing. The ombudsman has a well-publicised policy on the topic. He will only hold an oral hearing in [specified]cases ...
        Over and above these conditions, the ombudsman reserves an entitlement to hold an oral hearing, if he considers that it is right and proper to do so."

[177] [2010] IESC 30 at p.44. The relevant legislation is the Central Bank Act 1942 Pt VIIB (as inserted by s.16 of the Central Bank and Financial Services Authority of Ireland Act 2004). For a more general discussion of the scrupulous rule mentioned in the text, see further, paras 14–25 and 14–32.

"I note that [the legislation] dealing with the appointment of the Ombudsman ... provides that the [Financial Services Ombudsman] Council shall appoint ... a suitably qualified person, presumably a person with knowledge and experience of the financial services sector. It must be presumed that in carrying out [his] functions [he] will avail of such knowledge and experience and, if ... so, any decision [he reached] would not automatically be condemned as a breach of fair procedures."

9–80 The final argument made by the applicant concerned the fact that, in reaching his finding against the applicant, the Ombudsman had not identified the specific statutory ground on which the complaint was found to be substantiated. Here the applicant was drawing on the general law relating to reasons, which is considered at Chapter 14, Part D. This argument was rejected but only on the basis that, in line with that law, since the applicant had not applied to the Ombudsman to enquire which ground had been relied upon, the applicant had not been prejudiced by this omission.

9–81 This may or may not be a significant case, so far as the Public Service Ombudsman is concerned. Whilst there are some references in the judgment to the need to respect the fact that, in general, an Ombudsman operates informally and the Supreme Court reversed the High Court on some points, the concern shown for the conventional legalities of administrative law, is striking. However, it by no means follows that the same would be true in respect of the Public Service Ombudsman. In principle, there is no reason why it should not be followed. Yet, in practice, judges are not used to deploying fair procedure to protect public bodies and might lean against doing so (unless an investigation, unusually, involved the reputation of an identified public servant). And there is a flavour of this in McMahon J.'s observation in *Square Capital v Financial Services*[178]:

"... the office of the Ombudsman is different from an ordinary court and the provisions of the legislation ... mean that the Ombudsman has greater flexibility and choice in fashioning an appropriate remedy ... The relevant provision enables him, for example, to mitigate or change the conduct complained of ... [I]t is important, therefore that appropriate latitude should be given to the Ombudsman in determining the appropriate remedy ...".

9–82 While in this case, the specific issue was the remedy, it is suggested that the character of the Ombudsman is such that the dictum can be given a wider interpretation. Further, there is a significant point of distinction between the FSO and the (Public Service) Ombudsman in that the latter makes only recommendations (though in other areas—see para.14–117—this sort of argument has not been allowed much purchase).

The Ombudsman's general reforming role

9–83 Prevention is better than cure. A significant part of the Ombudsman's focus now goes on trying to improve the general level of public administration, with an individual complaint being used as a springboard to encourage general reform. As

---

[178] [2010] 2 I.R. 514. The quotation is at para.55.

with the individual cases, many of these changes will be of most benefit to the poorer sections of the community. This is appropriate since other, better-off groups are often well-equipped to make their own representations to the administrative machine, for example, accountants' organisations lobbying the Revenue Commissioners for extra-statutory concessions or farmers' groups negotiating with the Department of Agriculture in regard to grants.

9–84   There are two broad aspects. The first is that the Ombudsman has encouraged public bodies to develop and publicise their own internal complaints procedure,[179] so that, when complaints do arise, they are dealt with within the public body in which they occur[180]; thereby honouring the traditional legal axiom, "exhaust your local remedy first". The Ombudsman has a second role, namely to act as a critic and catalyst to encourage general improvement in administrative law structures and practices[181]; "I will always highlight ... systemic weakness as, once corrected, they can lead to long term improvements in service across a range of public bodies."[182] She has published lists of legislative policy changes which have come about partly, or entirely, as a result of recommendations of the Ombudsman.[183] The following five examples illustrate constitutional, or at least far-reaching, principles which the Ombudsman has supported:

> (i)   The Ombudsman was early in the fray[184] (which culminated in *Re Article 26 and the Health (Amendment) (No. 2) Bill 2004*)[185] in relation to the unlawful deductions from certain pension books of those in publicly funded residential homes, despite the fact that they had a statutory entitlement to free in-patient services under the Health Acts.
>
> (ii)   The Ombudsman has a long-held objection, on which see paras 9–20 to 9–22, to secondary legislation, because it is not scrutinised by the Houses of the Oireachtas.[186]

---

[179]   1985 Report, p.30; 1987 Report, p.34; 1996 Report, p.24. See also, 1994 Report, p.42 (appointment of a Premium Rate Service Regulator); 2004 Report, p.5.

[180]   In 1998, the Ombudsman published a guide to internal complaints systems, *Settling Complaints*. See also, 1998 Report, p.28; 2002 Report, pp.5, 32–33; 2004 Report, pp.23–25; 2006 Report, pp.29–30. In her 2004 Report, p.24, the Ombudsman announced that she would "produce no more than one or two such reports each year". The first body to come under the microscope was the newly established Health Service Executive (Report by the Ombudsman, *Complaints Against the Health Service Executive*, March 2006).

[181]   See, e.g. 1994 Report, pp.1–5.

[182]   1996 Report, p.16.

[183]   e.g. 2006 Report, pp.34–37; 1999 Report, pp.13–14; 1996 Report, pp.19–20; 1993 Report, pp.9–16; 1989 Report, p.16; 2006 Report, pp.32–33 (accountability). For other examples, see Third Edition, pp.391–393.

[184]   1989, 1992; and 2004 Report, pp.29–30; *Report on Nursing Home Subventions* (2001). See also, 2002 Report, pp.21–22 (application by health board of wrong set of regulations to a nursing home patient). In a similar case, a complainant's late husband had incurred a hospital bill of £120. The complainant was the recipient of a pension from the North Eastern Health Board. The Board deducted £20 a fortnight from her pension to make up the amount owed by her late husband. The complainant protested that this was a matter between the Board and her late husband's estate but the Board wrote her that it would be "incongruous" to pay her pension in full while the debt was outstanding. On the intervention of the Ombudsman, the monies deducted were repaid.

[185]   [2005] 1 I.R. 105.

[186]   In his *Report on Nursing Home Subventions* (January 2001), the Ombudsman complained that the regulations at issue were drawn up not with regard to the dictates of good administrative

(iii) In a serious example of malfeasance, Galway County Council had a policy of refusing to accept representations from anyone other than elected members of Galway County Council and not, for instance, from a lower-tier councillor in County Galway. The Ombudsman criticised this practice as conferring an "unfair advantage" on its own elected members and had no doubt that it was an "abuse of the democratic process" aimed at reducing competition from would-be elected representatives.[187] The Council ceased the practice on the Ombudsman's intervention.[188]

(iv) "[A]nother area in which the failure of legislation to keep pace with actual circumstances may give rise to unfairness is that of tax relief for medical expenses".[189] This statement was the lead-in to the upholding of a complaint regarding the refusal of tax relief for the cost of psychotherapy. The Ombudsman also criticised the Finance Bill 2000 for its failure to contain a proposal to this effect.[190]

(v) As can be seen at paras 9–64 to 9–65, the Ombudsman has taken a particular interest in local authorities' failure to enforce planning controls.

9–85 In such ways, the Ombudsman makes a contribution to upholding the Rule of Law, in a modern administrative state.

---

practice or principles of statutory interpretation but to cut the administrative cloth to suit the financial measure. The Ombudsman commented: "The report raises serious issues in regard to the relationship, on the one hand, between the Oireachtas and the Executive and, on the other, the relationships within the Executive between the political and administrative levels. These issues include the effective vetting of secondary legislation, the relationship between Ministers and senior civil servants, the funding of entitlements and human rights issues in relation to the elderly": 2000 Report, pp.12, 37.

[187] 2000 Report, pp.9–10; 2001 Report, p.9. A related example was in the reception of representations from members of the public. Leitrim County Council, for example, had adopted a policy of replying only to representations from elected members of the Council or other elected officials within the Sligo/Leitrim constituency: 2000 Report, pp.9–10.

[188] 2000 Report, pp.9–10.

[189] 1999 Report, pp.27–28.

[190] 1999 Report, pp.27–28. There are a number of other situations where the social welfare or tax code has been deemed to discriminate against married couples or cohabitees, for instance 1999 Report, pp.23, 28. At the same citation, there is a criticism of social welfare legislation for its outdated assumptions regarding the nature of part-time employment.

CHAPTER 10

FUNDAMENTAL PRINCIPLES OF JUDICAL REVIEW I

10–01   In the earlier editions of this book, what is now Chapters 10 and 11 formed a single chapter. The equivalent in this work would have been unbearably long. The present chapter accordingly deals with the central spine of judicial review, namely ultra vires and its seed, breed and generation. This leaves over to Chapter 11 some other topics relevant to the judicial review process before the High Court; as well as certain topics of substantive judicial review, which are not particular to constitutional justice or the control of discretionary powers and so have no home in specialised chapters on those subjects.

A. The Doctrine of Ultra Vires

Common law powers

10–02   The following elementary points should be made. First, public bodies are often endowed by statute with the legal power to perform certain acts which is not given to ordinary private persons. Examples include the power to make regulations, issue licences under statute and to make grants. As will be seen presently, the ultra vires doctrine requires that in exercising those powers, the public body may not go beyond the limits (vires) fixed, explicitly or implicitly, by the empowering statute. In addition, however, to these specific and special powers, public bodies will usually also enjoy what are sometimes (for shorthand) described as "common law powers" in that these powers are not bestowed by statute and are common to public bodies and ordinary citizens.[1] These powers include, for example, the power to make contracts, employ staff, hold land, sue and be sued and borrow or spend money. In some cases, these powers exist simply by virtue of the fact that the public body enjoys (artificial) legal personality.[2] However, despite what has

---

[1]   The terms "express", "implied" and "common law" are used to describe the three categories of powers. There may be overlaps between the three and we recognise that others may prefer to employ different terminology. However, for the avoidance of confusion, we confine ourselves to the three terms listed.

[2]   For a helpful discussion, see *Halsbury's Laws of England*, 4th edn (London: Butterworths,

just been said, in some cases, the Oireachtas prefers to ensure that these powers are explicitly spelt out in the constituent statute.[3]

10–03 Even in the case of "common law" powers, the public body will usually only be empowered to perform a legal action, so far as this is necessary to its statutory objectives or reasonably incidental thereto. Thus, in *Doherty v South Dublin County Council*,[4] although the Equality Authority had no statutory power to act as an amicus curiae in a judicial review of the provision of accommodation for members of the travelling community, Fennelly J. was satisfied, having regard to the Authority's mandate, that such an action would fall "well within the scope of the general power of the Authority".[5]

10–04 To return to a public body's statutory powers, up to the 1980s at least, it was generally accepted that the constitutional foundation for judicial review was (apart from error of law on the face of the record[6]) the ultra vires doctrine. Subsequently, in many common law jurisdictions, there has been a definite change in doctrine and practice, which is usually put under the slogan of "a rights-based approach", which we shall consider briefly in Part B.

10–05 The High Court possesses an inherent jurisdiction to supervise the activities of inferior courts,[7] tribunals and other public authorities. This is implemented by way of the ultra vires doctrine. To put briefly, something which is elaborated on below, the doctrine means that the power of review may be exercised only in circumstances where the inferior body has exceeded its jurisdiction. In other words, the High Court is not concerned with the merits, but rather with the legality, of the decision under review. To mention a point of terminology: the language of vires is used when the entity whose decision is under review is a Minister, local authority or other administrative agency; whereas the equivalent concept for a tribunal or lower court is "jurisdiction". But frequently the terms are used interchangeably.

10–06 The leading authorities do not disclose a governing principle which facilitates the classification of errors as "jurisdictional" as opposed to being within jurisdiction and consequently—unless they appear on the face of the record[8]— immune from correction. Because we are dealing with statutory powers, at least traditionally, the common law doctrine of ultra vires is based on the artifice of

---

2001), Vol.1(1). For some of these points in the context of local government, see paras 5–57 to 5–60.

[3] See, e.g. Local Government Act 2001 s.11.

[4] [2006] IESC 57; [2007] 1 I.R. 246.

[5] *Doherty v South Dublin County Council* [2006] IESC 57; [2007] 1 I.R. 246 at 256. Fennelly J. also rejected (at 256) the suggestion that the power was "merely ancillary or incidental".

[6] See below, Part G.

[7] The inferior courts are the District Court, the Circuit Court and the Special Criminal Court. The High Court, Court of Criminal Appeal and the Supreme Court are all superior courts of record and are not subject to judicial review: see *People (DPP) v Quilligan (No. 2)* [1989] I.R. 46 at 57 per Henchy J. and *Blackall v Grehan* [1995] 3 I.R. 208. But the Supreme Court retains an inherent jurisdiction to revisit and set aside its own judgments in exceptional circumstances: see, e.g. *Re Greendale Developments (No. 3)* [2000] 2 I.R. 514; *P v P* [2001] IESC 76; [2002] 1 I.R. 219; *Abbeydrive Developments Ltd v Kildare County Council (No.2)* [2010] IESC 8. Cf. the interesting case of *R. v Bow Street Magistrates Ex p. Pinochet (No. 2)* [1999] UKHL 1; [2000] 1 A.C. 119.

[8] See generally, paras 10–101 to 10–105.

statutory interpretation.[9] This body of law includes the court's presumption that the Oireachtas did not intend that the donee of a statutory power should exercise that power in an unfair or arbitrary fashion.[10] Thus, the courts will intervene not only to restrain administrative action which contravenes some express statutory provision, but also where some implied condition of the Act—for instance, adherence to the rules of constitutional justice, or the doctrine of reasonableness—has been infringed.

10–07 The modern tendency has been to increase the range of errors which affect the jurisdiction of administrative bodies and lower courts, almost to the point where all errors of law are assumed to destroy that jurisdiction. But this tendency—which is doubtless prompted by a judicial desire to protect the citizen against legally unjustifiable administrative actions—is often at odds with the legislative policy of allocating tasks to a specialised public body, which is trusted to deal with (possibly) thousands of routine cases.

10–08 In view of this tension, and given the inherent difficulty in distinguishing satisfactorily between matters bearing on the merits and those relating to vires (or jurisdiction), the entire doctrine of jurisdictional review has become increasingly artificial and complex. It may be useful, therefore, in paras 10–09 to 10–16, to separate out by way of introduction the seven heads of judicial review. Three of these heads—(a), (b) and (c)—will be examined here. The other four heads will only be mentioned in this Part since three of them—(d), (e) and (f)—will be dealt with more extensively elsewhere in this book and the fourth—(g)—falls more properly into the field of constitutional law. It should be emphasised too that, as we shall see when we turn to Parts E and F, the troubled borderline between jurisdiction and merits (para.10–56) applies to each of areas (a) to (d). (As noted, there is one other ground of judicial review—error on the face of the record—which is not based on jurisdiction or ultra vires and, consequently, is left over until Part G.)

(a) Conditions precedent to jurisdiction

10–09 An administrative authority can exercise its powers only over subject matter which falls within the description, as to law, facts and circumstances, specified in the authority's field of competence. For example, in *Keogh v Galway Corporation*[11] Carney J. quashed a purported amendment to a development plan: the amendments were "material", in the language of the legislation, and the respondents had failed to comply with their statutory duty[12] to publish in Iris Oifigiúil and in one newspaper circulating in the area. Again, where the error is one on a point of fact, its existence must be established before the authority has power to act. Thus if the facts in question are truly collateral or pre-conditions to jurisdiction, their existence can and will be reviewed in judicial review proceedings. As Keane J. commented in *Killeen v Director of Public Prosecutions*, "[i]t is clearly not possible for any tribunal, including the District Court, upon which a particular jurisdiction has been

---

[9]   See below, Part D.
[10] The presumption is capable of being overridden where the unconstitutionality is plain on the face of the statute. See *Loftus v Attorney General* [1979] I.R. 221; *Blehein v Minister for Health and Children* [2008] IESC 40; [2009] 1 I.R. 275.
[11] [1995] 3 I.R. 457.
[12] As imposed by the Local Government (Planning and Development) Act 1963 s.21A(2).

conferred by statute ... to extend or confine the boundaries of that jurisdiction by an erroneous determination of fact".[13] Moreover it is no answer for the deciding body to plead that its conclusion as to whether it had jurisdiction is a reasonable one, albeit incorrect, for the reviewing court must make a *de novo* assessment of whether the fact existed.[14] On the other hand, if the deciding authority correctly satisfies the statutory pre-conditions as to jurisdiction, its subsequent conclusions on mixed questions of law and fact will not lightly be disturbed, especially if the body in question is a specialist one.[15]

(b) Correct authority

10–10 A sub-species of the rule that all conditions precedent must be fulfilled prior to the exercise of statutory power is that the power may only be exercised by the administrative authority in which it was vested by the Oireachtas. One aspect of this is the *delegatus non potest delegare* principle[16]: a power may only be delegated to a body or person other than that designated by the Oireachtas if this is authorised, expressly or by implication, by the legislation in question.[17] If a particular power is delegated, it must be exercised by the delegate and not some other person. Other good examples of "correct authority" include *State (Walshe) v Murphy*,[18] in which a conviction was invalidated because, on appointment, the District Justice had not practised as a solicitor for the number of years specified in the Courts (Supplemental Provisions) Act 1961. Again, in *Thompson v Minister for Social Welfare*,[19] O'Hanlon J. quashed a decision of a social welfare appeals officer, as that officer had not sat with the two assessors required by s.298(12) of the Social Welfare (Consolidation) Act 1981 and the appellant had not consented to this course of action. Next, in *Hegarty v Governor of Limerick Prison*,[20] Geoghegan J. held that orders made by an irregularly constituted Special Criminal Court were invalid. Finally, in *DPP v Hamill*[21] the applicant was charged with an offence under s.7 of the Offences Against the State Act 1939 and was returned for trial to Dublin Circuit Court. However, the Courts (Supplemental Provisions) Act 1961 provides that all offences under s.7 are to be tried in the Central Criminal Court. Accordingly, the return for trial order was quashed by the High Court.

---

[13]   [1998] 1 I.L.R.M. 1 at 8.

[14]   *Shannon Regional Fisheries Board v An Bord Pleanála* [1994] 3 I.R. 449 at 456 per Barr J.; *Lambert v An tÁrd Chláraitheoir* [1995] 2 I.R. 372 at 384 per Kinlen J.; *Radio Limerick One Ltd v Independent Radio and Television Commission* [1997] 2 I.L.R.M. 1. This complex matter is considered further in Part F.

[15]   *Harte v Labour Board* [1996] 2 I.R. 171; *Radio Limerick One Ltd v Independent Radio and Television Commission* [1997] 2 I.L.R.M. 1; *Ryanair v Flynn* [2000] IEHC 36; [2000] 3 I.R. 240 at 265 per Kearns J.; *Scrollside Ltd v Broadcasting Commission of Ireland* [2006] IESC 24; [2007] 1 I.R. 166 at 175 per Denham J; *McCarron v Kearney* [2008] IEHC 195.

[16]   This is considered further in Ch.11, Part E.

[17]   The point is made, slightly obliquely, in *Brennan v Donnellan* [2003] IEHC 58. See also, *Dubsky v Ireland* [2005] IEHC 442; [2007] 1 I.R. 63; *Badri v Refugee Applications Commissioner* [2005] IEHC 452; [2006] 1 I.R. 503 at 513.

[18]   [1981] I.R. 275.

[19]   [1989] I.R. 618.

[20]   [1998] 1 I.R. 412. A Circuit Court judge had continued to sit on the Special Criminal Court following his "de-listing" from that Court, because officials had never informed him that the Government had made the appropriate order under s.39 of the Offences Against the State Act 1939.

[21]   [1999] IEHC 242; [2000] 1 I.L.R.M. 150.

10–11   The capacity of a decision-maker to carry out of his functions may also be relevant under this head, as is clear from *Joyce v Minister for Health*.[22] The chairman of a disciplinary committee of a health board appeared to be inebriated and unwell. The plaintiff, a consultant surgeon, issued proceedings challenging his suspension by this committee, and was granted an interlocutory injunction restraining the entire committee from resuming its hearing. O'Neill J. held in the first place that the plaintiff had an entitlement to have his case considered by a tribunal "all of whose members had the capacity at all times during the course of the hearings and in reaching a conclusion or recommendation, to properly discharge their function".[23] In addition the ordinary reasonable person would not have been confident of the chairman's ability to discharge his function in a fair and competent manner.

(c) *Within the power conferred by statute*

10–12   As mentioned at the start of this chapter, administrative action taken without either express or implied statutory authority will be found to be ultra vires. This head is the purest and most basic aspect of the ultra vires principle. Further examples of its operation are given throughout this chapter. Here the following modern[24] example illustrates the far-flung operation of the principle. In *Eastern Health Board v Farrell*,[25] the respondent coroner was investigating the death of a young man with cerebral palsy. The applicant sought to restrain the coroner from investigating whether the death was linked to a vaccine administered in the man's youth, in order to discover whether it was this which may have caused his mental handicap, without which he would never have suffered the fatal illness. The key provision was s.30 of the Coroners Act 1962, which limits a coroner "to ascertaining the identity of the person in relation to whose death the inquest is being held and how, when and where the death occurred". The question was: did the administration of the vaccine pertain to "how ... the death occurred"? Keane C.J. rejected the possibility of such a wide-ranging inquest as being:

> "... wholly at odds with the general policy underlying the legislation, as reflected in the definition of the circumstances in which a coroner is obliged or entitled to hold an inquest, the restrictions on his powers to summon medical witnesses and the limited financial resources available to him in conducting the inquest."

It was also at odds with the need for inquests to be held "as expeditiously as possible".[26] It is also an aspect of this principle that, where statutory authority has been removed, accidentally or otherwise, the State cannot continue to take action under it.[27]

22   [2004] IEHC 158; [2004] 4 I.R. 293.
23   [2004] IEHC 158; [2004] 4 I.R. 293 at 302.
24   A number of older examples are given in earlier editions. See Third Edition, pp.400–402.
25   [2001] IESC 96; [2001] 4 I.R. 627. See also, *Independent Star Ltd v O'Connor* [2002] IEHC 109; [2002] 4 I.R. 166.
26   [2001] IESC 96; [2001] 4 I.R. 627 at 644. See also, *Serco Services Ireland Ltd v Labour Court (Technical Engineering and Electrical Union)* [2001] IEHC 125; unreported, High Court, July 12, 2001; *Fuller v Minister for Agriculture* [2005] IESC 14; [2005] 1 I.R. 529.
27   *Grealis v DPP* [2001] IESC 50; [2001] 3 I.R. 144; *Cummins v McCartan* [2005] IESC 67; [2005] 3 I.R. 559.

10–13 Finally, we must notice two recent innovations, the first of which has been said to be introduced by the Constitution: in some cases the validity of actions taken without express statutory authority will be upheld on the ground that such actions were necessary to vindicate the personal rights of the citizen as required by Art.40.3.1°. A remarkable instance of this free-standing jurisdiction is supplied by *DG v Eastern Health Board*,[28] where a majority of the Supreme Court upheld a High Court order committing a seriously disturbed—but innocent—juvenile to a penal institution for a short period in the absence of any alternative secure accommodation. Hamilton C.J. held that, in the very special circumstances of the case, the detention was justifiable—even in the absence of any statutory authority for this course of action—as necessary to vindicate the child's welfare.[29]

In addition, it has been held recently[30] that central-level public bodies are endowed with legal powers which flow from the character of the executive organ in a democratic polity. However this novel doctrine has been received with some reserve by the Supreme Court.[31]

(d) Other formal and procedural requirements (Chapter 11, Part B)

10–14 This and the following two topics are the subjects of later chapters, as indicated:

(e) Discretionary powers (Chapter 15)

(f) Constitutional justice (Chapters 12–14)

(g) Unconstitutionality

10–15 The presumption of constitutionality requires that a constitutional interpretation be given to the impugned statutory provisions if this is at all possible. The presumption extends to proceedings, procedures, discretions and adjudications which are permitted, provided for or prescribed by an Act of the Oireachtas and, it means that, in these contexts, a statutory provision is entitled to the presumption:

> "... that what is required, or allowed to be done, for the purpose of its implementation, will take place without breaching any of the requirements, express or implied of the Constitution. If [the donee of the statutory power] exercised his discretion or his powers capriciously, partially or in a manifestly unfair manner it would be assumed that this could not have been contemplated or intended by the Oireachtas and his action would be restrained and corrected by the Courts."[32]

---

[28] [1997] 3 I.R. 511. See also, *N v Health Service Executive* [2006] IESC 60; [2006] 4 I.R. 374; *JH v Clinical Director of Cavan General Hospital* [2007] IEHC 7; [2007] 4 I.R. 242.

[29] The court expressly reasoned that on these facts the court's constitutional duty to protect the child's welfare took precedence over his constitutional right to liberty.

[30] *Prendergast v Higher Education Authority* [2008] IEHC 257; [2009] 1 I.L.R.M. 47. For another executive power case, but this time involving very particular facts, see the immigration case of *Bode v Minister for Justice, Equality and Law Reform* [2007] IESC 62. This new and strange idea is analysed at H & M, paras 10–86 to 10–92.

[31] For an indication of how novel it is, see *Gama Construction (Ireland) Ltd v Minister for Enterprise* [2010] 2 I.R. 85 at paras [24]–[27].

[32] *Loftus v Attorney General* [1979] I.R. 221 at 238–241 per O'Higgins C.J. This is an oft-affirmed

10–16   To elaborate: this presumption has been taken to mean that, where a statute is ambiguous, with one possible meaning which is constitutional and one which is unconstitutional, the courts will choose the former. This will usually have the effect of narrowing the power of a public body and so making its action ultra vires the governing statute under which it was purporting to act. It will also have the happy consequence of avoiding a direct conflict between the legislature and the courts, while, at the same time, keeping the public body under the law. In this context, one might note that the judges have been sharp-eyed in discerning ambiguity, where the untutored may have thought it perfectly clear that such statute was indeed unconstitutional.[33] In summary, the courts have used this principle to hold that the exercise of administrative discretion in an improper fashion,[34] or in a manner contrary to constitutional justice[35] is ultra vires the principal Act, while at the same time upholding the constitutionality of the parent legislation.[36]

B. Present Status of the Ultra Vires Doctrine in Ireland

10–17   The reason for the qualified character of the heading is that here we are offering an Irish view of a debate[37] which has been raging in other common law

---

principle; see, e.g. *Murphy v GM* [2001] IESC 82; [2001] 4 I.R. 113 at 135 per Keane C.J.
[33]   See the comments on *State (Lynch) v Cooney* [1982] I.R. 337. See paras 15–11 to 15–12.
[34]   See, e.g. *Irish Family Planning Association Ltd v Ryan* [1979] I.R. 295; *O'Callaghan v Ireland* [1994] 1 I.R. 555; *Holland v Governor of Portlaoise Prison* [2004] IEHC 97; [2004] 2 I.R. 573; *O'Brien v Personal Injuries Assessment Board (No. 3)* [2008] IESC 71; [2009] 2 I.L.R.M. 22.
[35]   *O'Brien v Bord na Móna* [1983] I.R. 255; *Barry v Medical Council* [1998] 3 I.R. 368; *Murray v Commission to Inquire into Child Abuse* [2004] IEHC 225; [2004] 2 I.R. 222; *Burns v Governor and Company of the Bank of Ireland* [2007] IEHC 318; [2008] 1 I.R. 762.
[36]   In addition, any administrative authority which acts in an unconstitutional fashion will exceed its jurisdiction. See the comments of Henchy J. in *State (Holland) v Kennedy* [1977] I.R. 193 at 201 and *State (Byrne) v Frawley* [1978] I.R. 326 at 345 and those of Walsh J. in *Shelly v Mahon* [1990] 1 I.R. 36 at 45. In *Coughlan v Patwell* [1993] 1 I.R. 31 a District judge was held to have exceeded jurisdiction when he refused to entertain an argument that particular evidence should be excluded for breach of constitutional rights. See also, *O'Brien v Personal Injuries Assessment Board (No. 3)* [2008] IESC 71. Also, acting pursuant to an unconstitutional law will cause a body to exceed its jurisdiction. Examples include *M v An Bord Uchtála* [1975] I.R. 81; *Cox v Ireland* [1992] 2 I.R. 503; *Lovett v Minister for Education* [1997] 1 I.L.R.M. 89; *McCann v Monaghan District Court* [2009] IEHC 276; [2009] 4 I.R. 200.
[37]   Principal protagonists in favour of traditional ultra vires review include Wade and Forsyth, *Administrative Law*, 9th edn (Oxford: OUP, 2004), pp.38–40; Forsyth, "Of Fig Leaves and Fairy Tales: The *Ultra Vires* Doctrine, the Sovereignty of Parliament and Judicial Review" (1996) C.L.J. 122; Elliott, "The Ultra Vires Doctrine in a Constitutional Setting: Still the Central Principle of Administrative Law" (1999) C.L.J 129; Elliott, *The Constitutional Foundations of Judicial Review* (Oxford: OUP, 2001). Principal antagonists include Oliver, "Is the Ultra Vires Rule the Basis of Judicial Review?" (1987) *Public Law* 543; Laws, "Law and Democracy" (1995) *Public Law* 72; Craig, "Ultra Vires and the Foundations of Judicial Review" (1998) C.L.J 63; Craig, "Public Law; Political Theory and Legal Theory" (2000) *Public Law* 211; Joseph, "The Demise of Ultra Vires – Judicial Review in the New Zealand Courts" (2001) *Public Law* 353; Barber, "The Academic Mythologians" (2001) 21 O.J.L.S. 369; and Laws, "Illegality: the Problem of Jurisdiction" in Supperstone, Goudie and Walker (eds), *Judicial Review*, 3rd edn (London: Lexis Nexis, 2005), p.91. A spin-off debate between Craig and Allan about the latter's attempt to reconcile his general theory with constitutional orthodoxy may also be of interest. See Craig and Bamforth, "Constitutional Analysis, Constitutional Principle and Judicial Review" (2001) *Public Law* 763; Allan, "The Constitutional Foundations of Judicial Review: Conceptual Conundrum or Interpretive Inquiry" (2002) 61 C.L.J. 87; Craig,

jurisdictions, especially the United Kingdom, for the past 20 years. Even if, as we do, one takes the view that it is not directly relevant here, one ought to say why this is so and set the debate in its own context. To a large extent, the issue arises out of the wider "British Question" which flows from the UK's lack of a written Constitution and the nineteenth century doctrine of parliamentary sovereignty. Accordingly, we must include a skein of British constitutional history.[38]

10–18   In finding a place in the UK's (unwritten) constitution for judicial review, it was necessary to reconcile the sovereignty of Parliament with the significant amount of political authority which judicial review necessarily vests in the hands of the higher judiciary (however much this may be either concealed or genuinely restricted by the observance of legal principles). In order to achieve this accommodation, in the U K and beyond, for the past nearly two centuries, the central spine from which judicial review has been hung is the ultra vires doctrine. However, by the late twentieth century, in the era of "rights-based jurisprudence", shares in the sovereignty of Parliament were at a discount. The question which jurists in many common law jurisdictions faced was how to reconcile individual rights with the ultra vires doctrine. The new rights-based jurisprudence presumes that there are certain fundamental values, grounded independently of Parliamentary intention, and consequently not susceptible of justification by the ultra vires doctrine. One can attempt a bald summary of this debate as follows.

10–19   First, the "traditionalists"—champions of sovereignty of Parliament—insist that Parliament may, by statute, impose whatever changes it wishes on the principles or details of public administration, while at the same time accepting that "[u]nless Parliament clearly indicates otherwise, it is presumed to intend that decision-makers must apply the principles of good administration drawn from the common law as developed by the Judges in making their decisions".[39] This is often called the "modified ultra vires" approach, which draws heavily on the rule of law as elaborated by judges: "statutory construction is a function of context and ... the rule of law forms a fundamental part of that context".[40]

10–20   The revisionists' response, which is less clear-cut is that judicial review is grounded in the common law and holds a status, even in the unwritten UK constitution which goes beyond the traditional mantra that "the common law exists only as far as it is not uprooted by statute". In particular, judicial review is a central and independent element of government which can be traced back at least to the seventeenth century, that is, to a period before the sovereignty of Parliament achieved its later ascendancy. Thus it is unnecessary to try to cast the values which

"Constitutional Foundations, the Rule of Law and Supremacy" (2003) *Public Law* 92; Allan, "Constitutional Dialogue and the Justification of Judicial Review" (2003) 23 O.J.L.S. 563; Craig, "The Common Law, Shared Power and Judicial Review" (2004) 24 O.J.L.S. 237; Allan, "Legislative Supremacy and Legislative Intent: a Reply to Professor Craig" (2004) 24 O.J.L.S. 563; and Craig, "Legislative Supremacy and Legislative Intention: a Reply to Professor Allan" (2004) 24 O.J.L.S. 583. See also, Forsyth (ed.), *Judicial Review and the Constitution* (Oxford: Hart Publishing, 2000) which reproduces several of the leading articles.

[38]   For an excellent discussion of the key issues see Allison, *The English Historical Constitution: Continuity, Change and European Effects* (Cambridge: Cambridge University Press, 2007).

[39]   Forsyth, "Heat and Light: A Plea for Reconciliation" in Forsyth (ed.), *Judicial Review and the Constitution* (Oxford: Hart Publishing, 2000), p.396.

[40]   Elliott, *The Constitutional Foundations of Judicial Review* (2001), p.111.

judicial review adds to the law as some sort of delegation, by omission, by the legislature. In addition, by today its values are fortified by the international *zeitgeist* in favour of human rights.

10–21   Here is a most important point: the revisionists distinguish between ultra vires in the narrow sense comprehended earlier as heads (a), (b) and (c) that a public body must not do an act that it does not have the legal capacity to do, and the wider sense of ultra vires, as teased out in sub-heads (e)–(g), namely, that a public body must not act unreasonably, in bad faith or without taking relevant factors into account, and must observe fair procedures and constitutional constraints.[41] The correctness of the narrow notion of ultra vires is (perhaps) inevitably accepted by the revisionists. By contrast, their radical contribution is that the last-mentioned requirements—which, as shorthand, we may call principles of good public administration—are to be grounded not on some (largely fictional) assumption about what the legislation intended. Rather, it should be frankly admitted that "courts impose standards of lawful conduct upon public authorities as a matter of common law and it is arguable that the power to impose such standards is a constitutional fundamental".[42]

10–22   This approach naturally leads to the question: "Where do the judges find their authority to do this?" On this issue, some English judges have adopted revisionist positions which a generation ago would be regarded as very radical. In *X Ltd v Morgan-Grampian (Publishers) Ltd*[43] Lord Bridge of Harwich advanced the notion of "twin sovereignties":

> "The maintenance of the rule of law is in every way as important in a free society as the democratic franchise. In our society the rule of law rests upon twin foundations: the sovereignty of the Queen in Parliament in making the law and the sovereignty of the Queen's courts in interpreting and applying the law."[44]

10–23   Lord Woolf of Barnes made similar reference to "twin sovereignties" in *Hamilton v Al Fayed*.[45] He referred to the "wider constitutional principle of mutuality of respect between two constitutional sovereignties",[46] denoting the Queen-in-Parliament and the superior Courts of Justice. A more decisive shift in favour of the courts was suggested in *Jackson v Attorney General*[47]; although Lord Bingham of Cornhill struck a blow for orthodoxy with his expression of the view that parliamentary sovereignty remained the "bedrock" principle of English law,[48] other members of the House strongly hinted in obiter remarks that Parliamentary sovereignty was not absolute and had to be qualified by reference to the rule of

---

[41] Head (d) perhaps has a foot in both camps.
[42] Wade and Bradley, *Constitutional and Administrative Law* (1985), p.594. See also, Joseph "Parliament, the Courts and the Collaborative Enterprise" (2004) 15 *King's College Law Journal* 321 at 329–330.
[43] [1991] 1 A.C. 1.
[44] [1991] 1 A.C. 1 at 48.
[45] [1999] 3 All E.R. 317.
[46] [1999] 3 All E.R. 317 at 320.
[47] [2005] UKHL 56; [2006] 1 A.C. 262.
[48] [2005] UKHL 56; [2006] 1 A.C. 262 at 274.

law. Lord Hope of Craighead, for example, took the view that the rule of law is the central element of the English Constitution:

> "The rule of law enforced by the courts is the ultimate controlling factor on which our constitution is based."[49]

10–24 One might ask in response: how can there be two sovereigns? In reply, Professor Joseph prefers the term "Collaborative Enterprise" and offers the status and arrangement of the (NZ) Bill of Rights Act 1990, on which the (Irish) European Convention on Human Rights Act 2003 is modelled, as a meaningful example of such collaboration.[50]

Relevance in Ireland?

10–25 As useful Irish examples of the values mentioned in sub-heads (e)–(f) which the common law has injected into public administration, we can refer to such presumptions of statutory interpretation as that the legislature does not extend to exclude the jurisdiction of the courts without very clear words indeed. Such presumptions were significant in Ireland, not just before the present era of strong judicial review but even before Independence. They are faithfully and vividly recorded in that early fruit of Irish legal scholarship, AG Donaldson's *Some Comparative Aspects of Irish Law*.[51] This summarises pre-1922 case law, in which legislative provisions, apparently excluding the courts from exercising judicial review ("no certiorari" clauses), were simply not followed.

10–26 However, in contemporary Ireland, there is no need to join in the strenuous contest between the traditionalists and the revisionists. Indeed, the Dublin observer may feel like the superior neighbour with a fancy car in the garage, who looks over the fence to find his neighbours admiring their car because it does not require a starting handle. To put it in simple terms, much of the difficulty which has engaged the attention of contemporary British legal thinkers stems from the need to fit the modern motor of individual rights into a chassis devised for a by-gone century. By contrast, in Ireland, the unequivocal status of the Constitution as a higher law makes it clear that the values which it establishes possess an incontestable status such that statute law must bow before them and there is no need for any sophistry to justify this result. This may explain why there has been little or no mention of the ultra vires debate in Irish judgments or writing.

10–27 However, it is a relevant question to ask: has the contribution of the Constitution given rise to judicial review principles of a different character from those in the UK? The short answer is "no". Undoubtedly, several different Articles of the Constitution have made an impact at a number of points in the

---

[49] [2005] UKHL 56; [2006] 1 A.C. 262 at 304.
[50] See also, Dyzenhaus, Hunt and Taggart, "The Principle of Legality in Administrative Law: Internationalisation and Constitutionalisation" (2001) 1 *Oxford University Commonwealth Law Journal* 5; Allan, *Constitutional Justice: a Liberal Theory of the Rule of Law* (Oxford: OUP, 2001).
[51] (Durham N.C: 1957), Ch.5 "Administrative Law", especially p.209.

public administration system. Here it is sufficient to give only the following examples[52]:

- The extension of procedural protection, in large part because of the establishment of constitutional justice.
- The notion of substantive constitutional values to control discretionary power.
- The use of Art.34.3.1° to prohibit the exclusion of judicial review and to restrain time limits in this field.
- The use of Art.34.1 to restrict executive privilege against the disclosure of official evidence.

10–28   But these significant though ad hoc controls do not add up to a single unifying principle of control of the administration. Rather, each has developed within its own context and usually by building on a substantial foundation already provided by the common law. Thus, for instance, constitutional justice is the offspring of natural justice. But the closest we have come to any coherent unifying principle is the deduction, just mentioned, from Art.34.3.1°, to the effect that judicial review of administrative action cannot be excluded by Act of the Oireachtas. However, the judiciary has not specified the form of judicial review which is protected by Art.34.3.1°. Thus one is left to infer from the silence that it is indeed common law judicial review (with its usual limitations) as traditionally developed here by the Irish and other common law courts. In summary, the Irish system of judicial review remains, in essence, common law ultra vires, coupled with discrete constitutional fortification, in response to particular problems.

C. Implied Powers

10–29   In this Part, we deal with implied (sometimes called "incidental") powers, whose effect is usually to extend the express, statutory powers; whereas, in Part D, we shall consider certain rules of interpretation, whose effect is usually to narrow the scope of the power beyond what a bare, literal, interpretation would have mandated.

10–30   In many of the reported cases, the real issue is whether the impugned administrative action is so closely related to the express powers that it falls within the implied powers envisaged by statute. The general rule remains that stated by Lord Selborne in *Attorney General v Great Eastern Railway Co*[53]:

"Whatever may fairly be regarded as incidental to or consequential upon, those things which the legislature has authorised, ought not (unless expressly prohibited) to be held by judicial construction to be *ultra vires*."[54]

---

[52]   For a fuller list, see paras 2–32 to 2–34.
[53]   (1880) 5 App. Cas. 473.
[54]   (1880) 5 App. Case 473 at 478. See also, *In re the Worth Library* [1995] 2 I.R. 301 (health board's express power "to acquire any estate or interest in land" extends to an implied power to become the custodian of a library).

In more recent times, it has been suggested that a such power "... could only ever be implied where (1) that is justified by the statutory context; (2) the power contended for is not of such a nature that one would expect to see it set out specifically and (3) the power contended for is consistent with the statutory scheme".[55]

10–31 A simple example of the doctrine in action is *Moke v Refugee Applications Commissioner*.[56] Here, the respondent did not accept an asylum seeker's claim that he was under the age of 18. However, there was no express statutory provision permitting the respondent to make an assessment as to the applicant's age. Finlay Geoghegan J. was satisfied, however, that because of the "explicit power and duty to inform the Health Service Executive of the arrival of an unaccompanied child under the age of 18 years" the Commissioner had as a consequence "the power to determine whether a person who claims to be a child under the age of 18 years and not in the custody of any person is such".[57]

10–32 A recent Supreme Court decision points in a slightly different direction from classical theory. In *Edobor v Refugee Appeals Tribunal*,[58] a member of the respondent Tribunal, to whom a number of appeals had been assigned, had failed to make decisions after holding oral hearings in two cases, even though a significant amount of time (a year, and 10 months, respectively) had elapsed since the hearings. The member had, in fact, built up a significant backlog of decisions yet to be rendered and the chairman of the Tribunal reassigned a number of cases, including the two which were at issue here, to other members. Under the relevant legislation, the chairman had the power to "assign to each [member] the business to be transacted".[59] There was also a provision pertaining to the "expeditious dispatch" of cases.[60] Fennelly J. criticised the terminology used by the High Court judge, who had suggested that any power of reassignment must have been an implied power. In fact, Fennelly J. held that "the chairperson has general power ... to assign and to reassign cases already assigned" because the legislation "is clearly designed to enable the chairperson to pursue the objective of the expeditious dispatch of business".[61] Ultimately, it was not difficult "to envisage that hearing rosters may need to be adjusted on an *ad hoc* basis in response to levels of business, the speed or slowness of disposal of particular cases or types of cases, the relative efficiencies of individual members, their personal circumstances, the availability of interpreters, vacations and any number of other banal daily circumstances".[62] Interestingly, Fennelly J. eschewed the usual categorisation of powers that are not expressly granted as implicit or reasonably incidental. He suggested[63] that the power found

---

[55] *Magee v Murray* [2008] IEHC 371 per Birmingham J. But cf. the comments of Fennelly J. on this point in *McCarron v Kearney* [2010] IESC 28.

[56] [2005] IEHC 317; [2006] 1 I.R. 476.

[57] [2005] IEHC 317; [2006] 1 I.R. 476 at 485. See also, *Dublin Corporation v Raso* [1976–1977] I.L.R.M. 139.

[58] [2005] IESC 15; [2006] 2 I.R. 11. See, similarly, *Casey v Minister for Arts* [2004] IESC 14; [2004] 1 I.R. 402.

[59] Refugee Act 1996 Sch.2 para.13, as substituted by the Immigration Act 1999 s.11(1)(t).

[60] Refugee Act 1996 Sch.2 para.1(b). The Supreme Court's reliance on this provision could be objected to, as it refers only to the Minister's appointment of sufficient members to conduct the public body's business, not to the chairman's powers.

[61] [2006] 2 I.R. 11 at 20.

[62] [2006] 2 I.R. 11 at 20.

[63] [2006] 2 I.R. 11 especially at 15. Obviously, any such power has to be exercised in accordance

is to be identified as an express power. This seems contrary to classical theory: to be described as express, the power must be explicitly provided for in the parent legislation. Implied powers, or necessarily incidental powers, are inferred from the structure of the parent legislation and/or express powers. However, little of consequence hangs on this semantic distinction.

10–33 The "reasonably incidental" principle is often supplemented by the allied principle of effectiveness: *ut res magis valeat, quam pereat* (literally, "that the thing may have effect rather than be destroyed"). This principle was applied in *McGlinchey v Governor of Portlaoise Prison*[64] in order to uphold the validity of the government order establishing the Special Criminal Court. Part V of the Offences against the State Act 1939 contains detailed requirements prescribing the composition, jurisdiction and procedure of the Special Criminal Court but it does not actually specify by whom the members of the court are to be appointed. While Lynch J. acknowledged that the relevant statutory provisions could have been more "felicitously drafted", he invoked the principle of effectiveness in order to uphold the validity of the order:

> "I have no doubt at all ... but that a necessary inference arises that the Government is given power to establish the first Special Criminal Court following the making of the [Government's] proclamation, having regard to the mandatory terms of section 38(1) [of the 1939 Act] that such court should be established ...".[65]

10–34 It will be seen, therefore, that often the ultra vires principle is not applied with unnecessary strictness and the courts will only intervene where the administrative action cannot fairly be said to be reasonably incidental to the statutory provisions.

10–35 The Oireachtas, moreover, frequently endeavours to legislate for implied powers by inserting what an English judge has called "commonly found 'sweep up' jurisdictional provision[s]".[66] Thus, for example, s.54(2) of the Personal Injuries Assessment Board Act 2003 grants the Board "all such powers as are necessary or expedient for, or incidental to, the performance of its functions under this Act".[67]

---

with basic principles of public law. The concern of Finlay Geoghegan J. in the High Court and of Kearns J., dissenting, in the Supreme Court, had been that a power to reassign *after* an oral hearing had taken place could give rise to impropriety or the suspicion of impropriety. Fennelly J. noted, however, that the questions of the scope of a statutory power and the principles governing its exercise are separate. As to the latter any decision-maker is presumed (in accordance with the well-established principles laid down in *East Donegal*) to carry out his or her functions in a manner conforming to the rules of constitutional justice. In the present circumstances there was no suggestion that these had actually been breached.

[64] [1988] I.R. 671. The principle of effectiveness was also present, perhaps *sub silentio*, in a trio of cases involving tribunals of inquiry: *Bailey v Flood* [1998] IEHC 74; *Haughey v Moriarty* [1999] 3 I.R. 1 at 75; *Lawlor v Flood* [1999] IESC 67; [1999] 3 I.R. 107 at 131, 133, 136.

[65] [1988] I.R. 671 at 681.

[66] *R. (Roberts) v Parole Board* [2005] UKHL 45; [2005] 2 A.C. 738 at 773 per Lord Woolf C.J.

[67] But see *O'Brien v Personal Injuries Assessment Board (No. 3)* [2005] IEHC 100; [2007] 2 I.R. 1, where the respondent had failed to demonstrate that a policy of refusing to deal with solicitors was necessary, expedient or incidental to its function. The respondent, indeed, had to positively "demonstrate how the approach comes within the Act of 2003": [2005] IEHC

But note that even "any implicit powers ... must also be construed in the context of the purposes for which powers are expressly given under [the legislation]".[68]

Limits to the scope of the implied powers doctrine

10–36 There are, of course, definite limits to the scope of the implied powers doctrine. In *Howard v Commissioners of Public Works*,[69] Costello J. held that the Commissioners had no implied power to build a visitors' centre at certain areas of natural beauty, as these powers were not either incidental to or consequential upon the certain specific statutory powers to construct public works such as roads, bridges and the maintenance of public monuments.[70]

10–37 The litigation in *Gama Construction Ireland Ltd v Minister for Enterprise, Trade and Employment*[71] arose out of a public controversy surrounding the alleged under-payment by the applicant company of non-national workers. After the matter was raised in the Dáil, the respondent directed that an investigation be carried out by a labour inspector under, inter alia, the Employment Acts, Industrial Relations Acts, Organisation of Working Time Act 1997, and National Minimum Wage Act 2000. Pursuant to the investigation, a report was prepared for publication but the applicant sought an order restraining the report's publication. The applicant successfully argued that there was no power to prepare a report for publication. Finlay Geoghegan J. carefully analysed the various statutory powers in issue and concluded that each of them was specific and limited in nature, such that no incidental power to publish the results of an investigation into a given employer was implied by any of the statutory frameworks. Finlay Geoghegan J. did accept that there was an incidental power to collate and pass to the Minister information gathered, because "[i]t would render almost useless the express powers conferred on an inspector to gather and obtain information for the purposes of enforcing the obligations imposed by the Acts unless he had a power to pass on the information gathered".[72] But this incidental power could only be used "for the purpose of those authorities enforcing, by the authorised civil procedures, obligations imposed on the applicants by the relevant Employment Acts or to prosecute alleged breaches thereof".[73] Preparing a report for the purpose of publication was ultra vires the inspector.

100; [2007] 2 I.R. 1 at 19. This would severely limit the utility of s.54. The Supreme Court, [2008] IESC 71 at paras 50–54, affirmed MacMenamin J.'s High Court judgment on this point.

[68] *Gama v Minister for Enterprise, Trade and Employment* [2005] IEHC 210; [2007] 3 I.R. 472 at 485 per Finlay Geoghegan J. Her reasoning on this point was affirmed by the Supreme Court: [2009] IESC 37; [2010] 2 I.R. 85.

[69] [1994] 1 I.R. 101. See also, *Q v Mental Health Commission* [2007] IEHC 154; [2007] 3 I.R. 755.

[70] The Oireachtas acted speedily on foot of this decision and such a general power was conferred by the State Authorities (Development and Management) Act 1993.

[71] [2005] IEHC 210; [2007] 3 I.R. 472. The Supreme Court ([2009] IESC 37) affirmed this analysis, although the Minister's appeal was allowed on other grounds. See below, paras 15–28 to 15–29 (plurality of purposes) and paras 11–26 to 11–28 (severance).

[72] [2005] IEHC 210; [2007] 3 I.R. 472 at 487.

[73] [2005] IEHC 210; [2007] 3 I.R. 472 at 489.

D. Specialised Rules of Statutory Interpretation

10–38   Pulling in the opposite direction to the "reasonably incidental" principle are certain specialised rules of statutory interpretation such as the presumption against unnecessary interference with vested or property rights, the strict construction of penal statutes and the need for express language in the case of taxing or revenue-raising statutes. These rules are in part but specialised examples of a more general principle of statutory interpretation: the presumption against unclear changes in the law. However, it will be convenient if the case law is considered under separate headings.

Presumption against interference with common law or vested rights

10–39   This presumption is often applicable in the case of regulatory or licensing statutes.[74] As Murray C.J. explained in *BUPA Ireland Ltd v Health Insurance Authority (No. 2)*[75]:

> "... where the Legislature is enacting provisions, however sound the reasons for them may be, which have potentially serious implications for legal rights, including constitutional rights, of persons or corporations, one must expect that the intended ambit or application of such provisions will be expressed in the legislation with reasonable clarity."

10–40   Likewise, legislation imposing duties or obligations on private citizens must not only be interpreted with "some rigour", but the *BUPA* principle extends so as to "include not only the ambit of a duty imposed, but also ... the ambit of Ministerial power to bring an entity within an Act such as that under consideration".[76]

10–41   A strict construction approach also clearly emerges from the judgment of Murphy J. in *O'Neill v Minister for Agriculture*.[77] Here a licensing scheme operated by the Minister divided the country into nine geographical areas in each of which only one licence to practice artificial insemination would be granted. While the Minister was entitled to introduce regulations to control the practice of artificial insemination, the decision that the regulations were ultra vires the Livestock (Artificial Insemination) Act 1947 was partly motivated by the fact that the Act did not provide express authority for so confining this otherwise perfectly lawful activity:

> "The scheme manifestly affects the right of citizens to work in an industry for which they may be qualified and the rights of potential customers to avail

---

[74]   An example from the planning field is *Ashbourne Holdings Ltd v An Bord Pleanála* [2003] IESC 18; [2003] 2 I.R. 114. See also, *CW Shipping Ltd v Limerick Harbour Commissioners* [1989] I.L.R.M. 416.

[75]   [2008] IESC 42; [2009] 1 I.L.R.M. 81.

[76]   *Central Applications Office Ltd v Minister for Arts, Gaeltacht and Community Affairs* [2008] IEHC 309 per MacMenamin J. (at para.44) (nonetheless upholding designation order under the Official Languages Act 2003). See also, the judgment of the Supreme Court: [2010] IESC 32.

[77]   [1997] 2 I.L.R.M. 435. See also, *Carrigaline Community Television Broadcasting Co Ltd v Minister for Transport, Energy and Communications (No. 2)* [1997] 1 I.L.R.M. 241.

of such potential services. It is not that there is any reason to doubt that the scheme ultimately devised by the Minister was desirable, and may well have operated in the national interest, it is simply that such a scheme is so radical in qualifying limited number of persons and disqualifying all others who may be equally competent from engaging in business ... I would be unwilling to accept that in using general words the Oireachtas contemplated such a far reaching intrusion on the rights of citizens."

Presumption against unnecessary interference with property rights

10–42 A particularly strong case of the presumption against interference with vested rights exists where there is interference with property or other proprietary rights. This traditional common law presumption was placed in a constitutional perspective by Budd J. in *Dunraven Estates Ltd v Commissioners of Public Works*,[78] where speaking in the context of the validity of an arterial drainage scheme which the Commissioners proposed to carry out on the plaintiff's lands under the Arterial Drainage Act 1945, he said:

> "In the course of elucidating the interpretation of these sections, one has to bear in mind the constitutional position of the plaintiffs with regard to their lands, fisheries, and other proprietary rights ... [T]he delimitation of property rights which is constitutionally permissible must be made with regard, as far as possible, to the property rights of citizens ... The Act of 1945 should be construed on the basis that it was not the intention of the legislature to deprive the plaintiffs of their property or interfere with it save and in so far as that was necessary for the common good and was in accordance with the Constitution."[79]

10–43 Starting from this rule of construction, Budd J. went on to hold that s.6 of the Act, which required the Commissioners to provide the owner of the lands with full details of the proposed works so that he could make observations on these proposals), was mandatory. Accordingly, since the Commissioners had not provided sufficient details of their proposals, the impugned decision was held to be ultra vires.[80]

---

[78] [1974] I.R. 113.

[79] [1974] I.R. 113 at 132, 134. This passage represents a perfect statement of the proportionality principle as it applies to interference with property rights, but before that term or concept ever came into vogue. But cf. *Crosbie v Custom House Dock Development Authority* [1996] 2 I.R. 531.

[80] This principle of strict construction was also applied in *Arthur v Kerry County Council* [2000] IEHC 164; [2000] 3 I.R. 407 at 417; *Hussey v Irish Land Commission*, unreported, Supreme Court, December 13, 1984; *Meaney v Cashel U.D.C. (No. 2)* [1937] I.R. 54; *Hendron v Dublin Corporation* [1943] I.R. 566; *Ashbourne Holdings Ltd v An Bord Pleanála* [2003] IESC 18; [2003] 2 I.R. 114. *A contra*: *Crosbie v Custom House Docks Authority* [1996] 2 I.R. 531 where, on the facts, it might be argued that in effect the Authority had exercised its statutory powers (or the threat of the exercise of such powers) in order to "landbank" once its original plans for the land had fallen through; and *Clinton v An Bord Pleanála* [2007] IESC 19; [2007] 4 I.R. 701.

Presumption against taxing or revenue-raising powers

10-44 In this jurisdiction, this presumption is probably given express constitutional underpinning by the Money Bill provisions of Arts 21 and 22 of the Constitution, which ensure that general taxation or charges may not be levied save by means of an Act of the Oireachtas. But, apart from the Constitution, the same policy informs one of the more deeply rooted presumptions of the common law, namely that taxes or charges may not be levied by the State or public authorities, in the absence of express words. As Atkin L.J. explained in a classic passage in *Attorney General v Wilts United Dairies Ltd*[81]:

> "The circumstances would be remarkable indeed which would induce the courts to believe that the Legislature had sacrificed all the well-known checks and precautions, and, not in express words, but merely by implication, has entrusted a Minister with undefined and unlimited powers of imposing charges upon the subject for purposes connected with his department."[82]

10-45 This question arose in *Humphrey v Minister for the Environment*.[83] The legislation at issue here permitted the imposition of charges in respect of licences for public service vehicles. Rather than relating the charges to, say, the costs of administration, Dundalk U.D.C. had introduced a charging scheme that calculated the licence fee based on the capital value of the subject of a licence. Murphy J. agreed that the scheme amounted to a tax, which could not be imposed absent clear statutory authority, and quashed the scheme.[84]

10-46 The effect of this presumption is that even statutes authorising local taxation or charges must be couched in express language.[85] Several good examples of the use of express language are provided by the Planning and Development Act 2000[86] s.48(i), which states:

---

[81]   (1921) 37 T.L.R. 884 (affirmed by the House of Lords (1922) 38 T.L.R. 781). See also, *Liverpool Corporation v Maiden (Arthur) Ltd* [1938] 4 All E.R. 200; *R. v Richmond-upon-Thames Ex p. McCarthy & Stone (Developments) Ltd* [1992] 2 A.C. 48.

[82]   (1921) 37 T.L.R. 884 at 886. This judgment was cited with approval by Murphy J. in *O'Neill v Minister for Agriculture* [1997] 2 I.L.R.M. 435 at 450 as illustrating the wider proposition that even in jurisdictions "where the separation of powers is not governed by the requirements of a written constitution a presumption appears to arise that in delegating legislation Parliament did not intend to confer radical powers of a legislative nature"—a proposition which, Murphy J. considered, applied a fortiori to this jurisdiction.

[83]   [2000] IEHC 149; [2001] 1 I.R. 263.

[84]   But see *Ryanair Ltd v Aer Rianta* [2003] IESC 19; [2003] 2 I.R. 143 where the Supreme Court distinguished *Wilts United Dairies* and upheld the validity of a charge imposed by Aer Rianta designed to recover certain additional costs following the introduction of new regulations. Keane C.J. saw this as simply "[a] perfectly normal response by a trading company to particular commercial constraints and the court is satisfied that it was in no sense the unauthorised exaction by them of a charge for the performance of their statutory functions".

[85]   See, e.g. *Inspector of Taxes v Kiernan* [1981] I.R. 117 and *Kinsale Yacht Club v Commissioner of Valuation* [1994] 1 I.L.R.M. 457 (where Finlay C.J. held that the occupier of an hereditament was not to be rated where the rating statute sought to impose a liability "by the use of oblique or slack language"); *The Adroit Company v Minister for Environment, Heritage and Local Government* [2004] IEHC 397; [2005] 2 I.L.R.M. 96; *Health Service Executive v Commissioners of Valuation* [2008] IEHC 17; *Nangles Nurseries v Commissioners of Valuation* [2008] IEHC 72.

[86]   The need for strict compliance with such statutory requirements in the planning field is

conditions for requiring the payment of a contribution in respect of public infrastructure and facilities benefiting development in the area of the planning authority and that is provided, or that it is intended will be provided, by or on behalf of a local authority.

10–47   The operation of this presumption can also be seen in the context of the cases arising under the Local Government (Financial Provisions) (No. 2) Act 1983, which authorises local authorities to charge for certain services provided by them. This legislation has been strictly construed by the courts and service charges have been held invalid where there is no clear statutory authorisation for the charge in question.[87] These cases are considered elsewhere.[88]

Presumption against penal statutes

10–48   At common law there is a particularly strong presumption in favour of a statutory construction which protects individual liberty. This common law presumption is now reinforced by the constitutional provisions protecting such fundamental rights. A modern restatement of this presumption (in which the notion of constitutionally protected personal rights appears to be implicit) is to be found in the judgment of Henchy J. in *Director of Public Prosecutions v Gaffney*[89] where, speaking in the context of a statutory power of arrest, he said:

> "The right of arrest without warrant given by section 49(4) of the Road Traffic Act 1961 [is a] substantial [invasion] of the personal rights enjoyed before the enactment of those provisions and there should not be attributed to Parliament an intention that such personal rights were to be curtailed further than the extent expressed in the statute."

10–49   Surprisingly, perhaps, this principle is not confined to decisions with implications for personal liberty. Thus, in *HMIL Ltd v Minister for Agriculture and Food*,[90] Barr J. ruled that an attempt by the Minister to impose administrative fines for alleged infractions of EU agricultural regulations was ultra vires in the absence of express legislative authority for this course of action.[91] In *Albatros Feeds v Minister for Agriculture and Food*[92] the Supreme Court, likewise, held that clear statutory authority was necessary in order to provide a valid legal basis for the detention of animal feed.

10–50   Special considerations apply in the case of legislation dealing with mental

---

illustrated by *Bord na Móna v An Bord Pleanála and Galway County Council* [1985] I.R. 205. See also, 2000 Act s.34(3).
[87]   See, e.g. *Athlone U.D.C. v Gavin* [1985] I.R. 434; *Louth County Council v Mathews*, unreported, High Court, April 14, 1989; *Ballybay Meat Exports Ltd v Monaghan County Council* [1990] I.L.R.M. 864.
[88]   See paras 5–107 to 5–110.
[89]   [1987] I.R. 181 at 181.
[90]   Unreported, High Court, February 8, 1996.
[91]   Barr J.'s decision was reversed by the Supreme Court ([2002] IESC 3) after a preliminary reference to the European Court of Justice seeking a ruling on the correct interpretation of the regulations. It was held that Barr J. had wrongly interpreted the regulations. However, his general point holds.
[92]   [2006] IESC 51; [2007] 1 I.R. 221.

health, where the courts' desire to safeguard personal liberty may be tempered by the necessity to construe legislation providing for the detention of patients in a purposive fashion.[93] Even then, however, statutory safeguards designed to protect the patients will be strictly upheld.[94]

Presumption against unclear changes in the law

10–51   As mentioned, the over-arching presumption, of which those previously listed are specific applications, is that the courts will lean against any interpretation of a statutory provision which would have the effect of reversing settled law or legal principles unless the language used is plain and unmistakeable. Thus, in *Minister for Industry and Commerce v Hales*,[95] Henchy J. held that regulations which sought to give the word "workers" an extended meaning so as to cover insurance agents working under contracts of service were ultra vires. The Oireachtas could not be presumed to have intended by means of a "loosely drafted sub-section" to effect "such radical and far-reaching changes in the law of contract".[96] In some cases, even where plain language has apparently been used, the courts will, following a restrictive interpretation of the statutory language, deem certain actions to be ultra vires. The presumption may also have been in operation in another case concerning the powers of a coroner. In *Morris v Farrell*,[97] the respondent was conducting an inquest into the shooting dead of a man in Dublin. Members of An Garda Síochána had been involved in the events leading up to the man's death. Prior to the holding of the inquest, a threat was made by a subversive organisation against the lives of the Gardaí concerned. The coroner decided, as a result, to permit the members to testify anonymously, even though as Keane C.J. recognised:

> "Although the [Coroners] Act of 1962 does not expressly require the holding of inquests in public, it cannot be inferred from the absence of such a provision that the Oireachtas intended to alter the principle apparently established at common law that, in general, the court of the coroner was a public court."[98]

10–52   Indeed, the Act expressly provides that a coroner must take the names and addresses of witnesses and that the list be made available to members of the public.[99] Keane C.J. sought a harmonious reconciliation of the traditional position and the need for the coroner to take certain measures to ensure that the inquest could go ahead. Thus, he held, it would be permissible for the coroner to allow the Gardaí to identify themselves in open court as "Garda A", "Garda B" and so on but that their full names and addresses would have to be entered into the record as required by the Act.

---

[93]   See, e.g. *Re Philip Clarke* [1950] I.R. 235; *Gooden v St Otteran's Hospital* [2005] 3 I.R. 617; *JB v Director of Central Mental Hospital* [2007] IEHC 201; [2007] 4 I.R. 778.

[94]   See, e.g. *WQ v Mental Health Commission* [2007] IEHC 154; [2007] 3 I.R. 755; *AM v Kennedy (Mental Health)* [2007] IEHC 136; [2007] 4 I.R. 667; *JB v Director of Central Mental Hospital* [2007] IEHC 201; [2007] 4 I.R. 778.

[95]   [1967] I.R. 50.

[96]   [1967] I.R. 50 at 77. See also, *BUPA Ireland Ltd v Health Insurance Authority (No. 2)* [2008] IESC 82; [2009] 1 I.L.R.M. 81.

[97]   [2000] IESC 24; [2000] 3 I.R. 592.

[98]   [2000] IESC 24; [2000] 3 I.R. 592 at 607.

[99]   Coroners Act 1962 ss.28 and 29.

E. ERROR OF LAW

10–53   Seven heads of jurisdictional error have already been listed in Part A. Here we must go in a little more detail into an issue which usually arises in the context of any of the heads (a)–(d) as identified in para.10–08. The crucial point is that, traditionally, not every error committed by an administrative body or lower court is regarded as affecting the jurisdiction of that body and thus as being subject to judicial review. The question of which errors are jurisdictional is an intractable one and is intrinsically linked to questions of statutory interpretation and judicial policy. While the various theories of jurisdictional error provide some guide to the extent of review, the matter is nonetheless not one of abstract logic, but, at root, judicial policy, for it depends upon what degree of supervision the courts wish to exercise over decisions of administrative bodies and of lower courts. To put it rather simplistically: where a court wishes to intervene, it is likely to classify the error as affecting jurisdiction; where it does not, the error is classified as going to "merits". As a preliminary to a survey of some rather dense case law, one should note that in each of the cases, the issue is whether the error is such that the court is empowered to review it; the fact that there is an error is taken for granted.

10–54   There have been several judicial suggestions, in line with the general notion of curial deference,[100] that the courts will be reluctant to interfere with decisions of specialist tribunals or decisions taken pursuant to expert advice.[101] Moreover, where it is the decision of a lower court which is under review, the advent in 1924 of District and Circuit Courts, staffed by professional judges, seems to have made the High Court reluctant to interfere with decisions of these lower courts.[102]

10–55   On the other hand, it is important that tribunals and lower courts do not wrongfully usurp jurisdiction and that errors of law must not go uncorrected. While not stating so openly, the courts have by and large sought to strike intuitively what they regard as the proper balance as between these competing considerations, rather than seeking to decide by reference to any set formula or theory of jurisdictional review. The question of whether the decision of the tribunal or lower court goes to jurisdiction or not can arise in regard to a decision about law (mainly points of statutory interpretation), fact or "mixed questions of law and fact". We return to these differences later.[103] Before considering the Irish jurisprudence on the question, something must be said about the general Anglo-Irish evolution of various theories of jurisdiction.

The pure jurisdiction doctrine

10–56   This theory held sway from the first half of the nineteenth century until relatively recently.[104] The crucial feature of this theory is that jurisdiction

---

[100]   On curial deference, see further, paras 15–64 to 15–72.
[101]   See, e.g. *O'Keeffe v An Bord Pleanála* [1993] 1 I.R. 39; *Ryanair v Flynn* [2000] IEHC 36; [2000] 3 I.R. 240; *Scrollside Ltd v Broadcasting Commission of Ireland* [2006] IESC 24; [2007] 1 I.R. 166.
[102]   *State (Attorney General) v Durcan* [1964] I.R. 279 at 288–289. See also, the comments of Gannon J. in *Clune v Director of Public Prosecutions* [1981] 1 I.L.R.M. 17 at 20.
[103]   See below, paras 10–66 to 10–80.
[104]   For an historical account of these developments, see Rubinstein, *Jurisdiction and Illegality*

is determined at the "commencement, not at the conclusion of, the inquiry".[105] If an administrative authority or lower court has "subject matter" or "original" jurisdiction, it does not lose such jurisdiction even if (since the same distinction applies even more so, as we shall below, where the error is one of fact, rather than law) there is no evidence to support its findings of fact.[106] This was decided by a very strong Divisional Court in *R. (Martin) v Mahoney*[107] where it was held that a conviction under s.1 of the Betting House Act 1853 which was (admittedly) based on insufficient evidence could not be quashed on certiorari, since the absence of sufficient evidence did not affect the jurisdiction of the convicting magistrate; as Lord O'Brien L.C.J. remarked:

> "To grant certiorari merely on the ground of want of jurisdiction, because there was no evidence to warrant a conviction, confounds want of jurisdiction with error in the exercise of it. The contention that mere want of evidence to authorise a conviction creates a cesser of jurisdiction, involves the unwarrantable proposition that a magistrate has ... jurisdiction only to go right; and that, though he had jurisdiction to enter upon an inquiry, mere miscarriage in drawing an unwarrantable conclusion from the evidence, such as it was, makes the magistrate act without and in excess of jurisdiction."[108]

10–57   The wealth of erudition displayed in the judgments of Lord O'Brien, Palles C.B. and Gibson J., coupled with the reputation of these judges, seems to have almost hypnotised successive generations of judges, since the authority of the reasoning in this case remained unquestioned until very recently.[109] Indeed, the emphasis on the original jurisdiction theory in *Mahoney's* case appears to have been so influential that even today many judges are reluctant to classify an error made in the course of exercising jurisdiction (such as misconstruing a statutory provision or admitting inadmissible evidence) as one which destroys that jurisdiction.

10–58   There are numerous Irish cases in which this doctrine has been followed

---

(Oxford: Clarendon Press, 1965), Ch.4; Jaffe and Henderson, "Judicial Review and the Rule of Law: Historical Origins" (1956) 72 L.Q.R. 345; and Jaffe, "Judicial Review: Constitutional and Jurisdictional Fact" (1957) 70 Harv. L. Rev. 953.

[105] *R. v Bolton* (1841) 1 Q.B. 66 at 74 per Lord Denman C.J.

[106] *R. (Martin) v Mahoney* [1910] 2 I.R. 695. Such was the influence of the "original jurisdiction" theory that in *McDonald v Bord na gCon (No. 3)*, unreported, High Court, January 13, 1966, Kenny J. held that the defendants had acted invalidly in breaching the *audi alteram partem* rule, but since they had original jurisdiction in that matter, they did not thereby exceed jurisdiction.

[107] [1910] 2 I.R. 695. See generally, Costello, "*R. (Martin) v Mahoney*: The History of a Classical Certiorari Authority" (2006) 27 *Journal of Legal History* 267. This remarkable and elegantly written essay provides a very valuable insight into nineteenth-century certiorari law and demonstrates that the doctrine regarding what constitutes an error as to jurisdiction was not based on abstract logic but (then as now) based on wider policy considerations regarding the breadth of the High Court's supervisory jurisdiction.

[108] [1910] 2 I.R. 695 at 707. For an interesting discussion of this passage, in the context of the decision to grant leave to apply for judicial review, see *Buckley v Kirby* [2000] IESC 18; [2000] 3 I.R. 431.

[109] In Northern Ireland, *Martin* was regarded as "the accepted authority on certiorari" by Lord Lowry L.C.J. in *R. v Belfast Recorder Ex p. McNally* [1992] N.I. 217 at 229. But see now *Re Belfast City Council* [2008] N.I.Q.B. 13; [2008] N.I. 277. It continues to be cited with approval in Ireland. See, e.g. *Killeen v Director of Public Prosecutions* [1998] 1 I.L.R.M. 1; *Buckley v Kirby* [2000] IESC 18; [2000] 3 I.R. 431.

and a representative example from the mid-1950s serves to illustrate how, as a result, the scope of review was narrowed for a substantial period. In *State (Batchelor & Co (Ireland) Ltd) v Ó Floinn*[110] the applicants sought to quash a search warrant issued under s.12 of the Merchandise Marks Act 1887. It was said that there was insufficient evidence before the respondent District judge to justify the warrant. But O'Daly J. for the Supreme Court disposed of this argument by stating that it was well settled that, providing the error did not appear on the face of the record, questions as to the sufficiency of evidence amounted to errors within jurisdiction and consequently could not be considered on judicial review: the District judge clearly had jurisdiction to make an order under the Act, and he did not lose jurisdiction by making an error of this nature. In the view of O'Daly J., questions as to the sufficiency of evidence were the very matters committed to the jurisdiction of the District judge. The result of this and other similar decisions was that the scope of review was rather narrow, and this could often lead to injustice, particularly in criminal cases.[111]

"Conditions precedent to jurisdiction"

10–59   One method of escaping the confines of the pure jurisdiction doctrine was to classify certain findings as "collateral" or as "conditions precedent to jurisdiction"[112]: see head (a) in para.10–09. Administrative authorities do not possess an inherent jurisdiction; sometimes their jurisdiction depends upon factual (or legal) preconditions, laid down in legislation, which must have an objective existence before the authority has power to act. Hence, any decision of the authority as to the boundaries of its jurisdiction could not be conclusive, as otherwise it would usurp power never conferred on it by the Oireachtas. If, for example, the Circuit Court has jurisdiction to hear ejectment cases where the rateable valuation of the premises does not exceed £60, that court cannot acquire jurisdiction by reason of an erroneous conclusion as to the rateable valuation of the premises.[113] In other words, an administrative authority cannot give itself a jurisdiction which it cannot have, and the High Court will enforce the ultra vires doctrine by insisting on the objective existence of certain circumstances upon which some jurisdiction depends.

10–60   Here, one should interpolate that these cases are sometimes complicated by the invocation by the reviewing court of the principle of the "grant of jurisdiction"[114]:

---

[110] [1958] I.R. 155. See also, *R. (Limerick Corporation) v Local Government Board* [1922] 2 I.R. 76; *R. (Dillon) v Minister for Local Government* [1927] I.R. 474; and *McDonald v Bord na gCon (No. 3)*, unreported, High Court, January 13, 1966.

[111] See, e.g. *State (Lee-Kiddier) v Dunleavy*, unreported, High Court, August 17, 1976, where McWilliam J. held that the question of whether there was sufficient evidence to support a conviction was not reviewable in certiorari proceedings, absent error on the face of the record. Contrast this with the observations of Kenny J. in *State (Holland) v Kennedy* [1977] I.R. 193 where he doubted whether the rule in *Mahoney* was compatible with Art.38.1 of the Constitution which requires a trial "in due course of law".

[112] Thus, in *State (O'Neill) v Shannon* [1931] I.R. 691 it was held that the principle of *Martin's* case only applied to decisions arrived at on the merits and was not relevant in the case of preliminary objections to jurisdiction.

[113] *State (Attorney General) v Durcan* [1964] I.R. 279; *Harrington v Judge Murphy* [1989] I.R. 207.

[114] *Union des employés de service, local 298 v Bibeault* [1988] 2 S.C.R. 1048 at 1086 per Beetz J. For comment on grant of jurisdiction, see *R. v Special Commissioners of Income Tax* (1888) 21 Q.B.D. 313; Wade and Forsyth, *Administrative Law*, 9th edn (2004), pp.257–262. For

that is, while some of these matters may well have been collateral, yet they may have been committed by the legislature to the decision-maker in question for determination: "Parliament is sovereign and in theory it can give the task of determining the meaning of a term to, for example, an inferior court or tribunal."[115] Similar logic pertains to findings of preliminary fact. In short, everything depends on what the statute says. This does not mean that a decision will be entirely unreviewable,[116] but that review is limited to grounds such as reasonableness and relevancy of considerations, rather than permitting the High Court to determine de novo whether the condition precedent has been satisfied.

10–61   In *State (Davidson) v Farrell*,[117] Kingsmill Moore J. followed this approach and sought to resolve the conundrum by referring to the jurisdiction conferred—whether expressly or by necessary intendment—by statute on the authority concerned. In this case the applicant, a tenant in a controlled dwelling, sought to quash decisions of the District and Circuit Courts awarding her landlord certain sums as allowances in respect of the repair of the premises. She claimed that these decisions were flawed by jurisdictional error as a result of the misconstruction of the phrase "premises", as defined by the Rent Restrictions Act 1946. A majority of the Supreme Court concluded following an examination of the 1946 Act that the Oireachtas had intended to vest the District Court with jurisdiction to determine the basic rent and allowances. It was not a precondition to jurisdiction that the word "premises" be correctly construed, and as Kingsmill Moore J. explained:

> "The [District] Court may make an error in law in interpreting the word 'premises', or an error in fact in determining that money has been expended when it has not, but these are errors within the jurisdiction conferred."[118]

10–62   To return to the main theme, a good example of a condition precedent can be found in s.2 of the Industrial Relations (Amendment) Act 2001,[119] which allows the Labour Court to investigate a "trade dispute", if four criteria are satisfied. In *Ryanair v Labour Court*,[120] the Supreme Court held that the existence of a "trade dispute" was a "vital precondition to jurisdiction",[121] the resolution of which could not be left to the substantive investigation. An uncontroversial example of a jurisdictional error may be seen in *Bank of Scotland (Ireland) v Employment Appeals*

---

theoretical discussion, see Daly, "Explaining Jurisdiction" (2007) 25 I.L.T. 72; Mulcahy, "Jurisdictional Errors of Fact in Judicial Review" (2008) 26 I.L.T. 298; and, in the English context, Craig, *Administrative Law*, 6th edn (London: Sweet & Maxwell, 2008), pp.437–452.

[115]   Craig, *Administrative Law* (2008), p.445.

[116]   This would probably be a violation of Art.34.3.1° in any event.

[117]   [1960] I.R. 438. See also, *State (Attorney General) v McGivern*, unreported, Supreme Court, July 25, 1961; and *State (Attorney General) v Durcan* [1964] I.R. 279, which has a useful judicial discussion of this question.

[118]   [1960] I.R. 438 at 455. This approach is unlikely to be followed today. See below, paras 10–72 to 10–78. But cf. *Hughes v Garavan* [2003] IESC 65; [2004] 1 I.L.R.M. 401 for another seemingly approving reference to *Davidson*.

[119]   As amended by s.2 of the Industrial Relations (Miscellaneous Provisions) Act 2004.

[120]   [2007] IESC 6; [2007] 4 I.R. 199. For a similarly vigorous line towards the fulfilment of a condition precedent, see *Fitzwilton v Mahon* [2007] IESC 27; [2008] 1 I.R. 712. The paternalistic approach of the High Court regarding cases arising in the area of mental health provides a contrast: *JH v Lawlor* [2007] IEHC 225; [2008] 1 I.R. 476.

[121]   [2007] IESC 6; [2007] 4 I.R. 199 at 216.

Tribunal.[122] Section 8(2)(a) of the Unfair Dismissals Act 1977 (as amended by s.7 of the Unfair Dismissals (Amendment) Act 1993) provides that any claim made under the Act must be made within six months of the dismissal (save where exceptional circumstances explain the delay). Here, the dismissed employee had made the claim six months and one day after the dismissal but the Tribunal nonetheless concluded that it had jurisdiction, apparently because it took the view that the dismissal had actually taken place one day later. Ó Caoimh J. held, however, that the making of a claim within the six-month period was a condition precedent to the holding of a substantive hearing by the Tribunal and accordingly quashed its determination that it had jurisdiction in the present case.[123]

10–63 *Kennedy v Hearne*[124] is another instance of a case in which certain facts were treated as jurisdictional. Here, through an administrative error, the Revenue Commissioners caused an enforcement notice in respect of unpaid income tax to be sent to the sheriff under s.485 of the Income Tax Act 1967 (now s.942 of the Taxes Consolidation Act 1997). The Supreme Court held that such a notice was invalid, as the powers contained in that section could only be validly activated upon the condition that there was an actual default in the payment of a levied tax. As Finlay C.J. explained:

> "The section must be construed as vesting in the Revenue Commissioners ... the power to issue a notice to the sheriff ... only in the case where an actual default in the payment of a levied tax has occurred. Where, as happened in this case, they issued such a notice where that default had not continued up to the time that the notice was issued, what they did was a nullity."[125]

10–64 It is easy to understand why the Supreme Court should hold that an actual default in the payment of tax was a condition precedent to the operation of a section with such potentially far-reaching consequences. The seriousness of the consequences may also have influenced the High Court in *Foley v Judge Murphy*.[126] Here the applicant had been convicted by the District Court of criminal damage and assault. The applicant was ordered to do 40 hours of community service, but before passing sentence, the District judge did not inquire into the appropriateness of a sentence of imprisonment. This inquiry seemed to be compelled by s.2 of the Criminal Justice (Community Service) Act 1983, according to which a community service order may be made where "the appropriate sentence would but for this Act

---

[122] [2002] IEHC 119. See also, *O'Rourke v Governor of Cloverhill Prison* [2004] IESC 29; [2004] 2 I.R. 456, where a warrant had not been "produced" to the Garda Commissioner, Deputy Commissioner or Assistant Commissioner in accordance with the Extradition Act 1965.

[123] In *Payne v Brophy* [2006] IEHC 34; [2006] 1 I.R. 560, Clarke J. suggested that the hearing of a challenge to the District Court's jurisdiction, on the basis that a summons was invalid, was itself a condition precedent to the exercise of jurisdiction by the District Court. Failure to consider the challenge if it raised "serious issues ... as to the jurisdiction of the court" ([2006] IEHC 34; [2006] 1 I.R. 560 at 566) was a species of jurisdictional error. A challenge based on technical errors in a summons would be defeated by the accused's presence in court, but the respondent was at least obliged to consider whether the challenge was technical, or touched on the jurisdiction of his court and if so, to hear evidence on the point.

[124] [1988] I.R. 481. See also, *Greene v Governor of Mountjoy Prison* [1995] 3 I.R. 541.

[125] [1988] I.R. 481 at 491. See also, *O'Connor v Giblin*, unreported, Supreme Court, December 19, 1994.

[126] [2005] IEHC 332; [2005] 3 I.R. 574. See similarly, *Simple Imports Ltd v Revenue Commissioners* [2000] IESC 40; [2000] 2 I.R. 243.

be one of penal servitude …". Dunne J. considered that s.2 made a consideration of whether a penal sentence would be appropriate, a condition precedent to the making of a community service order. Unless the order gave "a clear indication of what the appropriate term of imprisonment would be but for the making of a community service order" the District Court would have no jurisdiction to impose a community service order.[127] Here, a formal recitation that the "appropriate sentence would be one of imprisonment for the period of zero" was insufficient and Dunne J. granted an order of certiorari.

10–65 These cases have been presented as straightforward applications of the "conditions precedent" (or "collateral fact") doctrine. However, many if not all of them could have been decided the other way (i.e. as falling within the decision-maker's jurisdiction). This illustrates the fact that the basic difficulty is that the concept of "collateral fact" is a malleable one—virtually any fact may be classified as "collateral" to jurisdiction. However, "[t]he theoretical basis of this idea is … unimpeachable—which may explain why it has never been squarely repudiated"[128] and used quite frequently by Irish courts. Moreover, this issue is not solely one of statutory interpretation. For the essential legal policy behind the ultra vires doctrine is that it is vital that administrative authorities respect the principle of legality and have due regard to constitutional precepts of fairness. For these reasons the courts have recently tended to turn away from this theory of jurisdiction in order to increase the scope of review, while retaining it in the armoury in case of emergency. In general, the former, complicated position—that a reviewing court could consider de novo whether a condition precedent was satisfied, except where the decision as to the existence of the condition precedent had been committed to the original decision-maker—can be contrasted with the modern doctrine, that all errors of law can be corrected by a reviewing court. Complicated questions of the balance of power between the original decision-maker and the reviewing court have apparently been replaced by a simpler inquiry: did the original decision-maker make an error of law?

The modern doctrine of jurisdictional error

10–66 Contemporary courts have reached the furthest extreme from the "pure theory of jurisdiction", for the modern trend is to treat all errors of law committed by lower courts or administrative tribunals as jurisdictional in character. But the law in this area is far from settled. Contradictory opinions have been expressed by eminent judges and the Supreme Court has yet to give a fully authoritative and comprehensive exposition on the subject of jurisdictional error. Earlier authorities such as *Farrell's* case have never been formally overruled, and are still on occasion relied on as good law.[129] Moreover, it is not clear whether traditional doctrine can safely be relied on where the errors in question involve infringements of constitutional rules or principles.

---

[127] [2005] IEHC 332; [2005] 3 I.R. 574 at 584.

[128] *UES Local 298 v Bibeault* [1988] 2 S.C.R. 1048 at 1086 per Beetz J.

[129] *State (Lee-Kiddier) v Dunleavy*, unreported, High Court, August 17, 1976; *State (Cole) v Labour Court* (1984) 3 J.I.S.S.L. 128. But cf. the comments of Keane J. in *Killeen v Director of Public Prosecutions* [1997] 3 I.R. 218; [1998] 1 I.L.R.M. 1 for a suggestion that *Farrell's* case might no longer represent good law.

10–67 The leading Irish authority of what we have called "modern" doctrine probably remains *State (Holland) v Kennedy*.[130] The Children Act 1908 forbade the imposition of a prison sentence on a young person between the ages of 15 and 17 unless it was shown that he was of such an "unruly character" that he could not be detained in an approved place of detention. In this case the defendant had been convicted of a particularly serious assault. He was certified as of unruly character by the respondent District judge, and she sentenced him to a period of imprisonment.

10–68 The Supreme Court held that the bare facts of this assault, unrelated to any previous evidence of a behavioural pattern, could not justify a conclusion that this young person would not be amenable to detention in a suitable institute. In ruling that an error of this nature was reviewable, Henchy J. observed:

> "Having considered the authorities, I am satisfied that this error was not made within jurisdiction ... [I]t does not necessarily follow that a court or tribunal, vested with powers of a judicial nature, which commences a hearing within jurisdiction will be treated as continuing to act within jurisdiction. For any one of a number of reasons it may exceed jurisdiction and thereby make its decisions liable to be quashed on certiorari. For instance, it may fall into an unconstitutionality, or it may breach the requirements of natural justice, or it may fail to stay within the bounds of the jurisdiction conferred on it by statute. It is an error of the latter kind that prevents the impugned order in this case from being held to have been made within jurisdiction ... It was necessarily the statutory intention that a legally supportable certificate ... is to be a condition precedent to the exercise of jurisdiction to impose a sentence of imprisonment. Otherwise the sentencing limitation imposed by the statute could be nullified by disregarding what the law regards as essential for the making of the certificate. In the present case, the certificate, having been made without evidence, is as devoid of legal validity as if it had been made in disregard of uncontroverted evidence showing that the young person was not what he had been certified to be."[131]

10–69 The precise significance of *Holland* is difficult to assess. The above passage contains some reasoning reminiscent of the collateral fact approach.[132] However, the judgment of Henchy J. suggests that errors of law committed by a lower court or tribunal in the course of a hearing will be deemed—almost as of course—to go to jurisdiction. Yet other passages in the judgments of Henchy and Kenny JJ. give the impression that the existence of a legally supportable certificate was a collateral fact—a condition precedent to jurisdiction which the District judge had failed to satisfy. If the latter interpretation had proved to be correct, *Holland* would have represented no more than an application of principles approved in earlier

---

[130] [1977] I.R. 193.

[131] [1977] I.R. 193 at 201–202.

[132] As Henchy J. said (at 201): "It was necessarily the statutory intention that a legally supportable certificate to that effect is to be a condition precedent to the exercise of the jurisdiction to impose a sentence of imprisonment." See, e.g. *Greene v Governor of Mountjoy Prison* [1995] 3 I.R. 541, a case with facts identical to *Holland*, where the certificate under the Children Act 1908 was regarded a condition precedent to the District Court's jurisdiction to send a young person to prison.

decisions such as *State (Davidson) v Farrell*, and the case could hardly have been said to have broken new ground. On the whole, however, *Holland* is regarded as having made the same breakthrough in this jurisdiction as *Anisminic Ltd v Foreign Compensation Commission*.[133]

10–70   While this case law appeared to presage the abolition of the time-honoured distinction between errors which go to jurisdiction and those which do not, nothing of the kind immediately happened. The old distinctions retained an exiguous vitality and the courts veered from one direction to another without ever once reproaching themselves for their lack of consistency in this matter.

10–71   This point is well illustrated by the Supreme Court's next pronouncement on this topic. In *State (Abenglen Properties Ltd) v Dublin Corporation*,[134] the Supreme Court refused to quash a planning permission where the developer claimed that the respondents had acted ultra vires in attaching restrictive conditions to the grant of permission, and that the entire permission rested on an erroneous identification of the relevant development plan. Different judges took different routes to reach the same result in what was undoubtedly a very result-oriented case. Henchy J.'s response was to state:

> "The alleged errors arose in the course of identifying and construing the relevant development plan. There is no doubt but that on a true reading of the relevant Acts and Regulations, the Corporation had jurisdiction to identify and construe the relevant Dublin City development plan in its relation to Abenglen's application. If, therefore, they erred in either respect, they erred within jurisdiction, and any error they may have made does not appear on the face of the record."[135]

---

[133] [1969] 2 A.C. 147. For other examples of where "asking the wrong question" (as contrasted with giving the right answer), which was the *Anisminic* test, was held to be a jurisdictional error, see *State (Cork County Council) v Fawsitt*, unreported, High Court, March 13, 1981; *State (Cork County Council) v Fawsitt (No. 2)*, unreported, Supreme Court, July 28, 1983; *State (McMahon) v Minister for Education*, unreported, High Court, December 21, 1985; *Killeen v Director of Public Prosecutions* [1998] 1 I.L.R.M. 1; and *Ryanair v Labour Court* [2007] IESC 6; [2007] 4 I.R. 199.

For a very clear analysis, see Daly, "Judicial Review of Errors of Law in Ireland" (2006) 41 Ir. Jur. (N.S) 60. See, e.g. the comments of Keane J. in *Harte v Labour Court* [1996] 2 I.R. 171; *Killeen v Director of Public Prosecutions* [1998] 1 I.L.R.M. 1; and *Farrell v Attorney General* [1998] 1 I.R. 203. In the latter case Keane J. observed (at 224–225) that historically a coroner's verdict could only be quashed where "… there was fraud by the coroner, or an error by him going to jurisdiction, or where an error of law appeared on the face of the record. Today, however, the jurisdiction to review judicially the proceedings in a coroner's court is significantly wider and will extend to the circumstances identified by the House of Lords in *Anisminic Ltd v Foreign Compensation Commission* and by this Court in *State (Holland) v Kennedy*."

[134] [1984] I.R. 381. Hederman J. joined in the judgment of Henchy J. The other three members of the court reserved their position on this question.

[135] [1984] I.R. 381 at 399–400. This passage has served to resuscitate the distinction in this jurisdiction between errors of law affecting jurisdiction and those which do not. See, e.g. the High Court judgment of Blayney J. in *State (Keegan) v Stardust Compensation Tribunal* [1986] I.R. 642 at 649–650, where this passage of Henchy J. was quoted with approval. Cf. Daly, "Judicial Review of Errors of Law in Ireland" (2006) 41 Ir. Jur. (N.S) 60.

Recent developments

10–72 The decisions which we have just been discussed mainly date from a period in the early 1980s when this area of the law was in a constant state of flux, both here and in England. This pervasive judicial inconsistency[136] and the lack of clear general principles governing the question of jurisdictional error have not really abated. Indeed, this lack of consistency has been so prevalent that one suspects that the courts are prepared to characterise an error of law as being jurisdictional (or not) depending on whether the court considers it appropriate (to use a vague formulation) to upset the decision under review.[137]

10–73 As with all difficult legal questions, the matter is often one of degree. Thus, in *Sweeney v Judge Brophy*,[138] the Supreme Court appeared to suggest that the legal error in question must be decisive and that "routine mishaps" would not give rise to jurisdictional error. In this case a District judge with original jurisdiction to try an assault case committed a number of "fundamental irregularities" in the course of convicting the applicant. Hederman J. considered that such errors destroyed the jurisdiction of the District judge:

> "... *certiorari* is an appropriate remedy to quash not only a conviction bad on its face or where a court or tribunal acts without or in excess of jurisdiction but also where it acts apparently within jurisdiction but where the proceedings are so fundamentally flawed as to deprive an accused of a trial in due course of law. I take this opportunity of emphasising that *certiorari* is not appropriate to a routine mishap which may befall any trial; the correct remedy in that circumstance is by way of appeal. However, if there be a breach of the fundamental tenets of constitutional justice in the hearing or a failure to hear the evidence in the case the trial can properly be categorised as one which has not been held in due course of law ...".[139]

---

[136] Contrast, e.g. *Attorney General v Sheehy* [1990] 1 I.R. 70 in which it was assumed by the Supreme Court that the error would be reviewed as jurisdictional (without even a discussion to the contrary) with *State (Daly) v Ruane* [1988] I.L.R.M. 117, where a very restrictive approach to the scope of review was taken by O'Hanlon J. in the High Court.

[137] See, e.g. *Re Riordan* [1981] I.L.R.M. 2; *Killeen v Director of Public Prosecutions*, unreported, High Court, May 18, 1994 (reversed by the Supreme Court [1997] 3 I.R. 218; [1998] 1 I.L.R.M. 1). In both cases a finding of invalidity was perceived as being potentially unjust to private parties affected thereby, so the court in each case conveniently classified the error as one not affecting jurisdiction. This approach is also clearly evident in the judgment of Barrington J. in *Irish Permanent Building Society v Cauldwell* [1981] I.L.R.M. 242.

[138] [1993] 2 I.R. 202. The distinction drawn here had been anticipated in the decision of Lynch J. in *Gill v Connellan* [1987] I.R. 541.

[139] [1993] 2 I.R. 202 at 211. These principles have been applied in a number of subsequent decisions, though it should be noted that each of the following authorities involves the criminal jurisdiction of the inferior courts—rather than public administration more generally—and may have been affected thereby, since criminal jurisdiction is regarded as involving the most severe impact on individual rights. The authorities are: *McNally v Martin* [1995] 1 I.L.R.M. 350 (where the Supreme Court ruled that while the District judge had erred in law in a manner affecting jurisdiction in refusing to allow the defence to raise a legal argument, she had "behaved impeccably" in relation to a second charge, so that the second conviction was not tainted by the error in the first case); *Byrne v McDonnell* [1996] 1 I.L.R.M. 543 (wrongful refusal to grant adjournment affected jurisdiction in criminal prosecution); *Farrelly v Devally* [1998] 4 I.R. 76 (any irregularity in method of arrest of suspect did not deprive the court of jurisdiction); *Nevin v Judge Crowley* [2000] IESC 47; [2001] 1 I.R. 113 (where a failure to allow legal representatives to make submissions before sentence was imposed was held to

10–74   A similar preoccupation with the "severity" of the error under review might be said to have persisted in a number of recent High Court cases. For example, in *Ruttledge v Clyne*[140] a certificate noting the concentration of alcohol in the accused's breath printed the name of the prosecuting Garda rather than the accused's. At trial, the District judge amended the certificate, an action which both sides agreed before the High Court was an error of law. Dunne J. held, however, that the error was "of such a trivial nature that it should not give rise to a conclusion that the entire proceedings become a nullity".

10–75   On the other side of the line, in *Cork County Council v Shackleton*,[141] Clarke J. corrected an error of law committed by a property arbitrator who was exploring how property developers might fulfil their obligations to provide social and affordable housing under s.96 of the Planning and Development Act 2000. Clarke J. held in favour of a particular construction of the legislation, a construction that had not been applied by the arbitrator. Here, because the arbitrator was acting under statute and performing a public law function, the usual heightened deference to his findings would not be appropriate. Accordingly, Clarke J. quashed the arbitrator's determination because there was a "significant error in the interpretation of a material statutory provision leading to a decision of the property arbitrator being wrong in law".[142] The significance of Clarke J.'s emphasis on the severity of the arbitrator's error is debatable: on the one hand, Clarke J. may have been indicating that severity is always a relevant issue when a reviewing court is called upon to correct an error of law; but on the other hand, he may have been reacting to the traditional narrow scope of judicial review of arbitration decisions and may have felt compelled to provide an unimpeachable basis for his judgment. In another recent case, *McKernan v Employment Appeals Tribunal*,[143] Feeney J. referred to Clarke J.'s judgment in *Shackleton* as highlighting "the necessity to have regard to whether or not the error identified is significant relating to a material matter

---

be in excess of jurisdiction); *Orange v Director of Telecommunications (No. 2)* [2000] IESC 79; [2000] 4 I.R. 159 (where Murphy J. suggested at 244 that "the combination of error and an unsatisfactory trial" could lead to the quashing of a decision even where a judge was not, strictly speaking, biased); *Gilmartin v Murphy*, unreported, High Court, February 23, 2001 (where a failure to advise defendant of his right to legal representation rendered a conviction void ab initio); *O'Mahony v Ballagh* [2002] 2 I.R. 410 (where the failure of a District judge to rule specifically on a motion for non-suit saw him fall "into an unconstitutionality" and outside jurisdiction; but cf. *People (Director of Public Prosecutions) v Murphy* [2005] IECCA 1; [2005] 2 I.R. 125 holding that a judge is not compelled to rule on every single point that arises in the course of a hearing); *Landers v Patwell*, unreported, High Court, May 2, 2003 (inappropriate questioning by the trial judge justifying the granting of an order restraining any further trial of the applicant before the judge); *Bates v Judge Brady* [2003] IEHC 20; [2003] 4 I.R. 111 (where the respondent's decision to recall after the close of prosecution case a Garda witness who had failed to give a crucial piece of evidence going to the merits of the case rendered the conviction unsound; but cf. *Carey v Hussey* [1999] IEHC 71; [2000] 2 I.L.R.M. 401); *Duff v Dunne* [2004] IEHC 151; unreported, High Court, Herbert J., July 6, 2004 (where permitting a prosecution witness "to give new and very significant evidence" after all the evidence had been heard was fatal to the fairness of the proceedings); *Payne v Brophy* [2006] IEHC 34, [2006] 1 I.R. 560 (where the failure by a District Court judge to consider a challenge to the validity of a summons resulted in a jurisdictional error).

[140]   [2006] IEHC 146. In *Farrelly v Devally* [1998] 4 I.R. 76 at 82, Morris J. referred to the possibility of an "extreme example of an error of law" justifying High Court intervention.

[141]   [2007] IEHC 241.

[142]   [2007] IEHC 241 at para.9.7.

[143]   [2008] IEHC 40.

leading to the decision".[144] This interpretation of *Shackleton*, however, would not necessarily support any proposition that the significance (or magnitude) of the error of law is critical: Feeney J. was concerned, rather, with the materiality of the error and whether it affected the decision-maker's conclusion. In *McKernan*, though there was an error, it had no effect on the outcome of the decision-maker's hearing, because both parties proceeded on the same mistaken premises. Thus the error was not material. It might be objected that the nature or severity of such defects should go to the court's discretion to grant relief (rather than the basis of the court's power to intervene). This would be preferable to introducing a potentially confusing distinction between "severe" errors of law and "ordinary" errors of law. It is also difficult to see what the theoretical basis of such a distinction might be. If an error is not relevant or not material it can be dealt with at the relief stage. This is the path effectively taken in *McKernan*.[145]

10–76 After a series of decisions with contrasting—and not always reconcilable—reasoning, the judgment of Keane J. in *Killeen v Director of Public Prosecutions*[146] strongly suggested a rationalisation of the authorities along the lines of *Anisminic* and *Holland*. However, even here uncertainties abounded and no further rationalisation has occurred. In *Killeen*, a District judge discharged the applicants and, the Supreme Court held, erroneously refused to order their return for trial[147] on the ground that the arrest warrant was defective. On the question of whether the error was within jurisdiction, Keane J. first observed that:

> "It may be that an error of law committed by a tribunal acting within its jurisdiction is not capable of being set aside on certiorari: see *State (Davidson) v. Farrell*. It is otherwise where the error of law has its consequence the making of an order which the tribunal had no jurisdiction to make … *State (Holland) v. Kennedy* …".[148]

10–77 Having referred with approval to the speech of Lord Reid in *Anisminic* and the judgment of Henchy J. in *Holland*, Keane J. summarised the net question thus:

> "If the District judge in the present case discharged the applicants because he considered he was precluded from sending them forward for trial by reason of the defect in the warrant, was that an error of law which it was within his jurisdiction to make? I am satisfied that it was not. If the District judge was of that view, it follows that he failed to determine the precise question assigned for decision to the District Court i.e., as to whether, on the materials before the court, there was a sufficient case to put the applicants on trial. If that was

---

[144] [2008] IEHC 40 at para.4.6.

[145] cf. Cane, *Administrative Law* (Oxford: OUP, 2004), p.93.

[146] [1998] 1 I.L.R.M. 1. Cf. *Harte v Labour Court* [1996] 2 I.R. 171 where the applicant claimed that the respondent had exceeded jurisdiction by, inter alia, taking into account the existence of male comparators in an equal pay case taken by certain female part-time workers. Keane J.'s judgment rather curiously points in two directions.

[147] Keane J. acknowledged that this had the same status in law as an acquittal.

[148] [1998] 1 I.L.R.M. 1 at 8.

his decision, it constituted an error of law which rendered his order a nullity in accordance with the legal principles already set out."[149]

10–78   The effect of this decision is to restore some order and consistency to judicial views on the scope of jurisdictional error. It is clear that decisions such as *State (Daly) v Ruane*[150] which advocate a restrictive approach to the scope of jurisdictional review cannot now stand in the light of this decision.

Conclusions

10–79   No clear picture emerges from a consideration of the modern Irish cases, save that there is a trend towards treating all decisive errors of law as jurisdictional.[151] Part of the problem is that many of the Irish judges formerly used the word "jurisdiction" in the narrow sense of "original jurisdiction" and were disinclined to accept the argument that this jurisdiction might have been lost by reason of a serious error of law. And, while it has been long accepted by the Supreme Court since *State (Holland) v Kennedy*[152] that a tribunal may lose its jurisdiction by reason of legal error, with the possible exception of Keane J.'s authoritative judgment in *Killeen v Director of Public Prosecutions*,[153] there has, as yet, been no elaborate judicial statement of principle on this difficult issue, as has occurred in England in cases such as *Anisminic v Foreign Compensation Commission*[154] and *R. v Hull University Visitor Ex p. Page*.[155] Indeed, one of the other major judicial pronouncements—that of Henchy J. in *State (Abenglen Properties Ltd) v Dublin Corporation*[156]—based as it was on incorrect analysis of the post-*Anisminic* English authorities, only served to revive the old distinction and gave inconsistent signals as to the scope of jurisdictional review. While Keane J.'s judgment in *Killeen* goes a long way towards bringing coherence to Irish law, a fully comprehensive review of these issues is clearly required. It is disappointing that the Supreme Court has not seen fit to grapple with this problem even when the opportunity has clearly presented itself.[157]

10–80   Some indications of possible future developments in this area of the law are provided by *Tormey v Attorney General*.[158] Henchy J. observed that the High Court's "full original jurisdiction [over] all ... questions ... of law or fact, civil or criminal" under Art.34.3.1° might be invoked so as to ensure that "the hearing

---

[149] [1998] 1 I.L.R.M. 1 at 8, 10.
[150] [1988] I.L.R.M. 117. For a suggestion that the courts' power of review in Article 40.4.2° proceedings is even broader than in judicial review proceedings, see *Russell v Fanning* [1988] I.R. 505. This seems questionable, since the extent of the courts' power of review should not turn on the form of the proceedings or the (fortuitous) fact that the applicant happens to be in custody.
[151] Daly, "Judicial Review of Errors of Law in Ireland" (2006) 41 Ir. Jur. (N.S) 60, arguing that there is now a sufficient basis to recognise error of law as a ground of review in all cases in Ireland, at least where the errors are "clear".
[152] [1977] I.R. 193.
[153] [1998] 1 I.L.R.M. 1.
[154] [1969] 2 A.C. 147.
[155] [1993] A.C. 682.
[156] [1984] I.R. 381.
[157] See *Ryanair v Labour Court* [2007] IESC 6; [2007] 4 I.R. 199.
[158] [1985] I.R. 289.

and determination *will be in accordance with law*".[159] The context of this obiter observation was an explanation that, even though the High Court did not have original jurisdiction, it nevertheless retained a complete supervisory control over lower courts and tribunals. Accordingly, even if one does not, for policy reasons, wish to interpret Art.34.3.1° literally, this remark can be taken to mean that the High Court's power of review must be broad enough to allow it to quash at least for major errors of law committed by a lower court or administrative authority. It may also be that the High Court may review decisions of lower courts or administrative authorities which have been based on insufficient evidence. Alternatively, similar results might well be achieved through an extension of the constitutional principles of fair procedures and the right of access to the courts.[160] In any event, despite some recent inconsistent signals, our courts will probably find the trend towards increasing the scope of jurisdictional review to be well nigh irresistible.[161]

F. ERROR OF FACT AND MIXED QUESTIONS OF FACT AND LAW

10–81 Most of the errors in the cases just discussed have been errors on points of law, specifically statutory interpretation. And the distinctions between fact, law or mixed questions of fact and, on the other hand, law are rarely, if at all, discussed. Some limited discussion takes place in the context of appeals on points of law,[162] but discussion is conspicuous by its absence in the ever-growing output of judicial review decisions.[163]

10–82 It remains to deal now with the fate, in judicial review proceedings, of an argument that there has been an error of fact; and, later in this Part, with an error as to a mixed question of fact and law. Traditionally, among the most definite rocks of the island of immunity impregnable to judicial review,[164] has been error of fact.[165] It is easy to see why this should be so. First, constellations of facts, of their

---

[159] [1985] I.R. 289 at 297 (emphasis added).
[160] e.g. it could be argued that the constitutional guarantee of fair procedures requires that a decision be based on adequate, probative evidence, and Henchy J. has already argued along these lines in *M v M* [1979] I.L.R.M. 160. There are also hints of this in *State (Daly) v Minister for Agriculture* [1987] I.R. 165.
[161] Daly, "Judicial Review of Errors of Law in Ireland" (2006) 41 Ir. Jur. (N.S) 60.
[162] See, e.g. the illuminating Supreme Court discussion of what constitutes "mining operations" in *O'Connell (Inspector of Taxes) v Tara Mines* [2002] IESC 67; [2002] 3 I.R. 438. See also, *National University of Ireland, Cork v Ahern* [2005] IESC 40; [2005] 2 I.R. 577.
[163] Daly, "Judicial Review of Errors of Law in Ireland" (2006) 41 Ir. Jur. (N.S) 60.
[164] The *locus classicus* is *R. (Martin) v Mahoney* [1910] 2 I.R. 695. This view is also borne out by modern authorities: *State (Power) v Moran* [1976–1977] I.L.R.M. 20; *State (Shinkaruk) v Carroll*, unreported, High Court, December 15, 1976; *Memorex World Trade Corporation v Employment Appeals Tribunal* [1990] 2 I.R. 184; *Stokes v O'Donnell* [1999] 3 I.R. 218. As was said in *Lennon v Clifford* [1992] 1 I.R. 382 at 386 (O'Hanlon J.), the High Court does not act "… as a court of appeal from decisions of other tribunals". This statement was expressly approved by the Supreme Court on appeal: [1996] 2 I.R. 590 at 593 per Murphy J. Similar comments may be found in, e.g. *Chief Constable of the North Wales Police v Evans* [1982] 1 W.L.R. 1155 at 1173 per Lord Brightman (a frequently quoted passage); *Garda Representative Association v Ireland* [1994] 1 I.L.R.M. 81 at 88 per Finlay C.J.; *Devlin v Minister for Arts, Culture and the Gaeltacht* [1999] 1 I.R. 47 at 58 per Murphy J.
[165] One proviso is that exercises of discretionary powers must be factually justified. See, e.g. *State (Lynch) v Cooney* [1982] I.R. 337; *State (Daly) v Minister for Agriculture* [1987] I.R. 165; *Kiberd v Hamilton* [1992] 2 I.R. 257. The old orthodoxy no longer prevails in England: see *E*

nature, are unique and erroneous decisions in relation to them leave no precedents. Secondly, the body whose decision is under review will have heard the witnesses and sifted the documents, and will often be a specialised body with expertise and experience in the particular field.

10–83   These considerations justify the traditional position that a court will not review for error of fact. In *Ryanair Ltd v Flynn*,[166] Kearns J. commented on the general unavailability of judicial review for errors of fact:

> "There is no body of jurisprudence in this jurisdiction which suggests that it would be desirable for the Courts to interfere where errors within jurisdiction are made ... [A] very high threshold must be met ... before the Court can or should intervene."[167]

10–84   The background to this case was a dispute between the applicant airline and a trade union, which caused the temporary closure of Dublin Airport. The Minister for Enterprise, Trade and Employment invoked s.38(2) of the Industrial Relations Act 1990 and appointed the respondents, industrial relations experts, to conduct an inquiry into the dispute. The question for resolution was whether Ryanair's remuneration of baggage handling staff was below the industry norm. The applicant was unhappy with the conclusions reached and sought judicial review, inter alia, on the basis that errors of fact had been made by the respondent. The disagreement was rather heated: the parties could not even agree on companies with which comparisons could be drawn. As it happened, British Midland and Servisair were deemed the most appropriate comparators. The first task undertaken by the respondents was to establish the relevant factual matters, such as how much Ryanair staff were paid for ordinary working hours, overtime and holidays and how much British Midland and Servisair staff were paid for the same types of work. In the light of these facts Kearns J. made some general comments:

> "[V]ery considerable difficulties can and do arise when the dispute is in a specialised area and the facts themselves are in dispute and the subject matter of claim and counterclaim. In the instant case not merely are the facts in dispute, but differences of opinion exist as to the appropriate methodology for establishing the facts and as to the inferences to be drawn therefrom. When, as suggested by the inquiry report, the issue of pay comparability caused staff both in the applicant and members of [a trade union] considerable confusion, that is of itself a reason suggesting the court should be slow to enter the arena of fact finding. When that confusion is added to by the claims and counterclaims of those who profess superior knowledge and insight into the situation, it strongly suggests that the court should not engage in fact finding where mistake of fact is alleged unless it is absolutely necessary to do so. When placed in such a situation, it is my view that the court should

---

v *Secretary of State for the Home Department* [2004] EWCA Civ 49; [2004] Q.B. 1044; Craig, *Administrative Law* (London: Sweet & Maxwell, 2008), Ch.15; Woolf, Jowell and Le Sueur, *De Smith's Judicial Review*, 6th edn (London: Sweet & Maxwell, 2007), pp.564–569.
[166]   [2000] IEHC 36; [2000] 3 I.R. 240.
[167]   [2000] IEHC 36; [2000] 3 I.R. 240 at 264–265.

first determine whether or not the application is capable of being resolved on discrete and separate grounds as its first task."[168]

10–85 As a last resort, Kearns J. suggested, the court would usually exercise its discretion to refuse a remedy as a means of avoiding entangling itself in the protracted dispute under review. The position in this passage is a little confused, because the situation under review in this case was not a dispute as to basic facts, but, because of the comparability element, was very much at the mixed law and fact end of the scale. It is notable though that in *Aer Rianta Cpt v Commissioner for Aviation Regulation*,[169] O'Sullivan J. rejected the suggestion that the High Court had any power whatever to correct errors of fact:

"I would share Kearns J.'s marked reluctance to endorse the notion of jurisdiction to correct for error [of fact] as expressed in his judgment in *Ryanair*. Insofar as his obiter dicta in that case may appear to acknowledge the existence of such a jurisdiction I would respectfully decline to agree."[170]

10–86 This remains substantially the present position. However, there has been significant blurring at the edges. In a number of decisions in the last decade, the superior courts have quashed errors of fact in judicial review proceedings.[171] Pressure in favour of a shift from orthodoxy has come mainly from cases brought by those who had applied, unsuccessfully, for refugee status. Again, it is not hard to see why this should be so. Inevitably, the factual disputes in such cases usually centre on events in a far-off country which the tribunal member has never visited and in a society of which they have had no experience. In this predicament, an unusually high proportion of the bases of the facts, as found by the relevant tribunal, depend not on the informed hearing of witnesses or perusal of comprehensive documentation; but rather on the drawing of inferences, from incomplete data, by reference to that subjective and uncommon thing, common sense. In addition, the bodies charged with assessing asylum applications have been the subject of significant public controversy.[172] Not surprisingly, in some cases, the High Court may feel that its grasp on common sense is as secure as that of the tribunal. But

---

[168] [2000] IEHC 36; [2000] 3 I.R. 240 at 266–267.
[169] [2003] IEHC 707.
[170] cf. Delany, "Judicial Review in Cases of Asylum Seekers" (2002) 24 D.U.L.J. 1 at 24, describing this language as "unnecessarily strong".
[171] See, e.g. *BM(A) v Minister for Justice* [2001] IEHC 110; unreported, High Court, O'Donovan J., July 23, 2001; *Gulyas and Borchardt v Minister for Justice* [2001] IEHC 100; [2001] 3 I.R. 216; [2004] IEHC 219; [2004] 2 I.R. 607; *DVTS v Minister for Justice, Equality and Law Reform* [2007] IEHC 305; unreported, High Court, Edwards J., July 4, 2007; *Keagnene v Minister for Justice, Equality and Law Reform* [2007] IEHC 17; unreported, High Court, January 31, 2007. Such errors must be material to the decision if relief is to be available—see, e.g. *KK v Minister for Justice* [2007] IEHC 148; unreported, High Court, McGovern J., May 22, 2007. See Mulcahy, "Jurisdictional Errors of Fact in Judicial Review" (2008) I.L.T. 298.
[172] "Members of refugee appeal body considered taking legal action", *The Irish Times*, March 8, 2008; *PPA v Refugee Appeals Tribunal* [2006] IESC 53; [2007] 4 I.R. 94; *Nyembo v Refugee Appeals Tribunal* [2007] IESC 25; [2008] 1 I.L.R.M. 289. See also, Byrne, "Expediency in Refugee Determination Procedures" (2000) 35 Ir. Jur. (N.S) 149. For discussion and references in the English context, see Rawlings, "Review, Revenge and Retreat" (2005) 68 M.L.R. 378 at 387–388.

these decisions are exceptional[173] and are capable of being rationalised in a manner that fits the prevailing orthodoxy on factual error.[174]

10–87   One should emphasise, too, that there is a substantial overlap, in that this development affects not only errors of basic fact, but also errors of mixed fact and law and those involved in the exercise of a discretionary power. For historical reasons, these blocs of law have developed in separate streams of authority and, consequently, are treated in separate Parts of this book. However, by now, recent case law, which may be modifying the law in this area, seems to be couched in judicial language which straddles all three categories. For this reason, the reader is referred to discussion of a possible reduction in "curial deference", which affects administrative agency decisions, not only as to facts, but also as to mixed questions as to law and low-level exercises of discretionary power. This is a wider topic which will be discussed further at paras 15–64 to 15–72.

10–88   There is one particular exception to the general principle against re-agitating facts in judicial review proceedings: if the jurisdiction of the body under review is dependent on the existence of a collateral fact, there must be sufficient evidence on which the court can conclude that its jurisdictional requirements have been satisfied. This may be illustrated by *State (Holland) v Kennedy*.[175] In that case the District Court's jurisdiction to sentence a young person to prison was contingent on evidence that the accused was "depraved". Henchy J. concluded that the District judge erred in law in a manner going to jurisdiction when she wrongly concluded that this statutory requirement was satisfied by one single aberrational incident. In other words, there was no, or insufficient, evidence to enable the District Court to conclude that this jurisdictional requirement had been satisfied.

Determining the facts

10–89   In line with this point of principle, there remains the practical consideration that judicial review proceedings are not designed to deal with factual disputes. First, following the general rule, the applicants must make their case. In *GK v Minister for Justice*[176] in which the applicants were claiming that their representation for leave to remain in the State had not been considered, the Minister had responded with a letter stating that the representations had been considered. In face of this, the applicant sought to argue the contrary. This argument was rejected by Hardiman J. (writing for the Supreme Court)[177]:

> "A person claiming that a decision making authority has, contrary to its express statement, ignored representations which it has received must produce some evidence, direct or inferential of that proposition before he can be said to have an arguable case."

---

[173]   For the very particular case of *AMT v Refugee Appeals Tribunal* [2004] IEHC 219; [2004] 2 I.R. 607, see H & M, paras 10–136 to 10–137.
[174]   See Daly, "Judicial Review of Factual Error in Ireland" (2008) 30 D.U.L.J. 187.
[175]   [1977] I.R. 193. See also, *Greene v Governor of Mountjoy Prison* [1995] 3 I.R. 541.
[176]   [2002] 2 I.R. 418.
[177]   [2002] 2 I.R. 418 at 425. See further, *P v Minister for Justice, Equality and Law Reform* [2002] 1 I.R. 164 at 175.

10–90 The second limitation, which is discussed in detail at paras 16–27 to 16–28, stems from the essential character of judicial review: normally evidence may not be heard by a reviewing court[178]; and a related point is that "[i]t is not always helpful and indeed it is frequently unhelpful to have large tracts of technical and/or expert evidence, since the court is being asked to condemn the decision on the basis that there was no proper consideration at all of the application on its merits".[179] On that understanding of the law, detailed evidence should not be necessary. But, despite this general position, in the High Court, various resources are available, and have recently been strengthened, to settle disputes on the facts. These include: the minutes of a decision-making meeting; affidavits of participants at such a meeting; or public statements made by the responsible authority. And, in a characteristic passage in *East Donegal Co-Operative Ltd v Attorney General*, Walsh J. noted the existence of such devices as discovery and interrogatories and then issued the following warning:

"... [T]he resources of the Courts ... are not so limited that they could facilitate ... the concealment of an infringement of constitutional rights or the masking of injustice."[180]

10–91 One should add that it might be thought that a distinction could be drawn between a dispute on the substantive facts before the public body respondent and, on the other hand, the facts as to how the public body had gone about its decision-making process. (*GK* provides an example of the second category.) In fact, no such distinction has been drawn.[181]

10–92 Finally, to go one step further, it has long been regarded as axiomatic that a court in judicial review proceedings will not receive evidence which post-dates the decision under review.[182] This view was confirmed (albeit with a twist) in one of the few cases in which judicial attention has been paid to this point, *Efe v Minister for Justice, Equality and Law Reform*.[183] The High Court (Hogan J.) held that to receive such evidence would be to cross the line between appeal and review, in

---

[178] For discussion, see *Orange Ltd v Director of Telecoms (No. 2)* [2000] 4 I.R. 159 at 190, 238–241 and 266. In *Oguekwe v Minister for Justice, Equality and Law Reform* [2008] 3 I.R. 795 at paras 66–69 and 72, it was stated, in an analogous situation to that of a reviewing court, that even "... the Minister should consider in a general fashion the situation in the country where the child's parents may be deported; it is not necessary to do a specific analysis of the education and development opportunities that may be available to the child".

[179] *Bemis v Minister for Arts, Heritage, Gaeltacht and the Islands* [2007] 3 I.R. 255 at para.41. See also, *Orange Ltd v Director of Telecoms (No. 2)* [2000] 4 I.R. 159 at 238–241, 266, 272. See also, *Ni Eili v Environmental Protection Agency*, unreported, Supreme Court, July 30, 1999 at pp.17–18.

[180] [1970] I.R. 317 at 349. See also, *State (McGough) v Louth County Council* (1973) 107 I.L.T.R. 13 at 25; *Breen v Minister for Defence* [1994] 2 I.R. 34; *Brennan v Minister for Justice* [1995] 1 I.R. 612; *Gavin v Criminal Injuries Compensation Tribunal* [1997] 1 I.R. 132; and *Padfield v Minister for Agriculture* [1968] A.C. 1032 at 1061. (These authorities are analysed in the 3rd edn, pp.625–626.) But *a contra*, see *P&F Sharpe Ltd v Dublin County Council* [1989] I.R. 701.

[181] See, e.g. *AA and EP v Minister for Justice, Equality and Law Reform* [2005] 4 I.R. 564 at 574, para.32.

[182] *ISOF v Minister for Justice, Equality and Law Reform* [2010] IEHC 457.

[183] [2011] 2 I.L.R.M. 411 at paras 36–44, from which paragraphs the quotations in the text are taken.

that the court would be acting on the basis of new information which was never before the decision-maker.[184]

Mixed questions of law and fact

10–93   The tangled issue of the type of error which attracts the supervisory jurisdiction of the High Court has just been considered, first with reference mainly to errors of law and, thereafter, more briefly with regard to errors of fact. It remains in this section to consider the even more difficult marshland which runs between the two extremities. For the categories of law, fact and mixed law and fact are not hermetically sealed and tend to cross-pollinate and sow confusion with rare abandon. Although this unwelcoming terrain has not yet been fully judicially recognised, it is worth making some preliminary comments since the case law is likely to increase in the future. We may start with the following helpful account:

> "Perplexing problems may, however, arise in analysing the nature of the process by which a tribunal determines whether a factual situation falls within or without the limits of a category or standard prescribed by a statute or other legal instrument. Every finding by a tribunal postulates a process of abstraction and inference, which may be conditioned solely by the adjudicator's practical experience and knowledge of affairs, or partly or wholly by his knowledge of legal principle. He hears evidence and, by satisfying himself as to its reliability, finds what were the 'true' facts; it may then be necessary for him to draw a series of inferences from these primary findings in order to determine what were the material facts on which he has to base his decision; in order to draw certain of these inferences correctly he may need to apply his knowledge of legal rules. At what point does an inference

---

[184] In addition to this consideration, another broader constitutional reason was given by Hogan J. in *Efe*. This was that immigration and deportation "squarely involved the executive power". Coupled with this: "Any attempt to vest the judicial branch with functions in the immigration sphere akin to the determination and application of purely policy questions would, however, represent an unconstitutional violation of the separation of powers, as it would be tantamount to vesting the judicial branch with decision making powers of a type, style and nature which Art. 28 reserves to the executive branch."

This passage would require considerable study and may receive some judicial refinement in the future. All that can be said here is that the conventional view is that "the executive power of the State", which is the subject matter of Art.28, is a very narrow category; and secondly that non-judicial functions could be vested in the judiciary.

Hogan J. continued this line of thought, by another striking statement, which tells in the opposite direction : "Given that, subject to limited exceptions, immigration decisions can be challenged only by way of judicial review … I agree that if there were no mechanism whereby material facts which post-date the initial decision could not be acted on by the executive, such a lacuna would have represented a failure by the State to provide a procedure whereby applicants' constitutional rights could be adequately vindicated. Had there been such a lacuna, then in line with the Supreme Court's decision in *Carmody v Minister for Justice, Equality and Law Reform* [2009] IESC 71 … the applicants would in principle have been entitled to a declaration to this effect. The need for a mechanism whereby new facts can be assessed might be especially true in the general sphere of family rights under Art. 41 … but, as it happens, there is such a mechanism. In the immigration sphere, the applicants have a tailor-made remedy which can address new post-decision facts, namely the power to revoke the deportation order under s.3(11) of the Refugee Act, 1999 …".

This is a radical use of the Constitution to shift one of the foundation stones of judicial review (such as has been done by few other judges; see paras 10–27 to 10–28).

drawn from facts become an inference of law? Is the application of a statutory norm to the material facts always to be classified as the determination of a question of law? And where in this spectrum lie questions of policy?"[185]

10–94 Fairly typical examples of what De Smith calls "a category or standard prescribed by a statute ..." include the issue of "domicile" (which was at the heart of *Lambert v An tÁrd Chláratheoir*),[186] "political end" (in *Colgan v Independent Radio and Television Commission*)[187] or "sow" (in *Shannon Regional Fisheries Board v An Bord Pleanála*),[188] of which the first will be analysed below. These are classic examples of questions of mixed law and fact, because they involve the decision-maker applying statutory criteria to facts, but might equally well be classified as jurisdictional questions, in that the existence of "domicile", "political end" and "sow" are in a sense pre-conditions to the exercise of the jurisdiction conferred.

10–95 With these examples in mind and drawing in part on the above passage, we can say that the characteristic decision in this area may require the decision-maker to follow up to four stages of reasoning. First, a basic finding (or set of findings) of fact will be required, and this was considered earlier in this Part. Secondly, inferences will be drawn from these facts so as to reach a result at an appropriate level of abstraction for the statutory category. Thirdly, the decision-maker must compare the result of this second stage with the statutory category. Fourthly, it will sometimes be necessary to interpret the statutory category in the light of these facts. (In practice, some of these stages will be conflated or taken out of sequence so that it will not be clear at which stage the error lies.) In any case, we can say that stages one and four involve fact and law, respectively. Stages two and three—where the decision-maker is appraising and characterising the facts in the light of his understanding of the statutory category—is the difficult area marked "mixed law and fact", which involves the exercise of a discretionary power. Accordingly the same rules of control should be applied, a point which is brought out in the excellent analysis in *Ashford Castle Ltd v SIPTU*,[189] which arose out of the Labour Court's determination of pay rates. In the High Court, Clarke J. stated:

> "The tasks which administrative bodies are given under statute vary significantly ... At one end of the spectrum are issues which involve the same sort of mixed questions of law and fact with which the courts are frequently faced. A person may for example be entitled to a Social Welfare benefit provided that a certain set of facts, as specified by statute, are found to exist ... At the other end of the spectrum, expert bodies may be required to bring to bear upon a situation a great deal of their own expertise in relation to matters which involve the exercise of an expert judgment. Bodies charged with, for

---

[185] De Smith, Woolf and Jowell, *Judicial Review of Administrative Action*, 5th edn (London: Sweet & Maxwell, 1995), p.297. This quotation does not appear at as great a length in the latest edition.

[186] [1995] 2 I.R. 372. See paras 10–98 to 10–99.

[187] [2000] 2 I.R. 490. See H & M, para.10–148.

[188] [1994] 3 I.R. 449. See H & M, para.10–149.

[189] [2007] 4 I.R. 70. The quotation is at paras 36–42. The case was an appeal on a point of law to the High Court, from the Labour Court, regarding the Labour Court's determination in relation to rates of pay in the plaintiff's hotel. While the precise issue was the scope of an appeal on a point of law from an expert tribunal, it was accepted that the High Court's jurisdiction in this situation is similar to that in judicial review.

example, roles in the planning process are required to exercise a judgment as to what might be the proper planning and development of an area … [A] great deal of the expertise of the body will be concerned with exercising planning judgment independent of questions of disputed fact. In such cases the underlying facts are normally not in dispute … Some of the cases use terminology such as 'evidence' and 'findings of fact' which are borrowed from the approach of the courts. That terminology is entirely apposite where the issue which the statutory body has to decide is towards the end of the spectrum [first] identified above … Where applied to decisions towards the end of the spectrum, language such as 'evidence' and 'findings of fact' has, in my view, a capacity to mislead … It may, in those circumstances, be more appropriate to speak of 'materials' rather than 'evidence'. It may also be more appropriate to speak of 'conclusions' rather than 'findings of fact'. In those circumstances it seems to me that the Labour Court [in fixing pay rates] is very much towards the edge of the spectrum where it is required to bring to bear its own expert view on the overall approach to the issues … [A] very high degree of deference indeed needs to be applied to decisions which involve the exercise by a statutory body, such as the Labour Court, of an expertise which this court does not have."

10–96   The distinction between a dispute as to basic facts and the appraisal of them made by the expert statutory body is a useful one. As indicated in this passage, the appraisal—as, for instance, in the case of fixing pay rates or (say) determining what is "proper planning and development" of an area—is really a "covert" example of an exercise of discretionary power and should be treated as such.[190]

10–97   As regards the issue of whether errors in this area can be reviewed by the High Court, very little can be said since the matter has yet to be fully confronted by the Irish courts. This issue arises most frequently in appeals on a point of law. The reason is obvious: if a court has authority only to answer a question of law, by definition it does not have authority to answer either questions of mixed law and fact or questions of fact, and so requires some means of distinguishing law from fact and from mixed law and fact.[191]

10–98   The more difficult of these two borderlines is the second, that is where what the applicant is urging the High Court to review is an administrative body's evaluating of the facts in the light of an interpretation of the law. A case in point is *Lambert v An tÁrd Chláraitheoir*.[192] In this case the applicant sought to compel the Registrar-General to grant him a licence enabling him to re-marry. Permission was refused on the ground that the foreign divorce would not have been recognised here and this in turn raised the question of whether the parties to the first marriage had been domiciled in England at the relevant time. Kinlen J. first rejected the argument that the Registrar-General's conclusion on the issue of domicile could only be assailed on irrationality grounds:

---

[190]   At para.15–72, we criticise the modern tendency to conflate the rules for control of discretionary powers with those for error of basic fact, which is a different matter.
[191]   See the discussion of "Administrative Appeals" at Ch.11, Part D.
[192]   [1995] 2 I.R. 372.

"This case is not concerned with a situation where an administrative tribunal has been afforded a discretion in an administrative matter ... The present case turns on the determination of [the] legal issue of domicile ... It is clear that the determination of a person's domicile involves consideration of a legal issue; the Registrar-General cannot enjoy any discretion in the determination of this matter. The determination of the Registrar-General of an issue of law need not be treated with the same deference as the determination of a specialised tribunal on an issue of fact."[193]

10–99 As Kinlen J. was satisfied that the relevant party was domiciled abroad, the Registrar-General's conclusion was thereby set aside. It is worth emphasising that in *Lambert* the facts were not at issue; the Registrar-General appears to have misdirected himself in law and the incorrect inferences were drawn from the primary facts. It seems clear that a wrong inference of this kind will be classified as a jurisdictional error; what was not clear is whether the issue in *Lambert* was one of law[194]: domicile, as Kinlen J. acknowledged, is a mixed question of law and fact,[195] which would suggest that the High Court should have been slow to interfere. However, as against this, the issue seems to be more one of law than discretion. In addition, the Registrar General had no special expertise which is not also available to the High Court, and there was no reason, therefore, to accord any deference to his decision. In other words, it is respectfully suggested that the result is correct.

G. Error on the Face of the Record

10–100 The jurisdiction to review for error on the face of the record is an anomalous one since the power to review is not based on jurisdiction or ultra vires. Nevertheless, this power of review enables the High Court to quash a decision, otherwise within jurisdiction, if that decision contains an error of law,[196] on the face of the record.[197] It has fallen out of use in England, since all errors of law are now reviewable there regardless of where they appeared, but given the uncertainty about the High Court's jurisdiction to correct errors of law in this jurisdiction, some discussion is warranted.

---

[193] [1995] 2 I.R. 372 at 384.

[194] But cf. *Harte v Labour Court* [1996] 2 I.R. 171 for a suggestion that determinations of mixed questions of law and fact were not amenable to review on grounds of jurisdictional error. The wider problem was also in view in a case involving the meaning of the word "advertising" in s.10 of the Radio and Television Act 1988: *Radio Limerick One v Independent Radio and Television Commission* [1997] 2 I.L.R.M. 1 at 24.

[195] [1995] 2 I.R. 372 at 384. See also, *KED v MC*, unreported, High Court, September 26, 1984, cited in *MEC v JOC* [2001] IEHC 68; [2001] 2 I.R. 399 at 404; *RB v AS* [2001] IEHC 83; unreported, High Court, February 28, 2001. A similar conflation of questions of law and questions of mixed law and fact may have occurred in *Colgan v Irish Radio and Television Commission* [1998] IEHC 117; [2002] 2 I.R. 490.

[196] *Solomon v Nicholson* [2006] IEHC 29; unreported, High Court, Herbert J., February 7, 2006. But this jurisdiction does not extend to errors of fact. See *State (CIÉ) v An Bord Pleanála*, unreported, High Court, Carroll J., February 12, 1984.

[197] Thus, in *R. v Knightsbridge Crown Court Ex p. International Sporting Club Ltd* [1982] Q.B. 304 a Divisional Court was evenly divided as to whether a particular error of law went to jurisdiction, but held that, as they were agreed the error of law appeared on the record, the decision could be quashed.

10–101 What is the record? One traditional definition is that of Denning L.J.:

"[T]he record must contain at least the document which initiates the proceedings; the pleadings, if any; and the adjudication; but not the evidence, nor the reasons, unless the tribunal chooses to incorporate them. If the tribunal does state its reasons, and the reasons are wrong in law, certiorari lies to quash the decision."[198]

10–102 To this it may be objected that a court or tribunal could avoid review for error on the face of the record by the High Court by the simple expedient of refusing to make a judgment part of the final order or refusing to give any reason for a decision at all. But it is clear that English law, at any rate, has now progressed to the point whereby the reasons given orally for a decision are now regarded as forming part of the record, which is, when thus augmented, known as a "speaking order".[199] Moreover, the English courts have strongly hinted that they have jurisdiction, at least in appropriate cases, to call for reasons to be given for the decision by the tribunal or lower court,[200] so that if these reasons exhibit an error of law, the resulting decision may be quashed as appearing on the "face" of the record, irrespective of whether that error would otherwise affect jurisdiction.

10–103 In Ireland, we are lacking good, recent authority in this area. Older authorities[201] might suggest that the scope of review for error of law on the face of the record does not appear to be quite as broad as that suggested by recent English and Northern Irish authorities,[202] at any rate outside the particular field of criminal procedure.[203] However, it seems likely that a wider approach would be taken by the modern Supreme Court, comparable to the British authorities.

10–104 For the key feature determining the potency of this jurisdiction lies in the width of the "record" which is available. And, in Ireland, there has probably been an expansion of what constitutes the record, due to two reasons. First, the supporting documentation (pleadings, transcripts, written reasons for decisions, etc) is generally now more elaborate than was the case in the early part of the twentieth century, when the jurisdiction to review for error on the record had

---

[198] *R. v Northumberland Compensation Appeal Tribunal Ex p. Shaw* [1952] 1 K.B. 338 at 352. In *Ryan v Compensation Tribunal* [1997] 1 I.L.R.M. 194 at 200 Costello P. approved this passage as a correct statement of the extent of the record in civil cases. In a powerfully written article, "Documentary Error as a Ground of Judicial Review in Irish Law" (1993–1995) 28–30 Ir. Jur. (N.S) 145 at 150 Costello has disputed the historical basis for Denning L.J.'s conclusion.

[199] See, e.g. *R. v Chertsey JJ. Ex p. Franks* [1961] 2 Q.B. 152; *R. v Supplementary Benefits Commission Ex p. Singer* [1973] 1 W.L.R. 713; *R. v Knightsbridge Crown Court Ex p. International Sporting Club Ltd* [1982] Q.B. 304; *a contra*: Costello, "Documentary Error as a Ground of Judicial Review in Irish Law" (1993–1995) 28–30 Ir. Jur. (N.S) 145 at 150.

[200] "The Court has always had power to order an inferior tribunal to complete the record"; per Denning L.J. in *R. v Medical Appeal Tribunal Ex p. Gilmore* [1957] 1 Q.B. 574 at 582–583. See also, *R. v Knightsbridge Crown Court Ex p. International Sporting Club* [1982] Q.B. 304. This view is also implicit in the Supreme Court's judgment in *State (Creedon) v Criminal Injuries Compensation Tribunal* [1988] I.R. 51.

[201] See, e.g. *Walsh v Minister for Local Government* [1929] I.R. 377.

[202] Surveyed in H & M at paras 10–162 to 10–165.

[203] For the particular field of criminal procedure, see H & M, paras 10–168 to 10–71. Note that the necessity for official orders to demonstrate jurisdiction on their face is covered in H & M, paras 10–169 to 10–171.

fallen into decline. In addition, the facilities for recording spoken judgments is also nowadays far superior.[204] Secondly, there has been, especially because of Freedom of Information legislation, as noted in Chapter 14, Part D, a deepening of the duty to give reasons for a decision. Secondly, the courts are nowadays loath to allow a decision containing an error of law to survive review and will tend to classify such error as either going to jurisdiction or appearing on the face of the record.

10–105 In *State (Attorney General) v Binchy*,[205] the former Supreme Court implied that the record in a criminal trial on indictment was confined to the formal record of the trial (i.e. only the official court documents, the verdict and record of conviction, if any). Yet, some three years later, the Supreme Court held in *Re Tynan*[206] that the record in such a case included the court orders and the transcript (thus rendering a conviction liable to be quashed if, for example, the judge erred in law in his summing-up). Finally, in one of the few Irish cases on this point where an administrative order was quashed for error on the face of the record, *Bannon v Employment Appeals Tribunal*,[207] an error of law appearing in the Tribunal's decision was held to have appeared on the record and it was accordingly quashed.[208] And, in *Royal Dublin Society v Revenue Commissioners*,[209] a letter to the applicant stating reasons for refusal of a licence application was held to be part of the record.

---

[204] See the comments of Griffiths L.J. in *R. v Knightsbridge Crown Court Ex p. International Sporting Club* [1982] Q.B. 304. However, the presence of a stenographer in the District Court is a rare occurrence.

[205] [1964] I.R. 395.

[206] Unreported, Supreme Court, December 20, 1963.

[207] [1993] 1 I.R. 500.

[208] cf. *Amadi v Minister for Justice, Equality and Law Reform* [2005] IEHC 338; unreported, High Court, October 13, 2005, albeit in the context of an application for leave, where O'Neill J. held that a report sent to the Minister and underlying the decision to make a deportation order was not part of the record.

[209] [1999] IESC 45; [2000] 1 I.R. 270 at 280.

FUNDAMENTAL PRINCIPLES OF JUDICIAL REVIEW II

11–01   Chapter 10 had a strong unifying theme, namely the ultra vires doctrine, that is, for any administrative action, there must be a statutory authorisation and that the focus in judicial review is on whether such authorisation exists. However, the present Chapter is miscellaneous, dealing in Parts A–D with adjunct matters relating to the judicial review process before the High Court such as: statutory restriction of judicial reveiw, the practical consequences of invalidity, severance or the contrasts with appeals; and in the remaining Parts, with substantive rules, such as the "no delegation" principle.

A. STATUTORY RESTRICTION OF JUDICIAL REVIEW

Full ouster clauses

11–02   The courts have never looked favourably on legislative attempts to curb the High Court's supervisory jurisdiction over decisions of lower courts and administrative bodies.[1] Even at common law, both the High Court[2] and the

---

[1]   See the strict manner in which the Supreme Court has construed such clauses in cases such as *Pine Valley*; *State (Finglas Industrial Estates Ltd) v Dublin County Council*, unreported, Supreme Court, February 17, 1983; and *KSK Enterprises Ltd v An Bord Pleanála* [1994] 2 I.R. 128. The courts have declined to apply such clauses retrospectively, as to do so would unconstitutionally infringe on vested rights. See *Child v Wicklow County Council* [1995] 2 I.R. 447.

[2]   *State (O'Duffy) v Bennett* [1935] I.R. 70; *State (Hughes) v Lennon* [1935] I.R. 128; *Murren v Brennan* [1942] I.R. 466; and *State (Horgan) v Exported Livestock Board Ltd* [1943] I.R. 581. See also, *R. (Conyngham) v Pharmaceutical Society of Ireland* [1894] 2 I.R. 132; *Commissioners of Public Works v Monaghan* [1909] 2 I.R. 718; *R. (Sinnott) v Wexford Corporation* [1910] 2 I.R. 403; and *Waterford Corporation v Murphy* [1920] 2 I.R. 165. For a variation on the theme, see Carroll J.'s consideration in *Serco Services Ireland Ltd v Labour Court* [2001] IEHC 125; unreported, High Court, Carroll J., July 12, 2001. For a survey, which includes pre-Independence jurisprudence, see AG Donaldson, *Some Comparative Aspects of Irish Law* (London: Cambridge University Press, 1957), Ch.5.

Supreme Court[3] when confronted with widely drafted statutory[4] ouster clauses (sometimes known as "no certiorari" clauses) have affirmed on many occasions that such clauses will not protect a decision which is ultra vires. However, it may be that an ouster clause will have the limited effect of preventing the High Court from granting certiorari where the alleged defect is a non-jurisdictional error of law only,[5] very much a booby prize for the legislature.

11–03 More fundamentally, the constitutionality of legislative attempts to oust the High Court's power of review must be doubtful in light of the decision of the Supreme Court in *Tormey v Attorney General*.[6] In that case Henchy J. observed that Art.34.3.1°, when read in conjunction with Art.34.3.4° and Art.37,[7] permitted the Oireachtas to vest lower courts or administrative tribunals[8] with exclusive jurisdiction in respect of certain justiciable controversies, but where this had been done:

> "[The] full jurisdiction [of the High Court] is there to be invoked – in proceedings such as habeas corpus, certiorari, prohibition, mandamus, quo warranto, injunction or a declaratory action – so as to ensure that the hearing and determination will be in accordance with law. Save to the extent required by the terms of the Constitution itself, no justiciable matter or question may be excluded from the range of the original jurisdiction of the High Court."[9]

Partial ouster clauses: brief limitation periods

11–04 A more live issue at present concerns partial ouster clauses—legislative provisions which, instead of attempting to effect a complete ouster of the High Court's judicial review jurisdiction, purport to impose brief limitation periods.[10] It is worth noting that apart from such particular legislative regimes, the general rules of court for judicial review permit a limitation period of, in principle, only three months. Thus the analysis given here[11] might also be relevant in respect of this general regime.

11–05 Partial ouster clauses (which generally take the form of very short limitation periods) may be defended—at least in some cases—on the ground that, in the case

---

[3] *State (McCarthy) v O'Donnell* [1945] I.R. 126; *Brannigan v Keady* [1959] I.R. 283.
[4] This reasoning applies a fortiori to non-statutory ouster clauses: *Casey v Minister for Agriculture*, unreported, High Court, McCarthy J., February 6, 1987.
[5] *R. v Medical Appeal Tribunal Ex p. Gilmore* [1957] 1 Q.B. 574. But in *Gilmore* it was decided that the court may still intervene to quash for error of law on the face of the record even where the tribunal's decision is expressed to be final.
[6] [1985] I.R. 289.
[7] Article 34.3.1° vests the High Court with "full original jurisdiction" in respect of all matters and questions "whether of fact or law, civil or criminal". Article 34.3.4° goes on to permit the Oireachtas to establish courts of "local and limited jurisdiction" and Art.37 enables tribunals to exercise judicial functions of a limited nature in non-criminal matters.
[8] Any doubt on this point was laid to rest by the Supreme Court in *Criminal Assets Bureau v Hunt* [2003] IESC 20; [2003] 2 I.R. 168 at 183 per Keane C.J.
[9] [1985] I.R. 289 at 296–297. See also, *Criminal Assets Bureau v Hunt* [2003] IESC 20; [2003] 2 I.R. 168; *Doherty v South Dublin County Council* [2007] IEHC 4; [2007] 2 I.R. 696.
[10] See para.16–61. See also, Delany, "The Constitutionality of Limitation Periods Without Savers" (2004) I.L.T. 262.
[11] See further, paras 16–45 to 16–63.

of certain types of administrative decisions, there is an overwhelming need for a swift determination and finality.[12] Such clauses are now quite common.[13] Two of the most significant of these clauses are contained in the fields of planning and immigration and have prompted important judicial discussion. Section 50(4)(a) of the Planning and Development Act 2000 is the successor provision to s.82(3A) of the Local Government (Planning and Development) Act 1963,[14] which provided for a two-month time limit in any case where it was sought to challenge a decision of a planning authority or An Bord Pleanála. The new time limit is eight weeks; but, as we shall see, subject to the possibility of extension.[15]

11–06 Serious constitutional doubt was cast on the validity of the time limit restriction in the 1963 Act by Costello J. in *Brady v Donegal County Council*.[16] While his decision was set aside by the Supreme Court on factual grounds[17] (and not on the merits), his reasoning was essentially adopted by the Supreme Court in *White v Dublin City Council*.[18] In *Brady*, it appeared that the advertisement placed by the applicant for planning permission had not been published in a newspaper circulating in the area, as required by art.14 of the 1977 Planning Regulations. Some neighbours (who were, because of this flaw, unaware of the development) sought to quash this permission, but found that they were a few days out of time to challenge its validity. Costello J. held that the absence of any saver to permit a wrong-footed plaintiff to appeal out of time gave rise to a fundamentally unfair state of affairs:

> "[I]f the plaintiff's ignorance of his rights during the short limitation period is caused by the defendant's own wrong-doing and the law still imposes an absolute bar unaccompanied by any judicial discretion to raise it, there must be very compelling reasons indeed to justify such a rigorous limitation on the exercise of a constitutionally protected right. The public interest ... could well justify the imposition of stringent time limits for the institution of court proceedings ... Certainly the public interest would not be quite as well served by a law with the suggested saver as by the present law, but the

---

[12] See Finlay C.J. in *KSK Enterprises Ltd v An Bord Pleanála* [1994] 2 I.R. 128 at 135; Costello J. in *Brady v Donegal County Council* [1989] I.L.R.M. 282 at 289; Kelly J. in *Ní Éilí v Environmental Protection Agency* [1997] 2 I.L.R.M. 458 at 464 (in the latter case concerning the analogous (but not identical) two-month limitation period prescribed by s.85(8) of the Environmental Protection Agency Act 1992); and the Supreme Court in *In re Article 26 and the Illegal Immigrants (Trafficking) Bill 1999* [2000] IESC 19; [2000] 2 I.R. 360 at 392–393.

[13] See, e.g. Environmental Protection Agency Act 1992 s.87(10)(a), as inserted by Water Services Act 2007 s.107(e)(iii); Roads Act 1993 s.55A(2)(a), as inserted by Roads (Amendment) Act 1998 s.6; Commission to Inquire Into Child Abuse Act 2000 s.26A(2)(a), as inserted by Commission to Inquire Into Child Abuse (Amendment) Act 2005 s.19; Planning and Development Act 2000 s.50(4)(a); Illegal Immigrants (Trafficking) Act 2000 s.5(2)(a); Transport (Railway Infrastructure) Act 2001 s.47(2)(a).

[14] As inserted by the Local Government (Planning and Development) Act 1992 s.19(3).

[15] Planning and Development Act 2000 s.50(4)(a).

[16] [1989] I.L.R.M. 282.

[17] Costello J. had not reached a final determination as to whether the planning notice itself was invalid. The Supreme Court pointed out, however, that if the facts were such that it was valid, then the applicants' challenge to the validity of the permission would fall *in limine* and there would be no need for the courts to pronounce on the constitutionality of s.82(3A) of the 1963 Act. The finding of unconstitutionality was therefore vacated and the matter remitted back to the High Court. The case appears to have proceeded no further.

[18] [2004] IESC 35; [2004] 1 I.R. 545.

loss of the public interest by the proposed modification would be slight while the gain in the protection of the plaintiff's constitutionally protected rights would be very considerable. I conclude, therefore, that the present serious restriction on the exercise of the plaintiff's constitutional rights imposed by the two-month limitation period cannot reasonably be justified."[19]

11–07 This reasoning would also seem to apply a fortiori to cases of permission obtained in bad faith or, even, perhaps, where the requirements of the regulations were manifestly disregarded. On the basis of these assumed facts, Costello J. concluded that the subsection was unconstitutional. A difference worth noting between Costello J.'s reasoning in *Brady* and the Supreme Court's in *White* is that in the latter case, the legislation was held to infringe the plaintiffs' right of access to a court,[20] rather than, as in *Brady*, their property rights.

11–08 A key reform has been made to address these criticisms: s.50(4)(a)(iii) of the Planning and Development Act 2000 allows the High Court to extend the time limit if "it considers that there is good and sufficient reason for doing so". The constitutionality of an analogous provision, in immigration law, was considered by the Supreme Court in *In re Article 26 and the Illegal Immigrants (Trafficking) Bill 1999*.[21] Here, s.5(2)(a) of the Bill provided that an application for leave to apply for judicial review of any of a number of specified matters would have to be lodged within 14 days of notification of the decision or matter concerned. However, s.5(2)(a) also allowed the High Court to extend the time period for "good and sufficient reason". Having accepted that non-nationals have a right of access to the Superior Courts to challenge adverse decisions, which was infringed by the time limit, the Supreme Court considered whether the infringement was proportionate to the aim sought to be achieved. Here, for similar reasons of policy to those outlined in *KSK*,[22] the State had "a legitimate interest in prescribing procedural rules calculated to ensure or promote an early completion of judicial review proceedings of the administrative decisions concerned"[23] which justified the imposition of a stringent time limit. Although the court recognised the force of counsel's arguments that asylum seekers, hampered by unfamiliarity with the language and legal system and the problems in accessing legal advice, as well as other factors, would find it difficult to meet the 14-day limit, it held that such matters could be considered by the High Court in deciding whether to extend the limit:

> "[T]he discretion of the court to extend the time to apply for leave where the applicant shows 'good and sufficient reason' for so doing is wide and ample enough to avoid injustice where an applicant has been unable through no fault of his or hers, or for other good and sufficient reason, to bring the application within the fourteen-day period."[24]

11–09 Thus, in principle, strict time limits are permissible, provided that the High

---

[19] [1989] I.L.R.M. 282 at 288–289.
[20] Specifically, "a right to litigate", protected by Art.40.3.1° of the Constitution: [2004] IESC 35; [2004] 1 I.R. 545 at 567. See also, *Tuohy v Courtney* [1994] 3 I.R. 1.
[21] [2000] IESC 19; [2000] 2 I.R. 360.
[22] See *KSK Enterprises Ltd v An Bord Pleanála* [1994] 2 I.R. 128, 135 (Finlay C.J.).
[23] [2000] IESC 19; [2000] 2 I.R. 360 at 393.
[24] [2000] IESC 19; [2000] 2 I.R. 360 at 393–394.

Court must have discretion to extend the prescribed period.[25] The saver provisions now typically included[26] give the Superior Courts relatively wide power to grant extensions of time,[27] but naturally their discretion is not absolute.[28] In particular, the applicant must demonstrate an objective reason for extension and an explanation for the delay. In *Kelly v Leitrim County Council*,[29] the applicant was late by 19 days in applying for leave to seek judicial review. Illness to a family member and dissatisfaction with legal advice received were cited as the reasons for the delay. On a detailed analysis of the case law, Clarke J. considered that the following factors should be taken into consideration by the High Court in deciding whether or not there was "good and sufficient reason" to extend time:

"(a) The length of time specified in the relevant statute within which the application must be made ... Obviously the shorter the period of time which a person has to make application to the court, the easier it may be to show that despite reasonable diligence that person has been unable to achieve the time limit.

(b) The question of whether third party rights may be affected ... in particular, a person who had obtained planning permission should be put, within a short period of time, in a position where that planning permission, if not challenged, was absolute.

(c) [T]here is nonetheless a clear legislative policy involved in all such measures which requires that, irrespective of the involvement of the rights of third parties, determinations of particular types should be rendered certain within a short period of time as part of an overall process of conferring certainty on certain categories of administrative or quasi-judicial decisions. Therefore while it may well be legitimate to take into account the fact that no third party rights are involved, that should not be regarded as conferring a wide or extensive jurisdiction to extend time in cases where no such rights may be affected. The overall integrity of the processes concerned is, in itself, a factor to be taken into account.

(d) Blameworthiness. It is clear from all the authorities to which I have been

---

[25] See also, *Dekra Éireann Teo v Minister for the Environment* [2003] IESC 25; [2003] 2 I.R. 270, where a three-month time limit for review of the awarding of public contracts was held to reflect the objectives of Community law and policy, an essential feature of which is "a policy of urgency and rapidity which is required in such judicial reviews": ([2003] IESC 25; [2003] 2 I.R. 270 at 283 per Denham J.). See also, Irish Takeover Panel Act 1997. Section 13(3)(a) sets a seven-day time limit, but s.13(5) allows the High Court to extend time if it is satisfied that specified conditions are satisfied.

However, the more recent tendency seems to be simply for the legislation to provide that the High Court can extend the time for "good and sufficient reason". See, e.g. Environmental Protection Agency Act 1992 s.87(10)(b), as inserted by Water Services Act 2007 s.107(e)(iii); Commission to Inquire Into Child Abuse Act 2000 s.26A(3), as inserted by Commission to Inquire Into Child Abuse (Amendment) Act 2005 s.19.

[26] However, as Delany notes in "The Constitutionality of Limitation Periods Without Savers" (2004) I.L.T. 262 at 263, several statutes (listed (2004) I.L.T. 262 at fn.21) do not include savers and "considerable uncertainty must surround the question of their constitutionality".

[27] See the discussion in *Dekra Éireann Teo v Minister for the Environment* [2003] IESC 25; [2003] 2 I.R. 270 at 287–289.

[28] For the courts' general power to extend time, see paras 16–53 to 16–60.

[29] [2005] IEHC 11; [2005] 2 I.R. 404. See also, *CS v Minister for Justice* [2004] IESC 44; [2005] 1 I.L.R.M. 81; *GK v Minister for Justice* [2001] IESC 205; [2002] 2 I.R. 418; *Casey v An Bord Pleanála* [2004] 2 I.L.R.M. 296.

referred in each of the areas to which stricter rules in respect of judicial review have been applied that one of the issues to which the court has to have regard is the extent to which the applicant concerned may be able to explain the delay and in particular do so in circumstances that do not reflect any blame upon the applicant …[30]

(e) The nature of the issues involved. Both this court and the Supreme Court in *C.S. v. Minister for Justice*[31] seem to have had regard to the severe consequences of deportation to a State where fundamental rights might not be vindicated. The consequences of being excluded from challenging a planning or public procurement decision, while significant, are not in the same category.

(f) The merits of the case."[32]

11–10   In the instant case: the eight-week period was not "unduly harsh"; the nature of the decision was not one touching fundamental human rights; no significant third party rights were involved; the delay of 19 days was "significant having regard to the necessity to bring finality to all planning matters …"; and the applicant's explanations seemed unconvincing.[33] In the circumstances, only the absence of an effect on third-party rights pointed towards granting the extension of time and, accordingly, Clarke J. refused the application.

Conclusive evidence provisions: indirect exclusion of judicial review

11–11   These constitutional developments call into question the validity not only of ouster clauses, but also of the many other statutory provisions which seek to exclude or restrict judicial review, indirectly,[34] by providing that an administrative decision shall be "conclusive evidence" of the existence of certain facts or of the status of specified legal entities. Some important, miscellaneous examples of this legislative device include: s.2(1) of the Trade Union Act 1913[35] (which provides that the certificate of the Registrar of Friendly Societies is conclusive evidence of the status of a trade union); s.20(6) of the Civil Service Act 1956, as amended (which provides that the question of whether a person is a civil servant shall be determined by the Minister for Public Expenditure and Reform); s.104 of the Companies Act 1963[36] (which provides that the Registrar of Companies' certificate that a particular charge has complied with the registration requirements of Pt IV of the 1963 Act shall be conclusive evidence of this fact); and s.31(1) of the Registration of Title

---

[30]   However, Clarke J. noted the comments of McGuinness J. in *CS v Minister for Justice* [2004] IESC 44; [2005] 1 I.L.R.M. 81 at 101.

[31]   [2004] IESC 44; [2005] 1 I.L.R.M. 81.

[32]   [2005] 2 I.R. 404 at 412–413.

[33]   [2005] 2 I.R. 404 at 415–416.

[34]   For an excellent analysis of this topic, see Pye, "The Section 104 Certificate of Registration – An Impenetrable Shield No More?" (1985) 3 I.L.T. 213. See also, Hogan, "Reflections on the Supreme Court's Decision in *Tormey v. Attorney General*" (1986) 8 D.U.L.J. 31.

[35]   See Kerr and Whyte, *Irish Trade Union Law* (Abinsdon: Professional Books, 1985), pp.42–48 where the constitutionality of this and other similar conclusive evidence clauses is discussed.

[36]   *Lombard & Ulster Banking Ltd v Amurec Ltd* (1978) 112 I.L.T.R. 1. Courtney, *The Law of Private Companies*, 2nd edn (Dublin: Butterworths, 2002), pp.1220–1225. See also, the discussion of s.5(4) of the Companies (Amendment) Act 1983, a conclusive evidence provision in respect of certificates of incorporation, in Courtney, *The Law of Private Companies* (2002), pp.152–160.

Act 1964[37] (which states that the Register shall be "conclusive evidence" of title, subject to the right of the Circuit or High Court to order rectification on the grounds of actual fraud or mistake).

11–12 There would seem, however, to be a real risk that such "conclusive evidence" provisions will be held either to be unconstitutional or otherwise ineffective, at least in certain types of cases. In *Maher v Attorney General*,[38] the Supreme Court held that a "conclusive evidence" clause contained in the Road Traffic Act 1968 was unconstitutional,[39] as it attempted to oust the jurisdiction of the courts to determine an essential ingredient (alcohol levels) of a criminal prosecution.[40] All of this would seem to point to one of two conclusions. Either the "conclusive evidence" does not preclude judicial review, or, should it do so, it is unconstitutional as inconsistent with the High Court's jurisdiction under Art.34.3.1°.

11–13 The only judgment directly on this issue, however, points in the other direction. In *Sloan v Special Criminal Court*,[41] the applicant challenged the validity of s.19(4) of the Offences against the State Act 1939, in so far as it provided that a suppression order made by the Government shall be "conclusive evidence" of the suppressed organisation's illegality. Costello J. could not accept this submission, saying that: "If an order is made under [s.19(4)] then the justiciable dispute is whether an accused is a member of an illegal organisation and not whether the organisation itself is illegal."[42]

11–14 It may be thought, however, that this analysis is incomplete and does not cater for the case where the accused admits membership of the suppressed organisation, but says that, by virtue of the changed circumstances of the organisation, it should

---

37 Wylie, *Irish Land Law*, 3rd edn (Dublin: Butterworths, 1997), p.1045. See also, *Rhatigan and Rhatigan v Gill* [1999] IEHC 105; [1999] 2 I.L.R.M. 427; *Persian Properties Ltd v Registrar of Titles* [2003] IESC 12; [2003] 1 I.R. 450. For a recent example, see s.17(5) of the Sea Fisheries and Maritime Jurisdiction Act 2006.

38 [1973] I.R. 140. Though admittedly, in this case, the decision depended upon the particular circumstances in that a court was involved (since the main part of this case concerned a criminal trial) and, hence, Art.34.1 and the separation of powers were engaged. In *Criminal Assets Bureau v PS* [2004] IEHC 351; unreported, High Court, Finnegan P., October 19, 2004, Finnegan P. held that the use of certificates under s.488 of the Income Tax Act 1967 to establish prima facie evidence of certain matters was constitutional. Finnegan P. held that the proceedings in question were civil in nature but suggested that if conclusive evidence provisions had been at issue, they would have been of doubtful constitutionality. See also, *Criminal Assets Bureau v Kelly* [1999] IEHC 172; [2000] 1 I.L.R.M. 271. Cf. *Fitzgerald v DPP* [2003] IESC 46; [2003] 3 I.R. 247 at 255 per Keane C.J., suggesting that conclusive evidence provisions would be unconstitutional "in particular" in criminal proceedings.

39 Similar thinking prevailed with the European Court of Justice in *Johnston v Chief Constable of the Royal Ulster Constabulary*, where a "conclusive evidence" certificate issued by the Chief Constable pursuant to the provisions of art.53(2) of the Sex Discrimination (Northern Ireland) Order 1976 purported to establish that the conditions for derogating from the equal treatment directive had been satisfied: [1987] Q.B. 129 at 147.

40 The practice now seems to be to make such certificates rebuttable, but it may be the case that a trial judge will have to permit the defence to inspect the equipment which rendered the certificate. See Road Traffic Act 1994 s.21(1) and *Whelan v Kirby* [2004] IESC 17; [2005] 2 I.R. 30; *McGonnell v Attorney General* [2006] IESC 64; [2007] 1 I.R. 400.

41 [1993] 3 I.R. 528.

42 [1993] 3 I.R. 528 at 532.

no longer be regarded as illegal. The effect of the "conclusive evidence" provision of s.19(4) is that the accused is not permitted to raise this argument, yet, were it not for this purported statutory ouster, the justiciable controversy would be whether the organisation had, in fact, illegal objectives. Accordingly, it is difficult to see how this type of statutory provision (assuming it precludes judicial review) would survive constitutional challenge, either on the ground that it infringes the High Court's full original jurisdiction as conferred by Art.34.3.1° (as this provision was interpreted in *Tormey v Ireland*)[43] or that (assuming a lower court is involved and following *Maher*) it constitutes an impermissible invasion of the judicial domain, which is protected by Art.34.1. Despite the remarks of Costello J. in *Sloan*, it remains to be seen, therefore, whether this form of "conclusive evidence" provision will survive future challenges.

"Substantial grounds"

11–15   Occasionally, legislation, in a particular field, specifies that an applicant must have "substantial grounds" when applying for leave.[44] In general, such provisions do not raise constitutional difficulties.[45] Carroll J. in *McNamara v An Bord Pleanála (No. 1)*[46] suggested that "substantial grounds" equate to grounds that are reasonable, arguable and weighty and not trivial or tenuous. Any possible constitutional doubt was erased by the Supreme Court in *In re Article 26 and the Illegal Immigrants (Trafficking) Bill 1999.*[47] In brief, conclusive terms, the court commented that:

> "[T]he imposition of a requirement to show 'substantial grounds' in an application for leave to apply for judicial review is one which falls within the discretion of the legislature. It is not so onerous, either in itself or in conjunction with a fourteen-day limitation period, as to infringe the constitutional right of access to the courts or the right to fair procedures."[48]

11–16   However, one provision, though a most unusual one, which failed to pass constitutional muster is s.260 of the Mental Treatment Act 1945,[49] which was invalidated by the Supreme Court in *Blehein v Minister for Health and Children.*[50] However, the provision was unusual in that it prohibited anyone from taking civil proceedings in respect of any act under the Act, unless the applicant is able to demonstrate "substantial grounds for contending that the person against whom

---

[43] [1985] I.R. 289.
[44] See, e.g. Electricity Regulation Act 1999 s.32(2)(b), as substituted by Gas (Amendment) Act 2000 s.15; Aviation Regulation Act 2001 s.38(2); Prisons Act 2007 s.27(3).
[45] Indeed, s.50(4)(b) of the Planning and Development Act 2000 requires that an applicant has a "substantial interest" in the matter as well as "substantial grounds" for contending that the decision is invalid or ought to be quashed, but no constitutional difficulties appear to have arisen. See *Harding v Cork County Council* [2008] IESC 27; [2008] 2 I.L.R.M. 251. Difficulties in determining whether "substantial grounds" are present in an individual application, however, abound. See *McNamara v An Bord Pleanála (No. 1)* [1995] 2 I.L.R.M. 125; *Kenny v An Bord Pleanála (No. 1)* [2000] IEHC 146; [2001] 1 I.R. 565; *Arklow Holidays Ltd v An Bord Pleanála* [2006] IEHC 15; unreported, High Court, Clarke J., January 18, 2006.
[46] [1995] 2 I.L.R.M. 125.
[47] [2000] IESC 19; [2000] 2 I.R. 360.
[48] [2000] IESC 19; [2000] 2 I.R. 360 at 395.
[49] As amended by s.2(3) of the Public Authorities Judicial Proceedings Act 1954.
[50] [2008] IESC 40; [2009] 1 I.R. 175.

proceedings are to be brought acted in bad faith or without reasonable care". The restriction to these limited grounds of review was held to be a disproportionate interference with the applicant's right of access to the courts and his right to personal liberty.[51]

B. Practical Consequences of Invalidity

11–17   This Part concerns the law's response to a most practical problem. In theory, if an administrative action is ultra vires, it has no effect in law. Yet there is a hiatus of typically one or more years (assuming that there is no appeal) between the time at which the action is "purportedly" taken and the time when a court authoritatively pronounces the action ultra vires. During this period, the decision looks official and (to a layperson and many lawyers) "legal": few would be bold enough to ignore it altogether. It is to likely have some consequences, if only negative. The question is: how should the law accommodate such reasonable assumptions (even though they turn out later to have been unwarranted)?

General principles: the effect of unconstitutionality

11–18   As a general rule—which is subject to major exceptions—ultra vires decisions are null and void and have no legal consequences. The two important Irish cases where there has been an extended discussion of the nature of invalidity, *Murphy v Attorney General*[52] and *A v Governor of Arbour Hill Prison*,[53] arose in the special context of constitutional law. In both cases, a majority of the Supreme Court had little difficulty in holding that legislation found to be unconstitutional must be deemed to be void ab initio, and then proceeded, with substantially more difficulty, to avoid the natural consequences of the initial ruling.[54] Henchy J. described this principle as one which was "inherent in the nature of such limited powers".[55]

11–19   The cases described so far have concerned laws which have been held to be unconstitutional. The conventional view is that an analogous principle and exceptions (considered below) apply both to this situation and to the position in which an administrative action (or, for that matter, delegated legislation) has been held to be ultra vires a statute. As Costello J. remarked pregnantly in *O'Keeffe v An Bord Pleanála*,[56] "[i]t is usual to say that an ultra vires decision is void and a nullity but it is clear that it is wrong to conclude that such decisions are completely devoid of legal consequences."[57] The significant point here is that, with the very rare exception of a flagrantly invalid decision, invalidity can only be established

---

[51]   [2008] IESC 40; [2009] 1 I.R. 175 at para.18 per Denham J. The offending provision has now been repealed and replaced by s.73 of the Mental Health Act 2001, which substitutes "reasonable grounds" for "substantial grounds". In *Blehein's* case, the constitutionality of the provision was still relevant to an outstanding claim for damages.

[52]   [1982] I.R. 241.

[53]   [2006] IESC 45; [2006] 4 I.R. 88.

[54]   See also, *McDonnell v Ireland* [1998] 1 I.R. 134 (O'Flaherty J.).

[55]   [1982] I.R. 241 at 308–309.

[56]   [1993] 1 I.R. 39.

[57]   [1993] 1 I.R. 39 at 49. This meant that an appeal could be taken from an ultra vires administrative decision, which even though ultimately adjudged to be void, was not legally non-existent.

in legal proceedings.[58] Thus, until a court sets aside an impugned decision, the decision will enjoy a presumption of validity and the decision will be regarded as binding.[59] Moreover, even if invalidity is established in the appropriate, subsequent proceedings, the court may, as has often happened, refuse to grant relief on public policy or discretionary grounds.[60] Thus, an invalidity may, in effect, be "cured" by a failure to raise it in a timely manner before an appropriate body. In addition, the possibility always remains that a decision will be invalid but that no person has standing to take a judicial review.[61] In short, invalidity is a relative concept and the courts have refrained from pushing that concept to extremes.

11–20   Again, there are sometimes statutory provisions which specifically address the consequences of invalidation.[62] Or, rather similarly, the statutory context may be such that, as Costello J. said in *O'Keeffe*, the court must give legal efficacy to even an ultra vires decision "if the construction of the statute so requires".[63]

11–21   Perhaps it is because the Irish courts have, in general, taken such a pragmatic approach that the void/voidable controversy which has plagued English administrative law has not given rise to the same difficulties in this jurisdiction.[64]

---

[58]   *Smith v East Elloe RDC* [1956] A.C. 736; *State (Abenglen Properties Ltd) v Dublin Corporation* [1984] I.R. 381; *CW Shipping Ltd v Limerick Harbour Commissioners* [1989] I.L.R.M. 426; *McDonnell v Ireland* [1998] 1 I.R. 134; *Wicklow County Council v Wicklow County Manager* [2010] IESC 49; *Boddington v British Transport Police* [1999] 2 A.C. 143.

[59]   *Hoffman-La Roche & Co v Secretary for Trade and Industry* [1975] A.C. 295; *Campus Oil v Minister for Industry and Energy (No. 2)* [1983] I.R. 88 at 107 per O'Higgins C.J.; *State (Abenglen Properties Ltd) v Dublin Corporation* [1984] I.R. 381; and, in the special context of constitutional law, *State (Llewellyn) v Ua Donnachada* [1973] I.R. 151; *Pesca Valentia Ltd v Minister for Fisheries* [1985] I.R. 193.

[60]   See, e.g. *State (Cussen) v Brennan* [1981] I.R. 181; *Murphy v Attorney General* [1982] I.R. 341; *A v Governor of Arbour Hill Prison* [2006] IESC 45; [2006] 4 I.R. 88. Although the reasoning in *A* was controversial, it was expressly approved by the UK Supreme Court in *Cadder v Her Majesty's Advocate* [2010] UKSC 43.

[61]   See Ch.16, Part E.

[62]   See, e.g. Adoption Act 1976 s.6 (no child to be removed from custody of its adoptive parents solely on the grounds that the adoption order was invalid); Irish Takeover Panel Act 1997 s.15 (takeover which has not been conducted in accordance with the 1997 Act is not to be regarded as necessarily thereby invalid); Local Government Act 2001 s.27(6) (local election not conducted in accordance with regulations not necessarily invalid); Mental Health Act 2001 s.18(1)(a)(ii) (failure to comply with specified provisions of the legislation does not necessarily invalidate an admission or a renewal order in a review by a mental health tribunal); Garda Síochána Act 2005 s.8(6)(b) (nothing done by a member in instituting or conducting a prosecution is invalid solely because of a failure to comply with s.8 or a direction made thereunder).

[63]   [1993] 1 I.R. 39 at 50. Thus, Costello J. held that even if the planning authority's decision was void and a nullity, this did not mean that An Bord Pleanála had no jurisdiction to entertain an appeal against this decision. See also, *State (Abenglen Properties Ltd) v Dublin Corporation* [1984] I.R. 381 per Walsh J.

[64]   See, e.g. *DPP v Head* [1959] A.C. 83; *R. v Paddington Valuation Officer Ex p. Peachey Property Corporation Ltd* [1966] 1 Q.B. 380; *Hoffman-La Roche & Co v Secretary of State for Trade and Industry* [1975] A.C. 295; *R. v Environment Secretary Ex p. Ostler* [1977] Q.B. 122. However, the English courts no longer view nullity as an absolute concept: *Calvin v Carr* [1980] A.C. 574 and *London & Clydeside Estates Ltd v Aberdeen DC* [1980] 1 W.L.R. 182; *Bugg v DPP* [1993] Q.B. 473; *Boddington v British Transport Police* [1999] 2 A.C. 143. See generally, Cane, "A Fresh Look at *Punton's* Case" (1980) 43 M.L.R. 266; Forsyth, "The Metaphysics of Nullity – Invalidity, Conceptual Reasoning and the Rule of Law" in Forsyth and Hare (eds), *The Golden Metwand and the Crooked Cord* (Oxford: Clarendon Press, 1998);

Irish Permanent Building Society v Cauldwell[65] provides an interesting example of this pragmatic judicial attitude. Here Barrington J. refused to accept that the incorporation of a building society could be nullified by reason of an error on the part of the Registrar of Building Societies in construing the relevant legislation. Such a result would be "catastrophic",[66] and the judge could not believe that the Oireachtas intended that "an honest mistake" could have such drastic consequences.[67]

11–22   The problems endemic in this area were also plainly visible in *Hegarty v Governor of Limerick Prison*,[68] where the issue arose as to whether the Minister for Justice was correct in directing the release of certain remand prisoners, once it transpired that the Special Criminal Court which had made the orders for their detention had been irregularly constituted.[69] It was argued that there was no necessity for the Minister to apply to the High Court for such an order of release since:

> "[T]he relevant committal warrant ... was not just a bad order made by a lawfully constituted court but was an order which was bad because it was made by an unlawfully constituted court."[70]

11–23   Geoghegan J. did not find it necessary to resolve this issue—as it could not have affected the legality of the prisoner's re-arrest and consequent detention—but he agreed that "the legal position was by no means clear and that there are legitimate arguments both ways".[71] Yet the order of the Special Criminal Court bore no "brand of invalidity" on its face. If the Minister were free, as it were, to disregard the court's order, where would this stop?[72] Could, for example, an ordinary member of the Gardaí have similarly disregarded such an order and released a prisoner of his own volition? Or could the prisoner have fought his way free, using whatever force was necessary, on the basis that he had been falsely detained? Such questions have only to be asked to demonstrate that in this area, the law must take account of reality.

11–24   The very fact that the courts have found themselves obliged in appropriate cases to grant interlocutory relief to a person affected by the consequences of an administrative decision pending a challenge to its legality is significant. It indicates that in this interim period there may be legal consequences of the fact that a decision has been taken, even though this may ultimately prove to be ultra vires. Thus, in *Pesca Valentia Ltd v Minister for Fisheries*,[73] Finlay C.J. said that

---

Forsyth, "The Legal Effect of the Invalid Administrative Act: the Theory of the Second Actor Revisited" (2006) *Acta Juridica* 209.

[65]   [1981] I.L.R.M. 242. See also, *Re Riordan* [1981] I.L.R.M. 2 for a similar approach. See also the treatment of this issue in the important judgment of O'Donnell J. in *Wicklow County Council v Wicklow County Manager* [2010] IESC 49.

[66]   [1981] I.L.R.M. 242 at 270.

[67]   [1981] I.L.R.M. 242 at 269.

[68]   [1998] 1 I.R. 412.

[69]   One of the judges of that court had sat after his removal from the Special Criminal Court by order of the Government because the judge in question had not been informed of the Government's decision.

[70]   [1998] 1 I.R. 412 at 431.

[71]   [1998] 1 I.R. 412 at 431.

[72]   cf. the comments of O'Flaherty J. in *McDonnell v Ireland* [1998] 1 I.R. 134 at 143–144.

[73]   [1985] I.R. 193. See also, *Hoffman-La Roche & Co v Department of Trade* [1975] A.C.

the courts had power, in an appropriate case, to grant an interlocutory injunction restraining the implementation of administrative action which derived its authority from statutory provisions "which might eventually be held to be invalid having regard to the Constitution".[74] From this it may be inferred that the Supreme Court recognised that administrative action which is not patently illegal will be presumed to be valid and if there is no such interim order, the administrative action will have legal consequences during this period for the individual, pending a decision as to its invalidity.[75]

11–25 However, if an administrative act which is not flagrantly invalid enjoys a presumption of validity and has the force of law until quashed, how is it possible to assert, once that presumption has been displaced, and the decision quashed as ultra vires, that it was a legal nullity? The traditional answer is that when administrative decisions are invalidated by the courts, this invalidation has retrospective effect. A more sophisticated answer preferred by modern English commentators starts from the basis that "while unlawful administrative acts (the first acts) do not exist in law they clearly exist in fact. Those unaware of their invalidity (the second actors) may take decisions and act on the assumption that these (first) acts are valid. When this happens the crucial question is whether these second acts are valid."[76] The best approach to this issue is based on the notion that "the validity of [any second] acts ... depends on the legal powers of the second actor ... This issue will be determined by looking at the relationship between the two sets of acts".[77] In other words, the making or doing of an administrative act is a fact which may carry legal consequences. Sometimes the factual existence of a particular act, although later determined to be ultra vires, can act as the basis for the invocation of another statutory provision. The extent of the consequences of an invalid act will be determined by looking at the statutory framework in issue. In this difficult area, however, it must always:

"... be recognised that the empowering statute will normally provide little if any guidance as to this issue, and that it will be for the reviewing court to decide whether any of the acts done pursuant to the initial unlawful act can be regarded as valid."[78]

---

295 and, in the special context of European Community law, *R. v Transport Secretary Ex p. Factortame Ltd* (C-213/89) [1990] E.C.R. I-2433.

[74] [1985] I.R. 193 at 201. Cf. *Riordan v An Taoiseach* [2002] IESC 70; [2002] 4 I.R. 404 at 407 per Murphy J.

[75] In *O'Keeffe v An Bord Pleanála* [1993] 1 I.R. 39 at 50, Costello J. appeared to hint that he agreed with this proposition but said that he could decide the issue which arose in that case by reference to a construction of the relevant provisions of the Planning Acts without having to deal with this larger issue. Cf. the comments of O'Flaherty J. in *McDonnell v Ireland* [1998] 1 I.R. 134 at 143–144.

[76] Wade and Forsyth, 10th edn (2009), pp.253–254.

[77] Craig, *Administrative Law*, 6th edn (London: Sweet & Maxwell, 2008), p.768, citing Forsyth, "The Metaphysics of Nullity – Invalidity, Conceptual Reasoning and the Rule of Law" in Forsyth and Hare (eds), *The Golden Metwand and the Crooked Cord* (Oxford: Clarendon Press, 1998). For further details on the theory of the second actor, see Forsyth, "The Legal Effect of the Invalid Administrative Act: the Theory of the Second Actor Revisited" (2006) *Acta Juridica* 209.

[78] Craig, *Administrative Law*, 6th edn (2008), p.768. See, e.g. *R. v Wicks* [1998] A.C. 92.

C. Severance

General principles

11–26 In some cases, the condemned legislation or administrative decision may only be partially invalid. The question (common to constitutional and administrative law) arises as to whether it is open to the court to excise offending sections of the Act, order or decision, leaving the remainder valid. The classic statement of the Irish courts' attitude to the question of severance is to be found in the judgment of Fitzgerald C.J. in *Maher v Attorney General*,[79] where, speaking in the context of an unconstitutional statute, he said that, if, following the deletion of an unconstitutional portion of a statute:

> "... [T]he remainder may be held to stand independently and legally operable as representing the will of the legislature [then effect will be given to it]. But if what remains is so inextricably bound up with the part held invalid that the remainder cannot survive independently, or if the remainder would not represent the legislative intent, the remaining part will not be severed and given constitutional validity ... If, therefore, the Court were to sever part of a statutory provision as unconstitutional and seek to give validity to what is left so as to produce an effect at variance with legislative policy, the Court would be invading a domain exclusive to the legislature and thus exceeding the Court's competency."[80]

Administrative decisions

11–27 While these principles were enunciated in the context of an unconstitutional statute, it would seem that they also apply to the issue of whether it is possible to rescue some element of an administrative decision, the remainder of which has been held to be ultra vires.[81] For instance, in *Cassidy v Minister for Industry and Commerce*,[82] the Supreme Court severed the application of an invalid maximum prices order for alcoholic drink by means of "horizontal severance".[83] As a result, its scope did not apply to public bars and, in contrast to the order as made by the

---

[79] [1973] I.R. 140.

[80] [1973] I.R. 140 at 147–148. For an example of what amounts to the de facto application of this principle, see *Desmond v Glackin (No. 2)* [1993] 3 I.R. 67. See also, *An Blascaod Mór Teo v Commissioners for Public Works (No. 3)* [1999] IESC 4; [2000] 1 I.R. 6, affirming Budd J.'s analysis in the High Court, unreported, February 27, 1998; *Gorman v Minister for the Environment* [2001] IEHC 47; [2001] 2 I.R. 414 at 424 per Carney J.

[81] See the elaborate discussion of this point in *Desmond v Glackin (No. 2)* [1993] 3 I.R. 67 and *Mallon v Minister for Agriculture and Food* [1996] 1 I.R. 517. See also, *Kennedy v Law Society of Ireland* [2006] IEHC 172. Recently, in extending the principle to cases of omissions as well as inclusions, Sedley L.J. has vividly captured the underlying rationale of severance: "If an omission can be made good without disrupting the existing, presumptively lawful, text, and if so far the omission appears to have done no harm, I see no good reason why, instead of permitting the rule-maker to insert the missing brick, the entire structure should be pulled down": *R. (National Association of Health Stores) v Health Secretary* [2005] EWCA Civ. 154 (February 22, 2005) at para.20.

[82] [1978] I.R. 297.

[83] [1978] I.R. 297 at 313. This was defined by Henchy J. (at 312) as severing the order "... in the range of [its] application, so that [it] may be preserved and implemented in so far as [it is] *intra vires* and ruled inoperable only in so far as [its] application would run into the area of *ultra vires*." See also, *Ulster Transport Authority v James Brown & Sons* [1953] N.I. 79;

Minister, it excluded lounge bars. Similarly, in *State (McKeown) v Scully*,[84] that part of the record which recorded a verdict of suicide was quashed as ultra vires, leaving untouched the other aspects of the verdict. Finally, in *Glencar Explorations Plc v Mayo County Council*,[85] Blayney J. quashed only such portion of a development plan as contained a ban on mining. No injustice would be done by simply removing the ban and leaving the rest of the plan intact. The ban was not contained in the plan as originally drafted and the Council was perfectly free to review the terms of the development plan at any time.[86]

11–28 This question has also assumed relevance in planning cases where an invalid condition had been attached to the grant of a planning permission. In these cases, the court will quash the entire permission if, but only if, what remains when shorn of the invalid condition is such that the planning authority would not have been willing to grant it in the first instance.[87]

D. Appeals From Administrative Decisions

11–29 In some contexts the Oireachtas provides for a statutory right of appeal from a decision of an administrative body. The right of appeal is usually confined to an appeal on a point of law, although this need not necessarily be the case.[88] The appeal will usually,[89] but by no means always,[90] lie to the High Court, and it seems as if both the procedure by which the impugned decision was reached, as well as

---

Belfast Corporation v OD Cars Ltd [1960] A.C. 490; *Burke v Minister for Labour* [1979] I.R. 354; and *Kennedy v Law Society of Ireland (No. 3)* [2001] IESC 103; [2002] 2 I.R. 458.

[84] [1986] I.L.R.M. 133. See also, *State (Moloney) v Minister for Industry and Commerce* [1954] I.R. 253 (severance of ministerial order). But severance is not possible in the case of a criminal conviction: *State (Kiernan) v de Burca* [1963] I.R. 348; *Bowes v Judge Devally* [1995] 1 I.R. 315.

[85] [1993] 2 I.R. 237.

[86] Local Government (Planning and Development) Act 1963 s.20(1). See now, Planning and Development Act 2000 s.13.

[87] *Bord na Móna v An Bord Pleanála and Galway County Council* [1985] I.R. 205 at 211. See also, to like effect, *Killiney and Ballybrack Development Association v Minister for Local Government (No. 2)*, unreported, High Court, McWilliam J., April 1, 1977.

[88] e.g. some administrative bodies have power to state a case for the High Court: see Adoption Act 1952 s.20 (An Bord Uchtála); Freedom of Information Act 1997 s.42(5) (Information Commissioner); Planning and Development Act 2000 s.50(1) (An Bord Pleanála).

[89] See, e.g. Competition Act 2002 s.15(1); Residential Tenancies Act 2004 s.123(3) (appeal on point of law); Central Bank Act 1942 s.57CL (as inserted by s.16 of the Central Bank and Financial Services Authority of Ireland Act 2004).

[90] See, e.g. Casual Trading Act 1995 s.6(8) (appeal to the District Court against the making of casual trading bye-laws); Taxes Consolidation Act 1997 s.942(1) (appeal by way of rehearing to the Circuit Court); Equal Status Act 2000 s.8(8)(a) (appeal to the Circuit Court against a suspension of certificate of registration); Mental Health Act 2001 s.19(1) (appeal to the Circuit Court against a decision to affirm an order made on the basis that a person is suffering from a mental disorder); Taxi Regulation Act 2003 s.35(3) (appeal to the District Court against the refusal to grant, the revocation or the suspension of a taxi licence); Veterinary Practice Act 2005 s.113(3) (registered person may appeal to the District Court against a decision to grant or renew subject to conditions or to refuse to grant or renew a certificate of suitability); Water Services Act 2007 s.80(3) (appeal to the District Court against the decision that a particular service requires a water services licence).

its substantive merits, can be considered in the appeal proceedings.[91] Where it is a right of appeal to the lower courts which is granted by statute, the decision of the lower court, on appeal, may itself be quashed upon an application to the High Court for judicial review.[92]

11–30   The nature and scope of the court's jurisdiction on an appeal is in all cases a matter of statutory construction and will often be different from that of judicial review.[93]

11–31   In contrasting appeal and judicial review, three general points are relevant. First, an appeal usually carries with it the power to alter or vary an administrative decision. By contrast, in judicial review proceedings, these options are restricted. Traditionally (save where the order is severable), the court was faced with the stark question: to quash or not to quash. (Since 1986, however, there has been the possibility of both remittal and an award of damages.[94])

11–32   Secondly, even when an appeal is allowed, this will only have a prospective effect and will not call into question the legality of earlier administrative decisions in respect of the period between the actual decision and the appeal. Thirdly, there is the distinction between "legality" which is all that can be examined on review and "merits" which are the proper province of an appeal. It has already been explained that in practice there may not be a great deal of difference between the reach of the High Court's jurisdiction to hear appeals where these appeals are confined by statute to an appeal on a point of law, and, on the other hand, the scope of judicial review now that the reach of jurisdictional error has been so greatly expanded.[95] In addition, other important differences remain. In the first place, the remedies available on an application for judicial review are discretionary in nature. Next, a finding of invalidity has effect *erga omnes*. In other words, there may be a large category of persons who, being similarly affected by the impugned legislation or administrative act, will be permitted to rely on this finding of invalidity.[96] In contrast, because of the nature of the circumstances in which an appeal has been created, a decision of the High Court on appeal is a ruling in an inter partes matter between the appellant and the administrative body concerned and, its precedential valve aside, it need not necessarily have much wider significance for third parties.

11–33   Three issues now arise for discussion: first, how to determine the scope of an appeal in a given case; secondly, how to determine how closely the appellate court will examine the decision under appeal; and thirdly, at what point in the decision-making process does the appellate court undertake its examination.

---

[91]   *Teahan v Minister for Communications* [2008] IEHC 194; unreported, High Court, Laffoy J., June 18, 2008.

[92]   See, e.g. *Kiely v Minister for Social Welfare (No. 2)* [1977] I.R. 267; *State (McEldowney) v Kelliher* [1983] I.R. 289.

[93]   *Dunne v Minister for Fisheries* [1984] I.R. 230 at 237.

[94]   See paras 16–05 and 16–29 to 16–32.

[95]   See Ch.10, Part E. See *E v Secretary of State for the Home Department* [2004] EWCA Civ. 49; [2004] Q.B. 1044, where Carnwath L.J. held that the principles governing judicial review for error of law and appeal on a point of law were the same.

[96]   For a more extended discussion of the difference between appeal on the merits and judicial review, see Hogan, "Remoulding Certiorari" (1982) 17 *Ir. Jur.* (N.S) 32 at pp.48–54.

Determining the scope of appeal

11–34   Certain statutory provisions confer broader powers on the courts than simply an appeal on a "point of law". The question as to the scope of statutory provisions that provide for wider appeals[97] has been explored in a number of important decisions, principally *M&J Gleeson v Competition Authority*,[98] *Orange Communications Ltd v Director of Telecommunications Regulation*,[99] *Carrickdale Hotel v Controller of Patents*,[100] *Manorcastle Ltd v Aviation Commissioner*[101] and *Rye Investments Ltd v Competition Authority*.[102] To these superior court decisions may be added the important ruling of the (former) Electronic Communications Appeal Panel[103] in *Hutchinson 3G Ireland Ltd v Commission for Communications Regulation*.[104]

11–35   In *M&J Gleeson*, the plaintiffs, who were drinks wholesalers, had appealed against a decision of the Competition Authority to grant a licence to Guinness Ireland Group Ltd in relation to an agreement to acquire a 100 per cent stake in a drinks distribution company, on condition that it reduce its stake in another drinks distribution company. This appeal was brought under s.9 of the Competition Act 1991, which provided that "[a] person aggrieved by a license or a certificate of the Authority … may appeal to the High Court … and on the hearing of any such appeal the Court may confirm, amend or revoke the license so appealed against …". Kearns J. referred extensively to the decision of the Supreme Court of Canada in *Canada (Director of Investigation and Research) v Southam*,[105] in which it held that the greater the level of expertise and specialised knowledge which a particular tribunal has, the greater the reluctance there should be on the part of the court to substitute its own view for that of the authority. Thus the amplitude of the statutory provision of an appeal was to be qualified by the expertise of the respondents.[106]

11–36   Although consistency is naturally important,[107] a further aspect of the case law is that similarity of statutory wording cannot be determinative of the scope of the appeal. Factors such as the purpose of the appeal and the statutory context are

---

[97]   It seems, generally, as if the statute will have to provide expressly for an appeal for these principles to apply. See *Robert McGregor & Sons (Ireland) Ltd v Mining Board* [2002] IESC 28.

[98]   [1999] 1 I.L.R.M. 401.

[99]   [2000] IESC 79; [2000] 4 I.R. 159.

[100]   [2004] IEHC 17; [2004] 2 I.L.R.M. 401. See also, *Ulster Bank Ltd v Financial Services Ombudsman* [2006] IEHC 323.

[101]   [2008] IEHC 386.

[102]   *Rye Investments Ltd v Competition Authority* [2009] IEHC 140.

[103]   Which has subsequently been disbanded; see European Communities (Electronic Communications Networks and Services) (Framework) (Amendment) Regulations 2007 (S.I. No. 271 of 2007), which transfers the Panel's jurisdiction to the High Court.

[104]   ECAP Decision No. 01/05, Appeal No. 2004/01, February 10, 2005. For an earlier consideration of this issue see *Dunne v Minister for Fisheries* [1984] I.R. 230.

[105]   [1997] 1 S.C.R. 748. The *Southam* case was an important development in the overarching "pragmatic and functional" approach used by the Canadian courts. See generally, Delany, "Recent Developments in Administrative Law in Canada: the Implications of *Dunsmuir v New Brunswick*" (2008) 30 D.U.L.J. 100.

[106]   See also, *Orange* [2000] IESC 79; [2000] 4 I.R. 159 which, in effect, confirms *M&J Gleeson*.

[107]   *Ulster Bank Investment Funds Ltd v Financial Services Ombudsman* [2006] IEHC 323; unreported, High Court, November 1, 2006 per Finnegan P.

more relevant. While words such as "confirm", "annul", and "modify" are often used
by the draftsman, this use tends to be somewhat promiscuous and interchangeable.
As the Electronic Communications Appeal Panel observed in *Hutchinson 3G*:

> "The reality is that in the *Gleeson, Orange* and *Carrickdale* cases the wording
> of 'confirm' 'annul' or otherwise was not *of itself* determinative of the scope
> of the appeal or the standard of review. Other factors were more prevalent
> such as the purpose behind the legislative code and the principle of deference
> when the court is hearing an appeal from an expert body."[108]

11-37   These questions were re-examined[109] by Cooke J. in *Rye Investments
Ltd v Competition Authority*,[110] a case concerning the scope of the appeal to the
High Court granted by s.24 of the Competition Act 2002 against a decision of
the Competition Authority to prohibit a merger. The following passage may be
regarded as an authoritative exposition of many of the factors which are relevant
in considering the scope of the appeal:

> "   ...
>
> (b)   In principle and subject to the important limitation mentioned below, an
>   appeal may raise 'any issue of law or fact' concerning the determination.
>   The procedure before the High Court is not therefore confined to an
>   appeal on a point of law and thus contrasts with the further limited review
>   which is possible before the Supreme Court as provided for in ss. (9) of
>   s. 24. It follows, accordingly, that the appeal includes, but is wider than,
>   a review of the substantive and procedural legality of a determination.
>   To paraphrase the words quoted from Wade's Administrative Law by
>   Costello J. in *Dunne v. Minister for Fisheries* (above) the appeal may
>   raise both the question 'is it lawful or unlawful?' and the question 'is it
>   right or wrong?'
>
> (c)   On the other hand, it is equally clear that the procedure is not expressly
>   an appeal by way of rehearing of the original notification in which the
>   decision of the court fully replaces that of the Authority and, in this
>   respect, the provision can be contrasted with, for example, the procedure
>   for review of an application for planning permission decided by a

---

[108] ECAP Decision No. 01/05, Appeal No. 2004/01, February 10, 2005 at para.7.2. See also,
Carrickdale Hotels Limited v Comptroller of Patents [2004] IEHC 86; [2004] 2 I.L.R.M. 404
at 410 per Laffoy J; *Glancré Teo v Cafferkey* [2004] IEHC 34; [2004] 3 I.R. 401 at 405 per
Finnegan P. See also, the comments of Costello J. in *Dunne v Minister for Fisheries* [1984]
I.R. 230 at 237, where he said that it did not follow from the provision of an appeal that "in
every case the court's jurisdiction on a statutory appeal is the same: in every case the statute
in question must be construed". Cf. the suggestion of Barron J. in *Orange* [2000] 4 I.R. 159
at 238 that "the test for competition cases cannot be a guide for other codes".
[109] There is another judicial restatement of the factors relevant in determining the scope of the
High Court's jurisdiction on an appeal in *Manorcastle Ltd v Aviation Commissioner* [2008]
IEHC 386; unreported, High Court, Charleton J., November 28, 2008. See also, O'Reilly,
"Curial Deference in Ireland" (2007) 7(2) J.S.I.J. 196. Note also the comments of McMahon
J. in *Square Capital Ltd v Financial Services Ombudsman* [2009] IEHC 467: "The appeal
here, while having some of the characteristics of the traditional judicial review, including
some deferential recognition for the expertise of the Ombudsman, will also have to bear in
mind the nature and functions of the Financial Services Ombudsman as laid down by the
Oireachtas."
[110] [2009] IEHC 140.

local authority when appealed to the Planning Board under s. 37 of the Planning and Development Act 2000 (see in particular ss. (1)(g) of that section).

(d) That an appeal of limited scope is envisaged is also suggested by the duty imposed on the court by ss. (6) of s. 24 (so far as practicable) to hear and determine the appeal within two months. (That such a time limit involves considerable restraint upon the scope of an appeal can be seen from the fact that the present case, which is unlikely to be untypical, has involved an investigation lasting some five months, a determination comprising more than 150 pages and covering five product markets, appeal papers comprising more than 20 lever arch files and a hearing which has lasted eight days.)

(e) Most significantly, however, ss. (4) of s. 24, while permitting any issue of fact to be raised on the appeal, requires the court to presume, unless it is considered unreasonable to do so, that matters of fact have been correctly accepted or found by the Authority in its determination. The court is precluded from hearing any witness evidence on any issue of fact unless it has first been satisfied that the Authority was unreasonable in its finding or acceptance of that fact.

(f) It necessarily follows, therefore that, on the one hand, the court is required not to re-open or interfere with findings of fact so long as that presumption stands, thereby limiting in a significant degree the scope of the procedure as an appeal directed at the correctness of the determination on its merits, as opposed to one confined to its substantive and procedural legality.

(g) It also follows, on the other hand, that the court can in those limited circumstances where the presumption of reasonableness is rebutted, re-open and re-decide specific issues of fact. Accordingly, in so far as the court may thus have to make a new finding on an issue of fact material to the validity of the Authority's determination, the section clearly envisages that the court may in principle and exceptionally substitute its own new findings of primary fact for those of the Authority."

11–38 On occasion, the amplitude of an appeal will be considerable, to the extent that there may be a re-consideration of the evidence by the High Court and a de novo adjudication thereon. Thus, in *Glancré Teo v Cafferkey*,[111] Finnegan P. held that not to hold a full appeal as to what constitutes exempted development for the purposes of s.5 of the Local Government (Planning and Development) Act 1963 "would create an inherent contradiction within the planning code".[112]

The applicable standard of review

11–39 On an appeal, what is the appropriate standard of review, or intensity of the judicial scrutiny of the original decision? The issues here are: how badly must the administrative body err; and how closely must the appellate court examine the record? As to the standard of review, the definitive test is as stated by Keane C.J.

---

[111] [2004] IEHC 34; [2004] 3 I.R. 401. See similarly, *Esat Digifone v South Dublin County Council* [2002] IEHC 173; [2002] 3 I.R. 585.
[112] [2004] 3 I.R. 401 at 405.

in *Orange Communications Ltd v Director of Telecommunications Regulation*. The applicant must show:

> "[A]s a matter of probability that, taking the adjudicative process as a whole, the decision reached was vitiated by a serious and significant error or a series of such errors. In arriving at a conclusion on that issue, the High Court will necessarily have regard to the degree of expertise and specialised knowledge available to the first defendant."[113]

11–40 However, given the highly variable statutory frameworks at issue, the many different types of decision that might fall to be appealed and the great divergences in the expertise and composition of the bodies rendering the decisions, a monolithic standard of review seems inappropriate. If the possibilities allowed are a choice only between de novo review and the *Orange* test, this might not give effect to the intentions of the Oireachtas. The Oireachtas has established different decision-making bodies under different statutory frameworks and entrusted them with varying levels of power, which suggests that the standard of review should vary to reflect any nuances of the various statutory schemes. Thus, following a review of the case law the Electronic Communications Appeal Tribunal took a slightly different view of this issue:

> "It seems therefore that what is envisaged by the Regulations (as interpreted in the light of Article 4.1 [of the Framework Directive])[114] is an examination of the *decision* of the Regulator as opposed to a reassessment *de novo* by the Panel of whether the Appellant is a 'significant market power in the wholesale voice call termination market on individual mobile networks.' This will mean that Panel can focus on evidence and materials upon which the Regulator based its decision and look at the inferences and conclusions it drew from those materials. Whilst the Panel has appropriate expertise, and has expertise available to it, it is not the type of expertise which the Regulator itself has, for example, in collating data and information on the

---

[113] [2000] 4 I.R. 136 at 185. Compare *Orange* with *M&J Gleeson v Competition Authority* [1999] 1 I.L.R.M. 401 at 410–411 and the more stringent formulation in *Carrickdale Hotels Limited v Comptroller of Patents* [2004] IEHC 86; [2004] 2 I.L.R.M. 401 at 411 per Laffoy J. The formulation of the standard of review by Keane C.J. is notably different from that favoured by the Canadian Supreme Court in *Southam* [1997] 1 S.C.R. 748 at para.56: "An unreasonable decision is one that, in the main, is not supported by any reasons that can stand up to a *somewhat probing examination*." (Emphasis added.) Comparing the two tests textually, the Irish standard seems friendlier to the public body. The *Orange* test was effectively adopted by the legislature in the Anglo Irish Bank Corporation Act 2009 s.31(6).

[114] Article 4.1 of the Directive provides: "Member States shall ensure that effective mechanisms exist at national level under which any user or undertaking providing electronic communications networks and/or services who is affected by a decision of a national regulatory authority has the right of appeal against the decision to an appeal body that is independent of the parties involved. This body, which may be a court, shall have the appropriate expertise available to it to enable it to carry out its functions. Member States shall ensure that the merits of the case are duly taken into account and that there is an effective appeal mechanism. Pending the outcome of any such appeal, the decision of the national regulatory authority shall stand, unless the appeal body decides otherwise."

  The substance of this sensible provision may, indeed, be required by art.6 of the European Convention on Human Rights. A body that formulates and then implements policy may not be an independent and impartial tribunal for the purposes of art.6. See *R. (Alconbury) v Environment Secretary* [2001] UKHL 23; [2003] 2 A.C. 295 at 318.

market and carrying out an investigation and analysis of that market. Rather it is the type of expertise which allows the Panel to understand the specialist or technical matters which the Regulator has regard to in carrying out its functions and making its decision. To this extent, a degree of deference can be shown but not the same degree which the court in *Orange* or *Gleeson* would have shown.

The Panel is of the view, therefore, that the standard as envisaged by the Regulations is broader than the standard as set out in *Orange*, *Gleeson* and *Carrickdale*. The Regulations envisage that the Panel can annul, or annul in part, the decision of the Regulator if, on an examination of the Regulator's decision and the decision-making process, there are errors of fact or law (which includes erroneous inferences of fact, or errors as to jurisdiction and procedure) such as would vitiate the decision. In practical terms, therefore, the error (or errors) would need to be ... one which, when objectively assessed, had a bearing on the decision reached by the Regulator. However, the error(s) need not go to the root of the decision either ... In coming to this conclusion, the Panel will take into account the view of the Regulator given its expertise on certain technical matters, but ultimately can substitute its own opinion if it takes a different view in respect of these matters."[115]

11–41 At this point, a comparison may be useful. The test thus adumbrated in *Hutchinson 3G* is, to all intents and purposes, not materially different from that employed by the EU Court of Justice in merger cases coming on appeal from the Commission. As that Court said in *Petrolessence SA*[116]:

"... [R]eview by the Community Courts of complex economic assessments made by the Commission ... must be limited to ensuring compliance with the rules of procedure and the statement of reasons, as well as the substantive accuracy of the facts, the absence of manifest errors of assessment and of any misuse of power. In particular, it is not for the Court of First Instance to substitute its own economic assessment for that of the Commission."[117]

And there are numerous cases in which assessments made by the Commission in complex merger cases have been set aside on grounds of "manifest error".[118]

Stage of assessment

11–42 In adjudicating on an appeal, a court must choose a point in time at which to assess the evidence. A range of possibilities exist, from the time the decision-maker actually takes the decision, to the time of the court hearing itself. On the one hand, it may be desirable, in areas of regulation that move with considerably rapidity, to permit the court to assess the matter from the latest possible vantage point. On the other hand, a desire for consistency and certainty in judicial control of regulation counsels focusing on the time of the initial decision. Considerations of fairness and efficiency may also enter the equation.

---

[115] ECAP Decision No. 01/05, Appeal No. 2004/01, February 10, 2005 at paras 10.1 and 10.2.
[116] (T-342/00) [2003] E.C.R. II-1161.
[117] (T-342/00) [2003] E.C.R. II-1161 at para.101.
[118] (T-342/99) [2002] E.C.R. II-2585 at para.294.

11–43   An initial indication that the more flexible approach would be taken was provided by *Balkan Tours Ltd v Minister for Communications*.[119] Section 3 of the Transport (Tour Operators and Travel Agents) Act 1982 gives the Minister power to revoke a tour agent's licence. This power had been exercised by the Minister in the present case, since there had been a history of a "careless, unbusinesslike approach" on the part of the applicants, as far as the observance of their trading licences was concerned. One of the more serious breaches of these conditions lay in the fact that the applicants had apparently circulated their travel brochures to the public without ensuring that the correct tour operator's licence had been reproduced in the brochures. Since no satisfactory explanation had been forthcoming, Lynch J. concluded that the Minister had been correct "to revoke the licences at the time and in the circumstances when he did so". However, further evidence had come to light at the hearing before Lynch J., showing that this error had been principally the fault of the applicants' printers, who had "acted on their own initiative and without any instructions". This evidence had not been before the Minister. Lynch J. concluded that the effect of s.9(4) of the 1982 Act was that "the High Court is to ascertain all the relevant facts of the case whether they were before the Minister or not and to give effect to them".[120] The judge accordingly relied on the new evidence.

11–44   However, the more recent trend appears to be towards limiting the consideration of evidence to that available at the time of the original decision, at least as a "general rule".[121] Otherwise, "the hearing in [the High Court] would be an appeal in name only".[122] Nevertheless, Finnegan P. has advocated a more flexible approach:

> "The Court ... has a discretion on application to permit further evidence to be introduced where it is satisfied that this is necessary or appropriate in the interest of justice ... In determining whether or not additional evidence should be admitted regard should be had to the principles on which the Supreme Court [hearing a High Court appeal] admits additional evidence[123] ... However in the interests of justice regard should be had to the nature of the deciding body whose decision is being appealed: the proceedings before that body may well lack much of the formality which will attend a hearing before the High Court with which the Supreme Court will principally be concerned. An issue may arise on appeal which could not arise at a hearing for example an issue as to the extent of expertise of the deciding body. Thus a more flexible approach than that adopted by the Supreme Court on the admission of further evidence will be required."[124]

---

[119]   [1988] I.L.R.M. 101.

[120]   [1988] I.L.R.M. 101 at 107.

[121]   *Murray v Pensions Ombudsman* [2007] IEHC 27; [2007] 2 I.L.R.M. 196 per Kelly J.

[122]   *Murray v Pensions Ombudsman* [2007] IEHC 27; [2007] 2 I.L.R.M. 196 per Kelly J.

[123]   *Murphy v Minister for Defence* [1991] 2 I.R. 161. See also, *Carrickdale Hotels Limited v Comptroller of Patents* [2004] IEHC 86; [2004] 3 I.R. 410 at 429–430.

[124]   *Ulster Bank Investment Funds Ltd v Financial Services Ombudsman* [2006] IEHC 323; unreported, High Court, Finnegan P., November 1, 2006. See also, *Dunne v Minister for Fisheries and Forestry* [1984] I.R. 230 at 239 per Costello J.; *Glancré Teo v Cafferkey* [2004] IEHC 34; [2004] 3 I.R. 401 at 407 per Finnegan P.; *Murray v Pensions Ombudsman* [2007] IEHC 27; [2007] 2 I.L.R.M. 196.

E. *DELEGATUS NON POTEST DELEGARE*

11–45   The general principle here is that a power must be exercised by the authority (*delegatus*) in which it has been vested by the legislature. It cannot be transferred (*delegare*) to any other person or body.[125] A straightforward example is *Lawlor v Flood*.[126] In this case, the chair of a tribunal of inquiry had ordered the applicant to answer in private session questions posed by counsel for the Tribunal. However, the governing legislation only provided for the examination of witnesses by the Tribunal itself, and thus the Supreme Court held that the power could not be delegated to counsel for the Tribunal:

> "[W]hen it comes to the formal exercise by the Tribunal of its powers to examine witnesses this must be done by the Tribunal itself and ... must be done in public."[127]

11–46   In principle, the maxim may apply to all types of decision whether quasi-judicial, legislative, administrative or policy (discretionary) (which is why the subject is treated in this general chapter and not in the chapter on the control of discretionary powers). However, the nature of the decision is undoubtedly one of the factors conditioning whether the rule applies in any particular situation.

11–47   The principle is at its strictest in the case of court proceedings.[128] It is also fairly stringently applied in the case of legislative, quasi-judicial or wide discretionary powers. At the other end of the spectrum, naturally, the courts allow greater latitude in the case of routine administrative matters.[129] The essential point is

---

[125]   Another aspect is that the authority must be properly appointed, properly constituted and, where relevant, properly qualified: *State (Walshe) v Murphy* [1981] I.R. 275; *Shelly v Mahon* [1990] 1 I.R. 36 (convictions imposed by an improperly qualified District judge quashed); *Glavin v Governor of Mountjoy Prison* [1991] 2 I.R. 421; *Carroll v Law Society of Ireland (No. 2)* [1999] IEHC 85; [2003] 1 I.R. 284.

[126]   [1999] 3 I.R. 107.

[127]   [1999] 3 I.R. 107 at 133 per Hamilton C.J. However, it was permissible for the Tribunal to "retain persons to act on its behalf, both in the gathering of evidence and its adduction before the Tribunal or to carry out the administrative requirements of the Tribunal": [1999] 3 I.R. 107 at 133. See similarly, *O'Neill v Beaumont Hospital* [1990] I.L.R.M. 419; *Motor Distributors Ltd v Revenue Commissioners*, unreported, High Court, Kearns J., February 2, 2001; *J&E Davy v Financial Services Ombudsman* [2008] IEHC 256; [2008] 2 I.L.R.M. 507. For unsuccessful *delegatus* arguments, see *Flynn v An Post* [1987] I.R. 68 at 75, 80–81; *Heneghan v Western Regional Fisheries Board* [1986] I.L.R.M. 225 at 228; *Brennan v Donnellan* [2003] IEHC 58; *Dubsky v Ireland* [2005] IEHC 442; [2007] 1 I.R. 63 at 86; *Riordan v Ireland* [2006] IEHC 312.

[128]   In regard to courts, the decision of the Supreme Court in *State (Clarke) v Roche* [1986] I.R. 619 at 640 is relevant. (There is a critique in H & M, at para.11–137.) *A contra*: *O'Keeffe v Governor of St Patrick's Institution* [2006] 1 I.R. 228 at 241.

[129]   *State (Keller) v Galway County Council* [1958] I.R. 142 at 148 (chief medical officer can delegate physical examination of applicant for a grant, but not duty of forming the necessary opinion as to whether the applicant was substantially handicapped); *Ward v Governor of Portlaoise Prison* [2006] IEHC 297 (no need for proof of delegation where an assistant governor certified grounds for detention following an application for an inquiry under Art.40.4.2° of the Constitution by a prisoner, although the person making the certification had to be "a person of senior managerial rank within the prison"). In the case of routine tasks performed by servants of a public authority, foreign courts have sometimes achieved this result by characterising the situation as involving the creation of an agency and so evading the *delegatus* principle.

that the maxim is merely a rule of statutory construction, rather than a constitutional rule and, in predicting its operation it has been said that:

> "Whether a person other than that named in the empowering statute is allowed to act will be dependent upon the entire statutory context. The nature of the subject-matter, the degree of control retained by the person delegating and the type of person or body to whom the power is delegated, will all be taken into account."[130]

11–48   However, even with the tolerance which the attitude summarised in this passage evinces, the *delegatus* principle has immense and often unwelcome implications. For one should emphasise that this principle is, as might be guessed from its formulation, a survival from Roman law. It found a ready welcome in the very small British governmental units, which pre-dated the coming of big government in the mid-nineteenth century. However, by today, we have mass government, which is executed in practice largely by anonymous public servants, rather than the chieftains in whom the function has been formally vested.[131] Thus, fairly substantial exceptions to the principle have been developed in an attempt to reconcile it with modern conditions. The first of these applies only to the special, though common, case of the relationship between Ministers and civil servants: it is covered in the next Part of this chapter.

11–49   Then there are numerous statutory exceptions,[132] before which the *delegatus* principle has to bow. First, a government order may be made on the request of a government Minister, delegating to the particular Minister of State either all the Minister's powers and duties under a particular Act or, more narrowly, any particular statutory power.[133] Secondly, a statute or statutory instrument may provide for a specific delegation of power: from the Government to a Minister[134]; from a Minister to another body[135]; or from various other specified persons or entities vested with

---

[130] Craig, *Administrative Law*, 6th edn (London: Sweet & Maxwell, 2008), p.503. See generally, Willis, *"Delegatus Non Potest Delegare"* (1943) 21 Can. B.R. 257.

[131] A point recognised by the Supreme Court in *Re Article 26 and the Health (Amendment) (No. 2) Bill 2004* [2005] IESC 7; [2005] 2 I.R. 105 at 172: "When public officials are charged with administering a statutory scheme it may be difficult, if not impossible, for the Oireachtas to prescribe in legislation for every special circumstance of individuals who find themselves on the margins of such a scheme."

[132] On the other hand, alternatively a statute may expressly circumscribe an official's authority to delegate. See, e.g. Education Act 1998 s.13(13) (as amended by Education (Miscellaneous Provisions) Act 2007 s.3 (consent of Minister must be obtained before delegating a function)); Vocational Education (Amendment) Act 2001 s.13(8) (semble).

[133] Ministers and Secretaries (Amendment) (No. 2) Act 1977 s.2. See respectively, e.g. Health and Children (Delegation of Ministerial Functions) Order 2004 (S.I. No. 842 of 2004); Public Service (Delegation of Ministerial Functions) Order 1978 (S.I. No. 117 of 1978) art.2(2).

[134] Criminal Justice Act 1951 s.23A(1) (as inserted by s.17(b) of the Criminal Justice (Miscellaneous Provisions) Act 1997). See *Whelan v Minister for Justice, Equality and Law Reform* [2007] IEHC 374; [2008] 2 I.R. 142. See also, *Geraghty v Minister for Local Government* [1976] I.R. 153 at 154, 160.

[135] See, e.g. National Cultural Institutions Act 1997 s.51; Education Act 1998 s.31(2); National Treasury Management Agency (Amendment) Act 2000 ss.9, 21(2), 23(1) and 28; Dormant Accounts Act 2001 s.12(3)(c); Social Welfare Consolidation Act 2005 s.289. For an example of such an order see National Treasury Management Agency (Delegation of Claims Management Functions) Order 2005 (S.I. No. 503 of 2005). Difficulties may arise where the statutory source

a statutory power to some other person or entity.[136] Thirdly, at local government level, the manager is empowered to delegate any of his functions to an employee of the local authority.[137] There are numerous other statutory restrictions of the principle, one of which is a formula which is often included in the constituent statutes of public bodies: "[the Agency] may perform any of its stated functions through or by any of its officers and servants duly authorised by [the Agency] in that behalf."[138]

11–50 However, such statutory dispensations are usually fairly specific and narrow. Thus it may happen that there is a gap in the statutory patchwork, at which point the *delegatus* principle will operate to strike down an administrative action, for no better reason than legislative omission, coupled with actions by lay administrators which are out of line with the (antiquarian and unrealistic) law in this area.

11–51 Finally, two incidental points may be made, which involve the operation of the general principles of administrative law in association with an act of delegation.[139] In the first place, there is the possibility of a waiver being deemed to authorise a delegation. For example, in *Flanagan v University College, Dublin*,[140] a University committee of discipline, in which the duty of disciplining students had been vested, took action solely on the recommendation of an independent expert from another institution from whom it had commissioned a report on an alleged case of plagiarism. This amounted, Barron J. held, to an improper delegation of its function by the committee of discipline. What is striking is that Barron J. appeared to suggest that if the student had given her "informed consent"[141] to the committee's total reliance on the opinion of the independent expert, then the delegation would have been proper. This appears to be the first suggestion that the *delegatus* principle may be waived. In its favour is the fact that, in an appropriate case, it appears to meet the justice of the situation. As against this, however, it may be argued that the *delegatus* principle is supposed to be a bulwark of good public administration, having wider implications than its effects upon any particular individual.[142]

---

of the delegation changes. See the unusual case of *Dunnes Stores Ireland Co Ltd v Houlihan* [2003] IEHC 619.

[136] See, e.g. Vocational Education (Amendment) Act 2001 s.16; Personal Injuries Assessment Board Act 2003 s.67(3); State Examinations Commission (Establishment) Order 2003 (S.I. No. 373 of 2003) art.20(1); Child Care (Special Care) Regulations 2004 (S.I. No. 550 of 2004) art.5(6); Civil Registration Act 2004 s.8(6); Garda Síochána Act 2005 ss.31 and 75; National Economic and Social Development Office Act 2006 s.21(2); Health Act 2007 ss.14(2) and 23. See especially the rules in relation to An Bord Pleanála (Planning and Development Act 2000 s.111(6)); and planning conditions: 2000 Act s.34; *Boland v An Bord Pleanála* [1996] 3 I.R. 435; *Kenny v Dublin City Council* [2009] IESC 19.

[137] Local Government Act 2001 s.154(2). See *Cassels v Dublin Corporation* [1963] I.R. 193.

[138] See, e.g. Companies (Auditing and Accounting) Act 2003 s.27(4). By way of contrast, see Child Care Act 1991 s.23 (as amended by Children Act 2001 s.16 and Health Act 2004 Sch.7), which prevents the delegation by the Health Service Executive of the power to apply for care orders.

[139] For delegation coupled with the rule against rubber stamping, see paras 15–152 to 15–153.

[140] [1988] I.R. 724.

[141] [1988] I.R. 724 at 732.

[142] For analogous arguments in the context of whether the infractions of the rule against bias could be waived, see paras 13–67 to 13–79.

11–52   Secondly, where there is a statutory authority to delegate, then it will usually happen that this power will be discretionary. As such, like any substantive or, for that matter, procedural, discretionary power, it is subject to the general controls upon the exercise of discretionary powers, e.g. the requirement of reasonableness.[143] An illustration of this occurred in the Northern Irish case of *Re Curran and McCann's Application*.[144] Here the Craigavon Borough Council had exercised its power, under s.18(d) of the Local Government Act (Northern Ireland) 1972, to appoint a committee consisting of all the council members, apart from the two Sinn Féin councillors: and then delegated almost all the functions of the Council to that committee. The object of this device was to exclude the Sinn Féin councillors from the work of the Council. However, Hutton J. held that the legislative intendment of the delegation provision was to promote the better management and regulation of the Council's business. Accordingly, in reliance on the general principle that a power given for one purpose cannot be exercised for another, Hutton J. struck down the resolution effecting the delegation, since the purpose behind the resolution was not to further the better management of business.[145]

F. THE *CARLTONA* PRINCIPLE: THE DELEGATION OF MINISTERIAL POWERS TO CIVIL SERVANTS

11–53   Following on from the point made in the previous Part, it would plainly be an impossible state of affairs if the law required a Minister, even with the assistance of his Minister for State, to keep in personal contact with each of the hundreds of decisions taken in his department each day. In most cases, the *delegatus* doctrine can be side-stepped by regarding each civil servant as the *alter ego* of the Minister at the head of the department. This is a principle which is known as the "*Carltona* doctrine".[146] The principle that the powers vested in a Minister may be exercised, without any express act of delegation, by responsible officials on his behalf is according to an English authority "a common law constitutional power".[147] Even

---

[143] See, e.g. *Casey v Minister for Arts, Heritage and the Gaeltacht* [2004] IESC 19; [2004] 1 I.R. 402 at 425–429.

[144] [1985] N.I. 26.

[145] Another point worth noting is that at the basic level, uncertainty may arise as to the body in which the decision was originally vested. For example, in *McGabhann v Incorporated Law Society of Ireland* [1989] I.L.R.M. 854 at 865, a query was raised by Blayney J. (though he did not determine the issue, since it had not been argued by the parties) as to the particular entity in which the power had been vested in the first place. Similar issues were touched upon in *Dubsky v Ireland* [2005] IEHC 442; [2007] 1 I.R. 63.

[146] *Carltona Ltd v Commissioners of Works* [1943] 2 All E.R. 560. In that case, private property had been requisitioned under defence regulations by an official purporting to act on behalf of the responsible minister. Lord Greene rejected (at 563) the argument that the requisition was invalid on this ground: "In the administration of government in this country the functions which are given to ministers ... are functions so multifarious that no minister could ever personally attend to them. To take the example of the present case, no doubt there have been thousands of requisitions in this country by individual ministers. It cannot be supposed that this regulation meant that, in each case, the minister in person should direct his mind to the matter. The duties imposed upon ministers and the powers given to ministers are normally exercised under the authority of the ministers by responsible officials of the department. Public business could not be carried on if that were not the case."

[147] *R. v Secretary of State for the Home Department Ex p. Oladehinde* [1991] 1 A.C. 254 at 282 per Lord Donaldson M.R. This statement of principle was expressly approved by Hamilton C.J. in *Devanney v Minister for Justice* [1998] 1 I.L.R.M. 81.

more to the point, the Ministers and Secretaries (Amendment) Act 1939 s.6(3) contains what may be regarded as a statutory affirmation of the *Carltona* doctrine, although this view has not yet received consideration before a court. (The doctrine is buttressed, anyway, by the notion that the Minister bears political responsibility to the Dáil and legal responsibility, under the Ministers and Secretaries Act 1924, for all actions going on within his Department.)[148] Yet the extent to which the *Carltona* doctrine formed part of Irish law had been the subject of some uncertainty[149] prior to the decisions of the Supreme Court in *Tang v Minister for Justice*[150] and *Devanney v District Judge Shields*.[151]

11–54 Before turning to these authorities, however, we should note that the practical policies underlying the two approaches (*Carltona* versus *Delegatus*) are manifested in the following quotations. In *Murphy v Dublin Corporation*,[152] Walsh J. stated:

> "[The Minister] is *persona designata* in that the holder of the office of the Minister for Local Government is the person designated for that function. If the Oireachtas had so enacted, the Act could just as easily have assigned the functions to the chairman of Córas Iompair Éireann or to the chairman of the Electricity Supply Board."[153]

11–55 By contrast, in a passage which has its relevance also in relation to the previous Part, Lord Diplock said in *Bushell v Secretary of State for the Environment*[154]:

> "To treat the Minister in his decision-making capacity as someone separate and distinct from the department of government of which he is the political head and for whose actions he alone in constitutional theory is accountable to Parliament is to ignore not only practical realities but Parliament's intention. Ministers come and go; departments, though their names may change from time to time, remain. Discretion in making administrative decisions is conferred on a Minister not as an individual but as the holder of an office in which he will have available to him in arriving at his decision the collective knowledge, experience and expertise of all those who serve the Crown in the department of which, for the time being, he is the political head. The collective knowledge, technical as well as factual, of the civil

---

[148] See Ch.3, Part B. See also, National Treasury Management Agency (Amendment) Act 2000 s.9(3)(f), which specifically provides that "the delegation or declaration shall not remove or derogate from the responsibility of any Minister of the Government to Dáil Éireann or as a member of the Government for the performance of functions of that Minister of the Government thereby delegated or to which the declaration relates".

[149] The high water mark of this zeal for the principle is represented by *Geraghty v Minister for Local Government (No. 2)* [1976] I.R. 153 at 171 (Walsh J.); at 174–175 (Henchy J.); and at 181–182 (Gannon J.); and *Murphy v Dublin Corporation* [1972] I.R. 215 at 238.

[150] [1996] 2 I.L.R.M. 46. See also, *Agrichem BV v Minister for Agriculture and Food* [2005] IEHC 99; *Rimsa v Governor of Cloverhill Prison* [2008] IEHC 6.

[151] [1998] 1 I.L.R.M. 81.

[152] [1972] I.R. 215.

[153] [1972] I.R. 215 at 238. This passage was quoted with approval by O'Higgins J. in the High Court in *Geraghty* [1976] I.R. 153 at 160–161.

[154] [1981] A.C. 75.

servants in the department and their collective expertise are to be treated as the Minister's own knowledge, his own expertise. It is they who in reality will have prepared the draft scheme for his approval; it is they who in the first instance will consider the objections to the scheme and the report of the inspector by whom any local inquiry has been held and it is they who will give to the Minister the benefits of their combined experience, technical knowledge and expert opinion on all matters raised in the objections and the report. This is an integral part of the decision-making process itself; it is not to be equiparated with the Minister receiving evidence himself, expert opinion or advice from sources outside the department after the local inquiry has been closed."[155]

11–56 As noted, recent Irish case law appears to have come down in favour of what is submitted is the commonsensical view expressed in this passage In a deportation case, *Tang v Minister for Justice*,[156] a senior official refused to grant Hong Kong immigrants who breached the terms of their entry conditions permission to reside in the State. The official had responsibility for the immigration and citizenship section in the Department of Justice and acted in the name of the Minister when making the decision: the Minister was not, however, consulted about the decision. The Supreme Court was not impressed by the argument that this decision ought to have been made by the Minister personally. Hamilton C.J. explicitly endorsed the *Carltona* doctrine and added:

> "Having regard to the *extensive powers* conferred on the Minister by the Aliens Act 1935 and the regulations made thereunder, *it cannot be supposed that it was the intention of the legislature that the Minister personally should exercise these powers*. The duties imposed upon the Minister and the powers given to the Minister can be artificial and are normally exercised under the authority of the Minister by responsible officials of the Minister's Department."[157]

11–57 *Tang* was reinforced by the Supreme Court's decision in *Devanney v District Judge Shields*.[158] Here the issue was whether the Minister was personally obliged to consider the appointment of each District Court clerk having regard to the provisions of s.46(2) of the Court Officers Act 1926.[159] In the High Court McCracken J. held that the purported appointment of a District Court clerk by a civil servant was invalid, as the *Carltona* principle had no application to such appointments. The clerks had important statutory responsibilities, held office at the will of the Minister and there were relatively few such appointments. In these circumstances, it was—in contrast to the situation in *Tang*—"perfectly practical" for the Minister personally to appoint such clerks. This decision was reversed on appeal by the Supreme Court which unanimously affirmed the general applicability

---

[155] [1981] A.C. 75 at 95. See also, *McKernan v Governor of HM Prison Belfast* [1983] N.I. 83.
[156] [1996] 2 I.L.R.M. 46.
[157] [1996] 2 I.L.R.M. 46 at 60–61 (emphasis added). The executive power/*persona designata* question was not addressed in this case.
[158] [1998] 1 I.L.R.M. 81.
[159] Which provides in relevant part that "every District Court clerk shall be appointed by the Minister and shall ... hold office at the will of and may be removed by the Minister".

of the *Carltona* principle. Hamilton C.J. stressed the comparative importance of such an appointment compared to the decision in *Tang*:

> "The appointment of a District Court clerk is, no doubt, an important matter. But it is not more important than many of the decisions which fall to be made by civil servants, in the name of the Minister, under the Aliens Act 1935. Yet the Aliens Act 1935 was expressly approved by this Court in the *Tang* case as being a correct application of the *Carltona* principle. Logically, therefore, it seems to me that the Court must regard what happened in this case as being also a correct application of the *Carltona* principle."[160]

11–58 It would seem, therefore, that while the *Carltona* principle is one of general application (certainly as far as the exercise of routine bureaucratic powers is concerned), its scope depends in the last analysis on statutory interpretation.[161] To amplify: *Tang* is explicable on the basis that the Minister could not be expected to decide every immigration case personally, but there could well be certain exceptional types of cases where the statutory context is such that it was clear that the Oireachtas must have intended that the decision would be personal to the Minister.[162]

G. Acting under Dictation by Another Body

11–59 In the field next to the delegation of a decision by an authorised body to another body lies a case in which the authorised body does, in form, take the decision, but in substance is merely rubber stamping an instruction from another body.[163] A straightforward example of this occurred in *State (Rajan) v Minister for Industry and Commerce*.[164] This case arose out of "directives" issued by the Controller of Patents, Designs and Trade Marks to members of his professional staff which were designed to reduce the arrears of applications in the Patent Office. These directives stated, inter alia, that if exactly the same patent application had already been accepted in another European Patent Office then that specification should be accepted in Ireland without any further checks as to matters such as "patentability" and "novelty", which the Act requires to be tested. The crucial point here is that the duty to make such checks was vested not in the Controller but in members of his staff known as "examiners". For s.11(1) of the Patents Act 1964 stated:

---

[160] [1998] 1 I.L.R.M. 81 at 102.
[161] Thus in *DPP v O'Rourke*, unreported, High Court, Finlay P., July 25, 1983, Finlay P. held that the assigning of a District Court clerk to a specific District Court area was not a matter which required the personal decision of the Minister. In *Devanney*, McCracken J. said that *O'Rourke* concerned a "purely administrative matter and one to which the *Carltona* principle clearly applies".
[162] As McCracken J. said in *Devanney v District Judge Shields* [1998] 1 I.L.R.M. 81 at 92, the *Carltona* principle "arose out of practical necessity" and therefore "must be considered in relation to specific ministerial functions both in the light of the practicality of the Minister personally exercising those functions and in the light of the importance of each individual decision".
[163] The two classes plainly overlap. For instance, *Geraghty v Minister for Local Government* [1976] I.R. 300 could have been classified under the present heading.
[164] [1988] I.L.R.M. 231.

When the complete specification has been filed in respect of an application for a patent, the application shall be referred by the Controller to an examiner for examination.

11–60 In the light of this, Barron J. held that the Controller's instruction was doubly invalid. First, he found that there is a statutory obligation to examine all applications for both patentability and novelty, irrespective of anything done abroad. Secondly, Barron J. states that it was "erroneous" for the Controller to believe:

> "... that he has a general power of control over the Examiners even extending to telling them the extent of the investigation of applications which they are to perform. The examination is a statutory function and there is nothing in the relevant statutory powers giving him such a right either as persona designata or as head of the Patent Office".[165]

The point was strengthened by the fact that the 1964 Act, in effect, provided for an appeal from an examiner to the Controller, so making it even less appropriate for an examiner to be subject to instructions from the Controller.[166]

11–61 At issue more recently, in *Dunne v Donohoe*,[167] was s.4(b) of the Firearms Act 1925, which provides that a Garda superintendent must, before granting a firearms certificate, be satisfied that the applicant "can be permitted to have in his possession, use, and carry a firearm or ammunition without danger to the public safety or to the peace". The Garda Commissioner had introduced a directive, binding on all superintendents, to the effect that certificates in respect of shotguns and rifles up to .22 calibre should not be issued unless the applicant had a "properly constructed and locked firearms cabinet". The Supreme Court held that power had been conferred on a Garda superintendent as a *persona designata* who accordingly could not "be required to exercise it in any particular manner by any other body or authority".[168]

11–62 While on the purely legal plane, the result of the case was plainly correct, on the level of common sense, there may be more to be said. One strong general point which emerges from this case concerns one of the respondent's arguments. This was to the effect that the Garda Síochána naturally has "the established hierarchical structure of a disciplined force"[169] whose constitutional statute, the Police Forces (Amalgamation) Act 1925 s.8(1) states that "the general direction and control of the amalgamated force shall ... be vested in the Commissioner ...". The argument founded on this provision was not explicitly addressed by

---

[165] [1988] I.L.R.M. 231 at 240.

[166] See similarly, *J&E Davy v Financial Services Ombudsman* [2008] IEHC 256; [2008] 2 I.L.R.M. 507 at 535–537.

[167] [2002] IESC 35; [2002] 2 I.R. 533. It happens quite frequently that a situation arises in which both the present principle and the rule against an inflexible policy are engaged: see for instance *Dunne v Donohoe* [2002] 2 I.R. 533 or *McCarron v Kearney* [2010] 3 I.R. 302 at paras 15–138 to 15–142.

[168] [2002] IESC 35; [2002] 2 I.R. 533 at 542 per Keane C.J. The same rule would apply, Keane C.J. held, in respect of powers conferred on Garda superintendents by, for instance, the Betting Act 1931, the Public Dance Halls Act 1935, the Gaming and Lotteries Act 1956 or the Intoxicating Liquor Acts.

[169] [2002] IESC 35; [2002] 2 I.R. 533 at 539.

the judge, though he evidently rejected it, perhaps influenced by the argument of counsel for the applicant, to the effect that s.8 applied only to operational matters, not a regulatory power conferred on a *persona designata*. Nevertheless, when most people (whether Gardaí or laypeople) see a police force, they think of it as a single, disciplined entity observing common standards, in areas such as the security of weapons. It is appropriate for the law to follow the reasonable expectations of practitioners in the field, and not to impose unexpected technicalities like the *persona designata*, unless there is a very good reason for a departure. Similarly, the notion of a personage (in this case, a Garda superintendent) wearing two hats is well known to lawyers, but other people are not so conversant with what is, whether metaphorically or literally, a rather unlikely fashion.

11–63   Next, the notion of the *persona designata* is also unrealistic if it says that the duty of acting as a gun-licensing agency could have been vested as well in, say, a local Mother Superior, as in a Garda Superintendent. There are sound reasons for vesting it in the Gardaí, in that this is a force which disposes of substantial "collective knowledge, expertise and experience".[170] Moreover, stolen guns may be used outside the police district in which the licence was granted. It would be realistic, therefore, to regard the issue of licence holders keeping guns secure as requiring nationwide co-ordination and a common set of standards. On the level of common sense, this consideration does militate in favour of allowing some authority to the Commissioner, as head of the nationwide service, to issue guidelines.

11–64   In the cases mentioned so far, the decision-maker regarded itself as "bound" by the "direction" of another body. As a result, there could be said to have been an "abdication" by the decision-maker in question. But what of a situation in which the views of the other body are regarded merely as advice? For the decision-maker must take into account all relevant considerations, including public policy and, in an appropriate context, these could include the policy of a Minister or other public body. *State (Kershaw) v Eastern Health Board*[171] presented facts which were closer to this line than the cases considered so far. The case concerned the National Fuel Scheme which, pursuant to the Social Welfare (Consolidation) Act 1981, was operated by the respondent Health Board. However, without statutory authority, the then Minister for Social Welfare had issued a circular excluding from the Scheme persons who were in receipt of certain categories of social welfare payments. Finlay P. stated:

> "The Minister has, of course, in addition a general administrative function with regard to the administration of the scheme for supplementary benefits which he himself has prescribed in the Regulations of 1977 [the Social Welfare (Supplementary Welfare Allowances) Regulations 1977]. In so far, therefore, as the circulars issued on his behalf on June 22, 1983, form advice and guidance to health boards carrying out the National Fuel Scheme it is clearly a proper and valid administrative act."[172]

---

[170] *Bushell v Secretary* of *State for the Environment* [1981] A.C. 75 at 95 per Lord Diplock. See also, *McCarron v Kearney* [2008] IEHC 195.
[171] [1985] I.L.R.M. 235.
[172] [1985] I.L.R.M. 235 at 239.

11–65   However, the High Court went on to find for the applicant on the basis that the circular "purports to exclude absolutely from the discretion of the deciding officer ... the discretion to grant such an allowance to a person in receipt of [the specified social welfare payments]".[173]

11–66   It follows that there is a practical difficulty in this area, namely determining whether on the one hand, the line has been crossed between seeking advice and then genuinely exercising discretion and on the other hand, acting automatically under another's dictation. This aspect of the rule against delegation is increasingly important because of the propensity of Ministers to seek expert advice. The decision in *Genmark Pharma v Minister for Health*[174] partly concerned the ability of a Minister (including, in this term, his civil servants: see previous Part) to take a decision based on expert advice.[175] The body at issue was the National Drugs Advisory Board,[176] which advised the respondent Minister[177] on, amongst other things, applications for product authorisation for medicinal products. Under the relevant Regulations, the Minister could refuse an application if, inter alia, "the therapeutic efficacy of the preparation is lacking or is insufficiently substantiated by the applicant ...". Here, the Board engaged in substantial correspondence with the applicant before recommending rejection of the application. Some of this correspondence had been sent to the Minister by the applicant but no opportunity to rebut the findings of the Board had been provided. The Board's recommendation was eventually affirmed by the Minister, who simply stated that he had refused the application. While this was not exactly a case of "rubber stamping"[178] of the Board's recommendation, the manner in which the Minister had relied on the Board's advice was improper because:

> "... while the Minister was entitled to seek advice, he was not entitled to rely
> on advice in the form of conclusions without reference to the basic material
> on which those conclusions were based ... As the competent authority the
> Minister must be in a position to make his own evaluation of the advice
> received based on relevant documentation submitted. This he failed to do.
> Neither the documentation furnished by the applicant to the [Board] nor
> a reasonable summary of it was forwarded to the Minister ... It seems to
> me that the advice did not relate specifically to the documentation so that
> the Minister could evaluate the advice at the same time as he evaluated the
> submissions of the applicant. The Minister should have been sent whatever
> documentation was relevant to enable him to evaluate the advice and the
> submissions".[179]

11–67   Carroll J. seems to have struck the correct balance. She held first that Ministers are entitled to rely on advice prepared by independent agencies:

---

[173] [1985] I.L.R.M. 235 at 239.
[174] [1998] 3 I.R. 111.
[175] There were also aspects of constitutional justice and "rubber stamping".
[176] Established by the National Drugs Advisory Board (Establishment) Order 1966, under the authority of the Health (Corporate Bodies) Act 1961, but abolished by the Irish Medicines Board Act 1995 s.34 and replaced by the Irish Medicines Board.
[177] In fact, the functions of the Minister had been delegated to the Minister of State at the Department of Health but nothing of import turns on this delegation.
[178] See paras 15–152 to 15–153.
[179] [1998] 3 I.R. 111 at 127–128.

"An application for product authorisation for a medicinal product is by definition very technical and any Minister would require assistance to know what the salient points were. The applicant's solicitors ... did not dispute that the Minister was entitled to and, as a matter of common sense, ought to obtain expert advice."[180]

11–68   Yet, while it is unrealistic and unworkable to expect elected politicians (or even some senior officials) to be, or to become, scientific experts, the importance of a Minister or his civil servants having access to relevant information before taking the final decision cannot be gainsaid. Regulatory policy is not an area which can be simply handed over to experts on the basis that they know more about certain subjects. At the very least, the Minister should be in a position to know if further consultation and dialogue with the applicant would be worthwhile and, consequently, able to refer the matter back for further discussion.

Search warrant cases

11–69   This issue has also arisen in a series of cases dealing with search warrants, where, typically, applicants seeking to quash the warrants allege that the District judge or Peace Commissioner has simply signed the warrant at the say-so of the requesting Garda officer, without having carefully examined the nature of the order sought. A good example of this is supplied by *People (Director of Public Prosecutions) v Kenny,*[181] where McCarthy J. observed:

"There was no evidence that the Peace Commissioner inquired into the basis of the Garda's suspicion. On the contrary, on the evidence adduced at the trial the only conclusion is that the Peace Commissioner ... acted purely on the say-so of [the Gardaí]. In doing so, he failed to exercise any judicial discretion: he failed to carry out his function under the section and, accordingly, the warrant is invalid."[182]

11–70   It follows that the District judge or Peace Commissioner must be personally satisfied that there is, for example, reasonable ground for suspicion before granting the warrant, and is not entitled to rely on the mere assertion or even sworn averment of the person applying for the warrant (such as a member of the Gardaí or the Customs and Excise) that he or she had reasonable grounds for such suspicion.[183]

H. FORMAL AND PROCEDURAL REQUIREMENTS

11–71   As demonstrated in the previous chapter, nearly every issue pertaining to jurisdiction turns on a question of statutory interpretation. This is especially true in the case of the disregard of procedural and formal requirements laid down by statute.

---

[180] [1998] 3 I.R. 111 at 127. See similarly, *O'Leary v Maher* [2008] IEHC 113.

[181] [1990] 2 I.R. 110.

[182] [1990] 2 I.R. 110 at 117. See also, *Rederei Kennermerland NV v Attorney General* [1989] I.L.R.M. 821 (identical principle).

[183] See, e.g. *Byrne v Grey* [1988] I.R. 31; *Rederei Kennermerland NV v Attorney General* [1989] I.L.R.M. 821; *Hanahoe v District Judge Hussey* [1998] 3 I.R. 69.

When the Oireachtas stipulates that certain formal and procedural requirements must be observed before an administrative decision is arrived at, it rarely states what consequences follow non-compliance with these statutory requirements. Of course, to this general observation there are exceptions: s.5 of the Adoption Act 1976, for example, suggests that an adoption order shall not be declared invalid solely on the ground that certain statutory prerequisites have not been satisfied[184]; s.8(6)(b) of the Garda Síochána Act 2005 provides that a failure by a prosecuting Garda to comply with certain statutory provisions or a direction of the Director of Public Prosecutions does not invalidate the prosecution[185]; and s.37(3) of the Planning and Development Act 2000 provides that an appeal received by the Board after the expiration of the appropriate period shall be invalid as not having been made in time.[186]

11–72   Nevertheless, it is true to say that the courts are, for the most part, left to their own devices as far as the consequences of non-compliance with procedural requirements are concerned. The test which has been developed depends on the statutory intent and whether compliance with the provision can fairly be said to be essential to the general object intended to be secured by the Act.[187] The relevant test has been stated in the following terms:

> "If the requirement which has not been observed may fairly be said to be an integral and indispensable part of the statutory intendment, the courts will hold it to be truly mandatory, and will not excuse a departure from it. But if, on the other hand, what is apparently a requirement is in essence merely a direction which is not of the substance of the aim and scheme of the statute, non-compliance may be excused."[188]

11–73   However, even in the case of directory provisions, the courts will not readily sanction a radical departure from what the legislature has ordained, since to do otherwise would frustrate the legislative intent. As MacMenamin J. observed in *JB v Director of Central Mental Hospital*:

> "[T]he best interests of a person suffering from a mental disorder are secured by faithful observance of, and compliance with, the statutory safeguards put into [the Mental Health Act 2001] by the Oireachtas and only those failures

---

[184]   See similarly, Building Societies Act 1989 s.51(2); Credit Union Act 1997 s.70(3).

[185]   See similarly, Irish Takeover Panel Act 1997 s.15.

[186]   See similarly, Farm Tax Act 1985 s.23(2) (repealed by the Local Government Act 1994). In *McCann v An Bord Pleanála* [1997] 1 I.L.R.M. 314 (a case where, through an oversight, the appeal was received a day late), Lavan J. held that the language of the predecessor provision, s.17(1)(a) of the Local Government (Planning and Development) Act 1992 ("shall be invalid"), reflected clearly the "statutory intendment" and that, accordingly, the statutory requirements were mandatory and non-compliance with them could not be excused (in this case, at least) on a de minimis basis. See also, *Graves v An Bord Pleanála* [1997] 2 I.R. 205 and *Murphy v Cobh Town Council* [2006] IEHC 324.

[187]   *Monaghan U.D.C. v Alf-a-Bet Promotions Ltd* [1980] I.L.R.M. 64; *State (Elm Developments Ltd) v An Bord Pleanála* [1981] I.L.R.M. 108; *Brown v Board of Management of Rathfarnham Parish National School* [2006] IEHC 178; [2008] 1 I.R. 70.

[188]   *State (Elm Developments Ltd) v An Bord Pleanála* [1981] I.L.R.M. 108 at 110 per Henchy J. But in *Connolly v Sweeney* [1988] I.L.R.M. 483, McCarthy J. said (at 488) that he "would be slow to accept the underlying principle [in *Elm Developments*] in criminal matters".

of compliance which are of an insubstantial nature and do not cause injustice can be excused by such a tribunal."[189]

Thus, even provisions which are directory as to precise compliance are generally mandatory as to substantial compliance.[190]

11–74 On the other hand, as indicated in *JB*, courts will often excuse an irregularity where the "requirements of justice and the substance of procedure have been observed".[191] Thus, in *Veterinary Council v Corr*,[192] the appellants had requested a case stated from a decision of the Circuit Court. The relevant statutory provisions required that the case stated be served on the respondents "at or before the time" that the case stated was transmitted to the High Court. On the day that the case stated was lodged in the High Court, a representative of the appellant's solicitors was delayed in court and found that the respondents' offices had closed. The case stated was, however, delivered the following day. While the Supreme Court accepted that these statutory requirements were mandatory, Maguire C.J. held that, on these facts, there was sufficient compliance with the terms of the section.[193] One feature which is illustrated by, amongst other cases, *Corr* is that the courts are more prepared to excuse non-compliance on the part of a private litigant rather than the public body. The reason given for this is that it often happens that the public body is exercising a power which involves an interference with property or other vested rights and, consequently, the rules of interpretation explained in Chapter 10, Part D require strict interpretation.

11–75 There is a further point. In the decided cases so far, the outcomes appear always to have been either a finding of invalidity or no sanction whatsoever. Theoretically, there is a third possibility, namely that the court characterises the situation as involving a directory provision, yet the applicant is able to show some loss. The possibility exists that in these circumstances the courts may become

---

[189] [2007] IEHC 201; [2007] 4 I.R. 778 at 794. Cf. also the comments of Peart J. in *AM v Kennedy* [2007] IEHC 136; [2007] 4 I.R. 667 at 677 in respect of bona fides mistakes made by "busy personnel" administering the Mental Health Act 2001: "… But to pretend that nothing wrong occurred is to deny the right to liberty other than in due course of law, and that is a slippery slope down which I cannot bring myself to venture".

[190] *State (Doyle) v Carr* [1970] I.R. 87.

[191] *O'Mahony v Arklow U.D.C.* [1965] I.R. 710 at 735 per Lavery J. See also, *State (Toft) v Galway Corporation* [1981] I.L.R.M. 439; *State (Elm Developments Ltd) v An Bord Pleanála* [1981] I.L.R.M. 108; *State (Coveney) v Special Criminal Court* [1982] I.L.R.M. 284; *McGlinchey v Governor of Portlaoise Prison* [1988] I.R. 671 at 695 per Lynch J.; *Rhatigan v Textiles y Confecciones Europeas SA* [1990] 1 I.R. 126; *Schwestermann v An Bord Pleanála* [1994] 3 I.R. 437; *Blessington & District Community Council Ltd v Wicklow County Council* [1997] 1 I.R. 273; and *Devlin v Minister for Arts, Culture and the Gaeltacht* [1999] 1 I.R. 47.

[192] [1953] I.R. 12. There is an interesting analysis of this case in *Hughes v Viner* [1985] 3 All E.R. 40.

[193] See also, *Attorney General v Wallace*, unreported, High Court, Geoghegan J., June 18, 1996. But cf. the approach of Kelly J. in *Graves v An Bord Pleanála* [1997] 2 I.R. 205, and the comments of Budd J. in *People (Director of Public Prosecutions) v Canavan* [2007] IEHC 46; [2007] 3 I.R. 160 at 163, where Budd J. described the "procedural hurdles" erected by the case-stated provisions of s.2 of the Summary Jurisdiction Act 1857 (as amended by s.51 of the Courts (Supplemental Jurisdiction) Act 1961) as "arcane", "anachronistic" and containing "pitfalls and oubliettes" that created "a legal heffalump-trap for the unwary … Over the centuries time after time in these islands appellants have been caught out by this pitfall and disappeared into an oubliette created by this strict time limiting prerequisite".

more alive to the possibility of damages as a sanction, and, significantly, may less frequently reach a finding of invalidity.

11–76   In addition, in view of the fact that in nearly all cases the remedy sought will lie in the discretion of the court, it is increasingly the case that the crucial factor is not the abstract terms of the provision which has been breached, but rather whether, in the circumstances of the instant case, the irregularity will cause real prejudice.[194] If the party aggrieved cannot show that he has been "wrong-footed or damnified" or that the "spirit and purpose" of the statutory provisions have not been breached, then relief may be withheld on discretionary grounds.[195]

11–77   Thus, the conventional distinction between mandatory and directory provisions has been somewhat blurred in three Supreme Court decisions, even though the traditional language is employed in all cases. For instance, in *Monaghan U.D.C. v Alf-A-Bet Promotions Ltd*,[196] the respondent developer sought planning permission which would enable him to convert a drapery store into a betting office and an amusement arcade. The relevant regulations required the developer to publish a notice in a newspaper stating the "nature and extent of the development". The developer's notice referred only to "alterations and improvements". The Supreme Court held that the notice did not convey the nature and extent of the proposed development. Inclusion, in the notice, of information as to the nature and extent of the proposed development was vital to the statutory scheme for the grant of planning permission because it was the way of publicising the development. The misleading notice that was published was held not to comply with a mandatory provision, and such non-compliance was fatal to the developer's case. Planning permission could radically affect the rights and amenities of others, and substantially benefit or enrich the grantee of the permission and, so, Henchy J. considered that the courts should not countenance deviation from that which had been deemed obligatory by the Oireachtas, save on an application of the de minimis rule[197]

---

[194] See, e.g. the comments of Geoghegan J. more or less to this effect in *McCarthy v An Garda Síochána Complaints Tribunal* [2002] 2 I.L.R.M. 341 at 358.

[195] *State (Elm Developments Ltd) v An Bord Pleanála* [1981] I.L.R.M. 108; *State (Coveney) v Special Criminal Court* [1982] I.L.R.M. 284; *Blessington Heritage Trust Ltd v Wicklow County Council* [1998] IEHC 8; [1999] 4 I.R. 571; *Carroll v Minister for Defence* [2006] IEHC 334; unreported, High Court, Herbert J., November 10, 2006. But *a contra: R. v Governor of Maghaberry Prison Ex p. Gallagher* [1992] N.I. 155 at 158 and *Walsh v An Garda Síochána Complaints Board* [2010] IESC 2, where the Supreme Court held that a complaint which was made one hour after the six-month statutory time limit for the making of a complaint was out of time and the Board had no jurisdiction in the matter. De minimis-style arguments based on substantial compliance do not appear to have been advanced.

[196] [1980] I.L.R.M. 64. The other two cases are: *State (Elm Developments Ltd) v An Bord Pleanála* [1981] I.L.R.M. 108; and *Rhatigan v Textiles y Confecciones Europeas SA* [1990] 1 I.R. 126, each analysed in H & M, paras 11–27 to 11–30.

[197] [1980] I.L.R.M. 64 at 69. In *McDonagh & Sons Ltd v Galway Corporation* [1995] 1 I.R. 191, the applicant company was wrongly described on a planning application as the owner, whereas an associated company was, in fact, the true owner. Finlay C.J. (at 202) did not consider that this misdescription affected the validity of the application as it was one "which was not intentional, which did not have the effect of misleading anyone and which could not possibly have been in any way to the disadvantage either of the planning authority or of the public who would have a right to object …".

For further applications of the *Alf-a-Bet* principles, see *Schwestermann v An Bord Pleanála* [1994] 3 I.R. 437; *Littondale Ltd v Wicklow County Council* [1996] 2 I.L.R.M. 519;

11–78   Having stated what appear to be the general principles, it will be convenient if we now consider three particular categories of legislation laying down formal and procedural requirements.

Legislation promoting fair procedures

11–79   Where legislation requires that an administrative or judicial body must follow a set of prescribed procedures before arriving at its decision, non-compliance will usually be fatal to the validity of an order, if the prescribed procedure is designed to ensure compliance with the requirements of a fair hearing:

> "It is because of [the] potentially devastating consequences [of an adverse finding] that the legislature has laid down firm and definite rules which are designed to protect and safeguard, not only members of the public, but also members of the [organisation] itself."[198]

11–80   Take, for example, *Thompson v Minister for Social Welfare*[199] in which a social welfare appeals officer sat without the assessors required by s.298(12) of the Social Welfare (Consolidation) Act 1981. This failure to comply with an imperative statutory requirement was sufficient to warrant the quashing of the appeals officer's decision. Again, in *Dunraven Estates Ltd v Commissioners of Public Works*,[200] the Supreme Court held that the defendants were obliged to tender full particulars of their proposed arterial drainage works on the plaintiff's lands, as was required by ss.5 and 6 of the Arterial Drainage Act 1945. As Budd J. observed, the object of these sections was to enable an owner of land "to know precisely what is proposed to be done to his property". If he was not made aware of the proposals, he would not be in a position to make "observations of any worth"[201] on these proposals and his statutory right to do so would be defeated. The Supreme Court accordingly concluded that these provisions were mandatory and had to be strictly complied with.[202]

An Blascaod Mór Teo v Commissioners of Public Works [1996] IEHC 45; unreported, High Court, Kelly J., December 18, 1996.

[198] *O'Driscoll v Law Society* [2007] IEHC 352 per McKechnie J.

[199] [1989] I.R. 618.

[200] [1974] I.R. 113.

[201] [1974] I.R. 113 at 134.

[202] There is some dispute as to whether the requirements of art.8 of the Garda Síochána (Discipline) Regulations 1989 (S.I. No. 94 of 1989) (which state that alleged breaches of discipline must be investigated as "soon as practicable") are directory or mandatory. In *McNeill v Garda Commissioner* [1997] 1 I.R. 469, Hamilton C.J. stated that they were mandatory, but in *McCarthy v Garda Síochána Complaints Tribunal* [2002] IESC 18; [2002] 2 I.L.R.M. 341 Geoghegan J. suggested "that when Hamilton C.J. used the word 'mandatory' in the *McNeill* case it cannot be regarded as certain that he was doing so in contradistinction to 'directory.' I take the view that 'as soon as may be' means as soon as may be reasonably practicable in all the circumstances and if I am right about that then it may not make very much difference whether on a theoretical basis the words requiring expedition in the 1986 Act or indeed in the Garda Discipline Regulations are to be regarded as mandatory or directory".

Geoghegan J. went on to hold that whether delay was unreasonable would depend on the circumstances and "striking the balance which one must do between the rights of the complainant and the rights of the persons complained about ...": [2002] IESC 18; [2002] 2 I.L.R.M. 341 at paras 58–59. See similarly, *Kennedy v Commissioner of An Garda Síochána* [2008] IEHC 72 and *Ryan v Commissioner of An Garda Síochána* [2009] IEHC 424, but cf. *Ruigrok v Commissioner of An Garda Síochána* [2005] IEHC 439; unreported, High Court,

11–81 On the other hand, if the formal requirements do not affect individual rights and are simply prescribed for the convenience of the authorities and for good administration generally, then (since the courts have not been as much concerned with community interests, like good administration, as with individual interests) they are likely to be classified as directory only. Thus, a Divisional High Court held in *McGlinchey v Governor of Portlaoise Prison*[203] that the provisions of the Special Criminal Court Rules 1975, giving the court power to determine when and where to sit, etc. were administrative only and did not confer enforceable legal rights on persons coming before that court.

11–82 It is important to note, finally, that in some cases a failure of strict compliance with certain procedures within a decision-making process may be cured, or validated, if the remaining procedures are properly complied with.[204] The reasoning is that, on the whole, the decision-making process was fair.

Time limits

11–83 A large proportion of the cases raising non-compliance with formal requirements occur in the context of time limits.[205] No universal principles can be stated as to the consequences of non-compliance with such time limits, but four guiding principles in relation to time limits were stated as being relevant by Lord Lowry L.C.J. in *Dolan v O'Hara*.[206] It will be convenient if we examine the case law in the light of these four principles.

"A time limit is likely to be imperative where no power to extend time is given and where no provision is made for what is to happen if the time limit is exceeded."

11–84 An example of this principle was given by Henchy J. in *State (Elm Developments Ltd) v An Bord Pleanála*,[207] where, commenting on the 21-day appeal period for appeals prescribed by s.26(5) of the Local Government (Planning and Development) Act 1963, he said:

> "The decision of a planning authority to grant a development permission … will become final if an appeal is not lodged within the time fixed by the Act. Since an extension of time is not provided for, the requirement as to time is mandatory, so that a departure from it cannot be excused."[208]

Murphy J., December 19, 2005, where Murphy J., citing *McCarthy*, held it mandatory to investigate alleged breaches of discipline as soon as "the investigation is feasible or doable", but that no inexcusable delay had occurred on the facts of the instant case.

[203] [1988] I.R. 671. See, to same effect, *Cahill v Governor of Mountjoy Prison* [1980] I.L.R.M. 191.

[204] See, e.g. *RL v Clinical Director of St Brendan's Hospital* [2008] IEHC 11 (failure to comply with s.13 of the Mental Health Act 2001 did not vitiate the decision to detain the applicant).

[205] Note the divergence between the Irish and English courts on the correct method of computing a time limit. For discussion and references see *McCann v An Bord Pleanála* [1997] 1 I.L.R.M. 314; *DPP (Clarke) v Stafford* [2005] IEHC 187; [2005] 2 I.R. 586.

[206] [1975] N.I. 125.

[207] [1981] I.L.R.M. 108.

[208] [1981] I.L.R.M. 108 at 111. For a striking application of this principle (albeit without discussion of the mandatory/directory issue), see *Walsh v Garda Síochána Complaints Board* [2010]

11–85 Of course, these are but working principles which, as might be expected, will not cater for every case and will sometimes have to bow to other principles in this series. Thus, as regards the first principle, in *Irish Refining Plc v Commissioner of Valuation*,[209] the Supreme Court held that a six-month time limit prescribed by s.10 of the Annual Revision of Rateable Property (Ireland) (Amendment) Act 1860 was merely directory, despite the absence of any power to extend the time limit, since a contrary conclusion might produce an injustice.[210]

"Requirements in statutes which give jurisdiction are usually imperative."

11–86 This principle was illustrated in *Dolan v O'Hara*[211] itself, where an obligation on the appellant to transmit a case stated within a 14-day period was held to be mandatory, by the Northern Ireland Court of Appeal. Both Lord Lowry L.C.J. and Jones L.J. observed that, as the section itself conferred jurisdiction and as there was no provision for an extension of time, only impossibility could excuse non-compliance with this mandatory provision. This principle has also been applied to other statutory provisions, such as s.26(5) of the Local Government (Planning and Development) Act 1963[212] and s.8 of the Unfair Dismissals Act 1977.[213]

"Where the act is to be done by a third party for the benefit of a person who will be damnified by non-compliance, the requirement is more likely to be directory."

11–87 This principle appears to have been operative in *Curley v Governor of Arbour Hill Prison*.[214] Here the applicant prison officer had been accused of sexual harassment by female colleagues. He sought to restrain the respondent from holding

---

IESC 2 (complaint received one hour after six-month time limit was held to be invalid). See also, *McCann v An Bord Pleanála* [1997] 1 I.L.R.M. 314; *Browne v Kerry County Council* [2009] IEHC 552 (two-year time limit contained in s.261 of the Planning and Development Act 2000 on the right of Council to impose conditions on quarry owner held to be mandatory in the absence of a power to extend time).

In *A v Minister for Justice, Equality and Law Reform*, unreported, High Court, Smyth J., March 19, 2002 the applicant had failed to lodge an appeal against an adverse decision within the applicable time limit. However, the applicant argued that the Refugee Appeals Tribunal had the power to extend the time because of a provision in a statutory instrument: "The Tribunal shall, in arranging its business, have record to the desirability of disposing of appeals with due expedition consistent with fairness and natural justice." (Refugee Act 1996 (Appeals) Regulations 2000 (S.I. No. 324 of 2000) reg.3.) Smyth J. rejected this proposition, because "the terms of the statutory instrument cannot take precedence over the express terms of the statute".

[209] [1990] 1 I.R. 568.

[210] See similarly, *Cork County Council v Valuation Tribunal* [2007] IEHC 311, where the risk of "administrative absurdity and chaos" motivated Dunne J. to hold a six-month time limit for dealing with appeals to be directory rather than mandatory.

[211] [1974] N.I. 125.

[212] *State (Elm Developments Ltd) v An Bord Pleanála* [1981] I.L.R.M. 108; *McCann v An Bord Pleanála* [1997] 1 I.L.R.M. 314. See now, Planning and Development Act 2000 s.37(1).

[213] *State (IBM Ltd) v Employment Appeals Tribunal* [1984] I.L.R.M. 31.

[214] [2004] IEHC 189; unreported, High Court, Smyth J., May 5, 2004. The principle is also illustrated by cases involving the six-month time limit for the signature of a case stated by a District Judge, prescribed by the District Court Rules 1955 r.17. See *Irish Refining Plc v Commissioner of Valuation* [1990] 1 I.R. 568. See also, *Prendergast v Porter* [1961] I.R. 440; *McMahon v McClafferty* [1989] I.R. 68.

a disciplinary hearing because the allegation of breach of discipline had been made outside the prescribed seven-day period. Smyth J. refused relief:

> "Given the nature of the complaints (e.g. allegations of sexual harassment), the construction of the word 'shall' as mandatory rather than directory where a limit of seven days might well have the effect of preventing any complaint of that nature from being investigated would, in my view, not be a correct approach to the law. Very often such incidents are accompanied by shame, trauma, confusion and denials of reality. Stale claims or undue delay should not be permitted but compliance with the spirit of the law is paramount."[215]

"Impossibility may excuse non-compliance even where the requirement is imperative."

11–88 Clearly, the courts will not readily countenance arguments such as impossibility (or force majeure) in the face of imperative statutory provisions, so it is hardly surprising that there are few authorities on this point. However, it does seem that this principle may apply where it has proved impossible to effect service on the other side within the requisite period or where every effort has been made to comply with the statutory provisions. In *Veterinary Council v Corr*,[216] for example, the appellants attempted to serve a case stated on the respondents on the last day permitted by the legislation, but found that the offices had closed. This was held by the Supreme Court to be a sufficient compliance with the (mandatory) statutory requirements.[217]

11–89 Apart from these rules, interesting series of High Court habeas corpus cases have addressed the application of the Mental Health Act 2001 since its coming into force in 2006.[218] Two of these concern time limits and also touch on the suggestion that if procedures, on the whole, are fair, then a decision will not be quashed for failure to comply with the procedural requirements. Section 18 of the 2001 Act obliges a mental health tribunal to review the detention of a patient and affirm or revoke an admission or renewal order (as the case may be). Interestingly, s.18(1)(a)(ii) states that, in detaining a patient, if there has been a failure to comply with one of a list of provisions of the 2001 Act, but "the failure does not affect the substance of the order and does not cause an injustice", the order may be affirmed.[219]

---

[215] See however, *Director of Consumer Affairs v Bank of Ireland* [2003] 2 I.R. 217.

[216] [1953] I.R. 12. See also, *Attorney General v Wallace*, unreported, High Court, Geoghegan J., June 18, 1996 (non-availability of District judge excused non-compliance with obligation to bring applicant before the court as soon as practicable).

[217] But for a strict approach, see *Graves v An Bord Pleanála* [1997] 2 I.R. 205; *McCann v An Bord Pleanála* [1997] 1 I.L.R.M. 314 at 319; *Rowan v An Bord Pleanála*, unreported, High Court, Feeney J., May 26, 2006.

[218] Mental Health Act 2001 (Commencement) Order 2006 (S.I. No. 411 of 2006).

[219] The provision must be invoked expressly by the tribunal in order for it to become operative. See *JH v Lawlor* [2007] IEHC 225; [2008] 1 I.R. 476 at 485–486 per Peart J. See also, the obiter comments of Hardiman J. in *D v Clinical Director of St Brendan's Hospital* [2007] IESC 37, on the importance of following the procedures laid down in the 2001 Act.

The High Court has given this provision a broad reading,[220] on the basis that, for habeas corpus to issue, the applicant would have to demonstrate:

"... a reckless failure to fulfil the statutory scheme, either as regards the time limits set out in the relevant sections or through ignoring the dignity of the patient or in failing to make decisions concerning his or her care which have, as the principal consideration, the best interests of that person with due regard being given to the interests of those other persons who may be at risk of serious harm if a decision to detain is not made."[221]

Where non-compliance might affect third-party rights or the rights of the public

11–90   Where the non-compliance might affect third-party rights or the rights of the general public, then the provisions will generally be regarded as mandatory and the courts will be even more reluctant to excuse anything less than full and precise compliance with the statutory requirements. This is especially true of statutory requirements contained in planning, licensing and other regulatory legislation designed to protect the participation or other rights of third parties and the general public. Conversely, where there has been substantial compliance and no interested party has been misled by any error, a reviewing court is unlikely to intervene.[222]

11–91   In *Monaghan U.D.C. v Alf-A-Bet Promotions Ltd*,[223] the plaintiffs (who claimed to have secured planning permission by default under s.26(4) of the Local Government (Planning and Development) Act 1963)[224] had failed—whether by inadvertence or otherwise—to state the true nature of the proposed development in their advertisement in the local newspapers, as required by art.14 of the Local Government (Planning and Development) Regulations 1977. The Supreme Court held that the application was invalid, as the plaintiffs, whose notice under the heading of proposed developed has said merely "alterations and reconstructions", had not sufficiently complied with a mandatory provision.[225]

---

[220] *TOD v Kennedy* [2007] IEHC 129; [2007] 3 I.R. 689; and *JH v Lawlor* [2007] IEHC 225; [2008] 1 I.R. 476.

[221] [2007] IEHC 129; [2007] 3 I.R. 689 at 705.

[222] See, e.g. *Director of Consumer Affairs v Bank of Ireland* [2003] 2 I.R. 217; *Watson v Environmental Protection Agency* [1998] IEHC 148; [2000] 2 I.R. 454 (delay in publishing a newspaper notice pertaining to the release of genetically modified organisms did not cause any disadvantage to the applicant who relied on a later notice to submit a representations); *Ní Chonghaile v Galway County Council* [2004] IEHC 317; [2004] 4 I.R. 138 (error in a map relating to a planning application was of such a minor nature as to be de minimis).

[223] [1980] I.L.R.M. 64. See Cooney, "An Aspect of Planning Appeal Procedures" (1982) 17 Ir. Jur. (N.S) 346 and Scannell, "Planning Control: Twenty Years On" (1982) 4 D.U.L.J. 41. See also, *Dunne Ltd v Dublin County Council* [1974] I.R. 45; *McCabe v Harding Investments Ltd* [1984] I.L.R.M. 105; and *State (Multi-Print Labels Systems Ltd) v Neylon* [1984] I.L.R.M. 545.

[224] See now, Planning and Development Act 2000 s.34(8)(f).

[225] [1980] I.L.R.M. 64 at 69. See also, *R. (Byrne) v Dublin JJ.* [1904] 2 I.R. 190 (21 days' notice in Licensing Acts mandatory, as otherwise "there might be frequent disputes as to whether the notice was given within a reasonable time or not", thus prejudicing the interests of the members of the public who might otherwise wish to lodge an objection in licensing matters). But see *State (Toft) v Galway Corporation* [1981] I.L.R.M. 439 (no certiorari to quash planning permission granted to a company which had been innocently misdescribed in the planning application); *Schwestermann v An Bord Pleanála* [1994] 3 I.R. 437; *Littondale Ltd v Wicklow*

11–92 A strict approach was also taken by the Supreme Court in *Fitzwilton v Mahon*,[226] a case in which important private rights and interests were at stake. Here, the respondent Tribunal had, by not recording its decision, failed to fulfil a condition precedent to the exercise of jurisdiction, which pertained to holding public hearings into allegations, inter alia, that the applicant company had made a corrupt political donation. The respondent argued in the alternative that the failure to record a decision should not be deemed a vitiating error because there had been "substantial compliance" with the condition precedent. The Supreme Court rejected this proposition and quashed the purported decision. As Kearns J. put it:

> "Having regard to the [major] encroachment on the rights of those citizens or bodies subjected to public hearings, I am satisfied that there must be strict compliance with those requirements of the terms of reference which go to the heart of jurisdiction."[227]

11–93 A strict approach may be taken where the Oireachtas has "prescribed very carefully the procedure which has to be followed"[228] in any particular case. The High Court in *Blessington Heritage Trust Ltd v Wicklow County Council*[229] was faced with a case in which a public body had failed to follow a carefully prescribed statutory procedure. Under the previous planning regime, local authorities were required to make development plans on a regular basis, but could apply to the Minister for the Environment for an extension of time to make the plan. Here an amended development plan had been adopted by the respondent three days after the expiry of the last relevant extension of time. McGuinness J. described the planning legislation as "an integral and carefully balanced system", noted that the extremely controversial rezoning amendments in question were "no mere formality", and held that the requirement to abide strictly by the time periods was mandatory.[230]

11–94 The suggestion that public bodies will be held to a higher standard than the private individual, as to compliance with statutory conditions, also holds true under this head; and it may be objected that the courts have been overly concerned with form rather than substance. For instance, in *McAnenley v An Bord Pleanála*,[231] a planning authority had failed to submit a copy of its decision to the respondent as required by statute. The planning authority argued that it had sent a notification of its decision to grant permission to the Board, which necessarily included a copy of its decision and that its non-compliance should be treated as de minimis. Kelly J. rejected this submission:

> "It is difficult to treat non-compliance with an express statutory requirement on a *de minimis* basis. The notification of a decision of a planning authority will in all cases contain the essence of the decision itself. Notwithstanding

---

County Council [1997] 1 I.L.R.M. 519; *O'Connor v An Bord Pleanála* [2008] IEHC 13; *Murphy v Cobh Town Council* [2006] IEHC 324; unreported, High Court, MacMenamin J., October 26, 2006 (similar principles).

[226] [2007] IESC 27; [2008] 1 I.R. 712.
[227] [2007] IESC 27; [2008] 1 I.R. 712 at 730.
[228] *Graves v An Bord Pleanála* [1997] 2 I.R. 205 at 214.
[229] [1998] IEHC 8; [1999] 4 I.R. 571.
[230] [1998] IEHC 8; [1999] 4 I.R. 571 at 603–604.
[231] [2002] IEHC 60; [2002] 2 I.R. 763. In *O'Connor v An Bord Pleanála* [2008] IEHC 13, a rather similar infringement, but by the private individual, was overlooked.

that, Parliament has ordained that both should be provided to the respondent. I cannot disregard this statutory requirement."[232]

11–95 Even where strict compliance is deemed to be necessary, it may be possible to find other means of ensuring that minor errors of compliance need not be fatal. In *O'Connor v An Bord Pleanála*,[233] Finlay Geoghegan J. accepted that a requirement that an individual lodging an appeal with the Board state his or her name and address was of a mandatory nature.[234] However, the appeal was saved by compliance with another statutory requirement. Section 127(1)(e) of the Planning and Development Act 2000 required the appellant to include acknowledgement from the planning authority that submissions or observations had been lodged as to the initial planning application. The acknowledgement submitted in the present case referred to the appellant's name and address, which Finlay Geoghegan J. held was sufficient to meet the statutory requirement to provide a name and address.[235]

I. WAIVER AND CONSENT

11–96 The fundamental rule is that waiver and consent cannot confer jurisdiction. The rule is grounded in the fundamental public policy that a jurisdiction laid down by statute for the good of the community cannot be altered. It thus applies irrespective of whether the waiver emanates from the public body or the private individual affected. In the present chapter, the issue is how the fundamental rule with its many exceptions (as prevalent as the holes in gruyère cheese) applies, where the waiver emanates from the private individual affected. The precept, as it applies in cases where the waiver comes from the public body, will be further considered in the context of legitimate expectations in a later chapter.[236]

11–97 Many of the exceptions to the principle that waiver cannot confer jurisdiction rest, in varying degrees, on the idea that a plaintiff cannot "approbate and reprobate"; it would be "obviously inconsistent with the due administration of justice" if a plaintiff were allowed to reserve unto himself the right to argue later a point touching on the validity of a decision should that decision prove adverse to his interests.[237] But, at any rate in the case of planning (or other forms of licensing),

---

[232] [2002] IEHC 60; [2002] 2 I.R. 763 at 765.

[233] [2008] IEHC 13; unreported, High Court, Finlay Geoghegan J., January 24, 2008. See, to same effect, *Murphy v Cobh Town Council* [2006] IEHC 324; unreported, High Court, MacMenamin J., October 26, 2006.

[234] Planning and Development Act 2000 s.127(1)(b).

[235] On the latter point, as to whether an appeal (or a referral) to An Bord Pleanála must form one coherent document, Finlay Geoghegan J. applied *O'Reilly Bros v Wicklow County Council* [2006] IEHC 363; [2008] 1 I.R. 187.

[236] See paras 19–06 to 19–19.

[237] *Corrigan v Irish Land Commission* [1977] I.R. 317 at 326 per Henchy J. But see *State (Gallagher, Shatter & Co) v de Valera* [1986] I.L.R.M. 3 where a solicitors' firm permitted a taxation of costs to proceed while maintaining an objection to the Taxing Master's jurisdiction. The Supreme Court per McCarthy J. held (at 9) that there had been no waiver of jurisdictional objection: "[I]t does not appear to me that justice is served by determining a case of this kind against a solicitor because, whilst maintaining his objection, he thought it more practicable to allow the taxation to proceed, in the hope that the result would, in any event, be satisfactory. When, far from being short of satisfactory, it held him guilty of making a gross overcharge, in my view he is not to be defeated by a plea of waiver."

there may be a counter-argument, namely that a waiver might, in certain instances, make an unfair impact on third parties. For example, Hardiman J. suggested in *Ashbourne Holdings Ltd v An Bord Pleanála*[238] that acquiescence in the imposition of a condition on a planning application should not, as a general rule, debar the applicant from later asserting that the condition is ultra vires. This was because if a planning authority was to be permitted to take advantage of acquiescence in ultra vires conditions:

> "[T]hat fact will become known to professional people in the relevant area. They, in turn, seeing that such offers or acquiescence had produced a successful outcome in previous cases, will advise clients with new business to consider similar offers or acquiescence. If this process continued, it may lead to the situation in which a body's apparent jurisdiction, conferred by law, is only a very imperfect guide to its actual practice. Only an insider or a shrewdly advised person would know the true position and only a wealthy applicant could take advantage of it ... Firstly, it would mean that an applicant for a licence who was well provided financially would be at an advantage as against one who had no surplus after he had bought the premises and applied for the licence. Secondly, it would involve a serious absence of transparency in the licensing process: the real requirements for a licence would not be those laid down in the publicly available legislation but those on which the licensor and a wealthy applicant might agree after a process not unlike a form of auction. Thirdly, if such a practice were permitted it would involve the licensing authority or similar bodies using a statutory power to exact a form of payment in cash or kind which the legislature did not envisage."[239]

11–98   But in general Irish courts have been reluctant to commit themselves unequivocally to such a position.[240] Thus, in *Corrigan v Irish Land Commission*,[241] while acknowledging that a totally new jurisdiction[242] could not be created by means of an estoppel, Henchy J. stated that the crucial test was whether the court or tribunal had initial jurisdiction to enter upon the inquiry. For once such jurisdiction was present, any errors committed in the course of the inquiry could be waived. In *Corrigan* itself, it was clear that the Appeals Tribunal of the Land Commission plainly had jurisdiction to hear the plaintiff's appeal. The question was whether two particular lay commissioners were debarred from exercising that jurisdiction by reason of their prior dealings with the case. Henchy J. found that the point could

---

See also, *O'Neill v Irish Hereford Breed Society Ltd* [1992] 1 I.R. 431; *Bula Ltd v Tara Mines Ltd* [2000] 4 I.R. 412; *O'Callaghan v Mahon* [2007] IESC 17; [2008] 2 I.R. 514. It is doubtful, however, that this principle is entirely appropriate in the present context. The concern here is not that the applicant might seek a more favourable result by having the case re-heard, but that a public body might exceed its jurisdiction, thereby offending the rule of law.

[238]   [2003] IESC 18; [2003] 2 I.R. 114.

[239]   [2003] IESC 18; [2003] 2 I.R. 114 at 138–139. See also, *State (Byrne) v Frawley* [1978] I.R. 326 at 342 per O'Higgins C.J.; Macken, "Planning Gain in Ireland and the Old Head of Kinsale" [2004] B.R. 217.

[240]   *State (Byrne) v Frawley* [1978] I.R. 326; *Corrigan v Irish Land Commission* [1977] I.R. 317; and *State (Cronin) v Circuit Judge for the Western Circuit* [1937] I.R. 34.

[241]   [1977] I.R. 317. See also, *Re Creighton's Estate*, unreported, High Court, D'Arcy J., March 5, 1982; *Graham v Racing Board*, unreported, High Court, O'Hanlon J., November 22, 1983.

[242]   *Corrigan v Irish Land Commission* [1977] I.R. 317 at 325–326.

be, and indeed had been, waived by the plaintiff when he accepted the tribunal as he found it composed on the day of the hearing.

11–99   In other cases, waiver and estoppel have been regarded as a bar to discretionary relief.[243] In *R. (Kildare CC) v Commissioner for Valuation*,[244] the applicants sought to quash a revised valuation order made on appeal by a County Court. The applicants had allowed the appeal to proceed on the basis that there was jurisdiction in the County Court to revise the valuation: it was only when the decision of the court did not prove as favourable to their interests as they had expected that they sought to question the jurisdiction of the tribunal. The former Irish Court of Appeal agreed that the adjudication of the County Court was ultra vires, but held, nevertheless, that the applicants were precluded by their conduct from obtaining the relief sought.

11–100   There are two more practical points which apply even if in principle, effect could have been given to a waiver. First, in the field of constitutional justice, the waiver principle may only apply if the person making the waiver had "knowledge of all the relevant circumstances".[245] Secondly, it is sometimes difficult to know whether given behaviour actually constitutes a waiver. In *Gama Construction Ireland Ltd v Minister for Enterprise, Trade and Employment*,[246] for example, letters sent by the applicant indicating a willingness to co-operate with an investigation by a labour inspector, and public comments made by a senior employee of the applicant, were held not to constitute acquiescence in the ultra vires publication of a report. This was, in part, because objections were promptly raised to the publication. But a litigant will generally be deemed to have waived objections based on the composition of a tribunal[247] or the procedure adopted, if the jurisdictional question is not raised at the appropriate time in the proceedings. Persons who attend court hearings are deemed to have waived any possible irregularities which might exist.[248]

---

[243] *Dada v Minister for Justice, Equality and Law Reform* [2006] IEHC 166; unreported, High Court, MacMenamin J., January 31, 2006; *Byrne v Director of Public Prosecutions* [2003] IEHC 115; unreported, High Court, Ó Caoimh J., March 20, 2003; *Jacobs v Brophy* [2003] IEHC 626; unreported, High Court, Ó Caoimh J., March 21, 2003.

[244] [1901] 2 I.R. 215. See also, *State (Cronin) v Circuit Judge for Western Circuit* [1937] I.R. 34; *State (McKay) v Cork Circuit Judge* [1937] I.R. 650; *R. (Dorris) v Ministry of Health* [1954] N.I. 79; *State (Byrne) v Frawley* [1978] I.R. 326; *Whelan v R.* [1921] 1 I.R. 310; *Director of Consumer Affairs v Bank of Ireland* [2003] 2 I.R. 217 . For cases where the plea of waiver was disallowed, see *State (Redmond) v Wexford Corporation* [1946] I.R. 409; *State (Cole) v Labour Court* (1984) J.I.S.L.L. 128; *State (Gallagher, Shatter & Co) v de Valera* [1986] I.L.R.M. 3; and *Browne v An Bord Pleanála* [1991] 2 I.R. 209.

[245] *Corrigan v Irish Land Commission* [1977] I.R. 317 at 326.

[246] [2005] IEHC 210; [2007] 3 I.R. 472.

[247] *Corrigan v Irish Land Commission* [1977] I.R. 317.

[248] *Whelan v R.* [1921] 1 I.R. 310; *Graham v Racing Board*, unreported, High Court, O'Hanlon J., November 22, 1983.

FAIR PROCEDURE

12–01 Fair procedure looms especially large in the field of administrative law. The reason for this importance is that administrative law is directed to public authorities. One of the cardinal features distinguishing public authorities from private persons is that public authorities should be non-partisan and open to persuasion provided that all the relevant facts and arguments are placed before them. With a fair procedure, the relevant matters are more likely to emerge and to be properly weighed by the decision-maker. Accordingly, there is a causative link between proper procedure and the quality of the decision. In short, "[t]he whole theory of 'natural justice' is that ministers, though free to decide as they like, will in practice decide properly and responsibly once the facts have been fairly laid before them".[1]

12–02 By today, the justifications offered for fair procedure have gone beyond the "instrumental end" of accuracy. To some extent, procedural rectitude has been regarded as compensation for the latitude which the courts have traditionally allowed to the merits of an administrative action. There are other reasons too for the importance of procedure and we shall return to this basic question in Chapter 14, Part F.

12–03 Next, take a fundamental point, namely, whether it is appropriate for the courts to have moulded the procedure to be followed by public administrators so closely to their own form of procedure. (The truth of this observation may be tested against the case law, to be described in the course of this and the following chapter.) This question has also been raised in the context of English law where it has been remarked:

> "What is of immediate importance is the realisation, often lost sight of when discussing procedure, that adjudication is but one form of decision-making. As has been evident, our procedural rules are sown in an adjudicator frame-work ... [T]here has been little thought directed to the broader question of whether adjudication is the correct decision-making process on which to be fashioning procedures. The vital point, brought out forcefully by Fuller, is that just as adjudication is distinguished by the form of participation that it confers so are other types of decision-making, and just as the nature of adjudication shapes the procedures relevant to its decisional form, so do other species of decision-making. Nine categories are listed by Fuller: mediation;

---

[1] Wade, "Quasi-Judicial and its Background" (1949) 10 Camb. L.J. 216 at 217.

property; voting; custom; law officially declared; adjudication; contract; managerial direction; and resort to chance. In each of these instances the relationship between the type of decision-making, and the procedural rules which are attendant thereon, can be presented in the following manner. The procedural rules will be *generated* by, and *will* protect the integrity of, the type of decision-making which is in issue ... What relevance has all of this? The answer, at least in outline, is simple. There may well be situations when the procedures modelled on adjudication are not the most effective or appropriate."[2]

We shall pursue this theme no further here, since there is no sign that any Irish judge has questioned the view that what is good for a court is (in a somewhat modified way) good for a public administrator.

A. Procedural Rights Other than Constitutional Justice

12–04   It should be emphasised that the over-arching concept of constitutional justice does not comprehend the whole of the procedural law in the field of public administration. For, in addition, in the first place each decision may have its own particular procedural rules. Some examples of such rules have already been given in Chapter 11, Part H (under the heading of "Formal and Procedural Provisions")[3] and in Chapter 5, Part F (dealing with Planning Law).[4] Occasionally, these simply establish what would anyway have followed from the application of constitutional justice in the particular context.[5] Because of this overlap, it is not always clear whether a judgment relied on constitutional/natural justice or on particular statutory provisions.[6] But, in addition, procedural rules often serve a different policy, for instance, to establish an orderly timetable or provide an authoritative record of what occurred. Apart from the particular rules just mentioned and the all-embracing span of constitutional justice, covered in the following two chapters, there are also five[7] general sources of procedural law. These are outlined next.

---

[2]   Craig, *Administrative Law,* 3rd edn (London: Sweet & Maxwell, 1994), pp.302–303. The reference to Fuller is to his seminal article, "The Forms and Limits of Adjudication" 92 Harv. L. Rev. 353 at 364. For the equivalent in the fifth edition of Professor Craig's book, see pp.411–412.

[3]   See paras 11–71 to 11–95.

[4]   See paras 5–111 to 5–150.

[5]   See *Rajpal v Robinson* [2005] 3 I.R. 385 at 393–394. (By regulations made under the Health Act 1970, the Chief Executive of the Health Board is under a procedural obligation to notify the doctor of the intention to remove and of the reasons, and to consider any representations made by the doctor within seven days.) For other examples, see Planning and Development Act 2000 s.137 (where An Bord Pleanála takes into account matters other than those raised by the parties, it must so inform the parties and elicit their comments); and Adoption Act 1998 s.4 (right of father who wishes to be consulted).

[6]   *VU v Refugee Application Commissioner* [2005] 2 I.R. 537 at 546; *South Western Area Health Board v Information Commissioner* [2005] 2 I.R. 547 at 556; *Brown v Rathfarnham* [2008] 1 I.R. 70 at para.81.

[7]   In addition, the Third Edition, p.494, referred to the long-anticipated Administrative Procedure Bill, which would have set out a number of principles of good administration to which public bodies would be expected to adhere. These would have included: the fixing of minimum response times; the provision of adequate information; and the establishment of appeal or other grievance mechanisms. However, this comprehensive Bill has now been dropped.

(1) European Convention on Human Rights article 6(1)

12–05   As a result of the European Convention on Human Rights Act 2003, the Convention is now part of the domestic law of the State and in Chapter 2, Part C, we gave a general account of its impact on the Irish legal system. Here, we focus only on procedure. The most important provision is art.6(1) of the European Convention, which states that "in the determination of his civil rights and obligations ... everyone is entitled to a fair and public hearing within a reasonable time by an independent and impartial tribunal established by law ...". In relation to this provision, there are three general points for discussion.

(a) "Civil rights and obligations"

12–06   As can be seen from the text of art.6, just quoted, this phrase settles the field of the provision's operation. Originally, the phrase was intended to encompass only private law matters, but the ECtHR soon extended it[8] and the jurisprudence has now taken art.6 deeply into the field of public law. On this point, De Smith writes[9]:

> "... it appears that Art. 6 applies to the determination of all rights of a pecuniary nature, including for example rights to real and personal property, the right to engage in a commercial activity, the right to practice a profession, and the right to compensation for illegal state acts. Disciplinary proceedings resulting in professional suspension; questions relating to children taken into care; decisions relating to planning and the environment; conditions of detention and an application for release from detention in a prison psychiatric wing also engage Art. 6. Even a first-time applicant for a licence may be entitled to Art. 6 protection. In addition Art. 6 applies in the field of social insurance, not only to assistance linked to private employment contracts, but also where the benefit is non-contributory, provided it is not entirely discretionary. By contrast, however, it appears as if the Strasbourg court is reluctant to extend the protection of Art. 6 to certain non-pecuniary benefits; and school exclusions, asylum or citizenship applications and questions regarding tax liability generally do not engage Art. 6."

12–07   Plainly, this is a continuing story. Lord Bingham has offered the somewhat tantalising remark:

> "The narrower the interpretation given to 'civil rights', the greater the need to insist on review by a judicial tribunal exercising full powers. Conversely, the more elastic the interpretation given to 'civil rights', the more flexible must be the approach to the requirement of independent and impartial review if the emasculation (by over-judicialisation) of administrative welfare schemes is to be avoided."[10]

---

[8]   *Ringheisen v Austria* (1971) 13 E.H.R.R. 90; *Lecompte v Belgium* (1981) 4 E.H.R.R. 533. See the overview in Wade and Forsyth, *Administrative Law*, 10th edn (Oxford: OUP, 2009), pp.375–378.
[9]   Woolf, Jowell and Le Sueur (eds), *De Smith's Judicial Review*, 6th edn (London: Sweet and Maxwell, 2007), para.7–035.
[10]   *Begum v London Borough of Tower Hamlets* [2003] UKHL 5; [2003] 2 A.C. 430 at para.5.

The remark shows a responsible concern for the implications for public administrators of a tight article 6 regime, which is illustrated in the summary of English case law, given below.

(b) "Fair hearing by an independent and impartial tribunal"

12–08   The Strasbourg Court has not always been clear in its development of the concepts of independence and impartiality:

> "The notion of 'independence' refers to the lack of any connection between the tribunal and other parts of government, whereas the 'impartiality' must exist in relation to the parties to the suit and the case at issue. However, the Court has not always drawn a clear borderline between the two concepts, and often considers both concepts together ..."[11]

12–09   The reason that the borderline between the concepts can become blurred is that the institutional position of the decision-maker (its independence or otherwise) may sometimes cast a pall of doubt about the impartiality of its decision in a particular case. Broadly speaking, however, the common law on bias tracks the law of impartiality for Convention purposes and is considered further below. As regards independence, the test developed by the Strasbourg Court is in the following terms:

> "In order to establish whether a body can be considered 'independent' regard must be had, *inter alia*, to the manner of appointment of its members and their term of office, to the existence of guarantees against outside pressures and to the question whether the body presents an appearance of independence."[12]

12–10   Several decisions of the Strasbourg Court amplify this principle. Certain aspects of the Slovakian administrative system were found to breach art.6 because "[t]he appointment of the heads of [the relevant] bodies is controlled by the executive and their officers ... have the status of salaried employees".[13] Similarly, in *Findlay v United Kingdom*,[14] it was held that the British court martial system violated Art.6(1); since the prosecuting officer appointed the members of the court and they generally fell within his chain of command, concerns about the independence of the tribunal were objectively justified. In the planning field, the possibility of a Minister being able to revoke the power of an inspector to decide an appeal also violated art.6.[15] However, the mere fact that the Dutch Council of State had an advisory capacity (vis-à-vis the legislature) as well as a judicial capacity did not violate art.6.[16]

12–11   It would be interesting to assess the compatibility of certain Irish administrative apparatus with art.6. In a previous chapter, the position of decision-

---

[11] Van Dijk et al (eds), *Theory and Practice of the European Convention on Human Rights,* 4th edn (Intersentia Publishers, 2006), p.613.

[12] *Langborger v Sweden*, Judgment of June 22, 1989, para.32.

[13] *Lauko v Slovakia*, Judgment of September 2, 1998, para.64.

[14] (1997) 24 E.H.R.R. 221.

[15] *Bryan v United Kingdom* (1996) 21 E.H.R.R. 342.

[16] *Kleyn v Netherlands*, Judgment of May 6, 2003.

makers in the social welfare appeals system was criticised[17] and it is arguable, particularly with regard to terms of appointment, that the system is not compatible with the independence requirement of art.6. However, one should note that in the only Irish case to discuss the matter (briefly), a fairly relaxed standard for independence was set. In *Lovejoy v Attorney General*,[18] an asylum case, Birmingham J. stated:

> "I think the applicant may have been driving at an Art. 6 [of the Convention] point about the Minister not being independent and impartial. She also, unsuccessfully, ran an argument about the Office of the Refugee Applications Commissioner and the Refugee Appeal Tribunal also failing the independence and impartiality test. So far as the question of independence from the Executive is concerned, the position is that the statute itself, in respect of both bodies, states in terms that the bodies will be independent in the exercise of their functions. Sections 5(2) and 15(2) [of the Refugee Act 1996] respectively put this matter beyond doubt. It is quite clear that the Minister and the Executive are not in a position to determine how individual applications are processed and dealt with and what conclusions are reached in relation to them."

12–12 One may tentatively deduce from this ex tempore judgment that art.6.1 does not mean that a judicial-style tribunal must always be provided, replacing many ad hoc pieces of administrative machinery. The opposite conclusion would certainly have had far-reaching constitutional and financial implications for the Irish public service.[19]

12–13 Here one might briefly draw a comparison. Doubts about the independence of tribunals were probably part of the inspiration for the constitutional rule, Art.34.1, which provides that (subject to certain exceptions) "justice shall be administered in courts established by law by judges ..." and not by tribunals. Recently—to summarise what is said in Chapter 6, Part C—the judiciary has pulled in the horns of Art.34.1. But there is compensation for this withdrawal in the rather more sensible requirements which have been deduced from art.6(1) of the Convention.

(c) Does judicial review (or a statutory appeal) satisfy the requirements of "a fair hearing by an independent and impartial tribunal"?

12–14 The question here is whether an imperfect procedure before (say) a Minister or local authority would be cured, in the eyes of art.6, by the availability of judicial review or, where it is provided for, an appeal to a court or tribunal. In other words, would judicial review or statutory appeal add up to "a fair and public hearing ... by an independent and impartial tribunal ...?" Take first the easier question of the appeal. Here the answer will depend upon the terms of the particular appeal.

---

[17] See para.9–96.

[18] [2008] IEHC 225; High Court, ex tempore, Birmingham J.

[19] See McKechnie, "Article of the ECHR, Administrative Tribunals and Judicial Review" (2002) *Bar Review* 333 and 364; Wade and Forsyth, *Administrative Law*, 10th edn (2009), p.387 remark: "[The ECtHR's jurisprudence] has provided the means, particularly in regard to independence and impartiality, whereby the application of Article 6(1) is reconciled, without grave disruption, to existing administrative practice and law."

However, where the appellate agency is a court it will invariably, and where it is a tribunal it will usually, be the case that the requirement of "an independent and impartial tribunal" will be satisfied, assuming that the scope of the appeal is full enough to satisfy art.6. Where there is a de novo rehearing, for instance before An Bord Pleanála, the Appeal Commissioner of Income Tax or Valuation, this test would certainly be satisfied.

12–15 The answer is in greater doubt where no appeal is provided and it is judicial review on which the public body must rely as the safety net. Plainly, the High Court is "an independent and impartial tribunal". But the difficulty which arises here is that, because of the limitations attached to judicial review, it may not provide a sufficiently wide and intensive form of scrutiny to satisfy art.6(1). One should, however, note that the English case law, reviewed in the following paragraphs, seems to suggest that judicial review should be taken into account, *together with* the initial stage before the Minister or local authority, etc (as well as any appeal). In short, the entire package should be considered.[20]

12–16 Take first *R. v Secretary of State for the Environment, Transport and the Regions Ex p. Holdings and Barnes Plc*[21] ("the Alconbury litigation"). Here under the statute the respondent Minister had to consider an appeal against the decision of a local authority to enforce a breach of planning law. Objection was made to the Minister's involvement on the basis that he was not "independent or impartial" because of his prior commitment to policies which led to enforcement in the instant case. The House of Lords held that since this decision involved substantial considerations of policy and public interest, it did not need to be taken by a judicial-style tribunal. Moreover, the overall decision-making process was said to be fair: it included the investigation of the facts by a departmental inspector, who had advised the Minister, on the basis that the facts found by the inspector had to be accepted by the Minister (unless he had notified the objectors and allowed them an opportunity to make representations). In addition, the House of Lords relied on the fact that it had been accepted by the ECtHR in *Bryan v UK*[22] that the fact-finding procedures in a subsequent judicial review of the Minister's decision would provide a sufficiency of review to satisfy the article.

12–17 In another case, *Begum v Tower Hamlets LBC*,[23] a local authority had decided that the accommodation offered to the appellant was "suitable" under the relevant legislation. This decision was reviewed by a rehousing officer of the same local authority and it was held that, in order to satisfy art.6, it was not necessary for the reviewing officer to be an independent tribunal, because the questions of fact involved were part of broader considerations concerning local conditions and requiring specialist knowledge and experience. In addition, the review process contained adequate safeguards that the applicant's representations would be taken into account. Finally, there was an appeal to a county court from the reviewing officer's decision and it was held, as in *Bryan*, that this would provide sufficiency of review. In the wider dimension, Lord Hoffman also considered that, in schemes

---

[20] A *vagary* which one might mention at this point would be whether the existence of the Ombudsman, whose jurisdiction is almost always available, could help to satisfy art.6.
[21] [2003] 2 A.C. 295.
[22] (1996) 21 E.H.R.R. 342.
[23] [2003] 2 A.C. 430.

of social welfare, the values of "democratic accountability, efficient administration and the sovereignty of Parliament"[24] entitled Parliament to take the view that it was not in the public interest that an excessive proportion of the funds available should be consumed in administration and legal disputes. Similarly, Lord Bingham took the opportunity to warn against emasculation of administrative schemes by over-judicialisation.

12–18   However, the High Court in *R. (on the application of Bewry) v Norwich CC*[25] reached the opposite conclusion from this line of authority. This case arose out of the review of a challenge to a decision by a local authority on entitlement to housing benefit. Significantly, the review body consisted of three councillors from the same council which had made the initial decision, advised by a lawyer from the council's legal department. The High Court held that the situation was different from the other decisions in that it was largely not based on policy but on a finding of fact. Consequently, any judicial review proceedings would exercise only "limited control" since it could not substitute its views as to the weight of evidence.

Irish law

12–19   This important topic as to whether the availability of judicial review suffices to satisfy art.6 has not yet been squarely addressed by an Irish court and so we have included this brief survey of English authorities. What emerges from it is first, that to some extent, a court (as in *Holdings and Barnes Plc* and *Begum*) will look at all elements of the decision-making process, including judicial review or (where applicable) an appeal to a court or tribunal, as an entire package in order to assess whether the applicant has had a fair hearing. This may do some violence to the language of Art.6 but one can see its attraction. At a general level, the question of whether judicial review will satisfy Art.6 is really a decision critiquing the levels of judicial review which are currently applied in the Irish courts, so far as concerns the particular flaw about which the applicant is complaining. Thus our discussion of whether the availability of judicial review would satisfy Art.6 needs to consider the position in relation to each of the heads of judicial review. We may do this briefly by adopting Lord Diplock's classification of judicial review under three heads: illegality; irrationality; and procedural impropriety.[26] But, to this list significantly one has to add a fourth head, namely, error of fact. It may be useful to summarise the four separately:

(a) As to procedural impropriety, our view is that there is not usually very much to choose between the standards of procedure required by Art.6 and that already afforded by constitutional justice. Accordingly, one would expect judicial review to afford a satisfactory safety net in respect of procedural unfairness.

(b) The English authorities, as summarised above, distinguish between an initial decision the facts of which were disputed and one in respect of

[24] [2003] 2 A.C. 430 at para.36. The entirety of Lord Hoffman's judgment would repay reading.
[25] [2002] H.R.L.R. 2. For another case about facts, where the decision-maker's independence was held to be a crucial flaw and where the High Court's power of review was in the circumstances inadequate, see, to same effect, *Tsfayo v United Kingdom* [2007] B.L.G.R. 1.
[26] *CCSU v Minister for the Civil Service* [1985] A.C. 385 at 410.

which the policy was disputed. The former will require a more formal judicial-style proceeding. But it is just the decision turning on facts which cannot be redeemed by the availability of traditional review because of the elementary point that judicial review affords scarcely any check upon the correctness of the facts found by the initial decision-maker.[27] Thus, in respect of this flaw, judicial review might not be regarded as an adequate remedy in the eyes of art.6(1).

(c) Where the applicant is complaining about a policy choice/discretion, then it might seem that the extent to which judicial review provides a satisfactory safety-net is uncertain because of the current debate over the standards in regard to the control of discretionary power, analysed in Chapter 15, Parts B and C. However, the English article 6 ECHR cases reviewed above seem to have found ways around this, by virtue of their approach of considering all aspects of the initial decision (as well as judicial review) as a package.

(d) As regards "illegality" there does not appear to be much English (much less Irish) case law on this point. However, given that the Irish courts have, one way or another, been prepared to review errors of law, then it would seem likely that Art.6 would accept that judicial review afforded a satisfactory safety net in respect of this flaw.

(2) "Equality of arms"

12–20 This is a useful term which has been developed mainly in European Human Rights Convention jurisprudence, examples of which have nevertheless been glimpsed in Irish law. It connotes the idea that the individual and the official side should each be allowed the same opportunity to make their case. The question may be raised: what does "equality of arms" add which is not already to be found in the broader notions of no bias or possibly (where the applicant was disabled from making the best possible case) the *audi alteram partem* principle? The answer is that, under the equality of arms principle, the weight is on the private individual not being put at a disadvantage, compared to the public body.[28] By contrast, an individual's rights, established by the *audi alteram partem* rule, are independent, rather than having to be comparable with the rights actually enjoyed by the public body. Thus, often (but not always) the *audi alteram partem* rule will be of more use to the individual.[29]

---

[27] It is worth noticing that a recent English Court of Appeal decision has openly increased the level of review for error of fact, which traditionally was the lowest of all the heads of review. There was in the judgments no express link with what one might now call the "external examiner" of Art.6, but bearing in mind the English authorities, some of which are summarised above, it is a reasonable guess that this element was lurking in at least the judicial subconscious. See also, *E v Secretary of State for the Home Department* [2004] Q.B. 1044.

[28] Article 40.1 of the Constitution, which guarantees equality before the law, might also have a role to play here: see *Murphy v GM* [2001] 4 I.R. 113 at 134.

[29] For instance, in *JF v Director of Public Prosecutions* [2005] 2 I.R. 174 at 187, Hardiman J. stated: "… the provisions of Article 6 are also, and obviously, fatal to the abandoned argument that an expert called on behalf of the respondent should be accorded some presumptive superior status. I believe the respondent acted very wisely in withdrawing this contention." But Hardiman J. also stated ([2005] 2 I.R. 174 at 187): "I do not believe, however, that the Convention in this instance supplies rights lacking in the constitutional regime of trial in due course of law; I am quite satisfied that the rights are afforded by domestic law." See also, *Miggin v Health Service Executive* [2010] 4 I.R. 338 which arose out of a civil case for medical

12–21 There may be situations which do fit very snugly within the "equality of arms" category. An example of this is a situation (on the borderline between the two rules of constitutional justice) in which the governing statute is itself unbalanced, in that its terms put the applicant at a disadvantage in making his case, as compared with the public body against him. A statutory example forms the subject matter of *Law Society of Ireland v Competition Authority*, in which O'Neill J. stated[30]:

> "I am satisfied that were a tribunal empowered to veto a choice of lawyer made by a party appearing before it, invariably this would give rise to a perception of unfairness on the part of the person denied freedom of choice. Where a tribunal was in effect the adversary, as in the position of the respondent, that perception would be very strong indeed."

12–22 Another possible example would be the situation in *O'Brien v PIAB*, which Denham J. described in this way[31]:

> "PIAB dealt with the respondents' agents and insurers rather than the respondents themselves. Thus [for PIAB] to deal with a claimant and not their agent was onesided. An equal approach is fair."

(3) Freedom of Information Acts 1997–2003

12–23 The main purpose of the Freedom of Information Act 1997[32] (as amended in 2003) is to provide individuals with a legal right of access to information held by public bodies. This bloc of law falls outside the scope of this work. However, three of the Act's subsidiary provisions are relevant here, since they set down proper procedures which must be followed by "public bodies". Before turning to these provisions, the key term "public body" must be explained. This is defined widely in s.2 and Sch.1, to embrace not only the Departments of State, local authorities and the HSE; but also, following the extension in 2003 and 2006,[33] more than 500 entities, mainly public bodies, including the Director of Public Prosecutions, the Medical Council and several Ombudsmen and non-commercial state-sponsored bodies. But there remain various restrictions and exclusions: the Act has not been

---

negligence, in respect of which the defendant doctor knew everything which had occurred at the earlier hearing before the Fitness to Practice Committee of the Medical Council. The High Court (Hanna J.) accordingly ordered that discovery of the Committee's transcript be given to the plaintiff, despite the fact that this involved some infringement of the right to confidentiality for the Committee.

    See also, *Kiely v Minister for Social Welfare (No. 2)* [1977] I.R. 267 at 282 ("… natural justice is not observed if the scales of justice are tilted against one side …"), though this case was decided on the basis of constitutional justice with no reference to the ECHR; and *Murphy v GM* [2001] 4 I.R. 113 at 134, 155.

[30] [2006] 2 I.R. 262 at 282 and 290.
[31] [2009] 2 I.L.R.M. 22 at para.50. See also, para.59. Macken J. at paras 55–56 gave a possibly more historically accurate account, based on the jurisprudence of the ECtHR text and it should be emphasised that the formulation, quoted in the text was not expressly labelled as "equality of arms" in Denham J.'s judgment. Nevertheless, in this book the phrase "equality of arms" is used in the more popular, non-classical sense, which was rejected by Macken J.
[32] See generally, McDonagh, *Freedom of Information* (Dublin: Thomson Round Hall, 2006), especially Chs 4 and 6.
[33] The Freedom of Information Act 1997 (Prescribed Bodies) Regulations 2003 (S.I. No. 643 of 2003), and (S.I. No. 297 of 2006).

extended to the Garda Síochána and also does not cover the DPP's decision to prosecute.[34] A ministerial certificate may be issued to exclude particular sensitive information from the Act.[35]

12–24 The first of the three obligations mentioned is defined as follows, in s.15(1):

> A public body shall cause to be prepared and published and to be made available ... a reference book containing:
>
> (a) a general description of its structure and organisation, functions, powers and duties, any services it provides for the public and the procedures by which any such services may be availed of by the public,
>
>   ...
>
> (c) a general description of the matters referred to in paragraphs (a) and (b) of section 16(1) [see below]
>
>   ...
>
> (e) the names and designations of the members of the staff of the body responsible for carrying out the arrangements aforesaid
>
>   ...
>
> (g) appropriate information concerning:
>   (i)   any rights of review or appeal in respect of decisions made by the body (including rights of review and appeal under this Act), and
>   (ii) the procedure governing the exercise of those rights and any time limits governing such exercise,
> (h) any other information that the head of the body considers relevant for the purpose of facilitating the exercise of the right of access, and
> (i) information in relation to such other matters (if any) as may be prescribed [by the Minister for Finance].

12–25 In relation to this provision, one should notice the following points. First, the phrase "the rights of review or appeal" referred to in s.15(1)(g)(i) include, but are not restricted to, rights under the 1997 Act itself. Secondly, in preparing "the reference book", referred to at the start of the extract, the public body must have regard to "the fact that the purpose of the book is to assist members of the public ...".[36] Thirdly, the Minister for Finance must ensure that public bodies take appropriate measures to train staff and make arrangements to ensure compliance with the Act.[37]

12–26 The next obligation is contained in s.16(1), which provides:

---

[34] *Deely v Information Commissioner* [2001] 3 I.R. 439.
[35] 1997 Act s.25.
[36] Section 15(3).
[37] Section 15(5).

A public body shall cause to be prepared and published and to be made available in accordance with subsection (5)

> (a) the rules, procedures, practices, guidelines and interpretations used by the body, and an index of any precedents kept by the body, for the purposes of decisions, determinations or recommendations, under or for the purposes of any enactment or scheme administered by the body with respect to rights, privileges, benefits, obligations, penalties or other sanctions to which members of the public are or may be entitled or subject under the enactment or scheme, and
> (b) appropriate information in relation to the manner or intended manner of administration of any such enactment or scheme.[38]

12–27   Plainly, in respect of the category of "decisions, determinations ..." to which it applies, this is a far-reaching provision. Notice though that certain consequences of failure to follow the provision are stated in such a way as to suggest that breach of the obligation will not always lead to any form of compensation or other remedy for the person affected. For even if there has been a breach, the person affected must show that he was not aware of the "rule, procedure ..."; and that but for such non-publication he or she would have been aware of it. In addition, the public body must be unable to show that "reasonable steps [as an alternative to publication] were taken by it to bring the rule or requirement to the notice of those affected". However, even where all these conditions are satisfied, then the consequence is rather unspectacular:

> [T]he public body concerned shall, if and in so far as it is practicable to do so, ensure that the person is not subjected to any procedure (not being a penalty imposed by a court upon conviction of an offence).[39]

12–28   Probably a court order could be obtained to enforce obedience with this provision. However, plainly a good deal remains to be worked out in regard to both the practical operation and the consequences of breach of ss.15(1) and 16(1).

12–29   The third significant element of the 1997 Act (contained in s.18) establishes "a right to reasons", which is considered below.[40]

(4) "Charters"

12–30   A number of public bodies (among them, the Departments of Health and Agriculture, the Revenue Commissioners, Iarnród Éireann, Eircom, ESB) and indeed some private companies have now published "Customer Charters" or "Charters of Right". Whilst these lack the coherency of their British counterparts,[41] they are certainly intended to improve the quality of public services and to make them more responsive to their users. Much of their content is substantive, and for this reason, they are treated in the "Sources" Chapter 2, Part F. However, some of the advantages

---

[38]   See also, s.15(d)(iii).
[39]   All quotations in this paragraph are from s.16(4)(3).
[40]   See Ch.14, Part D.
[41]   For the British position, see Drewry, [1993] *Public Law* 248; Barron and Scott (1992) 55 M.L.R. 526.

they offer are procedural in character, and therefore, are briefly mentioned here. Thus they deal with such matters as prompt service; openness and accessibility; courtesy; privacy; and a right to complain. They also include target times for schemes, programmes and repayments. These charters are usually published with a fanfare of trumpets (copy to each consumer, etc). The fact that a charter sets a standard to which a public body has committed itself means that it may be judged fairly according to that standard, by citizens, politicians and media, and pilloried where it falls short of the standard promised. For our purpose, the interesting conceptual question is whether these charters have legal effect. Given their variety, generalisation poses difficulties. However, it can be said that they certainly do not have direct legal effect partly because of their generally imprecise language and mostly because they fall into the fuzzy category of "soft law".[42] Nevertheless, the doctrine of legitimate expectations might also provide the conceptual springboard from which to launch a legal claim. Another way in which they could have an indirect effect is in fixing the factors by which, on a judicial review application, a public body could be held to have behaved unreasonably or overlooked a relevant consideration (for example—in the case of the Revenue Commissioners' Charter of Rights—confidentiality, compliance costs or a presumption that the taxpayer would be honest). In addition, the charters restate what is already a legal right, for example, privacy or a duty not to mislead.

12–31   Again, apart from the law, assuming that the public body involved is within the Ombudsman's jurisdiction, failure to honour a charter commitment could amount to maladministration, which would attract censure under the Ombudsman Act 1980.[43]

12–32   There has been little case law in this area. One exception, however, is *Keogh v Criminal Assets Bureau and Revenue Commissioners*,[44] which centred on s.933 of the Taxes Consolidation Act 1997, by which any person aggrieved by any assessment to income tax is entitled to appeal to the Appeal Commissioners, provided that they give notice in writing to the Inspector of Taxes within the specified time limit. In the instant case, the applicant had indicated that they wished to appeal within the time limit, but failed to comply with all the necessary procedures before the time limit had expired. However, significantly, a letter from the second respondent had failed to notify the applicant of this requirement. In this case, the applicant relied successfully on the "Taxpayers Charter" issued by the second respondent, which provided that the Revenue Commissioners would make every reasonable attempt to give taxpayers timely information. In view of this, the Supreme Court accepted the applicant's argument that the time for bringing an appeal had not commenced. Giving the court's judgment, Keane C.J. stated[45]:

---

[42]   See Ch.2, Part E.
[43]   e.g. Ombudsman's Report 2001, p.41.
[44]   [2004] 2 I.R. 159.
[45]   [2004] 2 I.R. 159 at 175–176. As regards any doctrinal question which might seem to arise, Keane C.J. stated that it was unnecessary to decide whether the justification for this approach was breach of a legitimate expectation, or "simply the recognition of the duty on the respondents to observe the procedures they had undertaken to apply" ([2004] 2 I.R. 159 at 175). See analogous use made of the "Von Arnim" letter in *Fakih v Minister for Justice, Equality and Law Reform* [1993] 2 I.R. 406 at 423.

"It is undoubtedly the case that documents such as the Charter of rights under consideration in the present case ... frequently contain what are no more than praiseworthy statements of an aspirational nature designed to encourage members of the organisation concerned to meet acceptable standards of behaviour in their dealings with the public ... [By contrast in] this case, we are concerned with a specific undertaking to give taxpayers full, timely and accurate information as to the provisions of a notoriously opaque and difficult code. While it is manifestly not the function of the second respondents ... to give gratuitous advice ... it was not asking too much of the Revenue Commissioners in the present case not to respond to a letter such as that from the applicant in a manner in which they must have known could have left him in the dark as to his rights."

(5) Procedure of a deliberative body

12–33   One example of this category is the City and County Management (Amendment) Act 1955 s.10(1), which came up for discussion in *Ahern v Kerry County Council*.[46] This case concerned the internal proceedings of a local authority. The provision states that "an estimate of expenses shall be considered by the local authority at a meeting ...". At the meeting, the chairman had confined discussion to the first group of estimates, with the remaining groups being immediately put to the vote together with no further discussion and the rate being thereby struck. Blayney J. held that the procedure did not comply with s.10(1) of the 1955 Act (since "it would at least be necessary that each programme group should come up for discussion").[47]

12–34   A case which was grounded on a wider basis than *Ahern* in that it turned not on a specific statute, but, it seems (though nothing precise is stated in the judgment), on the judge's understanding of free speech and democratic process in a deliberative body, is *Farrell v South Eastern Health Board*,[48] a case which may have some potential for growth. The case grew out of a long-running controversy concerning the location of the acute general hospital for South Tipperary, support being divided between Clonmel and Cashel. The applicant complained of two aspects[49] of the way the dispute was treated, both at and before a meeting of the respondent health board. First, he had been frustrated in collecting information regarding fire safety standards at Clonmel Hospital. Secondly, he had been allowed by the chairman only two minutes in which to put his views before the meeting. Barron J. stated:

"The function of the Board is an administrative one and the members vote in accordance with their views as to the appropriate course which the Board should follow. As such, there is no place for the principles of [constitutional] justice."[50]

---

[46] [1988] I.L.R.M. 392.
[47] [1988] I.L.R.M. 392 at 397.
[48] [1991] 2 I.R. 291. *Doyle v Croke*, unreported, High Court, May 6, 1988. See to similar effect, *Rodgers v ITGWU* [1978] I.L.R.M. 51. (*Doyle* is covered in the Third Edition at p.499.)
[49] A further point in *Farrell* was that no details of the cost of the scheme were put before the meeting for the purpose of the resolution, as required by standing order 4.2.
[50] [1991] 2 I.R. 291 at 295.

However, the judge went on to find for the applicant. The central passage in the judgment is as follows[51]:

"[The applicant] was entitled to a reasonable opportunity to express his views on the motion and to put before the Board evidence in support of those views. It was a matter for the chairman to place reasonable fetters on the exercise of that right. Did the first applicant get that opportunity? Unfortunately, the essential facts in this case are blurred by the unnecessary confrontation which occurred ... But what must not occur is the stifling or attempted stifling of any member or group of members. By this I mean preventing unfairly that member from expressing his, her or their views."

B. Fair Procedure, Constitutional Justice and Natural Justice

Natural justice

12–35 There has recently been a substantial, though unstated, change in the terminology in this area, to which we return at para.12–43. However, the best way of explaining fair procedure is to follow the chronology of the case law and to start with natural justice, which consists of two fundamental procedural rules, namely: that the decision-maker must not be biased (*nemo iudex in causa sua*); and secondly, that anyone who may be adversely affected by a decision should not be condemned unheard: rather, he should have the best possible chance to put his side of the case (*audi alteram partem*).

12–36 The title, in particular the epithet "natural", has attracted a certain amount of attention. According to Costello J. in *Nolan v Irish Land Commission*:

"[T]he adjective 'natural' before justice was not used to describe justice by reference to man in a state of nature or in primitive society. Rather it has been employed as part of a phrase which developed from a philosophical view of man's nature as that of a being endowed with reason and capable of ascertaining objective moral values. As pointed out by De Smith, *Judicial Review of Administrative Action* ...: 'The term expresses the close relationship between the common law and moral principles and it has an impressive ancestry.'"[52]

12–37 The universality of natural justice can also be illustrated by the inclusion of the two principles of natural justice in Art.6(1) of the European Convention of Human Rights, already discussed; or by the African customary law principle of

---

[51] [1991] 2 I.R. 291 at 295–296.

[52] [1981] I.R. 23 at 34. Costello J. was countering criticism of the term "natural justice", contained in *Green v Blake* [1948] I.R. 242. See also, the lyrical passage of Gavan Duffy J. in *Maunsell v Minister for Education* [1940] I.R. 213 at 234: "[Natural justice is] ... elementary justice ... The principle cannot be more tersely expressed than in the lines of Seneca: '*Quicunque aliquid statuerit, parte inaudita altera, Aequum licet statuerit, haud aequus fuerit.*'" Dr Cronin of the UCC Classics Department translates Seneca as follows: "Whoever has made a decision, the second party not having been heard, although he has decided justly, will not have been just."

the Barotse people (of western Zambia) who follow a precept which translates as: "one does not ask a monkey to decide an affair of the forest", which is plainly a statement of the *nemo iudex* principle.

Constitutional justice: "... more than the two well-established principles"

12–38   In 1965, natural justice in Ireland was reincarnated as constitutional justice. In what was obviously intended to be a seminal obiter dictum, Walsh J. stated:

> "In the context of the Constitution, natural justice might be more appropriately termed constitutional justice and must be understood to import more than the two well-established principles that no man shall be judge in his own cause, and *audi alteram partem*."[53]

12–39   But we should note briefly that Walsh J. emphasised that constitutional justice is supposed to go beyond the two well-established principles. In fact, there has been little progress in divining what these additional factors comprise and the courts have sometimes appeared reluctant explicitly to draw upon this reservoir, in that, when new extensions to the law have been made, for example, barring delay[54] or requiring reasons,[55] it has not been indicated whether they are to be regarded as a development of the compendius *audi alteram partem* principle or as aspects of the "x factor" in constitutional justice.

12–40   It used to be generally assumed that the two rules of natural justice were co-extensive in their application.[56] This assumption was questionable, given the differing nature and function of the rules. Bias is a particularly heinous defect likely to lead to a general erosion of confidence in the administrative system, whereas the failure to grant a hearing does not appear to be such a fundamental flaw, since (if a decision-maker is biased) fairness becomes impossible and the decision loses all claim to legitimacy; whereas, with a breach of the other rule, a competent decision-maker could take into account all relevant facts and arguments, without these having to be pointed out by the applicant.

Foundation in the Constitution

12–41   There is another point of contrast between constitutional and natural justice,[57] namely that natural justice remains a mere common law (and therefore rebuttable) presumption to be applied, in appropriate contexts, in the interpretation

---

[53]   Per Walsh J. in *McDonald v Bord na gCon* [1965] I.R. 217 at 242. See Casey, "Natural and Constitutional Justice – The Policeman's Lot Improved" (1979–1980) 2 D.U.L.J. 95 and Hogan, "Natural and Constitutional Justice: *Adieu* to *Laissez-Faire*" (1984) 19 Ir. Jur. 309.

[54]   See, e.g. *Bosphorus Hava Yollari Turism ve Tickaret Anonim Sirketi v Minister for Transport (No. 2)*, unreported, High Court, January 22, 1996; *McNeill v Garda Commissioner* [1997] 1 I.R. 469; and *Re Gallagher's Application (No. 2)* [1996] 3 I.R. 15. See paras 14–67 to 14–74.

[55]   See, e.g. *State (Creedon) v Criminal Compensation Tribunal* [1988] I.R. 51; *Gavin v Criminal Injuries Compensation Tribunal* [1997] 1 I.R. 132; and *McCormack v Garda Síochána Complaints Board* [1997] 2 I.L.R.M. 321.

[56]   Clarke, "Natural Justice: Substance or Shadow?" [1975] *Public Law* 27.

[57]   For a discussion of the idea that constitutional justice only applies where a possible breach of some constitutionally protected interest, for example, a property right is involved, whereas

of statutes. By contrast, constitutional justice is judicially regarded as implicit in the Constitution (Art.40.3.1°).[58] The reasoning seems to be that words and phrases like "respect" and "protect … from unjust attack" in Art.40.3.1°[59] refer not only to substantive protection but also mean that even where substantive interference is permitted, it must be accompanied by a fair procedure. This difference in the sources of constitutional and natural justice is important. A British statute can, if it uses clear enough words, exclude the rules of natural justice because of the absence of a written constitution.[60] By contrast, an Irish statute attempting to exclude the rules of constitutional justice in a situation where they would be appropriate would be unconstitutional. A recent strong example is afforded by *McCann v Monaghan District Court*,[61] in which the High Court held that the Enforcement of Court Orders Act 1940 s.6 was unconstitutional, in that it conferred jurisdiction to order the arrest and imprisonment of an impecunious debtor in violation of the debtor's constitutional guarantee of procedural protection. In particular, the order for the debtor's arrest and imprisonment could be made in the debtor's absence; there was no provision for legal aid; and the onus of disproving refusal or neglect to pay was placed on the debtor.

12–42 Although constitutional justice has been grounded in Art.40.3 of the Constitution which confers rights explicitly on "citizen[s]", it has nevertheless been held by Barrington J. in *State (McFadden) v The Governor of Mountjoy Prison (No. 1)*[62] (a case arising out of extradition proceedings), that the duty to observe "basic fairness of procedures" applies even where aliens are involved.

"Fair procedure"

12–43 In the 2000s, however, there have been radical, though unacknowledged, changes in terminology in this area. In the first place, most judges speak of the "no bias" principle under that title and no longer associate it with constitutional justice, as if to suggest that constitutional justice should embrace only what is described here as the *audi alteram partem* principle.[63] This seems to have been

---

natural justice continues to exist to protect other, rights or privileges created by statute, common law or contract, see Third Edition, pp.510–511. This nuance no longer seems significant.

[58] *Re Haughey* [1971] I.R. 217; *Glover v BLN Ltd* [1973] I.R. 388; *Kiely v Minister for Social Welfare (No. 2)* [1977] I.R. 267; *Garvey v Ireland* [1981] I.R. 75; *Ryan v VIP Taxi Co-operative Ltd* (High Court, ex tempore), *Irish Times Law Report*, April 10, 1989; *Halal Meat Packers v EAT* [1990] I.L.R.M. 293 at 307–309.

[59] Although Art.40.3.1° confers rights explicitly on "citizen[s]", it was been held by Barrington J. in *State (McFadden) v The Governor of Mountjoy Prison (No. 1)* [1981] I.L.R.M. 113 at 122 (a case arising out of extradition proceedings) that the duty to observe "basic fairness of procedures" applies even where aliens are involved.

[60] See, e.g. Keane J. in *O'Brien v Bord na Móna* [1983] I.R. 255 at 270–271.

[61] [2010] I.L.R.M. 17 at 65–66. For another example, see *Jaggers Restaurant Ltd v Ahearne* [1988] I.R. 308. See also, *O'Cleirigh v Minister for Agriculture* [1996] 2 I.L.R.M. 12; *Madden v Minister for Marine* [1997] 1 I.L.R.M. 136 at 146; *State (Haverty) v An Bord Pleanála* [1987] I.R. 485.

[62] [1981] I.L.R.M. 113 at 122.

[63] *BFO v Govenor of Dochas Centre* [2005] 2 I.R. 1 at 24–26. See also, *Spin v IRTC* [2001] 4 I.R. 411 at 443 (and see 439), contradistinguishing the "no bias" rule from "fair procedure"; and *Beades v Dublin Corporation* [2005] IEHC 406. In England, *De Smith's Judicial Review*, 6th edn (London: Sweet and Maxwell, 2007) uses the term "procedural fairness" to cover the two limbs, with natural justice seldom mentioned; Wade and Forsyth, *Administrative Law*,

done unconsciously, without any explanation or acknowledgment of any change. In particular, there has been no inquiry as to whether this change would mean that the "no bias" principle is no longer grounded in the Constitution (a matter examined in the next section). This would be a grave change requiring substantial justification and so our working assumption is that, given their centrality, both legs of constitutional justice remain grounded in the Constitution, as stated in *McDonald*: for this reason, we use "constitutional justice" to refer to either or both limbs. As a conclusion to the last few paragraphs, the view may be expressed that more clarity, precision and consistency in this area, in particular a judicial indication of the appropriate vocabulary, would be useful.

Enforcing the rights

12–44 As ever, the practical question of implementation (or "remedies" as the law usually puts it) is under-developed. The first question here is whether, if either of the rules of constitutional justice is violated, the applicant can be given a remedy apart from the quashing of the decision: for example, damages. At common law, a breach of natural justice was not in itself tortious.[64] But it now seems probable that an infringement of the constitutional right to fair procedure may sound in damages and such awards have in fact been made by the courts.[65]

12–45 Another general question arises where the reason why either of the constitutional justice principles has not been followed is that the relevant legislation appears not to allow this to be done. In this situation, what is the court to do? Can it, for example, require the public body concerned to implement the rule, by invoking the Constitution? This is part of the subject of whether a court can go beyond the minimalist use of the Constitution to strike down laws, and instead, develop new positive rules to implement the constitutional provisions. As such, it is really part of broad constitutional discourse and so outside the province of this book. All we shall do here, therefore, is to mention the few cases in which this problem has been addressed in the constitutional justice field. In fact, those judgments which do treat this area have been fairly brief and pragmatic. Each of these two points is elaborated in later chapters.[66]

C. Fair Procedure in Court Cases

12–46 Whilst it is true that most fair procedure cases[67] emanate from the executive branch of government, it is an aspect of the rules' universality that they can apply, in appropriate circumstances, to each of the three arms of government: legislature;

10th edn (2009) uses the general title "natural justice" but organises most of the material into two chapters, headed "The rule against bias" and "The right to fair procedure".

[64] *Dunlop v Woollahra MC* [1982] A.C. 158.

[65] See, e.g. *Healy v Minister for Defence*, unreported, High Court, July 7, 1994; *McAuley v Garda Commissioner* [1996] 3 I.R. 208 at 232.

[66] See paras 13–61 and 14–04 to 14–05, respectively.

[67] For examples covered in the Third Edition at pp.505–506 and omitted here, see *S v S* [1983] I.R. 68; *O'Domhnaill v Merrick* [1984] I.R. 151; *Toal v Duignan (No. 1)* [1991] I.L.R.M. 135; *Toal v Duignan (No. 2)* [1991] I.L.R.M. 140; *Tuohy v Courtney* [1994] 3 I.R. 1 at 48; *Primor Plc v Stokes Kennedy Crowley* [1996] 2 I.R. 459 at 475; *Director of Public Prosecutions v Doyle* [1994] 2 I.R. 286 at 300; *State (McKeown) v Scully* [1986] I.L.R.M. 133; *Davitt v*

judicature; or executive. The rules regulate decisions affecting individuals directly and these are just the sort of decisions which are usually not taken by the Oireachtas. However, in appropriate circumstances constitutional justice has been extended even to the Oireachtas, as was demonstrated in the multi-faceted case of *Re Haughey*.[68] The aspect of the case which is relevant here is that it applied the *audi alteram partem* rule to an investigation by a committee of the legislature (specifically, the Dáil Public Accounts Committee). More recently, the rules have been applied even when it was a member of the Oireachtas who was under investigation by a Committee.[69]

12–47   At the opposite pole from the legislative function is the judicial function, which deals almost exclusively with individual decisions. But here procedure is largely regulated by a minute specialised code of procedural and evidential law. For example, at the pre-trial stage in the Superior Courts, provision is made by the Rules of the Superior Courts as to pleadings, interrogatories, discovery, etc in order to ensure that litigants have an adequate opportunity to meet their opponent's case. Fair procedure in the courts is underpinned by such specialised constitutional provisions as Arts 38.1 and 34.1, as well as Art.40.3.[70] These and the more detailed procedural rules often draw on similar policies and values to those which underlie constitutional justice. However, it is not usual to classify procedural law or the law of evidence as part of constitutional justice.

12–48   Nevertheless, in a growing number of cases, which form the subject matter of this Part, constitutional or natural justice has been invoked, by name, to augment procedural law often with unexpected and radical consequences. For instance, in *N v K*,[71] Henchy J. suggested that constitutional justice may require separate representation for children in appropriate cases where their welfare is at stake. In addition, it is likely that in suitable cases, constitutional justice could

---

Minister for Justice, unreported, High Court, February 8, 1989. On particular features of bias in regard to judges, see Ch.13, Part E.

[68] [1971] I.R. 217 at 263–264. Another episode involving a House of the Oireachtas occurred in 1991. The Senate Committee on Procedure and Privileges recommended to the House that Senator Norris be disciplined by being suspended from the service of the Senate for one week (T. 279 (Pl. 7181), March 14, 1990) and this recommendation was adopted: 124 *Seanad Debates* Cols 772–804 (March 15, 1990). The basis of Senator Norris' offence was an allegation he had made against the Cathaoirleach. Notwithstanding this, it was the Cathaoirleach who, in line with the usual practice, chaired both the Committee and the Senate at the relevant times. In addition, the Committee refused the Senator's request that he be allowed legal representation, to call witnesses, etc. Senator Norris was then granted leave by the High Court to apply for a judicial review of his disciplining by the Senate on the ground of violation of both the first and second rules of constitutional justice. As a result of the order made by the High Court, Senator Norris was reinstated and eventually his action was withdrawn before it had received a substantive hearing: see especially, 124 *Seanad Debates* Cols 1039–1145; 125 *Seanad Debates* Cols 381–385 (May 25, 1990).

[69] *Callelly v Moylan & Others* [2011] IEHC 2.

[70] Article 38.1 provides that: "No person shall be tried on any criminal charge save in due course of law." For a case (involving a jury) in which the "no bias" rule was grounded on Art.38, see *People (Director of Public Prosecutors) v Tobin* [2001] 3 I.R. 469 at 473, in which the Court of Criminal Appeal (Fennelly J.) stated: "… the right to a fair trial [is] guaranteed by Article 38 … The right of an accused to be tried by a jury free from any suspicion or taint of bias is one of the cornerstones of the criminal justice system". Article 34.1 states that: "Justice shall be administered in courts established by law …" For Art.40.3, see paras 12–41 to 12–42.

[71] [1985] I.R. 733 at 749.

be used or to make good the omission of the Rules of Court which provide no system of discovery of documents before the District Court.[72] Such examples draw attention to the continuum which exists between the principles of constitutional justice and the right of access to the courts, something which was acknowledged in the following passage from *S v S*:

> "The combined effect of Articles 34.1, 38.1 and 40.3 [of the Constitution] appears to me to guarantee (*inter alia*) something equivalent to the concept of 'due process' under the American Constitution in relation to causes and controversies litigated before the Court ... Just as the parties have a right of access to the courts when this is necessary to defend or vindicate life, person, good name or property rights, so they have a *constitutional right to fair procedure* when they get to court ... Because the rule in *Russell v. Russell* ran counter to [the] paramount public policy [of ascertaining truth and doing justice] and was calculated to defeat the due and proper administration of justice, I would hold that it ceased to have legal effect in the State after the enactment of the Constitution in 1937."[73]

12–49 Another question suggested by this passage, yet which appears not to have received much attention, concerns the long-established principle excluding hearsay. On the one hand, this may be said to be required by the *audi alteram* in that the character of hearsay is such as to exclude effective cross-examination. Yet, equally, the effect of the rule is to deny the party needing to rely on the hearsay the opportunity to put forward their best case. Thus, there will be many situations in which greater harm is done, in terms of the *audi* principle, by the hearsay exclusion rule than by its absence, or at any rate, radical reform.[74]

12–50 The point has been made that there is no discovery in criminal proceedings as there is for civil litigation, and for this reason, it has been recommended[75] that a preliminary hearing be held before the trial judge in all indictable cases[76] to identify whether full disclosure has been made because, in certain circumstances, the absence of any such procedure could give rise to unfairness.

12–51 Another example of constitutional justice in operation concerns the fact that when a court makes a final order which affects the rights of interested parties, fair procedure means that both sides must be heard. Thus, to take but one case

---

[72] See *Nolan v Irish Land Commission* [1981] I.R. 23 at 33, 39–40; *Director of Public Prosecutions v Doyle* [1994] 2 I.R. 286.
[73] [1983] I.R. 75 at 80 per O'Hanlon J.
[74] This argument is analysed more fully at para.14–46.
[75] By the *Working Party on the Jurisdiction of the Courts*, May 2003.
[76] This possibility was glimpsed in, though it did not arise on the facts of, *PG v Director of Public Prosecutions* [2007] 3 I.R. 39 at 42–43, 53, 54. (This concerned statements of psychologists who had examined the complainant who had allegedly been sexually abused. The accused claimed that he needed to see these statements in order to make a case against justification for the delay.) See also, *Braddish v Director of Public Prosecutions* [2001] 3 I.R. 127 at para.49; *JR v Minister for Justice* [2007] 2 I.R. 748. Four of the five Supreme Court judges in *PG* opined that matters of disclosure are within the province of the trial judge and are not matters for judicial review, except to the extent that the accused can show that there is real risk of an unfair trial.

among many, in *State (O'Sullivan) v Buckley*,[77] the Supreme Court quashed an order of a District judge where he had purported to grant, ex parte, an enlargement of time to allow an appeal to be taken to the Circuit Court. The court added that, save for purely procedural orders (of which this was not one), persons discharging judicial functions must hear both sides before proceeding to make a final order. In some cases, the principle will be held to mean that a particular person is entitled to separate representation.[78]

12–52 In this respect, there are significant observations in *DK v Crowley*.[79] Here the Supreme Court struck down a provision of the Domestic Violence Act 1996 which authorised the grant of an interim barring order on an ex parte basis. However, what is significant, given the diversity of ex parte orders which lurk in the thickets of court civil procedure, is that Keane C.J. was at pains to mark the *ne plus ultra* of the decision. As an overarching proposition, he stated[80]:

"The issue in this case is not as to whether the Oireachtas was entitled to abridge, even in a relatively drastic fashion, the right of the applicant to be heard, in order to protect spouses and dependent children from domestic violence. That the legislature was entitled to effect such an abridgment of the rights of individual citizens in order to deal with the social evil of domestic violence is beyond dispute. The question for resolution in this case is as to

---

[77] (1967) 101 I.L.T.R. 152. See also, the comments of Hamilton C.J. in *Balkanbank v Taher*, unreported, Supreme Court, January 19, 1995, pp.39–40. See *State (Rogers) v Galvin* [1983] I.R. 249 at 253; *Re Zwann's Application* [1981] I.R. 395 at 404. Though in *Butler v Ruane* [1989] I.L.R.M. 159, the Supreme Court sanctioned the making ex parte of certain purely procedural orders, such as giving the respondents additional time to file affidavits in judicial review matters.

[78] e.g. *Z and Y, X v An tArd Chláraitheoir, Ireland and the Attorney General*, unreported, High Court, Laffoy J., May 23, 2008, pp.7–8 (held that, in the proceedings concerning the registration of the birth of a minor, the minor had the right to be a party). See also, *FN and EB v CO (Guardianship)* [2004] 4 I.R. 311 at para.29.

For one of many examples of constitutional justice to be found in the Rules of Superior Courts 1986, take Ord.84 r.22(2) by which: "The notice of motion or summons [in a judicial review application] must be served on all persons directly affected ..."

A striking breach of the *audi alteram partem* rule occurred in *Bloomer v Law Society of Ireland* [1995] 3 I.R. 14. Here, Northern Ireland law students claimed that they were being discriminated against, in that the law graduates of (Southern) Ireland's universities were granted an exemption from entry examinations to the solicitors training course, while this advantage was not extended to Northern law graduates. Having found, in principle, in favour of the Northern law graduates, the High Court went on to rule, on separation of powers grounds, that it could not re-write the rules to extend the advantage to the Northern graduates. Instead, however, it quashed the regulations which bestowed this advantage on graduates of Irish universities. The amazing feature is that this was done despite the fact that no Irish graduates were before the court; nor had they been alerted to what was to happen. Next, the Law Society of Ireland appealed against the entire judgment to the Supreme Court. At this point, the Irish graduates sought to be heard; but were refused. This was on the basis of the rule of practice: that they ought to have been a party to the case at the High Court stage, before they could be allowed to participate at the Supreme Court level. No attention was paid to their fundamental right to be heard. (One of the present authors was involved in the case, on the side of the Southern law graduates.)

[79] [2002] 2 I.R. 744.

[80] [2002] 2 I.R. 744 at 758. This case and the subsequent legislation is discussed in H & M, para.12–71.

whether the manner in which the abridgment of the right to be heard has been effected is proportionate in the sense already indicated."

12–53   There were many ways in which the legislation involved might have been modified in order to make it "proportionate" to the needs of the situation and this judicial invitation was taken up in the amending legislation (the Domestic Violence (Amendment) Act 2002).

12–54   A major question in this context is the entire subject of substituted service. The only authority we have in the area is *Brennan v Windle*[81] which, admittedly, is a criminal case. The applicant had been convicted of driving without insurance and sentenced to four months' imprisonment. The central point was that the applicant had been unaware of the charge or hearing at which he was convicted. The case for the respondent rested on the Courts Act 1991 s.22(1) which states that:

> ... service of a summons upon a person pursuant to subs (1) of this section shall upon proof that a copy of the summons was ... delivered in accordance with the provision of the said subs. (1) be deemed to be good service of the summons upon the person unless it is proved that the person did not receive notice of the summons or of the hearing to which the summons relates.

12–55   The court found in favour of the applicant. The judgment of Hardiman J. (with whom Murray J. concurred; the thrust of Geoghegan J.'s separate assent was similar) was based on the interpretation of the Act. However, a good deal of judicial *saevo indignatio* came through, on the ground that the applicant was imprisoned as a result of proceedings "in which he was denied due process, fair procedure and natural and constitutional justice".[82]

12–56   Finally, in the case of an unrepresented party, a court has to strike a delicate balance. Notice the following observation of Keane C.J. from a custody case in which one of the parties was unrepresented before the High Court and had made an unsuccessful appeal to the Supreme Court based in part on unfair procedure[83]:

> "The trial of cases involving lay litigants thus requires patience and understanding on the part of trial judges. They have to ensure, as best they can, that justice is not put at risk by the absence of expert legal representation on one side of the case. At the same time, they have to bear constantly in mind that the party with legal representation is not to be unfairly penalised because he or she is so represented. It can be difficult to achieve the balance which justice requires and the problem is generally at its most acute in a family law case, such as the present."

12–57   This passage brings out the fact that a lay litigant creates a tension between

---

[81]   [2003] 2 I.L.R.M. 520. For another case in which notice was not given (this time of an application to the District Court under the "slip rule" to correct errors in the return for trial to the Special Criminal Court), see *Murphy v DPP* [2009] 2 I.R. 168.

[82]   [2003] 2 I.L.R.M. 520 at 527–528. For a rather similar case, see *DK v Crowley* [2002] 2 I.R. 744.

[83]   *RB v AS* [2002] 2 I.R. 428 at 435. See also, *Talbot v McCann Fitzgerald* [2009] IESC 25, paras 24–31.

the two rules of constitutional justice. On the one hand, the lay litigant must be facilitated in putting forward his best case. On the other hand, the judge must not be, or appear to be, partial.

CHAPTER 13

THE PRINCIPLE
AGAINST BIAS

A. CHARACTER OF BIAS

13–01   The principle that no person shall be a judge in his own cause[1] is fundamental and "as old as the common law itself".[2] It is a far-reaching concept, which applies not only in public administration but in the procedure of courts, the latter point being elaborated in Part E. In addition, "the attitude [engendered by bias] may be one of goodwill or ill will."[3] Bias may be conscious or unconscious and does not necessarily mean "a corrupt state of mind".[4] This is one of the features which distinguishes bias from bad faith (covered at paras 15–24 to 15–26) though admittedly there is a great deal of overlap between the two concepts.

Typology

13–02   In the past decade or so, there has been substantial development of categorisation in this area, which is noted at this point. But one should observe that, while this may (or may not) be useful from a descriptive point of view, in most cases, nothing turns on these distinctions. And it should be emphasised that we have used the term "bias" to embrace all members of the family. In the case of *Orange v Director of Telecoms (No. 2)*,[5] four of the five Supreme Court judges who heard the case ranged interestingly, though obiter, over a good deal of territory on the "no bias" principle—probably more than in any other Irish authority. Geoghegan J. offered the following typologys on the rule:

> "(1) The rare case of proved actual bias. For such bias to be established, it would be necessary actually to prove that the judge of the Tribunal or

---

[1]   For an excellent treatment of both rules of constitutional justice/fair procedure, see Delany, *Judicial Review of Administrative Action*, 2nd edn (Dublin: Round Hall, 2009), Ch.5. See also, Rayment, "Bias: recent developments" (2001) J.R. 93; Sheehan, "Bias Judgments: are Irish courts too lenient?" (2005) 23 I.L.T. 235.

[2]   *O'Reilly v His Honour Judge Cassidy* [1995] 1 I.L.R.M. 306 at 318.

[3]   *Orange Communication Ltd v Director of Telecoms (No. 2)* [2000] 4 I.R. 159 at 221 (Barron J.).

[4]   *R. (de Vesci) v Queen's Co. JJ.* [1908] 2 I.R. 285. For mala fides, see paras 15–24 to 15–26.

[5]   [2000] 4 I.R. 159.

the adjudicator ... was deliberately setting out to mark or hold against a particular party ...

(2) A situation of apparent bias where the adjudicator has a proprietary or some other definite personal interest in the outcome of the preceding competition or other matter on which he is adjudicating. In that case, there is a presumption of bias without further proof ...

(3) Even in cases where there is no evidence of actual bias, and no evidence of the adjudicator having any proprietary or other interest in the outcome of the matter, there was still to be held on the apparent bias. If a reasonable person might have apprehended that they might be biased because of some particular proven circumstance external to the matters to be decided in the case, such as for instance a family relationship in circumstances where objection may be taken."

13–03 Category (1)—"actual bias", sometimes known as "conscious bias"—is clear.[6] The other two categories are collectively known as "objective", "unconscious" or "perceived". The distinction between categories (2)[7] and (3) calls for explanation. It seems to hark back to the traditional notion of financial or material bias being the most heinous kind and thus the source of bias which is singled out as being the easiest to establish. In other words, to quote from category (2) in the passage, "... there is a presumption of bias without further proof." However, despite the separate identification of category (2) in this judgment, the Irish courts have not adopted the notion of "automatic disqualification".[8] The emphasis on appearance in categories (2) and (3)[9] seems to assume the centrality of the reasonable suspicion test, a point discussed in Part C.

13–04 Theoretically, there are two aspects to the "no bias" principle. The first is for the applicant to prove that the particular association or past involvement actually exists. This is a matter of fact (which, as it happens, has seldom been contested in the cases). The second question requires the applicant to establish, as a matter of law, that it is reasonable to expect the decision-maker to be influenced by the past association, etc.[10]

13–05 As regards the second question, there is now developing, here and in England, a strong line of authority that not every happenstance, common association between a decision-maker and party will suffice to ground reasonable suspicion. For example, "[a]ttendance at the same school by judges and lawyers does not establish objective bias. Having a spouse who many years before was a member of a law firm which is [a solicitor for the] respondent in a case does not establish

---

[6]   For a rare, though unsuccessful, claim of actual (also known as "subjective") bias, see *Hygeia Chemicals Ltd v Irish Medicines Board* [2010] IESC 4.

[7]   Category (2) is anyway out of line with the other two, in that it is a source of bias rather than a distinct type of approach to the facts.

[8]   See H & M, para.13–24.

[9]   In *Orange (No. 2)* [2000] 4 I.R. 159 at 222, the other judge to offer a classification, Barron J., conflated categories (2) and (3). Barron J. stated: "Bias can be of two types: conscious—which in the cases has also been referred to as actual or subjective; and perceived—also referred to as objective or unconscious."

[10] See *Orange (No. 2)* [2000] 4 I.R. 159 at 221–222 (Barron J.), and at 241 (Murphy J.).

objective bias by a judge."[11] The line seems to run between the fact that both the decision-maker and one of the parties are middle-class Catholics from Dublin; and, on the other hand, factors which are impermissible because they are less common and are likely to be more influential, such as family relationships.

13–06   On this, the wisest authority is *O'Ceallaigh v An Bord Altranais*[12] which emphasises that, while a good deal depends on the relationship, the bigger factor is the circumstances of the particular situation. The facts in *O'Ceallaigh* were instructive: the case concerned the relationship between the Chairperson (T) of a disciplinary inquiry and the independent expert witness (H), in that each was employed at the same hospital. But, as Hedigan J. stated, "… [this relationship] of itself is not of course sufficient. I must determine if there is some element or factor in respect of that relationship … which would give rise to a reasonable apprehension that the inquiry could have been affected."[13]

13–07   One might ask, how far could these linkages go? For example: would there be bias if the professional adviser to a party before a Tribunal were married to the bank manager of a son of the Tribunal Registrar? The answer may be that the line to be drawn depends upon the basic test of reasonable suspicion, considered below.

13–08   We ought to note too that *O'Ceallaigh* was one of those cases in which the connection lies between the decision-maker and a witness (or, as in other cases, a professional adviser), rather than directly with a party.[14] As regards the difference

---

[11]   *Talbot v Hermitage Golf Club* [2009] IESC 26 at para.19 (Denham J.). See also, *Rooney v Minister for Agriculture (No.1)* [2001] 2 I.L.R.M. 37.

[12]   [2009] IEHC 470. At para.29, Hedigan J. cited, with approval, the Court of Appeal authority, *Locabail (UK) Ltd v Bayfield Properties Ltd* [2000] Q.B. 451, in which Lord Bingham, writing for the Court of Appeal, stated that "… it would be dangerous and futile to attempt to define or list the factors which may or may not give rise to a real danger of bias."
        He then continued in a classical passage: "Everything will depend on the facts, which may include the nature of the issue to be decided. We cannot however conceive of circumstances in which an objection could be soundly based on the religion, ethnic or national origin, gender, age, class, means or sexual orientation of the judge. Nor, at any rate, ordinarily, could an objection be soundly based on the judge's social or education or service or employment background or history, nor that of any member of the judge's family; or previous political associations; or membership of social or sporting or charitable bodies, or Masonic associations; or previous judicial decisions; or extra curricular utterances (whether in text books, lectures …); or previous receipt of instructions to act for or against any party … or membership of the same Inn, circuit … By contrast, the real danger of bias might well be thought to arise if there were personal friendship or animosity between the judge and any member of the public involved in the case; or if the judge were closely acquainted with any member of the public involved in the case, particularly if the credibility of the individual could be significant in the decision of the case … or if on any question at issue in the proceedings before him the judge had expressed views, particularly in the course of the hearing, in such extreme and unbalanced terms as to throw doubt on his ability to try the issue with an objective judicial mind …"
        The High Court decision was affirmed in *O'Ceallaigh v An Bord Altranais* [2011] IESC 50 (December 21, 2011).

[13]   This and the following quotation are from [2009] IEHC 470 at paras 39–41. Notice also that Hedigan J. (at paras 17, 42) distinguished *Kudelska v An Bord Altranais*, unreported, High Court, Hedigan J., February 10, 2009, in that, in *O'Ceallaigh*, there was nothing untoward in the relationship between the adjudicator and the expert witness which would affect the adjudicator's impartiality.

[14]   This is a feature which, as we shall see below at paras 13–18 to 13–19, may arise with any of the sources of bias.

between a relationship with a witness rather than a party, Hedigan J. stated that "[w]here the impugned relationship concerns a witness or other person, not a party, who does not have a stake in the outcome of the proceedings, the threshold to establish objective bias will necessarily be higher [than in the case of a party]."[15] However, it may be commented that this observation should be seen in the context of the facts of the particular case in which the fortune of the expert witness was not affected by the outcome. As noted earlier, the particular circumstances are most significant and the position may be different where, say, the witness or other non-party is a young practitioner seeking to establish a reputation.

13–09 Two further preliminary points are worth raising. First, overwhelmingly, the concern of judicial review is to protect the individual immediately and adversely affected by some act of illegality by a public body. Or, to state the point from the opposite direction, there are few cases in which the argument presented is that there was partiality which told in favour of the individual affected; but against a public body or some third party. To take a rare example, in *Re Solicitors*[16] one of the less well-known points is that it was argued that the Disciplinary Committee may have been prejudiced against the solicitor whose disciplining was under consideration. Yet, no one even suggested a more likely source of bias, namely that, since members of the Disciplinary Committee were all solicitors, they might have been moved by some fellow-feeling for a member of the fraternity in trouble: a natural "there by the grace of God go I" sentiment. (However, *Vakauta v Kelly*[17] is an Australian case affording a rare example in which it was the official side which succeeded in a "no bias" claim.) A related point is that while, in principle, judicial review is against some public body, there will frequently be indirect consequences against another private party, who will seldom be able to claim compensation for the loss which they have suffered, by virtue of the delay caused by a voyage to the Superior Courts, or reputational damage.[18]

13–10 Secondly, the remainder of this chapter focuses on the element of a public body which is, or may be thought to be, biased. But, is it not relevant that many members or staff of the public body may be free of all such taint? Frequently, this

---

[15] [2009] IEHC 470 at para.37. On this point, see also *Bane v GRA* [1997] 2 I.R. 449 at 472, in which Kelly J. stated: "… take a homely example. Suppose that a member of the judiciary had a dispute with his or her neighbour which resulted in legal proceedings in which both gave evidence. Suppose further that there was a conflict of evidence between them which was resolved in favour of the judge and the neighbour was later prosecuted for giving false evidence to the court. Would it be appropriate for that criminal trial to be presided over by the judge …? I venture to think not." The strongest lesson which emerges from this example (which, with respect, is plainly correct) is that the circumstances are all-important; the circumstances in the example were rather extreme and the position of the judge-witness was a long way from the position of the nurse-witness in *O'Ceallaigh*.

[16] [1960] I.R. 239 at 272.

[17] (1989) 167 C.L.R. 568 at 585. The case arose out of a very aggressive comment made by a trial judge to an expert witness in a case of assessment of damages for personal injury. The judge, before hearing the evidence of the appellant's medical witnesses, referred to them as "an unholy trinity." He continued that they belonged to "the usual panel of doctors who think you can do a full week's work without arms or legs" whose "views are almost inevitably slanted by the [Government Insurance Office] by whom they have been retained consciously or unconsciously". The High Court of Australia, with one dissenting judgment, ordered that the judgment of the trial judge be set aside.

[18] *Bula Ltd v Tara Mines (No. 6)* [2000] 4 I.R. 412.

difficulty will not arise because, to take the extreme case, the entity under review may be made up of only one person, as is often the case in a court of law. But, even if the decision is taken by a multi-member board or committee, it has always been assumed that, where only one member is suspected of bias, decisions of the entire entity are invalid.[19] Many variations might be conjectured. For example, if appeals officer A, in Donegal, has a personal grudge against an applicant for Social Welfare Benefit, whose claim is rejected in County Cork by appeals officer X, then (leaving aside the unlikely possibility that the applicant reasonably believes that A had something to do with the decision), presumably the applicant has nothing of which to complain. The broad point is that the test is whether a reasonable person, in the position of the applicant, would have had a suspicion of bias. As yet, we have had no case going into this issue. But a case could quite easily arise in which a court would have to decide what level of knowledge to impute to the applicant, regarding the workings of a public body. This would depend, amongst other things, upon the level of information regarding its work which the body involved had given to the public.

B. Sources of Bias

13–11   So far, we have focused mainly on the differences drawn between subjective bias, that is whether the person affected could reasonably suspect bias, or, on the other hand, "objective" (or "actual" or "real" bias). Later, we consider what the substantive difference is between these two approaches. But meanwhile we turn to the underlying question of the possible sources of bias. These are infinitely varied and the list of (four) categories given below is certainly not exhaustive. Moreover, the list is only intended for descriptive purposes since, with the possible exception of the first category, no legal consequences turn on the particular pigeon-hole to which a case is allocated.

Material interest

13–12   The most obvious source of bias is financial (or material) interest of which *People (Attorney General) v Singer*[20] is a straightforward example. In this case, the Court of Criminal Appeal ordered a re-trial on a fraud charge because the foreman of the jury had been an investor in the company which was the vehicle for the alleged fraud and was thus one of the victims. Interest was also found to have been present in *Connolly v McConnell*,[21] a case arising out of the dismissal of a general secretary of a trade union on the authority of the executive council

---

[19] *O'Driscoll v Law Society of Ireland* [2007] IEHC 352 at para.56. In *Dublin and County Broadcasting v IRTC*, unreported, High Court, May 12, 1989, Murphy J. noted that, under the Act, the Commission must have seven to 10 members; yet he stated that if even one of the members were affected by bias, this would invalidate the Commission's decision. See, to similar effect, *Connolly v McConnell* [1983] I.R. 172.

[20] [1975] I.R. 408 (decided in 1963). In some cases, there is a statutory disqualification: see, e.g. s.856(1), Pt 37 of the Taxes Consolidation Act 1997 (special commissioner for income tax disqualified from adjudicating on his own personal tax liability).

[21] [1983] I.R. 172. Interest was found not to exist on the facts in *State (Divito) v Arklow U.D.C.* [1986] I.L.R.M. 123, where the respondent's refusal of a gaming licence to the applicant company was under challenge. Henchy J. found that there were no "financial or other connections" between the council and a rival company such as "would be likely to deflect

of the union. This dismissal was found to be void, as some of the members of the council had financial or other interests in the outcome of the disciplinary hearing. For example, one of the charges involved the defendant's disobedience to an order of the plaintiff trade union to pay a recoupment of expenses to a member of the executive council.

13–13 Again, in *Doyle v Croke*[22] an employer, whose company was drifting towards liquidation, paid £360,000 in settlement of an official strike. The strike committee decided that this fund was to be divided equally among the former employees, who had adequately performed picket duty. As a result, the committee drew up a list of 150 persons (out of a workforce of about 270) who were to participate in the distribution of these monies. However, in a case brought by 83 of the disappointed employees, the procedure was held to be invalid because, inter alia, according to Costello J., "[a]ll the members of the strike committee were former employees of Irish Meat Producers Limited and as such had a financial interest in the settlement …".[23]

13–14 An unsuccessful claim occurred in the case of *Dublin and County Broadcasting Ltd v Independent Radio and Television Commission*[24] which arose out of the allocation of contracts to provide sound broadcasting services, under the privately owned broadcasting régime created by the former Radio and Television Act 1988. To discharge the duty of selecting contractors, the Act constituted the Independent Radio and Television Commission (the precursor of the Broadcasting Association of Ireland), which was chaired by a former Supreme Court judge, Mr Justice Henchy. In the present action, which was brought by the only serious contender among the unsuccessful applicants for a contract, the plaintiff's major argument was that the Commission's decision in regard to the contract was void because Mr O'Donovan, one of the ordinary members of the Commission, was biased.

13–15 Mr O'Donovan's interest stemmed from the fact that he had been involved with E-Sat Television Ltd. The pecuniary aspect of Mr O'Donovan's alleged involvement lay in the fact that he had owned some £30,000 worth of shares in E-Sat which owned 70 per cent of the shares in one of the successful companies. However, about a year before the contract was awarded, he had sought to transfer these shares. In fact, as a matter of strict law concerning the assignment of shares, Murphy J. accepted that, unknown to Mr O'Donovan, he had retained some residual legal (but not beneficial or equitable) rights in the shares. However, Murphy J.'s crucial ruling was that:

> "Mr. O'Donovan had sought to divest himself of his shares in E-Sat, and he bona fide believed he had successfully done so. I would also accept that the

---

the council from fairness or even-handedness in their dealings with the applicant – or such as would be likely to lead a reasonable person to think that the Council would thus act."

[22] Unreported, High Court, May 6, 1988.
[23] Unreported, High Court, May 6, 1988 at 19–20. Cp. *Henry V* (the evening before the Battle of Agincourt): "The fewer men, the greater share of glory".
[24] Unreported, High Court, May 12, 1989.

vast majority of people would believe that such was the case and he could not as a matter of law or honour resile from the action he had taken."[25]

13–16   A theme which has not yet been fully developed but which may have some potential for growth applies where, for example, an applicant for planning permission, effectively as part of the transaction, gives some land or money to the local planning authority. Is there not a potential for bias here? This point was raised in Hardiman J.'s judgment in *Ashbourne Holdings v An Bord Pleanála*.[26]

Personal attitudes, relationships, beliefs

13–17   Bias may arise from the decision-maker's personal attitudes, relationships, or beliefs in the case. However, as noted in paras 13–05 to 13–07, there is developing a strong line of authority, to the effect that the fact that a party and a decision-maker happen incidentally to belong to the same grouping, will not suffice to ground a suspicion of bias, unless it is accompanied by particular circumstances. Nevertheless, in a number of clear cases, personal hostility has been found to be present. For example, in *R. (Donoghue) v Cork County JJ.*[27] a conviction imposed by a magistrate who had remarked shortly after a case that he "would not leave any member of the [accused's] family in the district" was quashed on this ground. Similarly, in *R. (Kingston) v Cork County JJ.*[28] an evicted farmer brought charges of assault against the purchaser of the farm. The charges arose out of a boycott which had been imposed on the purchaser by the United Irish League. The purchaser was convicted of assault by a magistrates' bench of four, including two members of the League, who had attended the meeting where the decision to impose the boycott had been taken. The High Court had little difficulty in quashing the conviction. In another case, a conviction in a rape trial was quashed on the basis that the jury had drawn the trial court's attention to the fact that one of the jurors had suffered a similar experience of sexual abuse.[29]   One type of association which might be suspect is where the decision-maker is a former professional adviser to one of the parties. Since this has arisen—so far—only where the decision-maker was a judge, who was formerly the lawyer of one of the parties, it is discussed below at Part E.

13–18   Family relationships have produced surprisingly few cases. However, *O'Reilly v Judge Cassidy (No. 1)*[30] involved a situation in which a Circuit Court judge was the father not of a party but of counsel for a party who was objecting

---

[25]   Unreported, High Court, May 12, 1989 at 16–17.

[26]   [2003] 2 I.R 114 at 138–139. See also, *North Wall v Dublin Docklands Development Authority* [2008] IEHC 305 at para.101.

[27]   [1910] 2 I.R. 271. For a case where judicial conduct was thought to "reasonably give rise in the mind of an unprejudiced observer to the suspicion that justice was not being done", see *Dineen v Delap* [1994] 2 I.R. 228 at 234 per Morris J. See also, *McDonough v Minister for Defence* [1991] I.L.R.M. 115 at 120 per Lavan J.: "… the Commanding Officer's decision to delegate Captain Holmes to conduct the interview [was unreasonable] having regard to the applicant's complaints against that Officer."

[28]   [1910] 2 I.R. 658. See also, *R. (Harrington) v Clare JJ.* [1918] 2 I.R. 116. For cases on the other side of the line, see *R. (Findlater) v Dublin JJ.* [1904] 2 I.R. 75 and *R. (Tavener) v Tyrone JJ.* [1909] 2 I.R. 763. For other examples occurring during the course of the famous *Sinn Féin Funds* case, see Hogan, "The *Sinn Féin Funds* judgment 50 years on" (1997) *Bar Review* 375 at 379.

[29]   *People (Director of Public Prosecutions) v Tobin* [2001] 3 I.R. 469 at 478–479.

[30]   [1995] 1 I.L.R.M. 306 at 309. Surprisingly, in *O'Reilly (No. 1)*, leave to apply for judicial

to the grant of a liquor licence. Although in the circumstances granting leave to apply for judicial review, Finlay C.J. remarked, surprisingly, that "[i]f no objection is taken to any (such) relationship ... there could be no conceivable impropriety in a judge continuing to hear a case."

13–19 There were subsequent proceedings in the High Court, *O'Reilly v Cassidy (No. 2)*[31] and in these proceedings Flood J. noted that, apart from the relationship, there were other factors present, including the respondent's behaviour in court. In finding for the applicant, Flood J. remarked that "... the mere fact of the judge's daughter being briefed before him is (not) sufficient to give rise to the possibility of a reasonable man considering that bias could follow ... To accept [this submission] would be to derogate [*sic*] from the oath made ... by every judge on appointment to a totally empty formula." One might comment that young advocates need to build up a practice and that the reasonable person may take the view that blood is thicker than water.[32] It seems likely that these judicial pronouncements will not represent the last word on this subject.[33]

13–20 A different type of what (the Supreme Court held) may have appeared to an "unprejudiced onlooker" as personal involvement occurred in *State (Hegarty) v Winters*.[34] Here an arbitrator appointed under the Acquisition of Land (Assessment of Compensation) Act 1919 was assessing the amount of compensation to be awarded to the applicant land owner for damage done to his land by a county council. The arbitrator went to inspect the land himself and was accompanied by the county council engineer with nobody to represent the applicant. The court quashed the arbitrator's award.

13–21 Another obvious instance of bias would be party political advantage in the context of a Minister (usually the Minister for Environment) taking decisions in regard to elections. The point was made obliquely but clearly in *Dillon v Minister for Posts and Telegraphs*[35] in which the plaintiff was a Dáil candidate yet the Minister would not allow him to circulate his election brochure free of charge to the voters on the ground that some of the material which it contained did not relate to the election. Henchy J. said:

> "[T]he expression 'matter relating to the election only' should be liberally

---

review had been refused by the High Court and it was necessary for the applicant to appeal (successfully) to the Supreme Court.

[31] *O'Reilly v Cassidy (No. 2)* [1995] 1 I.L.R.M. 311. The quotation is at 319.

[32] The Irish version is slightly different, "Fuilngeann fuil fuil i ngorta ach ni fhuilngeann fuil fuil a dhortadh" translates as "blood allows blood to go hungry but blood will not allow blood to be spilt". We are indebted to Professor Seán Ó Coileáin for this.

[33] See also, the rather extreme facts of *O'Brien v Tribunal of Inquiry* [2010] 4 I.R. 761, in which the applicant contended that the respondent was objectively biased in retaining M as their counsel, on the basis that M had conflict of interest arising out of his former capacity as a member of the Dáil and a Government Minister. The court held that, given the nature of adversarial proceedings, it was only in the most exceptional circumstances that barristers might be excluded under the rules relating to bias.

[34] [1956] I.R. 320. See also, *State (Horgan) v Exported Livestock Insurance Board* [1943] I.R. 600; *State (Fagan) v Governor of Mountjoy Prison*, unreported, High Court, March 6, 1978.

[35] Unreported, Supreme Court, June 3, 1981. The type of point discussed in the text does not appear to have been canvassed in *State (Lynch) v Cooney* [1982] I.R. 337.

construed. This is particularly so when, as in this case, the person seeking to block the free postal circulation of the plaintiff's election brochure is a member of the Dáil and whose party leader is seeking re-election to the Dáil in the same constituency as the plaintiff has chosen to contest."

13–22 The idea that a pre-determined belief or outlook[36] might give rise to a reasonable suspicion of bias was successfully invoked in *Dublin Well-Woman Centre Ltd v Ireland*.[37] In this case the plaintiff applied in the High Court to have an earlier injunction (restraining them from providing information about abortion services abroad) lifted in the light of the enactment of the Fourteenth Amendment of the Constitution Act 1994.[38] When the action came on for hearing before Carroll J. in the High Court, the judge refused to discharge herself from the hearing of the action, despite the fact that, in her capacity as Chairwoman of the Commission for the Status of Women (an official body), she had made a written submission to the government regarding the availability of abortion information. When Carroll J. refused to discharge herself, the notice party appealed successfully to the Supreme Court.

Loyalty to the institution and its policy

13–23 In this section, we deal, first, with situations involving broad policies, before turning to cases concerning narrower institutional interests. An aspect which, at first sight, might have been expected to attract more attention than it has received arises from the fact that many administrative agencies involve an intermingling of governmental functions. Thus, they are responsible for developing and executing policy in a significant field of public administration; and the policy would be very much "their policy", on the success or failure of which they might be judged, possibly at an election. At the same time, they must adjudicate on situations in which there is a tension between the smooth running of the administrative machine in implementing the policy; and the interests of individuals whose rights are adversely affected.[39]

13–24 The most unequivocal way of avoiding any such conflict would be to vest the policy function in one body and adjudication in an independent body. The best known example of this is in the field of land use planning. Here, the policy function is vested in a local planning authority (reserved function), whilst the (appellate) adjudicator is An Bord Pleanála. But, frequently, such a split will not be adopted, either on the grounds of cost or the convenience of having all the expertise in a single public body. Also important is the fact that the two functions sometimes go

---

[36] This is distinguished from the cases covered below (in "(iii) Prior involvement and pre-judgment of the issues"), on the basis that the decision-maker was involved in the particular case coming before him, rather than the general "cause" of the institution. Admittedly, this is a fine line.

[37] [1995] 1 I.L.R.M. 408; [1999] 2 W.L.R. 272. See also, Jones, "Judicial bias and disqualification in the *Pinochet* case" (1999) *Public Law* 391; Williams, "Bias; the judges and the separation of powers" (2000) *Public Law* 45. But, *a contra*, see *McNally v District Judge Martin* [1995] 1 I.L.R.M. 350.

[38] This provides that nothing in Art.40.3.3° (the "pro-life" provision) shall limit "freedom to obtain or make available, in the State, subject to such conditions as may be prescribed by law, information relating to services lawfully available in another State."

[39] Several examples were given in Ch.6 on Tribunals at paras 6–24 to 6–28.

well together, in that policy is often best made not as a separate operation but rather on a case by case basis: it is easier to work out policy in the context of actual cases, in order to know where the shoe pinches. And this no doubt is the reason why there are so many of what may be regarded as "policy-orientated" tribunals. In addition, it bears emphasis that a public administrator (in contrast to, say, a private individual or company) is, directly or indirectly, responsible to all members of the public, including the individual whose rights may be adversely affected. Thus, its policy and the way that it is administered will usually be sensitive to individual rights, even if this interferes with the institution's own interests, so that no reasonable suspicion of bias will usually arise.

13–25   However (without dragging in the separation of powers), the following type of argument has occasionally come before a court: would the fact that a public body has devised and applies a policy make it so impatient of anyone whose interests stand in the way of the policy that it would be incapable of giving a fair hearing to applicants affected? In other words, would the "no bias" principle be violated? The short answer is: "no" (or "only in extreme cases"). In cases where this issue has been addressed, expressly or implicitly, the courts have shown themselves to be sensitive to the difficulties faced by a public body pursuing a broad policy which has been designed to balance up a number of interests. In addition, if the courts were to intervene, the effect would be that the courts could be required to impose their views to divert a policymaker from applying a considered policy, with all types of knock-on effects from such a judicial ruling.[40]

13–26   An argument of the type under consideration here was rejected by Keane C.J. in *Mulcreevy v Minister for the Environment*.[41] The facts were that the validity of ministerial consents (under the National Monuments Acts 1930–1994) to the carrying out of works (construction of a motorway) impacting on archaeology at Carrickmines Castle was challenged. The ground for the challenge was that the ground for the procedure involved the Minister granting an approval in respect of his own order. However, despite the fact that this was only an application for leave, it was rejected (again) by Keane C.J. brusquely[42]:

---

[40]   One should note that this suspicion of bias might be claimed to arise at either of two stages, first where the policy is being made and secondly where it is being applied. The classic case of the first type is *Franklin v Minister of Town and Country Planning* [1948] A.C. 87, discussed in Wade and Forsyth, *Administrative Law*, 10th edn (Oxford: OUP, 2009), pp.411–412; Wade, "'Quasi-judicial' and its Background" (1949) 10 C.L.J. 216. This case arose out of the establishment of Stevenage as the first of the post-war new towns under the New Towns Act 1946. Before the Minister confirmed the designation order, he had addressed a hot public meeting in Stevenage. Responding to vigorous heckling including the epithet "Gestapo" he responded, "It is no good your jeering, it is going to be done". The English courts reached the conclusion that this did not necessarily mean that the Minister would be biased, at the time when he returned to his desk to consider signing the order.
[41]   [2004] 1 I.L.R.M. 419.
[42]   [2004] 1 I.L.R.M. 419 at 437. In this passage, Keane C.J. was presumably referring to his own decision in *O'Brien v Bord na Móna* [1983] I.R. 255 at 269, quoting O'Higgins C.J. in *Loftus v Attorney General* [1979] I.R. 229. The present argument—"no bias"—was not mentioned in the Supreme Court in *O'Brien*, where the plaintiff won the case on a different (*audi alteram partem*) point.
       With respect, the last part of the passage in the text (from "accordingly, the power …" onward) seems to go much further than is warranted by O'Higgins C.J.'s reasoning in *O'Brien*. This difficult passage, in *O'Brien*, seems to conflate the Art.34.1 issue and the "no bias" principle. Having concluded that Bord na Móna was not exercising the judicial function,

"That argument, however, is wholly at variance with the law as stated by this court in *O'Brien v Bord na Móna* [1983] IR 255; [1983] ILRM 314. In that case, it was held that Bord na Mona, in deciding whether to reject objections to a compulsory purchase of lands on which they had decided and which they were bound by statute to consider before proceeding with the acquisition were not exercising a judicial power within the ambit of Article 34 of the Constitution and that, accordingly, the power given to the board was not vitiated, since the *nemo iudex* principle had no necessary application to administrative procedures of that nature."

13–27   *Lovejoy v Attorney General*[43] offered a further example of an argument founded on a danger of a public body being swayed by loyalty to its own policy. The applicant challenged provisions of the Refugee Act 1996 on the basis, inter alia, that the Minister for Justice was an inappropriate person to have powers in the area of refugees, because he also controls immigration and other related areas. Birmingham J. rejected the submission (in a paragraph which seems to overlook the fact that constitutional justice has been grounded in the Constitution):

"The question of an asylum system is, therefore, an integral part of the immigration policy of this State or any other state. In those circumstances, the international experience is that it is not at all unusual for Ministers for Justice or Ministers for the Interior or Home Secretaries – however they are described – to be the member of government charged with responsibility in this area. Even as we speak, the newspapers report today that the Ministers for Justice of the European Union are gathering to discuss these issues in Cannes."

13–28   Turning away from questions of broad policy, we find that the other cases in this area have been founded on a claim that the respondent has some narrower institutional interest of its own, which would mean that the "no bias" principle has been violated. Circumstances have been rather varied and the outcomes of the cases hard to reconcile, though it can be said that, with some exceptions,[44] the judges have been sensitive to the difficulties of public bodies in this matter.[45] A typical

---

O'Higgins C.J. did state that it would have a duty "to act fairly and properly" (at 282; see also, 283). This would seem to mean at most a reduced level of the "no bias" principle.

[43]   [2008] IEHC 225; High Court, ex tempore, Birmingham J.

[44]   *Ó Cléirígh v Minister for Agriculture* [1996] 2 I.L.R.M. 12 at 15, critiqued in the Third Edition, pp.519–520. See also, *Davitt v Minister for Justice*, unreported, High Court, Barron J., February 8, 1989 at pp.7–8. *Ardagh v Maguire* [2002] 1 I.R. 385; *Application of Sean Leonard*, unreported, High Court, D'Arcy J., June 30, 1981; unreported, Supreme Court, December 15, 1982. But see now the Registration of Deeds and Titles Act 2006 s.69(b). See further, McAllister, *Registration of Title* (Dublin: Incorporated Council of Law Reporting for Ireland, 1973), p.302; Fitzgerald, *Land Registry Practice* (Dublin: Round Hall Press, 1989), p.248. See, also, *Damache v DPP*, unreported, Supreme Court, Denham C.J., February 2012, para.54: "A member of An Garda Síochána who is part of an investigating team is not independent on matters related to the investigation." (The case centred on the issue of a warrant by a superintendent, under the Criminal Law Act 1976 s.29).

[45]   See Keane J. in *State (Comer) v Minister of Justice*, unreported, High Court, December 19, 1980 (where he said that the principle of *nemo iudex* "could not be literally applied" to an adjudication by the prison authorities as to whether a prison officer was guilty of neglect of his duties); *Collins v County Cork VEC*, unreported, High Court, May 26, 1982; and *State*

case, *Corcoran*,[46] is outlined in Chapter 6. The facts were that the Garda Síochána Complaints Board had issued a press release complaining about the lack of co-operation it had received from Gardaí, in an investigation into Garda behaviour in quelling a demonstration. It was held, nevertheless, that the Garda Disciplinary Tribunal, which was under the auspices of the Board, was not biased against the actual Gardaí before it.

13–29 There is one rather narrow and particular group of cases[47] in which it has been unsuccessfully submitted that various categories of prosecutor were biased, because of their links with a public body, which public body had been the alleged victim of a crime by the applicant. This was an attempt to extend the doctrine, inasmuch as it was the prosecutor, rather than the actual decision-maker, who was involved; and whilst this was not mentioned in the judgments, this consideration may have been regarded as the reason why these claims failed.[48]

Prior involvement and pre-judgment of the issues

13–30 This source will often be interwoven with "(iii) Loyalty to the institution and its policy" above (since prior involvement will often arise because some institution is so structured that the same person is concerned at two stages of the decision-making process); or even with "(ii) Personal attitudes, relationships, beliefs".[49]

(McEldowney) v Kelleher [1983] I.R. 289 at 299 (High Court); *BFO v Governor of Dochas Centre* [2005] 2 I.R. 1 at 25.

[46] *Corcoran v Holmes* [2007] 1 I.L.R.M. 23. See further, paras 6–27 to 6–29 and 6–64.

[47] In *Scariff v Taylor* [1996] 1 I.R. 242 at 262–263, Denham J. stated that the *audi alteram partem* rule does not apply to a decision to prosecute. See too, *Flynn v Director of Public Prosecutions* [1986] I.L.R.M. 290 at 295 (but see also later proceedings, arising out of the same episode, *Flynn v An Post* [1987] I.R. 68, in which McCarthy J., who had sat on the bench in the earlier proceedings remarked (at 84): "[i]n my view, [the present] case shows that [the DPP's retention of An Post's solicitor] though legally proper, may, in practice, be unwise"). See also, *Hughes v Garda Commissioner*, unreported, High Court, July 23, 1996 (appointment of investigating officer under Garda Síochána (Discipline) Regulations 1989 by a Chief Superintendent who was also the complainant was held by McCracken J. to be "quite undesirable", but did not of itself invalidate the inquiry). See also, the comments of O'Sullivan J. in the subsequent judicial review arising from this case: *McAuley v Chief Superintendent Keating*, unreported, High Court, July 8, 1997; *Barry v Medical Council* [1998] 3 I.R. 368 at 382–387, 397–398.

In this context, see also environmental legislation: Local Government (Water Pollution) (Amendment) Act 1990 s.26; Environmental Protection Agency Act 1992 s.10 in which encouragement is given to prosecute for an offence, by a provision that, on the application of the prosecuting authority, any fine must be paid to the prosecutor.

[48] A rather tenuous claim of bias failed in *Murray v Commission to Inquire into Child Abuse* [2004] 2 I.R. 222 at para.173, where it was suggested that bias arose when a public inquiry gave advice in regard to the drafting of the legislation which governed its constitution and procedures.

[49] An example of this may be the hypothetical case mentioned by McMahon J. in *State (Fagan) v Governor of Mountjoy Prison*, unreported, High Court, March 6, 1978. Confusion is further confounded by the fact that, in certain circumstances, there may be pre-judgment because the decision is regarded as having been more or less taken by some other body, e.g. a sub-committee as in *Clancy v IRFU* [1995] 1 I.L.R.M. 193 at 199–200. On a further point of characterisation, it is even difficult to know whether to classify this flaw under the present rubric or under that of failure to exercise a discretion, by virtue of delegation or acting under the dictation of another body.

13–31   The situation in which an institution is so structured that the same person is involved at two stages of the same serpentine bureaucratic process is illustrated by *Heneghan v Western Regional Fisheries Board*,[50] in which the dismissal of a fisheries inspector was set aside because the prime mover in the dismissal process had acted as "witness, prosecutor, judge, jury and appeal court."[51] A slightly less extreme case is *Flanagan v University College Dublin*.[52] Before the three-member committee of discipline, the Registrar of the University acted as prosecutor. The accused student and her two representatives were then asked to retire. The Registrar and his principal assistant remained with the Committee. When the student and her representatives returned, they were informed that the alleged plagiarism would be sent to an independent expert to assess, a course to which she agreed. The choice of an independent assessor was left to the Registrar as was both the consultation with the relevant Professors who assisted in this choice and the correspondence with the assessor. The applicant was not involved in the selection process. All this was stigmatised as bias by Barron J. in the High Court. And in *Prendiville v Medical Council*,[53] the principle of "no bias" was held to be violated when the five members of the Fitness to Practice Committee took part in the meeting of the Medical Council (of which they were also members) which confirmed the Committee's recommendation regarding professional misconduct.[54]

13–32   As a matter of principle, it seems objectionable that a decision-maker exercising quasi-judicial functions should sit with an appellate body to hear an appeal against his own decision.[55] Statutory recognition of this is to be found in s.24 of the Courts of Justice Act 1924 which prohibits the judge who heard a case from sitting as a member of the court of appeal when the case at which he presided is being considered.[56]

---

[50]   [1986] I.L.R.M. 225 (upheld in the Supreme Court). See also, *O'Neill v Irish Hereford Breed Society Ltd* [1992] 1 I.R. 431 at 452. *A contra: McAuley v Chief Superintendent Keating*, unreported High Court, July 8, 1997.

[51]   [1986] I.L.R.M. 225 at 229. See also, *O'Donoghue v Veterinary Council* [1975] I.R. 398 and *Bane v Garda Representative Association* [1997] 2 I.R. 449, in each of which the charges against the applicant were actually instigated by the decision-maker.

[52]   [1988] I.R. 724. For a similar factual situation to *Flanagan*, with a similar outcome, see *Prendiville v Medical Council* [2008] 3 I.R. 122 at paras 122–125 and 130–144. See, rather similarly, *Khan v Health Service Executive* [2008] IEHC 234 at 3, 8.

[53]   [2008] 3 I.R. 122 at paras 122–125, 144. The statutory arrangements have been changed by the Medical Practitioners Act 2007 ss.70–71, so that it is now the Fitness to Practice Committee which takes the decision regarding professional misconduct, leaving only the penalty to the Medical Council.

[54]   For another case in which objective bias was held to exist, see *Tomlinson v Criminal Injuries Compensation Tribunal* [2006] 4 I.R. 321 at para.18 (discussed at H & M, para 13–51). For cases on the other side of the line, see *Philips v Medical Council* [1992] I.L.R.M. 469 at 475 and *Barry v Medical Council* [1998] 3 I.R. 368 at 382–387, 397–398.

[55]   For a rather strange example of this, see Irish Horseracing Industry Act 1994 s.45, as commented on at ICLSA Rel. 18–28.

[56]   Section 14 of the (former) Charities Act 1961 provided that any judicial members of the Commissioners for Charitable Bequests and Donations are not to be disqualified, on that account, from hearing charity cases. However, there is no equivalent of this provision in the new regime established by the Charities Act 2009; although, under the scheme established by the 2009 Act, a judge may be involved both as a member of the Charity Appeals Tribunal, and as a member of a court hearing an appeal from the Tribunal: 2009 Act s.75(2). Any difficulty of the type discussed here would thus have to be settled by general law.

13–33   There are a number of administrative mechanisms in which it has been found convenient that a selection of personnel to deal with one stage of an administrative process is made by a personage who is also directly involved at another stage of the same process. The example which came up in *O'Reilly v Lee*[57] was that, under the Solicitors Acts 1954–2002, it is for the President of the High Court, as part of his supervision of certain aspects of the discipline of solicitors, to appoint, from among a group formally nominated by the Law Society, certain solicitor members of the Solicitors Disciplinary Tribunal. In *O'Reilly*, the applicant submitted that, because of this connection, the President of the High Court might be regarded as objectively biased in hearing an appeal from a decision of that Tribunal. Rejecting this argument rather tersely, Macken J. (on behalf of the Supreme Court) stated:

> "[the President of the High Court] carries out his function as the properly named appointing party pursuant to legislation, and on no other basis. The mere fact that he does so could not, and would not in my view, lead a reasonable person to have a reasonable apprehension that the appellant would not get a fair hearing on an appeal from the Solicitors Disciplinary Tribunal …".[58]

13–34   It may be significant that what is at issue at the initial stage is often only whether a prima facie case has been made out. This was the situation in *O'Callaghan v Disciplinary Tribunal*[59] in which the same person sat at both the prima facie and substantive stages of the Solicitors Disciplinary Tribunal. The Supreme Court rejected the applicant's claim of apparent or objective bias fairly readily.

Reconsideration of invalid decisions

13–35   There is a problem which commonly confronts the legal adviser to a public body in the wake of successful judicial review proceedings. If, for example, it was a procedural point on which the applicant succeeded, it was quite likely that repeat proceedings will come before the same forum which has already heard and decided the initial proceedings. In this situation, is there not a danger of prejudice arising from prior involvement and pre-judgment against an applicant who has dragged the public body through a judicial review? This can be substantially reduced, if it can be arranged that the personnel of the forum is different from that of the initial hearing.[60]

---

[57]   [2008] 4 I.R. 269. See also, *Kelly v Visitors of Trinity College Dublin* [2007] IESC 61; unreported, Supreme Court, December 14, 2007, referred to in *O'Reilly* at para.28.

[58]   [2008] 4 I.R. 269 at para.29.

[59]   [2002] 1 I.R. 1. (One of the precedents examined in *O'Callaghan* was *Corrigan v ILC* [1977] I.R. 317, which is discussed in the Third Edition, p.527.) See also, *Tomlinson v Criminal Injuries Compensation Tribunal* [2006] 4 I.R. 321.

[60]   As, for instance, when Mrs Kiely's three appeals were each heard by different appeals officers, in order to avoid the danger contemplated in the text. See *Kiely v Minister for Social Welfare (No. 2)* [1977] I.R. 267 at 270, 276. See also, *Doyle v Kildare County Council* [1995] 2 I.R. 424 at 432. In *Potts v Minister for Defence* [2005] 2 I.L.R.M. 517 at 527, it was noted that, to avoid any perception of bias, if a disciplinary matter arises in the Defence Forces in which the accused's commanding officer would be the arbiter, it is normal practice, where a commanding officer has a prior involvement in the case, for the accused to be attached to a

13–36 But circumstances may be such that this is not possible. In this situation, further proceedings may or may not be lawful. A case in which this difficulty was discussed (though necessarily only obiter) is *McAuley v Garda Commissioner*,[61] a case where a trainee Garda had his contract terminated in a manner which clearly violated the guarantee of fair procedure. The Supreme Court declined to restrain the Garda authorities from conducting a fresh inquiry. Hamilton C.J. observed that such an order would have the effect of:

> "... depriving the Commissioner of the power to and responsibility of terminating the training of the applicant if after an inquiry or investigation conducted in accordance with fair procedure he formed the opinion that the applicant was unsuitable for continued employment as a trainee by reason of misconduct ... It cannot be assumed that such an inquiry would not be conducted in accordance with fair procedure. If it were, the decision made on foot thereof would be subject to judicial review."[62]

It seems probable that there was a generous measure of the necessity doctrine hanging over *McAuley*.

C. Standards for Bias: The "Reasonable Suspicion" Test

13–37 The Third Edition of this book remarked, rather confidently,[63] that "[t]wo formulations of the test vie with each other in the common law world. The test which is more difficult for the applicant to satisfy is whether there is a real likelihood of bias. The alternative test is whether there is a reasonable suspicion of bias." The difference in principle between the tests was that the reasonable suspicion test is concerned centrally with the question of the confidence of the public in the integrity of their courts, tribunals or public administrators. Thus, the perspective from which the possibility of bias is examined is not what is likely to have happened, but rather the reasonable observer's perception of what happened. In other words, a particular "window",[64] through which the conduct must be viewed, is interposed.

13–38 But, as mentioned, of its nature, establishing "actual bias" directly must be very rare.[65] In most circumstances, even if one applies the real likelihood test,

---

different unit of the Defence Forces, so that the charge can be dealt with by the commanding officer of that unit.

[61] [1996] 3 I.R. 208. See also, *O'Shea v Garda Commissioner* [1994] 2 I.R. 408; *McAuley v Commissioner of An Garda Síochána* [1996] 3 I.R. 208; but contrast *Bane v Garda Representative Association* [1997] 2 I.R. 449 at 478, analysed in the Third Edition, pp.531–532.

[62] [1996] 3 I.R. 208 at 232. See, to similar effect, *Garvey v Minister for Justice, Equality and Law Reform* [2006] 1 I.R. 548 at 559.

[63] Third Edition, p.530. A good deal of the material in the Third edition, pp.525–534, has been omitted from the present edition.

[64] *Muir v Commissioner of Inland Revenue* [2007] 3 N.Z.L.R. 495 at 508.

[65] One of the few cases on record was identified by Geoghegan J. in *Orange (No. 2)* [2000] 4 I.R. 159 at para.14, where he referred to *Berger v United States* 255 U.S. 22 at 28–29 in which a trial judge had said about the accused, who was of German origin, "... one must have a very judicial mind indeed not be prejudiced against German-Americans in this country". One should add that the extreme situations which arise in the criminal world whereby an actus reus does not always prove a mens rea are inherently unlikely in the sphere of public administration.

the relevant evidence as to likelihood would, in most cases, be the circumstances, for example financial interest or family relationship, which would also give rise to reasonable suspicion. Thus, the two tests are not very different in result: most factors which would be relevant to one would be relevant to the other.[66] The only exceptions would be matters which a court establishes not to be so; although their intentions would not be known to a reasonable observer. The difference between the two would depend on how well-informed the reasonable observer is: the more well-informed the observer is conceived to be, the less difference between the two tests. But the reasonable observer, as explained below, is one of the law's gallery of lay figures; so that, while there may be some difference in angle, each test would be very much under the court's control. We shall return to this discussion, after considering some of the case law.

13–39 Traditionally, the preferred test was the "real likelihood" test[67]; more recently, the tide seems to have turned very strongly in favour of the reasonable suspicion test.[68] We consider first *Bula Ltd v Tara Mines Ltd (No. 6)*,[69] because it was in this case that the Supreme Court gave the most thorough consideration to the policy choice between the two tests. In *Bula (No. 6)*, the facts of which are given below, the Supreme Court came down in favour of the reasonable suspicion formulation. The two judges, Denham J. and McGuinness J., who gave substantive judgments, agreed that this test represents the law in Ireland. In the first place, each judge noted that the House of Lords in *R. v Gough*[70] had plumped for the "real danger of bias" test. The contrast between this test and the "reasonable suspicion" test had also been identified in the High Court of Australia case of *Webb v R* and in *Bula Ltd (No. 6)*. Denham J. quoted, with approval, from the passage in *Webb*, in which Mason C.J. and McHugh J. stated[71]:

> "In *Gough*, the House of Lords rejected the need to take account of the public perception of an incident, which raises an issue of bias except in the case of pecuniary interest. Behind this reasoning is the assumption that public confidence in the administration of justice will be maintained because the public will accept the conclusions of the judge. But the premise on which the decisions in *this* Court are based is that public confidence in the administration of justice is more likely to be maintained if the Court adopts a test that

---

[66] It is suggested that in the reverse situation—that is, where a factor suggesting bias, which had not been known earlier, has come to light at the judicial review stage, it should be taken into account: public confidence would naturally be affected by matters which were disclosed even at this late stage.

[67] *R. (Ellis) v Dublin Justices* [1894] 2 I.R. 527; *R. (Findlater) v Dublin Justices* [1904] 2 I.R. 75; *R. (Kingston) v Cork Justices* [1910] 2 I.R. 658.

[68] *State (Horgan) v Export Livestock Insurance Board* [1943] I.R. 600; *O'Donoghue v Veterinary Council* [1975] I.R. 398; *O'Neill v Beaumont Hospital Board* [1990] I.L.R.M. 419; *Dublin Wellwoman Centre v Ireland* [1995] 1 I.L.R.M. 408 at 420–421; *Bane v Garda Representative Association* [1997] 2 I.R. 449; *McAuley v Chief Superintendent Keating* [1998] 4 I.R. 138.

[69] [2000] 4 I.R. 412.

[70] [1993] A.C. 646. But note that recently there has been a modest adjustment to the *Gough* test to bring English law closer to other common law jurisdictions. For a good summary of law in this area, see Delany, *Judicial Review of Administrative Action* (Dublin: Round Hall, 2009), pp.231–233.

[71] (1993–1994) 181 C.L.R. 41 at 79. The passage is quoted in Denham J.'s judgment at [2000] 4 I.R. 412 at 439–440.

reflects the reaction of the ordinary reasonable member of the public to the irregularity in question."

13–40   In supporting the Australian Court's policy choice as between these two options, Denham J. stated[72]:

"The submissions in relation to the test to be applied roved worldwide. However, there is no need to go further than this jurisdiction [Ireland] where it is well established that the test to be applied is objective, it is whether a reasonable person in the circumstances would have a reasonable apprehension that the applicants would not have a fair hearing from an impartial judge on the issues. The test does not invoke the apprehension of the judge or judges. Nor does it invoke the apprehension of any party. It is an objective test – it invokes the apprehension of the reasonable person.

The requirement of a 'cogent and rational link' between the judge's past associations and the capacity of those associations 'to influence the decision to be made' seems to me to fulfil the requirement that the applicants' apprehension should be both reasonable and realistic and I respectfully adopt it as a correct analysis test in the present case."

13–41   While agreeing, McGuinness J. emphasised that the applicant's apprehension must be "reasonable and realistic".[73] This represents something of a bow in the direction of the "real likelihood" test and shows that there is some common ground between the two tests. And, by way of final observation, it may be said that whatever the wording of the test in the area of bias, in the actual results of such cases as *Dublin & County Broadcasting*, *Chestvale* and *Huntsgrove*, and the *Land Commission* cases,[74] most Irish judges have proved charitable towards the difficulties of public authorities. In relatively few of the cases cited in this Part has the applicant succeeded.

13–42   The question arises as to whether the standard set in the case applies generally to tribunals and other public bodies, or whether it should be confined to courts. It is true that, as regards the question of policy, on one view a higher standard should apply to judges who are the ultimate guardians of rectitude in the entire system of State laws and institutions. However for the following reasons, we are inclined to the view that it applies generally. First, this has been the view taken by the courts in later cases.[75] It is noticeable, too, that in *Bula (No. 6)* itself, the Supreme Court referred promiscuously to earlier precedents involving either tribunals or courts and certainly made no express distinction.[76] In addition,

---

[72]   [2000] 4 I.R. 412 at 441. For McGuinness J.'s view, to the same effect, see [2000] 4 I.R. 412 at 485. See also, *Orange (No. 2)* [2000] 4 I.R. 159 at 186 (Keane C.J.).

[73]   [2000] 4 I.R. 412 at 510.

[74]   See paras 13–20, 13–69 and 13–110.

[75]   *Spin Communications Ltd v IRTC* [2001] 4 I.R. 411 at 431, quoted with approval in *North Wall v Dublin Docklands Development Authority* [2008] IEHC 305 at paras 97–99. See also, *P v Judge McDonagh* [2009] IEHC 316; unreported, High Court, Clarke J., July 10, 2009 at para.7.5: "… nothing which I say should be considered as presenting any barrier to adjudicators (and in that context adjudicators includes judges), giving indications as to questions … which are causing concern to the adjudicator …".

[76]   *Bula Ltd (No. 6)* [2000] 4 I.R. 412 at 518.

McGuinness J., in *Bula Ltd v Tara Mines Ltd (No. 6)*,[77] rejected the submission of counsel for the respondents that (because of the terms of the judicial oath) the public would be less ready to suspect bias in the case of a judge. But perhaps the clinching argument—against making any difference between the law, as it relates to judges and other decision-makers—is the practical fact that the rules are so broadly stated that it would be difficult to articulate a precise difference of standards. As indicated, in the next section, there is anyway something of a dual standard for different institutions, without dragging in a third level.

Limits to scope of "reasonable suspicion" test

13–43 Before going on to consider further detail in respect of the reasonable suspicion standard, one should notice a probable qualification of the scope of the principle: there has been significant judicial support for the notion of distinguishing between judicial or quasi-judicial functions and, on the other hand, administrative functions. The significance of this distinction would be that a less strict form of the rule against bias would apply in the case of administrative functions. This point is illustrated by *Aziz v Midland Health Board*,[78] where Barr J. stated that while the Health Board was obliged to abide by fair procedure, a non-judicial body "such as a ... health board has no obligation to apply formal court procedures in the investigation and determination of disciplinary charges brought against an employee or officer holder."

13–44 Similarly, in *O'Brien v Bord na Móna*,[79] the plaintiff challenged the compulsory acquisition of a large portion of his farm. In the system of compulsory acquisition created by the Turf Development Act 1946, both the drawing up of a provisional list of land to be acquired and the hearing of objections to the inclusion of land on that list was vested in the defendant. It was argued that the fact that the Board had drawn up the provisional list meant that it might be thought of as prejudiced at the second stage of the hearing. However, following a review of the provisions of the Act, the Supreme Court concluded that the Board's functions were administrative in nature as they entailed the "balancing of the desirability of the production of turf on the one hand, and the interest of an individual owner of land on the other ...". Accordingly, whilst the Board could not act from "an indirect or improper motive or without due fairness of procedure", a less stringent standard was required than in the case of persons or bodies exercising judicial function A related trend at any rate used to hold that the less stringent, real likelihood, test (or something like it) should be operated, where the source of bias impacts at an early stage of what may be a protracted administrative process.[80]

---

[77] [2000] 4 I.R. 412 at 512. Though this argument had been accepted in *O'Reilly v Judge Cassidy (No. 2)* [1995] 1 I.L.R.M. 311 at 319.

[78] [1995] E.L.R. 48 at 56.

[79] [1983] I.R. 255. (See Coffey, "Procedural Curbs on powers of Compulsory Acquisition" (1984) 6 D.U.L.J. 152.) See also, *Collins v Cork County VEC*, unreported, High Court, May 26, 1982. This decision was affirmed by the Supreme Court on March 18, 1983, but this point was not dealt with. For other authority along the same lines, see *McCann v Racing Board* [1983] I.L.R.M. 67; *O'Neill v Beaumont Hospital Board* [1990] I.L.R.M. 419 at 437; *Aziz v Midland Health Board* [1995] E.L.R. 48 at 56; and *Radio Limerick v IRTC* [1997] 2 I.L.R.M. 1 at 25–56 per Keane J., which was followed in *M&J Gleeson v Competition Authority* [1999] 1 I.L.R.M. 401 at 423.

[80] *Huntsgrove Developments Ltd v Meath County Council* [1994] 2 I.L.R.M. 36. See, to similar

13–45   It is hard to reconcile the tone of these authorities with that of *North Wall v Dublin Docklands Development Authority*.[81] Here, the High Court (Finlay Geoghegan J.) ruled that the same test applied to both judicial and administrative bodies. This point had indeed been conceded by counsel for the respondents, with the consequence that the *Huntsgrove* line of authority was not argued. The case centred on the Dublin Docklands Development Authority Act 1997 s.25 (as amended), which empowers the Authority to issue a certificate to the effect that the carrying out of specified categories of development would be consistent with the relevant planning scheme. This carries the consequence that the developer might be able to go ahead without needing to go through the normal process, including objections from members of the public. The critical point here was that, just before a certificate was granted to a notice party in the case, who was a competitor of the applicant, the respondent Authority had entered into an agreement with the third party. This agreement was to the effect that, in the event of the respondent granting a certificate, the notice party agreed to transfer to the respondent some land to be used as a public open space.

13–46   As mentioned, the High Court ruled that "… the same 'reasonable apprehension' test applies to both judicial and administrative bodies",[82] and then went on to hold that the existence of the agreement gave rise to a reasonable apprehension that the respondent might have been biased. Yet, at the same time, Finlay Geoghegan J. went out of her way to emphasise that "… administrative bodies are subject to some limitation or exception in favour of a bias of necessity or structural bias, by reason of relevant statutory provisions." Because of this and because the earlier authorities were not referred to in this judgment, there remains a good deal to be resolved in future cases.

The "reasonable person": how well informed should he or she be taken to be?

13–47   A significant practical question is how well-informed[83] that rather hazy beastie, the "reasonable person", must be taken to be. On the one hand, according to Murphy J., they must not be "ill informed". But, on the other hand, it seems that there are certain "matters of fact"[84] which they must be taken not to know. Where is the line to be drawn? The passage quoted earlier from the *Dublin Well Woman Centre* case speaks sensibly enough of "a person in the position of the appellant", which suggests that it is only the facts which should have been known to the particular

---

effect, *Chestvale Properties v Glackin* [1993] 3 I.R. 35, outlined in the Third Edition, pp.528–529.

[81]   [2008] IEHC 305.

[82]   [2008] IEHC 305 at paras 98, 106. Notice also the following comment at paras 97 and 113: "There is, I recognise, a thin line between what appears permissible, namely discussions under which a developer might seek to ascertain from the executives whether or not they perceive any inconsistency with what is being applied for, [and, on the other hand] … the type of formal commitment by the executives to make a particular recommendation which appears impermissible."

[83]   Atrill, "Who is the 'Fair-Minded Observer': bias after *Magill*" [2003] C.L.J. 279.

[84]   *Dublin and County Broadcasting Ltd v Independent Radio and Television Commission*, unreported, High Court, May 12, 1989. The matters of fact referred to in the text included the fact that the supposed bias in this case did not actually exist. On this question, see also *Kenny v Trinity College Dublin* [2008] 2 I.R. 40 at 45.

applicant which may be taken into account. And in *Ryan v Law Society of Ireland*,[85] where the alleged bias lay in relation to the Solicitors Disciplinary Committee, the test enunciated in the High Court, was whether any reasonable solicitor could have thought that the Disciplinary Committee might have been influenced. Herbert J. focused on "… a reasonable person in the position of the applicant, with his special advantages of legal training and experience …".[86]

13–48 Further assistance in mapping out the lineaments of the reasonable person are to be found in Denham J.'s judgment in *Bula Ltd v Tara Mines Ltd (No. 6)*, the facts of which are given at para.13–59. The relevant passage is entitled "An independent bar" and includes an explanation of the detached position of a barrister, who is approached not directly by clients but via solicitors; and also of "the cab rank principle". The judge concluded,[87] "[t]he reasonable person would know that barristers are independent … They would know that they act for opposing sides in different cases e.g. for an accused one day and the Director of Public Prosecutions the next day." It may be asked whether a good deal is being expected of the "reasonable person" here: many people, for instance, are hazy even about the difference between solicitors and barristers. However, on the other hand, it may be reasonable and realistic to cast the hypothetical reasonable person as well informed, on the basis that the parties involved will usually have professional advisers to guide them.

13–49 At a general level, what the cases outlined in this section show is that the reasonable person is a hypothetical lay figure, designed by the judges to implement the policy of public confidence in the notion of judicial and public administration. How well-informed to make this personage represents a major policy choice. If they are too well informed, then the test is dragged in the direction of the "real likelihood" test and sacrifices the merit of maintaining the confidence of the lay public. On the other hand, if the observer created is badly informed, efficient administration is impaired, some undeserving applicant is given an unwarranted advantage, and incidentally public confidence is again lost. A final point is that our account has assumed that the facts, which become known to the reviewing court yet which were not known to the applicant, are facts which would reduce or remove the suspicion. What if the reverse is the case? Presumably, the facts should still be taken into account.

Bias must be "extraneous" to the decision

13–50 The principle here is that neither the egregious conduct of a decision-maker at a hearing, nor the perversity of their decision, may be taken as evidencing bias.[88]

---

[85] [2002] 4 I.R. 21 at 29, 37–38, 41–43.

[86] [2002] 4 I.R. 21 at 38.

[87] [2000] 4 I.R. 412 at 444. For McGuinness J., see [2000] 4 I.R. 412 at 517. No mention is made of the fact that a barrister's first duty, which is of honesty to the court, comes above that to the client. Presumably, the reasonable person is not to be taken to know this.

[88] *Orange v Director of Telecoms (No. 2)* [2000] 4 I.R. 159 at 250 (Geoghegan J.). See also, Barron J. at 271–272; and *Beades Construction v Dublin Corporation* [2005] IEHC 406; unreported, High Court, McKechnie J., September 7, 2005 at para.63. See also, *Radio Limerick v IRTC* [1997] 2 I.R. 291 and *Spin Communications Ltd v I.R.T.C.* [2001] 4 I.R. 411; [2002] 1 I.L.R.M. 98; *North Wall v Dublin Docklands Development Authority* [2008] IEHC 305 at para.101.

The reasoning underlying this precedent is that, by the basic principle of judicial review, a review court may not take cognisance of every minor or intermediate procedural flaw. The reasoning runs that if an applicant were allowed to rely upon the behaviour of the respondent during the process or hearing to deduce that there has been bias, then, in effect, this would be to allow entry at the side door, when the front portal is barred.

13–51   The reason for this rule is shown by the case of *O'Callaghan v Mahon (No. 2)*.[89] The applicants were seeking to restrain the Mahon Tribunal from investigating them, on the basis of bias. The background to the case was the earlier judicial review proceedings of *O'Callaghan v Mahon (No. 1)*.[90] Here the Supreme Court had held, unanimously, that despite the Tribunal's policy of confidentiality, documents and materials generated during the Tribunal's information-gathering phase must be disclosed to the applicant, since they were essential to carry out a worthwhile cross-examination of a witness who was in effect giving evidence against the applicant.

13–52   Basing themselves on the facts at the centre of *O'Callaghan (No. 1)*, the applicants in *O'Callaghan v Mahon (No. 2)*[91] submitted that the Tribunal's refusal to disclose documents was evidence upon which it could be established that the Tribunal was biased against the applicants. Accordingly, the applicants sought an order restraining the respondents from investigating them further. Thus, in the instant case, the applicant urged the court to examine the earlier decision of the respondent, refusing to disclose matters, in order to establish that the respondent's decision was of such a quality as to indicate pre-judgment. One of the majority judges in *O'Callaghan (No. 2)*, Denham J., noted that the applicant's grounding affidavit took some 14 pages and 48 paragraphs to detail a large number of individual complaints regarding the decisions of the Tribunal. Likewise, the other majority judgment, given by Fennelly J., noted that for a court to base its review on these complaints would[92] "… involve the Court in conducting a 'mini-tribunal'".

Appraisal

13–53   This rule is a newish doctrine which seems (as indicated earlier) to have been deduced from first principles, in the late 1990s. As representative of the earlier law, take two lower court cases. In *McNally v District Judge Martin*,[93] it was held that the respondent had displayed bias in that "*at the hearing* … the applicant had been deprived of his basic rights of justice at his trial." Likewise, in *O'Reilly v Judge Cassidy (No. 2)*,[94] the basic fact was that counsel for an objector to the granting of a liquor licence was the daughter of the Circuit Court judge who had

---

See also, *Nyembo v Refugee Appeals Tribunal* [2007] IESC 25 (which only involved a preliminary issue) in which the basis of the applicant's claim was that, despite having determined hundreds of cases, one member of the Tribunal had never found in favour of an appellant. The issue under discussion in the text was not addressed. The case seems to have been settled.

[89]   [2008] 2 I.R. 514.
[90]   [2006] 2 I.R. 32.
[91]   [2008] 2 I.R. 514.
[92]   [2008] 2 I.R. 514 at para.85. See also, para.9.
[93]   [1995] 1 I.L.R.M. 350 at 351–352 (emphasis added).
[94]   [1995] 1 I.L.R.M. 311 at 318.

heard the licensing case. The High Court (Flood J.) stated that the mere fact of the father–daughter relationship would not have carried the day for the applicant. Rather, what turned the scales was that, at the trial, when counsel for the applicant referred to the relationship between counsel for the objector and the respondent judge, the respondent's reply was that "… it was an impertinence and would be a matter that he would report to the Bar Council." And even in many post-*Orange* cases (though without consideration of the "prevailing wind" in the Supreme Court), it has been accepted that the behaviour in the courtroom of a District or Circuit Court judge[95] could be taken into account as evidencing bias in a number of criminal cases.

13–54 It must be accepted that, as the facts of *O'Callaghan (No. 2)* show, without some restraint of this type, the extent of a reviewing court's power would be significantly widened. But this logic has perhaps been taken further than necessary: it would be possible to limit the impact of the new rule by reference to the facts in these cases, namely that the applicant's claim was founded on the outcome or substance of the case, not procedure. One could then go on to emphasise that *McNally* and *O'Reilly (No. 2)* were both cases in which the error was in regard to procedure, as opposed to merit. However, in fact this distinction has not been used to restrict the scope of the rule. In addition, a practical feature of operating this rule is that it is necessary to ask at what stage an episode must occur before it can be taken into account as showing bias. This is something which it is often difficult to settle.[96]

13–55 One way out of the doctrinal difficulty, which the law seems to have got itself into, would be simply to hold that a serious breach of fair procedure amounts to a violation of the wide-ranging *audi alteram partem* rule, rather than trying to lug in the "no bias" principle. This possibility was alluded to, but curiously not pursued, when Murray C.J. stated in *Spin v IRTC*[97]:

> "If Dr. Kenny had taken into account these matters as evidence of bad character … without giving the applicant an opportunity to meet the case against it … it would not be a case of bias but a case of breach of fair procedure."

Yet, curiously, this logic and these hints have never been followed through. Possibly this may be an occasion to call up the "Equality of Arms" doctrine, discussed in paras 12–20 to 12–22.

13–56 These criticisms apart, there is one exception to this principle under discussion, which (if it is upheld by the Supreme Court) would establish a limit to

---

[95] See also, *Fogarty v O'Donnell* [2008] IEHC 198; *Balaz v Judge Kennedy* [2009] IEHC 110; unreported, High Court, Hedigan J., March 5, 2009 at paras 27–29; *Landers v Director of Public Prosecutions* [2004] 2 I.R. 363 at 365; *Joyce v Minister for Health* [2004] 4 I.R. 293 at 302.

[96] This cut-off, and the difficulties of operating it, is illustrated by the High Court's (McKechnie J.'s) analysis in the case of *Beades Construction v Dublin Corporation* [2005] IEHC 406, covered in H & M, para.13–87.

[97] [2001] 4 I.R. 411 at 443 (and see 439). See also, Barron J. in *Orange (No. 2)* [2000] 4 I.R. 159 at 225; *Kiely v Minister for Social Welfare (No. 2)* [1977] I.R. 267 at 281.

the scope of the rule and would make sense of several of the situations in this area. *In P v Judge McDonagh*,[98] Clarke J. convincingly found an exception where the source of the bias was pre-judgment. The facts of the case were that, in a divorce case, a Circuit Court judge had refused to accept a settlement agreed by the parties as to the financial terms for the division of their assets. In the judicial review, the applicant husband claimed that this surprising refusal amounted to bias, in that it created a reasonable apprehension that the adjudicator had not considered all appropriate matters before reaching what appeared to be a final view on the issue. In reply, the respondent submitted that, according to the principle under discussion here, the bias must pre-date the hearing. The High Court, however, held that (in the particular case of pre-judgment) this is not necessary. What is distinctive about pre-judgment, in the view of Clarke J., is that, of its nature, it must arise out of "… what happens at, rather than prior to, the hearing concerned. The form of pre-judgment which I have sought to analyse can only happen at a hearing and arises from the adjudicator creating … an impression that a premature rush to judgment has occurred …".

"Making a clean breast of it"

13–57   Openness[99] by a decision-maker regarding a possible source of bias is a factor which has often told against a ruling of bias.[100] However, no one has teased out exactly why this should be so. There seem to be two possibilities. The first of these is that openness of itself would, in the eye of a reasonable observer, tend to undermine a suspicion of bias. Probably *Bula (No. 6)* and *Dublin and County Broadcasting Ltd v Independent Radio and Television Commission*, discussed earlier, are examples of this first factor.

13–58   Secondly, depending on the circumstances, openness may assist a respondent in arguing that sufficient information is available to the applicant to sustain a defence of waiver. An indisputable form of waiver occurs where the person whose bias might have been in issue declares openly, to the person who might be disadvantaged, the facts which might be thought to constitute bias and indicates that s/he will, if asked to do so, withdraw (or "recuse him or herself".) Where this occurs, and the applicant indicates that proceedings may go ahead, then they have surely waived any right to object at any later stage.

13–59   More usually, there is no such explicit exchange as is contemplated in the previous paragraph; yet the applicant knows some or all of the relevant facts and fails to protest before the decision is made. For example, in *Bula Ltd v Tara*

---

[98]   [2009] IEHC 316; unreported, High Court, Clarke J., July 10, 2009. The quotation is from para.7.6.

[99]   There is a link between this topic and the material on withdrawal/recusal, covered below. Bias is a matter peculiarly within the knowledge of the deciding authority, giving rise in other contexts to a duty to declare an interest (*R. (Malone) v Tyrone JJ.* 3 N.I.J.R. 77; *State (Cole) v Labour Court* (1984) 3 J.I.S.L.L. 128).

   For examples of disclosure of interest provisions, see Environmental Protection Agency Act 1992 ss.37, 38; Ethics in Office Act 1995 ss.5–7; Personal Injuries Assessment Board Act 2003 s.71.

[100]   Although it has been said that where a matter does not amount to objective bias, it does not become so by reason of not having been disclosed: *O'Ceallaigh v An Bord Altranais* [2011] IESC 50; unreported, Supreme Court, December 21, 2011 at para.57.

Mines Ltd (No. 6),[101] it was submitted that there was objective bias because of Barrington J.'s earlier involvement, as counsel, in advising the parties to this long-running dispute. As indicated earlier, the Supreme Court held that the issue turned on the fact that a reasonable person in the position of the applicant would not have apprehended bias. And, to come to the present point, McGuinness J. regarded it as an argument against a ruling of bias that the applicants had "prior knowledge, even if limited".[102] Here, there is a hint that the judge regarded the applicant's failure to protest as amounting to a waiver.

D. Two Defences

13–60   Here, we outline two defences against a complaint of bias: necessity and waiver.

Rule of necessity

13–61   Throughout the common law world, the "no bias" rule gives way to necessity in as much as the disqualification of the adjudicator will not readily be permitted to destroy the only tribunal with power to decide. Consider, for example, *O'Byrne v Minister for Finance*[103] in which the members of the High Court and

---

[101]   [2000] 4 I.R. 412. In *Bula Ltd (No. 6)* at 518, McGuinness J. stated: "[Barrington J.'s] behaviour was at all stages open … [he] consulted with Hamilton CJ as to the propriety of his sitting in the security for costs proceedings and was reassured by him. He sat both in the security for costs proceedings and in the nearly contemporaneous proceedings of *Crindle Investments v Wymes* [1998] 4 IR 567 without any query being raised. After the judgment in the appeal he replied to queries from *The Sunday Independent* in a situation where many judges would have refused to discuss such matters with a journalist. When inquiries were made by the Chief State Solicitor's office he replied in a frank and open letter setting out all his memories of communications with any of the respondent parties. At no stage did he endeavour to conceal any relevant facts."
    Some of these elements illustrate a common difficulty here: are there not assumed to be some limits on the reasonable person's sources of information? Possibly, they may be assumed to read *The Sunday Independent*. But surely they would not have seen the letter to the Chief State Solicitor? For the test can hardly assume an all-knowing reasonable applicant, since the entire basis of this part of the law is the need to assuage the fears of the reasonable person, who will not know everything.
[102]   [2000] 4 I.R. 412 at 506. See also, *Dublin and County Broadcasting Ltd v Independent Radio and Television Commission*, unreported, High Court, May 12, 1989.
[103]   [1959] I.R. 1, where the doctrine was applied, if not expressly invoked. In *Collins v County Cork VEC*, unreported, High Court, May 26, 1982, Murphy J. said that it was the "clear constitutional duty" of the Supreme Court to decide the *O'Byrne* case, "notwithstanding the interest which the members of the Court had in the outcome." See also, Hogan and Whyte, *JM Kelly: The Irish Constitution*, 4th edn (Dublin: LexisNexis Butterworths, 2003), paras 6.1.65 to 6.1.66 for an explanation of the composition of the Supreme Court in *State (Killian) v Minister for Justice* [1954] I.R. 207. *O'Byrne* was followed in *O'Neill v Irish Hereford Breed Society Ltd* [1992] 1 I.R. 431 at 449 and, in less acute circumstances, in *Flynn v Allen*, unreported, High Court, May 2, 1988. In *Flynn*, noting that the defendants in the action were Benchers of Kings Inn, Lynch J. stated (at p.3): "I am, of course, as is every other High Court Judge and Judge of the Supreme Court, a Bencher of the King's Inns and I am conscious of the fact that in one sense I myself could be said to be a defendant in these matters. Be that as it may, the matter has to come to be decided by some Judge of the High Court and it has come before me and I must not shirk my duty of dealing with it … I have been referred to the decisions of the High Court and the Supreme Court in the case of *O'Byrne v Minister for Finance and the Attorney General* [1959] I.R. 1 [and] of course the difficulty that arises

Supreme Court were obliged to pass judgment on the constitutionality of legislation rendering them (and their judicial brethren) liable to income tax on their salaries.

13–62 A more typical example is afforded by *O'Neill v Beaumont Hospital Board*.[104] In this case, as a result of a finding of bias, the Supreme Court granted an injunction restraining the Chairman and two other members of the Hospital Board from taking part in any meeting which would consider whether to retain the plaintiff as a consultant.[105] The court declined, however, to grant an injunction in the terms sought by the plaintiff, which would have restrained any meeting of the Board. The reason for this was that the other members of the Board had not committed themselves to a fixed position as much as had the Chairman and the other two members who were enjoined. This was coupled with the doctrine of necessity, whose application in the instant case was explained by Finlay C.J. as follows:

> "It is not a dominant doctrine, it could never defeat a real fear and a real reasonable fear of bias or injustice but it is a consideration in relation to the question of the entire Board being prohibited, for if that were to be done there can be no other machinery by which something which is of great importance both to the Board of the Hospital and to the plaintiff and I might add, to the public who will attend the Hospital, namely the continuance or noncontinuance of the plaintiff's services in the hospital, can be determined in accordance with the terms of the probationary agreement."[106]

13–63 Other employee disciplinary situations (especially in the private law field) may pose an even graver necessity than that in *O'Neill*. This broad point was recognised by both Keane J. and the Supreme Court in *Mooney v An Post*,[107] a case concerning the dismissal of a postman for alleged misconduct, when the former remarked that:

> "... the *nemo iudex* requirements cannot be literally applied to every employer confronted with a decision as to whether or not he should dismiss a particular employee. If it were, an employer could never dismiss an employee, since

---

here arose there. The necessity for proceeding notwithstanding that unfortunate difficulty was emphasised and I accept that that is so and that I should and must deal with the matter."
    Another example occurred in *Attorney General (Humphreys) v Governors of Erasmus Smith's Schools* [1910] 1 I.R. 325, a relator action involving a charitable trust administered by the defendants. Cherry L.J. commenced his judgment in the Irish Court of Appeal with the following apologia (at 332): "I am in a rather difficult position in adjudicating upon this case, in as much as I was Attorney-General when the writ was fiated. I would have preferred not to have been a member of the Court which had to decide this appeal, but as all the Judges of the Court except Lord Justice Holmes and myself are Governors of the Schools, a Court could not otherwise have been formed."
[104] [1990] I.L.R.M. 419. See the rather similar examples of *CW Shipping v Limerick* [1989] 1 I.L.R.M. 416 at 427; *Radio Limerick v IRTC* [1999] 2 I.L.R.M. 1 at 25 and *Allman v Minister for Justice, Equality and Law Reform* [2002] 3 I.R. 540 at 548–549, 552–553.
[105] Followed, on this point, in *O'Neill v Irish Hereford Breed Society Ltd* [1992] 1 I.R. 431 at 448–449 per Murphy J.
[106] [1990] I.L.R.M. 419 at 440. Followed in *O'Neill v Irish Hereford Breed Society Ltd* [1992] 1 I.R. 431 at 451.
[107] [1994] E.L.R. 103.

he would always be an interested party in the decision by a particular employee."[108]

13–64 Clearly, the existence of a necessity depends, in substantial measure, upon the content of the particular statute. To take a simple example, see *State (Curran) v Irish Land Commission*[109] in which Doyle J. opined, obiter, that the argument of necessity could not have excused the respondents in certain circumstances, e.g. ill health—for the reason that the Land Act 1950 allowed for the appointment of a temporary replacement where a lay commissioner is temporarily disabled from fulfilling his function on account of illness, absence "or other sufficient reason". Similarly, in *Potts v Minister for Defence*,[110] the High Court stated that "... it is normal practice, where a commanding officer has a prior involvement in a case, for the accused person to be attached to a different unit of the Defence Forces so that the charge against the person can be dealt with by a commanding officer in that unit".

13–65 The rule of necessity is probably compatible with constitutional justice. For, as has been seen, constitutional justice is grounded in Art.40.3, the rights contained in which are not absolute but qualified by such phrases as "far as practicable" and "as best it may". As Murphy J. observed in *Collins v County Cork VEC*,[111] since the courts cannot conjure up a new tribunal to take the place of an existing tribunal if it were held unconstitutional, in some cases chaos would result if the "no bias" rule were applied at its full width. The difficulty with this logic is that it would come close to undermining the "no bias" rule.

13–66 Accordingly, the question arises: how vigorously ought the doctrine of necessity be applied? On the one side, as a matter of practicality, it must be recalled that the present area will often involve part-time and/or unpaid committees or boards composed of members who do not live in an ivory tower and must earn their living elsewhere as professionals or business people, with several linkages or associations. Thus, all kinds of linkages and associations are possible which may suggest the possibility of bias. On the other hand, the values implemented by the "no bias" principle are undoubtedly significant and a sharp reminder of that

---

[108] [1994] E.L.R. 103 at 116. For the agreement of the Supreme Court, see unreported, Supreme Court, March 20, 1997.

[109] Unreported, High Court, June 12, 1978. See also, *R. (Snaith) v Ulster Polytechnic* [1981] N.I. 28. The dismissal procedure laid down in the University statutes required, first, that the initial decision should be taken by a sub-committee of 11 Governors and secondly, that on appeal, this decision must be upheld by a two-thirds majority of the Governors of whom there were 42 in all. This arrangement plainly breached the "no bias" rule. Given the numbers of Governors involved at each level, it would have been very difficult if not impossible to work this system without some overlap of personnel. However, Hutton J. ruled that the necessity doctrine did not apply because the difficulty arose "from the scheme for termination of appointments which the Governors themselves had provided [in the statutes]" rather than from some externally imposed instrument.

[110] [2005] 2 I.L.R.M. 517 at 527–528. Notice that in *O'Callaghan v Mahon (No. 2)* [2008] 2 I.R. 514 at 642, 647, the dissenting judge, Hardiman J., implicitly adverted to the doctrine of necessity.

[111] Unreported, High Court, May 26, 1982.

was given recently by the European Court of Human Rights in *Kingsley v United Kingdom*.[112]

Waiver

13–67 The right to object to a breach of the *nemo iudex* principle may be waived by a party with full knowledge of the facts which entitle him to raise a complaint.[113] The rule has been stated to be as follows:

> "[W]here a decision is challenged on the grounds of bias in the tribunal which gave it, [the] Court will not interfere where it appears that the fact or suspicion of bias was present to the mind of the challenging party at the hearing before the tribunal, and the point as to bias or suspected bias was not made by or on his behalf at the hearing by the tribunal."[114]

13–68 The commonsensical policy underlying this rule is presumably that an applicant may not wait to see whether a decision goes in their favour and then, if it does not do so, turn around and complain that the decision-maker was biased. In other words, the applicant cannot have his cake and eat it.[115]

13–69 On the other hand, this is plainly a door which could open very wide. Accordingly, qualifications exist. The first concerns the consent itself. For effective consent, the applicant must be aware of the bias, and not so taken by surprise that he omits to make an objection. Here, it should be borne in mind that it is a particularly embarrassing matter to have to raise the issue of bias in front of the person whom it is alleged is biased.

13–70 Secondly, even with a consent, the court may deem it proper to interfere because of the scandalous state of affairs involved.[116] Thus, in *DD v Gibbons*,[117] having given an explanation of objective bias, the High Court (Quirke J.) then went on to say by way of contrast, that "[i]t is unnecessary to state that a risk of actual bias requires a judge to disqualify himself/herself whether asked to do so or otherwise." There is a strong, though very much obiter, suggestion here that, in a case of actual bias, even if an applicant failed to object, they would not be deemed to have waived the right to do so.[118]

---

[112] (2001) 33 E.H.R.R. 13 at paras 52–59; (2002) 35 E.H.R.R. 10 at para.177. See generally, Toy-Cronin, "Waiver of the rule against bias" (2002) 9 Auckland U.L. Rev. 850.
[113] *Corrigan v Irish Land Commission* [1977] I.R. 317 at 326, distinguished in *O'Neill v Irish Hereford Breed Society Ltd* [1992] 1 I.R. 432 at 455 on the ground that the plaintiff did not have knowledge of all the relevant circumstances. *State (Cole) v Labour Court* (1984) 3 J.I.S.L.L. 128.
[114] *R. (Harrington) v Clare JJ.* [1918] 2 I.R. 116 per Sir James Campbell C.J. See also, *Corrigan* case, above, and *State (Graham) v Racing Board*, unreported, High Court, November 22, 1983.
[115] See, e.g. *O'Reilly v Cassidy (No. 2)* [1995] 1 I.L.R.M. 311 at 318.
[116] *R. (Giants Causeway Tram Co) v Antrim JJ.* [1895] 2 I.R. 603; *R. (Poe) v Clare JJ.* (1906) 40 I.L.T.R. 121; *R. (Harrington) v Clare JJ.* [1918] 2 I.R. 116.
[117] [2006] 3 I.R. 17 at 23. *O'Reilly v Cassidy* [1995] 1 I.L.R.M. 306 at 309; *McCarthy v Keane*, unreported, High Court, Lavan J., July 24, 2003 at 10–11.
[118] See the dissenting judgment of Kenny J. in *Corrigan v Irish Land Commission* [1977] I.R. 317 at 326.

13–71 In the case law considered so far, waiver occurs because of some action (or inaction) of the plaintiff at the time of the dispute. A distinct category of waiver exists where in the case of, for example, a trade union or other so-called voluntary association, the plaintiff is regarded as having consented to the defect of which he wishes to complain, simply by virtue of having joined the union or association in the first place. This may be a rather far-reaching and unrealistic notion, but it was nevertheless adopted by Lardner J. in *IDATU v Carroll*.[119] The facts of the case are described below: it concerned not the situation under consideration here, that is a trade union and a member, but the parallel situation of the ICTU and a member union. Lardner J. stated[120]:

> "In the present case, the court is concerned with Congress, an association of trade unions and its members who are trade unions who have negotiated and freely accepted its rules. There is nothing in the evidence before me to suggest that there was any inequality between the plaintiff union and Congress at the time this constitution was adopted. Having regard to the fact that the clause complained of is part of the Constitution of Congress, which was freely accepted by the plaintiff, I am not satisfied by [plaintiff's] counsel's submission that this clause is contrary to natural justice."

13–72 The relationship between the reasonable suspicion test (explained in Part C) and waiver is this. The reasonable suspicion centres on what a person in the position of the applicant would have thought if (as a hypothetical supposition) they had had all the relevant facts before them. By contrast, a waiver is directed at a situation in which the applicant actually did (or may be deemed to) have all the facts, and yet failed to protest at the time.

Withdrawal/recusal of suspect members

13–73 One obvious way of avoiding trouble, which may be available where the decision has yet to be taken and where the deciding body has a number of members, is for the suspect members[121] not to sit, as was suggested by *IDATU v Carroll*.[122] Here the General Secretary of the plaintiff union had made a number of derogatory references to other trade unions. Accordingly the plaintiff had been informed that it would be required to show cause before the Irish Congress of Trade Unions who were, in effect, the defendants, as to why it should not be suspended from Congress. The plaintiff's response was to seek an injunction to restrain the defendant from passing or considering any sanction upon the plaintiff.

13–74 One of the plaintiff's submissions was grounded on bias, in that the Irish Transport and General Workers Union and the Federated Workers Union of Ireland who were each members of ICTU cater to some extent for the same category of workers as are catered for by the plaintiffs. One of the reasons why Lardner J. rejected this argument was that:

---

[119] [1988] I.L.R.M. 713.
[120] [1988] I.L.R.M. 713 at 719. This was an ex tempore judgment.
[121] See earlier section on "Making a clean breast of it", at paras 13–57 to 13–59.
[122] [1988] I.L.R.M. 713. See also, *Radio Limerick v IRTC* [1997] 2 I.L.R.M. 1 at 25.

"... the executive council consists of [27 members] ... Seven is a quorum. When this matter was raised, counsel on behalf of the defendants undertook that no member of the executive council who had any direct interest in the matter ... would sit or take part in the deliberations of the executive council dealing with this matter."[123]

13–75   More recently, Keane C.J., in *Rooney v Minister for Agriculture and Food (No.1)*,[124] made a significant statement in what was formally a judgment but, from its subject matter, was more like a judicial circular. He stated:

"Where one or the other party does invite a judge to disqualify himself, the established and prudent practice has been for the judge concerned to disqualify himself if he has any reservations about the matter. *On the other hand a judge cannot permit a scrupulous approach by him to be used to permit parties to engage in forum shopping under the guise of challenging the partiality of the court. The need to ensure the appearance, as well as the reality, of impartiality must be reconciled with the proper functioning of the judicial system.* The dilemma to which these conflicting demands give rise might be resolved in cases of difficulty by the judge concerned referring the issue – perhaps on the basis of a memorandum prepared by him or her – to the senior available judge of the court of which he is a member. Such a course would be acceptable in cases of particular difficulty but I do not believe that this procedure should develop into common practice. The disclosure of possible grounds for concern and the sensible reaction of the parties, advised by their lawyers, has usually been sufficient to dispose of any such difficulty and I do not doubt this will continue to be the case."

13–76   It is worth teasing out this important passage a little. First, where a judge recuses him/herself, the "no bias" rule is plainly honoured. Then, the only danger concerns the possibility that a too scrupulous application of the "no bias" rule would allow the applicant to forum shop (as Keane C.J. put it; see the first sentence

---

[123] [1988] I.L.R.M. 713 at 718–719. See also, *Bane v The Garda Representative Association* [1997] 2 I.R. 449 where the applicant succeeded in part, because the committee of the respondent could have been constituted by persons other than those who had given evidence in the earlier proceedings, and so the necessity doctrine applied. See [1997] 2 I.R. 449 at 474.

[124] [2001] 2 I.L.R.M. 37 at 40 (emphasis added). One situation in which the judge did recuse himself at the request of a party, without judicial review, involved Keane C.J. The case concerned the question whether Hepatitis C victims who had accepted Hepatitis C Compensation Tribunal awards were precluded from appealing these awards to the High Court. The victims were invoking their constitutional rights, whilst the State relied upon Superior Court Rules. The significant point was that the judge had been a member of the committee which had drafted the Rules: *The Irish Times*, December 20, 2000.

For a case in which counsel for the applicant had made an application to the Fitness to Practice Committee to discharge itself from hearing her case on the basis of bias, and the Committee considered this application in the absence of the chairperson who was the member most nearly involved, see *O'Ceallaigh v An Bord Altranais* [2009] IEHC 470 at paras 10–16, 10–43.

And for an instructive example of a judge, in a measured, articulate and good humoured way, recusing himself, see *EPI v Minister for Justice, Equality and Law Reform* [2009] 2 I.R. 254 at paras 10–18. These passages include the observation at para.10 that "[j]udges should not lightly recuse themselves of their responsibility to hear cases that come before them" (Hedigan J.).

italicised in the passage quoted). This is a countervailing factor which has not always received the attention it deserves.[125]

13–77   The second issue suggested in the passage from *Rooney* is: what happens where, despite a request to recuse himself or herself, the judge declines to do so? The outcome then would depend on the circumstances. The circumstances might be such that the need to avoid the appearance of forum shopping (or, perhaps, some other disadvantage like delay) would mean that no reasonable person could suspect bias. The other alternative would be that, with all relevant facts being out in the open, the judge remained and the objector continued with the case before the same judge. In that case, it would be a well-balanced question whether a reviewing court would be prepared to hold that an applicant had waived their right to seek judicial review. The remaining possibility would be if the applicant withdrew and sought judicial review. The issue of bias would then squarely arise, with waiver not being an issue.

13–78   Thirdly, the notion of withdrawal embraces bodies other than courts. Even where the decision-maker is not a court, it might be wise to regard these remarks as applying mutatis mutandi. Keane C.J. in *Rooney* stated[126] that "[i]t has long been the practice for judges in this State *and other persons exercising quasi-judicial functions* to disclose the existence of any factor which either party might consider was capable of affecting the reality or the appearance of an impartial administration of justice".

13–79   One practical point: in *Baker v Quantum*,[127] it was stated that "[i]t is not open to a party which thinks it has grounds for asking for recusal to take a leisurely approach to raising the objections. Applications for recusal go to the heart of the administration of justice and must be raised as soon as is practicable."

E. The Particular Case of Judges

13–80   An increasing number of alleged bias cases[128] involve judges.[129] Some of the points raising issues peculiar to judges are summarised in the present section. As

---

[125]   But see *Curran v Finn* [2001] 4 I.R. 248 at 254–255.

[126]   [2001] 2 I.L.R.M. 37 at 40 (emphasis added).

[127]   [2009] EWCA Civ. 499. (This case centred on an unsuccessful submission that a judge with mild tinnitus, for that reason, should not hear a case on noise-induced deafness.)

[128]   In *District Judge MacMenamin v Ireland* [1996] 3 I.R. 100, the Supreme Court adjudicated on the substantive question of the constitutionality of judicial pension arrangements. O'Flaherty J. alluded (at 143) to the doctrine of necessity in this way: "I appreciate we do well when dealing with judicial colleagues to preserve a certain Caesarean detachment: *what touches us ourselves should be last serv'd*. (Shakespeare: *Julius Caesar*, Act III, Sc. 1). Nonetheless, judges of the District Court are entitled to the same measure of justice as anyone else in the land who appears in this Court: no more and no less ...". For an interesting hypothetical example, see *Bane v Garda Representative Association* [1997] 2 I.R. 449 at 472. For the special case of jurors, see "Apprehended Bias: the case of Jurors" (2010) 32 D.U.L.J. 121, covering *People (DPP) v Norris* [2009] IECCA 27.

[129]   It is, or used to be, the case that imputing bias against a judge could amount to a contempt of court: *Attorney General v Connolly* [1947] I.R. 213; *State (DPP) v Walsh* [1981] I.R. 412; *R. v Editor of New Statesman Ex p. DPP* (1928) 44 T.L.R. 301. See Walker, "Scandalising in the Eighties" (1985) 101 L.Q.R. 359.

Professor Le Sueur has remarked in Britain,[130] "[o]f all the changes in the make-up of [Public Law's] contributors over the past 50 years, the most significant has been the rise of the judge-scholar, willing to express views about the future direction of the law outside the pages of the law reports". There has been a similar development involving some members of the Irish judiciary and it remains to be seen whether this will throw up cases involving the "no bias" principle.

13–81   The commonest situation is where a former client of the judge's—in the days when the judge was a practitioner—manifests himself or herself as a party in the judge's court. One of the leading cases of this type, *Bula Ltd v Tara Mines Ltd (No. 6)*,[131] grew out of the long-running mining saga. It was an application to the Supreme Court to set aside an earlier judgment (dated January 15, 1999) of a three-member Supreme Court on grounds of objective bias, in that, when they were counsel, two members of the court had professional links with one of the parties. A good summation of the judgments in the case, which also gives an indication of the type of case in which such an application might succeed, is contained in the headnote[132]:

> "... barristers were independent and did not become espoused to a litigant's ambitions in providing the litigant with legal services. The reasonable person would be aware of that. A prior relationship of legal advisor and client did not generally disqualify the former advisor from becoming a member of a court sitting in proceedings to which the former client is a party. There must be additional factors establishing a cogent and rational link between the association and its capacity to influence the decision to be made in the particular case. A long, recent and varied connection may disqualify a judge. A reasonable apprehension would also arise where the judge as counsel had previously given legal services to a party on issues alive in the case to be heard by the court."

13–82   In one of the two substantive judgments given in the case, McGuinness J. stated, in a detailed passage[133]:

> "In applying the test of a person's reasonable apprehension of bias to the facts of this case, the following factors ought also to be taken into account.
>   1.   The importance of the judicial oath;
>   2.   the independence of the bar;
>   3.   the time factor, all of the professional work was done before 1980;
>   4.   the application was not made in advance of the hearing but after this court's decision;

---

[130] (2006) *Public Law* 2. For a sensible and at times entertaining analysis of Scalia J.'s refusal to recuse himself from a case involving a party with whom he had just gone duck-hunting, see Olowofoyeuku, "Subjective Objectivity: Judicial Impartiality and Social Intercourse in the US Supreme Court" (2006) *Public Law* 15.

[131] [2000] 4 I.R. 412. See also, *Rooney* [2001] 2 I.L.R.M. 37 and *Talbot v Hermitage Golf Club* [2009] IESC 26 at para.19.

[132] [2000] 4 I.R. 412 at 413.

[133] [2000] 4 I.R. 412 at 518. The claims involving Keane C.J. were said to be "not reasonable or realistic". The other substantive judgment, which was given by Denham J., was broadly in line with that of McGuinness J.

5. [The applicant] was aware of the existence of [Mr Barrington SC's] boundary opinion, prior to the hearing of the appeal;
6. [The applicant] in his affidavits was somewhat less than candid in revealing the advice given ... in regard to Keane and Barrington JJ."

13–83 McGuinness J. went on to emphasise the time factor ((3) above) as being of "great importance: a reasonable person would realise that Barrington J would be unlikely to have a clear memory of work done twenty years ago, let alone be influenced by it".[134]

13–84 Although none has yet emerged, the same situation could arise in an analogous way, in respect of an administrative agency, of which a member is a professional or business person who has links with a party before him (e.g. an estate agent on the Private Residential Tenancies Board or an engineer on An Bórd Pleanála). Indeed, the situation here might be so much more acute, in that appointments to an administrative agency are usually part time and for a limited period of five or seven years. The dangers of links with past, or (since the member's practice may well continue in being, even without him or her) future, clients are far more likely to be realistic than in the case of a judge, since the judge will not be returning to practice.

13–85 A claim with even less merit than that in the previous line of authority is illustrated by *DD v District Judge Gibbons*.[135] The applicant was the mother of two children, and she had separated from her husband. Custody orders were made on a number of occasions by the respondent in the District Court, in respect of the children of the family. Finally, the husband made an application for a full care order in respect of one child and a guardianship order in respect of the second. This was heard by the respondent. On the second day of the hearing, the applicant requested the respondent to disqualify himself on the basis that he had, in earlier proceedings, restricted the applicant's access to one of the children.

13–86 The request was refused and the High Court (Quirke J.) upheld this refusal on an application for judicial review. Quirke J. noted that judges frequently heard and determined *ad interim* applications and then proceeded to make final determinations and orders concerning the similar issues and the same parties, particularly in the context of custody of, and access to, children. The making of an *ad interim* order unfavourable to the interests of a party would not cause an objective and informed person in the position of that party to apprehend that the judge who made the order would not bring an impartial mind to bear on a final determination.

13–87 Another possible flashpoint arises from the fact that the notion that a judge must observe a high standard of detachment is the corner-stone of the accusatorial

---

[134] [2000] 4 I.R. 412 at 528. Thus, the applicant's case failed. Nevertheless, the judge stated (at 518): "The question remains as to whether Barrington J. should have disclosed the various connections set out above in open court prior to the hearing of the appeal. It might well have been more prudent for him to have done so, in so far as he actually remembered them."
This is a rather unexpected comment: the issue for a court is whether the law has been obeyed, not whether a judge has behaved prudently, politely or anything else.
[135] [2006] 3 I.R. 17.

trial structure (especially a criminal trial). It means that the judge must not take an active part but must remain above the forensic contest rather like a tennis umpire monitoring the play. This axiom was illustrated in *Magee v O'Dea*.[136] This was an extradition application. At the conclusion of the evidence, the presiding District judge was not satisfied as to the question of identity. Accordingly, he returned to court and recalled, of his own motion, a witness as to the identity of the plaintiff. He did this, without informing either the plaintiff's solicitor or the state solicitor as to what he intended to do. Holding the order of the District Court invalid, Flood J. stated:

> "... our system of justice is an adversarial system. The State presents its case ... I accept that a judge has a right to recall, or in fact call, on his own motion, a witness. All the authorities would suggest that this is a practice which should be sparingly used, and in particular, sparingly used in criminal matters, where the onus of proof is a strict onus of proof, as otherwise it may appear that he is descending into the arena and becoming partisan."[137]

13–88   What is perhaps more surprising is that the same notion—the idea of the accusatorial trial—was drawn upon in the context of *Kiely v Minister for Social Welfare (No. 2)*[138] which involved an appeals officer in the Department of Social Welfare. (Strangely, similar language had been used in *Kiely* to that in the *Magee* judgment although there was no reference to *Kiely* in *Magee*.) The particular feature of *Kiely* which is relevant here concerned the behaviour of the medical assessor who had sat with the appeals officer and had asked questions (of a medical nature) of the applicant's expert medical witness. Henchy J. stated:

> "It ill becomes an assessor who is an affiliate of the quasi-judicial officer, to descend into the forensic arena ... the taint of partiality will necessarily follow if [the appeals officer or assessor] intervenes to such an extent as to appear to be presenting or conducting the case against the claimant."[139]

13–89   However, perhaps one may comment that, while *Kiely (No. 2)* is a Supreme Court authority, it was decided right at the start of the modern period of administrative law and it is difficult to reconcile this rather dogmatic line of thought with *Idiakheua v Minister for Justice, Equality and Law Reform*,[140] in which Clarke J. (on an application for leave) made a remark which is full of common sense:

> "... it was suggested on behalf of the Refugee Appeals Tribunal that it would be inappropriate for the Tribunal either to direct the line of questioning which should be adopted on behalf of the Commissioner or to engage in questioning itself (on the ground that such questioning might give rise to an appearance of bias). I am afraid I cannot agree. If a matter is likely to be important to the determination of the Refugee Appeals Tribunal then that matter must be fairly put to the applicant ...".

---

[136] [1994] 1 I.R. 500.
[137] [1994] 1 I.R. 500 at 507.
[138] [1977] I.R. 267.
[139] [1977] I.R. 267 at 283. *A contra*: Keane J. in *Rajah v The Royal College of Surgeons* [1994] 1 I.R. 384 at 394.
[140] [2005] IEHC 180; unreported, High Court, Clarke J., May 10, 2005. The quotation is at 9–10.

CHAPTER 14

THE RIGHT TO BE HEARD:
AUDI ALTERAM PARTEM

14–01   Part A of this chapter covers miscellaneous introductory questions, some of them echoing themes developed at the start of Chapter 10. The right to be heard (*audi alteram partem*)[1] embraces two fundamental obligations (although nothing turns on the distinction). First—and this is the subject of Part B—the person affected by the decision must have notice of it, that is, must be alerted to it and given details. Secondly, Part C examines particular aspects of the complementary principle that the person affected must be allowed appropriate facilities to make the best possible case in reply. Part D treats an issue of growing importance, the right to reasons for a decision. Part E, which is relevant to this and the previous two chapters, considers which types of decision attract the right to be heard, and which do not. As a conclusion, Part F weighs the advantages and disadvantages of the rules. Finally, one should add that throughout this chapter, indeed this book, the term "hearing" is used more widely than an "oral hearing"; and embraces any form by which a decision-maker entertains the arguments advanced by a person affected by the decision.

A. PRELIMINARY MATTERS

14–02   As might be expected from the range of decisions to which it applies (as indicated in Part E), the standard of the right to be heard is plastic, varying with the circumstances, for "domestic and administrative tribunals take many forms and determine many different kinds of issues and no hard and fast rules can be laid

---

[1]   See Kelly, "*Audi Alteram Partem*" (1964) 9 *Natural Law Forum* 1.

down …".[2] The consequence of this wide span is that, as Costello J. has stated, at one end of the scale[3]:

> "The courts must not interfere officiously in the affairs of private associations such as trade unions and must only do so in clear cases to prevent or remedy some manifest injustice. And when considering what procedures can properly be regarded as fair it must consider procedures which would be appropriate to the type of organisation or association which is to adopt them and the nature and scope of the decision to which they relate."

14–03 In parenthesis, one could add that the law reports offer several examples[4] of what might almost be called a culture clash between the courts and the staff of certain tribunals or administrative agencies,[5] whose performance sometimes suggests that they have not taken on board this principle of fair procedure. In particular, the public body may make the (incorrect) assumption that, if all the points in the applicant's favour are actually taken into account, then that suffices. But, rightly or wrongly, the law has established the tenet that the applicant has to be in a position to make his or her own case.

14–04 Likewise, the opportunities and facilities which the *audi alteram partem* rule requires to be granted to the applicant raise the question: what if the respondent of the body has not been endowed with the necessary statutory powers to make arrangements to satisfy the applicant's right to fair procedure, for example, to call witnesses or to order disclosure? A case in point is *Davy v Financial Services Ombudsman*.[6] The particular issue here was that a complaint had been made to

---

[2]   *Russell v Duke of Norfolk* [1949] 1 All E.R. 109 at 118. This passage has been several times quoted with approval by Irish judges, e.g.: *Kiely v Minister for Social Welfare (No. 2)* [1977] I.R. 267 at 283; *State (Haverty) v An Bord Pleanála* [1987] I.R. 485 at 493; *Gallagher v Revenue Commissioners* [1995] 1 I.L.R.M. 241 at 259; *Tang v Minister for Justice* [1996] 2 I.L.R.M. 46 at 61; *McAuley v Garda Commissioner (No. 1)* [1996] 3 I.R. 208.

[3]   *Doyle v Croke*, unreported, High Court, May 6, 1988. See, to like effect: *State (Keegan) v The Stardust Victims Compensation Tribunal* [1986] I.R. 642; *McGowan v Wren* [1988] I.L.R.M. 744; *Ryan v VIP Taxi Co-operatives Ltd*, unreported, High Court, January 20, 1989 (reported in *The Irish Times*, Law Report, April 10, 1989); *Mooney v An Post* [1994] E.L.R. 103 at 106; *Grant v Garda Síochána Complaints Board*, unreported, High Court, June 12, 1996; *International Vessels Ltd v Minister for Marine (No. 2)* [1991] 2 I.R. 93 at 102. Keane J. echoed these views in *Mooney v An Post* [1994] E.L.R. 103. See also, *Menolly Homes v The Appeal Commissioners* [2010] IEHC 49 at para.42: "I would caution against any tendency towards applying the rules of civil plenary procedure within an administrative context in an unthinking or uncircumcised way"; *Ezeani v Minister for Justice, Equality and Law Reform* [2011] IESC 23 at paras 44–45.

[4]   For striking examples, see: *Flanagan v University College Dublin* [1988] I.R. 724; *State (Williams) v Army Pensions Board* [1983] I.R. 308 which is analysed in the 2nd edn of this book, pp.445–446. See also, *Maunsell v Minister for Education* [1940] I.R. 213; *State (Hussey) v Irish Land Commission* [1983] I.R. 23 at 36. In the criminal field, see *DPP v Doyle* [1994] 2 I.R. 286 at 296–302 and *Maher v O'Donnell* [1996] 2 I.L.R.M. 321 at 326–327 (considering the right of an accused to statements in advance of a trial).

[5]   For a British attempt to meet this difficulty, see Treasury Solicitor Department, *The Judge Over Your Shoulder*, 3rd edn (2000), available under "Other Publications" on the T. Sol. website at *http://www.treasury-solicitor.gov.uk*. See [1987] *Public Law* 485.

[6]   [2008] 2 I.L.R.M. 507 at para.51 (rev. though not on this point at [2010] 2 I.L.R.M. 305); *Gallagher v Revenue Commissioners (No. 2)* [1995] 1 I.R. 55 at 79, 87; *LD v Refugee Appeals Tribunal* [2006] 3 I.R. 439 at paras 5–7; *Ryan v VIP*, unreported, High Court, Gardner J., January 10, 1989; *O'Shea v Commissioner of Garda Síochána* [1994] 2 I.R. 408; *Beirne v*

the Financial Services Ombudsman by a credit union, arising out of advice which the applicant stockbroker had allegedly given to the credit union. However, the Ombudsman refused a request from the applicant to disclose documents which the credit union had sent to the Ombudsman. The essential point is that while the relevant legislation (the Pensions Act 1990) gives a power of disclosure as against the financial service provider, there was no power under the Act to order disclosure by a complainant. However, Charleton J. stated that, in an appropriate case, such as the present, he was prepared to interpret the general statutory requirements, that a complainant must cooperate with the Financial Services Ombudsman and that the Ombudsman must be satisfied that the complainant is acting in good faith, so as to require the disclosure of relevant documents by the complainant.[7] Such first aid will often be possible, but not always. And, if not, the question would arise as to whether the court would be prepared to deduce the necessary powers from the implied requirement in the Constitution, regarding constitutional justice. Alternatively, will the court simply strike down the legislation on the basis that, on the facts before it, there is a conflict with the Constitution?

14–05   In *Burns v Governor of Castlerea Prison*,[8] the Supreme Court went further. The question was whether a prison officer, against whom complaints had been made of alleged breaches of the disciplinary code, was entitled to legal representation at an oral hearing before the Governor of the prison. The relevant point here was that the disciplinary rules made no reference to legal representation. Nevertheless, writing for the Supreme Court, Geoghegan J. stated:

> "… the learned High Court judge [Butler J.] quite rightly was of the view that the absence of reference to legal representation in the rules did not necessarily preclude it … While that observation is valid, the Constitution itself might require legal representation in exceptional cases irrespective of the wording."

14–06   The question of waiver,[9] by the individual affected, is another important issue which has received less attention in the context of the *audi alteram partem* rule than the no bias principle.[10] The issue was treated briefly in *Carroll v State (D) v Groarke* procedure, the local veterinary inspector declared one of the applicant's cows to be a reactor and his farm to be a restricted holding. Rejecting the applicant's claim that he had not received a fair hearing, Blayney J. held:

Commissioner of An Garda Síochána [1992] I.L.R.M. 699 at 707–708; [1993] I.L.R.M. 1 at 9 per Finlay C.J.; *WS v Adoption Board* [2010] 1 I.L.R.M. 417.

[7]   A similar impatience with dogma to that manifest in *Davy* was evident in Murray C.J.'s judgment in *Curtin v Dáil Éireann* [2006] 2 I.L.R.M. 99.

[8]   Unreported, Supreme Court, April 2, 2009. The quotation is at pp.7–8 (emphasis added). For another illustration, see *O'Brien v Moriarty (No. 3)* [2006] 2 I.R. 474 at paras 71–74.

[9]   For cases on a criminal trial and waiver, see *State (D) v Groarke* [1988] I.R. 187 (High Court); [1990] I.R. 305 at 310–311 (Supreme Court). For a case on a criminal trial and waiver, see *Leonard v Garavan* [2003] 4 I.R. 60 at 84–85.

[10]   For a case in which it could be said that Clarke J. in substance held that the plaintiff, although being absent, had not waived his right to be present at his disciplinary hearing, see *Carroll v Bus Átha Cliath* [2005] 4 I.R. 184 at paras 42–44, 64–65. On the issue of waiver or the problem of an absence of statutory provisions by which to meet the difficulty, in relation to the "no bias" principle, see paras 13–67 to 13–72.

"... The applicant's criticism of the manner in which Mr. Lynch [a veterinary surgeon] carried out the test is not really relevant. No such criticism had been made by the applicant at the time [when the local veterinary inspector] made his decision. Accordingly, [the Minister] was perfectly entitled to act on Mr. Lynch's finding. There was no reason why he should have any doubt about its accuracy. There was no obligation on him to investigate how Mr. Lynch had carried out the test. The position might have been different if, before making his decision, the applicant had questioned the manner in which Mr. Lynch had carried out the test. In the absence of any such complaint it was perfectly normal for him to rely on Mr. Lynch's finding."[11]

14–07   In *State (D) v Groarke*,[12] the Supreme Court held that a District judge's warrant for the removal of a child, who had allegedly been abused, to a "place of safety" (Children Act 1908 s.24(i)) was procedurally flawed. The aspect of the case which is relevant for present purposes is that the prosecutor had failed to complain about these flaws. As to this omission, Finlay C.J. remarked:

"... If the proceedings in the District Court in this case were fully adversarial in character, then the absence of any application for a further adjournment; the absence of any complaint about the late delivery of medical or other professional reports and the failure to request the showing of the video on behalf of the prosecutors would almost certainly make these complaints unsustainable on behalf of the prosecutors. These proceedings were not, however, in the view of this Court, fully adversarial in nature, since a dominant issue in them which had to be investigated was the welfare of this child."

14–08 As noted earlier, constitutional justice has been located as one of the unenumerated rights established by Art.40.3.1° of the Constitution and it is characteristic of these rights that they are not unqualified. Surprisingly, little case law has yet emerged on this point; but it was at the centre of *O'Brien v Moriarty (No. 3)*[13] (which arose out of a public inquiry into the running by the Department of Communications of a competition for a mobile phone licence). The consultancy services in connection with the evaluation of the competitors for the licence had been provided to the Department by AM International. But AM was a Danish company which was reluctant to come to give evidence to the respondent and the respondent was advised by Danish lawyers that it would not be possible to secure AM's attendance, even by invoking the Danish court system. In these circumstances, the High Court (Quirke J.) had no hesitation in holding that the respondent's failure

---

[11]   [1991] 1 I.R. 230 at 234–235. See also, *Flanagan v UCD* [1999] I.L.R.M. 469 at 476 ("informed consent"); *O'Brien v Bord na Móna* [1983] I.R. 255 at 276 (Keane J.) and at 287 (Finlay P.). In *Gammell v Dublin County Council* [1983] I.L.R.M. 413 (for facts on which see para.14–155. No point was taken about the need to notify the plaintiff (see 2nd edn of this book at pp.470–471). The issue of waiver was expressly left open in *Glover v BLM* [1973] I.R. 388 at 425. cf. *State (Boyle) v General Medical Services (Payments) Board* [1981] I.L.R.M. 14 at 15.

[12]   [1990] 1 I.R. 305. The quotation is at 310–311.

[13]   [2006] 2 I.R. 474 at paras 125–139. See also, *Goodman v Hamilton (No. 2)* [1993] 3 I.R. 307 at 317; *Mahon v Air New Zealand* [1984] A.C. 808 at 814; *Ryan v VIP*, unreported, High Court, January 10, 1989; *McGonnell v Attorney General* [2007] 1 I.L.R.M. 321 at 337.

to take further steps to seek the witness' evidence was neither unreasonable (i.e. irrational) nor in breach of fair procedure.

14–09 Another feature of the *audi alteram partem* rule is that it probably does not extend as far as the protection given to an accused in criminal proceedings.[14] For example, it was stated in *Mooney v An Post*[15] that it does not include the right to silence. As was firmly pointed out by Barrington J. (writing for the Supreme Court):

> "The plaintiff raised no issue of fact which needed to be referred to a civil tribunal. It is important to emphasise that the dismissal proceedings were not criminal proceedings and it was not sufficient for a person in the position of the plaintiff simply to fold his arms and say: 'I'm not guilty. You prove it.'"

14–10 Like the "no bias" rule, the *audi alteram partem* rule has been invoked almost invariably to protect the individual from the exercise of state power. The question arises whether, in appropriate circumstances, it could operate in the opposite direction. It seems doubtful whether the passage just quoted may be taken so far as to sustain the proposition that (say) in a case before the Appeal Commissioner of Tax, the taxpayer is under a duty to disclose information to the Revenue Commissioners. But an argument which has succeeded (see paras 14–33 to 14–35) would be that, in a situation in which there is a third party, for instance, a contest between a licence applicant and an objector, the developer (licence applicant) would be obliged to make a disclosure to the objector.

B. PERSON AFFECTED MUST HAVE NOTICE

14–11 A stark illustration of the most basic right of all—the right to be alerted to the fact that some unfavourable official act is in the offing—is contained in *Davitt v Minister for Justice*.[16] Here, the High Court quashed an inquest's verdict

---

[14] The very particular field of criminal procedure is heavily weighted in favour of the accused, with such principles as the right to silence which certainly trumps the *audi alteram partem* rule. Nevertheless, Hogan and Whyte, *JM Kelly: The Irish Constitution*, 4th edn (Dublin: LexisNexis Butterworths, 2003), para.6.5.205 (see also, para.6.5.199) somewhat surprisingly remark, in the field of criminal procedure, that "[t]he State's right to the benefit of the *audi alteram partem* rule (in criminal as in other contexts) has also been acknowledged, both generally and in the special area of Article 40.4.2°".

[15] [1998] 4 I.R. 288 at 300. On the other hand, it is well established that details must be given by the decision-maker (see, e.g. *Atlantean Ltd v Minister for Communications and Natural Resources* [2007] IEHC 233 at para.3.2). One way of understanding the quotation in the text is to take it as emphasising at least that the criminal standard of proof does not apply outside the criminal field. But, in all fields of law, there is a principle that "he who asserts must prove". Like many points of evidence, this has not yet been well worked out in the administrative law field. The courts have also deprecated attempts to import principles of criminal procedure into civil disciplinary proceedings: *O'Laoire v Medical Council*, unreported, Supreme Court, July 23, 1997. (Further, as Keane J. said in that case in the High Court (unreported, January 27, 1995), a notice of inquiry convening a statutory disciplinary inquiry was not to be construed as if it were an indictment in a criminal case.)

[16] Unreported, High Court, Barron J., February 8, 1989. See, to similar effect, *State (Philpott) v Registrar of Title* [1986] I.L.R.M. 499 (Registrar must give notice to title owner, before

of suicide, following the death by drowning of a sea fisherman, despite the fact that the inquest had been held almost 18 years earlier. The flaw in the inquest's procedure was that there had been a failure to inform the next-of-kin about the inquest. (Ironically, this seems to have arisen because the responsible Garda liked such communication to be made as gently as possible and had left it to the skipper of the deceased's fishing boat to tell the deceased's family.) A more straightforward example of the principle is afforded by *Atlantean v Minister for Communications and Natural Resources*.[17] The Minister had purported to reduce the mackerel fishing quota allocated to the applicant. This was grounded on the alleged involvement of the applicant in undeclared landing of mackerel in Scotland. The flaw in the procedure followed by the Minister was that, despite requests from the applicant's solicitor, the Minister had failed to give any particulars of the landings.

14–12   One might ask: of what exactly must the person be given notice? In response to this question the following typology may be offered (although these are overlapping categories and nothing turns on the distinction: they are mentioned merely for the purpose of analysis):

> (i)   a notification that a decision adverse to the person affected is in contemplation;
> (ii) the grounds upon which the action is to be taken;
> (iii) all information relevant to the issue, including details of the case against and (probably) in favour of the person affected;
> (iv) the possible consequences of the decision—sanctions, etc.[18]

14–13   What if a deciding agency is motivated by a number of reasons about only some of which the applicant has been appraised or given an opportunity to be heard? This situation materialised in *International Fishing Vessels v Minister for Marine (No. 2)*[19] where the respondent had set forth, in a letter, a number of grounds for refusing to grant the applicant's request for a renewal of his sea-fishing licence. But there were other grounds of which the applicant had not been notified. McCarthy J. held[20]:

> "... I am satisfied that if the Minister intends to take into consideration a variety of different factors in making his decision, he must notify the person or body seeking the renewal of a sea-fishing licence of each of the matters; if

---

making an Inhibition); *Eircell v Leitrim County Council* [2001] 1 I.R. 479 (planning authority must give notice of intention to revoke a planning permission); *Balaz v Judge Kennedy* [2009] IEHC 110 (Hedigan J.) at paras 23–26.

[17]   [2007] IEHC 233; unreported, High Court, July 12, 2007. At para.3.2, Clarke J. noted that the applicant's solicitor's letter to the Minister stated in somewhat colourful terms that the behaviour of the Minister's Department "would decorate the actions of the great Mogul Hordes". See also, though in more prosaic terms, *Carroll v Bus Átha Cliath* [2005] 4 I.R. 184 at paras 15–17. For another good example, see *TV3 v IRTC* [1994] 2 I.R. 439.

[18]   For a case in which notice of each of these elements was given, see *Downey v O'Brien* [1994] 2 I.L.R.M. 130 at 150. See also, *Cahill v DCU* [2009] IESC 80 at p.6 per Geoghegan J.: "[t]he fair procedure that was required here was a warning that a notice of termination would follow if within a specified reasonable period the appellant did not clarify his position as to whether or when he was leaving the university".

[19]   [1991] 2 I.R. 92. See also, Part D below on reasons.

[20]   [1991] 2 I.R. 92 at 103. Each of the other two judges agreed with McCarthy J.

he fails to notify the applicant of a matter which, on its own, causes him to make his decision, then his decision must be quashed. If, however, there are valid reasons for his decision based upon matters of which he has notified the applicants and given them ample opportunity to make representations, the fact that there are other reasons of which he had not given them notice, does not, in my view, invalidate his decisions."

Right to see relevant information

14–14   This is a gate which could open very wide and we ought to acknowledge that, in this area, there are major practical and doctrinal difficulties. On the one side, traditionally the common law has always included (for good reason), throughout private and public law, such policies as "ignorance of the law is no defence". These ideas were consistent with the general idea that the law seldom imposed positive duties. But by now substantial differences have developed between public and private law; though it remains uncertain how far the present right has gone.

14–15   The free-wheeling Ombudsman has imposed a duty on public authorities to provide citizens with all relevant information regarding their rights.[21] But the courts, with a greater sense of both precedent and the wider ramifications of their decisions, have been more nuanced. For instance, in *Keogh v Criminal Assets Bureau*,[22] Keane C.J., while finding for the applicants on the basis of the taxpayers' Charter of Rights, was careful to point out that "… it is manifestly not the function of the second respondents … to give gratuitous advice, in all circumstances, to members of the public as to their legal position".[23] Accordingly, we can probably say that the law has not reached a stage where there is a general duty on a public body to give information even though not asked for. (The point may be raised here that an applicant who was ill-informed and not legally advised would not be able to ask the right questions. We have no case law on this sort of point.) What can be said is that, provided they ask for it, a person affected has a wide entitlement to relevant[24] information (a phrase elaborated below), since "… both parties [must be able] to approach the trial with all the cards faced upwards on the table".[25] An area of uncertainty here is that it may be significant that the information sought is already in the public domain (leaving aside exactly what is meant by "the public domain"). If a public body has to give to each individual information which is already conveniently available (e.g. on the website), its work would be unreasonably enlarged.[26]

14–16   To elaborate: the entitlement extends beyond the bare case against the applicant, and embraces other relevant documents and contextual material. Take,

---

[21]   See H & M, paras 9–48 to 9–52.

[22]   [2004] 2 I.R. 159.

[23]   [2004] 2 I.R. 159 at 176.

[24]   But not, of course, if the information sought is irrelevant: *Melton v Censorship of Publications Board* [2004] 1 I.L.R.M. 260.

[25]   See *Nolan v ILC* [1981] I.R. 33 at 39–40.

[26]   See *VU v Refugee Application Commissioner* [2005] 2 I.R. 536 at 546, in H & M, para.14–23. In *Re Mountcharles's Estate* [1935] I.R. 163 at 166, the only notice of the Land Commission decision which determined the ownership of mining rights was that published in *Iris Oifigiúil*.

for instance, *OO v Minister for Justice, Equality and Law Reform*.[27] (The respondent had refused to revoke a deportation order against the applicant, despite there being grounds to believe the applicant would take his own life. The Minister's decision was struck down because it had been taken without allowing the applicant any opportunity to read and comment on the report of the psychotherapist's report on him.) Again, in *O'Callaghan v Mahon (No. 1)*,[28] the Supreme Court had held, unanimously, that despite the Tribunal's policy of confidentiality, documents and materials generated during the Tribunal's information-gathering phase must be disclosed to the applicant, since they were essential to carry out a worthwhile cross-examination of a witness who was in effect giving evidence against the applicant. In addition, in an appropriate case, this entitlement would include information which was (or should have been) taken into account, in setting the merits of the person affected in a proper context. An example would be if a probationer public servant was not confirmed in his post, because of inadequate progress. He might be entitled to see the records of performance of other probationers.

14–17 An important practical point is that the right also extends to ensuring that the applicant is aware of what is bothering the respondent.[29] In addition, any policy or principles in the light of which the case is to be decided must be communicated to the applicant so as to allow them "the opportunity of conforming with or contesting such a principle or policy".[30] In this broad context, a case with considerable potential for growth is the Supreme Court decision in *PPA v Refugee Appeals Tribunal*.[31] Here the simple fact was that the applicants, in advance of the

---

[27]   [2004] 4 I.R. 426. See also, *State (Williams) v Army Pensions Board* [1981] I.L.R.M. 379; [1983] I.R. 308; *De Roiste v Minister for Defence* [2005] 3 I.R. 494 at 513.
       As a matter of statute law, objectors to a planning application have a right to see the planning file: Planning and Development Act 2000 s.38.

[28]   [2006] 2 I.R. 32. For the equivalent possible development regarding discovery in criminal procedure, see Ch.12, Part C. See also, *Huntstown v An Bord Pleanála* [1999] 1 I.L.R.M. 281 at 287 (respondent refused to order production of internal reports of objector to grant of planning permission. Judicial review of refusal failed on ground of prematurity).

[29]   To take some examples: (i) when an issue had been resolved in the applicant's favour by the Refugee Applications Commissioner at first instance, the Refugee Appeals Tribunal could not revisit the matter, on appeal, without putting the applicant on notice that the issue would be reopened: *NN v Refugee Appeals Tribunal* [2008] 1 I.R. 501; (ii) in *JGM v Refugee Applications Commissioner* [2009] IEHC 352 at paras 42–48, Clarke J. stated: "… if the [Officer of the Refugee Applications Commissioner] had taken the view that the acquisition of Mozambique nationality derived from his father's origins would or could debar the applicant from protection, then it was incumbent on the Officer to tease out the issue a little further, if only to establish the correctness of this view"; (iii) *Mishra v Minister for Justice* [1996] 1 I.R. 189 per Kelly J.: an applicant for citizenship was turned down because of a general assumption that he would later emigrate, despite his solemn declaration to the contrary. Kelly J. said that if the applicant were to be turned down on this basis, "fundamental fairness" required "he be given an opportunity to clarify his position".

[30]   *State (McGeough) v Louth County Council* (1973) 107 I.L.T.R. 13 at 28 per O'Daly J. See also, *Mahon v Air New Zealand* [1984] A.C. 808. (These authorities may be contradicted by *Corcoran v Minister for Social Welfare* [1991] 2 I.R. 175 at 184 per Murphy J.)

[31]   [2007] 1 I.L.R.M. 288. The quotations in the text are from 298–299, 301 and 302–303. (Notice that Geoghegan J. also stated in *PPA* (at 299): "It is not that a member of a tribunal is actually bound by a previous decision but consistency of decisions based on the same objective facts may, in appropriate circumstances, be a significant element in ensuring that a decision is objectively fair rather than arbitrary.") See also, *AA and EP v Minister for Justice, Equality and Law Reform* [2005] 4 I.R. 564 at para.39; *and PS and LS v Minister for Justice, Equality and Law Reform* [2011] 1 I.L.R.M. 206 at paras 38–42.

holding of their appeal before the Refugee Appeals Tribunal, had sought, but been denied, access to previous relevant decisions of the Tribunal. Writing on behalf of a unanimous, five-judge Supreme Court, Geoghegan J. stated[32]:

> "As to what kind of fair procedures the Constitution may require in any given instance, this will always depend on the particular circumstances … The refugee appeals are heard by single members of the tribunal taken from a large panel … It is of the nature of refugee cases that the problem for the appellant back in his or her country of origin which is leading him or her to seek refugee status is of a kind generic to that country or the conditions in that country. Thus, as in these appeals, it may be a problem of gross or official discrimination against homosexuals; enforced female circumcision; some concrete form of discrimination against a particular tribe. Where there are such problems it is blindingly obvious, in my view, that fair procedures require some reasonable mechanisms for achieving consistency in both the interpretation and the application of the law in cases like this of a similar category. Yet, if relevant previous decisions are not available to an appellant, he or she has no way of knowing whether there is such consistency …
>
> Previous decisions of the tribunal may be ones which if applied in the appellant's case would benefit the appellant but if there is no access, he has no knowledge of them and indeed he has no guarantee that the member of the tribunal has any personal knowledge of the previous decisions made by different colleagues … [S]uch a secret system is manifestly unfair. The unfairness is compounded if, as in this jurisdiction, the presenting officers as advocates against the appellants have full access to the previous decisions. That raises immediately an 'equality of arms' issue."

14–18   Among the most significant aspects of a significant decision is the fact that Geoghegan J. emphasised that "… the jurisprudential basis for the obligation to provide such reasonable access is not the new subsection [Immigration Act 2003 s.7] but the general constitutional requirement of fair procedures". This means that the new principle applies generally and not just to refugees. Thus, the new principle could be seen as part of a wide trend which also embraces the Freedom of Information Act 1997 s.16 (obligation on a public body to publish "rules, procedures … and an index of any precedents kept by the body"), as well as a stream of decisions by the Ombudsman. Given the twilight world which some public bodies allow to obscure their previous decisions, the strong tide in favour of open government on this front may have significant consequences.

14–19   But notice that Geoghegan J. also made a considerable qualification of this principle:

> "It would be wrong for this court, certainly in these proceedings, to hold that there was any statutory or constitutional obligation to provide some open library containing redacted previous decisions … [It suffices if] each of those applicants is given reasonable access, in whatever form the tribunal considers fit, to previous decisions which are being reasonably required for legal relevance …

---

[32] [2007] 1 I.L.R.M. 288 at 298–299.

> Finally, I should make it clear that this judgment relates only to the rights
> of persons who in advance of a hearing by the tribunal have requested access
> to relevant precedents and have been refused ...".

The final sentence of this quotation from *PPA* is significant: the applicant must
ask.[33]

14–20   One should note, too, that a distinction has been drawn between information
or evidence and, on the other hand, argumentation. As it was put in *Davy v Financial
Services Ombudsman*,[34] "where submissions [are] requested of the argument as
to right and wrong, there is no need to exchange such arguments. The parties can
make whatever arguments they wish. By contrast, where any factual material is
presented that may fairly be said to be of influence to adjudication, the respondent
to a complaint must be able to reply". Likewise, in the *National Maternity Hospital
v The Information Commissioner*,[35] it was contended by the Hospital that there was
a failure by the Information Commissioner to provide fair procedures in that the
Information Commissioner had relied upon submissions made by two complainants,
without giving the Hospital the opportunity to consider those submissions. Quirke
J. stated:

> "I know of no principle of natural or constitutional law or justice [*sic*],
> which confers upon parties who make submissions to a decision-making
> body, the right to respond to the submissions made by every other party who
> participates in the process."

Perhaps, the key difference between facts and argument is that it should be
possible to anticipate counter-arguments, whereas new facts cannot be predicted.
Admittedly, Quirke J. noted that he was dealing with the specific statutory context
of the Commissioner, who was intended to be inquisitorial rather than adversarial
in nature. However there is such practical commonsense in the notion that there
must be some end to the entitlement to debate that one would expect it also to
apply more generally. This rule does not contradict the general obligation described
earlier that, if requested, a public body may be under a duty to give information as
to relevant facts or policy: the ratio of *Davy* and *National Maternity Hospital* is that
this obligation does not extend to particular arguments, which are drawn from the
facts or policy. A further characteristic of the two authorities is that the situations
involved each conform to an accusational (or triangular) model; in other words,
there was a party on each side. We have not yet had a case of this type involving
just a decision-maker and an applicant.

Person affected "well knew"

14–21   It will often happen that, in reality, the person affected will have a pretty
fair idea of the case against them, although they have not actually been explicitly
informed about it by the public body. The law accommodates this feature of

---

[33]   See similarly, *Fairyhouse Club Ltd v An Bord Pleanála*, unreported, High Court, Finnegan J.,
       July 18, 2001. See also, *Stack v An Bord Pleanála*, unreported, High Court, O'Neill J., July
       11, 2000 at p.10.
[34]   [2008] 2 I.L.R.M. 507 at para.50.
[35]   [2007] 3 I.R. 643. The quotation is at 669.

common experience by the notion that the applicant "well knew" of the particular aspect of the case against him about which he claimed he should have had explicit notice. This pregnant phrase was used by Blayney J. in *Gallagher v The Revenue Commissioners (No. 1)*,[36] which arose out of the suspension of a Customs and Excise officer. Accepting that "natural justice" required that the person suspended be informed as to the grounds why he had been suspended, Blayney J. made an exception because the circumstances were such that the plaintiff "well knew why he had been suspended".[37]

14–22 By contrast, certain cases have set a rather high standard of explicitness and formality in regard to the warning which the public authority must give to the person affected. An example is *Gallagher v Corrigan*[38] which centred on the need to give notice of the likely consequences. The case arose out of the purported disciplining of four prison officers—the applicants in the case—following on the escape of a prisoner from St Patrick's Institution. Blayney J. posed the following question:

> "The applicants may have had reason to believe that if they did not give a satisfactory explanation of how they had performed their duties on the day of the escape, they might be charged with negligence, but *they had no reason to believe that such a charge had been preferred against them.*"[39]

14–23 The length to which the last sentence goes is clear when one bears in mind the detailed content of the reports which each applicant had received. In the face of this, it might be assumed, by a lay person of average intelligence who had some explanation of his conduct to offer that it would be prudent to offer it. However, Blayney J. rejected such a commonsensical approach and required something more akin to a formal charge. One might add that there is only a very fine line of distinction between this line of law and the doctrine of waiver which would have afforded an argument for the respondent; yet this was not mentioned in the judgment.

---

[36] [1991] 2 I.R. 370. Yet, in *TV3 v Independent Radio and Television Commission* [1994] 2 I.R. 439, Blayney J. stated that "[i]t was submitted on behalf of the Commission that the 31st August, 1991 was the deadline ... and that Mr Morris should have known that if the required information was not submitted in time that was the end of the negotiations. I accept Mr Morris' evidence that he was unaware of this ...". There was no mention here of the possibility that Mr Morris should have known. See also, *Doran v An Garda Síochána* [1994] 1 I.L.R.M. 303 at 311.

[37] [1991] 2 I.R. 370 at 374. See also, *Doupe v Limerick Corporation* [1981] I.L.R.M. 456 at 464; *O'Laoire v Medical Council*, unreported, High Court, January 27, 1995; *Lang v Government of Ireland* [1993] E.L.R. 234 at 245 per O'Hanlon J.; *Deegan v Minister for Finance* [2000] E.L.R. 190 at 204–205.

[38] Unreported, High Court, Blayney J., February 1, 1988.

[39] The quotation is from pp.13–14 of the judgment (emphasis added). See to similar effect, *Quirke v Bord Luthchleas na hÉireann* [1988] I.R. 83 at 87–88.

Misleading statements by public body

14–24   Worse than a failure to give notice of relevant information is a situation in which the public body misleads the person affected. In the decided cases[40] on this theme (in none of which was there any mention of legitimate expectations or estoppel), a misleading impression had been given as to the state of the public body's mind as to how the case was going. In the earliest case, *Kiely v Minister for Social Welfare (No. 1)*,[41] K succeeded on the ground (which was put on the basis of constitutional justice) that the appeals officer, at an oral hearing in respect of a death benefit claim, had given K the impression that her claim was likely to succeed. In consequence, K's solicitor did not persist with his request for an adjournment to enable him to call a medical witness who would have fortified K's case. Later, in *Madden v Minister for the Marine*,[42] one of the minor grounds for the applicant's success was that "... the Minister appears to have taken his decision in respect of the foreshore licence and had taken it at a time when he was still representing ... that he was considering the objections in this matter ...".[43] In each case, the point on which the public authority misled the applicant was procedural rather than substantive; but no-one regarded this as a significant distinction. Nor was the question raised as to whether the applicant had acted upon the misleading statement to their detriment.

Information obtained outside the hearing

14–25   One form of denial of *audi alteram partem* occurs when, although some type of hearing (whether oral or written) has been allowed, the decision-maker relies upon information or argument which has been obtained outside that hearing and not disclosed to the party adversely affected by it. It is useful to distinguish three sub-categories, before making some general comments.

(a) Information gathered specifically

14–26   The most straightforward category is where the evidence or information is gathered specifically for that case. Here there is no doubt that the principle has been violated. A straightforward illustration is *Killiney and Ballybrack v Minister for Local Government (No. 1)*[44] which arose from a planning appeal in which one of the factual issues was whether the sewerage disposal facilities in the area of the proposed development were already overloaded. There was a direct conflict of evidence at the oral inquiry as to whether raw sewerage was to be found on the foreshore near the development. After the inquiry had been concluded, the inspector examined the foreshore on his own and included a record of his findings in his report

---

[40]   Apart from the cases in the text, see *Beirne v Commissioner of An Garda Síochána* [1992] I.L.R.M. 699 at 707–708 (HC); [1993] I.L.R.M. 1 at 9 (SC); *Frenchurch v Wexford County Council* [1992] 2 I.R. 268, considered in the Third Edition, pp.544–545. *Frenchurch Properties* was distinguished by Laffoy J. in *Littondale Ltd v Wicklow County Council* [1996] 2 I.L.R.M. 519 at 537.

[41]   [1971] I.R. 21.

[42]   [1993] I.L.R.M. 436.

[43]   [1993] I.L.R.M. 436 at 448–449.

[44]   (1978) 112 I.L.T.R. 9. See also, *State (Hegarty) v Winters* [1956] I.R. 320; *Horan v An Post*, unreported, High Court, January 18, 1991 at 9–11; *O'Brien v An Garda Síochána, Irish Times Law Report*, November 18, 1996.

to the Minister who was, at the time of the case, responsible for deciding planning appeals. In the High Court, Finlay P. invalidated the Minister's decision because it was based on evidence which had not been disclosed to the party disadvantaged by it, who thus had no opportunity to reply to it.

(b) Information gathered specifically which consists of a legal opinion

14–27   Here, as with the first category, the information is gathered specifically for the particular case; but, in contrast to the first category, the information consists of a legal opinion; and the public body fails to show it to the applicant (or perhaps fails to allow an opportunity for rebuttal by the applicant). An example is afforded by *State (Polymark Ltd) v ITGWU*[45] in which an employer had made a submission before the Labour Court that, in the circumstances of the particular case, the court had no jurisdiction to entertain an appeal from the Equality Officer. In response to this submission, the Labour Court adjourned the case in order to seek legal advice from the registrar and, having received it, continued with the case. In the High Court, the applicant employer complained of the fact that his counsel before the Labour Court had not been made aware of the advice given or afforded an opportunity of commenting upon it. Blayney J. decided the case on the basis that, even if this were correct he would, since no useful purpose would be served, exercise his discretion against granting a remedy. However, Blayney J. evidently felt that the applicant's contention was correct in principle. In a passage (which has however, been substantially glossed in *Georgopolous*, as explained in the next paragraph), he stated[46]:

> "It might be of assistance for the future, however, if I were to indicate what procedure the Labour Court could safely adopt if similar circumstances arise again. They should first inform the parties of their intention to ask the registrar for legal advice; then, having obtained the advice, they should, at a resumed hearing, inform the parties of the nature of the advice they had obtained and give the parties an opportunity of making submissions in regard to it, and finally, having heard the submissions, the members of the court should, on their own, without further reference to the registrar, arrive at their own conclusion on the issue."

14–28   There was, however, a distinct, but possibly temporary, change of direction in *Georgopolous v Beaumont Hospital Board*[47] which admittedly concerned what the High Court characterised as the relatively informal procedure involved in terminating a contract of employment. One feature of the procedure about which the applicant complained was that the legal assessor, who was advising the lay Hospital Board, had given his advice in the absence of the applicant and without the advice being disclosed to him. In both the High Court and the Supreme Court, *Polymark* was distinguished rather unconvincingly[48] and the plaintiff's argument

---

[45]   [1987] I.L.R.M. 357.
[46]   [1987] I.L.R.M. 357 at 363. But cf. the gloss put on this decision by the Supreme Court in *Georgopolous v Beaumont Hospital Board* [1998] 3 I.R. 132 at 138, 154–156 and in *Cronin v Competition Authority* [1998] 1 I.R. 265 at 274; on each of which, see H & M, para.14–38.
[47]   [1998] 3 I.R. 132.
[48]   [1998] 3 I.R. 132 at 154–156. Kelly J., in *Prendiville v Medical Council* [2008] 3 I.R. 122 at para.138, states that "I agree with [Hogan and Morgan, *Administrative* Law, Third ed. p.556]

rejected, on the basis that the Board had to determine a question of fact only; whereas the advice from the assessor concerned points of law. One could question the logic of this distinction in the light of the fact that there will certainly be times when the termination of a contract will involve points of law and the legal advice would have been open to contention by the applicant, if they had been allowed the opportunity.

14–29   However, in *Prendiville v Medical Council*[49] legal advice was given to the Medical Council, in a professional disciplinary case, in circumstances unknown to the applicant who was given no opportunity of addressing the correctness of this advice. Citing *Polymark* with—and *Georgopolous* without—approval, the High Court regarded this omission as a ground of invalidity. Here is a point which awaits an authoritative Supreme Court decision.

(c) Evidence drawn from public bodies general experience and expertise

14–30   Unlike the other two categories, here the evidence is not specific to that case but is gleaned from the public body's general experience and expertise. This situation is illustrated by *Kiely v Minister for Social Welfare (No. 2)*[50] which arose after the appellant's husband had suffered an accident at work which caused severe burns and led eventually to depression. A few months later he died and the appellant, K, claimed a death benefit under the Social Welfare (Occupational Injuries) Act 1966 and this was rejected by the appeals officer in the (then) Department of Social Welfare. Before the appeals officer, the principal issue—on which the medical expert giving evidence for K disagreed with the Minister for Social Welfare's medical adviser—was whether it was possible for a heart attack to have been caused by depression and, thus, to be connected with her husband's employment. This question was settled against K by the appeals officer. K appealed successfully to the Supreme Court on a procedural ground, namely that, during the interval between the hearing of the appeal and the notification of the decision nearly two months later, the medical assessor had written a letter to the appeals officer giving new evidence as to why depression could not cause a heart attack. This letter, with its attachment, was not shown to K. In holding that this evidence had been obtained in breach of the rules of constitutional justice, Henchy J. stated briefly that the assessor's function is "to act as a medical dictionary and not as a medical report".

14–31   Such cases illustrate a difficulty which is likely to loom large in the future. For a large part of the raison d'être of specialised tribunals is that the tribunal has the ability and opportunity to accumulate a wealth of specialised knowledge, information and expertise. This indeed is said to be one of its advantages over a court. To some extent, therefore, a tribunal's decision is the result not only of the evidence adduced by the parties at a particular hearing; it is also the product of

which states that in the Supreme Court [in *Georgopolous*], *Polymark* was distinguished rather unconvincingly". Kelly J. goes on to say that the facts in *Prendiville* were "more like those in *Polymark* than *Georgopolous*" and went on to rule in favour of the applicant on this point.

[49]   [2008] 3 I.R. 122 at para.138. This was not the only thing the matter with the procedure: the source of the advice was the Registrar who had been the "prosecutor" of the applicant; see para.13–31.

[50]   [1997] I.R. 267. The quotation is at 284.

the tribunal's own expertise, which has been brought to bear upon the evidence. However, this attitude collides with a rule which is central to all judicial or quasi-judicial adjudication, namely that a decision must be made in accordance only with evidence introduced at the hearing, tested by the opposing sides and forming part of the record (this is the reason why the categories of material of which a court may take judicial or official notice are severely limited).

14–32   Outside Ireland, various tests have been proposed for resolving these conflicting tensions.[51] First, a distinction has been made according to whether a tribunal is using its expertise as a substitute for evidence or only for the purpose of evaluating the evidence that has already been presented. This test, which of course involves a difficult question of degree, would seem to accord with the distinction drawn in *Kiely (No. 2)* between a medical dictionary and a medical report. However, it might be argued that the court misapplied its own test in *Kiely*, in that a medical report is personal to a specific patient, whereas the issue in that case (whether depression is capable of causing a heart attack) was a general question which could have been appropriately dealt with in a medical dictionary. Another test, also used outside Ireland, distinguishes between the general accumulated experience of the decision-maker, which need not be shown to an applicant, and material obtained from an identifiable source. Comparing the Irish cases with this test, it may be argued, in regard to category (iii) that the material relied on by the appeals officer in *Kiely (No. 2)* ought to have been classified as "accumulated experience".[52] In short, it would be appropriate to treat cases in category (iii) differently from those in the other two.

Third-party rights

14–33   Where a public body is exercising its authority, e.g. in the grant of a licence, fair procedures must be afforded not only to the applicant who would benefit if the licence were granted, but also to the objector who would suffer thereby. This was the case in *Madden v Minister for the Marine*[53] which arose out of the grant of licences to construct fish farming facilities in Ballyvaughan Bay in Co. Clare. The significant feature of the case was that the licence had been granted pursuant to s.15 of the Fisheries (Consolidation) Act 1959 rather than s.54 of the Fisheries

---

[51] Contrast De Smith, *Judicial Review of Administrative Action*, 4th edn (London: Sweet & Maxwell, 1980), pp.203–207 and the Fifth Edition of the same book (1995) at pp.444–447. The change from the fourth to the fifth editions in this authoritative work may be characterised as a shift in an "Irish direction". But significantly, this appears to be due not to any Irish or recent English case law but, presumably, because of the new editors' views.

[52] Broadly speaking this was the conclusion reached in *Davy v Financial Services Ombudsman* [2010] 2 I.L.R.M. 305, where admittedly the court seemed to regard the respondent as a special case.

[53] [1993] I.L.R.M. 436 at 447–448 (HC); [1997] 1 I.L.R.M. 136 at 146 (SC). *Madden* was followed on this point, and more generally, in a similar case under the Fisheries (Consolidation) Act 1959, namely *Mulcahy v Minister for the Marine*, unreported, High Court, November 4, 1994. A somewhat similar situation arose in *South West Area Heath Board v Information Commissioner* [2005] 2 I.R. 547, where an adopted child sought information from the Board about her adoption, under the Freedom of Information Act 1997 and the High Court held that the birth mother ought to be given an opportunity to make representations before the Board took its decision. See also, *JF v Director of Public Prosecutions* [2005] I.R. 174 at para.27; *State (Haverty) v An Bord Pleanála* [1987] I.R. 485 at 493 (holding that the rights of an objector fall at the lower end of the register).

Act 1980. The latter avenue requires notice to be given and permits public inquiry and recourse to the High Court; whereas the former lacks each of these features. It was argued for the Minister that he was free to utilise either provision. However, the High Court (Johnson J.) and, on appeal, the Supreme Court held against this contention—in part, it is true, on a point of statutory interpretation; but also, to a greater degree, on the general doctrine of constitutional justice. In consequence of this, it was held that the would-be objectors who were the applicants for judicial review "had an absolute right to see and deal with the case being made for the applicant [for the licence] and this is particularly so when the minister decided not to have a public inquiry". Later in his judgment, Johnson J. also referred to the fact that "the Minister appears to have taken his decision ... without having made available to the applicants the information upon which he had based his decision".

14–34 Plainly *Madden* was correct on the facts. However, one may query the limits of the doctrine which it has brought to the surface. In the first place, whilst it may sometimes happen that an objector will have the same legal and/or moral interest as an applicant—or, even, in rare cases, a greater interest—the contrary will usually be the case: for an applicant for a licence will necessarily have sufficient legal interest to carry out the activity authorised by the licence, whereas the interest of an objector will vary. To take an example, an objector to an application for planning permission may be the owner of the house next door to the site of the proposed development; or the tenant of the next door house; or merely a concerned passer-by. The question which arises is whether each of these different levels of objectors should have a right to the same quantum of constitutional justice as the applicant, who will usually own the land to be developed. This line of comment leads ultimately to the question: at what point does the objector's interest become so insubstantial that s/he is not entitled to be heard?[54] It is perhaps an indication of some element of hedging of bets that the High Court's judgment in *Madden* uses such vague and circumlocutious formulations as "an obligation to act fairly and judicially in accordance with the fair principles of constitutional justice".[55]

14–35 Secondly, as a matter of administrative practicability, it is always easier for a public body to grant constitutional justice to an applicant because it is inherent in the process of (say) granting a licence that the public body will be in contact with the applicant. Thus in the planning field, if the movement towards some element of constitutional justice[56] at the local authority stage continues, then the argument is likely to be heard that there should be a parallel development for objectors. And this may prove difficult to implement. For example, frequently negotiations regarding planning permission go on between developers and planners *after* the advertisement has appeared at the site and hence at a time when it would be hard to inform potential objectors about them. In another context, the same line of possible

---

[54] For this question, in the particular statutory context of the Tribunal of Inquiry, see *Boyhan v Beef Tribunal* [1993] 1 I.R. 210. The query in the text is similar to the question of locus standi. The reason is that an applicant will usually have locus standi before a court regarding an *audi alteram partem* point, if, but only if, he had a right to be heard. Thus, the substantive hearing argument and the locus standi argument are usually effectively the same. For this reason, very few of the cases labelled "locus standi" involve *audi alteram partem*.

[55] *Madden v Minister for the Marine* [1993] I.L.R.M. 436 at 447.

[56] On which developments, see Third Edition, pp.544–545.

future development might ground a stronger form of victims' rights in a criminal trial than is now available.

C. PERSON AFFECTED MUST BE FACILITATED TO MAKE THE BEST POSSIBLE CASE

14–36 In Part B, we covered the obligation to alert the person affected, and to give details of the case against them. Here we consider the complementary requirement that the person should have the necessary opportunities and facilities to make the best possible case on his behalf.

Failure to entertain the argument

14–37 A basic principle is that the decision-maker must be made aware of, and really entertain, the applicants' arguments, so that they are fully and fairly considered.[57] Most of the cases illustrating this principle are so particular that they need only be mentioned in a footnote.[58] However, in a sensible departure in the opposite direction, it has been held[59] that, if material had been put forward by the applicant which had already been considered by the public body in the same context, then there is no need for it to be considered a second time.

14–38 Another question of interest here is whether the same person has to be involved at all stages of a decision. In large organisations, often routine decisions have to be shared among a number of different officials with similar qualifications and experience and guided by the same rules. In such situations, it may be convenient for the same decision to be dealt with by different persons at different stages. The legal question which arises here is whether there is any general principle precluding such an arrangement. In the first place, it goes almost without saying that this arrangement is forbidden if it causes the procedure to be unfair, most obviously because of some failure of communications between the two decision-makers.[60] But, otherwise, there is no modern authority to suggest that this administratively convenient, or even essential, practice is unlawful.[61]

---

[57] This principle is also related to the cases grouped under the title "Deciding without Hearing", considered at paras 14–59 to 14–66.

[58] (i) In *BFO v Governor of Dochas Centre* [2005] 2 I.R. 1, at the time when the applicant had applied for residency, there was a strong likelihood that she would achieve it by virtue of the fact that she had an Irish-born child who thus had Irish citizenship. However, after this time, the Supreme Court decided *AO and DL v Minister for Justice, Equality and Law Reform* [2003] 1 I.R. 1, which made a significant impact on the applicant's case. Finlay Geoghegan J. stated in *BFO* (at 27): "... as a matter of fair procedure the applicant was entitled to an opportunity of having the ... judgments [in the new case] considered by her lawyers ...", and making submissions thereon; (ii) In *JN v Minister for Justice, Equality and Law Reform* [2009] 1 I.R. 146 at para.8, the High Court ruled that "... the [Refugee Appeals Tribunal] member erred in refusing to permit submissions", seemingly on the basis that he and the presenting officer were taken by surprise.

[59] *FN v Minister for Justice, Equality and Law Reform* [2009] 1 I.R. 88 at para.70.

[60] A case in which this sort of argument did succeed, albeit in particular circumstances, is *Hession v Irish Land Commission* [1978] I.R. 322, analysed in the Third Edition, pp.564–565.

[61] A similar situation was upheld even in the case of the District Court: *O'Keeffe v Governor of St Patrick's Institution* [2006] 1 I.R. 228 at 241.

Right to an oral hearing, right to give evidence and right to cross-examine

14–39   Where there is a right to an "oral hearing", what this means is usually taken to be a series of rights, spelt out in the seminal case of *Re Haughey*.[62] This arose out of the Dáil Committee of Public Accounts' investigation into the expenditure of the grant in aid for Northern Ireland relief. During the course of the Committee's investigations, a senior Garda Officer made a number of serious allegations against the applicant. These accusations lay at the heart of the Committee's investigation, so much so, the court considered, that he might be regarded as being in an analogous position to a party in a court case, at any rate, so far as his good name was concerned. Emphasising this factor, Ó Dálaigh C.J., writing for the Supreme Court majority, held, in a much-cited passage, that the Committee ought to have granted Mr Haughey the following procedural safeguards:

> "(a) that he should be furnished with a copy of the evidence which reflected on his good name; (b) that he should be allowed to cross-examine, by counsel, his accuser or accusers; (c) that he should be allowed to give rebutting evidence; and (d) that he should be permitted to address, again by counsel, the Committee in his own defence."[63]

14–40   These rights have normally been applied as a package—in other words: "all or nothing". But there is no reason in principle why, in appropriate circumstances, some only of the rights would be applied: for example (as indicated in the following paragraphs) because of its character, certain evidence might have to be subject to cross-examination; while other evidence could be given in documentary form.

14–41   There are many authorities which testify that, depending on the circumstances, the *audi alteram partem* rule does not always require an oral hearing.[64] One of the bases for such a ruling was illustrated in *Mooney v An Post*.[65] The Supreme Court held that the plaintiff had raised no issue of fact which required that he be given an oral hearing before his dismissal as a postman. In these circumstances, said Barrington J., the plaintiff "had raised no issue of fact which needed to be referred to a civil tribunal".[66]

14–42   A case on the other side of what it is suggested is the same line is the Supreme Court decision in *Gallagher v Revenue Commissioners (No. 2)*.[67] This decision arose out of the purported dismissal of an officer of customs and excise

---

[62]   [1971] I.R. 217. For a recent illustration of the right to cross-examination, also in the context of a parliamentary committee of inquiry, see *Maguire v Ardagh* [2002] 1 I.R. 385 at 429–433, 547–550, 630–646, 704–707 where the applicant's rights were held to be wrongly restricted in that: (i) it was sought to postpone cross-examination until the conclusion of the evidence of all the witnesses; (ii) cross-examination of a witness was conditional on the committee's permission; and (iii) the time-frame for cross-examination was very restrictive.

[63]   [1971] I.R. 217 at 263. Failure to permit cross-examination was also held to be a breach of *audi alteram partem* in *Kiely v Minister for Social Welfare* [1977] I.R. 287, but this was a very particular situation in that this right had been granted to the other side.

[64]   *Potts v Minister for Defence* [2005] 2 I.L.R.M. 517 at 527.

[65]   [1998] 4 I.R. 288.

[66]   Another case in which a plea for an oral hearing failed on similar grounds is the immigration case of *VZ v Minister for Justice, Equality and Law Reform* [2002] 2 I.R. 135 at 161–162.

[67]   [1995] 1 I.R. 55: "... without an oral hearing, it would be extremely difficult, if not impossible to arrive at a true judgment on the issues which arose in this case". For a similar case to

for allegedly deliberately undervaluing vehicles which had been imported illegally into the State. The central fact in the case against the applicant was the value of the second-hand vehicles. Yet (notwithstanding vigorous requests from the applicant's legal advisers) the witnesses on this point were not called before the inquiry for cross-examination; all the evidence on the point was hearsay. The framework within which the Supreme Court set their decision on the point was that, to quote Hamilton C.J., "… while tribunals exercising quasi-judicial functions … are given a certain latitude … in the circumstances of the case, they may not act in such a way as to *imperil a fair hearing or a fair result*".[68] Here "the circumstances of the case" included the gravity of the consequences for the applicant (dismissal for misconduct, in something like disgrace, after 20 years' service), and the fact that the issue involved (the price of a particular second-hand vehicle) was both the essence of the entire case, and a matter of peculiar subjectivity and volatility.

14–43   Another pair of cases which illustrate the same contrast is *State (Boyle) v General Medical Services (Payment) Board*[69] and *Borges v Fitness to Practice Committee*.[70] *Boyle* stemmed from an investigation which had established that the applicant doctor's claims for remuneration, under the "choice of doctor" scheme, were excessive. Under the agreement on which the scheme was based, the applicant could, as he did, complain to an appeal committee. His appeal was rejected following an oral hearing. The committee based its decision on, inter alia, statistical data concerning the average number of home visits in the particular area. The applicant requested that the expert who had compiled the data should be made available for cross-examination before the committee. Keane J. held that the refusal of this request did not constitute a violation of constitutional justice because, when the applicant received a copy of the data, he had not raised any specific issue as to its reliability, which required oral evidence in order to be resolved.

14–44   On the opposite side of the line is *Borges v Fitness to Practice Committee*. The applicant had earlier been struck off the (British) medical register for professional misconduct, including inappropriate touching of female patients. He was also registered as a doctor in Ireland and the respondent was going to proceed with an inquiry into the same actions which had grounded his striking off in the UK. The important point is that the respondent had been asked to accept as evidence the transcript of proceedings before the British General Medical Council. The applicant's successful argument was that to admit such evidence, denying him the right to cross-examine, would violate his right to constitutional justice. The general point is that it is of the nature of transcript evidence, that the capacity of the respondent to arrive at a different conclusion from the British authorities, even as to the level of seriousness of the conduct, was drastically reduced.

14–45   Giving judgment for the Supreme Court, Keane C.J. (the same judge who had decided *Boyle*) accepted that there were exceptions to the rule excluding

---

Gallagher (No. 2), see *Galvin v Chief Appeals Officer* [1997] 3 I.R. 240, in the Third Edition, p.559.
[68]   [1995] 1 I.R. 55 at 76 (emphasis added). Denham J. concurred with Hamilton C.J.
[69]   [1981] I.L.R.M. 14. In effect, agreeing with *Boyle*, Charleton J. has articulated the test by reference to the reasonableness standard in *Menolly Homes v The Appeal Commissioners* [2010] IEHC 49 at paras 40–41.
[70]   [2004] 1 I.R. 103.

hearsay. In explaining why the present situation did not fall within any of the exceptions, Keane C.J. emphasised: that the accusations against the applicant were very serious in that they exposed him to the possibility of being struck off; that the Committee's decision turned largely on the issue of fact in the transcript; and that there was no difficulty in the complainants giving evidence, except that they were unwilling to do so. (The last point, of course, was not the fault of the respondent, much less Irish patients who might be treated by the applicant.)

14–46   What is the comparison between the question, when is there a right to cross-examination, and the nearby issue of whether a tribunal must adhere to the standard exclusionary rules of evidence, developed by and for courts, often sitting with juries? The long-established evidential rule excluding hearsay evidence (save where an exception applies) is obviously grounded on the same policy as the constitutional justice rule requiring an oral hearing in certain circumstances. But it is probably correct to take the law, in regard to (say) tribunals, to be that hearsay evidence is not as such excluded; but rather that, where the circumstances are that the absence of this opportunity would be unfair, a person adversely affected by evidence must be allowed an opportunity to test it by cross-examination. In other words, the cash value in the difference lies in the fact that the common law rule operates inflexibly; whereas, where an applicant is relying on the constitutional justice principle, they must be able to demonstrate that, in the circumstances, the lack of an opportunity to cross-examine would produce unfairness.

Right to a lawyer

14–47   Where there is an oral hearing, its practical value may depend on whether the individual is represented by an experienced advocate.[71] As was said in a deportation case (though probably without being confined to that context), "the right of access to a lawyer and to legal advice is a fundamental one".[72] Moreover, Denham J. stated that "… even in many situations which are not adjudicative … [a person] may wish to have a lawyer by his side".[73]

14–48   On the other hand, there might be thought to be a counter-policy here, namely that legal representation (apart from its advantages) will often complicate, prolong and make more expensive any proceedings. There is a substantial overlap between this issue and the broader question of whether any form of constitutional justice, not merely legal representation, should be barred or restricted because it undermines discipline or thwarts any other important policy.[74]

14–49   This counter-policy against legal representation has undoubtedly had some influence on Irish law. For example, in *Barry v Sentence Review Group and the*

---

[71]   *O'Brien v Personal Injuries Assessment Board* [2009] 2 I.L.R.M. 22 at paras 44, 58–60, 66 (Supreme Court holding that legal representation is a right of special importance in common law jurisdictions where the legal system is adversarial). See also, *McCann v Monaghan District Court* [2010] I.L.R.M. 17 at 65–66.

[72]   *Agao v Minister for Justice, Equality and Law Reform* [2007] 2 I.R. 492 at para.28.

[73]   *O'Brien v Personal Injuries Assessment Board* [2009] 2 I.L.R.M. 22, holding that it was ultra vires the power of PIAB to bar an applicant for damages from communicating with the Board by way of a solicitor.

[74]   This broader question is discussed at paras 14–180 to 14–183.

Minister for Justice, Equality and Law Reform,[75] while holding that the applicant was entitled to disclosure of material to be considered by the respondent, the High Court ruled that he was not entitled to legal representation. Butler J. stated:

> "As indicated, the applicant has at all material times had the benefit of independent legal advice and representation and his entitlement thereto is not as issue. What is at issue is whether he should be entitled to representation at an oral hearing before the first respondent. I do not believe that this is necessary to satisfy the requirements of fair procedures. The function of the first respondent is purely an advisory one and it exercises no power akin to a disciplinary body. It meets for the purpose of coming to a recommendation in a non-adversarial way. To introduce full legal representation at an informal hearing would, in my view, be disproportionate and would have the effect of changing the whole character of the procedure set up by the second respondent."

14–50 Furthermore, in *Corcoran v Minister for Social Welfare*[76]—which arose out of a social welfare appeal before an appeals officer of the Department of Social Welfare—the contention that there was a right to representation was also rejected (though, admittedly, representation had in fact been allowed). Again, in two (middle-aged) disciplinary cases, *Smullen* and *Gallagher*,[77] a claim for representation was refused, but it should be said that these were disciplinary cases and there is a particular counter-policy which holds that too much constitutional justice is bad for discipline. And there have also been weighty statements in the opposite direction. In a prison officer discipline case, Geoghegan J. stated[78] that "… there could be no automatic right to legal representation but, on the other hand, I would be of the opinion that in an important enough case where a prison officer's employment was at stake the requirement of fair procedures may include an entitlement to legal representation."

14–51 In the light of this knotty case law, it seems that the best synthesis may be to say only that the deciding authority must consider whether in all the circumstances (especially the seriousness of the consequences for the applicant), representation is necessary in the interests of justice.

14–52 Assuming that a right to representation exists, is there any limit to its extent in particular circumstances? For instance, can the administrative agency control the scale and nature of the legal representation? This point arose in *McGrath and Ó Ruairc v Trustees of Maynooth*[79] which involved the dismissal of two University lecturers. The Supreme Court ruled that there was a right to be represented by a

---

[75] [2001] 4 I.R. 167. The quotation is at 169–170.

[76] [1991] 2 I.R. 175 at 183. See also, *People (DPP) v Healy* [1990] 2 I.R. 73 at 81; *O'Neill v Iarnród Éireann* [1991] E.L.R. 1; *Aziz v Midland Health Board* [1995] E.L.R. 48 at 58; *Scariff v Taylor* [1996] 2 I.L.R.M. 278 at 287, 289; *Galvin v The Chief Appeals Officer* [1997] 3 I.R. 240.

[77] *State (Gallagher) v Governor of Portlaoise Prison*, unreported, High Court, May 18, 1977 (prison discipline); *State (Smullen) v Duffy* [1980] I.L.R.M. 46 (school expulsion).

[78] *Garvey v Minister for Justice, Equality and Law Reform* [2006] 1 I.R. 548 at 559, para.21. See also, *Potts v Minister for Defence* [2005] 2 I.L.R.M. 517 at 527.

[79] [1979] I.L.R.M. 166. The Supreme Court here may have taken the paternalistic view that it knew best that the plaintiffs would be better off if represented by lawyers. For a case stating

lawyer; but not by the lecturers' trade union representative. *Flanagan v University College Dublin*[80] may be regarded as presenting the reverse case: under the relevant procedural regulations, a student could only be represented by the Dean of Women's Studies and/or the President of the Students' Union. In *Flanagan*, given the grave consequences for the applicant, the High Court regarded the offer of representation by these personages as inadequate and considered that a lawyer should have been permitted. In this situation, where the applicant was seeking a lawyer, the applicant succeeded.

14–53　In a more recent cases in the same broad area, there was also a strong preference for permitting the party themselves to determine the extent of their representation. In *Law Society of Ireland v Competition Authority*,[81] the respondent Authority had a policy that the integrity of its processes could be compromised if the same lawyer represented more than one person in any particular matter. The High Court found for the applicant. The central passage in the judgment was[82]:

> "The appropriate balance between the constitutional right of a person facing a tribunal to freely choose their legal representatives and the right and duty of the tribunal to control its proceedings so as to discharge its function in accordance with the Constitution and the law, is achieved by [a] strong presumption in favour of a freedom of choice of legal representation, but with the retention in the tribunal of a discretion to deny that freedom of choice where it is apparent that to permit a particular legal representative to act would have the likely result of frustrating or impeding the tribunal discharging its lawful function.
>
> It would have to be observed that in all types of proceedings and in particular proceedings of a civil nature, the likelihood of a choice of legal representative being an obstacle to the proper conduct of the proceedings will be rare indeed."

Financial assistance to pay for representation?

14–54　Given that legal representation is necessary, the question then arises as to whether there is any obligation on the State or its agencies to provide any form of financial assistance towards payment for legal costs, arising from representation before tribunals, public inquiries or any other agency of public administration. The answer is "no"; while there are a few exceptions, the general principle applicable to administrative cases is that legal costs may not be claimed. This principle has been strongly articulated in two recent authorities. First, in *Magee v Farrell*,[83] writing for the Supreme Court, Finnegan J. stated that "[t]he [constitutional right to state-

---

　　obiter that there is a right to a "McKenzie friend" to assist a lay litigant before a court, see *RD v District Judge McGuinness* [1999] 2 I.R. 411 at 422–423. See also, H & M, para.14–84.

[80]　[1988] I.R. 724. *Flanagan* was followed in *Gallagher v The Revenue Commissioners (No. 1)* [1991] 2 I.R. 370 (at 377–378).

[81]　[2006] 2 I.R. 262. For another case which went very far in the same direction, see *Re Commission to Inquire into Child Abuse* [2002] 3 I.R. 459 at 476.

[82]　[2006] 2 I.R. 262 at 282. As an alternative ratio, the High Court also found for the applicant on the basis of art.6 of the European Convention on Human Rights.

[83]　[2009] 2 I.L.R.M. 453. See, to similar effect, *Corcoran v Minister for Social Welfare* [1991] 2 I.R. 175 at 183 and paras 6–27 to 6–28.

funded legal aid] has not been extended further than the criminal courts ...".[84] He went on to distinguish the authorities relied on by the respondent, mainly on the basis that they depended on some statutory or administrative scheme. Secondly, in *Grogan v The Parole Board*,[85] the relevant law is usefully surveyed and the following conclusion reached:

> "... Although attempts have been made to extend the occasions when the State has a constitutional obligation to grant free legal aid to persons who have no means, the occasions in which the courts are willing to do so ... are very few. Where the courts have recognised the State's obligation in non-criminal situations, it has done so only in very serious situations where the constitutional rights of individuals are clearly involved and failure to grant aid in the circumstances will amount to a breach of its constitutional responsibilities."

14–55 In *Grogan,* the following exceptional cases in which the State did have such an obligation were identified as, first, *Kirwan v Minister for Justice, Equality and Law Reform*[86] which arose from the detention, in the Central Mental Hospital, of an applicant who had been found guilty but insane in relation to a murder charge and was thereafter detained in the hospital. Secondly, in *Stevenson v Laney*,[87] the High Court held that an impecunious litigant had the constitutional right to civil legal aid, where she was contesting wardship proceedings taken by the State in respect of her child. Finally, in *Magee v Farrell*,[88] Gilligan J. held that the plaintiff, as the mother and next-of-kin of a man who died in Garda custody, was entitled to legal aid for the purpose of being adequately represented at the inquest.

14–56 In addition to the exceptions identified in *Grogan*, the following may be added. First, a statute may provide expressly for the payment of costs.[89] Secondly, in a rather surprising case,[90] the legal costs of representation at an inquiry were held to be payable as damages by CIÉ, consequential on a negligent act by CIÉ. Thirdly, in the case of a criminal trial (even in the absence of statute), there may be a constitutional right to legal assistance, depending on "the seriousness of the charge having regard to the person charged ... the nature of the penalty ... and his capacity ... to speak for and defend himself adequately".[91] It has been held,

---

[84] [2009] 2 I.L.R.M. 453 at 459–460.

[85] Unreported, High Court, McMahon J., June 27, 2008. The quotation is at 15. The facts in *Grogan* itself were that the applicant, who had been convicted and sentenced to 22 years' imprisonment by the (English) Central Criminal Court and then repatriated to Ireland to serve his sentence, had become eligible to have his sentence reviewed by the respondent Parole Board. He was now seeking legal aid to retain a solicitor to prepare legal submissions to the respondent. McMahon J. identified a number of features of the application which meant that it was outside the narrow category of exceptional cases in which the State has a constitutional obligation to grant legal aid.

[86] [1994] 2 I.R. 417.

[87] Unreported, High Court, Lardner J., February 10, 1993.

[88] Unreported, High Court, Gilligan J., October 26, 2005.

[89] See, e.g. para.6–88 (social welfare). Note that the Civil Legal Aid Act 1995 s.27(2)(b) gives the Minister for Justice, Equality and Law Reform the power to extend the scope of the legal aid scheme to cover tribunals.

[90] *Condon v CIÉ*, unreported, High Court, November 22, 1984. See Third Edition, p.306.

[91] *State (O) v Daly* [1977] I.R. 312 at 315 per O'Higgins C.J., qualifying *State (Healy) v Donoghue*

however, that this does not extend to "the earlier or ancillary stages of criminal proceedings".[92]

Hearing in public

14–57   There was, until recently, little Irish authority on the question of whether fair procedures dictates that an oral hearing must be held in public. The *zeitgeist* in favour of open government militates in favour of such a requirement; on the other hand, certainly in particular situations, there may be good reason to exclude from the hearing those with no interest (however defined) in the issue. This issue did, however, arise in *Barry v Medical Council*[93] where Costello P. appeared to suggest that the guarantee of fair procedures contained in Art.40.3 of the Constitution bestowed a qualified right to an open hearing, although the existence of a right of appeal to a court sitting in public "was a factor to be taken into account when determining whether the absence of public hearings before the [Fitness to Practice] Committee should be regarded as being unfair". In this case the Fitness to Practice Committee of the Medical Council had ruled that, under its constituent statute, it had discretion to hold public hearings, but decided not to do so in the present case, otherwise "the most intimate private matters would be disclosed to public scrutiny should the hearings be public". Costello P. held that the Committee had exercised their discretion fairly in arriving at this conclusion. He had regard, inter alia, to the complainants' constitutional right to privacy, bearing in mind the particular complaint (that the applicant had been photographing female patients in a state of undress) which it would have been embarrassing to have bruited in public; and the qualification contained in art.6(1) of the Convention.[94]

14–58   In *Barry*, the applicant's unsuccessful argument centred on a claim that the hearing be open to the public generally. A more common scenario is that a party wishes a particular person to be admitted, who is outside the usual category of tribunal or court members or staff or lawyers. One case of this type, *O'Ceallaigh v Fitness to Practice Committee*,[95] concerned an inquiry into the fitness to practice of an applicant nurse, on the grounds of alleged professional misconduct, under s.38 of the Nurses Act 1985. The respondent committee exercised its discretion to hold the inquiry in private and it was not really challenged on this issue. The point

---

[1976] I.R. 325. The passage quoted is from *Daly*. See also, *McSorley v Governor of Mountjoy Prison* [1996] 2 I.L.R.M. 331 at 338, and *Kirwan v Minister for Justice* [1994] 2 I.R. 417.
   Carmody v Minister for Justice, Equality and Law Reform [2009] IESC 71; [2010] 1 I.R. 635 arose when a farmer was prosecuted by the District Court for 42 offences relating to animal diseases. In the context of a request for legal aid for representation by counsel (and not merely a solicitor), which had been refused by the District Court, the Supreme Court held that legal aid for counsel should be provided to defend the case.

92   *State (O) v Daly* [1977] I.R. 312 at 315.

93   [1998] 3 I.R. 368. Both quotes are at 379. The High Court judgment was confirmed on this point by the Supreme Court (at 391). While the position regarding the Fitness to Practice Committee is now regulated by the Medical Practitioners Act 2007 s.65(2) (which requires a public hearing unless someone objects and the Committee "is satisfied that it would be appropriate in the circumstances to hold a hearing ... otherwise than in public"), Costello P.'s analysis remains of interest from the point of view of other tribunals.

94   Which, inter alia, permits the exclusion of the press where this is necessary for the protection "of the private lives of the parties".

95   [1999] 2 I.R. 552. But see the more particular case of *RD v District Judge McGuinness* [1999] 2 I.R. 411 at 422–423.

of contention concerned the refusal of the applicant's request to the respondent to be allowed to have two expert witnesses present throughout the inquiry to assist in assessing and cross-examining medical and midwifery witnesses. The Supreme Court by a majority accepted the argument, thereby overruling the High Court. Giving the leading judgment, O'Flaherty J. commenced by distinguishing *Barry* on the basis that there "[t]he publication of the proceedings could be nothing more than of prurient interest to the public".[96] Next, he held, in a slight development of the law, that "since persons are indubitably entitled to give evidence in their defence and to call witnesses in defence of a complaint of professional misconduct—prima facie they should be entitled to have present at the hearing ... any person who may assist their defence".[97]

Deciding without hearing: the intersection of the *audi alteram partem* rule and the "no delegation" principle

14–59 It frequently happens that the decision-making and information-gathering functions are divorced from each other, as for instance where the body in which a decision has been vested either instructs its officials,[98] or constitutes a sub-committee, to conduct interviews, examine records, etc. Two principles intersect here and, consequently, the public body is caught in a fork. The first principle is the *audi alteram partem* principle, which includes the central requirement that the decision-maker must be made aware of the applicant's arguments, and the facts which sustain them. This would be violated if the arguments and facts are properly examined only by the officials or sub-committee, even if the decision is actually taken by the body in which it is legally vested. But, the second principle—the no delegation rule—provides that, subject to substantial exceptions, the decision-maker may not delegate to officials or sub-committee. If (as has sometimes happened) the courts insist on an inflexible interpretation of each of these two principles, the public body is put in a considerable difficulty in performing duties in a practical way, to nobody's legitimate advantage.

14–60 Let us illustrate this observation by assuming that (in accord with the "no delegation" principle) a decision is not delegated, but that the legal decision-maker has not personally heard the evidence. The question arises: how far can this process go before it is held that the individuals affected have not been allowed a fair hearing because the decision-maker has not itself heard the case? One context in which this situation arose in early case law concerned the decision on a planning appeal, which is vested in An Bord Pleanála (or, before 1977, the (then) Minister for Local Government). The decision often requires a hearing at the site, which is chaired by an inspector and is not attended by the Board. Nevertheless, it was

---

[96] [1999] 2 I.R. 552 at 557. As to how far this right goes, giving a separate assenting judgment, Barron J. stated (at 574): "... the person before the first defendant should not be hampered in any way in his defence to the matters of complaint. That should basically be a subjective test and any application to allow persons to remain in the hearing should be granted unless it is seen to be unreasonable". He, like O'Flaherty J., ruled that to allow in expert witnesses did not mean that the hearing ceased to be private in character.

[97] [1999] 2 I.R. 552 at 560.

[98] For an acceptable delegation of fact collection and recommendation to an official, see *Mooney v An Post* [1998] 4 I.R. 288 at 298–299.

held (even before the statutory dispensation which presently operates)[99] in the *Murphy–Geraghty* line of cases,[100] that this procedure was valid, provided that the inspector gives the Minister "if not a verbatim account … at least a fair and accurate account of what transpired and one which gives accurately to the Minister the evidence and the submissions of each party …".[101]

14–61   Another example of this fork occurred in *O'Brien v Bord na Móna*[102] which involved the compulsory acquisition of the plaintiff farmer's bog land. The plaintiff had submitted to one of the Board's officials that the Board need only take a leasehold interest, with the land reverting to him after all the turf had been removed. Because of the Board's long-established policy of acquiring the fee simple interest, the official did not even bother to transmit this information to the Board. The Supreme Court dealt first with the argument that there had been no breach of the *audi alteram partem* rule because the decision had been delegated to the official who had received the plaintiff's submission. It held that even had there been an attempt at a delegation (though there was, on the facts, no sign of one) the decision would still have been invalid because determinations regarding compulsory acquisition are not capable of being delegated to officials. The court then turned to the alternative issue and held that the *audi alteram partem* rule had been broken by the official's failure to relay the plaintiff's submission to the board of Bord na Móna (in which the decision was vested).[103]

14–62   *O'Brien* was distinguished by Carroll J. in the High Court in *ESB v Gormley*[104] which involved the placing of an electric line upon the defendant's land. The defendant relied, inter alia, upon the fact that her objections had not been relayed to the ESB Board. Carroll J. rejected this argument and distinguished *O'Brien* primarily because the line had already been finally decided by the Board before the defendant acquired the land; but also because—and this is a point of more general significance—it was permissible for the Board to delegate to its officials negotiations with landowners and decisions regarding the relatively minor issue of the position of intermediate pylons. Unfortunately, in none of these cases have any guidelines been given as to what conditions (e.g. as regards control, reporting, etc) must be satisfied in order to legitimate the delegation.

14–63   A case of high constitutional importance, which also, incidentally, involved the intersection between the "no delegation" rule and the *audi alteram partem*

---

[99]   See Local Government (Planning and Development) Act 1983 s.11(6), now Planning and Development Act 2000 ss.111–112.
[100]   *Murphy v Dublin Corporation* [1972] I.R. 215. See, to like effect, *Murphy v Dublin Corporation (No. 2)* [1976] I.R. 143; *Geraghty v Minister for Local Government* [1976] I.R. 153; *O'Brien v Bord na Móna* [1983] I.R. 255. For another example, see *Genmark Pharma Ltd v Minister for Health* [1998] 3 I.R. 111 at 128. The essential point in *Genmark* was that the Minister in effect delegated his decision to the National Drugs Advisory Board (now the Irish Medicines Board), but "neither the documentation furnished by Genmark to the NDAB nor a reasonable summary of it was forwarded to the Minister".
[101]   *Murphy v Dublin Corporation* [1972] I.R. 215 at 239. This view is in line with the well-known Privy Council case of *Jeffs v New Zealand Dairy Board* [1967] 1 A.C. 551.
[102]   [1983] I.R. 255.
[103]   The court rejected the argument that since the plaintiff's argument would have been so unlikely to sway the Board, this breach did not matter. See further, para.14–193.
[104]   [1985] I.R. 129. Carroll J. was reversed, on other grounds, by the Supreme Court: see [1985] I.R. 144.

principle, was *Curtin v Dáil Éireann*.[105] This case arose out of proceedings, which, if they had not been discontinued, could well have led, for the first time ever, to the removal of a (Circuit Court) judge for stated misbehaviour. The point of relevance here is that, as a matter of practicality, it would not have been feasible for each House of the Oireachtas to hear and assess all the evidence against Judge Curtin. Accordingly, a Joint Oireachtas Preparatory Committee was established to hear evidence. However, the relevant law states that a judge may be removed only upon resolutions passed by each House.

14–64 These circumstances created a fork for the Oireachtas. On the one hand, it would not have been practical to leave all aspects of the investigation and inquiry to the full Dáil (166 members) and Seanad (60 members). On the other hand, if too much authority were left to the Committee, then it would have been argued that the decision had not been taken by the Houses; in other words, that there had been a breach of the "no delegation" principle. The Oireachtas sought to respect the "no delegation" principle by the insertion, in Dáil and Seanad Standing Orders, of the following key provision: "… provided that the Select Committee shall make no findings of fact, nor make any recommendations in respect of same …". Because of this tilt, the applicant judge attacked more or less along the *audi alteram partem* principle line, submitting that the Joint Oireachtas Committee should have had more authority. Thus, he submitted,[106] "… it is necessary, in order to assure the basic fairness of the procedures proposed, that the Houses appoint a committee to investigate, gather evidence and report their findings and conclusions to the Houses". The argument continued that this requirement was not fulfilled by the "undigested" evidence, which was envisaged in the Standing Orders, because it was "highly unsatisfactory to expect all the members of each House to consider, absorb and adjudicate upon the great mass of evidence which would be placed before them".

14–65 Giving judgment on behalf of the Supreme Court, Murray C.J. rejected this argument. He remarked, very much obiter, that it might have been "more satisfactory for the Houses to have opted for the type of committee [advocated by the applicant]". Murray C.J. then went on to make the following statement[107]:

"In the opinion of the Court, it would have been open to the Houses to have chosen such a committee, but they have not done so. It may well be that the Houses were concerned that such a committee would not validly be appointed, having regard to the decision of this Court in *Maguire v Ardagh* [2002] 1 IR 385. If so, it should be said that, so far as the power to appoint a committee was concerned, that case related to the question whether the Oireachtas possessed inherent implied power to appoint a committee to investigate the behaviour of individuals. It has no application to a case where

---

[105] [2006] 2 I.L.R.M. 99.

[106] [2006] 2 I.L.R.M. 99 at 143.

[107] [2006] 2 I.L.R.M. 99 at 145. Since the case concerned a Circuit Court judge, the relevant law was the Court of Justice Act 1924 s.39, and not the Constitution which makes no mention of Circuit Court judges. Curiously, this point, which could have had immense consequences for the result of the case, went unnoticed: see the last sentence of the passage quoted, which refers to the Constitution.

the Oireachtas is acting in the exercise of a power expressly conferred on it by the Constitution."

14–66   As can be seen, this practical approach is broadly in line with that taken in the more prosaic administrative situations, which have been summarised.[108]

Delay before disciplinary proceedings

14–67   The cases in this section centre on the situation in which what is delayed is disciplinary proceedings.[109] It is perfectly possible that judicial review might be attempted where some other official decision[110] is delayed and there have certainly been complaints of this type to the Ombudsman.[111] In addition, there is a volume of case law relating to delay in the context of criminal proceedings, which is not covered here.[112] These apart, the judicial review cases so far have overwhelmingly concerned disciplinary proceedings and, consequently, the subject of this section is confined as indicated.

14–68   It seems likely—though the case law does not permit one to be dogmatic about the point—that even unjustified[113] delay by the respondent public body in holding a disciplinary hearing is a ground of invalidity if, but only if, a plaintiff can point to some prejudice which flows from it. The issue of what happens where the delay is justified, but does prejudice the applicant, has not been thoroughly discussed. However, there is also some minority judicial support[114] for the view that, even without prejudice to the applicant, absence of justification for the delay by the public body will be significant, either as a supplementary factor or possibly even as a ground of invalidity in its own right.

14–69   The majority approach was adopted in the *ex tempore* judgment of Gannon J. in *McGowan v Wren*.[115] The facts were that in September 1985 a sworn inquiry,

---

[108]   However *Prendiville v Medical Council* [2008] 3 I.R. 122 at paras 94–121 stands out against this trend. It concerned the disciplining of the applicant doctor, by the Medical Council, acting under the Medical Practitioners Act 1978. The pre-*Prendiville* practice of the Medical Council is in effect now made legal by the clear words of the Medical Practitioners Act 2007 ss.70, 71, by which, if the Fitness to Practice Committee finds that the allegation is not substantiated, the complaint must be dismissed; whereas, if the allegation is proved before the Committee, then (subject to confirmation by the High Court) the Council has no discretion save to impose whatever sanction it considers appropriate.

[109]   cf. "The longest river winds somewhere safe to sea"; Tennyson's *The Brook*. For a court's discretion to refuse a remedy where the litigant delays, see paras 16–45 to 16–63.

[110]   Recently, for instance, there have been cases in the immigration field: see *KM v Minister for Justice, Equality and Law Reform* [2007] IEHC 234; unreported, High Court, July 17, 2007; *Nearing v Minister for Justice, Equality and Law Reform* [2010] 4 I.R. 211 at paras 22–31.

[111]   For the Ombudsman's decisions involving delay, see para.9–46.

[112]   *DPP v Byrne* [1994] 2 I.R. 236 at 375, quoted with approval in *McNeill v Commissioner of An Garda Síochána* [1994] 2 I.R. 426 at 436. Delay in advance of a criminal trial is considered in the Third Edition, pp.585–586, but not here.

[113]   In *Philips v Medical Council* [1991] 2 I.R. 115 at 143, Costello J. said that the Council was under a "statutory duty to determine the plaintiff's application [for registration] within a reasonable time. *It ... has no lawful excuse which justifies this failure.* I think a reasonable time for the consideration of the application was three months" emphasis added).

[114]   An example is the High Court judgment in *McNeill v Commissioner of An Garda Síochána* [1994] 2 I.R. 426 (the Supreme Court judgment focussed on a different point).

[115]   [1988] I.L.R.M. 744. See, to like effect, *Gallagher v The Revenue Commissioners (No. 1)*

under the Garda disciplinary regulations, was held to examine allegations that the plaintiff Gardaí had committed a breach of discipline (the date of which is not given in the report). Owing to certain irregularities in the documents before it, the inquiry was discontinued. Another fresh inquiry to examine the same allegation was fixed for September 1987. The plaintiffs then applied unsuccessfully to the High Court to quash the Garda Commissioner's decision to appoint the second Board of Inquiry. On the delay point, Gannon J. said:

> "[The applicants] are not suggesting that they are failing in recollection since the alleged events occurred. If there is any disadvantage in the delay, it must lie in the presentation of the investigation and is not a disadvantage to the applicants. I do not think that there are any grounds in delay upon which the applicants may rely for the relief sought."[116]

14–70 Another claim based on delay succeeded in the rather extreme circumstances of *Flynn v An Post*[117] (though without, it will be suggested, contradicting *McGowan*). The plaintiff had been suspended from duty without pay in May 1984 because he was suspected of stealing letters and parcels. He had remained suspended for nearly three years until the Supreme Court decision in the instant case, in 1987. He lived on social welfare benefits and a distress fund organised by his union. In July 1984 the Director of Public Prosecutions decided to prosecute the plaintiff on indictment. The solicitor for An Post, who was also acting for the DPP, then wrote to the plaintiff to say that An Post would not bring the disciplinary action against the plaintiff until the criminal trial was over. A significant fact was that, at this and all other stages, the plaintiff wished to press ahead with the disciplinary investigation. However, An Post decided to postpone the proceedings until the criminal trial was concluded; in order, as they thought, to protect the plaintiff's right to silence. McCarthy J., with whose judgment three of the other judges concurred, stated:

> "In the High Court [in the instant case] it was held that the plaintiff's right to silence might be lost ... in the criminal trial if the investigation had proceeded. Without expressing any view as to the nature of an alleged right to silence, in my judgment, if an accused in a criminal proceeding wishes to embark upon a course which may damage him in the manner suggested, it is no function of his employer, who is not the prosecutor ... to protect him from the consequences of such a course."[118]

[1991] 2 I.R. 370 at 375–376 per Blayney J. (where a person is charged with the disciplinary offence of grave misconduct in the performance of his duty, the court may not restrain the proceedings on the ground of inordinate delay in conducting the hearing but the delay is relevant in assessing the plaintiff's defence and to the imposition of any disciplinary measures should the charges be made out). See also, *Gallagher v Revenue Commissioners (No. 2)* [1995] 1 I.L.R.M. 241 at 245; *Curley v Governor of Arbour Hill Prison* [2005] 3 I.R. 308 at 320; *Morgan v TCD* [2003] 3 I.R. 157 at 175.

[116] [1988] I.L.R.M. 744 at 745–746.

[117] [1987] I.R. 68. See also, *C v The Legal Aid Board* [1991] 2 I.R. 43 at 56 where Gannon J. granted a declaration that the Board was obliged to consider the applicant's claim for civil legal aid within a reasonable time. See also, *Re Gallagher's Application (No. 2)* [1996] 3 I.R. 15 and *HMIL Ltd v Minister for Agriculture*, unreported, High Court, February 8, 1996 (similar principles); and *McNeill v Commissioner of An Garda Síochána* [1994] 2 I.R. 426, which is analysed in the Third Edition, p.581.

[118] [1987] I.R. 68 at 82.

14–71   McCarthy J. went on to hold that the suspension ceased to be valid in August 1984, which was the date when An Post should have been ready to proceed with the formal investigation if they had not. Yet, the plaintiff's criminal trial, which resulted in his acquittal on all charges, was held in November 1985. Accordingly he made a declaration to that effect and a consequential order for the payment of the plaintiff's salary from August 1984 to date.

14–72   *Flynn* could be read as supporting the proposition that any unjustifiable delay renders a decision or procedure invalid. Alternatively, it could be taken as confirming the narrower view hazarded at the start of this section, namely that delay renders a decision invalid only where the delay has caused prejudice to the applicant. On this latter analysis, the way in which the applicant in *Flynn* had been prejudiced is that his suspension had forced him to live without wages for a long period. *Flynn* was interpreted by Costello J. in this second sense and then distinguished, on the facts, in *Myers v Commissioner of the Garda Síochána*.[119] The factual background to *Myers* was similar to that in *Flynn*. But the applicant's claim, following *Flynn*, was that his continued suspension for over two years pending the outcome of the criminal prosecution was unconstitutionally unfair. This submission was rejected—and *Flynn* distinguished—on two grounds. In the first place, in *Myers* the applicant has been receiving suspension pay of two-thirds of his basic salary, whereas the applicant in *Flynn* had received nothing from his employers. Secondly, (as mentioned) it was a cardinal point, in *Flynn*, that the suspended employee had demanded that an internal inquiry might have prejudiced his defence in the pending criminal prosecution. By contrast, in *Myers*, there was no request that an immediate disciplinary inquiry be held.[120]

14–73   But a recent High Court authority confirms the view that prejudice must be shown. In *Ryan v Law Society of Ireland*,[121] the facts were that the respondent had commenced an investigation into the applicant's practice as a solicitor, including the fact that his apprentice had presented himself to the public as a qualified solicitor in 1993. The hearing of any formal charges was delayed pending an investigation into the conduct of the apprentice by the respondent's Education Committee and a number of applications to the courts in connection with it. The result was a delay of seven years, during which period, be it noted, the applicant continued to practice. Herbert J.'s judgment includes an unusually thorough survey of the authorities. Herbert J. stated[122] that, "the weight of judicial authority in this jurisdiction favours the principle that, save where some [law] contained an express time-frame[123] ... delay is not in itself a ground of invalidity in proceedings before

---

[119]   Unreported, High Court, January 22, 1988.

[120]   Unreported, High Court, January 22, 1988 at p.6 of the judgment.

[121]   [2002] 4 I.R. 21.

[122]   [2002] 4 I.R. 21 at 32. Herbert J. referred, with qualified approval, to Denham J.'s judgment in *O'Neill v Commissioner of An Garda Síochána* [1997] 1 I.R. 469. (Denham J. was dissenting, but not on this point.)

[123]   *Van Nierop v Commissioners for Public Works* [1990] 2 I.R. 189, which involved a notice of compulsory acquisition under the Fishery Harbour Centres Act 1968. There had been about 15 years' delay between the first notice and the present action and it was conceded, even by the Commissioners, that this could mean that the notices ceased to be valid (even though no time limit was fixed by the Act). This appears to have been grounded on the basis of equity and/or the intention of the legislature. See, to similar effect, *Grace Grice v Dudley Corporation* [1958] Ch. 329 at 339. *A contra*: *PJ Smyth v Dublin Corporation* [1955] 89 I.L.T.R. 1.

domestic disciplinary tribunals and the applicant must, in addition to establishing delay, be in a position to point to some specific prejudice flowing from it". On the facts, Herbert J. ruled that there was no prejudice since the inquiry would be based exclusively upon documents.

14–74 In summary, one could say that the majority of Irish cases have taken the view that, for a claim of unjustifiable delay to succeed, actual prejudice must be shown. However, as indicated in the passage quoted from *Ryan*, different considerations plainly apply where something is said regarding timeliness, in the Act or procedural rules, regulating the decision.[124]

D. Duty to Give Reasons and Supporting Materials

14–75 It used to be the law,[125] and probably still is in England,[126] that an administrative body (or possibly even a court; a point discussed below) was under no obligation to give reasons for its final[127] decision.[128] However, by today, as we shall see, this is no longer true. Unfortunately, because of its historical development, the explanation of the sources of the obligation is rather complicated and only a simplified account can be given here.[129] After we have explained, in (1), the sources of the duty, we turn, in later sections to a discussion of the meaning of the obligation to give reasons. Thus, section (2) deals with how cogent the reasons must be, and (3) with how and where the reasons must be stated. Section (4) deals with the findings, facts and materials available to public bodies, including note-taking; and (5) considers the pros and cons of the duty to give reasons. In each

---

[124] *McNeill v The Commissioner of An Garda Síochána* [1997] 1 I.R. 469 at 482 involving a delay of seven years. *McNeill* was distinguished, on the facts, in *McAuley v Chief Superintendent Keating*, unreported, High Court, July 8, 1997, in which the delay was only one year.

[125] See De Smith, *Judicial Review of Administrative Action*, 4th edn (2007), paras 7–087 to 7–115; Wade and Forsyth, *Administrative Law*, 10th edn (Oxford: OUP, 2009), pp.436–442 ("the principles of natural justice do not as yet, include any general rule that reasons should be given for decisions"). For monographs, see Flick, "Administrative Adjudications and the duty to give reasons" (1978) *Public Law* 16; Craig, "The Common Law, Reasons and Administrative Justice" [1994] C.L.J. 282. For the interaction between the right to reasons and substantive reasonableness, see para.13–17.

[126] Elliott, "Has the Common Law Duty to Give Reasons come of age yet?" [2011] *Public Law* 56 at 56.

[127] As contrasted with the duty to give reasons for a provisional decision which may arise as part of the narrow *audi alteram partem* rule. As an example of this distinction, take *Sherlock v Governor of Mountjoy Prison* [1991] 1 I.R. 451, which arose out of a decision not to grant a fresh period of temporary release in respect of a person to whom 15 continuous periods of temporary release (totalling 12 years) had already been granted. Condemning this decision, Johnson J. stated ([1991] 1 I.R. 451 at 453) that the applicant should have been "given an explanation as to [why he was not being given a further renewal] and be given an opportunity to be heard in that regard". This makes it clear that this was an example of the narrower, traditional duty rather than the duty to give reasons for a final decision.

[128] *Kiely v Minister for Social Welfare (No. 2)* [1977] I.R. 267 at 274; *State (Cole) v Labour Court* (1984) 3 J.S.L.L. 128 (though here there appears to have been a significant qualification: a party could "request the Court to give its decision in such a way that an appeal on a point of law could be taken"); *Pok Sun Shum v Ireland* [1986] I.L.R.M. 593 at 598. For a different tone in a later naturalisation case, see *Mishra v Minister for Justice* [1996] 1 I.R. 189 at 202–203.

[129] For a fuller story, see H & M, paras 14–108 to 14–170.

of sections (2)–(5), unless the contrary is indicated, we assume that the law is the same, regardless of the particular source.

(1) Sources

14–76   A right to reasons may be drawn from any of three[130] domestic[131] sources:

> (a) Constitutional justice.
> (b) Freedom of Information Act 1997.
> (c) Specialised legislation, for example the Planning and Development Act 2000.

14–77   In Ireland, at first, change was left to the judges. During the 1980s–1990s, the courts developed source (a), by tapping a vein of constitutional justice. More recently an ever more far-reaching development has come about through source (b), the Freedom of Information Act 1997, as a result of which there is an obligation on most[132] of our public bodies to give a reason for their decisions to the individual affected. A few specific institutions are within the scope of source (c).

14–78   While much of the judicial discussion of the reasons for the duty has been in relation to the constitutional source (a), "… [n]obody suggests that these decisions do not apply with equal force to the statutory obligations imposed under the Act of 2000, s. 34(10)",[133] and the courts frequently do not bother to identify which source is being used and apply precedents interchangeably. It seems probable, therefore, that apart from certain limitations particular to source (b), noted below, the scope of the duty is the same irrespective of the source. Although few new cases are now being decided in source (a), it remains of interest because it applies in the few areas which sources (b) and (c) do not reach.

(a) Constitutional justice

14–79   The first case in this line of authority is *State (Daly) v Minister for Agriculture*[134] which dealt with the dismissal of a probationer civil servant under s.7 of the Civil Service Regulation Act 1956, as amended by s.3 of the Civil Service

---

[130] In addition, the courts probably have an inherent jurisdiction to compel an administrative body to give a full account of the manner in which it arrived at its decision. In any event, a respondent opposing an application for judicial review is required by Rules of the Superior Courts Ord.84 r.22(4) to file a statement "setting out concisely the grounds for such opposition and, if any facts are relied on therein, an affidavit verifying such facts", so that in an appropriate case the High Court could probably compel a respondent to file an affidavit containing a fuller explanation than a mere laconic denial of any impropriety or illegality. On this point, see *State (Creedon) v Criminal Injuries Compensation Tribunal* [1988] I.R. 51 at 54–55 (Finlay C.J.). *Creedon* was distinguished by Murphy J. in *O'Donoghue v An Bord Pleanála* [1991] I.L.R.M. 751 at 759.

[131] For an ECJ case in which it was held that the reasons given were sufficient, see *Adia Interim SA v Commission of the European Communities* [1996] E.C.R. 321.

[132] Over 500 public bodies of one sort or another come within the scope of the 1997 Act: significant exclusions are the courts themselves or (to a limited extent) the DPP.

[133] *Mulholland v An Bord Pleanála (No. 2)* [2006] 1 I.L.R.M. 287 at 295 (Kelly J.).

[134] [1987] I.R. 165.

Regulation (Amendment) Act 1958. This provision states that where a civil servant is serving a probationary period, if the "appropriate authority is satisfied that he has failed to fulfil the conditions of probation ...", the authority shall terminate the service of such civil servant. Here the applicant had been dismissed with no indication of the ground for his dismissal; nor had any been given during the hearing before the High Court. The State's strongest authority was *Broomfield v Minister for Justice*[135] which concerned the dismissal of a civil servant, under the same statutory authority. In *Broomfield*, Costello J. had stated that in contrast with an office-holder, a probationer's service may be ended because "... his employing authority may consider the probationer unsuited for permanent employment and, without any specific charge of any acts of misconduct, the employing authority keeps to himself the right not to appoint the probationer on a full-time basis".[136]

14–80 However, in *Daly*, Barron J. held that *Broomfield* had been implicitly overruled by O'Higgins C.J.'s observation in *State (Lynch) v Cooney*[137] that "... [any] opinion formed by the Minister [under the statutory authority] must be one which is bona fide held and factually sustainable and not unreasonable". After this quotation, Barron J. went on to state:

> "The court must ensure that the material upon which the Minister acted is capable of supporting his decision. Since the Minister has failed to disclose the material upon which he acted or the reasons for his action there is no matter from which the court can determine whether or not such material was capable of supporting his decision. Since the Minister continues to refuse to supply this material, it must be presumed that there was no such material."

14–81 In *International Fishing Vessels Ltd v Minister for the Marine*[138] what was at stake was the Minister's refusal to renew the applicant's sea-fishing boat licence. The applicant had breached a condition which had been attached to its previous licence and which provided that at least 75 per cent of its crew should be either Irish citizens or nationals of an EC state. In response to a solicitor's letter asking for more detailed reasons, the Minister had refused "as a matter of policy" to give any reasons. Counsel for the Minister argued that while the Minister was obliged to act fairly, this did not include a duty to give reasons. However, Blayney J. followed *Creedon*[139] (although characterising the Minister's function as "not quasi-judicial") and *Daly* and held that the Minister was under a duty to give reasons.[140] However many later cases, albeit in their own particular circumstances,[141] have rejected a claim for reasons.

---

[135] Unreported, High Court, Costello J., ex tempore, April 10, 1981.

[136] Unreported, High Court, Costello J., ex tempore, April 10, 1981 at p.5 of the judgment.

[137] [1982] I.R. 337 at 361 quoted in *Daly* [1987] I.R. 165 at 170–171.

[138] [1989] I.R. 149. For the sequel to this case, see *International Fishing Vessels Ltd v Minister for the Marine (No. 2)* [1991] 2 I.R. 92.

[139] *State (Creedon) v The Criminal Injuries Compensation Tribunal* [1988] I.R. 51. For a more detailed discussion of *Creedon*, see the Second Edition of this book, p.459.

[140] [1987] I.R. 329. For another appeal case, see *Golding v The Labour Court* [1994] E.L.R. 153. See also, *Garda Representative Association v Ireland* [1989] I.R. 193; *Pok Sun Shum v Ireland* [1986] I.L.R.M. 593 at 599 (confining itself to cases where rights of appeal exist under statute); *Breen v Minister for Defence* [1994] 2 I.R. 34 at 41.

[141] *McCormack v Garda Complaints Board* [1997] 2 I.L.R.M. 321 at 332–333; *Manning v Shackleton* [1994] 1 I.R. 397 at 403 405; *Rajah v Royal College of Surgeons* [1994] 1 I.R. 384

14–82   The striking feature is that, even in those authorities that are most favourable to the applicant, the right to reasons was grounded in the fact that the decision for which reasons were sought was either reviewable or subject to appeal. For example, in *Daly*, Barron J. stated "… the Minister was entitled to dispense with the services of the applicant without warning him that he proposed to act in that manner. However, *once his decision was challenged*, he was obliged to disclose to the applicant the material and to give his reasons for so doing".[142]

14–83   The link between the right to reasons and their utility in facilitating judicial review on substantive grounds (in this case jurisdiction) was eloquently put in *Clare v Kenny*,[143] where MacMenamin J. stated:

> "… a court in judicial review proceedings cannot act on … a hypothesis as to the possible rationale for the [Circuit Court judge's] decision, particularly so in the context of the array of possible reasons, some of which would go beyond jurisdiction … The situation required a decision so that all the parties would be aware precisely of their positions. The reason or rationale for the decision as to jurisdiction unfortunately cannot be inferred from what was said by the respondent."

(b) Freedom of Information Act 1997

14–84   The 1997 Act establishes a far-reaching duty to give reasons. The central provision is s.18(1) which states:

> The head of a public body shall on application to him or her in that behalf, in writing or in such other form as may be determined, by a person who is affected by an act of the body and has a material interest in a matter affected by the act or to which it relates, not later than 4 weeks after the receipt of the application, cause a statement, in writing or in such other form as may be determined, to be given to the person—
> (a) of the reasons for the act, and
> (b) of any findings on any material issues of fact made for the purpose of the act.[144]

---

at 395. In the first of these cases, *H v Director of Public Prosecutions* [1994] 2 I.L.R.M. 285 at 290–291 (O'Flaherty J.); *Flood v Garda Complaints Board* [1997] 3 I.R. 321 at 341–343; *Stanley v Garda Síochána Complaints Board* [2000] 2 I.L.R.M. 121.

[142] [1987] I.R. 165 at 172 (emphasis added). See to similar effect, *State (Sweeney) v Minister for Environment* [1979] I.L.R.M. 35; *Anheuser Busch Inc v Controller of Patents, Design and Trade Marks* [1987] I.R. 329 at 331 (right of appeal); Finlay C.J. in *Creedon* [1988] I.R. 51 at 54–55 and *International Fishing* [1989] I.R. 149 at 155; and Carroll J. in *Gavin v Criminal Injuries Compensation Tribunal* [1997] 1 I.R. 132.
  Curiously, in at least one case, the same process of reasoning has also been used in reverse. In other words, if finality is taken to be among the objectives sought to be achieved by the involvement of an expert tribunal, then this militates against a requirement for reasons to be given, which facilitate judicial review: *Manning v Shackleton* [1996] 3 I.R. 85 at 96–97 (Keane J.).

[143] [2009] 1 I.R. 22 at para.53.

[144] In s.18(2) and (3), there are three statutory exceptions to the obligations contained in s.18(1). These obligations are foreshadowed in the *Devlin Report on Public Services Organisation Review* (Prl. 792), Appendix 1, p.456.

14–85   The key term here is "public body" because it is this term which determines the scope of the Act. In fact, as already discussed,[145] the term is now defined so widely that very few of what may reasonably be regarded as public bodies fall outside its scope. Moreover, where it applies, the Act goes beyond the previous obligation to give reasons deduced from constitutional justice, since (as noted above) this is restricted in various ways.

(c) Specialised legislation

14–86   Planning was among the earliest fields[146] to have specialised legislation. The present formulation is in the Planning and Development Act 2000 s.34(10)(a) which states: "A decision [in relation to the grant of planning permission] ... shall state the main reasons and considerations on which the decision is based ...". A leading authority on this provision (though with wider reverberations) is Kelly J.'s decision in the High Court in *Mulholland v An Bord Pleanála (No. 2)*.[147] The facts were that the applicants sought leave for judicial review to quash a decision of the respondent granting planning permission to retain a development. The grounds advanced included the contention that the respondent had not proffered sufficient reasons for departing from its inspector's recommendation, which was not to grant permission.

14–87   While ruling for the applicant, Kelly J. rejected the particular submission that the Planning and Development Act 2000 s.34(10) (quoted above), which had replaced the Local Government (Planning and Development) Act 1963 s.26(8), required more by way of reasons than its predecessor. Kelly J. stated[148] that, "... the pre-existing case-law on adequacy of reasons ... continues to apply". (It is possible to see in this bald observation impatience with any attempt to set up split-level standards for the adequacy of reasons, presumably on the common sense basis that such a thing would be so difficult to state precisely.) Justifying his view, Kelly J. stated that a lesser standard than "clear and cogent" would be inadequate and more would be superfluous. This broad attitude could be relevant, too, in regard to any attempt to argue that a different standard is required where the obligation to give reasons is derived from statute (sources (b) and (c)) rather than the Constitution (source (a)).

14–88   A second piece of specialist legislation, containing an obligation to give reasons, is the Immigration Act 1999 s.3(3)(a) (as amended by the Illegal Immigrants (Trafficking) Act 2000 s.10) which provides that, in making a deportation order, the Minister must give "reasons" (that is all) for it. This was interpreted in *Dimbo v Minister for Justice, Equality and Law Reform*[149] to mean "grave and substantial

---

[145]   See para.12–23.

[146]   Other examples include: an arbitrator's duty to give reasons, see *Vogelaar v Callaghan* [1996] 1 I.R. 88 at 93 and *Doyle v Kildare County Council* [1995] 2 I.R. 424 at 431; Solicitors (Amendment) Act 1994 s.15(4)(e) (adjudicator in respect of complaints "shall give reasons ... in every report to the Society"); Environmental Protection Agency (Licensing) Regulations 1994 (S.I. No. 85 of 1994) reg.28.

[147]   [2006] 1 I.R. 453, accepting the recommendations of the Board's inspector.

[148]   [2006] 1 I.R. 453 at 464.

[149]   Unreported, Supreme Court, Denham J., May 1, 2008 at p.19. See also, *Oguekwe v Minister for Justice, Equality and Law Reform* [2008] 2 I.L.R.M. 481 at 502–503, where Denham J. gave the breach of this obligation as a ground for striking down a deportation order.

reason[s]". Although no explanation of this phrase was given and no comparison with the duty to give reasons from any other source drawn in the judgments, this formulation sounds as if it was intended to go beyond the normal standard (though as to this, see the comments in the last paragraph).

Comparison of the three sources

14–89   It is convenient at this point to identify the situations in which the right to reasons arising from the various sources, (a), (b) and (c), would apply. While there will naturally be a good deal of overlap, the basic point here is that sources (b) and (c) apply only to specified public bodies or specified situations; though, in the case of (b), the 1997 Act covers most bodies and situations. Next, as just indicated in regard to (a), there are three restrictions on the scope of the constitutional justice right to reasons. First, it is subject to a requirement (canvassed above) that the reasons be required in order to facilitate a judicial review or appeal, which has no equivalent in the Act. Secondly, as we have also seen, the most recent cases evidence a tendency to restrict (admittedly, rather darkly) the type of decision and circumstances to which the right is attracted. There is no equivalent of these in the legislation and sources (b) and (c).

14–90   The third restriction[150] concerns a decision which involves preferring one situation or individual to another; for example, the selection of one area of the country rather than another for a grant scheme or post in the public service. In this category of decision, reasons have, classically, not been required on the ground that, since it is always difficult to prove a negative, to impose such a duty on the responsible public body would be to impose too heavy a burden. However, in the case of the Act, the scope of the duty is defined, in s.18, by reference to an "act" which includes a decision. This may include both negative and positive acts; as well as policy and administrative decisions.

14–91   In summary, in respect of the public bodies to which they apply, the right established by sources (b) and (c) are somewhat wider and more definite than that from source (a). What vitality does the Act leave to the constitutional justice obligation to give reasons? The main category would be where the decision-maker is a public body which is not within the scope of the Act. But, most public bodies are now within the scope of the Freedom of Information legislation and more may be brought in by order. As of 2009, a small number of significant public bodies were not included, among them the courts, Judicial Appointments Advisory Board, the Central Bank and Financial Services Authority of Ireland, the Refugee Applications Commissioner and the Refugee Appeals Tribunal.

14–92   But the big exception from the Act are the courts. This leads on to the broader question: are judges[151] themselves under an obligation to give reasons? Plainly, they are not within the scope of sources (b) and (c). However, it seems

---

[150]   See *Maigueside Communications v IRTC* [1998] 1 I.R. 265 at 274, analysed in H & M, paras 12–136 to 12–138.

[151]   In 2009, the European Court of Human Rights held at first instance, in *Taxquet v Belgium* (App. No.926/05), that a person had not received a fair trial under art.6(1), because there was a jury in the case and the jury, as is usually the way with juries, had given no reasons for its decision. In advance of the appeal to the Grand Chamber, the Irish Government submitted a

likely that they would come within the scope of the constitutional justice duty to give reasons, since the administration of justice in courts is essentially a matter of openness, reasoning and consistency. Its legitimacy or claim on the respect of the citizenry depends vitally on these qualities. In addition, given that the obligation to give reasons has been deduced from the notion of constitutional justice, one would expect that the obligation to give reasons would catch judges, since it applies in the case of a judicial or quasi-judicial decisions.[152]

14–93 Curiously, until recently, authority on this point was wanting. Perhaps, in view of what has just been said, it was regarded as "axiomatic". Perhaps no-one liked to take the case. In any event, by now there is some case law indicating that reasons must be given.[153] In *Foley v Murphy*[154] in the High Court, on review, McCarthy J. stated that it was not contested that judges must give reasons for their decisions (and a number of English and Irish authorities in favour of the proposition were usefully summarised). McCarthy J. went on to consider the standard which the reasons should meet:

> "The authorities go to show that there is no need in making an order for costs to address each argument advanced on the issue and the extent to which reasons may be offered will differ from case to case. However … where the matter is being dealt with at the more considered or leisurely pace appropriate for a criminal trial [in contrast to the trial of a minor offence in the District Court] as well as the engagement with the evidence by counsel for the prosecution …and, finally, the correspondence (which was a further exceptional feature of the case) it was appropriate for [the judge] to afford more detailed reasons than she did. Of course the evidence, the correspondence and the submissions were the only relevant matters upon which the first respondent could (and obviously did) base her decision but I think that the level of generality of the reasons is too high such that one does not know to what extent evidence or any particular piece of evidence or the correspondence or the submissions or the legal issues as to costs or otherwise gave rise to her conclusion … There was insufficient engagement in the judgment with the material before her … She was not dealing with a 'straightforward factual dispute' but rather 'something in the nature of an intellectual exchange with reasons and analysis advanced on either side' (see Henry LJ in *Flannery v Halifax Estate Agencies* [2000] 1 WLR 377 …".

---

document, emphasising the nature, purpose and constitutional importance of the jury, under the Irish Constitution, Art.38: *The Irish Times*, February 6, 2010, p.4.

[152] *Flood v Garda Síochána Complaints Board* [1999] 4 I.R. 560 at 569.

[153] *State (Creedon) v Criminal Injuries Compensation Tribunal* [1988] I.R. 51 at 55 (obiter); *O'Mahony v Judge Thomas Ballagh* [2002] 2 I.R. 410 at 415–416; *Clare v Judge Kenny* [2009] 1 I.R. 22 at paras 54–59; *The Working Group on the Jurisdiction of the Courts: the Criminal Jurisdiction of the Courts* (2003), para.368; *Report on Penalties for Minor Offences* (LRC 69–2003), para.3.06–12; *Consultation Paper on Penalties for Minor Offences* (LRC CP18–2002), para.6.25 states: "[i]f administrative bodies are bound to give reasons, where they exercise judicial power, it is obvious that the same applies to the judges themselves".

[154] [2008] 1 I.R. 619 at para.20. The facts of the case were that, at a criminal trial, the Circuit Court had failed to give reasons for refusing an award of the applicant's costs, costs being regarded as falling "into the category of substantive rights" because of the burden an accused person would otherwise face. It is not quite clear what, if anything, turned on this categorisation.

14–94   The gist of this carefully reasoned passage is that there were particular features of the situation before the court which called for fairly detailed reasons and that this standard was not met, a theme which we take up in a more general form in the following section.

(2) How cogent must the reasons be?

14–95   In other words, how exact and comprehensive a statement of reasons is necessary in order to satisfy the duty? According to Finlay C.J., "… the unsuccessful applicant … should be made aware in general and broad terms of the grounds".[155] The reasons must be "proper, intelligible and adequate".[156] Keane J. has remarked that, "… the determination by the Labour Court need not … take any particular form: what is essential is that the manner in which it is expressed leaves no room for doubt as to the reasons which led to the decision, thus ensuring that neither the appellate nor the supervisory jurisdiction of this Court is frustrated by an inadequate indication of reasons"[157]; "a mere formalistic mantra"[158] will not do. Apart from certainty and precision, the reasons should also be cogent (though these various qualities have not usually been distinguished).

14–96   But, despite these formulations, in terms of the actual results, there have been very few cases in which a reason, however peremptory, has been held not to suffice. Thus, for instance, in the Supreme Court case of *Faulker v Minister for Industry and Commerce*,[159] the applicant had complained to the Labour Court that she has been the victim of sexual discrimination (as regards promotion in the civil service). Yet, all that the Labour Court had given by way of reasons for rejecting the applicant's claim was "having examined in detail the claimant's assessment records, the Court is satisfied that the Department had reasonable grounds other than sex or marital status for her non-promotion in April 1989".[160] Ruling that this sufficed, O'Flaherty J. stated:

> "… administrative tribunals … should be required only to give the broad gist of the basis for their decisions. We do no service to the public in general, or to particular individuals, if we subject every decision of every administrative tribunal to minute analysis."[161]

---

[155] *State (Creedon) v The Criminal Injuries Compensation Tribunal* [1988] I.R. 51 at 55. See also, *JN v Minister for Justice, Equality and Law Reform* [2009] 1 I.R. 146 at para.16 ("no lengthy discursive judgment is required but an applicant should not be left perplexed as to why he or she failed, and someone else succeeded on the same facts").

[156] *Ní Eilí v EPA*, unreported, Supreme Court, Murphy J., July 30, 1999, quoting *MJT Securities v Secretary of State for the Environment* [1998] J.P.L. 138 at 144.

[157] *Golding v The Labour Court* [1994] E.L.R. 153 at 159.

[158] *P v Minister for Justice, Equality and Law Reform* [2002] 1 I.L.R.M. 16 at 32.

[159] [1997] E.L.R. 107. For another example, see *FP v Minister for Justice* [2002] 1 I.L.R.M. 16.

[160] [1997] E.L.R. 107 at 110.

[161] [1997] E.L.R. 107 at 111. See also, the similar comments of Murphy J. in the High Court [1993] E.L.R. 187 and also *Anisimova v Minister for Justice, Equality and Law Reform* [1998] 1 I.R. 186, and those of Keane J. in *Manning v Shackelton* [1996] 3 I.R. 85 at 97. *A contra*: Finlay C.J. in *North Western Health Board v Martyn* [1987] I.R. 565 at 568 and 579; *O'Donoghue v An Bord Pleanála* [1991] I.L.R.M. 750 at 757 per Murphy J.

14–97   Also of interest is the following observation from the High Court's (Smyth J.) judgment in *P v Minister for Justice, Equality and Law Reform*[162]:

> "Much argument focused on the extent to which the Minister in stating in the letter of notice that he had regard to the factors set out in s. 3(6) [of the Immigration Act 1999], failed to say what weight he attached to each particular heading for each particular applicant and that there ought to have been some form of points or other system applicable to each heading so that each applicant could know under which heading he fell short ... of success. He might then perhaps make a further application to the Minister or the court and have the Minister's decision adjusted or altered. There is no such statutory requirement upon the Minister and the court must not seek to legislate to obligate him so to do."

14–98   While, as can be seen, the general judicial consensus has been to set a rather low standard for the cogency of reasons, this approach has been challenged by some judges and commentators. For example, *Deerland Construction v Aquatic Licensing Appeals Board*[163] arose out of the grant by the respondent of an aquaculture licence to a trade rival of the applicant under the Fisheries Act 1997 s.40 (as amended by the Fisheries (Amendment) Act 2001 s.10). Kelly J.'s judgment gives a useful review of the case law, in Ireland and England. In particular, he quoted, with approval, the following passage, from *South Bucks County Council v Porter*,[164] in which Brown L.J. stated:

> "The reasons for a decision must be intelligible and they must be adequate. They must enable the reader to understand why the matter was decided as it was and what conclusions were reached on 'the principal important controversial issues', disclosing how any issue of law or fact was resolved ... The reasoning must not give rise to a substantial doubt as to whether the decision maker erred in law, for example by misunderstanding some relevant policy or some other important matter, or by failing to reach a rational decision on relevant grounds. But such adverse inference will not readily be drawn. Reasons need refer only to the main issues in the dispute, not to every material consideration. They should enable disappointed developers to assess their prospects of obtaining some alternative development permission, or, as the case may be, their unsuccessful opponents to understand how the policy or approach underlying the grant of permission may impact upon future such applications. Decision letters must be read in a straightforward manner, recognising that they are addressed to parties well aware of the issues involved and the arguments advanced. A reasons challenge will only succeed if the party aggrieved can satisfy the court that he is genuinely being substantially prejudiced by the failure to provide an adequately reasoned decision."

14–99   This is well balanced guidance and, in particular, the second half of this nuanced passage gives some (legitimate) advantage to the public body involved: it

---

[162]   *P v Minister for Justice, Equality and Law Reform* [2002] 1 I.L.R.M. 16 at 33.
[163]   [2009] 1 I.R. 673. Another case in which the reasons were not to be sufficiently cogent is *Hurley v Motor Insurance of Ireland* [1993] I.L.R.M. 886 at 890.
[164]   [2004] 1 W.L.R. 1953 at para.36.

is made clear that the technique of literal interpretation which has sometimes been applied to statements of reasons, as if they were Acts of the Oireachtas, should not be followed. In addition, the party aggrieved must show genuine prejudice, bearing in mind that they are "well aware of the issues involved".

14–100 It has been said that a higher degree of cogency is required where the administrative decision affects constitutional or human rights and obligations. This was stated in *Meadows v Minister for Justice, Equality and Law Reform*,[165] a deportation case where the applicant claimed that she ran the risk of being subjected to female genital mutilation if she were returned to her country of origin. A majority of the Supreme Court found for the applicant, albeit on slightly different grounds. Murray C.J., however, based his decision on the view that the Minister's reasoning (with its statement that non-refoulement was not an issue) was unsatisfactory:

> "An administrative decision affecting the rights and obligations of persons should at least disclose the essential rationale on foot of which the decision is taken. That rationale should be patent from the terms of the decision or capable of being inferred from its terms and its context. Unless that is so then the constitutional right of access to the Courts to have the legality of an administrative decision judicially reviewed could be rendered either pointless or so circumscribed as to be unacceptably ineffective. In my view, the decision of the Minister in the terms couched is so vague and, indeed, opaque that its underlying rationale cannot be properly or reasonably deduced."

14–101 There is thus a definite divergence[166] between the majority line of cases in this field, which have been fairly indulgent towards the public body, and a minority line, which is represented by the two judgments summarised in paras 14–98 to 14–100.

14–102 One should also note that the Information Commissioner has been fairly articulate[167] as to what constitutes a sufficient reason to satisfy the Freedom of Information Act 1997 and it is possible that her standards would indirectly affect the standards required at common law.

(3) How and where must the reasons be stated?

14–103 As regards the form in which reasons may be given, take first a right to reasons grounded in constitutional justice. *In McCormack v Garda Complaints Board*,[168] Costello P. noted "[t]here may also be circumstances in which (a) no unfairness arose by a failure to give reasons when the decision was made but (b) the concept of fair procedures might require that reasons should subsequently be

---

[165] [2010] IESC 3.
[166] Indeed, it should be noticed that Kelly J., in *Deerland Construction v Aquaculture Licences Appeals Board* [2009] 1 I.R. 673 at para.83, admitted that his decision on this point was at odds with his own earlier decision in *Mulholland (No. 2)*, which, he said, "... was heavily influenced by the approach of Finnegan P. in the *Fairyhouse Club* case ... in which no account was taken of a whole body of case law in England".
[167] McDonagh, *Freedom of Information Law*, 2nd edn (Dublin: Thomson Round Hall, 2005), paras 3–48 to 3–51.
[168] [1997] 2 I.L.R.M. 321 at 332.

given in response to a *bona fide* request". Secondly, in regard to the FOI obligation, all we have by way of guidance are the words of s.18(1). (The reasons must take the form of "… a statement in writing …". Does this mean that a single, coherent document is contemplated?) It seems reasonable to assume that, before the duty arises, the applicant must first ask for reasons, since s.18(1) of the Act uses the phrase "… on application".

14–104   A judicial consensus appears to be building up to the effect that reasons do not have to be given in a single, direct, discrete form: the message, to generalise from a number of cases seems to be that it suffices if the reasons may be deduced from whatever (presumably reliable) source or sources are available. Take, for example, *O'Keeffe v An Bord Pleanála*,[169] in which Finlay C.J. noted that "… there is no substance in the contention … that the Board should be prevented from relying on a combination of the reason given for the decision and the reasons given for the conditions, together with the terms of the conditions … [S]uch a rigid approach would be contrary to common sense and to fairness".

14–105   A big question here is how resourceful an applicant is expected to be, in first collecting information as to reasons from possibly disparate sources or deducing information by "putting two and two together".[170] For example, in *Orange Ltd v Director of Telecoms (No. 2)*,[171] Barron J. stated that "[t]he plaintiff made various calculated decisions as to what it would or would not offer in its bid. When it received the summary report, it knew perfectly well that its decisions were a mistake and were the cause of its losing the licence". Similarly, in *O'Keefe v An Bord Pleanála*, Finlay C.J. stated that "[w]hat must be looked at is what an intelligent person who had taken part in the appeal or been appraised of the broad issues which had arisen in it would understand from the document, these conditions and these reasons".[172]

14–106   As regards the stage at which reasons must be given, there seems to be a good deal of latitude. In *McAlister v Minister for Justice, Equality and Law Reform*,[173] which was a High Court case arising out of the respondent's failure to

---

[169] [1993] 1 I.R. 39 at 76. In *Foley v Murphy* [2008] 1 I.R. 619 at para.14, it was stated that "reasons must be apparent, whether expressly or by implication, or indeed by deduction".

[170] There is much in common between this issue and the questions, examined at paras 14–21 to 14–23, about how much information must be given to the person affected, in advance of the decision, and how far he is taken to "well know".

[171] [2000] 4 I.R. 159 at 219.

[172] [1993] 1 I.R. 39 at 76, quoted with approval in *Village Residents v An Bord Pleanála (No. 3)* [2001] 1 I.R. 441 at 451–452, which is itself an interesting case in its field. See, to similar effect, *Doran v An Garda Síochána* [1994] 1 I.L.R.M. 303 at 311; *Manning v Shackleton* [1996] 3 I.R. 85 at 95; *Ryanair Ltd v An Bord Pleanála* [2004] I.R. 334 at paras 62–63; and *Flood v Garda Síochána Complaints Board* [1997] 3 I.R. 321 at 343 (Kelly J.).

[173] [2003] I.L.R.M. 161. It seems from the last sentence, in *McCormack v Garda Síochána Complaints Board* [1997] 2 I.R. 489, that it suffices if the reasons are supplied even as late as the argument before the court. See also, *Village Residents v An Bord Pleanála (No. 3)* [2001] 1 I.R. 441 at 455–456. *A contra*: *Deerland Construction v Aquaculture Licences Appeals Board* [2009] 1 I.R. 673 at paras 84 and 94 and *Nash v Chelsea College of Art and Design* [2001] EWHC Admin. 538. See, to similar effect, *Gavin v Criminal Injuries Compensation Tribunal* [1997] 1 I.R. 132 at 142, in which the High Court (Carroll J.) refused to accept reasons given in the form of an affidavit signed by the Secretary to the Tribunal, remarking that "[i]t is for the respondent to speak for itself". Yet, it is quite normal for a senior official

allow a prisoner temporary release or to give reasons for this refusal, Finnegan P. stated[174]:

> "In the present case the criteria against which an application is considered had been set out in a policy not communicated to the applicant ... [But the] respondent exhibited in the replying affidavit of John Kenny at Exhibit JK1, the matters which were taken into account in arriving at the decision to refuse the application namely ...
>
> The applicant now knows the reasons for the refusal. Accordingly I do not propose to grant relief related to the failure to give reasons."

14–107   It seems rather odd if, as happened here, a person is to be required to take High Court proceedings to secure their right to reasons. As can be seen, however, there was no adverse comment from the judge.

14–108   One issue which has never been teased out expressly is the relationship of this right to reasons with the main channel of the *audi alteram partem* principle. For this precept, of course, requires that, as part of the obligation to facilitate the person likely to be affected by a decision in making his case, certain types of information should be given to him.[175] Among this information will often be what might amount to the provisional reasons why it is anticipated that the issue may go against him. Where this is the case, it will frequently be clear that the reasons which finally motivated the deciding authority were the same as those mentioned or implied at the earlier stage of the decision-making process. Oddly enough, the link between the duty to give a person affected notice of the case against him and the duty to give reasons for the final decision has seldom, if ever, been authoritatively scrutinised in this jurisdiction. The question is whether an adequate performance of the duty to give notice of the case against a person will, on the assumption that the reasons are the same at each stage, also satisfy the duty to give reasons at the final stage. This question is obviously part of the wider issue of how extensive must be the source of information regarding reasons, of which the applicant is expected to take account.

(4) Findings of fact and materials available to public bodies

14–109   Closely related to the duty to give reasons is a requirement that a decision-making authority should, in order to facilitate judicial review of its decision, indicate to the person affected the materials which were before it when the decision was taken. This is required by s.18(1)(b) of the Freedom of Information Act 1997[176] quoted above ("...any findings on any material issues of fact made for the purposes of the ... Act"). What seems to be the same requirement was anyway necessary under the head of constitutional justice, as an aspect of constitutional justice, as

---

to act as a channel of communication for a public body. Accordingly, perhaps the point really being made concerns the suspicion that, at such a late stage, self-justificatory reasons would be manufactured.

[174]   [2003] I.L.R.M. 161 at 170.

[175]   See paras 14–14 to 14–20.

[176]   As regards the Planning and Development Act 2000 s.34(10), the obligation is to state "the considerations on which a condition is based".

seems to be recognised in the judgment of Finlay C.J. in *P&F Sharpe v Dublin City and County Manager.*[177] The passage is as follows:

> "The necessity for the elected members in the case of any direction under section 4 [of the City and County Management (Amendment) Act 1955] concerning the granting or refusing of a planning permission to act in a judicial manner would *inter alia* involve an obligation to ensure that an adequate note was taken, not necessarily verbatim but of sufficient detail to permit a court upon review to be able to ascertain the material on which the decision had been reached."[178]

14–110 These themes were taken up in *NWR FM Limited v Broadcasting Commission of Ireland,*[179] which arose out of the respondent's refusal to grant the applicant a sound broadcasting contract. A number of the applicant's arguments were directed to note-taking at the respondent's meeting. The applicant had been furnished with a feedback report and a minute of the board meeting but the contemporaneous handwritten note of what took place at the meeting was destroyed once the minute had been approved. In this situation, the applicant made two arguments before the High Court (Peart J.). In response to the first of these, the court held that there was no statutory provision, whether under the Freedom of Information Act 1997 or the Radio and Television Act 1988 (nor presumably was there any constitutional obligation), requiring the respondent to take a handwritten note of meetings at which decisions are made: the statutory provisions to which the applicant referred obliged the respondent only to provide reasons for its decision to refuse an application; but this was not to be extended in the way sought by the applicant. Secondly, "an adequate record had been kept of sufficient detail to permit a court upon review to be able to ascertain the material on which the decision had been reached".

(5) Pros and cons

14–111 Here, we briefly examine the advantages and disadvantages of a duty to give reasons. First, "a decision is apt to be better if the reasons for it have to be set out in writing because the reasons are then more likely to have been properly thought out".[180] Secondly, reasons would give, to the person immediately affected and the public generally, confidence that the decision had been properly taken.

---

[177] [1989] I.L.R.M. 565 at 579. See also, *McLoughlin v Minister for Social Welfare* [1958] I.R. 1; *Kiely v Minister for Social Welfare (No. 1)* [1971] I.R. 21; *Kiely v Minister for Social Welfare (No. 2)* [1977] I.R. 297; *McKinley v Minister for Defence* [1988] I.R. 139 at 142; *Thompson v Minister for Social Welfare* [1989] I.R. 618; *De Roiste v Judge Advocate General* [2006] 1 I.L.R.M. 200 at 237–240. A ruling that a public body should, in order to facilitate judicial review, record the material before it was also made in the very particular circumstances of *Brennan v Minister for Justice* [1995] 1 I.R. 612 at 629. The Planning and Development Act 2000 s.34(10) requires a planning decision to state the "main reasons and considerations on which it is based". For puzzlement at what added meaning is given by "considerations", see *Ryanair Limited v An Bord Pleanála* [2004] 2 I.R. 334.

[178] [1989] I.L.R.M 565 at 579.

[179] [2004] 4 I.R. 50. The quotation is at 71.

[180] *The Franks Report,* 1957 (Cmnd. 218), para.98: "Notice that the requirement of reasons is of real significance in ensuring that other objectives of administrative law are not frustrated. If, for example, we decide to grant consultation rights in certain areas, then a duty to furnish

14–112   The advantages were explained by Finnegan P. in *McAlister v Minister for Justice, Equality and Law Reform*[181]:

> "Reasons will enable the person adversely affected by a decision who has a right of appeal to determine whether he has good grounds for an appeal and will inform him of the case he will have to meet if he does decide to appeal. Reasons will make an inferior tribunal or a decision-maker more amenable to the supervisory jurisdiction of the court: Wraith & Hutcheson, *Administrative Tribunals* (1973) at p. 150. Reasons will ensure that a tribunal is acting within its powers: *Westminster Bank Ltd. v. Beverley Borough Council* [1969] 1 QB 499 at p.508. Reasons will inform a person why a decision has been made and will make manifest any errors of law. They provide additional guidance to the person to whom a decision was adverse and to his legal advisors as to their future conduct. It is important that justice should be seen to be done and this will very often require that a person affected by a decision should know why that particular decision has been taken: *Breen v. Amalgamated Engineering Union* [1971] 2 QB 175 at p. 191."

14–113   There has been no equivalent Irish judicial discussion of the disadvantages, but an Australian authority has written:

> "At least two arguments have been advanced against the giving of reasons. First, the giving of reasons would impose additional administrative burdens and might well be an undue drain on the resources of an agency. Such burdens may even result in the giving of canned reasons. Secondly, reasons may hinder the manner in which a discretion is exercised and it may be thought that some discretions should be uncontrollable. But considerations of administrative expediency should not mitigate principles of fairness and few, if any, discretions should be uncontrollable."[182]

---

reasons will make it more difficult for the decision-maker merely to go through the motions of hearing interested parties without actually taking their views into account."

[181]   [2003] 1 I.L.R.M. 161 at 169–170. See also, *State (Sweeney) v Minister for the Environment* [1979] I.L.R.M. 35 at 37; *O'Donoghue v An Bord Pleanála* [1991] I.L.R.M. 751 at 757. See also, *Save Britain's Heritage v Secretary of State for the Environment* [1991] 2 All E.R. 10 at 24, where Lord Bridge states: "[The single and indivisible question in my opinion ... whenever a planning decision is challenged on the ground of the failure to give reasons is whether the interests of the applicant have been substantially prejudiced by the deficiency of the reason given ... I could expect that normally such prejudice should arise from one of three causes. First, there would be substantial prejudice to the developer whose application for permission has been refused or to an opponent of the development when permission has been granted, when the reasons for the decision are so inadequately or obscurely expressed as to raise a substantial doubt whether the decision was taken within the powers of the Act. Secondly, a developer whose application for permission is refused may be substantially prejudiced where the planning considerations on which the decision is based are not explained sufficiently clearly to enable him reasonably to assess the prospect of succeeding in any application for some alternative form of development. Thirdly an opponent of development ... may be substantially prejudiced by a decision to grant permission in which the planning considerations on which the decision is based, particularly if they relate to planning policy, are not explained sufficiently clearly to indicate what, if any, impact they may have in relation to the decision of future applications."

[182]   Flick, "Administrative Adjudications and the Duty to Give Reasons" (1978) *Public Law* 16 at 19.

14–114   Finally, one might remark that the duty to give reasons may have significant consequential effects in such neighbouring fields as: the control of discretionary powers (paras 15–13 to 15–17); estoppel and res judicata (paras 19–03 to 19–08), and the following of precedent in regard to administrative actions (para.6–21).

E. TYPES OF DECISIONS WHICH ATTRACT
THE RULES OF CONSTITUTIONAL JUSTICE

14–115   The arrangement adopted in this Part is, first, to pigeon-hole the case law into a number of categories in which the rules (case law here is from either rule; so that Chapter 13 may also be relevant) have been held to apply; and, subsequently, to enumerate several other categories in which they have usually (though with some exceptions) been held not to apply. In each of the two groups, there is a certain amount of overlap, as is the way with pigeon-holes.

14–116   A legitimate query here is whether there is any general principle which would indicate the common ground shared by these cases and so assist a lawyer advising a client to predict whether the principles apply to new areas. Formerly, the English courts invoked the quasi-judicial/administrative distinction to try to solve this problem".[183] This classification has been used fitfully in the Irish case law, principally, as we have seen,[184] in regard to the "no bias" principle, but also occasionally in regard to the *audi alteram partem* rule as, for example, in *State (Williams) v Army Pensions Board.*[185] It is significant that, in *Williams*, Keane J. in the High Court had differed from the Supreme Court in that he classified the relevant function as "administrative" yet then went on to say that "... it is clear from an abundance of recent authority, that even purely administrative acts of persons such as [the Army Pensions Board and the Minister for Defence] may be affected by the requirements of natural and constitutional justice".[186]

14–117   The former line of law which drew a distinction between an administrative and a quasi-judicial function reached its high-water mark in the view that it is only where some legal right is affected by a decision that the rules of constitutional justice are engaged. But this view is not probably part of contemporary Irish judicial review. Rather, the modern trend has been to recognise any interest as a

---

[183]   *R. v Gaming Board Ex p. Benaim and Khaida* [1970] 2 Q.B. 417 at 430. See further, De Smith, *Judicial Review of Administrative Action*, 5th edn (London: Sweet & Maxwell, 1995), Appendix.

[184]   See paras 13–43 to 13–46.

[185]   [1983] I.R. 308 (SC). For other examples, see *Re Roscrea Meat Products Estate* [1958] I.R. 47; *State (Shannon Atlantic Fisheries Ltd) v McPolin* [1976] I.R. 93 at 98; *Geraghty v Minister for Local Government* [1976] I.R. 153; *Connolly v McConnell* [1983] I.R. 172; *State (Genport Ltd) v An Bord Pleanála* [1983] I.L.R.M. 12; *State (Gallagher) v Governor of Portlaoise Prison*, unreported, High Court, April 25, 1983. In some cases the courts have not used the term quasi-judicial, but have spoken instead of "a duty to act judicially": *McDonald v Bord na gCon* [1965] I.R. 217; *O'Brien v Bord na Móna* [1983] I.R. 255. This is only a terminological difference.

[186]   [1981] I.L.R.M. 379 at 382 (HC). See, to similar effect, *Flanagan v UCD* [1988] I.R. 724 at 730 (University disciplinary committee "not a judicial body [but] under a duty to act judicially").

"right"[187] and, in line with this extension, reputation has been steadily accepted as warranting the protection of fair procedure. This is so even in a situation in which any defamation claim has been removed by constitutional immunity. Thus, in *Maguire v Ardagh*,[188] the Supreme Court held that constitutional justice applied to an Oireachtas Committee investigation into the fatal shooting of an unarmed man by members of the Gardaí.[189]

14–118 De Smith[190] gives the following sensible summary of the state of development, as regards the scope of fair procedure, in England and Wales:

> "The term 'natural justice' has largely been replaced by a general duty to act fairly, which is a key element of procedural propriety. On occasion, the term 'due process' has also been invoked. Whichever term is used, the entitlement to fair procedures no longer depends upon the adjudicative analogy, nor whether the authority is required or empowered to decide matters analogous to a legal action between two parties. The law has moved on; not to the state where the entitlement to procedural protection can be extracted with certainty from a computer, but to where the courts are able to insist upon some degree of participation in reaching most official decisions by those whom the decisions will affect in widely different situations, subject only to well-established exceptions. Procedural fairness is therefore not these days rationed at its source – blocked at the outset on the ground of a decision being administrative rather than judicial, of governing a privilege rather than a right. It may, in exceptional circumstances, be diverted during the course of its flow where special circumstances, such as national security, excuse a right to a fair hearing and the breadth of the [procedural protection afforded] will depend upon the circumstances surrounding the decision ... Increasing resort to the open textured standard of fairness is not, though, without its drawbacks. There is a point at which the benefits of its flexible application may be outweighed by the costs of uncertainty. The courts are perhaps creating 'a surrogate political process to ensure the fair representation of a wide range of affected interests in the administrative process'. Doubts have been expressed as to whether the courts are institutionally equipped for such tasks, and whether the unconstrained expansion of participation might paralyse effective administration."

---

[187] *Barry v Sentence Review Group and the Minister for Justice, Equality and Law Reform* [2001] 4 I.R. 167 at 169; and *Clarke v Judge Hogan* [2001] 4 I.R. 167 at 169: "what is done must be seen to be fair. What is fair in any given situation depends upon *the consequences for the person adversely affected by the exercise of the power*. Here it may not, in law, be a punishment, but it would certainly be perceived as being such" (emphasis added).

[188] [2002] 1 I.R. 385 at 511. See, to similar effect, the patriarch of this line of authority, *Re Haughey* [1971] I.R. 217 at 264.

[189] *De Roiste v Minister for Defence* [2005] 3 I.R. 494 at 509 (*arguendo*).

[190] Woolf, Jowell and Le Sueur (eds), *De Smith's Judicial Review of Administrative Action*, 6th edn (London: Sweet & Maxwell, 2007), para.7–003 (footnotes omitted). In *Dellway Investments Ltd v NAMA* [2010] IEHC 375; unreported, High Court April 12, 2010; [2011] IESC 14; unreported, Supreme Court, April 12, 2011 at p.65, Hardiman J. stated that he would adopt the law summarised in this passage in this jurisdiction. But in general, it is kinder not to go into the confusion engendered by the judgments in *Dellway*, which are effectively skewered in Kenny, "Fair Procedures in Irish Administrative Law" (2011) 34 D.U.L.J. 47.

14–119   As can be seen, Irish law appears (in many respects) to be moving in the direction indicated in the first part of this particular passage; and indeed is in the advance column, though with little concern about the note of warning sounded in the later sentences.

14–120   One contrast may be noted between these fair procedure cases and the authorities, described later, dealing with substantive reasonableness. As we shall see, the later group of cases have sometimes held (broadly on Separation of Powers grounds) that review for reasonableness is precluded, save in extreme circumstances. By contrast, such preclusion has happened much less frequently in the case of complaints that fair procedure is violated. One example of this contrast is the cases involving parole. Another example (though in a less clear-cut way, because of developments in regard to substantive reasonableness) is the field of immigration–deportation.[191]

14–121   Let us now list the categories of decision which have been held—or, more usually, assumed—to attract the rules of fair procedures (though one should say that there are situations in which their application has been unquestioned, although their extent may have been at issue).

Public and private employment

14–122   Historically, there were two distinctions of crucial importance for employment law. Office-holders (or officers) were distinguished from employees (servants), and, secondly, the category of office-holders was divided into two classes according to whether the holder was dismissible at pleasure or whether he could only be removed for cause. It was only the office-holder removable for cause who enjoyed the protection of the natural justice principles.

14–123   It seems plain that the second distinction is no longer part of the law. In *Garvey v Ireland*[192] the Commissioner of the Garda Síochána argued successfully that his summary dismissal from office by the Government was contrary to natural justice. Of the four judges who comprised the majority, O'Higgins C.J. (with whom Parke J. agreed) decided that the office was not held merely at pleasure, but also concluded that this distinction was no longer significant. Henchy and Griffin JJ. classified the office as one held at pleasure, yet found that the rules of natural justice applied to any decision to dismiss.

14–124   It seems, too, that the distinction between an office-holder and an employee has ceased to be significant in the present context   The continuing validity of the distinction was questioned by the Supreme Court as far back as *Glover v BLN Ltd*,[193] which arose from the dismissal of a company director for alleged misconduct and was, thus, in the field of private law. The dismissal was invalidated as the plaintiff had not been given a fair hearing by the board of the company. Writing on behalf of the Supreme Court majority, Walsh J. stated:

---

[191] Contrast H & M, paras 14–201 to 14–202 and paras 15–274 to 15–275.
[192] [1981] I.R. 75.
[193] [1973] I.R. 388. See O'Reilly, "The Constitution and the Law of Contract" (1973) 8 Ir. Jur. (n.s) 197.

"[O]nce the matter is governed by the terms of a contract between the parties, it is immaterial whether the employee concerned is deemed to be a servant or an officer [because] public policy and the dictates of constitutional justice require that statutes, regulations or agreements setting up machinery for taking decisions which may affect right or impose liabilities should be construed as providing for fair procedures."[194]

14–125 Initially, several High Court decisions[195] showed judicial reluctance to follow this innovatory approach. However, the Supreme Court in *Gunn v Bord na Choláiste Náisiúnta Ealaine is Deartha*[196] appears finally to have extirpated the distinction between an employee and an office-holder: *Glover* and *Gunn* have frequently been followed.[197]

14–126 So much for authority. As regards policy, too, it is submitted that the *Glover–Gunn* line represents the appropriate outcome. For the modern policy is that all means of livelihood are so important to the person to whom they belong that dismissal should require a fair procedure. On the technical plane, the distinction between an office-holder and a servant is "abstruse and verging on the asinine or bizarre".[198] Indeed in *Gunn*, the Supreme Court reversed the High Court on the question of whether the plaintiff was an officer, without either court offering a very rigorous analysis of the problem. Moreover, it is usually the case that even with an office-holder, the bulk of the terms of employment are fixed by contract, rather than statute, deed of trust, etc.—a factor which erodes the basis of the distinction. In short, whilst the great majority of cases happen to have occurred in the public (rather than the private) field, in principle the obligation to observe fair procedure applies to private, as well as public, employment.

14–127 However, the distinction between public and private may retain some second-order importance. First, the form of proceedings through which a remedy is sought may differ, principally in that judicial review would apply to removal from public employment, though not from private employment. However, now that most of its servants are subject to the Unfair Dismissal legislation,[199] they might have an option as to which form of proceedings they select. Secondly, in regard to the level of procedural protection, this varies considerably from one type of employment to another. The circumstances of private employment may be different and, in particular, likely to engender the type of difficulties which arose in *Mooney*[200] (though in fact this was a public service case). In *Mooney*, in the High

---

[194] [1973] I.R. 388 at 425. See, to like effect, the comments of McWilliam J. in *Garvey v Ireland* [1981] I.R. 75 at 82.
[195] *Heneghan v The Western Regional Fisheries Board* [1986] I.L.R.M. 225 at 228; *Connolly v McConnell* [1983] I.R. 172 at 178; *Lupton v Allied Irish Banks Ltd* (1983) 2 J.I.S.S.L. 107; *NEETU v McConnell* (1983) 2 J.I.S.S.L. 97; and *Connolly v McConnell* [1983] I.R. 172. These authorities are critiqued in the Second Edition of this book at pp.273–274.
[196] [1990] 2 I.R. 168.
[197] e.g. *O'Neill v Beaumont Hospital Board* [1990] I.L.R.M. 419; *Cooney v An Post*, unreported, High Court, April 6, 1990; *Hickey v Eastern Health Board* [1991] 1 I.R. 208 at 211. See also, the classic authority of *Maunsell v Minister for Education* [1940] I.R. 213 in which this distinction was not mentioned.
[198] De Smith, *Judicial Review of Administrative Action*, 4th edn (1980), p.228.
[199] See para.3–68.
[200] *Mooney v An Post* [1994] E.L.R. 103 at 116.

Court, Keane J. (writing in slightly more general terms than Barrington J. in the Supreme Court) remarked:

> "The two great central principles *audi alteram partem* and *nemo iudex in causa sua* cannot be applied in a uniform fashion to every set of facts. To take the most obvious example, the *nemo iudex* requirement cannot be literally applied to every employer confronted with a decision as to whether or not he should dismiss a particular employee. If it were, an employer could never dismiss an employee, since he would always be an interested party in the decision."

14–128   This observation may be taken as an application of the necessity doctrine, described in paras 13–61 to 13–66.

14–129   Here we cannot go into details regarding procedural protection against dismissal[201]; but we can note only that, apart from the overriding principle of constitutional justice, there are the following three sources of fair procedure. Which of them applies will depend upon the particular situation:

(a)   As illustrated by *Glover*, there may be a contract with an express or (more usually) implied term establishing fair procedure.

(b)   It is now accepted, at any rate to some extent, that, under the Unfair Dismissals Acts 1977–2001, a fair dismissal requires the observance of the rules of fair procedure. There are, however, certain restrictions on the impact of these Acts. Those public servants still outside the legislation, who may therefore have to rely on category (c) or (a) rights, include: the members of the defence forces and of the Gardaí[202]; and a few rare birds such as local authority managers[203]; or persons employed by or under the State who are still dismissable by the Government.[204]

(c)   Most of those public servants excluded from category (b) have some particular statutory form of procedural protection against dismissal. Thus, for instance: officers of local authorities have a special statutory fair dismissal system under the Local Government Act 1941.[205]

Membership of trade unions, professional bodies or clubs

14–130   As the relationship between the member and the institution concerned is often grounded ultimately in contract, or some cognate concept, one is again faced with the question of how the rules of constitutional justice may be interpolated. A conceptually satisfactory answer to this difficult question has yet to be given, but for the moment the courts are content to construe the contract of membership as

---

[201] On this, see Redmond, *Dismissal Law in Ireland* (Dublin: Tottel Publishing, 2007), Ch.7; Forde, *Employment Law* (Dublin: Round Hall, 2001), Ch.13; and Madden and Kerr, *Unfair Dismissal Cases and Commentary* (Dublin: Federation of Irish Employers, 1990), Ch.6.

[202] Unfair Dismissals Act 1977 s.2(1)(d), (e).

[203] Local Authorities (Officers and Employees) Act 1926.

[204] Civil Service Regulation (Amendment) Act 2005 s.2.

[205] Sections 24 and 25. See 294 *Dáil Debates* Col.480 (November 23, 1976). For an example of the 1941 Act in operation, see *O'Mahony v Arklow U.D.C.* [1965] I.R. 710 (dismissal by the Government (2005 Act s.2)).

containing an implied term that fair procedures will be observed.[206] Clauses in the constitutions or rules of trade unions, etc. which purport to provide for automatic forfeiture of membership, are probably void as contrary to public policy.[207] This has been the conclusion of the English courts, and given that the Constitution may inform notions of public policy, such reasoning would also seem to apply a fortiori in this jurisdiction. In the case of professional bodies exercising *statutory powers*, there can be no question but that the rules of constitutional justice are applicable to the exercise of such powers.

14–131   As illustrated earlier in this and the previous chapter, the content and stringency of the rules of constitutional justice vary enormously depending on "the circumstances". It is clear, however, that disciplinary action by a trade union,[208] professional body[209] or club[210] cannot be conducted on a summary, ex parte basis and the courts have set aside disciplinary actions either because it did not observe the rules of natural justice or because the requirements of the association's own constitution or rules relating to notice had not been complied with.[211]

14–132   This has been extended even to suspension from a sporting organisation provided that it "involv[ed] the imposition of a substantial sanction"[212] which was, in the case from which this quotation was taken, the disqualification of an international shot-putter from all competition, including the Olympic Games, for 18 months. But, in a later case,[213] it has been explicitly stated that this principle is confined to discipline (frequently involving drug testing) and not to extend to selection for, or retention on, the national team (save in the case of egregious injustice).

Licensing and commercial regulation

14–133   The application of the rules of natural justice in this area[214] stems from the desire to protect an individual's livelihood and business interests. Thus, the rules of constitutional justice have been applied, without controversy,[215] to: the revocation

---

[206] *Fisher v Keane* (1878) 11 Ch D 853; *Dawkins v Antrobus* (1881) 17 Ch D 615; *Flynn v Grt N Ry Co.* (1955) 89 I.L.T.R. 46; *Doyle v Croke*, unreported, High Court, May 6, 1988.

[207] *Edwards v SOGAT* [1971] Ch. 354. But cf. *Moran v Workers Union of Ireland* [1943] I.R. 485.

[208] *Kilkenny v Irish Engineering and Foundry Worker's Union* (1939) Ir. Jur. Rep. 52; *NEETU v McConnell* (1983) 2 J.I.S.L.L. 97; *Connolly v McConnell* [1983] I.R. 172. See also, Kerr and Whyte, *Irish Trade Union Law* (Abingdon: Professional Books, 1985), pp.113–121.

[209] *Manning v Incorporated Law Society for Ireland*, unreported, High Court, March 8, 1980; *Re M, a Doctor* [1984] I.R. 479; *State (Boyle) v General Medical Services (Payment) Board* [1981] I.L.R.M. 14; *O'Donoghue v Veterinary Council* [1975] I.R. 398; *K v An Bord Altranais* [1990] 2 I.R. 396.

[210] *Forde v Fottrell* (1930) 64 I.L.T.R. 89; *Goggins v Feeney* (1949) 83 I.L.T.R. 181; *Ahern v Molyneux* (1965) Ir. Jur. Rep. 59; *Cotter v Sullivan*, unreported, High Court, April 23, 1980.

[211] *Doyle v Griffin* [1937] I.R. 93.

[212] *Quirke v Bord Luthchleas na hÉireann* [1988] I.R. 83 at 88.

[213] *Jacob v Irish Amateur Rowing Union* [2008] 4 I.R. 731 at para.26.

[214] On licensing and fair procedure, see paras 7–06 to 7–10.

[215] However, see *Melton v Censorship of Publications Board* [2003] 2 I.L.R.M. 18 at 31.

or suspension of a taxi driver's licence[216] or a betting permit for a bookmaker[217]; the licensing of agricultural marts[218]; the censorship of publications[219]; the granting of a liquor licence in substitution for demolished licensed premises[220]; the renewal of an annual fishing licence[221]; and the granting of product authorisations for pharmaceutical drugs.[222]

Discipline

14–134   A number of what might be called trail-blazing cases on fair procedure has been in the field of discipline. For example, in *State (Gleeson) v Minister for Defence*,[223] the applicant had been summarily dismissed from the Defence Forces following an incident involving a group of soldiers of which he was one. This discharge was quashed by the Supreme Court, as the applicant had not been given an opportunity to meet the case against him or of dealing with the reason for his discharge. To take another example from a rather different field: it has been long established that the rules apply to the local government auditor's jurisdiction in the field of local government.[224]

14–135   One particular feature, which nevertheless frequently arises in this area, is the doubt over the notion that in a disciplined organisation the need for unquestioning obedience to the commands of a superior was regarded as outweighing the advantages of constitutional justice.[225] Even the question of what is a "disciplined organisation" for this purpose is not clear-cut; but it may reasonably be regarded as constituting a spectrum running from (at one extreme) the prisons and the Defence Forces and taking in, next, the Gardaí, the fire services and schools or colleges. However, over-precision in this area would be very unrealistic. The most that can be said is that, while there is no longer anything like a firm rule, this notion still retains some vitality; at least, it is a factor which, in certain circumstances,

---

[216] *Ingle v O'Brien* (1975) 109 I.L.T.R. 7; *Moran v Attorney General* [1976] I.R. 400; *International Fishing Ltd v Minister for the Marine (No. 2)* [1991] 2 I.R. 93; *TV3 v IRTC* [1994] 2 I.R. 439; *Shanley v Galway Corporation* [1995] 1 I.R. 396; *Slevin v Shannon Regional Fisheries Board* [1995] 1 I.R. 460; *Madden v Minister for the Marine* [1997] 1 I.L.R.M. 136; *Dunne v Donohue* [2002] 2 I.R. 533; *NWR FM Ltd v Broadcasting Commission of Ireland* [2004] 4 I.R. 50; *Goodison v Sheahan* [2008] IEHC 127; *McCarron v Kearney* [2008] IEHC 195.

[217] *McDonald v Bord na gCon* [1965] I.R. 217; *State (Graham) v Racing Board*, unreported, High Court, November 22, 1983.

[218] *East Donegal Co-Operative Ltd v Attorney General* [1970] I.R. 317. See also, *Gammell v Dublin County Council* [1983] I.L.R.M. 413 (licensing of temporary dwellings).

[219] *Irish Family Planning Association v Ryan* [1979] I.R. 295.

[220] *Jaggers Restaurant Ltd v Ahearne* [1988] I.R. 308.

[221] *Slevin v Shannon Regional Fisheries Board* [1995] 1 I.R. 460.

[222] *Genmark Pharma Ltd v Minister for Health*, unreported, High Court, July 11, 1997.

[223] [1976] I.R. 280. This decision has been applied in *Hogan v Minister for Justice* [1976–1977] I.L.R.M. 184 and *State (Furey) v Minister for Defence* [1988] I.L.R.M. 89. See also, *McDonough v Minister for Defence* [1991] 2 I.R. 33; *McGrath v Commissioner of An Garda Síochána (Nos 1 and 2)* [1990] I.L.R.M. 817; [1993] I.L.R.M. 38; *McNamara v South Western Area Health Board* [2001] IEHC 24; *Deegan v Minister for Finance* [2000] E.L.R. 190 at 198–199.

[224] *Downey v O'Brien* [1994] 2 I.L.R.M. 130 at 150.

[225] *R. v Army Council Ex p. Ravenscroft* [1917] 2 K.B. 504; *Ex p. Fry* [1954] 1 W.L.R. 730; *State (Jordan) v Garda Commissioner* [1987] I.L.R.M. 107 at 115 per O'Hanlon J. On this consideration, see also, paras 14–180 to 14–183. Cf. "Theirs not to make reply, | Theirs not to reason why, | Theirs but to do and die" (Tennyson, *The Charge of the Light Brigade*).

will influence certain judges. For example, in *Donnelly*[226] the applicant had been discharged from the Defence Forces as he was considered to have been a security risk, because of the theft of a machine gun. Finlay P. agreed that the fact that, at the outset of the investigation, the disciplinary officer had drafted an application for Donnelly's discharge was "suspicious", but he was satisfied that this was simply a recommendation and that the matter would not have been carried any further if the applicant had given a satisfactory explanation. Accordingly, Finlay P. ruled that there was no bias or prejudgment on the part of the commanding officer. The judge also took the view that, in the subsequent interviews, the applicant had been given an adequate opportunity to make his own case. Finlay P. stated that there was a "clear public necessity" that the military authorities should have the discretion to remove persons considered to be a security risk. In its context, this may be taken as authority for applying a lower standard of constitutional justice.

14–136 As against this, in *Garvey v Ireland*, the Supreme Court majority firmly rejected the argument:

> "... [t]hat the confidential and sensitive relationship that must necessarily exist between the Government of the day and the head of the national police force requires that the statutory right to remove a Commissioner from office at any time should not be interpreted as being shackled by an obligation to give a reason for its exercise ...".[227]

14–137 A compromise on the application of constitutional justice in the field of discipline is to say that the rules apply but with a relaxed standard. For example, in *Scariff v Taylor*,[228] Carroll J. quoted with approval the following passage from Finlay C.J.'s judgment in *C v The Court Martial*[229]:

> "... the Court can and should pay particular respect to the fundamental importance ... of the disciplinary machinery ... of the defence forces, but ... that respect and, in a sense, reluctance to intervene can never possibly interfere with a duty of the court to do justice ...".

14–138 Finally, it is, or used to be, questionable whether the rules of natural justice apply at all, where the punishment involved is the involuntary transfer of

---

[226] *State (Donnelly) v Minister for Defence*, unreported, High Court, Finlay P., October 9, 1979.

[227] [1981] I.R. 75 at 102 per Henchy J. See, to rather similar effect, *Gallagher v Corrigan*, unreported, High Court, February 1, 1988 at 11.

[228] [1996] 1 I.R. 242 at 249. See also, *State (Gallagher) v Governor of Portlaoise Prison*, unreported, High Court, May 18, 1977; *State (Gallagher) v Governor of Portlaoise Prison*, unreported, High Court, April 25, 1983. Though note that in *Murtagh v Board of Management of St Emer's National School* [1991] 1 I.R. 482, in spite of the extreme facts, Barron J. appeared to accept that the rules applied to a three days' suspension (though it indicated that the court might exercise its discretion to refuse relief on the ground of the trivial nature of the complaint). In the context of summary procedures in a military case, it was said obiter by Clarke J. in *Potts v Minister for Defence* [2005] 2 I.L.R.M. 517 at 527 (a leave case) that "certain [sc. minor] matters do not warrant the intervention of the court at all".

[229] Unreported, Supreme Court, February 15, 1994 at 2. Finlay P. also referred to the "partly magisterial" nature of the prison governor's functions and seemed to imply that it would be wrong for the courts to impose anything but the most rudimentary procedural standards in the context of prison discipline.

personnel. Such transfers are regarded as administrative decisions, and this fact when coupled with the public interest in maintaining the efficiency of the security forces, meant that it would probably require something akin to bad faith before such an administrative decision could be successfully challenged.[230]

Detention

14–139   Unsurprisingly, given the importance of the individual interest at stake, the detention of the person attracts the rules. Thus in *LK v Clinical Director, Lakeview Unit*[231] it was held that, where a person is challenging his involuntary detention under the Mental Treatment Acts 1945–2001, in the absence of special circumstances, someone acting on his behalf is entitled to access relevant medical records. As has been remarked, "[i]t is inherent in the constitutional scheme that persons may only be deprived of their liberty for good reasons embodied in law and in accordance with fair procedures. The European Convention [on Human Rights, Art.5(1)] goes somewhat further than the Constitution ...".[232]

Temporary release and parole

14–140   Three cases, with differing results, concerned the parole/release of prisoners, under the Prisoners (Temporary Release) Rules 1960.[233] Possibly, the reason for this was that the fundamental right of liberty was involved. In the first of these cases, *State (Murphy) v Kielt*,[234] the applicant-prisoner had, after serving four months, been released for the remainder of his sentence. The release was subject to certain conditions including keeping the peace and being of good behaviour during the period of his release. However, whilst on release, the applicant was arrested and charged with attempted murder. The Governor, "probably acting in a common-sense manner",[235] treated the arrest on this serious charge as automatically terminating the temporary release. The High Court and, on appeal, the Supreme Court, held that this termination was invalid for failure to observe the *audi alteram partem* rule, especially bearing in mind that charges are frequently dropped or not proceeded with. McCarthy J. remarked that while the suspicion regarding the person arrested must be assumed to be based on reasonable grounds, nevertheless the prisoner should be allowed the opportunity of contesting those grounds. Griffin J. agreed but added that "[the grant and termination of a temporary release] are clearly acts which are administrative in nature. An informal procedure is all that is required provided that such procedure is conducted fairly".[236]

14–141   By contrast, what had happened in *Ryan v Governor of Limerick*

---

[230]   *State (Boyle) v Governor of the Military Detention Barracks* [1980] I.L.R.M. 242; *State (Smith and Fox) v Governor of Military Detention Barracks* [1980] I.L.R.M. 208 (prison transfer cases); *Corliss v Ireland*, unreported, High Court, July 23, 1984 (transfer of Garda).

[231]   [2007] 2 I.L.R.M. 69 at 79–80.

[232]   Forde, *Constitutional Law*, 2nd edn (Dublin: First Law, 2004), p.314.

[233]   S.I. No. 167 of 1960. In none of these cases was anything said about the notion, just examined, that constitutional justice should be applied in a less stringent form in certain types of disciplinary case.

[234]   [1984] I.R. 458.

[235]   [1984] I.R. 458 at 462.

[236]   [1984] I.R. 458 at 472. See also, *Sherlock v Governor of Mountjoy Prison* [1991] 1 I.R. 451.

Prison[237] was not that a release was terminated, but that no release was granted. The applicant had been granted a series of brief temporary releases, after the last of which the applicant's release was not renewed (because, as he was informed by the Governor, there had been a rise in the crime rate in Limerick). In one of the very few cases in which it has ever been held that the rules of constitutional justice did not apply, Murphy J. distinguished sharply between the termination of a release and the refusal of a release (as on the facts here). In the latter case, no right to constitutional justice arose because "[t]he temporary release is a privilege or concession to which a person in custody has no right and indeed it has never been argued ... that he should be heard in relation to any consideration given to the exercise of such a concession in his favour".[238] Although quoting *Ryan* with approval, Finnegan P. in *McAlister v Minister for Justice*[239] nevertheless went on to hold that, on an application for temporary release, there was a right to constitutional justice, including reasons, but falling short of a right to a hearing. It is difficult to reconcile *McAlister* and *Ryan*.

Property and planning

14–142   Even at times and in jurisdictions where the bounds of natural justice have been narrowly set, there has never been any doubt that the rules of natural justice apply to state interference with property rights.[240] Thus, the rules have been applied to compulsory purchase orders, and land acquisition procedures; the taking over by the National Asset Management Agency of a loan owed to a bank[241]; decisions of An Bord Pleanála[242] and even, on one occasion, of local planning authorities[243]; the making of a preservation order by the Commissioners of Public Works[244]; and the award of a broadcasting contract by the IRTC.[245] Another example occurred

---

[237] [1988] I.R. 198.

[238] [1988] I.R. 198 at 199.

[239] [2003] 1 I.L.R.M. 161, esp. at 171.

[240] *Re Mountcharles' Estate* [1934] I.R. 754; *Foley v Irish Land Commission* [1952] I.R. 118; *Re Roscrea Meat Products Estate* [1958] I.R. 47; *State (Costello) v Irish Land Commission* [1959] I.R. 353; *Clarke v Irish Land Commission* [1976] I.R. 375; *Nolan v Irish Land Commission* [1981] I.R. 23; *State (Hussey) v Irish Land Commission* [1983] I.L.R.M. 407; *O'Brien v Bord na Móna* [1983] I.R. 255. See also, *Irish Land Commission v Hession* [1978] I.R. 322

[241] *Dellway Investments Ltd v NAMA* [2010] IEHC 375; unreported, High Court, April 12, 2010; [2011] IESC 14; unreported, Supreme Court, April 12, 2011: the borrower argued successfully that, because of various differences in the position of NAMA and the banks, as creditor, he was in a more unfavourable position because of the change. See also, *Daly v NAMA* [2011] IEHC; unreported, High Court, September 12, 2011.

[242] *Killiney and Ballybrack Residents Association v Minister for Local Government (No. 1)* (1978) 112 I.L.T.R. 69; *Geraghty v Minister for Local Government* [1976] I.R. 153; *State (Genport Ltd) v An Bord Pleanála* [1983] I.L.R.M. 12; *State (Boyd) v An Bord Pleanála*, unreported, High Court, February 18, 1983; *State (CIÉ) v An Bord Pleanála*, unreported, Supreme Court, December 12, 1984; *State (Hussey and Kenny) v An Bord Pleanála*, unreported, Supreme Court, December 20, 1984 (where Lynch J. said that generally a planning authority "is not obliged to enter into a dialogue ... or to indicate in advance to an applicant the authority's thinking or views before deciding on the application". However, the judgment then goes on to qualify this remark.)

[243] *Frenchurch Properties Ltd v Wexford County Council* [1992] 2 I.R. 268; *Eircell v Leitrim County Council* [2000] 1 I.R. 479 at 494 (revocation of planning permission).

[244] *O'Callaghan v Commissioners of Public Works* [1985] I.L.R.M. 364.

[245] *Dublin and County Broadcasting Ltd v IRTC*, unreported, High Court, May 12, 1989; *TV3 v IRTC* [1994] 2 I.R. 439.

in *State (Philpott) v Registrar of Titles*[246] in which the respondent had entered an inhibition on the folio, which prevented all dealings with the land save with the consent of the respondent and had done so—and here is the important point—without consulting the applicant, who was the registered owner of the property. This decision is of significance, not only to the Land Registry, but also for other systems of registration.[247]

Payments of grants, benefits and pensions

14–143 There used to be a notion (held, at any rate, in England) that the rules of constitutional justice did not apply to *privelegia*, i.e. discretionary payments, such as grants, benefits or pensions, to which the applicant had no statutory entitlement. To judge by a steady line of case law[248] in which the point has not even been raised and the rules were applied, the Irish courts have no interest in this restriction (which might not be relevant anyway, since many of these benefits have now been made matters of statutory right).

Deportation and other decisions affecting the residency of aliens

14–144 It seems to have been generally accepted[249] that the rules of constitutional justice apply in this context. Indeed, successive counsel for the State appear to have thought it not even worth running any argument grounded on deportation being inherently an area in which the Minister must be allowed a free hand.[250]

Tribunals

14–145 It is an element of a Tribunal that, irrespective of its subject matter, it should observe a fairly formal procedure. It follows—indeed, given the definition of a tribunal offered at paras 6–08 to 6–09, the point is almost circular—that a tribunal should observe the precepts of constitutional justice. Indeed as we have seen in Chapter 6, many of the cases on, for example, discipline, involve tribunals.

14–146 One can note here that, though it is not a point peculiar to tribunals, the

---

[246] [1986] I.L.R.M. 499. See also, *Clancy v Ireland* [1988] I.R. 326.

[247] e.g. the registration of company charges under Pt IV of the Companies Act 1963. See *R. v Registrar of Companies Ex p. Easal Commodities Ltd* [1986] Q.B. 1114 and Pye, "Certificate of Registration – An Impenetrable Shield No More?" (1985) 3 I.L.T. (n.s) 213.

[248] *State (McConnell) v Eastern Health Board*, unreported, High Court, June 1, 1983. See also, *McLoughlin v Minister for Social Welfare* [1958] I.R. 1; *Kiely v Minister for Social Welfare* [1971] I.R. 21; *Kiely v Minister for Social Welfare (No. 2)* [1977] I.R. 297; *McKinley v Minister for Defence* [1988] I.R. 139 at 142; *State (Hoolahan) v Minister for Social Welfare*, unreported, High Court, July 23, 1986; *Thompson v Minister for Social Welfare* [1989] I.R. 618; *Corcoran v Minister for Social Welfare* [1991] 2 I.R. 175. See further, paras 6–81 to 6–89.

[249] *Abdelkefi v Minister for Justice* [1984] I.L.R.M. 138; *Ghneim v Minister for Justice, Irish Times*, September 2, 1989 (although here there was also a large element of legitimate expectation); *Anisimova v Minister for Justice*, unreported, Supreme Court, November 28, 1997; *Stefan v Minister for Justice, Equality and Law Reform* [2001] 4 I.R. 203; *PPA v Refugee Appeals Tribunal* [2007] 1 I.L.R.M. 288 at 298–299. *A contra*: *Pok Sun Shum v Ireland* [1986] I.L.R.M. 593 at 599.

[250] See para.15–164.

audi alteram partem rule has been applied not only to substantive issues, but also to procedural questions, such as whether to grant an adjournment.[251]

Inquests

14–147   The extent to which fair procedure applies to an inquest was explicitly considered in *Ramsever v Mahon*.[252] The respondent coroner contended that an inquest was an inquisitorial procedure and hence constitutional justice did not apply. In line with this, the applicant, who was the deceased's sister, had been denied, by the respondent, statements or draft depositions made by potential witnesses, which she claimed were needed in order to enable her to participate fully in the inquest. However, writing for the Supreme Court, Fennelly J. stated[253]:

> "It is in no way inconsistent with the inquisitorial character of an inquest that persons with a legitimate interest should propound a version of the facts which accords with those interests. One may wish to seek to establish facts tending to deflect blame; one may wish to pursue a version which tends to suggest that the death occurred other than due to mere accident or natural causes ... It follows that persons represented at an inquest are entitled to an appropriate level of fair procedures. They are entitled to be present, to call witnesses and to cross-examine. But all of this is subject to the overriding consideration that they are assisting in an inquiry into the facts and are not either responding to or making a charge. They are subject to the directions of the coroner who is entitled to conduct the hearing in his discretion, while respecting the legitimate interests of interested persons to pursue lines of inquiry."

14–148   Given this balance, Fennelly J. accepted the view that a person in the position of the applicant is not entitled to "the full panoply of natural justice requirements of disclosure in advance of the hearing".[254] However, Fennelly J. went on to hold[255]:

> "... the applicant has expressed to the coroner a specific concern as to how the death of the deceased occurred ... In these circumstances her ability to address that issue at the inquest could be unduly prejudiced by the refusal to provide copies of the documents ...
>
>   I accept that the [coroner] has a discretion to decline to disclose sensitive material such as photographs of the body."

Multi-stage proceedings

14–149   There is a possibility that, where there are multiple stages to a process, there might need to be an application of constitutional justice at more than one

---

[251] *CG v Appeal Commissioner* [2005] 2 I.R. 472 at 473; *Kiely v Minister for Social Welfare (No. 1)* [1971] I.R. 21.

[252] [2006] 1 I.R. 216.

[253] [2006] 1 I.R. 216 at 225.

[254] This is a passage from Kelly J.'s judgment in *Northern Area Health Board v Geraghty* [2001] 3 I.R. 321 at 335, which Fennelly J. quoted with approval.

[255] [2006] 1 I.R. 216 at 226–227.

stage. The only general guidance which may be offered here is that a court will decide according to what fair procedure requires in the particular circumstances. These will include the character of constitutional justice granted at an earlier stage. To take an easy example: it may be the case that the person affected will have—or should have—put forward all their relevant arguments at an earlier stage, so that there is no need for them to be subsequently repeated. This, in effect, is what was decided in relation to an (unsuccessful) argument that fair procedure should be followed afresh, at the stage of sentencing.[256]

Legitimate expectations

14–150 The most common case of this type discussed at greater length at paras 19–30 to 19–35, is where the court finds that there has been an implicit commitment by a public body to a particular course of action, and holds that, consequently, the public body may not resile from this position, without granting the applicant a hearing. A striking example is *Slevin v Shannon Regional Fisheries Board.*[257] This arose out of the refusal to renew an annual fishing licence which had been granted to the applicant for the previous 25 years. Barron J. stated that "… it seems to me that if the Board wished to alter the stance which it had taken year by year by granting the licences, it ought to have informed the applicant why it was so doing".[258]

14–151 There have been only a few cases in which a public body has given an explicit commitment to consult in specified circumstances. These have involved development plans (for planning control) which, when zoning an area for use in the traveller accommodation programme, also include the following commitment, to quote from the plan in *Byrne v Fingal*[259]: "the council is committed to follow a consultation with the travelling community and with the local community in the neighbourhood of any such proposed site". But, in *Byrne*, the manager went ahead with the development of such a site without consultations. In the High Court, McKechnie J. granted a declaration that such a development would be in material contravention of the development plan.

Where there is an appeal, rather than confirmation

14–152 In paras 16–72 to 16–77, we consider whether the High Court should exercise its discretion not to grant a remedy in the circumstances in which an appeal would have been available to the applicant. We reach the conclusion that a great deal depends on the particular flaw of which the applicant complains and that, if the flaw is in breach of constitutional justice, then probably the availability of an appeal will not be a ground for exercising the court's discretion to refuse an order. However, the applicant also has a hurdle to jump at an earlier stage of the court's reasoning process, namely does the availability of an appeal, at which constitutional

---

[256] e.g. *Georgopolous v Beaumont Hospital Board* [1998] 3 I.R. 132 (citing *Graham v The Racing Board*, unreported, High Court, November 22, 1983 at 7); *Curtin v Dáil Éireann* [2006] 2 I.L.R.M. 99 at 147.

[257] [1995] 1 I.R. 460. Notice that the judgment does not actually use the phrase "legitimate expectations", but this appears to be the substance of the point.

[258] [1995] 1 I.R. 460 at 465.

[259] [2001] 4 I.R. 565. Contrast *Wilkinson v Dublin* [1991] I.L.R.M. 605, in which Costello P. ruled against the applicant, in part because there was no agreement.

justice would be available, mean that the applicant does not need to establish their case and so does not reach the discretion stage?

14–153 The Irish rule is probably that, subject to a substantial qualification considered in the following paragraphs, where a right of appeal is available, at which, if an appeal had been taken, the rules of constitutional justice would have been observed, this does not cure a want of constitutional justice at the original stage[260]: the view appears to have been taken that the applicant is entitled to constitutional justice at the initial stage, without being put to the trouble of taking an appeal. This is illustrated by *Stefan v Minister for Justice, Equality and Law Reform*[261] which centered on the Hope Hanlan appeal procedure, which predated the procedure set up by the Refugee Act 1996 (as amended). At the time of this case, the structure of the process for administering applications for refugee status consisted of two stages. In the first place, a decision was taken by a duly authorised officer in the Department of Justice, Equality and Law Reform. Then, secondly, there was an appeal to the Refugee Appeals Authority. The Supreme Court held that the process involved "two separate distinct decisions" (the significance of which is explained in the following paragraphs). The original decision had breached constitutional justice and "… the applicant is entitled to a primary decision in accordance with fair procedures … A fair appeal does not cure an unfair hearing". But, as against this, consider *Carroll v Bus Átha Cliath*,[262] which arose out of disciplinary proceedings in which there was a breach of constitutional justice in that the plaintiff was not present at the hearing and the issue was whether this breach could be cured by the provision of an internal disciplinary appeal. Clarke J. took a fairly nuanced approach, based on the notion of whether, considering the process as a whole, the applicant would have been afforded fair procedures.

14–154 The qualification, mentioned above, which takes longer to explain, was first expressly noted in *Gammell v Dublin County Council*[263] (the facts of which are given below). *Gammell* held that certain categories of "appeal" can be treated as part of the initial decision. Thus, where a "provisional" decision is taken without observing the *audi alteram partem* rule, this defect can be remedied if the person affected has the chance to put his side of the case before the decision is made

---

[260] *Leary v National Union of Vehicle Builders* [1971] Ch. 34; *Ingle v O'Brien* (1975) 109 I.L.T.R. 7; *Moran v Attorney General* [1976] I.R. 400; *Irish Family Planning Association v Ryan* [1979] I.R. 295; *Halal Meat Packers Ltd v EAT* [1990] I.L.R.M. 293 at 309; *McDonough v Minister for Defence* [1991] 2 I.R. 33 at 41.

[261] [2001] 4 I.R. 203. The quotations from the judgment are at 211 and 218.

[262] [2005] 4 I.R. 184 at 212–213. See also, *State (Stanbridge) v Mahon* [1979] I.R. 217; *Calvin v Carr* [1980] A.C. 574; and *State (Collins) v Ruane* [1984] I.R. 105 at 124 per Henchy J. (See, obiter, *Bane v Garda Representative Association* [1997] 2 I.R. 449 at 477–478 (where the alternative was not an appeal but a libel action).)

At the same time, it must be said that the Irish authorities on the general point are now rather middle aged and the view has been taken in other common law jurisdictions that "… a prior hearing may be better than a subsequent hearing but a subsequent hearing is better than no hearing at all"; De Smith, *Judicial Review of Administrative Action*, 6th edn (2007), para.8.024. Paragraph 8.03 of the same work states: "[t]he common law and the ECHR permit a public authority to make decisions which do not comply fully with procedural fairness requirements if the person affected has recourse to a further hearing or appeal which itself provides fairness". On the ECHR and this point, see paras 12–14 to 12–19.

[263] [1983] I.L.R.M. 413. See also, *State (Duffy) v Minister for Defence* [1979] I.L.R.M. 65.

permanent.[264] In short, for the purpose of constitutional justice, the process can sometimes be characterised as a single decision (as opposed to a discrete decision, followed by an appeal). The effect of this characterisation would be to avoid the principle explained at the start of this section.

14–155 *Gammell v Dublin County Council*[265] involved an order prohibiting the erection of temporary dwellings which had been made under the Local Government (Sanitary Services) Act 1948, in respect of the plaintiff's caravan site, by the defendant council. The plaintiff was not aware of the inspection of her site by the local authority and health board experts on whose certificate the local authority relied in making the order. Following the procedure under the 1948 Act, a notice that the order had been made and that any person aggrieved had 14 days in which to apply to the Minister for the Environment, asking for the order to be annulled, was published in a newspaper circulating locally. On such an application the order could then be annulled or confirmed by the Minister. Carroll J. held that this opportunity to make representations to the Minister sufficed for compliance with the *audi alteram partem* rule.

14–156 In *Gammell* the confirmation was to be given by a body other than the body which had taken the initial decision. This made the confirmation look more like an appeal and required the High Court (Carroll J.) to draw an important distinction in the following passage:

> "However, in this case we are not dealing with an order effective when made and an appeal therefrom to an appellate body. Under section 31 of the [1948] Act the order has no effect until the person aggrieved has been given an opportunity of stating reasons why it should not come into effect. There is no 'appeal' to the Minister from an operative order. There is machinery set up under the section whereby an aggrieved party can make representations why the order should not come into operation. If successful, the order is annulled by the Minister and it never becomes operative ...
>
> The fact that the representations are to be made to the Minister and not to the body making the order does not seem to me to be invidious in any respect. In fact, even though the County Council would not appear to be inhibited from acting, it seems preferable that representation should be made to the Minister who can avoid the criticism which might be levelled at the County Council that they are judges in their own cause."[266]

14–157 This distinction can also be applied in other areas. Take, for instance, applications for planning permission[267]: considered in isolation, the procedure before

---

[264] A somewhat similar, if more nuanced, position has been adopted by the Privy Council in *Calvin v Carr* [1980] A.C. 574 at 592.

[265] [1983] I.L.R.M. 413. It is suggested that a broadly similar approach was followed in a different field (courts-martial) in *Scariff v Taylor* [1996] 2 I.L.R.M. 278. For the application of art.6(1) of the Convention to courts-martial, see *Findlay v United Kingdom* (1997) 24 E.H.R.R. 221.

[266] [1983] I.L.R.M. 413 at 417–418.

[267] The actual planning situation should be considered in the light of the *Frenchurch Properties* case [1992] 2 I.R. 268 discussed at pp.544–545 of the Third Edition. Notice also that it might be made a point of distinction between the *Gammell* and the planning situation that in the planning situation, it is the private individual rather that the public body (as in *Gammell*) which is denied permission to do something.

a local planning authority might appear to violate the *audi alteram partem* rule in that (confining the discussion to the applicant for planning permission and not examining the position of objectors)[268] the applicant is not told of the authority's provisional thinking on his application, much less allowed any opportunity to make representations in regard to it. On the other hand, there is ample constitutional justice at the rehearing, on appeal, to An Bord Pleanála. The crucial question thus is whether the initial application stage is to be examined in isolation or whether it is to be considered together with the proceedings before An Bord Pleanála. In other words, is the structure of the decision-making system analogous to that involved in *Gammell*? It is submitted that the two systems are similar and thus that the planning application system does not violate the *audi alteram partem* rule. The key factor is that (as with the prohibition order) a local planning authority decision granting permission does not come into effect until the appeal has been heard or, if no appeal is taken, until the period for appealing has elapsed.[269]

14–158 Finally, one should note that (to take the reverse situation to that just discussed) it is probably the case that constitutional justice does not create any right to an appeal. This issue arose in the case of *Carroll v Minister for Agriculture and Food*[270] which concerned the basic fairness of the procedure for testing cattle for "reactors". The applicant had submitted that, because the procedure did not incorporate any appeal mechanism and did not enable the applicant to challenge the test or have an independent re-test in the event of a disputed finding, it was invalid. Blayney J. rejected this argument. One should add that this result seems to follow not least from the basic separation of powers consideration that for a full-blown appellate system to spring from the brow of a court would involve a substantial trespass on the legislative function.[271]

The rules do not (usually) apply

14–159 The law on decisions which, are—or may be—exempt from the rules may be put under the following heads:

Legislation

14–160 It has been stated earlier that the rules apply where any individual interest is *directly* affected. But what is the position where legislative decisions are concerned? The fact that the principal type of legislation is an Act of Parliament, made by a body where all interests are supposedly represented and which is traditionally not subject to control by the courts during the process of legislation, has traditionally encouraged courts to avoid this area. (As a matter of practice rather than law, Departments of State customarily consult interest groups about the content of draft bills.)

14–161 The rationale usually given for excluding legislative decisions from

---

[268] On which see *State (Stanford) v Dun Laoghaire Corporation*, unreported, Supreme Court, February 20, 1981.
[269] Planning and Development Act 2000 s.34(11).
[270] [1991] 1 I.R. 230 at 235. See, to similar effect, *Quinn v King's Inns* [2004] I.R. 344 at para.43.
[271] Wade and Forsyth, *Administrative Law*, 10th edn (Oxford: OUP, 2009), p.442.

the scope of the rules is that the *audi alteram partem* rule, at any rate, is more appropriate where a compact range of facts is in issue—for example, in a dismissal case, whether an employee was dishonest—and less appropriate when a broader range of acts and divergent considerations, for example, the economy or some other national interest, is concerned.[272] Traditionally, legislative decisions were taken as being beyond the reach of the rule.[273] This orthodoxy was confirmed by McMahon J. in the High Court in *Cassidy v Minister for Industry and Commerce*[274] where he held, without discussion, that the rule did not apply to require consultation with a vintners' association before the making of a statutory instrument fixing maximum prices for the sale of intoxicating liquor in the Dundalk area. In *Gorman v Minister for the Environment*[275] after an unusually thorough discussion of the basic principle considered here, Carney J. stated that "[l]egislative decisions, on grounds, *inter alia*, of practicability, have traditionally been taken not to attract the rules of constitutional justice".[276] He went on to hold that there was no duty to consult taxi drivers before the Minister made a statutory instrument deregulating the taxi industry, despite the capital loss that would be caused to existing licence holders.

14–162   On the other hand, in some cases involving delegated legislation, it has been assumed (although, surprisingly, without any discussion of the point and certainly with no reference to the authorities mentioned here) that the maker was under a duty to consult interested parties.[277] Recently, in a case concerning fisheries bye-laws,[278] the major point of controversy in the judgment concerned the extent of the High Court's powers on a statutory appeal. However, it was assumed that "fair procedures" (meaning that the persons affected ought to be consulted) applied to the making of a bye-law, although the principle under consideration here was

---

[272] This passage from our Third Edition was cited in *Gorman v Minister for the Environment* [2001] 2 I.R. 414 at 437.

[273] *Bates v Lord Hailsham* [1972] 1 W.L.R. 1373; *Essex CC v Minister for Housing* (1967) 66 L.G.R. 23.

[274] [1978] I.R. 297. This point was not dealt with by the Supreme Court, who found for the plaintiff on another ground.

[275] [2001] 2 I.R. 414.

[276] [2001] 2 I.R. 414 at 437. On the question of whether the rule applies to legislation, see also, *Association of General Practitioners v Minister for Health* [1995] 1 I.R. 382 at 388, followed in *Collooney Pharmacy Limited v North Western Health Board* [2005] 4 I.R. 124 at paras 46–49 (no right to be consulted when a mass contract is being negotiated).

[277] *Burke v Minister for Labour* [1979] I.R. 354 at 361–362. In *State (Lynch) v Cooney* [1982] I.R. 337 the Supreme Court appears to have accepted that the Minister could have been under a duty to consult with interested parties prior to the making of a banning order by way of statutory instrument under s.31 of the Broadcasting Authority Act 1960. However, the Minister's failure to do this was excused by the Supreme Court in view of the fact that, in the circumstances of the case, there was no time to hear the other side. In *US International Tobacco Co. Ltd v Attorney General* [1990] 1 I.R. 394, Hamilton P. reserved the question of whether the plaintiff company (whose products were the subject of an ultra vires banning order under the Health Act 1947) were entitled to be heard in advance of the making of such a statutory instrument. See also, *HML Ltd v Minister for Agriculture*, unreported, High Court, Barr J., February 8, 1996.

[278] *Re South Western Fisheries Region (No. 7), Kerry District Conservation of Salmon and Sea Trout Bye-law, Teahan v Minister for Communications, Energy and Natural Resources (No. 1)* [2008] IEHC 194 (Laffoy J.). See similarly, *Teahan v Minister for Communications, Energy and Natural Resources (No. 2)* [2009] IEHC 399 at paras 33–38 (Hedigan J.), which also assumed that there had, as a matter of "natural and constitutional justice", to be consultation in the adoption of a fishing bye-law.

not really considered. In short, this is one of many areas where a well-reasoned Supreme Court decision is sorely needed.

14–163 An even wider vista is opened up when one considers the situation arising when a public body, acting under legislation of a public regulation or public betterment character, makes an order which potentially applies to the property or business of inter alia the applicant, even though it may have no direct or immediate effect. To take the most obvious and significant example of this type of control—land-use planning—if land is being re-zoned,[279] for the purposes of planning permission, from (say) industrial to agricultural use, would the general advert in a local circulating newspaper suffice, as notice to a person whose land is affected? Or is the landowner entitled to actual notice or something approaching it? One fundamental line of defence which might be available to the public body is that such an order is so large in both its scope and its socio-economic and public policy characteristics as to be legislative or policy-making in character, and thus immune from the rules of constitutional justice. However this argument was not advanced in the only (rather brief) judgment in this field: *MacPharthaláin v Commissioners of Public Works*,[280] in which it was accepted, but again without the point being argued, that the applicant landowner should have been given notice of an intention to consider designating his land as an area of international scientific interest, under EU legislation, such designation carrying adverse consequences for the landowner.[281]

Policy

14–164 In regard to the question of whether the *audi alteram partem* rule does or should apply, much the same issues are raised if the decision being taken involves policy rather than legislation (as might be expected since legislation is of course a special category of policy). Some of the underlying issues, which have been little discussed here, are teased out in the following passage by a New Zealand writer, Peter Cane, who began by summarising the work of Lon Fuller who had advanced the view that natural justice was not suitable for dealing with what Professor Fuller called "'polycentric' disputes, that is disputes requiring account to be taken of a large number of interlocking and interacting interests and considerations". Professor Cane stated:

> "Fuller gave several examples of polycentric problems: how to divide between two art galleries 'in equal shares' a collection of paintings left by will; the task of establishing levels of wages and prices in a centrally controlled economy ...

---

[279] For this procedure, see para.5–118.

[280] [1992] 1 I.R. 111 at 118. Notice that in *MacPharthaláin*, no reference was made to *Wilkinson v Dublin County Council* [1991] I.L.R.M. 605 at 611 in which the applicant's case failed. However it is suggested that *Wilkinson* could have been distinguished on the ground that it held that there was no need for a local authority to consult as to what it did with its own property. *McPharthaláin* was appealed to the Supreme Court ([1994] 3 I.R. 353 at 359) where the present point was not seriously disputed by the respondent.

[281] See also, *Keogh v Galway Corporation* [1995] 1 I.L.R.M. 142; *Keogh v Galway Corporation (No. 2)* [1995] 2 I.L.R.M. 312 at 317–318. Here the applicants had been misinformed as to the detail of the material change to the development plan, and consequently it was held they had the right to make submissions.

The essential feature of the judicial process which makes it unsuitable to deal with polycentric problems is its bipolar and adversary nature. It is designed for one party to put forward a proposition which the other party denies or opposes. For example, the plaintiff asserts that he owns Blackacre and the defendant denies it; or the plaintiff asserts that he is entitled to compensation from the defendant and the latter denies it. None of Fuller's examples lends itself to being dealt with in this all-or-nothing way. For example, one of the galleries might want the Picasso if it also gets the Cezanne but not the Turner; but it would not insist on the Picasso if it got the Turner; but would want both if it did not get the Cezanne. The other gallery might have an equally complex set of preferences, and the greater the number of works involved, the more complex the preference sets might become. Again, the workers in an industry might claim a wage increase of £X, and their employers might resist it and offer £Y; but the interests of another part of the economy might be affected in such a way by either proposal that neither is acceptable.

... A good example in the administrative law context of a polycentric problem is provided by a motorway inquiry. The ramifications of the decision whether to build a motorway or not are enormous. At stake are not only the interests of potential motorway users and of persons whose land might be compulsorily acquired to provide a path for the motorway; also involved are the inhabitants of villages and towns which will be relieved of through-traffic by the motorway; British Rail may have an interest in inhibiting the development of alternative means for the transport of goods; improved transport and communications facilities provided by the motorway may benefit some businesses at the expense of others; and motorways have, of course, serious environmental effects which lovers of the countryside and people who live near the proposed route will be anxious to avoid. Not only would accommodation and compromise between these various interests be desirable, but also it may be that the best solution would be some alternative to a motorway, or some alternative route not already considered. The complexity of the issues involved makes the model of bipolar adversary presentation of fixed positions by parties in conflict seem inappropriate to the sound resolution of the issues involved. And since the adversary model of dispute settlement is inappropriate, so too is a standard of the validity of particular decisions on such issues which rests on the rules of natural justice."[282]

14–165   A policy question may arise either in regard to a specific single case (as, for instance, in the example discussed in the passage on the paintings) or in regard to a potentially unlimited category of persons or situations which happen to come within the boundaries of the decision (as, for instance, the wages example) because, while it concerns only one motorway, a nearly unlimited category of interest is offered. However, we can say that cases within the second category look, and are, rather closer to legislation than individual decisions and thus, as a general principle, should be less likely to attract the rules of fair procedure. However, in the case of decisions of a deliberative body as to policy, which do not have a direct effect on

---

[282]   *An Introduction to Administrative Law* (Oxford: Clarendon Press, 1986), pp.100–101. Professor Fuller's article will be found at (1978) 92 *Harv. L. Rev.* 353.

an individual, it seems, as mentioned in a previous chapter,[283] that sometimes a concept of fair procedure has been applied.

14–166 In regard to policy decisions which affect only individuals (as distinct from quasi-legislative actions) it seems that it is now too late in the day to argue that such decisions do not attract the rules. For instance, even in regard to the deportation of a (non-European Community) alien, it seems that the *audi alteram partem* rule has to be followed.[284]

Trivial cases

14–167 One of the most fundamental ideas in the law is that the courts, especially the High Court will not interfere where the individual interest affected by a decision is too trivial to warrant such attention (a notion expressed in the maxim *de minimis non curat lex*). This principle might seem to have an obvious application in opposing an attempt to invoke fair procedure to control the operation of (say) a sports or social club. It has, however, not been much considered[285] in Irish law.[286]

14–168 A particular example of this category is where the step being taken is preliminary. For instance, *Dunnes v Maloney*[287] concerned the appointment of an "authorised officer" by the Minister for Enterprise, Trade and Employment, under the Companies Act 1990 s.19, to gain information regarding the affairs of the applicant companies. The High Court (Laffoy J.) held that the Minister was not obliged to give either advance notice of the appointment or an opportunity to the applicants to make representations in respect of it. In part this was because, if the company were to be required to produce specified documents, there would at that stage have to be an opportunity to make representations. In addition, the learned judge relied on the rule that all that an "authorised officer" does is to collect information and make a private report. Laffoy J. stated[288]:

> "The risk that the [authorised officer's] investigation will become public knowledge and that the company may be perceived as being 'tarred with

---

[283] See paras 12–33 to 12–34. See also, *Association of General Practitioners v Minister for Health* [1995] 1 I.R. 382 at 388–392. Here it was held by O'Hanlon J. that where terms of employment for a group of doctors are being fixed, there is no obligation at common law or under the Constitution on the defendant to consult with an organisation representing his employees. Something similar could be said of *Shanley v Galway Corporation* [1995] 1 I.R. 396 at 407 which concerned an apparently general decision taken by the defendant in regard to an area which had been designated as a casual trading area under the Casual Trading Act 1980. (This decision was to the effect that there was a condition prohibiting trading in food of any kind which should be included in all such licences.)

[284] See para.14–144.

[285] It was not, for example, discussed in *Rochford v Storey*, unreported, High Court, November 4, 1982—it would not, of course, have been relevant in *Quirke v Bord Luthchleas na hÉireann* [1988] I.R. 83 for the reason that what was involved in that case was the disqualification of an international athlete.

[286] But see the comments of Hederman J. in *Murtagh v Board of Management of St Emer's National School* [1991] 1 I.R. 482 at 488: "A three day suspension for an admitted breach of discipline would be no more revisable by the High Court than, for example, the ordering of a pupil ... to write out lines ...".

[287] [1999] 3 I.R. 542. See similarly, *Scariff v Taylor* [1996] 1 I.R. 242 at 262–263.

[288] [1999] 3 I.R. 542 at 560.

the same brush' as other companies which have been subject to the s.19 procedure ... is part of the price which the company's proprietors pay for the benefits of incorporation."

"Holding-suspension"

14–169   As a matter of practicality, it will sometimes happen, when some indiscipline is suspected, that a delay of possibly months or longer may be required to prepare for a formal inquiry. During this hiatus, it may be inappropriate (or worse) for the employee or licence holder to continue as normal. In consequence, there will have to be a "holding-suspension", that is a suspension of the employment or licence, pending the outcome of the inquiry (in contrast to a suspension as punishment). In principle, this period can do only trivial harm, in that it would seem that any error can be rectified at a substantive hearing. Thus, for instance, in *Deegan v Minister for Finance*,[289] Keane C.J. stated that the rules of constitutional justice do not apply where "... suspension was being imposed so that an inquiry could be undertaken as to whether disciplinary action should be taken against the person concerned and, if so, the nature of such a sanction".

14–170   But in practice it may not be so simple: lost income and/or reputation may never be recovered, however complete the vindication at the full hearing. In response to these considerations, some recent cases have been decided which have muddied the water. These cases have suggested that the rules may apply where the suspension would have the effect of interfering with the affected individual's livelihood or reputation, as where he is suspended without pay or where the suspension imputes grave misconduct.[290]

14–171   The first of the Supreme Court cases, *Ó Ceallaigh v An Bord Altranais*,[291] arose out of the suspension of a nurse without pay, pending a formal inquiry. The Supreme Court referred to two opposing policy positions which were adopted in the works of the two leading English authorities, in passages each of which was quoted in Hardiman J.'s judgment, with the judge's own comments between the two quotations. He stated[292]:

---

[289] [2000] E.L.R. 190 at 198–200, quoted with approval in *Morgan v Trinity College Dublin* [2003] 3 I.R. 157 (Kearns J.). See also, *Rochford v Storey*, unreported, High Court, November 4, 1982; *McHugh v Garda Commissioner* [1985] I.L.R.M. 606 at 609–610; *Quirke v Bord Luthchleas na hÉireann* [1988] I.R. 83 at 87; *Scariff v Taylor* [1996] 2 I.L.R.M. 278 at 287 per Hamilton C.J.; *Cahill v Dublin City University* [2007] IEHC 20 at paras 7.1–7.5.

[290] *Flynn v An Post* [1987] I.R. 68; *Ní Bheoláin v Dublin VEC*, unreported, High Court, January 28, 1983; *Collins v Cork VEC*, unreported, Supreme Court, March 18, 1983; *State (Donegal VEC) v Minister for Education* [1985] I.R. 56. On a distinct point, which could often arise in the context of a holding-suspension, in *Morgan v Trinity College Dublin* [2003] 3 I.R. 157 at 171, Kearns J. remarked tellingly: "... the inevitable consequence of any suggestion that an employee who has been suspended is thereby and without more, irredeemably, prejudiced, and *ipso facto* cannot then get a fair hearing, would mean that there could never be a holding suspension as one of the steps in a disciplinary process. That in turn would mean that an employer, possibly faced with a situation where work colleagues are the complainants in a given case, would have to suffer the prejudice instead".

[291] [2000] 4 I.R. 54.

[292] [2000] 4 I.R. 54 at 123. The quotations are from De Smith, *Judicial Review of Administrative Action* (1980), p.199 and Wade, *Administrative Law* (1988), pp.570–571. (It is not known why out-of-date editions were used.)

"[Professor De Smith writes] 'Where an act or proposal is only the first step in a sequence of measures which may culminate in a decision detrimental to a person's interests, the courts will *generally* decline to accede to that person's submission that he is entitled to he heard in opposition to this initial act, *particularly* if he is entitled to be heard at a later stage.'

It is clear that Professor De Smith does not purport to lay down a rigid rule, but a statement of what will usually occur. There is a difference, at least of emphasis, in another distinguished academic treatment of the same topic by Sir William Wade in '*Administrative Law*':

'Natural justice is concerned with the exercise of power, that is to say, with acts or orders which produce legal results and in some way alter someone's legal position to his disadvantage. But preliminary steps, which in themselves may not involve immediate legal consequences, may lead to acts or orders which do so. In this case the protection of fair procedure may be needed throughout, and the successive steps must be considered not only separately but also as a whole. The question must always be whether, looking at the statutory procedure as a whole, each separate step is fair to the persons affected.'"

14–172   The dissenting judge, Murphy J., in effect adopted the De Smith view. Murphy J. noted that counsel for Ms Ó Ceallaigh had made[293] "... the simple and not unattractive point that there 'could not be too much *audi*'. I would venture to disagree: There is, or would be, a strange air of unreality if the Committee was required as a matter of statutory interpretation or constitutional necessity to conduct a preliminary inquiry as to whether they should conduct a substantive inquiry." In addition, a member of the majority, Geoghegan J., seems to have accepted De Smith's proposition as a general rule.

14–173   Another point which was significant is that it was said that, in a holding-suspension, only a low standard of *audi alteram partem* was required. Hardiman J. stated[294]:

"She ought to have been told about the allegations made to the Board and given a chance to deal with them – not necessarily by oral hearing but in whatever way was necessary for her reasonably to make her reply. That is not to say that there may not be circumstances in which the Board will have to act so rapidly that it is not a practical possibility to give notification of the complaints."

In respect of an earlier complaint, it had been accepted by the applicant that the Board had satisfied the standard by simply writing to inform her of the complaint and seeking certain documentation.

14–174   The next case is *O'Callaghan v Disciplinary Tribunal*,[295] a solicitor's

---

[293] Denham J. and Barron J. agreed with Hardiman J.'s judgment. Geoghegan J., whilst stating that he agreed with Hardiman J., added a few comments of his own. Murphy J. dissented; [2000] 4 I.R. 54 at 111–112. Murphy J.'s judgment, which is full of commonsense, made a number of points which went unanswered by the majority.

[294] [2000] 4 I.R. 54 at 130.

[295] [2002] 1 I.R. 1 at 6. For a broadly similar case to *O'Callaghan* and *Ó Ceallaigh* with a similar

discipline case. One significant point is that, in giving judgment for the Supreme Court, Geoghegan J. adopted (strictly speaking obiter) the view that "in general, no special natural justice procedures are required for a decision to set up a body or tribunal to carry out a function which itself would involve requirements of natural justice". In short, he took the De Smith line. However, he went on to state that there is an exception to this general principle, in the case of a professional body dealing with a complaint which could lead to a practitioner being struck off. This was based on the Privy Council case of *Rees v Crane*[296] which was "the principal persuasive authority" in both *Ó Ceallaigh* and *O'Callaghan*. However, in *O'Callaghan*, it was held that, on the facts, the fairly low standard of constitutional justice which is required in these circumstances had been satisfied.

14–175 At High Court level, there have recently been three strong, even extreme, decisions,[297] going beyond the Supreme Court, and ruling that, in the words of the earliest of them, *McNamara v South Western Area Health Board*,[298] "... the suspension was open ended and non-specific in duration. It seems to me that the suspension of a Senior Consultant without pay must be seen as something more than the mere 'holding operation' contended for by [counsel for the respondent]". But, in contrast to *McNamara*, in the later two cases—*O'Donoghue* and *Khan*—the suspension was with full pay, though in *O'Donoghue* it was stated (rather surprisingly)[299] that, "... that a suspension with pay is [no] less serious, onerous or potentially damaging than one with pay". And, in *O'Donoghue* and *Khan*, the precedent set in *McNamara* was followed. In none of these cases was the consideration that ample constitutional justice would be available at the full inquiry thoroughly considered. And, as regards authority, there was not very much acknowledgment of the more nuanced attitude taken by the Supreme Court in *Ó Ceallaigh* and *O'Callaghan*. For instance, there is no reference to the concession made by Hardiman J. in *Ó Ceallaigh*, namely that only a basic standard of fair procedure is necessary at the suspension stage.[300]

14–176 In summary, reading (and re-reading) *Ó Ceallaigh*, *O'Callaghan*, *Rees v Cane*, with the trio of High Court cases, leaves the law by no means as clear as it should be.

Criminal investigations

14–177 The principle that constitutional justice does not apply to criminal investigation by the Gardaí is long established. Writing obiter about Garda investigations, Denham J. remarked in *Brady v Haughton*[301]:

---

   outcome, see *Rajpal v Robinson* [2005] 3 I.R. 385 at paras 27–28.

[296]   [1994] 2 A.C. 173.

[297]   *McNamara v South Western Area Health Board* [2001] IEHC 24 (Kearns J.); *O'Donoghue v South Eastern Health Board* [2005] 4 I.R. 217 (Macken J.); *Khan v HSE* [2008] IEHC 234 (McMahon J.).

[298]   [2001] IEHC 24 at para.62

[299]   *O'Donoghue v South Eastern Health Board* [2005] 4 I.R. 217 at para.53.

[300]   Indeed, in *O'Donoghue*, Macken J. gave little attention to the copious communications which the respondent had had with the applicant, which might have been held to amount to rudimentary fair procedure.

[301]   [2006] 1 I.R. 1 at para.151 (and see para.75).

"In general, fair procedures do not require a person to be informed of steps being taken by a member of An Garda Síochána who is investigating a crime. Thus, if the property in issue was being considered by a forensic authority in Ireland for the purpose of an investigation here, the applicant would not be given, or be entitled to be given, notice of the steps being taken during such an investigation. Of course, later he could query any such steps in a trial if such evidence is presented to the court."

14–178   A question which might seem to arise here is: how *Brady* can be reconciled with the *Ardagh*–public inquiries line of authority mentioned at the start of this Part. It would seem, from the final sentence in this quotation and other passages in the case that the answer is that where there is a criminal investigation, an accused will usually have ample opportunity to put their side of the case at the trial. An alternative policy reason would be that importing constitutional justice into Garda investigations, beyond what is already required by traditional criminal procedure, would paralyse them.

Margin of appreciation

14–179   In any particular situation, constitutional justice is not the only source of fair procedure: in addition, other specific rules may be set by the parent Act for regulation or by the inveterate practice of the deciding agency. Furthermore, in respect of any particular case, it has been accepted that it is for the deciding agency itself to exercise "a certain discretion as to the manner in which it conducts the proceedings".[302] The question, which has not received as much judicial attention as might have been expected, is: what happens where, in a particular case, there is a difference between constitutional justice and one of these specific sources? There are three possibilities:

(a) The specific rule may not cover the particular situation which has arisen. In that situation, the Irish courts have shown themselves to be adroit in injecting the generalised concept of constitutional justice.[303] As McCarthy J. has remarked, "[i]f the proceedings derive from statute, then, in the absence of any set of fixed procedures, the relevant authority must create and carry out the necessary procedures; if the set or fixed procedure is not comprehensive, the authority must supplement it in such a fashion as to ensure compliance with constitutional justice, for which proposition there is a wealth of authority".[304]

(b) There may be a direct conflict between constitutional justice and the specific rule and it is the specific rule which offers a greater advantage to the individual affected. In this situation, the important point is that the

---

[302] *State (Boyle) v General Medical Services (Payments) Board* [1981] I.L.R.M. 14 at 16 per Keane J. See also, *State (Genport Ltd)* [1983] I.L.R.M. 12 at 16; *Scariff v Taylor* [1996] 2 I.L.R.M. 278 at 289 per Denham J. For a rather surprising decision, against an exercise of discretion by a Commission chaired by a High Court judge, see *Re Commission to Inquire into Child Abuse* [2002] 3 I.R. 459.

[303] See, e.g. *East Donegal Co-Operative Ltd v Attorney General* [1970] I.R. 317; *Kiely v Minister for Social Welfare (No. 2)* [1977] I.R. 267; *McKeen v Meath County Council* [1997] 1 I.R. 299.

[304] *State (Irish Pharmaceutical Union) v EAT* [1987] I.L.R.M. 36 at 40. As authority, *O'Brien*, *Loftus* and *East Donegal* were cited.

Constitution usually gives no positive right to the public body against the individual, but only creates exceptions to the individual's rights of which advantage may be taken, as the Constitution usually puts it, "by law". Thus, the result would be that the specific procedural rule should prevail and the applicant would succeed.

(c) The more difficult situation is where the specific procedural rule does apply and would have the effect of reducing the level of procedural protection granted. In England, the relevant principle is that, where a tribunal or other public authority has formulated a comprehensive, detailed code of procedure, the onus on a person who seeks to establish that this code is inconsistent with natural justice is very heavy.[305] However, in Ireland, constitutional justice is not just a general norm of statutory interpretation; but enjoys the support of the Constitution. At the same time, constitutional justice remains a fluid concept and, as a matter of commonsense, in deciding how it operates in a particular context, some respect would be given to the specific rule, or the "custom and practice" of the tribunal. For, as is demonstrated at several points in this chapter, the constitutional justice rules allow a considerable margin of appreciation. Thus, Barrington J. remarked in *Barry v Medical Council*,[306] "[i]t is not the function of the Court to monitor procedure as it unfolds. Only in the most exceptional circumstances will this Court interfere. For the same reason, I would not like anything in this judgment to inhibit any authority in the disciplinary proceedings from exercising any appropriate discretion". However, such a discretion must be genuinely exercised and it must be exercised fairly and reasonably.[307]

Countervailing factors

14–180 In a number of cases, countervailing factors have been said to justify a failure to observe the rules of constitutional justice (or, more correctly, just the *audi alteram partem* limb). The most common types of such countervailing policies are that observing the rules would cause a delay and so defeat the object of the public authority's action[308]; or that it was impossible for the public authority to contact the person affected to elicit his representations.[309]

14–181 There must, however, be a proper (and proportionate) balance between

---

[305] Evans, "Some Limits to the Scope of Natural Justice" (1973) 36 M.L.R. 439. There is some Irish support for this point of view (see, e.g. *State (Fagan) v Governor of Mountjoy Prison*, unreported, High Court, March 6, 1978).

[306] *Barry v Medical Council* [1998] 3 I.R. 368 at 398, quoted by Barron J. (one of the assenting judges) in *Ó Ceallaigh v Fitness to Practice Committee* at [1999] 2 I.R. 552 at 575. See, to similar effect, Murphy J. (dissenting) in *Ó Ceallaigh* at 572.

[307] *Irish Family Planning Association v Ryan* [1979] I.R. 295 at 309, 313.

[308] *Ó Ceallaigh v An Bord Altranais* [2000] 4 I.R. 54 at 64–65, 134. See also, *O'Callaghan v Commissioners of Public Works* [1985] I.L.R.M. 364; *State (Lynch) v Cooney* [1982] I.R. 337 at 365; *Irish Family Planning Association v Ryan* [1979] I.R. 295 at 313; *State (Smullen) v Duffy* [1980] I.L.R.M. 46; *State (Philpott) v Registrar of Titles* [1986] I.L.R.M. 499 at 507. However, "mere administrative difficulties in securing the attendance of witnesses before a tribunal" do not warrant suspension of the rules: *Gallagher v Revenue Commissioners (No. 2)* [1995] 1 I.R. 55 at 79 per Hamilton C.J.

[309] *Irish Family Planning Association Ltd v Ryan* [1979] I.R. 295 at 313–314 per O'Higgins C.J.; *WS v Adoption Board* [2001] 1 I.L.R.M. 417 (O'Neill J.).

the need for speed and the applicant's rights, as is illustrated by *DK v* Crowley[310] concerning s.4(3) of the Domestic Violence Act 1996 which authorised the grant by a District Court of an interim barring order. The significant factor was that the order was made ex parte so that the respondent had no opportunity to be heard by the court before the order was granted. As Keane C.J. said[311]:

> "… the procedures prescribed by s.4 of the Domestic Violence Act, 1996, in failing to prescribe a fixed period of relatively short duration during which an interim barring order made *ex parte* is to continue in force, deprived the respondents to such applications of the protection of the principle of *audi alteram partem* in a manner and to an extent which is disproportionate, unreasonable and unnecessary."

14–182 Another countervailing factor which has been accepted as justification for not observing the rules is the need to keep confidential the identity of witnesses, in certain circumstances. For instance, it was held, in *People (DPP) v Matthews*,[312] that the admissibility of "belief evidence" and the limitation on the ability to cross-examine the senior Garda officer as to the evidence for his belief did not breach constitutional justice or Art.38.1 of the Constitution ("due process") or art.6 of the European Convention on Human Rights. The reason was that the limitation was both necessary and the least invasive approach in the circumstances, which included the practice of the courts in not convicting on the *uncorroborated* belief evidence of a senior officer.

14–183 Pushing the boat out, in *Carroll v Minister for Agriculture*,[313] it was held that, in assessing the basic fairness of the procedure for testing cattle for "reactors", the great importance of the eradication of bovine tuberculosis in the public interest should be taken into account. Other cases have relied on the need to maintain confidence in the integrity of members of the Defence Forces and Gardaí,[314] and the need to curtail drink-driving.[315] These authorities suggest that there is a reservoir of discretionary power to identify situations in which the principles of constitutional justice do not apply, which is wider than any of the specific examples so far identified. It is also noteworthy that the courts have chosen to create a distinct ground of exemption rather than simply to exercise their long-established discretion to refuse to grant relief.[316] At the same time, it has been emphasised that any exception to fair procedures based on exigent circumstances

---

[310] [2002] 2 I.R. 744. See further, paras 12–52 to 12–53 on the significance of this decision and its limitations for other ex parte orders. In response to this decision, the law was changed by the Domestic Violence (Amendment) Act 2002.

[311] [2002] 2 I.R. 744 at 762.

[312] [2007] 2 I.R. 169 at paras 36–46. See also, *People (DPP) v Kelly* [2006] 3 I.R. 115; *Melton v Censorship of Publications Board* [2004] I.L.R.M. 260 at 276; *McAlister v Minister for Justice, Equality and Law Reform* [2003] 1 I.L.R.M. 161 at 171 (seemingly).

[313] [1991] 1 I.R. 230. At 235, Blayney J. stated: "… the cattle, beef and dairy industry in the country … account for over 70% of farm output and some 20% of Irish manufacturing output. The combined value of these exports in 1987 came to 2.3 billion pounds. The existence of bovine tuberculosis creates problems in that intra-community [sc. EU] trade in cattle or beef showing any signs whatsoever of bovine tuberculosis is prohibited".

[314] *State (Donnelly) v Minister for Defence*, unreported, High Court, October 9, 1979; *State (Jordan) v Garda Commissioner* [1987] I.L.R.M. 107.

[315] *McGonnell v Attorney General* [2007] 1 I.L.R.M. 321 at 330.

[316] On which, see Ch.16, Part D.

must be specific and not general. As Hardiman J remarked, "… it is the business of the law to identify such circumstances: otherwise the cry of 'emergency' would be sufficient to set all rights aside at the whim of the Executive."[317]

Private transactions and arrangements: "vertical application only?"

14–184   As illustrated earlier,[318] there is no doubt that the constitutional justice precepts apply to cases of loss of employment even in the private law field. This fact suggests the question of whether constitutional justice applies generally to private law transactions and arrangements. A mechanism for its importation is readily available in the form of the well-established notion that constitutional justice can be regarded, in appropriate circumstances, as an implicit term in a contract and this could presumably, with equal logic, be extended to other purely private law transactions such as an instrument constituting a settlement. Even more powerful is the fact that constitutional justice is part of the Constitution and the Constitution applies against private persons or companies as much as against the State. However, whilst this area is without much authority, judicial or academic, it is suggested that, at present, apart from loss of employment cases, constitutional justice does not apply in the private law arena. Take, for example, *Carna Foods Ltd v Eagle Star*,[319] in which it was contended unsuccessfully that, since the absence of reasons for the cancellation of their insurance cover made it virtually impossible for them to obtain alternative cover, it was contrary to constitutional justice for the insurer to cancel their cover without giving reasons. McCracken J. swept away this contention:

> "… where a decision is taken to exercise a function in the public realm, the person affected is entitled to know the reasons for the decision. This is because statutory powers must be determined and exercised reasonably. The plaintiffs here seek to extend this principle into the realm of private contractual relationships. To decide that any principle of natural justice or constitutional justice applies would be a serious interference in the contractual position of parties in a commercial contract and with very wide-ranging consequences. To take two examples, if a person applied for a job and was refused it, is he entitled to be told the reasons? Secondly, if a manufacturer decided to change his supplier of raw materials, is the supplier entitled to know the reasons? Surely not."[320]

---

[317]   *Dellway Investments Ltd v NAMA* [2011] IESC 14; unreported, Supreme Court, April 12, 2011 at p.65. NAMA's claim of a need for urgency failed on the facts.

[318]   See paras 4–122 to 4–129.

[319]   [1995] 1 I.R. 526.

[320]   [1995] 1 I.R. 526 at 530–531. It is testimony to the plaintiffs' lack of faith in any line of argument founded on constitutional justice that when the case was appealed, unsuccessfully ([1997] 2 I.L.R.M. 499) their arguments were principally based not on constitutional justice, but on the private law grounds of implied terms and the Competition Act 1991. In *Zockoll Group Ltd v Telecom Éireann*, unreported, High Court, November 28, 1997, a case concerning the withdrawal of telephone numbers, Kelly J. said that he was not persuaded that public law principles of fair procedures applied "to the commercial relationship which exists between the defendant and its customers". However, the judge went on to hold that as the defendant had not acted "fairly and reasonably" in withdrawing the numbers, the plaintiff was entitled to mandatory relief. This seems to amount to an application of the principles of judicial review, by the back door.

14–185   It has also been stated, emphatically, in a Northern Irish case that "[a]s a matter of company law, the rules of natural justice have no application to the decision of the members in general meeting. Such members are free to vote as their own individual interests and inclinations may require".[321] Again, in *Hounslow LBC v Twickenham Garden Developments Ltd*,[322] a case in which an architect had given notice, under the normal term in a building contract, that the contractor had failed to proceed with the work regularly and diligently, the English High Court found that the principles of natural justice did not apply to an architect's notice. Megarry J. stated that "[t]he principles of natural justice are of wide application and great importance but they must be confined within proper limits and not allowed to run wild".[323] This last quotation suggests that short shrift would be given to suggestions for instance that: objects of a power of appointment must be heard before the donee of the power chooses among them; a testator should solicit representations from a fond relative whom he intends to "leave out" of the will; or that a tenant must be heard before a landlord issues a notice to quit. For the essential point is that the imposition of a formalised fair procedure is thought to be more appropriate when one is dealing with a powerful public or quasi-public body than with a private company or individual.

14–186   There is a broader point supporting this observation: as mentioned in Chapter 12, Part A, there is an intimate connection between natural or constitutional justice and, on the other hand, substantive controls imposed upon a decision-maker, as regards for example, "reasonableness" (covered in the next chapter). If, as is the case, persons governed exclusively by private law are not subject to these substantive controls—indeed absent the Constitution or special stature, may be as whimsical or capricious as they wish—then it would be anomalous if they were to be subjected to constitutional justice.

F. Concluding Comment: Advantages and Disadvantages

14–187   Whilst there may be some variation in degree from one judge to another,[324] there is no doubting the significance which the Irish judiciary has assigned to constitutional justice. Take, for instance, *Khan v Health Service Executive*,[325] where McMahon J. offered the following observation:

> "... the HSE must comply with rules which adhere to fair procedure/standards. The [HSE] might like it to be otherwise. To those involved in administration, adherence to fair procedure standards may appear cumbersome, irritating and even irksome on some occasions. Undoubtedly, the necessary adherence may slow down the administrators and may not be conducive to efficiency. But that is the way it is. The battle between fair procedures and efficiency has

---

[321] *Hawthorn v Ulster Flying Club Ltd* [1986] N.I.J.B. 56 at 94. However, on the facts of the case, Murray J. held that the rules applied to a decision to expel a member; *a contra*: *Gaiman v National Association for Mental Health* [1970] 2 All E.R. 362.

[322] [1970] 3 All E.R. 326.

[323] [1970] 3 All E.R. 326 at 347.

[324] See, e.g. *Rajah v Royal College of Surgeons* [1994] 1 I.R. 384 and *Corcoran v Minister for Social Welfare* [1991] 2 I.R. 175.

[325] [2008] IEHC 234 at 7.

long since been fought and fair procedures have won out. Insistence on fair procedures governs all decision-makers in public administration. It governs the courts as well. None of us can ignore the principle. We might wish it were otherwise. We might like to cut through procedural niceties to secure what we perceive as justice in a more expeditious way … It is not sufficient that we justify our decision by alleging that we were focusing on the ultimate objective. It is not sufficient that we were doing our best. It is not sufficient to say that we were motivated by public health and safety objectives."

14–188   Yet, on the other hand, as illustrated throughout this Chapter, the form which constitutional justice may take may vary. In addition, in the previous Part, the growth of the notion of "countervailing factors" was emphasised.

Disadvantages and advantages

14–189   Neither the advantages nor the disadvantages of constitutional justice have yet been researched empirically in Ireland. In the first place, however, it seems reasonable to take it that there are the following disadvantages: first, that greater procedural complexity increases delay and expense.

14–190   It is useful to illustrate these difficulties by way of the *Kiely* saga. Mrs Kiely's claim for a widow's benefit was rejected by a deciding officer and, on appeal, by the appeals officer in the Department of Social Welfare. The appeals officer's decision was struck down, on appeal, by the High Court.[326] Next, the case was reheard by a second appeals officer who decided against the claimant; this decision was struck down in the Supreme Court.[327] The question was then decided by a third appeals officer, who reached the same decision as his two colleagues, and this time there was no review so that the decision was effective. It might well be asked rhetorically: who benefited from this substantial expenditure of legal costs and court time? Nor is the *Kiely* saga unique. The law reports are replete with judicial statements, offered, as consolation prizes, in cases in which some administrative action has been condemned for violation of constitutional justice, to the effect that the public authority may repeat the process, even reaching the same conclusion, provided only that the proper procedure is followed on the subsequent occasion.[328] (At the same time, when we come to consider the advantages, it will be seen that at least the appellant was satisfied, in that she had her day in court.)

14–191   Secondly, the rules promote excessive caution among public servants, particularly at the lower levels where the officials cannot reasonably be expected to be familiar with the novel, and sometimes rather unexpected, requirements of constitutional justice.[329] To take the example of an official charged with the duty of

---

[326] *Kiely v Minister for Social Welfare* [1971] I.R. 21.

[327] *Kiely v Minister for Social Welfare (No. 2)* [1977] I.R. 267.

[328] See, e.g. *Quirke v Bord Luthchleas na hÉireann* [1988] I.R. 83 at 88 per Barr J.

[329] cf. the comments of Murphy J. in *Anisimova v Minister for Justice* [1998] 1 I.R. 186: "With hindsight the proceedings of any and every tribunal, however formal or exalted, may well admit of improvement but it is of the utmost importance, particularly in the context of natural and constitutional justice, to test the attainment of the basic standards by reference to substance and reality rather than technicalities or ingenuous argument. If that position were otherwise, people of business affairs and those engaged in domestic or social tribunals of

awarding a licence: he will know that it is more likely that the refusal of a licence will be challenged by a disappointed applicant than that an erroneous award of a licence will be challenged by a competitor or other member of the public. In view of this, there is a pressure upon the administrator, which is contrary to the public interest, to grant the licence. One of the consequences of the constitutional justice rules is to increase this pressure by imposing something analogous to the procedures of a law court in the very different circumstances of a tribunal or public authority. A British Government lawyer has remarked that "while presently public administration is honest there is a risk that, as a result of judicial review, people will go through a charade: applicants to put themselves in the best possible position and the authority to defend themselves".[330] Recently, an Irish judge has remarked "[i]t is very necessary to adapt a famous phrase, that sound law and sound administrative practice should rhyme".[331]

14–192   As against this, constitutional justice is taken to carry four advantages. In the first place, an impartial decision-maker and an opportunity for the person affected to put forward his comments both help to promote an "appropriate" result. (The decision may be too subjective to speak of the *correct* result.) As Megarry J. remarked in a notable passage:

> "As everyone who has anything to do with the law well knows, the path of the law is strewn with examples of open and shut cases which, somehow, were not; of unanswerable charges which, in the event, were completely answered; of inexplicable conduct which was fully explained; of fixed and unalterable determinations that, by discussion, suffered a change."[332]

14–193   For instance, in *JGM v Refugee Applications Commissioner*,[333] Clarke J. stated that, "... if the [Officer of the Refugee Applications Commissioner] had taken the view that the acquisition of Mozambique nationality derived from his father's origins would or could debar the applicant from protection, then it was incumbent on the Officer to tease out the issue a little further, if only to establish the correctness of this view". It ought to be emphasised that this first and most obvious consideration is by no means the only one. A sceptic might ask: does a failure to follow fair procedure matter, if the outcome be correct? As to this, the dominant judicial view, by a considerable margin, is represented by the majority judges in *Glover v BLN Ltd*,[334] who brushed aside the submission that, if a hearing had been held, there was nothing the plaintiff could have said anyway, with Walsh J. remarking that, "[t]his proposition only has to be stated to be rejected. The

---

every description called upon to apply this important principle would be forced to abdicate their functions to lawyers who could select more appropriate terminology and invoke forms and formulae which might defy criticism, but not necessarily achieve justice."

[330] Referred to in Woolf, *Protection of the Public – A New Challenge* (London: Stevens, 1990), p.18. We are informed that, in Cork, junior staff in the Department of Social Protection are warned that they are "walking through a legal minefield".

[331] *Meadows v Minister for Justice, Equality and Law Reform* [2010] IESC 3 at p.14.

[332] *John v Rees* [1970] Ch. 345 at 402. The passage from which this extract is taken was quoted with approval in *Gallagher v Revenue Commissioners (No. 2)* [1995] 1 I.R. 55 at 82 (O'Flaherty J.). See also, *Keady v Garda Commissioner* [1992] 2 I.R. 197 at 213; and *Dawson v Irish Brokers Association*, unreported, Supreme Court, February 27, 1997.

[333] [2009] IEHC 352 at paras 42–48.

[334] [1973] I.R. 388.

obligation to give a fair hearing to the guilty is just as great as the obligation to give a fair hearing to the innocent".[335]

14–194 Secondly, the duty to give reasons for a public authority's proposed decision (covered in Part D) might disclose to the person affected that the decision was being taken on grounds, or in circumstances, which rendered it invalid in substance. In such a case, the rule would assist the person affected by giving him information which would enable him to launch an action for judicial review on substantive grounds or, perhaps, to refer the matter to the Ombudsman or a TD or to seek some other sanction.[336] The point was put eloquently in the following passage from Henchy J.'s judgment in *Garvey v Ireland*[337]:

> "If, by maintaining an obscuring silence, a Government could render their act of dismissal impenetrable as to its reasons and unreviewable as to its method, an office-holder such as the plaintiff could have his livelihood snatched from him, his chosen career snuffed out, his pension prospects dashed and his reputation irretrievably tarnished, without any hope of redress, no matter how unjustified or unfair his dismissal might be. I doubt if it would be even contended that the statutory power of removal from office could validly be used to dismiss a person for an unconstitutional reason (for example, because of his race, creed or colour); yet if such were to happen, and suddenness and silence were to be allowed to curtain off the dismissal from judicial scrutiny, the dismissed person, far from getting the constitutionally guaranteed protection from unjust attack, would be abandoned to the consequence of an unjust, unconstitutional and ruinous decision."

14–195 Thirdly, it is a matter of satisfaction and dignity to the individual that he should have his say before a decision is taken against him by a governmental agency. (This is the equivalent, in the administrative sphere, of "the day in court".) In *R. (Smyth) v Co. Antrim Coroner*[338] it was sought to quash the verdict returned by a coroner's jury on the grounds that, in breach of the relevant regulations, the coroner had failed to sum up the evidence to the jury. Quashing the verdict, Kelly J. conceded that another jury, hearing the same evidence and assisted by a proper and adequate summing up of it by the coroner, might come to exactly the same verdict; but held that the next of kin were entitled "to have their unhappiness tempered by the knowledge that such a verdict was reached by a considered and regular inquiry".[339]

14–196 Finally, an open consistent procedure in which the state agency taking the decision is seen to be impartial is necessary to maintain the confidence of the general public in the institutions of government. For example, in a case where the

---

[335] [1973] I.R. 388 at 429. See similarly, *O'Brien v Bord na Móna* [1983] I.R. 255 at 266, 287; *Maunsell v Minister for Education* [1940] I.R. 213; *General Medical Council v Spackman* [1943] A.C. 627; *Ridge v Baldwin* [1964] A.C. 40; *State (Crothers) v Kelly* [1978] I.L.R.M. 167; and see generally, Clark, "Natural Justice: Substance or Shadow?" (1975) *Public Law* 27.

[336] On this point, in the context of reasons, see Part D of this chapter.

[337] [1981] I.R. 75 at 101. But cf. *McDonnell v Ireland*, unreported, Supreme Court, July 23, 1997.

[338] [1980] N.I. 123.

[339] [1980] N.I. 123 at 125. See to similar effect, *John v Rees* [1970] 1 Ch. 345 at 402.

failure of a Joint Labour Committee to hear certain relevant evidence was found to be contrary to the principle of *audi alteram partem*, Henchy J. stated that, "… even if such evidence would have made no difference, the Committee by rejecting it unheard and unconsidered, left themselves open to the imputation of bias, unfairness and prejudice".[340]

14–197   To end on a very practical note, it is, of course, always possible for a court to avoid laying down any general principle and, instead, to determine the outcome of the case by refusing relief on discretionary grounds and this approach has often been adopted.[341]

---

[340] *Burke v Minister for Labour* [1979] I.R. 354 at 362. See also, the comments of O'Donnell L.J. in *R. (Hennessy) v Department of the Environment* [1980] N.I. 109.

[341] *Fulbrook v Berkshire Magistrates' Courts* (1970) 69 L.G.R. 75; *Ward v Bradford Corporation* (1971) 70 L.G.R. 27; *Glynn v Keele University* [1971] 1 W.L.R. 487; *R. (McPherson) v Department of Education* [1980] N.I. 115. On the question of the discretionary character of the remedies, see further, Ch.16, Part D.

CHAPTER 15

CONTROL OF
DISCRETIONARY POWERS

A. Discretionary Power: A Summary

15–01　There is a distinction[1] between decisions involving the application of pre-existing law (or, at least, a guideline) and, on the other hand, those involving the exercise of discretionary power. The first type of decision is quintessentially the domain of a court or tribunal, though often, and on a quite random basis, it may be vested in a Minister or local authority.[2] The second type of decision—that is where a discretionary or policy function is being exercised—may be illustrated by the following examples:

> "On the application of … a person who proposes to carry on the business of a livestock mart … the Minister may, at his discretion, grant or refuse to grant a licence authorising the carrying on of the business of a livestock mart …"[3]

> "A sanitary authority may by order prohibit the erection … of temporary dwellings on any land or water in their sanitary district if they are of opinion that such erection … would be prejudicial to public health …".[4]

15–02　In spite of the apparent *carte blanche* which expressions like "… may, at his discretion …" or "… if they are of opinion …" appear to bestow, discretionary powers are subject to the general requirements requiring the decision-maker to observe both the vires of the parent statute (explained in Chapter 10, Parts A and B) and also subject to certain additional controls which form the subject matter of this chapter.

---

[1]　These distinctions are discussed in Ch.1.
[2]　On this choice, see Ch.6, Part B.
[3]　Livestock Marts Act 1967 s.3(1), examined in *East Donegal Co-Operative Ltd v Attorney General* [1970] I.R. 317.
[4]　Local Government (Sanitary Services) Act 1948 s.31(1), involved in *Listowel U.D.C. v McDonagh* [1968] I.R. 312 and *Corporation of Limerick v Sheridan* (1956) 90 I.L.T.R. 59.

15–03   The law in relation to the control of discretionary power is in a state of change, with the result that the layout of this chapter has to be somewhat complicated. But one should also emphasise that, on one level, the policy considerations underlying the law are very straightforward and have not changed: on the one hand, courts do not wish to intervene too far in fields which have been vested in public bodies, comprising expert administrators, usually working (directly or indirectly) under elected heads; on the other hand, some independent detached body—the courts—must safeguard individual rights against excessive state interference. Part A covers basic topics which are common to each of the particular controls described in the later Parts. Then Part B goes on to consider the first generation of rules to control the exercise of discretionary power, which were identified in the classic exposition given in Lord Greene's celebrated passage in *Associated Provincial Picture Houses Ltd v Wednesbury Corporation*,[5] which is quoted below. He identified three facets of abuse of discretionary power: bad faith, taking irrelevant factors into account and unreasonableness. We shall deal with each of these, together with two other flaws: uncertainty and inconsistency. However, the law has not stood still since *Wednesbury*, at any rate, in the way in which it is presented and we conclude Part B with two major cases from the 1980s, one Irish and one English,[6] which were, in their day, regarded as representing a further stage of evolution.

15–04   However, by now, the law depends upon the tension between three divergent lines of policy which emerged in the 1990s: curial deference; the effect of the interests of the community; and the impact of the Constitution and ECHR/EU law. Part D offers a concluding comment on the troubled area of law described in A–C. An entirely separate range of controls, examined in Part E, operate when an administrator's failure has gone beyond an abuse of discretion and amounts to a complete failure to exercise a discretion. Finally, Part F offers some comments on the judicial march away from any unreviewable discretionary powers, which has taken place over the past few decades.

15–05   Here, we offer the following preliminary observations. First, control of discretionary powers is a difficult area of law. The formulation of a precise test is especially difficult because it has been made to apply to such a wide range of subject matter, so militating in favour of a high level of generality, the alternative being a horrendous degree of specificity which would attempt to capture all possible situations. Indeed, Fennelly J. has recently remarked that:

"... at one level [all this controversy concerning the appropriate test for a control of a discretionary power] is no more than semantics; what is irrational or unreasonable depends on the subject matter and the context".[7]

15–06   There are numerous illustrations of the point that the same framework of rules has been applied to the control of discretionary powers set in a number

---

[5]   [1948] 1 K.B. 223 at 230.
[6]   *Council of Civil Service Unions v Minister for the Civil Service* [1985] A.C. 374 at 410; *State (Keegan) v Stardust Compensation Tribunal* [1986] I.R. 642 at 658.
[7]   *Meadows v Minister for Justice, Equality and Law Reform* [2010] IESC 3 at para.67. See, to similar effect, Hardiman J. at p.16. Murray C.J. at p.26 of his judgment offered the term "semantic maze".

of different subject areas.[8] For example, they have been applied variously to procedural[9] as well as substantive questions. Again surprisingly, the same set of rules has also been applied without much discussion to: a tribunal of inquiry's refusal to hold a preliminary session in private[10]; a decision to grant representation at a tribunal[11]; the Minister for Justice's discretion to transfer to his home country a convicted life prisoner[12]; NAMA's decision to take over a loan from a bank[13]; the chairman of the Garda Conciliation Council's ruling as to whether a particular change in conditions of work could be considered by the Council; the Garda Review Board's decision to penalise an erring member of the Gardaí; the Irish Coursing Club's award of a greyhound trophy; whether an unreasonable workload had been imposed on a public servant[14]; the outcome of an arbitration[15;] or even a discretion exercised by a court,[16] even though such a discretion—"a judicial discretion"—has traditionally been considered sui generis.

15–07 Notice that the same framework law has been applied: whether the exercise of discretionary power is to make delegated legislation[17] or settle a large policy with wide repercussions in a number of cases, or whether it is merely to make a judgment between two competing courses of action in an individual case. Pondering the diversity of this kingdom, an early edition of De Smith offers a generalisation which is still of value:

> "The scope of review may be conditioned by a variety of factors: the wording of the discretionary power, the subject-matter to which it is related, the character of the authority to which it is entrusted, the purpose for which it is conferred, the particular circumstances in which it has in fact been exercised,

---

[8] For further discussion, see para.15–133.

[9] e.g. *White v Dublin City Council* [2004] 1 I.R. 545 at para.50.

[10] e.g. *Finnegan v Flood* [2002] 3 I.R. 47 at 65. See also, *Kiberd v Hamilton* [1992] 2 I.R. 257; *Desmond v Glackin (No. 2)* [1993] 3 I.R. 67 (ministerial appointment of inspector under Companies Act 1990 valid where decision made bona fide, was not unreasonable and was factually sustainable); *Dunnes Stores v Maloney* [1999] 3 I.R. 542; and *Dunnes Stores v Ryan* [2002] 2 I.R. 60 (the exercise by the Minister for Enterprise, Trade and Employment of her supervisory powers under the Companies Act 1990).

[11] *Boyhan v Beef Tribunal* [1993] 1 I.R. 210 at 221. See also, *O'Brien v Moriarty (No. 3)* [2006] 2 I.R. 474 at paras 125–148.

[12] *Nascimento v Minister for Justice, Equality and Law Reform* [2011] 1 I.R. 1.

[13] *Dellway Investments v NAMA* [2011] IESC 14; unreported, Supreme Court, April 12, 2011.

[14] The four decisions alluded to are: *Garda Representative Association v Ireland* [1989] I.L.R.M. 1 (HC); [1994] 1 I.L.R.M. 81 at 88–90 (SC); *Stroker v Doherty* [1991] 1 I.R. 23; *Mathews v Irish Coursing Club* [1993] 1 I.R. 346; and *Greaney v Dublin Corporation* [1994] 3 I.R. 384 at 391 (obiter).

[15] For reasonableness, in the context of arbitration, see *Greaney v Dublin Corporation* [1994] 3 I.R. 384 at 389 and *Doyle v Kildare County Council* [1995] 2 I.R. 424 at 430.

[16] *Cumann Lúthchleas Gael Teo v Judge Windle* [1994] 1 I.R. 525 at 540–541 (the test applied to a District judge's exercise of a statutory discretion as to whether an offence was a minor offence). See also, *DPP v District Judge Maughan* [2003] 1 I.L.R.M. 155 at 160 which involved both the judiciary and a procedural point.

[17] See *Philips v Medical Council* [1991] 2 I.R. 115 at 139–142. See also, *Clancy v IRFU* [1995] 1 I.L.R.M. 193 at 198; *Donegal Fuel and Supply Co. Ltd v Londonderry Port and Harbour Commissioners* [1994] 1 I.R. 24 at 40; *McCann v Minister for Education* [1997] 1 I.L.R.M. 1.

the materials available to the court, and in the last analysis whether a court is of the opinion that judicial intervention would be in the public interest."[18]

15–08 It should be emphasised that, while it is in the nature of a discretion that (subject to what has been said) it may be exercised as and when the decision-maker determines, once the discretion has been exercised, then in many circumstances it will not be lawful to change it. Accordingly, a good deal may depend upon the reviewing court's interpretation of what exactly has or has not been determined. A good example is *Dowling v Minister for Justice, Equality and Law Reform*[19] which centred on the Minister's decision to grant temporary release to the applicant, who was serving a term of imprisonment. The Supreme Court characterised this temporary release as "a privilege accorded ... at the discretion of the Executive".[20] Moreover, the letter announcing the release said that it was "grant[ing] monthly renewable temporary release". However, finally, the court was more impressed by the fact that the letter, in a valedictory way, offered the applicant best wishes for his future. According to the court (Murray C.J.), "[t]he reality is, and the particular words convey, that the applicant was going to be indefinitely on temporary release, provided he was of good behaviour. The Minister was not going to reconsider the matter each month". Thus, it followed that it was not open to the respondent to terminate the applicant's temporary release because he had been questioned in relation to another crime. The message of this case is that a court will interpret meticulously the terms of a decision.

15–09 However, one should add the qualification that, even if the statutory words, by which either a power is conferred or the conditions for its exercise are defined, are cast in subjective terms, they would be understood by a court as being objective. The major statement[21] of this source of judicial review is to be found in Henchy J.'s separate, assenting judgment in *State (Lynch) v Cooney*. Henchy J.'s judgment took a wide view based on constitutional personal rights (though, from the expansiveness of the thinking, it is possible that it is not confined to personal rights which are protected by the Constitution). The seminal passage is as follows:

> "I conceive the present state of evolution of administrative law in the Courts on this topic to be that when a statute confers on a non-judicial person or body a decision-making power affecting personal rights, conditional on that person or body reaching a prescribed opinion or conclusion based on a subjective assessment, a person who shows that a personal right of his has been breached ... the High Court [has] jurisdiction to give a ruling as to whether the pre-condition for the valid exercise of the power has been complied with in a way that brings the decision within the express, or necessarily implied, range of the power conferred by the statute. It is to be presumed that when it conferred the power, Parliament intended the power to be exercised only in a manner that would be in conformity with the Constitution and within the limitations of the power as they are to be gathered from the statutory scheme

[18] De Smith, *Judicial Review of Administrative Action*, 4th edn (London: Stevens & Sons, 1980), pp.281, 297.
[19] [2003] 2 I.R. 535.
[20] All quotations are from Murray C.J.'s judgment ([2003] 2 I.R. 535 at 543).
[21] See also, *Garvey v Ireland* [1981] I.R. 75 at 97; *State (Daly) v Minister for Agriculture* [1987] I.R. 165 at 172 (Barron J.).

or design. This means, amongst other things, not only that the power must be exercised in good faith, but that the opinion or other subjective conclusion set as a precondition for the valid exercise of the power must be reached by a route that does not make the exercise unlawful–such as by misinterpreting the law, or by misapplying it through taking into consideration irrelevant matters of fact, or through ignoring relevant matters. Otherwise, the exercise of the power will be held to be invalid for being *ultra vires*."[22]

15–10 Next, there is a distinction, in principle, between the exercise of a discretionary power and a statutory duty imposed on a public authority.[23] But, in practice, there are intermediate stages at which the two tend to run into each other. Speaking broadly, there may be either of two reasons for this. First, the situation may be that the specified statutory duty[24] is so broad and vague that the judicial task of determining its extent, in order to decide whether there has been a breach, comes close to the exercise of a statutory power. Alternatively and from the opposite direction, the conditions for the exercise of a discretionary power may be so specific as to leave little room for discretion and to bring the function close to a statutory duty.[25]

15–11 A court reviewing an administrative action for abuse of discretionary power must not substitute its own view of the merits for that of the public body. Rather, it is concerned with the path of reasoning followed by the respondent. Take, for example, *Stroker v Doherty*,[26] which involved an unsuccessful attempt to overturn a decision of the Garda Disciplinary Appeals Board. The Board had affirmed a decision that the applicant had been guilty of a breach of discipline of bringing the Gardaí into disrepute in that, when off duty in a public house, he had made lewd statements about his wife to an acquaintance. Here it was necessary for the Supreme Court to reverse the High Court. Writing for the Supreme Court, McCarthy J. stated:

> "Applying that test to the circumstances of this case, I am not prepared to hold that the conclusion of the Appeal Board involved a rejection or disregard of fundamental reason or common sense. There are, no doubt, many who would consider the incident in question as tasteless and offensive but irrelevant to An Garda Síochána as such, whatever about its relevance to the individual Garda; ... there are others who would consider that, in a small country community, members of the Gardaí should be setting an example of decent conduct. *Quot homines tot sententiae.* It follows that the appeal in respect of this breach should be allowed."[27]

15–12 One should emphasise that the logic of this area of the law, as indicated

---

[22] [1982] I.R. 337 at 380–381. The liberal sentiment in this passage was put under a cloud by *O'Keeffe*; see paras 15–64 to 15–66.

[23] The question of damages for breach of statutory duty, or for negligent exercise of a discretionary power, is considered at Ch.18, Parts A and D.

[24] e.g. see *O'Reilly v Limerick Corporation* [1989] I.L.R.M. 181 at 189–191.

[25] *Garda Representative Association v Minister for Finance* [2010] IEHC 78 at paras 18–20. See also, *University of Limerick v Ryan*, unreported, High Court, Barron J., February 21, 1991.

[26] [1991] 1 I.R. 23. For a similar case to *Stroker*, with a similar outcome, see *Doran v Commissioner of An Garda Síochána* [1994] 1 I.L.R.M. 303 at 311–312.

[27] [1991] 1 I.R. 23 at 29. See to similar effect, Griffin J. at 26.

in the passage from McCarthy J.'s judgment, is that, if the respondent Appeal Board's decision had happened to go in the opposite direction—that is in favour of the Garda—and a "concerned citizen" had brought judicial review, the concerned citizen's application would equally have failed. For the question is not what the court itself would have done had it been taking the initial decision, but rather whether no reasonable public body could have reached such a decision. In other words, a reviewing court is supposed not to trespass on the issue of the merits of a decision, which is reserved for the public body involved. Yet, at the same time, a court reviewing for unreasonableness (or any of its present-day equivalents) is to some extent engaged with the merits. We return at paras 15–111 to 15–112 to the question of how far this review is taken.

Reasons and abuse of discretionary power

15–13 Elsewhere, we deal with the obligation to give reasons,[28] insofar as this can be disentangled from the present topic. Here we address a question which has not received the attention it warrants, namely whether, in review proceedings, a court is permitted to argue from the fact that no reasons were given for a decision to the conclusion that the decision was invalidated by unreasonableness (or one of the other sub-heads of abuse of discretionary power).

15–14 At the outset, one might ask: why does the question matter? Why is it an advantage to an applicant to succeed on the basis of unreasonableness, rather than a failure to give reasons? One answer may be that, where an applicant's victory is grounded on a failure to provide reasons, this is a procedural ground and the only (necessary) consequence is that the matter may be remitted to the public body which then takes a fresh decision, accompanied by reasons, which this time may pass muster. By contrast, if the court's decision is based on reasonableness, any later decision in the same sense would almost certainly be struck down. In short, a court decision based on unreasonableness would be much more certain to bring advantage to the applicant. The question then arises: may a court automatically infer unreasonableness merely from an absence of reasons?

15–15 One of the few Irish cases[29] to have focused on the relationship between reasons and unreasonableness is *Meadows v Minister for Justice, Equality and Law Reform*.[30] The main theme in *Meadows*—control of discretionary power—is examined below. Here, we consider a minor chord, namely the critical link between reasons and reasonableness. The majority and minority judges drew opposing conclusions from this link; but each noted its importance. Indeed, it was the central theme in Murray C.J.'s judgment[31]:

[28] See Ch.14, Part D.
[29] For a summary of the case law, see H & M, paras 15–27 to 15–38. See also, *Abuissa v Minister for Justice, Equality and Law Reform* [2011] 1 I.R. 123 at para.[32]; *Brennan v An Bord Altranais* [2010] IEHC 193; *Cullen v General Medical Council* [2005] EWHC 353 (Admin.).
[30] [2010] IESC 3. For comment, see Daly, "Standards of Review in Irish Administrative Law After *Meadows v Minister for Justice, Equality and Law Reform*" (2010) 32 D.U.L.J. 379.
[31] [2010] IESC 3 at p.32. (Of the other majority judges, Denham J. did not mention this point, but it was an auxiliary reason for Fennelly J., at para.79.) Murray C.J.'s strong statement made no reference to whether the Minister for Justice, Equality and Law Reform had been asked

"In my view the decision of the Minister in the terms couched is so vague and indeed opaque that its underlying rationale cannot be properly or reasonably deduced … This decision is open to multiple interpretations."

15–16 The dissenting judges were also alert to the critical link between reasons and reasonableness, but they turned the argument on its head. Hardiman J.[32] stated:

"… the test now proposed to be applied has quite the contrary effect [to *O'Keeffe* or *Wednesbury*]: it looks for explanation and justification from the decision-maker which I believe to be inconsistent with the proper principles of judicial review and … that the onus of proof remains on the applicant."

15–17 On one view, one could respond to this stricture by saying that what Murray C.J. was insisting on was merely a strict application of the existing law. This perhaps misses the point, which was that, in Hardiman J.'s view, a requirement of a sharper articulation of reasons cannot fail to shine a more searching light on the substantive merits of a decision and, thus, to facilitate a successful judicial review. This, of course, has always been offered as the principal justification[33] for the right to reasons.

General policy assumptions

15–18 Many of the policy assumptions with which a judge approaches a statute are couched as rules of statutory interpretation, which take effect by way of fixing the vires (or limits) of the statutory power, so as to protect the individual. Most of these have been examined at Chapter 10, Part D. Others are constitutional in character and these are considered at paras 15–97 to 15–102. Another policy is pro-competition and this has given birth to the presumption that a statutory power may not be used to restrict the number of practitioners or businesses in the particular field, unless express words are used, and this is considered in the chapter on Licensing at Chapter 1, Part C.

15–19 In most of the policies just mentioned the net effect is to favour the individual. Next, we draw attention to a few policy assumptions (not covered elsewhere) which in contrast to those referred to elsewhere are of what might be called a pro-public institution and/or community character. First, any financial cost to the public body is obviously a factor to be taken into account. (In the case of local authorities, this notion used to be grounded on the basis that local authorities were regarded as being somewhat in the position of "trustees" in relation to their ratepayers and, hence, as owing them a "fiduciary" duty to observe business-like principles in regard to the expenditure of money.) This principle has now been established by statute.[34] It has been relied upon, for example, in cases establishing

---

by the applicant to provide reasons. In other authorities, such a request has been said to be necessary. See further, at para.14–103.
[32] [2010] IESC 3 at pp.15–17 per Hardiman J. See, to similar effect, Kearns J. at p.2.
[33] See paras 14–111 to 14–114.
[34] See Local Government Act 2001 s.69, discussed at paras 5–64 to 5–68.

that (even before the era of Public Procurement Rules)[35] in deciding to which contractor to award a public works contract, a local authority is obliged to take at least some account of the prices of the various tenders submitted to it.[36] A case in which this principle was treated as axiomatic is *Donegal Fuel and Supply Co. Ltd v Londonderry Port and Harbour Commissioners.*[37] Here an argument that some bye-laws, which permitted the use of part only of a harbour, were consequently ultra vires was repulsed on the ground of cost. Costello J. stated:

> "The harbour commissioners have a statutory duty to raise income and to apply it in fulfilment, *inter alia*, of the powers to maintain and repair quays and piers. That income may not be sufficient to repair and maintain every part of their undertaking and the harbour commissioners must have a discretion as to how its income is to be used. This means that the statutes must be construed so as to permit them to discontinue, or reduce, the use of part of their undertakings should financial constraints so require. This is what has happened in this case. It seems to me that the harbour commissioners have not acted unreasonably in proposing to limit in the way proposed in the draft bye-laws the use of the pier of Carrickarory."[38]

15–20   Particular structural features in which the decision-making machinery is set may also be relevant.[39] The simplest example of a structural feature would be when an appeal is available, as an alternative to judicial review for unreasonableness. Elsewhere[40] we consider whether the existence of an appeal is a discretion on which to refuse review, and conclude that much depends upon the particular flaw which would have been the subject of a review. And, since review for reasonableness/proportionality has much in common with review on the merits, it is suggested that, where it is this flaw of which the applicant complains, the availability of appeal should certainly act as a bar.

15–21   Another factor which would strengthen the applicant's case in getting a decision struck down would be where the decision created by the statutory framework is a sieve, designed only to filter out more or less "hopeless" cases with the remaining cases being sent on for the substantive decision, often by a different body. An example of this type is provided by *COI v Minister for Justice, Equality and Law Reform.*[41] Under the relevant legislation, the permission of the Minister was necessary to enable a person who had already been refused refugee status to make

[35] On which, see H & M, Ch.4, Part J.
[36] See generally, *State (Raftis) v Leonard* [1960] I.R. 381; *Bromley LBC v GLC* [1983] 1 A.C. 768; Street, *Law Relating to Local Government* (Dublin: Stationery Office on behalf of Incorporated Council of Law Reporting for Ireland, 1955), pp.1263–1264 and cases cited therein; Kelly, "Local Authority Contracts, Tenders and Mandamus" (1967) 2 Ir. Jur. (N.S) 7.
[37] [1994] 1 I.R. 24.
[38] [1994] 1 I.R. 24 at 40.
[39] An out-of-date British instance would be where the decision-maker is the Minister and he is "responsible to Parliament" and it is therefore deduced that judicial review is unnecessary. But compare *Brennan v Minister for Justice* [1995] 1 I.R. 612 at 629, which turns this argument on its head.
[40] See paras 16–79 to 16–80. In *Ferris v Dublin County Council*, unreported, Supreme Court, November 7, 1990, Finlay C.J. rejected a submission that a higher standard of reasonableness should be set for a public body if no appeal is provided.
[41] [2007] 2 I.L.R.M. 471 at 477–480.

a further application to the Refugee Applications Commissioner/Refugee Appeals Tribunal. In *COI*, it was indicated by the High Court that, because the substantive issue was a matter for the RAC/RAT, a relatively higher standard of substantive review would be applied to what is, in effect, the Minister's power to filter.

B. *Wednesbury* Unreasonableness: the Sub-heads

15–22 The classic exposition of the traditional principles traditionally restraining abuse of power by public authorities was given in Lord Greene's celebrated passage in *Associated Provincial Picture Houses Ltd v Wednesbury Corporation.*[42] As we shall see in Part C, the contemporary law has changed the jargon and, possibly, the substance set down in this seminal case. Nevertheless, this is where the modern law began and a lot of the concepts remain relevant today. One still occasionally hears the term "*Wednesbury* unreasonableness". In the central passage, quoted below, Lord Greene identified three facets of abuse of discretionary power: bad faith, taking irrelevant factors into account and unreasonableness. The opening lines allude to the fact that these principles, like the rules of natural justice, are cast in the mould of specialised rules of statutory interpretation:

"When an executive discretion is entrusted by Parliament to a body such as the local authority in this case, what appears to be an exercise of that discretion can only be challenged in the courts in a strictly limited class of case. As I have said, it must always be remembered that the court is not a court of appeal. When discretion of this kind is granted the law recognises certain principles upon which that discretion must be exercised, but within the four corners of those principles the discretion, in my opinion, is an absolute one and cannot be questioned in any court of law ... I am not sure myself whether the permissible grounds of attack cannot be defined under a single head. It has been perhaps a little bit confusing to find a series of grounds set out. Bad faith, dishonesty – those, of course, stand by themselves – unreasonableness, attention given to extraneous circumstances, disregard of public policy and things like that have all been referred to, according to the facts of individual cases, as being matters which are relevant to the question. If they cannot all be confined under one head, they at any rate, I think, overlap to a very great extent. For instance, we have heard in this case a great deal about the meaning of the word 'unreasonable.' ... It has frequently been used and is frequently used as a general description of the things that must not be done.

---

[42] [1948] 1 K.B. 223 at 230. The facts of the case were that the defendant was a local authority which was empowered, under the Sunday Entertainments Act 1932, to grant licences for Sunday entertainment at the cinema subject to such conditions as it thought fit. The plaintiff picture-house owner was granted a licence but subject to the condition that no children under 15 be admitted to a Sunday performance with or without an adult. This condition was challenged. The challenge failed and the Court of Appeal evidently regarded it as a very feeble case. Given the wide social and religious difference between Britain in the 1940s (with its Lord's Day observance tendency) and Ireland in the 2010s, the issue is difficult to discuss in contemporary terms. However, there seems at least a possibility that the plaintiff would have succeeded had he come before a present day Irish court with the same facts. The reasons for this surmise are that, as described in Part E, the respondent Council had imposed a blanket ban, preventing any person below the age of 15, even if accompanied by an adult, from watching any film, however innocuous.

For instance, a person entrusted with a discretion must, so to speak, direct himself properly in law. He must call his own attention to the matters which he is bound to consider. He must exclude from his consideration matters which are irrelevant to what he has to consider. If he does not obey those rules, he may truly be said, and often is said, to be acting 'unreasonably.' Similarly, there may be something so absurd that no sensible person could ever dream that it lay within the powers of the authority. Warrington L.J. in *Short v. Poole Corporation*[43] gave the example of the red-haired teacher, dismissed because she had red hair. That is unreasonable in one sense. In another sense it is taking into consideration extraneous matters. It is so unreasonable that it might almost be described as being done in bad faith; and, in fact, all these things run into one another."

15–23   At this point, we turn to deal with the three segments of the abuse of discretion which were highlighted in *Wednesbury,* and then briefly mention another two other flaws, "uncertainty" and "inconsistency".

Bad faith (mala fides)

15–24   Fraud (frequently known as mala fides or bad faith) exists where a public body intends to achieve an object other than that for which he believes the power to have been conferred. Thus, bad faith includes, but is wider than, the concept of "malice", which should be used only where the repository of the discretionary power is motivated by personal animosity against a person or persons affected by it. In the other direction, bad faith may be distinguished from bias (covered in Chapter 13, Parts A and B) in that bias may have an objective existence, without any element of consciousness similar to the *criminal* law concept of mens rea, whereas the essence of bad faith is dishonesty.

15–25   Straightaway, two features emerge: first, cases in which bad faith is established are inevitably rare. Courts naturally shrink from labelling elected representatives and/or public officials as dishonest.[44] Moreover, public bodies are often made up of groups of people with differing levels of information about the subject matter and with varying outlooks, motivations and political allegiances. Against this background, it will often be difficult to bring home a charge of bad faith because of the need to prove something akin to the criminal law concept of mens rea. Secondly, if a court concludes that a discretionary decision is the product of the consideration of irrelevant factors or is unreasonable, then it will be held invalid, even if there is no element of bad faith. Thus it will usually be otiose to try to establish bad faith. One exception to this observation would occur in an action where a plaintiff is suing for the (as yet undeveloped) tort of misfeasance of public office since bad faith is a necessary element of this tort.[45] Again, bad faith is regarded as particularly heinous so that the consequences of such a finding are

---

[43]   [1926] Ch. 66 at 90–91.
[44]   See *Smith v East Elloe U.D.C.* [1956] A.C. 736 at 767 quoted with approval in *Listowel U.D.C. v McDonagh* [1968] I.R. 312 at 317 and *P&F Sharpe v Dublin City and County Manager* [1989] I.L.R.M. 565 at 570.
[45]   See also, *Roncarelli v Dupleiss* (1959) 16 D.L.R. (2d) 689 at 705; *Dunlop v Woollahra MC* [1982] A.C. 158; *Bourgoin SA v Ministry of Agriculture* [1986] Q.B. 716; *Pine Valley Developments Ltd v Minister for Environment* [1987] I.R. 23.

more far-reaching than with other defects and this may tell in the applicant's favour. Thus, for example, where the subject matter of the power and other circumstances are such that exercise of the power is beyond the reach of judicial review, for "honest abuse of power", the courts might be prepared to intervene if bad faith could be established.[46]

15–26 Irish case law tends to bear out these general propositions. It is uncommon for bad faith[47] to be alleged before a court, never mind established. However, the Supreme Court made it clear in *Listowel U.D.C. v McDonagh*[48] that mala fides is "a well recognised ground of challenge". By the Local Government (Sanitary Services) Act 1948 a sanitary authority is empowered "[to] prohibit the erection … of temporary dwellings … if they are of opinion that such erection … would be prejudicial to public health …". Purporting to act under this power, Listowel U.D.C. made an order banning the construction of temporary dwellings on a number of named streets. The defendant was convicted and fined 10 shillings for contravening this order. His principal line of defence was to argue that the order had not been made bona fide in that the sanitary authority did not genuinely hold the necessary opinion. In effect finding for the defendant, the Supreme Court held that the defendant was free to adduce evidence before the Circuit Court (to which the case had gone on appeal) as to: what transpired at the council meeting which considered the passing of the bye-law; what views were expressed by members and officials of the Council; and the veracity of the opinion they expressed. In the result, the Circuit Court found as a matter of fact, that the order had been made bona fide.[49]

Improper purposes and irrelevant considerations

15–27 "Improper purpose" in this context refers to the fact that, in enacting a statute, the legislature is assumed to have had a definable purpose(s) or object(s). True to the traditional idea that they are implementing the mandate of the legislature, the courts seek to ensure that the power contained in the measure is used only for the "proper purpose". A simple example is afforded by *McDonough v Minister for*

---

[46] For an example of this, see *Kennedy v Law Society of Ireland (No. 3)* [2002] 2 I.R. 458 at 490–491, outlined at para.15–29.

[47] For other examples, see *State (Hully) v Hynes* (1966) 100 I.L.T.R. 145 (real purpose of securing prosecutor was to charge him with revenue offences); *Ellis v O'Dea* [1990] I.L.R.M. 87 at 93 (real purpose to make applicant available for interrogation: hypothetical remark); *State (O'Mahony) v South Cork Board of Public Health* [1941] Ir. Jur. Rep. 79; and *State (Cogley) v Dublin Corporation* [1970] I.R. 244 at 249–250.

For a case in which what looked like at least a prima facie case of bad faith received short shrift, see *State (Divito) v Arklow U.D.C.* [1986] I.L.R.M. 123. (Respondent local authority passed a resolution under the Gaming and Lotteries Act 1956, the result of which was that anyone with premises in the relevant area was entitled to apply to the District Court for a Gaming licence. The applicant applied unsuccessfully for a licence, his application being opposed by the local authority. Before he could reapply, the local authority revoked its resolution under the 1956 Act.)

[48] [1968] I.R. 312 at 318. For other likely examples, see *McDonough v Minister for Defence* [1991] 2 I.R. 33 at 41 and *Hoey v Minister for Justice* [1994] 3 I.R. 329. The quotation is at 344.

[49] The applicants put in evidence a council memorandum entitled "The itinerant problem". However, nine councillors swore that they were concerned only with health matters and their evidence was accepted.

Defence[50] which concerned the disciplining of a naval driver by being "grounded", i.e. being barred from driving any vehicle other than a tractor—with a resultant loss of pay. Lavan J. held that the applicant's disqualification should have been considered not from the perspective of punishing the applicant but from the distinct basis of what risks would be involved for the public in permitting the applicant to go on driving.[51]

15–28 One practical question here lies in establishing the purpose which underlies the particular action of the public body. The question is essentially mental and, consequently, a peculiarly difficult issue of fact. It is nowhere more difficult than where the administrative authority is moved by a number of different purposes. Where an authority has sought to achieve unauthorised as well as authorised purposes, the question of what test should be used to determine the validity of its act has been characterised as "a legal porcupine which bristles with difficulties as soon as it is touched".[52] A straightforward example occurred in *Cassidy v Minister for Industry and Commerce*[53] in which the plaintiff's case, on the present point, failed because, as Henchy J. stated:

> "The evidence forces me to the conclusion that the primary and dominant purpose of the Minister in making these orders was to eliminate unwarranted price increases (a proper purpose) and that, while he also had as his aim the return of the publicans to the voluntary practice of not making price increases without giving him prior notice (an improper purpose) that aim was merely subsidiary and consequential to the dominant and permitted purpose."[54]

---

[50] [1991] 2 I.R. 33 at 41. See to similar effect, *People (DPP) v McCaughey*, unreported, Supreme Court, November 20, 1989, in the context of a punishment fixed by a court for an offence of dangerous driving. On the general point, see *Cassidy v Minister for Industry and Commerce* [1978] I.R. 297. See also, planning cases surveyed in Ch.5 on Local Government.

[51] For other examples, see *Cassidy v Minister for Industry and Commerce* [1978] I.R. 297 at 310; *Minister for Industry and Commerce v White*, unreported, High Court, Finlay P., February 16, 1981; *Latchford v Minister for Industry and Commerce* [1950] I.R. 33 (disqualification from baking subsidy on ground of criminal conviction, which was held to be an irrelevant factor); *State (Keller) v Galway Co. Co.* [1958] I.R. 142 (disabled person's allowance refused on ground that the applicant not incapable of doing any job; yet the proper test was whether he could do job of same kind for which he would be suited, if he were not handicapped); *State (Melbarien Enterprises Ltd) v Revenue Commissioners* [1986] I.L.R.M. 476 at 482 (tax clearance certificate refused because a company with connections with the applicant company owed arrears of tax); *Ambiorix Ltd v Minister for the Environment (No. 2)* [1992] 2 I.R. 37 (in regard to the test of whether there was a "special need to promote urban renewal" in an area, Minister had taken into account the relevant factors); *Maher v An Bord Pleanála* [1993] 1 I.R. 439 (depreciation in value of property in vicinity of development amounted to a relevant planning factor); *Gutrani v Minister for Justice* [1993] 2 I.R. 427 at 438–439 (deportation of alien); *Madigan v RTÉ* [1994] 2 I.L.R.M. 472 at 477–479 (allocation of party political broadcasts); *Kweder v Minister for Justice* [1996] 1 I.R. 381 (Minister improperly refused entry visa merely because the applicant had been deported from the United Kingdom and this fact *in itself* was held by Geoghegan J. to be an irrelevant consideration); *Keane v An Bord Pleanála* [1997] 1 I.L.R.M. 508 (impact of development outside of the State held to be a relevant consideration in the planning process).

[52] De Smith, *Judicial Review of Administrative Action,* 4th edn (1980), p.340.

[53] [1978] I.R. 297. See also, *Murphy v Dublin Corporation* [1976] I.R. 143; *Hussey v Irish Land Commission*, unreported, Supreme Court, December 13, 1984; *State (Bouzagou) v The Station Sergeant, Fitzgibbon St Garda Station* [1986] I.L.R.M. 95; and, in regard to criminal procedure, *People (DPP) v Howley* [1989] I.L.R.M. 624, analysed in the Third Edition, pp.627–628.

[54] [1978] I.R. 297 at 308–309. The facts were on the other side of the same line in the Northern

15–29 A slightly different test was applied in *Kennedy v Law Society of Ireland (No. 3).*[55] The applicant was suspected by the first respondent of involvement in a number of fraudulent personal injury claims. However, at an earlier stage of the proceedings, it had been held by the Supreme Court that the investigation of fraudulent claims was not an authorised purpose under the Solicitors' Accounts Regulations. The net result was that the court held, in the instant case, that the appointment of the accountant had been made for two purposes, one of which (the fraudulent claims) was ultra vires and the other (compliance with the Solicitors' Accounts Regulations) was intra vires. Giving judgment on the Supreme Court's behalf, Fennelly J. stated[56]:

> "The pursuit of the impermissible objective was as important to the first respondent as the permissible one. Such an exercise of delegated power cannot be allowed to stand."

15–30 The two labels—"improper purpose" and "irrelevant consideration"—are used interchangeably in the judgments and here. For it is only by virtue of a decision as to what is the proper purpose (a difficulty to which we return below) that the court then deduces the considerations which are relevant in exercising a discretionary power created by the measure. It follows, therefore, that there is a close similarity between the rules that relevant considerations must be taken into account and irrelevant considerations excluded, and, on the other hand, the rule that the proper purpose must be observed when a discretionary power is being exercised.[57] Accordingly, there seems to be little point in discussing the cases in separate compartments. Instead, our selection of specimen cases is arranged according to the criterion of whether or not the statute creating the discretionary power gives (explicit or implicit) guidance as to its purpose and so identifies the considerations which must be taken into account in exercising the discretion.

Statutory guidance

15–31 One example of a statutory power, the relevant factors in relation to which were fairly plainly indicated, was considered in *State (Cussen) v Brennan.*[58] This case arose out of the selection, by the Local Appointment Commissioners (of whom Mr Brennan was one) of a consultant paediatrician. It was established that, as far as paediatrics was concerned, the LAC had judged the applicant to be slightly ahead of his nearest rival but that the rival candidate's knowledge of the Irish language had tipped the balance in his favour. According to the relevant statutory provision (Health Act 1970 s.18), it was for the Minister for Health to lay down the qualifications for the job. The Minister had duly done this and a knowledge of

---

Irish case of *Re Murray's Application* [1987] 12 N.I.J.B. 2.
[55]   [2000] 2 I.R. 104; [2002] 2 I.R. 458 at 488. A different test was ordered in *Director of Corporate Enforcement v DCC Plc* [2009] 1 I.L.R.M. 124, where Kelly J. stated: "I am not satisfied that the *sole* motivation of the Director in seeking the appointment of inspectors is with a view to obtaining a report which will do no more than appraise him of facts already known [which would have been an improper purpose under the relevant legislation]".
[56]   [2002] 2 I.R. at 485. See also 488.
[57]   This ground of distinction is explored in Taylor, "Judicial Review of Improper Purposes and Irrelevant Consideration" (1976) Camb. L.J. 272 at 277.
[58]   [1981] I.R. 181.

Irish was not among the qualifications which he had specified. Consequently, the LAC had taken irrelevant considerations into account.[59]

15–32   The most sophisticated formulation of factors which are to guide the exercise of a discretionary (it may be better to style it "a semi-discretionary") power is to be found in the Planning Code. According to the Planning and Development Act 2000 s.34(2), a local planning authority in dealing with a planning application is restricted to the factors specified therein. On this provision and judicial review cases in relation to it, see paras 5–127 to 5–132.

15–33   Other schemes of statutory guidance are less precise than in the planning field. An example is broadcasting where, in awarding certain types of contracts, the Broadcasting Authority of Ireland "shall have regard to" inter alia the following factors[60]:

> (a)   the character, expertise and experience of the applicant ...;
> (b)   the adequacy of the financial resources ... and the extent to which the application accords with good business and economic principles;
> (c)   the quality, range and type of the programmes proposed to be provided ...;
> (k)   any other matters which the Contract Awards Committee considers to be necessary to secure the orderly development of sound broadcasting services.
> (l)   where directed by the Authority ... the amount of a single cash payment which the applicant is willing to pay to the [Broadcasting Authority of Ireland].

15–34   In addition, by s.65(1) of the Broadcasting Act 2009, "... the Contracts Awards Committee shall ... assign a score" to each of the criteria (of which some examples are given in the list just quoted) and give these scores to each applicant.[61]

15–35   Another somewhat imprecise catalogue of relevant factors is to be found in regard to deportation which specifies the factors to which the Minister must pay regard in deciding whether to make a deportation order. Among these factors are a number of specific considerations focussed on the individual circumstances of the person who is the subject of the order, as well as "the common good".[62] This

---

[59]   However, the court exercised its discretion not to grant an order because of undue delay on the part of the applicant. The Local Authorities (Officers and Employees) Act 1983 s.2 effectively reversed the legal rule established in *Cussen* by providing that the LAC may take into account a knowledge of the Irish language.
[60]   Broadcasting Act 2009 s.66(2) (formerly Radio and Television Act 1988 s.6(2)).
[61]   On this general question of assigning a score, see H & M, paras 14–147, 15–66 to 15–68.
[62]   Section 3(6) of the Immigration Act 1999, as amended by the Illegal Immigrants (Trafficking) Act 2000 s.10, states:
>   The Minister shall have regard to—
>   (a)   the age of the person;
>   (b)   the duration of residence in the State of the person;
>   (c)   the family and domestic circumstances of the person
>   ...
>   (j)   the common good

element, it was held by the Supreme Court in *FP v Minister for Justice*,[63] "entitled the respondent to have regard to the State's policy in relation to the control of aliens".[64]

15–36 Next, the way in which the statutory test is formulated is obviously significant. It may, for instance, state that a specified public agency "shall" take the specified action, provided that specified conditions are satisfied. Some eventuality may arise which seems to the public agency to require a refusal to take the action, yet which is not listed among the conditions. In this situation, a refusal would be wrongful, because the use of the word "shall"[65] removes any discretion, to take or not to take the specified action, on any grounds other than those specified in the legislation. A straightforward example is *O'Donovan v Chief Superintendent of An Garda Síochána Cork*.[66] Here the central provision stated:

> Where an applicant for the grant of a licence to drive small public service vehicles is duly made, the Commissioner shall grant the licence if he is satisfied that the applicant
> (a) is a fit and proper person to hold a licence ...

15–37 The applicant had been refused a licence by the respondent because he was in receipt of a disability allowance for a back injury. There was then an appeal to the District Court and, at this point, the District Court submitted a case stated to the High Court asking whether it would be lawful to grant a licence to the applicant, in view of his welfare benefit. The High Court's response was that, in view of the wording of the legislation, the answer turned solely on whether the applicant was "a fit and proper person" to hold a PSV licence. If this condition were satisfied, then the obligation would be mandatory. In other words, there was no reservoir of discretion or public policy, outside the conditions specified in the statute, which could justify the refusal of the licence (as was the case, for example, in the broadcasting legislation, quoted earlier). It was significant here perhaps that what was at issue was an individual right, rather than a matter of high policy. In any case, one moral is that draftspersons should be prepared for the unexpected.

15–38 Another rather different example of statutory guidance would be where the public body is enjoined by the legislation "to have regard to" some specified matter, policies, guidelines or recommendation set by another public body. Given

---

(k)   considerations of national security and public policy.
For further comment, see *Garda Representative Association v Minister for Finance* [2010] IEHC 78 at paras 18–19.

[63]   [2002] I.R. 164.

[64]   [2002] I.R. 164 at 174. See also, Denham J.'s helpful analysis of this topic in *Dimbo v Minister for Justice, Equality and Law Reform*, unreported, Supreme Court, May 1, 2008 at pp.21–22. For "a non exhaustive list of matters which may assist" when the Minister is considering whether to deport the non-national parents of an Irish born child, see *Oguekwe v Minister for Justice, Equality and Law Reform* [2008] 3 I.R. 795 at para.85. See also, *Cirpaci v Minister for Justice, Equality and Law Reform* [2005] 2 I.L.R.M. 547 at 557.

[65]   Assuming that "shall" does not mean "may": see H & M, Ch.11, Part A.

[66]   [2005] 1 I.R. 407 at 414. The central provision in this case was the Road Traffic (Public Service Vehicles) Regulations 1963 (S.I. No. 191 of 1963) reg.34(3) (as substituted by reg.8 of S.I. No. 200 of 1970).

the proliferation of public bodies in Ireland,[67] such intersections are likely to arise with increasing frequency. The question of what force the words quoted have will usually arise in a situation in which a decision-maker has diverged from the course which seems to be directed by the other public body.[68]

Little or no statutory guidance

15–39   Thus far cases have been examined in which the relevant statute provided an explicit statement of the factors which the public authority must take into account. In situations in which even this limited assistance is not available, little judicial assistance has been given as to the process of teasing out "the relevant considerations" from the general tenor of the statute creating the discretionary power. A rare example of a judicial attempt to articulate how this process should be approached emerges from the well-known case of *East Donegal Co-Operative Ltd v Attorney General*,[69] in which the Supreme Court scrutinised the Livestock Marts Act 1967, in order to decide a claim by a group of agricultural mart owners that the Act was unconstitutional. The Act bestows considerable discretionary power on the Minister for Agriculture enabling him to control marts, through the grant (whether absolutely or subject to conditions), or the revocation, of licences. In spite of the wide discretionary language in which these powers are couched, Walsh J. stated that:

> "The words of the Act, and in particularly the general words, cannot be read in isolation and their content is to be derived from their context. Therefore words or phrases which at first sight might appear to be wide and general may be cut down in their construction when examined against the objects of the Act which are to be derived from a study of the Act as a whole including the long title."

15–40   Specifically:

> "The provisions of section 6 [of the 1967 Act] throw considerable light upon the purposes, objects and scope of the Act because they refer specifically to the power of the Minister for Agriculture and Fisheries being directed towards the proper conduct of the businesses concerned, the standards in relation to such places and to the provision of adequate and suitable accommodation and facilities for such auctions. Section 6 also provides for the making of regulations dealing with what might be referred to as the mechanics of sale such as book-keeping, accommodation, hygiene, etc. ... The type of conditions which the Minister may impose [on the grant of a mart licence] would include the site of the mart so as to ensure that, for example, it was not too near a place of worship or a particular road traffic hazard, or conditions

---

[67]   As Yeats wrote, "Much hatred, little room".
[68]   For recent cases, see *Glencar Exploration v Mayo County Council (No. 1)* [1993] 2 I.R. 237 at 248; *Glencar v Mayo County Council (No. 2)* [2002] 1 I.R. 84 at 142; and *McEvoy v Meath County Council* [2003] 1 I.R. 208 at 224; analysed in H & M, paras 16–72 to 16–78.
[69]   [1970] I.R. 317. See also, *Doupe v Limerick Corporation* [1981] I.L.R.M. 456 at 461 per Costello J.; *Gilmore v Mitchell*, unreported, High Court, April 16, 1988 (the court accepted that the locality in which a Garda was stationed may be a relevant factor in determining a charge of conduct likely to bring discredit on the force).

aimed at the restriction of the carrying on of business at certain hours or on certain days so as to prevent interference with the activities of persons not connected with the mart, or conditions which indeed might be designed to facilitate the carrying on of business at the particular mart by preventing it being carried on at times which, by reason of particular local conditions or activities, would be detrimental to the business itself and to the persons having stock for sale at the mart or to persons resorting there for the purpose of purchasing livestock."[70]

15–41 Frequently, the relevant considerations will be particular to the statutory and factual context.[71] No general principles have emerged in this area. And, notoriously, common law draftspersons (in contrast to their civilian counterparts) used not to provide informative preambles; though this practice may be changing in Ireland: see below. Nor have explanatory memoranda been found useful. Thus, each judge approaches the task of divining relevant considerations in their own way, making what use they can of the general content and surroundings of the legislation.

15–42 In this field, the argument has been made recently—and probably rejected, though a little unclearly—that a parent statute must contain guidance as to how a discretionary power is to be exercised, at any rate where a constitutional right is under attack. In *Dellway Investments v NAMA*,[72] it was said that the power given to the National Assets Management Agency to take over loans to banks was unconstitutional. This submission was put on the basis that the regulations used to determine bank assets gave NAMA a discretion so untrammelled and unguided as to represent an unjust and disproportionate attack on the borrower's property rights.[73] This submission was rejected on alternative grounds. First, Irish draftsmen now, in anticipation of the sort of argument considered here, sometimes adopts the civil law style, rather than the silence of the common lawyer, in stating explicitly the purposes, at any rate, of novel public law legislation. Thus, the National Asset Management Agency Act 2009 ss.2 and 84 set out the grounds upon which the power to acquire bank assets must be exercised. These include "the need to address a serious threat to the stability of credit institutions and the need for the maintenance and stabilisation of the financial system in the state". Alternatively, there is a general precept in Irish law, as it was put in an earlier classic authority, which was quoted earlier here and with approval by the court, namely that "[i]t is to be presumed that, when it conferred a statutory power, parliament intended the power to be exercised only in a manner that would be in conformity with the constitution and within the limitations of the power as they are to be gathered from

---

[70] [1970] I.R. 317 at 341–343. See also, *Byrne v O'Leary* [2006] IEHC 412 (in regard to the findings of a public inquiry into the affairs of Ansbacher (Cayman) Ltd, under the Companies Act 1990, the trust law of the Cayman Islands was an irrelevant factor and so it did not matter that it had not been taken into account).

[71] The considerations involved might include (real or potential) knock-on effects affecting third parties. An example is *O'Shea Fishing Company v Minister for Agriculture, Fisheries and Food* [2008] IEHC 91 at paras 5.7–5.10.

[72] [2011] IESC 14; unreported, Supreme Court, April 12, 2011 per Murray C.J. at pp.9, 13–14.

[73] Compare unsuccessful challenge by shareholders to British state takeover, as being interference with property rights under art.1, First Protocol.

the statutory scheme or design."[74] This view is also supported by the passage just quoted from *East Donegal*.

Reasonableness

15–43   As Lord Greene pointed out in the extract from his judgment in *Wednesbury Corporation*—quoted above—reasonableness can be used, widely, to cover almost all forms of abuse of power. Used more narrowly and, therefore, more usefully, it refers to a decision which departs so radically from the normal standards of cost, convenience, morality, respect for individual rights, etc that no reasonable public authority could have come to it. In this sense, reasonableness was traditionally seldom used by the courts because it entails deciding questions of judgment in highly political areas, where courts prefer not to tread. Accordingly, there is often a substantial overlap between the present and the previous sub-heads.[75] However, sometimes unreasonableness will result from a different flaw, namely too little weight being given to a relevant factor.

15–44   An example of an unreasonableness argument succeeding[76] is provided by *Ashbourne v An Bord Pleanála*.[77] The applicant had developed the Old Head of Kinsale as a golf club and planning permission had been granted to retain the development. However, the permission was accompanied by many conditions, which appeared to be a response to public indignation over the termination of what was claimed to be a long-standing public amenity. The thrust of these conditions, to which the developer objected, was to permit limited public access to the golf course. In particular, despite the fact that no public right of way existed, these conditions included requirements that access be provided first "at all times during daylight hours to the lighthouse and the area marginal to the neck and the northern rim of the headland", and secondly, "to the cliff face and cliff edges for interest groups ...".

---

[74]   *State (Lynch) v Cooney* [1982] I.R. 337 at 338. See para.15–09.

[75]   Notice, for example, the following extract from *O'Keeffe v An Bord Pleanála* [1993] 1 I.R. 39 where Costello J. said (at 60): "It seems to me that I am driven to the conclusion that the Board acted *ultra vires* because either (a) it took matters into consideration which, although, perhaps furnishing a rational explanation for its decision were not connected with considerations relating to the proper planning and development of the area, or alternatively, (b), it reached a conclusion which no reasonable planning authority applying the standards of reason and commonsense as laid down by the Supreme Court could have reached, namely that the proposed development was consistent with the proper planning and development of the area. It follows that its decision must be quashed." But the Supreme Court took a different view of the underlying facts, and so did not reach this point.

[76]   For other cases on unreasonableness, see *Limerick Corporation v Sheridan* (1956) 90 I.L.T.R. 59 at 64; *Cassidy v Minister for Industry and Commerce* [1978] I.R. 297; *Greaney v Scully* [1981] I.L.R.M. 340; *Doyle v An Taoiseach* [1986] I.L.R.M. 693; *Lawlor v Minister for Agriculture* [1988] I.L.R.M. 400 at 418; *State (Kugan) v Station Sergeant, Fitzgibbon St Garda Station* [1986] I.L.R.M. 95 (deportation arose from refusal of entry based on the applicant's inadequate knowledge of English); *State (Bouzagou) v Station Sergeant, Fitzgibbon St Garda Station* [1985] I.R. 426 at 428; *McGabhann v Incorporated Law Society of Ireland* [1989] I.L.R.M. 854 at 862–863; *Stroker v Doherty* [1991] 1 I.R. 23; *Harvey v Minister for Social Welfare* [1990] I.L.R.M. 185; *Belfast Corporation v Daly* [1963] N.I. 78; and *Philips v The Medical Council* [1991] 2 I.R. 115 (requirement that seven years' practice as a doctor must be consecutive to entitle applicant to full registration under the Medical Practitioners Act 1978 held to involve "manifest injustice" (at 141)).

[77]   [2002] 1 I.L.R.M. 321.

15–45 In the Supreme Court, the case was treated primarily as one of the vires of the planning legislation and is covered in Chapter 5, Part F on Planning Law. But, in this general chapter, it is of interest that the High Court (Kearns J.) held that the two public access conditions were classic examples of unreasonableness. He stated[78]:

> "The first part of the first condition is ... completely untrammelled and unrestricted. By deleting the reference to 'the existing roadway', access for the public is no[t] ... via a designated route so that 'at all times during daylight hours', members of the public can access the lighthouse at the southern tip by whatever route or direction they choose. The small map of the golf course ... shows all too clearly how such a condition has the capacity to completely frustrate and/or render inoperable the use of the headland as a golf course. The two users are clearly inimical to each other and, if allowed to co-exist, could result in either injury or conflict between members of the public and golfers using the facilities of the course.
>
> Furthermore, the terms of the condition as imposed obliges the golf course operator to keep this facility open, regardless of weather conditions, regardless of whether the course is open or closed and regardless of whether or not the golf development continues. I do not believe that any reasonable authority would have attached such a condition to a development of this nature."

Uncertainty

15–46 "Uncertainty" is not mentioned in the classic *Wednesbury* judgment quoted earlier. However, it seems that, since it is a prime requirement of the Rule of Law (explained in Chapter 2, Part A) it ought to be a feature of judicial review. The initial (English) proposition was that "a regulation or bye-law whose meaning cannot be ascertained with reasonable certainty is *ultra vires* and void"[79]; thus, a bye-law which ordained that "no person shall wilfully annoy passengers in the street" was held void, as was one which forbad the flying of hang-gliders over a pleasure ground but failed to specify the height below which the offence was committed.[80] Next, there was an extension to cover conditions and grants of planning permission. This extension probably stemmed from the fact that the original rule was most commonly used, in the field of local government, against bye-laws. But it also makes sense on the basis of the policy that the extent of a decision should be known to the person affected. For it would be a Kafka-esque world if the person affected (as well as third parties including even the persons enforcing the decision) were uncertain regarding the precise limits of, for instance: the extent of a licence; or the terms of temporary release from prison; or the grant of asylum. At the same time, it should be emphasised that, at the moment, the only Irish cases appear to be planning permission cases.

15–47 A straightforward recent example of uncertainty is *Ashbourne Holdings v An Bord Pleanála*, which has just been mentioned in a different context. The point

---

[78] [2002] 1 I.L.R.M. 321 at 344–345.
[79] Wade and Forsyth, *Administrative Law* (2009), p.749.
[80] See *Nash v Findlay* (1901) 85 L.T. 682 and *Staden v Tarjanyi* (1980) 78 L.G.R. 614.

relevant here concerned a condition attached to permission for development as a golf club, which condition required the club to allow "access to the cliff path and cliff edges for interest groups". The High Court (Kearns J.) held[81]:

> "[This condition is] ... void for uncertainty. 'Interest groups' are not defined, there is no dedicated route or routes for them, the areas they are to approach are contiguous to many of the greens on the golf course and, of course, the condition contains no restriction as to numbers. Again, it is not difficult to envisage unpleasant altercations arising on the headland ... [F]urther no details have been agreed as to the composition of such groups or the time or times when they may go on the headland ..."

15–48   A more complex case is *Dublin City Council v Liffey Beat Ltd,*[82] in which a "planning injunction" under s.160 of the Planning Development Act 2000 was sought by the applicant Council. In the High Court, Quirke J.'s conclusion was that the word "nightclub" (used in the planning permission which had been granted and, it was contended, violated) was not sufficiently clear cut for judicial enforcement. The net result of the vagueness of the drafting and the lack of any later guidance from the local authority was that, if the injunction had been granted, the weasel would have been passed to the court.

15–49   A slightly different point here was well put in another authority[83]: "... it is not the function of the courts to seek to resolve questions involving planning policy by acting in effect as a form of planning tribunal". In other words, administrators should not attempt, by the use of vague language, either to avoid the duty of taking a decision or to retain a discretion after they have purported to exercise it. There are thus two policies underlying this judicial dislike of uncertainty: first, it leaves the property owner or other person affected possibly in a quandry; secondly, it throws a policy decision into the lap of the court.

15–50   But all this said, it is also the case that, in determining whether the terms of an administrative rule or action are sufficiently certain, the courts should take (as they have not always done) what might be called a constructive attitude to the interpretation of (say) planning conditions or regulations. The Interpretation Act 2005 ss.2(1) and 5(2), which apply widely to all manner of statutory rules and orders, enjoin the courts to take, where appropriate, a purposive, rather than a literal, destructive approach to interpretation.

(5) Inconsistency

15–51   In traditional judicial review, there is no separate category of "inconsistency". While there have not been many explicit sightings of inconsistency in Irish judicial review, there have certainly been a few cases in which the idea

---

[81] *Ashbourne Holdings v An Bord Pleanála* [2002] 1 I.L.R.M. 321 at 345 (HC). See also, [2003] 2 I.L.R.M. 446 at 462 (SC).

[82] [2005] 1 I.R. 478.

[83] *Grianan an Aileach Centre v Donegal County Council (No. 2)* [2004] 2 I.R. 625 at 635 (Supreme Court).

was drawn upon.[84] *State (Kenny) v Minister for Social Welfare*[85] was a case of this type. The Social Welfare (Consolidation) Act 1981 provided that a welfare payment should be made to an "unmarried mother". The central point in the case was that this expression had then been defined, by the relevant regulations, to cover a woman, "if, not being or *having been* a married woman, she is the mother of a child ..." (emphasis added). The consequence of this was to create an anomaly: the intention of the legislation, taken as a whole, appeared to include all unmarried women; yet the result of the definition was to draw an unjustifiable distinction: while mothers who were deserted wives, prisoner's wives, or unmarried were entitled to these payments, by contrast, mothers who had been married but whose marriage had been dissolved were excluded from this bounty. The applicant was a member of this latter category. Finding in her favour and striking down the regulation, Egan J. stated:

> "Could Parliament have intended that one single class of mother should be excluded from the same benefits as those to which other classes of mother would be entitled? Was it intended that such a mother should be punished together with her child or children because her marriage had been dissolved? I think not. To repeat the words of Henchy J. it would be 'oppressive' and 'unfair'."[86]

---

[84] For instance, in *COI v Minister for Justice, Equality and Law Reform* [2007] 2 I.L.R.M. 471 at 477–480, the applicant claimed successfully that the respondent had acted in denial of his constitutional right to equality of treatment within the asylum process. His submission was based on the fact that his case was treated by the Refugee Appeals Tribunal differently from that of his sister-in-law, despite the fact that there was similar country-of-origin information.

Counsel for the respondent had quoted from *TNF v Refugee Appeals Tribunal* [2005] IEHC 423; unreported, High Court, O'Leary J., December 21, 2005 at p.8: "... *the decision of a body in a particular case is neither evidence in another case nor does it create a binding authority for future cases*". In response, McGovern J. in *COI* quoted with approval from *PPA v Refugee Appeals Tribunal* [2007] 1 I.L.R.M. 288, in which Geoghegan J. stated (at 298): "... it is not that a member of a Tribunal is actually bound by previous decisions but consistency of decisions based on the same objective facts may, in appropriate circumstances, be a significant element in ensuring that a decision is objectively fair rather than arbitrary".

In conclusion, McGovern J. stated ([2007] 2 I.L.R.M. 471 at 479): "[i]t seems to me to be quite unjust that the applicant cannot go back to the RAC and the RAT on the same facts and with the information that his sister-in-law's application has been granted so that a general review of his case can take place". In short, the judge held that inconsistency in factual findings required the RAC, at least to review its initial finding against the applicant. This is a classic use of judicial review.

For other examples of what, in substance, may be regarded as inconsistency, see *Goodman v Sheehan* [2008] IEHC 127 (holding that, where the applicant had held a gun licence for several years, without mishap, it was unlawful not to renew the licence): *JN v Minister for Justice, Equality and Law Reform* [2009] 1 I.R. 146 at para.16 ("consistency is as desirable in the asylum world as it is in other areas of the legal world").

See also, e.g. *McHugh v Minister for Social Welfare* [1994] 2 I.R. 139 at 156, 159. *Cassidy v Minister for Industry and Commerce* [1978] I.R. 297; *Purcell v Attorney General* [1995] 3 I.R. 287 at 293–294; *NWR FM LTD v Broadcasting Commission of Ireland* [2004] 4 I.R. 50 at para.68.

[85] [1986] I.R. 693. Previous to this decision the Ombudsman had received complaints from a number of divorced women who had been refused a Deserted Wife's Allowance. In the then existing state of the law, he had been unable to make a finding of maladministration. However, as a result of *Kenny*, in cases where the divorce was recognised in Ireland, some of these women were able to claim Unmarried Mother's Allowance: see *Annual Report of the Ombudsman for 1987* (P. 5258), p.20.

[86] [1986] I.R. 693 at 696.

15–52   The notion of inconsistency falls readily under such other established rubrics as: unreasonableness; discrimination; bias; or even bad faith; or, in some situations, legitimate expectations. There is an obvious way, too, in which inconsistency could be given a constitutional footing: Art.40.1[87] provides that "all citizens shall, as human persons, be held equal before the law".

GCHQ–Keegan

15–53   Before going to the contemporary Irish law, in Part D, we consider, as a necessary stage of evolution, certain developments, here and in the UK, in the late 1980s. *Wednesbury* was reported in 1948 and, in its diffidence and vagueness, it is very much a product of its time, which may be regarded as the pre-Renaissance era in judicial review of administrative action. It was to be expected then that a later generation of English judges would attempt at least a restatement of the *Wednesbury* principles and this duly came (along with much else) in the *GCHQ* case. In the first place, Lord Diplock re-classified the entire of substantive judicial review under three heads, namely: "… 'illegality,' [= ultra vires], 'irrationality' [= unreasonableness] and 'procedural impropriety' [= constitutional justice, etc]."[88]

15–54   It is the second head—irrationality—which concerns us in this chapter. Lord Diplock went on to say of it:

> "By 'irrationality' I mean what can by now be succinctly referred to as '*Wednesbury* unreasonableness'. It applies to a decision which is so outrageous in its defiance of logic or of accepted moral standards that no sensible person who had applied his mind to the question to be decided could have arrived at it. Whether a decision falls within this category is a question that judges by their training and experience should be well equipped to answer, or else there would be something badly wrong with our judicial system …"

15–55   The British fall-out from the *GCHQ* case[89] is worthy of brief examination here, because post-*GCHQ* developments may be of indirect influence (via the ECHR) in the future tenor of Irish law. In Britain (where the judges lack what an Irish judge (speaking extra-judicially) has called "the nice secure foothold" of a written Constitution), traditionally the major constitutional foundation is the "sovereignty of Parliament" doctrine. It is this dogma which has inspired the conceptual strait-jacket of the ultra vires doctrine within which, until *GCHQ*, all judicial restrictions on administrative actions (save for error of law on the face of the record) had to be accommodated. Thus, all such restrictions had to be justified by reference to an imputed legislative intent. Against this background, it was more

---

[87]   See para.15–85.

[88]   *Council of Civil Service Unions v Minister for the Civil Service* [1985] A.C. 410 (also "*GCHQ*").

[89]   De Smith, *Judicial Review of Administrative Action* (1980), paras 11–073 to 11–086; Walker, "Unreasonableness and Proportionality" in Supperstone, Goudie and Walker (eds), *Judicial Review*, 3rd edn (London: Butterworths, 2005), Ch.8; Le Sueur, "The Rise and Ruin of Unreasonableness?" [2005] J.R. 32; Jowell and Lester, "Beyond *Wednesbury*: Substantive Principles of Administrative Law" (1987) *Public Law* 368; Gearty, "Administrative Law in the 1980s" (1987) 9 D.U.L.J. (N.S) 91. This last article has an over-generous review of the First Edition of the present book.

awkward for a court to invoke, as a controlling factor upon an administrative action, any factor which could not, however artificially, be justified by reference to the particular legislation involved.

15–56 Accordingly, it was felt by some British commentators that *GCHQ* afforded more appropriate, comprehensive and precise principles, by which to police the exercise of a discretionary power and so would enable a court to give a better-reasoned explanation as to why a decision was struck down or upheld. There would be less suspicion of judicial subjectivity than within the *Wednesbury* cocoon: a court would be better able than if it were wielding the blunt instrument of *Wednesbury* unreasonableness to articulate reasons which would repulse the accusation of (consciously or unconsciously) following its own beliefs.

15–57 Thus, some commentators emphasised the reclassification of the relevant law into (to use the vocabulary of the quotation from *GCHQ*) "illegality" and "irrationality". They used the contrast between these two factors to deduce that, whilst "illegality" is concerned with the infidelity of an official action to a statutory purpose and, thus, is tied to the intention of the legislature, by contrast, "irrationality", fortified by classification as an independent and distinct category, provides a device which emancipates a reviewing court to give greater weight to objectively significant considerations. Among these considerations are: bad administrative practice, such as unfairness or unjustifiable inconsistency; vagueness or lack of certainty in the effect of a decision or standard; and unjustifiable violation of fundamental rights. The sources of such fundamental rights include the European Convention on Human Rights and European Union law.

15–58 In short, a major feature of the *GCHQ* departure was that it represents a new way of articulating the boundary between the needs and interests of the public administrative body, and those of the private individual. Previously the way in which this had been expressed had pivoted around the public body: on the one hand its interests and those of the public which it served; and on the other hand, the need for safeguards against abuse of its power. Post-*GCHQ*, there was more focus on the positive interests of the individual adversely affected by the decision (often known, as a shorthand, as "a rights-based culture"). At first sight, this might appear to be merely a matter of whether one describes the same boundary from one side rather than another. However, in practice, this new formulation had consequences: the articulation of individual rights probably shifts the boundary in their favour and against the public body. As we shall see in Part C, this development has been taken further, following the adoption of the ECHR into English domestic law, by way of the Human Rights Act 1998.

15–59 In Ireland, in terms of direct response, the *GCHQ* reformulation fell on stony ground; the wording of the redefinition was implicitly rejected in the judgment of Henchy J. (with whom the other members of the court agreed on this point) in *State (Keegan) v The Stardust Victims Compensation Tribunal*.[90] Here, Henchy J. offered his own reformulation of *Wednesbury* unreasonableness:

> "The *Wednesbury* test of unreasonableness or irrationality has been considered

---

[90] [1986] I.R. 642.

in a number of subsequent cases and has been qualified to some extent. For example, in [*GCHQ*] Lord Diplock said of the *Wednesbury* test:

'It applies to a decision which is so outrageous in its defiance of logic or of accepted moral standards that no sensible person who had applied his mind to the question to be decided could have arrived at it.'

For my part, I would be slow to test unreasonableness by seeing if the decision accords with logic. Many examples could be given of reputable decisions and of substantive laws which reject logic in favour of other considerations. I think in any event that it is only a particular aspect of logic that could be applicable in testing the validity of a decision when it is subjected to judicial review on the ground of unreasonableness, namely, whether the conclusion reached in the decision can be said to flow from the premises. If it plainly does not, it stands to be condemned on the less technical and more understandable test of whether it is fundamentally at variance with reason and common sense.

As to the suggestion that the unreasonableness of a decision should be decided by the extent to which it fails to accord with *accepted moral* standards, I would be equally slow to accept that criterion. The concept of accepted moral standards represents a vague, elusive and changing body of standards which in a pluralist society is sometimes difficult to ascertain and is sometimes inappropriate or irrelevant to the decision in question (as it is to the decision in question in this case). The ethical or moral postulates of our Constitution will, of course, make certain decisions invalid for being repugnant to the Constitution, but in most cases a decision falls to be quashed for unreasonableness, not because of the extent to which it has departed from accepted moral standards (or positive morality), but because it is indefensible for being in the teeth of plain reason and common sense. I would myself consider that the test of unreasonableness or irrationality in judicial review lies in considering whether the impugned decision plainly and unambiguously flies in the face of fundamental reason and common sense. If it does, then the decision-maker should be held to have acted *ultra vires*; for the necessarily implied constitutional limitation of jurisdiction in all decision-making which affects rights or duties requires, *inter alia*, that the decision-maker must not flagrantly reject or disregard fundamental reason or common sense in reaching his decision."[91]

15–60   In commenting on this passage, it should be emphasised that reasonableness or irrationality (and each term has been used in Ireland, with the same meaning as was explained in *Keegan)*[92] will not always be a matter merely of sensible reasoning; not infrequently there will have to be a component based on morals or values. Such a component can, as Henchy J. stated, be drawn from the Constitution, augmented by what he called "common sense",[93] which can be taken to include community

---

[91] [1986] I.R. 642 at 658. Commenting on the various formulations in this passage, in *O'Keeffe v An Bord Pleanála* [1993] 1 I.R. 39, Finlay C.J. stated at 70: "I am satisfied that these ... different methods of expressing the circumstances under which a court can intervene are not in any way inconsistent one with the other, but rather complement each other and constitute not only a correct but a comprehensive description of the circumstances under which a court may, according to our law, intervene in such a decision on the basis of unreasonableness or irrationality."

[92] In *NWR FM v Broadcasting Commission of Ireland* [2004] 3 I.R. 50 at 83–84, 86, the expression "irrational or unreasonable" is used on the apparent assumption that there is no difference.

[93] cp. Oscar Wilde, "that uncommon thing called commonsense".

values. As we shall see, Henchy J.'s reformulation in *Keegan* has been quoted with approval, especially in the 1990s.[94] But, by the 2000s, it has been largely overtaken by the complicated law outlined in the next Part.

C. CONTEMPORARY IRISH LAW: "CURIAL DEFERENCE"; COMMUNITY INTERESTS; FUNDAMENTAL RIGHTS

Summary of this Part

15–61 Against this background, we can summarise the contemporary law, which is explained in this Part. As we noted at the outset of this chapter, the law is in flux. The base line remains what is conveniently known as *Wednesbury* unreasonableness, with its three sub-heads of bad faith, taking irrelevant factors into account and unreasonableness (in the narrow sense). But the law is also changing and, to some extent, has been overlaid by three other lines of law which, as explained below, are in tension with each other. Thus, this Part is organised as follows:

(1) "Curial deference"[95];
(2) Countervailing Community interests and qualification to individual rights;
(3) Constitution, ECHR and European Union Law.

15–62 The basic policies in this field—the notion that the courts must respect the knowledge and experience of public administrators, while at the same time respecting the rights of persons affected by the exercise of discretionary powers— have not changed. Consequently, there are great similarities between *Wednesbury* and the new developments under examination in this Part. Notably, the *Wednesbury* notion that it is only in extreme cases that a court may intervene on a substantive point in review proceedings is represented by "Curial deference" in (1) below, or the *Keegan* principle mentioned at the end of Part B. In most situations, the impact made by significant individual rights is qualified by (2), countervailing community interests. Thus, as explained below, in most cases, the net effect of (2) would be to reinforce (1).

15–63 Pulling in the opposite direction is source (3), comprising the constitutional

---

[94] e.g. *Breen v Minister for Defence* [1994] 2 I.R. 34 at 42; *O'Keeffe v An Bord Pleanála* [1993] 1 I.R. 39; [1992] I.L.R.M. 237; *Ferris v Dublin County Council*, unreported, Supreme Court, November 7, 1990 at pp.9–10. See also, *Garda Representative Association v Ireland* [1994] 1 I.L.R.M. 81 at 89; *Doran v Commissioner of An Garda Síochána* [1994] 1 I.L.R.M. 303 at 311; *Matthews v Irish Coursing Club* [1993] 1 I.R. 346; *Ryan v Compensation Tribunal* [1997] 1 I.L.R.M. 194 at 199; and *Dietacarbon v An Bord Pleanála* [2005] 1 I.L.R.M. 32 at 50. This also mentions the interaction between ultra vires and irrationality.

 In *McAlister v Minister for Justice* [2003] 1 I.L.R.M. 161 at 168, Finnegan P. stated: "[t]he applicant has urged ... that I should substitute for the test in [*Keegan*] the test of proportionality enunciated in *R(Daly) v. Home Secretary* [2001] 2 WLR 1622. [*Keegan*] is a decision of the Supreme Court and has been consistently applied by the Supreme Court (See, e.g. *Z v. Minister for Justice, Equality and Law Reform* [2002] I.L.R.M. 215). It is not open to this court to set the same aside".

 See also, the list of approving authorities compiled by counsel at *Ryanair v Flynn* [2000] 3 I.R. 240 at 259–260.

[95] Sayeed, "Beyond the Language of Deference" [2005] J.R. 111.

and other higher rights, the explanation of which is sufficiently complicated to require division into three sections. At first, what might be called a significant minority of judges were of the view that, where the individual rights which were trenched upon by the exercise of the discretionary power were established by the Constitution, then the exercise of the power should be subjected to "anxious scrutiny". How the recently decided case of *Meadows v Minister for Justice, Equality and Law Reform*[96] has affected the position is not yet entirely clear. As we argue at paras 15–103 to 15–112, the "steer" which it appears to have given the law is to shift the focus from constitutionally protected rights to any rights which, in the circumstances, have significant value for the individual. In addition, the *Meadows* majority expressed a preference for the proportionality test, as a means of balancing the loss to the individual against the gain to the community or public body. The net result seems to have been a cautious increase in the extent to which a discretionary power may be reviewed. In Part D, we offer a comment on the tangled area of law described in Parts B. and C.

(1) "Curial deference"

15–64 Over the past two decades, running from *Keegan* and its predecessor *Sharpe*[97] to *Meadows*, the Supreme Court appears to have kept narrow the grounds on which the exercise of a discretionary power will be struck down. This definite mood-swing against judicial review, for unreasonableness or any of its sub-heads or successors, was made express first in *P&F Sharpe v Dublin City and County Manager*, and then, in very similar terms, in *O'Keeffe v An Bord Pleanála*.[98] This has now been subjected to considerable, though rather indefinite, swing back, represented by *Meadows*. For the moment, we focus on what is often referred to as the *Keegan–O'Keeffe* phase. In *O'Keeffe*, the respondent had granted planning permission for the erection of a long wave radio transmitting station, including a 300-metre-high mast. This permission had been given in the face of recommendations against the grant of permission, contained in reports, drawn up by the Board's inspector and a technical inspector, respectively. The reports emphasised the effects of electromagnetic interference on an area of radius seven kilometres around the development, in which 5,000 people lived. The outcome of the case is not especially significant since on the view of the facts, adopted by the Supreme Court, there was ample evidence in the reports which justified the Board in rejecting the inspector's recommendations. Much more striking is the tone of the following passage, from Finlay C.J.'s judgment:

> "[T]he circumstances under which the court can intervene on *the basis of irrationality with the decisionmaker involved in an administrative function* are limited and rare. It is of importance and, I would think, of assistance to consider not only as was done by Henchy J. in [*Keegan*] the circumstances under which the court can and should intervene, but also … the circumstances under which the court cannot intervene.
>
> The Court cannot interfere with the decision of an administrative decision-making authority merely on the grounds that (a) it is satisfied that on the facts as found it would have raised different inferences and conclusions, or

---

[96]   [2010] IESC 3; [2010] 2 I.R. 710.
[97]   *P&F Sharpe v Dublin City and County Manager* [1989] I.R. 701 at 718–719. On *Sharpe*, see H & M, para.15–107.
[98]   [1993] 1 I.R. 39.

(b) it is satisfied that the case against the decision made by the authority was much stronger than the case for it.

...

I am satisfied that in order for an applicant for judicial review to satisfy a court that the decision-making authority has acted irrationally in the sense which I have outlined above so that the court can intervene and quash its decision, it is necessary that the applicant should establish to the satisfaction of the court that *the decision-making authority had before it no relevant material which* would support its decision."[99]

15–65 This policy continued under Finlay C.J.'s successor, Hamilton C.J. He felt so strongly on the point that, although not himself giving a full judgment, he offered an eleven-line "preface" to the court's judgment in *Denny v Minister for Social Welfare*,[100] which included the following statement: "... tribunals have been given statutory tasks to perform and exercise their functions ... with a high degree of expertise and provide coherent and balanced judgments on the evidence and arguments heard by them, [and] it should not be necessary for the courts to review their decision ...". It has even been said that "... to be reviewable [as irrational] it is not sufficient that a decision-maker goes wrong or even hopelessly and fundamentally wrong: he must have gone completely and inexplicably mad; taken leave of his senses and come to an absurd conclusion".[101]

15–66 Despite these strong statements, a number of cases, even from the *Keegan–Meadows* era, attest to the fact that, even leaving aside Constitutional rights, the doctrine of unreasonableness retains some vitality. One example is *Matthews v Irish Coursing Club Ltd.*[102] The respondents (who are given statutory

[99] [1993] 1 I.R. 39 at 71–72 (emphasis added). See also, *Maher v An Bord Pleanála* [1993] 1 I.R. 439; *Boyhan v Beef Tribunal* [1993] 1 I.R. 217 at 221; *Schwestermann v An Bord Pleanála* [1994] 3 I.R. 437 at 447; *Littondale v Wicklow County Council* [1996] 2 I.L.R.M. 519 at 534; *O'Reilly v O'Sullivan*, unreported, High Court, Laffoy J., July 25, 1996 at p.19, quoted with approval in *Ashbourne v An Bord Pleanála* [2002] 1 I.L.R.M. 321 at 342; *Crofton v Minister for the Environment, Heritage and Local Government* [2009] IEHC 114 (Hedigan J.) at paras 34–35.
  Contrast the observation quoted in the text above with the very different passage in the High Court judgment in *P&F Sharpe Ltd v Dublin City and County Manager* [1989] I.R. 710; [1989] I.L.R.M. 565 at 571, which is quoted in the Second Edition of this book at pp.506–507.
[100] [1998] 1 I.R. 34 at 37–38.
[101] *Aer Rianta Cpt v Commissioner for Aviation Regulation*, unreported, High Court, O'Sullivan J., January 16, 2003 at p.48, cited with approval in *Kildare County Council v An Bord Pleanála* [2006] IEHC 173; unreported, High Court, MacMenamin J., March 10, 2006 at para.78. However, in *Neurendale Ltd (t/a Panda Waste Services) v Dublin City Council* [2009] IEHC 588 at para.181, McKechnie J. remarked tartly: "[i]n my view it is not possible to have, as a requirement of reasonableness, insanity before the courts may intervene ... were this test to be applied generally, there could be a risk of it offending the Remedies Directive (89/665/EEC). [See *SIAC Construction v Mayo County Council* [2002] 3 I.R. 148 at para.176]".
  The quotation in the text recalls Virgil's classical metaphor about piling Ossa on Pelion, each of these Greek mountains being about 2,000 metres in height.
[102] [1993] 1 I.R. 346. Note, however that in regard to a different aspect of the case, O'Hanlon J. stated: "While one might quarrel with the decision to overrule the sub-committee and to relieve the notice party from the fine ... and also to lift the suspension of the greyhound ... I would accept that this was a legitimate exercise of the discretion vested in the executive committee and should not be interfered with by the court."
  For another example of a successful plea of unreasonableness, see *Musheva v Minister*

responsibility for greyhound meetings) found that the winning dog at a coursing meeting had been drugged. Having found the owner of the winning dog guilty, the Club simply imposed a fine, but allowed her to keep the trophy. The owner of the runner-up dog was successful in his application to have this decision set aside as being unreasonable. Here, it is worth noting that the Club's decision would have affected what was close to being the legal right of an individual (the owner of the runner-up) and this could have been a particular factor impelling the court to intervene to ensure that the innocent dog had its day. Again, in *O'Leary v Maher*[103] it was held that even the *Keegan* test was satisfied and the refusal to grant a new gun licence was quashed on the grounds of "irrationality and illogicality". The particular feature on which Clarke J. focused was that the licensing agency was prepared to grant a licence for a different heavy-calibre gun, but not the one applied for, simply because the gun applied for was of the same calibre as the weapons used by the national forces: in view of this motivation "... the safety argument becomes illogical". What these decisions—in each of which the applicant did succeed—have in common is that they concerned situations which were of great importance to the individual affected; but much less for the wider purposes of the public body. Nevertheless, the *Keegan* line of curial deference[104] has been followed and cited with approval on several occasions.[105]

---

for Justice, Equality and Law Reform, unreported, High Court, Finlay Geoghegan J., July 25, 2003 (reason advanced by the Minister to justify a refusal to revoke a deportation was that the spouses had not been residing together, but this state of affairs arose from the fact that the wife had been deported: this reasoning was described by Finlay Geoghegan J. as "Catch 22"); *Carrigaline Co. Ltd v Minister for Transport* [1997] 1 I.L.R.M. 241 at 297.

[103] [2008] IEHC 113; unreported, High Court, April 24, 2008 at paras 47–49.

[104] Some authorities refer to it thus, while others speak of "*Keegan*" or "*O'Keeffe*": the difference is not significant.

[105] See, e.g. *McEvoy v Meath County Council* [2003] 1 I.R. 208 at 227; *Garda Representative Association v Ireland* [1994] 1 I.L.R.M. 81, confirming the High Court (Murphy J.) at [1989] I.L.R.M. 1; *ACT Shipping Ltd v Minister for Marine* [1995] 3 I.R. 406; *Fairleigh Ltd v Temple Bar Properties Ltd* [1999] 2 I.R. 508. (For more discussion, see Third Edition, pp.646–647.) In *McCarron v Superintendent Kearney* [2008] IEHC 195 at para.18, Charleton J. stated: "To interfere on any lesser test [than *Keegan*] would cause this Court to trespass on an executive function and so infringe the separation of powers doctrine."

Even where the proceedings take the form of a statutory appeal rather than judicial review, curial deference must still be observed: see *M&J Gleeson v Competition Authority* [1999] I.L.R.M. 401 at 409–410 (a statutory appeal from a decision of the Competition Authority).

Tellingly, in *Scrollside v Broadcasting Commission of Ireland* [2007] 1 I.R. 166, the successful applicant had been broadcasting illegally for 12 years, and yet the Commission allowed them to count this period as experience, in opposition to the lawful competitor. In judicial review proceedings, the Supreme Court majority, nevertheless, upheld the Commission's decision. The court thus allowed a good deal of latitude to the Commission. Writing for the majority, Denham J.'s ruling (at para.124) on this point seems to have been dictated by her view that it was the respondent's policy to consider applications from former pirates and that "... this policy is not irrational, it is a type of decision that a specialist body might arrive at in light of all the circumstances in the industry. Indeed, a policy of enticing persons who have been acting outside the law into legal processes is not unknown in other aspects of Irish life".

Scrollside is an unusual case, in that it was the applicant rather than, as usually, the respondent who (in effect) sought to rely on public policy. The applicant failed because the Supreme Court, applying the policy of judicial deference, took the deferential view that a lot of latitude should be allowed to the respondent. (Incidentally, this seems to mark a further widening of the scope of the irrational–unreasonable test, in that public policy has usually, for instance in other fields, such as contract or trusts, been regarded as a matter on which the courts need not be deferential.)

Less deference for deference?

15–67 In justifying the *Keegan* line against judicial review, as we have seen in the quotations just given, certain judges have emphasised the expertise of the bodies whose decisions are under review and the lack of expertise of judges in such area.[106]

15–68 But, as against this, it has been argued that it is bad policy for such consideration to apply to *all* tribunals.[107] One way of discriminating among public bodies, in the treatment accorded on judicial review, would be to distinguish public bodies which are under democratic control (most commonly, a Minister) from executive agencies, whose members are all appointed by the Government or a Minister (this type of justification being referred to as "legitimacy-deference". A second basis (referred to as "fact-deference") would discriminate according to whether or not the public body under review had a special expertise relevant to the issue in the review, which was not available to the High Court.

15–69 This category is illustrated by *Efe v Minister for Justice, Equality and Law Reform*,[108] in which the applicants were a Nigerian family, of which one spouse had been given permission to remain in the state but this permission had been denied to the other and the applicants were challenging the validity of the consequential deportation. The judgment of Hogan J. in *Efe* contains interesting observations concerning the need for a more discriminatory approach to curial deference, which should probably be taken as applying to decisions relating not only to facts, but also at least low-level questions of judgement. The judge notes, first of all, that decision which emanate from agencies with technical and administrative skills have long[109] enjoyed a special degree of deference. Hogan J. then goes on to remark that:

> "18. Quite independently of questions of technical expertise, there are naturally certain types of issues which do not admit of easy resolution if ordinary legal standards and principles ... are to be employed. Thus, in the sphere of planning and development, the resolution of questions involving technical engineering assessments, sustainability, and even taste probably admit of limited judicial involvement. This is, as Denham J. pointed out in

[106] *O'Keeffe v An Bord Pleanála* [1993] 1 I.R. 39 at 71–72 (emphasis added). See also, *Orange v Director of Telecommunications Regulations* [2000] 4 I.R. 159 at 238.
[107] In *Meadows v Minister for Justice, Equality and Law Reform* [2010] IESC 3, Denham J., while placing substantial emphasis (at paras 7 and 24) on *Keegan*, also stated that "... the application of the strict nature of the test in *O'Keeffe* ... is limited to decisions of skilled or otherwise technically competent decision-makers ... such as planning and development". But see Hardiman J.'s riposte, at 20, which states: "I would not withhold this description [*sc.* skilled ... decision-maker] from the Minister ...". See, supporting the Denham line, Hogan, "Judicial Review, the doctrine of reasonableness and the immigration process" [2001] *Bar Review* 329, commenting on *Camara v Minister for Justice, Equality and Law Reform*, unreported, High Court, Kelly J., July 26, 2000. One should add that in *Camara*, the issue in dispute was on the facts rather than the reasonableness of the decision. (For this distinction, see para.15–72.) Despite the involvement of constitutional rights, Kelly J. used the language of *O'Keeffe* unreasonableness.
[108] [2011] 2 I.L.R.M. 411. In *O v Refugee Appeals Tribunal* [2012] IEHC 48; unreported, High Court, February 2, 2012 the court quashed a decision of the RAT on a point of fact, admittedly in rather extreme circumstances.
[109] See, e.g. *Philadelphia Storage Battery Co. v Controller of Industrial and Commercial Property* [1935] I.R. 575.

Meadows, quintessentially the kind of decision attracting the specialised deference which the Supreme Court had in mind in *O'Keeffe* ... At the other end of the spectrum, for example, the question of whether the compulsory acquisition of land was objectively necessary in the public interest squarely engages the substantive protection of property rights and, as Geoghegan J. so carefully explained in *Clinton (No.2)*, these rights would not be adequately protected by a test which was satisfied by showing that there was a reasonable basis for the decision.

19. So far as asylum and immigration decisions are concerned, much might depend ... on the experience and expertise of the particular decision-maker in the context of the decision at hand ... Issues arising from Albanian blood feuds are perhaps a good case in point ... If, in this sort of unusual case, the decision-maker was shown to have this type of expertise, then of course the courts should generally defer to it."

15–70   In contrast to the last mentioned hypothetical situation, on the facts in the instant case, the decision-maker was not called upon to make a judgment upon the plausibility of an asylum claim by reference to specific internal events in the country of origin. Rather what was fundamentally at issue was the likely effect of the deportation on the applicant's family, in particular children, and whether it was realistic to expect the remainder of the family to travel to Nigeria, if the deportation order were upheld. Accordingly, "[i]t cannot be said that administrative decision-makers enjoy a specialist knowledge or expertise in relation to such matters. Besides, these decisions engage fundamental rights under Art. 41 of the Constitution the protection of which is the solemn duty of this court."

15–71   At the same time, while there is a good deal of force in these criticisms, any refinement of the law carries with it the seeds of over-complication. For instance, would a reviewing court really want to drill down into the actual stated knowledge or experience of the entity before it, as compared with the level of either, which might be available to the court from expert witnesses? Once the High Court departs from the simplicity of the "no evidence" rule, it could find itself on a slippery slope. In an appropriate case, would members of the Refugee Appeals Tribunal be cross-examined as regards their knowledge of Albanian blood-feuds? And, even if their knowledge turns out to be at a high level, might they then be said to be biased? In addition, beyond the field of primary facts, a good deal of the work of many tribunals, such as Bord Pleanála or the economic and sectoral regulatory authorities[110] consists of building up and administering a consistent policy line, against which primary facts are assessed. Judges, who see only random cases in the particular field, whose formation is in favour of the actual individual visible before them and whose main work will usually lie elsewhere, are not in a good position to develop such expertise. Finally, any development along the lines under consideration here would fly in the face of four centuries of judicial review and release a torrent of applications: "be careful what you wish for".

15–72   Finally, one should flag up an organisational-jargon point. A number of

---

[110]   On policy-orientated tribunals, see para.6–17.

modern judgments[111] appear to conflate two streams of law which have traditionally been regarded as distinct. These streams are: the law relating to the control of discretionary power; and that concerning the extent to which the High Court, in review proceedings, can consider whether the decision before it includes any factual error (on which see Chapter 10, Part F). In commenting on this sweeping together of blocs of law which have traditionally been separate, one must concede that the two had always had a good deal of underlying policy in common: namely that each engages the same sort of compromise as between respect for the autonomy of the tribunal or other public body, and the desire to see justice done in an individual case. Nevertheless, the classic tests did involve different standards, that for facts ("no evidence") being even more stringent than the discretionary powers test. At the very least, it would be useful if there were to be an express judicial declaration of this change. That said, one should add that the borderline between the two areas, which is being championed here, is frequently muddied, in that the test before the tribunal or the body is not always one of basic fact, but may be called future fact. One example, common in deportation cases such as *Efe*, is that the test may turn on what may happen to the applicant if they are deported to their home country. The view taken on this, by a tribunal or Minister, depends, in part, on a finding on a claim made by the applicant about what had happened to them earlier, in their home country, coupled with a prediction as to what may happen in future.

(2) Countervailing community interests and qualification to individual rights

15–73 The heading "Countervailing community interests" is not a term to be found in any judgment. We are taking it to refer to cases in which an applicant has sought to rely upon damage to their individual interest, but has failed because the court has given greater emphasis to the needs of the administrative arrangement or scheme under attack. In other words, "Community interests" refer simply to such interests as the general community interest in the provision of some smooth-running, economic and non-discriminatory public service or system.[112] The impact of curial deference and of community interest usually each pull in the same direction,[113] which happens to be against individual rights. It is true that there is a theoretical difference between deference and community interests, namely that the thrust of deference is to restrain the courts from exercising jurisdiction altogether. By contrast, if the community interest principle were to be properly applied, it would require some scrutiny of the alleged community interest to evaluate it properly.[114]

---

[111] e.g. *O'Keeffe v An Bord Pleanála* [1993] 1 I.R. 39 at 71–72; *Dumbrell v Governor of Mountjoy*, unreported, Supreme Court, December 2, 1993.

[112] See McAuslan, "Administrative Law, Collective Consumption and Judicial Policy" (1983) 45 M.L.R. 1.

[113] An exception would be where it happened that it was the applicant, rather than the respondent public body, whom it suited to rely on community interest. This is illustrated by the unsuccessful argument in *Scrollside v Broadcasting Commission of Ireland* [2007] 1 I.R. 166, summarised in fn.105.

[114] There was a sign of such scrutiny in *Mahon Tribunal v Keena* [2009] IESC 64, in which the Supreme Court held for the respondent newspaper in a case in which a tribunal of inquiry sought an order requiring the newspaper to identify the source of a leak regarding an investigation being carried out by the tribunal. One part of the court's judgment emphasised the strength of the freedom of expression interest, which was the constitutional or ECHR right at stake. But

But, in practice, a court might not feel qualified to do this, so that the two principles become, in effect, the same thing.

15–74 Until recently, the notion of community interest had not been given its due acknowledgement in review proceedings; probably because these focus on the position of the individual who happens to be before the court. By contrast, they do not always take into account the wider public interest which the respondent public body, with its definite existence, must serve. It is true that the celebrated passage from *Wednesbury*, quoted earlier, does throw out a reference to "public policy"; but this has received little attention. One case in which the term "public policy" was used (with the approximate meaning of community interest) is *LC v Minister for Justice, Equality and Law Reform*,[115] in which the applicant had stated that she would commit suicide if she were deported. The respondent's submission was that "no one can say whether such a threat will be effected or not ... however, public policy cannot be such that the law will not be applied in the face of such a threat". Adopting this argument, Hanna J. stated:

> "... a Minister is entitled, not just to look at cases in total isolation, although each case must be dealt with on its own merits. He can, and indeed should apply his mind to matters of public policy. Such an exercise is integral to its executive and administrative functions."

15–75 At a broader level, the message of this case is that a decision-maker is legitimately concerned with the broader reaches of public policy and may take into account considerations beyond the individual case of the applicant before the court. In other cases, too, the need for a balance between, on the one hand, the interests of an immigrant and, on the other, the State's "legitimate interest in the control of immigration"[116] has been acknowledged.

15–76 *Prendergast v Minister for Education*[117] is a graphic example, from another field of public administration, of a situation in which it was sought to use a constitutional right to invalidate a wide-reaching collectivist scheme established as a matter of high policy. At issue in *Prendergast* was a scheme by which a limit had been imposed on the numbers of places at medical schools reserved for Irish or other EU students, whilst there was a different quota of places to be filled by non-EU citizens paying a premium rate of fees. The conditions stated that no Irish students could apply for these places in this latter quota. It should be emphasised

---

another aspect of the judgment queried the strength of the harm actually done to the tribunal's investigation by the publication.

[115] [2007] 2 I.R. 135. The quotations in the passage are at paras 36 and 10 respectively. For another exception which does use the term "public policy", see *Scrollside v Broadcasting Commission of Ireland* [2007] 1 I.R. 166.

[116] *TC v Minister for Justice* [2005] 4 I.R. 109 at 111. See also, *AA and EP v Minister for Justice, Equality and Law Reform* [2005] 4 I.R. 564 at para.29; *Cirpaci v Minister for Justice, Equality and Law Reform* [2005] 2 I.L.R.M. 547 at 556–557. Fennelly J. repeated this passage in another deportation case: *TC v Minister for Justice* [2005] 4 I.R. 109 at 119; *AO and DL v Minister for Justice, Equality and Law Reform* [2003] 1 I.R. 1 at 155.

[117] [2009] 1 I.L.R.M. 47. The quotation is at paras 66 and 67. See also, *Garda Representative Association v Minister for Finance* [2010] IEHC 78, in which the facts were rather extreme, in that the GRA was claiming that it was unreasonable of the Minister not to exempt them from financial emergency measures.

here, as it was in the judgment, that the Minister's scheme was squarely based on the report into medical education, prepared by a committee, chaired by Dr Fottrell (former President of University College Galway).

15–77 The plaintiff put his case on the basis that he was being unconstitutionally discriminated against by an exercise of the Minister's discretion. In the High Court, Charleton J.'s approach was that:

> "[W]ere I to strike down the existing Fottrell scheme as an unconstitutional inequality, I must consider the effect that it would have. I am not entitled to act in an unthinking way. Furthermore, I am only entitled to act within the limit of my authority, which is to correct legal wrongs and not to set government policy ... Is the court ... to strike down a carefully thought through government policy based merely on looking at one side of the situation?"

15–78 In deciding whether in effect to strike down the scheme, the judge took into account the various wider consequences of doing so, among them the fact that admitting Irish students to the fee-paying quota would be likely to lead to an over-supply of Irish medical graduates, and to constitute discrimination against those Irish students who would not be able to afford the premium-rate fees.

15–79 Charleton J. also decided a broadly similar case, albeit with rather extreme circumstances, namely *Garda Representative Association v Minister for Finance*.[118] The facts centred on the deductions from public service pay authorised by the Financial Emergency Measures in the Public Interest Act 2009, in particular s.8 which allows the Minister for Finance to exempt a particular class of public servants from deductions. The applicant claimed that there were special features of a Garda's employment (for instance, the facts that they were not permitted legally to strike, and were under an obligation to do overtime) which rendered it unreasonable of the Minister not to exempt them. Rejecting this argument, the judge opened by stating[119]:

> "The Government has the power to set policy on areas of national interest and to disperse funds in accordance with that policy. These decisions are, in my view, in a category beyond the scope of judicial review: *Prendergast* ... [W]here on the other hand rights and obligations are set out by statute whereby funds may be made available to those applying in particular circumstances, or where a licence to conduct an otherwise prohibited activity may be made available, the executive power is limited in its operation by the wording of the statute."

---

[118] [2010] IEHC 78. Section 8 of the Act was drafted in rather extreme terms: "Where the Minister is satisfied that there is a particular class or group of public servants who, by reason of exceptional circumstances ... which, in the Minister's opinion, are materially distinguished from other classes or groups, then the Minister, if he or she considers it to be just and equitable in all the circumstances to do so, may by direction ...". Hardly surprisingly, the judge rejected the applicant's argument, at para.25. See, to broadly similar effect, *Unite the Union v Minister for Finance* [2010] IEHC 354; unreported, High Court, October 8, 2010.

[119] [2010] IEHC 78 at paras 15–16.

15–80 In the context of this typology, the judge located the Government's decision in the instant case at the earlier end of the spectrum, that is low intensity of judicial review, if any. Charleton J. emphasised the subject matter and its surrounding context, about which he remarked: "[the 2009 Act] is both policy based and fiscal".[120] Unsurprisingly, the applicant failed.

15–81 A broadly analogous situation may be conjectured in the planning field. Let us assume that planning permission is sought for the establishment of a large supermarket on the perimeter of a medium-sized town. The effect of this development would be to suck the economic life out of the traditional commercial centre and heart of the town, with: the bankruptcy of small to medium-sized shops; increase in unemployment; degeneration or loss of amenities in what may have been an historic centre. The question is whether these significant consequences could lawfully be taken into account by the local planning authority or An Bord Pleanála, so as to empower them to refuse permission for the large supermarket. It is suggested that cases like *Prendergast, Garda Representative Association* and those in the field of immigration have widened the range of factors which a planning authority may lawfully rely upon.[121] Consequently, the factors mentioned in the previous paragraph could be regarded as intra vires.

(3) Constitution, ECHR and European Union law

15–82 Part B examined the question of whether a discretionary power has been exercised within what may be called "common law judicial review". The other form of control, outlined here, tests whether the action or its parent legislation is in line with the Constitution (with assistance from the ECHR and European Union law). In broad terms, there are two ways in which the Constitution[122] has been used, in regard to the control of discretionary power: proportionality and constitutional or fundamental rights. Proportionality is directed at the level of protection; while constitutional rights concern the character of the individual right/interest which is protected. These two elements are outlined in (a) and (b) below; while in (c), the two are brought together in our analysis of *Meadows*. Unfortunately, the linkage between the two leaves a lot of unanswered questions, of which the main one (elaborated below) is whether the proportionality doctrine applies where non-constitutional rights are engaged. Finally, in (d), there is a brief survey of the impact of European Union and ECHR law.

(a) Proportionality

15–83 The usual use of proportionality has been to balance the gains of a public body against the harm to an individual, caused by the particular administrative action. (Essentially this is the "*ends v means*" equation.) However, it has occasionally been used to test the reasonableness of a decision, from the perspective of the public body, and to take into account, for instance, the inconvenience or labour created by a particular procedural protection for an individual. Thus, in *Barry v Sentence*

---

[120] [2010] IEHC 78 at para.23.
[121] This, of course, would represent a reversal of the pure doctrine of *State (Flanagan) v Galway County Council* [1990] 2 I.R. 66.
[122] For a summary of all the uses of the Constitution in administrative law, see para.2–32.

Review Group and the Minister for Justice, Equality and Law Reform[123] in regard to a procedural point, it was held that, subject to privilege, "... the applicant must *prima facie*, be entitled to sight of all documents, which are considered by the first respondent in coming to a decision on a recommendation to the second respondent. This is not in any way an onerous requirement and is proportionate".[124]

15–84   Another form in which proportionality may be used, which has not, however, received much attention in Irish case law, would be to compare the costs of the method which has been adopted by the public body to secure the objective, with the costs which would be entailed by some possible alternative method of achieving the same objective. With this exercise, it might be necessary to enter in the balance not only the costs of the alternative method to the individuals affected but also, as a set off, those which would be incurred by the public body. All this evaluation and balancing could impose considerable demands upon a judge—demands which s/he might not be qualified to meet, either by experience or capacity, or by virtue of the information available.

15–85   The principle of proportionality[125] offers, as we shall see, a refined and more applied version of equality[126] in Art.40.1, by which "[a]ll citizens shall, as human persons, be held equal before the law [subject to certain specified exceptions] ...".[127] The connection, between Art.40.1 and the doctrine of proportionality, is that the idea of equal treatment before the law draws with it the idea that, if there are any differences in treatment, these are only justifiable if they bear some sensible proportion to differences in circumstances. And this is, in a nutshell, the principle of proportionality.

15–86   In addition we ought to note that, apart from Art.40.1, wherever substantive rights given by the Constitution are concerned, some notion of proportionality is always involved. An example is the ban on religious discrimination in Art.44.2.3°, which states that the State, in providing aid for schools, must not "discriminate" between schools.[128] This arises from the fact that some constitutionally authorised exemption from the right will usually also be at issue and, in reconciling the two, it is always assumed that there must be a balance between the significance of the purpose served by the law or administrative action and, on the other hand, the damage to the constitutional right which is caused.[129]

---

[123] [2001] 4 I.R. 167.

[124] [2001] 4 I.R. 167 at 169.

[125] Buckley, "Merging Principles of Public Law: Towards Proportionality in an Irish Context" (2004) 39 Ir. Jur. 161; Foley, "The Proportionality Test: Present Problems" (2008) 1 *Judicial Studies Institute Journal* 61; Sales and Hooper, "Proportionality and the Form of Law" (2004) 120 L.Q.R. 426.

[126] *cp. CCSU v Minister for Civil Service* [1985] A.C. 374 at 410 (Lord Diplock).

[127] Blayney J. had Art.40.1 in mind in *Purcell v Attorney General* [1995] 3 I.R. 287, a case in which it was held to be invalid to enforce a taxing statute (Farm Tax Act 1985) against some only of the persons within its scope. For cases involving equality under EU law, see *Bloomer v Incorporated Law Society of Ireland* [1995] 3 I.R. 14 at 45–51 and *Re Colgan* [1997] 1 C.M.L.R. 53.

[128] See, e.g. *Quinn's Supermarket v Attorney General* [1972] I.R. 1; *Mulloy v Minister for Education* [1975] I.R. 88; *M v An Bord Uchtála* [1975] I.R. 81.

[129] See *Heaney v Ireland* [1994] 3 I.R. 593 at 607, 608–609. For comment, see Hogan, "The Constitution, Property Rights and Proportionality" (1997) 32 *Irish Jurist* 373.

15–87   The initial question is whether the doctrine of proportionality applies to judicial review of administrative actions, as well as to constitutional review of laws. After an initial wobble,[130] it is plain that it does. For example, in *Warnock v The Revenue Commissioners*[131] the plaintiff accountants claimed that a notice issued by the Revenue Commissioners (under s.59 of the Finance Act 1974) to provide certain information regarding the accountants' clients' affairs was unduly "burdensome and oppressive" in that compliance would involve an excessive amount of the accountants' staff time. The claim failed on the facts, although Costello J. appears to have accepted that, in extreme enough circumstances, the claim would have succeeded. Another example is the case of *Balkan Tours v Minister for Communications*.[132] This case was an appeal to the High Court from the Minister's revocation of a tour operator's licence. The rather brief basis of Lynch J.'s decision was that "the revocation of the licences would cause damage to the plaintiffs which would be disproportionate to their default …".[133]

15–88   Two questions then arise. First, does the doctrine apply only where it is some "constitutionally protected", rather than merely "legally protected", interest of the applicant which is at stake? Secondly, where it is applied, what difference would the proportionality doctrine make: would it lead to a more "anxious" scrutiny than *Wednesbury* unreasonableness?[134] As we shall see below, the cause of proportionality has recently received a blood transfusion, in the form of the majority judgments in *Meadows v Minister for Justice, Equality and Law Reform*.[135] They plumped for an infusion of *Keegan* by the principle of proportionality; and—to go back to the first point raised above—may have indicated that this should be so, regardless of whether constitutional rights were involved. This point will be explored further at paras 15–27 to 15–28. However, here, we need to raise another point.

Does "proportionality" take the law beyond "reasonableness"?

15–89   The present emphasis on "proportionality" naturally provokes the question:

[130]   cp. the comments of Keane J. in *Radio Limerick One Ltd v Independent Radio and Television Commission* [1997] 2 I.L.R.M. 1 at 20 (though, at 20, the judge also states: "… in some cases, at least, the disproportion between the gravity or otherwise of a breach of a condition attached to a statutory privilege and the permanent withdrawal of the privilege could be so gross as to render the revocation unreasonable within the *Wednesbury* or *Keegan* formulation").
[131]   [1986] I.L.R.M. 37. See also, *Re Gallagher's Application (No. 2)* [1996] 3 I.R. 10 at 63–65, where Kelly J. expressly applied the principle of proportionality in considering the validity of an executive decision, albeit one which impacted on a constitutional right, viz, liberty. See also, *Fajujonu v Minister for Justice* [1990] I.L.R.M. 234 ("… an action which can have the effect of breaking up this family [*sc.* deportation must] not [be] so disproportionate to the aim sought to be achieved as to be unsustainable"); and *McCann v Minister for Education* [1997] 1 I.L.R.M. 1 at 11 (Costello P. was prepared to make this assumption "for the purposes of this judgment").
[132]   [1988] I.L.R.M. 101. Another example is *Hand v Dublin Corporation* [1989] I.R. 26 at 31 and 32. Although Barron J.'s reasoning is sometimes unclear, the judgment does involve some discussion of the doctrine of proportionality in the context of judicial review. For analysis of *Hand*, see the Second Edition, pp.542–544. The Supreme Court judgment appears to agree very briefly with the view that the doctrine of proportionality could not have been relevant on the facts of *Hand*: [1991] I.R. 409 at 418.
[133]   [1988] I.L.R.M. 101 at 108.
[134]   See Hoffman, "A sense of proportion" (1997) 32 *Ir. Jur.* 49 at 49–58.
[135]   [2010] IESC 3. See paras 15–103 to 15–113.

what exactly does the concept do for the law that reasonableness does not do?[136] This is a pertinent question, since the difficulties in this field are endemic and always going to involve some judicial subjectivity and imprecision, because of the compromise between the decision-maker's autonomy and the view of the High Court as to what is appropriate. No amount of fresh jargon can alter this fact. Moreover, on any general dictionary definition, the words "reasonableness" and "proportionality" have a good deal in common with each other.

15–90 It is suggested, nevertheless, that, as understood, though not always expressed, in modern judicial review discourse, they may be contrasted on two bases. The first is on the hierarchy of intensity of review. This may be expressed in the form of a scale showing an ascending level of intensity: at the minimum reasonableness; then anxious scrutiny; and at the more intense level, proportionality.

15–91 Secondly, one may focus on what exactly is the element of the reasoning process which is being tested, according to the standard of proportionality. One convenient way of analysing this, which has been offered, is to break down the reasoning process being followed by the administrator, into the following elements[137]:

> "1. The objective of a measure limiting a fundamental right must be deemed to be legitimate (*legitimate objective*).
>
> 2. The measure must be rationally connected to the legitimate aim (*rational connection*).
>
> 3. ... the measure must not limit the fundamental right any more than is necessary to achieve the legitimate objective (*minimal impairment*).
>
> 4. There must be an overall proportionality between the achievement of that legitimate objective and the impact on the fundamental right (*overall balance*)."

15–92 It may well be said that there is nothing here that a devotee of reasonableness would regard as beyond its ken. However, if only because of the increased level of judicial and academic discourse in the present historical era, as compared to the Wednesbury—or even Keegan—eras, the virtue of proportionality is that the more comprehensive, explicit and precise catalogue of reasoning stages and desiderata has become firmly attached to it. Nevertheless, it must not be supposed that the adoption of the proportionality principle solves all the problems in this area, since courts purporting to apply this principle have reached widely differing conclusions on whether a given set of circumstances has given rise to a disproportionate interference with individual rights.[138] In addition, as explained, proportionality, as

---

[136] For a defence of *Wednesbury*, see Daly, "*Wednesbury*'s Reason and Structure" [2011] *Public Law* 238.

[137] Brady, "Proportionality, deference and fundamental rights in Irish administrative law: the aftermath of *Meadows*" (2010) 32 D.U.L.J. 136 at 146. Dr Brady has based this formulation on the proportionality test, set out in *Heaney v Ireland* [1994] 3 I.R. 593 at 607 (Costello J.).

[138] A striking example of this is *Bosphorus Hava Yollari Turizm Ve Tickaret Anonim Sirketi v Minister for Transport* [1994] 2 I.L.R.M. 551, a case where the High Court quashed a decision of the Minister to impound, pursuant to Regulation No. 990 of 1993 (the Serbian sanctions regulations), an aircraft which was about to leave from Dublin airport. The evidence showed that the aircraft, owned by Yugoslav Airlines, had been leased to a Turkish airline. The lease was

it has come to be understood, promotes more open systematic and, consequently, objective reasoning.

(b) Individual rights protected by the Constitution

15–93   The net question here is whether, when a significant individual right protected by the Constitution is affected by the exercise of a discretionary power, a more intense form of judicial review should be applied. However, before addressing this, we should mention a preliminary point with theoretical and practical significance: where the exercise of a discretionary power involves the infringement of an important right, this feature may be articulated in the law in either of two ways. The first, which is under discussion here, is by increase of the intensity of judicial review which is applied to the exercise of the discretionary power. The other way, examined in Chapter 10, Part D focuses on the question of the vires of the statutory power and considers—and this is the important point—whether the statutory provision should be interpreted in the light of (say) the presumption against interference with property or other vested rights. It is suggested that, although the law treats these areas in discrete blocs, they are in large measure, different ways of approaching the same point.

15–94   The comment may be made that the case law on the presumptions just explained has usually been rather peremptory. In particular, in contrast to the discussion in the present chapter on the first of these alternatives (intensity of judicial review), the case law on presumptions fails to consider whether the right under consideration is subject to a qualification in the public interest.[139] Because of this omission, there is an advantage to the applicant in taking this line of argument, rather than the type of argument based directly on the control of a discretionary power. Yet, surely this is wrong: in either case the policy objective is the same, or similar, namely to establish a viable compromise between an important individual right and any qualification necessary to it in the public interest. Thus, the legal outcome ought to be the same.

15–95   It is relevant to mention here one policy choice, which has not yet received much attention, namely the comparison between proportionality in the contexts of constitutional judicial review and of common law judicial review. But Dr Brady has remarked that[140]:

> "There are reasons to think that rights-based proportionality review should

---

entirely bona fide and Murphy J. struck down the Minister's action on grounds which may be regarded as involving the proportionality precept. Yet, the Court of Justice of the EU (C-84/95) [1996] 3 C.M.L.R. 257 at 295) was equally strong in the opposite direction and concluded that the interference with the airline operator's property rights was proportionate.

See also, *Air Canada v United Kingdom* (1995) 20 E.H.R.R. 150, which involves a similar contrast (to that in *Bosphorus*) between the Irish Supreme Court and, in this case, the European Court of Human Rights, which contrast is described in the Third Edition, p.662.

[139] McKechnie J.'s judgment in *Neurendale Ltd (t/a Panda Waste Services) v Dublin City Council* [2009] IEHC 588 is interesting in this context, in that it considers different sets of rights, of which one is treated as a matter of statutory interpretation (at paras 154–157); while the other is treated as a matter of reasonableness and proportionality (at paras 190–193).

[140] Brady, "Proportionality, deference and fundamental rights in Irish administrative law: the aftermath of *Meadows*" (2010) 32 D.U.L.J. 136 at 138–139.

be even more appropriate for administrative law than for challenges to legislation. Legislation is debated in public and enacted by the democratically elected Oireachtas. Legislation is prospective and potentially affects every citizen. In such circumstances the normal political processes may provide a means of remedying any fundamental rights difficulties ... The same is not true of administrative action. The number of people directly affected by a specific administrative decision is often very narrow, indeed administrative decisions are often directed at a single individual. Furthermore, executive decision-makers have substantially less democratic accountability than does the Oireachtas and their decision making process is not necessarily transparent and open ... On this basis, judicial supervision of administrative action which affects fundamental rights would seem as important, if not more important, than the existing supervision of legislation."

15–96 Following on from this suggestion, one context in which a difference of the type conjectured here would matter would be where an applicant was making a claim of invalidity, by reference to the constitutionality of the parent legislation, rather than by directly reviewing the constitutionality of the administrative action. If the difference conjectured were adopted by a court, the consequence would be to make the applicant's task harder, if they chose to attack the parent legislation.

15–97 To return to the main question here: when an individual right protected by the Constitution is affected by the exercise of a discretionary power, should a higher standard of judicial review be applied? This question was at the centre of the recent Supreme Court case, *Meadows v Minister for Minister for Justice, Equality and Law Reform.*[141] The court, by a three-to-two majority, supported a strengthened doctrine of proportionality. Nevertheless, this is a major issue which attracted significant debate during the decade preceding *Meadows*. Accordingly, before turning to this landmark, we shall survey some of the earlier case law on either side of the argument.

15–98 As had been justly remarked,[142] "[i]n recent years, a conflict ha[d] arisen between different High Court judges regarding which standard to apply [when a constitutional right was engaged]". Probably one could extend this to Supreme Court judges too. Thus, for example: in a case engaging the constitutional property right, *Clinton v An Bord Pleanála*,[143] writing for the Supreme Court, Geoghegan J., while ruling on the facts that the compulsory purchase order before him was proportionate, observed that the making and confirming of a CPO entails an invasion of property rights which are constitutionally protected. He went on to suggest that "it would

---

[141] [2010] IESC 3. For discussion of *Meadows*, see paras 15–103 to 15–111.

[142] See Donnelly, "Grounds for Judicial Review: New Developments", paper delivered at a conference at Trinity College Law School, June 27, 2009, para.48.

[143] [2007] 2 I.L.R.M. 81 at 99. See also, *Bailey v Mr Justice Flood*, unreported, High Court, Morris P., March 6, 2000: "The court may not interfere with the exercise of an administrative discretion on substantive grounds save where the court is satisfied ... that it is beyond the range of responses open to a reasonable decision-maker. But in judging whether the decision-maker has exceeded this margin of appreciation the human rights context is important. The more substantial the interference with human rights, the more the court will require by way of justification before it is satisfied that the decision is reasonable in the sense outlined above." On the facts, the applicants failed to establish that the decision was unreasonable. The decision was affirmed on narrower grounds by the Supreme Court, April 14, 2000.

insufficiently protect constitutional rights if the court, hearing a judicial review application, merely had to be satisfied that the decision was not irrational or was not contrary to fundamental reason and commonsense". Again, in *Holland v Governor of Portlaoise Prison*[144] (which concerned a prisoner's right to communicate with a journalist about the alleged injustice of his conviction), in finding for the applicant, McKechnie J. stated unequivocally: "I do not believe when the exercise of a fundamental right such as the right to communicate is at the core of an application, that [the *Keegan–O'Keeffe*] test is either proper or appropriate".

15–99   Yet, in *Green Party v RTÉ*[145] the *Keegan–O'Keeffe* principles were followed, in face of the constitutional rights to expression and equality. Here, the applicant unsuccessfully sought judicial review of the respondent's decision not to provide any live coverage of the applicant's Party Conference. In the High Court, Carroll J. went out of her way to show that, on many relevant bases, the applicant had a political stature that was at least the equivalent of the Progressive Democrat Party, whose Conferences had been covered. Nevertheless, she concluded that, "[t]he respondent did have criteria which existed for several years. They could be criticised ... but again, it is not for the court to lay down the criteria. The criteria which have been adopted ... cannot be said to be illogical or untenable. There is no suggestion that the respondent acted *mala fides*".

15–100   The principal forum for this debate, as to whether the *Keegan* principles should be modified where constitutional rights are affected, has been provided by a number of immigration or deportation cases, mainly in the 2000s,[146] in which Arts 41 and 42 of the Constitution (The Family and Education) have been invoked. Many of these cases have involved the same basic factual situation, namely that a deportation order (or a refusal to rescind a deportation order) would mean that the applicant's (and their family's) constitutional right to reside together, in Ireland, as a family would be violated. In these cases, while it was accepted that the family's right to reside in Ireland is not absolute and the Minister has a discretion to decide that the applicant should be deported, it was also contended that more weight should be given to the right of the family than would be the case if no constitutional right were engaged. As mentioned, different judges have taken different views on

---

[144] [2004] 2 I.R. 573 at paras 17–19. On the facts, the applicant's case was quite a strong one, probably stronger than that of the applicant in *Green Party* (explained in the text), in that the legitimate public interest at issue in *Holland* was security and this was not affected by a prisoner communicating with a journalist.

[145] [2003] 1 I.R. 558 at 566.

[146] *State (Bouzagou) v Fitzgibbon St Garda Station* [1986] I.L.R.M. 98; *Pok Sun Shum v Ireland* [1986] I.L.R.M. 593; and *Osheku v Ireland* [1987] I.L.R.M. 330 were relatively early immigration or deportation cases in which the plaintiffs relied unsuccessfully on the right to the family. See, however, *Fajujonu v Minister for Justice* [1990] I.L.R.M. 234, now effectively reversed by *Lobe and Osayende v Minister for Justice, Equality and Law Reform* [2003] 1 I.R. 1.

this fundamental choice.[147] For example, in favour of "anxious scrutiny", Clarke J. stated[148]:

"In a case where a valid deportation order has been made and where the first respondent is requested to revoke that deportation order by virtue of the existence of new circumstances in the form of family rights (under the Constitution) or rights deriving from a permanent relationship (under the Convention) of Human Rights, the first respondent is obliged to consider the rights of all concerned. Indeed, it would appear that it is possible that, in certain circumstances, for the reasons outlined by the Supreme Court (Fennelly J) in *Cirpaci v Minister for Justice* [2005] IESC 42, [2005] 2 ILRM 547 the first respondent may even be obliged in some cases to come to a conclusion in favour of acting so as to permit the parties to reside together in the State."

15–101   Naturally, even where constitutional rights are given a special weight, how much will vary with the circumstances. For example, in the case of immigration Fennelly J stated[149]:

"It is legitimate for the Minister to have regard to the duration of the marriage relationship when weighing in the balance the family rights in question. At one extreme an Irish citizen might contract a marriage, valid under the laws of a remote jurisdiction, while on holiday there. Could such a person, within days of the marriage, insist … that the brevity of the marital relationship was irrelevant, that his or her new spouse be granted a visa admitting him or her to reside in the State? At the other extreme would be an Irish citizen, who had lived abroad for many years, perhaps for his or her entire working life. Such a person has, as a citizen, an undoubted right to return to reside in Ireland on retirement or earlier. It is not necessary to pose the constitutional

---

[147] The authorities on the side of *Keegan–O'Keeffe*, even where constitutional rights are engaged, include *Meadows v Minister for Justice, Equality and Law Reform* [2003] IEHC 79; unreported, High Court, Gilligan J., November 19, 2003; *N v Minister for Justice, Equality and Law Reform* [2008] IEHC 8 (McCarthy J.); *Mwiza v Refugee Appeals Tribunal*, unreported, High Court, McCarthy J., August 22, 2008; *L v Minister for Justice, Equality and Law Reform* [2009] IEHC 107 (McCarthy J.).
    By contrast, in favour of anxious scrutiny, are *Gashi v Minister for Justice, Equality and Law Reform*, unreported, High Court, Clarke J., December 3, 2004; *Fitzpatrick v Minister for Justice, Equality and Law Reform* [2005] IEHC 9; unreported, High Court, Ryan J., January 26, 2005; *Idiakheua v Minister for Justice, Equality and Law Reform* [2005] IEHC 180; unreported, High Court, Clarke J., May 10, 2005 at 6–7, referring also to *Itare v Minister for Justice, Equality and Law Reform*, unreported, High Court, McGovern J., March 2, 2007; *COI v Minister for Justice, Equality and Law Reform* [2007] 1 I.R. 718 at paras 28–38; *KCC v Minister for Justice, Equality and Law Reform* [2007] IEHC 176 (McGovern J.); *N v Minister for Justice, Equality and Law Reform*, unreported, Charleton J., High Court, April 24, 2008; *FN v Minister for Justice, Equality and Law Reform* [2009] 1 I.R. 88 at paras 57–59.
    In the Supreme Court, in *AO v Minister for Justice, Equality and Law Reform* [2003] 1 I.R. 1, Murray J. (at 192) and Hardiman J. (at 165) were in favour of *O'Keeffe*; whereas McGuinness J. (at 127) and Fennelly J. (at 203) were against. Geoghegan J. (at 166) reserved his position.
[148] *AA and EP* [2005] 4 I.R. 564 at para.29.
[149] *Cirpaci v Minister for Equality, Justice and Law Reform* [2005] 2 I.L.R.M. 547 at 557. See, to broadly similar effect, in the field of licensing and the constitutional property right, *Hanrahan Farms Ltd v EPA* [2006] 1 I.L.R.M. 275 at 279.

question whether that person would have the right to be accompanied by his or her foreign spouse of many years. For my own part, I have no doubt that such a right exists. It would not, of course, be absolute. The foreign spouse might be a notorious criminal. It is enough to say that, in the most benign of such circumstances, the Minister would be entitled and possibly bound, in exercising the statutory powers applicable to such situations, to give favourable consideration to a claim that such a person be permitted to be accompanied by his or her spouse."

15–102   The outcome of the authorities just briefly summarised was that some Supreme Court and many High Court judges had frequently indicated that curial deference remained the law; though often with an indication that the possibility of change in the future was not shut out.[150]

(c) "Came the dawn": Meadows v Minister for Justice, Equality and Law Reform

15–103   The case which has, more or less, settled the controversy is *Meadows*.[151] The applicant in *Meadows* applied for asylum on the basis that, if returned to her home state, she was in danger of a forced marriage and female genital mutilation. She applied initially to the Department (first to an official and then to the asylum appeals unit) and then appealed to the Refugee Appeals Tribunal. She was unsuccessful at each stage, essentially on the basis that she was held not to have established a credible connection between herself and these dangers. A person in her position is then allowed, by statute,[152] one further opportunity to make representations to the

---

[150]   *VZ v Minister for Justice, Equality and Law Reform* [2002] 2 I.R. 135 at 158 (McGuinness J.). (Even in regard to this tentative passage, Denham J. considered it necessary to give, at 138, a short judgment which merely repeated that McGuinness J. had indicated that the issue of a test to be applied "was not fully argued ... and that further consideration must await a fuller argument".)

For another expression of judicial impatience with a situation in which "to use layman's language, in some cases you look hard and in others harder still", see *LC v Minister for Justice, Equality and Law Reform* [2007] 2 I.R. 133 (Hanna J.).

[151]   [2010] IESC 3; [2010] 2 I.R. 710. The Supreme Court handed down five separate judgments, of which that of Kearns J. is three pages long, with the other four averaging 27 pages. Kearns J. made it clear that he agreed entirely with the other dissenting judge, Hardiman J.

In a sense, the circumstances of the case were inauspicious for clarifying the law, in that it was an application for leave, rather than a substantive ruling, albeit it was necessary for the applicant to establish "substantial grounds": Illegal Immigrants (Trafficking) Act 2000 s.5(2)(b). Plainly, before leave is granted, there must be some understanding of what standard would be required at the substantive hearing. But, as against this, the understanding which the court has at the leave stage need not be as precise as would be required at the substantive stage. Indeed, Fennelly J., at para.82, remarked: "Equally this judgment implies no view on how the application for judicial review should be decided in the High Court, except in so far as it explains the applicable test for review on the ground of unreasonableness." Nevertheless, in the High Court, Gilligan J. certified the point as one of law for the Supreme Court and the Supreme Court recognised it as an opportunity to clarify the law.

Fennelly J., at para.1, notes that "The certified point of law is whether ... in determining the reasonableness of an administrative decision which affects ... constitutional rights ... it is correct to apply the standard set out in *O'Keeffe* ...". It would be true but misleading to say that all five of the judges answered this in the affirmative.

[152]   This opportunity arose under the Refugee Act 1996 s.5, which applies where life or freedom would be threatened by an expulsion to another State. Here, the criteria are similar to those already considered by the RAT. In addition, by the Immigration Act 1999 s.3(6), the Minister

Minister, as to why she should not be deported. *Meadows* was a judicial review of the exercise of the Minister's discretion against her.

15–104 Two of the judges—Denham J. and Fennelly J.—gave judgments which imposed a more stringent for the control of discretion than the established *Keegan–O'Keeffe* test. The two dissenting judges[153]—Hardiman J. and Kearns P.—vigorously reasserted *Keegan*. The fifth judgment—given by Murray C.J.—is more difficult to classify: after what human rights lawyers would have regarded as a promising start, Murray C.J.'s judgment seems to shy away from the broad channel followed by the two other members of the majority and to find for the applicant more on the basis of a different though related point (covered at para.15–15), namely that the Minister had failed to give reasons.

15–105 The more important reason why *Meadows* did not produce a clear victory for one view or the other is that there was a certain amount of common ground between all (or almost all) of the judges. In the first place, unsurprisingly, they accepted the logical links and inter-relationships between *Wednesbury*, *Keegan–O'Keeffe*, anxious scrutiny, proportionality, and the position of constitutional rights—more or less in the same sequence as they have been outlined in this chapter. (We are of course not saying here that the judges evaluated these major policy issues in the same way; rather that they were perceived similarly.)

15–106 A more significant reason for saying that there was some common ground is, first, that the "anxious scrutiny" test, which some English judges have espoused, has been rejected. The best explanation given for this was that it was an English solution to an English problem.[154] Fennelly J. stated that[155]:

> "… [anxious scrutiny would bring in] the English 'sliding scale' of review. In my view, it is neither appropriate nor necessary to have a different standard of review of cases involving an interference with fundamental constitutional or other personal rights. For example, it would be wrong and confusing to have

---

is required to take into account, as grounds for not deporting, specified humanitarian factors, including the personal circumstances of the person concerned, such as their duration of residence, family and employment history, and humanitarian considerations generally, as well as the common good and considerations of national security and public policy.

[153] Among the subsidiary points emphasised by the dissenting judges was the fact that the position of Ms Meadows had already been considered by the RAT, and the applicant had not sought review of the RAT's decision. In short, they emphasised that it is accepted that the intensity of judicial review varies with the circumstances, among which are whether there are other fora to which the aggrieved individual could have had recourse. And, secondly, that the Minister's decision was "*ad misericordiam*"—an expression intended to capture the fact that the Minister was exercising something like a prerogative of mercy, which has traditionally not been subject to much in the way of judicial control. While interesting, these are rather particular points.

[154] The summation in the text is not a quotation but our paraphrase of the judgment, in which it was indicated that the state of English law arose from the absence of fundamental rights established by a written instrument, before the ECHR was domesticated. *cp.* Hardiman J., [2010] IESC 3 at 14. Fennelly J., at para.17, stated: "… the principle of proportionality more fully developed in the judgments, which had been delivered by the Chief Justice and Denham J. at paras 19–22, can provide a sufficient and more consistent standard of review, without resort to vaguer notions of anxious scrutiny". No more justification is given for this view.

[155] [2010] IESC 3 at para.70. See also, paras 21, 64–65 and 71, 72, 82. Compare Hardiman J. at 8–9.

two different standards of judicial review for planning decisions, depending on whether the review is being sought by the applicant for permission (the owner of the land with constitutionally protected rights) or a third party applicant (with a merely legal right to object …). The holder of a licence may have a mere legal right, but will be entitled to expect not only fairness in any decision affecting his right to hold it but, in addition, it will not be taken from him for trifling reasons."

Hardiman J.[156] also regarded a dual test as undesirable for the same reason; but, in a rather dramatic judgment, he appeared to understand (misunderstand?) the majority judgments as establishing such a dual system.

15–107   In view of this rejection, where then is the epicentre of the judgments? Among the majority judges, there was heavy infusion of reasonableness by proportionality. As Daly remarks[157]:

"Amidst the confusion, one constant … theme was that proportionality was an aspect of unreasonableness and could function within the *Keegan* test … Proportionality for all three of the majority judges would have to operate within the confines of the *Keegan* test. Murray C.J. and Fennelly J. seemed to favour the narrower approach of viewing proportionality simply as an aspect of unreasonableness, relevant in extreme cases, whereas Denham J. seemed to favour a full proportionality analysis within the test of reasonableness, required in all cases where relevant rights are implicated."

15–108   Probably fearing that the law might be changed in substance, behind cover of retention of the same formula, the two dissenting judges were at extreme pains to portray the majority judgments as subverting sound law. Hardiman J. stated that[158]:

"… the test now proposed to be applied has quite the contrary effect [to *O'Keeffe* or *Wednesbury*]: it looks for explanation and justification from the decision-maker which I believe to be inconsistent with the proper principles of judicial review and with a view that the onus of proof remains on the applicant."

15–109   Nevertheless, even Hardiman J. remarked that "… the established [*O'Keeffe–Keegan–Wednesbury*] test is more flexible than its critics allow". And "[w]here fundamental human rights are at stake, the courts may and will subject administrative decisions to a particularly careful and thorough review, but within

---

[156] [2010] IESC 3 at 9. Fennelly J. remarked, at para.57, apparently approvingly: "[The UK's] variable approach has been characterised as a 'sliding scale' of review … There is for example less intense scrutiny where economic or property rights are at stake". It is possible that a narrow category of human rights would emerge. But, if not, then the difficulties alluded to by Hardiman J. seem very likely.

[157] Daly, "Standards of Review in Irish Administrative Law" (2010) 32 D.U.L.J. 379.

[158] [2010] IESC 3 at 16; [2010] 2 I.R. 710 at para.[336]. See also, [2010] IESC 3 at 6; or [2010] 2 I.R. 710 at para.[299]. There is a striking contrast between the approach of Hardiman J.'s judgment (in favour of narrowing judicial review) in *Meadows* as compared with such cases as *O'Callaghan v Mahon (No. 2)* [2008] 2 I.R. 514 at para.13–86.

the parameters of the *O'Keeffe* reasonableness review".[159] Fennelly J. remarked, almost identically[160]:

> "It is natural ... for any decision-maker to be the more hesitant, the more deliberate, the more cautious as the decision he or she is considering will the more gravely trench on the rights or interests of those likely to be affected."

15–110 Also, in a conciliatory spirit, Fennelly J.,[161] from the majority, remarked:

> "[T]his judgment is not intended to express or imply any view as to how the Minister should decide cases involving deportation of persons relying on a risk or a danger of infringement of their human rights. Matters of policy are for the Minister ... He might for example decide as the Refugee Appeals Tribunal had done in this case that all of the degree of risk to the individual was outweighed by the need to protect the integrity of the system. The Minister would be entitled to take account of the entirety of the problem of which an individual person is merely one example and the feasibility for the State of offering refuge to a large number of people from other countries."

This passage affords strong support for the line of legal policy, which we explained above, under the head of (2) "Countervailing community interests ...".

15–111 It is hard to summarise the effect of *Meadows*. Probably, the best that can be done is to say that the effect of *Meadows* is to confirm the *Keegan–O'Keeffe* standard, but to give it what may be called a liberal tone. The quotations given above suggest if not exactly a consensus (something which Hardiman J. was at pains to avoid), at least that the positions of both the majority and the minority judges were, to varying degrees, some distances from the excesses to which earlier courts had taken the *Keegan–O'Keeffe* test. Taken together, the judgments seem to reject the notion of "anxious scrutiny" for sharply defined "constitutionally protected" rights; yet, to acknowledge that there will be a more intensive scrutiny as the right affected is more important or, perhaps, is more severely curtailed. Either way, this comes rather close to the "sliding scale" which was condemned by Fennelly J. How this will operate in practice may depend on the particular field and circumstances involved, a point to which we return at paras 15–133 to 15–134.

---

[159] [2010] IESC 3 at 6, (or [2010] 2 I.R. 710 at para.[374]). The next quotation is at [2010] IESC 3 at 24, (or [2010] 2 I.R. 710 at para.[377]). See also, [2010] IESC 3 at 16, 22.

[160] [2010] IESC 3 at paras.65, (or [2010] 2 I.R. 710 at para.[443]) and [2010] IESC 3 at 54–58, (or [2010] 2 I.R. 710 at paras [432]–[436]). See also, Denham J. at 38–51, (at paras [149]–[162]). Murray C.J. states similarly, at 33, (at para.[101]): "This is quintessentially a discretionary matter for the Minister in which he has to weigh competing interests and only the Minister, who has responsibility for public policy ... is in principle in a position to decide where that balance lies."

[161] [2010] IESC 3 at para.82, (or [2010] 2 I.R. 710 at para.[460]). See also, [2010] IESC 3 at paras 65 and 71–72, (or [2010] 2 I.R. 710 at paras [443] and [449]–[450]).

Post-Meadows Developments

15–112   So far as one can tell, given the nuanced character of the judgments and the occasionally cavalier attitude of many judges to the precedent doctrine, it seems that the legal community has accepted the majority judgments. Academic commentary,[162] of which there has been quite a lot, has been pro-majority, if with varying nuances. More important, the majority has been followed in later High Court cases. For example, in *ISOF v Minister for Justice, Equality and Law Reform*,[163] Cooke J. stated:

> "If constitutional rights are in issue (whether absolute or qualified) it is the function and duty of the High Court to vindicate them. The same can be said for rights entitled to protection under the European Convention on Human Rights ... The common law remedies of judicial review and judicial practice in their application have, in the view of this Court, evolved differently in the constitutional framework of this State ... as compared with other common law jurisdictions and particularly that of the United Kingdom both before and since the enactment there of the Human Rights Act 1998. Nevertheless the potential for evolution of the criteria can be seen as reflected in, for example, judgments such as that in which the House of Lords ... held in the context of judicial review procedures ... that ... 'the intensity of review is greater than was previously appropriate ... and thus goes beyond that traditionally adopted [in] judicial review in a domestic setting ...' In this jurisdiction the Supreme Court has, of course, rejected the need to alter the 'intensity' or the level of review applied by the Court ... It remains the case however, as illustrated by ... the judgment of Fennelly J. [in Meadows] that judicial practice ... is capable of adapting to accommodate the need to examine the substantive content of a decision having impact on fundamental rights in order to evaluate the lawfulness of its encroachment on those rights without thereby supplanting the administrative decision with a new decision of its own."

(d) EU Law and ECHR

15–113   It frequently happens that there is an overlap in the sense that the same individual rights sound in both Constitution and Convention, or, less often, EU law. Thus, frequently the applicant's claim includes the contention that, if the court does not lift the standard of rights—protection above the austerity diet offered by *O'Keeffe*—Ireland will be in breach of international obligations.[164] This type of argument was manifest in *ISOF* and *Efe* and only slightly less so in *Meadows*. Thus one ought to flag the EU approach,[165] not merely as a comparative influence but as a source of law which must be applied by Irish courts, in regard to the exercise

---

[162] Daly, "Standards of Review in Irish Administrative Law" (2010) 32 D.U.L.J. 379; Brady, "Proportionality, deference and fundamental rights in Irish administrative law: the aftermath of *Meadows*" (2010) 32 D.U.L.J. 136 at 138–139; Delany and Donnelly, "The Irish Supreme Court inches towards proportionality review" (2011) *Public Law* 9.

[163] [2010] IEHC 457. See also, *JB v Minister for Justice, Equality and Law Reform* [2010] IEHC 296 (Cooke J.). *Efe v Minister for Justice, Equality and Law Reform* [2011] 2 I.L.R.M. 411 at para.34 (Hogan J.).

[164] Craig, "The Courts, the Human Rights Act and Judicial Review" (2003) 118 L.Q.R. 551; Barendt, "Free Speech and Human Rights" (2003) *Public Law* 580.

[165] Craig, *EU Administrative Law* (Oxford: OUP, 2006), Ch.13 "Law, Fact and Discretion".

of discretionary powers which affect rights derived from EU law. Thus, in *SIAC Construction Ltd v Mayo*,[166] the applicant had submitted a tender in respect of a major sewerage works at Ballinrobe. The tender was two to three per cent lower than that of the contractor whose tender was accepted. Despite this fact, the respondent's engineer recommended—and the recommendation was accepted—that the contract go to a rival contractor on the basis that its tender could prove the most economically advantageous in terms of the ultimate cost to the respondent of the completed works.

15–114   The key question in the case was whether the High Court had been correct to apply the Irish domestic standard of review. The response of the Supreme Court was that it was not the Irish standard but the EU standard which should have been applied. It is worth quoting from the court's judgment at unusual length because it articulates the EU principles of judicial review in terms which a common lawyer can understand and brings out the substantial amount which the two systems have in common. Giving judgment for the court, Fennelly J. (who was formerly an Advocate General at the European Court of Justice) stated[167]:

"There are obvious common threads which run through any system of review of administrative decisions, especially where the primary decision making function is administrative or governmental. The function of the courts is to guarantee legality, though that notion itself has a number of elements, some procedural and some substantive. The passages which I have cited speak of 'manifest' error as the test for judicial review adopted by the community courts. This is the standard which applies to the appreciation of facts by the decision maker. They do not say that this test must be adopted by the national courts. I would observe, however, that the word, 'manifest', should not be equated with any exaggerated description of obviousness. A study of the case law will show that the community courts are prepared to annul decision, at least in certain contexts, when they think an error has clearly been made.

The decisive additional consideration in the area of the public procurement is the explicit concession of a wide margin of discretion to awarding authorities.

I do not think, however, that the test of manifest error is to be equated with the test adopted by the trial judge [when this case was referred to the ECJ. See [2001] E.C.R.I. 33], namely that, in order to qualify for quashing, a decision must 'plainly and unambiguously fly in the face of fundamental reason and common sense.' It cannot be ignored that the Advocate General thought the test should be 'rather less extreme'."

However, on the facts, it was held that the respondent county council had remained within its margin of discretion, having followed objective and objectively verified criteria.

15–115   Another discussion of the comparison between Irish and EU standards

---

[166] [2002] 3 I.R. 148. See also, H & M, paras 4–191 to 4–193.
[167] [2002] 3 I.R. 148 at 175–176.

is contained in *Sweetman v An Bord Pleanála*.[168] The case was decided only at leave stage and it was concerned particularly with public participation in respect of the drawing up of certain plans relating to the environment. The applicant claimed (in the context of the approval by the first respondent of a road scheme to be undertaken by Clare County Council) that the relevant Directive had not been properly implemented in Irish law. In particular, it was submitted that the confining of the standard of review to the traditional *O'Keeffe* irrationality test would contravene the provisions of the Directive.

15–116   In response, Clarke J. stated, in effect, that the substantive review of a discretion which may be made by a court goes beyond the so-called *O'Keeffe* test. In the first place, he noted that, as has been long accepted, the court must consider whether all proper factors were taken into account and other factors were not taken into account. What is more significant is the way in which Clarke J. contemplated the means by which "anxious scrutiny" might be accommodated in Irish law. He stated[169]:

> "The courts of the United Kingdom, which apply a largely identical regime in respect of judicial review, have evolved the doctrine of 'anxious scrutiny' whereby a higher level of scrutiny is applied to cases involving fundamental human rights. That level of scrutiny has been applied, in appropriate cases, within the rubric of the existing judicial review system. While there has not, as yet, been a definitive determination of the matter in the courts in this jurisdiction, same has been the subject of some comment. In particular in the area of immigration law, this court has accepted that there are substantial grounds for arguing that a higher level of scrutiny needs to be applied in cases involving fundamental human rights in that field."

15–117   Clarke J. continued[170]:

> "[I]t might well be that Irish judicial review law could not accommodate a complete appeal on the merits. However, for the reasons which I am about to address, I am not satisfied that such a review is required by the Directive … The Directive does not require that there be a judicial review of the

---

[168] [2008] 1 I.R. 277 at paras 66–76. The EU law referred to in the text is art.10a of Directive 85/337, as inserted by art.7 of Directive 2003/35.

[169] [2007] 2 I.L.R.M. 328 at para.68. This passage cites as authority for this approach *Gashi v Minister for Justice, Equality and Law Reform* [2004] IEHC 394; unreported, High Court, Clarke J., December 3, 2004. Apart from the substantive point covered in the text, the *Sweetman* judgment also considered whether the requirement, under the Planning and Development Act 2000 s.50 that an applicant for judicial review show a substantial interest and the requirement to obtain leave, violated EU standards.

[170] [2007] 2 I.L.R.M. 328 at paras 71–73. The facts in *Sweetman* were that development was being undertaken by a local authority, so that (unusually) the application for planning permission was made, at first instance, to An Bord Pleanála, with the consequence that the only recourse available against the resulting decision was judicial review. *Sweetman* was distinguished in *Cáirde Chill v An Bord Pleanála* [2009] 2 I.L.R.M. 89 at paras 19, 32–34. This was on the basis that what was required by the Directive was "a review of procedure before a court of law or another independent and impartial body", and that while, in most cases, including the instant case, the grant of permission was determined by the local planning authority, the appeal to An Bord Pleanála satisfied the requirement of review by an independent and impartial body.

substance of the decision itself but rather of the 'substantive legality' of the decision."

15–118 Most of the ECHR cases have been in the field of immigration/residence.[171] Usually too, the ECHR has been applied in tandem with the Irish Constitution. A good example is *Yang v Minister for Justice, Equality and Law Reform*.[172] The issue was whether the Minister, in making deportation orders in respect of the non-national parents of Irish-citizen children, had applied the wrong test. In granting leave to seek judicial review, Charleton J. stated:

> "[The applicant child and parents] are part … of a stable family unit that is recognised under Article 8 of the European Convention on Human Rights, but it seems to me that ordinary considerations of humanity under Article 40 would lead to the conclusion that she also has the right under our Constitution to the society and assistance of both of her parents as that is what is ordained by nature in terms of children growing up … and looking at this decision [of the Minister] and asking myself whether substantial grounds have been shown, I cannot get over the fact that a completely wrong test [imposed by the Minister] of insurmountable obstacle to the family living together in their country of origin replaces what was the very careful reasoning of Ms Justice Denham [in *Oguekwe*] whereby she not only included reason but also included proportion in that regard."

15–119 Apart from the EU or the ECHR, there may be a similar source of privileged individual rights which has the effect of requiring a stricter test than that required by the *Keegan* standard, which is thus more in accord with the *Meadows* majority. This is where the discretionary power has been created under legislation implementing the State's obligation under an international convention. Thus it has been held, though only at High Court level, that a higher standard of review should apply in regard to the Minister for Justice, Equality and Law Reform's decision to permit an alien to make a further application for a declaration of refugee status pursuant to the Refugee Act 1996 s.17. This proposition was laid down in *COI v Minister for Justice, Equality and Law Reform*,[173] in which the applicant was an asylum seeker who, on the basis of fresh evidence, had sought but been denied by the Minister the necessary permission to make a further application. The High Court (McGovern J.) was pressed, by counsel for the respondent, with the view that the

---

[171] See *Oguekwe v Minister for Justice, Equality and Law Reform* [2008] 3 I.R. 795 at paras 70–72. *N v Minister for Justice, Equality and Law Reform* [2008] IEHC 8 is notable in that it is the only Irish case we have been able to find in which an applicant argued that the *O'Keeffe* test does not afford the applicant an effective remedy against a decision contrary to art.13 of the ECHR. This argument was rejected by McCarthy J., who refused to distinguish between decisions affecting constitutional rights and other decisions. He went on to note that constitutional rights can be implicated in almost all administrative law cases. For case law before the European Convention was incorporated into Irish law, see *Kavanagh v Ireland* [1996] 1 I.R. 321, and *Re Curran and McCann's Application* [1985] N.I. 261.

[172] Ex tempore judgment of Charleton J., February 13, 2009, which is quoted in Brazil, "Recent Developments in Asylum and Immigration Judicial Review", TCD Law School, June 27, 2009, p.17. The judgment of Denham J., to which Charleton J. referred, is *Oguekwe v Minister for Justice, Equality and Law Reform* [2008] 3 I.R. 795 at paras 70–72. See also, *Holland v Governor of Portlaoise Prison* [2004] 2 I.R. 573 at para.33 (a prisoners' rights case).

[173] [2007] 2 I.L.R.M. 471 at 476 and 480.

standard *O'Keeffe* test of irrationality applied. The judge responded by stating that the relevant legislation was enacted to implement the State's obligations under the Geneva Convention on the Status of Refugees. In holding that a stricter standard than *Keegan* was required, McGovern J. seems to have been impressed both by the gravity of the interests at stake and the fact that an international obligation was involved.

D. Conclusions

15–120   The law is difficult to appraise, because it is currently in a state of flux, and not alone in Ireland. Of the two leading texts in England and Wales, one states that "the default position is still, at the time of writing, that of the *Wednesbury* formulation"[174]; while the other remarks, "notwithstanding the apparent persuasiveness of these views [*sc.* that *Wednesbury* is a dead man walking], the *coup de grâce* has not yet fallen".[175]

15–121   In Ireland, at present, there are various levels of difficulty. The first issue which plainly is on the agenda concerns the transition between two systems of law—the traditional *Wednesbury* scheme (charted in Part B) and the three modern divergent rules explained in Part C. As to this, we may say that this difficulty need not be exaggerated, since the use of the *Wednesbury* vocabulary by the judiciary seems to have declined in the 2000s, as compared to the 1990s. And, in any case, at base the two systems have a good deal in common (in that both *Wednesbury* and *Keegan* allow substantial latitude to the public body).

15–122   The other and greater difficulty concerns the reconciliation between the three diverse lines of policy just surveyed in this Part. One thing that they have in common is that they cut against the grain of the rather bogus certainty of the ultra vires principle, with its emphasis on the nice techniques of statutory interpretation. Instead, they point the judiciary in the direction of the most basic question of expressly identifying and weighing up both individual rights and countervailing community interests. Thus, the new technique is more likely to bring even the latter factor to judicial attention and perhaps to subject it to critical scrutiny.

15–123   In favour of the *Keegan* principle, in the first place, is the feeling, articulated particularly by judges themselves, that they are not qualified, by expertise, experience or the kind of limitations imposed by the formal, accusatorial arrangement of a court, to settle major issues of public policy. A related consideration is that maintaining a difference between review and appeal is important in marking the boundary which, under the separation of powers, should remain between the judiciary and the elected organs of government. The alternative is "… a substantial transfer of power from the politically responsible organs of government to an unelected judiciary".[176]

---

[174]   *De Smith, Judicial Review of Administrative Action*, 6th edn (2007), para.11–097.
[175]   Wade and Forsyth, *Administrative Law*, 10th edn (2009), p.314. The passage is headed "Goodbye to *Wednesbury*?"
[176]   Hardiman J., in *Meadows* at 10; see also, at 23. See, to same effect, Kearns P. at 3, stating that the majority judgments would mean a significant "hiking up of judicial activism".

15–124   Secondly, there is the fear that to relax the stringent test for substantive reasonableness would be to release a torrent of judicial review applications, which might well swamp the High Court and paralyse public administration:

> "[This] would be a dangerous exercise in judicial adventurism … To adopt such a course might quickly bring in its wake an endless stream of judicial review applications in cases where human rights might to any degree be said to be affected by some ministerial or administrative decision."[177]

15–125   Thirdly, where an expert, independent tribunal has been provided, is it not appropriate that (extreme cases apart) any complaints on the substantive merits of the decision should be left to the tribunal? If so, then two conclusions follow. To elaborate; if a tribunal is not working satisfactorily,[178] the comprehensive remedy is not to widen judicial review but to address the failure of that particular tribunal, including, most of all, care in selecting their members and disciplining any misconduct, including conflict of interest.[179] Another improvement would be for the courts to work out a clear dividing line to settle what sorts of issue may be brought up on review, even where an appeal has been provided by statute: see paras 16–79 to 16–80. These three considerations are by no means paper tigers and it is natural that successive Chief Justices should have been influenced in favour of strict *Keegan* by them.

15–126   As against this, many critics of *Keegan* have pointed out, first, the individual injustice to which it may lead, in that it is probably no exaggeration to say that an applicant who has a substantive case would have a better chance of success before an Ombudsman than before a court. Secondly, "… by ruling that the courts should not get involved on the substantive merits … except in limited and rare instances, the Supreme Court has fettered the judicial power to contribute to the development of any general principles of law which might guide administrators … in the future".[180]

15–127   What then is the alternative to strict *Keegan*? In the first place, pre-*Meadows*, as we have seen, there was significant, though minority, judicial support for adopting a higher level of scrutiny in respect of only those rights protected by the Constitution/EU/ECHR. But, substantial, practical problems would arise from

---

[177] *Nash v Minister for Justice, Equality and Law Reform* [2004] 3 I.R. 296 at 311 (Kearns J.). See, to similar effect, Kearns P. in *Meadows* at 3; *Rajah v The College of Surgeons* [1994] 1 I.R. 384, where O'Hanlon J. stated that "… the High Court should not be turned into a Court of Appeal from decisions of administrative tribunals generally …".

[178] See, e.g. *The Irish Times*, April 21, 2012 (on the Refugee Tribunal).

[179] Yet, in fact, tribunals (using that term in the sense in which it is understood in this book) have not received a share of attention commensurate with their importance, from either politicians, the media or academia. It seems probable that academic researchers have allowed tribunals to fall into the gap between the boundaries of recognised disciplines, such as public law, social administration or applied economics. Also, there is a divide between substance and machinery/procedure issues, with the latter securing the lion's share of attention.

[180] Cox, "Aspects of the Judicial Review Process in Planning Law", paper given at Trinity College Dublin, Judicial Review Conference, June 27, 2009, p.19.

such a two-level[181] system of law[182] in that there would be certain rights established merely by statute, which would be left to the tender mercies of *Keegan*. Examples would include rights in the fields of health, education, welfare, and employment. On the other hand, the property right and the right to do business would be stringently protected, covering trades licences, the right to appear (at any rate on state-owned media), and immigration/deportation.

15–128   A second big difficulty would arise where a decision had gone in favour of the Constitution/ECHR right-holder and a third-party applicant was assailing the decision, in the interest of (say) the environment or the local community. An example would be where a third party was arguing that a licence should not have been granted to a particular holder, perhaps because of his or her bad character. In this case, the third party would be subject to the *Keegan* regime; despite the fact that, if the licence had been refused, a disappointed applicant would have had a much easier wicket on which to bat. Thus, one result could be that there would be one law for the "haves" and another law for the "have-nots".

15–129   As regards the impact of *Meadows*, following our earlier survey, we argued that the idea of a dual system, according to whether or not a right is constitutionally protected, is not part of the law.   As to what message on the positive side emerges, notice that Fennelly J. remarked[183]:

> "It is natural … for any decision-maker to be the more hesitant, the more deliberate, the more cautious as the decision he or she is considering will the more gravely trench on the rights or interests of those likely to be affected."

15–130   To find common ground with the minority judgment is difficult, given the vigour of the dissenting judgments. However, earlier we argued that, although the two minority judges at some parts of their judgments contended against any extension of substantive judicial review, at other points they accepted that "… the established [*Keegan–O'Keeffe*] test is more flexible than its critics allow". And, "[w]here fundamental human rights are at stake, the courts may and will subject administrative decisions to a particularly careful and thorough review, but within the parameters of *O'Keeffe* the reasonableness review".[184] One may take from such quotations the notion that, while a right or its infringement will often be regarded as the more serious, simply because it is constitutionally protected, even a non-constitutional right may also be important. Whether this is so will naturally depend upon the particular circumstances of the case. In addition, the majority judges in *Meadows* adopted proportionality as a principle by which to balance the loss to

---

[181] We are making the commonsensical assumption that a broadly uniform test would apply whether the Constitution or ECHR or EU law were engaged; no one would suggest four levels of review.

[182] Compare *Nash v Minister for Justice, Equality and Law Reform* [2004] 3 I.R. 296; *McCarron v Superintendent Kearney* [2008] IEHC 195 at paras 16–17.

[183] [2010] IESC 3 at 65. See also, paras 54–58 and Denham J. at paras 38–51. Murray C.J. states similarly, at 33: "This is quintessentially a discretionary matter for the Minister in which he has to weigh competing interests and only the Minister, who has responsibility for public policy … is in principle in a position to decide where that balance lies."

[184] The first quotation is at [2010] IESC 3 at 6 of Hardiman J.'s judgment; and the second at 24.

the individual against the gain to the community. One may take it, that the present law is probably *Keegan*, tempered by "proportionality" and flexibility.

15–131   One should interpolate here that little or nothing was said in *Meadows* as to the position of rights protected by EU law. However, because of the distinctive legal status of EU law, the position as regards respecting such rights, by stringent judicial review, is more definite than a situation in which Irish constitutional rights are engaged. And it seems that the infringement of an EU right will probably always attract anxious scrutiny. One cannot be as sure regarding rights which are protected by the ECHR: there is no reason to give them a different status from rights protected by the Constitution.

15–132   The weight of divergent precedents and arguments, as well as the inherent difficulty of articulating a precise guideline in the present varied and nuanced context, mean that the way forward is most difficult. However, the following considerations and distinctions may be of assistance in trying to develop sensible and predictable law. In the first place, as noted at para.15–07, broadly speaking, the same framework has been applied to decisions of all categories, in which discretion is involved. A better approach might be for the law to take into account certain real differences. The first of these would be the strength and nature of the individual right which is affected by a particular exercise of power,[185] something which has already been discussed.

15–133   On the other side of the equation, there is the interest of the public body (representing the members of the community whom it is supposed to serve). This would mean that a distinction would be drawn according to whether the implication of the decision for the public body would or would not have extensive knock-on effects. To take examples from the opposite ends of the spectrum: an individual decision such as the refusal of a grant or the dismissal of an individual is at a different point, in terms of knock-on effects, from legislative or quasi-legislative decisions, such as the content of a bye-law or regulation or a development plan; or major infrastructural decisions, like the construction of a dam or the line of a road. Another related difference is that, where there is a high-policy element in a decision, then, given the limitations on the experience and information available to a court, it will usually make little sense for a court to review the decision of experts. In line with this view, we have mentioned cases from diverse areas—immigration, university places, licensing and Garda salaries—in which the court indicated that the respondent public body was entitled to take into account legitimate aspects of the community interest, even though these weighed against individual constitutional rights.

15–134   Addressing the central question and bringing together many of the themes touched on here, De Smith remarks:

---

[185]   It is noticeable that most of the judicial controversy on these points has arisen from a single field—the immigration/deportation area; for instance, *Meadows* did indeed involve possibly a case of life or death or at any rate human freedom, traditionally and rightly regarded as the most highly valued of the law's range of rights. Moreover, this is an area in which international human rights norms are especially closely involved. This could suggest perhaps that the judicial disputes in this field are not as far-reaching as might be feared, at first sight.

"Whether a court carries out substantive review of a decision by reference to the concept of unreasonableness or proportionality, two questions arise: to what extent should the courts allow a degree of latitude or leeway to the decision-maker? and to what extent should it be uniform? The answers to these questions depend in large part on the respective constitutional roles of the court and the primary decision-maker (the impugned public authority), but also on practical considerations. The willingness of the courts to invalidate a decision on the ground that it is unreasonable or disproportionate will be influenced in part by the administrative scheme under review; the subject matter of the decision; the importance of the countervailing rights or interests and the extent of the interference with the right or interest."[186]

15–135 It must be emphasised that this passage is a summation of how distinguished authors believe that the (English) law should be, rather than necessarily how it is. This passage also demonstrates the many variables at play here; and the thought necessary to bring them all appropriately into the mix.

E. FAILURE TO EXERCISE A DISCRETION

15–136 Whereas "abuse of discretion" (examined in one form or another, in all the preceding Parts) refers to a wrongly exercised discretion, failure to exercise a discretion means that a public body vested with a discretionary power has incapacitated itself from being able to exercise its discretion at all. More specifically, there are at least seven ways in which this prohibited result may be brought about, namely by:

- delegating the decision to another body;

- acting on the dictation of another body;

- some previous agreement, representation, etc;

- a general blanket policy in the area;

- taking the decision over such a broad area that all elements of it cannot have been adequately scrutinised;

- "rubber-stamping" a decision; or

- failing to acknowledge that there is any discretion to be exercised.

15–137 The first two heads have already been discussed at Chapter 11, Parts E and G, since they apply generally to all types of decision and are not peculiar to discretionary powers. The third head will be examined in paras 19–44 to 19–46. Accordingly, here we shall deal only with the remaining four ways in which a body may disable itself from exercising its discretion freely and fully.

Adhering to an inflexible policy-rule

15–138 Various dangers attend on a discretionary power, for instance, the danger

---

[186] *De Smith, Judicial Review of Administrative Action*, 6th edn (2007), para.11–08.

of being, or seeming, arbitrary, partial or inconsistent. One way—and it might seem an eminently reasonable way—of avoiding the danger of a public administrator being arbitrary, is to proclaim and follow some precise and rational policy-rule[187] in the exercise of the discretion. However, such a solution carries its own difficulty, namely that, to the extent that the rule is rigidly followed, it emphasises a single policy and shuts out consideration of all others and thus neutralises the discretion which it was the intention of the legislature to create. Thus, on some pure plane, one would expect that where a discretionary decision is taken in accordance with a rule, it would therefore be invalid. One straightforward illustration of the principle occurred in *Dunne v Donoghue,*[188] *in which* Keane C.J. stated that, "… a superintendent who imposed a precondition in the case of *all* applications for the grant or renewal of firearm certificates that the applicant should … install a gun safe … would be acting *ultra vires* the provisions of the [Firearms Acts]".[189]

15–139   On the other hand, as mentioned, common sense suggests that, in view of the desirability of avoiding arbitrariness and the other defects mentioned, and especially where one is dealing with a large number of usually routine decisions, taken by fairly junior staff, the law should lean far over to accommodate such rules of practice. The result of these conflicting tensions is that there is a principle banning policy rules, but only in a fairly relaxed form, namely, "what the authority must not do is to refuse to listen at all".[190] Or, as the test was put more recently in *Crofton v Minister for the Environment, Heritage and Local Government,* "… there is no evidence … to suggest that the respondent has irrevocably closed his mind to the issue of hunting on this territory at some future date".[191]

15–140   In other words, it is permissible for a public body to guide the implementation of its discretion by means of a policy or a non-statutory set of rules, provided that it is open to an exception in a deserving case. Another simple illustration is afforded by *Farleigh Ltd v Temple Bar Renewal Ltd.*[192] The facts were that the respondent had refused to grant approval of the applicant's building with the consequence that the use of the building did not qualify for a tax advantage. One of the applicant's arguments was that the respondent had used its guidelines

---

[187]   There is a good recent discussion of the law in *McDonagh v Clare Co. Co.* [2002] 2 I.R. 634 at paras 52–54. See also, *Holland v Governor of Portlaoise Prison* [2004] 2 I.R. 573 at paras 37–40; *Cirpaci v Minister for Justice, Equality and Law Reform* [2005] 2 I.L.R.M. 547 at 557. For condemnation of a blanket refusal to grant licences of a particular type, see *Bemis v Minister for Arts, Sport and Tourism* [2007] 3 I.R. 255 at para.62. In *Dunne v Donohoe* [2002] 2 I.L.R.M. 200 at 207, 209, counsel even suggested, without success, that such a policy rule would violate Art.15.2.1° (presumably only if it introduced a new principle not to be found in principal legislation); for a case on plea bargains and fettering discretion, see *People (DPP) v Heevy* [2001] 1 I.R. 736.
[188]   [2002] 2 I.R. 533. For other examples, see *Re N, a solicitor,* unreported, High Court, Finlay P., June 30, 1980. See also, *Rice v Dublin Corporation* [1947] I.R. 425 at 455–456; *East Donegal Co-Operative Ltd v Attorney General* [1970] I.R. 317 at 344; *Norris v Attorney General* [1984] I.R. 36 at 81 (McCarthy J.); *MC v Legal Aid Board* [1991] 2 I.R. 43; *Frenchurch Properties Ltd v Wexford County Council* [1992] 2 I.R. 268 at 282–283; *State (McGeough) v Louth* (1973) 107 I.L.T.R. 13 at 19; *Mishra v Minister for Justice* [1996] 1 I.R. 189, analysed in the Third Edition, pp.669–670; *Garda Representative Association v Minister for Finance* [2010] IEHC 78 at para.19; *Duff v Minister for Agriculture* [1997] 2 I.R. 22 at 74–75.
[189]   [2002] 2 I.R. 533 at 543 (emphasis added).
[190]   *British Oxygen v Minister for Technology* [1971] A.C. 610 at 625.
[191]   [2009] IEHC 114 at para.27 (Hedigan J.).
[192]   [1999] 2 I.R. 508.

in such a way as to fetter its discretion. The argument failed because, while the applicant had taken into account the guidelines, it was "clear from the last paragraph of the respondent's [decision] letter that the respondent had proceeded to consider whether the applicant's case was an 'exceptional case' and was of the view that there were no grounds for doing so".[193]

15–141   The facts were on the other side of the line in *McCarron v Superintendent Kearney*,[194] where the applicant had applied for, and been refused, a licence to import a rifle. In the Supreme Court, Fennelly J. quoted from *Dunne*, with approval, and went on to state (in a passage whose opening sentence refers to another ground of invalidity,[195] which may however often arise in the same situation):

> "It follows from this passage that a decision reached by a superintendent in compliance with a general instruction or directive from a superior officer [is an unlawful act] and his decision may be set aside on that ground. In addition however the same result may follow where the decision maker himself lays down a rigid policy from which he does not permit himself to depart. On the other hand, it would be wrong to preclude a decision maker from formulating guidelines by reference to which he makes it clear that he will make his decisions. It would be inimical to good administration and to consistency and decision making to oblige all decision makers to treat each decision entirely on its own without reference to previous decisions or to criteria designed to serve the public interest ... Clearly, it would be difficult to draw the line between permissible guidelines and impermissible rigid and inflexible policies."

15–142   The administrator would certainly say "amen" to the final sentence. However, Fennelly J. continued by saying that, to use the language of the passage, on the facts, the policy was "inflexible" in that no opportunity had been offered to a licence applicant "to address the possibility of any exception to the policy or the merits of the particular firearm". Accordingly, he quashed the refusal of the licence.

15–143   A policy-rule may, by its express terms, have some built-in flexibility as in *TC v Minister for Justice, Equality and Law Reform*,[196] in which the High Court stated that "... the respondent has not been shown to have adopted a fixed or inflexible policy regarding the need for an appreciable period of cohabitation ... An 'appreciable period' is itself a flexible notion capable of adaptation to the facts of the individual case".

---

[193] [1999] 2 I.R. 508 at 515.
[194] [2010] 3 I.R. 302. The quotations are from paras 66–70. In the nature of things, it happens quite often that, as in the instant case, the same situation engages the present principle and the rule against "acting under dictation" covered at Ch.11, Part G. At first instance, the High Court ([2008] IEHC 195 at paras 19–20), taking a more tolerant view of the guidelines, had rejected the application.
[195] This is the principle against acting under dictation, described in Ch.11, Part G.
[196] [2005] 4 I.R. 109 at 119.

Examples of the rule in operation in particular contexts

15–144   Let us consider the principle against a policy-rule in the context of the commonly used (and generally perceived as fair) administrative arrangement of the "waiting list". Where limited resources, like corporation houses, are being distributed, the system often adopted is to give credit to those whose name has been longest on the waiting list. The question arises whether such a waiting list is valid, a question which was relevant in the related cases of *McDonald v Dublin Corporation*[197] and the later case of *McNamee v Buncrana U.D.C.*[198]

15–145   In *McDonald*, the Supreme Court, per O'Higgins C.J., had held that where a person is in need of housing, there is a duty on the relevant housing authority at least to consider whether their needs outweigh those of other applicants' even if the other applicants have been on the waiting list longer. However, O'Higgins C.J.'s later comment in *McNamee* on his own judgment in *McDonald* was to the effect that "… [i]t was not intended to suggest [in *McDonald*] that a housing authority need not have regard as a matter of priority to those in its functional area who have been resident or domiciled there for a particular period of time".[199] On this interpretation, what was really being said in *McDonald* was only that in a strong enough case—that is, strong in the context of the purposes of the Housing Act 1966—the housing authority must be prepared to override the dictates of the waiting list; and not that the waiting list may always, or even usually, be ignored. In short, a policy-rule was permitted, provided that the possibility of an exception was admitted. One might add the very general observation that one lesson which emerges from *McDonald–McNamee* is that, if the law is allowed to become too subtle, it will be open to misinterpretation by hard-pressed administrators.

15–146   Another field in which the principle against a blanket policy might seem to appear, at any rate on the horizon, is whether it is necessary for there to be a uniform contract between some public body and a number of independent service providers. What if one of the individual service providers challenges the validity of the terms negotiated between the public body and the representative professional organisation? This was essentially the position in both *Collooney Pharmacy Limited v North Western Health Board*[200] and *Association of General Practitioners Ltd v Minister for Health*.[201] In each of these High Court cases, a challenge, based on the argument that establishing common terms for all of the individual service providers involved fettering of the public body's discretion, failed.

15–147   The more thorough discussion is in the *Association of General*

---

[197]   Unreported, Supreme Court, July 23, 1980.
[198]   [1983] I.R. 213. This authority and *McDonald* are discussed at *McDonagh v Clare County Council* [2002] 2 I.R. 634 at 643–647.
[199]   [1983] I.R. 213 at 220. What happened is that, following on from *McDonald*, the Department of the Environment had issued a circular to all local housing authorities, stating (wrongly, but perhaps understandably) that *McDonald* had prohibited a waiting list, for Corporation houses, in any circumstances.
[200]   [2005] 4 I.R. 124 at paras 50–51. For a pair of contrasting cases, see *Cornish v Minister for Justice, Equality and Law Reform* [2000] 2 I.R. 548; *McAlister v Minister for Justice, Equality, and Law Reform* [2003] 1 I.L.R.M. 161, which are discussed in H & M, paras 15–219 to 15–221.
[201]   [1995] 1 I.R. 382.

Practitioners Ltd where O'Hanlon J. upheld the validity of an agreement, whereby the Minister had recognised one single organisation as the body for consultation and representation in respect of claims for doctors, as "a reasonable and permissible one", having regard especially to the fact that no other representative body had yet come forward. While to some extent the Minister had fettered his discretion in so acting, this was "quite defensible having regard to the importance of securing uniformity in terms and conditions of employment for all [participating] doctors, so far as it was possible to do so".[202] O'Hanlon J. further stressed that the agreement was for a comparatively short duration, which left scope for coping with "unexpected and unforeseen developments". If there were to be, for example, a mass exodus from the recognised organisation to the plaintiff, the Minister would need to have the necessary flexibility to recognise the new organisation, as the existing agreement was subject to review at regular intervals.

15–148   There are two rules which may arise together and may be confused,[203] namely the rule (presently under discussion) against an inflexible policy rule and the rules against abuse of a discretionary power, discussed in Parts A–D of this chapter; for designing the substance of a policy-rule is an exercise of discretion and, as such, distinct from its application. But, while conceptually distinct, these two principles may well operate together as in *McDonagh v Clare Co. Co.*[204] The applicants were travellers who had spent extended periods of time in Co. Clare and had put their names on the respondent County Council's housing list. However, the respondent had refused to consider their application, on the basis that they had not been resident in the county for at least three years prior to February 2000, as required by the respondent's Travellers' Accommodation Programme. The High Court (O'Sullivan J.) held, as regards the first point (reasonableness of the policy), that the inclusion of a "residents or indigenous policy" in a Travellers' Accommodation Programme is within the statutory power of a housing authority. However, the second point was that such a policy must not be applied with the rigidity of a rule, so that the housing authority refuses to listen *at all* to an application for accommodation. The eventual outcome took the form of an order directing the respondent:

> "[t]o consider the application of the applicants for accommodation generally … not [to] exclude the applicants *in limine* by reference to the indigenous policy. In so considering the applications, however, they are entitled to have regard to their indigenous policy …".[205]

Failing to address the specific issue[206]

15–149   Consider a discretionary power taking the following form: "If it appears

---

[202] [1995] 1 I.R. 382 at 393.
[203] There may be an example in *McAlister v Minister for Justice* [2003] 1 I.R.L.M. 161 at 168.
[204] [2003] 1 I.L.R.M. 36. For other examples of the coincidence of these two rules, see *State (McGeough) v Louth* (1973) 107 I.L.T.R. 13 at 19, 20, 24–26, 28; *McAlister v Minister for Justice* [2003] 1 I.R.L.M. 161 at 168; *Carrigaline Community Television Co. Ltd v Minister for Transport* [1997] 1 I.L.R.M. 241.
[205] [2003] 1 I.L.R.M. 36 at 52–53. By way of assisting the respondent in implementing the High Court's order, the court, at 53–54, gave a fairly detailed analysis of *Re N a Solicitor*, unreported, High Court, Finlay P., June 30, 1980, on which see the Third Edition, p.669.
[206] This rubric and that adopted in the two following sections have been coined by the present writers.

to the Minister that [a particular state of affairs exists] then the Minister may exercise [the specified power]." What the rule presently under discussion means is that the Minister will only be regarded as having properly exercised his discretion if he has genuinely considered whether the requisite state of affairs exists—and here is the important point—in relation to all the sectors which are affected by his exercise of the power. Thus, if the power is exercised over a very broad area, a court is liable to say that the Minister cannot be sure that the requisite state of affairs genuinely exists in relation to the entire area caught by the Minister's decision. Two examples[207] of this rule in operation may be cited of which the first is *Limerick Corporation v Sheridan*.[208] To summarise the facts: the relevant statutory provision allowed the Corporation to prohibit temporary dwellings on any land where their "erection would be prejudicial to public health". The Corporation made an order affecting almost the entire area of the county borough (which was nearly one square mile). One of the grounds on which the order was struck down was that the area covered was so large that the court considered it unlikely that the Corporation could have formed the requisite opinion with respect to *all* parts of the land caught by the order.

15–150   The second example is the case of *Roche v Minister for Industry and Commerce*[209] which concerned a mineral acquisition order made by the Minister in respect of "all minerals … under the land described in the Schedule to this Order …". The order was made under the Minerals Development Act 1940 s.14(1) by which:

> Whenever it appears to the Minister that there are minerals on or under any land and that such minerals are not being worked … and the Minister is of opinion that it is desirable in the public interest, with a view to the exploitation of such minerals, that the working of such minerals should be controlled by the State, the Minister … may by order … compulsorily acquire such minerals.

15–151   Dealing with the rule we are illustrating, Henchy J. said, in *Roche*:

> "[T]he Minister must make an appraisal of the situation in the light of the particular mineral substances which he invoked … and must consider whether it is desirable in the public interest, with a view to their exploitation, that the working of them should be controlled by the State … [T]he acquisition orders in question here [are] bad for they are blanket orders to cover 'all minerals' under the land … and thereby show a want of the discrimination and appraisal necessary on the part of the Minster to comply with the … prerequisites set out in the subsection."[210]

"Rubber stamping"

15–152   This rubric covers the straightforward notion that a discretionary power

---

[207] For another example, see *State (Minister for Local Government) v Ennis U.D.C.* [1939] I.R. 258 at 260.
[208] (1956) 90 I.L.T.R. 59.
[209] [1978] I.R. 149.
[210] [1978] I.R. 149 at 156.

must be exercised in substance and not merely in form. One illustration is provided by *Inspector of Taxes' Association v Minister for the Public Service*.[211] Up to 1960 a staff association known as the Association of Inspectors of Taxes represented Inspectors of Taxes (Technical). In 1960 the expansion of the PAYE scheme to cover all employees necessitated the appointment of extra staff to the Revenue Commissioners. A number of additional Inspectors of Taxes were appointed, who differed from the traditional (or "Technical") in that they: possessed no technical qualifications; were not granted a commission by the Minister; and were designated "Inspectors of Taxes (Clerical)". However, the Minister refused to create a separate personnel grade for these new Inspectors, with the result that the two categories of Inspector occupied the same grade. Later it became important to the applicant (in order to secure them representational rights in union negotiations) that there be a separate grade ("Technical Inspector"). The Minister declined to change the grades. In the instant case, the Association challenged this refusal. The submission was that the Minister had not really examined the possibility of re-grading, but instead had merely looked back to the refusal by the Minister for Finance (the predecessor of the Minister for the Public Service) in 1960 of an earlier (similar) request that a distinct grade for Clerical Inspectors be established. Rejecting this argument on the facts, but apparently accepting its correctness in law, Finlay C.J. held that before taking the 1980 decision, "[the Minister had gone] in detail into the existing situation in 1980 of the various categories of Inspectors of Taxes; the work that they carried out; and the material factors which might be appropriate if a re-grading of them had been contemplated".[212] Finlay C.J. concluded that the Minister had come to a considered decision on the application to re-grade, and that decision could not be attacked as unreasonable.

15–153   What is probably a further illustration of the notion that a discretionary power must be scrupulously exercised can be drawn from *Fajujonu v Minister for Justice*[213] (the facts of which concerned whether the alien parents of a minor child, who was an Irish citizen, could be deported). Here the review failed on the facts, but, at the same time, the Supreme Court fired a warning shot across the Minister's bows, as regards how the court expected the Fajujonu family to be treated in the future. Finlay C.J. stated:

> "[T]here is not any finding [of fact] that the existence of important family rights in the children of this marriage have been ignored ... Neither, however, is there a finding nor any evidence, it would appear to me, to support a finding of a careful consideration of those rights and a particular importance attached to them by reason of their constitutional origin ...
>
>   ... I am, however, satisfied also that if, *having had due regard to those considerations and having conducted such inquiry as may be appropriate ...*

---

[211] [1986] I.L.R.M. 296.

[212] [1986] I.L.R.M. 296 at 303.

[213] [1990] I.L.R.M. 234. See also, *State (Thornhill) v Minster for Defence* [1986] I.R. 1 at 12 (followed in *McKinley v Minister for Defence* [1988] I.R. 139; and also in *Breen v Minister for Defence* [1994] 2 I.R. 34 at 41–41; and *Rederij Kennemerland NV v Attorney General* [1989] I.L.R.M. 821 at 839. This issue has also been considered in a series of search warrant cases: *People (DPP) v Kenny* [1990] 2 I.R. 110 at 117; *Byrne v Grey* [1988] I.R. 31; *R. v Maidstone Crown Court Ex p. Waitt* [1988] Crim. L.R. 384; *R. v Southwark Crown Court Ex p. Sorsky Defries* [1996] Crim. L.R. 195 (far-reaching search warrant should not "be allowed to go through on the nod"); *Hanahoe v District Judge Hussey* [1998] 3 I.R. 69.

the Minister is satisfied that ... the residence of these parents within the State should be terminated ... that this is an order he is entitled to make ...".[214]

Failing to acknowledge that there is any discretion to exercise

15–154 Here, a public body is deemed to fail to exercise a discretion, by virtue of claiming (whether explicitly or implicitly) that there is no discretion to exercise. A typical example is *Sherwin v Minister for the Environment*.[215] The background to the case was that the Referendum Act 1994 s.26 provides that at a Referendum, all personation agents and agents who assist at the count are to be nominated by a member of the Oireachtas. Yet, in the case of the Fifteenth Amendment of the Constitution (No. 2) Bill 1995 (to remove the divorce ban) each of the parties represented in the Oireachtas were pro-divorce. The plaintiff who was an anti-divorce activist wrote to the Minister asking him to use his discretion under s.164(1) to make adaptations or modifications by ministerial order, where there is "an emergency or special difficulty". The essence of the letter in reply was that "the Minister has no power to alter [s.26] by regulations". Notwithstanding that the referendum was long over, at the time of the case, Costello P. ruled that "the Minister had misconstrued the section" and went on to make a declaration that "the Minister has jurisdiction to consider whether there exists circumstances of special difficulty ... [and if he so decides] to modify section 26 ...".

15–155 A second example is *Whelan v Kirby*[216] which arose out of a criminal prosecution for drunken driving. The solicitor for the accused made an application to have the intoximeter inspected by an independent expert. The District Court judge rejected this application with the words "I cannot get involved in this. The law is the law". In so saying, according to the Supreme Court, the judge failed to entertain the application and so failed to exercise his judicial discretion.

F. ARE THERE UNREVIEWABLE DISCRETIONARY POWERS?

15–156 Writing in 1966, Professor Kelly stated that:

"[P]rovided an authority entrusted with administrative discretion keeps inside its *vires* and (where appropriate) commits no open breach of natural justice it may act as foolishly, unreasonably or even unfairly as it likes and the Courts cannot (or at any rate will not) interfere."[217]

---

[214] [1990] I.L.R.M. 234 at 238–239 (emphasis added).

[215] [2004] 4 I.R. 279. Quotations in text are from paras 26–30. (The case was decided in 1997.) The Minister appears not to have taken the point that s.164 of the Referendum Act 1994 may have been unconstitutional by virtue of Art.15.2.1°. See, to analogous effect, *Abrahamson v Law Society of Ireland* [1996] 2 I.L.R.M. 481 at 499–500.

[216] [2005] 2 I.R. 30. The quotation is at 41–43.

[217] Kelly, "Administrative Discretion and the Courts" (1966) 1 Ir. Jur. (N.S) 209 at 210. Note however, such cases as *State (McGeough) v Louth CC* (1973) 107 I.L.T.R. 13 which was decided in 1956 but not reported until 1973, and *State (O'Mahony) v South Cork Board of Public Health* [1941] Ir. Jur. Rep. 79.

15–157   Commenting on this statement only five years later, the same writer made *amende honorable*:

> "In the light of four subsequent Irish decisions, it is clear that this point of view, whatever justification it may have had in 1966, does not now correctly state Irish law on the matter; ... the Courts have, within the last three years, explicitly marked out bridgeheads from which the exercise of statutory discretion can be controlled on more penetrating criteria than mere *vires* (as traditionally understood) or natural justice."[218]

15–158   The preceding parts of this chapter consist largely of an account of the break-out from these bridgeheads and we now offer a consideration of the few islands of immunity from judicial review which may continue to remain above the waterline.

15–159   At the outset, we ought to note that this is one of those common fields in administrative law in which a superfluity of jargon competes for a paucity of meaning. If an applicant is unsuccessful, then the High Court may articulate the ground in a number of different ways, though without acknowledging their real underlying similarity. Thus, the applicant may fail because the High Court: (a) holds that, because of the subject matter of the case, it (wholly or partly) lacks jurisdiction, which is the subject covered in this Part; (b) interprets normal judicial review principles as either not applying, or as applying with a reduced level of intensity, in the particular circumstances (paras 15–132 to 15–134); or (c) exercises its discretion not to send an order, because of one of a number of grounds summarised at Ch.16, Part D. Nevertheless, we continue to treat these barriers in discrete parts of this textbook, not only because this is the orthodox way of doing things, but also because each of these restrictions "sits" in its own context, with its own connections and comparisons, emphases and quirks.

15–160   As indicated, category (a) covers situations in which the courts' jurisdiction to review an administrative action is barred because the law considers (or in some cases used to consider) that the nature of the subject matter in particular fields is such that, irrespective of the normal technical categories of judicial review, some high public policy militates in favour of either immunity from judicial review or (more usually) review at a reduced intensity. Quite often, this bar is articulated in the form of some express or implicit constitutional restraint. These constitutional restraints include those which are intended to protect the autonomy of the Oireachtas, the President or (to a limited degree) the referendum process,[219]

---

[218] Kelly, "Judicial Review of Administrative Action: New Irish Trends" (1971) 6 Ir. Jur. (N.S) 40. The four subsequent Irish decisions referred to were: *Listowel U.D.C. v McDonagh* [1968] I.R. 312; *Central Dublin Development Association v Attorney General* (1975) 109 I.L.T.R. 69; *Kiely v Minister for Social Welfare* [1971] I.R. 21; and *East Donegal Co-Operative Ltd v Attorney General* [1970] I.R. 317.

[219] *Re Haughey* [1971] I.R. 217; *McKenna v An Taoiseach (No. 1)* [1995] 2 I.R. 1; and *McKenna v An Taoiseach (No. 2)* [1995] 2 I.R. 10. See Sherlock, "Constitutional Change, Referenda and the Courts in Ireland" (1997) *Public Law* 125; and *Maguire v Ardagh* [2002] 1 I.R. 385. It should be stressed that much recent case law has in the end gone against the autonomy of the Oireachtas, e.g. *Haughey*, *Ardagh*, *Norris* (for the abortive *Norris* proceedings in 1990, see Gwynn Morgan, *The Separation of Powers in the Irish Constitution* (Dublin: Round Hall Sweet & Maxwell, 1997) p.223, fn.5). See Murray, "Judicial Review of Parliamentary

or to curtain off foreign or international affairs.[220] Next, there are other areas which, without specific constitutional bars, are excluded because their character is regarded as unsuitable for judicial review. Sometimes, this sort of bar is justified by reference to the general notion of the Separation of Powers, in particular the notion that judges are not well situated or qualified to deal with the areas reserved for the legislature and the executive. (This is buttressed by its half-brother "the Political Question", which also overlaps with the shadowy area of "non-justiciability".)[221]

15–161   We are not going into these restraints, since they are covered in works of constitutional law. Instead, our focus is on the areas of public administration which are under review, or are excluded from review. The dominant judicial view would appear to be that all discretionary powers are reviewable. This may be illustrated by *Duff v Minister for Agriculture*.[222] Here the plaintiffs were a group of small farmers. The Minister, both on its own behalf and as agent for the European Commission, approved their plans to develop their farms (which included borrowing money) on the basis that there would be an expanded quota for the sale of their milk. However, subsequently the plaintiffs were not allocated any "reference quantity" to enable them to fulfil their development plan. They claimed damages to compensate them for this loss.

15–162   The plaintiff's claim failed before Murphy J. in the High Court who relied upon the older, more cautious, approach to judicial review. He stated:

"The Regulations deliberately chose to confer a discretion which though not absolute ... does not appear to have been restricted by any identifiable

---

Proceedings and Procedures under the Irish Constitution" in Doyle and Carolan (eds), *The Irish Constitution: Governance and Values* (Dublin: Thomson Round Hall, 2008).

　　On broad separation of powers principles, it has sometimes been said that the courts will refrain from interfering with the process of legislation: *O'Crowley v Minister for Finance* [1935] I.R. 536; *Halpin v Attorney General* [1936] I.R. 226; *Wireless Dealers Association v Fair Trade Commission*, unreported, Supreme Court, March 7, 1956; *O'Malley v An Ceann Comhairle* [1997] 1 I.R. 428; *Roche v Ireland*, unreported, High Court, Carroll J., June 17, 1983; and *Finn v Attorney General* [1983] I.R. 154. Yet judicial intervention will be forthcoming if the constitutionally required stages of law-making have not been carried out: *R. (O'Brien) v Governor of the North Dublin Military Barracks* [1924] 1 I.R. 32; *Victoria v Commonwealth* (1975) 7 A.L.R. 1; *Western Australia v Commonwealth* (1975) 7 A.L.R. 159.

　　In October 2011, a proposed constitutional amendment (Thirtieth Amendment of the Constitution (Houses of the Oireachtas Inquiries) Bill 2011) was rejected at referendum, probably because the public felt that it went too far in exempting Oireachtas' inquiries from judicial review.

[220] *Shortt v Ireland (No. 2)* [2006] 3 I.R. 297; *Horgan v An Taoiseach* [2003] 2 I.R. 468 at 515. But contrast *Crotty v An Taoiseach* [1987] I.R. 713.

[221] For an incisive analysis, see Daly, "'Political Questions' and Judicial Review in Ireland" (2008) 2 *Judicial Studies Institute Journal* 116; see also, Harris, "Judicial Review, Justiciability and the Prerogative of Mercy" (2003) 62 C.L.J. 631. (The title undersells the substance of this excellent article, which goes way beyond the prerogative.)

　　For a good example of an area in respect of which it is not apt for a court to adjudicate, see *Roche v Roche* [2009] IESC 82 at p.11, where Murray C.J. stated: "I do not consider that it is for a court of law, faced with the most divergent if most learned views available to it from the disciplines referred to, to pronounce on the truth of when human life begins". See also, *Abuissa v Minister for Justice, Equality and Law Reform* [2011] 1 I.R. 123 at paras 29–36 and 53–60 (Clarke J. declining to quash the Minister's refusal to grant a certificate of naturalisation in his absolute discretion, or to give reasons for the refusal).

[222] [1997] 2 I.R. 22.

objective or in any purposeful fashion. I can only infer that the discretion was granted to each Member State to be exercised in accordance with the national policy of that State rather than the attainment of particular objectives within the Council Regulations.

Even leaving aside any question of the application of the doctrine of the separation of powers it seems to me impossible for the Courts to review decisions based on questions of national policy."[223]

Yet, the striking point about these sentiments is their rarity; and, even more important, that the High Court decision was reversed in the Supreme Court.[224]

15–163   Next, to take a case from a very different field, in *Inspector of Taxes v Minister for the Public Service*,[225] the Supreme Court stated that a decision of the Minister in regard to grading, which affects the salary and career prospects of certain civil servants, is, like any other administrative action, open to review. Another major breakout was provided by the line of cases which established that it is open to a judge to overrule governmental claims to the non-disclosure of evidence before a court.[226] And, in *Gallagher v Corrigan*,[227] Blayney J. readily accepted, obiter, that judicial review would lie to control disciplinary decisions taken by prison authorities, whether it be in respect of prisoners or prison officers:

> "There is obviously a considerable difference between the Governor's exercising discipline over prisoners and his exercising discipline over his officers, but it seems to me that it would be anomalous ... that prisoners should be entitled to the protection of the rules of natural and constitutional justice, but that prison officers should not ... The Governor in exercising his powers of discipline over prison officers is also discharging a function which is partly magisterial and partly of a judicial or decision-making character, with the consequence that he must comply with the rules of natural and constitutional justice."[228]

15–164   There have been several cases, examined at paras 15–100 to 15–102, in

---

[223] [1997] 2 I.R. 22 at 43–44. For the facts in the case and the divergence between the minority and the majority, see H & M, paras 18–148 to 18–150.

[224] [1997] 2 I.R. 22. Notice that the two dissentients in the Supreme Court relied mainly on the principle that that Minister's decision did not defy fundamental reason and common sense. However, Keane J. also remarked that: "Ultimately [the Minister's decision] had to be made by a Minister responsible to Dáil Éireann and to the people in the electoral process." See also, similar comments of the other dissenting judge, Hamilton C.J., at 70–71.

[225] [1986] I.L.R.M. 296.

[226] It bears noting that, while this result was grounded on Art.34.1 of the Constitution by the Supreme Court, in *Murphy v Dublin Corporation* [1972] I.R. 215, the High Court in the same case had laid down the same principle (at 227) using the standard common law rules for the control of a discretionary power.

[227] Unreported, High Court, Blayney J., February 1, 1988. See also, the prison transfer cases. These include: *State (Smith and Fox) v Governor of the Curragh Military Barracks* [1980] I.L.R.M. 208 at 211–212 (Barrington J. distinguished the DPP's discretion to prosecute cases on the basis that the instant situation was "not of the same high order of importance and confidentiality as the opinion of the DPP ..."); *State (Boyle) v Governor of the Curragh Military Barracks* [1980] I.L.R.M. 242. See too, *Cornish v Minister for Justice, Equality and Law Reform* [2000] 2 I.R. 548; and *McAlister v Minister for Justice, Equality and Law Reform* [2003] 1 I.L.R.M. 161.

[228] Unreported, High Court, Blayney J., February 1, 1988 at pp.12–13 of the judgment.

the broad immigration–deportation–citizenship field, in which ordinary, or even in some cases an anxious scrutiny, level of judicial review has been operated, with no suggestion that this is a subject area in which judicial review either does not apply or is applied with less intensity than in other fields. However, something like this did occur in *Bode (a minor) v Minister for Justice, Equality and Law Reform*.[229] The situation in this case (which was said to be common to several thousand others) concerned the right to remain in Ireland of foreign nationals, who were the parents of children born here. The background to this case was an earlier Supreme Court decision of *Fajujonu v Minister for Justice*[230] which had held that, where a child had been born in Ireland thereby acquiring Irish citizenship, then (so long as the child was a minor) its parents (though foreign nationals) had a right to reside in Ireland. But, this ruling was substantially curtailed by another case, *Lobe & Osayende v Minister for Justice, Equality and Law Reform*.[231] The issue which then presented itself was what to do with those foreign national parents to whom a child had been born before the date of the earlier decision. To cater for them, an administrative scheme, the "Irish born child" had been established. This required the Minister to grant permission for the family to remain for two years, provided that the applicant's parents could demonstrate that they had remained in Ireland continuously since the birth of the child. In the instant case, the applicant was not in a position to satisfy this requirement. Nevertheless, he claimed that his deportation would be invalid by virtue of his constitutional and Convention rights. The Supreme Court's ruling rejecting this argument is not entirely clear. It seems to be based in part on the fact that the parents had not satisfied its requirement. Secondly and more relevant here, Denham J. relied on the notion that "[t]he inherent power of the state includes the power to establish an *ex gratia* scheme of this nature. Such an arrangement is distinct from circumstances where legal rights of individuals may fall to be considered and determined … [And thus the foreign nationals] were still entitled to have the Minister consider their constitutional and convention rights. The scheme enabled a fast, executive decision giving a benefit to very many people". The tone of this sounds as if, because of the circumstances of the case, the court applied a very reduced level of review.

15–165 One of the few situations in which a court seemed to regard itself as definitely not having jurisdiction was *State (Sheehan) v Government of Ireland*,[232] where the applicant sought judicial review of the Government's failure to make an order bringing into force s.60(1) of the Civil Liability Act 1961 (which abolishes the common law rule that a highway authority cannot be held liable for nonfeasance or non-repair of the public highway). Section 60(7)[233] provided that no commencement order could be made for a date prior to April 1, 1967. Reversing the High Court (Costello J.), the Supreme Court held that the subsection conferred

---

[229] [2008] 3 I.R. 663. Quotations are from paras 60–75.

[230] [1990] 1 I.L.R.M. 234.

[231] [2003] 1 I.R. 1.

[232] [1987] I.R. 550. See Hogan, "Judicial Review of an Executive Discretion" (1987) 9 D.U.L.J. 91.

[233] The same (or similar) formulae as that in the 1961 Act are still in use today. For example: s.2 of the Air Pollution Act 1987; s.2 of the Labour Services Act 1987; s.27(4) of the National Monuments (Amendment) Act 1987; and s.1(2) of the Safety, Health and Welfare (Off-Shore Installations) Act 1987 all provide that the relevant Minister "may" make an order bringing the Act into force.

on the Government what, in effect, is an unreviewable discretionary power. Henchy J stated:

> "The use of 'shall' and 'may,' both in the subsection and in the section as a whole, point to the conclusion that the radical law-reform embodied in the section was not intended to come into effect before the 1st April 1967 and thereafter only on such day as *may* be fixed by the Government. Not, be it noted, on such date as *shall* be fixed by the Government. Limiting words such as 'as soon as may be' or 'as soon as convenient,' which are to be found in comparable statutory provisions, are markedly absent ...
>
> [The] important law reform to be effected by the section was not to take effect unless and until the Government became satisfied that, in the light of factors such as the necessary deployment of financial and other resources, the postulated reform would come into effect. The discretion vested in the Government to bring the section into operation on a date after 1st April 1967 *was not limited in any way as to time or otherwise.*"[234]

15–166   This decision would seem to go against the tenor of modern administrative law,[235] and it seems best to regard it as confined to its own field; that is as a strong application of the Separation of Powers, in the mode of mandating judicial restraint in regard to the executive and legislature.

15–167   In some cases, the argument for saying that judicial review is excluded may appear to be strengthened by the use of such a statutory formula as "[t]he Minister may in his absolute discretion ...". These legislative attempts have been less frequent in recent decades and have most often involved procedural questions, such as whether an oral hearing should be held or costs awarded[236] rather than substantive matters.[237] But, in any case, these devices should be seen in the same light as the even more direct "ouster clauses" which were discussed earlier and said to be probably unconstitutional.[238]

15–168   Again major and long-established exemptions from the courts' jurisdiction to review traditionally existed in respect of decisions in the fields of security and prosecution. However, even though the general principle that these areas are exempt continues vital, its scope has been narrowed by a number of recent exceptions involving the DPP's discretion to prosecute.[239]

---

[234] [1987] I.R. 550 at 561 (emphasis added). But surely, the invocation (in the early part of this passage) of what amounts to the *expressio unius* principle seems misplaced in this statutory context. It was clearly intended that the Government should be given a discretion in the matter, but the use of the word "may" for this purpose probably results from the use of a convenient statutory formula to which no special significance should be attached. For more comment on *Sheehan*, see Third Edition, p.685.

[235] See Third Edition, pp.684–686.

[236] Local Government Act 2001 s.214; Tribunals of Inquiry (Evidence) (Amendment) Act 1997 s.3; Planning and Development Act 2000 s.134.

[237] Criminal Assets Bureau Act 1996 ss.8–9; Irish Nationality and Citizenship Act 2001 s.5; Mercantile Marine Act 1955 s.21.

[238] See para.11–14. See also, *State (Lynch) v Cooney* [1982] I.R. 337, analysed at para.15–09.

[239] e.g. *Eviston v DPP* [2002] 3 I.R. 260; *Carlin v DPP* [2003] 3 I.R. 547. See H & M, paras 15–250 to 15–276.

CHAPTER 16

APPLICATION FOR JUDICIAL REVIEW

A. INTRODUCTION

16–01 Because of the unique position of the State and its agencies, not only is there a unique body of substantive law for its control (described in Chapters 10–15); but the High Court procedure by which law is administered is also unique. This procedure is the subject of this and the following chapter. It is established by the 2011 Rules of Court[1] (in force from January 1, 2012), which (subject to exceptions noted below) are a word-for-word restatement of their 1986 precursors.[2] The 1986 Rules, however, marked a significant change, to understand which it is necessary to appreciate a little history.

16–02 Before 1986, a person seeking review of a decision of an administrative body or lower court was required to select the "correct" remedy from among a variety of remedies open to him (At paras 16–72 to 16–80, we deal with the question of how an aggrieved party chooses between review and an appeal, if available). In addition to the principal state side orders of certiorari, prohibition and mandamus,[3]

---

[1] Rules of the Superior Courts (Judicial Review) (S.I. No. 691 of 2011), Ord.84 rr.18–28. See generally, Donnelly, "Changes to Judicial Review Procedure", *Bar Review*, February, 2012. Although by no means all of the LRC's proposals were adopted, for the lead-up to the changes, see Law Reform Commission, *Judicial Review Procedure* (CP20–2003); *Report on Judicial Review Procedure* (LRC 71–2004).

[2] S.I. No. 15 of 1986. For an account of the pre-1986 State side practice, see Law Reform Commission Working Paper No. 8, *Judicial Review of Administrative Action: The Problem of Remedies* (1979), and Graham, "Judicial Review: Where to Reform" (1984) 6 D.U.L.J. 25. The Rules very largely follow the scheme of reform as proposed by the Law Reform Commission in their working paper.

[3] The other state side orders are habeas corpus (or an application under Art.40.4.2° of the Constitution as it is more properly described) and *quo warranto*. (There is "an inherent jurisdiction to convert a misdirected application for an enquiry under Art.40.4.2° to judicial review proceedings, and vice versa": see *Devoy v Governor of Portlaoise Prison* [2009] IEHC 288 per Edwards J.) The remedy of habeas corpus falls outside the scope of this book, but see Hogan and Whyte, *JM Kelly: The Irish Constitution*, 4th edn (Dublin: Lexis Nexis Butterworths, 2003), pp.1677–1706, and Costello, *The Law of Habeas Corpus in Ireland: History, Scope of Review and Practice under Article 40.4.2 of the Irish Constitution* (Dublin: Four Courts Press, 2006).
    While contrary to the LRC's recommendations (CP20–2003), p.139, *quo warranto* was retained in the 2011 Rules; the remedy is now virtually obsolete and there has been only

the private law remedies of the declaration and injunction could also have been invoked. These two sets of remedies differed in the scope of their application, depending on the nature of the decision, defect or public body involved. And if an applicant sought the wrong remedy, no relief could be granted because s/he would be deemed to have asked for an improper order. It is true that before 1986, the former state side orders could be awarded in lieu of each other, but they were not interchangeable with the private law remedies. What this meant, in practice, was that if an applicant had sought, say, certiorari, but the court was of the view that mandamus was more appropriate, then the latter remedy could be awarded. However, if on an application for certiorari it transpired that the applicant had a good case on the merits, yet the restrictions on the scope of certiorari were such that it was not available, then no alternative remedy such as a declaration or damages could be awarded. In such a situation the litigant would be required to brace himself for a fresh set of plenary proceedings, where the wider remedy of the declaration might be available. To take the converse example, the circumstances could be such that a litigant might initiate proceedings by way of plenary summons for a declaration, only to be turned away with the bitter-sweet news that although he had a good case on the merits, since one of the state side orders would have been available, he should have sought that order: the rationale for this rejection was that, since the state side orders were the specialised form of proceedings for a public law matter, the normally private law remedies of a declaration or injunction should only have been sought if no state side order was apt for the case. In practice, such blots on the legal system occurred but rarely.

16–03   However, post-1986, there has been a comprehensive procedure (known as an "application for judicial review") which enables an aggrieved party to test the legality of administrative action in the High Court. The major objective behind the creation of this new procedure was to obviate the possibility that a good case on the merits will be lost because of the wrong choice of remedy.[4] But despite this change, these formally distinct orders were retained and the question arises, does it ever matter which order is awarded? The answer is that it will be worth the applicant's time to argue for one order rather than another in very few situations. For instance, by now the time limit (three months)[5] is the same for each of the remedies. One of the few exceptional situations in which the remedy may matter concerns the fact that the declaratory order is not a coercive remedy and there may well be circumstances in which a coercive remedy is required in order, e.g. to expunge a conviction and other circumstances in which the declaratory remedy will be preferred.[6]

16–04   Thus, there seems to be very little to choose—in terms of practical consequences, as opposed to *amour propre*—between one remedy and another. And,

---

one reported case involving *quo warranto* since 1922: *State (Lycester) v Hegarty* (1941) 75 I.L.T.R. 121. The modern practice is to seek a declaration that an office holder has been invalidly appointed rather than to proceed by way of *quo warranto*: see *Glynn v Roscommon County Council* (1959) 93 I.L.T.R. 149.

[4]   Order 84 r.19.

[5]   Order 84 r.21. See para.16–47.

[6]   Unless necessary, the courts have a preference for granting declaratory relief rather than certiorari as a matter of "politeness" to the public body concerned. See, e.g. *District Judge MacMenamin v Ireland* [1996] 3 I.R. 100; *Doherty v Government of Ireland* [2010] IEHC 369.

as the early parts of this chapter illustrate, there would undoubtedly have been a gain, in terms of the simplicity of the law, if the six traditional remedies had been replaced by a single comprehensive remedy (which might have been called, like the principal remedy for judicial review in the United States Federal Courts, the "petition for review")?[7] Then, it may be asked: would anything have been lost? The answer would seem to be in the negative. Although some may have feared that if the traditional orders were amputated, violence might have been done to the substantive law of judicial review (which originally developed in the interstices of the prerogative writs), the previous chapters show that contemporary substantive law has become emancipated from its historical origins. Moreover, as Part E of the present chapter shows, the procedural law, for instance as to standing or discretion, is no longer different from one remedy to another.[8]

16–05 In addition to the major change of authorising the court to grant what it considered the "correct" order even though a different order had been sought, the 1986 Rules (as lightly amended in 2011) also made provision for such matters as time limits[9]; locus standi[10]; discovery and interrogatories[11]; and interim relief,[12] matters which are elaborated below. The Rules also established for the first time a right to claim damages in combination with an application for one of the public law remedies.[13] The rule-making power of the Committee is confined to rules dealing with "pleading and practice and procedure generally".[14] Accordingly, given the far-reaching dimensions of the changes brought about by Ord.84, it remains to be seen whether these changes can truly be said to be intra vires the Superior Court Rules Committee.[15]

---

[7] Wade and Forsyth, *Administrative Law*, 10th edn, (Oxford: OUP, 2009) p.500. Similar reforms have recently been made in New Zealand and Canada: Law Reform Commission (CP 20–2003), paras 5–01 to 5–09.

[8] This possible reform was considered by the Law Reform Commission in its Consultation Paper, *Judicial Review Procedure* (LRC CP20–2003), para.5.16 where it rejected the "single order" proposal: "The primary criticism of the proposal to abolish the separate orders and recommend their replacement with a single order is that such an approach would serve little purpose other than to encourage an amorphous approach to drafting in judicial review proceedings, whereby the papers as filed might not necessarily disclose the specific nature of the remedy sought. In the light of the emphasis on the issues of expedition and efficiency in judicial review proceedings, such a result would clearly be undesirable and in contradiction of much of the focus of this paper." But this paragraph assumes that the law of judicial review is somehow anchored in the character of the traditional remedies, which, it is suggested, is no longer the case. And note that the analogous Order 84A procedure employed in public procurement cases largely follows the "single order" method (described as an "application for review"): see Ord.84A r.3(x), established by Rules of the Superior Courts (No. 4) (Review of the Award of Public Contracts) 1998 (S.I. No. 374 of 1998).

[9] Order 84 r.21(1) imposes a general time limit of three months from the date "when grounds for the application first arose". The court has a discretion to extend these limits: see paras 16–53 to 16–61.

[10] Order 84 r.20(5) provides that the High Court shall not grant leave unless it considers that the applicant has a "sufficient interest" in the matter to which the application relates: see paras 16–81 to 16–107.

[11] Order 84 r.26(1). See paras 16–27 to 16–28.

[12] Order 84 r.20(8). See H & M, paras 16–80 to 16–81.

[13] See below, at paras 18–01 to 18–06. It was, of course, always the law that a plaintiff seeking declaratory and injunctive relief by means of a plenary hearing could also seek damages.

[14] Courts of Justice Act 1924 s.36 (as applied by ss.14 and 48 of the Courts (Supplemental Provisions) Act 1961).

[15] For discussion of the extent of changes which may be made by secondary legislation, such as

16–06   The High Court's power of judicial review is an inherent one which is designed to ensure that all forms of public body—Ministers, tribunals, public inquiries,[16] university visitors,[17] Oireachtas committees[18]—exercising public functions, do not exceed their jurisdiction. In addition, the sweep of judicial review extends to the decision of a lower court (District, Circuit or Special Criminal Court)[19]; but not of a Superior Court of record[20] (High Court, Court of Criminal Appeal and the Supreme Court).

B. DISTINCTIVE FEATURES OF PARTICULAR REMEDIES

16–07   It was traditionally the case—and remains so to some extent—that for an issue to be amenable to judicial review, two sets of conditions must be satisfied. In the first place, it must be a matter of public law. Secondly, each of the orders has its own characteristics. Most of the law in relation to these is artificial or even antiquarian and, as illustrated in the modern authorities quoted below, is probably of little significance in an age impatient of technicalities especially where, as here, they would generally favour the respondent public body. Moreover, there is also a substantial overlap between this law and the principles such as standing, which applies to all of the remedies and which is covered in Part E. Nevertheless, it is still worth mentioning some of this law, whether for reasons of historical context or of possible contemporary significance. It may be convenient to deal first with rules which are common to the three former state side orders, certiorari, prohibition and mandamus.

"Determining questions affecting the rights of citizens"

16–08   It was traditionally understood that these three public law remedies shared certain restrictive features. For instance, they would only lie to review something in the nature of a decision and there are older cases which held that a requirement that the decision be approved by another person or body prevented any order from issuing.[21] The modern tendency, however, is to eschew a rigid requirement

---

Rules of Court, see H & M, paras 16–07 to 16–12; Collins and O'Reilly, *Civil Proceedings and the State in Ireland* (Dublin: Round Hall Press, 1989), p.76.

[16]   See, e.g. *O'Callaghan v Mahon* [2005] IESC 9; [2006] 2 I.R. 32; *Fitzwilton Ltd v Mahon* [2007] IESC 27; [2008] 1 I.R. 712; *Ahern v Mahon* [2008] IEHC 119; [2008] 4 I.R. 704.

[17]   *Page v Hull University Visitor* [1993] 1 A.C. 682; *R. v Visitors to the Inns of Court Ex p. Calder* [1994] 3 Q.B. 1; *Kelly v Visitors of Trinity College Dublin* [2007] IESC 61 (semble).

[18]   *Maguire v Ardagh* [2002] 1 I.R. 385.

[19]   The Special Criminal Court ranks as an inferior court for this purpose: *Director of Public Prosecutions v Special Criminal Court* [1999] 1 I.R. 60; *Gilligan v Special Criminal Court* [2005] IESC 86; [2006] 2 I.R. 389.

[20]   "The High Court, whether sitting as the Central Criminal Court or otherwise, is not an inferior court subject to coercive orders such as mandamus", per Henchy J. in *People (DPP) v Quilligan (No. 2)* [1989] I.R. 46 at 57. For similar comments, see *CC v Ireland (No. 1)* [2006] 4 I.R. 1 at 54 per Fennelly J. However, judicial review will lie to quash decisions of officers such as the Master of the High Court or a Taxing Master, as it has been held that the High Court is not thereby making an order against itself or any other "Superior Court", but rather against an officer "attached" to the High Court. See *Elwyn (Cottons) Ltd v Master of the High Court* [1989] I.R. 14; *State (Gallagher, Shatter & Co.) v de Valera (No. 2)* [1991] 2 I.R. 198; *Gannon v Flynn* [2001] 3 I.R. 531.

[21]   *Re Local Government Board Ex p. Kingstown Commissioners* (1886) 18 L.R. Ir. 509.

that a determination must be "binding", "conclusive" or that the "legal rights" of the citizen have been affected. Rather, the courts are apt to examine whether the applicant has suffered a real or possible prejudice and would obtain a real benefit if the determination were quashed.[22] Significantly, here, the courts have declared themselves prepared to review decisions in cases involving questions of so-called "soft" law (e.g. decisions based on application of administrative circulars and guidelines) where questions of legal rights (at least in the strict sense of that term) may not necessarily arise.[23]

"Having the duty to act judicially"

16–09 Related to the requirement that for the remedy to be appropriate, legal rights must be at issue was the precept that the administrative body had to be under a duty to act judicially[24] before such remedies could be granted. Nowadays this requirement "is more honoured in the breach than in the observance" and, in practice, does not greatly restrict the scope of certiorari or prohibition. First, the duty to act judicially is implied where there is a power to affect rights or impose liabilities since "this is simply the automatic consequence of the power to determine questions affecting rights of citizens".[25] Secondly, even in cases where there is no duty to act judicially, mandamus will issue and this reflects the fact that until nearly the end of the nineteenth century, mandamus was used to enforce administrative and ministerial duties of every description.[26] Mandamus is, of course, the most appropriate remedy where the enforcement of a statutory duty is sought.[27] Certiorari traditionally enjoyed one distinct procedural advantage over and above the other remedies. It would lie to review not only ultra vires decisions, but it would also quash for error on the face of the record.[28]

---

[22] *MacPhartaláin v Commissioners of Public Works* [1994] 3 I.R. 353; *Dooner v Garda Síochána (Complaints) Board* [2000] IEHC 122 (semble); *Maguire v Ardagh* [2002] 1 I.R. 385; *de Roiste v Judge-Advocate General* [2005] 3 I.R. 494; *O'Shea Fishing Ltd v Minister for Agriculture, Fisheries and Food* [2008] IEHC 91.

[23] See, e.g. *Law Society of Ireland v Competition Authority* [2006] 2 I.R. 262 (official circular quashed on the ground that it violated constitutional rights of persons potentially affected thereby); *de Burca v Wicklow County Manager* [2009] IEHC 54 (unfair criticisms in an official report which "form[s] part of the public record of the State" impacted on her constitutional right to a good name and justified the quashing of the report).

[24] *State (Crowley) v Irish Land Commission* [1951] I.R. 250 at 265 per O'Byrne J. O'Higgins C.J. appeared to insist upon this requirement in *State (Abenglen Properties Ltd) v Dublin Corporation* [1984] I.R. 381 at 392, as did Hamilton P. in *Byrne v Grey* [1988] I.R. 31 at 40.

[25] *Ryanair Ltd v Flynn* [2000] 3 I.R. 240 at 256 per Kearns J. See also, *State (Crowley) v Irish Land Commission* [1951] I.R. 250; *Ridge v Baldwin* [1964] A.C. 40; *R. v Hillingdon BC Ex p. Royco Homes Ltd* [1974] Q.B. 720.
   It also appears that certiorari cannot be used to mount a direct challenge to the validity of a statute or delegated legislation, as no duty to act judicially arises in the case of the exercise of a legislative function: *Re Local Government Board Ex p. Kingstown Commissioners* (1886) 18 L.R. Ir. 509.

[26] Wade and Forsyth, *Administrative Law*, 10th edn (2009), pp.521–530.

[27] *State (Sheehan) v Government of Ireland* [1987] I.R. 550 at 562 per Henchy J. In *Minister for Labour v Grace* [1993] 2 I.R. 53 at 55, O'Hanlon J. said that for mandamus to issue for the enforcement of a statutory right: "[I]t must appear that the statute in question imposes a duty, the performance or non-performance of which is not a matter of discretion, and if a power or discretion only, as distinct from a duty exists, an order of mandamus will not be granted by the court."

[28] It is curious that the power to quash for error on the face of the record is nowadays so rarely

Certiorari, prohibition and mandamus: the distinctions

16–10   The demarcation lines between these three remedies are, broadly speaking, as follows. Certiorari lies to quash a decision of a public body which has been arrived at in excess of jurisdiction[29] (or where the error appears on the face of the record): whereas prohibition is sought to restrain that body from doing something which would be in excess of its jurisdiction. There is no real difference in principle between the two remedies, the distinction being almost exclusively one of tense. By contrast, the principal function of mandamus arises where a public body has failed to take action. Its purpose is to secure the performance of a public duty imposed on a public body either by statute or by common law.[30] In short, one can say (with some slight imprecision) that:

- Certiorari quashes an unlawful decision.
- Prohibition prevents an unlawful decision (which was anticipated).
- Mandamus instructs a public body which has unlawfully refused to take a positive decision to do so.[31]

Declaration and injunction

16–11   The remedies of the declaration and the injunction developed originally as private law remedies in the pre-Judicature Act Chancery Court. However, the declaratory action has come to occupy a special place, as a safety net, in our public law. This is chiefly because of the restrictions which hitherto limited the scope of the former state side orders, and hence left a gap in the courts' armoury. Indeed, it bears stating that a declaration would cover the ground of all of these remedies: it would apply to decisions taken, those to be taken or those which ought to have been taken. Furthermore, as to ripeness and standing it would go beyond this territory to cover—up to a limit patrolled by the standing rules[32]—anticipated or hypothetical decisions, in the field of public law.

---

invoked. But cf. *Bannon v Employment Appeals Tribunal* [1993] 1 I.R. 500 and *Simple Imports Ltd v Revenue Commissioners* [2000] 2 I.R. 243 for good modern illustrations of the utility of this jurisdiction.

[29]   There are some instances where the right to apply for certiorari is conferred by statute. Such legislation is principally to be found in nineteenth century local government statutes. Thus, s.12 of the Local Government (Ireland) Act 1871 gives persons aggrieved a right to apply to the High Court for certiorari to quash a charge or a surcharge. In *Downey v O'Brien* [1994] 2 I.L.R.M. 130, Costello J. held (at 135), following an earlier decision of a Divisional High Court in *State (Raftis) v Leonard* [1960] I.R. 381 to like effect, that in section 12 certiorari proceedings, the court may come "to a different conclusion on the evidence which was before the auditor and is not confined merely to considering whether there was evidence to support his findings of fact".

[30]   "The person or body against whom the order is sought must be shown to have neglected to perform some public duty imposed on him or them by law": *Minister for Labour v Grace* [1993] 2 I.R. 53 at 55 per O'Hanlon J. Prior to the enactment of the Judicature Acts, the courts regularly granted mandamus compelling private persons and bodies to perform duties imposed by statute (e.g. compelling company secretaries to make statutory returns). It seems safe to say, however, that mandamus "now belongs essentially to public law" and no longer serves this function: see Wade and Forsyth, *Administrative Law*, 10th edn (2009), p.523 and see also, Harding, *Public Duties and Public Law* (London: Clarendon Press, 1989), pp.86–87.

[31]   This brief statement overlooks the use of "certiorarified mandamus", explained in H & M, para.16–23.

[32]   See generally, *Osmanovic v Director of Public Prosecutions* [2006] 3 I.R. 504.

16–12 The declaratory action is of equitable origin, for the common law viewed non-coercive remedies with disfavour. Subsequently, it was given a statutory foundation, in the Chancery (Ireland) Act 1867 s.155 which stated that no action should be open to the objection that a merely declaratory decree or order was sought thereby, and that it should be possible for the court to make binding declarations of right whether any consequential relief is or could be claimed or not.[33] The wording of s.155 is substantially reproduced in Ord.19 r.29 of the Rules of the Superior Courts. Although the power to grant declaratory relief is of its nature very wide, the courts will generally refrain from doing so where this would be to usurp a function which in the first instance is committed to the decision of an administrative body.[34] Nor will interlocutory declarations be granted, save in the most exceptional of circumstances.[35]

16–13 The power of the High Court to grant an injunction has a similar source, namely s.28(8) of the Supreme Court of Judicature (Ireland) Act 1877,[36] which enabled the court to grant this remedy in all cases where it appeared just and convenient to do so. Despite the generality of the language used, this subsection did not extend the reach of the injunction to claims for which no remedy had previously existed either at law or in equity, nor were the principles governing the grant of an injunction substantially altered. Since the specialist public law remedies of prohibition and mandamus often fulfil the role which might otherwise be discharged by the injunction, applications for injunctions in public law are not very common.

Demarcation between former state side orders and equitable orders

16–14 A border-line may be drawn between the three former state side orders and the two orders which originated in the Courts of Equity, as to both their scope and their impact. As regards impact, a major feature is that a declaratory judgment merely declares the rights or the legal position of the parties to an action:[37] a declaratory judgment is not of itself coercive, although the litigant may safely assume that public bodies will respect and obey such a judgment. By contrast the effect of certiorari is positively to quash the impugned decision or order. This is a matter of some significance in practice in that the court will often simply grant a declaration as a matter of, as it were, politeness.[38]

---

[33] It may be noted that in *Guaranty Trust Co. of NY v Hannay & Co.* [1915] 2 K.B. 536 at 568, Bankes L.J. asserted that the courts had always possessed a residual jurisdiction to grant declaratory judgments. This statement was made, however, in the context of an action to have Rules of Court permitting the granting of declarations declared ultra vires. Naturally the Rules would have been ultra vires if they did not amount to procedural improvements of a jurisdiction which already existed.

[34] *Criminal Assets Bureau v Hunt* [2003] 2 I.R. 168 at 183 per Keane C.J. (semble); *Grianan an Aileach Interpretative Centre Co. Ltd v Donegal County Council (No. 2)* [2004] 2 I.R. 625 at 636–637 per Keane C.J.

[35] *St George's Healthcare NHS Trust v S* [1999] Fam. 26.

[36] As applied to the present High Court by s.8(2) of the Courts (Supplemental Provisions) Act 1961. Section 28(8) of the 1877 Act only refers in terms to the granting of an interlocutory order, but this subsection also encompasses the grant of a final order: *Beddow v Beddow* (1878) 9 Ch D 89 at 93 per Jessel M.R.

[37] Woolf and Zamir, *The Declaratory Judgment*, 2nd edn (London: Sweet & Maxwell, 1993).

[38] See, e.g. *Attorney General v Hamilton (No. 1)* [1993] 2 I.R. 250; *B v An Bord Uchtála* [1997] 1 I.L.R.M. 15; *Fitzwilton Ltd v Mahon* [2007] IESC 27; [2008] 1 I.R. 712.

16–15   There is also a difference in scope between the two sets of remedies in that, at any rate, the traditional view was that the declaration or the injunction were secondary remedies, that is, they were to be granted only, if because of the limitations noted earlier, none of the state side orders was available.

16–16   Nevertheless some element of differentiation remains. Ord.84 r.18(1) of the Rules of the Superior Courts states that: "An application for an order of certiorari [etc] shall be made by way of application of judicial review." By contrast, Ord.84 r.18(2) provides:

> An application for a declaration or an injunction may be made by way of an application for judicial review, and on such an application the Court may grant the declaration or injunction claimed if it considers that, having regard to—
>> (a) the nature of the matters in respect of which relief may be granted by way of an order of mandamus, prohibition, certiorari or quo warranto,
>> (b) the nature of the persons and bodies against whom relief may be granted by way of such order, and
>> (c) all the circumstances of the case,
> it would be just and convenient for the declaration or injunction to be granted on an application for judicial review.[39]

16–17   It is difficult, in the absence of any relevant case law, to interpret these provisions (which are unchanged in the 2011 Rules). However, it seems reasonably clear that the former state side orders still retain their pre-1986 premier position in that a declaration or injunction is to be granted only where there is some good reason under r.18(2)(a), (b) or (c). (This, of course, stems from the fact that the state side orders were the specialist remedies, whereas declaration and injunction were merely pressed into service, where necessary, in order to make up for the technical limitations borne by these three remedies.) Paragraphs (a) and (b) seem to direct the court to take into account the limitations of the former state side orders so far as the nature of the "matters" (i.e. function and defect in its exercise) or bodies, respectively, are concerned. And the wording of paragraph (c) would certainly be wide enough to embrace the fact that it is often considered politic to grant a non-coercive remedy against a public body.

C. Judicial Review Procedure

16–18   We do not attempt here even a comprehensive summary of the High Court procedure for judicial review.[40] Instead, we focus on five features of the procedure, which are particular to judicial review and result from its central role in governance. In addition, we should note that, as explained in Part D, the remedies are discretionary.

---

[39]   *Pandion Haliaetus Ltd v Revenue Commissioners* [1987] I.R. 309 provides a good example of the operation of Ord.84 r.18(2) in practice. For an example of where the court refused to grant declaratory relief on the ground that it would neither be just or convenient to do so, see *Shannon v McGuinness* [1999] 3 I.R. 274 at 284–285 per Kelly J.
[40]   See H & M, Ch.16, Part C.

The requirement as to leave

16–19 Order 84 r.20(1) requires that no application for judicial review shall be made unless the prior leave of the court has been obtained.[41] (Likewise, a court will generally not even entertain any arguments on the merits where no prior leave in respect of the ground in question has been granted.[42]) In other words, there are two stages: the application for leave to apply for judicial review ("the leave stage"), and the application for judicial review (known either as "the application stage" or "the judicial review stage"). The application for leave must be made by motion ex parte, by a notice containing, inter alia, details of the relief sought and the grounds on which it is sought, and an affidavit verifying the facts relied on.[43] While the applicant need not always be the deponent, care must be taken to ensure that any affidavit does not contain hearsay.[44] If the court grants leave,[45] it may impose such terms as to costs as it thinks fit, and may require an undertaking as to damages.[46]

16–20 As noted, the application for leave is generally ex parte, i.e. the respondent is not notified or present. However the (2011) Ord.18 r.24(1) now provides:

> The Court hearing an application for leave to apply for judicial review may, having regard to the issues arising, the likely impact of the proceedings on the respondent or another party, or for other good and sufficient reason, direct that the application for leave should be heard on notice and adjourn the application for leave on such terms as it may direct and give such directions as it thinks fit as to the service of notice of the application for leave (and copies of the statement of grounds, affidavit and any exhibits) on the intended respondent and on any other person, the mode of service and the time allowed for such service.

16–21 And r.24(2) goes on to accept the logic of this development, by providing for the possibility of treating the application for leave as if it were the application for judicial review. This may be done, on the consent of all the parties, or on the application of a party or on the court's own motion.

16–22 The requirement as to leave is a most important feature of the judicial review procedure. It serves as a "filtering device" and guards against unmeritorious

---

[41] See generally, Law Reform Commission, *Judicial Review Procedure* (LR CP 23–2003); Bradley, *Judicial Review* (Dublin: Round Hall, 2000), Ch.8; Collins and O'Reilly, *Civil Proceedings and the State*, 2nd edn (Dublin: Thomson Round Hall, 2003), Ch.5; de Blacam, *Judicial Review* (Dublin: Tottel Publishing, 2009), Ch.1; Delany, *Judicial Review of Administrative Action* (Dublin: Round Hall, 2009), Ch.7.

[42] *Shine v Fitness to Practice Committee of the Medical Council* [2008] IESC 41; [2009] 1 I.R. 283.

[43] Order 84 r.20(2).

[44] Save for statutory exceptions and affidavits filed in interlocutory applications, Ord.40 r.4 precludes the use of hearsay in affidavits: see generally, *FMcK v AF* [2002] 1 I.R. 242 at 246 per Geoghegan J. and *Grealish v An Bord Pleanála* [2007] 2 I.R. 536 at 546 per O'Neill J. (semble).

[45] Where leave is refused, Ord.58 r.13 provides that an application "for a similar purpose may be made to the Supreme Court *ex parte* within four days from the date of such refusal, or within such enlarged time as the Supreme Court may allow".

[46] For fortified undertakings, see para.16–38.

claims that a particular decision is invalid.[47] Three points are important here. First, the necessary standard—"satisfy[ing] the court in a *prima facie* manner"[48]—is the same for each of the issues which must be established, irrespective of whether it relates to facts or law, or is procedural (e.g. locus standi or delay), or is to do with the substance of the claim. (The Rules specifically state that leave will not be granted unless the applicant has a "sufficient interest in the matter" to which the application relates.[49]) Secondly, even though the applicant is successful, because only a prima facie test is applied at the leave stage, each of these issues can be brought up by the respondent at the judicial review stage. Finally, granting of leave to apply for judicial review will generally[50] operate as a stay of the proceedings to which the application relates.

16–23 The requirement for leave was comprehensively examined by the Supreme Court in *G v Director of Public Prosecutions*.[51] In this case the applicant sought an order of prohibition preventing his trial on a number of sex abuse charges on the ground of undue delay. In the High Court, Lavan J. had initially refused leave to apply for judicial review on the ground that indictable offences did not attract a specific time limit, but leave was granted on appeal by the Supreme Court. The following passage from the judgment of Finlay C.J.—wherein he set out the tests to be applied in considering whether leave should be granted—is of such importance that it deserves to be quoted in full:

> "An applicant must satisfy the court in a prima facie manner by the facts set out in the affidavit and submissions made in support of his application of the following matters:
>> (a) That he has a sufficient interest in the matter to which the application relates to comply with rule 20(4).
>> (b) That the facts averred in the affidavit would be sufficient, if proved, to support a stateable ground for the form of relief sought by judicial review.

---

[47] *G v Director of Public Prosecutions* [1994] 1 I.R. 374; *O'Reilly v Cassidy (No. 1)* [1995] 1 I.L.R.M. 306.

[48] In *Keane v An Bord Pleanála*, unreported, High Court, June 20, 1995, Murphy J. described the burden which the applicant must discharge at this stage as "modest" and in *TH v Director of Public Prosecutions* [2006] 3 I.R. 520 at 533, Fennelly J. observed that it was a "low threshold", comments which were also echoed by Kearns J. in *McFarlane v Director of Public Prosecutions (No. 2)* [2008] IESC 8. The Law Reform Commission's own statistical analysis of leave applications showed a success percentage of 61 per cent. Those figures date from the late 1990s and were admittedly dragged down by the figures for the statutory schemes where the percentage success rate for the grant of leave was much lower, at 36 per cent: Judicial Review Consultation Paper (CP20–2003), p.11.

[49] Order 84 r.20(5).

[50] Order 84 r.20(8)(b) (formerly r.20(7)(b)) provides that upon an application for judicial review by way of certiorari or prohibition, the grant of leave may, if the court so directs, operate as a stay of the proceedings until the determination of the application or until further order. Whatever relief is sought, Ord.84 r.20(8)(a) empowers the court to grant such interim relief "as could be granted in an action begun by plenary summons". For the scope of the court's jurisdiction to grant a stay, see *McDonnell v Brady* [2001] 3 I.R. 589 and H & M, paras 16–80 to 16–87.

[51] [1994] 1 I.R. 374. The quotations are at 377–378. *Digital Rights Ireland Ltd v Minister for Communications* [2010] 3 I.R. 251 at para.24 involved a different situation in that, in plenary proceedings, the plaintiff was arguing unsuccessfully that the issue of locus standi should not be determined as a preliminary.

(c) That on those facts an arguable case in law can be made that the applicant is entitled to the relief which he seeks.

(d) That the application has been made promptly and in any event within the three months or six months time limits provided for in Order 84, r.21(1), or that the Court is satisfied that there is a good reason for extending this time limit …

(e) That the only effective remedy, on the facts established by the applicant, which the applicant would obtain would be an order by way of judicial review or, if there be an alternate remedy, that the application by way of judicial review is, on all the facts of the case, a more appropriate method of procedure."

16–24   Finlay C.J. added that the above conditions were not "exhaustive" and he specifically drew attention to the discretionary character of the judicial review remedies. Applying those tests, he considered that leave should be granted, as the question of whether mere lapse of time created a presumption of prejudice was an "arguable" issue which could only be determined following a full hearing.[52]

The position of notice parties

16–25   Order 84 r.22(2) and (6) provide that, once leave has been granted, then service must be effected on any person "directly affected". The category of persons thereby entitled to notice of the proceedings is wider than in the purely private law setting, where the right to participate is strictly contingent on the prospect of orders which affect rights and obligations, as opposed to the fact that the litigation may have collateral consequences, such as implications for merely the reputational rights of persons not otherwise parties to the proceedings.[53] In public law cases, as Kearns J. said in *BUPA Ireland Ltd v Health Insurance Authority*,[54] the authorities:

"… demonstrate that where a party has a 'vital interest in the outcome of the matter' or is 'vitally interested in the outcome of the proceedings' or would be 'very clearly affected by the result' of the proceedings, it is appropriate for that party to be a notice party in the proceedings."

16–26   Thus, for example, any party directly affected by a challenge to the grant of a licence[55] or the operation of a statutory scheme[56] or the prosecutor in criminal cases[57] is entitled to be heard as a notice party.

Treatment of disputed facts

16–27   The traditional policy (which still largely holds good) was that High Court judicial review proceedings were not intended to reconsider disputed

---

[52]   [1994] 1 I.R. 374 at 378.

[53]   *Barlow v Fanning* [2002] 2 I.R. 593; *Yap v Children's University Hospital* [2006] IEHC 308; [2006] 4 I.R. 298 at 305; *Fitzpatrick v FK (No. 1)* [2007] 2 I.R. 406; [2008] 1 I.L.R.M. 68.

[54]   [2006] 1 I.R. 201; [2006] 1 I.L.R.M. 308.

[55]   *O'Keeffe v An Bord Pleanála* [1993] 1 I.R. 39; *Spin Communications Ltd v Independent Radio and Television Commission*, unreported, Supreme Court, April 14, 2000.

[56]   *BUPA Ireland Ltd v Health Insurance Authority (No. 1)* [2006] 1 I.R. 201.

[57]   *Fitzpatrick v FK (No. 1)* [2007] 2 I.R. 406; [2008] 1 I.L.R.M. 68.

issues of fact. Because of this limitation, especially prior to 1986, applicants often encountered formidable procedural difficulties in raising a factual dispute. One way to surmount these difficulties was to apply to cross-examine deponents on their affidavits, and this practice received the approval of the Supreme Court.[58] Similarly, while discovery was available,[59] there was no procedure for serving interrogatories, or for obtaining interlocutory relief pending the determination of the application. It was for these reasons that where issues of fact were raised in a challenge to the validity of administrative action, litigants tended to proceed by way of plenary hearing and seek an injunction or a declaration.[60] However, these procedural restrictions were swept away by the 1986 Rules and one may now apply for discovery or interrogatories.[61]

16–28   At the same time, there are special factors which have operated to limit the need for discovery in judicial review matters: first, as judicial review is normally concerned with procedure rather than substance, this inevitably will narrow the range of documents which are relevant. The result of these factors is that discovery in judicial review applications is generally confined to cases where information is improperly withheld or where there is a relevant and material conflict of fact on the affidavits.[62] Secondly, as a matter of law, disputes of facts are not usually agitated by way of judicial review, as emphasised in Chapter 10, Part F.

Remittal

16–29   A central feature of review is that it only quashes or prevents an unlawful action. It does not give the applicant what he would often want, namely the licence, grant, pension or benefit, which had been (unlawfully) denied the successful applicant. To obtain this, the applicant would have to return to the tribunal, Minister or lower court, whose decision had been found unlawful and require them to take the decision again, this time in accordance with the law. In practice, this restriction could be a great inconvenience. Accordingly, Ord.84 r.27(4) short-circuits the process, by providing:

> Where the relief sought is an order of certiorari and the Court is satisfied that there are grounds for quashing the decision to which the application relates, the Court may, in addition to quashing it, remit the matter to the Court, tribunal or authority concerned with a direction to reconsider it and reach a decision in accordance with the findings of the Court.

16–30   Rule 27(4) thus empowers the High Court to remit the matter to the court or tribunal concerned to decide the matter in accordance with law.[63] It is clearly

---

[58]   *State (Furey) v Minister for Defence* [1988] I.L.R.M. 89 at 92 per Griffin J.
[59]   See Ord.31 of the Rules of the Superior Courts 1962.
[60]   See the comments of Henchy J. to this effect in *M v An Bord Uchtála* [1977] I.R. 287 at 297.
[61]   Order 84 r.26(1).
[62]   *Kilkenny Broadcasting Co. Ltd v Broadcasting Authority of Ireland* [2003] 3 I.R. 528 at 538 per Geoghegan J.
[63]   But the High Court cannot use the power of remittal so as, in effect, to usurp the jurisdiction of the court or tribunal concerned: *McCarron v Kearney* [2008] IEHC 195.

a provision of utility which can obviate the need for an order of mandamus or, indeed, spare the parties the cost of instituting fresh proceedings.

16–31 An example of this may be demonstrated, by way of contrast, with the pre-1986 Rules case of *Bord na Móna v An Bord Pleanála and Galway County Council.*[64] Keane J. quashed a planning permission granted by An Bord Pleanála on appeal because of the existence of an invalid condition. Keane J. held that he had no jurisdiction to remit the matter to An Bord Pleanála and so the applicant for planning permission (who, after all, had won the action) was obliged to apply afresh to the local planning authority, with all the various procedural steps (including possible appeals to Bord Pleanála). Under the present Rules, the matter could simply have been remitted to An Bord Pleanála with an appropriate direction. It should be noted that this power is discretionary, so that the courts may, where it is just to do so, take into account third-party rights which could well be affected by the use of the power. There is no statutory grounding for this power and, again, it may be questioned as to whether this rule is, in fact, intra vires the powers of the Superior Court Rules Committee, although it has also been suggested that the High Court always had a jurisdiction to command a tribunal to rehear a case where its order has been quashed.[65] There is an understandably greater reluctance to use the power of remittal where the underlying dispute is criminal in nature. This is especially so where the original trial was unsatisfactory or where there was a significant error on the part of the trial judge[66] or, more generally, where it would now be oppressive or unfair to require the applicant to face a trial.[67] However, it should be emphasised that the making of Ord.84 r.27(4) "did not alter the general principles applicable to the re-trial of an accused person" or the right of such a person to plead the special pleas of autrefois convict or autrefois acquit in bar.[68]

Costs

16–32 While the costs of proceedings lie in the discretion of the court, these will usually follow the event.[69] There is, moreover, a jurisdiction to award costs

---

[64] [1985] I.R. 205.

[65] See Collins and O'Reilly, *Civil Proceedings and the State*, 2nd edn (2003), p.151; Costello, "Certiorari Followed by Remittal" (1993) *Irish Criminal Law Journal* 145; and the discussion of this point by Kelly J. in *Usk and District Residents Association Ltd v An Bord Pleanála* [2007] 2 I.L.R.M. 378 at 384–385. If, however, this is correct, then Keane J. was wrong to conclude in the *Bord na Móna* case that he had no such remittal jurisdiction.

[66] See, e.g. *Dineen v Delap* [1994] 2 I.R. 228; *Nevin v Crowley* [2001] 1 I.R. 113; *Stephens v Connellan* [2002] 4 I.R. 321; *Landers v Director of Public Prosecutions* [2004] 2 I.R. 363 at 373.

[67] See, e.g. *Dawson v Hamill (No. 2)* [1991] 1 I.R. 293 (unfair prosecutorial delay); *Sheehan v Reilly* [1992] 1 I.R. 368 (general oppression to applicant); *Director of Public Prosecutions v Kelly* [1997] 1 I.R. 405 (order of remittal ought not to be made where the fairness of a fresh trial might be imperiled by the absence of a key witness); *Noonan v Director of Public Prosecutions* [2007] IESC 36 (unfair prosecutorial delay) (semble). But see *Gilmartin v Murphy* [2001] 2 I.L.R.M. 442 for an example of where the prejudice was not considered sufficient to warrant the non-exercise of the discretion to remit.

[68] *Stephens v Connellan* [2002] 4 I.R. 321 at 359 per McKechnie J.

[69] Order 99 r.1(1). No court fees are payable in judicial review proceedings where certiorari or mandamus is sought in respect of a criminal matter: see para.8 of the Supreme Court and High Court (Fees) Order 1982 (S.I. No. 43 of 1982). The provisions of the Attorney General's scheme providing for legal aid in certain types of judicial review proceedings may also apply: see Collins and O'Reilly, *Civil Proceedings and the State*, 2nd edn (2003), pp.71–73.

to the notice parties,[70] as in private law actions. Where the case can properly be described as a test case with implications for significant numbers of other cases or for society in general, then this is a factor to which regard may be had so far as costs are concerned.[71] In some exceptional cases raising general points of importance the courts have even been prepared to award costs or a portion of the costs to the losing applicant.[72] But, beyond this, to varying degrees, there is, or has been, something of a judicial reluctance to award costs against an impecunious applicant in judicial review proceedings, even where no important point of principle is at issue.

16–33   In *Dunne v Minister for Environment (No. 2)*,[73] this issue of principle, as regards any exception to the normal rule that "costs follow the cause", was at last considered by the Supreme Court. Here the plaintiffs had unsuccessfully challenged the constitutionality of the National Monuments (Amendment) Act 2004 which had (in effect) disapplied the protections hitherto contained in the National Monuments Acts to Carrickmines Castle. In the High Court, Laffoy J. awarded the unsuccessful plaintiff his costs as she considered that the issues raised in the proceedings, were, adopting the words of Dyson J. in *Child Poverty Action Group*, "truly ones of general public importance. They were difficult issues of law. It was in the public interest that they be clarified".

16–34   The Supreme Court, however, set aside this decision. Murray C.J. acknowledged that the fact that a plaintiff "is not seeking a private personal advantage and that the issues raised are of special and general public importance are factors which may be taken into account". Nevertheless, he went on to enunciate the following general principles:

> "The rule of law that costs normally follow the event, that the successful party to proceedings should not have to pay the costs of those proceedings which should be borne by the unsuccessful party has an obvious equitable basis. As a counterpoint to that general rule of law the Court has a discretionary jurisdiction to vary or depart from that rule of law if, in the special circumstances of a case, the interests of justice require that it should do so. There is no predetermined category of cases which fall outside the full ambit of that jurisdiction. If there were to be a specific category of cases to which the general rule of law on costs did not apply that would be a matter for legislation since it is not for the Courts to establish a cohesive code according to which costs would always be imposed on certain successful defendants for the benefit of certain unsuccessful plaintiffs.
>
>   Where a Court considers that it should exercise a discretion to depart from the normal rule as to costs it is not completely at large but must do so on a

---

[70]   *Spin Communication v Independent Radio and Television Commission*, unreported, Supreme Court, April 14, 2000; *Eircom Plc v Director of Telecommunications Regulation* [2003] 1 I.L.R.M. 106; *Usk and District Residents Association Ltd v Environmental Protection Agency (No. 2)* [2007] IEHC 30 per Clarke J.

[71]   *O'Keeffe v Hickey (No. 2)* [2009] IESC 39.

[72]   Examples include *Norris v Attorney General* [1984] I.R. 36; *TF v Ireland* [1995] 1 I.R. 321; and *Curtin v Dáil Éireann (No. 2)* [2006] IESC 27. Note, however, that in *Curtin (No. 2)*, Murray C.J. stressed the limited value of past case law in this area.

[73]   [2007] IESC 60; [2008] 2 I.R. 775. The following High Court authorities may no longer be good law: *McEvoy v Meath County Council* [2003] 1 I.R. 208; *Sinnott v Martin* [2004] 1 I.R. 121.

reasoned basis indicating the factors which in the circumstances of the case warrant such a departure. It would neither be possible or desirable to attempt to list or define what all those factors are. It is invariably a combination of factors which is involved. An issue such as this is decided on a case by case basis and decided cases indicate the nature of the factors which may be relevant but it is the factors or combination of factors in the context of the individual case which determine the issue."[74]

16–35 Murray C.J. then concluded:

"Accepting that the appellant brought the proceedings in the interests of promoting compliance with the law and without any private interest in the matter I do not consider that the issues raised in the proceedings were of such special and general importance as to warrant a departure from the general rule. Undoubtedly it could be said that issues concerning subject matters such as the environment or national monuments have an importance in the public mind but a further factor for the Court is *whether the legal issues raised, rather than the subject matter itself,* were of special and general public importance. In this case nothing exceptional was raised in the issues of law which were before the Court so as to warrant a departure from the general rule."[75]

16–36 It followed, therefore, that there was nothing to justify a departure from the ordinary rule that costs should follow the event.[76] The decision in *Dunne* may be thus thought to presage a retreat from the more generous jurisdiction which had previously prevailed in major public law litigation, while at the same time not entirely excluding the possibility of an award of costs to a losing party in quite exceptional cases.

Pre-emptive costs orders

16–37 While there is a jurisdiction to make what is described as a "pre-emptive costs order" (by which, in advance of the case, the court orders that some or all of one party's costs must be paid by the other) the circumstances in which such a power could be exercised are truly "most exceptional".[77] In the pre-*Dunne* case of *Village Residents v An Bord Pleanála (No. 2),*[78] Laffoy J., following the approach of Dyson J. in *R. v Lord Chancellor Ex p. Child Action Poverty Group,*[79] held there was such a jurisdiction in cases where the applicant had no private interest and the application raised weighty issues of general public importance. Save that the application for costs was made *in advance* and not at the end of the hearing, the pre-emptive costs jurisdiction appeared to be similar, in terms of the relevant

---

[74] [2008] 2 I.R. 775 at 783.

[75] [2008] 2 I.R. 775 at 785 (emphasis added).

[76] This does not, however, mean that there are no circumstances in which such costs will not be awarded to a losing party, especially in an "exceptional" case where difficult and novel issues were clarified by the decision and where the court gave guidance to all relevant parties: see *Curtin v Dáil Éireann (No. 2)* [2006] IESC 27.

[77] *Friends of Curragh Environment Ltd v An Bord Pleanála* [2006] IEHC 243 per Kelly J.

[78] [2000] 4 I.R. 321. See generally, Costello, "Costs Principles and Environmental Judicial Review" (2000) 35 *Irish Jurist* 121.

[79] [1999] 1 W.L.R. 147.

criteria (such as no personal interest and the general importance of the issues), to the practice, already mentioned, which had emerged in some constitutional cases prior to *Dunne*. In the light, however, of the comments of the Supreme Court in *Dunne* it is hard to envisage the circumstances in which this pre-emptive costs jurisdiction might ever be exercised in practice, all the more so given that this involves making an order in advance of any hearing on the merits.

Damages

16–38   The situation under contemplation here arises where damages are claimed, by virtue of the fact that, at the leave stage, a party has been granted an interim injunction. During the time period before the full hearing (when, it may be that the injunction is terminated) the injunction may have a significant adverse effect on the respondent or a third party. An example might be if the result of the injunction would be to suspend a trading licence. In such instances the frustrated trader may claim damages. And, to go further, the court may require, in advance of the court hearing, a fortified undertaking as to damages,[80] which generally takes the form of an undertaking from a party with appropriate assets, even if that person is not actually a party before the court. Given the constitutional right of access to the courts, "the occasions on which the court might properly require ... a fortified undertaking ... must be very few".[81] If such an undertaking is sought, then the proper evidential basis must be set out to demonstrate that "the undertaking is either useless or worthless".[82]

D. The Discretionary Nature of the Remedies

General attitudes to the exercise of discretion

16–39   The public law remedies, including the declaration and injunction are all—and equally—discretionary remedies. There have been two schools of judicial thought[83] as regards the extent of this judicial discretion. The first is that, in the absence of good reason to the contrary, the court would grant relief to a "person aggrieved"[84] in respect of ultra vires administrative action. In other words, relief was

---

[80]   *Broadnet Ltd v Director of Telecommunications Regulations* [2000] 3 I.R. 281.

[81]   *O'Connell v Environmental Protection Agency* [2001] 4 I.R. 494 at 509 per Herbert J. Note also *Harding v Cork County Council* [2006] 1 I.R. 294 at 302, where Kelly J. endorsed these comments, saying that such an undertaking "is most unusual".

[82]   *Harding v Cork County Council* [2006] 1 I.R. 294 at 302 per Kelly J.

[83]   See generally, Hogan, "Remoulding Certiorari: A Critique of *State (Abenglen Properties Ltd.) v. Dublin Corporation*" (1982) 17 *Irish Jurist* 32; Jackson, "Certiorari, Alternative Remedies and Judicial Discretion" (1983) 5 D.U.L.J. 110; and Collins, "*Ex Debito Justitiae*" (1988) 10 D.U.L.J. 130. See also, Bingham, "Should public law remedies be discretionary?" (1991) *Public Law* 64.

[84]   A "person aggrieved" is defined as someone whose legal rights or interests are affected by the impugned order: see *de Roiste v Minister for Defence* [2001] 1 I.R. 190 at 200 per Fennelly J. See generally, *R. v Thames Magistrates' Court Ex p. Greenbaum* (1957) 55 L.G.R. 129; *State (Doyle) v Carr* [1970] I.R. 87; *State (Toft) v Galway Corporation* [1981] I.L.R.M. 439. As Fennelly J. noted in *de Roiste*, the court retains a discretion to quash an order at the behest of an applicant who "is not directly affected by the illegal acts which he attacks", but "applications of this sort are rare": [2001] 1 I.R. 190 at 200. One may indeed query whether this traditional common law position has survived the changes brought about by the modern law of standing in cases such as *Cahill v Sutton* [1980] I.R. 269.

said to issue *ex debito justitiae* (i.e. almost as a matter of right).[85] It was true that the applicant's right to relief might be lost on account of his delay, bad conduct, etc but, generally speaking, this would only happen where to grant relief would prejudice the rights or interests of the administrative body concerned or third parties.[86]

16–40 This formulation is, however, now generally regarded as somewhat inflexible. The alternative view, at present in the ascendant, is that the court must be satisfied "not only as to matters such as default in the performance of a public duty and jurisdictional error, but also that it would be just and proper in all the circumstances to grant [relief]".[87] Thus, the last two decades have witnessed a number of Supreme Court dicta and High Court decisions which suggest that the grant of relief should be purely discretionary.[88] And the grounds on which relief may be denied are, however, not closed, a point illustrated by the unusual facts of *Brennan v Minister for Justice*.[89] However, we may now proceed to examine separately the discretionary bars[90] to relief which are most frequently encountered.

---

[85] See, e.g. *State (Kelly) v District Justice for Bandon* [1947] I.R. 258; *State (Vozza) v O'Floinn* [1957] I.R. 227. It should be noted that both of these decisions involved applications to quash criminal convictions.

[86] As Fennelly J. stated in *de Roiste v Minister for Defence* [2001] 1 I.R. 190 at 220: "When the order is one to which the applicant is entitled *ex debito justititae*, i.e., one which affects him directly, that discretion can normally be exercised in only one way (i.e. in his favour.) That does not mean, however, that the behaviour of the applicant may not be such as to deprive him of his *prima facie* right to relief." In effect, *de Roiste* reversed *State (Furey) v Minister for Defence* [1988] I.L.R.M. 89.

[87] *State (Cussen) v Brennan* [1981] I.R. 181 at 195 per Henchy J.; *G v Director of Public Prosecutions* [1994] 1 I.R. 374 at 378 (Finlay C.J.). But relief will not lightly be refused where there has been a clear breach of the law or a violation of constitutional rights: see, e.g. *Haughey v Moriarty* [1999] 3 I.R. 1 at 76–77 per Hamilton C.J.; *Carr v Minister for Education and Science* [2001] 2 I.L.R.M. 272 at 288 per Geoghegan J.; *O'Keeffe v Connellan* [2009] IESC 24 per Hardiman J.; and *P v McDonagh* [2009] IEHC 316 per Clarke J.

[88] *Duff v Mangan* [1994] 1 I.L.R.M. 91 at 101 per Denham J.; *G v Director of Public Prosecutions* [1994] 1 I.R. 374 at 378 per Finlay C.J.

[89] [1995] 1 I.R. 612; [1995] 2 I.L.R.M. 206. In the substantive part of the case, Geoghegan J. held that it was wrongful for the Minister to have remitted fines imposed on a convicted offender. However, the judge declined on discretionary grounds to quash ministerial decisions which he found had improperly remitted certain fines and penalties imposed by the applicant District Court judge. Third parties in the case were convicted persons who had applied to the Minister for remission of the penalties in accordance with long-standing practice, and Geoghegan J. felt that it would be unfair to deprive them of the benefit of the decision in their own case, particularly as their cases had been selected on a more or less random basis in order to test the legality of a more general practice and as the declaratory relief actually granted was sufficient to clarify the law. It would seem that yet another pronouncement by the Supreme Court on this question will be necessary before the matter can be regarded as settled.

[90] At common law it was clear that the Attorney General could not be refused relief on discretionary grounds: see, e.g. *Re An Application for Certiorari* [1965] N.I. 67. Murnaghan J. made a similar observation in *State (Kerry County Council) v Minister for Local Government* [1933] I.R. 517 at 546. But, as Lord McDermott L.C.J. explained in *Re An Application for Certiorari* [1965] N.I. 67 at 70–71, this rule was derived from the fact that the Attorney General had a privileged position as representing the Crown. In view of this rationale and the general reasoning of the Supreme Court in *Howard v Commissioners for Public Works* [1994] 1 I.R. 101, not to speak of the injustice which might be caused to an individual litigant if discretionary bars such as delay could not be pleaded as against the Attorney General, it must be doubtful if such a rule survived the enactment of the Constitution.

Lack of good faith and general conduct of the applicant

16–41   All applications for judicial review require the utmost good faith and full disclosure of all material facts on the part of the applicant.[91] This is because the initial application is ex parte,[92] together with the fact that there is usually no oral evidence and because of the generally weighty issues raised by the application. Accordingly, relief may be withheld where the applicant has been guilty of gross exaggeration in his affidavits[93] or where relevant evidence has been suppressed[94] or where there has been a failure to make a proper disclosure.[95] In *GD v Minister for Justice, Equality and Law Reform*,[96] one of the applicants swore falsely that she was resident in Ireland at a particular time, in order to avail of what amounted to a quasi-amnesty for a large number of illegal immigrants with Irish citizen children. She later swore a supplementary affidavit admitting her deceit and it was argued that this fact alone disentitled her to discretionary relief. Finlay Geoghegan J. acknowledged that:

> "There may be exceptional circumstances in which the court will refuse to exercise its discretion in favour of granting such relief. The swearing by an applicant of a false affidavit is undoubtedly potentially such an exceptional circumstance. It is an extremely serious matter and one which might well disentitle an applicant to a relief to which he or she might otherwise be entitled."

16–42   Finlay Geoghegan J. nevertheless refused to find against the applicant on this ground, since the effect of such a refusal would fall disproportionately on an innocent party (namely her child) and the applicant had apologised to the court for her behaviour. The court was furthermore finding for the applicant on other grounds, so that the false affidavit did not, in fact, affect the outcome.[97]

16–43   The court will also have regard to the general conduct of the applicant,[98]

---

[91]   An applicant's legal representatives are under a duty to draw relevant authorities to the attention of the court which would suggest that an order of this type ought not to be made: see *Adams v Director of Public Prosecutions* [2001] 2 I.L.R.M. 401 at 416 per Kelly J. and *Fitzpatrick v FK (No. 2)* [2008] IEHC 104 per Laffoy J. A more forgiving attitude will, however, be taken in this respect of litigants in person: *Grimes v Cork County Council* [2005] IEHC 420.

[92]   Save, of course, in the case of the statutory schemes or where even in ordinary non-statutory Order 84 cases, the court has directed that the applicant be put on notice of the application.

[93]   See, e.g. the comments of Keane C.J. in *Shannon v McCartan* [2002] 2 I.R. 377 at 380.

[94]   See, e.g. *State (Vozza) v O'Floinn* [1957] I.R. 227 at 249–252; *de Roiste v Minister for Defence* [2001] 1 I.R. 190 at 220 per Fennelly J.; *AGAO v Minister for Justice, Equality and Law Reform* [2007] 2 I.R. 492 at 507 per MacMenamin J. (applicant disentitled to relief given that his "interactions with the various organs of the State were designed to mislead and deceive").

[95]   While the court must obviously have regard to all the circumstances of the case: *Bambrick v Cobley* [2006] 1 I.L.R.M. 81 at 89 (Clarke J.): *P v McDonagh* [2009] IEHC 316.

[96]   [2006] IEHC 344.

[97]   See also, *Atlantean Ltd v Minister for Communications and Natural Resources* [2007] IEHC 233 ("technical omission"). But where the deceit is central to the relief claimed, the court is less disposed to overlook this fact: see *CRA v Minister for Justice, Equality and Law Reform* [2007] 2 I.L.R.M. 209.

[98]   See, e.g. *Murtagh v Board of Governor of St Emer's National School* [1991] 1 I.R. 482; *Connolly v Collector of Customs and Excise*, unreported, High Court, October 5, 1992 (where Blayney J. hinted that he would have refused an order of mandamus compelling the respondent to grant a publican's licence having regard "to the very extraordinary conduct of the applicant

the reasons for the application[99] and whether the granting of relief would cause hardship to innocent third parties.[100] Thus, in *Ahern v Minister for Industry and Commerce (No. 2)*,[101] the applicant was placed on compulsory sick leave following his "unreasonable refusal to see a psychiatrist". Blayney J. held that this decision was invalid, but refused to quash the decision (in part, it would seem) because of the applicant's unreasonable behaviour, which was compounded by his persistent allegations (which Blayney J. found to be wholly unfounded) that his superiors were not acting bona fide.

16–44 Yet in another case, a different judge exercised his discretion in the opposite direction. In *Carr v Minister for Education and Science*,[102] the Supreme Court held that the Minister had no statutory power to withhold the salary of the applicant teacher. It was argued, however, that relief should be withheld on discretionary grounds, since it was claimed that the applicant had acted unreasonably by failing to co-operate with a mediator who had been appointed to endeavour to solve the differences between the parties. Geoghegan J. rejected this argument, saying:

> "It would seem to me that these are essentially procedural matters. In so far as the applicant was acting unreasonably it was procedural unreasonableness … It may well be that there are circumstances where that type of unreasonableness could deprive an applicant of the discretionary remedy but this is not one of them. For the Court to refuse *certiorari* would be to condone an open illegality by the Minister in the face of the wording of the statute. Put otherwise, the antecedent unreasonable behaviour of the applicant of which the Minister was fully aware, would confer on the Minister a statutory power which was not established by the section upon which the validity of his decision depended."[103]

Delay

16–45 Order 84 r.21(1) of the Rules of the Superior Courts 2011 provides that, subject to certain refinements explained below, all applications for judicial review shall be made within three months from the date when the grounds for the

---

in totally ignoring the licensing laws for almost six years before bringing this application"); *Mamyko v Minister for Justice, Equality and Law Reform* [2003] IEHC 75 (applicant "drip feeding" fresh grounds by submitting "eleventh hour" fresh applications for leave to remain in order to avoid deportation process).

[99] See, e.g. *State (Toft) v Galway Corporation* [1981] I.L.R.M. 439 (rival business seeking to exploit technical and non-prejudicial defect in the grant of an intoxicating liquor licence with a view to having the licence quashed for commercial advantage); *State (Abenglen Properties Ltd) v Dublin Corporation* [1984] I.R. 384 (attempt to obtain benefits "not contemplated" by the planning code); *Shannon v McGuinness* [1999] 3 I.R. 274 (attempt indirectly to seek judicial review of a decision of the Director of Public Prosecutions to withdraw a prosecution).

[100] See, e.g. *State (Cussen) v Brennan* [1981] I.R. 181 (unfair to quash statutory appointment where successful candidate had resigned from his earlier post to take up that appointment); *Minister for Education v Letterkenny RTC* [1995] 1 I.L.R.M. 438 (similar principle).

[101] [1991] 2 I.R. 462.

[102] [2001] 2 I.L.R.M. 272. Note also *Flynn and O'Flaherty Properties Ltd v Dublin Corporation* [1997] 2 I.R. 560; *Gama Endustri Tesisleri Imalat Montag AS v Minister for Enterprise, Trade and Employment* [2007] 3 I.R. 472; and *Carrigaline Community Television Ltd v Minister for Communications* [1997] 1 I.R. 241.

[103] [2001] 2 I.L.R.M. 272 at 288.

application first arose.[104] It should be emphasised that these are the Rules which apply to general judicial applications; whereas special regimes with their own time limits are covered at paras 11–05 to 11–10.

History

16–46 Before coming back to deal with the present position, we should refer briefly to the two earlier regimes regarding delay, namely during the pre-1986 era, and the 1986–2011 period. In each case, as we shall see, the direction of the changes has been towards a more stringent attitude regarding delay by the applicant. Pre-1986, the matter of delay was not addressed and under the 1962 (and earlier) Rules, the general attitude of the courts had been to ask whether the delay had been such as to affect prejudicially the rights of third parties: otherwise, delay was not of itself a ground for refusing relief.[105] The 1986 Rules brought in a number of changes, which, in broad outline, have been retained in the 2011 Rules. Since the 2011 Rules came into effect only on January 1, 2012 all the authorities interpreting the Rules given here are based on the 1986 (or earlier) Rules, so that a government health warning applies.

16–47 The 1986 and 2011 Rules each have three elements. First, a definite time limit is specified. Under the 1986 Rules, this was six months when the relief sought was certiorari and three months for each of the other remedies. The reason for the difference was that certiorari is the appropriate remedy to quash an invalid criminal conviction (though certiorari is not exclusively used in quashing invalid criminal convictions). However, under the 2011 Rules, the time limit is three months,[106] for each remedy.

---

[104] For the curiously neglected topic of the significance of a delay being due to the applicants legal advisor, see the analysis by Finnegan J. in *GK v Minister for Justice, Equality and Law Reform* [2002] 1 I.L.R.M. 61 at 86–87 (as approved by the Supreme Court in *CS v Minister for Justice, Equality and Law Reform* [2005] 1 I.R. 143). These were immigration cases where the courts would be more naturally tolerant, given the possible consequences for the applicant concerned. But vicarious liability for the failures of one's legal advisers loomed less heavily in immigration matters that it would in planning- or procurement-type cases, even before the amendments effected by s.13 of the 2006 Act: see *Kelly v Leitrim County Council* [2005] 4 I.R. 404 at 417 per Clarke J.

[105] *State (Furey) v Minister for Defence* [1988] I.L.R.M. 89. Here a majority of the Supreme Court held that the applicant, who had suffered an ignominious dismissal from the Defence Forces which had been imposed in clear breach of fair procedures, was entitled to an order of certiorari quashing the dismissal. This was despite a delay of over four years in commencing the proceedings, which delay was attributable to ignorance of his legal entitlements on the part of the applicant. While it is possible that *Furey* was correctly decided on its facts, the underlying principle—that delay in itself can never preclude a successful application for judicial review—is no longer good law and *Furey* was expressly overruled on this point in *de Roiste v Minister for Defence* [2001] 1 I.R. 190.

The difficulties inherent in relying on *Furey* as an authority in the wake of *de Roiste* were well summed up by Laffoy J. in *Minister for Finance v Civil and Public Service Union* [2006] IEHC 145 when she observed: "While the *ratio decidendi* of the *Furey* case was not disapproved of [in *de Roiste*, it is nonetheless] difficult to determine the extent to which the *ratio* was predicated on Mr. Furey's lack of knowledge of his legal and constitutional rights or the likelihood of success in the proceedings, as opposed to the efforts he had made to seek re-enlistment in the army during the period of delay."

[106] 2011 Rules (S.I. No. 691 of 2011) r.4 provides that "… an application for leave to apply for judicial review by way of certiorari may where the grounds for such application first arose on a date before [January 1, 2012] be made within six months from the date when the grounds for

16–48 The second element is that, even where the application is made within the time limit, there is a requirement of what the 1986 Rules called "prompt[ness]". But thirdly, and telling in the opposite direction, the court may extend the period for good reason. We turn to elaborate on each of these elements in the following paragraphs. Before doing so, however, one should note that, apart from the 1986 Rules directing a stricter attitude to the issue of delay, the courts "have, in recent years, applied much more severe scrutiny to delayed applications for judicial review than formerly".[107] In addition, there has been a series of cases arising from the statutory schemes in particular fields and, for instance, the authorities in relation to the procedures prescribed in Ord.84A for review of public procurement decisions have had an indirect influence in relation to the analogous procedures arising under Ord.84 simpliciter.

Time period: from what date does time run?

16–49 As mentioned, the time period is now three months. However, on the question of when time runs, the wording of (2011) Ord.84 r.21(i) remains that the period commences "… from the date when the grounds for the application first arose …". This would normally suggest time ran from the dates these grounds for challenge actually arose, irrespective of an applicant's state of personal knowledge.[108] However, if new facts came to light after time had begun to run, this would be a highly material factor so far as any decision to extend time is concerned. In addition, although time normally runs from the date of the decision under challenge,[109] the running of time may nevertheless in some special circumstances be postponed until the consequences of the decision effectively crystallise.   Thus, for example, time will start only from the date when the decision becomes effective.[110] Likewise, a litigant challenging the validity of an indictment is entitled to wait until the indictment has been served.[111] It is similarly permissible for an applicant to wait for the outcome of a review by the respondents of their original decision[112] or until there is a real danger that a particular statutory scheme is commenced and

---

the application first arose". See generally, Donnelly, "Changes to Judicial Review Procedure" *Bar Review*, February, 2012.

[107] *O'Brien v Moriarty* [2005] 2 I.L.R.M. 321 at 334 per Fennelly J. To the same effect, see the comments of Denham J. in *de Roiste v Minister for Defence* [2001] 2 I.R. 190 at 210, that "[t]ime is more of the essence, more urgent, in judicial review proceedings". See generally, Delany, "Extension of Time Limits in Judicial Review Proceedings" (2003) I.L.T. 156.

[108] *Veolia Water UK Plc v Fingal County Council* [2007] 1 I.L.R.M. 216 at 229.

[109] In *McIniry v Flynn*, unreported, High Court, May 6, 1998 the applicant sought judicial review of a decision of the Taxing Master. McCracken J. held that time ran from the date of the Master's certificate, as opposed to the date of the hearing before the Master himself.

Note that Ord.84 r.21(2) expressly provides that: "Where the relief sought is an order of certiorari in respect of any judgment, order, conviction or other proceeding, the date when grounds for the application first arose shall be taken to be the date of that judgment, order, conviction or proceeding."

[110] *Mulcreevy v Minister for Environment* [2004] 1 I.R. 74 at 80. Here the applicant commenced judicial review proceedings some three weeks after the end of the time period during which the relevant ministerial order might have been annulled by either House of the Oireachtas. The Supreme Court held that time commenced to run for Ord.84 purposes only after the time for annulment.

[111] *CC v Ireland (No. 1)* [2006] 4 I.R. 1 at 39 per Geoghegan J.

[112] *Brown v Rathfarnham National School* [2006] IEHC 178; [2008] 1 I.R. 70 at 83–84 per Quirke J.

will be applied adversely against them.[113] On the other hand a litigant wishing to challenge the validity of a rating valuation is not entitled to await the outcome of appeal proceedings in the District Court and Circuit Courts before commencing judicial review proceedings since those courts have no jurisdiction to set aside or quash a decision of the Commissioner of Valuation.[114]

The obligation to apply so as not to cause "prejudice to a respondent or third party"

16–50   Under the 1986 Rules, an applicant who had not moved "promptly" might find that s/he was turned away, even where the application had been brought within the relevant time limit. *Dekra Éireann Teo v Minister for the Environment*[115] is a significant decision, which Fennelly J. signalled was intended to apply generally and not merely in relation to its own field of public procurement. Although on the facts the application fell just outside the limitation period, there are judicial comments emphasising that the the time limits, as laid down in the Rules, will be stringently applied (whether the application is within or outside the time limit) and that the Supreme Court dicta[116] dating from the 1980s and early 1990s regarding delay *in itself* never being enough to defeat an application for judicial review should not now be followed. At the same time, Fennelly J acknowledged that "… a claim cannot normally be defeated for delay if it is commenced within the period. There would need to be some quite special factor such as prejudice to third parties [for this to occur]".[117] Under the 2011 Rules, this position is confirmed by the requirement in Ord.21(6) that, even if the applicant is within the three-month time period, "… the Court [may dismiss] the application on the ground that the applicant's delay in applying … has caused or is likely to cause prejudice to a respondent or third party".

16–51   Situations in which this prejudice has been found to exist include: where the prosecution authorities seek to quash rulings given by trial judges which are favourable to the accused[118]; or where the applicant is aware that the notice party has invested heavily on foot of a licence, the validity of which is now challenged.[119] There may also be special cases where a particular onus rests on accused persons seeking judicial relief to act with particular promptitude.[120]

---

[113]   *BUPA Ireland Ltd v Health Insurance Authority (No. 2)* [2006] IEHC 431.
[114]   *Slatterys Ltd v Commissioner of Valuation* [2001] 4 I.R. 91 at 99 per Keane C.J. Note also *Sloane v An Bord Pleanála* [2003] 2 I.L.R.M. 61; *John Paul Construction Ltd v Minister for Environment, Heritage and Local Government* [2006] IEHC 255 (time ran from the date the Minister clarified his position).
[115]   [2003] 2 I.R. 270.
[116]   See, e.g. the comments of McCarthy J. in *O'Flynn v Mid-Western Health Board* [1991] 2 I.R. 223 at 239.
[117]   [2003] 2 I.R. 270 at 302. See also, *O'Brien v Moriarty* [2006] 2 I.R. 221 at 237; *de Burca v Wicklow County Manager* [2009] IEHC 54.
[118]   See, e.g. *Director of Public Prosecutions v Macklin* [1989] I.L.R.M. 113; *Director of Public Prosecutions v Kelly* [1997] 1 I.R. 405.
[119]   *O'Connor v Minister for Marine, The Irish Times Law Report*, November 15, 1999.
[120]   In *Twomey v Director of Public Prosecutions* [2004] 3 I.R. 232, an applicant who was facing larceny charges claimed that he was prejudiced by reason of the failure of the Gardaí to preserve a video tape from a security camera on the premises. Yet he did not apply for leave for some 15 months after the discovery of the existence of the tape and just under three months

16–52 Under the 1986 Rules, there were held to be instances where it was incumbent on the applicant to move with great speed, especially where the challenge was to the award of licences to third parties[121]; or where the impugned decision affected "major infrastructural projects where huge expense and inconvenience inevitably may be expected to arise where delay occurs".[122] The substance and context of the application would thus often be material to the issue of delay. To take further examples, a stricter attitude will often be taken in: cases involving allegations of discrimination in employment[123] or affecting the public generally[124]; applications which concern a last-minute application to restrain the holding of an administrative hearing[125] or a criminal trial[126]; cases which raise major constitutional issues where the subject matter of the claim cannot properly be the subject of an adjudication in such a short time frame which has been caused by the applicant's delay[127]; cases where the applicant is seeking belatedly to take advantage of a purely technical invalidity[128]; or where the underlying merits of the application are weak.[129] As emphasised already, almost all of these authorities were based on the word "prompt" in the 1986 Rules. Under the 2011 Rules, the equivalent formulation is whether "… the applicant's delay has caused or is likely to cause prejudice to a respondent or third party". And it seems probable that most of the authorities can be fitted in under this heading.

Extensions of time beyond the specified time limits

16–53 We have just examined case law in which an applicant who, although within the specified time limits, has not been prompt in seeking judicial review and, therefore, may be required to explain this delay. The applicant's task is more uphill where the delay has been greater than three months and he or she is seeking an extension.

---

after it had been discovered that the tape had been misplaced. Quirke J. held that in these circumstances the applicant had not acted promptly.

[121] See, e.g. *O'Connor v Minister for the Marine, The Irish Times Law Report*, November 15, 1999; *Dekra Éireann Teo v Minister for the Environment and Local Government* [2003] 2 I.R. 270.

[122] *Noonan Services Ltd v Labour Court* [2004] IEHC 42 per Kearns J.; *Mulcreevy v Minister for Environment* [2004] 1 I.R. 74 at 80.

[123] *Minister for Finance v Civil and Public Service Union (No. 2)* [2006] IEHC 145. Although this was a statutory appeal, Laffoy J. held that the Order 84 principles applied by analogy to the question of whether any delay by claimants in asserting legal rights had been sufficiently excused.

[124] *Slatterys Ltd v Commissioner of Valuation* [2001] 4 I.R. 91 (quashing of rating valuation after many years' delay might have implication for third parties); *Noonan Services Ltd v Labour Court* [2004] IEHC 42 (where Kearns J. held that a five-month delay in the context of an application to quash a decision of the Labour Court affecting the entire contract cleaning industry was excessive).

[125] *O'Flynn v Mid-Western Health Board* [1991] 2 I.R. 223; *AA v Medical Council* [2003] 4 I.R. 302 at 319 per Hardiman J. (very belated application to stop disciplinary inquiry).

[126] *Buckley v Kirby* [2000] 3 I.R. 431; *Gilligan v Ireland* [2000] 4 I.R. 579; [2001] 1 I.L.R.M. 473; *Connolly v Director of Public Prosecutions* [2003] 4 I.R. 121; *Scully v Director of Public Prosecutions* [2005] 1 I.R. 242 at 259 per Hardiman J.; *Connolly v Director of Public Prosecutions* [2003] 4 I.R. 121 at 125–126.

[127] *Riordan v Ireland* [1999] 4 I.R. 343; *O'Doherty v Attorney General* [2001] IESC 206.

[128] *Connors v Delap* [1989] I.L.R.M. 93; *White v Hussey* [1989] I.L.R.M. 109.

[129] *GK v Minister for Justice* [2002] 1 I.L.R.M. 401 at 405–406 per Hardiman J.

1986 Rules

16–54   Before considering the new Rules, it is worth summarising the case law under the 1986 Rules, which used only the term "good reason" as the ground to justify an extension. Substantial use was made of this discretion, especially in criminal cases. But the longer the delay, the more that delay will require explanation and "explicable delays have usually been a matter of months and very rarely years".[130] In more recent years a stricter approach to delay has been in evidence and the Supreme Court's decision in *de Roiste v Minister for Defence*[131] represented a definite shift of judicial mood. Here the applicant sought to challenge the validity of his summary dismissal from the Defence Forces some 29 years after the event. There was—not surprisingly—ample evidence of prejudice on the part of the respondents, but the court took the opportunity to stress that *delay in itself* could be a ground for refusing relief and in the process disavowed the dictum of McCarthy J. in *State (Furey) v Minister for Defence*.[132] McCarthy J. had stated that he could see no reason "why delay, however long, should of itself disentitle to certiorari any applicant for that remedy who can demonstrate that a public wrong has been done to him".[133]

16–55   Denham J. listed five (non-exhaustive) factors to which the court could have regard in cases of this kind:

> "In analysing the facts of a case to determine if there is a good reason to extend time or to allow judicial review, the Court may take into account factors such as; (i) the nature of the order or actions the subject of the application; (ii) the conduct of the applicant; (iii) the conduct of the respondents; (iv) the effect of the order under review on the parties subsequent to the order being made and any steps taken by the parties subsequent to the order to be reviewed; (v) any effect which may have taken place on third parties by the order to be reviewed; (vi) public policy that proceedings relating to the public law domain take place promptly except when good reason is furnished. Such list is not exclusive. It is clear from precedent that the discretion of the Court has ever been to protect justice. When criminal convictions are in issue the matter of justice may be very clear."[134]

16–56   The courts will generally be impressed by evidence which showed that the applicant endeavoured to solve the problem through the political system[135] or

---

[130] *De Roiste v Minister for Defence* [2001] 1 I.R. 190 at 221 per Fennelly J. The same judge added however ([2001] 1 I.R. 190 at 221): "In the nature of things, a short delay might require only slight explanation. The judicial review time limit is not a limitation period. Prompt pursuit of a remedy is, however, a requirement of a judicial review application."

[131] [2001] 1 I.R. 190. For two major decisions from a significantly different era, see *State (Furey) v Minister for Defence* [1988] I.L.R.M. 89; *O'Donnell v Dun Laoghaire Corporation* [1991] I.L.R.M. 301.

[132] [1988] I.L.R.M. 89.

[133] [1988] I.L.R.M. 89 at 100.

[134] [2001] 1 I.R. 190 at 208. A comprehensive set of factors governing the question of an extension of time is set out in the judgment of Clarke J. in *Kelly v Leitrim County Council* [2005] 2 I.R. 404 at 412–413.

[135] *O'Donnell v Dun Laoghaire Corporation (No. 2)* [1991] I.L.R.M. 305.

through mediation[136] or where other legal avenues were pursued or explored.[137] This, however, has its limits. As McMahon J. observed in *McCarthy v Irish Prison Service*[138] (a case where the delay was some 14 months):

"... it cannot be the case that simply by corresponding with the respondents the applicant indefinitely extends the period within which he is obliged to commence proceedings under the Rules of the Superior Courts. If the case were otherwise, then an applicant could extend the time indefinitely, merely by engaging in letter writing. It must be remembered that O. 84, r. 21 (1) is not there simply for the convenience of the parties. It has a public dimension and it has been adopted to ensure the expeditious administration of justice."

16–57 In some circumstances the absence of knowledge of key facts may justify the courts taking a more lenient attitude to the issue of delay.[139] Moreover—and, in practice, this is most significant—in some circumstances, a delay which is attributable to the applicant's legal advisers may provide a justification, although in the nature of things this is a factor which will have more purchase in asylum type matters than it would in planning or public procurement matters.[140]

16–58 In contrast, delay was less likely to be excused where there was an established or potential prejudice to third parties,[141] or the delay: affects large segments of a particular industry[142] or major projects,[143] or impacts upon scarce public resources[144] or a pending referendum.[145] This would be the case, too, where the applicant belatedly applies for judicial review in order to stay a pending criminal trial,[146] or tribunal.[147]

---

[136] *Bane v Garda Representative Association* [1997] 2 I.R. 449.
[137] See, e.g. *Murphy v District Justice Wallace* [1993] 2 I.R. 138; *Quinn v O'Leary* [2004] 3 I.R. 128
[138] [2009] IEHC 311.
[139] *Veolia Water UK Plc v Fingal County Council* [2007] 1 I.L.R.M. 217 at 228–230 per Clarke J.
[140] *Kelly v Leitrim County Council* [2005] 2 I.R. 404 at 417 per Clarke J. This is not only because the courts are less tolerant of delay in these types of commercial (or quasi-commercial) cases, but also because of the potential consequences for the individual in the asylum cases, a point graphically made by Finnegan J. in *GK v Minister for Justice* [2002] 1 I.L.R.M. 81 at 86–87 (and subsequently approved by the Supreme Court in *CS v Minister for Justice* [2005] 1 I.R. 343 at 361 per McGuinness J.).
[141] *M v Judge O'Donnabhain* [2011] IESC 22 (July 12, 2011).
[142] See, e.g. *Noonan Services Ltd v Labour Court* [2004] IEHC 42.
[143] See, e.g. the comments of Denham J. in *Dekra Éireann Teo v Minister for the Environment* [2003] 2 I.R. 270 at 289 regarding a slightly belated challenge to the award of the national car testing contract: "The public contract in issue involved significant liabilities, obligations and expense which may raise important factors for the court."
[144] See, e.g. *Rock v Dublin City Council*, unreported, Supreme Court, February 8, 2006 (delay in seeking judicial review cases involving local authority lettings may affect "the management of the housing pool" which should be conducted "in an orderly and speedy manner" by the Council); *Atlantean Ltd v Minister for Communications and Natural Resources* [2007] IEHC 233 (allocation of limited amounts of fishing quota).
[145] *Riordan v Ireland* [1999] 4 I.R. 343; *O'Doherty v Attorney General* [2001] IESC 206.
[146] *Gilligan v Ireland* [2000] 4 I.R. 579 at 583; [2001] 1 I.L.R.M. 473 at 479–80 per Denham J.; *AA v Medical Council* [2003] 4 I.R. 302 at 319 per Hardiman J.
[147] *O'Flynn v Mid-Western Health Board* [1991] 2 I.R. 223 at 236.

2011 Rules

16–59   In the first place, under the 1986 Rules, the time could be extended by
the court, for "good reason" (Ord.84 r.21(1)). By contrast, the 2011 Rules (Ord.84
r.21(3)) are more precise and restrictive:

> (3) Notwithstanding sub-rule (1), the Court may, on an application for that
> purpose, extend the period within which an application for leave to apply for
> judicial review may be made, but the Court shall only extend [the prescribed
> period] if it is satisfied that:—
> >   (a) there is good and sufficient reason for doing so, and
> >   (b) the circumstances that resulted in the failure to make the application
> >   for leave within the [prescribed] period ... either—
> > >   (i)   were outside the control of, or
> > >   (ii)   could not reasonably have been anticipated by the applicant
> > >   for such extension.
> (4) In considering whether good and sufficient reason exists for the purposes
> of sub-rule (3), the court may have regard to the effect which an extension
> of the period referred to in that sub-rule might have on a respondent or third
> party.

16–60   One can summarise the new Rules, quoted above, by saying that it seems
that an applicant who is outside the three-month limit must, if their application
is to be considered, jump three hurdles. In the first place, there must be a "good
and sufficient reason" to extend the period. But, secondly, even if such exists, any
prejudice to "a respondent or third party" may be set off against the good reason.
Finally, in addition, the circumstances causing the failure to make the application
in time must have been either "outside the control of or could not reasonably have
been anticipated by" the applicant. This was not explicit in the 1986 Rules (though
it was a factor sometimes taken into account by a court). In connection with the
enforcement of each of these requirements, one should note that Ord.84 r.21(5) now
states that "an application for an extension ... shall be grounded upon an affidavit
sworn by ... the applicant which shall set out the reasons for the applicant's failure
to make the application for leave within the period prescribed ...".[148] Without
specifically appraising the former case law against the new Rules, it can, however,
be said generally that, if the new Order is faithfully followed, the applicant's task
would be more difficult than under the 1986 regime. The mass of case law just
summarised suggests that the situations thrown up are likely to remain a fertile
field for disputation, whatever form the Rules take.

Time limits in particular fields

16–61   As discussed in paras 11–04 to 11–10 there has been a series of

---

[148]   *O'Flynn v Mid-Western Health Board* [1991] 2 I.R. 223 at 236 indicates that, in practice, the
position was the same under the 1986 Rules. This duty is perhaps especially onerous where
the application is a last-minute application to restrain a criminal trial: see *Scully v Director
of Public Prosecutions* [2005] 1 I.R. 242 at 259 per Hardiman J. If time is extended ex parte
(whether at the leave stage or otherwise), this does not prevent the court from re-examining
the matter in an inter partes hearing: see *Slatterys Ltd v Commissioner of Valuation* [2001] 4
I.R. 91 at 98 per Keane C.J.

heterogeneous provisions in particular fields,[149] which have, in the interests of legal certainty,[150] imposed special time limits. However given the constitutional difficulties which would almost certainly ensue if there was an inflexible time limit,[151] there is nearly always a power to extend time, albeit that the circumstances in which time can be extended can vary.[152] While existence of a statutory time limit has meant that the courts have applied the existing case law on delay, albeit in a more rigorous and stricter fashion, the reasons justifying the delay are of the same character as those just surveyed.[153]

Delay and judicial review of criminal proceedings

16–62 So far, we have been speaking about delay in initiating judicial review. A related source of delay to be taken into account is the time consumed by the judicial review proceedings themselves, which, especially if there is an appeal, will be as much as one or two years. This inevitably means delay and dislocation in whatever proceedings are the subject matter of the review (indeed, it has sometimes been suggested that this is among the motivations for certain judicial reviews taken against tribunals of inquiry). Surprisingly, perhaps, this ground for the exercise of discretion has received judicial attention so far only in the context of criminal proceedings. The considerations were well explained by Hardiman J. in *Scully v Director of Public Prosecutions*[154]:

> "Firstly, a case which has a trial date attributed to it is displacing another case which might have been listed for the same day, thereby causing additional stress, anxiety and possibly worse to the parties in the other case. Secondly,

---

[149] See, e.g. s.33BF(a) of the Central Bank Act 1942 (application to quash decision of the Regulatory Authority must be made within two months after the date of notification of the decision); s.50(8) of the Planning and Development Act 2000 (as inserted by s.13 of the Planning and Development (Strategic Infrastructure) Act 2006) (applications to challenge planning decisions to be made within two months); Prisons Act 2007 s.27.

[150] See, e.g. the comments of Finlay C.J. in *KSK Enterprises Ltd v An Bord Pleanála* [1994] 2 I.R. 128 at 135 and those of Macken J. in *Openneer v Donegal County Council* [2006] 1 I.L.R.M. 106 at 150. In *AHP Manufacturing Ltd v Director of Public Prosecutions* [2008] IEHC 144; [2008] 2 I.L.R.M. 344, O'Higgins J. rejected (at 351) the argument that the eight-week time limits for judicial review provided for in s.87(10) of the Environmental Protection Agency Act 1992 (as amended) applied only to "a decision to grant a licence" and not to the imposition of conditions in respect of the licence: "[i]f the licence and conditions were taken disjunctively as contended for by the applicant, the clear intention of the legislature as expressed in s 87(10) would be entirely thwarted. The certainty and security of benefit both to the developer and to the objectors would simply not exist if the conditions to a licence were open to challenge many years later."

[151] Thus the former absolute two-month time limit contained in s.82(3A) of the Local Government (Planning and Development) Act 1963 was held to be unconstitutional by the Supreme Court in *White v Dublin City Council* [2004] 1 I.R. 545. Section 87(10) of the Environmental Protection Agency Act 1992 (as amended) contains an absolute eight-week period for challenge, a provision whose constitutionality must now be considered highly suspect in view of the decision in *White*.

[152] Section 33BF(b) of the Central Bank Act 1942 (High Court given general power to extend two-month period); s.50(8) of the Planning and Development Act 2000 (High Court given to extend time for "good and sufficient reasons" where default outside of the control of the applicant).

[153] *Openneer v Donegal County Council* [2006] 1 I.L.R.M. 106 at 150 per Macken J.

[154] [2005] 1 I.R. 242. See also, *Connolly v Director of Public Prosecutions* [2003] 4 I.R. 121 at 126 per Finlay Geoghegan J.

inconvenience or worse is inevitably caused to witnesses when the trial date is vacated at the last moment. Thirdly, a good deal of effort in ensuring that the case is ready to go on would be wasted if the date is lost. I would apply these strictures to the loss of a trial date regardless of which side brings it about. In the particular case of loss of an assigned trial date due to a very late application for judicial review the underlying reason will almost always be a failure to think seriously about the case until just before the date for which it is listed. I would not advocate an absolutely rigid attitude to such applications because experience shows that there can be circumstances which justify the delay. But if it is necessary to make a very late application of this sort I consider that the reasons for this necessity should be specifically addressed in the statement of grounds or the affidavit verifying it so that the Court can consider whether, in the exercise of its discretion, it should grant a very late application for leave."[155]

16–63 In effect, therefore, the onus on an applicant seeking leave to apply for judicial review which would have the effect of displacing a trial date is a particularly heavy one.[156]

Acquiescence and waiver

16–64 The courts will not allow the creation of a wholly new jurisdiction through acquiescence or waiver by the applicant.[157] But acquiescence or waiver may well be a ground on which a court may exercise its discretion not to grant relief. For example, in *R. (Kildare County Council) v Commissioner of Valuation*[158] the applicant appealed to the County Court against a valuation revision. It was only when the decision of the County Court proved not to be as favourable as expected that the applicant claimed that the County Court had no jurisdiction in the matter. The Court of Appeal ruled that, even assuming that the County Court had acted without jurisdiction, relief should be refused on discretionary grounds. Holmes L.J. said that he found it difficult to conceive of a "stronger case of estoppel by conduct".[159] Likewise, in the criminal procedure case of *A v Governor of Arbour Hill Prison*,[160] the Supreme Court held that the applicant's failure to raise the issue of the constitutionality of the offence with which he was charged *prior* to a plea of guilty in the Circuit Court meant that he was now precluded by his own

---

[155] [2005] 1 I.R. 242 at 259.
[156] There is, however, some uncertainty as to the date from which time runs for this purpose. In *Kennedy v Director of Public Prosecutions* [2007] IEHC 3, MacMenamin J. (reluctantly) concluded that he was bound by the decision in *CC* to rule that time ran from the date of the service of the indictment (which is frequently immediately before the trial) as opposed to the date of the return for trial. This meant that even though the application for leave had been made on the eve of the trial, time had yet to run as against the applicant, as the indictment had not yet been served.
[157] *Corrigan v Irish Land Commission* [1977] I.R. 317 at 325 per Henchy J.; *State (Byrne) v Frawley* [1978] I.R. 326 at 342 per O'Higgins C.J. On this subject, see also, para.14–06. The contrasting situation, where what is at issue is (broadly) acquiescence by the public body, is covered at Ch.19.
[158] [1901] 2 I.R. 215. See also, *State (Byrne) v Frawley* [1978] I.R. 326; *State (McKay) v Cork Circuit Judge* [1937] I.R. 650; *R. (Doris) v Ministry for Health* [1954] N.I. 79.
[159] [1901] 2 I.R. 215 at 213. The *Kildare* case was distinguished by Barron J. in *Browne v An Bord Pleanála* [1991] 2 I.R. 209 at 214.
[160] [2006] 4 I.R. 89.

conduct from challenging the validity of his conviction.[161] The right to object to an irregularity of procedure or breach of natural justice may also be lost by acquiescence and waiver.[162]

Where no useful and legitimate purpose would be served

16–65 The court will not make an order which cannot now be implemented or which would be either futile[163] or illegal.[164] Nor will relief be granted where this would: cause further delay[165]; lead the court into an uncertain area where it lacked appropriate expertise[166]; confer no practical benefit on the applicant; or serve no legitimate purpose.[167]

16–66 There have been several heterogeneous examples of where relief on this ground has been refused and which may be cited for purposes of illustration. For example, in *H v Director of Public Prosecutions*,[168] Barron J. refused to grant an order of mandamus compelling the Director of Public Prosecutions to reconsider a decision[169] he had taken five years previously not to prosecute certain members of the applicant's family in respect of alleged sexual offences against her son. Barron J. believed that it would not have been in the infant's interests to pursue this matter, "particularly after such a lapse of time". In *State (Abenglen Properties*

---

[161] For two powerful critiques (taking opposite views) of this highly controversial decision, see Fanning, "Hard Case, Bad Law? The Supreme Court decision in *A v Governor of Arbour Hill Prison*" (2005) 40 *Irish Jurist* 188; Murphy, "The Problem of Unconstitutionality and Retroactivity in Criminal Law: Ireland, The US and Canada Compared" (2007) 42 *Irish Jurist* 63. Following the decision of Laffoy J. in *McCann v Judges of the Monaghan District Court* [2009] IEHC 276 (where the court held that s.6 of the Enforcement of Court Orders Act 1940—which allowed for the imprisonment of civil debtors—was unconstitutional) it was reported that the Government had ordered the release of all persons detained pursuant to this section. But if the Government had not done so, could the *A* principles have been invoked to defend any Article 40 applications which such detained persons might have brought?

[162] *Corrigan v Irish Land Commission* [1977] I.R. 317; *Burns v Early* [2003] 2 I.L.R.M. 321; *Gorman v Martin* [2005] IESC 56; *Balaz v Kennedy* [2009] IEHC 110. In both *Burns* and *Gorman* the applicants were held to be precluded by their conduct in raising post-conviction jurisdictional points to challenge their convictions. See Ó Caoimh J. in *Burns* ([2003] 2 I.L.R.M. 321 at 332).

[163] *Minister for Labour v Grace* [1993] 2 I.R. 53 (where O'Hanlon J. refused to grant mandamus in circumstances where this would have been a "meaningless exercise"); *Ryan v Compensation Tribunal* [1997] I.L.R.M. 194 (where Costello P. refused to quash a decision awarding compensation which (it was claimed) failed to include a sum for home help payments as the law had since been changed to impose on health boards a statutory duty to provide such a service free of charge); *Healy v Minister for Communications* [2009] IEHC 258; [2009] 4 I.R. 186 (no practical benefit would accrue to applicant if decision quashed).

[164] *Kenny Homes & Co. Ltd v Galway City and County Manager* [1995] 1 I.R. 178 (no mandamus to compel the City Manager to comply with an invalid resolution).

[165] *State (Walshe) v Maguire* [1979] I.R. 372; *A v Eastern Health Board* [1998] 1 I.R. 464.

[166] *Ryanair Ltd v Flynn* [2000] 3 I.R. 240 at 273 per Kearns J. (applicant's claim would require High Court to make findings of fact in a contentious industrial relation dispute).

[167] See, e.g. *State (Doyle) v Carr* [1970] I.R. 77; *State (Toft) v Galway Corporation* [1981] I.L.R.M. 439 (orders of certiorari would be refused on discretionary grounds where the object of the quashing order was simply to cause difficulties for a business rival).

[168] [1994] 2 I.R. 589. See also, in the same vein, *Shannon v McGuinness* [1999] 3 I.R. 274.

[169] On the question of whether judicial review will lie for this purpose, see *Eviston v Director of Public Prosecutions* [2002] 3 I.R. 260; *Heaney v Commissioner of An Garda Síochána* [2007] 2 I.R. 69.

Ltd) v Dublin Corporation,[170] the Supreme Court refused to quash the granting of a planning permission when it became clear that the applicants could not obtain the default planning permission which they had sought. Likewise, as the Supreme Court made clear in *Blanchfield v Harnett*,[171] the courts will not quash even invalid orders made in the course of a criminal prosecution, if the sole purpose of the application is to seek to determine in advance the admissibility of evidence obtained pursuant to such orders and the court of trial has sufficient jurisdiction to deal with all such questions.[172]

16–67   Nevertheless, the courts have sometimes recognised in this context that it may serve a useful purpose to grant relief in order to clear an applicant's name. Thus, in *State (Furey) v Minister for Defence*[173] certiorari was granted to quash an ignominious dismissal from the Defence Forces. Even though the applicant's probationary period had long since expired, McCarthy J. rejected the argument that a quashing order would serve no useful purpose on the grounds that an order would allow him to vindicate his reputation.[174] However, the decision of the Supreme Court in *Barry v Fitzpatrick*[175] suggests a different approach. Here the applicant had been remanded in custody beyond the statutory eight-day period without his consent. While the court agreed that the remands were bad in law, a majority held that as the order was spent, no useful purpose would be served by quashing same. The difference between *Furey* and *Barry* is one of degree, and the fact remains that in the latter case the court refused to quash an order which related to the applicant's constitutional right to liberty.[176]

16–68   Relief will not be granted if the purpose is not regarded as legitimate. This ground of refusal is more difficult to define, but there have been cases where the courts have held that they will not facilitate a litigant who seeks relief for an unmeritorious or ulterior purpose. There are elements of such thinking in *Abenglen Properties* and also in the judgment of Henchy J. in *State (Doyle) v Carr*.[177] Here the applicant established that the District Court order providing for a transfer of a publican's licence on an interim basis was invalid. Moreover, the publican had

---

[170]   [1984] I.R. 381.

[171]   [2002] 3 I.R. 207.

[172]   See also, to the same effect, *Farrell v Farrelly* [1988] I.R. 210; *Berkeley v Edwards* [1988] I.R. 217; and *Byrne v Grey* [1988] I.R. 31.

[173]   [1988] I.L.R.M. 89.

[174]   [1988] I.L.R.M. 89 at 100. Note also the comments of Kelly J. in *Bane v Garda Representative Association* [1997] 2 I.R. 449 at 477 where, rejecting arguments that the remedy was inappropriate, he observed: "… even though the applicants are no longer members of the [Association], the fact remains that the record of that Association contains findings of guilt concerning serious misconduct on their part. Even though they may have no intention of ever again becoming involved in membership of the [Association], the mark remains against them". See also, *Clarke v Hogan* [1995] 1 I.R. 310 and *de Burca v Wicklow County Council* [2009] IEHC 54.

[175]   [1996] 1 I.L.R.M. 512.

[176]   The subsequent decision of the Supreme Court in *Howard v Early* [2006] IESC 34 suggests that *Barry v Fitzpatrick* will be largely be regarded as a decision turning on its own facts. Here the applicant had been remanded in custody for an offence the maximum penalty for which was only a monetary fine. Denham J. distinguished *Barry* on the basis that in the present case there were "consequences (custodial remand) from the unlawful order which may be relevant to the assessment of the penalty".

[177]   [1970] I.R. 69. See also, to like effect, *State (Toft) v Galway Corporation* [1981] I.L.R.M. 439.

long since acquired a perfectly valid full licence and this of itself was a ground for refusing to quash an order which was now spent. However, reading between the lines of the judgment of Henchy J., it may be that relief was refused also because it appeared that the application was simply a stratagem designed to discomfit a business rival.

Discretion and the issue of resources

16–69   Mandamus will not be granted if the respondent has not the resources to carry out its functions or where it is doing its best to perform its functions within a limited budget.[178] Thus, in *Brady v Cavan County Council*,[179] the applicants had sought mandamus to compel the County Council to repair a certain road. A majority of the Supreme Court held that, while the applicant was in breach of its statutory duty, the Council was proceeding to repair some 600 roads in a "rational and systematic order", having regard to a scheme of priorities identified by its engineers. The court was not, accordingly, prepared to make an order of mandamus where the respondent body did not have "the means to comply with the order" and where "its successful implementation depends on the co-operation of other bodies who are not before the court".[180]

16–70   However, this principle has not always been evenly applied. In *Hoey v Minister for Justice*[181] the respondents pleaded that excessive expense justified the Minister in failing to provide local authorities with sufficient resources to fulfill their statutory duties under the Courthouses (Provision and Maintenance) Act 1935. Lynch J. was unimpressed by this:

> "It is not open to the Executive by arrangements made with the local authority or by promises made to the local authority to relieve such local authority from the obligations expressly imposed upon it by the Act of 1935 … If the Executive wishes to limit or reduce such obligations, the Executive must introduce the appropriate legislation to the Oireachtas and must persuade the Oireachtas to enact the same."[182]

16–71   But even in cases where the court has been unimpressed with arguments based on lack of resources or administrative inconvenience, public authorities will frequently be given time and an opportunity to address the problem. Thus, in *Hoey v Minister for Justice*,[183] Lynch J. placed a stay on an order of mandamus directing

---

[178] *R. v Bristol Corporation Ex p. Hendy* [1974] 1 W.L.R. 498.

[179] [1997] 1 I.L.R.M. 390 (HC); [1999] 4 I.R. 99 (SC).

[180] [1999] 4 I.R. 99 at 106.

[181] [1994] 3 I.R. 329.

[182] [1994] 3 I.R. 329 at 343. See also, *FN v Minister for Education* [1995] 1 I.R. 409; [1995] 2 I.L.R.M. 297 at 303 (where Geoghegan J. said that the State was under a constitutional obligation to provide suitable methods of treatment for the applicant unless this would be so "impractical or prohibitively expensive as would come within any notional limit on the State's constitutional obligation").

[183] See also, the judgment of Barrington J. in *State (Richardson) v Governor of Mountjoy Prison* [1980] I.L.R.M. 82. Here the judge concluded that the hygiene facilities provided in the women's section of Mountjoy Prison were so inadequate that the State had failed in its constitutional duty to vindicate the applicant prisoner's right to bodily integrity. Nevertheless,

the Minister to perform her statutory duty to keep a particular courthouse in good repair to enable the necessary repair work to be performed in the interim period.

Availability of alternate remedies

16–72 Where an aggrieved party undertakes and completes an appeal, then he or she is deemed to have waived his/her right to a review of the original decision. However, the mere existence of an alternative remedy does not of itself debar an application for judicial review. The question of whether the availability of an appeal bars judicial review is essentially one for the discretion of the court[184] and regard will be had to the adequacy of the alternate remedy[185] and to all the circumstances of the case.[186] Where the issues in question are principally issues of fact or law not fundamentally going to jurisdiction and which can be dealt with on appeal, then the courts will invariably insist that the appellate remedy be availed of.[187] The more difficult questions arise where—as is often the case—the errors of law in question go to jurisdiction.

16–73 There is a vast modern jurisprudence on this topic, not all of it fully consistent. Thus, in *State (Abenglen Properties Ltd) v Dublin Corporation*,[188] the Supreme Court appeared to lean in favour of the "exhaustion of remedies" requirement. The applicant company had sought certiorari to quash certain conditions attached by the respondent to the grant of planning permission, thus by-passing the possible appeal to An Bord Pleanála which the relevant legislation made available for them. It was said that the applicants were entitled to a ruling by the High Court as to the vires of these conditions and that the legality of the conditions was not within the capacity of An Bord Pleanála. While it appears that the applicant's evident desire to obtain a benefit "not contemplated by the planning code" may have coloured the court's attitude, Henchy J. also stated that where the Oireachtas had provided "a self-contained administrative scheme",[189] the courts should not intervene by way of judicial review where—as in the instant case—the statutory appellate procedure was adequate to meet the complaint on which the

---

the judge granted a short adjournment to allow the recommendations for the improvement of facilities to be implemented.

[184] As Charleton J. put it in *Doherty v South Dublin County Council (No. 2)* [2007] 2 I.R. 696 at 724: "The fact that an appeal might be available as an alternative can, depending on the circumstances, bar the availability of a remedy, but it does not automatically exclude it."

[185] Thus, for example, in *Brennan v Windle* [2003] 3 I.R. 494 the Supreme Court held that the applicant had been convicted without any notice in the District Court, so that his conviction and sentence of four months' imprisonment were bad in law. The applicant had spent some time in custody before applying for judicial review and the Supreme Court firmly rejected any argument that he ought to have applied to the District Court to have the deemed good service set aside since this would have resulted in further delay.

[186] There may thus be special circumstances which would make it unfair or unrealistic to insist on the exhaustion of appellate remedies: see, e.g. *Bane v Garda Representative Association* [1997] 2 I.R. 449 at 447 per Kelly J. ("the relationship between the parties was so soured that the failure on the part of the applicants to exercise their right of internal appeal was not conduct such as would debar them from obtaining an order of certiorari"); *Maher v Minister for Social Welfare* [2008] IESC 15 (where the information regarding an internal appeal was "not easily discernible from the information provided" by the respondent).

[187] See generally, *O'Connor v Private Residential Tenancies Board* [2008] IEHC 205.

[188] [1984] I.R. 381.

[189] [1984] I.R. 381 at 405.

application was grounded. This approach was subsequently followed in a series of cases in the 1980s and 1990s.[190]

16-74 However, the more rigid approach taken in *Abenglen* and subsequent cases has now been more or less abandoned. In more recent times the courts have treated both the existence of an alternative appeal and even the actual exercise of that remedy as simply one factor to be considered in the exercise of the court's discretion. The modern approach was eloquently summarised thus by Barron J. in *McGoldrick v An Bord Pleanála*:

> "The true question is which [the appeal or the review] is the more appropriate remedy considered in the context of common sense, the ability to deal with the questions raised and principles of fairness; provided, of course, that the applicant has not gone too far down one road to be estopped from changing his or her mind."[191]

16-75 The first sign of unhappiness in the Supreme Court with the rigidity of *Abenglen* had come previously in *P&F Sharpe Ltd v Dublin City and County Manager*.[192] Here the applicant had sought permission to build an access road on to a new dual carriageway, but the respondent indicated that, for reasons of traffic safety, he was unwilling to accede to this request. He further declined to comply with a resolution passed under s.4 of the City and County Management (Amendment) Act 1955 on the grounds that it was unlawful. The applicants sought an order of mandamus compelling the respondents to comply with the resolution. The Supreme Court refused to grant an order of mandamus on the grounds that the resolution in question was a nullity, but did grant certiorari to quash the respondent's refusal to grant permission for the access road. The respondents had argued that as the applicants had commenced an appeal to An Bord Pleanála against the decision to refuse permission, they should be confined to that remedy and certiorari should be refused on discretionary grounds. Finlay C.J. did not accept this contention:

> "The powers of An Bord Pleanála on the making of an appeal to it would be entirely confined to the consideration of the matters before it on the basis of proper planning and development of the area and it would have no jurisdiction to consider the question of the validity, from a legal point of view, of the purported decision by the county manager. It would not, therefore, be just

---

[190] For examples from this period, see, e.g. *O'Connor v Kerry County Council* [1988] I.L.R.M. 660 (in a case where the applicant had challenged the validity of an enforcement notice served under the Local Government (Planning and Development) Act 1963, Costello J. refused the relief sought, saying that an appeal to An Bord Pleanála was a more appropriate remedy than judicial review); *Byrne v Grey* [1988] I.R. 31 (where Hamilton P. refused to grant certiorari to quash an invalid search warrant on the grounds that the real object of the application was to seek to exclude certain evidence and the ruling on admissibility was best left to the court of trial); *Nova Colour Graphic Supplies Ltd v Employment Appeals Tribunal* [1987] I.R. 426 (where Barron J. held that, as the issues arising out of an unfair dismissal case would be reheard de novo by the Circuit Court (where the applicant's appeal was pending), this procedure was more appropriate than an application for judicial review).

[191] [1997] 1 I.R. 497 at 509. This passage has subsequently been endorsed by the Supreme Court in a series of cases.

[192] [1989] I.R. 701. See, to like effect, *Mythen v Employment Appeals Tribunal* [1990] 1 I.R. 98 at 108–109; *SP v Residential Institutions Redress Board* [2006] IEHC 401.

for the [applicants] to be deprived of their right to have that decision quashed for want of validity."[193]

16–76   This, however, is precisely the argument which had been advanced by the applicants in *Abenglen* who had sought an authoritative ruling from the High Court as to the validity (as opposed to the merits) of the conditions attached by the planning authority. By contrast, in *P&F Sharpe* the issue related to the reasonableness of the local authority's decision and was thus even closer to the merits than the pure ultra vires issue raised in *Abenglen*. In addition, the argument against granting relief in *P&F Sharpe* was stronger than in *Abenglen*, inasmuch as the applicants had also concurrently sought to appeal to An Bord Pleanála in addition to commencing judicial review proceedings; whereas in *Abenglen* an appeal was available, but not actually exercised.

16–77   Two contemporary examples provide contrasting illustrations of how this discretionary approach is applied in practice. In *Tomlinson v Criminal Injuries Compensation Tribunal*[194] the applicant's husband had died following a criminal assault and she made a claim to the Tribunal for appropriate compensation. At first instance, a single member of the Tribunal had found for her on the issue of liability, but had deducted over half the award to take account of the financial benefits coming from other sources which had been paid to the family on her husband's death. The single issue in the judicial review proceedings was whether the Tribunal member had acted ultra vires in making such deductions, but in the High Court Kelly J. considered that this applicant ought to have exhausted her internal appellate remedies by way of appeal to a three member panel who would have heard the case de novo. The Supreme Court took a different view, although Denham J. admitted that the courts would normally "lean towards requiring" applicants to exhaust their appellate remedies. Here the situation was different: the decision of the single member on the deductions issue was in line with established practice of the Tribunal, so insisting on exhaustion seemed unnecessarily rigid. Moreover, any such appeal would be de novo, thus potentially re-opening the issue of liability to her ultimate prejudice. Finally, the fact that the case raised a net issue of law going to jurisdiction was "a factor in favour of a decision by a court".[195] By contrast in *O'Donnell v Tipperary (South Riding) County Council*[196] the Supreme Court held that it was more appropriate in the circumstances of that case that the applicant continue with his appeal to the Employment Appeals Tribunal. Here the applicant was dismissed from his position as a fire station officer for having allegedly made fraudulent claims. Following an internal disciplinary inquiry, the applicant appealed to the Employment Appeals Tribunal. Following two days of hearing before the Tribunal, that Tribunal adjourned to enable the applicant

---

[193] [1989] I.R. 701 at 721. Note also the comments of Kelly J. in *Harding v Cork County Council (No. 1)* [2006] 2 I.L.R.M. 392 at 399 where he observed (albeit not in the context of any exhaustion requirement) that points relating to "*vires*, fair procedures and bias ... should properly be determined by a court rather than by An Bord Pleanala".

[194] [2005] 1 I.L.R.M. 394.

[195] [2005] 1 I.L.R.M. 394 at 400.

[196] [2005] 2 I.R. 483. Note also the approach of Hedigan J. in *O'Connor v Private Residential Tenancies Board* [2008] IEHC 205 where, having examined each of the four complaints of the applicant, he concluded that each of them raised issues of law which could readily have been included in an appeal on a point of law under s.123 of the Residential Tenancies Act 2004 and that the appeal route was the most appropriate remedy.

pursue his judicial review remedy. While Denham J. held that the fact that the applicant had pursued an alternative remedy did not in itself debar him from now seeking judicial review, it was nonetheless a "weighty factor".[197] As, moreover, the substance of the case related to the merits of the disciplinary dispute and not to any issue of law or procedure, the most appropriate remedy was to enable the applicant to continue the appeal before the Tribunal. Denham J. stressed that no point of substance had been raised on the issue of fair procedures, the implication here being that the court would probably have taken a different view had the merits of this procedural point been stronger.

16–78 This last point refers to the fact that there is authority that the exhaustion requirement will not be insisted upon where the complaint relates to a breach of fair procedures[198]: because of the grievous nature of the error "a fair appeal does not cure an unfair hearing".[199] But there is also opposing authority to the effect that an applicant "must demonstrate a clear and compelling case that an injustice has been done that is incapable of being remedied on appeal ...".[200] Certainly, certiorari "is not appropriate to a routine mishap which may befall any trial".[201]

Concluding comment

16–79 In the light of these cross-currents of judicial authority and policy, three comments may be offered. In the first place, the two lines of authority are grounded on different policy views in that the *Abenglen* line takes the view that if the applicant has had a fair, full trial on the merits available to him, even if an appeal had been necessary, then he has little to complain about. The alternative *Sharpe* view is that the applicant is entitled to a proper decision at the initial stage without being put to the trauma, delay and expense of an appeal. The second comment is to suggest that, especially since the appellate body involved in both *Abenglen* and *Sharpe* was the same (An Bord Pleanála), these two cases seem hardly capable of being reconciled. However it may be that some consistency can be built upon a reasonable principle by considering, in the context of a given case and the alleged blemish, exactly how comprehensive and appropriate is the right of appeal which was provided—the approach which, judged by reference to the subsequent Supreme Court decisions such as *Tomlinson* and *O'Donnell*, is the one which has now found

---

[197] See also, the broadly similar analysis of this point by Clarke J. in *Payne v Brophy* [2006] 1 I.R. 560.

[198] See, e.g. *Gill v Connellan* [1987] I.R. 541 at 548 per Lynch J.; *Bane v Garda Representative Association* [1997] 2 I.R. 449 at 477 per Kelly J.; *Ronan v Coughlan* [2005] 4 I.R. 274 at 280 per Quirke J.

[199] This last point was strongly made in *Stefan v Minister for Justice* [2001] 4 I.R. 203 at 218. It is important to stress that, certainly in immigration cases, *Stefan* nonetheless remains the exception and not the rule.

[200] As Hedigan J. said in *N v Minister for Justice, Equality and Law Reform* [2008] IEHC 308. See also, to the same effect, *TTA v Minister for Justice, Equality and Law Reform* [2009] IEHC 215; *RLA v Minister for Justice, Equality and Law Reform* [2009] IEHC 2.

[201] *Sweeney v Brophy* [1993] 2 I.R. 202 at 211 per Hederman J.; *Grennan v Kirby* [1994] 2 I.L.R.M. 199 at 202 per Murphy J. These principles were applied by Laffoy J. in *Maher v O'Donnell* [1995] 3 I.R. 530 when she said that the non-attendance of a witness whom an accused expected to attend at a trial, but whose attendance he did not arrange for, was an error which "should be sought to be remedied by way of appeal and not by way of certiorari".

favour. The adequacy of the alternative remedy is a matter whose significance is attested to in many authorities.[202]

16–80   The third comment, in contrast to the first two, approaches the question not from the perspective of the individual but from the general interest of the legal system in ensuring that public bodies remain within their appointed bounds and securing authoritative rulings as to what these are. From this perspective, it would seem that even the availability of an alternate remedy would not militate against a court exercising its discretion to grant relief. *Tomlinson* offers a good illustration of this.[203]

E. Locus Standi

16–81   The law on locus standi, which is largely judge made, though with occasional legislative forays,[204] is currently in a state of flux. The modern tendency of the courts in common law countries is to move away from a technical approach to locus standi towards a rationalisation of standing requirements based on considerations relating to the general administration of justice, and the separation of powers.[205] Thus, there have been dicta to the effect that the standing rules are merely rules of practice (which may be relaxed if there are "weighty countervailing considerations" justifying a departure from the ordinary rules), and that these requirements are the same regardless of the form of the proceedings.[206] Following the 1986 reforms, Ord.84 r.20(4) now provides that leave to apply for judicial review shall not be granted unless the applicant "has a sufficient interest in the matter to which the application relates".[207] As noted at para.16–86, the effect of a similar

---

[202]   *Gill v Connellan* [1987] I.R. 541 at 548.

[203]   *Director of Public Prosecutions v O'C* [2006] 3 I.R. 238.

[204]   Section 50 of the Planning and Development Act 2000 represents a legislative attempt to tighten the standing requirements which had heretofore been liberally permitted by the courts. It provides that: "Leave [to apply for judicial review] shall not be granted unless the High Court is satisfied that there are substantial grounds for contending that the decision is invalid or ought to be quashed and that the applicant has a substantial interest in the matter the subject of the application." As Murray C.J. pointedly observed in *Harding v Cork County Council (No. 2)* [2008] IESC 27; [2008] 2 I.L.R.M. 251 at 259, no "substantive definition" of what constitutes a "substantial interest" is provided by the section.

[205]   See the judgment of Henchy J. in *Cahill v Sutton* [1980] I.R. 269.

[206]   *Cahill v Sutton* [1980] I.R. 269 at 285 per Henchy J.; *State (Lynch) v Cooney* [1982] I.R. 337 at 369 per Walsh J.

[207]   In the case of applications for leave in planning cases, s.50(4)(b) of the Planning and Development Act 2000 (as amended) requires that the High Court shall not grant leave unless it is satisfied that "the applicant has a substantial interest in the matter". While this is a somewhat stricter test than that which applies under Ord.84, this statutory requirement is not to be "applied in such a restrictive manner as would preclude the courts from checking 'a clear and serious abuse of process by the relevant authorities'": *Friends of the Curragh Environment Ltd v An Bord Pleanála* [2007] 1 I.L.R.M. 386 at 393 per Finlay Geoghegan J., quoting Macken J. in *Harrington v An Bord Pleanála* [2006] 1 I.R. 388. Nevertheless, "the fact that a member of the public may have an interest in seeing that the law is observed is not such as to amount to the existence of a 'substantial interest'" within the meaning of s.50(4) of the Planning and Development Act 2000: see *O'Shea v Kerry County Council* [2003] 4 I.R. 143 at 160 per Ó Caoimh J. This approach was endorsed by the Supreme Court in *Harding v Cork County Council (No. 2)* [2008] IESC 28; [2008] 2 I.L.R.M. 251. See also, the comments of O'Neill J. in *O'Brien v Dun Laoghaire Rathdown County Council* [2006]

change in the English Rules of Court has been stated to permit an *actio populatis* (or "citizen's action") in suitable cases and the Supreme Court has also appeared to take this view in respect of the standing requirements in Ord.84 r.20(4).[208] Nevertheless, as noted at paras 16–96 to 16–100, in addition to the rather extreme case of *Cahill v Sutton*,[209] there is also a line of contemporary case law emerging which shows a move away from what might be termed an ultra-liberal approach.[210]

The traditional standing rules

16–82 Traditionally, the standing rules varied depending on the character of the remedies. In theory the public law remedies of certiorari and prohibition always contained an element of the *actio populatis*, as the purpose of these remedies was not merely to avoid injustice inter partes, but also to maintain order in the legal system.[211] It was thus open to anyone—even a stranger to the proceedings—to apply for certiorari or prohibition. In practice, however, relief was hardly ever given to anyone other than a "person aggrieved".[212] Even, in theory, a stricter approach was taken in the case of the declaration and the injunction, because the standing rules reflected the fact that these remedies were derived from private law. An applicant was required to show the existence of a legal right or other cognisable interest which was affected or threatened. However, in respect of both sets of remedies, the law has long moved away from the stricter, technical requirement of a legal right and towards the (common) position that the applicant should have suffered some prejudice going beyond that felt by most other members of the community. That this is so was stated in the major Supreme Court case of *Cahill v Sutton*.[213]

16–83 Given this more liberal policy, why then retain a standing rule at all? The reasoning is based on the need to safeguard the proper administration of justice (against the officious man of straw); to prevent the abuse of the power of judicial

---

IEHC 177 ("passionate interest" in local planning issues is not in itself sufficient to satisfy the statutory test).

[208] See the comments of Keane C.J. in *Mulcreevy v Minister for Environment* [2004] 1 I.R. 72 at 78.

[209] [1980] I.R. 269.

[210] See, e.g. *Shannon v McGuinness* [1999] 3 I.R. 274; *Construction Industry Federation v Dublin City Council* [2005] 2 I.R. 496; [2005] 2 I.L.R.M. 256; *Lennon v Limerick City Council* [2006] IEHC 112; *John Paul Construction Ltd v Minister for Environment, Heritage and Local Government* [2006] IEHC 255; *O'Brien v Dun Laoghaire Rathdown County Council* [2006] IEHC 177; *Harding v Cork County Council (No. 2)* [2008] IESC 28; [2008] 2 I.L.R.M. 251.

[211] Yardley, "Certiorari and the Problem of *Locus Standi*" (1955) 71 L.Q.R. 388; "Prohibition and Mandamus and the Problem of *Locus Standi*" (1957) 73 L.Q.R. 534. The locus standi requirements for mandamus have traditionally been somewhat stricter than in the case of the other public law remedies: see *R. v Lewisham Guardians* [1897] 1 Q.B. 498 (existence of specific legal right); *R. (IUDWC) v Rathmines U.D.C.* [1928] I.R. 260 (where Hanna J. said that an applicant must demonstrate that a "legal right" was infringed and where O'Byrne J. said that a "specific interest in performance of duty" was required). But for a less restrictive approach, see *State (Modern Homes (Ire) Ltd) v Dublin Corporation* [1953] I.R. 202; *State (ACC Ltd) v Navan U.D.C.*, unreported, High Court, February 22, 1980.

[212] See, e.g. *State (Kerry County Council) v Minister for Local Government* [1933] I.R. 517; *State (Doyle) v Carr* [1970] I.R. 87; and *State (Toft) v Galway Corporation* [1981] I.L.R.M. 439. In all three cases certiorari was refused because the applicants were held not to be "persons aggrieved" in this sense.

[213] [1980] I.R. 269.

review; and to uphold the principle of the separation of powers. In addition, it was said in *Cahill* that a case brought by a litigant with no direct interest would tend to lack (in Henchy J.'s words) "the force and urgency of reality".[214] It has also been said that a standing rule is "constitutionally inspired but not constitutionally compelled".[215] It is among a package of devices which enable a judge to refuse to address the merits of a constitutional claim. At base then, the content of a standing rule depends upon a judge's view of the proper place of judicial review in a constitutional polity.

Preliminary points

16–84   However, before returning to explore this central issue further, we should attempt to clear away three preliminary points. In the first place, whatever about the historical position set out in the previous paragraph, the standing requirements are now the same whether the court is dealing with the three remedies which originated on the state side or the two which originated in the Courts of Equity. That this is so had been accepted even before the new system was introduced.[216] It has surely been put beyond any doubt by the advent of the new regime. The policy of the (1986 and 2011) Rules is to achieve uniformity between the remedies. This is confirmed by the fact that Ord.84 r.20(5) (which provides that the court "shall not grant leave unless it considers that the applicant has a sufficient interest in the matter") applies to each of the remedies, irrespective of the form of the proceedings. This must mean that the locus standi requirements do not vary from remedy to remedy.

16–85   Secondly, it has now been stated judicially on several occasions[217] that the standing requirements are the same, even though the application for judicial review involves the constitutionality of a law or an executive or administrative action, rather than merely the vires of an administrative action with no such constitutional issues. It is significant that whereas *Cahill v Sutton* was a case involving the

---

[214] [1980] I.R. 269 at 282–283. Though note that in *Norris v Attorney General* [1984] I.R. 36 at 91 McCarthy J. remarked apropos of what might be termed the "busybody" basis of *Cahill* that "from 1937 to 1980, I doubt if the court records reveal many, or even any, instances of such officious interference". But cf. the comments of Ó Caoimh J. in *Riordan v An Taoiseach (No. 5)* [2001] 4 I.R. 463 at 473 (where a challenge to the constitutionality of the Courts (Establishment and Constitution) Act 1961 brought by a plaintiff who was held to lack locus standi was described as "vexatious") and those of Smyth J. in *Riordan v Government of Ireland* [2006] IEHC 312 where a similar claim was held to amount to an abuse of the locus standi rules.

[215] See Kirby, "Deconstructing the Law's Hostility to Public Interest Litigation" (2011) 127 L.Q.R. 537; Sherlock, "Understanding standing: Locus Standi in Irish Constitutional Law" (1987) *Public Law* 345 at 366–369.

[216] See, e.g. *State (Lynch) v Cooney* [1982] I.R. 337 at 369 per Walsh J.

[217] *State (Sheehan) v Government of Ireland* [1987] I.R. 550 at 557 per Costello J.; *Duggan v An Taoiseach* [1989] I.L.R.M. 710 at 725 per Hamilton P. In *Sheehan*, Costello J. thought that it was "to be expected" that the test in each case should "be formulated somewhat differently". But it may be noted that in *Society for the Protection of Unborn Children (Ire) Ltd v Coogan* [1989] I.R. 734, both Finlay C.J. (at 742) and Walsh J. (at 746) give some cause to suggest that the standing requirement may be stricter where it is a law, rather than an administrative or executive action, whose constitutionality may be at stake. Humphreys and O'Dowd, "*Locus Standi* to Enforce the Constitution" (1990) 3 I.L.T. 14 suggest (at 15) that the fact that the courts cannot fulfill the statutory vacuum created by the invalidation of legislation argues in favour of stricter standing rules in cases challenging the constitutionality of legislation.

constitutionality of a law, yet the principle it laid down has been widely followed in cases falling within each of the other two categories.

16–86   The third and final preliminary point is the fact that the issue of standing is distinct from that of the merits or strength of an applicant's case. This orthodoxy would hardly be worth stating were it not for the fact that in Britain, in a very well-known case,[218] the House of Lords has seized upon the analogous changes to Ord.84 as a ground for rejecting the traditional view. There is no reason to expect the Irish courts to draw upon Ord.84 (which does expressly require "a sufficient interest") in order to follow this rather surprising English authority. Every Irish case has treated the issue of standing independently from the merits.[219]

Cahill v Sutton

16–87   The decision of the Supreme Court in *Cahill v Sutton* was the first modern Irish case thoroughly to address the issue of locus standi and, having been quoted with approval in almost every case on standing,[220] it remains, by some distance, the leading authority on the point. It involved a medical negligence claim in which the plaintiff was time barred under the Statute of Limitations 1957 s.11(2)(b). The plaintiff challenged the section on the ground that it contained no exception to protect the right to litigate of an injured person who had only become aware of the facts on which his claim was based after the period of limitation had expired. The essential point for present purposes was that the plaintiff was not herself such a person since at all material times she was aware of all the facts necessary to ground her claim. In sum, said Henchy J.:

> "[T]he plaintiff is seeking to be allowed to conjure up, invoke and champion the putative constitutional rights of a hypothetical third party, so that the provisions of s.11, subs. 2(b), may be declared unconstitutional on the basis of that constitutional *jus tertii* – thus allowing the plaintiff to march through the resulting gap in the statute."[221]

---

[218]   *Inland Revenue Commissioners v National Federation of Self-Employed and Small Businesses Ltd* [1982] A.C. 617.

[219]   See, e.g. the comments of Keane J. in *Lancefort Ltd v An Bord Pleanála (No. 2)* [1992] 2 I.R. 270 at 318. This point was also stressed by the Supreme Court in *Harding v Cork County Council (No. 2)* [2008] IESC 27 in the context of s.50 of the Planning and Development Act 2000. As Kearns J. put it, "… the 'substantial grounds' and 'substantial interest' requirements of s. 50 creates two fences, not one, and an applicant who fails to establish the latter has no entitlement to obtain leave merely because he has grounds which are substantial".
  But cf. the comments of Costello P. in *Kenny v Revenue Commissioners* [1996] 3 I.R. 315 at 318 where he said that a taxpayer has "no locus standi to challenge administrative decisions, including applications, made by the Revenue Commissioners relating to the duties and tax payable by another taxpayer". This may be true so far as it goes, but it could scarcely be suggested that a taxpayer could not challenge unfair preferential treatment accorded by the Revenue Commissioners to another taxpayer. This, it will be recalled, was the gravamen of the complaint in the *Self-Employed* case.

[220]   A notable exception being the dissent of McCarthy J. in *Norris v Attorney General* [1984] I.R. 36 at 91 where McCarthy J. described *Cahill v Sutton* as a case "he was bound reluctantly to follow".

[221]   [1980] I.R. 269 at 280. The converse of this principle is that the courts will, generally speaking, refuse to give the benefits of a finding of invalidity *retrospectively* to persons who would not have had standing in the first instance to challenge the constitutionality of the impugned measure: see *A v Governor of Arbour Hill Prison* [2006] 4 I.R. 88.

16–88   Only two of the five unanimous judges who heard *Cahill* gave substantive judgments. The tenor of O'Higgins C.J.'s fairly brief judgment and Henchy J.'s judgment are in accord. However, as Henchy J. gave the more elaborate consideration to the standing topic, it is his treatment which is generally regarded as the more authoritative. In holding that Ms Cahill had no standing to make the only argument which could assist her, Henchy J. stated:

> "[An applicant] must show that the impact of the impugned law on his personal situation discloses an injury or prejudice which he has either suffered or is in imminent danger of suffering.
>
>   This rule, however, being but a rule of practice must, like all such rules, be subject to expansion, exception or qualification when the justice of the case so requires. Since the paramount consideration in the exercise of the jurisdiction of the Courts to review legislation in the light of the Constitution is to ensure that persons entitled to the benefit of a constitutional right will not be prejudiced through being wrongfully deprived of it, there will be cases where the want of the normal locus standi on the part of the person questioning the constitutionality of the statute may be overlooked if, in the circumstances of the case, there is a transcendent need to assert against the statute the constitutional provision that has been invoked. For example, while the challenger may lack the personal standing normally required, those prejudicially affected by the impugned statute may not be in a position to assert adequately, or in time, their constitutional rights. In such a case the court might decide to ignore the want of normal personal standing on the part of the litigant before it. Likewise, the absence of a prejudice or injury peculiar to the challenger might be overlooked, in the discretion of the court, if the impugned provision is directed at or operable against a grouping which includes the challenger, or with whom the challenger may be said to have a common interest – particularly in cases where, because of the nature of the subject-matter, it is difficult to segregate those affected from those not affected by the challenged provision."[222]

16–89   Three comments may be made on this passage. First, given the entire range of public cases which the standing rule must accommodate, it is inevitable that the rule should be broad and flexible.[223] Secondly, what may be taken as the general rule, which is contained in the first paragraph, describes the plaintiff's title to sue as "injury or prejudice". Later in the judgment, it was said that he must "stand in real or imminent danger of being adversely affected". These formulations are, of course, much broader than the traditional standard (at any rate for the remedies of declaration or injunction). Finally, Henchy J. acknowledged that the rule was flexible and embraced a number of exceptions "when the justice of the case so

---

[222] [1980] I.R. 269 at 284–285. An example of this exception is provided by *Doorley and Martin v Legal Aid Board* [2007] 1 I.L.R.M. 481, a case where solicitor employees of the Board challenged a decision which would have permitted authorised officials to have access to client files on a more or less random basis. Laffoy J. rejected the argument that the plaintiffs lacked standing, saying ([2007] 1 I.L.R.M. 481 at 503): "... a solicitor who has privileged information must have sufficient interest to challenge an enactment which he believes has the effect of interfering with the privilege adversely to the interest of his client, because he has the duty to uphold that privilege."

[223] *State (Lynch) v Cooney* [1982] I.R. 337 at 369 per Walsh J.

requires". The leading example of this qualification or exception is where "there is an absence of a prejudice ... peculiar to the challenger ... but the impugned provision is directed against a grouping which includes the challenger ...". This category may be illustrated by the clutch of high-profile cases outlined at paras 16–101 to 16–107.

Post-*Cahill* cases

16–90 But this line of rather particular mega-constitutional cases apart, the question remains: how has *Cahill* fared in administrative law cases? In fact, the majority of the subsequent decisions have involved a straightforward application of the *Cahill* principle. In *Chambers v An Bord Pleanála*,[224] the applicant was a member of an environmental pressure group that had opposed the granting of planning permission for the erection of a pharmaceutical manufacturing facility. When permission was granted following an oral hearing before An Bord Pleanála, the plaintiffs (who were husband and wife) sought to set aside that decision. In the High Court, Lavan J. held that the plaintiffs lacked locus standi for this purpose, because they had not actually participated as objectors at an earlier stage.[225] The Supreme Court took a different view, with Egan J. holding that it was reasonable for the plaintiffs to have allowed the pressure group (of which they were members) to deal with the oral hearing. Furthermore, there was no question but that the plaintiffs did have standing in their own right. One of the plaintiffs was an asthmatic, both lived near the proposed site and both had indirectly participated in the appeal via membership of the pressure group in question. This conclusion would seem plainly in line with *Cahill v Sutton*. Possibly different considerations would arise had the plaintiffs lived in a different part of the State remote from the proposed factory and opposed the decision for purely ideological reasons.[226] Although the court did not have to address this wider issue, the rationale underlying the exceptional constitutional cases which afford a generous degree of standing to such public-spirited "ideological" plaintiffs would seem no less applicable to such a case, especially if there was no other obvious plaintiff at hand who could show that he personally would suffer in a special way from the proposed development.

16–91 The interesting case of *Bargaintown Ltd v Dublin Corporation*[227] raises

---

[224] [1992] 1 I.R. 134.

[225] But the approach of Lavan J. has been restored by the Oireachtas so far as planning cases are concerned: see s.50(2)(b) of the Planning and Development Act 2000 (as inserted by s.13 of the Planning and Development (Strategic Infrastructure) Act 2006), and *Harding v Cork County Council (No. 2)* [2008] IESC 27; [2008] 2 I.L.R.M. 251.

[226] It may be noted that in *Mulcreevy v Minister for Environment* [2004] 1 I.R. 72 the applicant was held to have standing to challenge the validity of a statutory instrument which permitted certain works to be carried out to a national monument located in Dublin, even though he himself lived in Kerry. Note, however, that in planning cases simpliciter "the fact that a member of the public may have an interest in seeing that the law is observed is not such as to amount to the existence of a 'substantial interest'" within the meaning of s.50(4) of the Planning and Development Act 2000: see *O'Shea v Kerry County Council* [2003] 4 I.R. 143 at 160 per Ó Caoimh J. Likewise in the same statutory context in *Harding v Cork County Council* [2008] IESC 27; [2008] 2 I.L.R.M. 251 at 272, Kearns J. rejected the idea that "a person with some knowledge of the local area who has moved away overseas, but nonetheless likes to fill in idle moments by tracking planning developments in Ireland ..." would have a sufficient interest for this purpose.

[227] [1993] I.L.R.M. 890.

novel standing questions. Here the applicant held the sub-lease of certain premises from Mr Foster. Mr Foster in turn held the head lease in the premises from the respondents and when the head lease expired, he applied to the Circuit Court for a reversionary lease. Although the respondents were well aware of the applicant's desire to buy out the premises, the proceedings were compromised with an agreement to sell the fee simple to Foster. The applicant then sought to challenge this disposal of the property on the ground, in effect, that since the respondent had failed to consult with it prior to completing the sale, it had acted unreasonably in law in failing to seek the highest possible purchase price for the property.

16–92   It is noteworthy that Morris J. first rejected the suggestion that the applicant had standing simply qua ratepayer, a view which is contrary to long-established law, at any rate in Britain.[228] Nor did he accept that, on the facts, it was aggrieved by the decision not to consider it as a potential buyer:

> "On my understanding of the law, this does not bring the applicant sufficiently far so as to confer on it a sufficient interest to maintain these proceedings. It does not establish an 'injury or prejudice' as stated in *Cahill v. Sutton*. It does not establish that any interest, which it might have, had been adversely affected by the sale, as referred to in *Duggan v. An Taoiseach*, nor does it establish that it has or may suffer a substantial amount of money as referred to in *State (Sheehan) v. Government of Ireland*. The furthest that the applicant can go in this case is to establish that it is bitterly disappointed by the fact that the Corporation failed to give it an opportunity to make a bid for the fee simple. The reality of the position is that the applicant is now in no worse position than it was before the sale of the fee simple to the notice party. It is in precisely the same position."[229]

16–93   With its implicit assumption that locus standi requires a pre-existing legal interest, this case appears to represent an unsupportable throw-back to an earlier era. It is more probable, however, that the judge was influenced, at some level, by the fact that the local authority was exercising not a statutory power, but rather its rights qua private land owner.

16–94   These fears have been ameliorated by the same judge's later decision in *Lancefort Ltd v An Bord Pleanála (No. 1)*.[230] In this case Morris J. had to consider whether a limited company which had been formed by a group of dedicated conservationists had locus standi to challenge a decision to grant planning permission. Although it had been argued that as the company (which had limited assets) had only been formed after the date of the grant of the permission in order to afford "the true applicants a shield against an award of costs", Morris J. was

---

[228] See *De Smith's Judicial Review*, 5th edn (1995), pp.133–134, 746. So far as this point is concerned, Morris J. responded ([1993] I.L.R.M. 890 at 895): "The applicant comes before the court in its capacity as a ratepayer who has a financial interest in the manner in which the Corporation conducts its affairs in relation to the disposal of the property. This would leave the applicant in no better position than many thousands of thousands of business houses in the city and if this were its only claim to be entitled to bring these proceedings, then … it would clearly fail."

[229] [1993] I.L.R.M. 890 at 896.

[230] [1997] 2 I.L.R.M. 508.

clearly impressed by the bona fides of the company's promoters.[231] He proceeded to hold that the applicant company did have the requisite standing and that the present case fell within one of the exceptions to *Cahill v Sutton*.

16–95 This judgment clearly takes a liberal view of standing requirements and provides considerable support for bona fide interest groups who wish to impugn administrative decisions of concern to them. To that extent, it is in harmony with the preponderance of authority, which either expressly or by implication has allowed standing in the case of corporate bodies.[232] This approach was more or less endorsed by the Supreme Court, in *Lancefort Ltd v An Bord Pleanála (No. 2)*[233] where Keane J. held that such bodies may well enjoy standing in cases of this nature.[234]

16–96 There are, nevertheless, some recent signs of a moderate judicial retreat from the ultra-liberal approach reflected in judgments such as *Riordan v An Tánaiste*.[235] An important aspect of this development has centred around cases in which a representative body brings a case on behalf of its members. On one side of the argument, it will be contended that it is more convenient and practicable for a representative body to bring a case. Thus, for example, in *Rafferty v Bus Éireann*,[236] Kelly J. held that a trade union had sufficient standing to bring a claim on behalf of its members concerning changes in work practices which were said to be ultra vires, noting that bringing the action in that form "rendered unnecessary the naming as individual applicants of all of the union's 600 members".[237]

---

[231] Morris J. described them ([1997] 2 I.L.R.M. 508 at 513) as "… genuinely and honestly concerned and have devoted significant efforts in the past for the protection of listed and historical buildings and have a legitimate concern for the historical building heritage of Dublin and throughout the country … I do not think that [any of the persons associated with the applicant] fall within the category of persons contemplated by Henchy J. in *Cahill v. Sutton* [1980] IR 269 at 284 which he described as 'the crank, the obstructionist, the meddlesome, the perverse [and] the officious man of straw'". But, of course, the difference between "the genuinely and honestly concerned" and "the crank" is very subjective; though, no doubt, it could be made more definite, with further elaboration.

[232] O'Neill, *Constitutional Rights of Companies* (Dublin: Thomson Round Hall, 2007). See to like effect regarding companies, *Digital Rights Ireland Ltd v Minister for Communications* [2010] 3 I.R. 251 at paras [32]–[38].

[233] [1999] 2 I.R. 270.

[234] Keane J. expressly agreed ([1997] 2 I.R. 270 at 317) with the following statement (although not its application in the present case) of McGuinness J. in *Blessington Heritage Trust Ltd v Wicklow County Council* [1999] 4 I.R. 571 at 595: "[The] blanket refusal to all such companies may tip the balance too far in favour of the large scale and well resourced developer."

[235] [1995] 3 I.R. 62 at 75 (HC); [1997] 3 I.R. 502 (SC) (plaintiff held to have sufficient standing to challenge the absence of both the Taoiseach and the Tánaiste from the State at the same time).

[236] [1997] 2 I.R. 424. In *State (King) v Minister for Justice* [1984] I.R. 169 (which actually pre-dates *Cahill*) the applicants obtained an order of mandamus commanding the Minister to exercise his statutory powers, under the Courthouses (Provision and Maintenance) Act 1935 to renew and repair Waterford Courthouse. Rather surprisingly, Doyle J. rejected the argument that the applicants (one of whom was President of the Waterford Law Society) had standing as representatives of the Society which Doyle J. noted was "an unincorporated body whose membership includes most, if not all, of the solicitors practising in the city and county of Waterford". However, Doyle J. went on to hold that the applicants had standing in their own right ([1984] I.R. 169 at 175): "Both gentlemen carry on an extensive practice in the Waterford court and may, therefore, be regarded as having a particular personal interest in the provision of proper court accommodation to enable them to earn their livelihood."

[237] [1997] 2 I.R. 424 at 441. Note, however, that even aspects of *Rafferty* may require to be re-considered in the light of the Supreme Court's decision in *Construction Industry Federation*

16–97   On the other side of the debate, there is an influential Supreme Court case which identifies some of the difficulties in this area, *Construction Industry Federation v Dublin City Council*.[238] The facts were that the respondent had decided to make a development contribution scheme. The applicant sought judicial review, on the substantive basis that the level of detail included in the scheme did not fulfil the requirements of s.48 of the Planning and Development Act 2000. The relevant issue here is that the respondent contended, successfully, that the applicant, an unincorporated trade association for builders and developers, which itself did not engage in any development, lacked the necessary standing. Writing for the court, McCracken J. stated:

> "In the present case, the applicant claims to have a sufficient interest on the basis that the proposed scheme affects all … of its members in the functional area of the respondent and, therefore, the applicant has a common interest with its members. However, it appears to me that to allow the applicant to argue this point without relating it to any particular application and without showing any damage to the applicant itself, means that the court is being asked to deal with a hypothetical situation, which is always undesirable. This is a challenge which could be brought by any of the members of the applicant who are affected and would then be related to the particular circumstances of that member. The members themselves are, in many cases, very large and financially substantial companies, which are unlikely to be deterred by the financial consequences of mounting a challenge such as this. Unlike many of the cases in which parties with no personal or direct interest have been granted *locus standi*, there is no evidence before the court that, in the absence of the purported challenge by the applicant, there would have been no other challenger. Indeed, the evidence appears to be to the contrary."

16–98   At the very least, this passage emphasises the need for a discriminating approach, focusing on the policy factors underlying the concept of standing.

16–99   Summing up, it may be said that, in the post-*Cahill* era, the few cases in which the rules of standing have prevented an issue from being examined on the merits are, on the whole, cases in which the claim may be regarded as opportunist and unmeritorious; or where the party is seeking some indirect benefit only[239]; or

---

v Dublin City Council [2005] 2 I.R. 496 regarding the locus standi of representative bodies. In *National Maternity Hospital v Information Commissioner* [2007] 3 I.R. 643 (a case concerning access to post-mortem records), Quirke J. held that a company limited by guarantee designed to represent the interests of parents had no locus standi to participate in a statutory appeal against a decision of the Information Commissioner to release such information. Quirke J. observed (at 655) that the normal rule was that such entities had no such locus standi, unless "individual constituent members of an association were financially incapable of mounting a challenge in their own right". As there was no evidence in the present case that the constituent members of the company were "incapable individually of financing the costs associated with the appeal", it followed that the company had no locus standi.

[238] [2005] 2 I.R. 496. The quotation is at 526–527. See, to broadly similar effect, *Harding v Cork County Council (No. 2)* [2008] IESC 27; [2008] 2 I.L.R.M. 251, though *Harding* was heavily influenced by the new statutory test contained in s.50(4)(b) of the Planning and Development Act 2000.

[239] See, e.g. *Shannon v McGuinness* [1999] 3 I.R. 274 (witness seeking judicial review of prosecution decision to withdraw prosecutions); *Lennon v Limerick City Council* [2006] IEHC 112 (agent seeking a declaration that his principal's planning application was valid and

as in *Construction Industry Federation*, where there is a realistic possibility of a person with their own concrete interest (which is regarded as the ideal option) taking action. As Murray C.J. observed when upholding the respondent's plea of no locus standi in *Riordan v Government of Ireland*[240]:

> "All citizens have a right of access to the Courts which, in other cases, the Courts have been sedulous in protecting. But this right of access is for the purpose of resolving justiciable issues and not for the purpose of constituting the Courts as a sort of debating society or deliberative assembly for the discussion of abstract issues."

16–100 It is suggested, then, that this review demonstrates that, subject to some possible exceptions,[241] the cases accord reasonably well with the flexible *Cahill* principles and sensibly accommodate:

> "… a tension between two principles which the courts have sought to uphold: ensuring on the one hand, that the enactment of invalid legislation or the adoption of unlawful practices by public bodies do not escape scrutiny by the courts because of an absence of indisputably qualified objectors and, on the other hand, that the critically important remedy provided by the law in these areas are not abused."[242]

Constitutional cases

16–101 We must now turn to a series of major constitutional cases, in which the circumstances have been regarded as falling within a qualification to the *Cahill* principles: *Society for the Protection of Unborn Children (Ireland) Ltd v Coogan*[243]; *Crotty v An Taoiseach*[244]; *McKenna v An Taoiseach (No. 2)*[245]; *Riordan v An Tánaiste*[246]; *Mulcreevy v Minister for Environment*.[247] These cases are very

---

where the agent's only interest was that his own fee would not be discharged unless planning permission was granted); *John Paul Construction Ltd v Minister for the Environment, Heritage and Local Government* [2006] IEHC 255 (applicant building contractor had no standing to argue that Minister wrongly withheld the grant of compliance certificate to developer, when the only benefit to the applicant would have been to assist it in defending an action for breach of contract which was being brought against it by the developer).

[240] [2009] IESC 44.

[241] See, e.g. *ESB v Gormley* [1985] I.R. 129 and *Construction Industry Federation v Dublin City Council* [2005] 2 I.R. 496.

[242] *Lancefort Ltd v An Bord Pleanála (No. 2)* [1999] 2 I.R. 270 at 308–309 per Keane J. See similarly, *Digital Rights Ireland Ltd v Minister for Communications* [2010] 3 I.R. 251 at para. [49].

[243] [1989] I.R. 734 (plaintiff Society sought an injunction restraining the dissemination of a student handbook containing information on abortion services, claiming that this booklet infringed Art.40.3.3°).

[244] [1987] I.R. 713 (where the plaintiff had challenged the validity of the ratification of the Single European Act).

[245] [1995] 2 I.R. 10 (a case where the plaintiff ultimately succeeded before the Supreme Court in establishing that the use of public monies in advocating a "Yes" vote at a referendum was unconstitutional).

[246] [1995] 3 I.R. 62 at 75 (HC); [1997] 3 I.R. 502 (SC) (a private citizen sought an order restraining the Tánaiste from leaving the jurisdiction and so acting in a manner which he claimed infringed Art.28.6.3°).

[247] [2004] 1 I.R. 72 (the applicant challenged the validity of the consents under the National

well known and concern the constitutionality of a law, rather than the legality of an administrative action (albeit that the standing rules are similar); in a word, they fall on the constitutional side of the line. Accordingly, we are not going into their facts or far into the reasoning of their judgments.

16–102   Each of these cases are examples of what Henchy J. in *Cahill* called a "transcendent need to assert against the statute the constitutional provisions".[248] This is clearly a door which could open very wide, in that it cannot be every constitutional point which warrants a suspension of the normal standing rules. The great question is what these cases have in common, as regards standing. In fact, two common threads may be discerned running through the cases under review.

16–103   First, it was reasonable to assume that there is no one who had standing in the classic sense of being directly and materially affected by the allegedly unconstitutional law. As Walsh J. remarked in *Coogan*:

> "[E]ven in cases where it is sought to invalidate a legislative provision the Court will, where the circumstances warrant it, permit a person whose personal interest is not directly or indirectly, presently, or in the future, threatened, to maintain proceedings if the circumstances are such that the public interest warrants it. In this context, the public interest must be taken in the widest sense."[249]

16–104   This was expressly recognised by Keane J. in *Iarnród Éireann v Ireland*[250] where he acknowledged that the courts were more likely to accord a generous view of standing where "the nature of the constitutional challenge is such that a plaintiff will not emerge whose interests may be said to be either immediately or prospectively affected in a manner specific to him or her".[251] Of its nature, this

---

Monuments Acts 1930–2004 which the Minister had granted in respect of a national monument which would be affected by the completion of a motorway scheme).

    For other cases where a generous approach to locus standi was adopted in practice (even though the standing of the plaintiff was not directly put at issue), see *Horgan v An Taoiseach* [2003] 2 I.R. 468 (challenge to the transiting of foreign troops in the absence of a war resolution under Art.28.3.3°); *Dunne v Minister for Environment, Heritage and Local Government* [2007] 1 I.L.R.M. 264 (challenge to the building of a motorway which impacted on a national monument). In the latter case, Murray C.J. described the position of the plaintiff ([2007] 1 I.L.R.M. 264 at 280) "as being that of the concerned citizen who seeks to exercise a supervisory role in relation to decision making by the executive or the legislature, such as arose in *McGimpsey v. Ireland* or in *Horgan v. An Taoiseach*".

[248] [1980] I.R. 269 at 285.
[249] [1989] I.R. 734 at 746–747.
[250] [1996] 3 I.R. 321.
[251] [1996] 2 I.R. 321 at 351. This view has been consistently advanced by Keane J.; see in that regard his judgments in *Riordan* and *Mulcreevy*. On the other hand, the decision of McCracken J. in *Construction Industry Federation* [2005] 2 I.R. 496 (where the plaintiff was held not to have standing) is probably best explained by the fact that the Federation represented members of each of whom individually would have had the requisite standing to challenge the development levy which Dublin City Council proposed to exact.

    The decision in *Construction Industry Federation* was distinguished by Gilligan J. in *Irish Penal Reform Trust Ltd v Governor of Mountjoy Prison* [2005] IEHC 305, a case where the plaintiff non-governmental organisation alleged that prisoners with psychiatric illness were systematically treated in a deficient manner by the prison authorities. Gilligan J. held that the plaintiff should be afforded standing as otherwise "those it represents may not have

exceptional head of standing is more likely to arise in cases where it is said that there has been a breach of constitutional provisions setting out the powers and functions of the State, rather than raising individual constitutional rights: *Crotty*, *McGimpsey*, *McKenna*, *Riordan* and *Mulcreevy* clearly fall into this category.[252]

16–105 The second requirement is that the litigants should have a serious concern with the matter, the formula used in *McGimpsey* being "patently sincere and serious" and in *Coogan* "bona fide concern and interest". Again in *Iarnród Éireann*, Keane J. stated:

> "... it cannot be said that, because every citizen has an interest in ensuring that the Constitution is observed, everyone is entitled to invoke its provisions, irrespective of actual or threatened injury to him or her resulting from the operation of the impugned statute."[253]

16–106 The assumption here is that if that dreaded figure, the meddlesome and crank litigant, is not to be excluded by the test of material interest, then he must be excluded in some other way. One way in which the seriousness of the litigant might be shown would be if the litigant were, or were a member of, a representative association, as in the *Coogan* case. Another possibility is that, as mentioned in *McGimpsey*, there should be a large number of persons, including the applicant, affected by the action or law, of which complaint was made.

16–107 Finally, one should also mention the notion that, where EU or ECHR rights are invoked, this an additional reason why a relaxed rule of standing should be applied. In *Digital Rights Ireland Ltd v Minister for Communications*,[254] it was held that "a more relaxed approach" may be necessary where the point at issue originates in EU law or the ECHR, "since there is an overriding obligation on the national court to uphold European law and national procedural law should not operate in such a way as to undermine a claimant's right to effective judicial protection".

Jus tertii

16–108 One further difficulty which was raised, without being determinative, by the Supreme Court in *McGimpsey v Ireland*[255] pertains to the relationship of the plaintiffs not only to the law or act of which they complain, but also to the character of the flaw which they perceive in it. Plainly, as distinguished members of the Ulster Unionist party of Northern Ireland, the plaintiffs had standing in the first, wider sense because they were concerned about the signing of the Anglo-Irish Agreement. The difficulty lies in the particular constitutional argument on

---

an effective way to bring the issues before the court. A potential plaintiff would not be in a position to command the expertise and financial backing of the Trust, a less well-informed challenge might ensue and justice may not be done".

[252] As Keane J. said in *Iarnród Éireann* ([1996] 3 I.R. 321 at 351): "Such claims typically arise in the context of purported changes to the structure of government itself or its relationship to other sovereign governments."

[253] [1996] 3 I.R. 312 at 349.

[254] [2010] 3 I.R. 251 at para.28.

[255] [1990] 1 I.R. 110 at 114–115.

which they principally relied. This argument depended upon the jurisdictional claim in respect of Northern Ireland contained in the (former) Arts 2 and 3 of the Constitution. Yet surely these were provisions which, as Unionists, they found offensive. Although the Supreme Court decided that their case should be heard on the merits, Finlay C.J. had considerable reservations as to whether a claim of this kind could be entertained:

> "As a general proposition it would appear to me that one would have to entertain considerable doubt as to whether any citizen would have the *locus standi* to challenge the constitutional validity of an act of the executive or of a statute of the Oireachtas for the specific and sole purpose of achieving an objective directly contrary to the purpose of the constitutional provisions invoked."

16–109   Indeed, one might observe that the McGimpseys' complaint in relation to Arts 2 and 3 was roughly analogous to that between Mrs Cahill and the defect which she wished to rely upon in the Statute of Limitations. This in turn raises the question of the distinction between locus standi and *jus tertii*.

16–110   In turning to a definition, one should note that the concept of *jus tertii* has not really yet been treated judicially as a separate category. The distinction between the two concepts is that locus standi involves the litigant's status in relation to the administrative action (or law) and its consequences, whilst *jus tertii* refers to his position vis-à-vis the particular defect in the administrative action or law, of which complaint is made and, in particular, whether it is competent for him to rely on the rights of a third party in order to advance his argument. The practical rationale for this rule was well put by Hardiman J. in *A v Governor of Arbour Hill Prison*[256]:

> "The *jus tertii* rule is a very necessary regulation of *locus standi* ... It prevents the proliferation of litigation and the expense and uncertainty it causes by requiring that each litigant must show that on the facts of his situation he is personally affected by the law he challenges. It prevents necessary and important laws from being struck down on a purely hypothetical supposition which may never arise in real life and avoids the taxpayer having to fund the holding of pointless moots."[257]

Strictly speaking, as is acknowledged in Henchy J.'s judgment in that case, *Cahill*,

---

[256] [2006] 4 I.R. 88.

[257] [2006] 4 I.R. 88 at 187. *A* was itself a striking case of *jus tertii*. A had been convicted on a plea of guilty of the unlawful carnal knowledge of a classmate of his young schoolgirl daughter in circumstances where he knew that she was under age. Following the invalidation of the unlawful carnal knowledge provisions of s.1(1) of the Criminal Law (Amendment) Act 1935 in *CC v Ireland* [2006] 4 I.R. 1 on the ground that it created a strict liability offence and did not allow for a defence of mistake of age, A sought his release on the ground that his continued detention was thus rendered unlawful. It was common case that A himself would have lacked the appropriate locus standi to challenge the constitutionality of the section on this ground since he at all times knew the age of his victim and this was a major factor in the Supreme Court's conclusion that he was precluded by his conduct from asserting the invalidity of his detention. For another example of a *jus tertii*, see *Norris v Attorney General* [1984] I.R. 36 at 90.

like *McGimpsey*, was a *jus tertii* case in that the plaintiff was certainly affected by the law, but not by the particular infirmity of which she complained.

Ripeness

16–111 The requirement of ripeness means that even a litigant whose interest is likely to be affected by an administrative action or law may not initiate proceedings until the threat has actually materialised or until the public body in question has taken concrete steps. In short, he may not take action in respect of an abstraction or a hypothesis.[258]

16–112 The issue of ripeness arose in *East Donegal Co-operative Ltd v Attorney General*[259] where it was, in fact, discussed under the heading of locus standi. The plaintiffs were mart owners who sought a declaration that the Livestock Marts Act 1967 which had established a licensing system for marts was unconstitutional. They clearly had the necessary locus standi (in the strict sense of the term) to challenge this regime, but the key issue was whether they had taken the action prematurely. Their licences had not been revoked, nor had the conduct of their business otherwise been interfered with. The Supreme Court, however, concluded that the plaintiffs did have a genuine apprehension that their business activities might be interfered with and that, accordingly, the action was not premature. The rationale for this decision was later expressed by Walsh J. in *State (Lynch) v Cooney*[260] in the following terms:

> "This Court in East Donegal expressly rejected the contention that it was necessary for a plaintiff to show that the provisions of the legislation impugned applied not only to the activities in which he was currently engaged but that their application has 'affected his interests adversely'. This decides that a person does not to have to wait to be injured. Once again, the question of sufficiency of interest will depend upon the circumstances of the case and

---

[258] cf. the unwillingness of Kearns J. in *Collooney Pharmacy Ltd v North Western Health Board* [2005] 4 I.R. 124 at 146 to address "problems and difficulties [which] are entirely hypothetical in nature insofar as no particular instance has been indicated to this court whereby the applicants, or, indeed, anyone else, have been adversely affected by any application of the clauses at issue".

Note also the unwillingness of Kelly J. in *John Paul Construction Ltd v Minister for Environment, Heritage and Local Government* [2006] IEHC 255 "to make an adjudication upon a hypothetical state of affairs which never came to pass" and the similar sentiments which were also expressed by Laffoy J. in *Fitzpatrick v FK (No. 2)* [2008] IEHC 104; [2009] 4 I.R. 7.

[259] [1970] I.R. 317; *Osmanovic v Director of Public Prosecutions* [2006] 3 I.R. 504; *Lythe v Attorney General (No. 2)* [1936] I.R. 549. Note, however, *Kennedy v Director of Public Prosecutions* [2007] IEHC 3, where MacMenamin J. declined to adjudicate on the merits of a challenge to the constitutionality of an evidential provision of the Prevention of Corruption (Amendment) Act 2001 on the ground that the court was being invited to rule on a hypothesis or a moot. The High Court could not anticipate how the evidence at a pending criminal trial might unfold and, depending on the extent to which prosecution evidence was challenged, it might never be necessary for the prosecution to rely on the provision in question. See, similarly, *Grace v Ireland* [2007] IEHC 90; [2007] 2 I.L.R.M. 283.

[260] [1982] I.R. 337.

upon what appears to be the extent or nature of the impact of the impugned law on the [applicant's] position."[261]

16–113   The issue of ripeness has also arisen in a number of cases where the applicant has sought to anticipate a certain course of conduct. This point is well illustrated by *Phillips v Medical Council*,[262] a case where the respondent's Fitness to Practice Committee had decided that there were prima facie grounds to warrant a statutory investigation into the conduct of certain doctors. To this end, the Committee commissioned a report from an independent expert and when his draft report appeared to exonerate the applicant in respect of any question of professional misconduct, the latter sought various orders by means of judicial review. In effect, the applicant sought to compel the Committee to discontinue the inquiry, but Carroll J. refused this relief on the ground that the application was premature:

> "Judicial review does not exist to direct procedure in advance but to make sure that bodies which have made decisions susceptible of review have carried out their duties in accordance with the law and in conformity with natural and constitutional justice. Since the High Court cannot anticipate or direct what the findings of the Committee will be, the application for an order of prohibition against holding the inquiry on the grounds that it must of necessity be a nullity must also fail."[263]

F. Relator Actions

16–114   The Attorney General may sue ex officio to enforce the law, in plenary civil proceedings, by way of declaration or injunction, without showing any special injury.[264] By extension, the Attorney General may also sue at the relation (i.e. at the instance) of some members of the public in order to restrain a breach of the

---

[261] [1982] I.R. 337 at 371. See also, the subsequent decisions of Carroll J. in *Curtis v Attorney General* [1985] I.R. 458 and that of the Supreme Court in *Osmanovic v Director of Public Prosecutions* [2006] 3 I.R. 504 for a similar approach.

[262] [1992] I.L.R.M. 469.

[263] [1992] I.L.R.M. 469 at 475. For a similar approach, see also *Donegal Fuel & Supply Co. Ltd v Londonderry Harbour Commissioners* [1994] 1 I.R. 24 (High Court cannot anticipate that Minister would necessarily approve bye-laws made by the Commissioners, which the applicants claimed were ultra vires); *Clune v Director of Public Prosecutions* [1981] I.L.R.M. 17 (High Court cannot anticipate that the District Court will not fairly adjudicate in respect of pending criminal charges); and *Kennedy v Director of Public Prosecutions* [2007] IEHC 3 (High Court cannot anticipate how newly enacted section dealing with evidential presumptions will be interpreted by trial judge at pending criminal trial). Note, however, that in *Martin and Doorley v Legal Aid Board* [2007] 1 I.L.R.M. 481 at 502, Laffoy J. rejected a prematurity argument in a case where two solicitor employees of the Board sought to challenge a decision of the Board to permit the inspection of client files by authorised persons, noting that "the manner of intended implementation of that specific decision has been established with sufficient clarity on the evidence to avoid any hypothetical or moot element". Note also, however, the theoretically unusual case of *Curtin v Dáil Eireann* [2006] IESC 14; [2006] 2 I.R. 556; [2006] 2 I.L.R.M. 99 in which Murray C.J. gave guidance to the Oireachtas regarding the conduct of a judicial impeachment hearing and the procedures to be followed. See similarly, *O'Donoghue v Veterinary Council* [1975] I.R. 398.

[264] *Attorney General (O'Duffy) v Appelton* [1907] 1 I.R. 352; *Attorney General v Paperlink Ltd* [1984] I.L.R.M. 373; *Attorney General v X* [1992] 1 I.R. 1; *Attorney General v Lee* [2000] 4 I.R. 298.

law or to enforce the rights of the public.[265] The use of the relator action enables a private individual to sue where he might otherwise not have the necessary locus standi.[266] In effect, the relator action is a form of *actio popularis*, which is subject to the control of the Attorney General and is part of his ancient role as *parens patriae*. The Attorney General (and not the relator) remains at all times the plaintiff in a relator action:

> "It has been settled beyond the possibility of question that the Attorney General alone is plaintiff. It is true that he generally permits the relator to select a solicitor to conduct the case; but such person is not the solicitor of the relator, but of the Attorney General, who remains *dominus litis* throughout the proceedings."[267]

16–115 Nevertheless, where an undertaking as to damages has been given by the relator, the relator alone will be liable on foot of that undertaking.[268] The grant of the Attorney General's consent (or *fiat*) to the relator action simply means that the relator has been conferred with the necessary standing in order to permit him to litigate an arguable case, and does not necessarily imply approval of the proceedings.

16–116 Because of the traditional stringency of the standing rule, until comparatively recent times, the Attorney General was regarded, in certain circumstances, as enjoying an exclusive role in the enforcement of public rights.[269] The decision in *Irish Permanent Building Society Ltd v Caldwell (No. 1)*,[270] which has been mentioned above, supplies a good example of this. In this case, Keane J. hinted very strongly that the plaintiff would have to be able to show that the decision infringed some private right which it enjoyed,[271] as the protection of

---

[265] It is important to note that where the Attorney is the plaintiff on the relation of a private citizen, the court will be concerned only with the rights of the public as distinct from the private rights of the relating party: see *Attorney General (OF Fishing Ltd) v Port of Waterford Company* [2007] 2 I.R. 156 at 166 per Fennelly J.

[266] For a recent example, see *Attorney General (OF Fishing Ltd) v Port of Waterford Company* [2007] 2 I.R. 156 where it was contended that the defendant port company had acted ultra vires in purporting to sell part of its port undertaking. The relator was, however, a company which had made extensive use of the port and was unhappy with the proposed move, and in these circumstances, it would presumably have had standing in its own right.

[267] *Attorney General (Humphreys) v Governors of Erasmus Smith's Schools* [1910] 1 I.R. 325 at 331 per Cherry L.J. (as the Attorney General alone is the plaintiff, a relator is not entitled to appear personally to argue the case).

[268] *Attorney General (Martin) v Dublin Corporation* [1983] I.L.R.M. 254.

[269] See, e.g. *Moore v Attorney General for Irish Free State* [1930] I.R. 471; *Gouriet v Union of Post Office Workers* [1978] A.C. 435; *Irish Permanent Building Society v Caldwell (No. 1)* [1979] I.L.R.M. 273; and Casey, *The Irish Law Officers* (Dublin: Round Hall Sweet & Maxwell, 1996), pp.157–167. Although the Attorney General still retains this exclusive role in the United Kingdom, "the liberalization of the court's approach to the sufficient interest test has more or less brought an end to the use of relator actions in the public law context as there is now no impediment on a citizen commencing a claim in his own name to enforce a public duty"; see Woolf, Jowell and Le Sueur, *De Smith's Judicial Review* (London: Sweet & Maxwell, 2007), pp.76–77.

[270] [1979] I.L.R.M. 273.

[271] The plaintiffs subsequently amended their pleadings to claim that the registration of the rival building society had caused them loss and damage: *Irish Permanent Building Society v Caldwell (No. 2)* [1981] I.L.R.M. 242.

public rights was the exclusive preserve of the Attorney General, or a plaintiff suing at his relation:

> "I cannot detect any fundamental difference between the law in this country and [the law as stated in England in *Gouriet*]. It is at least arguable that the limitations recognised by the common law on the right of a private citizen to assert a right, public in its nature, without the intervention of the Attorney General, were not in any way affected by the enactment of the present Constitution."[272]

16–117 However, despite this now middle-aged authority, the obverse of the widening of standing rules in the context of high constitutional matters established by cases such as *McGimpsey*, *Coogan*, *Mulcreevy* and the various *Riordan* cases is the termination of the Attorney's traditional monopoly on enforcing public rights. In other words, if the standing rules are widened, there is less need to call upon the Attorney General. And it is clear from recent cases that the traditional views expressed in *Caldwell* no longer hold sway.

16–118 The first of the modern cases to be considered is *Attorney General (Society for the Protection of Unborn Children (Ireland) Ltd) v Open Door Counselling Ltd*.[273] Here the plaintiff who had originally commenced proceedings without the intervention of the Attorney General sought to restrain the defendants' counselling activities which, it was claimed, provided active assistance for women seeking to avail of abortion facilities in Great Britain, contrary to Art.40.3.3° of the Constitution. The Attorney General was subsequently joined at the close of pleadings. It was clear that the plaintiff had locus standi *ex relatione* the Attorney General, but, in a subsequent judgment, Hamilton P. was required to decide the issue of the costs incurred—and here is the practical point—prior to the joining of the Attorney General. This in turn raised the question of whether the Society would independently have had standing without the benefit of the Attorney General's intervention. Hamilton P. ruled that it was not necessary for the Society to have obtained the Attorney's *fiat*:

> "[H]aving regard to the obvious fact that the unborn themselves cannot seek the protection of the court, the obligation which rests on all organs of government to support the right to life of the unborn must and should be extended to all persons, artificial and real. In bringing these proceedings, the Society was fulfilling this obligation and I have no doubt but that they had *locus standi* to maintain these proceedings."[274]

---

[272] [1979] I.L.R.M. 273 at 275–276. This view must now be regarded as having been superseded by the judgment of the Supreme Court in *Society for the Protection of Unborn Children (Ire) v Coogan* [1989] I.R. 734 and, indeed, by Keane J.'s own comments in *Riordan v An Tánaiste* [1997] 3 I.R. 502 at 510 and *Mulcreevy v Minister for Local Government* [2004] 1 I.R. 72 at 78.

[273] [1988] I.R. 593.

[274] Hamilton P. added ([1988] I.R. 593 at 604): "The public interests are committed to the care of the Attorney General. He is entitled to sue to restrain the commission of an unlawful act, to protect and vindicate a right acknowledged by the Constitution and to prevent the corruption of public morals. I am satisfied that the Attorney General has the *locus standi* to maintain these proceedings and that when the Attorney General sues with a relator, the relator need

16–119   This question was even more directly at issue in a subsequent case involving the Society: *Society for the Protection of Unborn Children (Ireland) Ltd v Coogan*.[275] Here the Society sought to restrain the dissemination of a student publication containing information on abortion services which again was said to infringe Art.40.3.3°. On this occasion the Society had not invoked the Attorney General's protection and Carroll J. ruled in a very short, ex tempore judgment that, without his *fiat*, the Society had no locus standi to maintain the proceedings.[276] The Supreme Court, however, took a different view. Finlay C.J. said that the contention that only the Attorney General could sue to protect a constitutional right of this nature would represent "a major curtailment of the duty and power of the courts to defend and uphold the Constitution".[277] Accordingly, the Society had the requisite standing, as it had a bona fide and legitimate interest in the outcome of the proceedings.

16–120   Walsh J. also drew attention to the fact that the Attorney General might, acting in his other role as Government legal adviser, be required to defend the actions of either the executive or the Oireachtas:

> "If some Department of State or some public health authority with the approval, if not the encouragement, of the executive power, were to engage in activities which this Court in the *Open Door Counselling* case restrained as being a violation of the Constitution, it would be an intolerable situation if the defence or vindication of constitutional rights was to be confined to the very officer of State who had been entrusted with the task of defending such impugned activities."[278]

16–121   It is clear from the judgment of Walsh J. that these observations are of general application and the decision in *Coogan* does not turn on the constitutional nature of the rights protected by Art.40.3.3°.

16–122   Indeed, O'Hanlon J. appeared to arrive at a similar conclusion in *Parsons v Kavanagh*,[279] where the plaintiff had sought an injunction to restrain the actions of the defendants who were apparently engaged in operating a bus service in competition with her, without having obtained the necessary licence under the Road Transport Act 1932. Although the 1932 Act was passed for the benefit of the public rather than individual licence holders, the plaintiff was entitled to an

---

have no personal interest in the subject except his interest as a member of the public: see *Attorney General v. Logan* [1891] 2 QB 100."
[275] [1989] I.R. 734.
[276] She said that ([1989] I.R. 734 at 737): "The plaintiff has assumed the self-appointed role of policing the Supreme Court judgment. In my opinion, it has no right to seek undertakings from citizens and it is the Attorney General who is the proper party to move in such a case."
[277] [1989] I.R. 734 at 742.
[278] [1989] I.R. 734 at 744. Barrington J. had also drawn attention to this possible anomaly in *Irish Permanent Building Society v Caldwell (No. 2)* [1981] I.L.R.M. 242. The Attorney General had refused his *fiat* to the plaintiffs, yet after the commencement of the proceedings they learned that the Attorney General had actually advised the defendants as to the conduct of the litigation. McCarthy J. also adverted to this in *State (Sheehan) v Governor of Ireland* [1987] I.R. 550 at 552–553, as did Keane J. in *Riordan v An Tánaiste* [1992] 3 I.R. 502 at 510.
[279] [1990] I.L.R.M. 560.

injunction restraining "unlawful activity which impaired in a significant manner the exercise of her constitutional right to her living by lawful means".[280] This view was also endorsed by the Supreme Court in *Lovett v Gogan*[281]—a case which also concerned an attempt by one licensed transport undertaking to obtain an injunction restraining the illegal activities of a competitor—where Finlay C.J. stated that the "true position" was that such a plaintiff was "entitled to such an injunction if he can establish that it is the only way of protecting him from the threatened invasion of his constitutional rights".[282] Thus, in *Pierce v Dublin Cemeteries Committee (No. 1)*[283] the Supreme Court held that the plaintiff (who competed with the defendant) had sufficient standing to seek a declaration that the defendant was acting ultra vires its statutory powers. In the High Court Laffoy J. had found for the plaintiff on this ground:

> "The correct analysis ... of the plaintiff's objectives is that he avers that his constitutional right to earn his living is being interfered with by reason of the committee engaging in an activity which he alleges is ultra vires its powers. There being no other way in which the plaintiff can protect the right he asserts and ... in my view, he has *locus standi* to bring an action for declaratory and injunctive relief."

In the Supreme Court, Macken J. expressly agreed with this analysis, noting also that the plaintiff had no obvious remedy under competition law.

16–123   A discordant note had previously been struck by the Supreme Court in *Incorporated Law Society v Carroll*[284] in holding (though without mentioning *Kavanagh* or *Gogan*) that the plaintiff society had no standing to seek an injunction restraining the defendant/solicitor from engaging in what was alleged to be unlicensed practice. Here Blayney J. observed that the Law Society did not have standing and that the enforcement of such public rights was a matter for the Attorney General alone. Leaving aside the fact that this decision goes against the trend of cases such as *Coogan*, it seems curious, in the wake of *Lovett v Grogan*, that an individual solicitor would appear to have the requisite locus standi to seek an injunction restraining an unqualified person acting in competition against him, while the statutory body responsible for regulating the profession in question has been held to have no such standing to enforce the law.

16–124   This[285] line of authority (with the exception of *Carroll*) establishes that

---

[280] [1990] I.L.R.M. 560 at 567.

[281] [1995] 3 I.R. 132.

[282] [1995] 3 I.R. 132 at 142. This was found to be necessary on the facts, having regard to the minimal penalties for infringement provided for in the 1932 Act, as otherwise the plaintiff's constitutional right to earn his livelihood by lawful means would have been interfered with. On the other hand, in *O'Connor v Williams* [1996] 2 I.L.R.M. 382 Barron J. refused to grant an injunction to taxi drivers the effect of which would have restrained the illegal activities of hackney drivers on the ground that the penalties were substantial and that the "criminal law is sufficiently strong to prevent the damage at present being caused to the plaintiffs".

[283] [2009] IESC 47; [2010] 2 I.L.R.M. 73.

[284] [1995] 3 I.R. 145.

[285] The question of whether an interested member of the public required the *fiat* of the Attorney General to sue in respect of a charities matter was expressly reserved by the Supreme Court in *Connolly v Byrne*, unreported, Supreme Court, January 23, 1997.

the relaxing of the standing rules has had the result that the Attorney General is now seldom left with an exclusive right to assert the public interest. In *Coogan*, Walsh J. said that he did not "subscribe to the view" that the Attorney General enjoyed an exclusive right to enforce public rights.[286]

16–125   On the other hand, the minority view in *Coogan* is worth noting: both Carroll J. in the High Court and McCarthy J. in the Supreme Court[287] expressed concern at the prospect of private individuals or pressure groups being equipped to police the activities of other private persons by commencing litigation which is founded on some political, ideological or religious motivation, rather than some personal grievance which is justiciable at law.

16–126   As the standing rules in regard to constitutional and public matters have been substantially relaxed, the Attorney's decision in this field is of less significance than formerly. Nevertheless, the question of whether, as is the case in England and Wales, the Attorney's decision to grant his consent is immune from judicial review remains of some potential significance. One can illustrate this by asking, hypothetically, whether Mrs Cahill could have either sought or compelled the Attorney General to intervene on her behalf to argue the constitutionality of s.11(2)(b) of the Statute of Limitations 1957? The answer may be that, in practice, the majority of such cases which fall outside the exceptions will not involve fundamental constitutional issues and are unlikely to be situations in which the Attorney General will feel impelled to intervene. However one can at least pose the question of whether, in an extreme enough case, judicial review proceedings would lie. In 1980 Professor Casey argued that it was open to the Irish courts to hold that the Attorney General's consent was no more unfettered than that of a Minister, and that if the Attorney General's consent was unreviewable, this will be "a situation unique in Irish law".[288] Given the absence of any authority on the point, it is not possible to predict with full confidence what attitude Irish courts will take to the question of the reviewability (or otherwise) of the Attorney General's decision. Nevertheless, the probability is that the courts will follow the approach which they have adopted in the case of review of the Director of Public Prosecutions, namely, that the courts will interfere only where he reaches a decision "mala fide or influenced by an improper motive or improper policy".[289]

---

[286] [1989] I.R. 734 at 743. See also, *Attorney General (McGarry) v Sligo County Council* [1991] 1 I.R. 99.

[287] [1989] I.R. 734 at 751. Note the contradiction between McCarthy J's views, on what is legally the same point, as between his judgments in *Coogan* and *McGarry*.

[288] *The Office of the Attorney General in Ireland* (Dublin: IPA, 1980), p.154. At the equivalent point in the Second Edition (1996), p.166, Professor Casey says that the issue is "not clear". Professor Casey rested his argument on cases such as *East Donegal Co-operative Ltd v Attorney General* [1970] I.R. 317 which stresses that all exercises of administrative discretion should, in principle, be open to review. Contrast *Macauley v Minister for Posts and Telegraphs* [1966] I.R. 345 at 346 where Kenny J. opined that the Attorney General "is free to grant or withhold his *fiat* for any reason and if he decides to withhold it, no proceedings to review his decision can successfully be brought in the courts". See also, discussion in H & M, Ch.15, Part F, "Are there unreviewable discretionary powers?"

[289] *State (McCormack) v Curran* [1987] I.L.R.M. 225 at 237 per Finlay C.J. See also, *H v Director of Public Prosecutions* [1994] 2 I.R. 589. Note that the Supreme Court has, in fact, set aside the exercise of a prosecutorial discretion by the Director: see *Eviston v Director of Public Prosecutions* [2002] 3 I.R. 260.

Chapter 17

THE SCOPE OF PUBLIC LAW

A. The Public–Private Divide in Irish Law

17–01 The expression "public law" is best defined simply by comparison with private law. Thus, whilst private law governs relations between private individuals (e.g. contract, tort, property law), by contrast, public law comprises rules which are particular to the relations between a public body and, on the other hand, private individuals or companies, or other public bodies.[1] One should note though, that the ordinary private law of, say, contract also applies in appropriate contexts to public bodies, a point which is developed below. Public law is more or less synonymous with administrative law, but it is used here in preference to administrative law because a wide, conceptual point is under consideration.

17–02 In France (and, by a transplantation, many other civil law jurisdictions) this public–private divide has been fundamental to the control of the organs of public administration since the time of Napoleon. In contrast, the common law with its dislike of special regimes traditionally rejected any such segregation. However, with the attempts in England and elsewhere in the common law world (in the 1970s and 1980s) to put the supervision of public administration upon a systematic and reformed basis, some element of demarcation beyond that required by the English prerogative writs seemed, to many people, to be inevitable.

17–03 The public–private dichotomy can arise in a number of particular contexts, many of them already considered.[2] The first arises in legislation which applies only to public bodies, such as the Borrowing Power of Certain Bodies Act 1996,[3] the Freedom of Information Acts 1997–2003, the Official Languages Act 2003, the European Convention of Human Rights Act 2003,[4] the Financial Emergency

---

[1]   For a more elaborate treatment of the distinction between public and private law, see paras 17–03 to 17–05.

[2]   Some of these have been covered, at a more general level, in H & M, Ch.4.

[3]   Section 2 of the 1996 Act provides that, subject to limited exceptions, it applies "to any body established by or under statute whose power to borrow money is, in some or all cases, subject to the consent of the Minister [for Finance]".

[4]   Thus, s.3(1) of the European Convention of Human Rights Act 2003 imposes a duty to comply with the Convention on every "organ of the State". This term is defined by s.1 as including "a tribunal or any other body (other than the President or the Oireachtas or either House of the

Measures in the Public Interest Act 2009, or the public procurement rules.[5] Other situations in which the public–private divide applies include legitimate expectations,[6] the privilege against disclosure of confidential evidence before a court,[7] the tort of misfeasance in public office,[8] and whether the entity in question constitutes an "undertaking" for the purposes of competition law.[9] The fact that a body has been classified as a public body in one of the contexts mentioned here or in the following paragraph may or may not be an indication as to the same classification, in another context.[10]

17–04 However, far and away the main forum in which the dichotomy may arise is the field of judicial review of administrative action. In this field, perhaps even more than any other, Irish law has developed at a considerable angle to English law. One reason is that, while the dictates of the principles underlying the common law system are, broadly speaking, the same here as in England; yet, as we shall see, the Irish judiciary have frequently turned a blind eye to the public–private divide. It is quite likely, however, that in the future, Irish law will move somewhat closer to the general common law position.

17–05 So far as judicial review is concerned, the public–private divide may arise in the following four distinct contexts:

(a) We have already covered the central topics in the judicial review of administrative action, the substantive bloc of law being treated in Chapters 10 to 15 (plus Chapter 19 on legitimate expectations and most of the procedural-machinery law in Chapter 16 ("The Application for Judicial Review").

Oireachtas or a Committee of either such House or a Joint Committee of both such Houses or a court) which is established by law or through which any of the legislative, executive or judicial powers of the State are exercised".

Note that in *R. (Heather) v Leonard Cheshire Foundation* [2002] EWCA Civ 366; [2002] 2 All E.R. 936, the English Court of Appeal held that a charitable foundation which had contracted with a local authority to provide accommodation to the claimants was not "a body certain of whose functions are functions of a public nature" within the meaning of s.6(3)(b) of the (UK) Human Rights Act 1998: see generally, Donnelly, "Leonard Cheshire Again and Beyond: Private Contractors, Contract and section 6(3)(b) of the Human Rights Act" (2005) *Public Law* 785.

[5] See H & M, paras 17–03 and 3–182 to 3–201.
[6] This forms the background to cases such as *Eogan v University College, Dublin* [1996] 1 I.R. 390; [1996] 2 I.L.R.M. 302.
[7] See generally, Ch.20, Part E.
[8] See generally, paras 18–08 to 18–10.
[9] See, e.g. *Easy Readers Ltd v Bord na Radharcmhastorí* [2003] IEHC 93 (Opticians Board not an undertaking for this purpose); *Kenny v Dental Council* [2004] IEHC 29 (Dental Council exercising public powers in the public interest and hence not an undertaking); and *Hemat v Medical Council* [2010] IESC 24 (similar principle). But note that where a public body engages in economic activity, it will generally be held to be an undertaking for this purpose, even if it is otherwise governed by public law: see, e.g. *Wouters* (C-309/99) [2002] E.C.R. I-1577 (Dutch Bar held to be an undertaking despite being given public interest powers by statute); and *Neurendale Ltd v Dublin City Council* [2009] IEHC 588 (local authority held to be an undertaking where it collected waste for a fee in competition with private service providers). For more on competition law and public bodies, see Ch.4.
[10] Thus, it seems implicit in Shanley J.'s judgment in *Eogan v University College Dublin* [1996] 1 I.R. 390; [1996] 2 I.L.R.M. 302 that if the decision of the respondent was not amenable to judicial review (which he held it was), then the public law doctrine of legitimate expectations would have had no application.

However, we have left over for this chapter the basic question of which bodies and which of their activities fall within the specialised régime of the application for judicial review. Before the reformation in procedure, described in Chapter 15, the general understanding was that in seeking to challenge decisions of certain types of entity on the fringe of the public body category (e.g. trade unions and universities), a litigant could not proceed by way of state side order (the forerunner of the judicial review application), but had to proceed by the less convenient method of plenary proceedings for a declaration or injunction. But now, the advent of the application for judicial review, with the declaration and injunction as part of its empire, raises the question of whether trade unions or universities were more or less automatically brought within its sweep.

(b) Here we need to amplify the distinction, mentioned in (a), between procedural judicial review, that is the procedural rules controlling the way in which judicial review is brought before the High (or Supreme) Court; and, on the other hand, substantive judicial review—the principles governing the public bodies and the way they exercise their powers. The question arises whether, in the case of a matter which could not have been heard by way of the application for judicial review (because either the respondent body or the function being exercised fell outside the scope of the application for judicial review), it follows that the substantive judicial review principles (ultra vires, constitutional justice, legitimate expectations, reasonableness, etc) should not be applied? A particular, practical, point arises in regard to cases concerning employment for a public body, because an employee who is confined to a private law remedy is generally restricted to damages (usually of a limited amount, under the Unfair Dismissals Acts 1977–1993).[11] Accordingly, it may make a hugely significant—even spectacular—difference[12] if the employee can utilise the application of judicial review and succeed in having his dismissal invalidated.

(c) The related question is whether the scope of judicial review (whether substantive or procedural, as explained in (b)) extends to a public law entity, even when exercising a private law function.

(d) As explained in the previous chapter, the possibility of agitating a public law matter by way of a declaration or injunction granted in the course of plenary proceedings sprung up because of the often arbitrary restrictions upon the scope of certiorari, prohibition, etc. Following the procedural changes of 1986, noted in (a), in which a declaration or injunction is available in an application for judicial review, a question arises which is, in a sense, the obverse of that canvassed in (a). That question is whether in the case of issues which could have been heard by way of judicial review, a litigant may instead apply for a declaration or injunction, in plenary proceedings.

17–06 So far, most Irish judgments have not identified issues (a) and (b) as being separate. This could be taken as a view that the policy issues in relation to each

---

[11] See generally, Redmond, *Dismissal Law in Ireland* (Dublin: Tottel Publishing, 2007).

[12] Take, for example, cases such as *Histon v Shannon Foynes Port Co* [2004] IESC 107 and *Cahill v Dublin City University* [2009] IESC 80. In both cases the Supreme Court held that purported terminations of contract were invalid by reason of procedural irregularity and granted declarations that the dismissals were invalid.

are broadly similar. In any case, in view of this overlap, it seems sensible to treat (a) and (b) together in Part B below. This leaves issues (c) and (d) to be dealt with in Parts C and D respectively.

B. The Importance of Being "Public"

17–07 As noted in the previous chapter, there are two sets of limitations upon the scope of applications for judicial review. The first of these (which was formerly of significance but is no longer) is based on the characteristics of the remedies themselves. It has already been briefly covered in Chapter 16, Part A. The second requirement, namely, that the issue should be public in nature, is now dealt with by outlining the Irish case law in this issue. In this Part, most of the cases involve situations in which the doubt is whether (given its legal status and general powers) the respondent is sufficient of a public body to attract judicial review. In Part C, we address situations in which the respondent is undoubtedly a public body, but the question is whether it is exercising private (common) law powers.

17–08 It may be useful, first of all, to set the scene by inquiring why in the light of the safeguards built into the application for judicial review procedure,[13] any properly advised litigant might want to argue his way on to the path of judicial review if the apparently easier road offered by plenary proceedings were open to him. The answer is that, depending on the circumstances, there may be definite advantages to be gained from following that which might seem, at first sight, to be the rockier road. Judicial review proceedings are, broadly speaking, speedier and less expensive[14] than the plenary procedure. Proceeding by way of judicial review may offer an applicant certain tactical advantages deriving from the fact that a High Court judge will determine at an early stage whether the case is sufficiently stateable to merit the grant of leave. In addition, when leave is granted the grant of leave often attracts wide publicity and this may have the effect of disadvantaging a potential respondent.[15] Equally, as we shall see in Part D, there may be advantages, most obviously regarding time limits, to be gained by casting what is naturally a public law claim in the form of plenary proceedings.

17–09 Divergent judicial views have been taken on the question of whether a

---

[13] See Ch.16, Parts C and D.

[14] The cost savings derive principally from the fact that most of the evidence in judicial review proceedings is given by way of affidavit, whereas oral evidence is still the norm in plenary cases.

[15] cf. the comments of O'Hanlon J. in *Desmond v Glackin* [1993] 1 I.R. 1 at 9: "Although the [judicial review] application was made *ex parte* it was not to be expected that it would escape the notice of the media when the interest of the public in the affair had already been whetted to an inordinate extent. The application was made in open court and reached the ears of the newsmen, giving rise to a flurry of activity on their part ... Press reports of orders made by the courts on *ex parte* applications, where only one side has been heard, and more particularly the headlines which accompany such reports, often convey the wrong impression that some issue between the parties has been finally determined. I consider that there is a real risk that the general public will be deceived as to the nature of the relief granted unless such applications are reported in a very accurate manner."
   See also, Murphy J.'s telling comments in *Geoghegan v Institute of Chartered Accountants in Ireland* [1995] 3 I.R. 86 at 101; Budd J. in *B v Director of Public Prosecutions* [1997] 1 I.R. 140 at 147.

body is public for the purpose of judicial review. In one of the first cases where the point arose in the wake of the new Rules, *Murphy v Turf Club*,[16] what might be regarded as the traditional British line was asserted. The applicant sought to challenge by way of judicial review a decision of the Turf Club not to renew a trainer's licence, on the ground that the decision had been arrived at in breach of fair procedures.[17]

17–10   While the Turf Club enjoys certain statutory powers,[18] these powers were held by Barr J. to be immaterial in this context as the Turf Board's disciplinary jurisdiction in respect of trainers was derived from contract. In the event, it was held that the applicant could not proceed by way of judicial review, but could only proceed in the ordinary way for breach of contract. As Barr J. said:

> "I have no doubt that the relationship between the applicant and the [Turf Club] derives from contract ... and the [latter's] duty to regulate the sport of horse-racing in Ireland, though having a public dimension, is not a public duty as envisaged by the Court of Appeal in *R. v. Take-Over Panel, Ex p. Datafin Plc*[19] and in purporting to revoke the applicant's training licence the respondent was not exercising a public law function. On the contrary, its decision was that of a domestic tribunal exercising a regulatory function over the applicant, being an interested person who had voluntarily submitted to its jurisdiction."[20]

17–11   This passage prompts a number of observations. First, it illustrates the fact that the Turf Club can be amenable to judicial review in respect of some of its functions (for example, excluding the members of the public from racecourses) and not for others. This is not simply a matter of procedure: if the applicant is not allowed to proceed by way of judicial review, then it is probable that the decision itself could only have been challenged on the private law ground that the Turf

---

[16] [1989] I.R. 172.

[17] The applicant would appear to have had a good case on the merits. Inspectors called to the applicant's stables and, as a result of their complaints, the licence was revoked without any form of hearing some two days later: see [1989] I.R. 171 at 172–173.

[18] Such as the power to exclude certain persons from race meetings: Racing and Racecourses Act 1945 s.39.

[19] [1987] Q.B. 815. See also, *Bowes v Motor Insurers' Bureau of Ireland* [1989] I.R. 225 at 228.

[20] In view of the fact that the Turf Club's disciplinary functions have now been subsumed into the functions of the Racing Regulatory Body established by Pt III of the Irish Horseracing Industry Act 1994 and since the latter body is now obliged by s.45(2) of that Act to provide for an appeals procedure to be conducted in a "fair and impartial manner", one may expect that *Murphy v Turf Club* would now be decided differently today in the light of the altered statutory background. *Murphy* was distinguished by the Supreme Court in *Walsh v Irish Red Cross Society Ltd* [1997] 2 I.R. 479, where the issue was whether a person who had been expelled from the Society could challenge that expulsion by means of judicial review. Blayney J. noted that the Society has been established by the Irish Red Cross Act 1938 and a statutory instrument made pursuant to that Act. Given that the statutory instrument provided that all Irish citizens had the right to become members of the Society on payment of the appropriate fee, Blayney J. said that he was satisfied that "membership of the Society is not consensual" and that on examination of the statutory background, "the manner in which the Society was established, its structure and rules" demonstrated that "membership of the Society is not governed by private law, but is in the public domain." *Walsh* was applied by Kelly J. in *Bane v Garda Representative Association* [1997] 2 I.R. 449.

Club was in breach of contract, as opposed to the wider public grounds based on reasonableness, irrationality and so forth. Secondly, is it not altogether unrealistic to regard the Turf Club's jurisdiction as "voluntary" given that it enjoys a monopoly in respect of the granting of a horse-trainer's licence?[21] Thirdly, the *Murphy* judgment fails to take account of the argument that in reality the Turf Club was exercising a quasi-governmental function.

17–12   A similar analysis was adopted in *Rajah v Royal College of Surgeons*.[22] Keane J. had to consider the submission that an academic appeals board was obliged to state its reasons for its decision. Keane J. held that it was not, since the decisions in question derived not from public law, "but from the contract which came into being when the applicant became a student in the College". The fact that RCSI derived its existence in law "from a charter or Act of Parliament is not a sufficient ground for bringing matters relating to the conduct and academic standing of its students within the ambit of judicial review".[23]

17–13   As a distinct ground on which the applicant would also fail,[24] Keane J. held that since the respondent was not a public law body, the relevant substantive judicial review principle, regarding the right to reasons, did not apply.

17–14   However the revisionist line of authority, as regards taking a wider view of the scope of judicial review, may be taken as commencing with *Murtagh v Board of Governors of St Emer's School*.[25] In this case, certiorari had been sought

---

[21]   It is true that in the not dissimilar *Aga Khan* case, *R. v Jockey Club Ex p. Aga Khan* [1993] 2 All E.R. 853 at 873, Farquharson L.J. dismissed this objection with these pithy remarks: "[Counsel for the applicant] has referred to the lack of reality in describing such a relationship as consensual. The fact is that if the applicant wished to race his horses in this country he had no choice but to submit to the Jockey Club's jurisdiction. This may be true but nobody is obliged to race his horses in this country and it does not destroy the element of consensuality."
       But cf. the comments of Pannick, "Who is Subject to Judicial Review and in Respect of What?" (1992) *Public Law* 1 where the author argued that the "source of power" test should no longer be conclusive on the issue of whether judicial review should lie, but that instead the courts should ask themselves whether "the respondent body has such a de facto monopoly over public life that an individual has no effective choice but to comply with their rules, regulations and decisions in order to operate in that area" (at 3).

[22]   [1994] 1 I.R. 384.

[23]   [1994] 1 I.R. 384 at 394.

[24]   Keane J. noted that the jurisdiction of the relevant college committees did not derive from public law, but instead derived solely from the contract which came into being when the applicant became a student in the college, and her agreement to be bound by the regulations of the college, including its procedures. Accordingly, the court had no jurisdiction to grant relief by way of judicial review. In so holding, Keane J. distinguished the approach which had been adopted by Finlay C.J. in *Beirne v The Commissioner of An Garda Síochána* [1993] I.L.R.M. 1, where it had been held that the functions of the Commissioner in admitting persons as trainees of An Garda Síochána were amenable to judicial review, as these were "matters of particular and immediate and public concern, directly relevant to the public question of the ordering of society and the regulation of discipline within society".
       It may be questioned, however, whether Keane J.'s view has survived the subsequent decision of the Supreme Court in *O'Donnell v Tipperary (South Riding) County Council* [2005] 2 I.R. 483. These comments would also have to be reconsidered in the light of the subsequent enactment of the Universities Act 1997.

[25]   [1991] 1 I.R. 482. The Supreme Court subsequently dismissed the applicant's appeal against Barron J.'s judgment. No clear ratio emerges from that judgment, but the court appears to have taken the view that, even assuming judicial review did lie, relief should be denied on

to quash a minor disciplinary punishment imposed on a schoolboy attending national school. The respondents raised the issue as to whether certiorari would lie, but Barron J. found for the applicant on this point. Stressing that the body whose decision it is sought to quash "must be discharging a function of a public nature affecting private rights" and must also be under a duty "to act fairly in arriving at the decision", Barron J. said that the question of discipline in national schools was not in the private domain:

> "The school is a national school under the Department of Education. Rules formulated by the Department with the concurrence of the Minister for Finance govern every aspect of its existence. This includes school discipline. The provisions for discipline [in the respondent school] are no different in character from any other of the Rules governing these schools. They are not consensual in nature. Nor do they become so because, where different schools may have adopted different codes of discipline, one code rather than another is chosen. In each case, the parameters of the code are governed by the Rules."[26]

17–15 Barron J.'s analysis of the public law element of the Rules for the National Schools is undoubtedly correct. And yet this public law–private law demarcation can give rise to serious anomalies. For example, does it follow from this demarcation that in the case of a student expelled from university, a declaratory action by way of plenary summons should be the only remedy, since this disciplinary jurisdiction is (arguably) consensual and (again arguably) does not have its origins in public law?[27] Yet, the gravity of this punishment of expulsion from university vastly exceeds that imposed in *Murtagh*, so it would be strange if the expeditious and cheaper remedy of judicial review were available in the latter case only.

17–16 Turning to a different subject area, the kernel of the Court of Appeal's reasoning, in a significant English case, involving the Panel on Takeovers and Mergers, has been well summarised as follows[28]:

> "While the Court excluded, from judicial review and 'publicness', bodies whose sole source of power was a consensual submission, it pointed out that the power of self-regulatory bodies such as the Panel is not exclusively consensual. Rather it is a system whereby a group of people acting in concert

---

discretionary grounds. Hederman J. clearly took the view that judicial review did not lie, as the punishment in question was governed by private law; McCarthy J. reserved his position and O'Flaherty J. said (at 490) that the proceedings "should have been dismissed as quite inappropriate for judicial review", without, however, indicating whether judicial review could ever lie in respect of such a punishment.

[26] [1991] 1 I.R. 482 at 486.

[27] Although this argument would have to be re-assessed in the light of the potential impact of the Universities Act 1997 and decisions such as *University of Cambridge* (C-380/98) [2000] E.C.R. I-8035.

[28] Beatson, "'Public' and 'Private' in English Administrative Law" (1987) 103 L.Q.R. 34 at 50–51. The case being referred to is *R. v Panel on Take-overs and Mergers Ex p. Datafin Plc* [1987] Q.B. 815, which concerned a self-regulating unincorporated association which devised and operated the City Code on Take-overs, a non-statutory scheme. The English Court of Appeal held that certiorari would issue to such a body.
    The Irish Takeover Panel has been established by statute and its decision may *only* be challenged by means of judicial review: Irish Takeover Panel Act 1997 ss.3 and 13.

use their collective power to force themselves and others to comply with a code of conduct of their own devising. But the existence of de facto power was insufficient in itself to make the Panel 'public' and amenable to judicial review. What was vital was that (a) the decision that there should be a central but non-statutory regulatory body for takeovers was a government decision and, (b) the non-statutory system was buttressed by a periphery of statutory powers and penalties which assume that the Panel is the centrepiece of the regulatory system. The test is thus whether de facto power is underpinned by either a government decision to have regulation by a non-statutory body or by statutory support or, as in the *Take-over Panel* case, by both."

17–17 Two points bear emphasis. In the first place, it will often happen that, even where (as in the case of the (British) Takeover Panel) there is an element, real or artificial, of consensus, nevertheless the body's activities will have an effect on those outside the consensus (e.g. shareholders, employees, customers). Secondly, it happened that in the two cases just mentioned there was an organisational link between the body and the Government. What is to happen if this link is absent, yet the body is performing governmental-type functions, such as, for example, the regulation of a sport or of some important community activity? In short, here one has a private body with public functions as opposed to the reverse which is discussed elsewhere.[29] Of bodies like the Gaelic Athletic Association and Bord Lúthchleas na hÉireann[30] it has been said, in England, that "[i]f they did not exist, the government might have to invent them".[31] Does it follow from this that they ought to be regarded as subject to public law, even though there is no element of government control? As a matter of policy, this question depends at a fundamental level upon whether one views judicial review as being primarily concerned to protect the rights of the individual or to discipline the agencies of the State. Traditionally, it has been regarded as the latter.[32]

---

[29] See paras 17–27 to 17–40.

[30] The Irish Athletics Board.

[31] It may be noted that the courts have been more prepared to intervene to review decisions of sporting and other voluntary associations involving disciplinary proceedings: see, e.g. *Quirke v Bord Luthchleas na hÉireann* [1988] I.R. 83; *Modahl v British Athletics Federation* [2002] 1 W.L.R. 1192. In other non-disciplinary cases, there is a far more studied reluctance to intervene. In *Jacob v Irish Amateur Rowing Union Ltd* [2008] IEHC 196; [2008] 4 I.R. 731 at 742, Laffoy J. wondered whether "… it is appropriate at all, in the absence of proof of mala fides, for a court to intervene in a decision of an organization governing a particular sport as to matters of selection and de-selection for competitive events of team members based on performance and fitness … The issues in this case, issues involving retention on the national team on the basis of performance and fitness, are radically different [from disciplinary proceedings] and, in the absence of obvious bad faith on the part of the defendant or some obvious egregious injustice to the plaintiff, it is difficult to countenance how the court's involvement could be warranted".
    On this topic, see Munro, "Sports in the Courts" (2005) *Public Law* 681. For a very thoughtful and comprehensive analysis of the courts' jurisdiction to review decisions of sporting bodies, see the judgment of Richards J. in *Bradley v Jockey Club* [2004] EWHC 2164, as affirmed by the English Court of Appeal ([2005] EWCA Civ 1056).

[32] Note the analysis of this issue by Kerr J. in *Re Kirkpatrick's Application* [2003] N.I.Q.B. 49, when he held that the licensing functions of a private society were amenable to judicial review: "Lough Neagh is the largest inland waterway in the United Kingdom. The conservation of its natural resources is a matter of intense public interest in my view. The public has a legitimate concern as to how fish stocks are maintained and how fishing activities are regulated in this substantial and important natural asset. The licensing system operated by the Society

17–18   But the modern law appears now to be represented by Denham J.'s judgment in *Geoghegan v Institute of Chartered Accountants*,[33] in which the applicant was facing disciplinary charges before the respondent. The issue was whether the respondent's decision would be amenable to judicial review. The Supreme Court appears to have been evenly divided on this question.[34] However, later decisions indicate a consensus in favour of Denham J. who was clearly of the view that judicial review would lie in respect of decisions of the Institute. She enumerated six separate factors which she thought pointed towards this conclusion:

> "(1) This case relates to a major profession ... with a special connection to the judicial organ of Government ...
> (2) The original source of the powers of the Institute is the Charter – through that and the legislation ... the Institute has a nexus with two branches of the Government of the State.
> (3) The functions of the Institute and its members come within the public domain of the State.
> (4) The method by which the contractual relationship between the Institute and the [member] was created is an important factor as it was necessary for the individual to agree in a 'form' contract to the disciplinary process to gain entrance to membership of the Institute.
> (5) The consequences of the domestic tribunal's decision may be very serious for a member.
> (6) The proceedings before the disciplinary tribunal must be fair and in accordance with the principles of natural justice ...".[35]

17–19   This approach seems compelling. After all, the *Geoghegan* case concerned the exercise of powers in relation to a regulated profession with statutory links to the administration of justice. In effect, the disciplinary procedures in question were agreed with the Government in lieu of legislation and against that background it would seem pure formalism to suggest that judicial review should not lie.[36]

17–20   At all events, in the first decision on this point delivered in the wake of *Geoghegan*, *Eogan v University College Dublin*,[37] Shanley J. clearly indicated his preference for the views of Denham J, which now seem to represent the modern law on the subject.[38] This case concerned a claim brought on behalf of

---

is supplemented by monitoring and regulating of fishing activities by bailiffs. But for the historical accident that fishing rights are privately owned by the Society one would expect that such an important natural resource would be controlled by a public agency accountable to government and ultimately the public. I am satisfied, therefore, that the licensing system for eel fishing in Lough Neagh is a matter of public law."

[33]   [1995] 3 I.R. 86.

[34]   O'Flaherty J. (with whom Blayney J. concurred) said in *Geoghegan v Institute of Chartered Accountants* [1995] 3 I.R. 86 at 121 that he was "inclined to agree" with the judgment of the High Court. Both Egan and Denham JJ. delivered separate judgments indicating their disagreement with Murphy J. Hamilton C.J. expressly reserved his position.

[35]   [1995] 3 I.R. 86 at 130–131.

[36]   See generally, Costello, "The Identification of Organisations Subject to Judicial Review" (1995) 17 D.U.L.J. 89 (N.S).

[37]   [1996] 1 I.R. 390; [1996] 2 I.L.R.M. 302.

[38]   See Kelly J. in *Rafferty v Bus Éireann* [1997] 2 I.R. 424 at 440 and in *Bane v Garda Representative Association* [1997] 2 I.R. 449 at 470; Carroll J. in *O'Donoghue v South Eastern Health Board* [2001] IEHC 165; and by the Supreme Court in *O'Donnell v Tipperary (SR)*

a retired professor that a new policy of refusing to extend tenure beyond the age of 65 years infringed his legitimate expectations. The College Statutes permitted serving professors to continue in office to the age of 70, providing that this was recommended by the governing body with the consent of the university senate. Shanley J. drew attention to the fact that the statutes in question had been made pursuant to the Irish Universities Act 1908 and that by s.5(2) of that Act, the statutes were required to be laid before both Houses of the Oireachtas. In the circumstances, as he was satisfied that the decision to appoint and not to continue in office "were decisions taken in substance pursuant to the statutory regime flowing from the 1908 Act", Shanley J. held that the decision in question could be challenged by means of judicial review.[39]

17–21   Taken at face value, *O'Donnell* greatly expands the scope of judicial review and certainly beyond the circumstances where no private law remedy is otherwise available.[40] The focus is less on the contractual relationship between the parties and more on questions whether the functions are performed in the public interest.

Concluding comment

17–22   The following general observations are also relevant to the discussion of "public function", examined in Part C, paras 17–35 to 17–40. There are a number of historical/political developments which have stretched public law from its pristine (and possibly unrealistic) simplicity to the uncertainties and anomalies of today. The first of these is that the scope of governmental power has increased so much that there are few islands of private right against which it does not, at least potentially, lap. In the dirigiste state, often this is effected not by way of traditional public law instruments, like delegated legislation, but through what are originally and conceptually private law devices, such as grants or "contracts".[41]

17–23   Secondly, governmental entities now take a variety of forms. A utility, for instance, may be operated in the form of a Department of State; a state-sponsored

---

County Council [2005] 2 I.R. 483 and *Brown v Board of Management of Rathfarnham Parish National School* [2006] IEHC 178; [2008] 1 I.R. 70.

    A contra: *Becker v Board of Management, St Dominic's Secondary School, Cabra* [2005] IEHC 169. This case law is analysed in H & M, paras 17–38 to 17–60.

[39]   The strict ratio decidendi of this decision appears to be authority for the proposition that only decisions made pursuant to the UCD statutes are amenable to judicial review and that different considerations might perhaps apply if, for example, the applicant had held a non-tenured post which was not governed by the statutes. On the other hand, the fact that the Universities Act 1997 now provides the legal basis for many decisions taken within the university sector means that the potential application of judicial review within that sector has probably been much extended.

[40]   i.e. the test subsequently articulated by O'Neill J. in *Becker v Duggan* [2005] IEHC 376; [2009] 4 I.R. 1.

[41]   Thus, e.g. holders of sound broadcasting licences under the Broadcasting Act 2009 are required to enter into contracts with the Broadcasting Authority of Ireland, and Pt 6 of this Act specifies the conditions attaching to such contracts. Another example is provided by Community Pharmacy Contractor's Contract which regulates the contractual relationship between health boards and the proprietors of community pharmacies to enable the latter to provide pharmacy services under the Health Act 1970: see, e.g. *Collooney Pharmacy Ltd v North Western Health Board* [2005] IESC 44; [2005] 4 I.R. 124; *Hickey v Health Service Executive* [2008] IEHC 290; [2009] 3 I.R. 156.

body; or a private company in which the State may have a shareholding. Again, a private company with monopoly power or a trade union with a closed shop may dispose of a reservoir of power greater than many State organs; for example, the Irish Aviation Authority Act 1993. The Irish Aviation Authority is cast as a private company,[42] but it may exercise quite far-reaching regulatory, licensing and related functions, including the power to detain aircraft.[43] Furthermore, it is "owned" and financed by the State. It would seem inconceivable that the owner of an airplane who claimed that its detention was unlawful would not have a remedy by way of judicial review against the Authority, its status as a private company notwithstanding.[44]

17–24 Yet, in contrast with this contemporary landscape, because of the nature and history of judicial review most of the actions to which it was traditionally directed, were actions, first, authorised by statute and, secondly, discharged by bodies constituted by statute. Plainly there are two types of restriction here. In the first place, as regards the body involved, the High Court could only exercise public law powers of control over a body which was grounded upon statute, statutory instrument or prerogative. Secondly, as to the particular function being discharged, control could only be exercised when the body was using statutory, as opposed to common law, powers. It remains to enlarge upon each of these two points , though we shall return to the second point in Part C.

17–25 As we have seen from the case law just summarised, times have changed and it may be that the best way forward is to ask simply whether abuses of power of the type illustrated should be subject to public law controls. We can answer this question briefly by considering the public–private divide, first in the context of the substantive principles of judicial review. If one takes the view that, for example the requirement of reasonableness should not be imposed promiscuously on all transactions and functions even if a public body or what may seem to be a public body is involved, then it would seem inevitable that some such borderline should be observed. Take, next, the question of the scope of the application for judicial review. The first point is that if an application for judicial review is being entertained, it is unthinkable that the substantive principles of judicial review would not be applied. In this way the issue raised earlier concerning the applicability of these substantive principles would have been automatically settled simply by permitting the judicial review application to proceed. Secondly, since there are major

---

[42] However, this rather disguises the essential nature of the company, since shareholders who are not Ministers of the Government are required to hold their shares in trust for the Minister for Finance: see s.24 of the 1993 Act. See generally, Hoy, "Annotation to The Irish Aviation Authority Act 1993" [1993] I.C.L.S.A. 29–01. The Irish Takeover Panel is another example of what in reality is a public law body, even though in form it is a public company formed and registered under the Companies Acts 1963–1990: see Irish Takeover Panel Act 1997 s.3(1). The public law character of the Panel is underscored by the fact that its decisions can only be challenged by means of judicial review: see s.13(1) of the 1997 Act.

[43] Thus, by virtue of s.67 of the Irish Aviation Authority Act 1993, the company may exercise powers of detention (formerly exercised by the Minister) in respect of aircraft for which certain aerodrome and route charges have not been paid.

[44] In *Matthews v Irish Coursing Club Ltd* [1993] 1 I.R. 346, O'Hanlon J. granted an order of certiorari quashing a decision of the respondent company. The company had been given certain statutory responsibilities under the Greyhound Industry Act 1958 and O'Hanlon J. observed (at 354) that it had been accepted that "the decision made by the respondent was an exercise of its discretionary powers as a body established by statute and having important public duties to perform".

advantages—notably expedition—in the judicial review route, it is axiomatic that there must be some principled criterion to determine which type of litigant should have the chance of these advantages. It is accepted even in the most expansive of judicial authorities that the criterion should be grounded upon the notion that the State's action in the public law field has a peculiarly significant effect upon the community. The conclusion would seem to follow that there has to be some concept of a public–private divide in order to ensure that only certain types of cases enjoy this special procedure.

17–26   At the same time great care needs to be taken in defining this borderline. Does it, for example, make any sense to distinguish between the decisions of, say, different educational institutions on the basis of their legal origin? The essential point is that in each case they wield a substantial degree of educational power over the individual and often do so on what is, in practice, close to a monopoly basis. On this view, it seems preferable, first, that they should all be subject to the same form of supervision by the courts, and secondly, that that form should be an application for judicial review.[45]

C. THE PRIVATE LIFE OF A PUBLIC BODY

17–27   So far, the nature of the body and its general powers and functions have been the main focus of discussion. The other question concerns the particular power which it is exercising. For while public law deals only with public bodies, it is also true that public bodies are sometimes governed by private law, in such fields as property, contract and tort. As has been said, "[l]ike public figures, at least in

---

[45]   This is a vexed question. So far as third-level institutions are concerned, in *Flanagan v University College Dublin* [1988] I.R. 724, certiorari was granted to quash such a disciplinary punishment and the procedural issue of whether judicial review would lie was not raised. The issue might also have been addressed in *Kenny v Kelly* [1988] I.R. 457 (a judicial review case involving UCD admissions policy), but this procedural objection was only raised at the hearing and Barron J. said that, at this stage, it was too late to raise this point. There have been some English cases where certiorari was said to lie to quash a punishment of this kind (e.g. *R. v Aston University Senate Ex p. Roffey* [1969] 2 Q.B. 538), but this was doubted by Russell L.J. in *Herring v Templeman* [1973] 3 All E.R. 569 at 585. There was a suggestion in *R. v Disciplinary Committee of the Jockey Club Ex p. Massingberd-Mundy* [1993] 2 All E.R. 207 that the fact that the Jockey Club was established by Royal Charter might be enough to make it amenable to judicial review. Perhaps the fact that both the University of Dublin and the constituent colleges of the National University of Ireland were established by Royal Charter (in the latter case by charter under the Irish Universities Act 1908) might be sufficient for this purpose. Yet a further approach is evident in the judgment of Shanley J. in *Eogan v University College, Dublin* [1996] 1 I.R. 390; [1996] 2 I.L.R.M. 302 where he held that decisions of the University, taken pursuant to its internal statutes which were promulgated under the Irish Universities Act 1908, were amenable to judicial review. All of these cases were, however, decided prior to the enactment of the Universities Act 1997 which would seem to have extended the reach of public law deep into this sector. The position with regard to the non-third-level sector is more complex: *Becker v St Dominic's Secondary School* [2005] IEHC 169; *Becker v Duggan* [2005] IEHC 376; *Brown v Rathfarnham Parish National School* [2006] IEHC 178; [2008] 1 I.R. 70; *Hand v Ludlow* [2009] IEHC 583. As of 2009, the new disciplinary regimes contemplated by s.23 of the Education Act 1998 have been put in place. Thus, it would seem that most disciplinary actions concerning teachers can be litigated by way of judicial review.

theory, public bodies are entitled to have a private life".[46] This is a long-established doctrine, which links up with the Diceyan view that, save in exceptional cases when there is some specific reason to justify the contrary, public bodies should be subject to the same law as private individuals. When Dicey enunciated this influential principle, he did so by way of contrast against his (erroneous) portrayal of the *droit administratif* which, supposedly, set a rather low standard by which to control the Executive. Now, paradoxically, what is happening is that the law has developed to such an extent that it frequently offers a more stringent control over public bodies than over private bodies. One straightforward example is the area of legitimate expectations,[47] which applies only where a public authority is the defendant and which has gone beyond the normal rules on the formation of a contract and contractual dealing.

17–28   Before turning to the case law, we should remark that the subversion of the boundary between public and private law has been assisted by developments in other fields, namely the draftsman's fear of the ultra vires rule, coupled with the judiciary's strict approach to statutory interpretation. The consequence of these developments has been that the amount of detail in constituent legislation, spelling out the powers of public bodies and the controls on them, has increased exponentially. The natural result has been a rapid rise in the number of cases, some of which are presented here, in which a public body's common law powers have been enhanced, qualified or otherwise intertwined with public law statutes. This has left it open to applicants to submit that, although the situation might seem to centrally involve the public body's common law powers, there is a sufficient statutory overlay to warrant judicial review (whether procedural and/or substantive). In many such cases, as we shall see below, the reasoning has been of the type: "Ah, statute; therefore judicial review!"—with scant attempt to think out a balanced judicial policy.

17–29   We may commence, however, with a straightforward judicial recognition of the distinction between public and private law, which is taken from the judgment of Peart J. in *Becker v Board of Management, St Dominic's Secondary School, Cabra*[48]:

> "I draw an important distinction between the various public functions of the school which are involved in the provision of education to the public, and what I might describe as the private functions of that body, such as the hiring and firing of a teacher. One could think of other private functions of a school, such as entering into a contract for the supply of food, or school books, or the building of an extension to the school, which have a similar private law element to the hiring and firing of a teacher. Disputes arising in such private contracts are to be dealt with under private law remedies, such as breach of contract, unless there is some particular public law element to the dispute.

---

[46]   Woolf, "Public Law–Private Law: Why the Divide?" (1986) *Public Law* 220 at 223.

[47]   See also, e.g. the readiness of the High Court in both *Deane v Voluntary Health Insurance Board (No. 2)*, unreported, High Court, April 22, 1993 and *Zockoll Group v Bord Telecom Éireann* [1997] IEHC 178; [1998] 3 I.R. 287 to conclude that public bodies exercising quasi-monopoly powers had acted unreasonably in law in dealing with particular customers.

[48]   [2005] IEHC 169.

Simply because a school may be established, and its functions and obligations set forth, in an Act of the Oireachtas, is not of itself sufficient to bring every dispute emanating from the school's activities within the reach of judicial review."

17–30 Despite the general principle, just explained, that public bodies are governed by private law in respect of their private law transactions, there have been cases where, seemingly, just because public bodies are involved, private law issues have been litigated by way of judicial review, and even examples of substantive judicial review precepts being applied to private law cases.[49]

17–31 An example is *Browne v Dundalk U.D.C.*[50] in which the representatives of the Sinn Féin party had contracted to hire a hall for their annual conference from the respondents. When the elected councillors learnt of this development, they passed a resolution recommending that the town clerk rescind the contract. The town clerk then sought to rescind the contract and the applicants sought judicial review of that decision. At the hearing it was not seriously disputed that the respondents were in breach of contract. While the applicants could well have sought specific performance of the contract, Barr J. held that judicial review would lie:

"In the instant case there is no doubt that the hiring of the town hall to the applicant by the town clerk with the authority of the county manager constituted a valid administrative contract in private law made on behalf the local authority. Prima facie, therefore, it is outside the realm of judicial review."

17–32 However, Barr J. held that there was an element in the purported rescission of the contract which was not derived "solely and exclusively" from the contract itself: "As the council's resolution was in terms politically motivated, it was clearly in the public domain." Yet, with respect, the test is not the motivation of the respondent, but the legal powers under which it acted: it might well have happened that the hall belonged to a private person or company which for political reasons preferred to break a contract rather than let Sinn Féin use its hall, but this would not let in the law or procedure of judicial review.

17–33 A more difficult case to call is *Neville v South Dublin County Council.*[51] A corporation house tenant sought a declaration that his eviction was invalid. As a preliminary point, the question arose regarding whether this was an appropriate matter for judicial review. The High Court (O'Neill J.) held that the local authority was not merely exercising its private law rights as a landlord, but was exercising a statutory function, to evict the applicant for anti-social behaviour, pursuant to s.20 of the Housing (Miscellaneous Provisions) Act 1997. Accordingly, the matter was amenable to judicial review.

---

[49] See, e.g. *Hickey v Health Service Executive* [2008] IEHC 290; [2009] 3 I.R. 156.
[50] [1993] I.L.R.M. 328 at 333–334.
[51] [2010] 4 I.R. 309 at paras 13–16; *a contra: Hunt v Dublin City Council* [2004] IESC 80, in which a local authority was taking possession of property that it owned, against a trespasser, and the local authority was exercising its rights as a landowner. The Supreme Court held that, therefore, the judicial review application was not appropriate.

17–34   It is submitted that the trend of such cases is unfortunate. In the first place, it would introduce uncertainty into a fairly settled area if, as features of some new public law of contract (perhaps derived from the notion of legitimate expectations) public authorities were made subject—to take a few hypothetical examples—to a particularly stringent doctrine of undue influence or remoteness of damage, or a duty of full disclosure. Secondly, such changes would be unfair to public authorities. For, while it is one thing to say, as Dicey did, that public authorities should not be above the law, it is another to state that public authorities should be at a disadvantage. In a constitutional democracy, public authorities should be—and to a substantial degree, are—merely embodiments of community interests and it would be wrong to suggest that—certainly, at least, as far as their financial dealings are concerned—they should be put in a worse position than private parties.

17–35   There is, of course, a case to be made for saying that, in exceptional circumstances (which may turn out to encompass a number of cases), public authorities should be subject to a strict régime, such that they should be governed in their common law activities by special principles of public law as well as the ordinary private law. This argument focuses upon the fact that public authorities dispose of huge reservoirs of economic power by way, largely, of making contracts and do so, moreover, in some sense, as a trustee for the community. They should not, therefore, be free to abuse the power given by freedom of contract in order, for instance, to achieve policy objectives which would normally be effected by the exercise of the discretionary powers, which are subject to public law controls. An example here may have been the case of *Crofton v Minister for Environment, Heritage and Local Government*,[52] where the applicant challenged a ban on hunting on the state holdings of woodlands (over 10 per cent of all woodlands). It is notable that Hedigan J. was prepared to apply the standard public law precepts of jurisdiction and reasonableness in order to determine the legality of the decision, even though on one view it simply concerned a decision by the Minister qua landowner and was quintessentially in the private law domain. A second example may be afforded by the terms of the Anglo Irish Bank Corporation Act 2009 which provides that the nationalised bank is governed in the public interest. This, of course, raises the question of the extent to which public policy objectives will inform the exercise of even traditionally private law powers by the bank and which, perhaps, may pave the way for the application of judicial law precepts.

17–36   The second exception would be where the use of a public body's common law powers would have the effect of altering the commercial or social ecology for others. Something like this occurred in *McCord v ESB*.[53] The subject of the obiter dictum (in these plenary proceedings seeking damages for breach of contract) was the ESB's standard form contract for the supply of electricity, of which Henchy J. stated:

> "… judicial self-control requires that I withhold adverse comments on certain terms of the contract, such as that which purports to give contractual force to the idea that notices of intended disconnection may be taken as having been delivered on the weekday following the day they were posted; or on

---

[52]   [2009] IEHC 114.
[53]   [1980] I.L.R.M. 153.

even the final term of the contract by which 'the Board reserves to itself the right to add to, alter or amend any of the foregoing terms and conditions, as it may think fit'."[54]

17–37 Commenting on this legal artefact, Henchy J. said:

"[The] contract made between the plaintiff and Board (incorporating the General Conditions Relating to Supply) is what is nowadays called a contract of adhesion: it is a standardized mass contract which must be entered into, on a take it or leave it basis, by the occupier of every premises in which electricity is to be used. The would-be consumer has no standing to ask that a single iota of the draft contract presented to him be changed before he signs it. He must lump it or leave it. But, because for reasons that are too obvious to enumerate, he cannot do without electricity, he is invariably forced by necessity into signing the contract, regardless of the fact that he may consider some of its terms arbitrary, or oppressive, or demonstrably unfair. He is compelled, from a position of weakness and necessity vis-à-vis a monopolist supplier of a vital commodity, to enter into what falls into the classification of a contract … The real facts show that such an approach is largely based on legal fictions. When a monopoly supplier of a vital public utility – which is what the Board is – forces on all its consumers a common form of contract, reserving to itself sweeping powers, including the power to vary the document unilaterally as it may think fit, such an instrument has less affinity with a freely negotiated interpersonal contract than with a set of bye-laws or with any other form of autonomic legislation. As such, its terms may have to be construed not simply as contractual elements but as components of a piece of delegated legislation, the validity of which will depend on whether it has kept within the express or implied confines of the statutory delegation and, even if it has, whether the delegation granted or assumed is now consistent with the provisions of the Constitution of 1937."

17–38 This type of situation is most likely to arise in monopoly or near monopoly conditions. And, by now, with the developments in (Irish and EU) competition law, a more refined and apt set of legal tools to deal with this type of situation could be drawn from competition law. Perhaps the best solution would be if contract law and competition law were to evolve to provide new controls of abuses of private law which would parallel—while remaining distinct from—similar developments in the field of public law. A good example here is provided by *Donovan v Electricity Supply Board*,[55] a case which concerned the membership rules of an electrical trade association. The ESB decided that it would permit electricity connection only on premises where the electrical work had been done by an electrician who was a member of a trade association. Costello J. held that the membership rules of the trade association had anti-competitive effects, because "… the imprecision of criteria for enrolment, the lack of objective standards for registration, the arbitrary power to refuse enrolment, the absence of any appeal procedure [all] imposed unjustified restrictions on enrolment on the register".[56]

---

[54] [1980] I.L.R.M. 153 at 161. For criticism of the High Court's failure in *Quinn v King's Inns* [2004] 4 I.R. 344 to follow the *McCord* principle, see H & M, paras 17–18 to 17–20.
[55] [1994] 2 I.R. 305.
[56] [1994] 2 I.R. 305 at 324.

17–39   One possible situation in which this approach might have seemed appropriate would have been judicial control over the dealings of the National Asset Management Agency, which is clearly both a statutory body enjoying public law functions and an "undertaking" for the purposes of competition law. The background to *Daly v NAMA*[57] is that a public body, the National Asset Management Agency, was set up, by statute, to acquire from commercial banks assets, mainly land and buildings, which had been mortgaged to them (the banks) by developers, as securities against loans. Under the National Asset Management Agency Act 2009, the ownership of these assets had been transferred to NAMA. The developers were now complaining regarding certain actions, taken under these loan transactions, by NAMA. And the respondent NAMA had argued that, since the applicant's claim was based on contract and property, it was private law in character. In short, the applicant was not entitled to proceed by way of judicial review. The High Court rejected this argument:

> "[T]hese proceedings are a matter of public law ... even though it is clear from section 99 of the Act that the rights and obligations in question are those deriving from '... the bank asset, and arising under any law or in equity or by way of contract'. Section 2 of the Act sets out purposes which are public, truly national in their scope, and aimed at securing some advantage to the State's economy and finances, and the stability of the banking sector. The Act has all the appearances of emergency legislation where a statutory body is established with unusual powers which would not, I would have thought, be contemplated as being necessary, desirable or perhaps even permissible in normal times ... Decisions made under such legislation with the capacity to affect the interests of persons in such a drastic way and supposedly in the interests of the State as a whole should be capable of judicial scrutiny, where, as contemplated by the Act itself, a substantial issue is raised as to the lawfulness of decisions ... The Act itself seems to anticipate that this should be the case since the Oireachtas has included the specific provisions of section 193, albeit that it has limited and defined the circumstances in which leave to seek relief may be granted."

17–40   One may comment that what was at issue here was not whether (as the passage puts it) there was to be no "judicial scrutiny", but rather whether the scrutiny was to be by way of judicial review or plenary proceedings. In any case, it was standard form judicial review which was applied here.

D. CAN A PUBLIC LAW ISSUE BE LITIGATED BY WAY OF PLENARY PROCEEDINGS?

17–41   In contrast to Ord.84 r.18(1) of the Rules of the Superior Courts (which, of course, relates to the purely public law remedies of certiorari, prohibition and mandamus), r.18(2) is couched in discretionary language. ("An application for a declaration may be made by way of an application for judicial review.") It might appear from this wording that the litigant is given a choice: he may apply for a declaration or an injunction by way of an application for judicial review or he may,

---

[57]   Unreported, High Court, Peart J., September 12, 2011, at 89, 95–96.

as in the pre-1986 era, commence the proceedings by way of plenary summons. But in fact, the litigant's choice is not an unrestricted one; in the first place, as discussed in Parts B and C, the application for judicial review is available only where the proceedings relate to the exercise of public law powers by a public body.

17–42 But in regard to the declaration and injunction, there is a further question which of its nature could arise in the case of only these two remedies (and not of the specialist public law remedies, certiorari, prohibition and mandamus), for the reason that they are available on a plenary summons. It is this: where declaration or injunction is sought to be raised in a public law matter, is the party aggrieved confined to an application by way of judicial review or may he or she litigate the case by way of plenary summons? The most likely reason why this apparently arcane issue could matter, in practice, arises from the fact, explained in paras 16–45 to 16–61, that in the case of judicial review, the equivalent of the period of limitation is so very short. Before addressing this issue further, it may be convenient to illustrate it, taking a private law function:

> A local authority fails to honour its contractual obligation to purchase certain products from X Company Ltd. X seeks a declaration that the local authority is in breach of contract. The outcome may be summarized as follows: X cannot proceed by way of an application for judicial review, for although the respondent is a public body, the matter does not relate to the exercise of the authority's public law functions,[58] but is governed by ordinary principles of contract. X must commence declaratory proceedings by way of plenary summons. If the company proceeds by way of an application for judicial review, the court, however, instead of refusing the application, may exercise the power bestowed by Ord.84 r.26, namely, to order that the proceedings continue as if they had been begun by plenary summons.

17–43 Secondly, consider the converse case, i.e. where public functions are involved:

> A local authority refuses to grant Y a statutory licence. Y seeks a declaration that this refusal is invalid. Since Y's claim relates to the exercise of public law powers by a public body, then of course, the declaratory action may proceed by way of an application for judicial review. To anticipate the discussion, which is the main subject of this Part, it appears that in this jurisdiction, Y may, as an alternative, commence the proceedings by way of plenary summons. There is, however, a qualification to this proposition, which is likely to be quite important in practice: questions of an abuse of process may arise where the litigant's motivation is to circumvent the stricter time limits and other safeguards provided for in Ord.84 by proceedings by way of plenary summons.[59]

17–44 Let us now enlarge on the subject matter illustrated by the second example. It should be noted that there is no converse power to that contained in Ord.84 r.26(5)

---

[58] cf. the comments of Peart J. in *Becker v Duggan* [2005] IEHC 376.
[59] *O'Donnell v Dun Laoghaire Corporation* [1991] I.L.R.M. 301; *Dublin City Council v Williams* [2010] IESC 7.

whereby proceedings, commenced by way of judicial review, may be ordered to continue as if they had begun by way of plenary summons.[60] It is not immediately obvious why the courts should not have been given the power to "convert" an action commenced by way of plenary summons into an application for judicial review. It may be that, were such a power to exist, it would facilitate litigants who wished to circumvent the inherent restrictions in the Order 84 procedure (the need for leave, strict time limits, etc) by commencing their action by way of plenary summons and for these reasons, the Superior Court Rules Committee deliberately elected to allow conversion in one direction only. If this is so, this would be another powerful argument in favour of the approach favoured by the English courts (and described below), namely that Ord.84 creates a special self-contained procedure for challenging administrative decisions and that, as a general rule, any challenges to such a decision must be brought in this fashion. It is to this important issue that we now turn.

Procedural exclusivity and the decision in *O'Reilly v Mackman*

17–45   The English law on this point was (originally) established by *O'Reilly v Mackman*,[61] in which certain prisoners commenced declaratory proceedings by plenary summons against a prison board of visitors. They sought declarations to the effect that the board of visitors had acted contrary to natural justice and that disciplinary punishments imposed by them were invalid. As this complaint was likely to raise many disputed issues of fact, it was decided to proceed by way of plenary action rather than by way of an application for judicial review. The proceedings had, however, been commenced some four years after the events in question, i.e. well outside the conventional time limits for judicial review.[62] The House of Lords held that the actions should be struck out as an abuse of process.

17–46   In his speech in the House of Lords, Lord Diplock noted first, that whereas formerly the courts had, by concession, encouraged the use of the declaration and injunction in public law cases in order to permit litigants to avoid the procedural limitations of scope which then attached to the purely public law remedies of

---

[60]   In *R. v East Berkshire Health Authority Ex p. Walsh* [1985] Q.B. 152 at 166, Sir John Donaldson M.R. described the equivalent English rule in the following terms: "This is an anti-technicality rule. It is designed to preserve the position of an applicant for relief who finds that the basis of that relief is private law rather than public law. It is not designed to allow him to amend and to claim different relief."

[61]   [1983] 2 A.C. 237. For largely critical comment, see Wade, "Procedure and Prerogative in Public Law" (1985) 101 L.Q.R. 180. Many will agree with Professor Jolowicz's observation that *O'Reilly v Mackman* represented a "singularly unfortunate step back to the technicalities of a by-gone age": see "The Forms of Action Disinterred" (1983) 15 Camb. L.J. 1. cf. the comments of Wade and Forsyth, *Administrative Law*, 10th edn (Oxford: OUP, 2009), p.579: "Lord Diplock's speech in *O'Reilly v. Mackman* was a brilliant judicial exploit, but it turned the law in the wrong direction, away from the flexibility of procedure and towards a rigidity reminiscent of the bad old days of the forms of action a century and a half ago. The well-intentioned reforms of 1977 became a classic example of the remedy being worse than the disease."

[62]   It is clear from the judgment that the plaintiffs launched the proceedings in the wake of the success of fellow prisoners in challenging similar prison disciplinary punishments in *R. v Hull Prison Visitors Ex p. St. Germain* [1979] Q.B. 425. Prior to that date it was not even clear whether such prison disciplinary decisions could be challenged by way of judicial review, a factor which at least explains the delay.

certiorari, prohibition and mandamus. However, Lord Diplock concluded that this concession should now be withdrawn in view of the removal of those procedural defects by the new Rules of Court. More importantly, the new judicial review procedures contained certain safeguards designed to protect public bodies from vexatious and unmeritorious claims. An applicant for judicial review must obtain leave from the High Court, and conditions may be attached to the grant of leave. The applicant must, from the outset, put his case on affidavit, and cannot rely on merely unsworn allegations in the pleadings. What is of special importance is that there is such a short time limit. This means that the judicial review procedure provides for a speedy and expeditious determination of the validity of administrative action, in contrast to the delays that may be caused in the case of an action commenced by plenary summons. Such delays would be particularly unwelcome in such diverse areas as extradition, planning or adoption.

17–47 Nevertheless, even if it is difficult to take issue with the principle underlying Lord Diplock's reasoning, its practical operation has wreaked havoc ever since. A whole new process of characterisation of claims became necessary and the decision in *O'Reilly* has been made subject to numerous exceptions.[63] It may even be said that the whole object of the reforms has been defeated by the decision. The new rules were designed to ease the path of public law litigants and to ensure that a meritorious application was not lost by reason of the wrong choice of remedy. In Britain, however, many litigants have found in the wake of *O'Reilly v Mackman* that their applications for judicial review have been struck out by reason of the wrong choice of proceedings.[64] In fact, this result is actually now more frequent than ever was the case prior to the introduction of the new Rules in England in 1977, when the procedural reforms, designed to avoid precisely this result, came into force. Furthermore, judicial unhappiness with this decision is growing and there are signs that the entire issue may have to be re-considered by the UK Supreme Court.[65] In summary, to import the *O'Reilly* gloss in Ireland would entail drawing a demarcation line between public and private law and thus admitting by the back door the curse of characterisation which had just been ceremoniously expelled at the front door. Moreover, it does not appear that, under the pre-1986 Rules, public authorities were, in fact, unduly troubled by the prospect of having to defend actions for declarations or injunctions commenced by plenary summons.[66] Finally, in those special cases where speed of decision and certainty

---

[63] The judicially created exceptions included the following: where there is no objection: *Gillick v West Norfolk Area Health Authority* [1986] A.C. 112; where the invalidity arises by way of defence: *Davy v Spelthorne B.C.* [1984] A.C. 264; *R. v Reading Crown Court Ex p. Hutchinson* [1987] Q.B. 384; where the Order 53 procedure is not well suited to the nature of the dispute: *Mercury Ltd v Director General of Telecommunications* [1996] 1 W.L.R. 48; where the issues arise collaterally in a claim for the infringement of a right of the plaintiff arising under private law: *Wandsworth L.B.C. v Winder* [1985] A.C. 461; *Roy v Kensington and Chelsea and Westminster F.P.C.* [1992] 1 A.C. 624.

[64] The procedural complexities arising from the *O'Reilly v Mackman* jurisprudence are well summarised by Wade and Forsyth, *Administrative Law*, 10th edn (2009), pp.570–581.

[65] In *Equal Opportunities Commission v Secretary of State* [1995] 1 A.C. 1, Lord Lowry commented (at 34) that he had never "been entirely happy with the wide procedural restriction for which *O'Reilly v. Mackman* is an authority, and I hope that that case will one day be the subject of your Lordships' further consideration". See also, his speech in *Roy v Kensington and Chelsea and Westminster Family Practitioner Committee* [1992] 1 A.C. 624.

[66] In *M v An Bord Uchtála* [1977] I.R. 287, the Supreme Court saw no obstacle to the plaintiff's choice of declaration in plenary proceedings to certiorari to quash a decision of the Adoption

are considered to be of critical importance, the Oireachtas may intervene by statute and legislate for a form of *O'Reilly v Mackman* rule, as has now been done by a variety of heterogeneous statutory provisions.

The partial rejection of *O'Reilly v Mackman* in Ireland

17–48   It was not until the judgment of Costello J. in *O'Donnell v Dún Laoghaire Corporation*,[67] in which the plaintiff had sought a declaration that a decision to levy certain service charges was invalid, that the problem received full consideration by an Irish court. Here the plaintiffs successfully established that certain water charges imposed by the defendants some years previously were invalid. It was argued that it was an abuse of process for the plaintiffs to proceed by way of plenary action, especially since the action had been commenced outside the three-month time limit prescribed by Ord.84 r.21(1). In *O'Donnell*, Costello J. explained that he could not follow the House of Lord's decision in *O'Reilly v Mackman* because:

> "Firstly, as a matter of construction, I cannot construe the new rules as meaning that in matters of public law, Ord.84 provides an exclusive remedy in cases where the aggrieved party wishes to obtain a declaratory order and that such a person abuses the courts' processes by applying for such an order by plenary action. Secondly, I do not think that the court is at liberty to apply policy considerations and conclude that the public interest requires that the court should construe its jurisdiction granted by the new rules in the restrictive way suggested ..."[68]

17–49   However, Costello J. then went on to address and, to a substantial degree, adopt the policy underlying *O'Reilly* (though it is likely that there will be further development in this area, before firm law is established). He held that the safeguards contained in Ord.84 should be applied, mutatis mutandis, to actions against public authorities commenced by plenary summons (writ of summons):

> "[I]n considering the effects of delay in a plenary action there are now persuasive reasons for adopting the principles enshrined in Ord. 84, r.21 relating to delay in applications for judicial review, so that if the plenary action is not brought within the three months from the date on which the cause of action arose the court would normally refuse relief unless it is satisfied that had the claim been brought under Ord. 84, time would have been extended."[69]

17–50   Because he felt that the Order 84 safeguards could be applied to plenary actions against public authorities, Costello J. concluded that:

Board. See also, the comments of Lord Slynn in *Mercury Ltd v Director General of Telecommunications* [1996] 1 W.L.R. 48.

[67]   [1991] I.L.R.M. 301. More recently, in *Dublin City Council v Williams* [2010] IESC 7, the Supreme Court has endorsed the *O'Donnell* view.

[68]   [1991] I.L.R.M. 301 at 314. A further consideration is that Ord.84 has not been given statutory backing and in the absence of equivalent statutory provisions, the Superior Court Rules Committee would probably have been acting ultra vires had it purported to prescribe an exclusive procedure for challenging the validity of an administrative decision.

[69]   [1991] I.L.R.M. 301 at 314.

"The apprehended use of plenary actions as a device to defeat the protections given by Ord. 84 is not a real danger and does not justify the court in concluding that the proceedings by plenary action for declaratory relief must be an abuse of process."[70]

17–51 The fact that a majority of constitutional actions have been begun by plenary proceedings and not by judicial review must also have influenced the conclusion in *O'Donnell*. For, in many of many of these cases, the plaintiff simply attacks the constitutionality of the impugned legislation and there is no administrative law "decision" which lends itself to being quashed.[71]

17–52 What is interesting is that, in a number of discrete areas, most notably planning and immigration—where the need for legal certainty and swift decision-making are thought to be paramount[72]—the Oireachtas has now expressly legislated for a form of the *O'Reilly v Mackman* rule. Thus, s.50 of the Planning and Development Act 2000 now provides as follows:

> (2) A person shall not question the validity of any decision made or other act done by—
>> (a) a planning authority, a local authority or the Board in the performance or purported performance of a function under this Act,
>> (b) the Board in the performance or purported performance of a function transferred under Part XIV, or
>> (c) a local authority in the performance or purported performance of a function conferred by an enactment specified in section 214 relating to the compulsory acquisition of land,
> otherwise than by way of an application for judicial review under Order 84 of the Rules of the Superior Courts (S.I. No. 15 of 1986) (the "Order").[73]

Public law element is collateral

17–53 The discussion thus far has focused upon a situation in which the applicant has sought a declaration in plenary proceedings, when he might have applied for a declaration by way of an application for judicial review. In other words, the circumstances are such that the proceedings are exclusively or primarily public law in character. However, the situation in which the public law element is subordinate

---

[70] [1991] I.L.R.M. 301 at 314.
[71] The examples here are too numerous to mention. For some recent examples, see, e.g. *Blehein v Minister for Health and Children* [2008] IESC 40; [2009] 1 I.R. 275; *McCann v Judges of the District Court for Monaghan* [2009] IEHC 276; [2009] 4 I.R. 200.
[72] This formula has proved popular with the Oireachtas: see, e.g. Transport (Dublin Light Rail) Act 1996 s.12; Irish Takeover Panel Act 1997 s.13; Roads Act 1993 s.55A (as inserted by Roads (Amendment) Act 1998 s.6(4)); Aviation Regulation Act 2001 s.38; Prisons Act 2007 s.27; National Assets Management Agency Act 2009 s.193.
[73] As inserted by s.42 of the Planning and Development (Strategic Infrastructure) Act 2006. Earlier versions of this provision date back to 1992: see s.82(3A) of the Local Government (Planning and Development) Act 1963 (as inserted by s.19 of the Local Government (Planning and Development) Act 1992). Further changes were made in 2000 (Planning and Development Act 2000 s.50) and 2002 (Planning and Development (Amendment) Act 2002 s.12). There is a discussion of this legislation in H & M, at paras 17–84 to 17–88.

and arises as a collateral issue in a criminal prosecution or a civil law action also needs to be considered.

17–54 A typical example of the former is *Listowel U.D.C. v McDonagh*,[74] in which an accused was permitted to raise the argument, as a defence to a prosecution for violating bye-laws, that the bye-laws were ultra vires. A typical example of the latter situation is *Cooper v Wandsworth L.B.C.*,[75] in which the plaintiff sued for trespass to land. The local authority's defence was founded upon a compulsory purchase order and the public law element was the validity of the compulsory purchase order. But as these decisions ante-date the major reforms of judicial review, one question which has troubled both the Irish and English courts, in the last 15 years or so, is whether there is any reason why such cases—or, at any rate, the public law element in such cases—would now have to be taken by way of judicial review.

17–55 In *Boddington v British Transport Police*,[76] the House of Lords firmly rejected the argument that a defendant charged with violating a transport bye-law was not entitled to raise the validity of that bye-law before the criminal court. In this jurisdiction, too, it is clear that in criminal cases an accused is entitled to raise the validity of the administrative decision (such as, for example, the validity of a search warrant) by way of defence, save that the ruling by the trial judge is not regarded as a pronouncement of invalidity *erga omnes*. In other words, while the ruling governs the legal rights of the parties, it does not have the status of a general declaration of invalidity such as the High Court might grant following an application in that behalf for judicial review. The existence of this jurisdiction was confirmed for very practical reasons by the Supreme Court in *Blanchfield v Harnett*.[77]

17–56 However, so far as civil cases are concerned, the preponderance of authority is now generally against collateral challenges to the validity of administrative decisions, since it is usually considered appropriate that the deciding authority ought to be given the opportunity of defending the validity of its own order.[78] In other words, the point may be raised only by way of judicial review in the High

---

[74] [1968] I.R. 312.

[75] (1863) 14 C.B. 180.

[76] [1998] UKHL 13; [1999] 2 A.C. 143; [1998] 2 W.L.R. 639; [1998] 2 All E.R. 203.

[77] [2002] IESC 41; [2002] 3 I.R. 207; [2002] 2 I.L.R.M. 435. See also, *Byrne v Grey* [1988] I.R. 31 (where the High Court declined to entertain a judicial review application on the ground that the ultimate issue raised—the admissibility of evidence obtained pursuant to a search warrant which was said to be invalid—was best dealt with by the court of trial).

[78] *Faulkner v Minister for Industry and Commerce* [1997] E.L.R. 107; *Slatterys Ltd v Commissioner of Valuation* [2001] 4 I.R. 91. In *Faulkner*, O'Flaherty J. hinted that it was for this reason that a challenge to a decision of the Labour Court for an alleged breach of the requirement to state reasons should not have been by way of appeal on a point of law where the Labour Court was not a party, but rather by way of judicial review where the Labour Court would have been a respondent to such proceedings. See also, to like effect the same judge's comments in *McSorley v Governor of Mountjoy Prison* [1997] 2 I.R. 258.

In *Slatterys*, Keane C.J. distinguished ([2001] 4 I.R. 91 at 100) *Listowel U.D.C.* on the basis that "the public authority concerned was a party to the proceedings". Note also the comments of Finlay P. in *Re Comhaltas Ceolteoirí Éireann*, unreported, High Court, December 5, 1977 where he held that the validity of a decision of a planning authority could not be challenged in the course of a case stated from the District Court, since "it would be contrary to natural justice for a court to be called upon to adjudicate on the validity of the acts of the planning authority in a case to which they were not a party".

Court. Where the defence is sought to be raised in the District Court or the Circuit Court, there is the additional point that the lower courts have no jurisdiction to adjudicate on the validity of administrative decisions.[79] Thus, in *Dublin City Council v Williams*,[80] the Supreme Court (Geoghegan J.) considered that the nature of a challenge to the validity of waste charges:

> "... clearly demonstrate that the issues in controversy are wholly inappropriate to be dealt with in the District Court by way of defence to a simple claim for the charges. In expressing this view, I am not in any way suggesting that these matters cannot be litigated in some other forum nor am I suggesting that they could only be litigated by way of judicial review. I accept that the exclusivity principle lay down by the House of Lords in *O'Reilly v. Mackman*[81] does not apply in this jurisdiction. This is quite clear from the well respected judgment of Costello J. in the High Court in *O'Donnell v. Corporation of Dún Laoghaire*.[82] I fully accept that a person with *locus standi* might be entitled to litigate the issue of whether 'the polluter pays principle' is not being lawfully implemented, by a declaratory action just as much as by a judicial review. I do not accept, however, that such an issue may properly be raised in the District Court by way of defence to a claim for a civil debt of a public nature albeit recoverable as a simply contract debt."

17–57 Thus, while the Irish courts have avoided one element of procedural exclusivity (i.e. by generally permitting an applicant to choose between Order 84 judicial review or plenary summons), they seem to be increasingly moving in the direction of excluding collateral challenges to an administrative decision, by way of defence in civil proceedings.

---

[79] *Slatterys Ltd v Commissioner of Valuation* [2001] 4 I.R. 91 (District Court had no jurisdiction to rule on validity of rates); *Dublin City Council v Williams* [2010] IESC 7 (District Court had no jurisdiction to rule on the validity of waste charges); *Menolly Homes Ltd v Appeal Commissioners* [2010] IEHC 49 (Appeal Commissioner had no jurisdiction to rule on validity of opinion of Inspector of Taxes).
[80] [2010] IESC 7; [2010] 1 I.R. 250.
[81] [1983] 2 A.C. 237.
[82] [1991] I.L.R.M. 301.

CHAPTER 18

DAMAGES IN TORT

A. Governmental Liability and Judicial Control of Administrative Action

18–01   By way of preliminary, we should emphasise that this chapter deals with particular public law features of the law of tort: we do not treat the general law of tort which is common to torts committed by public bodies or private individuals or companies. Secondly, as to contract, where a public body is a party to the contract, the rules are generally unaffected.[1] There are a few exceptions, for example, public bodies must observe certain formalities in making certain categories of contract ("public procurement"); may not contract so as to fetter their discretionary powers; or, if they exceed their statutory vires, may not create an estoppel?[2] Thirdly, the liability of public bodies for breach of EU law or for restitution is covered not here but in H & M, Chapter 18, Parts H and J.

18–02   We should also mention a point which follows from the character of judicial review. Irrespective of the change in the judicial review procedure made in 1986, it remains the fact that when a court annuls an administrative act on procedural grounds, that decision is deemed to be void ab initio. But it does not follow that a declaration of invalidity of an administrative decision in and of itself gives rise to a cause of action in damages.[3] This is because "'paralysis' of public authorities would inevitably follow if the exercise of statutory powers could readily, in the case of an *ultra vires* exercise of same and without more, attract an award of damages".[4]

18–03   However, the change to the judicial review procedure did have one

---

[1]   For a good recent example, see *Hickey v Health Service Executive (No. 1)* [2008] IEHC 290.
[2]   See below, paras 19–44 to 19–58.
[3]   See *Delargy v Minister for the Environment* [2006] IEHC 267 per Murphy J.
[4]   *Kennedy v Law Society of Ireland (No. 4)* [2005] 3 I.R. 228 at 237 per Kearns J. (HC). See also, *Glencar Exploration Plc v Mayo County Council* [2002] 1 I.R. 84 at 148–150 per Fennelly J. (SC).

practical consequence: prior to the introduction of the Rules of the Superior Courts in 1986,[5] even where a claim for damages did exist, it was not possible to combine this claim with an application for a state side order (although, in plenary proceedings, such a claim could be combined with an application for a declaration or injunction). If damages were sought, it was formerly necessary to commence separate proceedings.[6] The new Rules seek to rectify this procedural anomaly by providing for a new unified judicial review procedure. The new Ord.84 r.25 of the 2011 Rules empowers the court to grant damages in addition to, or in lieu of, certiorari or prohibition, or a declaration or an injunction. The effect of these changes has been to make it easier for applicants to recover damages in respect of wrongful administrative action and such claims are now made with increasing frequency.[7]

18–04 To return to substantive law, an invalid administrative act will sound in damages (only) if:

    (1) it happens also to constitute the commission of a recognised tort, such as false imprisonment, trespass or negligence;

    (2) where the invalid act was motivated by malice or the authority knew that it did not have the power which it purports to exercise, i.e. the tort of misfeasance of public office;

    (3) there is a breach of statutory duty;

    (4) the invalid act amounts to an infringement of a personal constitutional right;

    (5) a special statutory right to compensation has been established;

    (6) there is a negligent exercise of discretionary statutory power; or

    (7) there is a breach of the plaintiff's legitimate expectations.[8]

18–05 It remains to consider each of these categories: (1)–(3) in this Part, with categories (4)–(6) in Parts B to D, and, for reasons of length, category (7) is left until the following chapter. Certain defences peculiar to public bodies and the vicarious liability of the State are covered in Parts E to H of this chapter.

The commission of a recognised tort

18–06 There are many heterogeneous examples of cases where either the

---

[5] S.I. No. 15 of 1986; now S.I. No. 691 of 2011.

[6] To take an example, in the *State (Pine Valley Developments Ltd) v Dublin County Council* [1984] I.R. 407, the Supreme Court ruled that the Minister had no power to contravene the planning authority's development plan and granted certiorari. But it was then necessary for Pine Valley to institute separate proceedings, seeking damages in *Pine Valley Developments Ltd v Minister for the Environment* [1987] I.R. 23. See also, Law Reform Commission, *Judicial Review of Administrative Action*, Working Paper No. 8–1979 (December, 1979), pp.4–5.

[7] However, one practical problem which remains is whether it is possible to proceed via the Order 84 procedure, where the applicant's claim is solely for damages: see H & M, paras 18–03 to 18–06. See *Grimes v Cork County Council* [2005] IEHC 420, in which Dunne J. suggested that this question remained unresolved.

[8] In *Duff v Minister for Agriculture and Food* [1997] 2 I.R. 22, the Minister was held liable in damages for breach of legitimate expectations and in *Lett v Wexford Borough Corporation* [2007] IEHC 195, a legitimate expectation of compensation for loss of income was enforceable against a public authority.

State or public officials have been found liable for recognised torts such as false imprisonment,[9] trespass,[10] nuisance[11] or negligence,[12] following a finding that the relevant decisions in question have been held to be ultra vires.

18–07   In *Gildea v Hipwell*,[13] for example, the Governor of Sligo Prison was held liable in damages for false imprisonment for wrongfully detaining the plaintiff pursuant to an invalid arrest warrant. Likewise in *Walsh v Ireland*[14] the State was held vicariously liable for false imprisonment, following the wrongful arrest of the plaintiff by members of the Garda Síochána who did not realise that they had arrested the wrong person. There are also numerous examples where either an individual Garda[15] or the State itself has been liable for wrongful arrest. In *Farrell v Minister for Agriculture and Food*,[16] the Minister was held liable in trespass when, with the mantle of statutory Regulations (eventually held to be invalid) around him, he had the plaintiff's cattle slaughtered.

Misfeasance in public office

18–08 There are two "limbs" to the tort. The first is that the act is performed by a public official. Secondly, there are two alternative requirements: either "targeted malice by a public officer"[17]; or actual knowledge that it is committed without jurisdiction, and is so done with the known consequence that it would injure the plaintiff or a group to which s/he belongs.[18] Without these sorts of restrictions, the tort of misfeasance in public office would begin to bear an uncomfortable resemblance to the tort of negligence.

18–09   In respect of the second limb, the leading Irish case, *Kennedy v Law Society*

---

[9]   See, e.g. *McIntyre v Lewis* [1991] 1 I.R. 121.
[10]   cf. *Kennedy v Law Society of Ireland (No. 4)* [2005] 3 I.R. 228 at 252–254 (HC).
[11]   See, e.g. *Kelly v Dublin County Council*, unreported, High Court, O'Hanlon J., February 21, 1986; *Larkin v Joosub and Dublin City Council* [2006] IEHC 51; [2007] 1 I.R. 521.
[12]   See, e.g. *Siney v Dublin Corporation* [1980] I.R. 400; *Ward v McMaster* [1988] I.R. 337; *Hanahoe v Hussey* [1998] 3 I.R. 69; *Carey v Mould and Donegal County Council* [2004] IEHC 66; *Gray v Minister for Justice, Equality and Law Reform* [2007] IEHC 52; [2007] 2 I.R. 654.
[13]   [1942] I.R. 489.
[14]   Unreported, Supreme Court, November 30, 1994. See also, *McGowan v Farrell*, *Irish Times*, February 15, 1975 and *McIntyre v Lewis* [1991] 1 I.R. 121. See also, *Hanahoe v Hussey* [1998] 3 I.R. 69, a case where details of a highly sensitive Garda search of solicitors' offices were improperly "leaked" to the media in advance by an individual member of the Garda Síochána. Kinlen J. held that this amounted to negligence in the execution of the warrant and held the State vicariously liable. However, Kinlen J. refused to hold that the State was liable on the alternative claim of misfeasance of office on the part of the (unidentified) Garda in question, as the evidence was that "secrecy and discretion were fully impressed on the [search team] as part of their obligations", so that any such misconduct would be wholly outside the scope of his employment.
[15]   See, e.g. *Lynch v Fitzgerald* [1938] I.R. 382 where a detective was held personally liable in an action under the Fatal Accident Act 1846.
[16]   Unreported, High Court, October 11, 1995.
[17]   *Three Rivers DC v Bank of England* [2000] 2 W.L.R. 1220 at 1231 per Lord Steyn.
[18]   See also, *Kenny v Bord na gCon (No. 3)*, unreported, High Court, January 13, 1966; *McDonnell v Ireland* [1998] 1 I.R. 134 at 156 per Keane J.; and *Glencar Exploration Plc v Mayo County Council (No. 2)* [2002] 1 I.R. 84 at 98–99 (HC), where several different definitions are referred to by Kelly J.

of Ireland (No. 4),[19] Geoghegan J. held that the first alternative "necessarily involves bad faith in the exercise of the public power for an improper or ulterior motive".[20] As to the second alternative, the subjective standard of reckless indifference was applied: "a test of knowledge or foresight that a decision would cause damage".[21] In other words, a subjective, rather than objective, test would apply because "[i]f the 'reasonable foreseeability' test [were] permitted, it would introduce an objective element and, effectively, remove the requirement of bad faith".[22] In addition, the Supreme Court took the opportunity to emphasise in *Beatty v Rent Tribunal*[23] that "bad faith in the exercise of public powers ... is the essence of the tort".[24] Fennelly J. suggested that the necessary standard of recklessness "is something much more than gross carelessness. It requires clear advertence to the risk (for example, that there is no power to do the act) and not caring about the consequences".[25]

18–10 As a practical matter it is manifest that the motives necessary to ground an action for misfeasance in public office would be most difficult to establish. One[26] of the only two Irish cases where liability under this heading was established[27] was *Re "The La Lavia"*.[28] Following the quashing of a preservation order which had been made in respect of a maritime wreck, Barr J. awarded damages in misfeasance against the Office of Public Works, saying:

> "I am satisfied that the officials who were responsible for the making of the order knew, or strongly suspected, that there was no statutory authority under [the National Monuments Act 1930] for making it. It seems to me that the circumstances fall within the principle laid down by the Supreme Court

19 [2005] IESC 32; [2005] 3 I.R. 228.
20 [2005] 3 I.R. 228 at 260–261.
21 [2005] 3 I.R. 228 at 262.
22 [2005] 3 I.R. 228 at 262.
23 [2005] IESC 66; [2006] 2 I.R. 191.
24 [2006] 2 I.R. 191 at 200.
25 [2006] 2 I.R. 191 at 204. For a somewhat similar case in which the question of misfeasance did not arise, since the evidence showed that the Minister had acted on the basis of legal advice prior to granting the planning permission, see *Pine Valley Developments Ltd v Minister for the Environment* [1987] I.R. 23.
26 The other one is *Deane v Voluntary Health Insurance Board (No. 2)*, unreported, Supreme Court, July 28, 1994, in which the Supreme Court held that the VHI had wrongly exercised its statutory powers in withdrawing insurance cover from a hospital and went on, it appears, to classify this as misfeasance in public office. However, it is respectfully suggested that the decision may need to be reconsidered, to the extent that it appeared to suggest that a public body might be liable for misfeasance in public office, if its statutory powers were merely exercised "unreasonably and unfairly" in a manner which caused loss and damage.
27 In *Hanahoe v Hussey* [1998] 3 I.R. 69, Kinlen J. appeared to accept that the actions of an individual Garda who "leaked" details of a highly sensitive Garda search of solicitors' offices in advance to the media amounted to misfeasance in public office. However, he found that such misconduct was clearly outside the scope of employment of the member in question, so that the State could not be made vicariously liable. In *Gray v Minister for Justice, Equality and Law Reform* [2007] IEHC 52; [2007] 2 I.R. 654, Quirke J. held that the Gardaí had breached their duty of care to the plaintiffs, by leaking information to the media to the effect that the plaintiffs were sheltering a convicted rapist. However, Quirke J. applied the negligence test of *Ward v McMaster* rather than that in *Glencar Exploration Plc v Mayo County Council* (see below, paras 18–44 to 18–50) and did not consider whether the actions of the Gardaí amounted to misfeasance in public office, which, it is respectfully suggested, would have been more appropriate given the facts of the case.
28 Unreported, High Court, Barr J., July 26, 1994.

in *Pine Valley Developments Ltd v. Minister for Environment* that where it did not possess the power which it purported to exercise, it is answerable in damages to a person who is injured by the exercise of the power."

Breach of statutory duty

18–11   A plaintiff may also seek damages in respect of breach of statutory duty, a cause of action which although certainly not peculiar to public bodies is more likely to involve public bodies. Given that a showing of negligence has no bearing on the question of whether a plaintiff is entitled to succeed, the imposition of liability for breach of statutory duty is really a form of strict liability. The major problem in this area is whether breach of the statute gives rise to a private right of action. The test "is whether the legislature intended that private law rights of action should be conferred upon individuals where breaches of statutory duty are shown to have occurred".[29] Very occasionally the statute will state explicitly that breach of the statute does[30] or does not[31] do so. Generally, however, the statute will be silent on the matter, and the courts will engage in the imaginative exercise of imputing legislative intent, in order to determine whether breach of the statute will give rise to a civil action.[32]

18–12   As regards this difficult exercise, first it is clear that if the duty is owed to the public at large, then no action for breach of that duty will lie. As Fennelly J. put it in *Glencar Exploration Plc v Mayo County Council (No. 2)*,[33] "[a] duty imposed by statute on a public body will not be held to create a right to damages for its breach unless it can be shown to have within the scope of its intendment, a reasonably identifiable protective purpose and identifiable class intended to benefit".[34] In this case, the making of a draft development plan by the respondent local authority "constituted the purported exercise by it of a power vested in it by law for the

---

[29]   *Doherty v South Dublin County Council (No. 2)* [2007] IEHC 4; [2007] 2 I.R. 696 at 707 per Charleton J.

[30]   See, e.g. Electoral Act 1992 s.159; Competition Act 2002 s.14; Consumer Protection Act 2007 s.74(2).

[31]   See, e.g. Litter Pollution Act 1997 s.14 (no action for damages by reason of failure of local authority to exercise their statutory functions); Teaching Council Act 2001 s.17 ("no action shall lie against a member of the Council in respect of anything done by that member in good faith and in pursuance of [the] Act").

[32]   See, e.g. *Kenny v Dental Council* [2004] IEHC 29 (no mandatory duty on the Minister for Health under the Dentists Act 1985 to bring into force a registration scheme for "denturists"); *Breen v Ireland* [2004] IEHC 243; [2004] 4 I.R. 12 ("safe custody" in the Rules for the Government of Prisons 1983 meant "safe in the sense that [the prisoner] would remain in custody and could not escape therefrom" and not safety from attack). See generally, McMahon and Binchy, *The Irish Law of Torts*, 3rd edn (Dublin: Butterworths, 2000), pp.589–614.

[33]   [2002] 1 I.R. 84. See also, *Atlantic Marine v Minister for Transport* [2011] 2 I.L.R.M.12 at paras 6.6–6.15: even if the legislation could be said to impose a statutory duty on the Minister, it could not be said that the legislation was intended to cover such a person such as the plaintiff. The plaintiff was a supplier of life rafts, who had sold fewer life-saving pieces of equipment than he would otherwise have done, because of the Minister's failure to enforce the safety Code of Practice (see para.18–50).

[34]   [2002] 1 I.R. 84 at 150.

benefit of the public in general",[35] and the fact that the use of the power had been held invalid[36] did not give rise to an action for breach of statutory duty.[37]

18–13   On the other side of the line was *Moyne v Londonderry Port and Harbour Commissioners*,[38] where Costello J. found that the breach of the statutory duties imposed on the defendants, by the provisions of the Londonderry Port and Harbour Act 1854, to keep certain harbours open, gave rise to an action for damages, at the suit of members of the public living in the locality:

> "[It] is clear that the statute with which this case is concerned is strikingly different from that class of statutes which the courts held concerned *a duty to the public only*. Here it cannot reasonably be argued that the duty to maintain the pier was imposed for the benefit of the Irish public generally. The benefit which was being afforded by the pier was being conferred primarily on *a definable class of persons*, namely those living in the clearly defined geographical area of the Inishowen peninsula, and particularly those living and working on its eastern seaboard."[39]

The general test which emerges from such passages as these is that an action for breaching statutory duty will only arise where the plaintiff can establish that there is a definite class of persons for whose benefit the duty was imposed and that he is within that class.

18–14   A particular situation arises when the legislature establishes new rights to assist a specified (usually disadvantaged) section of the community and a special scheme, aside from the courts, is set up to administer the scheme. In these circumstances, an action for breach of statutory duty will usually not lie. In *Doherty v South Dublin County Council (No. 2)*,[40] which concerned an attempt to seek damages under the Equal Status Act 2000 before a court, Charleton J. held that the effect of the legislation was that:

> "… a specific legal obligation is created for the first time by statute, a mode of enforcement is set up through an agency which was thereby created and limited rights of access to the courts are created. In my judgment this amounts to the creation of a separate legislative and administrative scheme which does not create a series of private rights which are either enforceable in damages, or outside the context of that scheme."[41]

18–15   Charleton J. accordingly held that claims under the 2000 Act claims were to be addressed exclusively by the Equality Authority, with the High Court retaining a supervisory jurisdiction only:

---

[35]   [2002] 1 I.R. 84 at 127 per Keane C.J.
[36]   [1993] 2 I.R. 237.
[37]   See also, *O'Donoghue v Legal Aid Board* [2004] IEHC 413; [2006] 4 I.R. 204.
[38]   [1986] I.R. 299.
[39]   [1986] I.R. 299 at 314 (emphasis added). See similarly, *Waterford Harbour Commissioners v British Railway Board* [1979] I.L.R.M. 296. But cf. *John C Doherty Timber Ltd v Drogheda Harbour Commissioners* [1993] 1 I.R. 315 (no duty owed to users of quayside).
[40]   [2007] IEHC 4; [2007] 2 I.R. 696.
[41]   [2007] IEHC 4; [2007] 2 I.R. 696 at 707–708.

"Many of the rights and obligations created by modern statute were never justiciable until they were created by the passage of legislation. Some legislation consolidates existing rights in a code form while others interfered with the general freedom of contract by establishing, for instance, that particular terms of contracts in particular circumstances may be unfair. These Acts tag onto the existing law, by way of amendment or tidying up, and divert the law in a particular direction. Such legislation contemplates that the courts are to be used for the settling of controversies. Where, however, an Act creates an entirely new legal norm and provides for a new mechanism for enforcement under its provisions, its purpose is not to oust the jurisdiction of the High Court but, instead, to establish new means for the disposal of controversies connected with those legal norms. In such an instance, administrative norms, and not judicial ones are set: the means of disposal is also administrative and not within the judicial sphere unless it is invoked under the legislative scheme. In the case of the Planning Acts, in employment rights matters and, I would hold, under the Equal Status Acts 2000 to 2004, these new legal norms and a new means of disposal through tribunal are created. This expressly bypasses the courts in dealing with these matters. The High Court retains [only] its supervisory jurisdiction."[42]

18–16   Before considering in Part B the separate question of actions for breaches of constitutional rights where no statute is necessarily involved, it must be noted that the settled common law rules of statutory interpretation, just outlined, have yielded in some instances to over-riding constitutional considerations. The outcome is a kind of hybrid. Thus, in *Parsons v Kavanagh*,[43] the plaintiff was a licensed bus operator who faced competition on the same bus route from an unlicensed competitor. O'Hanlon J. first rejected the contention, based on the traditional rules of interpretation just noted, that the Road Transport Acts 1932–1933 were to be construed as statutes passed for the benefit of a limited class of the public, namely, licensed operators under the terms of the Acts. This would have led, according the traditional rules, to the result that the plaintiff would have had no cause of action. But O'Hanlon J. held that this result would have to yield to constitutional considerations:

"The right to earn one's living by any lawful means was recognised by Kenny J. in *Murtagh Properties Ltd v. Cleary*[44] [where] he granted an injunction to restrain picketing of licensed premises on the basis that it amounted to an unlawful interference with the constitutional right of the bar maids employed therein to earn their livelihood ... The Supreme Court in *Byrne v. Ireland*[45] was primarily concerned with the enforceability of civil claims against the State in situations where a right of action would arise against a private individual

---

[42]   [2007] IEHC 4; [2007] 2 I.R. 696 at 706. Cf. also the comments of Fennelly J. in *Maha Lingam v Health Service Executive* [2005] IESC 89 made in the context of a claim for damages which, in part, relied on the Protection of Employees (Fixed-Term Work) Act 2003.

[43]   [1990] I.L.R.M. 560.

[44]   [1972] I.R. 330.

[45]   [1972] I.R. 241.

but the judgments also stress that rights derived from the Constitution must be safeguarded by remedies to be provided by the courts."[46]

18–17   O'Hanlon J. then concluded that:

"The constitutional right to earn one's livelihood by any lawful means carries with it the entitlement to be protected against any unlawful activity on the part of another person which materially impairs or infringes that right."[47]

In the event, as the defendant had engaged in unlawful activity which significantly impaired the plaintiff's exercise of her constitutional right to earn a livelihood, O'Hanlon J. granted an injunction restraining the defendant from carrying on business as an unlicensed operator.

18–18   In future, therefore, the answer to the question of whether breach of statutory duty gives rise to an action in damages may depend not on the presumed legislative intent, as ascertained by a construction of the relevant statutory provisions, but rather on the issue of whether the absence of such a remedy would infringe the constitutional rights of the plaintiff. It is also critical to this question that the plaintiff has no other remedy realistically available to him.[48]

B. Breach of Constitutional Rights

18–19   We turn now to the more general use of the Constitution in the area of damages.[49] Article 40.3.1° provides that the State "guarantees in its laws to respect, and, as far as practicable, by its laws to defend and vindicate the personal rights of the citizen". The willingness of the courts to countenance a re-shaping of law in the light of the Constitution was nowhere more evident than in the context of torts,[50] though, as we shall see, high noon has probably passed. It must be observed, first of all, that the Constitution in general and Art.40.3.1° in particular may be used in either of two ways. The first, which will be described in Part G of this chapter, is as a device to render invalid some defence, established by statute or common law, on which a public body could otherwise rely. The other use is as a basis to establish some cause of action which would not otherwise exist. This section concentrates

---

[46]   [1990] I.L.R.M. 560 at 566. The result had already been anticipated by Barrington J. in *Irish Permanent Building Society v Caldwell (No. 2)* [1981] I.L.R.M. 242 at 254.

[47]   [1990] I.L.R.M. 560 at 566. See also, *Lovett v Gogan* [1995] 3 I.R. 132 (a case with very similar facts), where this approach was expressly affirmed by the Supreme Court. cf. *Law Society of Ireland v Carroll* [1995] 3 I.R. 145; *O'Connor v Williams* [2001] 1 I.R. 248 (relief through the criminal law, rather than by granting an injunction, more appropriate).

[48]   This point was made by the Supreme Court in *Pierce v Dublin Cemeteries Committee* [2009] IESC 47; [2010] 1 I.L.R.M. 349.

[49]   A brief interlude in which it seemed as if the European Convention on Human Rights might have a far-reaching effect on the law of negligence seems now to have passed: *Osman v United Kingdom* [1999] 1 F.L.R. 193, qualified (to the point of being overruled) by *Z v United Kingdom* (2001) 34 E.H.R.R. 97.

[50]   The best analysis of this problem is found in Binchy, "Constitutional Remedies and the Law of Torts" in O'Reilly (ed.), *Human Rights and Constitutional Law: Essays in Honour of Brian Walsh* (Dublin: Round Hall Press, 1992), pp.201–225. For an international contribution, see McLay, "Tort and Constitutional Damages" [2011] P.L. 27.

on the second usage, although, given the nature of the material, a certain degree
of overlap is inevitable.

18–20   In regard to the use of the Constitution to establish new causes of action,
there are essentially two schools of thought.[51] The first is that the Constitution
gives the courts a general licence to engage in an entire re-balancing exercise of
the competing rights involved so as to shape the existing contours of tort law[52]
(and, where necessary, to create entirely new torts)[53] in the light of constitutional
considerations. The second view is that the courts are entitled to intervene "only
where there has been a failure to implement or, where the implementation relied
on is plainly inadequate to effectuate the constitutional guarantee in question".[54]
There was a time in the 1980s when the first school of thought seemed to be in the
ascendancy, but the second view now seems firmly established.

18–21   In any case, the jurisprudence in this field, dealing with awards of damages
for breach of constitutional rights, starts with the much-quoted dictum of Ó Dálaigh
C.J. for the Supreme Court in *State (Quinn) v Ryan*,[55] where he said:

> "It was not the intention of the Constitution in guaranteeing the fundamental
> rights of the citizens that these rights should be set at nought or circumvented.
> The intention was that rights of substance were being assured to the individual
> and that the courts were the custodians of these rights. As a necessary
> corollary, it follows that no one can with impunity set these rights at nought
> or circumvent them, and that the court's powers are as ample as the defence
> of the Constitution requires."[56]

---

[51] See now, however, the comprehensive judgments of in *W v Ireland (No. 2)* [1997] 2 I.R. 141
      and *McDonnell v Ireland* [1998] 1 I.R. 134.
[52] See, e.g. *Byrne v Ireland* [1972] I.R. 241 (state immunity from suit inconsistent with
      constitutional obligation to vindicate legal and constitutional rights); *Ryan v Ireland* [1989]
      I.R. 177 (any common law rule preventing soldiers suing the State for negligence would be
      unconstitutional); and *McKinley v Minister for Defence* [1992] 2 I.R. 333 (common law rule
      confining loss of consortium actions to husbands only would infringe equality guarantee in
      Art.40.1, and hence the cause of action must be extended so as to permit wives to sue for
      loss of consortium).
[53] See, e.g. *Kearney v Minister for Justice* [1986] I.R. 116; *Kennedy v Ireland* [1987] I.R. 587;
      Healy v Minister for Defence, unreported, High Court, July 7, 1994; *Lovett v Gogan* [1995] 3
      I.R. 132 at 152; *Walsh v Ireland*, unreported, Supreme Court, November 30, 1994; and *Sinnott
      v Minister for Education* [2001] 2 I.R. 545.
[54] *Hanrahan v Merck, Sharp and Dohme (Ireland) Ltd* [1988] I.L.R.M. 626 at 636 per Henchy
      J. See also, *Murphy v Ireland* [1996] 2 I.L.R.M. 461 at 467 per Carroll J. and *Grant v Roche
      Products (Ireland) Ltd* [2008] IESC 35 per Hardiman J. However, in *McDonnell v Ireland*
      [1998] 1 I.R. 134, Keane J. said of Henchy J.'s comments in *Hanrahan* that there was nothing
      in this passage "… to suggest that where a plaintiff is obliged to have recourse to an action
      for breach of a constitutional right, because the existing corpus of tort law affords him no
      remedy, or an inadequate remedy, that action cannot in turn be described as an action in tort,
      albeit a tort not hitherto recognised by the law, within the meaning of, and for the purpose of,
      the [Statute of Limitations 1957]". Cf. However, the comments of Barrington J. in the same
      case (especially his remark, at 148, that "constitutional rights should not be regarded as wild
      cards which can be played at any time to defeat all existing rules") which effectively endorse
      the views of Henchy J.
[55] [1965] I.R. 70.
[56] [1965] I.R. 70 at 122.

18–22   This principle was further developed in *Meskell v CIÉ*.[57] Here the Supreme Court held that a plaintiff was entitled to sue his employer in damages for breach of his constitutional right to associate when he was in effect dismissed from his employment by reason of his failure to join a union. Walsh J. explained that:

> "A right guaranteed by the Constitution or granted by the Constitution can be protected by action or enforced by action even though such action may not fit into any of the ordinary forms of action in either common law or equity and ... the constitutional right carried within it its own right to a remedy or for the enforcement of it. Therefore, if a person has suffered damage by virtue of a breach of a constitutional right or the infringement of a constitutional right, that person is entitled to seek redress against the person or persons who have infringed that right ...".[58]

18–23   The real significance of *Meskell* is that it permitted a plaintiff to sue directly for damages for breaches of constitutional rights, where there was no other effective remedy available under statute or common law, even though the ordinary law did not provide for such a cause of action. While the Supreme Court subsequently clarified that the *Meskell* doctrine did not render the ordinary law of tort either unconstitutional or irrelevant,[59] it also stressed that the law of tort might also itself have to be modified in any given case, if this were necessary to ensure compliance with constitutional guarantees.[60] If, therefore, there is no existing cause of action in tort (whether at common law or by virtue of statute) or the existing tort is ineffective to protect and vindicate the constitutional right in question, then a plaintiff can sue directly for damages for breach of that right. Take, for example, *Kelly v Minister for Agriculture, Food and Forestry*[61]—a case where the plaintiff sought to sue the Minister for facilitating his prosecution for an offence of which he was innocent. Butler J. observed that if the alleged damage suffered by the plaintiff could not be redressed in tort, he would have a cause of action for breach of his constitutional right to liberty. The decision of Quirke J. in *Gray v Minister for Justice, Equality and Law Reform*,[62] where damages were awarded against the State for a breach of privacy occasioned by the leaking of confidential information by the Gardaí, is in the same vein.

18–24   Further examples from diverse fields of law where damages have been awarded for a breach of constitutional rights include: *Kearney v Minister for Justice*[63] (where Costello J. awarded the plaintiff prisoner damages for breach of his constitutional right to communicate when his mail was not delivered); *Kennedy v Ireland*[64] (where Hamilton P. awarded the plaintiffs damages for the invasion of their constitutional right to privacy as a result of unauthorised interception of their

---

[57]   [1973] I.R. 121.

[58]   [1973] I.R. 121 at 132–133.

[59]   See, e.g. *Hanrahan v Merck, Sharp & Dohme* [1988] I.L.R.M. 626; *McDonnell v Ireland* [1998] 1 I.R. 134.

[60]   See, e.g. *McKinley v Minister for Defence* [1992] 2 I.R. 333 (where the limits of common law of tort of action for loss of consortium were extended so as to make the tort gender neutral in order to comply with the equality guarantee in Art.40.1).

[61]   [2001] IEHC 86.

[62]   [2007] IEHC 52; [2007] 2 I.R. 654.

[63]   [1986] I.R. 116.

[64]   [1987] I.R. 587.

telephone conversations); *Conway v Irish National Teachers' Organisation*[65] (where the Supreme Court awarded damages against a teacher's union who had organised an unlawful and prolonged school strike for breach of the plaintiff's constitutional right to free primacy education); *Healy v Minister for Defence*[66] (where Barron J. awarded an army officer who was held to have been unfairly overlooked for promotion damages for breach of his constitutional right to fair procedures); *Walsh v Ireland*[67] (where the Supreme Court held that a wrongful arrest constituted "a breach of his constitutional right to liberty [Article 40.4.1° of the Constitution] and to his good name [Article 40.3.2°]"; *Sinnott v Minister for Education*[68] (where the Supreme Court upheld an award of damages to an autistic boy in circumstances where the State had failed adequately to meet its constitutional obligation to provide him with adequate primary education, contrary to Art.42.4); *Gulyas v Minister for Justice, Equality and Law Reform*[69] (where damages were awarded by Carroll J. to the plaintiff who was refused leave to enter the State, in breach of her constitutional right to fair procedures); *Delargy v Minister for the Environment*[70] (where Murphy J. held that an action based on a breach of Arts 40.1 and 40.3[71] would lie against the Minister by reason of the exclusion of certain categories of individual from insurance cover); *Redmond v Minister for Environment (No. 2)*[72] (where Herbert J. awarded damages to the plaintiff in respect of the—as it happens—minimal loss which he suffered by reason of the operation of an unconstitutional statute); *O'Donoghue v Legal Aid Board*[73] (damages awarded for two years' delay in granting a legal aid certificate, the delay being characterised as a breach of a constitutional right to legal aid[74]; and *Herrity v Independent Newspapers Ltd*[75] (damages awarded for egregious breach of the plaintiff's right to privacy).

18–25 It will be immediately appreciated—especially having regard to the large number of individual rights which merit constitutional protection and the relative frequency with which these rights are infringed both by the State or private individuals[76]—that these are dangerous developments. They could readily lead to the complete circumvention of the traditional restrictions imposed by the law of torts (for example, limitations requiring proof of negligence and so forth).[77] Accordingly, it might not be altogether surprising if, in order to avoid the creation

---

[65] [1991] 2 I.R. 305.
[66] Unreported, High Court, Barron J., July 7, 1994.
[67] Unreported, Supreme Court, November 30, 1994.
[68] [2000] IEHC 148; [2001] 2 I.R. 545.
[69] [2001] IEHC 100; [2001] 3 I.R. 216.
[70] [2005] IEHC 94; [2006] IEHC 267.
[71] In his substantive judgment Murphy J. also suggested that there may have been a breach of Art.15.2.1°.
[72] [2004] IEHC 24; [2006] 3 I.R. 1.
[73] [2004] IEHC 413; [2006] 4 I.R. 204.
[74] But the notion that legal aid is part of constitutional justice is controversial: see paras 14–54 to 14–56. The decision might have been cast as a delay in determining the claim, and so as a breach of an existing, statutory right to legal aid.
[75] [2008] IEHC 249.
[76] A plaintiff may, of course, recover damages in an appropriate case against a *private* defendant, for "uniquely the Irish Constitution confers a right of action for breach of constitutional rights against persons other than the State and its officials": *PH v John Murphy and Sons Ltd* [1987] I.R. 621 at 626 per Costello J. See also, *Grant v Roche Products (Ireland) Ltd* [2008] IESC 35; and *Herrity v Independent Newspapers Ltd* [2008] IEHC 249.
[77] See the comments of Henchy J. in *Hanrahan v Merck, Sharpe and Dohme Ltd* [1988] I.L.R.M. 626 at 636. See generally, McMahon and Binchy, *The Irish Law of Torts* (2000), pp.8–25.

of such an alternative system of quasi-tort law, we were to witness some form of judicial checks on the emergence of such a strict liability system.[78] One example of this would occur if the courts were to move away from the present strict liability system in actions for breach of constitutional rights in favour of some *via media* requiring proof of fault or knowledge of illegality. There is already a hint of this in some judgments.[79]

18–26 Again, consistently with this strand of judicial thinking, it appears that a plea of breach of constitutional rights cannot be used to circumvent the inherent limitations of the law of torts or the quasi-immunities enjoyed by persons discharging public office, if these limitations or immunities are in themselves justifiable by reference to accepted constitutional values. This emerges from the Supreme Court's decision in *Pine Valley Developments Ltd v Minister for the Environment*.[80] Here, the plaintiffs sued for damages in respect of a breach of their property rights following a ruling by the Supreme Court that a planning permission granted to them by the defendant Minister was invalid. However, Finlay C.J. observed that "… the State may have to balance its protection of the right as against other obligations arising from regard for the common good".[81]

18–27 In effect, the court appears to have created a quasi-immunity in favour of persons discharging public duties affecting the rights or liberties of others, thus effectively emasculating the potential scope of liability for breach of constitutional rights in this area. But what is the explanation for such immunity? Finlay C.J. said

---

[78] Compare. the comments of Binchy, "Constitutional Remedies and the Law of Torts" in O'Reilly (ed.), *Human Rights and Constitutional Law: Essays in Honour of Brian Walsh* (1992), pp.214–215: "In cases where a court holds that a defendant was not under a duty of care relative to the plaintiff, it is doing more than merely relieving the defendant of liability: it is holding that broad considerations of social and economic policy warrant the establishment of immunity in these circumstances … Of course, the determination in negligence proceedings that the case is one involving immunity from liability, on the basis of an absence of a duty of care can, and should, have no *necessary* implication that a similar determination should apply in the context of infringement of constitutional rights; but the public policy considerations leading to such a determination would in most instances have required the court to address the constitutional dimension, at least tacitly. A decision not to impose a duty of care in negligence is not lightly taken, without regard to the probable aftershocks throughout the legal system."

[79] See, e.g. *Moyne v Londonderry Port and Harbour Commissioners* [1986] I.R. 299, where Costello J. said (without elaborating) that the infliction of pecuniary loss by a State agent in the course of an illegal act did not of itself establish an infringement of the constitutional right to earn a livelihood; and *An Blascaod Mór Teo v Commissioners of Public Works (No. 4)* [2000] 3 I.R. 565 where the passing of a statute subsequently found to be unconstitutional did not, without more, justify the awarding of damages. In this regard the Irish courts might well be influenced by the attitude taken by the Court of Justice in the *Factortame* and *Brasserie du Pecheur* litigation with regard to State liability for infringement of the EC Treaty (discussed in H & M, paras 18–172 to 18–182). As against this, it should be noted that in (the admittedly very different) context of the exclusion of unconstitutionally obtained evidence, liability is strict and there is no good faith exception: *The People (DPP) v Kenny* [1990] 2 I.R. 110. Although the comments of Barrington J. in *Duff v Minister for Agriculture and Food* [1997] 2 I.R. 22 threw some doubt on the position adopted by Costello J. in *Moyne*, the Supreme Court clarified (per Fennelly J.) in *Glencar Explorations Plc v Mayo County Council (No. 2)* [2001] 1 I.R. 84 at 150 that it was not appropriate "to treat liability for damages as automatically flowing from a mistake of law".

[80] [1987] I.R. 23. See, to like effect, *W v Ireland (No. 2)* [1997] 2 I.R. 141.

[81] [1987] I.R. 23 at 38, quoting from the judgment of O'Higgins C.J. in *Moynihan v Greensmyth* [1977] I.R. 56 at 71.

that, were it otherwise, this would lead to "an inevitable paralysis of the capacity for decisive action in the administration of public affairs".[82] But this reasoning seems contrary to modern principles of liability. In most other areas of tort law, the imposition of higher standards is viewed as salutary, and several immunities in both public and private law have disappeared.[83] Moreover, where the doctrine of proportionality is applied to alleged breaches of constitutional rights, concepts such as bad faith and reasonableness could have been utilised within a proportionality test. This would have mitigated the possible harshness and stultifying effects on public administration of strict liability.[84]

18–28   A question of considerable practical and theoretical importance is whether, when a plaintiff's constitutional rights have been infringed by conduct which also amounts to a tort, the plaintiff may avoid the usual statutory periods of limitation by casting their action as being for the breach of constitutional rights. The Supreme Court was equivocal on this issue in *McDonnell v Ireland*.[85] In this case the plaintiff had forfeited his civil service post in 1974 pursuant to s.34 of the Offences Against the State Act 1939, following his conviction for membership of an illegal organisation. In 1991,[86] this provision was found to be unconstitutional in separate proceedings and it was only then that the plaintiff brought an action claiming damages for breach of constitutional rights. However, the Supreme Court held that insofar as he had a cause of action under the Constitution it was nonetheless statute barred, since this form of action was an action in tort, at least for the purposes of the Statute of Limitations.[87] Nor could it be suggested that there

---

[82]   [1987] I.R. 23 at 38.

[83]   Take, for instance, the principles of liability in general or professional negligence. In *Roche v Peilow* [1985] I.R. 232 the Supreme Court held that a solicitor was guilty of professional negligence, even though he had not departed from what was then accepted conveyancing practice, because he ought to have realised (per Henchy J. at 254) "that the practice in question was fraught with danger for his client and was readily avoidable or remediable". The thinking here is that the imposition of such liability will have a salutary effect on professional standards and will ensure that solicitors (and other professionals) are sufficiently careful in the discharge of their duties. Yet cases such as *Pine Valley* and *Glencar (No. 2)* show no willingness to accept that the potential imposition of such liability for negligent administrative errors might have a similar effect on administrators and others discharging public functions or quasi-judicial duties. As against this, one consideration here is that in the case of independent professional professions, a successful damages claim may have a more direct impact than in the case of a public servant: cf. the comments of Hardiman J. in *Shortt v Garda Commissioner* [2007] 4 I.R. 587.

[84]   See, e.g. *Devoy v Ireland* [2004] IEHC 404; [2004] 4 I.R. 481 (searches carried out by Gardaí under s.26(2) of the Misuse of Drugs Act 1977 in "a proportionate, reasonable, proper and constitutional manner").

[85]   [1998] 1 I.R. 134.

[86]   *Cox v Ireland* [1992] 2 I.R. 503.

[87]   Thus, referring to *Kennedy v Ireland* [1987] I.R. 587, Keane J. acknowledged in *McDonnell* ([1998] 1 I.R. 134 at 157–158) that "even in the absence of a written constitution, such a novel growth might, for all one knows, have flourished steadily in this jurisdiction. The fact that it did so in the form of an action for infringement of a constitutional right does not prevent it ... from being classified as a civil wrong: indeed, I do not know of any other category to which it could be assigned. Specifically, it can be classified as a civil wrong which is not a breach of contract but which is remediable by an action for unliquidated damages and/or an injunction". Both Barrington and Barron JJ. expressed some reserve on this point, with the former saying that it was not necessary to decide for the purposes of this case whether "all breaches of constitutional right are torts within the meaning of the Statute of Limitations. No

was any policy reason why a different limitation period should apply to actions for breach of constitutional rights.[88]

C. Statutory Right to Compensation

18–29   We have seen that, at common law, there is no general right to obtain compensation or damages in respect of administrative decisions which have been properly taken within jurisdiction: any right to compensation depends upon the action being tortious. And, even then, it may be that there is a defence by virtue of the principle (explained in paras 11–68 to 11–70) that where a statute authorises the doing of an act, no action will lie, provided that the damage was inevitable, given the act authorised.

18–30   However, torts apart, a right to compensation in respect of certain administrative decisions has often been granted by way of specific statute. Such a statutory right has been established, for example: where land has been acquired by an administrative body[89]; where the value of land has been reduced by certain types of planning decisions; or where a preservation order has been imposed under the National Monuments Acts 1930–2004. (Naturally, if the damage which materialises is not within the scope of the statutory claim, then no compensation may be recovered on this score; though it may well happen that an alternative action will lie in tort.[90]) There are many administrative decisions which affect legal rights or interests in respect of which no statutory right to compensation of this type exists: for example, the power of a local authority to require measures to be taken to prevent water pollution[91] or to order the demolition of a dangerous house[92]; and the refusal of most types of planning permission[93] fall into this category. It would be out of place to provide a full list of administrative decisions in respect of which

---

doubt the terms have been used as interchangeable by judges when the distinction was not of any great importance": [1998] 1 I.R. 134 at 147.

[88] Keane J. cited the policy reasons underlying the Statutes of Limitation identified by Finlay C.J. in *Tuohy v Courtney* [1994] 3 I.R. 1, adding (at 160): "I can see no reason why an actress sunbathing in her back garden whose privacy is intruded upon by a long-range camera should defer proceedings until her old age to provide herself with a nest egg, while a young man or woman rendered a paraplegic by a drunken motorist must be cut off from suing after three years. The policy considerations identified [in *Tuohy v Courtney*] are applicable to actions such as the present as much as to actions founded on tort in the conventional sense."

[89] See generally, McDermott and Woulfe, *Compulsory Purchase and Compensation in Ireland: Law and Practice* (Dublin: Butterworths, 1992).

[90] *Red Cow Service Station Ltd v Bord Gáis Éireann* (1985) I.L.T. (N.S) 15. In *Collins v Gypsum Industries Ltd* [1975] I.R. 321, the plaintiffs had claimed damages for personal injuries under the Mineral Development Act 1940. The Supreme Court held, however, that the 1940 Act provided for a scheme of compensation in respect of damage to land caused by mining operations and it did not extend to personal injuries. The proper forum for pursuing such a claim for personal injuries was that provided by the ordinary courts.

[91] Local Government (Water Pollution) Act 1977 ss.12(5) and 13(2) (as substituted by Local Government (Water Pollution) (Amendment) Act 1990 s.10) (permitting a local authority to take such steps as seem to it necessary and recouping the cost from the person whose act, omission or disregard of a notice issued under s.12 necessitated the steps in question).

[92] Local Government (Sanitary Services) Act 1964 ss.2 and 3.

[93] Planning and Development Act 2000 s.191.

no compensation is payable,[94] but the general principle on which the Oireachtas appears to operate is that no provision for compensation is made in respect of administrative decisions which can be objectively shown to be in the public interest, unless this would impose an undue burden on the individual citizen.

18–31 These principles may, however, have to be re-examined in the light of the provisions of Art.40.3 and Art.43 of the Constitution. Article 40.3 requires the State by its laws to protect "as best it may from unjust attack" and in the case "of injustice done" to vindicate the property rights of every citizen. Article 43, while protecting the institution of private property rights, permits the delimitation of such rights "with a view to reconciling their exercise with the exigencies of the common good".[95] The interpretation of these separate provisions is fraught with uncertainty, but the following propositions can be put forward:

1. If the action of the State authorities can be justified by reference to Art.43, then such action cannot by definition be regarded as an "unjust attack" on the individual's property rights as protected by Art.40.3.[96]
2. It is for the courts to say whether the delimitation of property rights is actually required by social justice and the exigencies of the common good, i.e. whether this general regulation of particular property rights can be justified under Art.43.[97]
3. The courts will test the validity of any such interference with property rights by reference to the principle of proportionality.[98]
4. It is not clear that compensation is a sine qua non of interference with property rights.[99]

18–32 These questions were examined by McGovern J. in *Rafferty v Minister for Agriculture, Food and Rural Development*,[100] where the constitutionality of an administrative scheme to compensate farmers for the culling of their flocks was at issue. During the foot and mouth crisis of 2001, when it was feared that an outbreak of the disease would occur in Ireland (as well as in the United Kingdom), flocks of sheep in border areas were culled, even though they were uninfected. Section

---

[94] See, e.g. National Monuments Acts 1930–2004 (imposition of preservation orders on national monuments).
[95] See generally, Hogan and Whyte, *JM Kelly: The Irish Constitution*, 4th edn (Dublin: Lexis Nexis Butterworths, 2003), pp.1969–2028.
[96] *Dreher v Irish Land Commission* [1984] I.L.R.M. 94; *O'Callaghan v Commissioners of Public Works* [1985] I.L.R.M. 364; *Lawlor v Minister for Agriculture* [1990] 1 I.R. 356. In *Chadwick v Fingal County Council* [2007] IESC 49; [2008] 3 I.R. 66 the Supreme Court held that there was no "unjust attack" on the plaintiff's property rights as a result of the accepted interpretation of s.63 of the Land Clauses Consolidation Act 1845.
[97] *Buckley v Attorney General* [1950] I.R. 64; *Electricity Supply Board v Gormley* [1985] I.R. 129.
[98] *Tuohy v Courtney* [1994] 3 I.R. 1; *Daly v Revenue Commissioners* [1995] 3 I.R. 1; *In re Article 26 and the Planning and Development Bill 1999* [2000] IESC 20; [2000] 2 I.R. 321; *In re Article 26 and the Health (Amendment) (No.2) Bill 2004* [2005] IESC 7; [2005] 1 I.R. 105.
[99] See *In re Article 26 and the Planning and Development Bill 1999* [2000] IESC 20; [2000] 2 I.R. 321 at 350; O'Donnell, "Property Rights in the Irish Constitution: Rights for Rich People or a Pillar of a Free Society" in Carolan and Doyle (eds), *The Irish Constitution: Governance and Values* (Dublin: Thomson Round Hall, 2008).
[100] [2008] IEHC 344.

17 of the Diseases of Animals Act 1966 permits the Minister to exercise a power of culling but requires that compensation be paid. An independent valuer assessed the compensation payable, which was more than the full market value of the flocks, but somewhat less than the consequential loss which was attendant upon a full replacement of the flock (e.g. the new animals might not have the same weaning rates as the culled animals or would be deprived of more experienced mentors to guide them away from the cliff's edge). As a result, the plaintiffs challenged the constitutionality of the scheme, which they alleged infringed their property rights. McGovern J. accepted that the State was obliged "to provide a scheme which is fair and reasonable and proportionate to the situation", but upheld the constitutionality of the scheme:

> "When calamities occur – whether they are natural disasters or outbreaks of disease in the human or animal population – it is inevitable that this will bring suffering and hardship on those who are affected. It is a matter for the State to take such steps as it can to ameliorate the effects of such calamities consistent with available resources ... If, as a matter of statutory provision or constitutional law, the State was obliged to compensate farmers by way of full consequential loss, this could have enormous implications for the Exchequer, and impose a serious and disproportionate burden on the taxpayer ... The purpose of such a scheme is to minimise the hardship suffered by those sheep farmers who, in this case, had to permit their flocks to be culled. In looking at the proportionality of the measures taken, one is entitled to consider that there are many other people who suffered financial losses as a result of the outbreak of foot and mouth disease for whom there was no scheme of compensation."[101]

Following the general constitutional precept, in *Arthur v Kerry County Council*[102] the High Court (McGuinness J.) stated that where the right of an applicant to compensation under a statutory scheme is at issue, the statute should be interpreted in favour of the property owner.[103]

18–33 The machinery for assessing compensation is also of some importance. Thus in *Electricity Supply Board v Gormley*,[104] the Supreme Court held that, where a statutory scheme of compensation was necessary to compensate landowners for an interference with their land, the constitutional property rights also required that such legislation provide for assessment by an independent arbitrator.

D. Liability for the Negligent Exercise of Discretionary Public Powers

18–34 As noted, public authorities are subject to broadly the same common law of tortious liability as private individuals or companies.[105] They (or their servants or

---

[101] [2008] IEHC 344 at para.38.
[102] [2000] 3 I.R. 407.
[103] See *Grange Developments v Dublin City Council* [1986] I.R. 246.
[104] [1985] I.R. 129.
[105] See, e.g. *Larkin v Joosub and Dublin City Council* [2006] IEHC 51; [2007] 1 I.R. 521.

agents) must (to take examples of what may be called straightforward, operational torts) drive carefully; observe the appropriate duties of an employer or occupier; or, if they dig a trench, ensure that it is guarded so that no one will fall into it. However, the negligent exercise of a statutory discretionary power, while it frequently brings in some operational elements, is also often concerned with discretion or policy (we are not distinguishing the two here).

18–35 That said, many of the cases decided so far fall within a rather small sub-field of the exercise of discretion, namely the regulation of private, commercial activity such as building and planning matters. This means that the wider aspects of a potentially vast field remain uncharted: we have not yet gone much beyond the range of policy decisions similar to those which may arise in the private law field where, for instance a hospital's policy is not to adopt a particular surgical technique, or a stockbroker's policy is not to buy a share in a particular type of undertaking. Thus, we have not yet encountered cases raising broader issues such as, for example, situations in which a victim of a motor accident claims that this accident was caused by the highway authority's failure to improve a junction[106]; or a trader argues that the decision to turn the road on which his shop is located into a one-way street was negligent, thereby causing him financial loss; or, to go even further, an exporter claims that a Government decision to withdraw export credit insurance, in respect of a country with which the exporter is trading was negligently arrived at. So far, however, as one can tell, extrapolating from the case law which we do have, it looks almost certain that this type of claim would be unsuccessful.[107]

18–36 It is as well to identify the underlying factors which make the shaping of the law in this area so different and difficult and to explain why it is so unsatisfactory. In the first place, as a matter of tort law, the damage caused by invalid administrative action will usually result in pure economic loss, without any physical damage. Secondly, often, the complaint will be that a public body has failed to prevent some third party from inflicting loss on the complainant. Thus the obligation which the plaintiff claims has been broken would be a duty to take positive action. Next, it may be thought that the imposition of discipline through the courts on a public body may have a chilling effect on the quality of the decisions of administrators,[108] who must be allowed a "margin of appreciation" to balance divergent factors, including economy, the allocation of scarce resources, and fairness to all members of the community and not just the plaintiff. And all this is at least as true where the discipline concerned is liability in tort rather than a finding of invalidity (in the context of the abuse of discretionary powers),[109] where we have already noted the major policy premise that a decision assigned to a public body should not be claimed by the judiciary.[110]

---

[106] Though see *Stovin v Wise* [1996] 3 All E.R. 801.

[107] See paras 18–60 to 18–67.

[108] This reasoning was very much to the fore in the judgments of Finlay C.J. in *Pine Valley Developments Ltd v Minister for Environment* [1987] I.R. 23; Costello J. in *W v Ireland (No. 2)* [1997] 2 I.R. 141; and Keane C.J. and Fennelly J. in *Glencar Explorations Plc v Mayo County Council (No. 2)* [2001] 1 I.R. 84.

[109] See above, paras 15–03 to 15–11.

[110] See generally, Woolf, Jowell and Le Sueur, *De Smith's Judicial Review*, 6th edn (London: Sweet & Maxwell, 2007), paras 19–65 to 19–80.

18–37 The law in this area has certainly been affected by these doubts and difficulties. In certain contexts, the courts used to be reluctant to hold that public authorities owe the general public a duty of care[111] and, even in the case of ultra vires acts, the courts are unwilling to impose liability where these public functions had been discharged in good faith.[112] Secondly, it is now evident that the question of whether a duty of care is to be imposed on the public body for the negligent exercise of a discretionary power depends, at least in part, upon the relevant statutory context.[113] This, in turn, has tended to assimilate the test for negligence to that of liability for breach of statutory duty, namely, was the plaintiff a member of the class of persons which the statute was designed to protect? Finally, it must be borne in mind in any analysis of the case law that the different approaches to this problem and the judicial pronouncements thereon cannot always be reconciled.

18–38 The issue as to what extent public bodies may be liable for the negligent exercise of their discretionary powers, as contrasted with a mere operational decision or action, is one which has beset the courts of the common law world for the last 35 years or so and, in particular, since the House of Lords landmark decision in *Anns v Merton L.B.C.*[114]

18–39 A wide variety of approaches have been taken by the Irish courts. In the first major case of its kind, *Siney v Dublin Corporation*,[115] the plaintiff had been allocated a flat by the defendant. It transpired that it was unfit for human habitation and that the inspection which had taken place was inadequate. In finding that the local authority was negligent, the Supreme Court appears to have applied the standard common law principles of liability—the neighbour principle enunciated in *Donoghue v Stevenson*[116]; so that, at first sight it might seem as if this judgment were a simple case of operational negligence (or more accurately, landlord's liability). However, what lifts it out of this category is that at common law,[117] a landlord was under no obligation, tortious or otherwise, to ensure that domestic premises were sound or fit for purpose. As a result, in an innovative judgment, this obligation was

---

[111] This is true, for example, of attempts to impose a duty of care upon regulators: see, e.g. *Pine Valley Developments Ltd v Minister for the Environment* [1987] I.R. 23; *Yuen Kun Yue v Attorney General for Hong Kong* [1988] A.C. 175; *McMahon v Ireland* [1988] I.L.R.M. 610.

[112] See, e.g. *Pine Valley Developments Ltd v Minister for the Environment* [1987] I.R. 23; *Rowling v Takaro Properties Ltd* [1988] A.C. 473; *Jones v Department of Employment* [1989] Q.B. 1; *Beatty v Rent Tribunal* [2005] IESC 66; [2006] 2 I.R. 191 per Fennelly J.

[113] This was the approach adopted by the House of Lords in *Governors of Peabody Donation Fund v Sir Lindsay Parkinson and Co.* [1985] A.C. 210 and *Stovin v Wise* [1996] 3 All E.R. 801; by McCarthy J. in *Sunderland v McGreavey* [1990] I.L.R.M. 658; by Keane J. in *Convery v Dublin County Council* [1996] 3 I.R. 153; and by Keane C.J. in *Glencar Explorations Plc v Mayo County Council (No. 2)* [2001] 1 I.R. 84.

[114] [1978] A.C. 726. *Anns* was substantially reversed in *Peabody Donation Fund v Sir Lindsay Parkinson & Co* [1985] A.C. 210. For the fate of *Anns*, see H & M, paras 18–122 18–127.

[115] [1980] I.R. 400. For an account of *Siney*, see Clark and Kerr, "Council Housing, Implied Terms and Negligence – A Critique of *Siney v. Dublin Corporation*" (1980) 15 Ir. Jur. (N.S) 32. See also, *Coleman v Dundalk U.D.C.*, unreported, Supreme Court, July 17, 1985; *Burke v Dublin Corporation* [1990] 1 I.R. 18; and *Howard v Dublin Corporation* [1996] 2 I.R. 235 at 239. It may be noted that s.22(1) of the Housing (Miscellaneous Provisions) Act 1992 now excludes liability in these circumstances.

[116] [1932] A.C. 562.

[117] But, see now, Residential Tenancies Act 2004 s.12.

deduced from an analysis of a housing authority's (i.e. local authority's) general obligations under the (then) Housing Act 1966.

18–40   The next judgment[118] requiring attention is that of Costello J. in *Ward v McMaster*.[119] In this case the plaintiff had purchased a new house which turned out to be grossly sub-standard structurally and a health risk. Proceedings were then instituted against the local authority (as well as the builder, with which proceedings we are not concerned). The plaintiff had applied to the Council for a loan of IR£12,000 under the provisions of the Housing Act 1966 to enable him to purchase the house.[120] The Council sent a valuer who reported that it was in good repair and that its market value was IR£25,000. Costello J. found that the valuer had no professional qualification relating to building construction. There were two aspects of the claim against the local authority. First, the plaintiff alleged that this valuation was negligently carried out and that the Council was vicariously liable. However, the court held that the Council had sent a valuer who was employed simply to place a market value on the property, and accordingly, the valuer was not negligent.

18–41   However, secondly, the plaintiff successfully alleged that the Council was directly (not vicariously) liable, in that it had broken the common law duty of care owed to the plaintiff borrower in carrying out its statutory functions. The Council had a statutory power under the 1966 Act to grant a loan to the plaintiff and a statutory duty by virtue of the relevant regulations to inspect the property before granting a loan. In carrying out the inspection, a duty to act with care arose, a duty which was broken by the Council's authorising an inspection by someone who lacked the necessary qualification to ascertain reasonably discoverable defects. Costello J. had no doubt that a common law duty of care, based on the principle established in *Donoghue v Stevenson*, might exist when statutory functions were being performed. Following a review of the relevant authorities Costello J. concluded that the relevant principles in cases of this kind were as follows:

> "(a) When deciding whether a local authority exercising statutory functions is under a common law duty of care the court must firstly ascertain whether a relationship of proximity existed between the parties such that in the reasonable contemplation of the authority, carelessness on their part might cause loss. But all the circumstances of the case must in addition be considered, including the statutory provisions under which the authority is acting. Of particular significance in this connection is the purpose for which the statutory powers were conferred and whether or not the plaintiff is in the class of persons which the statute was designed to assist.
>
> (b) It is material in all cases for the court in reaching its decision on the

---

[118]   The major decision of the Supreme Court which immediately followed *Siney—Weir v Dún Laoghaire Corporation* [1983] I.R. 242—has now been overruled: in *Convery v Dublin County Council* [1996] 3 I.R. 153, Keane J. said that *Weir* was "clearly irreconcilable" with the subsequent decision in *Sunderland v McGreavey* [1990] I.L.R.M. 658.

[119]   [1985] I.R. 29 (HC).

[120]   Section 39 of the Housing Act 1966 (repealed by the Housing (Miscellaneous Provisions) Act 1992) provided that a local authority may lend money to a person for the purpose of acquiring or constructing a house.

existence and scope of the alleged duty to consider whether it is just and reasonable that a common law duty of care as alleged should in all the circumstances exist."[121]

18–42   Applying these principles to the facts, Costello J. concluded that, although the plaintiff did not expressly inform any member of the Council's staff, he was relying on their valuation. Further, although the Council carried out the valuation for its own purposes and to comply with its statutory obligations, the Council ought to have been aware that it was probable that the plaintiff, a person of limited means, would not have gone to the expense of having the house examined by a professionally qualified person and would have relied on the inspection which he knew would be carried out for the purpose of the loan application. There was therefore a sufficient relationship of proximity and there was nothing in the dealings between the parties which restricted or limited the duties in any way. In particular, no warning against relying on the proposed valuation was given. As to the scope of the duty, Costello J. concluded that the Council should have ensured that the person carrying out the valuation would be competent to discover reasonably ascertainable defects which would materially affect its market value.

18–43   The judge did not attempt to draw any sharp distinction between "powers" and "duties" for the purposes of liability. He also declined to pay too much regard to the distinction between "discretionary" and "operational" decisions, concluding that the matter was essentially a question of whether it was "just and reasonable" in the circumstances that a common law duty of care as alleged should exist.

18–44   In 1988, the entire question was exhaustively examined by the Supreme Court when delivering judgment on the appeal from Costello J. in *Ward v McMaster*.[122] Henchy J. (with whom Finlay C.J. and Griffin J. concurred) considered that while the Council were plainly in breach of their public duty, it was for the plaintiffs to show that there was sufficient proximity between the parties to give rise to a duty of care. This they had done:

> "The consequences to the plaintiff of a failure on their part to value the house properly should have been anticipated by the council in view of factors such as that, in order to qualify for the loan, the plaintiff had to show that he was unable to obtain the loan from a commercial agency and that his circumstances were such that he would otherwise need to be re-housed by the council. A borrower of that degree of indigence could not have been reasonably expected to incur the further expense of getting a structural survey of the house done."[123]

18–45   But, in *Sunderland v McGreavey*,[124] the plaintiffs had purchased a house from a builder, who was the owner of the site. When the house proved to be hopelessly defective and unfit for human habitation due to flooding and a defective drainage system, the plaintiffs sued the local authority on the ground that it was

---

[121] [1985] I.R. 29 at 49–50.
[122] [1988] I.R. 337.
[123] [1988] I.R. 337 at 342.
[124] [1990] I.L.R.M. 658.

the authority which had granted both planning and retention permission for the house, and as such they owed him a duty of care. The Supreme Court dismissed the plaintiff's claim. In holding that planning authorities did not owe purchasers or occupiers a duty of care to ensure that a particular dwelling was structurally sound and suitable for human habitation, McCarthy J. distinguished between cases such as *Siney* and *Ward* on the one hand and the present case on the other:

> "The fundamental difference between what may be called planning and housing legislation is that the first is regulatory according to the requirements of the proper planning and development, but the second is a provision in a social context for those who are unable to provide for themselves. If they are unable to provide for themselves, then the duty on the provider reaches the role that would be taken by professional advisers engaged on behalf of the beneficiary. This is in marked contrast to the watchdog role that is created under the Planning Act, a watchdog role that is for the benefit of the public at large."[125]

18–46 If the plaintiff's argument were correct, McCarthy J. continued, it would mean that planning authorities and An Bord Pleanála would be under a duty of care to inspect dwelling houses before deciding to grant permission. These potential consequences were mentioned not "*in terrorem*", but rather to seek to identify "on a reasonable approach the intention of the legislature in enacting the relevant parts of the 1963 Act". The judge concluded that:

> "The Act in conferring statutory powers on planning authorities imposed on them a duty towards the public at large. In my view, in conferring these powers, the Oireachtas did not include a purpose of protecting persons who occupy buildings erected in the functional area of planning authorities, from the sort of damage which the plaintiffs suffered. That being so, the Council, in the exercise of those powers, owed no duty of care at common law to the plaintiffs."[126]

18–47 In *Duff v Minister for Agriculture*,[127] in the Supreme Court, the question centred on whether the Minister might be liable in damages in respect of his failure to allocate a milk quota to the development farmers whom he had promised to assist. Strangely, the minority appears to have characterised the situation as involving a policy decision which the Minister had taken reasonably.[128] By contrast, and it is suggested, more realistically, the majority drew a distinction between the Minister's decision to help the plaintiffs (which was a policy decision but one which had been taken in the plaintiffs' favour) and the unlawful means by which he sought to implement that decision. The critical reasoning is in the following extract from Barrington J.'s judgment:

> "But once the Minister had decided to give them a reference quantity out of the national quota the Minister had a duty, and they had a right to expect,

---

[125] [1990] I.L.R.M. 658 at 663.
[126] [1990] I.L.R.M. 658 at 663.
[127] [1997] 2 I.R. 22.
[128] O'Flaherty, Blayney and Barrington JJ.; Hamilton C.J. and Keane J. dissented.

that the Minister would implement this decision in a lawful manner. The Minister, in breach of his duty and of their rights, attempted to implement his decision in a manner which was unlawful. As a result the plaintiffs did not obtain the special reference quantities to which they were entitled and have, in consequence, suffered damage and loss.

The trouble is that the method which the Minister chose to provide for the development farmers was unlawful. He chose this method due to a mistake of law on his part. When he discovered his mistake … it was too late … to retrieve the situation … If, as appears to be the case, the plaintiffs have suffered loss and damage as a result of the Minister's mistake of law, it appears to me to be just and proper in the circumstances of this case, that the Minister should pay them compensation."[129]

18–48 This important passage is a little unclear. The plaintiffs appear to have succeeded on the ground of something like a negligent error of law in that the Minister had misunderstood the EC Directive which he was applying. This may be classified as a special case of operational negligence as opposed to the negligent exercise of a discretionary power.[130]

18–49 The leading case in this jurisdiction is now *Glencar Explorations Plc v Mayo County Council (No. 2)*.[131] In *Glencar (No. 1)*,[132] the High Court held that the respondent had acted ultra vires in imposing a mining ban through the medium of a development plan. In *Glencar (No. 2)*, the applicant plaintiffs claimed that they suffered damage as a result of this decision. Giving the leading judgment in the Supreme Court, Keane C.J. considered the leading Irish and English jurisprudence and set a three-condition test:

"There is, in my view, no reason why courts determining whether a duty of care arises should consider themselves obliged to hold that it does, in every case where injury or damage to property was reasonably foreseeable and the notoriously difficult and elusive test of 'proximity' or 'neighbourhood' can be said to have been met, unless very powerful public policy considerations dictate otherwise. It seems to me that no injustice will be done if they are required to take the further step of considering whether, in all the circumstances, it is just and reasonable that the law should impose a duty of a given scope on the defendant for the benefit of the plaintiff, as held by Costello J. at first instance in *Ward v. McMaster.* … As Brennan J. pointed out [in *Sutherland v Heyman*][133] there is a significant risk that any other approach will result in what he called a 'massive extension of a prima facie duty of care restrained only by undefinable considerations …'."[134]

18–50 In short, a three-condition test was laid down. On the facts, the first element of the three-stage test was established: the loss was reasonably foreseeable as it

[129] [1997] 2 I.R. 22 at 77–78 (Blayney J. agreed with Barrington J.).
[130] In this sense, the judgment is comparable to *Carbury Milk Products Ltd v Minister for Agriculture* (1993) 4 *Irish Tax Reports* 492.
[131] [2001] 1 I.R. 84.
[132] [1993] 2 I.R. 237.
[133] *Sutherland* is reported at (1985) C.L.R. 424.
[134] [2001] 1 I.R. 84 at 138–139.

followed naturally from the decision to impose a mining ban. However, the second element, that of proximity, was not met, because "the powers in question were exercisable by the respondent for the benefit of the community as a whole and not for the benefit of a defined category of persons to which the applicant belonged".[135] Another relevant authority here is *Atlantic Marine v Minister for Transport*,[136] where a Code of Practice had been established by the Minister requiring all fishing vessels within a particular category to carry a life raft meeting certain specifications. Yet, many of these vessels were carrying unapproved liferafts. The plaintiff was a certified seller of life rafts to vessels. He claimed that, as a result of the failure of the Minister to enforce the requirements of the Code of Practice, it had suffered financial loss. While the applicant succeeded on other grounds, the High Court held, on *Glencar (No. 2)* principles, that the Minister owed no duty of care to the plaintiff, which operated as a lifeboat provider, in relation to the operation of the licensing system for fishing boats.

18–51   As laid down in *Glencar (No. 2)*, the third element of the test is whether imposing a duty of care would be just and reasonable. In contrast to *Ward v McMaster* and *Siney v Dublin Corporation*, on the facts in *Glencar (No. 2)*, "this was not a case in which it could reasonably be said that the applicants, in incurring the expense of their prospecting activities, could be said to have been relying on the non-negligent exercise by the respondent of its statutory powers".[137] In other words, to satisfy the third element of the test, the applicants would have to demonstrate that they "might reasonably be said to have relied on the local authority ... taking reasonable care in the exercise of the statutory powers vested in them".[138]

18–52   The second and third elements were further considered by the High Court in *Kennedy v Law Society of Ireland (No. 4)*.[139] Here, Kearns J. drew on authorities from other common law jurisdictions to form the view that the respondent body exercised its powers in the interests of the general public, not individual solicitors. Thus, the second condition was not satisfied, in that no proximity arose between the plaintiff and the agents of the respondent, who had acted under an order that

---

[135] [2001] 1 I.R. 84 at 141. See also, *Flynn v Waterford Corporation* [2004] IEHC 335 (s.95(3)(a) of the Road Traffic Act 1961, as amended, confers a discretionary power and not an obligation on a road authority, and evidences no legislative intention to confer upon an individual a right to claim for damages).

[136] [2011] 2 I.L.R.M. 12 at para.6.15.

[137] [2001] 1 I.R. 84 at 141.

[138] [2001] 1 I.R. 84 at 141. In *Cotter v Minister for Agriculture*, unreported, Supreme Court, April 1, 1993, O'Flaherty J. observed that in *Ward* the court took "an especial account of the indigency of the plaintiffs in that case, together with the obligation that rested on the local authority not to do anything to encourage the existence of houses that would be unfit for human habitation which, in turn, would have been contrary to the relevant housing legislation". See also, *Convery v Dublin County Council* [1996] 3 I.R. 153. On the other hand, in *Hanahoe v Hussey* [1998] 3 I.R. 69, Kinlen J. accepted that the actions of an (unidentifiable) individual Garda who "leaked" details of a highly sensitive Garda search of solicitors' offices in advance to the media amounted to negligence. As it was readily foreseeable that such actions would cause the plaintiffs loss and damage, the plaintiffs could bring themselves within the passages of the judgment of McCarthy J. in *Ward v McMaster* which were relied upon in respect of this operational tort. Similarly, in *Gray v Minister for Justice, Equality and Law Reform* [2007] IEHC 52; [2007] 2 I.R. 654, Quirke J. held that the Gardaí had breached their duty of care to the plaintiffs by leaking information to the media to the effect that the plaintiffs were sheltering a convicted rapist.

[139] [2005] 3 I.R. 228.

was subsequently held to have been partially ultra vires. Kearns J. also suggested that it would not be just and reasonable to impose a duty of care:

"... to find that a duty of care existed to the solicitor, or to both the public and the solicitor, would be to uphold two incompatible duties and would completely undermine the capacity of the first respondent to exert proper supervisory and regulatory control of the profession."[140]

18–53 Upholding this decision in the Supreme Court, Geoghegan J. held that "a body such as the first respondent, carrying out a public function in pursuance of a public duty, is not liable to a private individual in tort unless the authority, in so acting, has committed the tort of misfeasance in public office".[141] He was concerned that imposing a duty of care too freely would undermine public administration by moving away from the subjective fault required by the tort of misfeasance in public office, and towards an objective standard.

18–54 Also relevant is Fennelly J.'s judgment in *Beatty v Rent Tribunal*.[142] Here, the alleged loss was said to flow from a breach of constitutional justice during a rent review and not by reason of an alleged negligent exercise of a discretionary power, although the same legal framework appears to have been applied. The original decision was quashed and the plaintiffs sought damages for the loss of rental income. As to the second element—proximity—which in his view was a question of fact in each case, Fennelly J. considered it important that in *Ward v McMaster* and *Siney* the local authority had not been under any conflicting duty to the general public. Similarly, the Rent Tribunal was primarily concerned with the interests of the parties before it:

"It would be difficult to say that the applicants in the present case do not satisfy the test of proximity taken in isolation. Both landlord and tenant come into a direct relationship with the respondent once the latter is asked to review and determine a rent. It has only those two parties in contemplation. I would not go so far as to accept the submissions of counsel that performance of the respondent's function is exclusively of interest to the parties. There is a clear public interest in ensuring that rents generally are fairly set and that the law is properly interpreted in doing so ... Nonetheless, in reality, the only parties with a direct and real interest in the outcome of the proceedings of the respondent are the landlord and the tenant respectively."[143]

18–55 However, considering the third of the requirements, Fennelly J. ruled that it would not be just and reasonable to impose liability. Here, even though there was little tension with the Tribunal's duty to serve the public interest, the Tribunal owed a duty both to landlord and tenant. Fennelly J. also noted that the remedy of damages was the only one available to the plaintiffs in *Ward v McMaster* and *Siney*, whereas in the instant case, judicial review of the Tribunal and an appeal on a point of law to the High Court were available. Moreover, there was no reliance on the

---

[140] [2005] 3 I.R. 228 at 251.
[141] [2005] 3 I.R. 228 at 259.
[142] [2005] IESC 66; [2006] 2 I.R. 191.
[143] [2006] 2 I.R. 191 at 210. See similarly, the judgment of McCracken J.: [2006] 2 I.R. 191 at 219.

Tribunal as there had been in *Ward v McMaster* and *Siney*, and imposing a duty of care could be detrimental to the performance of its functions by the Tribunal:

> "The respondent is necessarily required in every case to make a choice between conflicting submissions as to the amount of the rent. If a respondent were exposed to potential claims from either landlord or tenant where it favoured the submission of one over the other, it might tend towards compromise in every case. I believe that the independence of the respondent [and, by extension, other adjudicative bodies] would potentially be compromised by the existence of such a remedy."[144]

18–56 The "just and reasonable" requirement was again considered by the High Court in *Gaffey (A Minor) v Dundalk Town Council*.[145] Here, the plaintiff had suffered an injury while playing football in a green area near his home. The lid had been lifted off a fire hydrant (presumably by local people and not employees of the respondent's fire department) located in the grassy area and the plaintiff fell into the hole. It was alleged that the lid was frequently lifted off, but the respondent was unaware of this. The plaintiff sought damages for negligence. Peart J. was satisfied that the location of the fire hydrant was reasonable, considering the purposes it might have to serve in the event of an emergency, and regulations restricting where hydrants might be located. However, Peart J. went on to consider whether it would be just and reasonable to impose a duty of care on the respondent and commented as follows:

> "It would also be relevant to consider the nature and purpose of the statutory power being exercised by the local authority in placing the hydrant where it is located. In the present case the Council are clearly obliged to place hydrants sufficiently close to houses in the area so that the fire services can be effective in an emergency. Such a duty is an important one, given the capacity for a fire to cause loss of life and serious injury. The design of the lid facilitates the easy access to the water supply in such an emergency. That would need to be balanced against the risk of possible injury by placing the hydrant on this grassed area.
>
> It cannot be reasonable for the Council to have imposed upon it a duty to ensure that the lids are at all times in place on hydrants in the town – the more so in the absence of any information being given to them that lids are being removed. The Council has in place a system of inspection of hydrants on a routine basis to ensure that they are in working order, but it is quite unreal to expect that they could inspect all these installations on a daily basis. As I have stated there is no evidence that the hydrants are inherently dangerous or dangerously located. It requires the mischievous act of an intervening party to create the hazard."[146]

18–57 At this point, it is worth recalling that even where the three considerations set down in the *Glencar (No. 2)* test—duty of care; proximity; and "just and

---

[144] [2006] 2 I.R. 191 at 214–215.

[145] [2006] IEHC 436.

[146] While *Gaffey* is as much a case concerning the private law duties of a property owner as it is about the negligent exercise of a discretionary power, it is nonetheless illuminating in respect of the "just and reasonable" requirement.

reasonable"—are satisfied, this does not of itself lead to the imposition of liability. In addition (although it may involve duplication), the plaintiff must also demonstrate: a breach of the standard of care; causation; damage; and the absence of countervailing public policy. Much of these would be common to liability in the case of a private law defendant. But there is some case law of particular relevance here. In the Supreme Court's decision in *Hayes v Minister for Finance*,[147] the plaintiff was a pillion passenger on a motorbike which had crashed after being pursued by Gardaí. Kearns J. noted that the Gardaí were vested with numerous statutory and common law powers to preserve law and order:

> "Indeed in recent years the Oireachtas has seen fit to increase the penalties for dangerous driving and speeding. The Gardaí have a clear obligation to ensure that these laws are upheld and to detect, prevent or stop any breaches thereof."[148]

18–58 It also followed that the standard of care would vary according to the circumstances:

> "In complying with these obligations it is obvious that the Gardaí may owe different standards of care in a pursuit situation depending on the particular circumstances. For example, if there are good grounds for believing the perpetrator of a recent murder or bank robbery is attempting an escape, the standard of the duty owed to such a person may obviously be less than in the case of a trivial offender, particularly if the surrounding circumstances create particular risks in continuing the pursuit."[149]

18–59 The High Court ruled that the standard of care had not been breached in the crucial part of the pursuit:

> "Unless one took the view, which I do not take, that the Gardaí in the following vehicle should have opted out of any further interest in these events by halting their car, I do not believe there was any breach of duty which the occupants of the Garda vehicle owed, either to the driver of the motorcycle, or to the plaintiff pillion passenger, over these last few miles, even if the plaintiff is deemed to be no more than an involuntary participant in events at that stage."[150]

As to public policy (a concern which is anyway dancing around many of the other requirements), in *Lockwood v Ireland*[151] the plaintiff was the complainant in a prosecution for rape, in which the prosecution case collapsed when admissions made

---

[147] [2007] IESC 8; [2007] 3 I.R. 190.

[148] [2007] IESC 8; [2007] 3 I.R. 190 at 204.

[149] [2007] IESC 8; [2007] 3 I.R. 190 at 204. See similarly, the comments of Peart J. in *Keogh v Electricity Supply Board* [2005] IEHC 286; [2005] 3 I.R. 77 at 85.

[150] [2007] IESC 8; [2007] 3 I.R. 190 at 206. The English courts have also consistently refused to countenance the suggestion that the law enforcement agencies owed victims or potential victims of crime a duty of care. See, e.g. *Hill v Chief Constable of West Yorkshire* [1989] A.C. 53; *Osman v Ferguson* [1993] 4 All E.R. 344; *X (Minors) v Bedfordshire County Council* [1995] 2 A.C. 633; *Capital and Counties Plc v Hampshire County Council* [1997] Q.B. 1004; *OLL Ltd v Secretary of State for Transport* [1997] 3 All E.R. 897.

[151] [2011] 1 I.R. 374 at paras 20–25.

by the accused in Garda custody could not be placed before the jury. It was held by the High Court (Kearns P.) that even if there had been a sufficient relationship of proximity to the plaintiff, it would be contrary to public policy to impose a duty of care towards the plaintiff on the Gardaí. In short, *Hayes, Lockwood, Beatty* and *Gaffey* indicate that the law has a number of ways of accommodating their special difficulties.

Concluding comment

18–60   To return to the issue highlighted at the outset of this Part: the major question confronting the law is how to accommodate negligence in relation to discretion or policy choices At one extreme, they could be excluded altogether. Another possibility is the requirement that, for liability or negligence in this context, the action must at least be ultra vires. This was the requirement employed by Lord Wilberforce in *Anns*,[152] which was among the first generation of common law authorities to address the problem. But *Anns* is no longer in favour and the status of the ultra vires requirement in Ireland is unclear,[153] due in no small part to the unfortunate fact that in the most recent Irish authorities, the liability of public bodies has been discussed after an initial finding that the public body in question had acted ultra vires.[154] Equally, the policy–operations distinction has not featured prominently in recent case law, nor any distinction between statutory powers and statutory functions. Instead, as noted, in cases like *Glencar (No. 2)*, the courts have stated that the same formula is to be applied to the issue of whether there exists a duty of care in negligence in the exercise of a discretionary power regardless of whether discretionary or operational aspects are involved. And based on the limited case law, post-*Glencar (No. 2)* it appears that the relevant policy considerations will be brought into account under the heading of whether it would be "just and reasonable" to impose a duty of care.[155]

18–61   Granted that the same broad formula applies whether the issue claimed to

---

[152] Note that in *Graham v Minister for the Environment* [1998] 2 I.R. 88, Morris J. held that although a returning officer had wrongly denied the plaintiff the right to vote, there was no negligence as the officer had acted diligently and within the limits of her statutory discretion.

[153] In *Glencar (No. 2)*, Fennelly J. suggested (at 155) that the trial judge had fallen into error in assimilating vires to breach of duty: "Whether the mining ban was 'unnecessary' or 'contrary to the best interests of the county …' or lacked 'objective justification' are not in my view relevant to the question of negligence." However, Fennelly J. went on to ask, on the hypothesis that the planning authority had the power to impose the mining ban, "… could it have been liable to persons, natural or legal, to compensate them for economic damage suffered as the result of the incidence of the operation of the plan? In my judgment, the answer would clearly be in the negative. The development represents the culmination of a process designed to gather the views of all relevant interests, economic and social, and to give appropriate weight to them in the plan formally adopted. The authority is required to publish its proposals and receive representations from those affected or potentially affected."
    Drawing on this discussion, the Supreme Court in *McGrath v Minister for Justice, Equality and Law Reform* [2003] 1 I.R. 622 at 639 per Murray J. (obiter), described "the rational test" for breach of duty in respect of statutory functions as "whether the decision taken was one which no reasonable authority would have taken …".

[154] *Ward v McMaster* [1988] I.R. 337 at 346–347.

[155] This is borne out by developments in the general law of negligence: see, e.g. the important decisions in *Fletcher v Commissioners for Public Works* [2003] IESC 13; [2003] I.R. 465; *Wildgust v Bank of Ireland* [2006] IESC 19; [2007] 3 I.R. 39.

be negligent is policy or operational, the question arises: how has the formula been used in regard to policy decisions? One clear case is *Glencar (No. 2)*. Another is *McMahon v Ireland*,[156] in which the plaintiff had lost money following the collapse of a deposit-taking institution which, taking advantage of an exemption in the Central Bank Act 1971 which it then enjoyed, had carried on a form of banking business. It was claimed that both the Ministers for Finance and Industry and Commerce, on the one hand, and the Registrar of Friendly Societies, on the other, were negligent in failing to ensure that the legislation was amended so as to end this particular exemption. Blayney J. found that neither Minister was responsible for the initial exemption; nor did they owe the plaintiff a duty of care to bring a Bill before the Oireachtas to seek to have the 1971 Act amended.

18–62   The next case, *Convery v Dublin County Council*,[157] centred around a major policy decision. The plaintiff was seeking an injunction to compel the Council to take action to abate the huge increase of traffic volumes, which had "caused a serious interference with the normal amenities of life in a residential area as a result of a volume of traffic which is greatly in excess of the design capacities of the roads". Keane J. held that the action in negligence must fail, since the Council did not owe the plaintiff any duty of care:

> "The powers and duties of the County Council as planning authority and roads authority are vested in them in order to ensure the proper planning and development of their area and the provision and maintenance of an appropriate road network in that area. While the exercise of those powers and duties can be regulated by the High Court by means of the judicial review process so as to ensure that they are exercised only in accordance with law, the plaintiff does not belong to any category of persons to whom the Council, in the exercise of those powers, owed a duty of care at common law."[158]

18–63   The extreme example of cases involving an appraisal of policy choices is where the claim is for the improvement, in quantity or quality, of a public service. The defence by the recipient public body will inevitably be that satisfying this claim would involve expenditure of public monies, which are needed elsewhere. And this has resulted in the comprehensive application of public-policy type defence, under whatever label, to restrict liability. Given the growth of crime, the state of Gardaí–public relations and the reluctance of the Garda to investigate minor offences of dishonesty, it is perhaps unsurprising that two cases of this type, *Fowley v Conroy*[159] and *Heaney v Commissioner of Garda Síochána*,[160] concerned the investigation of crime (and, consequently, carry with them their own peculiarities). *Fowley*, especially, had its own very particular facts and so here we focus on *Heaney*. In *Heaney*, the applicants had made a complaint to the respondent about their neighbours' offensive conduct. While finding on the facts that certain Gardaí had not (as the applicant alleged) deliberately frustrated the investigation, and that

---

[156] [1988] I.L.R.M. 610. See McGrath, "Tort-Negligence – The Duty of Care and The World at Large" (1987) 9 D.U.L.J. (N.S) 163. But the Oireachtas is clearly taking no chances: see now s.17(9) of the Building Societies Act 1989.

[157] [1996] 3 I.R. 153.

[158] [1996] 3 I.R. 153 at 174.

[159] [2005] 3 I.R. 480. See H & M, paras 15–277 to 15–284.

[160] [2007] 2 I.R. 69.

it had been properly carried out, Quirke J. also quoted with approval the following statement from *Fowley*[161]:

> "There may be a whole series of legitimate reasons why there may not be an inquiry ... into a particular crime ... A police force may have legitimate policy reasons for not vigorously pursuing crimes of a particular type [or not investigating] a particular crime ... In the context of the manner in which the inquiry is actually conducted, it is accepted by counsel on both sides that, in virtually all cases, the court would have no jurisdiction to review operational matters such as the manner in which the inquiry is being conducted.
>
> In all these circumstances, it seems to me that it would be very difficult to formulate any form of positive entitlement on the part of the victim. However, I am satisfied that a victim may have an entitlement to ensure that an inquiry into the crime concerned is not dealt with in a capricious manner. For example, a refusal to investigate the crime for no good reason may be reviewable even though it must be clear that the courts would afford a very wide margin of appreciation to the Gardai ... Similarly, once embarked upon, the Gardai must enjoy a very wide margin of appreciation and indeed as to the manner in which the inquiry is conducted ..."

18–64   In *Heaney*, Quirke J. himself added:

> "It is not the function of the court to supervise the investigation of complaints made to the Gardai. It is not the function of complainants to do so either."[162]

18–65   A good part of the reasoning underlying the rejection of the applicant's case was concern for the operational efficiency of An Garda Síochána, a most important matter.[163] The majority of cases on the control of discretionary powers concern a situation in which the public body has taken some positive action which is inimical to the applicant's individual interest. However, there are a minority of cases of which these two are examples[164]—which, given contracting public expenditure, are likely to expand in number—in which the applicant's case is that it was unreasonable of the respondent public body to refrain from acting. And, in response, the public body

---

[161]   [2005] 3 I.R. 480 at paras 26–28 quoted in *Heaney* [2007] 2 I.R. 69 at para.53.

[162]   [2007] 2 I.R. 69 at para.60. At the same time he also remarked (at para.57): "The Garda authorities have an obligation to investigate complaints alleging the commission of a criminal offence." But this should probably be read in the context of a contrast with the following sentence: "[T]hey are not obliged however, to bring criminal prosecution proceedings ..." Earlier, in *State (McCormack) v Curran* [1987] I.L.R.M. 225 at 239, Walsh J. had stated that it was "[t]he common law duty of a policeman to bring criminals to justice and a refusal by a policeman on notice not to pursue a criminal [would be] a common law misdemeanour". For Finlay C.J.'s version of this, see [1987] I.L.R.M. 225 at 236. See also, *Norris v Attorney General* [1984] I.R. 36 at 81.

[163]   See earlier material on community interests, at paras 15–73 to 15–81.

[164]   So too is *Garda Representative Association v Minister for Finance* [2010] IEHC 78, which concerned the Minister's refusal to exercise his statutory discretion to make an exception from an austerity measure in favour of the Gardaí. Another case of this type is *State (Lynch) v Cooney* [1982] I.R. 337 at 381 in which Henchy J. stated: "... not only was the Minister's opinion [regarding the ban on Sinn Féin appearing on the airwaves, under s.31 of the Broadcasting Authority Act 1960, as amended] formed in good faith and justified by the facts ... but an opinion to the contrary would have been perverse."

contends, typically, that given all the competing claims, it simply did not have the resources to take the action demanded by the applicant. A straightforward example would be a complaint about the quality of a service which is being provided by some public body, like (to take hypothetical examples): doctors being instructed not to make house calls to a health card patient; a university lecturer not setting essays for his students; RTÉ not putting on enough Irish language programmes. A successful claim in this area would be likely to mean that the same resources could not be used elsewhere and it would be impossible for a court to make the necessary comparison. In such cases, the courts would be slow to accede to the applicant's argument.

18–66 As noted, the law now eschews a policy–operational distinction, preferring to use the same framework for each. Nevertheless the peculiarities of the exercise of discretionary power in respect of policy are such that they have to be taken into account and, as indicated, this is done by way of more than one element of the framework. In addition, we may use this distinction for the purposes of analysis. In an area where any test is bound to include a large margin of judicial appreciation, previous results may be a better guide to future decisions than any stated formula. So far as the results in the cases outlined here[165] are concerned, the following summary may be offered. There are several cases involving decisions which were close to the policy end of the spectrum in which the plaintiff lost. Of these cases, *McMahon*, *Convery* and *Heaney* were at the furthest end of the operational–policy spectrum in that negligence was alleged in respect of a major and far-reaching aspect of public policy. Then there were a group of cases involving an exercise of discretion but in respect of a situation involving one or a limited number of individuals: *Hayes* and *Gaffey*. Another group involved the particular field of a regulatory decision: *Sunderland*; *Glencar (No. 2)*; *Atlantic Marine*; *Kennedy (No. 4)*. Even in these, the plaintiff lost.

18–67 That leaves two cases—*Siney* and *Ward*—in which an impoverished plaintiff won. It is significant, perhaps, by way of contrast, that in a similar case to *Ward*—*Curran* in the House of Lords — the defendant local authority won. It may also be significant that subsequent decisions—such as *Cotter* and *Convery*—have sought to stress the special facts of *Ward* and have been wary of imposing new liabilities on public authorities. Such results as *Siney* or *Ward*—in which the tenor of the Irish decisions is often in contrast not only with British but with other foreign decisions—display the Irish courts' marked preference for the individual plaintiff. To take one of the few other cases in which the plaintiff won, *Duff*, at its root there lay no policy choice by the Minister but simply negligent legal advice.

---

[165] See also, *Ryan v Ireland (No. 2)*, unreported, High Court, October 19, 1989 (the sequel to *Ryan v Ireland* [1989] I.R. 177) where Barr J. found that officers of the Defence Forces had been negligent at an "operational level" in not taking adequate steps to protect Irish troops serving with the UN forces in Lebanon from the possibility of attack by militia groups. The plaintiff was awarded IR£198,354 in damages.

E. Defences in Tort

18–68   As a general proposition, it is true to say that, at common law, neither the State nor any other public authority enjoys any special position in the law of torts: we have seen, in earlier Parts, that the general law—trespass, negligence, nuisance, breach of statutory duty, etc—applies in substantially the same way as to a private person.[166] This is an important aspect of the rule of law, and damages actions are one effective means of securing judicial protection against unlawful administrative action.

18–69   But there are certain immunities and exemptions for public bodies and we deal in this Part with those which flow from the nature of the power being exercised (leaving until the following Part immunities defined by reference to the public body exercising the power). Most of these defences are statutory in origin. And it is a significant principle that where a statute authorises the doing of a particular act, then no action will lie at the suit of any person if the inevitable consequence of the act is to cause damage, provided, of course, that it is done without negligence.[167] The most common application of this principle is where public bodies are authorised to commit what might otherwise be a nuisance. One case in which this principle was considered is *Kelly v Dublin County Council*.[168] Here, the defendant local authority had made use of a vacant site beside the plaintiff's cottage for the purpose of storing vehicles and materials used in an extensive road construction project. The plaintiffs claimed that these activities amounted to an actionable nuisance, but the defendants argued that they enjoyed statutory protection under the Local Government Act 1925. O'Hanlon J. found that the activities in question amounted to a nuisance. Next, as to the question of the defence under examination here, he held that while the 1925 Act afforded protection to the defendant's road construction work, it did not extend to the provision and use of a depot for vehicles and materials.[169] In the alternative, O'Hanlon J. held that the defendants had not shown that the nuisance was an inevitable result of the exercise of the statutory powers for there was no evidence to show that the Council had no reasonable alternative but to use this particular site.

18–70   Take next a case which did involve negligence. In *Red Cow Service Station Ltd v Murphy International Ltd and Bord Gáis Éireann*[170] it was held that, while under s.27(1)(d) of the Gas Act 1976 Bord Gáis Éireann has the power to dig or break or interfere with any road, if it acted negligently, e.g. broke a telephone cable

---

[166] *Emerald Meats Ltd v Minister for Agriculture* [1997] 2 I.L.R.M. 275 at 295 per Blayney J. (adopting the above formulation as a correct statement of the law).

[167] *Allen v Gulf Oil Refining Ltd* [1981] A.C. 1001. See also, *Transco v Stockport Metropolitan Borough Council* [2003] UKHL 61; [2004] 2 A.C. 1.

[168] Unreported, High Court, O'Hanlon J., February 21, 1986.

[169] Although it might well have been contended that as these ancillary works were necessarily implied by the terms of the 1925 Act, the immunity should have also extended to them.

[170] (1985) 3 I.L.T. (N.S) 15. In *Collins v Gypsum Industries Ltd* [1975] I.R. 331, the plaintiffs had claimed damages for personal injuries under the Minerals Development Act 1940. The Supreme Court held, however, that the 1940 Act provided for a scheme of compensation in respect of damage to land caused by mining operations and it did not extend to personal injuries. The proper forum for pursuing such a claim for personal injuries was that provided by the ordinary courts.

and caused damage to the plaintiff beyond what was essential and necessary, it could not claim the protection of the Act.

18–71 The cases so far have not taken into account the Constitution. Its impact may be illustrated by utilising the fact of the English case of *Allen v Gulf Oil Refining Ltd.*[171] A private Act of Parliament had authorised the defendant to construct a refinery but it did not specifically authorise the operation of the refinery. Some neighbours complained of excessive smell, vibration and noise and sued in nuisance. Nevertheless, the House of Lords ruled that the operation of the refinery was authorised at least by necessary implication; and as a result the plaintiffs had no remedy in so far as the nuisance complained of was the inevitable result of the authorised operation.

18–72 However, given the strength of the Constitution, it may be queried whether an Irish court would reach the same conclusion[172]: the judge would probably rule that the statute amounted to an unconstitutional attack[173] on the plaintiff's rights to sue in tort[174] (which itself is a species of the property right protected by Art.40.3), or to recover compensation in respect of this State interference with property rights. Alternatively, if the statute were silent on the matter, an Irish court, applying the presumption of constitutionality, would probably rule that, as there was no overt legislative intention to act in an unconstitutional fashion, it must be presumed that the legislature did not intend to deprive the plaintiffs of their right to sue in respect of the nuisance.

F. Rules of Immunity for Particular Sectors

18–73 In addition, however, there are special rules creating immunity for particular areas of governmental action. As these exceptions (which, apart from the first two, are statutory in origin) are heterogeneous, they may be considered separately.

---

[171] [1981] A.C. 1001.

[172] See the very important decision of Laffoy J. in *Smyth v Railway Procurement Agency* [2010] IEHC 290. See also, *Duff v Minister for Agriculture* [1997] 2 I.R. 22 where a majority of the Supreme Court held that the plaintiff farmers should be compensated following a mistake of law on the part of the Minister. The basis for this conclusion is not entirely clear, but Barrington J. appeared to ground this finding on the basis of Art.40.3.2° and *Glencar Explorations Plc v Mayo County Council (No. 2)* [2001] 1 I.R. 84, where the Supreme Court, while clarifying that damages would not flow automatically from an ultra vires act, nonetheless gave a strong hint that Art.40.3 effectively requires *ubi jus, ibi remedium* where a wrongful act has caused a private wrong, unless, perhaps, there are compelling policy reasons which make such a course of redress impossible. See also, *Kelly v Dublin County Council*, unreported, High Court, February 21, 1986 (Council liable for damages caused by storing of vehicles in neighbouring depot, as nuisance not shown to have been the "inevitable result of the exercise of statutory powers").

[173] See, e.g. *In re Article 26 and the Health (Amendment) (No. 2) Bill 2004* [2005] IESC 7; [2005] 1 I.R. 105. See also, the discussion of this question in the important judgment of Laffoy J. in *Smyth v Railway Procurement Agency* [2010] IEHC 290.

[174] On the ground that otherwise existing tort law would be "plainly inadequate" (to use the language of Henchy J. in *Hanrahan v Merck, Sharp and Dohme (Ireland) Ltd* [1988] I.L.R.M. 629 at 636) to vindicate the landowner's constitutional rights.

Courts and tribunals

18–74 It is clear in this jurisdiction that courts and statutory tribunals[175] generally benefit from common law immunity from actions in negligence.[176] *Kemmy v Ireland*[177] offered a fairly typical and instructive set of facts. The applicant had been convicted of rape and had served some years in prison. His conviction was set aside on the basis that his trial was unfair, and in the instant proceedings he sought damages. In the first place, McMahon J. noted that if (as had not happened) the plaintiff had sued the judge personally, he would have failed, on the basis that "although frequently described as absolute, the judge may be successfully sued personally [only] in extreme cases, where for instance, he accepts a bribe ...".[178] But the plaintiff had other (unsuccessful) ways of formulating his claim, of which the first, against the State vicariously, is examined at paras 18–100 to 18–102.

18–75 In his final argument in *Kemmy*, the plaintiff argued that the State was directly liable for a trial judge's failure to respect his constitutional right to a fair trial. McMahon J. was satisfied that, given the robust appellate process which had been put in place, the State had discharged its obligation to respect, defend and vindicate the plaintiff's rights so far as practicable:

> "In the present context, I am of the view that the plaintiff's 'right to a fair trial' should more properly be referred to as an obligation on the State to provide a *fair legal system* within which the plaintiff's trial can take place. By providing an appeal system, the State has carried out its duty in this respect."[179]

18–76 The equivalent issue was considered by the Supreme Court in *Beatty v Rent Tribunal*.[180] The respondent body had, in a previous action, been found to have acted contrary to the rules of constitutional justice, in a manner adverse to the interests of the plaintiffs, who subsequently sought damages. Geoghegan J.'s majority judgment affirmed that the Rent Tribunal[181] was immune from actions in negligence:

> "Even though the respondent is a tribunal which essentially determines rent disputes as between private parties, it is a statutory body exercising statutory duties in the public interest. In these circumstances, I am quite satisfied that, provided it is purporting to act bona fide within its jurisdiction, it enjoys an

---

[175] For tribunals, see paras 6–75 to 6–77. For the special statutory immunity of the Special Criminal Court, see Offences Against the State Act 1939 s.53.

[176] *Deighan v Ireland* [1995] 2 I.R. 56 at 62 per Flood J. See also, *McIlwraith v Fawsitt* [1990] 1 I.R. 343; *O'Connor v Carroll* [1999] 2 I.R. 160; *Desmond v Riordan* [2000] 1 I.R. 505; *O'Q v Buttimer* [2009] IEHC 25; *O'F v Judge O'Donnell* [2009] IEHC 142; [2010] 1 I.L.R.M. 198.

[177] [2009] IEHC 178; [2009] 4 I.R. 74.

[178] [2009] IEHC 178; [2009] 4 I.R. 74 at para.23.

[179] [2009] 4 I.R. 74 at 104. (Emphasis in original.) It may be queried, however, whether a system of review or appeal which was not as robust as that provided in the criminal field would also be protected by McMahon J.'s reasoning, assuming that a similarly robust constitutional right were implicated: *McFarlane v Ireland* [2010] ECHR 1272. One could also point to the rather stern view taken in a comparable context that an appeal does not cure a want of constitutional justice at the initial stage: see paras 14–152 to 14–153.

[180] [2005] IESC 66; [2006] 2 I.R. 191.

[181] Housing (Private Rented Dwellings) (Amendment) Act 1983.

immunity from an action in ordinary negligence ... In this respect it is in no
different position from a court whether such court be traditionally categorised
as 'superior' or 'inferior'."[182]

18–77   Moreover, such an immunity would not have to be expressly granted by
statute: "the immunity of a statutory tribunal arises at common law and if it is to
be removed, the statute has to say so".[183] However, the immunity is not unlimited.
Although he did not express a "definitive view" on the question,[184] Geoghegan J.
suggested that, "if a judge or tribunal was to knowingly engage in behaviour that
was criminal or malicious ... the immunity to a claim for damages for misfeasance
[in] public office would not apply".[185] Equally, he had "considerable doubt" that
an action for misfeasance in public office would lie "in circumstances where the
court or tribunal was acting within jurisdiction".[186]

Roads

18–78   The principle that a local authority is not liable for an injury to a user of
the highway caused by a hole in the road resulting from failure to repair can be
traced back to *Russell v The Men Dwelling in the County of Devon*.[187] The basis
of this immunity is that at common law the duty of repairing highways fell on the
community (though by virtue of a statute of 1614[188] this duty was imposed on the
parish). Because the inhabitants were not a corporation, they could not be sued
collectively and therefore no action lay against them in respect of their failure to
carry out their duty. By contrast, in the case of misfeasance, someone has acted
and the local authority which employed that person may be liable.[189] Despite the
changes wrought by the Local Government (Ireland) Act 1898—most notably the
imposition, by s.82, on every county and district council of the duty of keeping
the road in good condition and repair—the position remained the same. The
distinction between nonfeasance and misfeasance has been judicially described as
both "unsatisfactory"[190] and "anomalous",[191] but was regarded as sufficiently well
established to warrant its abrogation by statute. Accordingly the next stage was
s.60(1) of the Civil Liability Act 1961, which provided that "[a] local authority
shall be liable for damages caused as a result of their failure to maintain adequately
a public road". Section 60(7) however provided that the section is to come into
operation on such day as might be fixed by order of the Government.

---

[182] [2006] 2 I.R. 191 at 195.
[183] [2006] 2 I.R. 191 at 196.
[184] [2006] 2 I.R. 191 at 200.
[185] [2006] 2 I.R. 191 at 199. The policy reasons underpinning the immunity are readily understood.
In Lord Denning M.R.'s typically colourful expression, a judge "should not have to turn the
pages of his books with trembling fingers, asking himself: 'If I do this, shall I be liable in
damages?'": *Sirros v Moore* [1975] Q.B. 118 at 132.
[186] [2006] 2 I.R. 191 at 200. cf. the concurring judgments of Fennelly and McCracken JJ.,
preferring to focus on the existence or non-existence of a duty of care.
[187] (1788) 2 T.R. 667.
[188] 11, 12 & 13 Jac. 1 c.7 (Ir.), following the lines of the 1555 English statute (2 & 3 Ph. & M.
c.8).
[189] *Harbinson v Armagh County Council* [1902] 2 I.R. 538. The reasons for this restrictive
approach were explained by Johnson J. ([1902] 2 I.R. 538 at 560–561).
[190] *Kelly v Mayo County Council* [1964] I.R. 315 at 324 per Kingsmill Moore J.
[191] *O'Brien v Waterford County Council* [1926] I.R. 1 at 8 per Murnaghan J.

18–79   No such order was made and Costello J. held in *State (Sheehan) v Government of Ireland*[192] that the Government had failed in its statutory duty and made an order of mandamus directed against the Government compelling them to bring s.60 of the 1961 Act into effect. A majority of the Supreme Court, however, took a different view, with Henchy J. holding in effect that the discretion vested in the Government was unreviewable.[193] The present law, established by s.19(4) and (5) of the Roads Act 1993, reaffirmed the common law, and provides that no action shall lie against the National Roads Authority or a local road authority in respect of a failure to maintain a road.

Treatment of the mentally ill

18–80   Section 73(1) of the Mental Health Act 2001 provides that:

> No civil proceedings shall be instituted in respect of an act purporting to have been done in pursuance of this Act save by leave of the High Court and such leave shall not be refused unless the High Court is satisfied:
> (*a*) that the proceedings are frivolous or vexatious, or
> (*b*) that there are no reasonable grounds for contending that the person against whom the proceedings are brought acted in bad faith or without reasonable care.

18–81   Thus a significant limitation is placed on the ability of an applicant to bring an action relating to the provisions of the 2001 Act. Its predecessor, s.260 of the Mental Treatment Act 1945,[194] was held to be unconstitutional by the Supreme Court in *Blehein v Minister for Health and Children*.[195] That provision differed from the current one in that it required the applicant to demonstrate "substantial grounds" for establishing that the person against whom proceedings were brought acted in bad faith or without reasonable care.[196] The restriction to these limited grounds of review was held to be a disproportionate interference with the applicant's right of access to the courts and his right to personal liberty.[197] In view, however, of the court's conclusion that the Oireachtas could not constitutionally limit the substantive *grounds* on which the proceedings could be commenced, it is, nevertheless, not easy to see how there is any difference in principle as between the old s.260 and the new s.73(1)(b); so that the latter subsection would appear to be equally vulnerable to a successful constitutional challenge.

---

[192] [1987] I.R. 550. This case is further discussed in H & M, at paras 15–247 to 15–249.
[193] [1987] I.R. 550 at 561. See also, *Brady v Cavan County Council* [1999] 4 I.R. 99, reaffirming this position. Note that in Northern Ireland this immunity was removed by the Roads (Liability of Road Authorities for Neglect) (Northern Ireland) Act 1966.
[194] As amended by s.2(3) of the Public Authorities (Judicial Proceedings) Act 1954. See *O'Dowd v North Western Health Board* [1983] I.L.R.M. 186; *Murphy v Greene* [1990] 2 I.R. 566; *O'Reilly v Moroney* [1992] 2 I.R. 145; *Bailey v Gallagher* [1996] 2 I.L.R.M. 433; *Croke v Smith*, unreported, Supreme Court, July 31, 1996; *Melly v Moran*, unreported, Supreme Court, May 28, 1998; *Kiernan v Harris and others*, unreported, High Court, May 12, 1998; *Blehein v Murphy (No. 2)* [2000] 3 I.R. 359.
[195] [2008] IESC 40; [2009] 1 I.R. 275. In *Blehein's* case the constitutionality of the provision was still relevant to an outstanding claim for damages.
[196] See Clarke J. in *L v Clinical Director of St Patrick's Hospital* [2010] IESC 62.
[197] See further, Ch.11.

Postal and telecommunications services

18–82 Special provision is also made by s.64 of the Postal and Telecommunications Services Act 1983[198] which provides that An Post shall be immune from all liability in respect of any loss or damage suffered by a person in the use of a postal service, by reason of: (i) failure or delay in providing, operating or maintaining a postal service; or (ii) failure, interruption, suspension or restriction of a postal service. Similarly, members of staff are immune from civil liability except at the suit of An Post itself in respect of any such loss or damage.

Defence Forces

18–83 In times past, there was said to be a common law immunity covering actions taken by the military in time of war. This immunity met its Waterloo in *Ryan v Ireland*,[199] when the Supreme Court was given the opportunity of considering the liability of the State in respect of tortious acts committed by officers while engaged in active service. The plaintiff was a member of the Irish contingent which formed part of the United Nations International Force serving in the Lebanon. In April 1979 a member of a Christian militia had been shot dead outside an Irish Army post and it appears that the militia were determined to seek revenge from the members of the Irish contingent. Although there were clear signals that such an attack was being planned, the plaintiff was ordered to take a rest in a portacabin shelter which had not been sandbagged. His position was attacked after he had gone to sleep and he was seriously injured by a mortar which struck his portacabin. There was evidence of negligent preparations to meet the attack. The State made the argument that Art.28.3 of the Constitution gives the Oireachtas extensive powers to deal with war and the preservation of the State in time of war and that the Constitution may not be invoked to invalidate "legislation expressed to be for such purpose". But in response to this submission, Finlay C.J. concluded that these provisions made it impossible to accept:

> "... the application of a common law doctrine arising from necessity to ensure the safety of the State during a period of war or armed rebellion which has the effect of abrogating constitutional rights. In so far, therefore, as the principle apparently supporting some of the decisions to which we have been referred is the question of the dominant priority in regard to the defence of the State, such decisions would not appear to be applicable and cannot be applied to the question of service with the United Nations force. I, therefore, conclude that an immunity from suit, or the negation of any duty of care to, a serving soldier in respect of operations consisting of armed conflict or hostilities has not been established as part of our common law."[200]

18–84 Finlay C.J. further held that, even if such an immunity had existed at common law, it would not have survived the enactment of the Constitution:

---

[198] Repealed in part by the European Communities (Postal Services) Regulations 2000 (S.I. No. 310 of 2000) art.3(2) which restricts the immunity to universal postal services as specified in art.6 of the 2000 Regulations.

[199] [1989] I.R. 177. See also, *Healy v Minister for Defence*, unreported, High Court, Barron J., July 7, 1994 (damages awarded to members of the Defence Forces for breach of constitutional right to fair procedures).

[200] [1989] I.R. 177 at 182.

"I conclude that in the blanket form which has been contended for [such an immunity] would be inconsistent with the guarantees by the State to respect, defend and vindicate the rights of the citizens contained in Article 40.3.1 and Article 40.3.2 of the Constitution."[201]

18–85   As regards statute law, s.111 of the Defence Act 1954 provides that, where any action is commenced against any person for any act done in pursuance, execution or intended execution of the Act or in respect of any alleged neglect or default in the execution of the Act, the action must be brought in the High Court and must be instituted within six months of the act, neglect or default complained of. In *Ryan v Ireland*[202] the Supreme Court held that this provision had no relevance to a case where it was alleged that officers of the Defence Forces had been guilty of common law negligence in the performance of their duties.

Fire services

18–86   A complete immunity is given by s.36 of the Fire Services Act 1981 to fire and sanitary authorities who are discharging their fire safety, fire fighting and fire protection functions under this Act. Section 36 provides:

> No action or other proceeding shall lie or be maintainable against the Minister, or against a fire authority or a sanitary authority or any officer or servant of, or person engaged by, any such authority for recovery of damages in respect of injury to persons or property alleged to have been caused or contributed to by the failure to comply with any functions conferred by this Act.

18–87   The wording of this section makes it clear that, in the words of Feeney J. in *Moran v O'Donovan*,[203] its object:

> "… is to provide immunity from civil claims. The use of the words 'no action' or 'other proceedings' makes this clear. The words of the section make it clear that the section does not seek to identify the type of action or cause of action or the legal basis for an action, but rather starts from the premise that no action or other proceedings shall be maintainable. The section provides immunity in respect of injury or property and that immunity arises if such injury is caused or contributed to by the failure to comply with any functions conferred by the Act. The immunity arises not just for any injury caused but also for one contributed to by failure to comply with the functions under the Act."

18–88   Sanitary authorities are also immune from actions in nuisance, on the basis of s.17 of the Public Health (Ireland) Act 1878.[204]

---

[201]   [1989] I.R. 177 at 182–183.
[202]   [1989] I.R. 177.
[203]   [2007] IEHC 178; [2010] 4 I.R. 338.
[204]   *Superquinn Ltd v Bray Urban District Council* [1998] 3 I.R. 542.

Investigating and prosecuting authorities

18–89 The initial question of whether a cause of action lies at the suit of a victim disappointed by the performance of the investigating or prosecuting authorities is considered tentatively at paras 18–63 to 18–65. The issue of whether the investigating and prosecuting authorities enjoy an immunity in respect of actions brought by either suspects or victims of crime is one which does not appear to have been judicially decided in this jurisdiction prior to Costello P.'s judgment in *W v Ireland (No. 2)*.[205] In England, wide-ranging immunities have been upheld in the case of investigations by social workers responsible for child care[206]; police investigations[207]; and prosecuting authorities.[208] In *W*, Costello P. held that the Attorney General enjoyed immunity from suit in negligence in respect of the discharge of his statutory functions under s.2 of the Extradition (Amendment) Act 1987.[209] Even if there was sufficient proximity between the parties to give rise to a duty of care,[210] there were compelling public policy reasons why such a duty of care should not be imposed. If such a duty were imposed on the Attorney (or, for that matter, other prosecuting authorities) there was an unacceptable risk of a conflict between "the proper exercise of his public function with the common law duty of care to the victim which might result in an improper exercise of his statutory functions".[211]

Regulatory authorities

18–90 Nearly all regulatory legislation enacted in recent times provides that the regulatory agency and its members enjoy either an absolute or qualified immunity.[212] Two representative examples may be given here. Section 86 of the Safety, Health and Welfare at Work Act 2005 provides that:

> No action or other proceedings shall lie or be maintainable against the Authority or [any prescribed person] ... for the recovery of damages in respect of any injury to persons, damage to property or other loss alleged to have been caused or contributed to by a failure to perform or to comply with any of the functions imposed on the Authority or [prescribed person] ...[213]

---

[205] [1997] 2 I.R. 141. In this case the plaintiffs (who were victims of child sexual abuse) had sued the State in respect of the emotional distress which had been caused to them by the failure to extradite promptly a notorious sex offender.

[206] *X (minors) v Bedfordshire County Council* [1995] 3 All E.R. 353.

[207] *Hill v Chief Constable for West Yorkshire* [1989] A.C. 53; *Alexandrou v Oxford* [1993] 4 All E.R. 328; *Osman v Ferguson* [1993] 4 All E.R. 344.

[208] *Elguzoli-Daf v Metropolitan Police Commissioner* [1995] Q.B. 335.

[209] Section 2 of the 1987 Act requires the Attorney General not to endorse a particular extradition warrant from the United Kingdom for execution unless he is satisfied that it is backed by sufficient evidence and that there is an intention to prosecute in respect of such evidence.

[210] And Costello P. in *W (No. 2)* thought that there was not: [1997] 2 I.R. 141 at 158.

[211] See also, the Constabulary (Ireland) Act 1836 s.19, which purports to limit recourse for damage done by a police officer in the execution of a warrant. In *Osbourne v Minister for Justice* [2006] IEHC 117; *People (Attorney General) v O'Brien* [1965] I.R. 142.

[212] See, e.g. Health Insurance Act 1994 s.35(1), as inserted by Health Insurance (Amendment) Act 2003 s.3; Irish Takeover Panel Act 1997 s.20; Copyright and Related Rights Act 2000 s.180; Companies (Auditing and Accounting) Act 2003 s.33; Chemicals Act 2008 s.13.

[213] See also, Environmental Protection Agency Act 1992 s.15; Radiological Protection (Amendment) Act 2002 s.10; Digital Hub Development Agency Act 2003 s.38; Dublin Transport Authority Act 2008 s.43.

18–91   Section 53 of the Investment Intermediaries Act 1995[214] is more typical in that it provides a qualified immunity where the regulatory authority acts in good faith:

> A supervisory authority or any employee or officer of a supervisory authority ... shall not be liable in damages for anything done or omitted in the discharge or purported discharge of any of its functions under this Act unless it is shown that the act or omission was in bad faith.

18–92   In line with the argument advanced in the following Part, it may be thought that the restricted immunity in the Investment Intermediaries Act 1995 is more likely to be in accord with the (qualified) guarantee of rights conferred by the Constitution than is the absolute immunity contained in the 2005 Act.

G. CONSTITUTIONALITY OF STATUTORY RULES OF IMMUNITY

18–93   The issue of whether it is competent for the Oireachtas to establish special rules of immunity is something which has never been directly judicially considered.[215] This issue clearly arises in the wake of *Byrne v Ireland*,[216] where the Supreme Court invalidated the common law rule whereby the State was deemed to be immune from suit. The court held, first, that none of the prerogatives which had hitherto attached to the Crown had survived the enactment of the Constitution[217]; and secondly, and more pertinently here, that (by virtue of its content, rather than its source) this particular prerogative was inconsistent with the plaintiff's constitutional rights to have access to the courts and to recover damages in respect of a legal wrong. As Budd J. observed, the constitutional rights given to citizens "would be quite meaningless, in so far as suing the State is concerned, unless they were in some way enforceable against the State".[218] This decision has had enormous repercussions: it abolished at one fell swoop a long-standing (common law or prerogative) immunity of the State and thus raised doubts about the constitutionality of certain of the statutory immunities conferred by statute and outlined in the previous Part.[219]

18–94   This doubt is reinforced by both *Ryan v Ireland*[220] (where the Supreme

---

[214] As amended by Central Bank and Financial Services Authority of Ireland Act 2004 Sch.3, Pt XI.

[215] A novel claim arose for consideration in *An Blascaod Mór Teo v Commissioners of Public Works (No. 4)* [2000] 3 I.R. 565 at 570.

[216] [1972] I.R. 241.

[217] See generally, Kelly, "Hidden Treasure and the Constitution" (1988) 10 D.U.L.J. 1; Lenihan, "Royal Prerogatives and the Constitution" (1989) 24 Ir. Jur. 1. See further, below, paras 20–01 to 20–04.

[218] [1972] I.R. 241 at 292.

[219] For example, s.64 of the Postal and Telecommunications Services Act 1983, discussed above. In *Ryan v Ireland* [1989] I.R. 177 at 183, the Supreme Court held that insofar as the common law provided for an immunity from suit in respect of an action for negligence taken by a soldier on active service, such a rule had not survived the enactment of the Constitution "since it would be inconsistent with the guarantees by the State to respect, defend and vindicate the rights of the citizen contained in Art. 40.3 of the Constitution".

[220] [1989] I.R. 177.

Court held that common law immunities relieving the Defence Forces from liability in respect of injuries to soldiers engaged on active service were unconstitutional) and *Blehein v Minister for Health and Children*[221] (where the Supreme Court held that a statutory provision which limited the grounds upon which a plaintiff could sue in civil proceedings was unconstitutional).

18–95   Accordingly, a shadow must hang over the validity of s.36 of the Fire Services Act 1981, at least in so far as it precludes a fireman from suing a fire authority in respect of the negligent discharge of their statutory duties under the 1981 Act. It is difficult to see how such an immunity could survive if an analogous common law immunity enjoyed by the Defence Forces has been condemned as unconstitutional. And while it is easy to understand the legislative intention to favour the rescue services and to ensure that they will not be hampered by the threat of legal action, the absolute nature of this immunity seems hard to justify. Again, what of the fire authority which, through some gross act of negligence on its part, failed to answer a distress call? Certainly major constitutional issues would be raised should the authority seek to fall back in such circumstances on the provisions of s.36 of the 1981 Act in order to defend itself against an action for negligence.[222]

18–96   One way of justifying such immunities might be to adopt the reasoning in *Pine Valley Developments Ltd v Minister for Environment*[223] and say that the personal rights guarantees contained in Art.40.3 are not absolute and that the Oireachtas has to balance the common good against them and that, in some instances, no action will lie for negligence or breach of duty. Such an immunity might, therefore, be justified on the basis of public policy grounds either in order to protect persons performing an essential social service (such as firemen) or some implied constitutional value (such as the independence of persons performing judicial or quasi-judicial functions).[224]

18–97   This conclusion is strongly suggested by Costello P. in *W v Ireland (No. 2)*[225] where an immunity in negligence in respect of the Attorney General's prosecutorial functions was upheld. Costello P. distinguished *Ryan v Ireland* on the basis that *Ryan* was not a decision in which an issue "relating to immunity from suit on public policy grounds arose". Nor was *Ryan* an authority for the proposition that:

> "[I]n no case could the law confer immunity from suit on a constitutional officer and ... the Irish courts have recognised the validity of such a rule in relation to judges carrying out their judicial functions. Laws may limit the exercise of protected rights and in each case when the claim is raised it is a

[221] [2008] IEHC 40; [2009] 1 I.R. 175.
[222] See *Moran v O'Donovan* [2007] IEHC 200. Of course it might be contended, quite irrespective of s.36 of the 1981 Act, that a fire authority owes no common law duty of care to respond to an emergency call. On this point, see *Capital and Counties Plc v Hampshire County Council* [1997] 2 All E.R. 865.
[223] [1987] I.R. 23.
[224] See [1987] I.R. 23 at 38 per Finlay C.J.
[225] [1997] 2 I.R. 141.

question for the court to decide where, in the interests of the common good, the balance should lie."[226]

18–98   This last sentence suggests the use of the proportionality doctrine in this area of immunity and quasi-immunity. Indeed, in recent times, the proportionality doctrine has been applied, with, in one instance, fatal effect, to statutes restricting the bringing of legal proceedings. The case referred to is *Blehein v Minister for Health and Children*,[227] in which it was held that the plaintiff's right of access to the courts had been infringed and the infringement was disproportionate to the aim sought to be achieved.[228] In the light of such cases, one possible compromise might be for the courts to hold that not all special rules of immunity or quasi-immunity are per se unconstitutional where such quasi-immunities were objectively justified, but a complete and absolute immunity (such as that contained in ss.64 and 88 of the Postal and Telecommunications Services Act 1983) would nonetheless seem susceptible to a successful constitutional challenge.

H. VICARIOUS LIABILITY OF THE STATE FOR ACTIONS OF JUDGES, GARDAÍ, PRISON OFFICERS AND THE DEFENCE FORCES

18–99   The general question of just who is a servant of the State has been considered elsewhere.[229] Here this question arises in a specific context, namely whether a particular official is a servant of the State for the purpose of attracting the State's vicarious liability, as employer. (This, in practice, often arises together with the question of special defences, covered in Part E, for in some cases, the servants will enjoy an immunity or quasi-immunity (usually statutory in origin) in their own right.) The question of vicarious liability naturally involves the issue of whether the person responsible for the conduct on which the plaintiff relies is a servant of the State. In most cases, this requirement may be taken for granted. But in some situations, notably where the action is based on the conduct of a judge, it draws in considerations of its own. A second query floating over this area is as to how wrong the official must go, before it may be said they have gone outside the scope of their employment, so that the State is not vicariously liable. So far this type of defence has succeeded only in the case of *O'Reilly v Devereux*.[230]

Judges

18–100   Clearly the judiciary are not civil servants nor employees of the Government. Even though the courts are organs of the State, arguments for some form of vicarious liability were rejected by McMahon J. in *Kemmy v Ireland*[231]:

---

[226]   [1997] 2 I.R. 141 at 161.

[227]   [2008] IESC 40; [2009] 1 I.R. 275.

[228]   cf. *In re Article 26 and the Illegal Immigrants (Trafficking) Bill 1999* [2000] IESC 19; [2000] 2 I.R. 360, where no disproportionate interference was established.

[229]   See Ch.4, Part C and H & M, Ch.3, Part C.

[230]   [2009] IESC 22. See para.18–112.

[231]   [2009] IEHC 178; [2009] 4 I.R. 74. Here the plaintiff had been convicted of rape following a trial which turned on the issue of consent. Following a request from the jury (who had been deliberating for a day and a half) to be allowed to see the transcript of the evidence of the complainant, the trial judge read his note of her evidence and her cross-examination. The

"From these [constitutional] provisions it is clear that the administration of justice can only be exercised by the judiciary and its administration is free from any other person, including the legislature or the executive. It is also clear that this is very different from the duty which a servant (employee) has towards his master (employer) and who must also carry out his master's orders at all times. Importantly, under the Constitution, the judge does not receive his power or authority from the State but from the people, is independent in the exercise of his functions and is free from interference from the State, particularly from other organs of government. The only limit or control on the judge is to be found in the Constitution itself or in the law. For these reasons too, it would be difficult to consider the judge to be part of the State 'enterprise' since his only function is to administer justice as mandated by the people.

For the above reasons it is wholly inappropriate to attempt to describe the relationship between the State and a member of the judiciary in the master/servant terminology developed for the purposes of imposing vicarious liability for tortuous acts or omissions. Accordingly, in my view, the State cannot be vicariously liable for the errors which a judge may commit in the administration of justice."

18–101   Similar sentiments are to be found in the judgment of Morris P. in *Desmond v Riordan*[232] when he noted that:

"[T]he immunity from suit enjoyed by the judiciary exists not for the benefit of the judge, but for the benefit of the community as a whole. This immunity is perceived to be necessary and desirable so that a judge may perform his functions the better free of concern that in the course of performing his functions the better, freed of concern that in the course of performing his duties he may defame a third party and be required to be answerable to that party in damages ... The granting of an immunity to the judiciary of necessity imposes a limitation upon the constitutional rights of the citizen to vindicate his good name and so the limitations placed upon the exercise of this right must be strictly limited to the degree to which the granting of the immunity may be necessary to achieve its objectives, namely to enable the judge to administer the law freed of the concern that he will be answerable for his actions."

18–102   Thus, at common law, judges, acting in their judicial capacity, are not liable in tort. Moreover, the defence of absolute privilege attaches to all statements made by judges during judicial proceedings, at least provided "that they do not

---

Court of Criminal Appeal allowed the appeal and did not order a re-trial on the ground that in the circumstances of the case and given the centrality of the consent issue, the reading of the complainant's evidence after an interval of a day and a half ran the risk "at least of emphasising the complainant's evidence at the expense of the evidence of the accused". See also, *Desmond v Riordan* [2000] 1 I.R. 505. There are many other statements to this same effect: see, e.g. *Macauley & Co. Ltd v Wyse-Power* (1943) 77 I.L.T.R. 61 at 63 per Maguire J. ("[t]he people were entitled to have the opinion of a judge without fear of his words being challenged elsewhere"); *Beatty v The Rent Tribunal* [2006] 2 I.R. 191 at 212 per Geoghegan J. ("The immunity of judges is based on public policy considerations").

[232] [2000] 1 I.R. 505 at 507 (although this was said in the context of coronorial functions).

deliberately and consciously act in excess of their jurisdiction".[233] This immunity might have been considered to be vulnerable to challenge, on *Byrne*-type grounds, as the State is required by Art.40.3 of the Constitution, by its laws, to defend and vindicate the personal rights of the citizen, which includes the right to litigate a justiciable controversy and to recover damages in respect of a tortious act.[234] As against this, the most fundamental rule of constitutional interpretation is that the Constitution must be read as a whole and that its several provisions "must not be looked at in isolation, but be treated as interlocking parts of the general constitutional scheme".[235] Immunity from suit in respect of judicial acts would appear to be latent in Arts 34 and 35, which guarantee the administration of justice by judges and judicial independence.[236] Given that the courts lean against an interpretation which perverts "any of the fundamental purposes of the Constitution", this constitutional right to litigate a justiciable controversy has had to give way to this judicial immunity from suit and such a possibility is accommodated in Art.40.3.1° by the words "as far as practicable". As McMahon J. explained in *Kemmy v Ireland*[237]:

> "The State cannot guarantee that no error will ever occur in the judicial process. The judges it appoints are human and inevitably will make mistakes. In these circumstances, it is incumbent on the State to provide a corrective mechanism to address these errors. This is the appeal process. In my view, failure by the State to do so would be a breach of its obligations to guarantee 'as far as practicable' the citizen's right to a fair trial. But by doing so, the State has fulfilled its obligations under the Constitution."[238]

---

[233] *O'Q v Buttimer* [2009] IEHC 25 per Edwards J. Note also the comments of McMahon J. in *Kemmy v Ireland* [2009] IEHC 178: "Although [the immunity is] frequently described as absolute, the judge may be successfully sued personally in extreme cases where, for example, he accepts a bribe to decide a case in a particular way." In *Redahan v Minister for Education and Science* [2005] IEHC 271, Gilligan J. held that arbitrators were entitled to the benefit of the common law judicial immunity, save where they are guilty of collusion or dishonesty.

[234] *Byrne v Ireland* [1972] I.R. 241; *O'Brien v Keogh* [1972] I.R. 142; *Blehein v Minister for Health and Children and Ors* [2008] IESC 40; [2009] 1 I.R. 275; and see generally, *JM Kelly: The Irish Constitution* (2003), pp.1446–1463.

[235] *Tormey v Ireland* [1985] I.R. 289 at 296 per Henchy J.

[236] As Murphy J. put it *EOK v DK* [2001] 3 I.R. 568 at 573: "The immunity from suit to which this appeal relates does not derive from any right or privilege enjoyed by a potential defendant. It is merely the by-product of conflicting constitutional rights and the impact of public policy on the administration of justice. The Constitution implicitly recognises that every citizen should have a right of access to the Courts to determine the existence or breach of a legal obligation owed to him by any potential defendant. On the other hand the Constitution expressly recognises the need for finality in the judicial process. Moreover it is recognised that justice is more likely to be achieved where persons participating in litigation whether as parties, witnesses, judges, jurors or lawyers can discharge their function without the fear of being held to account, at the suit of, perhaps, a disgruntled litigant for the manner in which he performs his role."

[237] [2009] IEHC 178; [2009] 4 I.R. 74.

[238] This point was also recognised by Murphy J. in *Looney v Bank of Ireland* [1996] 1 I.R. 157 in upholding the validity of common law rules conferring absolute privilege on witnesses giving evidence in court. The judge observed that in this instance the constitutional interest in the fair administration of justice took precedence over the constitutional right to a good name, saying that the privilege "derives from the necessity of affording to witnesses the opportunity of giving their evidence feely and fearlessly ... It derives from the very nature of the judicial process and the independent judiciary created by our Constitution".

18–103 However, it might be suggested that the requirements of judicial independence could be solved by the executive indemnifying individual members of the judiciary. This solution has been considered in *OF v O'Donnell*[239] in the context of an order for costs, though the difference between costs and damages does not seem to be significant here. Writing obiter, O'Neill J. stated:

> "... an indemnity for judges would merely expose the judiciary to continuous litigation in respect of the discharge of judicial office and apart from the onerous burden which defending this litigation would place on the judiciary with the consequent dilution of the endeavours of judges in the administration of justice, it is inevitable that such a constant process of litigious attack on the judiciary would erode public confidence in the judiciary and, in all probability weaken judicial independence itself, as few human beings could sustain such a process without suffering a serious consequent loss of confidence."

18–104 This passage draws attention to the fact that it frequently happens that the background to many of the cases in this area is a claim that the judiciary made an egregious mistake which created loss, often including legal costs. To adjudicate on such a claim, it would be necessary to rehear the case (something which would usually be unnecessary because of the availability of an appeal). In short, as the passage indicates, considerations pertaining to public confidence, judicial esteem and the very propriety of stigmatising another judicial decision as negligent may make it unlikely that this suggestion will ever be accepted. This view is partly borne out by the judgment of Flood J. in *Deighnan v Ireland*,[240] where the traditional common law rule was re-iterated without any concessions to modern constitutional thinking.

18–105 Save, therefore, in the plainest of cases,[241] judges enjoy a near complete immunity and cases such as *Kemmy* demonstrate that endeavours to impose direct or vicarious liability on the State will very probably fail.

The police and prison officers

18–106 Even before the Garda Síochána Act 2005, the State had been held responsible under the doctrine of *respondeat superior* for the wrongful acts of Gardaí and prison officers acting within the scope of their employment, in accordance with the principles enunciated in *Byrne*. Thus, in *McIntyre v Lewis*[242] the State was held vicariously liable for assault, false imprisonment and malicious prosecutions committed by Gardaí in the course of their employment. Likewise, in

---

[239] [2009] IEHC 142; [2010] 1 I.L.R.M. 198 at para.14.8.

[240] [1995] 2 I.R. 56. The plaintiff claimed that he had been wrongly convicted of contempt of court and he accordingly sought to sue Ireland, the Minister for Justice and the Minister for Finance on the ground that they were vicariously liable for the allegedly tortious act of the judge. See also, *Lopes v Minister for Justice, Equality and Law Reform* [2008] 4 I.R. 743 at 748–749 per Hanna J.

[241] It may be noted that in the cases of both witness immunity and judicial liability, the courts have held open the possibility of personal liability in extreme cases, such as bribery or other corrupt or mala fide behaviour: see, e.g. the comments of McMahon J. in *Kemmy v Ireland* [2009] IEHC 178; [2009] 4 I.R. 74 at 84.

[242] [1991] 1 I.R. 121.

Hanahoe v Hussey[243] the State was held to be vicariously liable for the wrongful acts of the Gardaí, where details of a planned police raid on a firm of highly reputable solicitors were improperly disclosed in advance to the media. An even more striking example is provided by *Shortt v Garda Commissioner*,[244] a case where the State was held vicariously liable for egregious and oppressive acts of members of the Gardaí which resulted in the wrongful imprisonment of the entirely innocent plaintiff for serious crimes.[245]

18–107   This matter was also considered by Costello J. in *Kearney v Minister for Justice*,[246] which concerned the liability of the State for constitutional wrongs committed by prison officers. In this case, the plaintiff's mail was stopped by reason of unofficial action taken by prison officials. Costello J. held that although these actions did not amount to a tort at common law, they did constitute a breach of the plaintiff's constitutional right to communicate. On the question of the State's vicarious liability, the judge had this to say:

> "The wrong that was committed in this case was an unjustified infringement of a constitutional right, not a tort; and it was committed by a servant of the State and, accordingly, Ireland can be sued in respect of it: see *Byrne v. Ireland*. The State is clearly liable for such a wrong when it can be shown that had the wrong been a tort, vicarious liability would attach to the State. The meaningful act in this case was obviously connected with the functions for which the prison officers or officers who committed it were employed, and even though the act was not authorised I cannot hold that it was performed outside the scope of his or their employment. The plaintiff is therefore entitled to be awarded damages against the State."[247]

18–108   This reasoning would appear to apply, mutatis mutandis, to the Gardaí and to ensure that the State is vicariously liable for torts or constitutional wrongs committed by members of the force within the scope of their employment and, indeed, *Walsh v Ireland*[248] provides direct authority for this proposition. Here the plaintiff had been wrongly arrested by members of the Garda Síochána following what Hamilton C.J. described as a "clear case of mistaken identity". The Chief Justice said that the arrest of the plaintiff was nonetheless unlawful and that it:

> "... was effected by members of the Garda Síochána acting in pursuance of their duties on behalf of the State, that such arrest was a breach of the constitutional right of the [plaintiff] to his personal liberty and a failure by the organs of State to defend and vindicate such right and that the defendants are liable in respect thereof."

---

[243] [1998] 3 I.R. 69.

[244] [2007] 4 I.R. 587.

[245] Which misconduct was described as "regrettably a stain of the darkest dye on the otherwise generally fine tradition of the institution of An Garda Síochána": [2007] 4 I.R. 587 at 593 per Murray C.J. It is scarcely surprising that the court awarded the plaintiff the sum of over €4.6 million, including the sum of €1 million by way of exemplary damages.

[246] [1986] I.R. 116.

[247] [1986] I.R. 116 at 122. Cf. *McHugh v Garda Commissioner* [1986] I.R. 228 at 233 where Finlay C.J. accepted that Ireland was vicariously liable for a breach of constitutional rights committed by the Garda Commissioner.

[248] Unreported, Supreme Court, November 30, 1994.

18–109 The Supreme Court rejected a defence based on s.50 of the Constabulary (Ireland) Act 1836,[249] since the action was not being brought against the Gardaí who had actually effected the arrest. Moreover, the arrest had not been effected "in obedience to [the] warrant", since the wrong person had actually been arrested.

18–110 So far as Gardaí are concerned, the law has been re-stated and, to some degree, clarified by s.48 of the Garda Síochána Act 2005 which provides that:

> (1) Where a member of the Garda Síochána commits an actionable wrong in the course of performing the member's functions under this Act—
>> (*a*) the State is liable to an action for damages in respect of damage resulting from the wrong as if the State were the employer of the member, and
>> (*b*) the member is, for the purposes of such liability, deemed to be the servant of the State in so far as the member was acting in the course of performing his or her functions under this Act.
> (2) In proceedings brought against the State by virtue of this section, the plaintiff need not name as a defendant the member or members of the Garda Síochána alleged to have committed the actionable wrong.
>> (3) Nothing in this section affects any right of the State to—
>> (*a*) join an individual member of the Garda Síochána as a defendant to proceedings in respect of an actionable wrong to which this section applies, or
>> (*b*) recover contribution or seek indemnity from an individual member of the Garda Síochána who is, or who, if sued at the time of the commission of that wrong, would have been, liable in respect of the same damage.[250]

As can be seen from s.(1)(a), this provision skirts around the issue of whether a Garda is a servant of the State, by the formula "as if the State were the employer".

Members of the Defence Forces

18–111 Members of the Defence Forces are regarded as servants of the State for the purposes of the *Byrne* decision, and in the series of cases which followed this decision, the State did not attempt to dispute this point.

18–112 But while *Ryan* establishes that the State no longer enjoys any traditional common law immunity vis-à-vis members of the Defence Forces, this does not mean that the State is automatically liable qua employer for any wrongful acts of

---

[249] Which provides that: "[W]hen any action shall be brought against any constable for any act done in obedience to the verdict of any magistrate, such constable shall not be responsible for any irregularity in issuing the warrant, or for any want of jurisdiction in the magistrate issuing the same, and such constable may plead the general issue and give such warrant and providing that the signature thereto is the handwriting of the person whose name shall appear subscribed thereto, and that such person is reputed to be and acts as a magistrate ... and that the acts or acts complained of were done in obedience to such warrant, the jury who shall try the said issue shall find a verdict for such constable, and such constable shall recover his cost of suit."

[250] Note, however, that s.48(5) provides that this provision does not apply "to a wrong committed by the use of a mechanically propelled vehicle belonging to the State".

a member of the Defence Forces. To put it simply, there are limits to vicarious liability, and in *O'Reilly v Devereux*,[251] the Supreme Court rejected the argument that the State could be vicariously liable for the sexual abuse perpetrated by one member of the Defence Forces on another, even where the abuser was a superior officer. As Kearns J. put it:

> "While undoubtedly the first named defendant exercised a supervisory and disciplinary role where the plaintiff was concerned, he was not in the same position as a school teacher or boarding house warden in relation to a child. Nor was the nature of the employment one which would have encouraged close personal contact where some inherent risks might be said to exist as, for example, might arise if the first named defendant had been a swimming instructor in close physical contact with young recruits. There was no intimacy implicit in the relationship between the plaintiff and the first named defendant nor was there any quasi-parental role or responsibility for personal nurturing which was found to exist in the cases where vicarious liability was established. To hold otherwise would be to extend to the Defence Forces a virtual new species of liability where the defendants would be liable for virtually every act or omission of an employee."

---

[251] [2009] IESC 22.

CHAPTER 19

LEGITIMATE EXPECTATIONS

A. INTRODUCTION

19–01   Put simply, the legitimate expectation doctrine means that, subject to exceptions considered later, a legal commitment exists when a public authority "makes a representation ... to an identifiable person or group ... [which] must be such as to create an expectation reasonably entertained by the person or group that the public authority will abide by the representation, to the extent that it would be unjust to permit the public authority to resile from it".[1] The justification for it has been grounded on the notion that "[g]ood government depends upon trust between the governed and the governor. Unless that trust is sustained and protected officials will not be believed and government becomes a choice between chaos and coercion". At the same time, "the [concept] must not be allowed to collapse into an inchoate justification for judicial intervention".[2] This concern, which has been echoed in Ireland,[3] means that a good deal of this chapter must be taken up with issues such as: the meaning of "legitimate"; when it is lawful for a public body to resile from a commitment; and whether the doctrine applies to a substantive

---

[1]   *Glencar Exploration v Mayo County Council (No. 2)* [2002] 1 I.R. 84 at 162–163. This definition is considered further at para.19–13. There has been a considerable amount of academic writing on this topic: see, e.g. Delany, "The Doctrine of Legitimate Expectations in Irish Law" (1990) 12 D.U.L.J. 1 (N.S), "The Doctrine of Legitimate Expectations: Recent Developments" (1993) 11 I.L.T. 192 (N.S) and "The Future of the Doctrine at Legitimate Expectations in Irish Administrative Law" (1997) 32 *Irish Jurist* 217; Craig, "Legitimate Expectations: A Conceptual Analysis" (1992) 108 L.Q.R. 79 and "Substantive Legitimate Expectations in Domestic and Community Law" (1996) Camb. L.J. 289; Brady, "Aspiring Students, Retiring Professors and the Doctrine of Legitimate Expectation" (1996) 31 *Irish Jurist* 133; Delany, "The Future of the Doctrine of Legitimate Expectations in Irish Administrative Law" (1997) 32 *Irish Jurist* 317; Barrett, "Granting Expectations" in Breen, Casey and Kerr (eds), *Liber Memorialis for James Brady* (Dublin: Round Hall Sweet & Maxwell, 2000); Buckley and McDermott, "Expecting too Much of Legitimate Expectation?" (2006) 11 *Bar Review* 184; Delany, "Legitimate Expectations and Substantive Effects: Recent Developments" (2007) 29 D.U.L.J. 413. The treatment in Craig, *Administrative Law*, 6th edn (London: Sweet and Maxwell, 2008), Ch.20, is excellent and appropriately nuanced.

[2]   Wade and Forsyth, *Administrative Law*, 10th edn (Oxford: OUP, 2009), p.446.

[3]   See, e.g. the comments of Costello J. in *Tara Prospecting Ltd v Minister for Energy* [1993] I.L.R.M. 771 at 783–784. In *Association of General Practitioners Ltd v Minister for Health* [1995] 1 I.R. 382 at 393–394, O'Hanlon J. observed that if the plea of legitimate expectations were "allowed its head", it could "introduce an unwelcome element of uncertainty into well-defined law concerning the rights of property ... contract and other matters." cf. also the comments of Kelly J. to similar effect in *Glencar Exploration Plc v Mayo County Council (No. 2)* [2002] 1 I.R. 84 at 109.

promise, rather than merely a procedural commitment to consult before a change of official mind.

19–02 When the first edition of this book was published in 1986, legitimate expectations received scarcely a mention. Yet this principle, which was to receive the imprimatur of the Supreme Court in its decision in *Webb v Ireland*[4] in 1987, has launched a host of subsequent cases.[5] Apart from the doctrine of proportionality, there is, perhaps, no other new principle which has so rapidly given rise to so much litigation or which has so quickly become embedded in the fabric of the legal system. Nevertheless, there continues to be uncertainty as to its exact parameters[6] and not all of the case law over the last quarter century is readily reconcilable.[7] Besides its native roots in estoppel and cognate equitable concepts (covered below),[8] the principle may also be traced[9] to the European Court of Justice[10] and, beyond that, to German administrative law. It is likely, therefore, that developments in the administrative law of the European Union will continue to have an influence on the future progress of this principle in this jurisdiction.[11]

Cognate concepts: res judicata, functus officio and the individual estopped

19–03 A very particular and specialised species of estoppel/legitimate expectation is res judicata. Put briefly, the distinction is that, for an estoppel, in principle any form of serious commitment will suffice. But res judicata requires something tantamount to a court judgment. It has been defined in the following manner by Holmes L.J.:

> "A judgment not appealed from binds the parties and privies for all time by what appears on its face; and if it can be shown that, in the course of the action that resulted in the judgment, a certain definite material issue not set forth in the judgment itself was raised by the parties and determined judicially or

---

[4] [1988] I.R. 353.

[5] See, e.g. *Glencar Exploration Plc v Mayo County Council (No. 2)* [2002] 1 I.R. 84; [2002] 1 I.L.R.M. 1; *Lett & Co. Ltd v Wexford Borough Corporation* [2007] IEHC 195; *Power v Minister for Social and Family Affairs* [2006] IEHC 170; [2007] 1 I.R. 543; [2007] 1 I.L.R.M. 109; *Curran v Minister for Education and Science* [2009] IEHC 378; [2009] 4 I.R. 300.

[6] *Keogh v Criminal Assets Bureau* [2004] 2 I.R. 159 at 175 per Keane C.J.

[7] As noted by McCracken J. in *Abrahamson v Law Society of Ireland* [1996] 1 I.R. 403 at 422.

[8] See Part G.

[9] "The doctrine of legitimate expectation … derives, it would seem, from the jurisprudence of the European Court of Justice, although some have seen it also constituting a development of the English doctrine of promissory estoppels": *Glencar Exploration Plc v Mayo County Council (No. 2)* [2002] 1 I.R. 84 at 129 per Keane C.J.

[10] See, e.g. *Commission v Council (Staff Salaries)* [1973] E.C.R. 575; *EVGF v Mackprang* [1975] E.C.R. 607; *Delacre v Commission* (C-350/88) [1990] E.C.R. I-395. The classic case is now, of course, *Mulder v Minister van Landbouwen en Visserij* [1988] E.C.R. 2321, where the Court of Justice held that a milk producer who had been encouraged by provisions of a Community Regulation to suspend the marketing of milk for a limited period could not, following the expiry of that period, be subjected to new restrictions which specifically prejudiced him as far as future milk production was concerned. See generally on this issue, Sharpston, "Legitimate Expectations and Economic Reality" (1990) 15 E.L. Rev. 103.

[11] Indeed, in *Skellig Fish Ltd v Minister for Transport* [2010] IEHC 190, O'Neill J. observed that in the light of recent developments in domestic administrative law regarding substantive legitimate expectations, "there is no substantial difference between E.U. and Irish law on legitimate expectations".

by consent, it would be contrary to public policy to allow the same parties to re-agitate the same matter in subsequent legal proceedings."[12]

19–04   The doctrine of res judicata has hitherto had a limited application in regard to administrative decisions.[13] Such decisions rarely fulfil the required *probanda* for res judicata in that they do not deal with matters of status[14] and generally do not involve a *lis* between private individuals.[15] More fundamentally, a rigid application of the doctrine might conflict with two essential principles of administrative law: that jurisdiction cannot be created by estoppel, and that statutory powers and duties may not be fettered.[16] Subject to all these qualifications, the doctrine of res judicata is not confined to courts of law but may also apply in certain circumstances to tribunals and administrative authorities with powers to make binding determinations.[17] What little case law there is on the subject is covered in H & M, Chapter 19, Part K.

19–05   There are at least four forms of res judicata. First, a "cause of action" estoppel precludes the same parties from re-litigating an action which has been finally determined by a court of competent jurisdiction—this is res judicata "in its most essential form".[18] Secondly, an "issue estoppel" (or "constructive res judicata") prevents the parties to the earlier proceedings litigating an essential feature—"a certain definite material issue"—of the earlier decision.[19] Thirdly, a judgment in rem binds not only the parties to the litigation, but conclusively determines the status of a particular res or thing.

19–06   Finally, one form of issue estoppel which has recently been relied on in *Arklow Holidays v An Bord Pleanála*[20] is known as the rule in *Henderson v Henderson*. The facts in *Arklow* were that the applicants were seeking to rely upon substantive points of law which—and here is the important point—could have been, but were not, taken in earlier proceedings brought by the applicant against the respondent. It was held that they were barred from relying upon such arguments.

---

[12]   *Irish Land Commission v Ryan* [1900] 2 I.R. 565 at 584. For a general discussion of this topic, see Spencer Bower, Turner, *Res Judicata* (London: Butterworths, 1969).
[13]   Ganz, "Estoppel and Res Judicata in Administrative Law" [1965] *Public Law* 237.
[14]   *McMahon v Leahy* [1984] I.R. 525 (prior extradition order).
[15]   *R. v Fulham Tribunal Ex p. Zerek* [1951] 2 K.B. 1 at 11 per Devlin J.
[16]   *Bradshaw v M'Mullan* [1920] 2 I.R. 412 (prior court settlement contrary to Local Government (Ireland) Act 1898; plea of res judicata failed as one cannot give "judicial effect to a transaction which the statute expressly forbids" (Lord Shaw)). See also, the comments of Walsh J. in *Kildare County Council v Keogh* [1971] I.R. 330 at 343: "It would be contrary to public policy that an erroneous construction of a statute should be perpetuated so as to decide successive claims between the same parties". See also, the judgment of Carroll J. in *Dublin County Council v Mahon* [1995] 3 I.R. 193 and the comments of Laffoy J. in *Minister for Finance v Civil and Public Service Union (No. 1)* [2006] 1 I.R. 254 at 358. However, this rationale has been rejected by Lord Bridge in *Thrasyvoulou v Secretary of State for Environment* [1990] 2 A.C. 273.
[17]   *Athlone Woollen Mills Ltd v Athlone U.D.C.* [1950] I.R. 1; *Thrasyvoulou v Secretary of State for Environment* [1990] 2 A.C. 273; *Crown Estate Commrs v Dorset County Council* [1990] 1 Ch. 297; and *Ashbourne Holdings Ltd v An Bord Pleanala* [2003] IESC 18; [2003] 2 I.R. 114; [2003] 2 I.L.R.M. 446.
[18]   Spencer Bower, Turner, *Res Judicata* (London: Butterworths, 1969), p.149; McDermott, *Res Judicata and Double Jeopardy* (Dublin: Butterworths, 1999).
[19]   *D v C* [1984] I.L.R.M. 173; *Hoystead v Federal Taxation Commissioner* [1926] A.C. 155.
[20]   [2011] IESC 29 (July 21, 2011).

19–07   The res judicata doctrine must not be confused with a situation where the decision-taker has become functus officio. If a public authority has statutory power to determine some question, its decision will generally be final and irrevocable.[21] This is not because of the operation of res judicata, but rather because the authority lacks jurisdiction to alter its original decision. In other words, it is said to have become functus officio.[22]

19–08   In almost all the cases considered in this chapter, it is the applicant who is contending that he or she has a legitimate expectation or that the public body is estopped. However, in principle, there is no reason why the circumstances should not be such that a public body could rely upon estoppel as against the private party. This topic has been briefly covered in Chapter 11, Part I.

B. The Development of the Legitimate Expectations Doctrine

Seminal cases from the 1980s

19–09   In Ireland, the two earliest major authorities are the decision of the House of Lords in *Council of Civil Service Unions v Minister for the Public Service* (the "*GCHQ* case") and that of the Supreme Court in *Webb v Ireland*.[23] In the former case, the majority of employees working at Government Communications Headquarters, a highly sensitive defence establishment, belonged to a trade union. There had been a long-standing practice whereby all matters pertaining to the terms and conditions of employment were the subject of prior consultation between the management and the unions. The British Government, fearing that industrial action at GCHQ was impairing defence readiness, unilaterally revised the conditions of employment for GCHQ employees by providing that they would no longer be eligible to join any trade union other than a departmental staff association recognised by the director of GCHQ. The speeches of Lords Fraser and Diplock were notable for the fact that they were willing (obiter) to classify the practice of the consultation as a legitimate expectation enjoyed by the GCHQ employees and to hold that where such an expectation was not going to be honoured, in principle, the rules of natural justice had to be followed. However, Lord Diplock went on to hold that, on the facts of the instant case, this prima facie right to consultation had to yield to the interests of national security.

19–10   In *Webb v Ireland*,[24] the plaintiffs were the finders of a hoard of treasure

---

[21]   Of course, there are some examples of the decision-maker being expressly given the statutory power to alter the original decision, for instance, s.301(1)(a) of the Social Welfare (Consolidation) Act 2005. Sometimes, an administrative tribunal is expressly given the power to review decisions on grounds of consistency, e.g. s.122 of the Residential Tenancies Act 2004.

[22]   *Re 56 Denton Road* [1952] 2 All E.R. 799. See also, *Re Lynham's Estate* [1928] I.R. 127.

[23]   [1985] A.C. 374 and [1988] I.R. 353 respectively. This was not the first time that the phrase "legitimate expectations" has been used by the English courts, but *GCHQ* is regarded as the first major case in which the concept received the seal of approval of the House of Lords.

[24]   [1988] I.R. 353 at 379. For an interesting account of some of the issues which arose in this multi-faceted case, see Kelly, "Hidden Treasure and the Constitution" (1988) 10 D.U.L.J. 5 (N.S).

containing exceptionally valuable specimens of early Christian art. These articles were handed over for safe-keeping to the Director of the National Museum. The plaintiffs had alternative claims. The first of these, which succeeded, was grounded on the Director's assurance to the plaintiffs that they would be honourably treated and that the State had failed to do this. Finlay C.J. put the matter thus:

> "It would appear that the doctrine of 'legitimate expectations', sometimes described as 'reasonable expectations' has not in those terms been the subject of any decisions of our courts. However, the doctrine connoted by such expressions is but an aspect of the well-recognised concept of promissory estoppel whereby a promise or representation as to intention may in certain circumstances be held binding on the representor or promisor. The nature and extent of that doctrine in circumstances such as those of this case has been expressed as follows by Lord Denning M.R. in *Amalgamated Property Co. v Texas Bank*:
>> 'When the parties to a transaction proceed on the basis of an underlying assumption – either of law or of fact – whether due to misrepresentation or mistake makes no difference – on which they have conducted the dealings between them – neither of them will be allowed to go back on that assumption when it would be unfair or unjust to allow him to do so. If one of them does seek to go back on it, the courts will give the other such remedy as the equity of the case demands.'"[25]

19–11 The plaintiffs had argued, in the alternative, that the long-standing practice of the National Museum of paying rewards to finders of such treasure was enough to create a legitimate expectation to fair compensation in their favour, but (because of the express assurance given by the plaintiffs) Finlay C.J. did not find it necessary to[26] decide whether the long-standing practice could of itself give rise to a legitimate expectation.

19–12 However, whichever alternative be taken, the *Webb* decision would seem to have been an instance of a generous application of the doctrine of promissory estoppel, rather than presaging a radical new development in the law[27] (and might indeed have occurred in a private law case in which the defendant was, for example, an insurance company). In addition, this was a case in which no statutory powers of the State were involved and, accordingly, where there was no potential conflict between the plaintiff's legitimate expectations and the doctrine that the exercise of statutory powers may not be fettered by estoppel, a point which has deservedly received attention in the subsequent case law.[28] Nevertheless, it is *Webb* which has captured the headline.

---

[25] [1988] I.R. 353 at 384. The quotation from Lord Denning is at [1982] Q.B. 84 at 122.

[26] [1988] I.R. 353 at 379. This principle was applied in somewhat similar circumstances by Barr J. in *Re the "La Lavia"*, High Court, July 26, 1994. Note, however, that the Supreme Court took a different view of these facts: [1996] 1 I.L.R.M. 194.

[27] "[The] roots [of *Webb*] were firmly planted in the soil of promissory estoppel": *Glencar Exploration Plc v Mayo County Council (No. 2)* [2002] 1 I.R. 84 at 106 per Kelly J.

[28] See, e.g. the comments of O'Flaherty J. in *Wiley v Revenue Commissioners* [1994] 2 I.R. 160, those of Costello J. in *Tara Prospecting Ltd v Minister for Energy* [1993] I.L.R.M. 771 and those of Kelly J. in *Glencar Exploration Plc v Mayo County Council (No. 2)* [2002] 1 I.R. 84.

The modern law from *Glencar Exploration* onwards

19–13   The leading case now is *Glencar Exploration v Mayo County Council (No. 1)*.[29] In this case the plaintiffs were mining companies who had prospected for valuable metals pursuant to licence, but this activity was then prohibited by Mayo County Council in their development plan. Following the invalidation of the ban, the plaintiffs sought damages for misfeasance (see paras 18–08 to 18–10) and for breach of legitimate expectations. Fennelly J. on behalf of the Supreme Court observed that the plaintiffs' case on this point was very weak, since it did not come "in any meaningful way at all within the concept of action or inaction by a public authority which an affected individual legitimately has the right to expect".[30] Thus, even though Fennelly J. did not think that this was "an appropriate case in which to delineate the contours of the principle of legitimate expectations", *Glencar Exploration* has since come to be regarded as the leading authority, by virtue of the following much-quoted passage from the judgment:

> "In order to succeed in a claim based on failure of a public authority to respect legitimate expectations, it seems to me to be necessary to establish three matters ... Firstly, the public authority must have made a statement or adopted a position amounting to a promise or representation, express or implied as to how it will act in respect of an identifiable area of its activity. I will call this the representation. Secondly, the representation must be addressed or conveyed either directly or indirectly to an identifiable person or group of persons, affected actually or potentially in such a way that it forms part of a transaction definitively entered into or a relationship between that person or group and the public authority or that the person or group has acted on the faith of the representation. Thirdly, it must be such as to create an expectation reasonably entertained by the person or group that the public authority will abide by the representation to the extent that it would be unjust to permit the public authority to resile from it. Refinements or extensions of these propositions are obviously possible. Equally they are qualified by considerations of the public interest including the principle that freedom to exercise properly a statutory power is to be respected."

19–14   These principles have been consistently applied in a series of subsequent decisions. A most important example is *Lett & Co. v Wexford Borough Council*,[31] a case where the Minister was held to be bound by the establishment of a compensation scheme to compensate mussel fishing companies in respect of losses caused by the operation of a waste water facility, in which Clarke J. stated:

> "... [O]n the current state of the development of the doctrine of legitimate expectation, it is reasonable to state that there are both positive and negative factors which must be found to be present or absent, as the case may be, in order that a party can rely upon the doctrine. The positive elements are to be found in the three tests set out by Fennelly J. in the passage from *Glencar Exploration (No 2)* [see above] ... The negative factors are issues which may either prevent those three tests from being met (for example the fact that, as

---

[29]   [2002] 1 I.R. 84.
[30]   [2002] 1 I.R. 84 at 160.
[31]   [2007] IEHC 195.

in *Wiley*,[32] it may not be legitimate to entertain an expectation that a past error will be continued in the future) or may exclude the existence of a legitimate expectation by virtue of the need to preserve the entitlement of a decision maker to exercise a statutory discretion within the parameters provided for in the statute concerned or, alternatively, may be necessary to enable, as in *Hempenstall v Minister for Environment*,[33] legitimate changes in executive policy to take place. I therefore propose to approach the contentions of the parties as to the existence of a legitimate expectation in this case by first considering the positive elements of the test.

The first issue which, therefore, arises is as to whether it has been shown that a public authority has made a statement or adopted a position amounting to a promise or representation. On the facts of this case it ... seems to me that the evidence establishes that the Minister did, indeed, at a minimum, adopt a position which amounts to a representation to the effect that an appropriate compensation scheme would be put in place ... The first test is, therefore, met.

The second matter that requires to be established is that the representation or promise must be conveyed either directly or indirectly to an identifiable person or group of persons. Again it seems to me that this test is met. The whole purpose of putting in place a scheme of compensation was expressly directed towards dealing with the concerns of the mussel fishermen. Letts are, therefore, within a group of clearly identifiable persons to whom the promise was made.

The third test is that the promise or representation must be such as to create an expectation, reasonably entertained, that the public authority will abide by the representation to the extent that it would be unjust to permit the public authority to resile from it. It is clear that the Minister was persuaded that, in balancing the various rights, entitlements and obligations which were at play in considering to grant the foreshore licence, it was appropriate, in the public interest, to give Wexford Council such a licence, provided that an appropriate compensation scheme was put in place. To resile from that obligation, certainly in the absence of some compelling alternative factor, would, in my view, be unjust."

19–15 Clarke J. went on to consider whether were any negative conditions, the existence of which would prevent a legitimate expectation from arising. Although he found none, the following statement of his approach is valuable:

"It is, therefore, necessary to turn to those factors which may limit the operation of the doctrine of legitimate expectation even though the three positive tests may be found to be met. As is clear from *Glencar* there are

---

[32] *Wiley v Revenue Commissioners* [1989] I.R. 350 (HC); [1994] 2 I.R. 160 (SC). See para.19–36.

[33] [1994] 2 I.R. 20. In this case the Minister had rescinded a previous moratorium on the grant of new taxi licences in the light of a new departmental report on the subject. Costello J. held (at 32) that no plea of legitimate expectations could prevail in such circumstances: "It seems to me that the law should not trammel the exercise by a Minister of his statutory functions even if, in the light of new information and advice, he exercises them in a manner contrary to an earlier statement of intent."

limitations on the operation of the doctrine so that it cannot be invoked to require that a statutory discretion be exercised in any particular way.

While the original decision of the Minister in this case was to the effect that a foreshore licence should be granted (and was, thus, an exercise of a statutory power) it does not seem to me that the question of the grant or otherwise of compensation (or a promise to that effect) was, in reality, a decision within a statutory framework. There is no legislation providing for compensation in this area. The Minister, in deciding whether it is appropriate or not to ensure that compensation be granted, is not, therefore, in my view, exercising a statutory discretion. It is not, therefore, the case that the limitations on the doctrine of legitimate expectation which preclude the Minister from being bound to exercise a statutory discretion in a particular way, have any application to the facts of this case."

C. Analysis

19–16   Here, we focus on some of the more specific issues thrown up by the case law. Broadly speaking, sections (1)–(4) are concerned with "positive factors" (to use the *Lett* terminology), whereas sections (5)–(11) deal with "negative factors".

(1) Must the promise have been communicated to the applicant?

19–17   In *Nolan v Minister for Environment*,[34] Costello J. held that the applicant could not rely on an alleged representation in a letter sent to her local residents' association in the absence of evidence that this representation was communicated to her at the relevant time. Likewise, in *Re "La Lavia"*,[35] O'Flaherty J. rejected the plea of legitimate expectations in the absence of an explicit representation causing the applicants to act to their detriment, as the "whole idea of a promise is that it has to make an impression on the mind of the promisee".[36] (It should be noted, however, that in that case O'Flaherty J. left open the possibility that a regular practice might in and of itself establish an entitlement to a legitimate expectation.)

19–18   But, as against these authorities, Fennelly J. in *Glencar Exploration* has remarked:

"I do not say that there must be a direct *nexus*. It may be sufficient that the claimant belongs to class or group of persons affected by an act which is accompanied by or implies an intention to follow an identifiable course of conduct by the public authority."[37]

---

[34] [1989] I.R. 357. See also, *Devitt v Minister for Education* [1989] I.L.R.M. 636 at 650–651 discussed at para.19–22.

[35] [1996] 1 I.L.R.M. 194.

[36] [1996] 1 I.L.R.M. 194 at 200.

[37] [2002] 1 I.R. 84 at 161. Fennelly J. has also articulated the view that the legitimate expectation must form part of a transaction or relationship between the public body and the citizen concerned: see, e.g. his comments to this effect in *Daly v Minister for the Marine* [2001] IESC 77; [2001] 3 I.R. 513 at 528.

Similarly, in *Fakih v Minister for Justice*,[38] the applicants (who were Lebanese asylum seekers) were held to be entitled to rely on the terms of (an admittedly solemn) commitment given regarding the treatment of asylum seekers contained in a letter written by the Minister to the United Nations High Commissioner for Refugees, but in respect of which the applicants could have had no advance knowledge prior to their illegal entry into the State. O'Hanlon J. then continued by saying:

"As the law has developed it has come to be applied in situations where the conventional plea of estoppel by conduct might not be available since the party seeking to rely on the plea of legitimate expectation may not be able to establish that he has been induced by the conduct of the other party to act to his own detriment."[39]

The judge, therefore, concluded that the applicants had acquired a legitimate expectation that their request for asylum would be dealt with in accordance with the 1985 procedures.

19–19 Perhaps the case law can be explained on the basis that it is in the interests of good and orderly administration that, in the absence of good reasons to the contrary, an administrator should be bound by agreed procedures. Since these cases the courts have consistently held that officially published statements of practice can give rise to an enforceable legitimate expectation.[40] A point of distinction is that in *Fakih*, *Lett & Co.* and *Curran* the Minister had intended to lay down binding procedures applicable to all appropriate cases or had published or circulated the documentation giving rise to the representation, whereas the documents in *Nolan* and *Devitt* were in the nature of internal memoranda which were not expressed to be for the benefit of the public at large, and by their nature were never intended to create an expectation on which the relevant class of the public could rely.

(2) Is an assurance or representation enough of itself or must there be reliance?

19–20 There have been some High Court decisions which hold that a mere representation of itself will not give rise to a legitimate expectation, as there must be something approaching reliance or change of circumstances so as to make it unfair or inequitable for the representor to renege on an assurance. In one of these cases, *Garda Representative Association v Ireland*,[41] the plaintiffs

[38] [1993] 2 I.R. 406. See, to similar effect, *Curran v Minister for Education and Science* [2009] IEHC 378; [2009] 4 I.R. 300 at 312.

[39] [1993] 2 I.R. 406 at 424.

[40] See, e.g. *Keogh v Criminal Assets Bureau* [2004] IESC 42; [2004] 2 I.R. 159 (taxpayer's charter); *Power v Minister for Social and Family Affairs* [2006] IEHC 170; [2007] 1 I.R. 543; [2007] 1 I.L.R.M. 109 (back to work scheme); *Curran v Minister for Education and Science* [2009] IEHC 378; [2009] 4 I.R. 300 (early retirement scheme for teachers).

[41] [1989] I.L.R.M. 1 (HC). This question did not feature on appeal to the Supreme Court which focused on the reasonableness issue: see [1994] 1 I.L.R.M. 81. For a similar view, see also, *Cosgrove v Legal Aid Board* [1991] 2 I.R. 43 (applicant may have acquired expectation that Legal Aid Board would deal promptly with her case, but this could not be enforced under the legitimate expectations doctrine as there was no evidence that she had acted to her detriment); *Glencar Exploration v Mayo County Council (No. 2)* [2002] 1 I.R. 84 at 162 (Fennelly J.).

sought to rely on an assurance given by the Minister for Justice in the Dáil that certain overtime payments would not be abolished without consultation with the representative associations. Murphy J. held that this could not form the basis of a legitimate expectation, "as there [was] no evidence that the plaintiffs relied upon the Minister's statement". Perhaps another way of looking at this matter is to say that this was simply a political statement which none of the parties understood to be absolutely binding.[42]

19–21 Two other decisions tentatively suggest that some form of reliance is necessary. In *Dunleavy v Dun Laoghaire Rathdown County Council*,[43] Macken J. held that, given its generality, the initial letter which had been designed to gauge the level of interest in potential sales of certain maisonettes could not in itself create a legitimate expectation. But there was additional correspondence which went further and conveyed a clear impression that the properties would be sold. This, coupled with the fact that the tenants had acted to their detriment by making arrangements to buy, was sufficient to create a legitimate expectation. Likewise, in *Curran v Minister for Education and Science*,[44] Dunne J. held that teachers who had acted on foot of a published department circular with regard to early retirement acquired a legitimate expectation in that regard. However, on the facts, the Minister was subsequently entitled to resile from that commitment due to abruptly declining State finances.[45]

(3) Terms of representation

19–22 Any representation, whether express or implied, must be unqualified and unambiguous. This point was made by Lardner J. in *Devitt v Minister for Education*[46]

---

[42] cf. the comments by Keane C.J. in *Keogh v Criminal Assets Bureau* [2004] 2 I.R. 159 at 175 with regard to the Revenue's Charter of Rights: "It is undoubtedly the case that documents such as the Charter of Rights under consideration in the present case, whether so described or called a 'mission statement' or given some other title, frequently contain what are no more than praiseworthy statements of an aspirational nature designed to encourage the members of the organisation concerned to meet acceptable standards of behaviour in their dealings with the public ... Statements of that nature would not normally give rise to causes of action based on the legitimate expectation doctrine."
        These considerations notwithstanding, Keane C.J. nonetheless held that the Revenue Commissioners' commitment in the Charter to give taxpayers access to "full, accurate and timely information about revenue law" was enforceable by means of the legitimate expectation doctrine.
[43] [2005] IEHC 381.
[44] [2009] IEHC 378; [2009] 4 I.R. 300.
[45] See para.19–43.
[46] [1989] I.L.R.M. 636 at 650–651. In *John M.P. Greaney Ltd v Dublin Corporation* [1994] 3 I.R. 384 Morris J. held (at 392) that a legitimate expectations plea failed on the facts as "nothing in the nature of a firm assurance was ever given to the first applicant as an integral part of the transaction under which it lodged the application".
        Returning to the applicant's acceptance that he had not acted to his detriment on foot of the letter of October 1, 1993, I would accept that there is a distinction between the doctrine of legitimate expectations and promissory estoppel. Legitimate expectations constitutes an accepted part of the principles of administrative law applied by our courts through the vehicle of judicial review. It is concerned essentially to see that administrative powers are not used unfairly. An expectation may be legitimate and cognisable by the courts even in the absence of the sort of action to the claimant's detriment that forms part of the law of estoppel. On the other hand, I would not accept that the mere fact of an expectation can suffice without some context relevant to fairness in the exercise of legal or administrative powers. Those who come

where the plaintiff had submitted that since the Minister had allowed her to apply for a permanent teaching post, she could not turn around and appoint the applicant to a mere temporary post. In the absence of an "unqualified assurance" (such as had been given in *Webb*), Lardner J. did not think that the applicant had acquired a legitimate expectation that she would be appointed to a permanent position.

19–23 *Atlantic Marine v Minister for Transport,*[47] too, illustrates the fact that a good deal may turn on what exactly are the terms of the expectation and, thus, what does compliance require. The facts were that a Code of Practice had been established by the Minister, requiring all fishing vessels within a particular category to carry a life raft meeting certain specifications. It was established in evidence that a significant number of these vessels were carrying unapproved life rafts, contrary to the code of practice. Plaintiff was a certified seller of life rafts to vessels. He claimed that, as a result of the failure of the Minister to enforce the requirements of the Code of Practice, it had suffered financial loss. The High Court (Clarke J.) found that, at least in general terms, a legitimate expectation arises that the Minister would:

> "... enforce the code of conduct through the licensing system to a reasonable extent. However, it does not seem to me that any such expectation could extend to an obligation on the Minister to ensure that the code is enforced in the circumstances. The Minister clearly retains a discretion as to how to deal with any failure of compliance ... Any representation that the Minister might impliedly be said to have made ... could only extend to reasonable enforcement having regard to the resources reasonably available ... and having regard to the need to act proportionately so far as the rights of individual fishing vessel operators are concerned."

19–24 Given this finding, the conclusion to the case was that the court would adjourn to allow the Minister to consider the judgment and formulate the action he would take.

(4) Circulars

19–25 The cases disclose that one of the most common ways in which legitimate expectations have been created is by way of an administrative circular. An example of this (from well before the era in which the concept received an identity and a label) is provided by *Latchford v Minister for Industry and Commerce,*[48] which concerned a ministerial scheme providing for the payment of subsidies to bakers. This published scheme contained certain conditions, with all of which the plaintiffs

---

within the ambit of an administrative or regulatory regime may be able to establish that it would be unfair, discriminatory or unjust to permit the body exercising a power to change a policy or a set of existing rules, or depart from an undertaking or promise without taking account of the legitimate expectations created by them. However, the very notion of fairness has within it an idea that there is an existing relationship which it would be unfair to alter.

[47] [2011] 2 I.L.R.M. 12 at para.7.6. The quotation is at paras 7.19–8.5.

[48] [1950] I.R. 33. For other cases on circulars, see *Staunton v St Lawrence's Hospital*, unreported, High Court, February 21, 1986. In *Donohue v Revenue Commissioners* [1993] 1 I.R. 172, Blayney J. suggested that had the defendants refused to pay certain allowances specified in a circular as payable to certain of its employees, the applicant employer would have been entitled to recover them.

had complied. The Minister refused to sanction the payment of the subsidy on the ground that the plaintiffs had been convicted of an offence relating to the sale of bread. The published conditions, however, did not disqualify a claimant on this ground. The Supreme Court accordingly made a declaration that the Minister was not entitled to withhold payment of the subsidy, with Murnaghan J. commenting:

> "After having made and published the conditions on which the payment of subsidy would be made, the Minister can alter these conditions from time to time; but until altered or withdrawn, the conditions apply, and persons who have complied with the conditions are entitled to claim that they have qualified for payment of the subsidy."[49]

19–26 This is a classic example of where an administrative circular may be said to have created legitimate expectations, although, of course, the Supreme Court did not use this language as such. Here the notion that there can be no estoppel in respect of the exercise of statutory powers could have no purchase, since the scheme in *Latchford* was a non-statutory administrative one. The expectation arose from a circular and circulars are—and are intended to—taken seriously by administrators and citizenry, few of whom readily appreciate the difference between a law and a circular.

19–27 The administration of our tax laws could prove a fertile source of legitimate expectation claims. For it is a significant feature of tax practice in this jurisdiction that the Revenue Commissioners will sometimes give what have come to be known as "advance rulings" on tax planning schemes, i.e. indicate their position in advance on whether a particular scheme will avoid a tax liability. A second practice is said to exist whereby the Revenue Commissioners will sometimes grant extra-statutory concessions to mitigate the rigour of the revenue code, although (in contrast to the practice prevailing in the United Kingdom) such concessions are not published. Thirdly, occasionally, the Revenue Commissioners do publish statements of practice, indicating what attitude they will take in regard to the interpretation of certain legislation.

19–28 There would seem to be room for the operation of the doctrine of legitimate expectations in any of these three areas, so as to prevent the Revenue officials from reneging on prior representations or from unilaterally altering settled practices or from treating similarly situated taxpayers in an inconsistent fashion. However, as in other areas, this doctrine must be reconciled with the conflicting principle that the Revenue Commissioners, like other public officials, cannot by their representation change the law. However the issue has not squarely arisen, on the facts.[50]

(5) What conduct or practice gives rise to an expectation or estoppel?

19–29 The situation covered here is where although the public body has said little or nothing directly, it has been pursuing an open and consistent practice, which a reasonable and informed person would regard as creating an expectation that it

---

[49] [1950] I.R. 33 at 40–41.
[50] *Pandion Haliaetus Ltd v Revenue Commissioners* [1987] I.R. 309 at 318.

would continue. At any rate, in certain circumstances, the courts will not permit a public body to depart without notice from an established practice.[51] Thus, for example, in *Glenkerrin Homes Ltd v Dun Laoghaire Rathdown Corporation*[52] a practice had evolved over the years whereby local authorities had given developers certificates of compliance, in respect of payment of planning contributions under the Planning and Development Act 2000. Although, strictly speaking, there was no statutory basis for the practice, it had nonetheless evolved as a key element of any conveyancing transaction. Accordingly, Clarke J. felt that, in these circumstances, it would be unfair if the Council could change the policy unilaterally without notice. In short, in the circumstances, the existence of such a well-established and significant practice amounted to an implied representation that the practice would be followed. Another aspect of this case related to the negative features identified in *Lett* (at paras 19–14 to 19–15) is that this was not a situation in which the public body had much discretion, nor one in which there had been a change of policy. Accordingly, Clarke J. held for the applicant.

(6) Substantive benefits or procedural requirements?

19–30 The legitimate expectations doctrine means, at least, that a public body is obliged to honour a commitment which it has given that some particular procedure must be followed.[53] Thus, straightforwardly, a public body must honour an explicit commitment as to the procedure which it will follow. In *Fakih v Minister for Justice*,[54] for instance, a number of Lebanese immigrants had illegally arrived in Ireland. Their applications for refugee status were summarily rejected and they were refused permission to enter the State. They asserted that their applications should have been dealt with on the basis of procedures to be followed prior to the making of any deportation order[55] which had been privately agreed between the Irish Minister for Justice and the United Nations High Commissioner for Refugees in 1985. O'Hanlon J. held that the applicants had acquired a legitimate expectation that they would be dealt with according to the terms of the 1985 agreement and he quoted the following passage from the speech of Lord Fraser in *Attorney General of Hong Kong v Ng Yuen Shiu*[56] with approval:

> "The justification [for the principle of legitimate expectations] is primarily that, when a public authority has promised to follow a certain procedure, it is in the interest of good administration that it should act fairly and should

---

[51] The practice must, however, be firmly established. Cf. the comments of Blayney J. in *Wiley v Revenue Commissioners* [1989] I.R. 350 at 356 (in the context of a legitimate expectations plea based on two separate decisions concerning the same applicant) that "the doing of something on two occasions only could not constitute a practice".

[52] [2007] IEHC 298.

[53] See, e.g. *Fakih v Minister for Justice* [1993] 2 I.R. 406; *Navan Tanker Services Ltd v Meath County Council*, unreported, High Court, December 13, 1996; *Anisimova v Minister for Justice* [1998] 1 I.R. 186; and *Keogh v Criminal Assets Bureau* [2004] 2 I.R. 159.

[54] [1993] 2 I.R. 406. See, to similar effect, *Gutrani v Minister for Justice* [1993] 2 I.R. 427; *Anisimova v Minister for Justice* [1997] IESC 72; [1998] 1 I.R. 186 (principles in *Fakih* tacitly approved, but legitimate expectations claim failed on the facts).

[55] The agreement set out the steps (such as personal interviews, etc) that would be taken by immigration officers in respect of applications for refugee status.

[56] [1983] 2 A.C. 629.

implement its promise, so long as the implementation does not interfere with its statutory duty."[57]

19–31   The second—and less straightforward—form which a procedural advantage may take occurs where no procedure is set down. Yet, depending on the circumstances, before the public body is free to resile from the commitment given a court may require either *some* form of notice of the impending change or even some form of hearing in that regard.[58] This form is illustrated by *GCHQ* (the facts of which were given at para.19–09).

19–32   For the first two decades or so since *Webb*, the general understanding was that the doctrine of legitimate expectations was concerned with procedural commitments only. Cases such as *Tara Prospecting* and *Gilheaney* show that the courts struggled to navigate a via media between, on the one hand, obliging public authorities to honour commitments given to the public, and ensuring that no estoppel could prevail as against the exercise of statutory powers on the other. Confining the legitimate expectations doctrine to procedural commitments seemed an ideal way of ensuring that the doctrine was kept in check; "judges feel far more comfortable telling public bodies what procedures they should follow rather than what outcomes they should pursue".[59]

19–33   Attractive as this reasoning is, it seems impossible to differentiate between procedural and substantive commitments on such an a priori basis. As was said in a celebrated English decision:

> "It is difficult to see why it is any less unfair to frustrate a legitimate expectation that something will or will not be done by the decision-maker than it is to frustrate a legitimate expectation that the applicant will be listened to before the decision-maker decides whether to take a particular step."[60]

19–34   The Supreme Court has reserved the question of whether the doctrine of

---

[57]   [1983] 2 A.C. 629 at 638.
[58]   See, e.g. *Eogan v University College Dublin* [1996] 1 I.R. 390; [1996] 2 I.L.R.M. 302 (applicant professor had acquired an expectation that he would be allowed to continue in office until the age of 70, but it was held that this expectation was defeated by a change of circumstances necessitating an earlier retirement age and where the applicant had been given every opportunity to make submissions); *Glenkerrin Homes v Dun Laoghaire Rathdown Co. Co.* [2007] IEHC 298 (third-party applicants relying on administrative practice generally entitled to notice of the change). But notice will not always be possible or feasible having regard to public interest considerations: see, e.g. *Curran v Minister for Education and Science* [2009] IEHC 378; [2009] 4 I.R. 300.
[59]   Steele, "Substantive Legitimate Expectations: Striking the Right Balance" (2005) 121 L.Q.R. 300.
[60]   *R v Minister for Agriculture, Fisheries and Food Ex p. Hamble (Offshore) Fisheries Ltd* [1995] 2 All E.R. 714 at 724 per Sedley J. This reasoning was strongly disapproved two years later by the English Court of Appeal in *R. v Secretary of State for the Home Department Ex p. Hargreaves* [1997] 1 All E.R. 397. But English law has moved on to the point where substantive benefits will be protected: see, e.g. *R v North and East Devon Health Authority Ex p. Coughlan* [2001] Q.B. 213; [2000] 2 W.L.R. 622; *R. (Nadarahah) v Home Secretary* [2005] EWCA Civ 1363.

legitimate expectations is capable of protecting substantive benefits.[61] Nevertheless, a consistent line of High Court authority on the law in this jurisdiction has now evolved to the point where the courts will protect substantive benefits by means of legitimate expectations, at any rate where either non-statutory powers are at issue[62] or where perhaps it is plain that there is no real conflict on the facts with the potential exercise of a discretionary power.[63] There remains, nevertheless, substantial life in the "procedural rights only" restriction. For instance, in *Lett & Co. v Wexford Borough Council*,[64] Clarke J. stated:

"I should emphasise that the existence of a longstanding practice does not give rise to any legitimate expectation that that practice will not change. However where third parties reasonably arrange their affairs by reference to such a practice it seems to me that such third parties are entitled to rely upon an expectation that the practice will not be changed without reasonable notice being given. The notice that would be required is such as would reasonably allow those who have conducted their affairs in accordance with the practice to consider and implement an alternative means for dealing with the issues arising. On the facts of this case a reasonable period would need to be given to enable those involved in conveyancing (and, in particular, the Conveyancing Committee of the Law Society) an opportunity to consider and make recommendations as to the manner in which conveyancing issues arising in relation to planning in respect of newly built homes should be dealt with in the absence of certificates of compliance."[65]

19–35 The most definite contribution to the "procedure only versus substantive right" debate is to be found in the following passage from *Atlantic Marine v Minister for Transport*,[66] in which the High Court (Clarke J.) made what, with respect, seems to be a statement of sound common sense:

"There is no reason in principle why the doctrine of legitimate expectation cannot be invoked to obtain a substantive, rather than a procedural, benefit. However, it does seem to me that the negative factors which I identified in *Lett* as being likely to prevent a legitimate expectation arising and are much more likely to apply, in practice, to cases where a substantive, rather than a procedural, benefit is asserted. There are likely to be very few cases where a legitimate expectation concerning compliance with a particular procedure could infringe the principles frequently invoked against recognising a legitimate expectation ... It is highly improbable that imposing an agreed procedure could for example lead to a party obtaining a right which they

---

[61] See, e.g. the comments of Keane C.J. and Fennelly J. in *Glencar Exploration Plc v Mayo County Council (No. 2)* [2002] 1 I.R. 84 at 131 and 162.

[62] See, e.g. *Power v Minister for Social and Family Affairs* [2006] IEHC 170; [2007] 1 I.R. 543 at 556 per MacMenamin J.; *Lett & Co. v Wexford Borough Council* [2007] IEHC 413 per Clarke J.; and *Curran v Minister for Education and Science* [2009] IEHC 378; [2009] 4 I.R. 300 at 313–316 per Dunne J. For an incisive analysis, see Delany, "Legitimate Expectations and Substantive Effects: Recent Developments" (2007) 29 D.U.L.J. 413.

[63] See, e.g. the comments of Quirke J. in *O'Leary v Minister for Finance* [1998] 2 I.L.R.M. 321.

[64] [2007] IEHC 195.

[65] Emphasis added.

[66] [2011] 2 I.L.R.M. 12 at para.7.6.

did not have [as in *Wiley*]. Likewise, the preservation of an entitlement of a decision maker to exercise a statutory discretion within the parameters provided for in the statute concerned, is most unlikely to be interfered with by requiring the relevant decision maker to comply with expectations legitimately arising in respect of the procedures to be followed. Other examples could be given."

(7) When is an expectation "legitimate"?

19–36   In *Wiley v Revenue Commissioners*,[67] pursuant to a statutory scheme, the applicant had obtained, on two occasions, substantial repayments of excise duty on the basis that he was a disabled driver, despite the fact that he was not sufficiently disabled to satisfy the statutory requirements. Next, the Revenue Commissioners, conscious that a scheme designed for the benefit of wholly disabled drivers had been availed of by ineligible persons, introduced more stringent evidential requirements, so as to ensure that the statutory requirements were met. The applicant was not aware of this until he had purchased a new motor vehicle in 1987, when he discovered that the medical certificates as to the extent of his partial disability were not accepted. He then claimed that he had acquired a legitimate expectation that the earlier arrangements should be continued in his case, or, failing that, that "if there was to be a change in the requirements of the Revenue Commissioners", he should have been told in advance of his purchase of a new motor car.[68] The major reason why the plaintiff failed in *Wiley* was Blayney J.'s finding that it was necessary for the applicant to show not only that he had an expectation that he would receive the refund, but also that such an expectation was a legitimate one. It is scarcely surprising that the applicant's appeal was rejected by the Supreme Court.[69]

(8) Reasons justifying a change of position

19–37   The public body is generally entitled to resile from its previous practice or representation where there actually exist in the particular case objective reasons which justify this change of position. At most then, the effect of the doctrine of legitimate expectations is only to protect the citizen against a sudden[70] or arbitrary change of position by a public authority. Thus, in *Egan v Minister for Defence*,[71] the plaintiff was an officer in the Air Corps. He sought the Minister's permission (as is required by the Defence Act 1954) for early retirement, in order to take up a position with a private airline. Barr J. found, as a fact, that there was no settled practice giving rise to a legitimate expectation on the part of the plaintiff. Significantly, however, Barr J. added that even if there had been such a settled practice, this would not have been either unfair or unjust in the circumstances.

---

[67]   [1989] I.R. 350; [1994] 2 I.R. 142.

[68]   [1994] 2 I.R. 160 at 168.

[69]   The European Court of Justice would scarcely have taken a different view, for, as was said in *Delacre v Commission* (C-350/88) [1990] E.C.R. I-395 at 462: "Traders cannot have a legitimate expectation that an existing situation which is capable of being altered by Community institutions in the exercise of their discretionary powers will be maintained."

[70]   See, e.g. *Glenkerrin Homes v Dun Laoghaire Rathdown County Council* [2007] IEHC 298.

[71]   Unreported, High Court, November 24, 1988.

19–38   More generally,[72] "the executive enjoys a constitutional entitlement to change policy". Thus, in *Tara Prospecting v Minister for Energy*[73] the applicant companies had been awarded mining prospecting licences under the Minerals Development Act 1940 in 1981 and 1984. The companies found some gold deposits in the areas covered by their licences and they re-applied for a renewal of their prospecting licences. These licences were granted, but large areas of territory included in the earlier licences were excluded. The Minister justified this exclusion on environmental, cultural and religious grounds.[74] The applicants challenged this aspect of the decision on the ground that it violated the principle of legitimate expectations; they asserted that the Minister had represented that their licences would be renewed in full if the prospecting had proved to be successful.

19–39   In *Tara*, Costello J. reached the following conclusions:

> "(1) There is a duty on a Minister who is exercising a discretionary power which may affect rights or interests to adopt fair procedures in the exercise of the power. Where a member of the public has a legitimate expectation arising from the Minister's words and/or conduct that (a) he will be given a hearing before a decision adverse to his interests will be taken or (b) that he will obtain a benefit from the exercise of the power then the Minister also has a duty to act fairly towards him and this may involve a duty to give him a fair hearing before a decision adverse to his interests is taken. There would then arise a co-relative right to a fair hearing which, if denied, will justify the court in quashing the decision.
>
> (2) The existence of a legitimate expectation that a benefit will be conferred does not in itself give rise to any legal or equitable right to the benefit itself which can be [judicially] enforced. However, in cases involving public authorities, other than cases involving the exercise of statutory discretionary powers, an equitable right to the benefit may arise from the application of the principles of promissory estoppel to which effect will be given by appropriate court order.
>
> (3) In cases involving the exercise of a discretionary statutory power the only legitimate expectation relating to the conferring of the benefit that can be inferred from words or conduct is a conditional one, namely, that a benefit will be conferred provided that at the time that the Minister considers that it is a proper exercise of the statutory power in the light of current policy to grant it. Such a conditional expectation cannot give rise to the benefit should it later be refused by the Minister in the public interest.
>
> (4) In cases involving the exercise of a discretionary statutory power in which an explicit assurance has been given which gives rise to an expectation that a benefit will be conferred no enforceable equitable or legal

---

[72]   *Glenkerrin Homes Ltd v Dun Laoghaire Rathdown Corporation* [2007] IEHC 298 per Clarke J. cf. the comments of Lord Diplock in *Hughes v Department of Health and Social Security* [1985] A.C. 776 at 788 to the effect that the liberty to change administrative policy was "inherent in our constitutional form of government". For particularly graphic examples, see *R. v Secretary of State for Health Ex p. US Tobacco International Ltd* [1992] 1 Q.B. 353 and *Clinton v Minister for Justice, Equality and Law Reform*, unreported, High Court, June 21, 2010.

[73]   [1993] I.L.R.M. 771.

[74]   Some of the lands were particularly scenic. One licence had also included Croagh Patrick, a traditional place of pilgrimage.

right to the benefit can arise. No promissory estoppel can arise because the Minister cannot estop either himself or his successors from exercising a discretionary power in the manner prescribed by Parliament at the time it is exercised."[75]

19–40   On the facts, Costello J. agreed that the applicants could reasonably have expected that if prospecting was successful, their licences would be renewed until such time as they were in a position to apply for a mining lease:

> "But this expectation could only be a conditional one as the Minister was exercising a discretionary power and the applicants should have been aware that the renewal of the licence was conditional on the Minister concluding at the time of renewal that renewal was in the public interest. This was the only 'legitimate expectation' that the applicants could entertain. As the Minister concluded that the renewal of licences was not in the public interest no enforceable right to them could possibly arise."[76]

19–41   Contrast *Tara Prospecting* with an earlier decision of Costello J., *Philips v Medical Council*.[77] In this case, a foreign doctor had sought registration under the terms of rules promulgated in September 1980. While that application was pending, the Council adopted new rules which it then sought to apply to the plaintiff's case. Costello J. would not, however, permit this:

> "The parties in this case had treated the September 1980 rules as those governing the plaintiff's application. The plaintiff had a reasonable expectation that his application would be determined in accordance with them. It would ... be grossly unfair to allow the Council to rescind the rules when an application was pending under these and adopt new ones which effectively made it impossible for the plaintiff to be registered."[78]

19–42   It is suggested that one way of reconciling cases like *Tara Prospecting* with such cases as *Philips* is that there is a world of difference between allowing a legitimate expectation to prevail against the exercise of a statutory power in cases where the exercise of that power is largely personal in its consequences to the applicant or a potentially small number of persons (as in *Philips*), and cases where

---

[75]   *Tara Prospecting v Minister for Energy* [1993] I.L.R.M. 771 at 789. This passage was approved and followed by Morris J. in *Dempsey v Minister for Justice* [1994] 1 I.L.R.M. 401. See, to like effect, the comments of Lardner J. in *Devitt v Minister for Education* [1989] I.L.R.M. 639 at 651 and those of Morris J. in *John M.P. Greaney Ltd v Dublin Corporation* [1994] 3 I.R. 384 at 392–393, and (in an English context) those of Laws J. in *R. v Secretary of State for Transport Ex p. Richmond upon Thames London B.C.* [1994] 1 W.L.R. 74.

[76]   [1993] I.L.R.M. 771 at 789. See, to like effect, Costello P.'s judgment in *Gilheaney v Revenue Commissioners* [1996] E.L.R. 25; [1998] 4 I.R. 150.

[77]   [1991] 2 I.R. 115.

[78]   [1991] 2 I.R. 115 at 138. See, to like effect, *O'Leary v Minister for Finance* [1998] 2 I.L.R.M. 321.

> However, note that in *Abrahamson v Law Society of Ireland* [1996] 1 I.R. 403, McCracken J. hinted that *Philips* must be regarded as an example of the furthest the courts have gone in permitting a plea of legitimate expectations to prevail in a case presenting a possible clash with the exercise of a statutory power, and suggested ([1996] 1 I.R. 403 at 496) that this case "must now be considered in the light of certain other decisions in which the courts have refused to interfere with the exercise of a statutory discretion".

this would retard the capacity of the Government or administrators to make new policy decisions affecting the community at large (as in *Tara Prospecting*).

(9) Crisis in public finances

19–43 As a result of measures taken by various public bodies to meet the current financial crisis, a great number of private individuals or companies have been disappointed, in multifarious ways, regarding expectations they held about the future conduct—mainly financial—of various public bodies. The question arises whether this disappointment could ground a claim for breach of legitimate expectations. This issue is discussed in its constitutional guise, at paras 19–59 to 19–65. Here, we outline a case in which the issue arose in the form of a claim that a Minister's administrative act amounted to a breach of a legitimate expectation and, not unexpectedly (for reasons explained below), the claim failed. In *Curran v Minister for Education and Science*,[79] in order to deal with the crisis, the Minister immediately terminated an early retirement scheme for teachers, even though this impacted on a number of teachers who had organised their affairs on the basis that the scheme would be available. Dunne J. held that the public interest considerations were so acute that they justified this sudden change.[80]

(10) No fettering of statutory discretion by legitimate expectations?

19–44 In a typical legitimate expectation situation, there is claimed to be an implicit assurance which had been broken. What if the reverse happens, namely, where there is an agreement, whether express or implied, which has been honoured and it is some third party who is thereby disadvantaged? Where the third party consequently seeks judicial review of the action honouring the agreement by claiming that it is not a free exercise of a statutory[81] discretionary power,[82] in principle, the third party should succeed. Just because of this, the law has traditionally taken the view that, if the public body has failed to honour the contract and the disappointed promisee brings an action for breach of contract, a public

---

[79] [2009] IEHC 378; [2009] 4 I.R. 300.

[80] See also, *Eogan v University College, Dublin* [1996] 1 I.R. 390; [1996] 2 I.L.R.M. 302, which was the product of the public financial crisis of the 1980s. Formerly, academic staff at UCD traditionally enjoyed the benefit of staying in office until aged 70, but this practice was changed in 1987 and extensions in office were no longer sanctioned in order to "achieve a reduction in the age profile of academic staff in UCD and to make financial savings". While Shanley J. agreed that the applicant had acquired a legitimate expectation in relation to the retirement age, this simply entitled him to comment on the proposed change and he had been given every opportunity of doing so. This is an example of the procedural point, already canvassed at paras 19–30 to 19–36. Furthermore, as UCD had rational grounds for altering its prior practice, it was held to be entitled to do so.

[81] But the courts seem prepared, in principle at least, to give effect to substantive rights by means of the enforcement of a legitimate expectation where the underlying right does not derive from statute: see, e.g. *Dunleavy v Dun Laoghaire County Council* [2005] IEHC 381; *Power v Minister for Social and Family Affairs* [2006] IEHC 170; [2007] 1 I.R. 543; *Lett & Co. v Wexford County Council* [2007] IEHC 195; *Curran v Minister for Education* [2009] IEHC 378; [2009] 4 I.R. 300. See generally, Delany, "Legitimate Expectations and Substantive Effects: Recent Developments" (2007) 29 D.U.L.J. 413.

[82] See the discussion of this by Clarke J. in *Rosborough v Cork County Council* [2008] IEHC 94; [2008] 4 I.R. 572 at 589 and by O'Keeffe J. in *Clinton v Minister for Justice, Equality and Law Reform*, unreported, High Court, June 21, 2010.

body must be allowed a defence.[83] (This bar on the fettering of future executive action is part of a wider principle[84] considered elsewhere).[85]

19–45 This reasoning was followed by FitzGibbon J. in *Kenny v Cosgrave*,[86] where the plaintiff sought to rely on a promise made to him by W. T. Cosgrave, then President of the Executive Council. Mr Cosgrave apparently represented to him that if the plaintiff (who was a builder) refused to compromise with his striking employees, then the Executive Council would reimburse him for any losses thereby incurred by him. The plaintiff acted on this assurance to his detriment, and duly sued Mr Cosgrave personally. Because he chose to sue Mr Cosgrave, his action was struck out as disclosing no reasonable cause of action. However, the relevant point here is that it was stated by the judge that, even if the action had been brought against the Executive Council, it would have been bound to fail on the ground that the Government cannot fetter its future executive action.[87] These principles were expressly applied in *Clinton v Minister for Justice, Equality and Law Reform*,[88] a case where the plaintiff prison officers sought to compel the Minister to give effect to a contractual commitment to re-introduce a particular statutory instrument dealing with the provision of medical assistance to prison officers and their families. Applying *Kenny v Cosgrave*, O'Keeffe J. refused to give effect to that agreement, since it was:

> "... an attempt to limit or restrict the discretion of the [Minister] in the manner which he legislates, whether by enactment or by statutory instrument. Such a limitation or restriction is ... a fetter on the [Minister's] discretion to act as he sees fit in the public interest for the common good."[89]

19–46 But at the same time as noting this well-established principle, it may be commented that it is one of the rules which became embedded in the law during

---

[83] See, e.g. *Stringer v Minister of Housing and Local Government* [1970] 1 W.L.R. 1281, where it was the agreement at local authority level which was at issue. Admittedly, there are few examples of this type.

[84] This issue also surfaced in a curious manner in the confidence debate in the Dáil in November 1994, arising out of the appointment of the then Attorney General as President of the High Court. The then Taoiseach (Mr A. Reynolds, T.D.) had asserted that, by convention, the Attorney had first claim on any judicial vacancy and that this convention was in the nature of a condition of employment of the Attorney General. This contention was, it is submitted, convincingly countered by the Tánaiste (Mr R. Spring, T.D.) speaking in the same debate (447 *Dáil Debates* Col.352, November 16, 1994): "Our Constitution reserves the right of appointment of members of the judiciary to the President of Ireland, acting on the advice of the Government ... Any promise of 'condition of employment' which guaranteed an appointment to the judiciary, thereby pre-empting the free and unfettered decision of the Government in the matter, would clearly have to be null and void ...".

[85] See Ch.15, Part E.

[86] [1926] I.R. 517. For a classic example of this type of case, see *Redereiaktiebolaget Amphitrite v The King* [1921] 3 K.B. 300 at 503.

[87] [1926] I.R. 517 at 523–528 per FitzGibbon J. Note also the comments of Costello P. in *Gilheaney v Revenue Commissioners* [1996] E.L.R. 25 at 37; [1998] I.R. 4 I.R. 150 at 165; *Re Parke Davis & Co.'s Trade Mark Application* [1976] F.S.R. 195; see *Rosborough v Cork City Council* [2008] 4 I.R. 572 at 589 per Clarke J.

[88] Unreported, High Court, June 21, 2010.

[89] O'Keeffe J. further stressed (at para.66) that such a commitment would significantly impair the Minister's freedom of action.

the pre-"Big Government" era.[90] It is not really appropriate in the modern era and a way forward, by which the State's proper discretion may be retained without doing injustice to the individual, may be to characterise the making of the representation or contract as itself being the exercise of the discretion.

(11) Mistake of law, contrasted with exercise of discretion

19–47 In *Carbury Milk Products Ltd v Minister for Agriculture*,[91] the plaintiffs had manufactured a certain type of milk product which they submitted to the defendants. The defendants classified the product as a milk protein product for Common Customs Tariff Classification purposes and this meant that the company was entitled to export refunds for third-country sales. On the strength of this classification the plaintiffs entered into contracts with third parties based outside the European Community, in the expectation that such export refunds would be payable. Some two years later, however, the defendants realised that, through no fault of the plaintiffs, an error had been made; the product was, in fact, to be classified as a whey powder which did not attract export refunds. The plaintiffs then claimed an entitlement to export refunds for the two years during which the product had been wrongly classified as being entitled to such payments. Hamilton P., in a judgment which (without much discrimination) drew upon both promissory estoppel and legitimate expectations under both Irish and European law, held that the Minister was estopped from denying the plaintiffs entitlement to the export refunds.

19–48 However one classifies the law in this case, it is plain that the company deserved to succeed in its claim, but one may criticise the characterisation of the case as involving legitimate expectations, in that this cuts across the notion that legitimate expectations cannot prevail against legislation, a notion examined in the following Part. In *Carbury*, the classification of the plaintiff's milk product depended in part on the legal definition (which had been negligently handled by the Minister's advisers). In other words it was a (negligent) mistake of law.

D. Legitimate Expectations Cannot Prevail Against Legislation

19–49 The legitimate expectations doctrine cannot be allowed to interfere with a major principle of law, namely that a public authority cannot alter the law, and in particular it cannot give itself a jurisdiction it does not possess. A public body cannot do this by a mistaken conclusion as to the extent of its own powers and neither can it do so by creating an estoppel or a legitimate expectation. There can thus be no legitimate expectation which is contrary to law.[92]

---

[90] Unlike some of the others, such as the *Delegatus* rule (see Ch.11, Part E), it is likely to be of advantage to the State, rather than the individual.
[91] (1988–1993) 4 *Irish Tax Reports* 492. For another case involving legitimate expectations in both EU and Irish law, see *Hagemayer Ireland Plc v Revenue Commissioners* [2007] IEHC 49.
[92] *Re Greendale Building Co.* [1977] I.R. 256 was followed in *Dublin Corporation v McGrath* [1978] I.L.R.M. 208; *Morris v Garvey* [1983] I.R. 319 at 324–325; and *Devitt v Minister for Education* [1989] I.L.R.M. 639. Similar views were expressed by Murphy J. in *Nova Media Services Ltd v Minister for Posts and Telegraphs* [1984] I.R. 161, by Blayney J. in *Power*

19–50   This principle is well illustrated by *Pesca Valentia Ltd v Minister for Fisheries*,[93] where it was argued that the conduct of certain public bodies such as the Industrial Development Authority gave rise to a legitimate expectation on the part of the plaintiffs that no fundamental legislative changes would be made affecting their right to fish.[94] Keane J. rejected this contention:

> "[W]hile the plaintiffs were undoubtedly encouraged in their project by semi-state bodies, they were not given any assurance that the law regulating fishing would never be altered so as adversely to affect them nor, if such an assurance had been given, could any legal rights have grown from it. *No such 'estoppel' could conceivably operate so as to prevent the Oireachtas from legislating or the executive from implementing the legislation when enacted.*"[95]

19–51   Keane J. was here drawing on two fundamental constitutional principles, each of which may be regarded, at some level, as stemming from the separation of powers and the rule of law. The first of these is that the executive arm of government (or as in the instant case, a state-sponsored body) cannot commit the legislature as to the laws it will or will not make. This is inherent in the nature of the organs of government. It is also implicit, in particular, in Art.15.2.1° ("The sole and exclusive power of making of making laws ... is hereby vested in the Oireachtas"). Secondly, there is also a reference to the precept that one cannot fetter a discretionary power.

19–52   Yet, there are cases which seem to contradict this principle. One of these is *Waterford Harbour Commissioners v British Railway Board*,[96] where the Supreme Court effectively held that a statutory provision had been allowed to fall into disuse. The facts were that the defendants were under a statutory duty imposed by s.70 of the Fishguard and Rosslare Railways and Harbours Act 1898 to provide a daily steamer service between Waterford and the Welsh coast. Political considerations, changed commercial trends and the advent of war all combined to undermine the viability of the provision of a daily service. The parties reached an agreement in 1939 by which the defendants agreed to provide a thrice-weekly service while the plaintiffs undertook not to sue for damages for breach of statutory duty. When the defendants gave notice of intention to discontinue the service in 1977, the plaintiffs sued for damages for breach of statutory duty and for breach of contract. A majority

---

     v Minister for Social Welfare [1987] I.R. 307, and by Costello J. in *Nolan v Minister for Environment* [1989] I.R. 357 and in *Galvin v Chief Appeals Officer* [1997] 3 I.R. 240.
[93]   [1990] 2 I.R. 305.
[94]   cf. also the facts of *R. v Secretary of State for Health Ex p. US Tobacco International Ltd* [1992] 1 Q.B. 353.
[95]   [1990] 2 I.R. 305 at 323 (emphasis added). See also, *Hempenstall v Minister for the Environment* [1994] 2 I.R. 20 at 32 per Costello J. (no legitimate expectation or promissory estoppel to prevent the Minister from making new regulations). This was also echoed by Laffoy J. in *Kavanagh v Government of Ireland* [1996] 1 I.R. 321.
     This is also the position with regard to legitimate expectations and EU law: see, e.g. *Hauptzollamt Hamburg-Jones v Firma P. Kruchen* (C-316/86) [1988] E.C.R. 2213; *Spa Alois Lageder v Administrazione delle Finanze dello Stato* (C-44/91) [1993] E.C.R. I-1761; *Hagemayer Ireland Plc v Revenue Commissioners* [2007] IEHC 49; *Duff v Minister for Agriculture (No. 2)* [1997] 2 I.R. 22 at 81.
[96]   [1979] I.L.R.M. 296. For other cases with the same flavour, see *Duggan v An Taoiseach* [1989] I.L.R.M. 710; and *Conroy v Garda Commissioner* [1989] I.R. 140. These cases do, however, depend on very particular facts: H & M, paras 19–85 to 19–89.

of the Supreme Court held that while the plaintiffs could sue for breach of contract, they were now estopped from pursuing the claim for breach of statutory duty, since by their conduct they had led the defendants to believe that their statutory obligations were "moribund or dead". Henchy J. added:

> "Thus, so far as the plaintiffs were concerned, from 1939 to 1977, *section 70 had been allowed to become a dead letter*. In the circumstances, the plaintiffs are estopped from reverting to the position they were in when they could justifiably have said that section 70 should be complied with."[97]

19–53 In respect of this surprising passage, the following three points of criticism or limitation may be adduced. First, this rare pre-*Webb* example of a successful plea of legitimate expectation was founded not upon practice but upon a formal agreement not to sue for damages, which had been renewed on several occasions over a 40-year period. Secondly, notwithstanding the language used in the passage quoted, the same result could have been reached by a holding that these particular parties had reached an agreement by which the plaintiffs promised not to enforce their statutory rights, i.e. in effect, an out-of-court settlement. This is a fairly common arrangement at any rate as between private parties and there appears no reason why it should be different where the defendant is a public body. It is altogether different from a commitment either to change or not to change the law. By "law" we mean an Act of the Oireachtas. (The reason for making this definitional point is that we assume that the position in regard to the making of a statutory instrument is the same as for the exercise of any other statutory discretionary power so that there are no distinctive features requiring discussion here.) Finally, the language of the judgment notwithstanding ("dead letter"), *Waterford Harbour* is not a case of desuetude and thus, following on from the second point, there was nothing to stop a person who was not a party to the agreement—for instance, the Attorney General—from enforcing the statutory rights in question.

19–54 At the same time, there is no doubt but that if the notion that a legitimate expectation cannot change the law is strictly applied, it is capable of causing considerable injustice. One stopping point, which was accepted obiter by Henchy J. in *Re Green Dale Building Co.*,[98] would be an exception which debarred a public authority from relying on a mere technicality which it ought in fairness to have overlooked.[99] Henchy J. did not explain why technicalities represented an exception to the rule. It might be an example of the application of the de minimis principle. But perhaps the exception represents a wider principle which would allow an estoppel in respect of ultra vires action where the injustice to the plaintiff was not outweighed by any tangible public benefit.[100] Indeed, the very fact that a public body sees fit

---

[97] [1979] I.L.R.M. 296 at 353 (emphasis added).

[98] [1977] I.R. 257 at 264.

[99] See, e.g. *Wells v Minister for Housing and Local Government* [1967] 1 W.L.R. 1000; *Lever Finance Ltd v Westminster L.B.C.* [1971] 1 Q.B. 222. But even these authorities are considered doubtful in light of more recent developments: see *Western Fish Products Ltd v Penwith District Council* [1981] 2 All E.R. 204 and *Rootkin v Kent County Council* [1981] 1 W.L.R. 1186.

[100] Craig, *Administrative Law*, 6th edn (London: Sweet & Maxwell, 2008), paras 20–41 to 20–52. In his judgment in *Ashbourne Holdings Ltd v An Bord Pleanála* [2003] 2 I.R. 114, Hardiman J. hinted that a more flexible approach might be adopted where the lack of vires was more "marginal" than "radical" in nature.

to resile from an earlier promise might itself amount to an abuse of discretionary powers and, hence, itself amount to an ultra vires act. Such a balancing of interests would surely be acceptable given that the object of the ultra vires rule is to protect the public interest. It could also be said that the mere fact that the public authority has acted ultra vires should not of itself be decisive, and that regard must be had to other considerations.[101] In line with this, the English Court of Appeal appears to have begun the retreat from the orthodox absolutist position.[102]

19–55 It has also been suggested that a public body should be bound by ultra vires representations when that body is acting in a proprietary rather than in a governmental or administrative capacity. This proposition has a certain superficial attractiveness, but its application involves the difficulty of distinguishing between a function as governmental rather than proprietary, a distinction which it is not easy to draw.[103]

19–56 Another broader possibility would be to compensate individuals who have relied to their detriment on an ultra vires representation. This could be done by finding the public authority liable in negligence for careless misrepresentations resulting in financial loss to the misrepresentee, in circumstances where, by reason of a change in position as a result of legitimate expectation, "it would be unjust not to provide the claimant concerned with some remedy".[104] In addition, such cases would seem to come within the ambit of the Ombudsman's power.[105]

19–57 There is another issue which often arises in this area. What if a representation is made which is beyond the powers of the official who gave the assurance but which is not actually ultra vires the public body itself? In this situation the doctrine of estoppel might be allowed to apply. Such an approach would have obvious affinities with the "internal management rule" in company law and appears to have been adopted—albeit without elaborate discussion—by Barron J. in *Kenny v Kelly*.[106] Here the applicant had sought a deferral of a place offered to her by University College Dublin. An administrative official informed the

---

[101] The courts regularly engage in such reasoning when considering whether to invalidate past administrative decisions: see, e.g. *Murphy v Attorney General* [1982] I.R. 241; *A v Governor of Arbour Hill Prison* [2006] IESC 45; [2006] 4 I.R. 88.

[102] *Rowland v Environment Agency* [2005] Ch. 1. Here the court recognised that in some instances an ultra vires promise might give rise to a legitimate expectation, albeit that the relief available might be conditioned by the nature of the public body's statutory powers. See generally, Hammett and Busch, "Ultra Vires Representations and Illegitimate Expectation" [2005] *Public Law* 729.

[103] The Supreme Court has subsequently hinted that a less absolute approach may be apposite where the invalidity relates to "something more marginal than the essence of the [administrative] action which is impugned – for example, its scope of extent rather than its nature – there may be greater scope for the operation of estoppel": *Ashbourne Holdings* [2003] 2 I.R. 114 at 137 (per Hardiman J.).

[104] *Atlantic Marine Suppliers Ltd v Minister for Transport* [2010] IEHC 194 per Clarke J. For earlier indications that damages might be an appropriate remedy for an infringement of a legitimate expectation, see *Abrahamson v Law Society of Ireland* [1996] 1 I.R. 403 and *Lett & Co. v Wexford Corporation* [2007] IEHC 195.

[105] The Ombudsman Act 1980 s.4(2), provides, inter alia, that the Ombudsman may investigate any action where it appears to him that the action was, or may have been, taken as "the result of negligence or carelessness".

[106] [1988] I.R. 457.

applicant's father that her request for a deferral for one year had been granted. As it happened, the official who had communicated that information had misconstrued her instructions, but, of course, the granting of such a deferral was not ultra vires the respondents. Barron J. held that this representation was binding, since if the official had misrepresented her instructions, this "does not entitle the respondent to deny her apparent authority to bind the respondent".[107]

19–58 Nevertheless, this approach would be of assistance only in a limited class of cases. In *Dublin Corporation v McGrath*,[108] for example, the defendant submitted that the planning authority was estopped from denying the existence of planning permission in respect of an unauthorised structure. It appeared that an agent of the authority had given verbal permission for the construction of a garage which was subsequently erected by the defendant. The plea of estoppel failed, for, as McMahon J. observed, not only did the agent not have power to make such a representation, but such a representation was also ultra vires the planning authority itself.

Unconstitutionality?

19–59 Although the issue had not, until recently, squarely arisen, legitimate expectations have apparently been regarded as a common law equitable doctrine. This would carry with it the consequence that the doctrine would have to bow before legislation, a point which was rather assumed in the preceding Parts. However, here we propose to address the question of whether the legitimate expectations principle can be regarded as being grounded in the Constitution because, if so, the the consequence would be that any legislation which purported to defeat a legitimate expectation would be unconstitutional. The obvious concrete situation in which this position arises at the moment is where the legislation—which is claimed to be unconstitutional—has been enacted to deal with the State's current financial difficulties. This has arisen in the form of a High Court (McMahon J.) case, *J. & J. Haire & Company Limited v The Minister for Health and Children*,[109] which is worth attention, before we focus directly on legitimate expectations. The central fact was that the Financial Emergency Measures in the Public Interest Act 2009 allowed for the reduction in amounts paid by the State to specified persons, including pharmacists. Pursuant to her powers under the Act, the Minister introduced Regulations[110] which reduced payments made to pharmacists under a pre-existing scheme. The plaintiff pharmacist brought proceedings challenging the constitutionality of both the 2009 Act and the Regulations.

19–60 Among the scatter-gun of arguments advanced by the plaintiff, the most significant, for present purposes, was that, arising from the contract between the plaintiff and the HSE, the plaintiff had a property right which was protected by the Constitution. There were two central points in the judge's reasoning (which are, as we shall see below, also relevant to whether legitimate expectations have a

---

[107] [1988] I.R. 457 at 462. Cf. the views of Costello J. in *Nolan v Minister for Environment* [1989] I.R. 357, who did not think that the Minister could be bound by the views expressed by a local authority engineer in the course of a planning inquiry.

[108] [1978] I.L.R.M. 208.

[109] [2009] IEHC 562; [2010] 2 I.R. 615.

[110] Health Professionals (Reduction of Payments to Community Pharmacist Contractors) Regulations 2009 (S.I. No. 246 of 2009).

constitutional basis). The first concerned whether the contract was a property right protected in the Constitution. It has certainly been held that, in general, property rights include contractual rights. However, addressing this point, McMahon J. stated[111]:

> "Insofar as a contractual right is a fundamental right in the Constitution, it has the protection of the common law rules of contract, developed over the centuries and ... it is this code that is the State's expression of its protection of these contractual rights. The principles of contract are well established and it must be assumed that they provide adequate protection for the contractual rights of the parties where contracts are involved. It is only where such protection is demonstrably inadequate that persons may come forward and make an independent argument based on the property rights in the Constitution."

McMahon J. held that, in view of the fact that the contract between the Minister and the plaintiff was so drafted as to allow the Minister to make a unilateral change in the rates under the scheme, in this case the varying of those rates pursuant to a statutory power did not infringe any property right of the plaintiff.

19–61   However, the judge's alternative line of reasoning is of more general significance because it was independent of the particular fact that the Minister was permitted to make a unilateral change. The alternative reason was that if there were property rights, the reduction of the pharmacists' pay rate was not (to use the language of Art.40.3.2°) "unjust". McMahon J. stated[112]:

> " ... 'unjust' in this sense, refers to matters such as retrospectivity, lack of fair procedures, unreasonableness and irrationality, discrimination, lack of proportionality and, in some cases, lack of compensation. Suffice it to say at this point not only do I consider that there has not been an attack on the plaintiffs constitutional rights but also I consider that what encroachment the plaintiffs might complain of could not be considered unjust ...".

19–62   The judge also noted that the Act of 2009 was a "measured, proportionate and carefully drawn piece of legislation",[113] which had been made, in response to an unprecedented economic crisis and included a number of significant safeguards. A further relevant point is that before varying the rates, the Minister had engaged in a consultation process with the pharmacists' professional body.

19–63   Turning now directly to legitimate expectations, a preliminary difficulty concerns the question of where precisely in the Constitution the doctrine might find a platform: might a legitimate expectation be regarded as a property right? As to this, there is a contrast between contract which, as McMahon J. noted in para.19–60, has long occupied a central position in law and the doctrine of legitimate expectations with its recent and somewhat cloudy origin. One of the major tenets of the Rule

---

[111] [2009] IEHC 562; [2010] 2 I.R. 615 at paras 93–96. For the ruling that property rights include contractual rights, see *Moynihan v Greensmyth* [1977] I.R. 55 at 71; *Condon v Minister for Labour (No. 2)*, unreported, High Court, McWilliam J., June 11, 1980 at 10–11.
[112] [2009] IEHC 562; [2010] 2 I.R. 615 at para.113.
[113] [2009] IEHC 562; [2010] 2 I.R. 615 at para.106.

of Law is that—substantial statutory and other exceptions aside—the State should keep within the same law as private individuals, including, most relevantly here, contract and tort. This view seems to accord with the earlier extract from McMahon J.'s judgment, in which he stated that it is only if contract law is demonstrably inadequate that the property rights may be invoked to fortify it. In the same way, one might reason that it would be subversive and the cause of massive uncertainty if some additional shadowy "contract-lite" body of law were to be imposed on the State and given constitutional status.

19–64 To turn, next, to the second point identified in the *Haire* judgment, it seems that in the same way as at sub-Constitutional level, there are significant qualifications of the legitimate expectations doctrine. The one relevant here allows the State to make "changes of policy". So far as this rather vague category can be understood, it is almost always the case that new legislation is the outcome of a "change of policy".[114] It seems likely, therefore, that most legislation would count as an exception.

19–65 If not the property right argument, is there some other foothold which the doctrine of legitimate expectations might secure in the Constitution? The most likely candidate might seem to be some notion of the rule of law, deduced from the general structure and assumptions of the Constitution, including Art.40.1 (equality before the law) and the capacious Art.40.3.1° (unenumerated rights). But the direction from which such a line of argument would come would be that legislation could make no discriminatory or arbitrary impact on a person's legitimate expectations. And discriminatory or arbitrary laws are forbidden anyway, irrespective of the need of a legitimate expectation. In summary, it seems unlikely that legitimate expectations would find a platform in the Constitution.

E. SUMMARY AND COMPARISON WITH ESTOPPEL

Summary of legitimate expectations

19–66 In view of the rollercoaster course taken by the law over the past decade and also by way of attempting to give some guidance for the future, it may be useful at this point to attempt a brief stock-taking:

1. A fixed and settled practice may of itself give rise to a legitimate expectation: see, e.g. *Eogan v University College, Dublin*[115] and *Glenkerrin Homes*.[116] Likewise, a formal commitment given by a public body which is communicated to an identifiable group of citizens is

---

[114] No reasonable person would hold such an expectation: given the vicissitudes of public finance (including uncertainties of both income and expenditure), would any reasonable person suppose that the Oireachtas could be committing itself to follow a fixed policy in this field? Cf. the comments of Clarke J. in *Lett & Co. v Wexford Borough Council* [2007] IEHC 195: "All investment is open to some risk including a risk that its value will be affected by subsequent regulatory developments and changes in policy. The fact of that investment, of itself, could not, without more, give rise to a legitimate expectation that compensation would be paid in respect of any measures which might affect the value of the investment."

[115] [1996] 1 I.R. 390.

[116] [2007] IEHC 298.

       capable in and of itself of giving rise to a legitimate expectation (see, e.g. *Fakih*,[117] *Keogh v Criminal Assets Bureau* and *Power*).

2.   Where procedural rights are concerned, it seems clear from cases like *Fakih v Minister for Justice* and *Glenkerrin Homes*, supported by similar cases in other jurisdictions, that the doctrine can be invoked to require the observance of such rights.

3.   In respect of substantive rights, the position is more qualified. Save where this would potentially clash with the exercise of a statutory power, the law has now evolved to the point where, in cases involving a non-statutory discretion, the courts will give effect to substantive rights by means of legitimate expectations: see, e.g. *Dunleavy*,[118] *Power*,[119] *Curran*,[120] *Glenkerrin Homes*,[121] and *Lett & Co.*[122]

4.   But, as against this in a large number of cases where there is a statutory discretion—examples include *Tara Prospecting*,[123] *Gilheany*,[124] *Abrahamson*,[125] *Glencar Exploration (No. 1)*,[126] and *Clinton*[127]—the traditional teaching that the executive cannot fetter its statutory discretion has reasserted itself, in preference to the legitimate expectations doctrine.

5.   A related ground on which a public body will be permitted to resile from an earlier commitment, is if there is a change of circumstances, which justifies a change of position: see, e.g. *Egan, Eogan, Abrahamson* and *Curran*.

6.   As explained in the discussion of *Carbury Products*,[128] cases may arise involving a misunderstanding or misapplication of the law. It may be best to treat them as (negligent) errors of law, without engaging legitimate expectations.

7.   The legitimate expectations doctrine cannot be invoked where honouring the expectation would necessitate a breach or change of the law: see, e.g. *Pesca Valentia*[129] and *Clinton v Minister for Justice, Equality and Law Reform*.[130]

8.   Probably the doctrine is not grounded in the Constitution.

Comparison of legitimate expectations and promissory estoppel

19–67 It will be readily appreciated that the doctrine of legitimate expectations has very close affinities with that of promissory estoppel and, indeed, there are

---

[117] [1993] 2 I.R. 427.
[118] [2005] IEHC 381.
[119] [2007] 1 I.R. 543.
[120] [2009] 4 I.R. 300.
[121] [2007] IEHC 298.
[122] [2007] IEHC 195.
[123] [1993] I.L.R.M. 771.
[124] [1998] 4 I.R. 150; [1996] E.L.R. 25.
[125] [1996] 1 I.R. 403.
[126] [2002] 1 I.R. 84.
[127] Unreported, High Court, June 21, 2010.
[128] Unreported, High Court, February 21, 1986.
[129] [1990] 2 I.R. 305.
[130] Unreported, High Court, June 21, 2010.

judicial dicta to the effect that these doctrines are more or less interchangeable.[131] However, these dicta probably go too far and do not recognise important differences between the two principles. The following analysis of these doctrinal differences between the principles of promissory estoppels and legitimate expectations is tentatively advanced:

1. Strictly speaking, the principle of promissory estoppel can only apply to suspend or vary the legal rights already existing between the parties by virtue of a contractual or other similar relationship. Such a relationship is not, however, essential for legitimate expectations, as is evidenced by cases where the plaintiff has sought to rely on the settled practices of a public body or representations made by it to the public in general and not necessarily to particular individuals.

2. Again, strictly speaking, promissory estoppel may be used as a "shield but not as a sword". By contrast, in the nature of things, in most legitimate expectations cases, the doctrine has been used as a sword.

3. There must be an element of reliance or acting to one's detriment in order to give rise to a promissory estoppel. This would not seem to be essential in the case of legitimate expectations, which rather focuses on the behaviour of the public body, emphasising consistency, good administration and equal treatment.

4. A claim of legitimate expectation applies to a wider category of cases than does a plea of estoppel, in that, of its nature, estoppel operates only if the author of the misrepresentation is himself involved in the case (usually, it happens, as the defendant). By contrast, with a legitimate expectation, the author of the misrepresentation who created the expectation may be a third party to the case.

5. By contrast, the next point of difference would seem to make it easier to establish a plea of estoppel. For, in estoppel, it would seem to be irrelevant that, subsequently, new factors have come to light since then which would, objectively speaking, justify the body in question in changing its position or resiling from its representation.[132]

6. It is quite clear that the doctrine of legitimate expectations is a principle whose operation is confined to the public law sphere. In other words, it cannot be invoked unless the defendant is a public authority, and probably (though Irish courts have been slow to take this point) only if the dispute is in the field of public law.

---

[131] See, e.g. the comments of Finlay C.J. in *Webb v Ireland* [1988] I.R. 353 at 384, of Murphy J. in *Garda Representative Association v Ireland* [1989] I.R. 193, and of O'Hanlon J. in *Association of General Practitioners Ltd v Minister of Health* [1995] 1 I.R. 382.

[132] As opposed to circumstances which were known to at least one of the parties at the date of the transaction which is said to give rise to the promissory estoppel: see, e.g. *D&C Builders Ltd v Rees* [1966] 2 Q.B. 617. Here the defendants (who were fully aware of the plaintiffs' precarious financial position) had unfairly extracted a promise from them to accept a smaller sum in respect of certain debts. The English Court of Appeal found that, in the circumstances, it would not be inequitable for the plaintiffs to go back on their promise and they could sue for the balance of the debts. The decision would almost certainly have gone the other way if the defendants could have shown: (i) that their precarious financial situation had arisen after the original promise had been made; and (ii) they had altered their circumstances in reliance on that promise.

CHAPTER 20

THE STATE IN LITIGATION

20–01   Historically, for no better reason than that the King (who was not then called the "State") owned the courts, he had a number of advantages in litigation.[1] The dismantling of these special rights and privileges so that the State in litigation was on the same level as a private person or company and, thereby affirming the Rule of Law is a story mainly of judicial initiatives,[2] some of which are recounted in this chapter. A number of the advantages stem from "the (Royal) Prerogative" whose fate is summarised in Part A. Parts B and C then deal with issues arising from state and ministerial liability flowing from the major case on the Prerogative. Parts D and E summarise central segments of public law, which although not formally part of the prerogative may be regarded as closely related to it.

A. PATRIMONY OF THE PREROGATIVE

20–02   In the United Kingdom, the prerogative has been said to embrace "those rights and capacities which the King alone enjoys in contradistinction to others".[3] In the United Kingdom many of the former prerogative rights have been uprooted, qualified or superseded by statute, or shrivelled by desuetude.[4] Nevertheless, the prerogative still covers a diverse bundle of rights, powers, privileges, etc most of which are exercised by the Crown on the advice of the responsible Ministers.[5]

20–03   In Ireland, by contrast, the former prerogative had been largely superseded in that much of the ground which the prerogative covers in the United Kingdom is regulated by the Constitution or, to a lesser extent, by statute.[6] Thus, for instance,

---

[1]   At common law the Crown, as plaintiff, enjoyed a variety of procedural privileges derived from the prerogative. Thus, neither *laches* nor delay could be imputed to the Crown and the courts would not deny relief on discretionary grounds to the Attorney General.
[2]   This is an achievement admired even by those who consider that in other fields judicial activism has been taken too far: Morgan, *A Judgement too Far* (Cork: Cork University Press, 2001), Ch.7.
[3]   Blackstone, *Commentaries* (Oxford: Clarendon Press, 1766–1769), Vol.1, p.239. See also, Wade, "Procedure and Privilege in Public Law" (1985) 101 L.Q.R. 180.
[4]   Wade and Forsyth, *Administrative Law*, 10th edn (Oxford: OUP, 2009), p.181.
[5]   Wade and Forsyth, *Administrative Law* (2009), p.182.
[6]   Thus, for example, the granting of passports (heretofore assumed to be a species of the prerogative power) is now regulated by the Passports Act 2008. Of course, even if that were not so, it might have been said that the right to issue passports was a species of executive power, derived variously from Art.28.2 and Art.29.4 of the Constitution. Wade and Forsyth,

when the President appoints or removes Ministers or dissolves the Dáil, s/he does so on the authority of Arts 13.1, 13.2 and 28.9.4°, respectively. Again, the prerogative of mercy has been overtaken by the right of pardon and remission of punishment vested in the President by Art.13.6; whilst the prerogative to declare war is now grounded in Art.28.3.1° (which reserves this right to the Dáil). In the case of certain of the other prerogatives, their content is such as actually to conflict with the Constitution. In the leading case of *Byrne v Ireland*,[7] where the plaintiff had been injured when she fell into a trench dug by, or, more probably, on the authority of the Minister for Posts and Telegraphs, the State sought to defend itself by calling in aid the supposed prerogative of immunity from tort action. However, the Supreme Court held this prerogative to be unconstitutional. According to the narrower alternative ratio (the other ratio is covered below), the reason for this was that this immunity interfered unjustifiably with the right to litigate a justiciable controversy (under Art.40.3.1°). Another example of a prerogative whose contents are in conflict with the Constitution is provided by a series of cases which held that, since the Central Fund of the Irish Exchequer does not have the character of a royal fund, it cannot attract the prerogative of priority of debts due to the State in case of an insolvency.[8] Again the prerogative of the Crown to enforce payment of a judgment debtor by securing the arrest and imprisonment of the debtor is scarcely compatible with Art.40.4.1°.[9]

20–04 Pre-*Byrne*, it had, however, been accepted—although without much discussion—that, save for cases where it had been superseded by, or was in conflict with, the Constitution or a statute, the prerogative had managed to navigate the rapids of 1922 and 1937. In short, it had been assumed that there was nothing in the nature or source of the prerogative to prevent its continued existence. However, *Byrne v Ireland*—which was subsequently confirmed by the Supreme Court in *Webb v Ireland*[10] and *Howard v Commissioners of Public Works*[11]—gave (or, at least, appeared to give) the quietus to that notion.[12]

    Administrative Law (2009) doubted (at p.182) whether the grant of a passport involved the prerogative at all, describing it as "more probably" as "merely an administrative practice involving no legal power at all".

[7] [1972] I.R. 241.

[8] *Re PC, an Arranging Debtor* [1939] I.R. 306; *Re Irish Mutual Insurance Association Ltd* [1955] I.R. 176. Preference for Revenue debts is now provided for by statute: see Companies Act 1963 s.285(2)(a).

[9] *State (Coombes) v Furlong*, unreported, High Court, Davitt P., February 1, 1963. Davitt P. appeared to doubt whether this particular prerogative had survived the "constitutional changes of 1922 and 1937". It may be noted that in *N(J) v K(T)* [2003] 2 I.L.R.M. 40, Kearns J. made an order restraining a debtor from leaving the State, but without any reference to this former prerogative right. He acknowledged that the constitutional right to travel could legitimately be constrained under certain circumstances, of which the desirability of preventing a debtor from absconding was one.

[10] [1988] I.R. 353. For analysis of this decision, see Kelly, "Hidden Treasure and the Constitution" (1988) 10 D.U.L.J. 5; Gwynn Morgan, "Constitutional Interpretation" (1988) 10 D.U.L.J. 24; Lenihan, "Royal Prerogatives and the Constitution" (1989) 24 *Irish Jurist* 1; Costello, "The Expulsion of Prerogative Doctrine from Irish Law: Quantifying and Remedying the Loss of the Royal Prerogative" (1997) 32 *Irish Jurist* 145.

[11] [1994] 1 I.R. 101. See Hogan, "The Mullaghmore Case" (1993) 15 D.U.L.J. 243.

[12] Although note the apparent qualification of O'Flaherty J. in *Geoghegan v Institute of Chartered Accountants in Ireland* [1995] 3 I.R. 86 at 118, which advocates "a more gradual approach in regard to the place of the royal prerogative in our constitutional scheme of things".

20–05   Nevertheless, since the prerogative represents such an important stage in the evolution of the law covered in the remainder of this chapter, a brief summary of these developments remains relevant.

20–06   The view that the prerogative had survived the enactment of the Constitution of the Irish Free State in 1922 was based, in the first instance, upon Art.49.1 of the Constitution which provides that:

> All powers, functions, rights and prerogatives whatsoever exercisable in or in respect of Saorstát Éireann immediately before the 11th day of December, 1936, whether in virtue of the Constitution then in force or otherwise, by the authority in which the executive power of Saorstát Éireann was then vested are hereby declared to belong to the people.

20–07   This provision makes the inquiry turn on the antecedent question of whether the prerogative existed in Saorstát Éireann before December 11, 1936. The significance of this date lies in the fact that it was the day when the Irish Free State Constitution was amended to extirpate the King (formerly the head of State in whom all executive authority was vested under Arts 41, 51, 55, 60 and 68 of the Irish Free State Constitution). Prior to *Byrne*, it had been assumed that the presence of the King drew with it the prerogative. This argument was rejected by the majority in *Byrne*. In response to the argument just summarised, it was said that the King's powers could be confined to those actually specified in the 1922 Constitution: there was no necessary reason why they had to be identical with those which the Crown enjoyed in the United Kingdom or in pre-independence Ireland. There is, however a different argument for saying that the prerogative survived the establishment of the State: "[The prerogative] was part of the common law which was applied to the Irish Free State by Article 73".[13] In response to this argument, the kernel of the court's argument is contained in the following extract from Walsh J.'s judgment:

> "[T]he basis of the Crown prerogative(s) in English law was that the King was the personification of the State. Article 2 of the Constitution of the Irish Free State[14] declared that all the powers of government and all authority, legislative, executive and judicial, in Ireland were derived from the people of Ireland and that the same should be exercised in the Irish Free State through the organisations established by or under and in accord with that Constitution. The basis of the prerogative of the English Crown was quite inconsistent with the declaration contained in that Article. The King enjoyed a personal pre-eminence; perfection was ascribed to him."[15]

20–08   This passage merits two observations. First, it might have seemed more realistic to regard Art.2 as a statement of political principle, in other words as a generalised warning to Irish governments that they held their power "on trust" for the People along the lines of the generally accepted Lockean, "social contract"

---

[13]   *Cork County Council v Commissioners of Public Works* [1945] I.R. 561 at 578 per O'Byrne J.

[14]   Article 2 is not quoted separately here since it is quoted practically verbatim in the above extract. The article is substantially reproduced in Art.6(1) of the present Constitution.

[15]   [1972] I.R. 241 at 272.

theory of limited government; and also as a warning to the British Crown that as governmental authority came ultimately from the People, it was not for the British to start trying to take power away from the Irish Free State or to interfere with it in any way.

20–09 Secondly, leaving aside this criticism, the effect of Art.2 is to stipulate (i) that all powers of government flow in some sense from the People and, (ii) that these powers may only be exercised by the independent Irish organs of government. As to the content of the powers of government, little is said. In view of this, Art.2 could have been interpreted as not affecting the content of these powers, but rather as relocating the basis of the State authority from the King to the People and as shifting the mode of its exercise from the King to the organs established by the Constitution.

20–10 At a broader level, Professor Kelly has criticised not so much the reasoning as the conclusion in *Byrne*. He summarises his views, characteristically cogently, in the following passage:

> "[T]he statutory usage of the Irish Free State, positive and negative, together with the opinions of judges who played a part in drafting its Constitution, together with the record of what actually was done in those years in such matters as pardons, passports, and precedence of counsel, suggest that the Crown and its prerogative were understood to have survived into the newly independent Irish State, as part of the common law, under Article 73, so far as such survival was not, in letter or in spirit, inconsistent with some specific dimension of the new Constitution. I think that for us today, 50 or 60 years later, to take the line that our fathers and grandfathers in legal and official life quite misunderstood the nature of the machine they were not only operating but had also in fact constructed is to adopt an unreal and intellectually unamiable position."[16]

20–11 Irrespective of such criticisms, however, it now seems—subject to some judicial hints that aspects of *Byrne* and *Webb* will have to be reconsidered—that the prerogative is not part of the Irish constitutional legal scene. This means, it might be thought, that the State is without certain pockets of legitimate authority the need for which is likely to arise unexpectedly or in an emergency, when there might be no time for the passage of legislation. Examples (drawn from English law) include the rules: permitting the seizure or destruction of private property, in time of war or imminent danger (albeit on payment of compensation); affording a

---

[16] Kelly, "Hidden Treasure and the Constitution" (1988) 10 D.U.L.J. 5 at p.14. In *Geoghegan v Institute of Chartered Accountants* [1995] 3 I.R. 86 at 118, O'Flaherty J. referred to this article and said that "[d]oubtless, in any future debate [this] essay which favours a more gradual approach in regard to the place of the royal prerogative in our constitutional scheme of things will prove of immense value". But cf. the comments of Barrington J. in *Eastern Health Board v MK* [1999] 2 I.R. 99 at 117: "... [T]he wardship jurisdiction itself survives in this country only insofar as it is not inconsistent with the provisions of the Constitution of 1937. The statement that the sovereign is '*parens patriae*' is probably a harmless piece of rhetoric and may describe the origins of the wardship jurisdiction in the royal prerogative. But it is a concept which has no place in a modern democratic republic."

significant component in martial law; and enabling the State to create corporations, without statutory authority.[17]

20–12 The question of the continued existence of the prerogative of treasure trove was squarely considered by the Supreme Court in *Webb v Ireland*.[18] The plaintiffs in this case were the finders of an exceptionally valuable hoard of early Christian objects who had handed over the artefacts to the National Museum for safe-keeping. They were dissatisfied with the compensation offered to them by the State and commenced proceedings seeking the delivery up by the State of these objects. The State pleaded that it was not a mere bailee, but that by reason of the prerogative of treasure trove, it had acquired a superior title to that of the plaintiffs.

20–13 In *Webb*, the Supreme Court, affirming the reasoning of Walsh J. in *Byrne*, held that none of the royal prerogatives had survived the enactment of the Constitution. Nor was it possible, said Finlay C.J., to distinguish between the prerogative of sovereign immunity "which could be traced to the royal dignity of the King" and a prerogative of treasure trove.[19] This meant that no part of the prerogative had survived and, indeed, it was on this basis that the plaintiffs had succeeded before Blayney J. in the High Court. This result was, however, avoided in the Supreme Court by the use of rather surprising reasoning. Finlay C.J. nevertheless held that the State did enjoy a right to a modern form of the treasure trove prerogative, by virtue of Art.5, which proclaims that "Ireland is a sovereign, democratic State".[20]

20–14 This trend was subsequently continued by the Supreme Court's decision in *Howard v Commissioners of Public Works*.[21] Here a majority of the court confirmed that none of the former Crown prerogatives had survived the enactment of the Constitution and that, as the former rule whereby it was presumed that the State was not bound by the application of statute could not be divorced from its prerogative origins, it too had failed to survive the enactment of the Constitution.[22] It may, however, be significant that (as with *Byrne*) there was an alternative ratio, which was the less dramatic principle that any law, whatever its sources, is of no effect if its content was in conflict with the Constitution. Thus, Denham J. ventured the unexceptionable proposition that Art.40.1 (equality before the law) was engaged in that the traditional rule gave the State an unwarranted advantage.

The *Geoghegan* case: some signs of retrenchment

20–15 The first hint that the Supreme Court might be prepared to draw back from

---

[17] See generally, Wade and Forsyth, *Administrative Law* (2009), pp.181–186.
[18] [1988] I.R. 353.
[19] [1988] I.R. 353 at 382.
[20] [1988] I.R. 353 at 383. But it is not easy to see why the State's ownership of such artefacts should be deemed to be an inherent feature of the State's sovereignty. As an alternative ratio a majority of the court (Finlay C.J., Henchy and Griffin JJ.) held that the phrase "all royalties" contained in Art.10.3 of the Constitution was broad enough to include artefacts such as the Derrynaflan Chalice.
[21] [1994] 1 I.R. 101; [1993] I.L.R.M. 665.
[22] Denham J. was satisfied that this rule of statutory construction ([1994] 1 I.R. 101 at 136–137) was "in fact so rooted in the prerogative and the Crown as the personification of the State that it is, in fact, inseparable from that concept …".

the absolutist position it had taken in cases such as *Webb* and *Howard* may be found in an obiter dictum in the judgment of O'Flaherty J. in *Geoghegan v Institute of Chartered Accountants*.[23] In this case, an accountant who was facing disciplinary charges before a disciplinary panel established by the Institute—which was itself a charter body established by exercise of the prerogative prior to 1922—raised the question of whether such bodies had actually survived the enactment of the Constitution. While the court appears implicitly to have acknowledged that the former prerogative power to establish a corporation by letters patent or by charter had not survived the enactment of the Constitution, O'Flaherty J. was decidedly unimpressed by the argument that bodies validly established prior to that date had also ceased to have existence:

> "If we were to attempt to declare that the charter did not exist since the establishment of the State, it would mean that in a suit brought by a person for the purpose of safeguarding his professional qualification we would be declaring that he had no qualification to safeguard because the Institute to which he thought that he belonged had no legal existence. I believe that it would be wrong even to entertain the possibility of such a nonsensical result."[24]

20–16   O'Flaherty J.—who incidentally had been the only dissenter in *Howard* on the question of whether the State exemption from statute had survived—then went on to hint that aspects of *Byrne* and *Webb* might need to be re-considered:

> "As regards the decisions in *Byrne* and *Webb* since each was concerned with a single question in respect of the royal prerogative ... it may be that if in a future case a wider question is raised concerning the royal prerogative the parameters of the judgments in these cases may need to be delineated. Doubtless, in any future debate Professor John M. Kelly's essay[25] which favours a more gradual approach in regard to the place of the royal prerogative in our constitutional scheme of things ... will prove of immense value."[26]

20–17   This must be regarded as a clear manifestation of judicial concern about the formidable legal and practical difficulties that would result in the straightforward disappearance of the prerogative. It is, however, scarcely accurate for O'Flaherty J. to describe *Byrne* and *Webb* as simply presenting issues as to the survival of individual prerogatives, since the entire thrust of these cases was that none of the prerogative's rights had survived the enactment of the Constitution.

20–18   In any event, the general effect of *Byrne*, *Webb* and *Howard* is that whilst

---

[23]   [1995] 3 I.R. 86.

[24]   [1995] 3 I.R. 86 at 118. Blayney J. agreed with O'Flaherty J. and the other members of the Supreme Court reserved their positions on this issue. Note also that in *Laurentiu v Minister for Justice, Equality and Law Reform* [1999] 4 I.R. 26 at 91 (a case concerning the nature of the deportation power), Keane J. observed that it was unnecessary to consider "the vexed question as to the extent to which and the form in which, the royal prerogative survived the enactment of the Constitution of 1922", suggesting, perhaps, that some doubts attached to this question, the language of cases such as *Webb* and *Howard* notwithstanding.

[25]   "Hidden Treasure and the Constitution" (1988) 10 D.U.L.J. 5.

[26]   [1995] 3 I.R. 86 at 118.

the prerogative has been formally expelled, certain former prerogatives may yet be indirectly admitted to the post-1922 polity. For this to occur, such prerogatives must comply with two conditions. The first of these has always existed. It is a rational and relatively predictable condition, namely, that the prerogative should not conflict with the Constitution. The effect of *Byrne, Webb* and *Howard* is to add a second—and, it is suggested—a vague and unnecessary condition. This has been articulated by reference to such subjective factors as the public interest (*Leen*) and sovereignty (*Webb*). And although this argument was not accepted by the majority in *Howard*, the rule whereby the State is presumed to be exempt from the application of statute might have been rationalised on the basis that although it was "sometimes called a prerogative right [it] is, in fact, nothing more than a reservation, or exception, introduced for the public benefit, and equally applicable to all governments".[27] These remarks had been anticipated in the case of public interest immunity (or "executive privilege") from disclosure of documents as early as 1925, by Meredith J. in *Leen v President of the Executive Council*.[28]

20–19   A narrower and more convincing example of the same phenomenon—the re-location of a former prerogative on a more acceptable basis—concerns the status of the right to a passport prior to the enactment of the Passports Act 2008. Whilst the right to a passport (arguably) has its origins from a common law perspective in the prerogative,[29] there seems little doubt but that the administrative arrangements which pre-dated the 2008 Act would have been upheld as a means of giving effect to the citizen's constitutional right to travel abroad. In any event, the passage of time has meant that this debate is becoming gradually less important from a practical point of view, in that individual prerogatives are being slowly replaced by new legislation.

B. THE STATE AS JURISTIC PERSON

20–20   In holding in *Byrne v Ireland* that the State could be sued in tort, the Supreme Court necessarily confirmed that the State had legal personality. It is true that the significance of this is reduced to some extent by the fact that most central government functions are vested in Ministers who have been designated as corporations sole by the Ministers and Secretaries Act 1924. In addition, Art.28.2 makes a grant of the executive power of the State to the Government, a body which is legally distinct from a Minister. However, this constitutional provision is carefully made "subject to the provisions of this Constitution", which suggests that the State retains in itself executive power for some purposes and this alone would be a ground on which to suggest that the State has some legal personality. It is also significant that it is the State and not the responsible Minister who is

---

[27]   *Byrne v Ireland* [1972] I.R. 241 at 287 per Walsh J., quoting from the judgment of Story J. in *United States v Hoar* (1821) 26 Fed. Cas. 329.
[28]   [1926] I.R. 456 at 463.
[29]   This is certainly the position in England: "[T]here is no doubt that passports are issued under the royal prerogative in the discretion of the Secretary of State", per O'Connor L.J. in *R. v Foreign Secretary Ex p. Everett* [1989] Q.B. 811 at 817. In *State (M) v Minister for Foreign Affairs* [1979] I.R. 73 at 76, Finlay P. took a similar view when he said that the "granting or withholding of a passport does not appear to have been of statutory origin but would appear to have derived originally from the Crown prerogative".

vicariously responsible for a tort committed by a civil servant (since it is the State which employs a civil servant), although the position in contract is less clear. The significance of this is that this common law responsibility is among the reasons why the State's legal personality is an important matter.

20–21 However, one further preliminary point which is of importance arises from the fact that in Britain two alternative means of defining the prerogative have been adopted. The first is to restrict the prerogative to those powers which are unique to the Crown. The alternative and wider approach is to treat the prerogative as embracing "every power of the Crown which is non-statutory".[30] If the latter approach were adopted,[31] certain difficulties would be presented by reason of the Supreme Court's decisions to the effect that the prerogative did not survive the constitutional changes after 1922. These would be that the State would be lacking in even the legal personality and attributes which are possessed by the ordinary artificial legal person, since, if one utilises the second definition, this very personality would derive from the prerogative.

20–22 Such a suggestion, however, would serve only to confuse the character of the Irish State with that of the United Kingdom. In the United Kingdom it is the Crown, a corporation sole, whose character and capacities were initially determined by the prerogative, which acts as the State. In Ireland, the State is the creation of the People and designed according to the (admittedly rather vague) specifications of the Constitution.[32] Next, again by virtue of the Constitution, Art.28.4.2° and Art.29.4, the executive power of the State is firmly vested in the Government. The most that could ever have been claimed for the prerogative in Ireland is that, entering the polity via the bridges of Art.73 of the 1922 Constitution and Art.49.1 of the present Constitution, it might have contributed certain auxiliary rights and privileges to the capabilities of the State, rather than actually establishing it and shaping it. However, as we have seen as a result of *Byrne*, *Webb* and *Howard* it has now been determined that the prerogative did not survive beyond 1922.

20–23 It seems clear, therefore, that the State's legal personality is independent of the prerogative and not in any sense contingent on its survival. The question then is whether the State has all the usual powers of a legal person to sue and be sued; establish companies; expend money; and generally bear similar legal rights and duties to those of an ordinary artificial person. These are now matters to be determined by the Constitution, as interpreted by case law. And it is true that:

---

[30] Wade and Forsyth, *Administrative Law* (2009), p.182.

[31] In *Re K, an Arranging Debtor* [1927] I.R. 260 at 270, Kennedy C.J. described the prerogative as "the residue of discretionary or arbitrary power which at any given time is legally left in the hands of the Crown". Similar views are to be found in *R. v Criminal Injuries Compensation Tribunal Ex p. Lain* [1967] 2 Q.B. 864 at 881 per Diplock L.J. and *Council of Civil Service Unions v Minister for the Public Service* [1985] A.C. 374. Note, however, that in *R. v Panel on Take-Overs Ex p. Datafin Plc* [1987] Q.B. 815 at 848, Lloyd L.J. accepted the narrower definition of the prerogative urged by Sir William Wade. It may be of interest that in *MF v Legal Aid Board* [1993] I.L.R.M. 797 Finlay C.J. said that the Board had been established by "executive act" of the Government, i.e. thereby implying that Art.28 of the Constitution provided sufficient authority for this decision. This view avoids any difficulties associated with the prerogative.

[32] *JM Kelly: The Irish Constitution*, 4th edn (Dublin: Lexis Nexis Butterworths, 2003), p.87.

"[T]he Constitution gives no express answer [to the question of the State's legal personality], nor to questions about the State's legal capacities or privileges. These answers must be elaborated from the narrow base of Article 5, with the help of some other indications."[33]

20–24   Nor does statute offer any real assistance, for the only statutory provisions even to allude to this matter are ss.10 and 11 of the State Property Act 1954, which confer extensive powers on the Minister for Finance in relation to the sale, exchange, transfer and leasing of State lands.[34] And insofar as the 1954 Act says anything about the present issue, it implies a lack of confidence about the State's capacity, at common law, to hold, lease and convey property. The 1954 Act was, however, passed in an era long before *Byrne v Ireland* and the rapid modern development of constitutional thought and the usage of statute could, in any event, be scarcely conclusive on this issue.

20–25   Another line of argument, which tends to confirm the view that in Ireland it is not necessary to invoke anything like the prerogative in order to sustain the view that the State is a juristic person, has found favour in the few cases on this topic. This argument is grounded in the rights and duties, on the high constitutional plane, with which the Constitution endows the State. These include the capacity to own natural resources, lands, minerals and waters (Art.10); the power to commit itself to international agreements and international organisations (Arts 29.4 and 29.5); the duty to provide for free primary education (Art.42.4); as well, of course, as the State's liability in tort, which was stated in *Byrne* to be founded on Art.40.3. Surely it would be strange, indeed, if the State—which, after all, *is* a juristic person—were not also endowed with an adequate legal personality on the mundane level of making grants, entering contracts, etc to equip it to implement these rights and bear these duties, in much the same way as if it were a corporation sole?[35] This line of thought finds expression in the following example of judicial statesmanship taken from the judgment of Kingsmill Moore J. in *Comyn v Attorney General*[36]:

"There is at least one point on which general agreement may be found, namely, the practical necessity of endowing the State with some form of legal personality. Ultimately, the nature and attributes of the State must be found in the wording of the Constitution. It is, however, not unreasonable to assume that those who framed, and those who debated, the Constitution were familiar with current opinions as to the nature of the State. The Constitution has told us a great deal about the State, its organisation, its rights, its obligations and its attributes; but still it has not attempted to define its juristic nature. Is it a corporation? Is it, as has been suggested, an unincorporated association? Is it neither of these, but a legal persona of a new type and *sui generis*? These questions may provide much food for discussion in future cases. It is not necessary, and it would be dangerous, to attempt a full or final answer.

---

[33] *JM Kelly: The Irish Constitution* (2003), p.87.

[34] As MacMenamin J. remarked in *Health Service Executive v Commissioners of Valuation* [2008] IEHC 178: "[I]n general, property rights inhering in the State are exercised through the State Property Act 1954, through Ministers or government departments."

[35] See also, the passing discussion of this by Finlay Geoghegan J. in *Gama Endustri Tesisleri Imalat Montaj AS v Minister for Enterprise and Employment* [2007] 3 I.R. 472 at 481–482.

[36] [1950] I.R. 142.

For the purposes of this case, all that is necessary is to find that the State is conceived of as a juristic person or entity having as one of its many attributes the capacity to hold property. It may; or may not, be a corporation. It may be a conception entirely new to English and Irish law; but I hold that it is a juristic person and can hold property."[37]

20–26 Thus, if—as has been judicially confirmed—the State is a juristic person (whether by virtue of Art.5 of the Constitution or otherwise), then it would seem to follow that the State must thereby enjoy the ordinary legal capacity of an artificial person. Accordingly, the State's right to make contracts, establish companies, etc would seem to be derived from this juristic status and the non-survival of the prerogative has no bearing on the issue.

20–27 A related question which sometimes arises is whether the Government, as distinct from the State, can sue and be sued and whether it has legal personality for this purpose. At one stage a practice had emerged whereby all individual members of the Government were sued in cases involving the actions of the Government: see, e.g. *Crotty v An Taoiseach*[38]; *Horgan v An Taoiseach.*[39] However, in *State (Sheehan) v Government of Ireland*[40] the Government was sued as such and no objection was taken to that course of action. Since then, practice in this regard has varied and there are prominent examples where both of these courses of action have been taken.[41]

C. Liability of the State and Ministers

20–28 The purpose of this Part is to outline the relationship between the State, Ministers and the civil service as these have been created (the word is used advisedly as some artificiality is involved here) by the courts in the context of tort and contract litigation.

---

[37] [1950] I.R. 142 at 160–161. See also, to the same effect, *Commissioners of Public Works v Kavanagh* [1962] I.R. 216 at 225–227 per Ó Dalaigh J. and *Health Service Executive v Commissioner for Valuation* [2008] IEHC 178.

[38] [1987] I.R. 713.

[39] [2003] IEHC 64; [2003] 2 I.R. 468; [2003] 2 I.L.R.M. 357.

[40] [1987] I.R. 550. See also, *Kavanagh v Government of Ireland* [1996] 1 I.R. 321, and *Breathnach v Government of Ireland* [2000] IEHC 53 in which Quirke J. noted: "The applicant, as a matter of law, is entitled to commence proceedings against the State and against the Law Officer of the State and whilst it might be useful to identify the Government of the State with greater particularity it has not been contended on behalf of the State or on behalf of the Law Officer of the State that the applicant is not entitled to bring proceedings seeking relief against the Government of the State and, when it is appropriate, to obtain such relief." This passage is not, however, included in the Irish Reports' version of the judgment: see [2000] 3 I.R. 467.

In *Dudley v An Taoiseach* [1994] 2 I.L.R.M. 321, Geoghegan J. granted liberty to the applicant to seek judicial review against the Government in respect of its failure to fulfil an alleged constitutional obligation (holding a Dáil bye-election within a reasonable period of time). Yet the judge refused leave to apply for judicial review in respect of Dáil Éireann, on the grounds that the courts "cannot mandamus the body of members of the Dáil as such to vote in a particular way on a particular motion". This, however, is not quite the same thing as saying that Dáil Éireann is not a juristic person without legal capacity.

[41] See, e.g. *Dubsky v Government of Ireland* [2005] IEHC 442; [2007] 1 I.R. 63.

20–29   There are two bases to the central executive organ's capacity to sue and to be sued, and the relationship between these two bases has not yet been clarified. The first basis is the Ministers and Secretaries Act 1924, s.2(1) of which provides:

> Each of the Ministers, heads of the respective departments of State shall be a corporation sole under his style or name aforesaid and shall have perpetual succession and an official seal and may sue and be sued.

20–30   The purposes of making each of the Ministers a corporation sole have been explained as follows by Sullivan P. in *Carolan v Minister for Defence*[42] (a case in which the plaintiff claimed damages for personal injuries sustained through the alleged negligence of a soldier driving an Army lorry):

> "1.   to secure continuity of title and obviate the need for the transfer of State property, rights and obligations from a Minister to his successor;
> 2.   to secure that persons contracting with the Government through any of its Departments should have the ordinary remedy of action available in case of breach of contract;
> 3.   to enable a Minister to be sued in his corporate capacity for a wrongful act done by him as such Minister or by his orders and directions. I cannot think that the legislature intended to go further and create by this section a liability in each Minister for all the wrongful acts or defaults of all the persons employed in his Department."[43]

20–31   Comment is unnecessary on the first of these functions; the third is considered below and the second will be examined immediately.

Contract

20–32   The second function mentioned in the quotation enables the Minister to be sued in contract in the ordinary way, rather than, as formerly, having to proceed by way of the Petition of Right (Ireland) Act 1873. At common law, the existence of the prerogative ensured that neither the Crown nor its servants could be sued upon a contract.[44]

20–33   As in private law, it is, of course, a precondition of the Minister's liability that the contract was actually made by a person (usually a civil servant) who could be regarded as the agent of the Minister. The question of agency featured in *Grenham v Minister for Defence*,[45] in which Hanna J. held that army officers, who had commandeered motor vehicles for military purposes during the Civil War,

---

[42]   [1927] I.R. 62.

[43]   [1927] I.R. 62 at 69.

[44]   Phillimore J. said in *Graham v Public Works Commissioners* [1901] 2 K.B. 781 at 789–790: "The Crown cannot be sued; and that being so, neither can the subject take action indirectly against the Crown by suing a servant of the Crown upon a contract made by the servant as agent of the Crown."
      But even at common law it was clear that public officials could, in Phillimore J.'s words, be designated as "agents of the Crown with a power of contracting as principals" (i.e. not merely as agents).

[45]   [1926] I.R. 54.

were not agents of the Minister so as to make him liable on the contract. However, because of the unusual facts of the case and the brevity of the judgment, *Grenham* cannot be regarded as having significant precedential value. This case does raise the more general question of whether an action arising out of a contract made by a civil servant should be brought against the State or against the Minister for the Department in which the civil servant worked. It would seem that the contract should be brought against the Minister and this is buttressed by the fact that government contracts are always made in the name of the appropriate Minister. In effect, the Minister is—to adapt Phillimore J.'s formulation, cited in footnote 44—an agent of the State but with the power of contracting as principal. Moreover, the fact that a civil servant is, in law, a servant of the State rather than the Minister, does not prevent him from also being the agent of his Minister (whose alter ego he is always said to be in the conventional and slightly imprecise usage). While the question is not of great significance, so long as it remains unresolved, the prudent plaintiff will join both the State and the relevant Minister as defendants.

Tort

20–34   *Byrne v Ireland*[46] is the basis of liability in tort. Until *Byrne v Ireland*, the general rule was that, statute apart, neither the State nor any of its organs could be liable for an action in tort. Historically, the British Crown was immune from actions in tort (whether directly or vicariously, through the behaviour of Crown servants),[47] both because of the principle that the King could do no wrong and because of the King's disability to command himself to appear before his own courts. In tort, in contrast to contract, this relic persisted into the twentieth century. In *Carolan v Minister for Defence*, Sullivan P. held that s.2 of the Ministers and Secretaries Act 1924 was intended not to alter the position because its objective was only to allow:

> "... a Minister to be sued in his corporate capacity for a wrongful act done by him as such Minister, or by his orders or directions, I cannot think that the Legislature intended to go further, and create by this section a liability in each Minister for all wrongful acts or defaults of all the persons employed in his Department."[48]

20–35   The evident injustice of this situation was ameliorated in particular areas by statute.[49] However, the most far-reaching developments were to come via the judiciary. In 1965, in *Macauley v Minister for Posts and Telegraphs*,[50] Kenny

---

[46]   [1972] I.R. 241.

[47]   See, e.g. *Murphy v Soady* [1903] 2 I.R. 213, where the Commissioners of Public Works were permitted to invoke Crown immunity to defeat an action for negligence.

[48]   [1927] I.R. 62 at 69. While this was probably a correct application of the principle against unclear changes in the law, the Dáil Debates reveal that the intention was to abolish the State's immunity from suit: see the comments of the then Attorney General (Hugh Kennedy, subsequently Chief Justice) at 5 *Dáil Debates* Col.1498 (December 16, 1923).

[49]   For instance, s.59 of the Civil Liability Act 1961 provides that where a wrong is committed through the use of a motor vehicle belonging to the State, and driven by a person acting in the course of his employment, then the Minister for Finance is liable. See *Murray v Minister for Finance*, unreported, Supreme Court, April 22, 1982 (accident caused by off-duty policeman).

[50]   [1966] I.R. 345.

J. said that in his view the State could be sued "whenever this is necessary to vindicate or assert the rights of a citizen". Accordingly, the requirement in s.2(1) of the Ministers and Secretaries Act 1924 (which required the fiat of the Attorney General before proceedings could be instituted against the Minister) was held to be unconstitutional.

20–36   In *Byrne*, it had not been open to the plaintiff to sue the Minister, since *Carolan v Minister for Defence*[51] had decided that both the Minister and civil servants were fellow employees of the State. The judgments in *Byrne* confirmed this rule and, consequently, a Minister (as distinct from the State itself) cannot be made vicariously liable for the tortious acts of civil servants in his Department. As Walsh J. explained:

> "All persons employed in the various Departments of the Government and the other Departments of State, whether they be in the civil service or not, are in the service of the State and the State is liable for damages done by such person in carrying out the affairs of the State so long as that person is acting within the terms of his employment."[52]

20–37   Unfortunately, *Byrne*, like many another epoch-making authorities, leaves many questions unanswered.[53] First, it would seem probable that this decision has not effected an implied repeal of the earlier statutory provisions which granted limited statutory rights to sue specified Ministers. For example, in the case of a person injured by the negligent use of a vehicle used in the service of the State, the aggrieved party may still either sue the Minister for Finance by virtue of the Civil Liability Act 1961,[54] or the State itself under the principle enunciated in *Byrne*. Secondly, is it possible to enact legislation which would modify the effects of the *Byrne* decision? Such legislation might provide, for example, that injured parties could sue only the Minister for Finance and not the State or that a special limitation period might apply to actions against the State. Such alternative arrangements would not, in principle, at least, unfairly impinge on a person's right to litigate a justiciable controversy. But, equally, it is doubtful whether legislation which sought to tamper with the fundamental principle enunciated in *Byrne*—such as legislation placing an upper limit on the quantum of damages recoverable in actions against the State or which precluded recovery in respect of certain types of economic loss which were otherwise recoverable—would survive constitutional challenge.

20–38   The major query raised by *Byrne* is the relationship between the new liability which the case created and the existing basis for suing the central state authority (i.e. the right to sue Ministers of State created by s.2 of the 1924 Act). Reference has already been made to one question raised by *Byrne*, namely, whether

---

[51]   [1927] I.R. 62.

[52]   *Byrne v Ireland* [1972] I.R. 241 at 285–286 per Walsh J. In addition, the Supreme Court has confirmed its unwillingness to extend the boundaries of vicarious liability beyond its traditional common law limits: see *O'Keeffe v Hickey* [2008] IESC 72; [2009] 2 I.R. 302; [2009] 1 I.L.R.M. 490 (holding that the State was not vicariously liable in respect of sexual abuse committed by a teacher in a State-recognised but Church-run school).

[53]   For useful discussion, see Osborough, "The Demise of the State's Immunity in Tort" (1973) 8 *Irish Jurist* 274 at 278–279.

[54]   Originally Road Traffic Act 1933 s.116. The Minister for Finance is not, however, liable where the state employee is not acting within the course of his employment.

breach of contract actions should be brought against the State or the responsible Minister. A similar question arises in relation to tort actions. In the first place, as stated already, it is quite clear that where the tort was actually committed by a civil servant, the Minister cannot usually be held to be responsible, so that the appropriate defendant would be the State.

20–39 However, Sullivan P. in *Carolan v Minister for Defence* acknowledged that one of the functions of s.2 was to enable the Minister to be sued "in his corporate capacity for a wrongful act done by him as Minister, or by his orders or directions".[55] What this probably means is that the Minister cannot be held vicariously liable for the torts of his civil servants, but this does not affect his direct liability in tort. For there is an important distinction between the direct liability of a Minister and the acts of his civil servants and vicarious liability for the torts committed by them. If a plaintiff contends that the Minister ordered or authorised the civil servant to commit the action complained of, or that the Minister was careless in selecting or supervising the employee, then this is an allegation of direct or personal liability on the part of the Minister and the action can proceed under s.2(1) of the 1924 Act.[56] On the other hand, vicarious liability arises when the law attaches liability to the employer for the employee's torts even where the employer is not personally at fault. For this more usual category of liability, as already mentioned, the appropriate defendant is the State.

Personal responsibility of Minister or public servant

20–40 It ought to be emphasised that the cardinal and historical principle that, if the plaintiff prefers, the responsible public servant or ministerial incumbent may be sued in tort personally (rather than the State or the Minister as corporation sole), remains correct.[57] Thus, in *Lynch v Fitzgerald*[58] the detectives who had unlawfully killed the son of the plaintiff during the course of suppressing a riot were found to be personally liable in an action under the Fatal Accidents Act 1846. It is, likewise, worth emphasising that the Minister, qua corporation sole,[59] is a separate legal entity from the incumbent at any particular time, and remains personally liable in tort. *Sheil v Attorney General*[60] is a good illustration of this principle. The plaintiff had been a train-bearer to the former Master of the Rolls, and upon the abolition of that judicial office in 1924, he was granted a declaration against the Attorney General to the effect that he was entitled to compensation under Art.10 of the Anglo-Irish Treaty 1921, to be paid out of monies voted by the Oireachtas. Costs of the action

---

[55] [1927] I.R. 62 at 68–69.
[56] In cases of direct liability, it is the Minister's negligence which is the basis of the action and it is not crucial that the employee in question was negligent. On this general question, see McMahon and Binchy, *Irish Law of Torts*, 3rd edn (Dublin: Butterworths, 2000).
[57] In the case of Gardaí, s.48(3) of the Garda Síochána Act 2005 provides that it is not necessary for the plaintiff to sue the individual member, although s.48(4) provides that this cannot of itself preclude an application by the State to join the member concerned to the proceedings.
[58] [1938] I.R. 382. This case was, of course, decided in the pre-*Byrne* era and so the State was still assumed to be immune from suit. And, for the reasons set out in *Carolan*, the plaintiff could not sue the Minister for Justice, as the Minister and the detectives were both fellow servants of the State and thus the doctrine of *respondeat superior* could not apply.
[59] On this point, see para.20–34.
[60] (1928) 62 I.L.T.S.J. 199. See further, Casey, *The Irish Law Officers* (Dublin: Round Hall, Sweet & Maxwell, 1996), pp.171–172.

were awarded against the Attorney General. And it was against Mr John Costello personally, the then holder of the office, that the plaintiff sought to enforce this part of the judgment. (However note that the original judgment was then rectified to make it clear that the costs, as well as the compensation, were also entitled to come from funds appropriated by the Oireachtas.)

20–41   By contrast, in contract there is no personal liability. In *Kenny v Cosgrave*[61] the President of the Executive Council had told an employer whose workers were on strike that it was essential that the strikers' demands be resisted. The President promised that the Executive Council would also indemnify him against any financial loss which resulted from this resistance. The action failed before the Supreme Court on a number of grounds, which included the fact that Mr Cosgrave had been sued personally and neither a Minister nor a civil servant can be held personally liable on a state contract.

Vicarious liability of the State

20–42   Irrespective of the fact that public servants will seldom be sued personally,[62] their formal liability is of obvious importance since (just as with any other employer) the State's liability is usually vicarious and is thus contingent upon proof of the employee's individual liability, usually in negligence. Public officials, while not as such carrying on a business or profession, necessarily hold themselves out as having special knowledge and authority in their field of activity. If they make a decision or give specific advice regarding the application of departmental or governmental policy, in circumstances where they should know that their advice will be relied on, it would be consistent with general principles of negligence for the courts to hold that they are under a duty to be reasonably careful. Nevertheless, assuming that such a duty of care does exist, it would seem that liability under this heading will be difficult to establish not least because of the various special defences which Ministers and other public officials have sometimes been held to enjoy. In *Pine Valley Developments Ltd v Minister for the Environment*,[63] the Supreme Court held that the defendant Minister must be acquitted of negligence where he had acted on the basis of legal advice. The plaintiffs had suffered considerable financial loss as a result of the invalidation of a planning permission which had been granted to them by the defendant. The evidence showed, however, that the Minister's legal advisers believed that he had power to grant such permission and the court held that, in such circumstances, no liability could attach. As Finlay C.J. said:

> "If a Minister of State, granted as a *persona designata* a specific duty and function to make decisions under a statutory code (as occurs in this case), exercises his decision *bona fide*, having obtained and followed the legal advice of the permanent legal advisers attached to his department, I can not see how he could be said to have been negligent if the law eventually proves to be otherwise than they have advised him and if by reason of that, he makes an order which is invalid or *ultra vires*."[64]

---

[61]   [1926] I.R. 517.
[62]   Although there have been instances where the State has indemnified civil servants in such circumstances.
[63]   [1987] I.R. 23.
[64]   [1987] I.R. 23 at 35.

20–43   The Supreme Court was, however, less than clear as to the precise extent of a Minister's duty in general. Henchy J. (with whom Griffin and Lardner JJ. agreed) expressly stated that the Minister's duty was to give "his decision with the care and circumspection to be expected from a reasonably careful Minister". But Finlay C.J. (Hederman J. concurring), with whom Griffin and Lardner JJ. also agreed, appeared to enumerate a different test, referring with approval to a dictum of Lord Moulton in *Everett v Griffiths*[65] to the effect that the Minister's duty was merely to make a decision honestly and in good faith.[66]

20–44   A further query which this case leaves unanswered, of course, is what is the position if the legal advice tendered to the Minister had itself been negligent? This, of course, was not the case in *Pine Valley*, because the advice then given to the Minister represented the common understanding of the legal profession at the time when it was given. However, had these facts been otherwise, and assuming that the negligent advice had been given by a civil servant (as opposed to a private practitioner), there would appear in principle to be no reason why the State should not have been made vicariously liable for the negligent advice.[67]

20–45   This matter was also considered by Blayney J. in *McMahon v Ireland*.[68] Here the suggestion was that the Minister for Finance and the Minister for Industry and Commerce were negligent in allowing an under-capitalised friendly society (which ultimately became insolvent, leaving unsecured and unpaid creditors) to continue to operate what in effect was a banking business outside the control of the Central Bank. Blayney J. found that there was no cause of action vis-à-vis the Ministers:

> "Neither [Minister] was responsible for the initial exemption [from the scope of the Central Bank Acts] of which the plaintiff complains. It was contained in a statute enacted by the Oireachtas. And it could not be contended that either Minister owed the plaintiff a duty of care to have the Central Bank

---

[65]   [1921] A.C. 631.

[66]   [1987] I.R. 23 at 38. Cf. *Jones v Department of Environment* [1989] Q.B. 1 where the English Court of Appeal held that a social security officer did not owe a claimant a common law duty of care in calculating social security entitlements. Glidewell L.J. said ([1989] Q.B. 1 at 22) that, as a matter of general principle: "[I]f a government department or officer, charged with the making of decisions whether certain payments should be made, is subject to a statutory right of appeals against his decisions, he owes no duty of care in private law. Misfeasance apart, he is only susceptible in public law to judicial review or to the right of appeal provided by the statute under which he makes his decision."
    Likewise, there can be no negligence where the statutory body simply lacks the resources to perform its task effectively: see *O'Donoghue v Legal Aid Board* [2004] IEHC 413 where Kelly J. observed: "Her claim in negligence against the Board must likewise fail. I am unable to identify any act of negligence on the part of the Board or its officers. They were simply being swamped with work and their cries for assistance went unheeded. The working conditions that they had to experience and the demands being made upon them are evidenced in the lengthy memoranda that were sent regularly by the Board's Chief Executive to the relevant department. The conditions under which the Board's personnel had to operate were woefully substandard and the reason for that was the failure to resource the Board properly."

[67]   See *Cotter v Minister for Agriculture*, unreported, High Court, Murphy J., November 15, 1991 (Minister liable for negligent advice given by officials, but claim failed on the facts); *Duff v Minister for Agriculture* [1997] 2 I.R. 22.

[68]   [1988] I.L.R.M. 610.

Act amended so as to prevent industrial provident societies from taking deposits."[69]

20–46   Blayney J. thus appears to have demonstrated at least an openness to testing the ministerial activity by reference to standard principles of negligence. However, he concluded his judgment by saying that the principles of quasi-immunity enjoyed by persons discharging quasi-judicial functions which were recognised by *Pine Valley* would have been applicable to the present case and would, in any event, have been enough to defeat the plaintiff's claim.[70]

D. State Exemption from Statute

20–47   As usually stated, this exemption meant that the State was not "bound" (i.e. affected to its disadvantage) by a statute unless it is referred to either expressly or by necessary implication. An early example is provided by *Galway County Council v Minister for Finance*,[71] where one of the issues was whether the defendant Minister was free to set off as against the plaintiff's claim an overpayment which he had made to them eight years earlier. The County Council submitted in reply that the Minister's claim was not statute barred. Johnson J. was unimpressed by this argument:

> "[T]he Minister relies on prerogative rights and contends that the sub-section has no applicability to a claim such as the present, there being no indication in the subsection that it was the intention of the Legislature to bind the Crown or the State. There has been no doubt and it has not been argued in the present case to the contrary, that the prerogative and prerogative right can be relied upon by the Irish Free State, and is part of the law of the land, I can see nothing in [the subsection] that suggests that it was intended to have any applicability to the Crown or the State and, I think, therefore, that the defendant is entitled to rely on this set-off."[72]

Even in *Byrne v Ireland*,[73] Walsh J. was prepared to contemplate the survival of this common law presumption on the ground that "… though this [exemption] is sometimes called a prerogative right, it is in fact nothing more than a reservation,

---

[69]   [1988] I.L.R.M. 610 at 612. Striking as it may seem to modern eyes, friendly societies had been exempted from the requirement to hold banking licences under the Central Bank Act 1971.

[70]   While Blayney J. only applied the *Pine Valley* principles in the case of a claim against the Registrar of Friendly Societies (who, it was said, had been negligent in failing to take action under s.16 of the Industrial and Provident Societies (Amendment) Act 1978 to direct the company to cease accepting deposits), it is implicit in his judgment that he would have been prepared to apply these principles to the case of the two Ministers had this been required.

[71]   [1931] I.R. 215.

[72]   [1931] I.R. 215 at 232. See now s.3(1) of the Statute of Limitations 1957 which provides that the Statute shall apply to "proceedings by or against a State authority in the same manner as if that State authority were a private individual". Note, however, that from time to time even contemporary statutes expressly state that the State will, or, as the case may be, will not be bound: see, e.g. s.3(2)(c) of the Residential Tenancies Act 2004 which provides that the Act does not apply to a "dwelling let by or to" a public authority.

[73]   [1972] I.R. 241.

or exception, introduced for the public benefit, and equally applicable to all governments".[74]

20–48 Nevertheless, this approach was rejected by a majority of the Supreme Court in *Howard v Commissioners of Public Works*.[75] In this case the defendants had proposed the construction of visitors' centres in three areas of outstanding scenic beauty. These proposals proved to be very controversial and the legality of the Commissioner's actions was challenged in the courts. Quite apart from the more specific question of whether the Commissioners, as a body corporate, had any power to construct interpretative centres, the major question was whether these proposals required planning permission. It was common case that these proposals would have required planning permission had the Commissioners been a private body and this raised the more fundamental question of whether the traditional rule presuming that the State was not bound by statute had survived the enactment of the Constitution.

20–49 A majority of the Supreme Court concluded that the rule could not be divorced from its historical origins. Both Finlay C.J. and Denham J. quoted from recent British authority to demonstrate this point, including the following passage from the judgment of Diplock L.J. in *BBC v Johns*:

"The question is, thus, one of construction of statutes. Since laws are made by rulers for subjects, a general expression in a statute such as 'any person' is descriptive of those upon whom the statute imposes obligation or restraints, it is not to be read as including the ruler himself."[76]

Accordingly, the rule had not survived the enactment of the Constitution. Even if the Supreme Court was wrong to condemn the rule as simply an outcrop of the now vanished prerogative, because of its discriminatory content the rule is unlikely to persist in a modern world, as is clear from other jurisdictions.[77]

The consequences of the *Howard* decision

20–50 A related question concerns the capacity of the Oireachtas expressly to exempt the State and state bodies from the scope of any legislation. Both Finlay C.J. and Denham J.[78] expressly contemplated the enactment of legislative exceptions of this kind. One example is the Planning and Development Act 2000—which re-enacted the provisions of the Local Government (Planning and Development) Act 1993 enacted in the immediate wake of the *Howard* decision. The Act provides

---

[74] [1972] I.R. 241 at 278, quoting Story J. in *United States v Hoar* (1821) 2 *Mason* 311 at 313. The US Supreme Court has accepted the survival of this rule of statutory construction, despite its origins as a Crown prerogative: *Guaranty Trust Co. v United States* 304 U.S. 126 (1938); *United States v Nardone* 338 U.S. 303 (1939).

[75] [1994] 1 I.R. 101. See generally, Hogan, "The Mullaghmore Case" (1993) 15 D.U.L.J. 243.

[76] [1965] Ch. 32 at 78–79. This passage was expressly approved by the House of Lords in *Lord Advocate v Dunbarton B.C.* [1990] 2 A.C. 580.

[77] The rule has been abandoned in India (*State of West Bengal v Corporation of Calcutta* [1967] A.I.R. 997) and relaxed in Canada (*Bropho v Western Australia* (1990) 171 C.L.R. 1).

[78] As Denham J. said ([1994] 1 I.R. 101 at 160): "… [T]he Oireachtas may legislate including or excluding the application of an Act to the executive in accordance with constitutional parameters."

that, subject to certain exceptions in favour of certain developments associated with or for the purposes of "public safety or order, the administration of justice or national security or defence",[79] the planning laws shall henceforth apply to all state development. Nevertheless, it is possible that there are limits to this form of exception and legislation which sought to confer unjustified and disproportionate advantages on state bodies by, e.g. creating certain immunities or exceptions in their favour might be open to challenge on constitutional grounds other than the non-importation of the prerogative.

E. PRIVILEGE AGAINST THE DISCLOSURE OF OFFICIAL EVIDENCE

Historical antecedents

20–51 It was formerly the law that Ministers could not be compelled by court order to produce documents for inspection or even to disclose the existence of a document. This applied in all litigation, irrespective of whether the Minister or the State were actually a party to it. All that was necessary for the exercise of this privilege was an affidavit claiming it, signed by the responsible Minister or one of his senior civil servants. There were, plainly, two elements to this privilege:

(i) There was a public interest in maintaining the confidentiality of certain official documents; and

(ii) It was for the responsible Minister, and not the court, to decide whether this interest outweighed the public interest in the fair administration of justice.

20–52 As has been remarked, "the newly independent State, having shaken off the yoke of the Crown, embraced with enthusiasm many of its privileges".[80] The privilege was invoked to protect: communications between the Executive Council and the Shaw Commission which investigated the destruction of Ballyheigue Castle[81]; advices and minutes given to the Minister for Local Government in regard to the Electoral (Amendment) Act 1959[82]; and, in a prosecution for "showing for gain an indecent and profane performance", the instructions given by their supervisors to the detectives who watched the play.[83]

---

[79] Planning and Development Act 2000 s.181(1)(a).

[80] Russell, "A Privilege of the State" (1967) 2 *Irish Jurist* 88. This prescient article reviewed the former law and predicted its demise. For a fine analysis of the development of the law in the United Kingdom, see Jacob, "From Privileged Crown to Interested Public" (1993) *Public Law* 121.

[81] *Leen v President of the Executive Council* [1926] I.R. 456.

[82] *O'Donovan v Attorney General* [1961] I.R. 114.

[83] *Attorney General v Simpson* [1959] I.R. 335. In *Kenny v Minister for Defence* (1942) 8 Ir. Jur. Rep. 81 (an action in contract concerning the construction of army huts), Maguire P. observed that the Minister was entitled to claim privilege in respect of "documents of a confidential nature". A prison governor was allowed to claim privilege in respect of confidential information concerning a planned prison escape: see *State (Comerford) v Mountjoy Prison* [1981] I.L.R.M. 86.

The modern law: the *Murphy* and *Ambiorix* decisions

20–53 The law was authoritatively changed in *Murphy v Dublin Corporation*,[84] a case which arose in the wake of objections raised by the plaintiff to a proposed compulsory purchase order in respect of his lands. A public inquiry was held in accordance with the usual procedure, and the planning inspector sent a report of the proceedings to the Minister. In dealing with the Minister's claim for privilege in respect of the report, Walsh J. stated:

> "Under the Constitution the administration of justice is committed solely to the judiciary in the exercise of their powers ... Power to compel the attendance of witnesses and the production of evidence is an inherent part of the judicial power of government of the State and is the ultimate safeguard of justice in the State. The proper exercise of the three powers of government ... is in the public interest. There may be occasions when the different aspects of the public interest 'pull in contrary directions' ... If the conflict arises during the exercise of judicial power then, in my view, it is the judicial power which will decide which public interest shall prevail. This does not mean that the court will always decide that the interest of the litigant shall prevail. It is for the court to decide which is the superior interest in the circumstances of the particular case and to determine the matter accordingly."[85]

20–54 The courts thus still retain a discretion to preserve the confidential nature of official evidence in the public interest, but this matter may not be constitutionally remitted to a non-judicial personage. The courts will, of course, be reluctant to overrule official claims for privilege, especially in sensitive areas concerning the security or safety of the State[86] or where an assurance of confidentiality has been given to third parties.[87] But as Walsh J. remarked:

> "It may well be that it would be rare or infrequent for a court after its own examination, to arrive at a different conclusion from that expressed by the Minister, but that is a far remove from accepting without question the judgment of the Minister."[88]

20–55 In 1991 the Supreme Court emphatically upheld the *Murphy* principles in *Ambiorix Ltd v Minister for Environment (No. 1)*[89] and rejected the suggestion that the earlier decision had been wrongly decided.[90] In this case the plaintiffs had claimed that the designation of certain lands under the provisions of the

---

[84] [1972] I.R. 215.

[85] [1972] I.R. 215 at 233–234.

[86] See, e.g. *State (Comerford) v Mountjoy Prison* [1981] I.L.R.M. 86; *O'Mahony v Ireland, The Irish Times*, July 28, 1989; *O'Brien v Ireland* [1995] 1 I.L.R.M. 22; *McDonald v Radio Telefís Éireann* [2001] IESC 6; [2001] 1 I.R. 355; [2001] 2 I.L.R.M. 1 (no disclosure of Garda file into ongoing murder inquiry).

[87] See, e.g. *O'Neill v An Taoiseach* [2009] IEHC 119; *Leech v Independent Newspapers (Ireland) Ltd* [2009] IEHC 259.

[88] [1972] I.R. 215 at 236.

[89] [1992] 1 I.R. 277.

[90] Thus, McCarthy J. observed ([1992] 1 I.R. 277 at 289) that "to depart, as we are invited to do, from the reasoning and the decision in *Murphy v. Dublin Corporation* would be to lessen or impair judicial sovereignty in the administration of justice".

Urban Renewal Act 1986[91] was ultra vires. To that end they sought discovery of certain memoranda for Government and other Cabinet documents which dealt with these issues. The defendants resisted discovery on class rather than content grounds, namely, that the discovery of these documents might prejudice the "necessary requirements of confidentiality of cabinet, government and ministerial communications and discussions" and the "confidentiality and the collective responsibility of the Government".[92] Finlay C.J. summarised the effect of the *Murphy* principles and then stated that:

> "(a) The Executive cannot prevent the judicial power from examining documents which are relevant to an issue in a civil trial for the purpose of deciding whether they must be produced.
>
> (b) There is no obligation on the judicial power to examine any particular document before deciding that it is exempt from production and it can and will in many instances uphold a claim of privilege merely on the basis of a description of its nature and contents which it (the judicial power) accepts.
>
> (c) There cannot, accordingly, be a generally applicable class or category of documents exempted from production by reason of the rank in the public service of the person creating them or the position of the individual or body intended to use them."[93]

20–56 Finlay C.J. emphasised that these principles stemmed directly from the constitutional requirements ordaining the separation of powers. In addition, focusing on the executive privilege, based on class grounds, which was the issue in *Ambiorix*, the Chief Justice nonetheless highlighted the consequences. If a privilege of this kind "were accepted as a general standard" it might mean that:

> "… a challenge to a decision made by the Government or a Minister of the Government, on the basis that it was made without material which supported it or having regard to the consideration of material which was wholly irrelevant, could never be mounted."[94]

20–57 There is a consistent line of authorities which has assumed that responsible ministers and civil servants will not be deterred by the prospect that their confidential deliberations will ultimately be disclosed by discovery in the course of civil litigation. Public interest immunity has frequently been claimed on the ground that the public servants concerned might henceforth be less than candid if the documents

---

[91] The owners of the properties in question would have obtained tax and other fiscal advantages by reason of this designation.

[92] [1992] 1 I.R. 277 at 280. Note that in *Gormley v Ireland* [1993] 2 I.R. 75 at 78, Murphy J. permitted discovery of what were "unquestionably confidential, sensitive documents recording for the greater part submissions and advices by senior civil servants to Minister and, indeed, to the Government".

[93] [1992] 1 I.R. 277 at 283–284.

[94] [1992] 1 I.R. 277 at 285. In his concurring judgment McCarthy J. drew attention (at 289) to the fact that the plaintiff had claimed that the tax concessions granted to one of the defendants were based on improper considerations: "[T]he exact nature of which must be contained in the documents for which privilege is claimed. Yet it is said that the plaintiffs are to be denied inspection of at least some of these documents. They would thus be precluded from identifying the strength of their case."

in question were required to be disclosed.[95] But, with the particular exception of *Hamilton (No. 1)* (considered at paras 20–60 to 20–61), the courts have, by and large, been less than sympathetic to this argument.[96] In *Fitzpatrick v Independent Newspapers Plc*,[97] Costello J. held that documents pertaining to a statutory inquiry carried out by Bord na gCon were not privileged, as he could not see "how the production of these particular documents would be adverse to the public interest" or how "their production would injure the proper functioning of the service which the Board is required by statute to provide". This trend was continued by both Lardner J. in *Ahern v Minister for Industry & Commerce*[98] and Blayney J. in *PMPS Ltd v PMPA Ltd*.[99] In *Ahern*, the applicant was an established officer in the Patent Office who sought judicial review to challenge certain disciplinary action taken by the Minister. The respondent objected to the production of confidential reports prepared by the applicant's immediate superiors on the grounds that:

> "[D]isclosure of them would considerably interfere with the day-to-day running of a Civil Service Department and would breach fundamental concepts of confidentiality which pertain to the ability of officers to report on the conduct of officers they supervise."

Lardner J. could not accept these submissions, as the reports in question were prepared simply with the particular applicant in mind. As the reports were highly relevant to the applicant's case and as Lardner J. was not satisfied that production of the reports would have the consequences feared by the respondent, he accordingly disallowed the claim of privilege.

20–58 In *PMPS Ltd v PMPA Ltd*, the liquidator of a friendly society sought discovery of documents pertaining to an investigation carried out on behalf of the Registrar of Friendly Societies prior to the collapse of the society in question. Blayney J. rejected the argument that the inspector's functions and civil service morale would be undermined if privilege could not be claimed:

> "Nobody interrogated by the inspector could be under any illusion that information obtained by him would be confidential. Nor can I accept that either that responsible civil servants would be any less likely to speak with the Registrar if the memorandum was disclosed to the liquidator."[100]

---

[95] In *Ambiorix Ltd v Minister for Environment (No. 1)* [1992] 1 I.R. 277 at 281, the argument was put thus by a senior official from the Department of the Taoiseach when it was averred that the production of Government memoranda would not be in the public interest as "officials might tend where possible to make their comments or suggestions or recommendations orally rather than in a written format, and such a tendency would not be in the interests of the public or in the efficiency of the public service".

[96] Note, however, the special circumstances of *Leech v Independent Newspapers (Ireland) Ltd* [2009] IEHC 259, where O'Neill J. refused to order disclosure of statements which had been given to an informal external inquiry into the award of a public contract, saying that "the viability of this form of public inquiry would almost certainly be defeated if there was a risk of disclosure, where confidentiality had been sought from and granted by the person conducting the inquiry".

[97] [1988] I.R. 132.

[98] Unreported, High Court, Lardner J., March 4, 1988.

[99] [1990] 1 I.R. 284.

[100] [1991] 1 I.R. 284 at 287. But cf. *Leech v Independent Newspapers (Ireland) Ltd* [2009] IEHC

20–59 Another example of the "no class" principle is *W v Ireland*,[101] a case where the plaintiff was suing the State for loss and damage arising from what was said to have been the failure of the State to secure the expeditious extradition of a particular suspect. To this end the plaintiff sought discovery of certain documents which had been supplied by the Office of the UK Attorney General to the Irish Attorney General. While Geoghegan J. accepted that these documents were supplied in confidence and that it was in the public interest that this confidence should be upheld, he referred to what Walsh J. had said in *Murphy* and rejected a claim for privilege based on class grounds. On the facts, Geoghegan J. held in favour of disclosure, largely because the criminal proceedings had long been disposed of and it was difficult to see any particular reason "why the U.K. Government would be concerned about the production of the particular documents" in question.

The Cabinet confidentiality case and the 17th Amendment of the Constitution

20–60 The Supreme Court's decision in *Attorney General v Hamilton (No. 1)*[102] arose in unusual circumstances. One of the issues which the Tribunal of Inquiry into the Beef Industry had been required to examine concerned allegations regarding the operation of the statutory export credit insurance scheme. There was a conflict of evidence as to whether the Government at a particular meeting had decided, in respect of beef exports to the Iraqi market, to confine the allocation of this very valuable insurance to two named companies. When Mr Ray Burke T.D., a former Minister for Industry and Commerce, appeared to give evidence before the Tribunal, counsel for the Attorney General objected, on grounds of cabinet confidentiality, to a line of questioning which sought to establish what had transpired at the Government meeting in question. When the Tribunal overruled the objection, the Attorney General sought judicial review of that decision.

20–61 O'Hanlon J. was unimpressed by this argument, stressing that it was inconsistent with the principles underlying *Murphy v Dublin Corporation*, while also drawing attention to what he considered to be the unacceptable corollaries of the Attorney General's submission.[103] A majority of the Supreme Court, however, upheld this submission. Finlay C.J. ruled that the *Murphy* and *Ambiorix* principles had no application to the present case:

> "[T]he principles laid down in these two cases derive, on consideration of the judgments in them, so clearly and unambiguously from the question of the exercise of the judicial power, that they cannot be, automatically, principles applicable to the question of the evidence adduced before the Tribunal of Inquiry."[104]

259, where an assurance of confidentiality was central to the inquiry in that case and was held to be a potent reason for not ordering discovery in that case.

[101] [1997] 2 I.R. 133.

[102] [1993] 2 I.R. 250. See generally, *JM Kelly: The Irish Constitution* (2003), pp.459–468.

[103] As he said ([1993] 2 I.R. 250 at 258–259), such an absolute rule would prevent a Tribunal of Inquiry investigating the conduct of "totally corrupt governments" or discussions at "cabinet level at which … a nefarious plot was being considered".

[104] [1993] 2 I.R. 250 at 270.

20–62 In *Hamilton (No. 1)* two distinct lines of law were perceived to intersect. The first is the principle under consideration here, namely that it is for a court to decide on executive privilege. (One might however, raise the objection that the principle is grounded on Art.34.1 and the "administration of justice", whereas *Hamilton (No. 1)* involved a tribunal[105] and it is unclear whether this principle would extend to a non-judicial body such as a tribunal.) The other issue is the content of the privilege. As to this, in *Hamilton (No. 1)* the essential premise of the majority was that absolute confidentiality was a corollary of the principle of collective responsibility provided for in Art.28.4 of the Constitution:

> "It is clear from the very nature of the collective responsibility of the Government that discussions among its members at their formal meetings must be confidential, otherwise its decisions are liable to be fatally weakened by disclosure of dissenting views … If it were permissible to compel in any circumstances the disclosure of the contents of discussions which take place at Government meetings the executive role of the Government as envisaged by the Constitution, perhaps, even de-stabilised."[106]

20–63 The insistence that the confidentiality which certainly flows from Art.28.4 must be absolute seems unpersuasive and would, if strictly applied, lead to striking anomalies. In the first place, it seems odd that government papers and documents of a highly confidential character may be discovered in the course of civil litigation, whereas discussions at government meetings are inadmissible before a tribunal of inquiry.[107] For if the declared objective of the absolute confidentiality rule is to protect the workings of Government, then this rule is subverted if highly confidential documentation revealing the thought processes of individual Ministers may be discovered in civil litigation.[108] Thus, the most that can be said by way of support for the majority in *Hamilton (No. 1)* is that it sets a particularly heavy premium on the Government's presenting a united phalanx to Dáil and public. By contrast, the *Murphy–Ambiorix* line of authority sets a heavy premium on the administration of justice before a court.

20–64 The ratio in *Hamilton (No. 1)* was unpopular, not least because it was feared that it might interfere with the operation of future tribunals of inquiry. Accordingly, at a time when two separate Tribunals of Inquiry had been established it was in effect partially reversed by the Seventeenth Amendment of the Constitution

---

[105] See Morgan, *The Separation of Powers in the Irish Constitution* (Dublin: Round Hall Sweet & Maxwell, 1997), pp.159–162.

[106] [1993] 2 I.R. 250 at 275 per Hederman J. Finlay C.J. also spoke (at 266) of the "necessity for full, free and frank discussion between members of the Government prior to the making of decisions, something which would appear to be an inevitable adjunct to the obligation to meet collectively and to act collectively".

[107] Byrne and Binchy, *Annual Review of Irish Law 1992* (Dublin: The Round Hall Press, 1993), comment (at p.216) that "undoubtedly, the majority decision is difficult to reconcile with the existing case-law, particularly the general thrust of the discovery cases".

[108] Byrne and Binchy, *Annual Review of Irish Law 1992* (Dublin: The Round Hall Press, 1993), conclude (at p.217) that "the precise circumstances [of the case] were, apparently, highly influential to the outcome", i.e. implying that this decision will not in practice prove to be an authority for the propositions that might seem logically to flow from the decision of the majority.

Act 1997 which inserted the following provision, as the new Art.28.4.3° of the Constitution:

> The confidentiality of discussions at meetings of the Government shall be respected in all circumstances, save only where the High Court determines that disclosure should be made in respect of a particular matter—
>   i.   in the interests of the administration of justice by a Court, or
>   ii.   by virtue of an overriding public interest, pursuant to an application in that behalf by a tribunal appointed by the Government or a Minister of the Government on the authority of the Houses of the Oireachtas to inquire into matters stated by them to be of public importance.

20–65   There are three features to this provision. First, as already mentioned, it reverses the effect of *Hamilton (No. 1)*, but only on the basis that it is for the High Court to determine whether "disclosure should be made ... by virtue of an overriding public interest". Secondly, it makes plain a point on which some doubt had arisen, namely, that where court proceedings (as opposed to a tribunal) were concerned, the *Murphy* and *Ambiorix* line of authority governs the question, even though discussions at a government meeting are in question. Here one should emphasise that, as with the first precept, it is the High Court[109] which must be involved, irrespective of whether the disclosure has arisen in the course of proceedings before a different court. Thirdly, the new Art.28.4.3°—which states that the confidentiality of Government meetings be respected "in *all* circumstances"— contains a remarkably strong statement of the confidentiality precept and certain (potentially unwelcome) consequences would appear to follow. If this is taken at face value, it would seem to bar a Minister who is resigning from the Government because he was not prepared to bear collective responsibility for a particular policy or decision from recounting relevant details from the government meeting. It would even appear to prevent a Minister from informing his senior civil servants of what happened at a particular government meeting. It might also interfere with publication of ministerial biographies and other historical memoirs where this recounted the background to the decisions of a government, however ancient the episodes involved. And here one should recall that Ireland has been called "a minor country, with a major country's history".

Examples of the privilege against disclosure being upheld

20–66   There have also been, of course, many instances of where the privilege has been upheld. In *O'Mahony v Ireland*[110] the plaintiff, who was a soldier with the Irish UN contingent in the Lebanon, claimed damages for negligence against the State. It was said that Irish army officers had permitted him and his two colleagues to be placed under the control of an officer who was not a member of the UN interim force, thereby causing him to fall into the hands of the irregular Christian militia. His colleagues were killed and he was seriously injured as a result. A separate court of inquiry was conducted by the Irish Defence Forces and by the UN force itself.

---

[109] Although Art.28.4.3° refers only to the High Court, an appeal would seem to lie to the Supreme Court by virtue of Art.34.4.3°.
[110] *The Irish Times*, July 28, 1989.

Barrington J. upheld the claim of public interest privilege in respect of the reports of these bodies. It was not unreasonable for the Minister for Defence to provide that the court of inquiry organised by the Defence Forces should be confidential, "having regard to the nature of the work which a court of inquiry could do and the possible security implications. The privilege, therefore, was properly claimed".

20–67 Again, with regard to the UN inquiry, Barrington J. said that the report had been passed on to the Irish Government in circumstances of confidentiality:

> "The Government had taken the view that it was under a duty to preserve the confidence. This was a reasonable attitude and the privilege was properly claimed."[111]

20–68 Thus, that privilege appears to have been extended—not unreasonably—to apply to documents emanating from third parties which the Government regards itself as under a duty to keep confidential: such cases may constitute instances of where "confidentiality is itself a public interest".[112] In the opposite direction, the force of an argument for confidentiality is eroded where it is evident that the material in question will, anyway, be made available to the public or otherwise enter the public domain.[113]

The procedure for adjudication on pleas of privilege and onus of proof

20–69 The procedure to be followed in adjudicating upon a claim for privilege is a most important matter. In the first place, where a document is relevant, the burden of proving that it is privileged rests on the State.[114] It may be possible for the court to decide the claim without an inspection. As Finlay C.J. said in *Ambiorix Ltd v Minister for Environment (No. 1)*:

> "There is no obligation on the judicial power to examine any particular document before deciding that it is exempt from production, and it can and will in many instances uphold a claim of privilege in respect of a document merely on the basis of a description of its nature and contents which it (the judicial power) accepts."[115]

---

[111] For other examples of where the privilege was upheld by reason of a duty of confidence owed to third parties, see *O'Brien v Ireland* [1995] 1 I.L.R.M. 22; *Leech v Independent Newspapers (Ireland) Ltd* [2009] IEHC 259.

[112] *D v National Society for the Protection of Cruelty to Children* [1971] A.C. 171 at 230 per Lord Hailsham and quoted with approval in *Goodman International v Hamilton (No. 3)* [1993] 3 I.R. 320 at 327 by Geoghegan J. and in *Leech v Independent Newspapers (Ireland) Ltd* [2009] IEHC 259 per O'Neill J.

[113] *Rooney v Skeffington* [1997] 1 I.R. 22; *McDaid v Minister for Marine* [1994] 3 I.R. 321.

[114] Once it has been established that the documents in question are relevant, then the "burden of satisfying the court that a particular document ought not to be produced lies upon the party, or the person, who makes such a claim": see *Murphy v Dublin Corporation* [1972] I.R. 215 at 235 per Walsh J. See also, *Breathnach v Ireland (No. 3)* [1993] 2 I.R. 458.

[115] [1992] 1 I.R. 277 at 284. See also, *Murphy v Dublin Corporation* [1972] I.R. 215 at 234–235. In other cases, the court itself will order inspection of the documents, especially where the decision as to whether to order disclosure cannot be made without having taken this step: see, e.g. *Director of Consumer Affairs v Sugar Distributors Ltd* [1991] 1 I.R. 225; *W v Ireland* [1997] 2 I.R. 133; *McDonald v RTE* [2001] IESC 6; [2001] 1 I.R. 355; [2001] 2 I.L.R.M. 1.

20–70 However, even before any inspection is ordered, the affidavit must plainly establish at least a prima facie case that the documents are privileged. In one case, McWilliam J. complained that to ask the court "to examine all these documents under the circumstances of the present case seems to me to be getting very close to asking the Court to prepare an affidavit of discovery".[116] In some cases it will, nonetheless, be necessary for the court to inspect the documents, possibly in camera, in order to decide whether to order discovery.[117]

20–71 There are a number of further points which require further elaboration.

Criminal proceedings

20–72 In *Murphy*, Walsh J. had been careful to refrain from expressing any opinion as to the scope of executive privilege in criminal proceedings. But if the balancing test is required in civil litigation, it is even more appropriate that such a test should be applied in criminal proceedings where "the applicant's reputation and freedom are at stake and where she is entitled to a fair trial under the Constitution".[118]

20–73 This very point was at issue in *Breathneach v Ireland (No. 3)*.[119] Keane J. first endorsed his earlier judgment in *Holly* and emphasised that no "class" claim of privilege could arise simply by reason of the fact that these were Garda documents. He then addressed the factors to be considered in the balancing process:

> "[T]he court ... is required to balance the public interest in the proper administration of justice against the public interest reflected in the grounds put forward for non-disclosure in the present case ... It is only where the first public interest outweighs the second public interest that an inspection should be undertaken or disclosure should be ordered. In considering the first public interest, it is necessary to determine to what extent, if any, the relevant documents may advance the plaintiff's case or damage the defendant's case or fairly lead to an enquiry which may produce either of these consequences ... [T]here may be documents the very nature of which is such that inspection is not necessary to determine on which side the scales come down. Thus, information supplied in confidence to the Gardaí should not in general be disclosed or at least not in cases like the present where the innocence of an accused person is not in issue ... Again, there may be material the disclosure of which would be of assistance to criminals by revealing methods of detection or combating crime, a consideration of particular importance today when criminal activity tends to be highly organised and professional. There

---

[116] *Hunt v Roscommon VEC*, unreported, High Court, McWilliam J., May 1, 1981. See also, the comments of Walsh J. in *Murphy v Dublin Corporation* [1972] I.R. 215 at 237.

[117] cf. the comments of Keane J. in *Skeffington v Rooney* [1997] 1 I.R. 22 at 35: "On occasions, these issues can be resolved by the judge by reference to the description of the documents contained in the affidavit of discovery. More frequently, it will involve an examination of some or all of the disputed documents. In any event, the procedure to be adopted must depend to some extent upon the circumstances of each case and the nature and extend of the disputed documents."

[118] *Traynor v Delahunt* [2008] IEHC 272; [2009] 1 I.L.R.M. 113 at 121 per McMahon J.

[119] [1993] 2 I.R. 448. The quotation is at 469. See also, *DPP (Hanley) v Holly* [1984] I.L.R.M. 149.

may be cases involving the security of the State, where even disclosure of the existence of the document should not be allowed. None of these factors – and there may, of course, well be others which have not occurred to me – which would remove the necessity of even inspecting the documents is present in this case."[120]

20–74 The judge concluded that, on the facts, the documents were likely to be of some assistance to the plaintiff in his malicious prosecution claim and this consideration overcame the competing public interest in maintaining the confidentiality of the documents in question. Dealing with a different form of privilege which, it might be thought, however, could often arise from the same situation as the privilege under discussion here, Keane J. continued by rejecting the suggestion that the documentation in question could attract legal professional privilege on the ground that the dominant purpose for its preparation was contemplated or pending litigation.[121] The documentation in question consisted of Garda files concerning an investigation into a train robbery, which had been submitted to the Director of Public Prosecutions so that a decision could be taken regarding a possible prosecution.

20–75 In subsequent cases the claim for privilege has generally been advanced on the basis that the identity of a source might be compromised[122] or where sensitive information regarding a Garda investigation might be compromised.[123] Thus, for example, in *McDonald v RTE*[124] the issue was whether disclosure should be ordered in respect of certain Garda documents which had been generated in the course of a murder investigation. Not surprisingly, the Supreme Court upheld the claim for privilege in respect of these key documents:

> "In addition the file has been assembled in connection with the investigation of a criminal offence of abduction and murder which on the evidence before the court is still a live investigation. I would accept the submission of [counsel] that in such a situation it might be of interest to various persons to discover not only what was on the file but what was not on the file. It seems to me that in principle it would be injurious to the public interest to bring some of the relevant documents into the public arena through the means of discovery."[125]

Extension of privilege to all public interest cases?

20–76 In *Murphy's* case, Walsh J. emphasised the point that "executive privilege"

---

[120] [1993] 2 I.R. 448 at 469. See also, *DPP (Hanley) v Holly* [1984] I.L.R.M. 149.

[121] Keane J. observed ([1993] 2 I.R. 448 at 472): "The fact that the documents in question may … be submitted by the investigating Gardai to the Director of Public Prosecutions in order to obtain his decision as to whether a prosecution should be instituted could not possibly give that material the same status as, to take an obvious example, a medical report obtained by a plaintiff in a personal injuries action solely for the purposes of his claim."

[122] See, e.g. *People v Eccles* (1986) 3 Frewen 36 (Garda Superintendent entitled to claim privilege in respect of both the source and the nature of the source of "sensitive, confidential information").

[123] See, e.g. *McDonald v RTE* [2001] IESC 6; [2001] 1 I.R. 355; [2001] 2 I.L.R.M. 1.

[124] [2001] IESC 6; [2001] 1 I.R. 355; [2001] 2 I.L.R.M. 1.

[125] [2001] 1 I.R. 355 at 376; [2001] 2 I.L.R.M. 1 at 20–21 per McGuinness J.

only applied to a Minister who was exercising "the executive powers of government of the State". If this observation were to be taken at its face value, it would appear narrowly to restrict the immunity to Ministers exercising their executive powers under Art.28 of the Constitution.[126] But if the immunity has now (in fact, since *Leen's* case in 1926) been severed from the prerogative, and put on the basis of public interest, it seems arbitrary and unnecessary to confine the immunity in this narrow fashion. In fact, the later case law makes it clear that the immunity is not so confined. For example, in *State (Williams) v Army Pensions Board*,[127] Henchy J. assumed that privilege could be claimed, in a suitable case, in respect of the Board's documents. Again, in *Geraghty v Dublin Corporation*,[128] the immunity was allowed to protect some of the documents for which it was claimed, although that case involved a Minister hearing a planning appeal, and thus taking a quasi-judicial—as opposed to executive—function. In *D v National Society for the Prevention of Cruelty to Children*,[129] the House of Lords held that the defendant body (a private, charitable body which did, however, enjoy official status to the extent of being an "authorised person" for the purpose of bringing child care proceedings under the relevant English legislation) was entitled to claim immunity on the grounds of public interest in respect of members of the public who had given information to them concerning child abuse.

Informer privilege

20–77   Informer privilege seems to form a category of its own. In any case, informer privilege has been applied in a number of cases,[130] quite apart from *Buckley*. This is not just confined to criminal proceedings, but is nowadays extended to a variety of statutory bodies and agencies, such as, for example, the Director of Consumer Affairs,[131] the Garda Síochána Complaints Board[132] and the Law Society of Ireland.[133] The immunity from disclosure under this head is not absolute and the courts may be prepared to permit disclosure if this will "tend to show that the defendant had not committed the wrongful acts alleged against him"[134] or where it has not been demonstrated that confidentiality was an essential feature of the complaints procedure operated by the statutory body in question.[135]

---

[126] As opposed to the cases where the Minister has acted merely as a persona designata, as in *Murphy v Dublin Corporation* [1972] I.R. 215.

[127] [1983] I.R. 308. In *Skeffington v Rooney* [1997] 1 I.R. 22, Keane J. similarly ruled that the Garda Síochána Complaints Board would be entitled to claim public interest immunity in respect of materials supplied to it in confidence.

[128] [1975] I.R. 300.

[129] [1978] A.C. 171.

[130] See, e.g. *State (Comerford) v Governor of Mountjoy Prison* [1981] I.L.R.M. 86 (prison governor allowed to claim privilege in respect of prison escape plan); *People v Eccles* (1986) 3 Frewen 36; *People v Reddan* [1995] 3 I.R. 560.

[131] *Director of Consumer Affairs v Sugar Distributors Ltd* [1991] 1 I.R. 225.

[132] *Skeffington v Rooney* [1997] 1 I.R. 22.

[133] *Buckley v Incorporated Law Society of Ireland* [1994] 2 I.R. 44.

[134] *Director of Consumer Affairs v Sugar Distributors Ltd* [1991] 1 I.R. 225 at 229 per Costello J.

[135] *Skeffington v Rooney* [1997] 1 I.R. 22 at 38 per Keane J. (routine documents, none of which suggested that the statements had been on a confidential basis).

Does the right to a fair hearing require the disclosure of documents?

20–78   While much of the foregoing discussion has been based upon separation of powers considerations, it should be recalled that the obligation to make disclosure of documents can just as readily be justified by reference to the requirements of fair procedures. The dictates of constitutional justice will often require the disclosure of relevant evidence, and this is especially so where the decision-maker is exercising quasi-judicial functions.

20–79   In *O'Leary v Minister for Industry and Commerce*,[136] a bridge in the neighbourhood of the plaintiff's farm had been submerged by the Electricity Supply Board in the course of the construction of a hydro-electric scheme. The Board was required by the relevant legislation to build a new bridge unless the defendant Minister determined that in the circumstances this was not necessary. Privilege was claimed in respect of memoranda and other communications exchanged between the Board and the Minister. Ó Dálaigh C.J. observed that the Minister had been cast in a quasi-judicial role and that he was required to make "an objective finding in effect as between the parties". The communications of the Board to the Minister were not those of an adviser in relation to the discharge of a statutory duty, but were rather "the representations of a party with an interest". The *audi alteram partem* principle therefore required that such circumstances be disclosed.

20–80   A related point is that very often the public authority in question will have in its possession all the relevant documentation and that without access to such documentation the applicant could not hope to be able to make out his case.[137] This very point was made by McCarthy J. in *Ambiorix Ltd v Minister for Environment (No. 1)*,[138] a case where the plaintiffs claimed that the Minister had acted on improper considerations in designating certain lands which would then benefit from certain urban renewal tax concessions:

> "The Constitution guarantees fair procedures in the administration of justice; discovery of documents is part of those procedures. The plaintiffs here allege a case of unfair competition, contending that tax concessions made to the fifth defendant were based on invalid considerations, the exact nature of which must be contained in the documents for which privilege is claimed. Yet, it is

---

[136]   [1966] I.R. 676.

[137]   cf. the celebrated comments of Sir John Donaldson MR in *R. v Lancashire County Council Ex p. Huddleston* [1986] 2 All E.R. 941 at 945: "[Counsel for the respondents] says that it is for the applicant to make out his case for judicial review and that it is not for the respondent authority to do it for him. This, in my judgment, is only partially correct. Certainly, it is for the applicant to satisfy the court of his entitlement to judicial review and it is for the respondent to resist his application, if it considers it to be unjustified. But it is a process which falls to be conducted with all the cards face upwards on the table and the vast majority of the cards will start in the authority's hands."
  Note also the comments to the same effect (in dissent, admittedly) of Lord Walker in *Belize Alliance v DOE* [2004] U.K.P.C. 6 (at para.86): "It is now clear that proceedings for judicial review should not be conducted in the same manner as hard fought commercial litigation. A respondent authority owes a duty to the court to co-operate and to make candid disclosure, by way of affidavit, of the relevant facts and (so far as they are not apparent from contemporaneous documents which have been disclosed) the reasoning behind the decision challenged in the judicial review proceedings."

[138]   [1992] 1 I.R. 277.

said that the plaintiffs are to be denied inspection of at least some of these documents. They would thus be precluded from identifying the strength of their case. It is accurately described as a 'Catch 22' situation."[139]

20–81   In other cases, the courts may be prepared to make adverse inferences if the public authority declines to make appropriate discovery or otherwise demonstrate the factors it took into account in reaching its decision.[140] However, the rule will not always require that such disclosure of relevant documents be made: there will be situations where the constitutional guarantee of fair procedures, which, of course, is not absolute, may have to yield to the need to preserve confidential information.[141]

Does the Constitution place limits on the power of the Oireachtas to create new categories of statutory privilege?

20–82   The extent to which the Oireachtas is free to create new forms of statutory public interest privilege is not entirely clear and has received scant judicial consideration. There are a number of diverse examples of such statutory privileges, including an immunity from disclosure for officials of the Central Bank[142]; the archives of United Nations[143]; findings and recommendations of military courts of inquiry[144]; records of An Bord Uchtála[145]; statements made to the Confidential Committee of the Commission to Inquire into Child Abuse[146]; and documents gathered by a Commission of Investigation.[147] Of course, the fact that officials or employees are statutorily prohibited from disclosing confidential information does not in itself serve to preclude an order for discovery, since clear words creating an immunity for documents are generally required.[148] Nevertheless, the courts have given effect to the absolute nature of these "no discovery" clauses as they have indicated that they feel compelled by statute to do so, absent a successful challenge to their constitutional validity.[149]

20–83   Here we are examining a different question from that considered earlier

---

[139] [1992] 1 I.R. 277 at 289. See also, the comments of Finlay C.J. to the like effect ([1992] 1 I.R. 277 at 285) and *O'Keeffe v An Bord Pleanála* [1993] 1 I.R. 39.

[140] See, e.g. the comments of Laws L.J. in *Quark Fishing Ltd v Secretary of State* [2002] EWCA 149 and those of Kerr L.C.J. in *Re Williamson's Application* [2008] N.I.C.A. 52.

[141] See, e.g. *O'Neill v An Taoiseach* [2009] IEHC 119.

[142] Central Bank Act 1989 s.16. In *Cully v Northern Bank Finance* [1984] I.L.R.M. 683, O'Hanlon J. held that he was compelled to uphold this absolute privilege against the production of documents by the statutory predecessor of this section "unless and until the validity of [the] section … is successfully challenged".

[143] Diplomatic Relations and Immunities Act 1967 s.9.

[144] Rules of Procedure (Defence Forces) 1954 (S.I. No. 243 of 1954) art.121. See *O'Brien v Ireland* [1995] 1 I.L.R.M. 22.

[145] Adoption Act 1976 s.8. See generally, *PB v AL* [1996] 1 I.L.R.M. 154.

[146] Commission to Inquire into Child Abuse Act 2000 s.27; *MB v Commission to Inquire into Child Abuse* [2007] 3 I.R. 541.

[147] This was held to arise by necessary implication from a number of provisions of the Commissions of Investigation Act 2004: see *O'Neill v An Taoiseach* [2009] IEHC 119.

[148] See, e.g. *Cully v Northern Bank Finance* [1984] I.L.R.M. 683; *O'Brien v Ireland* [1995] 1 I.R. 568; *MB v Commission to Inquire into Child Abuse* [2007] IEHC 1; [2007] 3 I.R. 541; and *O'Neill v An Taoiseach* [2009] IEHC 119.

[149] See, in particular, the comments of O'Hanlon J. in *Cully v Northern Bank Finance* [1984] I.L.R.M. 683 at 686.

in this Part in two respects. First, the source of the privilege is statutory rather than the common law prerogative (however presently defined). Secondly, the content of the privilege is, in some cases, defined by reasonably precise statutory rules (which it is for a court to apply) rather than allowing the judiciary a complete free hand, guided only by general principle and case law. In *O'Brien v Ireland*[150] O'Hanlon J. adverted to this issue, saying that neither *Murphy* nor *Ambiorix*:

> "... was intended to convey that the power of the legislature to intervene and confer the privilege of exemption from production on specified categories of documentary or other evidence was curtailed or restricted in any way, save insofar as any legislation enacted must not conflict with the overriding provisions of the Constitution."[151]

20–84 This, of course, leaves open the questions of what provisions of the Constitution would be engaged and also what types of "curtail[ment] or restrict[ion]" would survive constitutional challenge. However, it might be that legislation which, for example, purported to create a statutory privilege from immunity in all instances of litigation against the State or some commercial state body would presumably be open to challenge on the grounds that it infringed the right of access to the courts (Arts 34.1 and 40.3.1°) or equality (Art.40.1).

20–85 An interesting contemporary example of such a statutory provision—which is an exception to what was said earlier regarding the content of a privilege being defined precisely—is supplied by s.10(3) of the Interception of Postal Packets and Telecommunications Messages (Regulation) Act 1993. This subsection provides that in civil proceedings alleging an unlawful interception without proper authorisation of telecommunications or postal messages, a court must first determine whether such an interception has taken place as alleged and unless this has been affirmatively determined, no discovery can be made which would tend to disclose the existence of an official authorisation or any related matter. It is said that without such a safeguard, any person "wanting to find out whether his telephone had been tapped" might start proceedings with a view to compelling an official in Bord Telecom or An Post "to say whether there had been an interception".[152] Nevertheless, while the public interest in protecting the integrity of an official interception system must be very great, the constitutionality of such a far-reaching exclusion clause must, in the light of cases such as *Murphy* and *Ambiorix*, be open to question. In addition, without the benefit of discovery, a plaintiff who was the victim of an unlawful interception could not easily establish this fact. Here is the very type of "Catch-22" situation which, as we have already seen, was stigmatised by McCarthy J. in *Ambiorix* as a breach of fair procedures.

---

[150] [1995] 1 I.R. 568.
[151] [1995] 1 I.R. 568 at 575.
[152] 424 *Dáil Debates* Col.1201, per the Minister for Justice (Mr P. Flynn T.D.).

INDEX

plenary proceedings—*contd.*
  litigation of public law issue by, 17–05,
    17–41—17–57. *see also* **public
    law**
    O'Reilly v Mackman, 17–45—17–52
police. *see also* **Garda Síochána**
  investigations
    immunity from suit, 18–89
  torts or constitutional wrongs
    State's vicarious liability, 18–106,
      18–108—18–110
policy assumptions
  discretionary powers, control of,
    15–20—15–23
policy decisions
  administrative decisions and, distinction
    between, 1–09—1–11
  constitutional justice/fair procedure,
    applicability of, 14–164—14–166
  examples, 1–10, 1–11, 1–14
  individual policy decisions, 1–14
  judicial control over, 1–16
  legislative decisions, 1–14
  Ombudsman, jurisdiction of, 9–27—9–34
policy rules
  adherence to inflexible policy rule,
    15–138—15–143
  examples, 15–144—15–148
policy-oriented tribunals, 6–17
poor law, 5–02, 5–03, 5–05
postal and telecommunication services
  immunity provisions, 18–82
precedent, 6–78, 14–114, 15–112
pre-emption, doctrine of, 2–68
pre-emptive costs orders
  judicial review proceedings, 16–37
pre-judgment of issues
  bias, source of, 13–30—13–34. *see also*
    bias
prerogative, 4–28, 20–02—20–19
  British approach, 20–21—20–22
  charters, 20–15
  Constitution of Ireland, and, 20–03,
    20–11—20–14
    conflict with, 20–03, 20–18
    Geoghegan case, 20–15
    retrenchment from absolutist position,
      20–15—20–19
  Constitution of the Irish Free State, and,
    20–06—20–09
    Byrne v Ireland, 20–03, 20–07—
      20–11
  corporations, creation of, 5–57
  Crown prerogative, 20–02, 20–03
    survival of, 20–07—20–14
  judgment debt, enforcement of, 20–03
  mercy, of, 20–03
  priority of debts, 20–03
  public bodies, application to, 4–28
  sovereign immunity, 20–03, 20–13

prerogative—*contd.*
  State exemption from statute, 20–14,
    20–18, 20–47—20–50
    consequences of *Howard* decision,
      20–50
  State's legal personality, and, 20–20—
    20–26
  treasure trove: *Webb v Ireland,* 20–12—
    20–13, 20–16, 20–17, 20–18
  war, declaration of, 20–03
President of Ireland
  pardon, right of, 20–03
presumptions, statutory. *see* **statutory
  interpretation**
primary legislation. *see* **legislation**
principles and policies test. *see* **delegated
  legislation**
prior involvement
  as source of bias, 13–30—13–34, 13–35
prison officers
  State's vicarious liability, 18–106,
    18–107
prison service, 4–05
  fair procedure/constitutional justice
    disciplinary matters, 14–135
    temporary release and parole,
      14–140—14–141
Prisoners Appeals Tribunal, 6–01
private companies, 17–23
private employment
  constitutional justice, applicability of,
    14–122—14–129
private law, 1–02, 17–01. *see also* **contract;
  tort**
  constitutional justice, applicability of,
    14–184—14–186
  public bodies, application to, 17–10,
    17–27, 17–30
    judicial review, litigation by,
      17–30—17–40
  public–private divide in Irish law,
    17–01—17–26, 17–28, 17–29. *see
    also* public law
  tribunals, 6–03
Private Residential Tenancies Board,
  6–03, 6–56, 8–04
Private Security Appeals Board, 6–02
Private Security Authority, 6–02
privilege
  absolute privilege, 18–102
  public inquiries, 8–09
  public interest privileges, 20–82. *see also*
    executive privilege
  new categories, power of Oireachtas to
    create, 20–82—20–85
privilegia, 14–143
Privy Council, 1–04
**procedural and formal requirements,
  disregard of**, 11–71—11–78
  mandatory/directory requirements,
    11–72—11–77